SOUTHAMPTON INSTITUTE
Mountbatten Library

for reference only

DICTIONARY OF
COMPUTING
& INFORMATION TECHNOLOGY
English-German

Second edition

DICTIONARY OF
COMPUTING
& INFORMATION TECHNOLOGY

English-German

Second edition

S.M.H. Collin
Armin Mutscheller
Eva Torkar
Rupert Livesey

PETER COLLIN PUBLISHING

Second edition 1997

First Published in Great Britain 1991

By Peter Collin Publishing Ltd

1 Cambridge Road, Teddington, Middlesex, TW11 8DT

Second edition 1997

Reprinted 1998, 2000

British Library Cataloguing-in-Publication Data

A catalogue record for this book is available from the British Library

ISBN 1-901659-00-3

Text typeset by Create Publishing Services, Bath

Printed and bound in Great Britain by

Selwood Printing Ltd, Burgess Hill, West Sussex

Vorwort

Diese vollständig neubearbeitete und aktualisierte Auflage des Fachwörterbuchs Datenverarbeitung enthält etwa 10.000 englische Stichwörter und Wendungen sowie rund 12.000 deutsche Übersetzungen. Berücksichtigt werden Ausdrücke aus den Fachgebieten Software, Hardware, Netzwerke, Peripheriegeräte, Programmierung und Computeranwendungen, wie z.B. Desktop publishing, Grafik, Elektronik und Telekommunikation. Sowohl sämtliche Computerplattformen, wie die aktuellsten PDAs, PCs, Minicomputer und Großrechnersysteme, als auch die wichtigsten Softwareprodukte und die bekanntesten Computerunternehmen sind eingeschlossen.

Die ca. 10.000 Stichwörter und Wendungen werden in leicht verständlichem Englisch erklärt. Diese revidierte Ausgabe enthält zahlreiche neue, authentische Zitate, die die Verwendung der Fachterminologie im täglichen Gebrauch darstellen.

Im zweiten Teil des Wörterbuchs sind die deutschen Fachbegriffe noch einmal mit ihren englischen Entsprechungen in einem alphabetischen Register aufgelistet, so dass auch ausgehend von deutschen Begriffen nachgeschlagen werden kann. Der Anhang enthält weitere nützliche Informationen in Form von Illustrationen und Tabellen.

In dem PONS Fachwörterbuch Datenverarbeitung wird die neue deutsche Rechtschreibreform berücksichtigt.

Englisch-Deutsches
Wörterbuch

Aa

A = AMPERE base SI unit of electrical current; defined as the current flowing through an impedance of one ohm which has a voltage of one volt across it **A(mpere)**

A hexadecimal equivalent to decimal number 10 **A**

Å *see* ANGSTROM

A: (used in some operating systems) denotes the first disk drive on the system **A:**; *to see what is stored on your floppy disk, use the DOS command DIR A:*

A/UX version of the Unix operating system for the Apple Macintosh range of computers **A/UX**; *see also* UNIX

A-bus *noun* main internal bus in a microprocessor **Hauptübertragungsweg**

A programming language (APL) *noun* high-level programming language used for scientific and mathematical work **anwendungsorientierte Programmiersprache**

◊ **A1, A2, A3, A4, A5** *noun* ISO recommended international standard sizes of paper *or* sizes of screen **A1, A2, A3, A4, A5**; *you must photocopy the spreadsheet on A3 paper; we must order some more A4 headed notepaper; a standard 300 d.p.i. black and white A4 monitor* ⇨APPENDIX

A to D *or* **A/D** = ANALOG TO DIGITAL changing a signal from an analog form to a digitally coded form **Analog-Digital-Umwandlung; A to D converter** = (analog to digital converter) device used to convert an analog input to a digital output form which can be understood by a computer **Analog-Digital-Umsetzer;** *the speech signal was first passed through an A to D converter before being analysed; opposite is* DIGITAL TO ANALOG

abandon *verb* to clear a document or file or work from the computer's memory without saving it to disk or tape **abbrechen;** *once you have abandoned your spreadsheet, you cannot retrieve it again*

abbreviated address *noun* (in a network) user name that has fewer characters than the full name, making it easier to remember or type in **Kurzadresse;** *my full network address is over 60 characters long, so you will find it easier to use my abbreviated address;* **abbreviated addressing** *or* **abb. add.** = use of a smaller computer address word than normal which provides faster address decoding operations **Kurzadressierung; abbreviated installation** = (during installation) to install new hardware *or* software without restoring the previous backup settings of the operating system **abgekürzte Installation**

abbreviation *noun* short form of a word *or* command *or* instruction **Abkürzung;** *within the text, the abbreviation proc is used instead of processor*

ABD = APPLE DESKTOP BUS ™

abend *noun* = ABNORMAL END unexpected stoppage of a program being run, due to a fault *or* error *or* power failure **abnormales Ende; abend code** = special number (generated by the operating system) that identifies the type of error that has caused the problem **Abbruchcode;** *an interrupt from a faulty printer caused an abend;* **abend recovery program** = software that will reload a program (or system software) and restart it at the point where the abend occurred **Wiederanlaufprogramm nach abnormalem Ende;** *if a fault occurs, data loss will be minimized due to the improved abend recovery program*

aberration *noun*
(a) distortion of a light beam *or* image due to defects in the optical system **Aberration**
(b) distortion of a television picture caused by a corrupt signal *or* incorrect adjustment **Aberration;** *see also* SPHERICAL

ABIOS = ADVANCED BASIC INPUT/OUTPUT SYSTEM set of routines stored on a ROM chip in the IBM PS/2 range of personal computers **ABIOS**

COMMENT: the ABIOS is used in addition to the normal BIOS routines; ABIOS routines are used to control the MCA bus in an IBM PS/2 computer

ablation *noun* method of writing data to an optical storage device **Ablation**

COMMENT: a laser burns a hole or pit (that represents digital bits of data) into the thin metal surface of the storage device

ABM = ASYNCHRONOUS BALANCED MODE

◊ **ABME** = ASYNCHRONOUS BALANCED MODE EXTENDED

abnormal *adjective* not normal **anormal**; *its abnormal for two consecutive disk drives to break down abnormal error;* **abnormal end** *or* **abend** *or* **abnormal termination** = unexpected stoppage of a program being run, caused by a fault *or* error *or* power failure **anormaler Abbruch**

◊ **abnormally** *adverb* not as normal *or* not as usual **anormal;** *the signal is abnormally weak; the error rate with this disk is abnormally high*

abort *verb* to end a process (when a malfunction occurs), by switching the computer off manually *or* by an internal feature **abbrechen;** *the program was aborted by pressing the red button; abort the program before it erases any more files; see also* RESET; **aborted connection** = connection to a network or online service that has not been shut down correctly **Abbruch; abort sequence** = unique sequence of bits that indicates that the transmission will be abnormally terminated **Abbruchsequenz**

About... (in the SAA CUA front-end) menu selection that tells you who developed the program and gives copyright information **Über...**

above-the-line costs *plural noun* variable costs involved in making TV films (such as scriptwriters, actors, sets, etc.) as opposed to below-the-line costs (film crew, technicians, etc.) **Kosten über dem Strich**

AB roll *noun* (in a multimedia application) two video or music segments that are synchronised so that one fades as the second starts **AB-Ausblendung**

ABS = ABSOLUTE FUNCTION programming instruction that returns the magnitude of a number without the number's sign **ABS;** *the command ABS(-13) will return the answer 13*

absolute address *or* **actual address** *or* **machine address** *noun* (a) computer storage address that directly, without any modification, accesses a location *or* device **absolute Adresse;** *compare* INDEXED ADDRESS; *program execution is slightly faster if you code only with absolute addresses* (b) computer storage address that can only access one location **absolute Adresse; absolute addressing** = locating a data word in memory by the use of its absolute address **absolute Adressierung; absolute assembler** = type of assembly language program designed to produce code which uses only absolute addresses and values **absoluter Assemblierer; absolute cell reference** = spreadsheet reference that always refers to the same cell, even when copied to another location **absolute Bezugszelle; absolute code** = binary code which directly operates the central processing unit, using only absolute addresses and values (this is the final form of a program after a compiler *or* assembler pass) **absoluter Code;** *see also* OBJECT CODE; **absolute coordinates** = coordinates that describe the distance of a point from the intersection of axes **absolute Koordinaten;** *compare* RELATIVE COORDINATES; **absolute device** = input device such as a tablet or mouse that returns the coordinates of a pointer within specified axes **absolute Einheit; absolute error** = value *or* magnitude of an error, ignoring its sign **absoluter Fehler; absolute expression** = (in assembly language) value of an expression that is not affected by program relocation **absoluter Ausdruck; absolute instruction** *or* **code** = (i) instruction which completely describes the operation to be performed (no other data is required); (ii) graphics command that uses absolute coordinates (i) **endgültiger Maschinenbefehl;** (ii) **absolute Instruktion; absolute loader** = program that loads a section of code into main memory **Ladeprogramm für absolute Programme; absolute maximum rating** = maximum values or limits of a system **absolute Maximumwerte; absolute positioning** = position of an object in relation to an origin **tatsächliche Position; absolute priority** = (in the OS/2 operating system) priority of a process that cannot be changed by the operating system **absolute Priorität; absolute program** = computer program written in absolute code **absolutes Programm; absolute value** = size *or* value of a number, regardless of its sign **Absolutwert;** *the absolute value of −62.34 is 62.34; an absolute value of the input is generated*

absorb *verb* to take in (light *or* liquid) **absorbieren, aufsaugen**

◊ **absorptance** *noun* percentage of light that is absorbed by a material instead of reflecting it **Absorptionskonstante** NOTE: the opposite is **reflectance**

◊ **absorption** *noun* power loss of a signal when travelling through a medium, due to its absorptance **Absorption; absorption filter** = filter that blocks certain colours of light **Absorptionsfilter**

abstract
1 *noun* short summary of a document **Kurzdarstellung;** *it's quicker to search through the abstracts than the full text*
2 *verb*
(a) to remove something from something **entwenden**
(b) to make a summary of an article **zusammenfassen**

◊ **abstract data type** *noun* a general data type that can store any kind of information **abstrakter Datentyp;** *the stack is a structure of abstract data types, it can store any type of data from an integer to an address*

AC = ALTERNATING CURRENT electric current whose value varies with time in a regular, sinusoidal way **Wechselstrom**

COMMENT: the mains electricity supply uses alternating current to minimize transmission power loss, with a frequency of 50Hz in U.K., 60Hz in the USA

ACC *noun* = ACCUMULATOR most important internal CPU storage register, containing the data word that is to be processed **Akkumulator(register)**

acceleration time *noun*
(a) time taken for a disk drive to spin a disk at the correct speed, from rest **Beschleunigungszeit;** *allow for acceleration time in the access time*
(b) total time between an access instruction being issued (to a peripheral) and the data being transferred **Anlaufzeit**

◊ **accelerator** *see* ACCELERATOR KEY

◊ **accelerator board** *or* **card** *noun*

circuit board that carries a faster or more advanced version of the same processor that runs your computer; adding an accelerator card to your computer makes it run faster **Beschleunigerkarte**

◊ **accelerator key** *noun* combination of keys that, when pressed together, carry out a function that would otherwise have to be selected from a menu using a mouse **Schnelltasten, Shortcut;** *instead of selecting the File menu then the Save option, use the accelerator keys Alt and S to do the same thing and save the file*

accent *noun* mark above a character to indicate a different pronunciation **Akzentzeichen; acute accent** = accent above a character, which slopes upwards to the right **Akut; circumflex accent** = accent above a character, shaped like an upside down 'v' **Zirkumflex; grave accent** = accent above a character, which slopes upwards to the left **Gravis;** *see also* CEDILLA, TILDE, UMLAUT

◊ **accented** *adjective* (letter) with an accent on it **(Buchstabe) mit Akzent, betont**

accept *verb*
(a) to agree to do something **annehmen, akzeptieren;** *he accepted the quoted price for printing; she has accepted our terms; he did not accept the programming job he was offered*
(b) to take something which is being offered **annehmen, akzeptieren;** *the laser printer will accept a card as small as a business card; the multi-disk reader will accept 3.5 inch disks as well as 5.25 inch formats;* call accept signal = signal sent by a device showing that it is willing to accept (caller's) data **Rufannahmesignal**
(c) to establish a session or connection with another device **annehmen**

◊ **acceptable** *adjective* which can be accepted **annehmbar, akzeptabel;** *the error rate was very low, and is acceptable; for the price, the scratched case is acceptable*

◊ **acceptance** *noun* action of accepting something **Abnahme; acceptance angle** = angle of total field of view of a lens *or* optic fibres **Einfangwinkel;** *a light beam at an angle greater than the acceptance angle of the lens will not be transmitted;* **acceptance sampling** = testing a small random part of a batch to see if the whole batch is up to standard **Qualitätskontrolle mittels Stichprobe; acceptance test** *or* **testing** = method of checking that a piece of equipment will perform as required *or* will reach required standards **Abnahmeprüfung**

access

1 *noun* being allowed to use a computer and read *or* alter files stored in it (this is usually controlled by a security device such as a password) **Zugriff, Zugang; to have access to something** = to be able to get *or* examine *or* reach something **Zugang zu etwas haben;** *to have access to a file of data; he has access to numerous sensitive files;* **to bar access to a system** = to prevent a person from using a system **Zugang zu einem System verwehren;** *after he was discovered hacking, he was barred access to the system;* **access arm** = mechanical device in a disk drive used to position the read/write head over the correct track on a disk **(Platten)zugriffsarm;** *the access arm moves to the parking region during transport;* **access authority** = permission to carry out a particular operation on data **Zugriffsberechtigung; access barred** = to prevent a user accessing particular data **Zugriff verweigert; access category** = one of several possible predefined access levels; the category defines which files or data a user can access, and which he cannot **Zugriffskategorie, Zugriffsberechtigungsebene; access channel control** = (in Token-Ring network) protocols that manage the data transfer between a station and a medium access control (MAC) **Kanalzugriffssteuerung; access charge** = cost due when logging onto a system *or* viewing special pages on a bulletin board **Zugriffsgebühr; access code** = series of characters *or* symbols that must be entered to identify a user before access to a computer is permitted **Zugriffscode;** *see also* PASSWORD; **access hole** = opening in both sides of a floppy disk's casing allowing the read-write head to be positioned over the disk's surface **Zugriffsöffnung; access level** = various predefined access categories; the lowest access level might allow the user to only view data, the highest access level allows a user to do anything **Zugriffsebene; access line** = permanently connected communications line between a terminal and a computer **Anschlussleitung; access mechanism** = mechanical device that moves an access arm over the surface of a disk **Zugriffsmechanismus; access method** = means used for the internal transfer of data between memory and display *or* peripheral devices (differences in the methods used is often the cause of compatibility problems) **Zugriffsmethode; access method routines** = software routines that move data between main storage and an output device **Zugriffsroutinen; access name** = unique name that identifies an object in a database **Zugriffsbezeichnung; access path** =

description of the location of a stored file within a directory structure of a disk **Zugriffspfad; access path journalling** = recording changes to an access path in case of malfunction **Aufzeichnen des Zugriffspfads; access period** = period of time during which a user can access data **Zugriffszeitraum; access permission** = description of all the access rights for a particular user **Zugriffsberechtigung; access point** = test point on a circuit board *or* in software, allowing an engineer to check signals *or* data **Zugangspunkt; access privilege** = status granted to a user that allows them to see or read or alter files **Zugriffsprivileg; access rights** = permission for a particular user to access a particular file or data object **Zugriffsrechte; access unit** = (in Token-Ring networks) wiring concentrator **Zugriffseinheit; direct access storage device (DASD)** = storage medium whose memory locations can be directly read *or* written to **Direktzugriffsspeicher; direct memory access (DMA)** = direct, rapid link between a peripheral and a computer's main memory which avoids the use of accessing routines for each item of data required **direkter Speicherzugriff; disk access** = operations required to read from or write to a magnetic disk, including device selection, sector and track address, movement of read/write head to the correct location and access the location on disk **Plattenzugriff; disk access management** = regulating the users who can access stored data **Plattenzugriffsverwaltung; instantaneous access** = storage that has virtually no access time delay, such as access to RAM **unmittelbarer Zugriff;** *the instantaneous access of the RAM disk was welcome;* **parallel access** = data transfer between two devices with a number of bits (usually one byte wide) being sent simultaneously **paralleler Zugriff; public access terminal** = terminal which can be used by anyone to access a computer **Datenstation mit allgemeiner Zugriffsberechtigung; random access** = ability to access immediately memory locations in any order **wahlfreier Zugriff; sequential access** = method of retrieving data from a storage device by starting at the beginning of the medium (such as tape) and reading each record until the required data is found **sequenzieller Zugriff; serial access** = one item of data accessed by reading through all the data in a list until the correct one is found **serieller Zugriff**

2 *verb* to call up (data) which is stored in a computer; to obtain data from a storage

device **zugreifen auf**; *she accessed the employee's file stored on the computer*

◊ **access control** *noun* security device (such as a password) that only allows selected users to use a computer system *or* read files **Zugriffskontrolle; access control byte** = (in Token-Ring network) byte following start marker in the token that indicates if the station can access the network **Zugriffskontrollbyte**

| COMMENT: a good access control system should allow valid users to gain access and operate the computer easily with the minimum of checks, whilst barring entry to hackers *or* unauthorized users

◊ **accessible** *adjective* which can be reached *or* accessed **zugänglich**; *details of customers are easily accessible from the main computer files*

◊ **access time** *noun* (a) total time which a storage device takes between the moment the data is requested and the data being returned **Zugriffszeit**; *the access time of this dynamic RAM chip is around 200nS we have faster versions if your system clock is running faster* (b) length of time required to find a file *or* program, either in main memory *or* a secondary memory source **Ansprechzeit**

accession number *noun* (i) number in a record that shows in which order each record was entered; (ii) serial number used in a library indexing system (i) **Annahmezahl; (ii) Signatur**

◊ **accessions** *plural noun* new books which are added to a library **Neuerwerbungen**

accessor *noun* person who accesses data **Datenbenutzer, Zugriffsberechtigter**

accessory *noun* useful device which is attached to *or* used with another **Zubehör(teil)**; *the printer comes with several accessories, such as a soundproof hood; this popular home computer has a large range of accessories*

accidental *adjective* which happens by accident **zufällig**; *always keep backup copies in case of accidental damage to the master file*

accordion fold *or* **fanfold** *noun* method of folding continuous paper, one sheet in one direction, the next sheet in the opposite direction, allowing the paper to be fed into

a printer continuously with no action on the part of the user **Zickzackfaltung**

account
1 *noun* (in a network or online system) record of a user's name, password and rights to access a network or online system **Benutzerprofil;** *if you are a new user, you will have to ask the supervisor to create an account for you;* **account name** = unique name of a user on a network or online system **Benutzername;** *John Smith's account name is JSMITH*
2 *verb* to keep track of how much time and resources each user of a network or online system uses **verwalten**

accounting *or* **accounts package** *noun* software that automates a business's accounting functions **Finanzbuchhaltungsprogramm;** *we now type in each transaction into the new accounting package rather than write it into a ledger*

accumulate *verb* to gather several things together over a period of time **summieren, aufrechnen, anhäufen;** *we have gradually accumulated a large databank of names and addresses*

◊ **accumulator** *or* **ACC (register)** *noun* most important internal CPU storage register, containing the data word that is to be processed **Akkumulator(register);** *store the two bytes of data in registers A and B and execute the add instruction - the answer will be in the accumulator;* **accumulator address** = address accessed by an instruction held in the accumulator **Akkumulatoradresse; accumulator shift instruction** = command to shift the contents of an accumulator left *or* right by one bit **Befehl zur Stellenverschiebung im Akkumulator**

accuracy *noun* total number of bits used to define a number in a computer, the more bits allocated, the more accurate the definition **Genauigkeit;** **accuracy control character** = code that indicates whether data is accurate or whether the data should be disregarded by a particular device **Genauigkeitsprüfzeichen**

accurate *adjective* correct; without any errors **genau, akkurat;** *the printed bar code has to be accurate to within a thousandth of a micron*

◊ **accurately** *adverb* correctly *or* with no errors **genau, akkurat;** *the OCR had difficulty in reading the new font accurately; the error was caused because the data had not been accurately keyed*

COMMENT: most high level languages allow numbers to be represented in a more accurate form by using two or more words to store the number

ACD = AUTOMATIC CALL DISTRIBUTION specialised telephone system that can handle lots of incoming calls and direct them to a particular operator according to programmed instructions in a database **ACD-System**

ACDI = ASYNCHRONOUS COMMUNICATIONS DEVICE INTERFACE

acetate *noun* sheet of transparent plastic used for making overlays **Azetat;** *the graphs were plotted on acetate, for use on an overhead projector*

ACF = ADVANCED COMMUNICATIONS FUNCTION

achieve *verb* to succeed in doing something **leisten, erreichen;** *the hardware designers are trying to achieve compatibility between all the components of the system*

achromatic *adjective* (an optical device) that has been corrected for chromatic aberration **achromatisch; achromatic colour** = (grey) colour within the range between black and white displayed by a graphics adapter **achromatische Farbe**

ACIA = ASYNCHRONOUS COMMUNICATIONS INTERFACE ADAPTER circuit that allows a computer to transmit and receive serial data using asynchronous access **asynchroner Kommunikationsschnittstellenanschluss**

ACK = ACKNOWLEDGE; *the printer generates an ACK signal when it has received data*

Ackerman's function *noun* recursive function used to test the ability of a compiler to cope with recursion **Ackermann-Funktion**

acknowledge
1 *noun* signal that is sent from a receiver to indicate that a transmitted message has been received and that it is ready for the next one **positive Rückmeldung**
2 *verb* (i) to tell a sender that a message *or* letter has been received; (ii) to send a signal from a receiver to show that a transmitted message has been received (i) & (ii) **bestätigen; acknowledge character** = special code sent by a receiver to indicate to the transmitter that the message has been correctly received **Quittungszeichen**

◊ **acknowledged mail** *noun* function that signals to the sender when an electronic mail message has been read by the recipient **bestätigte Post**

◊ **acknowledgements** *noun* text printed at the beginning of a book, where the author *or* publisher thanks people who have helped **Danksagung, Anerkennung**

ACM = ASSOCIATION OF COMPUTING MACHINERY

acoustic *adjective* referring to sound **akustisch; acoustic delay line** = original data storage method that delays data (in the form of sound pulses) as it travels across a medium **akustische Verzögerungsleitung; acoustic hood** = soundproof hood placed over a printer to reduce the noise **Schallschluckhaube;** *the acoustic hood allows us to speak and print in the same room;* **acoustic panel** = sound-proofed panel placed behind a device to reduce noise **Schalldämpfkonsole; acoustic store** *or* **acoustic memory** = (old) regenerative memory that uses an acoustic delay line **akustischer Speicher**

◊ **acoustic coupler** *noun* device that connects to a telephone handset, converting binary computer data into sound signals to allow data to be transmitted down a telephone line **Akustikkoppler;** *I use an acoustic coupler with my lap-top computer*

COMMENT: the acoustic coupler also converts back from sound signals to digital signals when receiving messages; it is basically the same as a modem but uses a loudspeaker on which a handset is placed to send the signals rather than direct connection to the phone line. It is portable, and clips over both ends of a normal telephone handset; it can be used even in a public phone booth

◊ **acoustical feedback** *noun* distortion in an audio signal, due to a part of an amplified signal being picked up by the microphone and amplified again until the amplifier is overloaded **akustische Rückmeldung**

◊ **acoustics** *noun* study and science of sound waves **Akustik**

acquisition *noun* accepting *or* capturing *or* collecting information **Erwerb; data acquisition** = gathering data about a subject **Datenerfassung**

ACR = AUDIO CASSETTE RECORDER; **ACR interface** = interface which allows a cassette recorder to be linked to a computer **Schnittstelle zu einem Kassettenrekorder**

Acrobat *noun* file format (developed by Adobe Systems) that describes a graphics image and allows the image to be displayed on different hardware **Acrobat**

acronym *noun* abbreviation, formed from various letters, which makes up a word which can be pronounced **Akronym;** *the acronym FORTRAN means Formula Translator; the acronym RAM means Random Access Memory*

actinic light *noun* light which is able to cause chemical change in a material, such as film **aktinisches Licht**

action *noun*
(a) something which has been done **Tat, Aktion;** *action has been taken to repair the fault;* **to take action** = to do something **Schritte unternehmen, etwas tun**
(b) (in SAA CUA front-end) user event, such as pressing a special key, that moves the cursor to the action bar at the top of the screen **Aktion; action bar** = (in SAA CUA front-end) top line of the screen that displays the menu names **Aktionsleiste, Menüleiste; action bar pull-down** = (in SAA CUA front-end) when a user moves the cursor to a particular menu name on the action bar, the full menu is displayed below the menu name **Aktionsfenster, Menüfenster; action code** = (in SAA CUA front-end) single letter associated with a particular menu option to speed up selection; when the letter action code is pressed, the menu option is selected **Aktionscode; action cycle** = complete set of actions involved in one operation (including reading data, processing, storing results, etc.) **Aktionszyklus; action list** = (in SAA CUA front-end) list of choices **Aktionsliste; action message** = prompt given to inform the user that an action *or* input is required **Aktionsnachricht; action object** = (in SAA CUA front-end) object to which a user specifies an action should be applied **Aktionsobjekt**
(c) movement **Aktion, Bewegung; action field** = area to be photographed by a camera **Aktionsfeld; action frame** = camera field of view where the filmed action is taking place **Aktionsrahmen; action shot** = still photograph showing action taking place (such as a person running) **Schnappschuss**

◊ **activate** *verb* to start a process *or* to make a device start working **aktivieren, einschalten;** *pressing CR activates the printer*

◊ **active** *adjective* busy *or* working *or* being used **aktiv, wirksam; active application** = (in a multitasking operating system) application currently being used by a user **aktive Anwendung; active area** = (i) (in a spreadsheet program) the area that contains data bounded by the top left hand corner and the bottom right hand cell; (ii) (in a graphical window) an area that will start or select a function if the user moves the pointer into it with a mouse (i) & (ii) **aktiver Bereich; active cell** = spreadsheet cell which is currently selected with a cursor or pointer **aktiviertes Tabellenfeld; active code page** = code page currently in use by the system **aktive Codeseite; active database** = database file currently being accessed by a database management program **aktive Datenbank; active device** = electronic component that requires electrical power to operate and provides gain *or* a logical function **Aktivvorrichtung;** *compare with* PASSIVE DEVICE; **active file** = file which is being worked on **aktive Datei; active gateway** = (in a network) gateway that exchanges routing information, unlike a passive gateway **aktiver Gateway; active high** = electronic signal that is valid when it is high *or* logical one *or* at five volts **Positivsignal; active hub** = hub that selectively directs packets of data according to their address *or* content **aktiver Hub; active line** = line in a communications link *or* port that is being used to transfer data or carry control signals **aktive Leitung; active link** = link currently being used to transfer information **aktive Verbindungsstrecke; active low** = electronic signal that is valid when it is low *or* logical zero *or* at zero volts **Negativsignal; active node** = node on a network connected to *or* available to connect to another node **aktiver Knoten; active printer** = printer that is currently connected to the computer's printer port **aktiver Drucker; active program** = (in a multitasking system) program that is currently in control of the processor **aktives Programm; active record** = record that is being updated or accessed **aktiver Datensatz; active star** = network consisting of a central point with nodes branching out, in which a central processor controls and routes all messages between devices **sternförmiges Netzwerk; active state** = electronic state in which an action occurs **aktiver Status; active storage** = main storage, fast access RAM whose locations can be directly and immediately addressed by the CPU **aktiver Speicher; active window** = (i) area of display screen in which you are currently working; (ii) (in a GUI or SAA CUA front-end), the window that is currently the focus of cursor movements and screen displays **(i) & (ii) aktives Fenster;** see also WINDOW

◊ **activity** noun
(a) being active or busy **Tätigkeit, Aktivität; activity level** = maximum number of jobs that can run in a multitasking system **Auslastungsgrad; activity light** = small light or LED on the front of a disk drive or computer that indicates when the disk drive is reading or writing data to disk **Kontrollleuchte; activity loading** = method of organizing disk contents so that the most often accessed files or programs can be loaded quickly **LRU-(Speicher)methode; activity ratio** = number of files currently in use compared to the total stored **Bewegungshäufigkeit; activity trail** = record of activities carried out **Aktivitätenprotokoll** (b) activities = jobs or tasks which are being performed on a computer **Tätigkeiten, Bewegungen**

actual address or **absolute address** noun computer storage address that directly, without any modification, accesses a location or device **absolute Adresse, tatsächliche Adresse;** compare with INDEXED ADDRESS; **actual code** = binary code which directly operates the central processing unit, using only absolute addresses and values (this is the final form of a program after a compiler or assembler pass) **absoluter Code; actual data transfer rate** = average number of data bits transferred in a period of time **tatsächliche Datenübertragungsrate; actual instruction** = the resulting instruction executed after the modification of an original instruction **endgültiger Maschinenbefehl**

actuator noun mechanical device that can be controlled by an external signal (such as the read/write head in a disk drive) **Bestätigungsschaltstück**

ACU = AUTOMATIC CALLING UNIT device which allows a computer to call stations or dial telephone numbers automatically **automatische Anrufeinrichtung**

acuity noun
(a) ability of the eye to define between shades and shapes of an object **(Seh)schärfe**
(b) ability of the ear to detect frequency or volume changes **(Hör)schärfe**

acutance noun ability of a lens to produce clear edges **Randschärfe**

acute adjective
(a) very sharp or clear **scharf, spitz**
(b) **acute accent** = accent above a character, which slopes upwards to the right **Akut**

AD = ASSISTANT DIRECTOR, ASSOCIATE DIRECTOR

A/D or **A to D** = ANALOG TO DIGITAL; see ANALOG, A to D

ADA noun high-level programming language that is used mainly in military, industrial and scientific fields of computing **ADA (Programmiersprache)**

adapt verb to change to fit **anpassen;** can this computer be adapted to take 5.25 inch disks?

◊ **adaptation** noun ability of a device to adjust its sensitivity range according to various situations **Anpassungsfähigkeit;** the adaptation of the eye to respond to different levels of brightness

◊ **adapter** or **adaptor** noun device that allows two or more incompatible devices to be connected together **Adapter;** the cable adapter allows attachment of the scanner to the SCSI interface; the cable to connect the scanner to the adapter is included in the package; **adapter card** = add-on interface board that allows incompatible devices to communicate **Anschlusskarte; adapter plug** = plug which allows devices with different plugs (two-pin, three-pin, etc.) to be fitted into the same socket **Zwischenstecker; adapter unit** = device that interfaces a CPU to one or more communications channels **Datenadapter, Ferndatensteuereinheit; graphics adapter** = electronic device (normally on an expansion card) in a computer that provides converts software commands into electrical signals that display graphics on a connected monitor **Grafikadapter;** the new graphics adapter is capable of displaying higher resolution graphics; see also CGA, EGA, VGA; **network adapter** = add-in board that connects a computer to a network; the board converts the computer's data into electrical signals that are then transmitted along the network cable **Netzwerkadapter**

◊ **adaptive channel allocation** *noun* providing communications channels according to demand rather than a fixed allocation **adaptive Kanalzuordnung; adaptive differential pulse code modulation (ADPCM)** = CCITT standard that defines a method of converting a voice or analog signal into a compressed digital signal **adaptive differenzielle Pulscodemodulation (ADPCM); adaptive packet assembly** = method used by the MNP error correcting protocol to adjust the size of data packets according to the quality of the telephone line (the better the line, the bigger the packet size) **adaptive Paketierung; adaptive routing** = ability of a system to change its communications routes according to various events *or* situations such as line failure **adaptiver Leitweg; adaptive systems** = ability of a system to alter its responses and processes according to inputs *or* events *or* situations **anpassungsfähige Systeme**

adaptor *see* ADAPTER

ADC *noun* = ANALOG TO DIGITAL CONVERTER device used to convert analog input to a digital output form, that can be understood by a computer **Analog-Digital-Umsetzer**

add *verb*
(a) to put figures together to make a total **addieren, hinzufügen;** *in the spreadsheet each column should be added to make a subtotal;* **add register** = register which is an adder **Additionsregister; add time** = period of time taken to perform one addition operation (either of a CPU *or* adder) **Additionszeit**
(b) to put things together to form a larger group **zusammenfügen;** *the software house has added a new management package to its range of products; adding or deleting material from the text is easy using function keys*

◊ **added entry** *noun* secondary file entry in a library catalogue **zusätzlicher/sekundärer Eintrag**

◊ **addend** *noun* number added to the augend in an addition **Summand**

◊ **adder** *noun* device *or* routine that provides the sum of two *or* more (digital *or* analog) inputs **Addiereinrichtung; adder-subtractor** = device that can either add or subtract **Addier-/Subtrahiereinrichtung; full adder** *or* **three input adder** = binary addition circuit which can produce the sum of two inputs, and can also accept a carry input, producing a carry output if necessary **Volladdierer; half adder** *or* **two input adder** = binary addition circuit which can produce the sum of two inputs and a carry output if necessary, but will not accept a carry input **Halbaddierer; parallel adder** = a number of full adders arranged in parallel to add two words at once **Paralleladdierer; serial adder** = one bit full adder used to add two words one bit at a time **Serienaddierer**

| COMMENT: a parallel adder takes one clock cycle to add two words, a serial adder takes a time equal to the number of bits in a word

◊ **add-in** *noun & adjective* (something) which is added **Zusatz; Zusatz-;** *the first method is to use a page description language, the second is to use an add-in processor card; can you explain the add-in card method? processing is much faster with add-in cards*

◊ **addition** *noun & adjective* arithmetic operation that produces the sum of an addend and augend **Addition; zusätzlich, Zusatz-, zusatz-; addition record** = record with changes used to update a master record *or* file **Zusatzdatensatz; addition time** = time an adder takes to carry out an add operation **Additionszeit; addition without carry** = addition operation without any carry bits *or* words **Addition ohne Übertrag;** *same as* EXOR FUNCTION; **destructive addition** = addition operation in which the result is stored in the location of one of the operands used in the sum, so overwriting it **löschende Addition**

◊ **additional** *adjective* which is added *or* which is extra **zusätzlich;** *can we add three additional workstations to the network?*

◊ **additive colour mixing** *noun* mixing different coloured lights to produce the colour which is wanted **additives Farbmischen**

◊ **add-on** *noun & adjective* piece of software *or* hardware that is added to a computer system to improve its performance **Zusatz; Zusatz-;** *the add-on hard disk will boost the computer's storage capabilities; the new add-on board allows colour graphics to be displayed* (NOTE: the opposite is **built-in**)

address
1 *noun*
(a) details of number, street and town where an office is or a person lives **Adresse;** *my business address and phone number are printed on the card;* **cable address** = short address for sending cables **Telegrammadresse; home address** = address

of a house or flat where someone lives Privatadresse; *please send the documents to my home address;* address list = list of addresses Adressenliste; *we keep an address list of two thousand businesses in Europe* (b) number allowing a central processing unit to reference a physical location in a storage medium in a computer system Adresse; *each separate memory word has its own unique address; this is the address at which the data starts;* address access time = total time which a storage device takes between the moment the data is requested and the data being returned Adressenzugriffszeit; address base = part of an address that defines the origin to which the logical address is added Adressbasis; address book = (i) (in a network) list of node addresses; (ii) (in electronic mail) list of the network addresses of other users to which electronic mail can be sent (i) & (ii) Adressbuch; address bus = physical connection that carries the address data in parallel form from the central processing unit to external devices Adressbus; address code = special code that identifies the part of a document that is an address (i) & (ii) Adressierungscode; address computation = operation on address data (in an instruction) Adressrechnung; address decoder = logical circuit that will produce a signal when a certain address or range is placed on the address bus Adressendecodierer; address field or operand field = (i) (in networks) part of a packet that contains the address of the destination node; (ii) (in programming) part of a computer instruction that contains the location of the operand (i) & (ii) Adressfeld or Operandenfeld; address format = rules defining the way the operands, data and addresses are arranged in an instruction Adressformat; address mapping = virtual address translated to an absolute real address Adressabbild; address mark = special code on a disk that indicates the start of sector location data Adressmarke; address modification = changing the address field, so that it can refer to a different location Adressänderung, Adressmodifikation; address register = register in a computer that is used to store all the bits that make up an address which can then be processed as a single unit (in small micros, the address register is usually made up of two data bytes) Adressenregister; *see also* MAR; address resolution protocol (ARP) = protocol used within the TCP/IP standard to link one IP address to a low-level physical address Adressauflösungsprotokoll; *see also* TCP/IP;

address space = total number of possible locations that can be directly addressed by the program or CPU Adressraum; address strobe = signal (pulse) that indicates that a valid address is on the address bus Adressimpulseingang; address track = track on a magnetic disk containing the addresses of files, etc., stored on other tracks Adressenspur; address translation = an address produced by calculating an expression Adressumsetzung; address word = computer word, usually made up, in a small micro, of two data words that contain the address data Adresswort; absolute address or actual address or direct address = (i) computer storage address (within a CPU's address range) that directly, without any modification, accesses a location or device; (ii) computer storage address that can only access one location (i) & (ii) absolute Adresse; base address = initial address in a program used as a reference for others Grund-, Bezugs-, Basisadresse; destination address = address of the node to which data is being transferred or sent Zieladresse; initial address = address at which the first location of a program is stored Anfangsadresse; machine address = storage address that directly, without any modification, accesses a location or device Maschinenadresse, absolute Adresse; network address = unique number that identifies each device on a network Netzwerkadresse; relative address = location specified in relation to a reference (address) relative Adresse

2 *verb*
(a) to write the details of an address on an envelope, etc. adressieren; *to address a letter or a parcel; please address your reply to the manager; a letter addressed to the managing director; an incorrectly addressed package* (b) to put the location data onto an address bus to identify which word in memory or storage device is to be accessed adressieren; *a larger address word increases the amount of memory a computer can address*

QUOTE the world's largest open data network, the Internet, links more than 10,000 local networks and 3 million workstations in 50 countries. It has grown so fast that its address space is 'bust' and is being redesigned to allow further expansion

Computing

◊ **addressability** *noun* the control available over pixels on screen Adressierbarkeit

◊ **addressable** *adjective* adressierbar;

with the new operating system, all of the 5MB of installed RAM is addressable; **addressable cursor** = cursor which can be programmed to be placed in a certain position **adressierbarer Positionsanzeiger; addressable point** = any point *or* pixel in a graphics system that can be directly addressed **adressierbarer Punkt; addressable terminal** = terminal that will only accept data if it has the correct address and identification number in the message header **adressierbare Datenstation, adressierbarer Terminal**

◊ **addressee** *noun* person to whom a letter *or* package *or* communication is addressed **Adressat/-in, Empfänger/-in**

◊ **addressing** *noun* process of accessing a location in memory **Adressierung; abbreviated addressing** = use of a smaller address word than normal, which provides faster address decoding operations **Kurzadressierung; absolute addressing** = locating a data word stored in memory, by the use of its absolute address **absolute Adressierung; bit addressing** = selecting a register and examining one bit within it **Bitadressierung; deferred addressing** = indirect addressing where the location accessed contains the address of the operand to be processed **indirekte/ausgesetzte Adressierung; direct addressing** = method of addressing where the storage location address given in the instruction is the location to be used **direkte Adressierung; immediate addressing** = accessing data immediately because it is held in the address field itself **unmittelbare Adressierung; indexed addressing** = addressing mode, in which the storage location to be accessed is made up of a start (base) address and an offset (index) word, which is then added to it to give the address to be used **indizierte Adressierung; indirect addressing** = way of addressing data, where the first instruction refers to an address which contains a second address **indirekte Adressierung; addressing capacity** = largest location that a certain program *or* CPU can directly address, without special features (such as virtual memory *or* memory banks) **Adressierkapazität; addressing level** = zero-level: operand is the address part of the instruction; first-level: operand stored at the address of the instruction; second-level: operand stored at the address given in the in-struction **Adressierebene; addressing method** = manner in which a section of memory is located **Adressiermethode; addressing mode** = way in which a location

is addressed, either sequential, indexed, direct, etc **Adressierungsart**

◊ **addressing machine** *noun* machine which puts addresses on envelopes automatically **Adressiermaschine**

adjacent *adjective* which is near *or* next to something **benachbart, angrenzend;** *the address is stored adjacent to the customer name field;* **adjacent domains** = two domains linked by two adjacent nodes **Nachbarbereiche; adjacent nodes** = two nodes connected by a path that does not connect any other node **Nachbarknoten**

adjunct register *noun* 32-bit register in which the top 16 bits are used for control information and only the bottom 16 bits are available for use by a program **adjunktives Register**

adjust *verb* to change something to fit new conditions *or* so that it works better **einstellen, einrichten, justieren, abstimmen;** *you can adjust the brightness and contrast by turning a knob*

◊ **adjustment** *noun* slight change made to something so that it works better **Angleichung, Abstimmung;** *the brightness needs adjustment; I think the joystick needs adjustment as it sometimes gets stuck*

administrator *noun*
(a) individual who is responsible for looking after a network; responsibilities include installing, configuring and maintaining the network **Administrator, Verwalter**
(b) control *or* supervisor *or* executive software *or* person **Administrator, Verwalter; data administrator** = control section of a database management system **Datenverwalter**

Adobe ᵀᴹ software company that developed products including Acrobat, ATM, and PostScript **Adobe** ᵀᴹ

◊ **Adobe Type Manager** *or* **ATM** ᵀᴹ standard for describing scalable fonts - used with Apple System 7 and Microsoft Windows to provide fonts that can be scaled to almost any point size, and printed on almost any printer **Adobe Type Manager** *or* **ATM** ᵀᴹ; *see also* OUTLINE FONTS

ADP = AUTOMATIC DATA PROCESSING data processing done by a computer **automatische Datenverarbeitung**

ADPCM = ADAPTIVE DIFFERENTIAL

PULSE CODE MODULATION CCITT standard that defines a method of converting a voice or analog signal into a compressed digital signal **ADPCM**

advance verb to move forward; to make something move forward **vorwärts bewegen**; *the paper is advanced by turning this knob; advance the cursor two spaces along the line*
◊ **advanced** adjective more complicated or more difficult to learn **erweitert, fortgeschritten**; **advanced program to program communications (APPC)** = set of protocols that allows peer-to-peer communication between workstations connected to an SNA network; also known as LU 6.2 protocols **erweiterte Programm-zu-Programm-Verbindung (APPC)**; **advanced peer-to-peer networking (APPN)** = extension to SNA that routes information around a network and dynamically adjusts the route if part of the network is damaged **Advanced Peer-to-Peer Networking**; **advanced run-length limited (ARLL)** = method of storing data onto a hard disk that is faster and more efficient than RLL **Advanced Run-Length Limited (ARLL)**; **advanced version** = program with more complex features for use by an experienced user **erweiterte Version**

adventure game noun game played on a computer, where the user pretends to be a hero in an imaginary land and has to get through various dangerous situations, fight monsters, etc. **Abenteuerspiel**

advisory lock noun (in a multitasking system) lock placed on a region of a file by one process to prevent any other process accessing the same data **Sperrverhinderung**
◊ **advisory system** noun expert system that provides advice to a user **Beratungssystem**

aerial
1 noun device for receiving or sending radio transmissions by converting electromagnetic impulses into electrical signals and vice-versa **Antenne**; **aerial cable** = wire stretched between poles which acts as an aerial **Luftkabel**
2 adjective in the air **Luft-, luft-**; **aerial image** = a view from high above a scene **Luftbild, Luftansicht**

affect verb to touch or to influence or to change something **beeinflussen, sich auswirken auf**; *changes in voltage will affect the way the computer functions*

affiliate verb to connect or join with **angliedern**
◊ **affiliated** adjective connected with or owned by another company **angegliedert**; *one of our affiliated companies*

affirmative adjective meaning "yes" **bejahend, positiv, affirmativ**; **the answer was in the affirmative** = the answer was "yes" die **Antwort war positiv**; **affirmative acknowledgement** = acknowledge signal from the receiver that it has accepted the message and is ready for the next one **positive Rückmeldung**

AFIPS = AMERICAN FEDERATION OF INFORMATION PROCESSING SOCIETIES

AFNOR in France Association Française de Normalisation (the French standards organization) **französische Normenorganisation**

AFP = APPLETALK FILING PROTOCOL ™ protocol used to communicate between workstations and servers in a network of Apple Macintosh computers **AFP**

afterglow see PERSISTENCE

after-image noun copy of a block of data that has been modified **Nachabbild**

AGC = AUTOMATIC GAIN CONTROL electronic device that provides a constant amplitude output signal from a varying input signal by changing its gain **automatische Verstärkungsregelung**

agenda noun (i) list of things to be discussed at a meeting; (ii) list of tasks or appointments or activities that have to be carried out on a particular day (i) **Tagesordnung**; (ii) **Tagesordnung, Programm**; *the conference agenda or the agenda of the conference; after two hours we were still discussing the first item on the agenda the secretary put finance at the top of the agenda; the chairman wants two items removed from or taken off the agenda;* **agenda item** = topic on an agenda to be discussed **Tagesordnungspunkt, TOP**; **electronic agenda** = software that allows a user to record appointments for each day **elektronischer Terminplaner**

agent noun
(a) program or software that runs on a workstation in a network; the software sends performance and statistical

information about the workstation to a central network management console **Agent**

(b) series of commands or actions that are carried out automatically on a particular file or data **Agent**

aggregate *noun* collection of data objects **Aggregat; data aggregate** = collection of items of data that are related **Datenverbund; aggregate bandwidth** = total bandwidth of a channel carrying a multiplexed data stream **aggregierte Bandbreite; aggregate function** = mathematical database function performed on a selected field in every record in a selected database **Datenverbundfunktion; aggregate line speed** = maximum speed at which data can be transmitted through a particular channel **kumulative Übertragungsgeschwindigkeit; aggregate operator** = command in a database management program that starts an aggregate function **Datenverbundoperator**

AI = ARTIFICIAL INTELLIGENCE the design and development of computer programs that attempt to imitate human intelligence and decision-making functions, providing basic reasoning and other human characteristics **künstliche Intelligenz;** *see also* EXPERT SYSTEM, IKBS

A & I = ABSTRACTING AND INDEXING making summaries and indexes for articles and books **Anfertigen von Kurzfassungen und Registern**

aid
1 *noun* help **Hilfe, Unterstützung;** *the computer is a great aid to rapid processing of large amounts of information;* **diagnostic aid** = hardware *or* software device that helps find faults **Diagnostikhilfe**
2 *verb* to help **helfen, unterstützen;** *industrial design is aided by computers; see also* COMPUTER-AIDED

aiming symbol *or* **field** *noun* symbol displayed on screen which defines the area in which a light-pen can be detected **Zielsymbol**

airbrush *noun* (in graphics software) a painting tool that creates a diffuse pattern of dots, like an mechanical airbrush **Sprühdose;** *we used the airbrush tool to create the cloud effects in this image*

air gap *noun* narrow gap between a

recording *or* playback head and the magnetic medium **Luftspalt**

◊ **air circuit breaker** *noun* mechanical device that has an electrical *or* manual switched circuit isolator **Luftschalter**

AIX ™ = ADVANCED INTERACTIVE EXECUTIVE version of UNIX produced by IBM to run on its range of PCs, minicomputers and mainframes **AIX** ™

alarm *noun* ringing or other sound which warns of a danger **Warnsignal, Fehlersignalisierung;** *all staff must leave the building if the alarm sounds; an alarm rings when the printer has run out of paper*

albumen plate *noun* photographic plate, with a light-sensitive coating **Albumin**

ALC = AUTOMATIC LEVEL CONTROL; *see* AGC

alert *noun* warning message sent from software to warn a person or application that an error or problem has occurred **Warnmeldung; alert box** = warning panel displayed on screen to warn a user about something **Warnfeld;** *the alert box warned me that I was about to delete all my files;* **alert condition** = status of a particular object *or* device that triggers an alarm **Alarmzustand; network alert** = message sent from the network operating system to the user warning that the network hardware is not working properly **Netzwerkalarm**

algebra *noun* use of letters in certain mathematical operations to represent unknown numbers *or* a range of possible numbers **Algebra; Boolean algebra** = rules set down to define, simplify and manipulate logical functions, based on statements that are true or false **boolesche Algebra**

◊ **algebraic language** *noun* context free language **algebraische Sprache**

ALGOL = ALGORITHMIC LANGUAGE high level programming language using algorithmic methods for mathematical and technical applications **algorithmische Programmiersprache**

algorithm *noun* rules used to define *or* perform a specific task *or* to solve a specific problem **Algorithmus**

◊ **algorithmic** *adjective* expressed using algorithms **algorithmisch; algorithmic language** = computer language designed to process and express algorithms, such as ALGOL **algorithmische Sprache**

QUOTE image processing algorithms are step by step procedures for performing image processing operations

Byte

QUOTE the steps are: acquiring a digitized image, developing an algorithm to process it, processing the image, modifying the algorithm until you are satisfied with the result

Byte

QUOTE the complex algorithms needed for geometrical calculations make heavy demands on the processor

PC Business World

alias *noun* representative name given to a file, port, device or spreadsheet cell or range of cells **Aliasname;** *the operating system uses the alias COM1 to represent the serial port address 3FCh;* **alias name** = (on a network) another name that is used instead of the user name **Aliasname**

◊ **aliasing** *noun* jagged edges that appear along diagonal or curved lines displayed on a computer screen caused by the size of each pixel **Aliasing; anti-aliasing** = (i) (in graphics) method of reducing the effects of jagged edges in graphics by using shades of grey to blend in along edges; (ii) (in sound) to add sound signals between the sound samples to create a smoother sound **(i) Konturenglättung, Antialiasing; (ii) Antialiasing**

alien *adjective* different *or* not fitting the usual system **fremd, anders; alien disk** = disk formatted on another system *or* containing data in a format which is in a form that cannot be read *or* understood **anders formatierte Diskette; alien disk reader** = add-on device which allows a computer to access data on disks from other computers *or* systems **Leser für anders formatierte Disketten;** *when you have an alien disk select the multi-disk option to allow you to turn the disk drive into an alien disk reader*

align *verb*
(a) (i) to make sure that the characters to be printed are spaced and levelled correctly, either vertically or horizontally; (ii) to arrange numbers into a column with all figures lined up against the right hand side (right-aligned) or the left-hand side (left-aligned) **(i) ausrichten; (ii) bündig ausrichten; align text** = (in a word-processor) to add spaces between words in a line to make sure that the line of text fills the whole line **spationieren;** *see also* JUSTIFY

(b) to ensure that a read/write head is correctly positioned over the recording medium **ausrichten**

◊ **aligner** *noun* device used to make sure that the paper is straight in a printer **Ausrichtungstransportbahn, Zeilen(ein)richter, Justierschiene**

◊ **aligning edge** *noun* edge of an optical character recognition system used to position a document **Führungskante**

◊ **alignment** *noun* correct spacing and levelling of printed characters **Ausrichtung; in alignment** = correctly aligned **richtig ausgerichtet; out of alignment** = not aligned correctly **nicht richtig ausgerichtet; alignment pin** = peg that fits in a hole to ensure that two devices are correctly aligned **Ausrichtungsnadel**

allocate *verb* to divide (a period of time *or* a piece of work) in various ways and share it out between users **zuteilen;** *the operating system allocated most of main memory to the spreadsheet program*

◊ **allocation** *noun* dividing memory *or* disk space *or* printer use *or* program *or* operating system time *or* device in various ways **Zuteilung;** *allocation of time or capital to a project;* **allocation routine** = short program that divides the memory resources of a system between the software and peripherals that use it **Zuteilungsroutine; allocation unit** = one or more sectors on a hard disk that are used to store a file or part of a file **Zuordnungseinheit; band allocation** = range of frequencies allocated to various users *or* for various purposes **Bandzuteilung;** *the new band allocation means we will have more channels;* **dynamic allocation** = system where resources are allocated during a program run, rather than being determined in advance **dynamische Zuteilung; memory allocation** = process in which an operating system provides an application with the memory it requires in order to run **Speicherzuordnung**

QUOTE IBM has issued a fix to correct bugs in the latest version of its OS/2 PC operating system which could cause screen crashes. The fix is meant to correct seven problems with OS/2 2.0, which began shipping just three months ago. They include problems with swapper files and DOS memory allocation

Computing

allophone *noun* smallest unit of sound from which speech can be formed **Allofon**

all points addressable (APA) mode *noun* graphics mode in which each pixel can be individually addressed and its colour and attributes defined **punktadressierbarer Modus (APA)**

ALPHA ™ *noun* processor chip developed by Digital Equipment Corporation; the ALPHA chip is a 64-bit RISC processor **ALPHA**

alpha *or* **alpha test** *noun* first working attempt of a computer product **Alphatest;** *the new software is still in an alpha product stage; see also* BETA TEST

◊ **alpha beta technique** *noun* (free structure) technique used in artificial intelligence for solving game and strategy problems **Alpha-Beta-Technik**

alphabet *noun* the 26 letters used to make words **Alphabet**

◊ **alphabetic character (set)** *noun* characters (capitals and small letters) that make up the alphabet **Buchstabe; alphabetic string** = string that only contains alphabetic characters **Buchstabenkette**

◊ **alphabetical order** *noun* arrangement of records (such as files, index cards) in the order of the letters of the alphabet (A,B,C,D, etc.) **alphabetische Reihenfolge**

◊ **alphabetically** *adverb* in alphabetical order **alphabetisch;** *the files are arranged alphabetically under the customer's name*

◊ **alphabetize** *verb* to put into alphabetical order **alphabetisch ordnen;** *enter the bibliographical information and alphabetize it*

alpha channel *noun* (in 32-bit graphics systems) the top eight bits that define the properties of a pixel; the lower 24 bits define the pixel's colour **Alphakanal**

alphageometric *adjective* (set of codes) that instruct a teletext terminal to display various graphics patterns *or* characters **alphageometrisch**

alphameric *(US)* = ALPHANUMERIC

alphamosaic *adjective* (character set) used in teletext to provide alphanumeric and graphics characters **Alphamosaik-, alphamosaik(-)**

alphanumeric *adjective* **alphanumeric characters** *or* **alphanumerics** = roman letters and arabic numerals (and other signs such as punctuation marks) **alphanumerische Zeichen; alphanumeric data** = data that represents the letters of the alphabet and the arabic numerals **alphanumerische Daten; alphanumeric display** = display device able to show characters as well as numbers **alphanumerische Anzeige; alphanumeric keyboard** = keyboard containing character keys as well as numerical keys **alphanumerische Tastatur; alphanumeric operand** = operand which can contain alphanumeric characters, such as a string **alphanumerischer Operand; alphanumeric string** = series of alphanumeric characters that are manipulated and treated as a single unit **alphanumerische Zeichenkette**

QUOTE geometrical data takes up more storage space than alphanumeric data
PC Business World

alpha particle *noun* emitted alpha radiation particle **Alphateilchen; alpha-particle sensitivity** = problem experienced by certain (MOS) memory devices exposed to alpha radiation, causing loss of stored charge (data) **Alphateilchenempfindlichkeit**

alphaphotographic *adjective* which represents pictures using predefined graphics characters, for teletext services **alphafotografisch**

alpha radiation *noun* naturally occurring radiation **Alphastrahlen**

alphasort *verb* to sort data into alphabetical order **alphabetisch ordnen**

alpha test *see* ALPHA

alpha wrap *noun* method used for feeding tape into a helical scan video recorder to make sure the alignment is correct **Alphawindung**

Alt key *noun* special key on a PC's keyboard used to activate special functions in an application **Alt-Taste;** *press Alt and P at the same time to print your document*

COMMENT: the Alt key has become the standard method of activating a menu bar in any software running on a PC; for example, Alt-F normally displays the File menu of a program, Alt-X normally exits the program

alter *verb* to change **ändern, abändern;** *to alter the terms of a contract; the program specifications have just been altered*

◊ **alterable** *adjective* which can be altered **veränderbar**; *see* EAPROM, EAROM

◊ **alteration** *noun* change which has been made **Änderung**; *the agreement was signed without any alterations; the new version of the software has many alterations and improvements*

alternate
1 *verb* to change from one state to another and back, over and over again **wechseln, alternieren**
2 *adjective* which change from one to another **abwechselnd, alternierend; alternate character set** = second set of special characters that can be accessed from a keyboard **alternativer Zeichensatz**; *we can print Greek characters by selecting the alternate character set*; **alternate key** = key in a database file that is not the primary key **Alternativschlüssel; alternate mode** = application for multi-user use, where two operators can access and share a single file at the same time **Ausweichmodus, Alternativmodus; alternate route** = backup path in a communications system, used in case of a fault *or* breakdown **Alternativweg, Ausweichleitweg**

◊ **alternately** *adverb* switching from one to the other **abwechselnd, alternierend**

◊ **alternating current** *or* **AC** *noun* electric current whose value varies with time in a regular, sinusoidal way (changing direction of flow each half cycle) **Wechselstrom**

◊ **alternation** *noun* logical function that produces a true output if any input is true **Wechsel**

◊ **alternator** *noun* device which produces an alternating current **Wechselstromgenerator, Lichtmaschine**

alternative
1 *noun* something which can be done instead of something else **Alternative**; *what is the alternative to re-keying all the data?*; **we have no alternative** = there is nothing else we can do **wir haben keine andere Wahl**
2 *adjective* other *or* which can take the place of something **alternativ; alternative denial** = logical function whose output is false if all inputs are true and true if any input is false **NAND-Funktion**

ALU = ARITHMETIC LOGIC UNIT; *see also* CPU

AM = AMPLITUDE MODULATION

A-MAC low bandwidth variation of MAC **A-MAC**

ambient *adjective* normal background (conditions) **umgebend, im Hintergrund; ambient noise level** = normal background noise level **Hintergrundgeräusch;** *the ambient noise level in the office is greater than in the library;* **ambient temperature** = normal average temperature of the air around a device **Umgebungstemperatur**

ambiguity *noun* something which is not clearly defined **Zwei-, Mehrdeutigkeit; ambiguity error** = error due to incorrect selection of ambiguous data **Fehler aufgrund von Uneindeutigkeit**

◊ **ambiguous** *adjective* which has two possible meanings **zweideutig, mehrdeutig, uneindeutig; ambiguous filename** = filename which is not unique to a single file, making it difficult to locate the file **uneindeutiger Dateiname**

ambisonics *noun* recording more than one audio signal to give the effect of being surrounded by sound **umgebender Schall**

amendment record *noun* record containing new information used to update a master record *or* file **Änderungssatz**

American National Standards Institute (ANSI) organization which specifies computer and software standards including those of high-level programming languages **amerikanische Organisation zur Erstellung von Industrienormen**

American Standard Code for Information Interchange (ASCII) code which represents alphanumeric characters as binary codes **ASCII-Code**

Amiga ™ range of personal computers developed by Commodore **Amiga ™**

COMMENT: Amiga computers are based on the Motorola 68000 range of CPUs and are not IBM PC compatible

AMM = ANALOG MULTIMETER multimeter that uses a graduated scale and a moving needle as a readout for voltage, current and impedance levels **Analogmultimeter**; *compare with* DMM

amount
1 *noun* quantity of data *or* paper, etc. **Menge**; *what is the largest amount of data which can be processed in one hour?*
2 *verb* **to amount to** = to make a total of **sich belaufen auf, betragen;** *the total keyboarded characters amount to ten million*

amp *or* **ampere (A)** *noun* base SI unit of electrical current; defined as the current flowing through an impedance of one ohm which has a voltage of one volt across it **Ampere** NOTE: used with figures: **a 13-amp fuse**

ampersand *noun* printing sign (&) which means "and" **Und-Zeichen (&)**

amplification *noun* the output-to-input signal strength ratio **Verstärkung;** *increase the amplification of the input signal; the amplification is so high, the signal is distorting*

◊ **amplifier** *noun* electronic circuit that magnifies the power of a signal **Verstärker; audio amplifier** = domestic amplifier that handles frequencies in the human hearing range **Tonverstärker; low noise amplifier** = high-quality amplifier placed very close to a receiving aerial to amplify the received signals before they are corrupted by noise **rauscharmer Verstärker; amplifier class** = way of classifying the design of amplifiers meant for different jobs **Verstärkerklasse**

◊ **amplify** *verb* to magnify a signal power *or* amplitude **verstärken;** *the received signal needs to be amplified before it can be processed;* **amplified telephone** = system to allow hands-off telephone conversations **lautverstärktes Telefon**

amplitude *noun* strength *or* size of a signal **Amplitude; amplitude distortion** = distortion of a signal due to uneven (non-linear) amplification (high levels amplified less than low) **Amplitudenverzerrung; amplitude modulation** = method of carrying data by varying the size of a carrier signal (of fixed frequency) according to the data **Amplitudenmodulation; amplitude quantization** = conversion of an analog signal to a numerical representation **(Amplituden-)Quantisierung**

analog *or* **analogue** *noun* representation and measurement of numerical data by continuously variable physical quantities, such as the size of electrical voltages **Entsprechung, Analog-;** *compare with* DIGITAL; **analog channel** = communications line that carries analog signals such as speech **Analogkanal; analog computer** = computer which processes data in analog form (that is, data which is represented by a continuously varying signal - as opposed to digital data) **Analogrechner; analog data** = data that is represented as a continuously variable

signal; speech is a form of analog data **Analogdaten; analog display** = display or monitor that can display an infinite range of colours or shades of grey (unlike digital displays that can only display a finite range of colours); VGA monitors are a form of analog display **Analoganzeige; analog gate** = logic gate whose output is proportional to an input signal **Analogschaltelement; analog input card** = all circuitry on one PCB required for amplifying and converting analog input signals to a digital form **analoge Eingabekarte; analog line** = communications line that carries analog signals, such as a telephone line **Analogleitung; analog loopback** = test mode on a modem used to test the serial port of the local computer or terminal **Analogschleife; analog loopback with selftest** = test mode on a modem used to test the serial port of the modem **Analogschleife mit Selbsttest; analog monitor** = display screen that uses a continuously variable input signal to control the colours display so it can display a near infinite range of colours **Analogbildschirm; analog multimeter** = multimeter that uses a graduated scale and a moving needle as a readout for voltage, current and impedance levels **Analogmultimeter;** *compare with* DMM; **analog output card** = all circuitry on one PCB required to convert digital output data from a computer to an analog form **analoge Ausgabekarte; analog recording** = storing signals in their natural form without conversion to digital form **Analogaufzeichnung; analog representation** = value *or* variable in analog form **Analogdarstellung; analog signal** = continuously varying signal **analoges Signal; analog transmission** = data transmission in which the data is sent as a series of changes in a continuously varying signal **analoge Übertragung; analog to digital (A to D** *or* **A/D)** = change a signal from an analog form to a digitally coded form **Analog-Digital-Umwandlung; analog to digital converter (ADC** *or* **A to D converter)** = device used to convert an analog input signal to a digital output form, that can be understood by a computer **Analog-Digital-Umsetzer; digital to analog converter (DAC** *or* **D to A converter)** = circuit that outputs an analog signal that is proportional to the input digital number, and so converts a digital input to an analog form **Digital-Analog-Umsetzer**

COMMENT: a DAC allows the computer to work outside the computer's environment, controlling machines, producing sound *or* speech, etc.; an ADC allows real-world signals to be processed by a computer

analyse or **analyze** verb to examine in detail analysieren, kritisch untersuchen; to analyse a computer printout; to analyse the market potential for a new computer

◊ **analysis** noun detailed examination and report Analyse, Untersuchung; market analysis; sales analysis; to carry out an analysis of the market potential; to write an analysis of the sales position; cost analysis = examination in advance of the costs of a new product Kostenanalyse; data analysis = to extract information and results from data Datenanalyse, Datenauswertung; systems analysis = analysing a process or system to see if it could be more efficiently carried out by computer Systemanalyse NOTE: plural is analyses

◊ **analyst** noun person who carries out an analysis of a problem Analytiker/-in; systems analyst = person who specializes in systems analysis Systemanalytiker

◊ **analyzer** noun electronic test equipment that displays various features of a signal Analysator; frequency analyzer = test equipment that displays the amplitudes of the various frequency components of a signal Frequenzanalysator

analytical engine noun mechanical calculating machine developed by Charles Babbage in 1833 that is generally considered the first general-purpose digital computer analytische Maschine

anamorphic image noun image which has been distorted in one direction Verzeichnung

ANAPROP = ANOMALOUS PROPAGATION distortion of transmitted television signals due to atmospheric conditions verzerrte Übertragung

anastigmat noun lens or optical device that has been corrected for astigmatism anastigmatische Linse

ancestral file noun system of backing up files (son to father to grandfather file), where the son is the current working file Dateivorfahre

anchor cell noun cell in a spreadsheet program that defines the start of a range of cells Ankerzelle

ancillary equipment noun equipment which is used to make a task easier, but which is not absolutely necessary Zusatzgeräte

AND or **coincidence function** noun logical function whose output is true if both its inputs are true UND-Funktion; AND or coincidence gate or circuit or element = electronic gate that performs a logical AND function on electrical signals UND-Schaltung; AND or coincidence operation = processing two or more input signals, outputting their AND function UND-Verknüpfung

COMMENT: if both inputs are 1, results of the AND will be 1 if one of the input digits is 0, then AND will produce a 0

anechoic adjective (room) that produces no echoes, used for testing audio equipment schalltot, echofrei

angle noun measure of the change in direction, usually as the distance turned from a reference line Winkel; wide-angle lens = lens which has a large acceptance angle Weitwinkelobjektiv

angstrom (Å) noun unit of measurement equal to one thousand millionth of a metre Ångström (Å)

ANI = AUTOMATIC NUMBER IDENTIFICATION telephone system which displays the telephone number of the caller ANI

animate verb to make a series of drawings which, when filmed, will create moving images beleben, (Film) animieren

◊ **animation** or **computer animation** noun creating the illusion of movement by displaying a series of slightly different images on screen; the images are displayed very rapidly to give the effect of smooth movement Animation

annotation noun comment or note in a program which explains how the program is to be used Bemerkung, Anmerkung; annotation symbol = symbol used when making flowcharts, to allow comments to be added Anmerkungszeichen

annunciator noun & adjective (signal) which can be heard or seen in order to attract attention Anzeige; Signal-

anode noun positive electrical terminal of a device Anode

NOTE: the opposite is **cathode**

anomalistic period *noun* time taken for a satellite to travel between consecutive maximum points in its orbit **anomalistischer Zeitraum**

ANSI *(US)* = AMERICAN NATIONAL STANDARDS INSTITUTE organization which specifies computer and software standards, including those of high-level programming languages **amerikanische Organisation zur Erstellung von Industrienormen;** ANSI C = standard version of the C programming language **ANSI C;** ANSI driver = (in a PC) small resident software program that interprets ANSI screen control codes and controls the screen appropriately **ANSI-Treiber;** ANSI escape sequence = sequence of ANSI screen control characters that controls the colours and attributes of text on screen; the sequence must begin with the ASCII character Esc (ASCII 27) and the character [(ASCII 91) **ANSI-Escapesequenz;** ANSI screen control = standard codes developed by ANSI that control how colours and simple graphics are displayed on a computer screen **ANSI-Bildschirmsteuerung**

answer
1 *noun* reply *or* letter *or* conversation coming after someone has written or spoken **Antwort;** *I am writing in answer to your letter of October 6th; my letter got no answer or there was no answer to my letter; I tried to phone his office but there was no answer* **2** *verb*
(a) to speak *or* write after someone has spoken or written to you **antworten; to answer a letter** = to write a letter in reply to a letter which you have received **einen Brief beantworten; to answer the telephone** = to lift the telephone when it rings and listen to what the caller is saying **das Telefon abnehmen**
(b) to reply to a signal and set up a communications link **beantworten;** *the first modem originates the call and the second answers it;* **answer back** = signal sent by the receiving end of a communications system to identify itself *or* to transmit a message **Antwort; answer mode** = mode of a modem that emits an answertone used to establish a connection with an originate modem **Antwortbetrieb; answer modem** = modem that is waiting to receive a telephone call and establish a connection **Antwortmodem;** *see also* MODEM; **answer time** = time taken for a receiving device to respond to a signal **Beantwortungszeit**

◊ **answering** *noun* **answering machine** = machine which answers the telephone automatically when someone is not in the office **automatischer Anrufbeantworter; answering service** = office which answers the telephone and takes messages for someone *or* for a company **Anrufbeantworterbüro**

◊ **answer/originate (device)** *noun* communications device, such as a modem, that can receive or send data **Empfangs-/Sendegerät**

◊ **answerphone** *noun* cassette recorder attached to a telephone, which plays a prerecorded message and records messages from people dialling the number **automatischer Anrufbeantworter**

◊ **answertone** *noun* tone an answering modem emits before the carrier is exchanged **Antwortton**

antenna *noun* aerial *or* device for receiving *or* sending radio transmissions by converting electromagnetic impulses into electrical signals and vice-versa **Antenne; antenna array** = series of small transmitting *or* receiving elements connected in parallel, that make up a complex antenna **Antennengruppierung; antenna gain** = transmitted signal power increase due to using a certain type of antenna **Antennenverstärkung**

anthropomorphic software *noun* (in artificial intelligence) software that appears to react to what a user says **anthropomorphe Software**

anti- *prefix* meaning against **anti-, gegen-, wider-; anti-aliasing** = method of reducing the effects of jagged edges in graphics by using shades of grey to blend in along edges **Konturenglättung, Antialiasing; anticoincidence circuit** *or* **function** = logical function whose output is true if either (of 2) inputs is true, and false if both inputs are the same **Antivalenzglied; anti-static mat** = special rubberised mat which dissipates static electricity charge through an electrical earth connection; an operator touches the mat before handling sensitive electronic components that could be damaged by static electricity **antistatische Unterlage; anti-tinkle suppression** = *(in a modem)* switch which prevents other telephones on a line ringing when a modem dials out **Unterdrückung des Telefonklingelns; anti-virus program** = software program that looks for virus software on a computer and destroys it before it can damage data or files **Antivirenprogramm, Virensuchprogramm, Virenscanner**

APA = ALL POINTS ADDRESSABLE

APD = AVALANCHE PHOTODIODE

aperture *noun* opening in a device that allows a certain amount of light *or* a signal to pass through it **Öffnung; aperture card** = method of storing microfilmed information with a card sur-round, that can contain punched information **Filmlochkarte; aperture illumination** = pattern generated from an aperture antenna **Aperturflächenausleuchtung; aperture mask** = mask used in colour televisions *or* monitors to keep the red, green and blue beams separate **Schattenmaske**

API = APPLICATION PROGRAMMING INTERFACE set of standard program functions and commands that allow any programmer to interface a program with another application **API**; *if I follow the published API for this system, my program will work properly*

APL = A PROGRAMMING LANGUAGE high-level programming language used in scientific and mathematical work **anwendungsorientierte Programmiersprache**

apochromatic lens *noun* optical lens that has been corrected for chromatic aberration **apochromatische Linse (gegen Farbabweichungen)**

apogee *noun* point in a satellite's orbit where it is at its maximum distance from the earth **Apogäum, erdfernster Punkt**

apostrophe *noun* printing sign ('), which generally indicates that a letter is missing *or* used in ('s), to indicate possession **Apostroph**

APPC = ADVANCED PROGRAM TO PROGRAM COMMUNICATION set of protocols that allows peer-to-peer communication between workstations connected to an SNA network; also known as LU 6.2 protocols **APPC**

append *verb* (i) to add data to an existing file *or* record; (ii) to add a file or data to the end of an existing file **(i) anhängen, anfügen,** ketten; (ii) anhängen; *if you enter the DOS command COPY A+B, the file B will be appended to the end of file A*

◊ **appendix** *noun* section at the back of a book, containing additional information **Anhang, Ergänzung;** *for further details see the appendices; a complete list is printed in the appendix* NOTE: plural is **appendices**

Apple Computer Corporation company (formed in 1975) which has developed a range of personal computers including the Apple II, Apple Lisa and, more recently, the Apple Macintosh **Apple Computer Corporation**

◊ **Apple-Desktop-Bus** *noun* serial bus built into Apple Macintosh computers that allows low-speed devices, such as the keyboard and mouse, to communicate with the processor **Apple-Desktop-Bus**

◊ **Apple file exchange** ™ *noun* software program that runs on an Apple Macintosh computer allowing it to read disks from a PC **Apple file exchange** ™

◊ **Apple filing protocol (AFP)** ™ *noun* method of storing files on a network server so that they can be accessed from an Apple Macintosh computer **Apple filing protocol (AFP)** ™

◊ **Apple Key/a/noun** special key on the keyboard of an Apple Macintosh that, when pressed with another key, provides a short-cut to a menu selection **Apple-Taste**

◊ **Apple Mac or Apple Macintosh** ™ **computer** *noun* range of personal computer developed by Apple Inc. that has a graphical user interface and uses the 68000 family of processors **Apple Mac oder Apple Macintosh** ™ **Computer**

◊ **Appleshare** ™ *noun* software that allows Apple Macintosh computers to share files and printers using a file server **Appleshare** ™

◊ **AppleTalk** ™ *noun* proprietary communications protocol developed by Apple Computer that carries data over network hardware between two or more Apple Macintosh computers and peripherals; similar to the seven-layer OSI protocol model; AppleTalk can link up to 32 devices, uses a CSMA/CA design and transmits data at 230Kbps **AppleTalk** ™; **AppleTalk Filing Protocol** ™ (AFP) = protocol used to communicate between workstations and servers in a network of Apple Macintosh computers **AppleTalk Filing Protocol** ™ (AFP)

QUOTE Apple Computer has fleshed out details of a migration path to the PowerPC RISC architecture for its 7 million Apple Macintosh users. Developments in the pipeline include PowerPC versions of the AppleTalk Remote Access networking protocol

Computing

applet *noun* (i) utility application program; (ii) (in Microsoft Windows) application started from the Control Panel **(i) Hilfsprogramm; (ii) Option (der Systemsteuerung);** *there are applets to help format your disk and configure your keyboard*

appliance *noun* machine, especially one used in the home **Gerät, Vorrichtung;** *all electrical appliances should be properly earthed*

◊ **appliance computer** *noun* ready to run computer system that can be bought in a shop, taken home and used immediately for a particular purpose **gebrauchsfertiger Computer;** *see also* TURNKEY

application *noun*
(a) asking for something, usually in writing **Antrag;** *application for an account on the system;* **application form** = form to be filled in when applying **Antragsformular;** *to fill in an application (form) for an account on the system*
(b) task which a computer performs *or* problem which a computer solves (as opposed to an operating system which is the way in which a computer works) **Anwendung; application developer** = programmer who designs the look of an application and defines its functions **Anwendungsentwickler; application file** = binary file stored on disk that contains the machine code instructions of a program **Programmdatei; application generator** = special software that allows a programmer to define the main functions and look of an application the generator then automatically creates the instructions to carry out the defined application **Anwendungsgenerator; application icon** = small image *or* graphical symbol that represents an application program in a graphical user interface stock control, tax, etc.) **Anwendungssymbol; application layer** = top layer in an ISO/OSI network, which requests a transmission (from a users program) **anwendungsbezogene Schicht; application orientated language** = programming language that provides

functions that allow the user to solve certain application problems **anwendungsbezogene Sprache; application package** = set of computer programs and manuals that cover all aspects of a particular task (such as payroll, stock control, tax, etc.) **Anwendungsprogrammpaket; application programming interface (API)** = set of standard program functions and commands that allow any programmer to interface a program with another application **Anwendungsprogrammierschnittstelle (API);** *if I follow the published API for this system, my program will work properly;* **application service element** = part of a program in the application layer of an OSI environment that interacts with the layers beneath it **Anwendungsdienstelement; application software** *or* **application program** = programs which are used by a user to make the computer do what is required, designed to allow a particular task to be performed **Anwendungsprogramm;** *the multi-window editor is used to create and edit applications programs;* **application specific integrated circuits (ASIC)** = specially designed ICs for one particular function *or* to special specifications **integrierte Schaltkreise für bestimmte Funktionen; application terminal** = terminal (such as at a sales desk) which is specially configured to carry out certain tasks **anwendungsorientierte Datenstation; application window** = application program running in a window displayed in a graphical user interface such as Microsoft's Windows **Anwendungsfenster;** *see also* GUI

QUOTE they have announced a fourth generation application development tool which allows users of PCs and PC networks to exchange data with mainframe databases

Minicomputer News

QUOTE how do users interact with a computer system? Via a terminal or PC. So what application layer OSI protocol do we need first? The Virtual Terminal. And what do we get? File Transfer Access and Maintenance

Computing

apply *verb*
(a) to ask for something, usually in writing **etwas beantragen, sich bewerben**
(b) to affect *or* to touch **betreffen;** *this formula applies only to data received after the interrupt signal*

APPN = ADVANCED PEER-TO-PEER

NETWORKING extension to SNA that routes information around a network and dynamically adjusts the route if part of the network is damaged **APPN**

appoint *verb* to choose someone for a job **einstellen, ernennen;** *to appoint James Smith (to the post of) manager; we have appointed a new computer services manager* NOTE: you appoint a person to a job

◊ **appointee** *noun* person who is appointed to a job **Ernannte(r)**

◊ **appointment** *noun*
(a) arrangement to meet **Termin, Verabredung;** *to make or; to fix an appointment for two o'clock; to make an appointment with someone for two o'clock; he was late for his appointment; she had to cancel her appointment;* **appointments book** = desk diary in which appointments are noted **Terminkalender**
(b) being appointed to a job **Ernennung; on his appointment as manager** = when he was made manager **bei seiner Ernennung zum Manager; letter of appointment** = letter in which someone is appointed to a job **Ernennungsschreiben**
(c) job **Stelle; staff appointment** = job on the staff **Anstellung; computer appointments vacant** = list (in a newspaper) of jobs which are available in the computer industry **freie Stellen in der Computerindustrie**

approval *noun*
(a) agreement that something can be used **Billigung, Zustimmung, Einverständnis;** *a BABT approval is needed for modems;* **certificate of approval** = document showing that an item has been approved officially **Anerkennungsurkunde, Genehmigungszertifikat**
(b) on approval = sale where the buyer only pays for goods if they are satisfactory **auf Probe, zur Ansicht;** *to buy a photocopier on approval*
NOTE: no plural

◊ **approve** *verb*
(a) to approve of = to think something is good **gutheißen, billigen;** *the new graphics monitor was approved by the safety council before being sold; I approve of the new editor - much easier to use*
(b) to agree to something **zustimmen;** *to approve the terms of a contract; the software has to be approved by the board; an approved modem should carry a label with a green circle and the words "Approved by ...."*

approximate *adjective* not exact, but almost correct **annähernd;** *we have made an*

approximate calculation of the time needed for keyboarding

◊ **approximately** *adverb* almost correctly **annähernd;** *processing time is approximately 10% lower than during the previous quarter*

◊ **approximating** *adjective* which is nearly correct **annähernd;** *using approximating A to D*

◊ **approximation** *noun* rough calculation **(An)näherung(swert);** *approximation of keyboarding time; the final figure is only an approximation;* **approximation error** = error caused by rounding off a real number **Näherungsfehler**

APT = AUTOMATICALLY PROGRAMMED TOOLS programming language used to control numerically controlled machines **Programmiersprache**

Arabic *adjective* **Arabic numbers** *or* **figures** = figures such as 1, 2, 3, 4, etc. (as opposed to the Roman numerals I, II, III. IV, etc.) **arabische Zahlen;** *the page numbers are written in Arabic figures*

arbitration *noun* **bus arbitration** = protocol and control of transmission over a bus that ensures fair usage by several users **Buszuteilung**

arcade game *noun* computer game played on a machine in a public place **öffentliches Computerspiel**

archetype *noun* document *or* book that illustrates the styles of a particular time and subject **Archetyp**

Archimedes *noun* personal computer developed by Acorn Computers; the Archimedes is based around a RISC central processor and is not compatible with either the IBM PC or Apple Macintosh **Archimedes**

architecture *noun* layout and interconnection of a computer's internal hardware and the logical relationships between CPU, memory and I/O devices **Aufbau, Architektur; onion skin architecture** = design of a computer system in layers, according to function *or* priority **Zwiebelschalenarchitektur;** *the onion skin architecture of this computer is made up of a kernel at the centre, an operating system, a* *low-level language and then the user's programs*

> QUOTE software giant Microsoft is also interested in using Xerox' Glyph technology as part of its Microsoft At Work architecture that seeks to unite office computers with fax machines and copiers
>
> *Computing*

archive

1 *noun* storage of data over a long period **Archiv; archive attribute** *or* **bit** *or* **flag** = special attribute attached to a file in DOS and OS/2 that indicates if the file has been archived since it was last changed **Archivbit;** *see also* ATTRIBUTE; **archive file** = file containing data which is out of date, but which is kept for future reference **Archivdatei**
2 *verb* to put data in storage **archivieren; archived copy** = copy kept in storage **Archivkopie**

◊ **archival quality** *noun* length of time that a copy can be stored before it becomes illegible **Archivierungsqualität**

> QUOTE on-line archiving is also used to keep down the interruption needed for archiving to seconds
>
> *Computer News*

ARCNET *or* **ARCnet** = ATTACHED RESOURCE COMPUTER NETWORK network hardware and cable standard **ARCNET** *or* **ARCnet**

> COMMENT: developed by Datapoint Corporation, ARCNET is a token bus network that transmits data at between 2.5 and 4Mbps; it uses a single token that moves from one workstation to the next carrying data, and uses a star-wired cable topology

area *noun*

(a) measurement of the space taken up by something (calculated by multiplying the length by the width) **Bereich;** *the area of this office is 3,400 square feet; we are looking for a shop with a sales area of about 100 square metres;* **type area** = space on a page which is taken up by printed characters **Satzspiegel; area composition** = organizing and setting up pages before photocomposition **Lay-out; area fill** = (in graphics) instruction to fill an area of the screen *or* an enclosed pattern with a colour *or* pattern **Bereichsfüllung; area graph** = line graph in which the area

below the line is filled with a pattern or colour **Fülldiagramm**
(b) section of memory *or* code that is reserved for a certain purpose **Speicherbereich; area search** = search for specific data within a certain section of memory *or* files **Bereichssuche; image area** = region of a display screen in which characters can be displayed **Bildbereich; input area** = section of main memory that holds data transferred from backing store until it is processed **Eingabebereich**
(c) part of a country *or* town **Gebiet;** *his sales area is the centre of the town; he finds it difficult to cover all his area in a week;* **area code** = part of a telephone number that allows the exchange to identify the part of the country required **Vorwahl;** *the area code for inner London is 0171;* **area exchange** = central point in a part of a country where telephone calls are directed to their correct destination inside the area *or* to another exchange **Telefonvermittlungsstelle**

◊ **area manager** *noun* manager who deals with a certain part of the country **Gebietsleiter**

arg *see* ARGUMENT

argue *verb* to discuss something about which you do not agree **diskutieren, argumentieren;** *they argued over or about the design of the cover; we spent hours arguing with the managing director about the layout of the new factory* NOTE: you argue **with** someone **about** *or* **over** something

◊ **argument** *or* **arg** *noun*
(a) discussing something without agreeing **Auseinandersetzung;** *they got into an argument with the customs officials over the documents; he was sacked after an argument with the managing director*
(b) variable acted upon by an operator *or* function **Parameter;** *if you enter the words 'MULTIPLY A, B', the processor will recognise the operator, MULTIPLY, and use it with the two arguments, A and B; see also* OPERAND; **argument separator** = punctuation mark or symbol that separates several arguments on one line **Argumenttrennzeichen;** *the command 'MULTIPLY A, B' uses a comma as the argument separator*

arithmetic *noun* concerned with mathematical functions such as addition, subtraction, division and multiplication **Arithmetik; arithmetic capability** = ability of a device to perform mathematical functions **arithmetische Fähigkeit; arithmetic**

check = further arithmetic operation carried out to ensure that a result is correct **Rechenprüfung; arithmetic functions** = calculations carried out on numbers, such as addition, subtraction, multiplication, division **arithmetische Funktionen; arithmetic instruction** = program instruction in which the operator defines the arithmetic operation to be carried out **Rechenbefehl;** compare with LOGICAL INSTRUCTION; **arithmetic logic unit (ALU)** or **arithmetic unit** = hardware section of a CPU that performs all the mathematical and logical functions **Rechenwerk im CPU; arithmetic operation** = mathematical function carried out on data **Rechenoperation; arithmetic operators** = symbol which indicates an arithmetic function (such as + for addition, x for multiplication) **Rechenzeichen; arithmetic register** = memory location which stores operands **Rechenregister; arithmetic shift** = word or data moved one bit to the left or right inside a register, losing the bit shifted off the end **arithmetische Stellenverschiebung;** compare with LOGICAL SHIFT; **external arithmetic** = arithmetic performed by a coprocessor **extern ausgeführte Rechnung; internal arithmetic** = arithmetic performed by the ALU **im Rechenwerk ausgeführte Rechnung**

arm
1 noun **access arm** = mechanical device in a disk drive used to position the read/write head over the correct track on a disk **(Platten)zugriffsarm**
2 verb (i) to prepare a device or machine or routine for action or inputs; (ii) to define which interrupt lines are active **(i) & (ii) vorbereiten; armed interrupt** = interrupt line which has been made active (using an interrupt mask) **absichtliche Unterbrechung**

ARP = ADDRESS RESOLUTION PROTOCOL protocol used within the TCP/IP standard to link one IP address to a low-level physical address **ARP;** see also TCP/IP

ARQ = AUTOMATIC REPEAT REQUEST error correction system used in some modems that asks for data to be retransmitted if it contains errors **ARQ**

array noun ordered structure containing individually accessible elements referenced by numbers, used to store tables or sets of related data **Anordnung, Feldgruppe; alphanumeric array** = array whose elements are letters and numbers **alphanumerische Feldgruppe; array bounds** = limits to the number of elements which can be stored in an array **Grenzen der Strukturgröße; array dimension** = number of elements in an array, given as rows and columns **Matrixdimension; array element** = one individual piece of data within an array **Matrixelement; array processor** = computer that can act upon several arrays of data simultaneously, for very fast mathematical applications **Vektorenrechner;** the array processor allows the array that contains the screen image to be rotated with one simple command; **string array** = array whose elements can be strings (of alphanumeric characters) **Anordnung einer Zeichenkette; three-dimensional array** = array made up of a number of two dimensional arrays, arranged in parallel, giving rows, columns and depth **dreidimensionale Matrix; two-dimensional array** = ordered structure whose elements are arranged as a table (of rows and columns **zweidimensionale Matrix**

arrow keys noun set of four keys on a keyboard that move the cursor or pointer around the screen; the four keys control movement up, down, left and right **Pfeiltasten**

arsenide see GALLIUM ARSENIDE

article noun
(a) section of a newspaper or magazine **Artikel;** he wrote an article about the user group for the local newspaper
(b) section of an agreement **Artikel, Paragraph;** see article 8 of the contract

artificial intelligence (AI) noun the design and device of computer programs that attempt to imitate human intelligence and decision making functions, providing basic reasoning and other human characteristics **künstliche Intelligenz**

artwork noun graphical work or images which are to be printed **Reprovorlage;** the artwork has been sent for filming
NOTE: no plural

ASA American Standards Association **ASA (amerikanische Normeninstitution); ASA exposure index** = one standard method used to code the sensitivity of film **Filmempfindlichkeitsangabe**

ascend verb to increase **zunehmen; ascending order** = to arrange data with the smallest value or date first in the list **aufsteigende Folge**

◊ **ascender** *noun* part of a character that rises above the main line of printed characters (as the 'tail' of a 'b', 'd', etc.) **Oberlänge**

ASCII = AMERICAN STANDARD CODE FOR INFORMATION INTERCHANGE code which represents alphanumeric characters in binary code **ASCII-Code;** ASCII **character** = character which is in the ASCII list of codes **ASCII-Zeichen;** ASCII **file** = stored file containing only ASCII coded character data **ASCII-Datei;** *use a word processor or other program that generates a standard ASCII file;* ASCII **keyboard** = keyboard which gives all the ASCII characters **ASCII-Tastatur;** ASCII **text** = letter and number characters with an ASCII code between 0 and 127 **ASCII-Text;** **ASCIIZ string** = (in programming) a sequence of ASCII characters followed by the ASCII code zero that indicates the end of the sequence **ASCIIZ-String;** *for full listing of ASCII codes see also* APPENDIX (NOTE: when speaking say 'as-key')

ASIC = APPLICATION SPECIFIC INTEGRATED CIRCUITS specially designed ICs for one particular function *or* to special specifications **integrierte Schaltkreise für bestimmte Funktionen**

aspect *noun* way in which something appears **Erscheinung, Aussehen, Aspekt;** **aspect card** = card containing information on documents in an information retrieval system **Aspektkarte; aspect ratio** = ratio of the width to the height of pixel shapes **Längen- und Seitenverhältnis; aspect system** = method of storing and indexing documents in a retrieval system **Aspektsystem**

ASR = AUTOMATIC SEND/RECEIVE device *or* terminal that can transmit *or* receive information **automatischer Sender/Empfänger;** *compare* KSR

| COMMENT: an ASR terminal can input information via a keyboard or via a tape cassette or paper tape. It can receive information and store it in internal memory or on tape

assemble *verb*
(a) to put a hardware *or* software product together from various smaller parts **zusammensetzen;** *the parts for the disk drive are made in Japan and assembled in France*
(b) to translate assembly code into machine code **assemblieren, umwandeln;** *there is a*

short wait during which time the program is assembled into object code; syntax errors spotted whilst the source program is being assembled
(c) to insert specific library routines *or* macros *or* parameters into a program **assemblieren**

◊ **assembler (program)** *noun* assembly program *or* program which converts a program written in assembly language into machine code **Assemblerprogramm; absolute assembler** = type of assembly language program designed to produce code which uses only absolute addresses and values **absoluter Assemblierer; assembler error messages** = messages produced by an assembler program that indicate that errors have been found in the source code **Assemblierer-Fehlermeldungen; cross-assembler** = assembler that produces machine-code code for one computer while running on another **Kreuzassemblierer; single-pass assembler** = object code produced in one run through the assembler of the source program **Assemblierer mit einem Durchlauf; two-pass assembler** = assembler that converts an assembly language program into machine code in two passes, the first pass stores symbolic addresses, the second converts them to absolute addresses **Assemblierer mit zwei Durchläufen**

◊ **assembly** *noun*
(a) putting an item together from various parts **Montage;** *there are no assembly instructions to show you how to put the computer together;* **assembly plant** = factory where units are put together from parts made in other factories **Montagewerk**
(b) converting a program into machine code **Umwandlung; assembly code** = mnemonics which are used to represent machine code instructions in an assembler program **Umwandlungscode; assembly language** *or* **assembler language** = programming language used to code information which will then be converted to machine code **Assembliersprache; assembly listing** = display of an assembly program ordered according to memory location **Assemblerliste; assembly (language) program** = number of assembly code instructions which perform a task **Assemblerprogramm; assembly routine** *or* **system** *see* ASSEMBLER; **assembly time** = (i) time taken by an assembler program to translate a program; (ii) period during which an assembler is converting a program from assembly language into machine code **(i) & (ii) Umwandlungszeit**

assertion *noun* (i) program statement of a fact *or* rule; (ii) fact that is true *or* defined as being true **(i) Behauptung; (ii) Beteuerung**

assign *verb*
(a) to give a computer *or* someone a job of work **anweisen**; *he was assigned the job of checking the sales figures; two PCs have been assigned to outputting the labels*
(b) (i) to set a variable equal to a string of characters *or* numbers; (ii) to reserve part of a computer system for use while a program is running **(i) zuordnen; (ii) freihalten; assigned frequency** = frequency reserved for one user *or* application **zugeordnete Frequenz**

◊ **assignment** *noun*
(a) transfer of a property *or* of a right **Übertragung, Übereignung, Abtretung;** *assignment of a copyright*
(b) particular job of work **Aufgabe;** *he was appointed managing director with the assignment to improve the company's profits; the oil team is on an assignment in the North Sea*
(c) setting a variable equal to a string of characters *or* a value **Zuordnung; assignment compatible** = (in the Pascal programming language) check to see if a value is allowed according to its type **zuordnungskompatibel; assignment conversion** = (in the C and Fortran programming languages) operation to change the type of a value **Zuordnungsänderung; assignment statement** = basic programming command that sets a variable equal to a value *or* string *or* character **Zuordnungsanweisung**

◊ **assignor** *noun* person who assigns something to someone **An-, Zuweiser; Abtretende(r); Zedent**

assist *verb* to help **helfen, assistieren;** *can you assist the stock controller in counting the stock? he assists me with my income tax returns* NOTE: you assist someone **in** doing something or **with** something

◊ **assistance** *noun* help **Hilfe, Unterstützung; financial assistance** = help in the form of money **finanzielle Unterstützung** NOTE: no plural

◊ **assistant** *noun* person who helps *or* an ordinary employee **Assistent/-in; personal assistant** = secretary who also helps the boss in various ways **persönlicher Assistent; shop assistant** = person who serves the customers in a shop **Bedienung, Verkäufer/-in; assistant manager** = person who helps a manager **stellvertretender Manager**

associate
1 *adjective* linked **zugehörig, verbunden, assoziiert; associate company** = company which is partly owned by another **Teilhaberfirma, Beteiligungsgesellschaft**
2 *noun* person who works in the same business as someone **Kollege, Partner;** *she is a business associate of mine*

◊ **associational editing** *noun* way of editing a film *or* video ·so as to present together scenes which are similar to others **Assoziativschnitt**

◊ **associative addressing** *or* **content-addressable addressing** *noun* location addressed by its contents rather than its address **Assoziativadressierung; associative processor** = processor that uses associative storage **Assoziativprozessor; associative memory** *or* **storage** *or* **content-addressable storage** = method of data retrieval that uses part of the data rather than an address to locate the data **Assoziativspeicher; associative storage register** = register that is located by its contents rather than a name *or* address **Assoziativspeicherregister**

astable multivibrator *noun* electronic current that repeatedly switches an output between two voltage levels **astabiler** *or* **instabiler Multivibrator**

asterisk *noun* (i) graphical symbol (*) used in programming as a sign for multiplication; (ii) graphical symbol used as a wildcard in many operating systems (including DOS) to mean any characters **Stern(chen) (*);** *to view all the files beginning with the letter 'L', use the DOS command DIR L*.*;* **asterisk fill** = to fill unused decimal places with the asterisk symbol **Sternfüllung;** *we have used asterisk fill to produce the answer of '***122.33'*

astigmatism *noun* optical lens disorder which prevents the light beams from converging properly **Astigmatismus**

asymmetric transmission *noun* method of data transmission used in high-speed modems **asymmetrische Übertragung**

> COMMENT: asymmetric transmission splits a communications channel into two, one that can support fast data transmission at 9,600bps or higher and a slower channel that can support transmission of around 300bps. The slower channel is used to carry control and error-correcting data, the high-speed channel used to transfer the bulk of the data

◊ **asymmetric video compression** *noun* using a powerful computer to compress video, allowing it to be played back on a less powerful computer **asymmetrische Videokompression**

async *(informal)* = ASYNCHRONOUS

asynchronous *adjective* serial data *or* equipment which does not depend on being synchronized with another piece of equipment **asynchron; asynchronous access** = communications using handshaking to synchronize data transmission **asynchroner Zugriff; asynchronous communications** = data transmission between devices that is not synchronized to a clock, but is transmitted when ready **asynchrone Übertragung; asynchronous communications interface adapter (ACIA)** = circuit that allows a computer to transmit and receive serial data using asynchronous access **asynchroner Kommunikationsschnittstellenanschluss; asynchronous computer** = (i) computer that changes from one operation to the next according to signals received when the process is finished; (ii) computer in which a process starts on the arrival of signals *or* data, rather than on a clock pulse **(i) & (ii) Asynchronrechner; asynchronous data transfer** = transfer of data between two devices that takes place without any regular or predictable timing signal **asynchrone Datenübertragung; asynchronous mode** = terminal linked to another piece of equipment in a way where the two need not be synchronized **Asynchronübertragung; asynchronous port** = connection to a computer allowing asynchronous data access **Asynchronanschluss;** *since asynchronous ports are used no special hardware is required;* **asynchronous procedure call (APC)** = (in a program) function that runs separately from the main program and will execute when a particular set of conditions exist **asynchroner Prozeduraufruf (APC); asynchronous transfer mode (ATM)** = (i) method of transferring data very rapidly (at up to 155Mbps) across an ISDN link or network; (ii) CCITT and ANSI standard defining cell relay transmission **(i) asynchroner Übertragungsmodus; (ii) Asynchronbetrieb;** *see also* CELL RELAY TRANSMISSION; **asynchronous transmission** = data transmission that uses handshaking signals

rather than clock signals to synchronize data pulses **asynchrone Übertragung**

> QUOTE each channel handles two forms of communication: asynchronous communication is mainly for transferring data between computers and peripheral devices, while character communication is for data transfer between computers
> *Electronics & Power*

AT *noun* standard of PC originally developed by IBM that uses a 16-bit 80286 processor **AT; AT-bus** = expansion bus standard developed by IBM that uses an edge connector to carry 16-bits of data and address information **AT-Bus; AT-keyboard** = standard keyboard layout for IBM AT personal computers; the keyboard has 102 keys with a row of 12 function keys along the top **AT-Tastatur**

> COMMENT: AT originally meant IBM's Advanced Technology personal computer, but is now used to describe any IBM PC compatible that uses a 16-bit processor

AT command set *noun* standard set of commands to control a modem, developed by Hayes Corporation **AT-Befehlssatz; AT mode** = mode of a modem that is ready to accept commands using the Hayes AT command set **AT-Modus**

Atari ST ™ range of personal computers developed by Atari Corp; Atari ST computers use the 68000 range of processor and are not compatible with IBM PC **Atari ST** ™

ATC = AUTHORIZATION TO COPY software publisher granting the user the permission to make a certain number of copies of a program **Kopiergenehmigung**

ATD = ATTENTION, DIAL standard command for compatible modems used to dial a telephone number; defined by Hayes **ATD**

ATE = AUTOMATIC TEST EQUIPMENT computer controlled testing facilities, that can check a complex circuit *or* PCB for faults *or* problems **automatische Prüfeinrichtung**

ATM = AUTOMATED TELLER MACHINE electronic machine in a bank that dispenses cash when you insert a magnetic card **Geldautomat, ATM**

◊ **ATM** *see* ADOBE TYPE MANAGER

◊ **ATM** = ASYNCHRONOUS TRANSFER MODE (i) method of transferring data very rapidly (at up to 155Mbps) across an ISDN link or network (ii) CCITT and ANSI standard defining cell relay transmission **(i) asynchroner Übertragungsmodus; (ii) Asynchronbetrieb;** *see also* CELL RELAY TRANSMISSION

atmosphere *noun* gas which surrounds the earth **Atmosphäre**

◊ **atmospheric** *adjective* referring to the atmosphere **atmosphärisch; atmospheric absorption** = energy loss of a radio signal due to atmospheric conditions causing dispersion of the signal **atmosphärische Absorption; atmospheric conditions** = state of the atmosphere (including clouds, pressures, etc.) **atmosphärische Bedingungen**

atom *noun*
(a) smallest particle of an element that has the same properties as the element **Atom**
(b) value *or* string that cannot be reduced to a simpler form **Atom**

◊ **atomic** *adjective* (i) referring to atoms; (ii) of an operation that returns data to its original state if it is stopped during processing **(i) Atom-, atomar; (ii) atomar; atomic clock** = very accurate clock which uses changes in energy of atoms as a reference **Atomuhr**

attach *verb* (i) to fasten *or* to link; (ii) to connect a node *or* login to a server on a network **(i) anschließen, befestigen; (ii) anmelden, einloggen;** *I issued the command to attach to the local server*

◊ **attached processor** *noun* separate microprocessor in a system that performs certain functions under the control of a central processor **Anschlussprozessor**

◊ **attached resource computer network (ARCNET)** *see* ARCNET

◊ **attachment** *noun*
(a) device which is attached to a machine for a special purpose **Anschluss, Zusatzgerät;** *there is a special single sheet feed attachment*
(b) named file which is transferred together with an electronic mail message **angehängte Datei;** *there is an attachment with my last mail message - it contains the sales report*

attack *noun* start of a sound **Einsatz; attack envelope** = shape of the initial section of a signal **Anfangskurve**

attend *verb* to be present at **anwesend sein**

◊ **attend to** *verb* to give careful thought to (something) and deal with it **Beachtung schenken, sich kümmern um;** *attend to this fault first - its the worst*

◊ **attended operation** *noun* process which has an operator standing by in case of problems **überwachter Ablauf**

◊ **attention** *noun* giving careful thought, especially to processing a particular section of a program **Aufmerksamkeit; Abruf, Unterbrechung;** *this routine requires the attention of the processor every minute;* **attention code** = the characters AT used within the Hayes AT command set to tell a modem that a command follows **Abrufcode; attention interruption** = interrupt signal that requests the attention of the processor **Abrufunterbrechung, Achtung Unterbrechung; attention key** = key on a terminal that sends an interrupt signal to the processor **Unterbrechungstaste, Abruftaste**

attenuate *verb* to reduce the strength *or* size of peaks (of a signal) **abschwächen, dämpfen**

◊ **attenuation** *noun* reduction or loss of signal strength; the difference between transmitted and received power measured in decibels **Abschwächung, Dämpfung**

attribute *noun*
(a) (i) field entry in a file; (ii) information concerning the display *or* presentation of information **(i) Eintrag; (ii) Attribut;** *this attribute controls the colour of the screen;* **screen attributes** = variables defining the shape, size and colour of text *or* graphics displayed **Bildschirmattribute;** *pressing Ctrl and B keys at the same time will set the bold attribute for this paragraph of text*
(b) in some operating systems (such as DOS and OS/2) each file is stored with a set of control data which control particular functions or aspects of the file **Attribut; archive attribute** = special attribute attached to a file in DOS and OS/2 that indicates if the file has been archived since it was last changed **Archivierungsattribut; read-only attribute** = special attribute attached to a file which, when switched on, only allows the contents of the file to be viewed, the contents cannot be changed **Read-Only-Attribut; system attribute** = special attribute attached to a file used by the operating system; the file is hidden from normal users **Systemattribut**

auctioneering device *noun* device that

will select the maximum *or* minimum signal from a number of input signals **Vorrichtung zum Auswählen der Extremsignale**

audible *adjective* which can be heard **hörbar, akustisch;** *the printer makes an audible signal when it runs out of paper*

audience *noun* people who watch a TV programme *or* listen to a radio programme **Publikum; Zuschauer; Zuhörer; audience rating** = rating of a programme by calculating the number of people who have watched it **Einschaltquote**

audio *adjective* referring to sound *or* to things which can be heard **audio-, Ton-;** **audio active** = system used in a learning laboratory, where the student can hear and respond to questions **audioaktiv; audio cassette** = reel of magnetic recording tape in a small protective casing inserted into a cassette recorder (for recording music *or* voice *or* data) **Tonkassette; audio cassette recorder (ACR)** = machine to transfer audio signals onto magnetic tape **Audiokassettenrecorder (ACR), Kassettenrecorder; audio compressor** = circuit that limits the maximum level of a signal by attenuating any peaks **Ton(frequenz)kompressor; audio conferencing** *see* TELECONFERENCING; **audio file** = digital sound sample stored on disk **Klangdatei; audio frequency** = frequency within the audio range that a human can hear **Tonfrequenz; audio range** = frequency range between 50-20000Hz **Ton(frequenz)bereich; audio response unit** = speech synthesizer that allows a computer to speak responses to requests **Sprachausgabeeinheit; audio slide** = photographic slide that has magnetic tape along an edge allowing sound to be recorded **Diapositiv mit Tonspur**

◊ **audiovisual (AV)** *adjective* which uses sound and images **audiovisuell; audiovisual aids** = equipment used in teaching, which includes both sound and pictures **audiovisuelle Hilfsmittel**

audit
1 *noun* noting tasks carried out by a computer **Protokoll, Revision; audit trail** = recording details of use of a system by noting transactions carried out (used for checking on illegal use *or* to trace a malfunction) **Buchungskontrolle**
2 *verb* to examine the state of a system and check that it is still secure *or* working properly **prüfen**

augend *noun* (*in an addition*) the number to which another number, the addend, is added to produce the sum **Augend, erster Summand**

augment *verb* to increase **erhöhen, vergrößern, erweitern, vermehren; augmented addressing** = producing a usable address word from two shorter words **erweiterte Adressierung**

◊ **augmenter** *noun* value added to another **zweiter Summand**

AUI connector *noun* D-connector used to connect thick Ethernet cable to a network adapter **AUI-Anschluss**

aural *adjective* by ear **aural, Hör-, hör-**

authentic *adjective* which is true **echt, authentisch**

◊ **authenticate** *verb* to say that something is true *or* genuine **bestätigen, authentifizieren**

◊ **authentication** *noun* making sure that something is authentic **Bestätigung, Authentifizierung; authentication of messages** = using special codes to identify the sender of messages, so that the messages can be recognized as being genuine **Echtheitsbestätigung von Meldungen**

author *noun* person who wrote a program **Verfasser, Autor**

◊ **authoring** *noun* creating a multimedia application by combining sound, video and images **Authoring; authoring language** = programming language used to write CAL and training programs **Autorensprache; authoring system** = set of tools normally used to develop multimedia applications; an authoring system provides special commands to control CD-ROM players, play sound files and video clips and display a user-friendly front-end **Autorensystem**

QUOTE the authoring system is a software product that integrates text and fractally compressed images, using any word-processor line editor, to create an electronic book with hypertext links between different pages
Computing

authority *noun* power to do something **Berechtigung, Vollmacht, Befugnis;** *he has no authority to delete your account;* **authority file** *or* **list** = list of special terms used by people compiling a database and also by the users of the database **Benutzerdatei**

authorization *noun*
(a) permission *or* power to do something
Berechtigung
(b) giving a user permission to access a
system **Zugriffsberechtigung; authorization
code** = code used to restrict access to a
computer system to authorized users only
Berechtigungscode

◊ **authorization to copy (ATC)** *noun*
software publisher granting the user the
permission to make a certain number of
copies of a program **Kopiergenehmigung**

COMMENT: some companies have
introduced ATC schemes which allow users of
certain software to make duplicates of the
companies' programs for a fee

◊ **authorize** *verb*
(a) to give permission for something to be
done **genehmigen;** *to authorize the purchase
of a new computer system*
(b) to give someone the authority to do
something **berechtigen, autorisieren,
ermächtigen**

◊ **authorized** *adjective* permitted
berechtigt, autorisiert; authorized user =
person who is allowed to access a system
berechtigter Benutzer

auto *adjective & prefix* automatic *or* which
works without the user needing to act **auto-,
automatisch; auto advance** = paper in a
printer that is automatically moved
forward to the next line at the end of a line
automatischer Zeilenvorschub; auto-answer
= (modem) that will automatically answer
a telephone when called **automatische
Anrufbeantwortung; auto-baud scanning**
circuit that can automatically sense and
select the correct baud rate for a line
automatische Baud-Abtastung; auto boot =
computer system that will initiate a
boot-up procedure when it is switched on
automatischer Urlader; auto-dial = to dial a
number automatically using stored data
selbst wählen; auto-login *or* **auto-logon** =
phone number, password and user's
number transmitted when requested by a
remote system to automate logon
automatische Anmeldung; *see also* LOGIN,
LOGON; **auto-redial** = (modem) that dials
a telephone number again if engaged, until
it replies **automatische Wählwiederholung;
auto repeat** = facility where a character is
automatically repeated if the key is kept
pressed down **Dauerfunktion; auto restart** =
feature of a computer that can initialize and
reload its operating system if there is a fault
or power failure *or* at switch on

Wiedereinschaltautomatik; auto save =
feature of some application programs, such
as word-processor or database software,
that automatically saves the file being used
every few minutes in case of a power failure
or system crash **automatische
Dateisicherung, Auto-Speichern; auto start** =
facility to load a program automatically
when the computer is switched on
automatischer Start; auto stop = feature of a
tape player which stops when it has reached
the end of a tape **Tonträger-Endabschaltung;
auto trace** = feature of some graphics
programs that will transform a bit-mapped
image into a vector image by automatically
locating the edges of the shapes in the
image and drawing lines around them **Auto-
Trace; auto verify** = verification procedure
carried out automatically, as soon as the
data has been saved **Selbstprüfung**

QUOTE expansion accessories include
auto-dial and auto-answer
Electronic & Wireless World

AUTOEXEC.BAT (in an IBM PC
running the MS-DOS operating system)
batch file that contains commands that are
executed when the computer is first
switched on or reset **AUTOEXEC.BAT;** *see
also* CONFIG.SYS, BATCH FILE

automate *verb* to install machines to do
work previously done by people
automatisieren; automated office = office
where many of the tasks are done by
machines **automatisiertes Büro; automated
teller machine (ATM)** = *(US)* automatic
telling machine *or* machine linked to a main
computer that allows cash to be taken out
of a bank account when a special card is
inserted and special instructions given
Geldausgabeautomat

◊ **automation** *noun* use of machines to
do work with very little supervision by
people **Automatisierung**
NOTE: no plural

automatic *noun & adjective* (machine)
which works by itself, without being
worked by an operator **Automat,
automatisch; automatic backup** = feature of
some application programs, such as word-
processor or database software, that
automatically saves the file being used
every few minutes in case of a power failure
or system crash **automatische Sicherung;
automatic call distribution (ACD)** =
specialised telephone system that can
handle lots of incoming calls and direct
them to a particular operator according to

programmed instructions in a database **automatische Anrufverteilung (ACD); automatic calling unit (ACU)** = device which allows a computer to call telephone numbers automatically **automatische Anrufeinrichtung; automatic carriage return** = system where the cursor automatically returns to the beginning of a new line when it reaches the end of the previous one **automatischer Wagenrücklauf; automatic checking** = error detection and validation check carried out automatically on received data **Selbstprüfung, automatische Prüfung; automatic data capture** = system where data is automatically recorded in a computer system, as it is input **automatische Datenaufzeichnung; automatic data processing (ADP)** = data processing done by a computer **automatische Datenverarbeitung; automatic decimal adjustment** = process of lining up all the decimal points in a column of figures **automatische Dezimalstellenausrichtung; automatic error correction** = correction of received data, using error detection and correction codes **automatische Fehlerkorrektur; automatic error detection** = use of an (alphanumeric) code, such as a gray code, that will allow any errors to be detected **automatische Fehlererkennung; automatic font downloading** = process in which special font information is sent to a printer by the application **automatische Zeichensatzladung; automatic gain control (AGC)** = electronic device that provides a constant amplitude output signal from a varying input signal, by changing its gain **automatische Verstärkungsregelung; automatic hyphenation** = feature of a software program that looks up in an electronic dictionary how to correctly split and hyphenate words **Silbentrennautomatik; automatic letter writing** = writing of form letters (using a wordprocessor) **automatisches Briefschreiben; automatic loader** = short program (usually in ROM) that will boot up a system and load a program **automatisches Ladeprogramm; automatic message accounting** = system of logging telephone calls automatically so that details of them can be given to the user **automatische Anrufaufzeichnung; automatic mode** or **frequency switching** = monitor that can adjust its internal circuits to the different frequencies used by different video standards **automatische Frequenzumschaltung; automatic number identification** = telephone system which displays the telephone number of the caller **automatische Rufnummernerkennung; automatic programming** = process of producing an optimum (operating) system for a particular process **automatisches Programmieren; automatic recalculation** = spreadsheet mode in which the answers to new formula are calculated every time any value or cell changes **automatische Neuberechnung; automatic repeat** = facility where a character is automatically repeated if the key is kept pressed down **Dauerfunktion; automatic repeat request (ARQ)** = error correction system used in some modems that asks for data to be retransmitted if it contains errors **automatische Wiederholungsanforderung (ARQ); automatic sequencing** = ability of a computer to execute a number of programs or tasks without extra commands **automatische Programmsteuerung; automatic speed matching** = ability of a modem to adjust its data rate to the speed of the remote modem **automatische Geschwindigkeitsangleichung; automatic telephone exchange** = telephone exchange operated by a computer rather than a human operator **computergesteuertes Fernsprechamt; automatic telling machine** or (US) **automated teller machine (ATM)** = machine which allows money to be taken out of a bank account when a special card is inserted and special instructions given **Geldausgabeautomat; automatic test equipment (ATE)** = computer controlled testing facilities, that can check a complex circuit or PCB for faults or problems **automatische Prüfeinrichtung; automatic vending machine** = machine which provides drinks, cigarettes, etc., when money is put in **Automat**

◊ **automatically** adverb (machine) working without a person giving instructions **automatisch;** *the statements are sent out automatically; addresses are typed in automatically; a demand note is sent automatically when payment is late; the compiler automatically corrected the syntax errors; a SBC automatically limits the movement of the machine the program is run automatically when the computer is switched on*

automation see AUTOMATE

autopositive noun photographic process that produces a positive image without a negative stage **Umkehrentwicklung**

AUX = AUXILIARY abbreviation for a serial communications port under the DOS operating system **AUX;** see also COM1 or SERIAL PORT

auxiliary adjective which helps

Hilfs-, zusätzlich; *the computer room has an auxiliary power supply in case there is a mains failure;* **auxiliary equipment** = backup *or* secondary equipment in case of a breakdown **Hilfs-, Zusatzgeräte; auxiliary processor** = extra, specialized processor, such as an array *or* numerical processor that can work with a main CPU to increase execution speed **Hilfsprozessor; auxiliary storage** *or* **memory** *or* **store** = any data storage medium (such a magnetic tape *or* floppy disk) that is not the main high speed computer storage (RAM) **Hilfsspeicher;** *disk drives and magnetic tape are auxiliary storage on this machine*

AV = AUDIOVISUAL

available *adjective* which can be obtained *or* bought **verfügbar;** *available in all branches; item no longer available; items available to order only;* **available light** = light which is present at a place where photographs are being taken, without needing additional artificial light **vorhandenes Licht, Tageslicht; available list** = list of unallocated memory and resources in a system **Liste freier Speicherplätze; available point** = smallest single unit *or* point of a display whose colour and brightness can be controlled **benutzbarer Punkt; available power** = maximum electrical *or* processing power that a system can deliver **Richt(leistungs)wirkungsgrad; available time** = time during which a system may be used **verfügbare Benutzerzeit**

◊ **availability** *noun* being easily obtained **Verfügbarkeit;** *the availability of the latest software package is very good;* **offer subject to availability** = the offer is valid only if the goods are available **solange Vorrat reicht** NOTE: no plural

avalanche *noun* one action starting a number of other actions **Lawine;** *there was an avalanche of errors after I pressed the wrong key;* **avalanche photodiode (APD)** = photodiode able to detect very low light levels (one photon received produces several electrons) **Lawinendiode, Avalanchediode**

average
1 *noun* number calculated by adding together several figures and dividing by the number of figures added **Durchschnitt;** *the average for the last three months or the last three months' average; sales average or average of sales;* **weighted average** = average which is calculated taking several factors into account, giving some more value than others **gewichteter Durchschnitt,**

Bewertungsdurchschnitt; **on an average** = in general **durchschnittlich;** *we sell, on an average, five computers a day*
2 *adjective* middle (figure) **durchschnittlich;** *average cost per unit; average price; average sales per representative;* **average access time** = the average time taken between a request being sent and data being returned from a memory device **mittlere Zugriffszeit; average delay** = average time that a user must wait when trying to access a communication network **mittlere Verzögerung;** *see also* MEAN; *the average delay increases at nine-thirty when everyone tries to log-in*
3 *verb* to produce as an average figure **den Durchschnitt ermitteln**

◊ **average out** *verb* to come to a figure as an average **durchschnittlich betragen;** *it averages out at 120 dpi·*

axis *noun* (i) line around which something turns; (ii) reference line which is the basis for coordinates on a graph **(i) Achse; (ii) Koordinate(nachse);** *the CAD package allows an axis to be placed anywhere;* **horizontal axis** = reference line used for horizontal coordinates on a graph **x-Achse, Abszisse(nachse); vertical axis** = reference line used for vertical coordinates on a graph **y-Achse, Ordinate(nachse)**
NOTE: plural is **axes**

azerty keyboard *noun* method of arranging the keys on a keyboard where the first line begins AZERTY (used mainly in Europe) **AZERTY-Tastatur;** *compare* QWERTY

azimuth *noun* angle of a tape head to a reference (such as a tape plane) **Azimut, Richtungswinkel; azimuth alignment** = correct horizontal angle of a tape head to the magnetic tape **Justieren des Richtungswinkels;** *azimuth alignment is adjusted with this small screw; azimuth alignment might not be correct for tape recorded on a different machine*

Bb

b *abbreviation* one bit **b** *or* **bt; bps (bits per second)** = number of bits transmitted or received per second **bps (Bit pro Sekunde);** *compare* B

B *abbreviation* one byte **B**; **KB (kilobyte)** = meaning equal to 1024 bytes **KB (Kilobyte)**

B hexadecimal equivalent to decimal number 11 **B**

B: (in personal computers) indicates the second disk drive, normally a floppy disk drive **B:**; *copy the files from the hard drive, C:, to the floppy drive, B:*

Babbage Charles Babbage (1792-1871) English inventor of the first automatic calculator and inventor of the forerunner of today's digital computers

babble *noun* crosstalk *or* noise from other sources which interferes with a signal **Nebensprechen**

BABT = BRITISH APPROVAL BOARD FOR TELECOMMUNICATIONS; **BABT approval** = independent organisation that tests and certifies telecommunications equipment **britische Telekommunikationsgenehmigung (BABT);** *if you design a new modem, you must have BABT approval before you can sell it*

back
1 *noun* **back panel** = panel at the rear of a computer which normally holds the connectors to peripherals such as keyboard, printer, video display unit, and mouse **Rückseite**
2 *verb* to help **unterstützen**; **battery-backed** = (volatile storage device) that has a battery backup **batterieunterstützt;** *the RAM disk card has the option to be battery-backed battery-backed CMOS memory replaces a disk drive in this portable*

QUOTE the V3500 has on-board Ethernet and SCSI interfaces, up to 32Mb local DRAM, two programmable timers, a battery-backed real-time clock with 32Kb RAM and four serial ports

Computing

back-end network *noun* a connection between a mainframe computer and a high-speed mass storage device or file server **Host-Netzwerk**

◊ **back-end processor** *noun* special purpose auxiliary processor **Nachschaltrechner**

◊ **back-end server** *noun* computer connected to a network that carries out tasks requested by client workstations **nachgeschalteter Server**

background *noun*
(a) past work *or* experience **Hintergrund, Werdegang;** *his background is in the computer industry; the company is looking for someone with a background of success in the electronics industry; what is his background or; do you know anything about his background?*
(b) part of a picture which is behind the main object of interest **Hintergrund;** *the new graphics processor chip can handle background, foreground and sprite movement independently;* **background colour** = colour of a computer screen display (characters and graphics are normally displayed in a different foreground colour) **Hintergrundfarbe;** *white background colour with black characters is less stressful for the eyes;* **background image** = image displayed as a backdrop behind a program or windows of a GUI; *the background image does not move and does not interfere with any programs* **Hintergrundbild; background noise** = noise which is present along with the required signal **Nebengeräusch;** *the other machines around this device will produce a lot of background noise; the modem is sensitive to background noise;* **background projection** *or* **back projection** = film projected onto the back of a screen, in front of which further action is filmed **Hintergrundprojektion; background reflectance** = light reflected from a sheet of paper that is being scanned or read by an optical character reader **Hintergrundspiegelung**
(c) system in a computer where low-priority work can be done in the intervals when very important work is not being done **Hintergrundprogrammbetrieb; background communication** = data communication activity (such as downloading a file) carried out as a low-priority task in the background **Hintergrundübertragung; background job** = low priority task **Hintergrundjob; background operation** = low priority process that works as and when resources become available from high-priority foreground tasks **Hintergrundprozess; background printing** = printing from a computer while it is processing another task **Nebenherdrucken;** *background printing can be carried out whilst you are editing another document;* **background program** = computer program with a very low priority **Hintergrundprogramm; background recalculation** = (in a spreadsheet program) facility that allows a user to enter new numbers or equations while the program recalculates the solutions in the

background **Neuberechnung im Hintergrund; background task** = process executed at any time by the computer system, not normally noticed by the user **Hintergrundtask**

◊ **background processing** *noun*
(a) low priority job which is executed when there are no higher priority activities for the computer to attend to **nachrangige Verarbeitung**
(b) process which does not use the on-line capabilities of a system **Hintergrundverarbeitung**
NOTE: opposite is **foreground**

backing *noun* **backing store** *or* **storage** *or* **memory** = permanent storage medium onto which data can be recorded before being processed by the computer *or* after processing for later retrieval **Hilfs-, Zusatzspeicher;** *by adding another disk drive, I will increase the backing store capabilities; paper tape is one of the slowest access backing stores; compare with* MAIN MEMORY

back-level *noun* earlier release of a product which may not support a current function **Backlevel; Vorgängerversion**

backlight *noun* light behind a liquid crystal display (LCD) unit that improves the contrast of characters on the screen and allows it to be read in dim light **Hintergrundbeleuchtung**

◊ **backlit display** *noun* a liquid crystal display (LCD) unit that has a backlight fitted to improve the contrast of the display **hinterleuchtete Anzeige**

backlog *noun* work *or* tasks that have yet to be processed **Rückstand;** *the programmers can't deal with the backlog of programming work; the queue was too short for the backlog of tasks waiting to be processed*
NOTE: no plural

back number *noun* old copy of a journal *or* periodical **alte Ausgabe**

backout *verb* to restore a file to its original condition before any changes were made **zurücksetzen**

backpack *noun* lightweight television recording equipment which the cameraman carries on his back when filming **Rucksack**

backplane *noun* part of the body of a computer which holds the circuit boards, buses and expansion connectors (the backplane does not provide any processing functions) **gedruckte Rückwandverdrahtung, Rückwandplatine;** *see* MOTHERBOARD, RACK

back pointer *noun* (in a tree structure) a pointer that holds the position of the parent node relative to the current node used in programming to search backwards through a file **Rückwärtszeiger**

back projection *noun* background projection *or* film projected onto the back of a screen, in front of which further action is filmed **Hintergrundprojektion**

backscatter *noun* reflected *or* scattered radio wave travelling in the opposite direction to the original signal **Rückstreuung**

backslash *noun* ASCII character 92, the sign \ which is used in MS-DOS to represent the root directory of a disk, such as C:\, or to separate subdirectories in a path, such as C:\APPS\DATA **Backslash**

backspace *noun* movement of a cursor *or* printhead back by one character **Rückwärtsschritt; backspace character** = code that causes a backspace action in a display device **Rücksetzungszeichen; backspace key** = key which moves the cursor back one space **Rücktaste;** *if you make a mistake entering data, use the backspace key to correct it*

backtab *verb* (in SAA CUA front-end) to move the cursor back to the previous field **mit dem Tabulator zurückspringen; den Tabulator zurücksetzen**

backtrack *verb* to carry out list processing in reverse, starting with the goal and working towards the proofs **zurückverfolgen**

back up *verb*
(a) to make a copy of a file *or* data *or* disk **sichern; eine Sicherungskopie anlegen;** *the company accounts were backed up on disk as a protection against fire damage; the program enables users to back up hard disk files with a single command*
(b) to support *or* to help **unterstützen; helfen;** *he brought along a file of documents to back up his claim; the printout backed up his argument for a new system*

◊ **BACKUP** *noun* (in MS-DOS)

command to backup data from a hard disk onto floppy disks or a tape drive **BACKUP**

◊ **backup** *noun & adjective*
(a) help(ing) **Unterstützung(s-);** *we offer a free backup service to customers*
(b) **backup** *or* **backup file** = copy of a file *or* set of data kept for security against errors in the original *or* master copy **Sicherungskopie; backup copy** = copy of a computer disk to be kept in case the original disk is damaged **Sicherungskopie;** *the most recent backup copy is kept in the safe;* **backup domain controller** = server in a network that keeps a copy of database of user accounts to validate login requests in case of a fault with the main server **Sicherungs-Domänen-Controller; backup path** = (in a Token-Ring network) alternative path for a signal around a network avoiding a malfunctioning device **Ausweichpfad; backup plan** = set of rules that take effect when normal operation has gone wrong **Notplan;** *the normal UPS has gone wrong, so we will have to use our backup plan to try and restore power;* **backup procedure** = method of making backup copies of files **Datensicherungsprozedur; backup server** = second computer on a network that contains duplicate files and up-to-date data in case of a problem with the main server **Ausweichserver; backup utility** = software that simplifies the process of backing up data; backup utilities often allow a user to backup files automatically at a particular time **Backup-Utility; Sicherungshilfsprogramm; backup version** = copy of a file made during a backup **Sicherungsversion; battery backup** = use of a battery to provide power to a volatile device (RAM chip) to retain data after a computer has been switched off **Batteriesicherung; memory backup capacitor** = very high capacitance (small) device that can provide power for volatile RAM chips for up to two weeks (used instead of a battery) **Sicherungskondensatorspeicher**

QUOTE the system backs up at the rate of 2.5Mb per minute
Microcomputer News

QUOTE the previous version is retained, but its extension is changed to .BAK indicating that it's a back-up
Personal Computer World

Backus-Naur-Form (BNF) system of writing and expressing the syntax of a programming language **Backus-Naur-Form**

backward *or* **backwards** *adjective &*

adverb towards the back *or* in the opposite direction **rückwärts; backward chaining** = method used in artificial intelligence systems to calculate a goal from a set of results **Rückwärtskettung; backward channel** = channel from the receiver to transmitter allowing the receiver to send control and handshaking signals **Hilfskanal; backward error correction** = correction of errors which are detected by the receiver and a signal is sent to the transmitter to request a re-transmission of the data **rückwärtige Fehlerkorrektur; backward LAN channel** = (in a broadband network) channel from receiver to sender used to carry control signals **LAN-Rückkanal; backward mode** = negative displacement from an origin **Rückwärtsmodus; backward recovery** = data retrieval from a system that has crashed **Wiederherstellungsverfahren; backwards search** = (in a word-processor or database) search for data that begins at the position of the cursor or end of the file and searches to the beginning of the file **Rückwärtssuche; Suche nach hinten; backwards supervision** = data transmission controlled by the receiver **Rückwärtssteuerung**

COMMENT: backward recovery is carried out by passing the semi-processed data from the crashed computer through a routine that reverses the effects of the main program to return the original data

BACS = BANKERS AUTOMATED CLEARANCE SYSTEM system to transfer money between banks using computer linked via a secure network **BACS**

bacterium *see* VIRUS

bad break *noun* hyphen inserted in the wrong place within a word; a problem sometimes caused by the automatic hyphenation feature of word-processing software **Silbentrennfehler**

◊ **bad copy** *noun* illegible *or* badly edited manuscript which the typesetter will not accept **schlechtes Manuskript**

◊ **bad sector** *noun* sector which has been wrongly formatted *or* which contains an error *or* fault and is unable to be correctly written to or read from **fehlerhafter Sektor;** *you will probably receive error messages when you copy files that are stored on bad sectors on a disk*

badge reader *noun* machine that reads data from an identification badge **Ausweisleser;** *a badge reader makes sure that only authorized personnel can gain access to a computer room*

baffle *noun* sections of material placed in a loudspeaker, used to prevent unwanted internal resonating frequencies **Resonanzwand**

bag *noun* number of elements in no particular order **Beutel**

BAK file extension *noun* standard three-letter file extension used in MS-DOS systems to signify a backup or copy of another file **Dateinamenerweiterung BAK**

balance
1 *noun*
(a) placing of text and graphics on a page in an attractive way **Ausgewogenheit**; *the dtp package allows the user to see if the overall page balance is correct;* **column balance** = (in a word-processor *or* DTP system) method of making sure that the ends of two columns of text are level **Spaltenausgleich**
(b) positioning of musical instruments so that they may be recorded to their best advantage **Ausgeglichenheit**
(c) amplitude control of left and right audio signals in a stereo system **Ausgewogenheit**; **balance stripe** = thin magnetic stripe on a cine film on the opposite side to the sound track, so that the whole film will lie flat when played back **Ausgleichsstreifen**
2 *verb* to plan something so that two parts are equal **ausgleichen, ausbalancieren**; **balanced circuit** = electronic circuit that presents a correct load to a communications line (the correct load is usually equal to the impedance of a line element) **ausgeglichener Stromkreis**; *you must use a balanced circuit at the end of the line to prevent signal reflections;* **balanced error** = the probability of any error occurring (from a number of errors) is the same for all errors **symmetrischer Fehler**; **balanced line** = communications line that is terminated at each end with a balanced circuit, preventing signal reflections **symmetrische Leitung**; **balanced routing** = method of using all possible routes through a network equally **ausgeglichene Leitungsausnutzung**

ball printer *noun* impact printer that uses a small metal ball on the surface of which are formed the characters **Kugelkopfdrucker**; *see also* GOLF-BALL PRINTER

balun *noun* transformer that matches two circuits which have different impedances **Impedanzwandler**; *we have used a balun to* *connect the coaxial cable to the twisted-pair circuit*

band *noun*
(a) range of frequencies between two limits **Band**; **base band** = frequency range of a signal before it is processed *or* transmitted **Basisband**; *voice base band ranges from 20Hz to 15KHz;* **base band modem** = communications circuit that transmits an unmodulated (base band) signal over a short distance **Gleichstrom-Datenübertragungseinrichtung für niedrige Sendespannung**; *do not use a base band modem with a normal phone line;* **base band local area network** = LAN using unmodulated signals transmitted over coaxial cable, often using a CSMA/CD protocol **Basisbandnetz**
(b) group of tracks on a magnetic disk **Band**

◊ **banding** *noun* **elastic banding** = method of defining the limits of an image on the computer screen by stretching a boundary round it **elastische Grenzen**; *elastic banding is much easier to control with a mouse*

◊ **bandlimited** *adjective* (signal) whose frequency range has been limited to one band **bandbegrenzt**

◊ **bandpass filter** *noun* electronic filter that allows a range of frequencies to pass, but attenuates all frequencies outside the specified range **Bandpassfilter**; *compare with* LOW PASS, HIGH PASS

◊ **band printer** *noun* printer in which the characters are located along a movable steel belt **Banddrucker**

◊ **bandwidth** *noun*
(a) range of frequencies **Bandbreite**
(b) measure of the amount of data that can be transmitted along a cable *or* channel *or* other medium **Bandbreite**; *this fibre-optic cable has a greater bandwidth than the old copper cable and so it can carry data at higher speeds*
(c) measure of the range of frequencies that a monitor or CRT will accept and display; high resolution monitors display more pixels per area so need high speed data input and so a higher bandwidth **Bandbreite**

bank *noun* collection of similar devices **Bank**; *a bank of minicomputers process all the raw data;* **bank switching** = selection of a particular memory bank from a group **Bankauswahl**; **memory bank** = collection of electronic memory devices connected together to form one large area of memory **Speicherbank**; *an add-on card has a 128KB memory bank made up of 16 chips;* see also DATABANK

COMMENT: memory banks are used to expand the main memory of a CPU (often above the addressing range of the CPU) by having a number of memory chips arranged into banks. Each bank operates over the same address range but is selected independently by a special code

bankers automated clearance system (BACS) *noun* system to transfer money between banks using computer linked via a secure network **automatisches Banküberweisungssystem (BACS)**

banner *noun (in printing)* heading *or* title extending to the width of a page **Balkenüberschrift; banner headlines** = large headlines on a newspaper running across the width of the page **Schlagzeilen**

bar
1 *noun* thick line *or* block of colour **Strich, Balken**
2 *verb* to stop someone from doing something **verbieten, ausschließen; to bar entry to a file** = to stop someone accessing a file **den Zugang zu einer Datei verwehren**

◊ **bar chart** *or* **bar graph** *noun* graph on which values are represented as vertical *or* horizontal bars **Balkendiagramm**

◊ **bar code** *or* (*US*) **bar graphics** *noun* data represented as a series of printed stripes of varying widths **Streifencode; bar-code reader** *or* **optical scanner** = optical device that reads data from a bar code **optischer Leser, optischer Abtaster**

COMMENT: bar codes are found on most goods and their packages; the width and position of the stripes is sensed by a light pen *or* optical wand and provides information about the goods, such as price, stock quantities, etc.

◊ **bar printer** *noun* printer in which the characters are on arms which strike the paper to print characters **Stabdrucker;** *see also* DAISY WHEEL

bare board *noun* circuit board with no components on it; usually refers to a memory expansion board that does not yet have any memory chips mounted on it **unbestückte Leiterplatine**

barrel *noun* conducting post in a terminal **Tonne**

◊ **barrel distortion** *noun* optical lens distortion causing sides of objects to appear curved **Tonnenverzeichnung**

◊ **barrel printer** *noun* type of printer where characters are located around a rotating barrel **Typenwalzendrucker**

barrier box *noun* device that electrically isolates equipment from a telephone line to prevent damage **Isoliersteg**

baryta paper *noun* coated matt paper used to produce final high quality proofs before printing **Barytpapier**

base
1 *noun*
(a) lowest *or* first position **Basis**
(b) collection of files used as a reference **Basisdateien;** *see* DATABASE
(c) place where a company has its main office or factory *or* place where a businessman has his office **Hauptquartier, Sitz, Standort;** *the company has its base in London and branches in all European countries*
(d) initial *or* original position **Grundposition; base address** = initial address in a program used as a reference for others **Grund-, Bezugs-, Basisadresse; base address register** = register (in a CPU) used to store the base address **Basisadressregister; base addressing** = relative addressing **relative Adressierung; base font** = default font and point size used by a word-processing program **Standardschriftart; base language** = assembly language **Assemblersprache; base line** = horizontal line along which characters are printed or displayed; the descenders of a character drop below the baseline **Grundlinie; base memory** *or* **conventional memory** *or* **base RAM** = (in an IBM-compatible PC) first 640Kb of random access memory fitted to the PC **Basisspeicher;** *compare* HIGH MEMORY *or* EXPANDED MEMORY; **base register** = register in a CPU (not usually in small computers) that contains the address of the start of a program **Bezugs-, Basisregister; base station** = fixed radio transmitter/receiver that relays radio signals to and from data terminals or radios **Funk-Basisstation**
(e) (notation) referring to a number system **Basis; base 2** = binary number system (using the two digits 0 and 1) **binäres Zahlensystem; base 8** = octal number system (using the eight digits 0 - 7) **oktales Zahlensystem; base 10** = decimal number system (using the ten digits 0 - 9) **dezimales Zahlensystem; base 16** = hexadecimal number system (using the ten digits 0 - 9 and six letters A - F) **hexadezimales Zahlensystem**

2 *verb*
(a) to start to calculate from a position ausgehen von; *we based our calculations on the basic keyboarding rate;* **based on** = calculating from ausgehend von; *based on last year's figures; the price is based on estimates of keyboarding costs*
(b) to set up a company *or* a person in a place stationieren, seinen Sitz haben; *the European manager is based in our London office; a London-based system serves the whole country*

◊ **baseband** *or* **base band** *noun* (i) frequency range of a signal before it is processed *or* transmitted; (ii) digital signals transmitted without modulation; (iii) information modulated with a single carrier frequency **(i)(ii) & (iii)** Basisband; **baseband local area network** = transmission method in which the whole bandwidth of the cable is used and the data signal is not modulated; Ethernet is a baseband network Basisband-Netzwerk; *base band local area networks can support a maximum cable length of around 300m;* **baseband signalling** = transmitting data as varying voltage levels across a link Basisband-Signalgebung

BASIC = BEGINNER'S ALL-PURPOSE SYMBOLIC INSTRUCTION CODE high-level programming language for developing programs in a conversational way, providing an easy introduction to computer programming BASIC

◊ **basic** *adjective* normal *or* from which everything starts grundlegend; *the basic architechture is the same for all models in this range;* **basic code** = binary code which directly operates the CPU, using only absolute addresses and values (this is the final form of a program after a compiler *or* assembler pass) Grundcode; **basic controller** = part of a communications controller that carries out arithmetic and logic functions Grundsteuereinheit; **basic control system satellite (BCS)** = system that runs dedicated programs *or* tasks for a central computer, controlled using interrupt signals Satellit für Grundsteuerungssysteme; **basic direct access method (BDAM)** = method of directly updating or retrieving a particular block of data stored on a direct access device Basisdirektzugriffsmethode; **basic exchange format** = standard method of storing data on a disk so that it may be accessed by another type of computer Basisaustauschformat; **basic input/output operating system (BIOS)** = system routines that interface between high-level program

instructions and the system peripherals to control the input and output to various standard devices, this often includes controlling the screen, keyboard and disk drives **BIOS (Ein-/Ausgabesystem des Betriebssystems)**; **basic instruction** = unmodified program instruction which is processed to obtain the instruction to be executed Grundbefehl; **basic mode link control** = standardized control of transmission links using special codes Verfahren der (Daten)übertragungssteuerung; **basic operating system (BOS)** = software that controls the basic, low-level running of the hardware and file management BOS (Basisbetriebssystem); **basic sequential access method (BSAM)** = method of storing or retrieving blocks of data in a continuous sequence Basic Sequential Access Method (BSAM); **basic telecommunications access method (BTAM)** = method to provide access (read *or* write operations) to a remote device BTAM-Zugriffsmethode; **basic weight** = weight of printing paper per 500 sheets Basisgewicht

◊ **basically** *adverb* seen from the point from which everything starts im Grunde, im wesentlichen; *the acoustic coupler is basically the same as a modem*

◊ **basis** *noun* point *or* number from which calculations are made Basis; *we calculated keyboarding costs on the basis of 5,500 keystrokes per hour*

bass *noun & adjective* low sound *or* sound with a low frequency Bass(-); **bass signal** = audio signals in the frequency range below 100Hz Bass-Signal; **bass control** = knob used to vary the strength of the bass frequencies in an audio signal Tiefenregler; **bass driver** *or* **speaker** = large loudspeaker able to produce low frequency sounds Basslautsprecher; **bass response** = characteristics of a circuit *or* device to bass signals Basswiedergabe

BAT file extension *noun* standard three-letter file extension used in MS-DOS systems to signify a batch file; a text file containing system commands Dateinamenerweiterung BAT

batch
1 *noun*
(a) group of items which are made at one time Stapel; *the last batch of disk drives are faulty*
(b) (i) group of documents which are processed at the same time (ii) group of tasks *or* amount of data to be processed as a single unit **(i)** Stapel; **(ii)** Stapelverarbeitung;

today's batch of orders; we deal with the orders in batches of fifty; **batch file** = file stored on disk that contains a sequence of system commands; when the batch file is run, the commands are executed, saving a user typing them in **Stapelverarbeitungsdatei, Batchdatei;** *this batch file is used to save time and effort when carrying out a routine task;* **(processing data in) batch mode** = (processing the data) in related groups in one machine run **(Daten im) Stapelbetrieb/Batchbetrieb (verarbeiten);** **batch region** = memory area where the operating system executes batch programs **Stapel-, Batchregion; batch system** = system that executes batch files **Stapelverarbeitungssystem; batch total** = sum of a number of batches of data, used for error checking, validation or to provide useful information **Zwischensumme pro Stapel**
2 *verb*
(a) to put data *or* tasks together in groups **stapeln; batched communication** = high-speed transmission of large blocks of data without requiring an acknowledgement from the receiver for each data item **Stapelübertragung**
(b) to put items together in groups **stapeln**

◊ **batch number** *noun* reference number attached to a batch **Bearbeitungs-, Stapelnummer**

◊ **batch processor** *noun* system able to process groups of tasks **Stapelverarbeiter; batch processing** = system of data processing where information is collected into batches before being processed by the computer in one machine run **stapelweise Verarbeitung, Batch-Betrieb**

COMMENT: batch processing is the opposite to interactive processing (where the user gives instructions and receives an immediate response)

battery *noun* chemical device that produces electrical current **Batterie; battery-backed** = (volatile storage device) that has a battery backup **mit Batterie abgesichert; battery backup** = use of a battery to provide power to volatile storage devices (RAM chips) to retain data after a computer has been switched off **Batteriesicherung; battery voltage level** = size of voltage being provided by a battery **Spannungsebene der Batterie**

baud *or* **baud rate** *noun* measure of the number of signal changes transmitted per second **Baudrate;** *the baud rate of the binary signal was 300 bits per second a modem with*

auto-baud scanner can automatically sense at which baud rate it should operate; see also (AUTO-BAUD) SCANNER; **baud rate generator** = device that produces various timing signals to synchronize data at different baud rates **Baudratengenerator; split baud rate** = modem which receives data at one baud rate but transmits data at another **geteilte Baudrate;** *the viewdata modem uses a 1200/75 split baud rate; see also* (AUTO-BAUD) SCANNING

COMMENT: baud rate is often considered the same as bits per second, but in fact it depends on the protocol used and the error checking (300 baud is roughly equivalent to 30 characters per second using standard error checking)

Baudot code *noun* five-bit character transmission code, used mainly in teletypewriters **Baudot-Code**

bay *or* **drive bay** *noun* space within a computer's casing where a disk drive is fitted **Laufwerksschacht**

B box *noun* register in a CPU (not usually in small computers) that contains the address of the start of a program **B-Register, Indexregister**

BBS = BULLETIN BOARD SYSTEM information and message database accessible by modem and computer link **Schwarzes-Brett-System**

BCC = BLOCK CHARACTER CHECK error detection method for blocks of transmitted data **Blockdatenprüfung**

BCD = BINARY CODED DECIMAL representation of single decimal digits as a pattern of four binary digits **binär codierte Dezimalzahl;** *the BCD representation of decimal 8 is 1000;* **BCD adder** = full adder able to add two four-bit BCD words **Addierer für binär codierte Dezimalzahlen**

BCH code = BOSE-CHANDHURI-HOCQUENGHEM CODE

BCNF = BOYCE-CODD NORMAL FORM; *see* NORMAL FORM **BCNF**

BCPL *noun* high level programming language **BCPL (Programmiersprache)**

BCS
(a) = BRITISH COMPUTER SOCIETY
(b) = BASIC CONTROL SYSTEM (SATELLITE)

beacon _verb_ signal transmitted repeatedly by a device that is malfunctioning on a network **Fehlersignal**

◊ **beacon frame** _noun_ special frame within the FDDI protocol that is sent after a network break has occurred **Beacon-Rahmen;** _see also_ FDDI

bead _noun_ small section of a program that is used for a single task **Perle**

beam _noun_ narrow set of light _or_ electron rays **Strahl;** _a beam of laser light is used in this printer to produce high-resolution graphics;_ **beam deflection** = (in a CRT) to move the electron beam with the CRT across the screen **Strahlenablenkung;** _a magnetic field is used for beam deflection in a CRT;_ **beam diversity** = using a single frequency communications band for two different sets of data **Frequenzbandaufteilung; beam splitter** = device to redirect a part of a beam **Strahlenteiler; beam width** = maximum size of a transmission beam which should not be exceeded if a constant received power is to maintained **Strahlenbreite**

beard _noun_ blank section between bottom of a character and the type face limit **Fleisch**

BEC = BUS EXTENSION CARD

beep
1 _noun_ audible warning noise **Piepton, akustisches Signal;** _the printer will make a beep when it runs out of paper_
2 _verb_ to make a beep **piepsen;** _the computer beeped when the wrong key was hit; see also_ BLEEP

beginning _noun_ first part **Anfang; beginning of file (bof)** = character _or_ symbol that shows the start of a valid section of data **Dateianfang; beginning of information mark (bim)** = symbol indicating the start of a data stream stored on a disk drive _or_ tape **Informationsanfangsmarke; beginning of tape (bot) marker** = section of material that marks the start of the recording area of a reel of magnetic tape **Bandanfangsmarke**

Beginner's All-Purpose Symbolic Instruction Code (BASIC) _noun_ high-level programming language for developing programs in a conversational way, providing an easy introduction to computer programming **BASIC (Programmiersprache)**

bel _noun_ unit used when expressing ratio of signal power in logarithmic form (P bels = Log (A/B) where A and B are signal power) **Bel**

BEL _noun_ bell character (equivalent to ASCII code 7) **BEL**

bell character _noun_ control code which causes a machine to produce an audible signal **Klingelzeichen**

Bell-compatible modem _noun_ modem that operates according to standards set down by AT&T **Bell-kompatibles Modem**

bells and whistles _plural noun_ advanced features or added extras to an application or peripheral **Raffinessen;** _this word-processor has all the bells and whistles you would expect - including page preview_

below-the-line _adjective_ **below-the-line expenditure** = exceptional payments which are separated from a company's normal accounts **Sonderausgabe, außerordentliche Aufwendungen; below-the-line costs** = costs of crew and technicians used in making a TV programme (as opposed to scriptwriters, actors, etc., who are above-the-line costs) **Kosten unter dem Strich**

benchmark _noun_
(a) point in an index which is important, and can be used to compare with other figures **Vergleichspunkt**
(b) program used to test the performance of software _or_ hardware _or_ a system **Test-, Referenzprogramm;** _the magazine gave the new program's benchmark test results_

◊ **benchmarking** _noun_ testing a system _or_ program with a benchmark **Testen mit einem Referenzprogramm**

◊ **benchmark problem** _noun_ task _or_ problem used to test and evaluate the performance of hardware _or_ software **Leistungsvergleichsaufgabe**

| COMMENT: the same task _or_ program is given to different systems and their results and speeds of working are compared

Berkeley UNIX (BSD) _noun_ version of UNIX operating system developed by the University of California, Berkeley **Berkeley UNIX (BSD)**

Bernoulli box _noun_ high capacity storage system using exchangeable 20MB cartridges **Bernoulli-Box**

QUOTE I use a pair of Bernoulli boxes for back up and simply do a disk-to-disk copy
PC Business World

best fit *noun* (i) (something) which is the nearest match to a requirement (ii) function that selects the smallest free space in main memory for a requested virtual page (i) **höchstpassend;** (ii) **Best Fit**

beta site *noun* company or person that tests new software (before it is released) in a real environment to make sure it works correctly **Betatester**

◊ **beta software** *noun* software that has not finished all its testing before release and so may still contain bugs **Betasoftware; Betaversion**

◊ **beta test** *noun* second stage of tests performed on new software just before it is due to be released **Betatest;** *the application has passed the alpha tests and is just entering the beta test phase*

◊ **beta version** *noun* version of a software application that is almost ready to be released **Betaversion;** *we'll try out the beta test software on as many different PCs as possible to try and find all the bugs*

> QUOTE the client was so eager to get his hands on the product that the managing director bypassed internal testing and decided to let it go straight out to beta test
> *Computing*

bezel *noun* front cover of a computer's casing or disk drive unit **Frontblende**

Bézier curve *noun* geometric curve; the overall shape is defined by two midpoints, called control handles **Bézierkurve**

> COMMENT: Bézier curves are a feature of many high-end design software packages; they allow a designer to create smooth curves by defining a number of points. The PostScript page description language uses Bézier curves to define the shapes of characters during printing

bias *noun*
(a) electrical reference level **Vorspannung**
(b) high frequency signal added to recorded information to minimize noise and distortion (the high frequency is removed on playback) **Vormagnetisierung**
(c) deviation of statistical results from a reference level **asymmetrischer Fehlerbereich**

◊ **biased** *adjective* which has a bias **voreingenommen, befangen; biased data** = data *or* records which point to one conclusion **tendenziöse Daten; biased exponent** = value of the exponent in a floating point number **kodierter Exponent**

bibliographic *or* **bibliographical** *adjective* referring to books *or* to bibliographies **bibliografisch; bibliographical information** = information about a book (name of author, number of pages, ISBN, etc.) which is used for library cataloguing **bibliografische Information**

◊ **bibliography** *noun*
(a) list of documents and books which are relevant to a certain subject **Bibliografie, Literaturverzeichnis;** *he printed a bibliography at the end of each chapter*
(b) catalogue of books **Bibliografie**

bid *verb* (*of a computer*) to gain control of a network in order to transmit data **ein Senderecht anfordern;** *the terminal had to bid three times before there was a gap in transmissions on the network*

bi-directional *adjective* (operation *or* process) that can occur in forward *or* reverse directions **zweiseitig gerichtet, in beiden Richtungen;** *bi-directional file transfer;* **bi-directional bus** = data *or* control lines that can carry signals travelling in two directions **zweiseitig gerichteter Übertragungsweg; bi-directional printer** = printer which is able to print characters from left to right and from right to left as the head is moving forward *or* backward across the paper (speeding up the printing operation) **Zweirichtungsdrucker;** *compare* OMNIDIRECTIONAL

bifurcation *noun* system where there are only two possible results **Gabelung**

Big Blue *informal name for* IBM

billion number equal to one thousand million *or* one million million **Milliarde** NOTE: in the US it means one thousand million, but in GB it usually means one million million. With figures it is usually written **bn: $5bn** (say 'five billion dollars')

BIM = BEGINNING OF INFORMATION MARK symbol indicating the start of a data stream stored on a disk drive *or* tape **Informationsanfangsmarke**

bin *noun* tray used to hold a supply of paper ready to be fed into a printer **Fach**

binary *adjective* (& *noun*) base 2 *or* number notation system which uses only the digits 0 and 1 **binär, dual; binary adder** = device that provides the sum of two or more binary digits **binärer Addierer; binary arithmetic** = rules and functions governing arithmetic operations in base 2

Binärarithmetik; **binary bit** = smallest single unit in (base 2) binary notation, either a 0 or a 1 **binärer Bit; binary cell** = storage element for one bit **binäre Zelle; binary chop** see BINARY SEARCH; **binary code** = using different patterns of binary digits to represent various symbols, elements, etc. **Binärcode; binary coded characters** = alphanumeric characters represented as patterns of binary digits **binär codierte Zeichen; binary coded decimal (BCD)** = representation of single decimal digits as a pattern of four binary digits **binär codierte Dezimalzahl; binary counter** = circuit that will divide a binary input signal by two (producing one output pulse for two input pulses) **Binärzähler; binary digit** or **bit** = smallest single unit in (base 2) binary notation, either a 0 or a 1 **Binärziffer, Bit; binary dump** = display of a section of memory in binary form **binärer Speicherauszug; binary encoding** = representing a character or element with a unique combination or pattern of bits in a word **binäre Verschlüsselung; binary exponent** = one word that contains the sign and exponent of a binary number (expressed in exponent and mantissa form) **binärer Exponent; binary file** = file that contains data rather than alphanumeric characters; a binary file can include any character code and cannot always be displayed or edited **Binärdatei;** *the program instructions are stored in the binary file; your letter is a text file, not a binary file;* **binary fraction** = representation of a decimal fraction in binary form **binärer Bruch;** *the binary fraction 0.011 is equal to one quarter plus one eighth (i.e. three eighths);* **binary half adder** = binary adder that can produce the sum of two inputs, producing a carry output if necessary, but cannot accept a carry input **binärer Halbaddierer; binary loader** = short section of program code that allows programs in binary form (such as object code from a linker or assembler) to be loaded into memory **Binärlader; binary mantissa** = fractional part of a number (in binary form) **binäre Mantisse; binary notation** or **representation** = base 2 numerical system using only the digits 0 and 1 **Dualschreibweise; binary number** = quantity represented in base 2 **Binärzahl, Dualzahl; binary operation** = (i) operation on two operands; (ii) operation on an operand in binary form **(i) Rechenoperation mit zwei Operanden; (ii) Binäroperation; binary point** = dot which indicates the division between the whole unit bits and the fractional part of a binary number **Binärkomma; binary scale** = power of two associated with each bit position in a word **Binärskala;** *in a four bit word, the binary scale is 1,2,4,8;* **binary search** or **chop** = fast search method for use on ordered lists of data (the search key is compared with the data in the middle of the list and one half is discarded, this is repeated with the remaining half until only the required data item is left) **binäres Suchen, Halbierungsverfahren; binary sequence** = series of binary digits **Binärsequenz; binary signalling** = transmission using positive and zero voltage levels to represent binary data **binäre Zeichengabe; binary split** = method of iteration in which the existing number is compared to a new value calculated as the mid-point between the high and low limits **Binäraufteilung; binary synchronous communications (BSC)** = (old) standard for medium/high speed data communication links **binär-synchrone Übertragungssteuerung; binary system** = use of binary numbers or operating with binary numbers **Binärsystem; binary-to-decimal conversion** = process to convert a binary number into its equivalent decimal value **Binär-Dezimal-Umwandlung; binary tree** = tree structure for data, where each item of data can have only two branches **binärer Baum; binary variable** = variable that can contain either a one or zero **binäre Variable**

> QUOTE with this type of compression you can only retrieve words by scanning the list sequentially, rather than by faster means such as a binary search
> *Practical Computing*

binaural *adjective* method of recording two audio channels **binaural, beidohrig**

|| COMMENT: separate sound tracks for the left and right ears are recorded to provide enhanced depth of sound

bind *verb*
(a) to link and convert one or more object code programs into a form that can be executed **verknüpfen; binding time** = time taken to produce actual addresses from an object code program **Verknüpfungszeit**
(b) to glue or attach sheets of paper along their spine to form a book **binden;** *the book is bound in laminated paper; a paperbound book; the sheets have been sent to the bindery for binding* (NOTE: **binding - bound**)

◊ **binder** *noun*
(a) program that converts object code into a form that can be executed **Bindungsprogramm**
(b) company which specializes in binding books **Binder(ei)**

◊ **bindery** *noun* factory where books are bound **Buchbinderei**

◊ **binding** *noun*
(a) action of putting a cover on a book **Binden; binding offset** = extra wide margin on the inside of a printed page (left margin on a right hand page, right margin on a left hand page) to prevent text being hidden during binding **Heftrandversatz**
(b) cover of a book **Einband;** *the book has a soft plastic binding*

Bindery *noun* special database used in a Novell NetWare network operating system to store user account, access and security details **Bindery**

BIOS = BASIC INPUT/OUTPUT SYSTEM system routines that interface between high-level program instructions and the system peripherals to control the input and output to various standard devices, this often includes controlling the screen, keyboard and disk drives **BIOS (Ein-/Ausgabesystem des Betriebssystems)**

biosensor *noun* device that allows electrical impulses from an organism to be recorded **Biosensor;** *the nerve activity can be measured by attaching a biosensor to your arm*

bipolar *adjective* with two levels **bipolar; bipolar coding** = transmission method which uses alternate positive and negative voltage levels to represent a binary one, with binary zero represented by zero level **bipolare Codierung; bipolar signal** = use of positive and negative voltage levels to represent the binary digits **bipolares Signal; bipolar transistor** = transistor constructed of three layers of alternating types of doped semiconductor (p-n-p or n-p-n) **bipolarer Transistor**

| COMMENT: each layer has a terminal labelled emitter, base and collector, usually the base signal controls the current flow between the emitter and collector

biquinary code *noun* decimal digits represented as two digits added together (for decimal digits less than 5, represented as 0 + the digit, for decimal digits greater than 4, represented as 5 + the digit minus 5) **Biquinärcode**

B-ISDN = BROADBAND ISDN

bistable *adjective* (device *or* circuit) that has two possible states, on and off **bistabil;**

bistable circuit *or* **multivibrator** = circuit which can be switched between two states **bistabile Kippschaltung**

bit *noun*
(a) = BINARY DIGIT smallest unit in binary number notation, which can have the value 0 or 1 **Bit, Binärzeichen**
(b) smallest unit of data that a system can handle **Bit; bit addressing** = selecting a register *or* word and examining one bit of it **Bitadressierung; bit blit** *or* **bitblt** = (in computer graphics) to move a block of bits from one memory location to another **Bitblockverschiebung, Blittern; bit block** = (in computer graphics) group of bits treated as one unit **Bitblock; bit block transfer** = (in computer graphics) to move a block of bits from one memory location to another **Bitblockverschiebung; bit bucket** = area of memory into which data can be discarded **Papierkorb; bit density** = number of bits that can be recorded per unit of storage medium **Bitdichte; bit error rate (BER)** = (normally referring to fibre optics) ratio of the number of bits received compared to the number of errors in a transmission **Bitfehlerrate (BER); bit flipping** = to invert the state of bits from 0 to 1 and 1 to 0 **Bithantierung; bit handling** = CPU commands and processes that allow bit manipulation, changing, etc. **Bitbearbeitung; bit image** = collection of bits that represent the pixels that make up an image on screen or on a printer **Bitbild; bit interleaving** = form of time domain multiplexing used in some synchronous transmission protocols such as HDLC and X.25 **Bitverschachtelung; bit manipulation** = various instructions that provide functions such as examine a bit, change *or* set *or* move a bit within a word **Bitverarbeitung; bit parallel** = transmission of a collection of bits simultaneously over a number of lines; the parallel printer port uses bit parallel transmission to transfer eight bits at a time to a printer **bitparallel; bit pattern** = certain arrangement of bits within a word, that represents a certain character *or* action **Bitmuster; bit plane** = (in computer graphics) one layer of a multiple-layer image; each layer defines one colour of each pixel **Bitebene; bit position** = place of a bit of data in a computer word **Bitstelle, Bitposition; bit rate** = measure of the number of bits transmitted per second **Übertragungsgeschwindigkeit; bit significant** = using the bits within a byte to describe something **bitsignifikant;** *testing bit six of a byte containing an ASCII character is bit significant and determines if the ASCII*

character is upper or lower case; **bit-slice design** = construction of a large word size CPU by joining a number of smaller word size blocks **Bitscheibenaufbau;** *the bit-slice design uses four four-bit word processors to construct a sixteen-bit processor;* **bits per inch (bpi)** = number of bits that can be recorded per inch of recording medium **Bits pro Inch; bits per pixel (BPP)** = number of bits assigned to store the colour of each pixel; one bit provides black or white, four bits gives 16 colour combinations, eight bits gives 256 colour combinations **Bits pro Pixel (BPP); bits per second (bps)** = measure of the number of binary digits transmitted every second **Bits pro Sekunde; bit stream** = binary data sequence that does not consist of separate, distinct character codes *or* groups **Bitreihe; bit stuffing** = addition of extra bits to a group of data to make up a certain length required for transmission **Bit-Füllung; bit track** = track on a magnetic disk along which bits can be recorded *or* read back **Bitspur;** *compare* LOGICAL TRACK; **bit wise** = action or operation carried out on each bit in a byte, one bit at a time **bitweise; check bit** = one bit of a binary word that is used to provide a parity check **Prüfbit; mask bit** = one bit (in a mask) used to select the required bit from a word *or* string **Maskenbit; most significant bit (MSB)** = bit in a computer word that represents the greatest power of two (in an eight-bit word the MSB is in bit position eight and represents a decimal number of two to the power eight, or 128) **größtes Bit; sign bit** = single bit that indicates if a binary number is positive or negative (usually 0 = positive, 1 = negative) **Vorzeichenbit;** *see also* BYTE

◊ **bitblt** *see* BIT, BLIT

◊ **bit-map** *verb* to define events *or* data using an array of single bits; (this can be an image *or* graphics *or* a table of devices in use, etc.) **als (digitales) Muster speichern; bit-mapped graphics** = image whose individual pixels can be controlled by changing the value of its stored bit (one is on, zero is off; in colour displays, more than one bit is used to provide control for the three colours - Red, Green, Blue) **als digitales Muster gespeicherte Grafik**

QUOTE it became possible to store more than one bit per pixel
Practical Computing

QUOTE the expansion cards fit into the PC's expansion slot and convert bit-mapped screen images to video signals
Publish

QUOTE it is easy to turn any page into a bit-mapped graphic
PC Business World

black *adjective* with no colour **schwarz; black and white** = (i) use of shades of grey to represent colours on a monitor *or* display; (ii) an image in which each pixel is either black or white with no shades of grey (i) **Graustufen-;** (ii) **schwarzweiß; black box** = device that performs a function without the user knowing how **Blackbox; black crush** = conversion of a television picture to one with no tones, only black or white **Schattenschwärzung; black level** = level of a TV signal that produces no luminescence on screen **Schwarzpegel**

◊ **blackout** *or* **black out** *noun* complete loss of electrical power **Gesamtausfall;** *compare* BROWNOUT, BROWN-OUT

◊ **black writer** *noun* printer where toner sticks to the points hit by the laser beam when the image drum is scanned **spezieller Laserdrucker;** *compare* WHITE WRITER

COMMENT: a black writer produces sharp edges and graphics, but large areas of black are muddy

blank
1 *adjective* empty *or* with nothing written on it **leer; blank cell** = empty cell in a spreadsheet **Leerzelle; blank character** = character code that prints a space **Leerzeichen; blank instruction** = program instruction which does nothing **leere Anweisung; blank tape** *or* **blank disk** = magnetic tape *or* disk that does not have data stored on it **leeres Band; leere Platte; blank string** = (i) empty string; (ii) string containing spaces (i) **leere Zeichenfolge;** (ii) **Zeichenfolge aus Leerzeichen**
2 *noun* space on a form which has to be completed **(Text)lücke;** *fill in the blanks and insert the form into the OCR*

◊ **blanking** *noun* preventing a television signal from reaching the scanning beam on its return trace **Austasten; blanking interval** = time taken for the scanning beam in a TV to return from the end of a picture at the bottom right of the screen to top left **Austastlücke; blanking pulse** = electrical signal used to start the blanking of a TV signal **Leerimpuls**

blanket agreement *noun* agreement which covers many items **Pauschalabmachung; blanket cylinder** = rubber coated cylinder in a offset lithographic printing machine that transfers ink from the image plate to the paper **Gummituchzylinder**

◊ **blanketing** *see* JAMMING

blast *verb*
(a) to write data into a programmable ROM device **einbrennen**
(b) to free sections of previously allocated memory *or* resources **Bereiche freimachen**

◊ **blast-through alphanumerics** *noun* characters that can be displayed on a videotext terminal when it is in graphics mode **Zeichen, die im Grafikmodus sichtbar gemacht werden können**

bleed
1 *noun* (i) line of printing that runs off the edge of the paper; (ii) badly adjusted colour monitor in which colours of adjoining pixels blend **(i) angeschnittener Satzspiegel; (ii) Verlaufen**
2 *verb* **the photo is bled off** = the photograph is printed so that the image runs off the edge of the page **das Foto ist angeschnitten**

bleep
1 *noun* audible warning noise **Piepton;** *the printer will make a bleep when it runs out of paper*
2 *verb* to make a bleep **piepsen;** *see also* BEEP

◊ **bleeper** *noun* device which bleeps (often used to mean radio pager) **Piepser;** *the doctor's bleeper began to ring, and he went to the telephone; he is in the factory somewhere - we'll try to find him on his bleeper*

blind *adjective* which will not respond to certain codes **blind, tot**

◊ **blind copy receipt** *noun* (in electronic mail) method of sending a message to several users, whose identities are not known to the other recipients **Blindkopieversand;** *compare* CARBON COPY

◊ **blind dialling** *noun* ability of a modem to dial out even if the line appears dead, used on certain private lines **blindes Anwählen; blind keyboard** = keyboard whose output is not displayed but is stored directly on magnetic tape *or* disk **unsichtbar schreibende Tastatur**

B-line counter *noun* address register that is added to a reference address to provide the location to be accessed **Zusatzadressregister**

blinking *noun* flashing effect caused by varying the intensity of a displayed character **Blinken**

blip *noun* small mark on a tape or film counted to determine the position **Markierung**

blister pack *noun* type of packing where the item for sale is covered with a thin plastic sheet sealed to a card backing **Schrumpffolienverpackung**

blit *or* **bitblt** *verb* (in computer graphics) to move a block of bits from one memory location to another **blittern, verschieben**

◊ **blitter** *noun* electronic component designed to process or move a bit-mapped image from one area of memory to another **Blitterchip;** *the new blitter chip speeds up the graphics display*

block
1 *noun*
(a) (i) series of items grouped together; (ii) number of stored records treated as a single unit **(i) & (ii) Satz, Block; block character check (BCC)** = error detection method for blocks of transmitted data **Blockzeichenprüfung; block code** = error detection and correction code for block data transmission **Blockcode; block compaction** *see* COMPRESS, COMPACT; **block copy** = (i) to duplicate a block of data to another section of memory; (ii) (in a word-processor) to copy a selected area of text from one part of a document to another **(i) & (ii) einen Block kopieren; block delete** = (in a word-processor) to delete a selected area of text **einen Block löschen; block device** = device that manipulates many bytes of data at once **Blockeinheit;** *the disk drive is a block device that can transfer 256bytes of data at a time;* **block diagram** = illustration of the way the main components in a system are connected, but without detail **Blockdiagramm;** *the first step to designing a new computer is to draw out a block diagram of its main components;* **block error rate** = number of blocks of data that contain errors compared with the total number transmitted **Blockfehlerhäufigkeit; block header** = information at the start of a file describing content organization and characteristics **Blockkopf; block ignore character** = symbol at the start of a block indicating that it contains corrupt data **Blockignorierungszeichen; block input processing** = input system that requires a whole error-free block to be received before it is processed **Blockeingabeverarbeitung; block length** = number of bytes of data in a

block **Blocklänge; block list** = list of the blocks and records as they are organized in a file **Blockliste; block mark** = code that indicates the end of a block **Blockmarke; block move** = (i) (in a word-processor) to move selected text from one area of a document to another; (ii) (in memory) to move the contents of an area of memory to another area of memory **(i) & (ii) einen Block verschieben; block operation** = process carried out on a block of data **Blockoperation; block parity** = parity error check on a block of data **Blockprüfung; block protection** = (in a word-processor) to prevent a selected block of text being split by an automatic page break **Blockschutz; block retrieval** = accessing blocks of data stored in memory **Blockzugriff; block synchronization** = correct timing of start, stop and message bits according to a predefined protocol **Blocksynchronisierung; block transfer** = moving large numbers of records around in memory **Blockübertragung, Blocktransfer; building block** = self-contained unit that can be joined to others to form a system **Baustein; data block** = all the data required for or from a process **Datenblock; end of block (EOB)** = code which indicates that the last byte of a block of data has been sent **Ende des (Datenübertragungs)blocks; (inter)block gap (IBG)** = space between two blocks of stored data **Blockzwischenraum**

(b) wide printed bar **Blockade (in Form einer Linie); block cursor** = cursor the shape of a solid rectangle that fills a character position **Blockcursor; block diagram** = graphical representation of a system or program operation **Blockdiagramm**

(c) block capitals or **block letters** = capital letters (such as A,B,C) **Großbuchstaben, Blockschrift;** write your name and address in block letters

2 verb
(a) to stop something taking place **aufhalten, stoppen, blockieren;** the system manager blocked his request for more CPU time
(b) to block in = to sketch roughly the main items of a design **andeuten, skizzieren**

◊ **blocking factor** noun number of records in a block **Blockungsfaktor**

bloom noun bright spot on the screen of a faulty television **Überstrahlen**

bloop verb to pass a magnet over a tape to erase signals which are not needed **Fehler löschen**

blow or **burn** verb to program a PROM

device with data **einen Festwertspeicher programmieren**

blueprint noun copy of an original set of specifications or design in graphical form **Blaupause**

◊ **blue-ribbon program** noun perfect program that runs first time, with no errors or bugs **erstklassiges Programm**

blur
1 noun image where the edges or colours are not clear **verschwommenes Bild; Schmitz**
2 verb to make the edges or colours of an image fuzzy **verwackeln;** the image becomes blurred when you turn the focus knob

BMP noun (in graphics) three-letter extension to a filename that indicates that the file contains a bit-mapped graphics image **BMP;** this paint package lets you import BMP files

bn = BILLION

BNC connector noun cylindrical metal connector with a copper core that is at the end of coaxial cable and is used to connect cables together; it attaches by pushing and twisting the outer cylinder onto two locking pins **BNC-Stecker**

◊ **BNC T-piece connector** noun T-shaped metal connector used to connect an adapter card to the ends of two sections of RG-58 'thin' coaxial cable used in many Ethernet network installations **BNC-T-Stecker**

BNF = BACKUS-NAUR-FORM system of writing and expressing the syntax of a programming language **Backus-Naur-Form**

board noun
(a) flat insulation material on which electronic components are mounted and connected **Platine; bus board** = PCB containing conducting paths for all the computer signals (for the address, data and control buses) **Buskarte; daughter board** = add-on board that connects to a system motherboard **Erweiterungsplatine; expansion board** or **add on board** = printed circuit board that is connected to a system to increase its functions or performance **Erweiterungsplatine; motherboard** = main printed circuit board of a system, containing most of the components and connectors for expansion boards, etc. **Hauptplatine; printed circuit board (PCB)** = flat insulating material that has conducting

tracks of metal printed *or* etched onto its surface, which complete a circuit when components are mounted on it **gedruckte Schaltkarte**
(b) people who run a company *or* group *or* society **Aufsichtsrat, Beirat, Firmenvorstand, Kommission; editorial board** = group of editors **Redaktionsausschuss**

QUOTE both models can be expanded to the current maximum of the terminals by adding further serial interface boards
Micro Decision

◊ **bulletin board system (BBS)** *noun* information and message database accessible by modem and computer link **Schwarzes-Brett-System**

body *noun* (i) main section of text in a document; (ii) main part of a program **(i) Haupttextteil; (ii) Hauptprogrammteil; body size** = length of a section of text from top to bottom in points **Schriftspiegel; body type** = default font and point size that is used for the main section of text in a document **Zeichenformatierung im Haupttextteil; Standardzeichenformat**

bof *or* **BOF** = BEGINNING OF FILE character *or* symbol that shows the start of a valid section of data **Dateianfang**

boilerplate *noun* final document that has been put together using standard sections of text held in a word processor **Schriftsatz (aus Standardtexten)**

◊ **boilerplating** *noun* putting together a final document out of various standard sections of text **Herstellung eines Schriftsatzes (aus Standardtexten)**

bold face *noun* thicker and darker form of a typeface **Fettdruck**

bomb
1 *noun* routine in a program designed to crash the system or destroy data at a particular time **Zeitbombe;** *the system programmer installed a bomb when they made him redundant*
2 *verb (informal) (of software)* to fail **abstürzen;** *the program bombed, and we lost all the data; the system can bomb if you set up several desk accessories or memory-resident programs at the same time*

bond paper *noun* heavy grade writing paper **Bankpost-, Bondpapier**

book
1 *noun*
(a) set of sheets of paper attached together **Buch;** *they can print books up to 96 pages; the book is available in paperback and hard cover*
(b) cheque book = book of new cheques **Scheckbuch; phone book** *or* **telephone book** = book which lists names of people *or* companies with their addresses and telephone numbers **Telefonbuch**
2 *verb* to order *or* to reserve something **buchen;** *to book a room in a hotel or a table at a restaurant or a ticket on a plane; I booked a table for 7.45*

◊ **booklet** *noun* small book with a paper cover **Broschüre**

◊ **bookseller** *noun* person who sells books **Buchhändler**

◊ **bookshop** *noun* shop which sells books **Buchhandlung**

◊ **bookstall** *noun* small open bookshop (as in a railway station) **Bücherstand**

◊ **bookstore** *noun (US)* bookshop **Buchhandlung**

◊ **bookwork** *noun*
(a) keeping of financial records **Buchführungsarbeit**
(b) printing and binding of books **Buchproduktion**
NOTE: no plural

bookmark *noun* code inserted at a particular point in a document that allows the user to move straight to that point at a later date **Lesezeichen; Textmarke**

Boolean algebra *or* **logic** *noun* rules set down to define, simplify and manipulate logical functions, based on statements which are true or false **boolesche Algebra;** *see* AND, NOT, OR; **monadic Boolean operation** = logical operation on only one word, such as NOT **monadische boolesche Operation**

◊ **Boolean connective** *noun* symbol *or* character in a Boolean operation that describes the action to be performed on the operands **boolescher Operator**

◊ **Boolean operation** *noun* logical operation on a number of operands, conforming to Boolean algebra rules **boolesche Operation; Boolean operation table** = table showing two binary words (operands), the operation and the result **Tabelle der booleschen Operationen; dyadic Boolean operation** = logical operation producing a result from two words, such as

AND dyadische *or* zweistellige boolesche Operation; **monadic Boolean operation** = logical operation on only one word, such as NOT **monadische oder einstellige boolesche Operation**

◊ **Boolean operator** *noun* logical operator such as AND, OR etc. **boolescher Operator**

◊ **Boolean value** *noun* one of two values, either true or false **boolescher Wert**

◊ **Boolean variable** *or* **data type** *noun* binary word in which each bit represents true or false, using the digits 1 or 0 **boolesche Variable**

boom
1 *noun*
(a) piece of metal which supports a microphone *or* antenna **Galgen**
(b) time when sales *or* production *or* business activity are increasing **Aufschwung, Boom; boom industry** = industry which is expanding rapidly **Aufschwungindustrie; the boom years** = years when there is a boom **die Jahre des Aufschwungs**
2 *verb* to expand *or* to do well in business **einen Aufschwung nehmen;** *sales are booming; a booming industry or company; technology is a booming sector of the economy*

boost
1 *noun* help received **Auftrieb;** *the prize was a real boost; the new model gave a boost to the sales figures*
2 *verb* to make something increase **anheben, verstärken;** *the extra hard disk will boost our storage capacity by 25Mb*

boot *verb* to execute a set of instructions automatically in order to reach a required state **laden; boot block** *or* **record** = first track (track 0) on a boot disk of an IBM-compatible floppy disk **Urladeprogrammblock; boot disk** = special disk which contains a bootstrap program and the operating system software **Startdiskette;** *after you switch on the computer, insert the boot disk;* **boot partition** = on a hard disk with more than one partition, the partition that contains the bootstrap and operating system **Boot-Partition; Startpartition**

◊ **boot up** *or* **booting** *noun* automatic execution of a set of instructions usually held in ROM when a computer is switched on **Laden**

◊ **bootleg** *noun* illegal copy of recorded material **Raubkopie**

◊ **bootstrap (loader)** *noun* set of instructions that are executed by the computer before a program is loaded, usually to load the operating system once the computer is switched on **Urlader;** *compare* LOADER

QUOTE the digital signal processor includes special on-chip bootstrap hardware to allow easy loading of user programs into the program RAM
Electronics & Wireless World

booth *noun* small place for one person to stand *or* sit **Kabine; telephone booth** = soundproof cabin with a public telephone in it **Telefonzelle; ticket booth** = place outdoors where a person sells tickets **Kartenhäuschen**

border *noun* area around printed *or* displayed text **Umgrenzung**

Borland software company which has developed a wide range of programming languages, database management systems and spreadsheet applications (including Turbo C++, Paradox, and QuatroPro) **Borland**

borrow *verb*
(a) to take something (such as money *or* a library book) from someone for a time, returning it at the end of the period **entleihen;** *he borrowed £1,000 from the bank; she borrowed a book on computer construction*
(b) operation in certain arithmetic processes, such as subtraction from a smaller number **borgen**

◊ **borrower** *noun* person who borrows **Entleiher;** *borrowers from the library are allowed to keep books for two weeks*

BOS = BASIC OPERATING SYSTEM software that controls the basic, low-level running of the hardware and file management **BOS (Basisbetriebssystem)**

Bose-Chandhuri-Hocquenghem code (BCH) *noun* error correcting code **Bose-Chandhuri-Hocquenghem-Code**

bot *or* **BOT** = BEGINNING OF TAPE; **BOT marker** = section of material that marks the start of the recording area of magnetic tape **Bandanfang**

bottom space *noun* blank lines at the bottom of a page of printed text **Fußsteg**

◊ **bottom up method** *noun* combining

low-level instructions to form a high-level instruction (which can then be further combined) **Bottom-Up-Verfahren**

bounce *noun* (error) multiple key contact caused by a faulty switch **Prellen; de-bounce** = preventing a single touch on a key producing multiple key contact **Entprellen**

boundary *noun* limits of something **Grenzen; boundary protection** = preventing any program writing into a reserved area of memory **Grenzenschutz; boundary punctuation** = punctuation which marks the beginning *or* end of a file **Grenzmarkierung; boundary register** = register in a multi-user system that contains the addresses for the limits of one user's memory allocation **Grenzenregister**

bounds *noun* limits *or* area in which one can operate **Grenzen; array bounds** = limits to the number of elements which can be given in an array **Matrixgrenzen**

box *noun*
(a) cardboard *or* wood *or* plastic container **Kasten;** *the goods were sent in thin cardboard boxes; the keyboard is packed in plastic foam before being put into the box;* **black box** = device that performs a function without the user knowing how **Blackbox**
(b) **box number** = reference number used in a post office or an advertisement to avoid giving an address **Postfachnummer;** *please reply to Box No. 209; our address is: P.O. Box 74209, Edinburgh*
(c) **cash box** = metal box for keeping cash **Geldkassette; letter box** *or* **mail box** = place where incoming mail is put **Briefkasten; call box** = outdoor telephone booth **Telefonzelle**
(d) square of ruled lines round a text *or* illustration **Kasten;** *the comments and quotations are printed in boxes*

◊ **boxed** *adjective* put in a box *or* sold in a box **verpackt (in einer Schachtel); boxed set** = set of items sold together in a box **in einer Schachtel verpacktes Set**

◊ **box in** *verb* to surround a section of text with ruled lines **(mit einem Kasten) einrahmen**

Boyce-Codd normal form (BCNF) *see* NORMAL FORM

BPI *or* **bpi** = BITS PER INCH number of bits that can be recorded per inch of recording medium **Bits pro Inch**

BPP = BITS PER PIXEL number of bits assigned to store the colour of each pixel;

one bit provides black or white, four bits gives 16 colour combinations, eight bits gives 256 colour combinations **BPP**

bps = BITS PER SECOND; **bps rate** = rate at which information is sent equal to the number of bits transmitted or received per second **Bitrate; bps rate adjust** = ability of a modem to automatically adjust the speed of its serial port to match the communications speed **bps-Anpassung**

Bps = BYTES PER SECOND

BRA = BASIC RATE ACCESS basic ISDN service that provides two data channels capable of carrying data at a rate of 64Kbps together with a signalling channel used to carry control signals at 16Kbps **BRA**

braces *noun* curly bracket characters { } used in some programming languages to enclose a routine **geschweifte Klammern**

bracket
1 *noun* printing sign to show that an instruction *or* operations are to be separated **Klammer; curly brackets** *or* **braces** = curly bracket characters { } used in some programming languages to enclose a routine **geschweifte Klammern; round brackets; square brackets** = different types of bracket ( ), [ ] **runde Klammern; eckige Klammern**
2 *verb* **to bracket together** = to print brackets round several items to show that they are treated in the same way and separated from the rest of the text **einklammern**

◊ **bracketed** *adjective* (characters) joined together with small lines between serif and main part **eingeklammert**

◊ **bracketing** *noun* photographing the same scene with different exposures to make sure there is one good picture **Belichtungsreihe**

Braille *noun* system of writing using raised dots on the paper to indicate letters, which allows a blind person to read by passing his fingers over the page **Blindenschrift;** *she was reading a Braille book; the book has been published in Braille;* **Braille marks** = raised patterns on equipment *or* in books to permit identification by touch **Blindenschrift**

branch
1 *noun*
(a) possible path *or* jump from one

instruction to another **Programmzweig, Verzweigung; branch instruction** = conditional program instruction that provides the location of the next instruction in the program (if a condition is met) **Verzweigungsbefehl; branch table** = table that defines where to jump to in a program depending on the result of a test **Verzweigungstabelle; program branch** = one or more paths that can be followed after a conditional statement **Programmzweig** **(b)** line linking one or more devices to the main network **Verzweigung;** *the faulty station is on this branch* **2** *verb* to jump from one section of a program to another **verzweigen**

◊ **branchpoint** *noun* point in a program where a branch can take place **Verzweigungspunkt**

COMMENT: in BASIC, the instruction GOTO makes the system jump to the line indicated; this is an unconditional branch. The instruction IF...THEN is a conditional branch, because the jump will only take place if the condition is met

brand *noun* make of product, which can be recognized by a name *or* by a design **Marke;** *the number one brand of magnetic tape; the company is developing a new brand of screen cleaner;* **brand name** = name of a brand **Markenname; brand image** = idea of a product which is associated with the brand name **Markenimage, Markenprofil; own brand** = name of a store which is used on products which are specially packed for that store **Geschäftsname als Markenbezeichnung**

◊ **branded** *adjective* **branded goods** = goods sold under brand names **Markenartikel**

◊ **brand new** *adjective* quite new *or* very new **brandneu**

breach *noun* failure to carry out the terms of an agreement **Verletzung, Verstoß; breach of contract** = failing to do something which is in a contract **Vertragsbruch; the company is in breach of contract** = it has failed to carry out the duties of the contract **die Firma ist vertragsbrüchig geworden; breach of warranty** = supplying goods which do not meet the standards of the warranty applied to them **Verletzung der Gewährleistung**

breadboard *noun* device that allows prototype electronic circuits to be constructed easily without permanent connections or soldering **Brettschaltung; Laborplatine**

break
1 *noun* action *or* key pressed to stop a program execution **Unterbrechung; Break key** = special key on an IBM-compatible keyboard that halts execution of a program when pressed with the Control key **Pause-Taste;** *I stopped the problem by pressing Ctrl-Break* **2** *verb* **(a)** to fail to carry out the duties of an agreement **brechen;** *the company has broken the agreement* **(b)** to decipher a difficult code **knacken;** *he finally broke the cipher system* NOTE: **breaking - broke - has broken**

◊ **break down** *verb* to stop working because of mechanical failure **ausfallen;** *the modem has broken down; what do you do when your line printer breaks down?*

◊ **breakdown** *noun* stopping work because of mechanical failure **Ausfall;** *we cannot communicate with our New York office because of the breakdown of the telex lines*

◊ **breaker** *noun* **circuit breaker** = device which protects equipment by cutting off the electrical supply **Stromkreisunterbrecher**

◊ **breakpoint** *noun* symbol inserted into a program which stops its execution at that point to allow registers, variables and memory locations to be examined (used when debugging a program) **bedingter Programmstop; breakpoint instruction** *or* **halt** = halt command inserted in a program to stop execution temporarily, allowing the programmer to examine data and registers while debugging a program **Stopbefehl; breakpoint symbol** = special character used to provide a breakpoint in a program (the debugging program allows breakpoint symbols to be inserted, it then executes the program until it reaches one, then halts) **Programmstopsignal**

◊ **breakup** *noun* loss *or* distortion of a signal **Verlust**

breezeway *noun* signal used to separate the colour information from the horizontal synchronizing pulse in a television signal **getrenntes Schalten von Ton und Bild**

B register *noun* (i) address register that is added to a reference address to provide the location to be accessed; (ii) register used to extend the accumulator in multiplication and division operations **(i) Zusatzadressregister; (ii) B-Register**

bridge
1 *verb* to use bridgeware to help transfer programs, data files, etc., to another system **überbrücken**

2 *noun* **bridge** *or* **bridging product** =
(a) device that connects two networks together; bridges function at the data link layer of the OSI network model **Brücke**; *see also* ROUTER; BROUTER
(b) matching communications equipment that makes sure that power losses are kept to a minimum **Brücke**
(c) hardware or software that allows parts of an old system to be used on a new system **Überbrückung**

> COMMENT: a bridge connects two similar networks, a gateway connects two different networks. To connect two Ethernet networks, use a bridge

◊ **bridgeware** *noun* hardware or software used to make the transfer from one computer system to another easier (by changing file format, translation, etc.) **Bridgeware**

◊ **bridging** *noun* the use of bridgeware to help transfer programs, data files, etc., to another system **Überbrückung**; *a bridging product is available for companies with both generations of machines*

> QUOTE Lotus Development and IMRS are jointly developing a bridge linking their respective spreadsheet and client server reporting tools. It will allow users of IMRS' Hyperion reporting tool to manipulate live data from Lotus Improv
> *Computing*

brightness *noun* luminance of an object which can be seen **Helligkeit**; *a control knob allows you to adjust brightness and contrast the brightness of the monitor can hurt the eyes;* **brightness range** = variation of reflected light intensity **Helligkeitsbereich**

> QUOTE there is a brightness control on the front panel
> *Micro Decision*

brilliant *adjective* very bright and shining (light *or* colour) **brilliant**; *the background colour is a brilliant red; he used brilliant white for the highlights*

◊ **brilliance** *noun* the luminance of an object as seen in a picture **Brillianz**

bring-up *verb* to start a computer system **starten**

British Standards Institute (BSI) organization that monitors design and safety standards in the UK **Britisches Normeninstitut**

broadband *or* **wideband** *noun*
(a) transmission channel whose bandwidth is greater than a voice channel (allowing faster data transmission) **Breitband**; **broadband radio** = radio communications link using a broadband channel **Breitbandradio**
(b) (in local area networks *or* communications) transmission method that combines several channels of data onto a carrier signal and can carry the data over long distances **Breitband**; *compare* BASEBAND

broadcast
1 *noun* (i) (radio communications) data transmission to many receivers; (ii) (in a network) message or data sent to a group of users (i) **Sendung, Ausstrahlung**; (ii) **Rundspruch**; **broadcast homes** = homes with at least one TV *or* radio receiver **Haushalt mit Radio- und/oder Fernsehgerät**; **broadcast message** = message sent to everyone on a network **Rundsendenachricht**; **Rundspruch**; *five minutes before we shut down the LAN, we send a broadcast message to all users;* **broadcast network** = network for sending data to a number of receivers **Rundspruchnetz**; **broadcast quality** = video image *or* signal that is the same as that used by professional television stations **Fernsehqualität**; *we can use your multimedia presentation as the advert on TV if it's of broadcast quality;* **broadcast satellite technique** = method of providing greatest channel bandwidth for a geostationary satellite **Rundfunksatellitentechnik**
2 *verb* to distribute information over a wide area *or* audience **senden, ausstrahlen**; *he broadcast the latest news over the radio or over the WAN;* **broadcasting station** = radio station that transmits received signals to other stations **Rundfunksendestelle**

broadsheet *noun* uncut sheet of paper *or* paper which has printing on one side only **einseitig bedrucktes Blatt, Einblattdruck**

broadside *noun* (*US*) publicity leaflet **Flugblatt**

brochure *noun* publicity booklet **Broschüre**; *we sent off for a brochure about holidays in Greece*

bromide *or* **bromide print** *noun*
(a) positive photographic print from a

negative *or* the finished product from a phototypesetting machine **Bromidsilberdruck;** *in 24 hours we had bromides ready to film*
(b) lithographic plate used for proofing **Bromidsilberplatte**

brouter *noun* device that combines the functions of a router and bridge to connect networks together **Brouter;** *the brouter provides dynamic routing and can bridge two local area networks; see also* BRIDGE; ROUTER

brown-out *noun* power failure (low voltage level rather than no voltage level) **Spannungsabfall;** *see also* BLACK-OUT

browse *verb*
(a) to view data in a database or online system **anzeigen**
(b) to search through and access database material without permission **stöbern**

brush *noun* tool in paint package software that draws pixels on screen **Pinsel;** *the paint package lets you vary the width of the brush (in pixels) and the colour it produces;* **brush style** = width and shape of the brush tool in a paint package **Pinselform;** *to fill in a big area, I select a wide, square brush style*

brute force method *noun* problem-solving method which depends on computer power rather than elegant programming techniques **Methode der rohen Gewalt**

BS = BACKSPACE

BSAM = BASIC SEQUENTIAL ACCESS METHOD

BSC = BINARY SYNCHRONOUS COMMUNICATIONS (old) standard for medium/high speed data communication links **binär-synchrone Übertragungssteuerung**

BSI = BRITISH STANDARDS INSTITUTE

BTAM = BASIC TELECOMMUNICATIONS ACCESS METHOD method to provide access (read *or* write operations) to a remote device **BTAM-Zugriffsmethode**

btree = BINARY TREE

bubble jet printer ™ *see* INK-JET PRINTER

bubble memory *noun* method of storing binary data using the magnetic properties of certain materials, allowing very large amounts of data to be stored in primary memory **Blasenspeicher; bubble memory cassette** = bubble memory device on a removable cartridge that can be inserted into a controller card (like an audio cassette) to provide high capacity, high speed, removable memory **Blasenspeicherkassette**

◊ **bubble sort** *noun* sorting method which repeatedly exchanges various pairs of data items until they are in order **Bubblesort (einfaches Sortierverfahren)**

bucket *noun* storage area containing data for an application **Sammelfeld**

buckling *noun* distortion and bending of a film due to heat *or* dryness **Wölbung**

buffer
1 *noun*
(a) (circuit) that isolates and protects a system from damaging inputs from circuits *or* peripherals **Puffer;** *see also* DRIVER
(b) temporary storage area for data waiting to be processed **Zwischenspeicher; buffer register** = temporary storage for data read from *or* being written to main memory **Pufferregister; buffer size** = total number of characters that can be held in a buffer **Puffergröße; data buffer** = temporary storage location for data received by a device that is not yet ready to process it **Datenpuffer; dynamic** *or* **elastic buffer** = buffer whose size varies with demand **elastischer Puffer; I/O buffer** = temporary storage area for data waiting to be input *or* output **Ein-/Ausgabepuffer**
2 *verb* using a temporary storage area to hold data until the processor *or* device is ready to deal with it **zwischenspeichern; buffered input/output** = use of a temporary storage area on input *or* output ports to allow slow peripherals to operate with a fast CPU **zwischengespeicherte Ein-/Ausgabe; buffered memory** = feature that allows instructions *or* data to be entered before the device has finished processing **Pufferspeicher; buffering** = using buffers to provide a link between slow and fast devices **Pufferung; double buffering** = two buffers working together so that one can be read while the other is accepting data **doppelte Pufferung**

COMMENT: buffers allow two parts of a computer system to work at different speeds (i.e. a high-speed central processing unit and a slower line printer)

> QUOTE the speed is enhanced by the 8K
> RAM printer buffer included

> QUOTE the software allocates a portion of
> cache as a print buffer to restore program
> control faster after sending data to the
> printer
>
> *Which PC?*

bug

1 *noun (informal)*
(a) error in a computer program which makes it run incorrectly **Programm-, Softwarefehler;** *(informal)* **Mucken; bug patches** = (temporary) correction made to a program; small correction made to software by a user on the instructions of the software publisher **Ausmerzung von Softwarefehlern;** *see also* DEBUG
(b) hidden microphone which records conversations secretly **Wanze**
2 *verb* to hide a microphone to allow conversations to be recorded secretly **verwanzen;** *the conference room was bugged*

◊ **buggy** *noun* small computer-controlled vehicle **computergesteuertes Fahrzeug**

build

noun particular version of a program **Version;** *this is the latest build of the new software*

building block

noun self-contained unit that can be joined to others to form a system **Baustein**

built-in

adjective (special feature) that is already included in a system **eingebaut;** *the built-in adapter card makes it fully IBM compatible; the computer has a built-in hard disk;* **built-in check** = error detection and validation check carried out automatically on received data **automatische Selbstprüfung; built-in function** = special function already implemented in a program **eingebaute Standardfunktion**

◊ **built into** *adjective* feature that is already a physical part of a system **fest eingebaut;** *there are communications ports built into all modems*
NOTE: opposite is **add on**

bulk

noun large quantity of something **große Mengen; in bulk** = in large quantities **in großen Mengen; bulk erase** = to erase a complete magnetic disk *or* tape in one action **vollständig löschen; bulk .storage medium** = medium that is able to store large amounts of data in a convenient size and form **Massenspeichermedium;** *magnetic tape is a reliable bulk storage medium;* **bulk**

update terminal = device used by an information provider to prepare videotext pages off-line, then transmit them rapidly to the main computer **Aktualisierungsdatenstation für große Datenmengen**

bullet *noun*

(a) solid area of typeset tone indicating the required image intensity **Blockade (als Maß der Farbintensität)**
(b) symbol (often a filled circle or square) in front of a line of text, used to draw attention to a particular line in a list **Bullet; Aufzählungszeichen**

> QUOTE for a bullet chart use four to six
> bullet points and no more than six to
> eight words each
>
> *Computing*

bulletin board system (BBS) *noun*

information and message database accessible by modem and computer link **Schwarzes-Brett-System**

> QUOTE the Council of European
> Professional Informatics Societies has
> instituted an experimental Bulletin
> Board System based at the University of
> Wageningen
>
> *Computing*

bundle

1 *noun*
(a) number of optic fibres gathered together **(Leitungs)bündel**
(b) package containing a computer together with software or accessories offered at a special price **Software im Bundle; mitgelieferte Software;** *the bundle now includes a PC with spreadsheet and database applications for just £999*
2 *verb* to market at a special price a package that contains a computer together with a range of software or accessories **bundeln; als Bundle anbieten**

◊ **bundled software** *noun* software included in the price of a computer system **im Kaufpreis inbegriffene Software; mitgelieferte Software**

bureau

noun office which specializes in keyboarding data *or* processing batches of data for other small companies **Büro;** *the company offers a number of bureau services, such as printing and data collection; our data manipulation is handled by a bureau;* **information bureau** = office which gives information **Informationsbüro; output bureau** = office that converts data from a

DTP program or a drawing stored on disk into typeset artwork **Setzerei; Satzanstalt; word-processing bureau** = office which specializes in word-processing **Textverarbeitungsbüro;** *we farm out the office typing to a local bureau*
NOTE: the plural is **bureaux**

> QUOTE IMC has a colour output bureau that puts images onto the uncommon CD-ROM XA format
>
> *Computing*

burner *noun* device which burns in programs onto PROM chips **Brenner**

◊ **burn-in** *noun* heat test for electronic components **Einbrennen, Voraltern**

◊ **burn in** *verb*
(a) to mark a (television *or* monitor) screen after displaying a high brightness image for too long **einbrennen**
(b) to write data into a PROM chip **einbrennen**

◊ **burn out** *noun* excess heat *or* incorrect use that causes an electronic circuit *or* device to fail **Ausbrennen**

burst *noun* short isolated sequence of transmitted signals **geschlossener Übertragungsblock; burst mode** = data transmission using intermittent bursts of data **Stoßbetrieb; error burst** = group of several consecutive errors (in a transmission) **Fehlerhäufung**

burster *noun* machine used to separate the sheets of continuous fanfold paper **Vereinzelungsmaschine**

bus *noun*
(a) communication link consisting of a set of leads *or* wires which connects different parts of a computer hardware system, and over which data is transmitted and received by various circuits in the system **Übertragungsweg, Bus; bus address lines** = wires, each of which carries one bit of an address word **Adressbusleitung; bus arbitration** = protocol and control of transmission over a bus that ensures fair usage by several users **Buszuteilung; bus board** = PCB containing conducting paths for all the computer signals **Busplatine; bus control lines** = wires, each of which carries one bit of a control word **Bussteuerungsleitung; bus data lines** = wires, each of which carries one bit of a data word **Busdatenübertragungsleitung; bus driver** = high power transistors *or* amplifier that can provide enough power to transmit signals

to a number of devices **Bustreiber; bus extender** *or* **bus extension card (BEC)** = (i) device that extends an 8-bit bus to accommodate 16-bit add-in cards; (ii) special board (used by repair engineers) that moves an add-in board up to a position that is easier to work on **(i) Buserweiterung; (ii) Buserhöhung; bus master** = data source that controls the bus whilst transmitting (bus master status moves between sending stations) **Bushauptkontrolle; bus master adapter** = adapter card that fits in a EISA or MCA expansion slot in a PC; the adapter can take control of the main bus and transfer data to the computer's main memory independently of the main processor **Buskontroller-Adapter;** *the bus master network adapter provides much faster data throughput than the old adapter;* **bus mouse** = mouse that plugs into the main data bus of a computer (using an interface card) rather than using a serial port **Busmaus; bus network** = network of computers where the machines are connected to a central bus unit which transmits the messages it receives **Busnetzwerk; bus slave** = data sink which receives data from a bus master **Busnebenstelle; bus structure** = way in which buses are organized, whether serial, parallel, bidirectional, etc. **Busstruktur; bus topology** = network topology in which all devices are connected to a single cable which has terminators at each end **Bustopologie;** *Ethernet is a network that uses the bus topology; token ring uses a ring topology;* **address bus** = bus carrying address data between a CPU and a memory device **Adressbus; bi-directional bus** = data and control lines that can carry signals travelling in two directions **bidirektionaler Bus; control bus** = bus carrying control signals between a CPU and other circuits **Steuerbus; daisy chain bus** = one communications bus that joins one device to the next, each device being able to receive *or* transmit *or* modify data as it passes through to the next device in line **verkettete Busstruktur; data bus** = bus carrying data between a CPU and memory and peripheral devices **Datenübertragungsweg; dual bus system** = way of linking different parts of a system which keeps the memory bus separate from the input/output bus **doppeltes Übertragungswegsystem; expansion bus** = data and address lines leading to a connector and allowing expansion cards to control and access the data in main memory **Erweiterungsbus; input/output data bus (I/O bus)** = links allowing data and control transfer between a CPU and external peripherals **Ein-/Ausgabedatenbus; memory bus** = bus carrying address data between a CPU and memory devices **Speicherbus** (b) central source of information which supplies several devices **Hauptverbindung, Sammelschiene**

QUOTE the slot controller detects when a new board is inserted, it activates power up and assigns a bus arbitration and card slot ID to the board

Computing

QUOTE mice can either be attached to the PC bus *or* a serial port

PC Business World

QUOTE both buses can be software controlled to operate as either a 16- or 32-bit interface

Electronics & Power

business *noun*
(a) work in buying *or* selling **Geschäft;** *business is expanding; business is slow; he does a good business in repairing computers; what's your line of business?;* **business computer** = powerful small computer which is programmed for special business tasks **Geschäftscomputer; business efficiency exhibition** = exhibition which shows products (computers, word-processors) which help a business to be efficient **anwendungsorientierte Fachausstellung; business system** *or* **business package** = set of programs adapted for business use (such as payroll, invoicing, customers file, etc.) **Programmpaket für geschäftlichen Gebrauch** (b) commercial company **Geschäft;** *he owns a small computer repair business; she runs a business from her home; he set up in business as an computer consultant;* **business address** = details of number, street and town where a company is located **Geschäftsadresse; business card** = card showing a businessman's name and the name and address of the company he works for **Visitenkarte; business equipment** = machines used in an office **Büroausstattung** NOTE: no plural for (a); (b) has the plural **businesses**

busy *adjective*
(a) (i) occupied in doing something *or* in working; (ii) electrical signal indicating that a device is not ready to receive data (i)

beschäftigt; (ii) **belegt, besetzt;** *when the busy line goes low, the printer will accept more data;* **the line is busy** = the telephone line is being used **die Leitung ist besetzt** (b) distracting *or* detailed (background to a film shot) **unruhig**

button *noun*
(a) (on a mouse or joystick) switch that carries out an action **Taste;** *use the mouse to move the cursor to the icon and start the application by pressing the mouse button* (b) square shape displayed that will carry out a particular action if selected with a pointer or keyboard **Schaltfläche;** *there are two buttons at the bottom of the status window, select the left button to cancel the operation or the right to continue*

buzz
1 *noun* sound like a loud hum **Summen**
2 *verb* to make a loud hum **summen**

◊ **buzzer** *noun* electrical device which makes a loud hum **Summer**

◊ **buzzword** *noun* (*informal*) word which is popular among a certain group of people **Jargon**

bypass *noun* alternative route around a component *or* device, so that it is not used **Nebenweg;** *there is an automatic bypass around any faulty equipment*

byte *noun* group of bits *or* binary digits (usually eight) which a computer operates on as a single unit **Byte; byte address** = location of data bytes in memory **Byteadresse; byte machine** = variable word length computer **Rechner mit variabler Wortlänge; byte manipulation** = moving, editing and changing the contents of a byte **Bytemanipulation; byte-orientated protocol** = communications protocol which transmits data as characters rather than as a bit-stream **byteorientiertes Protokoll; byte serial transmission** *or* **mode** = transmission of bytes of data sequentially, the individual bits of which can be sent in a serial *or* parallel way **byteserielle Übertragung; bytes-per-inch** = measure of data storage capacity of magnetic tape **Bytes pro Inch**

QUOTE if you can find a way of packing two eight-bit values into a single byte, you save substantial amounts of RAM or disk space

Practical Computing

Cc

C hexadecimal number equivalent to decimal 12 **C**

C high level programming language developed mainly for writing structured systems programs **C**

> QUOTE these days a lot of commercial software is written in C
> *PC Business World*

◊ **C++** high level programming language based on its predecessor, C, but providing object oriented programming functions **C++**

cable

1 *noun*
(a) flexible conducting electrical *or* optical link **Kabel; cable connector** = connector at either end of a cable **Kabelstecker; cable matcher** = impedance matching device that allows non-standard cable to be used with a particular device **Kabeladapter; cable plant** = all the cables, connectors and patch panels within a building or office **Kabelanlage; cable television** *or* **cable TV** = television system where signals are broadcast to viewers' homes over cables **Kabelfernsehen; cable tester** = test equipment used to find breaks *or* faults *or* cracks in cabling **Kabelprüfgerät, Kabelmessgerät; cable TV relay station** = receiving station which retransmits received television signals to a terminal point (where they are then distributed by cable to viewers' homes) **Relaisstation für Kabelfernsehen;** *see also* CATV
(b) telegram *or* message sent by telegraph **Telegramm;** *he sent a cable to his office asking for more money;* **cable address** = specially short address for sending cables **Telegrammadresse**
2 *verb* to send a message *or* money by telegraph **telegrafieren;** *he cabled his office to ask them to send more money; the office cabled him £1,000 to cover his expenses*

◊ **cablegram** *noun* telegram *or* message sent by telegraph **Telegramm**

◊ **cabling** *noun* cable (as a material) **Kabel;** *using high-quality cabling will allow the user to achieve very high data transfer rates; cabling costs up to £1 a foot;* **cabling diagram** = drawing showing where the cable runs throughout an office, including connection points **Verkabelungsplan**
NOTE: no plural

> QUOTE It has won a {500,000 contract to supply a structured voice and data cabling system to the bank and its stockbroking subsidiary.
> *Computing*

cache

1 *noun* **cache controller** = logic circuits that determine when to store data in the high-speed cache memory, when to access data in the cache and when to access data stored in the slower storage device **Cache-Controller; cache memory** = section of high-speed memory which stores data that the computer can access quickly **Cache-Speicher (schneller Pufferspeicher);** *file access time is much quicker if the most frequently used data is stored in cache memory;* **instruction cache** = section of high-speed memory which stores the next few instructions to be executed by a processor (to speed up operation) **Befehlsschnellspeicher**
2 *verb* to file *or* store in a cache **gesondert verarbeiten;** *this program can cache any size font; this CPU caches instructions so improves performance by 15 percent*

> QUOTE the first range of 5.25 inch Winchester disk drives to feature inbuilt cache
> *Minicomputer News*

> QUOTE a serious user might also want a tape streamer and cache memory
> *PC Business World*

> QUOTE The Alpha AXP PC runs at 150MHz and comes equipped with 256Kb of Cache RAM, 16Mb of RAM (upgradeable to 128Mb) and Microsoft Windows NT.
> *Computing*

CAD = COMPUTER AIDED DESIGN *or* COMPUTER ASSISTED DESIGN the use of a computer and graphics terminal to help a designer in his work **computergestützte Entwurf und Konstruktion (CAD);** *all our engineers design on CAD workstations;* **CAD/CAM** = CAD/COMPUTER AIDED MANUFACTURE interaction between computers used for designing and those for manufacturing a product **computergestützte Entwurf und Fertigung (CAD/CAM)**

QUOTE CAD software is memory-intensive

PC Business World

QUOTE John Smith of CAD supplier CAD/CAM Limited has moved into sales with responsibilities for the North of England. He was previously a technical support specialist.

Computing

CAI = COMPUTER AIDED INSTRUCTION *or* COMPUTER ASSISTED INSTRUCTION use of a computer to assist pupils in learning a subject **computergestützter Unterricht**

CAL = COMPUTER AIDED LEARNING *or* COMPUTER ASSISTED LEARNING use of a computer to assist pupils in learning a subject **computergestütztes Lernen**

calculate *verb*
(a) to find the answer to a problem using numbers **kalkulieren, berechnen**; *the DP manager calculated the rate for keyboarding; you need to calculate the remaining disk space*
(b) to estimate **schätzen**; *calculate that we have six months' stock left;* **calculated field** = field within a database record that contains the results of calculations performed on other fields **Resultatfeld**

◊ **calculation** *noun* answer to a problem in mathematics **Kalkulation, Berechnung; rough calculation** = approximate answer **grobe Berechnung;** *I made some rough calculations on the back of an envelope according to my calculations, we have six months' stock left*

◊ **calculator** *noun* electronic machine which works out the answers to numerical problems **Rechenmaschine;** *my pocket calculator needs a new battery; he worked out the discount on his calculator*

calendar program *noun* software diary utility that allows a user to enter and keep track of appointments **Terminplaner; multi-user** *or* **network calendar program** = software diary utility that allows many users to enter appointments and schedule meetings with other users **Mehrbenutzer-Terminplaner**

calibration *noun* comparing the signal from an input with a known scale to provide a standardized reading **Eichung**

call
1 *noun* conversation (between people or machines) on the telephone **Anruf; local call** = call to a number on the same exchange **Ortsgespräch; trunk call** *or* **long-distance call** = call to a number in a different zone *or* area **Ferngespräch; person-to-person call** = call where you ask the operator to connect you with a named person **vorangemeldetes Gespräch zu bestimmten Personen; transferred charge call** *or* *(US)* **collect call** = call where the person receiving the call agrees to pay for it **Rückgespräch; to make a call** = to dial and speak to someone on the telephone **telefonieren; to take a call** = to answer the telephone **das Telefon abnehmen; to log calls** = to note all details of telephone calls made **Anrufe aufzeichnen**
2 *verb*
(a) to transfer control to a separate program *or* routine from a main program **aufrufen;** *after an input is received, the first function is called up the subroutine call instruction should be at this point;* **call instruction** = programming instruction that directs control to a routine (control is passed back once the routine has finished; before the call, the program counter contents are saved to show the return instruction where to return to in the main program) **Aufrufbefehl**
(b) to try to contact another user by telephone **anrufen;** *I'll call you at your office tomorrow;* **call accepted signal** = signal sent by device meaning willing to accept caller's data **Rufannahme;; call back modem** = modem that, on answering a call, immediately hangs up and calls the user back to establish a connection (used to provide better security than a normal dial-up modem) **Rückrufmodem; call control signal** = signal necessary to establish and end a call **Verbindungssteuerungssignal; call diverter** = device that on receiving a call, contacts another point and re-routes the call **Anrufablenker; call duration** = length of time spent between starting and ending a call **Anrufdauer;** *call duration depends on the complexity of the transaction charges are related to call duration;* **call forwarding** = automatic redirection of calls to another user *or* station **Anrufumleitung;** *we are having all calls forwarded from the office to home;* **call scheduling** = (in a fax server) arranging calls so that long-distance calls are made at off-peak times **Anrufeinplanung; called party** = person *or* station to which a call is made **angerufene Seite**

◊ **call box** *noun* outdoor telephone booth **Telefonzelle**

◊ **caller** *noun* person who telephones *or* requests a call **Anrufer**

◊ **call in** *verb* to telephone to make contact **anrufen;** *we ask the representatives to call in every Friday to report the weeks' sales*

◊ **calling** *noun* signal to request attention, sent from a terminal *or* device to the main computer **Anruf; calling sequence** = series of program commands required to direct execution to or back from a subroutine **Aufruffolge von Unterprogrammen**

◊ **call up** *verb* to ask for information from a backing store to be displayed **abrufen;** *all the customers addresses were called up; call up the previous file*

callier effect *noun* scattering of light as it passes through one *or* more lenses **Callier-Effekt**

calligraphy *noun* art of handwriting **Kalligraphie**

calloc (in C programming) instruction to allocate memory to a program **calloc**

CAM
(a) = COMPUTER AIDED MANUFACTURE *or* COMPUTER ASSISTED MANUFACTURING use of a computer to control machinery *or* assist in a manufacturing process **computergestützte Fertigung (CAM)**
(b) = CONTENT ADDRESSABLE MEMORY memory that is addressed and accessed by its contents rather than a location **Assoziativspeicher**

Cambridge ring *noun* local area networking standard used for connecting several devices and computers together in a ring with simple cable links **Cambridge-Netz**

cameo *noun*
(a) reverse characters, that is, white on a black background **invertierte Zeichen**
(b) front-lit subject filmed in front of a dark background **Hell-auf-dunkel-Bild, Aufnahme vor neutralem Hintergrund**

camera *noun* (i) photographic device that transfers a scene onto a piece of film, usually via a lens; (ii) device that transforms a scene into electronic signals that can be displayed on a television **(i) Fotoapparat; (ii) Filmkamera; camera chain** = pieces of equipment necessary to operate a television camera **Kameraaggregat; camera-ready copy (crc)** = final text *or* graphics ready to be photographed before printing **reproreife Vorlage**

campus environment *noun* large area or location that has lots of users connected by several networks, such as a university or hospital **Campusumgebung**

cancel *verb* to stop a process *or* instruction before it has been fully executed **stornieren, abbrechen; cancel character** = control code used to indicate that the last data transmitted was incorrect **Ungültigkeitszeichen;** *the software automatically sends a cancel character after any error;* **cancel page** = extra printed page inserted into a book to take the place of a page with errors on it **Ersatz- und Ergänzungsblatt**

◊ **cancellation** *noun* action of stopping a process which has been started **Stornierung**

candela *noun* SI unit of measurement of light intensity **Candela, neue Kerze (NK)** ⇨APPENDIX

canonical schema *noun* model of a database that is independent of hardware *or* software available **kanonisches Schema**

capability *noun* being able to do something **Leistungsfähigkeit;** *resolution capabilities; electronic mail capabilities;* **capability list** = list of operations that can be carried out **Leistungslist**

◊ **capable** *adjective* able to do something **leistungsfähig;** *that is the highest speed that this printer is capable of the software is capable of far more complex functions* NOTE: a device is capable **of** something

capacitance *noun* ability of a component to store electrical charge **Kapazität**

◊ **capacitive** *adjective* something which has capacitance **kapazitiv**

◊ **capacitor** *noun* electronic component that can store charge **Kondensator; capacitor microphone** = microphone that uses variations in capacitance due to sound pressure to generate an electrical signal **Kondensatormikrofon; ceramic capacitors** = general purpose, non-polar small capacitors made from ceramic materials **Keramikkondensatoren; electrolytic capacitors** = polar, high-capacitance devices made in a variety of materials **elektrolytische Kondensatoren; non-electrolytic capacitors** = non-polar, low-capacitance devices made from a variety of materials **nichtelektrolytische Kondensatoren; variable capacitor** = device whose capacitance can be varied over a small range, used for tuning purposes **variabler Kondensator; capacitor storage** = device using capacititive properties of a material to store data **Kondensatorspeicher; memory backup capacitor** = very high-capacitance, small device that can provide power for volatile RAM chips for up to two weeks (used instead of a battery) **Speicherkondensator;** *see also* BATTERY BACKUP

capacity *noun*
(a) amount which can be produced *or* amount of work which can be done **Leistungsvermögen;** *industrial or manufacturing or production capacity;* **channel capacity** = maximum rate for data transmission over a channel **Kanalkapazität; to work at full capacity** = to do as much work as possible **mit voller Kapazität arbeiten; to use up spare** *or* **excess capacity** = to make use of time *or* space which is not fully used **Restkapazitäten ausnutzen**
(b) amount of storage space available in a system *or* on a disk **Kapazität; storage capacity** = space available for storage **Speicherkapazität;** *total storage capacity is now 3Mb*

capitals *or (informal)* **caps** *noun* large form of letters (A,B,C,D, etc.) as opposed to lower case (a,b,c,d, etc.) **Großbuchstaben;** *the word BASIC is always written in caps;* **caps lock** = key on a keyboard *or* typewriter that allows all characters to be entered as capitals **Feststelltaste;** *the LED lights up when caps lock is pressed*

◊ **capitalization** *noun* function of a word-processor to convert a line or block of text into capitals **Großschreibung**

capstan *noun* spindle of a tape player *or* tape backup unit that keeps the tape pressed against the magnetic read/write head *or* pinch roller **Capstan, Bandantrieb**

caption *noun* note *or* explanation above, below or next to a picture *or* diagram **Bildüberschrift, Bildunterschrift, Bilderläuterung;** *the captions are printed in italics*

capture
1 *noun* **data capture** = action of obtaining data (either by keyboarding *or* by scanning or often automatically from a recording

device *or* peripheral) **Datenerfassung;** *data capture starts when an interrupt is received*
2 *verb*
(a) to take data into a computer system **einlesen;** *the software allows captured images to be edited; scanners usually capture images at a resolution of 300 dots per inch (dpi)*
(b) (in a Token-Ring network) to remove a token from the network in order to transmit data across the network **entnehmen;** *see also* TOKEN-RING

QUOTE In July this year it signed a two-year outsourcing and disaster-recovery deal with Unisys for the operation and management of its Birmingham-based data-capture facility.
Computing

QUOTE images can then be captured, stored, manipulated and displayed
Electronics & Wireless World

carbon *noun*
(a) carbon paper **Kohlepapier;** *you forgot to put a carbon in the typewriter*
(b) carbon copy **Durchschlag;** *make a top copy and two carbons; see also* NCR

◊ **carbon copy** *noun* copy made with carbon paper **Durchschlag;** *give me the original, and file the carbon copy*

◊ **carbonless** *adjective* which makes a copy without using carbon paper **selbstdurchschreibend;** *our representatives use carbonless order pads;* **carbonless paper** = paper that transfers writing without carbon paper **selbstdurchschreibendes Papier**

◊ **carbon microphone** *noun* microphone that uses changes of resistance in carbon granules due to sound pressure to produce a signal **Kohlemikrofon**

◊ **carbon paper** *noun* thin paper with a coating of ink on one side, used to make copies in a typewriter *or* printer **Kohlepapier**

◊ **carbon ribbon** *noun* thin plastic ribbon, coated with black ink, used in printers **Karbonband;** *compare* FIBRE RIBBON

◊ **carbon set** *noun* forms with carbon paper attached **Formulare mit Kohlepapier**

◊ **carbon tissue** *noun* light-sensitive material used to transfer an image to the printing plate of a photogravure process **Pigmentpapier**

card *noun*
(a) stiff paper **Karton;** *we have printed the*

instructions on thick white card NOTE: no plural

(b) small piece of stiff paper *or* plastic **Karte; card reader** = device which reads data from the magnetic strip on the back of an identity or credit card **Magnetkartenleser; cash card** = plastic card containing the owner's details on a magnetic stripe, used to obtain money from a cash dispenser **Bargeldkarte; charge card** = plastic card which allows you to buy goods and pay for them later **Kreditkarte; credit card** = plastic card which allows you to borrow money *or* to buy goods without paying for them immediately **Kreditkarte; filing card** = card with information written on it, used to classify information in correct order **Karteikarte; index card** = card used to make a card index **Karteikarte; punched card** = card with holes punched in it that represent data **Lochkarte; smart card** = plastic card with a memory and microprocessor device embedded in it, so that it can be used for electronic funds transfer *or* for identification of the user **Chipkarte;** *smart cards reduce fraud; future smart cards could contain an image of the users fingerprint for identification*

(c) card code = combination of punched holes that represent characters on a punched card **Lochkartencode; card column** = line of punched information about one character, parallel to the shorter side of the card **Lochkartenspalte; card feed** = device which draws punched cards into a reader automatically **Kartenzuführung; card field** = part of a card column reserved for one type of data **Lochkartenfeld; card format** = way in which columns and rows are arranged to represent data fields *or* characters in a punched card **Kartenformat; card image** = section of memory that contains an exact representation of the information on a card **Dualkartenverarbeitung; card loader** = short program that transfers data from a punched card into main memory **Kartenlader; card punch (CP)** = machine that punches the holes in punched cards **Kartenlocher; card reader** *or* **punched card reader** = device that transforms data on a punched card to a form that can be recognized by the computer **Lochkartenleser; card row** = punch positions parallel to the longer edge of a card **Kartenzeile**

(d) sheet of insulating material on which electronic components can be mounted **Platine; card cage** = metal supporting frame for circuit boards **Platinengehäuse; card edge connector** = series of metal tracks ending at the edge and on the surface of a card, allowing it to be plugged into an edge connector to provide electrical contact (for data transmission, etc.) **Kartenrandverbindung; card extender** = card containing only conducting tracks, inserted between a motherboard connector and an expansion card, allowing the expansion card to be worked on and examined easily, outside the card cage **Platinenerweiterung; expansion card** *or* **expansion board** = printed circuit board that is connected to a system (expansion connector) to increase its functions *or* performance **Erweiterungsplatine; hard card** = board containing a hard disk drive and the required interfacing electronics, which can be slotted into a system (expansion connector) **Festplattenlaufwerksplatine; card frame** *or* **card chassis** = frame containing a motherboard into which printed circuit boards can be plugged to provide a flexible system **Kartenchassis**

◊ **cardboard** *noun* thick stiff brown paper **Pappe, Karton; cardboard box** = box made of cardboard **Pappkarton** NOTE: no plural

◊ **card index** *noun* series of cards with information written on them, kept in special order so that the information can be found easily **Kartei; card-index file** = information kept on filing cards **Katalogdatei**

◊ **card-index** *verb* to put information onto a card index **katalogisieren**

◊ **card-indexing** *noun* putting information onto a card index **Katalogisierung;** *no one can understand her card-indexing system*

QUOTE this card does not occupy system memory space and provides fifty functions including programmable character sets
Computing Today

QUOTE A smart card carries an encryption chip, which codifies your ID and password prior to their being transmitted across a network.
Computing

cardinal number *noun* positive integer **Kardinalzahl;** *13, 19 and 27 are cardinal numbers, −2.3 and 7.45 are not*

cardioid response *noun* heart shaped response curve of an antenna *or* microphone when a signal source is moved around it herzförmige **Empfangscharakteristik**

caret *noun* symbol ' ^ ' that is often used to mean the Control key **Winkelzeichen**

◊ **caret mark** *or* **sign** *noun* proofreading symbol to indicate that something has to be inserted in the text **Caretzeichen, Winkelzeichen**

carpal tunnel syndrome *see* RSI

carriage *noun* mechanical section of a typewriter *or* printer that correctly feeds *or* moves the paper that is being printed **Vorschub; carriage control** = codes that control the movements of a printer carriage **Vorschubsteuerung;** *carriage control codes can be used to move the paper forward two lines between each line of text;* **carriage return (CR)** = signal *or* key to move to the beginning of the next line of print *or* display **Wagenrücklauf(taste);** *the carriage return key is badly placed for touch-typists*

carrier *noun*
(a) substance that holds the ink for photocopying *or* printing processes **Träger**
(b) device that holds a section of microfilm **Träger; carrier detect (CD)** = signal generated by a modem to inform the local computer that it has detected a carrier from a remote modem **Empfangssignal, Carrier-Detect-Signal; carrier frequency** = frequency of the carrier signal before it is modulated **Trägerfrequenz; carrier signal** = continuous high frequency waveform that can be modulated by a signal **Trägersignal**
(c) continuous high frequency waveform that can be modulated by a signal **Trägerschwingung;** *he's not using a modem - there's no carrier signal on the line;* **carrier sense multiple access - collision detection (CSMA-CD)** = network communications protocol that prevents two sources transmitting at the same time by waiting for a quiet moment, then attempting to transmit **CSMA/CD (Verfahren zum Schutz, dass mehrere Sender in einem Netz nicht gleichzeitig senden); carrier signalling** = simple data transmission (by switching on and off a carrier signal according to binary data) **Trägersignal; carrier system** = method of transmitting several different signals on one channel by using different carrier frequencies **Trägerfrequenzsystem; carrier telegraphy** = method of transmitting telegraph signals via a carrier signal **Trägerfrequenztelegrafie; carrier wave** = waveform used as a carrier **Trägerschwingung; data carrier** = (i) any

device *or* medium capable of storing data; (ii) a waveform used as a carrier for data signals (i) **Datenträger;** (ii) **Datenschwingungsträger; data carrier detect (DCD)** = RS232C signal from a modem to a computer, indicating a carrier wave is being received **Empfangssignal eines Datenschwingungsträgers;** *the call is stopped if the software does not receive a DCD signal from the modem*

carry
1 *noun* (extra) digit due to an addition result being greater than the number base used **Übertrag;** *when 5 and 7 are added, there is an answer of 2 and a carry which is put in the next column, giving 12;* **carry bit** *or* **flag** = indicator that a carry has occurred **Übertragsbit; carry complete signal** = signal from an adder circuit indicating that all carry operations have been completed „**Übertragung beendet"-Signal; carry look ahead** = high speed adder that can predict if a carry will be generated by a sum and add it in, removing the delay found in an adder with ripple-through carry **Parallelübertrag; carry time** = period of time taken to transfer a carry digit to the next higher digit position **Übertragszeit; cascade carry** = carry generated in an adder from an input carry signal **Kaskadenübertrag; end-around carry** = most significant digit (the carry) is added into the least significant place (used in BCD arithmetic) **Übertrag des Überlaufs in die niedere Stelle; high speed carry** = when a carry into an adder results in a carry out, all produced in one operation **Schnellübertrag; partial carry** = temporary storage of all carries generated in parallel adders, rather than a direct transfer **Teilübertrag; ripple-through carry** = carry generated by a carry in to an adder **Schnellübertrag**
2 *verb* to move (something) from one place to another **hinübertragen;** *the fibre optic link carried all the data; the information-carrying abilities of this link are very good*

cartesian coordinates *noun* positional system that uses two axes at right angles to represent a point which is located with two numbers, giving a position on each **kartesische Koordinaten**

◊ **cartesian structure** *noun* data structure whose size is fixed and the elements are in (a linear) order **kartesische Struktur;** *compare with* AXIS, POLAR COORDINATES

cartridge *noun* removable cassette, containing a disk *or* tape *or* program *or* data (usually stored in ROM) **Kassette; data cartridge** = cartridge that contains stored data **Datenregister; disk cartridge** = removable hard disk **Plattenkassette; ink cartridge** = (for use in bubble-jet or ink-jet printers) plastic module that contains ink **Tintenkartusche; ROM cartridge** = sealed module (with electrical connections) which can be plugged into a computer and contains data *or* extra programs stored in a ROM chip **ROM-Kassette;** *the portable computer has no disk drives, but has a slot for ROM cartridges;* **tape cartridge** = cassette box containing magnetic tape **Magnetbandkassette; cartridge drive** = drive which uses a disk *or* tape in a cartridge **Cartridge-Laufwerk, Magnetbandkassettenlaufwerk; cartridge fonts** = ROM cartridge which can be plugged into a printer, providing a choice of new typefaces, but still limited to the typefaces and styles included in the cartridge **auswechselbare Zeichensätze;** *compare* RESIDENT FONTS; **cartridge ribbon** = printer ribbon in a closed cartridge **Kassettenfarbband**

◊ **cartridge paper** *noun* good quality white paper for drawing *or* printing **Zeichenpapier**

cascade carry *noun* carry generated in an adder from an input carry signal **Kaskadenübertrag**

◊ **cascade connection** *noun* number of devices *or* circuits arranged in series, the output of one driving the input of the next **Kaskadenverbindung**

◊ **cascade control** *noun* multiple control units, each controlling the next **Kaskadensteuerung**

◊ **cascading windows** *plural noun* (in a GUI) multiple windows that are displayed overlapping so that only the title bar at the top of each window is showing **überlappende Fenster**

case
1 *noun*
(a) protective container for a device *or* circuit **Gehäuse**
(b) box containing metal characters used in composing **Setzkasten; upper case** *or* **lower case** = capital letters *or* ordinary letters **Großbuchstaben; Kleinbuchstaben;** *he corrected the word "coMputer", replacing the upper case M with a lower case letter;* **case change** = key used to change from upper to lower case on a keyboard **Umschalttaste; case sensitive** = command *or*

operation that will only work when the characters are entered in a particular case **abhängig von Groß-/Kleinschreibung;** *the password is case sensitive;* **case sensitive search** = search function that succeeds only if both the search word and the case of the characters in the search word match **Suche mit Berücksichtigung der Groß-/Kleinschreibung**
(c) programming command that jumps to various points in a program depending on the result of a test **Case; case branch** = branch to a part of a program that is dependant upon the result of a test **Case-Verzweigung, Mehrfachverzweigung**
(d) cardboard cover for a book **Buchdecke;** *the library edition has a case and jacket; have you remembered to order the blocking for the spine of the case?;* **case binding** = stiff cardboard cover **fester Einband**
(e) cardboard *or* wooden box for packing and carrying goods **Schachtel, Kiste; packing case** = large wooden box for carrying items which can be easily broken **Kiste**
2 *verb*
(a) to bind a book in a stiff cardboard cover **fest binden; cased book** = book with a hard cover **fest gebundenes Buch**
(b) to pack in a case **in eine Kiste packen**

◊ **case-making machine** *noun* machine for cutting the cardboard which forms the cover of a book **Buchdeckenmaschine**

casing *noun* solid protective box in which a computer *or* delicate equipment is housed **Gehäuse**

cassette *noun* hard container used to store and protect magnetic tape **Kassette;** *you must back up the information from the computer onto a cassette;* **audio cassette** = small cassette containing a reel of narrow magnetic tape on which audio signal can be recorded (used to store data in small home computers) **Tonkassette; data cassette** = special high-quality tape for storing data **Datenkassette; video cassette** = large cassette containing a reel of wide magnetic tape on which video data can be recorded **Videokassette; cassette recorder** = machine to transfer audio signals onto magnetic tape **Kassettenrekorder; cassette tape** = narrow reel of magnetic tape housed in a solid case for protection **Tonbandkassette**

COMMENT: using cassette tape allows data to be stored for future retrieval; it is used instead of a disk system on small computers or as a slow, serial access, high-capacity back-up medium for large systems

cast *noun* (in a programming language) instruction that converts data from one type to another **Konvertierungsausdruck;** *to convert the variable from an integer to a character type, use the cast command*

caster machine *noun* machine that produces metal type **Gießmaschine**

◊ **cast off**
1 *noun* amount of space required to print a text in a certain font **geschätzter Satzumfang**
2 *verb* to calculate the amount of space needed to print a text in a certain font **Satzumfang schätzen**

◊ **casting off** *noun* calculating the amount of space required to print text in a certain font **Schätzen des Satzumfangs**

CAT
(a) = COMPUTER AIDED *or* ASSISTED TRAINING use of a computer to demonstrate to and assist pupils in learning a skill **computergestütztes Training**
(b) = COMPUTER AIDED *or* ASSISTED TESTING use of a computer to test equipment *or* programs to find any faults **computergestütztes Prüfen**

catalogue
1 *noun* list of contents *or* items in order **Katalog; disk catalogue** *or* **directory** = list of files stored on a magnetic disk **Plattenverzeichnis;** *all the terminals were catalogued, with their location, call sign and attribute table the entry in the disk catalogue is removed when the file is deleted*
2 *verb* to make a catalogue of items stored **katalogisieren;** *all the terminals were catalogued, with their location, call sign and attribute table*

◊ **cataloguer** *noun* person who makes a catalogue **Katalogisierer**

catastrophe *noun* serious fault, error *or* breakdown of equipment, usually leading to serious damage and shutdown of a system **Katastrophe**

◊ **catastrophic error** *noun* error that causes a program to crash *or* files to be accidentally erased **schlimmer Fehler; catastrophic failure** = complete system failure *or* crash **Totalausfall**

catena *noun* (i) number of items in a chained list; (ii) series of characters in a word **(i) Zahl der Kettenglieder; (ii) Kette**

◊ **catenate** *verb* to join together two or more sets of data **verketten**

cathode *noun* negative electrical terminal of a device *or* battery **Kathode** NOTE: opposite is **anode**

◊ **cathode ray tube (CRT)** *noun* device used for displaying characters *or* figures *or* graphical information, similar to a TV set **Kathodenstrahlröhre, Bildröhre; cathode ray tube storage** = a cathode ray tube with a long persistence phosphor screen coating that retains an image for a long time **Bildröhrenspeicher** NOTE: CRT is now often used to mean 'monitor'

COMMENT: cathode ray tubes are used in television sets, computer monitors and VDUs; a CRT consists of a vacuum tube, one end of which is flat and coated with phosphor, the other end containing an electron beam source. Characters *or* graphics are visible when the controllable electron beam strikes the phosphor causing it to glow

CATV = COMMUNITY ANTENNA TELEVISION cable television system using a single aerial to pick up television signals and then distribute them over a wide area via cable **Kabelfernsehen**

CB = CITIZENS BAND RADIO cheap popular system of radio communications, usually between vehicles **CB (Citizen-Band, Jedermannfunk)**

C band *noun* microwave communications frequency range of 3.9 - 6.2GHz **C-Band**

CBL = COMPUTER BASED LEARNING learning mainly using a computer **computergestütztes Lernen**

CBMS = COMPUTER BASED MESSAGE SYSTEM use of a computer system to allow users to send and receive messages from other users (usually in-house) **computergestütztes Nachrichtensystem;** *see also* BBS

CBT = COMPUTER BASED TRAINING use of a computer system to train students **computergestütztes Training**

CBX = COMPUTERIZED BRANCH EXCHANGE

CCD = CHARGE COUPLED DEVICE **CCD memory** = capacitors used (with MOS transistors) to store data, allowing either serial or random access **ladungsgekoppelter Speicher**

CCITT = Comité Consultatif International Téléphonique et

Télégraphique international committee that defines communications protocols and standards **CCITT**

CCP = COMMAND CONSOLE PROCESSOR software which interfaces between a user's terminal and system BIOS **CCP (Teil des Betriebssystems, der direkt mit dem Anwender kommuniziert, bei CP/M)**

CCTV = CLOSED CIRCUIT TELEVISION

CCU = COMMUNICATIONS CONTROL UNIT

CD
(a) = COMPACT DISC; **CD-I** = COMPACT DISC-INTERACTIVE hardware and software standards that combine sound, data, video and text onto a compact disc and allow a user to interact with the software stored on a CD-ROM; the standard defines encoding, compression and display functions **CD-I**; **CD-ROM** = COMPACT DISK-READ ONLY MEMORY small plastic disk that is used as a high capacity ROM device, data is stored in binary form as holes etched on the surface which are then read by a laser **CD-ROM**; **CD-ROM Extended Architecture** or **CD-ROM/XA** = extended CD-ROM format that defines how audio, images and data are stored on a CD-ROM disk **CD-ROM/XA**; **CD-ROM player** = disk drive that allows a computer to read data stored on a CD-ROM; the player uses a laser beam to read etched patterns on the surface of the CD-ROM that represent data bits **CD-ROM-Laufwerk**
(b) = CHDIR or CHANGE DIRECTORY system instruction in MS-DOS and UNIX that moves you around a directory structure **CHDIR**; *type in CD DOCS to move into the DOCS subdirectory*

QUOTE Customers' images will be captured, digitised, and stored on optical disk or CD-ROM, and produced if queries arise about responsibility for ATM transactions.

Computing

cedilla *noun* accent under a letter c, used in certain languages to change the pronunciation **Cedille**

cell *noun*
(a) single function or number in a spreadsheet program **Zelle**; **cell address** = (in a spreadsheet) code that identifies the position of a cell by row and column; the rows are normally numbered and the columns use the letters of the alphabet **Zellenadresse**; **cell definition** = (in a spreadsheet) formula that is contained in a cell **Zellendefinition**; **cell format** = (in a spreadsheet) way in which the result or data in a cell is displayed **Zellenformat**; *the cell format is right-aligned and emboldened;* **cell protection** = to prevent the contents of a particular cell or range of cells from being changed **Zellenschutz**; **cell reference variable** = register that contains the reference locating a certain cell that is being operated on **Zellreferenzvariable**; **current** or **active cell** = thicker line surrounding the border of the cell being edited **aktive Zelle**
(b) single memory location, capable of storing a data word, accessed by an individual address **Zelle**

◊ **cellphone** *noun short for* CELLULAR TELEPHONE

◊ **cellular** *adjective* **cellular telephone** = a portable telephone operated by cellular radio **Zelltelefon** or **Mobiltelefon**; **cellular radio** = radio telephone linked to a main telephone system, which uses a network of stations, each covering a certain area, to provide a service over a large area (the radio is switched from one station to another as it moves from area to area) **Zellradio**; **cellular service** = changing from one transceiver station to another as a cellular radio or cell phone user moves from area to area **Zelltelefon-Fernsprechdienst**

cellar *noun* temporary storage for data or registers or tasks, in which items are added and retrieved from the same end of the list in a LIFO order **Keller**

centi- *prefix* meaning one hundred or one hundredth **zenti-**; **centimetre** = one hundredth of a metre **Zentimeter**

central *adjective* in the middle **zentral, Haupt-, haupt-**; **central computer** = HOST COMPUTER; **central memory (CM)** = area of memory whose locations can be directly and immediately addressed by the CPU **Zentralspeicher**; **central processing element (CPE)** = short (2, 4 or 8 bit) word length module that can be used to produce large word CPUs using bit slice techniques **Zentralverarbeitungseinheit**; **central processing unit (CPU)** or **central processor** = group of circuits which perform the basic functions of a computer, made up of three parts: the control unit, the arithmetic and logic unit and the input/output unit **Zentraleinheit (CPU)**; **central terminal** =

terminal which controls the communications between a central *or* host computer and remote terminals **Hauptterminal**

◊ **centralized** *adjective* which is located in a central position **zentralisiert; centralized data processing** = data processing facilities located in a centralized place that can be accessed by other users **zentrale Datenverarbeitung; centralized computer network** = network with processing power provided by a central computer **zentrales Computernetz**

centre *or* *(US)* **center**
1 *noun* point in the middle of something **Mittelpunkt; centre holes** = location holes punched along the centre of paper tape **Vorschublöcher; centre operator** = person who looks after central computer operations **Rechenzentrumsoperator; centre sprocket feed** = centre (sprocket) holes that line up with coding hole positions on punched tape **Stachelbandführung**
2 *verb*
(a) to align the read/write head correctly on a magnetic disk *or* tape **zentrieren**
(b) to place a piece of text in the centre of the paper *or* display screen **zentrieren;** *which key do you press to centre the heading?*

◊ **centering** *noun* action of putting text in the centre of the screen **Zentrierung;** *centering of headings is easily done, using this function key*

Centronics interface *noun* parallel printer interface devised by Centronics Inc **Centronics-Schnittstelle**

CEPT standard *noun* videotex character standard defined by the Conference of European Post Telephone and Telegraph **CEPT-Norm**

ceramic *adjective* made from baked clay **keramisch;** *see* CAPACITOR

CGA = COLOUR GRAPHICS ADAPTER popular microcomputer medium-resolution colour display system **Farbgrafikadapter;** *see also* EGA

CGM = COMPUTER GRAPHICS METAFILE device-independent file format that provides one method of storing an image as objects **CGM**

chad *noun* waste material produced from holes punched in tape *or* card

Stanzrückstand; chadless tape = punched tape that retains chad by not punching holes through fully **Schuppenstreifen**

chain
1 *noun* (i) series of files *or* data items linked sequentially; (ii) series of instructions to be executed sequentially **(i) Kette; (ii) Kettenbefehl; chain code** = series of words, each word being derived (usually shifted by one bit) from the previous word **geketteter Code; chain delivery mechanism** = mechanical system to move paper from machine to machine **Kettenliefermethode; chain list** = list of data with each piece of information providing an address for the next consecutive item in the list **gekettete Liste; chain printer** = printer whose characters are located on a continuous belt **Kettendrucker; command chain** = list of commands (in a file) executed sequentially by a batch mode system **Befehlskette; daisy chain** = method of connecting equipment with a single cable passing from one machine *or* device to the next (rather than separate cables to each device) **Verkettung; daisy chain bus** = one communications bus that joins one device to the next, each device being able to receive *or* transmit *or* modify data as it passes through to the next device in line **verkettete Busstruktur**
2 *verb* to link files *or* data items in series by storing a pointer to the next file *or* item at each entry **(ver)ketten;** *more than 1,000 articles or chapters can be chained together when printing; see also* CATENA; **chained** *or* **threaded file** = file in which an entry will contain data and an address to the next entry that has the same data content (allowing rapid retrieval of all identical data records) **gekettete Datei; chained list** = list in which each element contains data and an address to the next element in the list **gekettete Liste; chained record** = data record in a chained file **geketteter Satz; daisy-chain** = to connect equipment using the daisy chain method **verketten;** *daisy-chaining saves a lot of cable*

◊ **chaining** *noun* execution of a very large program by executing small segments of it at a time, this allows programs larger than memory capacity to be run **Ketten; chaining search** = search of a file of elements arranged in a chained list **Suche in verknüpfter Liste; data chaining** = storing one record that holds the address of the next in the list **Daten(adress)kettung**

change *verb* to make something different; to use one thing instead of another **austauschen, verändern; change**

dump = printout of locations where data has been changed **Speicherauszug der Änderungen; change file** = file containing records that are to be used to update a master file **Änderungsdatei; change record** = record containing new data which is to be used to update a master record **Änderungssatz; change tape** = (magnetic) tape containing recent changes *or* transactions to records which is used to update a master file **Änderungsband**

◊ **change over** *verb* to switch from one computer system to another **überwechseln**

◊ **changer** *noun* device which changes one thing for another **Umwandler; gender changer** = two connectors, used to change a female connector to a male one (or vice-versa) **Geschlechtsumwandler;** *you can interconnect all these peripherals with just two cables and a gender changer;* **record changer** = device on a turntable which allows records to be changed automatically **Plattenwechsler**

channel
1 *noun*
(a) physical connection between two points that allows data to be transmitted (such as a link between a CPU and a peripheral) **Kanal; channel adapter** = interfacing device allowing different channels to be interconnected **Kanalanschluss; channel bank** = collection of a number of channels, and circuits to switch between them **Kanalbank; channel capacity** = maximum rate of data transmission over a channel **Kanalkapazität; channel command** = instruction to a channel *or* control unit, providing control information such as data selection *or* routes **Kanalbefehl; channel group** = collection of twelve channels, treated as one group in a multiplexing system **Kanalgruppe; channel isolation** = separation of channels measured as the amount of crosstalk between two channels (low crosstalk is due to good channel isolation) **Isolationseinrichtung für Kanäle; channel overload** = transmission of data at a rate greater than the channel capacity **Kanalüberlastung; channel synchronizer** = interface between a central computer and peripherals, providing a channel, channel command interpretation and status signals from the peripherals **Kanalsynchronisierer; channel queue** = (i) queue of requests to use a channel; (ii) queue of data that has yet to be sent over a channel **(i)** & **(ii) Kanalwarteschlange; channel-to-channel connection** = direct link between the main I/O channels of two computers, allowing

high speed data transfer **Kanal-zu-Kanal-Verbindung;** **data channel** = communications link able to carry data signals **Datenkanal; dedicated channel** = communications channel reserved for a special purpose **dedizierter Kanal; I/O channel** = link between a processor and peripheral allowing data transfer **Ein-/Ausgabekanal**
(b) way in which information *or* goods are passed from one place to another **Weg; to go through the official channels** = to deal with government officials (especially when making a request) **den Dienstweg gehen; to open up new channels of communication** = to find new ways of communicating with someone **neue Nachrichtenverbindungen erschließen; distribution channels** *or* **channels of distribution** = ways of sending goods from the manufacturer for sale in shops **Verteilungskanäle**
2 *verb* to send signals *or* data via a particular path **leiten**

◊ **channelling** *noun* protective pipe containing cables *or* wires **Kanalisierung**

chapter *noun*
(a) section of a main program that can be executed in its own right, without the rest of the main program being required **Kapitel**
(b) sequence of frames on a video disk **Kapitel; chapter stop** = code at the end of a video disk chapter that enables rapid location of a particular chapter **Kapitelende**
(c) section of a book *or* document **Kapitel; chapter heading** = special heading at the beginning of each printed chapter **Kapitelüberschrift;** *chapter headings are in 12 point bold*

character *noun* graphical symbol which appears as a printed *or* displayed mark, such as one of the letters of the alphabet, a number or a punctuation mark **Zeichen; alphanumeric characters** = roman letters and arabic numerals (and other signs such as punctuation marks) **alphanumerische Zeichen; cancel character** = control code used to indicate that the last data transmitted was incorrect **Ungültigkeitszeichen; character assembly** = method of designing characters with pixels on a computer screen **Zeichenrasterung; character blink** = character whose intensity is switched on and off (as an indicator) **blinkendes Zeichen; character block** = the pattern of dots that will make up a character on a screen *or* printer **Zeichenblock; character byte** = byte of data containing the character code and any error check bits **Zeichenbyte; character**

check = check to ensure that a character code protocol and format are correct **Zeichenprüfung; character code** = system where each character is represented by a unique number **Zeichencode;** *the ASCII code is the most frequently used character coding system;* **character density** = number of characters that can be stored *or* displayed per unit area **Zeichendichte; character display** = device that displays data in alphanumeric form **(alphanumerische) Zeichenanzeige; character fill** = writing one character to every location within an area of memory (for clearing and resetting the memory) **mit Zeichen füllen; character generator** = ROM that provides the display circuits with a pattern of dots which represent the character (block) **Zeichengenerator;** *the ROM used as a character generator can be changed to provide different fonts;* **character key** = word processor control used to process text one character at a time **Zeichentaste; character machine** = computer in which the number of bits which make up a word is variable, and varies according to the type of data **Computer mit variabler Wortlänge; character orientated** = computer that addresses character locations rather than words **zeichenorientiert; character printer** = device that prints characters one at a time **Zeichendrucker;** *a daisy wheel printer is a character printer;* **character recognition** = system that optically reads written *or* printed characters into a computer, using various algorithms to ensure that characters are correctly recognized **Zeichenerkennung;** *see also* OCR; **character repertoire** = list of all the characters that can be displayed *or* printed **Zeichenvorrat; character representation** = combination of bits used for each character code **Zeichendarstellung; character rounding** = making a displayed character more pleasant to look at (within the limits of pixel size) by making sharp corners and edges smooth **Zeichenrundungen; character set** = list of all the characters that can be displayed *or* printed **Zeichensatz; character skew** = angle of a character in comparison to its correct position **Zeichenneigung; character string** = storage allocated for a series of alphanumeric characters **Zeichenfolge;** *compare with* NUMERIC STRING; **characters per inch (cpi)** = number of printed characters which fit within the space of one inch **Zeichen pro Inch;** *you can select 10 or 12 cpi with the green button;* **characters per second (cps)** = number of characters which are transmitted *or* printed per second **Zeichen pro Sekunde;** **character**

stuffing = addition of blank characters to a file to increase its length to a preset size **Leerzeichenfüllung; check character** = additional character inserted into transmitted data to serve as an error detection check, its value is dependent on the text **Prüfzeichen; device control character** = special code sent in a transmission to a device to instruct it to perform a special function **Gerätesteuerzeichen**

◊ **characteristic**

1 *noun*
(a) value of exponent in a floating point number **Gleitpunktexponent;** *the floating point number 1.345 x 10³, has a characteristic of 3;* **characteristic overflow** = exponent value of a floating point number that is greater than the maximum allowable **charakteristischer Überlauf**
(b) measurements *or* properties of a component **Merkmal**
2 *adjective* which is typical *or* special **charakteristisch;** *this fault is characteristic of this make and model of personal computer;* **characteristic curve** = response curve of an electronic component *or* circuit **charakteristische Kurve**

> QUOTE the screen displays very sharp and stable characters, each cell occupying an 8 by 11 dot matrix
>
> *Computing Today*

charge *noun* (i) a quantity of electricity; (ii) the number of *or* excess of *or* lack of electrons in a material *or* component **(i) & (ii) Ladung; charge-coupled device (CCD)** = electronic device operated by charge **ladungsgekoppelter Elektronikbaustein; charge-coupled device memory** = capacitors used (with MOS transistors) to store data, allowing serial and random access **ladungsgekoppelter Speicher; electric charge** = a number of atoms that are charged (due to an excess *or* deficiency of electrons) **elektrische Ladung**
2 *verb* to supply a device with an electric charge **laden; battery charging** = to replenish the charge stored in a re-chargeable battery **Batterieaufladen**

◊ **chargeable** *adjective* which can be charged **aufladbar; re-chargeable battery** = battery that can be used to supply power, and then have its charge replenished **wiederaufladbare Batterie;** *a re-chargeable battery is used for RAM back-up when the system is switched off*

chart *noun* diagram showing information

chart 68 chip

as a series of lines *or* blocks, etc. **Abbildung, Diagramm; bar chart** = graph on which values are represented as vertical *or* horizontal bars of different heights *or* lengths **Balkendiagramm; flowchart** = diagram showing the arrangement of various work processes as a series of stages **Flussdiagramm;** *a flowchart is the first step to a well designed program;* **logical chart** = graphical representation of logic elements, steps, decisions and interconnections in a system **Logikplan; pie chart** = diagram where ratios are shown as slices of a circle **Kreisdiagramm;** *the memory allocation is shown on this pie chart;* **chart recorder** = mechanical device that records input values by drawing lines on a moving reel of paper **Kreisblattschreiber**

chassis *noun* metal frame that houses the circuit boards together with the wiring and sockets required in a computer system *or* other equipment **Gehäuse;** *see also* RACK

check
1 *noun*
(a) act of making sure that something is correct **Prüfung; character check** = check to ensure that a character code protocol and format are correct **Zeichenprüfung; check bit** = one bit of a binary word that is used to provide a parity check **Prüfbit; check character** = additional character inserted into transmitted text to serve as an (error detection) check for the text, its value is dependent on the text **Prüfzeichen; check digit** *or* **number** = additional digit inserted into transmitted text to monitor and correct errors **Prüfzahl; check indicator** = hardware *or* software device that shows that received text is not correct and a check has failed **Prüfanzeiger; check key** = series of characters derived from a text used to check for and correct errors **Prüfzeichen; check point** = point in a program where data and program status can be recorded *or* displayed **Prüfpunkt; check point dump** = printout of data and program status at a check point **Speicherauszug des Programmstops; check register** = temporary storage for received data before it is checked against the same data received via another path *or* method **Prüfregister; check total** = CHECKSUM; **desk check** = dry run of a program **Probelauf**
(b) short fault *or* pause in a process (that does not stop the process) **Kurzunterbrechung; data check** = error in reading data due to a fault with the magnetic medium **Datenprüfung**
2 *verb* to examine *or* to make sure than

something is in good working order **prüfen;** *the separate parts of the system were all checked for faults before being packaged;* he checked the computer printout against the invoices = he examined the printout and the invoices to see if the figures were the same **er verglich die Computerausdrucke mit den Rechnungen**

◊ **checkerboarding** *noun* (virtual page) memory organization that has resulted in odd pages *or* spread-out pages *or* segments of memory being filled, wasting memory by leaving unusable gaps in between **spezielle Speicherorganisation**

◊ **checking** *noun* examination **Überprüfung;** *the maintenance engineer found some defects whilst checking the equipment;* **checking program** = software that finds errors in program *or* data syntax, format and coding **Prüfprogramm, Diagnoseprogramm; self-checking code** = error detection code **Fehlererkennungscode** NOTE: no plural

◊ **checksum** *or* **check total** *noun* program which checks that data is correct, by summing it and comparing the sum with a stored value **Kontrollsumme;** *the data must be corrupted if the checksum is different*

chemical
1 *adjective* referring to the interaction of substances **chemisch; chemical reaction** = interaction between two substances *or* elements **chemische Reaktion**
2 *noun* product resulting from the interaction of other substances *or* elements **Chemikalie**

chip *noun* device consisting of a small piece of a crystal of a semiconductor onto which are etched *or* manufactured (by doping) a number of components such as transistors, resistors and capacitors, which together perform a function **Chip; chip architecture** = design and layout of components on a chip **Chiparchitektur; chip card** = plastic card with a memory and microprocessor device embedded in it, so that it can be used for electronic funds transfer *or* identification of a user **Chipkarte; chip count** = number of chips on a PCB *or* in a device **Chipanzahl;** *it's no good, the chip count is still too high;* **chip select line** = connection to a chip that will enable it to function when a signal is present **Chipverbindungsstelle;** *the data strobe line is connected to the latch chip select line;* **chip set** = chips which together will carry out a function **Chipsatz; diagnostic chip** = chip that contains circuits to carry out tests on circuits *or* other chips **Diagnosechip;** *they are carrying out research on diagnostic chips to test computers that contain processors;* **single chip computer** = complete simple computer including CPU, memory and input/output ports on one chip **Einzelchipcomputer; sound chip** = device that will generate a sound *or* tune **Tonteil**

choke *see* INDUCTOR

Chooser ™ operating system utility supplied with the Apple Macintosh that allows a user to select the type of printer, network and other peripherals that are connected **Chooser** ™, **Auswahl**

chop *see* BINARY

chord keying *noun* action of pressing two *or* more keys at the same time to perform a function **Tastenfolge**

| COMMENT: as an example, to access a second window, you may need to press control and F2 pressing shift and character delete keys at the same time will delete a line of text

chroma *noun* colour hue and saturation measure **Farbenreinheit, Farbenintensität; chroma control** = circuit in a TV that alters the colour saturation **Farbkontrolle; chroma detector** = television circuit that checks whether a signal is monochrome *or* colour **Farbdetektor**

◊ **chromatic** *adjective* referring to colours **Farb-, farb-, chromatisch; chromatic aberration** = optical lens that affects and focuses different colours in different ways **chromatische Abweichung, Farbabweichung, Farbaberration; chromatic dispersion** = uneven refraction index across an optic fibre causing signal distortion **chromatische Dispersion**

◊ **chromaticity** *noun* quality of light according to its most prominent colour and purity **Chromatizität**

◊ **chrominance signal** *noun* section of a colour monitor signal containing colour hue and saturation information **Farbsignal**

chronological order *noun* arrangement of records *or* files according to their dates **chronologische Anordnung**

CIM
(a) = COMPUTER INPUT FROM MICROFILM coordinated use of microfilm for computer data storage and the method of reading the data **CIM (Dateneingabe von Mikrofilm)**

(b) = COMPUTER INTEGRATED MANUFACTURE use of computers in every aspect of design and manufacturing **computerintegrierte Fertigung**

cine- *prefix* meaning moving pictures *or* film **Film-; cine camera** = camera that records motion pictures onto a roll of film **Filmkamera; cine orientated image** = data *or* graphics on a microfilm where the image is at right angles to the long edge of the roll of film **Zeilenanordnung quer (bei Mikrofilmen)**

◊ **cinema** *noun*
(a) the cinema = making of films for showing to the public **das Filmen**
(b) building where films are shown to the public **Kino**

◊ **cinematography** *noun* (i) motion picture photography; (ii) effects giving impression of motion **(i) Filmen; (ii) Cinematographie**

cipher *noun* system of transforming a message into an unreadable form with a secret key (the message can be read normally after it has passed through the cipher a second time) **Verschlüsselung;** *always use a secure cipher when sending data over a telephone line;* **cipher key** = secret sequence of characters used with a cipher system to provide a unique ciphertext **Chiffrierschlüssel; cipher system** = formula used to transform text into a secret form **Verschlüsselungssystem; public key cipher** = cipher that uses a public key to encrypt messages and a secret key to decrypt them (conventional ciphers use one secret key to encrypt and decrypt messages) **Verschlüsselungssystem mit bekanntem Chiffrierschlüssel; ciphertext** = data output from a cipher **verschlüsselter Text** NOTE: opposite is **plaintext**

CIR = CURRENT INSTRUCTION REGISTER CPU register that stores the instruction that is currently being executed **aktuelles Befehlsregister**

circuit *noun* connection between electronic components that perform a function **Schaltung, Stromkreis; circuit analyzer** = device that measures voltage *or* current *or* impedance *or* signal in a circuit **Schaltkreisanalysator; circuit board** *or* **card** = insulating board used to hold components which are then connected together (electrically) to form a circuit **Schaltkarte; circuit breaker** = device which protects equipment by cutting off the electrical supply when conditions are abnormal

Stromkreisunterbrecher; **circuit capacity** = information-carrying capacity of a particular circuit **Leistungsvermögen eines Stromkreises**; **circuit diagram** = graphical description of a circuit **Schaltbild**; *the CAD program will plot the circuit diagram rapidly;* **circuit grade** = ability of a communication channel to carry information (the grades are: wideband, voice, subvoice and telegraph) **Übertragungsmöglichkeiten eines Nachrichtenkanals**; **circuit noise level** = amplitude of noise in a circuit compared to a reference level **Leitungsgeräuschpegel**; **circuit switched network** = communications network in which each link can be linked to another at a switching centre **Durchschaltnetz**; **circuit switching** = method in which the link or path between two nodes is established at the time of calling for the exclusive use of this call rather than being a fixed, permanent link **Durchschaltevermittlung**; **data circuit** = circuit which allows bi-directional data communications **Datenverbindung**; **decision circuit** = logical circuit that operates on binary inputs, producing an output according to the function set in hardware **Entscheidungsschaltung**; **digital circuit** = electronic circuit that operates on digital information providing logical functions *or* switching **Digitalschaltung**; **logic circuit** = electronic circuit made up of various logical gates, such as AND, OR and EXOR **logische Schaltung**; **printed circuit board (PCB)** = flat insulating material that has conducting tracks of metal printed *or* etched onto its surface, which complete a circuit when components are mounted on it **gedruckte Schaltkarte**

◊ **circuitry** *noun* collection of circuits **Schaltlogik**; *the circuitry is still too complex* NOTE: no plural

QUOTE The biggest shock was to open up the PC and find the motherboard smothered in patch wires (usually a sign that a design fault in the printed circuit board was rectified at the last minute).
Computing

circular
1 *adjective* which goes round in a circle **kreisförmig**; **circular buffer** = computer-based queue that uses two markers, for top and bottom of the line of stored items (the markers move as items are read from *or* written to the stack) **Rundpuffer**; **circular file** = a data file that has no visible beginning *or* end, each item points to the location of the next item with the last pointing back to the

first **Runddatei**; **circular list** = list in which each element contains data and an address to the next element in the list with the last item pointing back to the first **Kreisliste**; **circular orbit** = orbit of a satellite that is always at a constant distance from the centre of the earth **Kreisumlaufbahn**; **circular reference** = (in a spreadsheet) error condition that occurs when two equations in two cells reference each other **Kreisbezug**; **circular shift** = rotation of bits in a word with the previous last bit inserted in the first bit position **Rundverschiebung**; **circular waveguide** = microwave beam carrying a channel, of circular cross-section, allowing high frequencies to be carried **Rundhohlleiter**

◊ **circulate** *verb*
(a) to go round in a circle, and return to the first point **kreisen**
(b) to send information to to in Umlauf bringen; *they circulated the new list of prices to all their customers*

◊ **circulating** *adjective* which is moving about freely **zirkulierend**; **circulating register** = shift register whose output is fed back to its input to form a closed loop **Kreislaufregister**; **circulating storage** = storage device that maintains stored data as a series of pulses, that move along the length of the medium, being regenerated and re-input when they reach the end **Umlaufspeicher**

COMMENT: circulating storage devices are not often used now, being slow (serial access) and bulky: typical devices are acoustic or mercury delay lines

◊ **circulation** *noun*
(a) movement **Umlauf**; *the company is trying to improve the circulation of information between departments*
(b) *(of a newspaper)* number of copies sold **Auflage(nziffer)**; *what is the circulation of this computer magazine? specialized paper with a circulation of over 10,000*

circumflex *noun* printed accent (like a small 'v' printed upside down) placed above a letter, which may change the pronunciation *or* distinguish the letter from others **Zirkumflex**

CISC COMPLEX INSTRUCTION SET COMPUTER CPU design whose instruction set contains a number of long, complex instructions, that makes program writing easier, but reduces execution speed **konventioneller Rechner**; *compare with* RISC

citizens band radio (CB) *noun* cheap

popular system of radio communications, usually between vehicles **Citizen-Band, Jedermannfunk (CB)**

cladding *noun* protective material surrounding a conducting core **Verkleidung**; *if the cladding is chipped, the fibre-optic cable will not functon well*

claim frame *noun* (in an FDDI protocol network) special frame which is used to determine which station will initialise the network **Claim Frame**

clamp *verb* to find the voltage of a signal **klemmen**

clapper *noun* mechanical part of a dot matrix printer that drives the printing needles onto the ribbon to print a character on the paper **Nadeldruckwerk**

clarity *noun* being clear **Klarheit**; *the atmospheric conditions affect the clarity of the signal*

class *noun* (in programming language) definition of what a particular software routine will do or what sort of data a variable can hold **Klasse**; **class interval** = range of values that can be contained in a class **Klassenintervall**

classify *verb* to put into classes *or* under various headings **klassifizieren**; *the diagnostic printouts have been classified under T for test results*; **classified directory** = book which lists businesses grouped under various headings (such as computer shops *or* newsagents) **Branchenverzeichnis**

◊ **classification** *noun* way of putting into classes **Klassifizierung**

clean
1 *adjective* not dirty *or* with no errors *or* with no programs **sauber, gereinigt**; *I'll have to start again - I just erased the only clean file*; **clean copy** = copy which is ready for keyboarding, and does not have many changes on it **Reinkopie**; **clean machine** = computer that contains only the minimum of ROM based code to boot its system from disk, any languages required must be loaded in **Computer mit minimalem ROM-basiertem Code**; **clean page** = page (of memory) that has not been changed since it was loaded **unveränderte Speicherseite**; **clean proof** = proof without any corrections **Reinkopie**; **clean room** = area where hard disks, wafers and chips are manufactured; the air inside has been filtered to ensure no

dust or particles are present which could damage a chip **Reinraum**
2 *verb* to make something clean **reinigen**; **data cleaning** = to remove errors from data **Datenreinigung**; **head cleaning disk** = special disk which will clean dirt from the read/write head **Kopfreinigungsdiskette**; *use a head cleaning disk every week; write errors occur if you do not use a head cleaning kit regularly*; **screen cleaning kit** = liquids and cloth which remove any static and dirt from a   VDU   screen **Bildschirmreinigungsausrüstung**

clear
1 *adjective* easily understood **klar verständlich**; *the program manual is not clear on copying files; the booklet gives clear instructions how to connect the different parts of the system; he made it clear that the system will only work on IBM-compatible hardware*
2 *verb*
(a) to wipe out *or* erase *or* set to zero a computer file *or* variable *or* section of memory **löschen**; *type CLS to clear the screen; all arrays are cleared each time the program is run; to clear an area of memory; to clear the data register*
(b) to release a communications link when transmissions have finished **freigeben**; **clear to send (CTS)** = RS232C signal that a line *or* device is ready for data transmission **sendebereit**

◊ **clearance** *noun* authority to access a file **Berechtigung**; *you do not have the required clearance for this processor*

click
1 *noun*
(a) short duration sound, often used to indicate that a key has been pressed **Klicken**
(b) pressing a key *or* button on a keyboard **Klicken**; *you move through text and graphics with a click of the button*; **double-click** = two rapid press-release actions on a mouse button; normally to start a program or select an option **Doppelklick**; **drag-and-click** = holding down a mouse button while moving the mouse, so moving the object selected **Ziehen und Klicken**
2 *verb* to press a key *or* a button on a keyboard *or* the mouse **drücken**; *use the mouse to enlarge a frame by clicking inside its border*

client *noun* (in a network) a workstation *or* PC *or* terminal connected to a network that can send instructions to a server and display results **Client**

◊ **client-server architecture** *noun*

distribution of processing power in which a central server computer carries out the main tasks in response to instructions from terminals or workstations; the results are sent back across the network to be displayed on the terminal, the client (the terminal or workstation) does not need to be able to directly access the data stored on the server nor does it need to carry out a lot of processing **Client-Server-Architektur**

◊ **client-server network** *noun* method of organising a network in which one central dedicated computer, the server, looks after tasks such as security, user accounts, printing and file sharing, while clients (the terminals or workstations connected to the server) run standard applications **Client-Server-Netzwerk;** *compare* PEER-TO-PEER NETWORK

clip
1 *noun* short piece of (live) film **Clip;** *there was a clip of the disaster on the news*
2 *verb*
(a) to attach papers together with a wire **heften;** *the corrections are clipped to the computer printout*
(b) to cut out with scissors **ausschneiden;** .**clipping service** = service which cuts out references to someone in newspapers *or* magazines and sends them to him **Presseausschnittdienst**
(c) to remove the peaks of a waveform **kappen;** *the voltage signal was clipped to prevent excess signal level*

clip-art
noun set of pre-drawn images or drawings that a user can incorporate into a presentation or graphic **Clipart;** *we have used some clip-art to enhance our presentation*

clipboard
noun (i) temporary storage area for data; (ii) (in Microsoft Windows and Macintosh Finder) utility that temporarily stores any type of data, such as a word or image **(i) Zwischenspeicher; (ii) Zwischenablage;** *copy the text to the clipboard, then paste it back into a new document*

clock
noun
(a) machine which shows the time **Uhr;** *the micro has a built-in clock; the time is shown by the clock in the corner of the screen;* **digital clock** = clock which shows the time using numbers (as 12:05) **Digitaluhr**
(b) circuit that generates pulses used to synchronize equipment **Taktgeber; clock cycle** = time period between two consecutive clock pulses **Taktzyklus; clock**

doubler = component that doubles the speed of the main system clock **Taktverdoppler;** *the new CPU from Intel has an optional clock doubler that will double performance;* **clock pulse** = regular pulse used for timing *or* synchronizing purposes **Taktsignal; clock rate** = number of pulses that a clock generates every second **Taktgeberrate; clock track** = line of marks on a disk *or* tape which provides data about the read head location **Taktspur; main clock** = clock signal that synchronizes all the components in a system **Haupttaktgeber; programmable clock** = circuit whose frequency can be set by the user **programmgesteuerter Zeittaktgeber**
2 *verb* to synchronize signals *or* circuits with a clock pulse **takten; clocked signals** = signals that are synchronized with a clock pulse **Synchronsignale**

clone *noun* computer *or* circuit that behaves in the same way as the original it was copied from **Klon;** *they have copied our new personal computer and brought out a cheaper clone; higher performance clones are available for all the models in our range*

> QUOTE On the desktop, the IBM/Motorola/Apple triumvirate is planning to energise a worldwide clone industry based on the PowerPC chip.
> *Computing*

close *verb* to shut down access to a file *or* disk drive **schließen; close file** = to execute a computer instruction to shut down access to a stored file **Datei schließen; closed bus system** = computer with no expansion bus that makes it very difficult for a user to upgrade **geschlossenes Bussystem; closed loop** = number of computer instructions that are repeated **Schleife ohne Ausgang; closed subroutine** = number of computer instructions in a program that can be called at any time, with control being returned on completion to the next instruction in the main program **abgeschlossenes Unterprogramm; closed user group (CUG)** = to restrict the entry to a database *or* bulletin board *or* system (about or on a certain topic *or* subject) to certain known and registered users, usually by means of a password **geschlossener Benutzerkreis;** *see also* USER GROUP

◊ **CLOSE** (in a programming language) command that means the program has finished accessing a particular file *or* device **CLOSE**

◊ **close up** *verb* to move pieces of type *or*

typeset words closer together **aufschließen;**
if we close up the lines, we should save a page

◊ **close-up** *noun* photograph taken very
close to the subject **Nahaufnahme**

CLS (in MS-DOS) system command to
clear the screen, leaving the system prompt
and cursor at the top, left-hand corner of
the screen **CLS**

cluster *noun*
(a) one or more sectors on a hard disk that
are used to store a file or part of a file **Cluster**
(b) number of terminals *or* stations *or*
devices *or* memory locations grouped
together in one place, controlled by a
cluster controller **Mehrfachdatenstation;**
cluster controller = central computer that
controls communications to a cluster of
devices *or* memory locations
Gruppensteuereinheit

◊ **clustering** *noun* series of elements,
occurring in a sequential line within a hash
table **Gruppierung**

QUOTE cluster controllers are available
with 8 or 16 channels
Microcomputer News

QUOTE these include IBM networking
and clustering hardware and software
Personal Computer World

CM = CENTRAL MEMORY area of
memory whose locations can be directly
and immediately addressed by the CPU
Zentralspeicher

C-MAC new direct-broadcast TV
standard using time division multiplexing
for signals **C-MAC**

CMI = COMPUTER MANAGED
INSTRUCTION

CMIP = COMMON MANAGEMENT
INFORMATION PROTOCOL protocol
officially adopted by the ISO used to carry
network management information across a
network **CMIP**

CMIS = COMMON MANAGEMENT
INFORMATION SPECIFICATION
powerful network management system
CMIS

CML = COMPUTER MANAGED
LEARNING

CMOS = COMPLEMENTARY METAL

OXIDE SEMICONDUCTOR integrated
circuit design and construction method
(using a pair of complementary p- and n-
type transistors) **CMOS (Halbleiterelement;**
Kombination von PMOS- und NMOS-Technik)

COMMENT: the final package uses very low
power but is relatively slow and sensitive to
static electricity as compared to TTL integrated
circuits; their main use is in portable computers
where battery power is being used

QUOTE Similarly, customers who do not
rush to acquire CMOS companion
processors for their mainframes will be
rewarded with lower prices when they
finally do migrate.
Computergram

CMOT = CMIP/CMIS OVER TCP use of
CMIP and CMIS network management
protocols to manage gateways in a TCP/IP
network **CMOT**

CMYK = CYAN-MAGENTA-YELLOW-
BLACK (in graphics *or* DTP) method of
describing a colour by its four component
colours **CMYK**

CNC = COMPUTER NUMERIC
CONTROL machine operated
automatically by computer **CNC**
(computergestützte, numerische
Werkzeugmaschinensteuerung); *see also*
NUMERICAL CONTROL

coalesce *verb* to merge two or more files
vereinigen

coat *verb* to cover with a layer (of clay,
paint or varnish) **beschichten, überziehen;**
coated paper = paper which has been
covered with a layer of clay to make it shiny
gestrichenes Papier

◊ **coating** *noun* material covering
something **Überzug; Streichmasse;** *paper*
which has a coating of clay

co-axial cable *noun* cable made up of a
central core, surrounded by an insulating
layer then a second shielding conductor
Koaxialkabel

COMMENT: co-axial cable is used for high
frequency, low loss applications such as TV
aerials

COBOL = COMMON ORDINARY
BUSINESS ORIENTED LANGUAGE
programming language mainly used in
business applications **COBOL**

code

1 *noun*

(a) rules used to convert instructions *or* data from one form to another **Code; code conversion** = rules used to change characters coded in one form, to another **Codeumsetzung; code page** = (in MS-DOS) table that defines the characters that are produced from each key **Codeseite, Zeichenumsetztabelle;** *in order to enter Swedish characters from an English keyboard, you have to change the system code page*

(b) sequence of computer instructions **Code; chain code** = series of words, each word being derived (usually shifted by one bit) from the previous word **Kettencode; code area** = section of main memory in which program instructions are stored **Befehlsbereich; code line** = one written *or* displayed computer program instruction **Codierzeile; code segment** = (in an IBM-compatible PC) an area of memory assigned to hold the instructions that form a program **Codesegment; computer** *or* **machine code** = programming language that consists of commands in binary code that can be directly understood by the central processing unit, without the need for translation **Maschinencode; direct** *or* **one-level** *or* **specific code** = binary code which directly operates the central processing unit, using only absolute addresses and values (this is the final form of a program after a compiler *or* assembler pass) **Direktcode; macro code** = one word that is used to represent a number of instructions, simplifying program writing **Makrocode; object code** = (i) binary code which directly operates a CPU; (ii) program code after it has been translated, compiled or assembled (into machine code) **(i) & (ii) Objektcode; optimum code** = coding system that provides the fastest access and retrieval time for stored data items **optimale Codierung; source code** = set of codes (as a program) written by the programmer which cannot be directly executed by the computer, but have to be translated into an object code program by a compiler *or* assembler *or* interpreter **Quellcode; symbolic code** = instruction that is in mnemonic form rather than machine code **symbolischer Code**

(c) system of signs *or* numbers *or* letters which mean something **Code; area code** = numbers which indicate an area for telephoning **Ortsnetzkennzahl, Vorwahl;** *what is the code for Edinburgh?;* **bar code** = data represented as a series of printed stripes of varying widths **Balkencode; bar-code reader** = optical device that reads data

from a bar code **Balkencodeleser; code bit** = smallest signalling element used by the physical layer (of an OSI model network) for transmission **Codebit; code element** = voltage *or* signal used to represent binary digits **Codeelement; code group** = special sequence of five code bits that represent an FDDI symbol **Codegruppe; cyclic code** = coding system in which the binary representation of decimal numbers changes by only one bit at a time from one number to the next **zyklischer Code; device code** = unique identification and selection code for a peripheral **Gerätekennung; error code** = code that indicates that a particular type of error has occurred **Fehlercode; error correcting code** = coding system that allows bit errors occurring during transmission to be rapidly corrected by logical deduction methods **Fehlerkorrekturcode; error detecting code** = coding system that allows bit errors occurring during transmission to be detected, but is not complex enough to correct them **Fehlererkennungscode; escape codes** = transmitted code sequence which informs the receiver that all following characters represent control actions **ESC-Codes (Codeumschaltung); international dialling code** = numbers used for dialling to another country **Auslandsvorwahl, Internationale Vorwahl; machine-readable codes** = sets of signs *or* letters (such as bar codes *or* post codes) which can be read by computers **maschinenlesbare Codes; post code** *or* **(US) zip code** = letters and numbers used to indicate a town *or* street in an address on an envelope **Postleitzahl; punched code** = combination of holes that represent characters in a punched card **Lochkartencode; self-checking code** = error detecting code **Fehlererkennungscode; stock code** = numbers and letters which refer to an item of stock **Lager-, Warencode**

2 *verb*

(a) to convert instructions *or* data into another form **umsetzen**

(b) to write a program in a programming language **codieren**

◊ **coder** *noun* device which encodes a signal **Codierer**

◊ **coding** *noun* act of putting a code on something **Codieren; coding sheet** *or* **coding form** = special printed sheet used by programmers to write instructions for coding a certain type of program **Programmschema**

CODEC = CODER/DECODER device which encodes a signal being sent *or* decodes a signal received (used in many advanced PABX systems) Codierer/Decodierer

coercivity *noun* magnetic field required to remove any flux saturation effects from a material **Koerzitivkraft**

coherent *adjective* referring to waveforms which are all in phase **zusammenhängend, kohärent;** *the laser produces coherent light;* **coherent bundle** = number of optical fibres, grouped together so that they are all the same length and produce coherent signals from either end **kohärentes Bündel**

coil *noun* number of turns of wire **Spule, Rolle;** *an inductor is made from a coil of wire*

coincidence circuit *or* **element** *noun* electronic circuit that produces an output signal when two inputs occur simultaneously *or* two binary words are equal **Koinzidenzschaltung, UND-Schaltung;** *see also* AND

cold *adjective*
(a) not hot **kalt;** *the machines work badly in cold weather*
(b) without being prepared **unvorbereitet; cold boot** = switching on a computer **Kaltstart; cold fault** = computer fault *or* error that occurs as soon as it is switched on **Kaltfehler; cold standby** = backup system that will allow the equipment to continue running, but with the loss of any volatile data **Cold-Standby-System;** *compare* HOT STANDBY, WARM STANDBY; **cold start** = switching on a computer *or* to run a program from its original start point **Kaltstart;** *compare* WARM START; WARM BOOT

collate *verb* (i) to compare and put items in order; (ii) to put signatures in order for sewing and binding **(i) sortieren; (ii) zusammentragen; collating marks** = marks printed on the spine of a signature so that the binder can see if they have been collated in correct order **Flattermarken; collating sequence** = (i) characters ordered according to their codes; (ii) order in which signatures are stacked for binding **(i) Kollationierungsfolge; (ii) Reihenfolge der Lagen**

◊ **collator** *noun* (i) software that collates data; (ii) device that collates punched cards **(i) Sortierer; (ii) Kartenmischer**

collect *verb* to receive *or* capture data **erfassen**

◊ **collection** *noun* (i) gathering together; (ii) series of items put together **(i) Sammeln; (ii) Sammlung; data collection** = act of receiving data from various sources (either directly from a data capture device *or* from a cartridge) and inserting correctly in order into a database **Datenerfassung; data collection platform** = station that transmits collected data to a central point (usually via satellite) **Datenerfassungsstation**

◊ **collect transfer** *verb* to load a register with bits from a number of different locations **sammelnd laden**

collision detection *noun* the detecting and reporting of the coincidence of two actions *or* events **Zusammenstoßerkennung; carrier sense multiple access-collision detection (CSMA-CD)** = network communications protocol that prevents two sources transmitting at the same time by waiting for a quiet moment on the channel, then attempting to transmit **Verfahren zum Schutz davor, dass nicht mehrere Sender in einem Netz gleichzeitig senden (CSMA/CD)**

colon *noun* printing sign (:), which shows a break in a string of words **Doppelpunkt; semi-colon** = printed sign (;) which marks the end of a program line *or* statement in some languages (such as C and Pascal) **Strichpunkt**

colophon *noun* design *or* symbol *or* company name, used on a printed item to show who are the publisher and the printer **Signet**

colour *noun* sensation sensed by the eye, due to its response to various frequencies of light **Farbe; colour balance** = TV control adjustment to provide a pleasant image *or* various frequencies of light in a signal **Farbabstimmung; colour bits** = number of data bits assigned to a pixel to describe its colour; one bit provides two colours, two bits give four colours and eight bits allow 256 colour combinations **Farbbits; colour burst** = part of a TV signal used to provide information about the hue of the colour **Farberkennungssignal; colour cell** = smallest area on a CRT screen that can display colour information **Farbzelle; colour decoder** = device which converts colour burst and picture signals so that they can be displayed on a screen **Farbdecodierer; colour display** = display device able to represent characters *or* graphics in colour **Farbbildschirm; colour encoder** = device that produces a standard TV signal from separate Red, Green and Blue signals **Farbcodierer; colour graphics adapter (CGA)** = popular microcomputer colour display system **Farbgrafikadapter;** *see also* EGA **colour monitor** = screen that has a demodulator which shows information in colour **Farbmonitor;** *the colour monitor is great for games;* **colour printer** = printer that can produce hard copy in colour; includes colour ink-jet, colour dot-matrix and thermal-transfer printers **Farbdrucker; colour saturation** = purity of a colour signal **Farbsättigung; colour separation** = process by which colours are separated into their primary colours **Farbauszug; colour shift** = (unwanted) change in colour **Farbverschiebung; colour temperature** = method of standardizing the colour of a body (at a certain temperature) **Farbtemperatur; colour transparency** = transparent positive film in colour, which can be used to project on a screen *or* to make film for printing **Diapositiv, Farbdia**

> QUOTE as a minimum, a colour graphics adapter (CGA) is necessary, but for best quality of graphic presentation an enhanced graphics adapter (EGA) should be considered
>
> *Micro Decision*

column *noun*
(a) series of characters, printed one under the other **Spalte;** *to add up a column of figures; put the total at the bottom of the column;* **card column** = line of punched information about one character, parallel to the shorter side of the card **Lochkartenspalte; column guide** = (in a DTP application) vertical line that indicates the position and width of a column **Spaltenlinie; column indicator** = (in word-processing software) status bar at the bottom of the screen that displays in which column the cursor is positioned **Spaltenanzeige; column parity** = parity check on every punched card *or* tape column **Spaltenparitätsprüfung; 80-column printer** = printer which has a maximum line width of 80 characters **80-Spalten-Drucker;** *an 80-column printer is included in the price*
(b) section of printed words in a newspaper *or* magazine **Kolumne, Spalte; column-centimetre** = space in centimetres in a newspaper column, used for calculating charges for advertising **Kolumnenzentimeter**

◊ **columnar** *adjective* in columns in **Spalten, spaltenweise; columnar graph** = graph on which values are shown as vertical

or horizontal bars **Tabelle, Säulendiagramm; columnar working** = showing information in columns in **Tabellen arbeiten**

COM = COMPUTER OUTPUT ON MICROFILM recording the output from a computer directly onto microfilm **COM (Datenausgabe auf Mikrofilm)**

◊ **COM file** *noun* (in operating systems for the PC) three-letter extension to a file name which indicates that the file contains a machine code in binary format and so can be executed by the operating system **COM-Datei;** *to start the program, type the name of the COM file at the MS-DOS prompt*

◊ **COM1** (in an IBM-compatible PC) name for the first serial port **COM1;** *see also* AUX

coma *noun* lens aberration **Koma**

COMAL = COMMON ALGORITHMIC LANGUAGE structured programming language similar to BASIC **COMAL (Programmiersprache)**

combine *verb* to join together **verbinden; combined head** = transducer that can read and write data from the surface of a magnetic storage medium, such as a floppy disk **kombinierter Lese-/Schreibkopf; combined station** = high-level data link control station that processes commands and responses **Hybridstation; combined symbol matching (CSM)** = efficient optical character recognition system **CSM (wirkungsvolles optisches Zeichenerkennungssystem)**

◊ **combination** *noun* several things which are joined together; series of numbers which open a lock **Kombination**

◊ **combinational** *adjective* which combines a number of separate elements **verbindend; combinational circuit** = electronic circuit consisting of a number of connected components **Schaltnetz; combinational logic** = logic function made up from a number of separate logic gates **Kombinatorik**

comma *noun* symbol (,) that is often used to separate data *or* variables *or* arguments **Komma; comma-delimited file** = data file in which each data item is separated by a comma **Datei mit Kommaabgrenzung, Comma-delimited-Datei;** *all databases can import and export to a comma-delimited file format*

command *noun*
(a) electrical pulse *or* signal that will start *or* stop a process **Befehl**
(b) word *or* phrase which is recognized by a computer system and starts *or* terminates an action **Befehl**; *interrupt command; the command to execute the program is RUN;* **channel command** = instruction to a channel *or* control unit, providing control actions such as data filtering *or* routes **Kanalbefehl**; **command code** = binary code that starts *or* stops an instruction *or* action in a CPU **Befehlscode**; **command console processor (CCP)** = software interface between a user's terminal and the BIOS **CCP (Teil des Betriebssystems, der direkt mit dem Anwender kommuniziert, bei CP/M)**; **command control language** = programming language that allows equipment to be easily controlled **Befehlssteuersprache**; **command-driven program** = program which requires the user to enter instructions at every stage **befehlsgetriebenes Programm**; **command file** = sequence of frequently used commands stored in a file **Befehlsdatei**; **command file processor** = execution of a user's command file, allowing the user to create a customized simple operating environment *or* to carry out a series of frequently used commands **Befehlsdateiprozessor**; **command interface** = cue and prompts used by a program to inform and accept from a user required inputs (this can be user-friendly such as a WIMP environment, or not so friendly, such as a question mark) **Kommandoschnittstelle**

◊ **COMMAND.COM** (in MS-DOS) program file that contains the command interpreter for the operating system; this program is always resident in memory and recognises and translates system commands into actions **COMMAND.COM**; *MS-DOS will not work because you deleted the COMMAND.COM file by mistake;* **command interpreter** = program within an operating system that recognises a set of system commands and controls the processor, screen and storage devices accordingly **Befehlsinterpreter**; *when you type in the command 'DIR', the command interpreter asks the disk drive for a list of files and instructs the monitor to display the list;* **command key** = (on an Apple Macintosh) special key that gives access to various special functions, similar in effect to the Control key on an IBM PC **Befehlstaste**; **command language** = programming language made up of procedures for various tasks, that can be called up by a series of commands

Kommandosprache; **command line** = (i) program line that contains a command instruction; (ii) command prompt and system command **(i) & (ii) Befehlszeile**; **command line argument** = additional items entered following a command **Befehls(zeilen)argument, Befehls(zeilen)parameter**; *use the command 'DIR' to view the files on disk, add the command line argument 'A:' to view the files on drive A:;* **command line operating system** = computer system software which is controlled by a user typing in commands (as in MS-DOS), now being replaced by GUI front-ends, such as Microsoft Windows, which allow a user to control the system through images **Befehlszeilenbetriebssystem**; **command prompt** = symbol displayed to indicate a command is expected **Befehlseingabeformat**; **command register** = register that stores the instruction to be carried out *or* that is being processed **Befehlsregister**; **command state** = state of a modem in which it is ready to accept commands **Befehlsstatus, Befehlsmodus**; **command window** = area of a screen where commands are entered **Befehlsfenster**; *the user can define the size of the command window;* **dot command** = method of writing instructions, with a full stop followed by the command, used mainly for embedded commands in a word-processing system **Punktbefehl**; **embedded command** = printer control command, such as indicating that text should be in italics, inserted into test and used by a word-processor when text formatting **eingebetteter Befehl**

> QUOTE This gives Unix a friendly face instead of the terrifyingly complex command-line prompts that make most users reach for their manuals.
>
> *Computing*

comment *noun* helpful notes in a program to guide the user **Kommentar**; *the lack of comments is annoying; BASIC allows comments to be written after a REM instruction;* **comment field** = section of a command line in an assembly language program that is not executed but provides notes and comments **Kommentarfeld**; **comment out** = temporarily to disable a command by enclosing it in a comment field **herauskommentieren**

◊ **commentary** *noun* spoken information which describes a film **Kommentar**

commercial *noun* advertising film on TV
Werbung, Werbespot

common *adjective*
(a) which happens very often **häufig**; *this is a common fault with this printer model*
(b) belonging to several different people *or* programs *or* to everyone **gemeinsam; common business orientated language (COBOL)** = programming language mainly used in business applications **verbreitetste problemorientierte Programmiersprache für kaufmännische Anwendungen (COBOL); common carrier** = (i) firm which carries goods *or* passengers, and which anyone can use; (ii) company which can provide information services to the public **(i) öffentliches Transportunternehmen; (ii) Informationsbüro; common channel signalling** = one channel used as a communications link to a number of devices *or* circuits **Zeichengabe mit gemeinsamem Zeichenkanal; common hardware** = hardware items that can be used for a variety of tasks **Mehrzweckhardware; common language** = data *or* program instructions in a standardized form that can be understood by other processors *or* compilers/interpreters **einheitliche Maschinensprache; common mode noise** = external noise on all power and ground lines **asymmetrische Störung; common pricing** = illegal fixing of prices by several businesses so that they all charge the same price **Preisabsprache; common software** = useful (routines) that can be used by any program **Mehrzwecksoftware; common storage area** = memory *or* storage area used by more than one program **allgemeiner Speicherbereich;** *the file server memory is mainly common storage area, with a section reserved for the operating system*

◊ **common management information protocol (CMIP)** *noun* protocol officially adopted by the ISO used to carry network management information across a network **Common Management Information Protocol (CMIP)**

comms *(informal)* = COMMUNICATIONS

communicate *verb* to pass information to someone **kommunizieren, übertragen;** *he finds it impossible to communicate with his staff communicating with head office has been quicker since we installed the fax;* **communicating word processor** = word

processor workstation which is able to transmit and receive data **Textfernverarbeiter**

communication *noun*
(a) passing of information **Nachrichtenverbindung;** *communication with the head office has been made easier by the fax*
(b) **communications** = process by which data is transmitted and received, by means of telephones, satellites, radio or any medium capable of carrying signals **DFV, Datenfernverarbeitung; communications buffer** = terminal *or* modem that is able to store transmitted data **DFV-Puffer; communications channel** = physical link over which data can be transmitted **Schaltbrücke; communications computer** = computer used to control data transmission in a network **Netzsteuerungscomputer; communications control unit** = electronic device that controls data transmission and routes in a network **Netzsteuerungseinheit; communications executive** = main set of programs that ensure that protocol, format and device and line handlers are correct for the type of device *or* line in use **DFV-Hauptsteuerprogramm; communications interface adapter** = electronic circuit that allows a computer to communicate with a modem **DFV-Schnittstellenanschluss; communications link** = physical path that joins a transmitter to a receiver **DFV-Verbindungsweg; communications link control** = processor that provides various handshaking and error detection functions for a number of links between devices **Steuerelement für DFV-Verbindungswege; communications network** = group of devices such as terminals and printers that are interconnected with a central computer, allowing the rapid and simple transfer of data **DFV-Netz; communications network processor** = processor that provides various interfacing and management (buffering *or* code conversion) between a computer and communications link control **DFV-Netz-Prozessor; communications package** = software that allows a user to control a modem and use an online service **DFÜ-Paket; communications port** = socket or physical connection allowing a device to communicate **Datenübertragungsanschluss, DFÜ-Anschluss; communications protocol** = parameters that define how the transfer of information will be controlled **Datenübertragungsprotokoll;** *the communications protocol for most dial-up online services is eight-bit words, no stop bit*

and even parity; **communications satellite** = satellite used for channelling radio *or* television *or* data signals from one point on the earth to another **DFV-Satellit; communications scanner** = line monitoring equipment to check for data request signals **DFV-Abtaster; communications server** = computer with a modem or fax card attached that allows users on a network to share the use of the modem **Datenübertragungsserver, DFÜ-Server; communications software** = software that allows a user to control a modem and use an online service **Datenübertragungssoftware, DFÜ-Software; data communications** = transmission and reception of data rather than speech *or* images **Daten(fern)übertragung, DFÜ; data communications buffer** = buffer on a receiver that allows a slow peripheral to accept data from a fast peripheral, without slowing either down **Datenübertragungspuffer; data communications equipment (DCE)** = equipment (such as a modem) which receives *or* transmits data **Datenübertragungseinrichtung**

> QUOTE it requires no additional hardware, other than a communications board in the PC
> *Electronics & Power*

community *noun* group of people living *or* working in the same place **Gemeinschaft; the local business community** = the business people living and working in the area **Geschäftsleute am Ort**

◊ **community antenna television (CATV)** *noun* cable television system using a single aerial to pick up television signals and then distribute them over a wide area via cable **Kabelfernsehen**

compact
1 *adjective* (thing) which does not take up much space **kompakt; compact cassette** = magnetic recording tape contained inside a standard plastic box, used in home personal computers for data storage **Kompaktkassette; compact code** = minimum number of program instructions required for a task **Kompaktcode; compact disc (CD)** = small plastic disc that contains audio signals in digital form etched onto the surface **CD (Compact Disc); compact disc player** = machine that reads the digital data from a CD and converts it back to its original form **CD-Spieler; compact disk ROM** *or* **CD-ROM** = small plastic disk that is used as a high capacity ROM device, data

is stored in binary form as holes etched on the surface which are then read by a laser **CD-ROM;** *the compact disk ROM can store as much data as a dozen hard disks;* **compacting algorithm** = formula for reducing the amount of space required by text **Komprimierungsalgorithmus; compact model** = memory model in the Intel 80x86 family of CPUs that allows only 64Kb of space for the code of a program, but 1Mb of space for the program's data **Kompaktmodell**
2 *verb* to reduce the space taken by something **komprimieren; data compacting** = reducing the storage space taken by data by coding it in a more efficient way **Datenkomprimierung**

companding = COMPRESSING AND EXPANDING two processes which reduce *or* compact data before transmission *or* storage then restore packed data to its original form **Kompandierung**

◊ **compandor** *noun* = COMPRESSOR/EXPANDER device used for companding signals **Kompandierer**

COMPAQ ™ US personal computer company (founded in 1983) that was the first manufacturer to produce a clone to the IBM PC **COMPAQ ™**

compare *verb* to check the differences between two pieces of information **vergleichen**

◊ **compare with** *verb* to put two things together to see how they differ **vergleichen mit**

◊ **comparable** *adjective* which can be compared **vergleichbar;** *the two sets of figures are not comparable*

◊ **comparator** *noun* logical device whose output is true if there is a difference between two inputs **Vergleicher**

◊ **comparison** *noun* way of comparing **Vergleich; there is no comparison between speeds of the two processors** = one of the two is much faster than the other **es ist kein Vergleich zwischen den Geschwindigkeiten der beiden Prozessoren**

compatible
1 *adjective* (two hardware *or* software devices) that function correctly together **kompatibel;** *is the hardware IBM-compatible?*
2 *noun* hardware *or* software device that functions correctly with other equipment

(i.e. is a clone and can run the same software as the other) **kompatibler Rechner; kompatible Software;** *buy an IBM PC or a compatible; this computer is much cheaper than the other compatibles*

> QUOTE the compatibles bring computing to the masses
>
> *PC Business World*

> QUOTE low-cost compatibles have begun to find homes as terminals on LANS
>
> *Minicomputer News*

> QUOTE it is a fairly standard feature on most low-cost PC compatibles
>
> *Which PC?*

> QUOTE this was the only piece of software I found that wouldn't work, but it does show that there is no such thing as a totally compatible PC clone
>
> *Personal Computer World*

compatibility *noun* ability (of two hardware *or* software devices) to function together **Kompatibilität; compatibility box =** window *or* session in an operating system that can execute programs written for a different, but related, operating system **Kompatibilitätsfenster;** *OS/2 has a compatibility box to allow it to run DOS applications*

> QUOTE The manufacturer claims that this card does not require special drivers on the host machine, as a flash-memory card does, and therefore has fewer compatibility problems.
>
> *Computing*

> QUOTE check for software compatibility before choosing a display or graphics adapter
>
> *PC Business World*

compile *verb* to convert a high level language program into a machine code program that can be executed by itself **übersetzen, kompilieren;** *compiling takes a long time with this old version; debug your program, then compile it; compiled BASIC programs run much faster than the intrpretor version;* **compile and go =** computer program not requiring operator interaction that will load, compile and execute a high level language program **kompilieren und verarbeiten; compile phase =** the time during a program run, when the instructions are compiled **Kompilierphase**

◊ **compilation** *noun* translation of an encoded source program into machine readable code **Kompilierung; compilation error =** syntax error found during compilation **Kompilierfehler;** *compilation errors result in the job being aborted;* **compilation time =** length of time it takes for a computer to compile a program **Kompilierzeit;** *compare with* DECOMPILATION

◊ **compiler (program)** *noun* piece of software that converts an encoded program into a machine code program **Kompilierer;** *the new compiler has an in-built editor; this compiler produces a more efficient program;* **compiler diagnostics =** features in a compiler that help the programmer to find any faults **Kompilierdiagnostik; compiler language =** high level language (such as C, Pascal) that will convert a source program that follows the language syntax into a machine code version, then run it **Kompilierersprache; cross-compiler =** assembler *or* compiler that compiles programs for one computer whilst running on another **Kreuzkompilierer;** *compare with* INTERPRETER; *we can use the cross-compiler to develop the software before the new system arrives;* **language compiler =** software that converts an encoded source program into another (machine code) form **Sprachkompilierer**

> QUOTE This utility divides the compilation of software into pieces and performs the compile in parallel across available machines on the network.
>
> *Computergram*

complement
1 *noun* (i) inversion of a binary digit; (ii) result after subtracting a number from one less than the radix **(i) & (ii) Komplement;** *the complement is found by changing the 1's to 0's and 0's to 1's;* **one's complement =** inversion of a binary digit **Einerkomplement; nine's complement =** decimal complement (equivalent to binary one's complement) formed by subtracting each digit in the number from nine **Neunerkomplement; ten's complement =** formed by adding one to the nine's complement of the number **Zehnerkomplement; two's complement =** formed by adding one to the one's complement of a number **Zweierkomplement**
2 *verb* to invert a binary digit **komplementieren; complemented =** (binary digit) that has had a complement performed **komplementiert**

◊ **complementary** *adjective* (two things) that complete each other *or* that go well together **komplementär; complementary colours** = two colours that when optically combined produce white **Komplementärfarben; complementary operation** = logical operation that results in the logical NOT of a function **negierte Operation**

◊ **complementary metal oxide semiconductor (CMOS)** *noun* integrated circuit design and construction method (using a pair of complementary p- and n-type transistors) **Halbleiterelement, Kombination aus PMOS- und NMOS-Technik**

◊ **complementation** *noun* number system used to represent positive and negative numbers **Komplementbildung**

complete
1 *adjective*
(a) finished *or* all ready **abgeschlossen, fertig;** *the spelling check is complete; when this job is complete, the next in the queue is processed*
(b) requiring nothing else (in order to function) **vollständig; complete operation** = operation that retrieves the necessary operands from memory, performs the operation, returns the results and operands to memory and reads the next instruction to be processed **vollständige Operation**
2 *verb* to finish a task **beenden;** *when you have completed the keyboarding, pass the text through the spelling checker*

◊ **completion** *noun* time when something is complete **Abschluss;** *completion date for the new software package is November 15th*

complex *adjective* very complicated *or* difficult to understand **komplex;** *the complex mathematical formula was difficult to solve; the controller must work hard to operate this complex network;* **complex instruction set computer (CISC)** = CPU design whose instruction set contains a number of long, complex instructions, that makes programming easier, but reduces execution speed **konventioneller Rechner;** *compare* REDUCED INSTRUCTION SET COMPUTER

◊ **complexity** *noun* being complicated **Komplexität; complexity measure** = measure of the system resources used in an operation *or* job **Komplexitätsmaß**

complicated *adjective* with many different parts *or* difficult to understand **kompliziert;** *this program is very complicated; the computer design is more complicated than necessary*

component *noun* (i) piece of machinery *or* section which will be put into a final product; (ii) electronic device that affects an electrical signal **(i) Teilbauelement; (ii) Komponente; component density** = number of electronic components per unit area on a PCB **Komponentendichte;** *component density increases with production expertise component density is so high on this motherboard, that no expansion connectors could be fitted;* **component error** = error introduced by a malfunctioning device *or* component rather than incorrect programming **Komponentenfehler**

compose *verb* to arrange the required type, in the correct order, prior to printing **setzen; composing room** = room in a typesetters *or* in a newspaper, where the text is composed by compositors **Setzraum, Setzerei**

◊ **composition** *noun* creating typeset text, either using metal type *or* by keyboarding on a computer typesetter **Setzen; composition size** = printing type size **Typengröße**

◊ **compositor** *noun* person who sets up the required type prior to printing **Setzer; electronic compositor** = computer that allows a user to easily arrange text on screen before it is electronically typeset **elektronische Setzmaschine**

composite circuit *noun* electronic circuit made up of a number of smaller circuits and components **kombinierter Schaltkreis**

◊ **composite display** *noun* video display unit that accepts a single composite video signal and can display an infinite number of colours *or* shade of grey **Kombinationsbildschirm; composite video** = video signal which combines the colour signals and the monochrome signal into one single signal **Farbbildsignalgemisch;** *most TV set and video players expect a composite video feed;* **composite video signal** = single television signal containing synchronizing pulse and video signal in a modulated form **Farbmischsignal**

compound *adjective* **compound logical element** = logical circuit *or* function that produces an output from a number of inputs **zusammengesetztes logisches Element; compound statement** = a number of program instructions in one line of program **zusammengesetzte Anweisung;** *the debugger cannot handle compound statements*

compress *verb* to squeeze something to fit into a smaller space **verdichten, komprimieren;** *use the archiving program to compress the file*

◊ **compression** *noun* varying the gain of a device depending on input level to maintain an output signal within certain limits **Verdichtung, Komprimierung; data compression** = means of reducing the size of blocks of data by removing spaces, empty sections and unused material **Datenverdichtung; disk compression software** = resident software that compresses data as it is written to disk and de-compresses it as it is read back **Festplattenkomprimierungssoftware, Online-Komprimierer**

◊ **compressor** *noun* (i) electronic circuit which compresses a signal; (ii) (program *or* device) that provides data compression **(i) Verdichter; (ii) Verdichtungsprogramm; audio compressor** = circuit which limits the maximum signal level **Tonkompressor**

comptometer *noun* machine which counts automatically **automatische Zählmaschine**

CompuServe ™ one of the largest US-based online information services **CompuServe** ™

compute *verb* to calculate *or* to do calculations **berechnen;** *connect charges were computed on an hourly rate*

◊ **computable** *adjective* which can be calculated **berechenbar**

◊ **computation** *noun* calculation **Berechnung**

◊ **computational** *adjective* referring to computation **Rechen-; computational error** = mistake made in calculating **Rechenfehler**

computer *noun*
(a) machine that receives *or* stores *or* processes data very quickly according to a stored program **Computer, Rechner; analog computer** = computer which processes data in analog form (that is data which is represented by a continuously variable signal - as opposed to digital data) **Analogrechner; business computer** = powerful small computer which is programmed for special business uses **Geschäftscomputer; digital computer** = computer which processes data in digital form (that is data represented in discrete form) **Digitalrechner; mainframe computer** = large scale powerful computer system that

can handle high capacity memory and backing storage devices as well as a number of operators simultaneously **Großrechner; microcomputer** *or* **micro** = complete small-scale, cheap, low-power computer system based around a microprocessor chip and having limited memory capacity **Mikrocomputer; minicomputer** *or* **mini** = small computer with a greater range of instructions and processing power than a microcomputer, but not able to compete with the speed or data handling capacity of a mainframe computer **Minicomputer; personal computer (PC)** *or* **home computer** = small computer which can be used in the home, in which the various sections (screen, keyboard, disk drives, processing unit, memory etc.) are in one or two small compact cases **Personalcomputer (PC); single board computer (sbc)** = micro *or* mini computer whose components are all located on a single printed circuit board **Einzelplatinencomputer, Minicomputer; single chip computer** = complete simple computer, including CPU, memory and I/O ports on one chip **Einzelchipcomputer; supercomputer** = very powerful mainframe computer used for high speed mathematical tasks **Großrechner**
(b) **computer animation** = making a series of computer-generated images displayed in sequence to emulate motion **Computeranimation; computer applications** = the tasks and uses that a computer can carry out in a particular field *or* job **Computeranwendungen; computer architecture** = (i) layout and interconnection of a computer's internal hardware and the logical relationships between CPU, memory and I/O devices; (ii) way in which the CPU, terminals, printers and network connections are arranged **(i) & (ii) Computerarchitektur; computer bureau** = office which offers to do work on its computers for companies which do not have their own computers **Computerbüro; computer code** = programming language that consists of commands in binary code that can be directly understood by the central processing unit, without the need for translation **Computercode; computer conferencing** = connecting a number of computers *or* terminals together to allow a group of users to communicate **Computerkonferenz; computer crime** = theft, fraud or other crimes involving computers **Computerkriminalität; computer dating** = use of a computer to match single people who may want to get married **computerisierte Heiratsvermittlung; computer department** = department in a company which manages

the company's computers **Computerabteilung; computer engineer** = person who maintains *or* programs *or* designs computer equipment **Computeringenieur; computer error** = mistake made by a computer **Computerfehler; computer file** = section of information on a computer (such as the payroll, list of addresses, customer accounts) **Computerdatei; computer graphics** = information represented graphically on a computer display **Computergrafik; computer graphics metafile (CGM)** = device-independent file format that provides one method of storing an image as objects **Computer Graphics Metafile (CGM); computer image processing** = analysis of information in an image, usually by electronic means *or* using a computer, also used for recognition of objects in an image **computergestützte Bildverarbeitung; computer independent language** = programming language that will operate on any computer that has a correct compiler *or* interpreter **computerunabhängige Programmiersprache; computer input microfilm (CIM)** = use of microfilm for computer data storage, and the method of reading the data **Computer Input Microfilm (CIM); computer language** = language (formed of figures *or* characters) used to communicate with a computer **Maschinensprache; computer listing** = printout of a list of items taken from data stored in a computer **Computerausdruck; computer literacy** = understanding the basic principles of computers, related expressions and concepts, and being able to use computers for programming *or* applications **Computerfachkenntnis; computer-literate** = (person) able to understand how to use a computer, the expressions and concepts used **computersachverständig;** *the managing director is simply not computer-literate;* **computer logic** = way in which the various sections of the CPU, memory and I/O are arranged (in hardware) **Computerlogik; computer mail** *or* **electronic mail** = messages sent between users of a bulletin board *or* network **elektronische Post; computer manager** = person in charge of a computer department **Computerverwalter; computer network** = number of computers, terminals and peripherals connected together to allow communications between each other **Computernetz; computer numeric control (CNC)** = control of a machine by computer **computergestützte, numerische Werkzeugmaschinensteuerung (CNC); computer office system** = computer and related peripherals used for office tasks

(filing, word processing, etc.) **Computerbürosystem; computer operator** = person who operates a computer **Computerbediener; computer organization** *see* COMPUTER ARCHITECTURE; **computer output** = data *or* information produced after processing by a computer **Computerausgabe; computer output on microfilm (COM)** = information output from a computer, stored directly onto microfilm **Ausgabe auf Mikrofilm; computer power** = measure of speed and capacity of a computer (several tests exist, such as FLOPS *or* benchmark timings) **Computerstärke, Computerleistung; computer program** = series of instructions to a computer, telling it to do a particular piece of work **Computerprogramm;** *the user cannot write a computer program with this system;* **computer programmer** = person who writes computer programs **Programmierer; computer run** = action of processing instructions in a program by a computer **Computer-Programmlauf; computer science** = scientific study of computers, the organization of hardware and development of software **Informatik; computer services** = work using a computer, done by a computer bureau **Computerservice; computer system** = a central processor with storage and associated peripherals that make up a working computer **Rechensystem; computer time** = time when a computer is being used (paid for at an hourly rate) **Rechenzeit;** *running all those sales reports costs a lot in computer time;* **computer virus** = program which adds itself to an executable file and copies (or spreads) itself to other executable files each time an infected file is run; a virus can corrupt data, display a message or do nothing **Computervirus, Virus; computer word** = number of bits that make up a standard word within a CPU (usually 8,16 *or* 32 bits long) **Maschinenwort**

◊ **computer generations** *noun* way of defining the advances in the field of computing **Computergenerationen**

COMMENT: the development of computers has been divided into a series of "generations": *first generation:* computers constructed using valves having limited storage *second generation:* computers where transistors were used in construction *third generation:* use of integrated circuits in construction *fourth generation:* most often used at present, using low cost memory and IC packages *fifth generation:* future computers using very fast processors, large memory and allowing human input/output

computer- *prefix* referring to a computer Computer-, computer-; **computer-based learning (CBL)** = learning mainly using a computer **computergestütztes Lernen; computer-based message system (CBMS)** = use of a computer system to allow users to send and receive messages from other users (usually in-house) **computergestütztes Nachrichtensystem; computer-based training (CBT)** = use of a computer system to train students **computergestütztes Training; computer-generated** = which has been generated by a computer **computergeneriert;** *computer-generated graphics;* **computer-integrated manufacturing (CIM)** = coordinated use of computers in every aspect of design and manufacturing **computerintegrierte Fertigung; computer-integrated systems** = coordinated use of computers and other related equipment in a process **computerintegrierte Systeme;** *this firm is a very well-known supplier of computer-integrated systems which allow both batch pagination of very long documents with alteration of individual pages;* **computer-managed instruction (CMI)** = using a computer to assist students in learning a subject **computergestützter Unterricht; computer-managed learning (CML)** = using a computer to teach students and assess their progress **computergestütztes Lernen**

◊ **computer-aided** *or* **computer-assisted** *adjective* which uses a computer to make the work easier **computergestützt; computer-aided** *or* **assisted design (CAD)** = the use of computer and graphics terminal to help a designer in his work **computergestützte Entwurf und Konstruktion (CAD); computer-aided** *or* **assisted engineering (CAE)** = use of a computer to help an engineer solve problems *or* calculate design *or* product specifications **computergestütztes Konstruieren; computer-aided** *or* **assisted instruction (CAI)** = use of a computer to assist pupils in learning a subject **computergestützter Unterricht (CAI); computer-aided** *or* **assisted learning (CAL)** = use of a computer to assist pupils to learn a subject **computergestütztes Lernen (CAL); computer-aided** *or* **assisted manufacture (CAM)** = use of a computer to control machinery *or* to assist in a manufacturing process **computergestützte Fertigung (CAM); computer-aided** *or* **assisted testing (CAT)** = use of a computer to test equipment *or* programs to find any faults **computergestütztes Prüfen (CAT); computer-**

aided *or* assisted training **(CAT)** = use of a computer to demonstrate to and assist pupils in learning a skill **computergestütztes Training**

◊ **computer-readable** *adjective* which can be read and understood by a computer **computerlesbar;** *computer-readable codes*

computerize *verb* to change from a manual system to one using computers **computerisieren, auf EDV umstellen;** *our stock control has been completely computerized; they operate a computerized invoicing system*

◊ **computerization** *noun* action of introducing a computer system *or* of changing from a manual to a computer system **Computerisierung, Umstellung auf EDV;** *computerization of the financial sector is proceeding very fast*

computing *adjective & noun* referring to computers *or* work done on computers **Rechen-; Computing; computing power** = measure of speed and ability of a computer to perform calculations **Rechenstärke; computing speed** = speed at which a computer calculates **Rechengeschwindigkeit**

CON (in IBM-PC compatible systems) name used to identify the console: the keyboard and monitor **CON**

concatenate *verb* to join together two or more sets of data **verketten; concatenated data set** = more than one file *or* set of data joined together to produce one set **verkettete Dateien**

conceal *verb* to hide *or* not display information *or* graphics from a user **verbergen;** *the hidden lines are concealed from view with this algorithm*

concentrate *verb* (i) to focus a beam onto a narrow point; (ii) to combine a number of lines *or* circuits *or* data to take up less space (i) **konzentrieren;** (ii) **komprimieren;** *to concentrate a beam of light on a lens; the concentrated data was transmitted cheaply*

◊ **concentrator** *noun* **(a)** (in a Token-Ring network) device at the centre of a Token-Ring network which provides a logical star topology in which nodes are connected to the concentrator, but connects each arm of the star as a physical ring within the device **Konzentrator**

(b) (in an FDDI network) node which provides access for one or more stations to the network **Konzentrator**
(c) (in an 10Base-T Ethernet network) the device at the centre of a star-topology 10Base-T Ethernet network that receives signals from one port and regenerates them before sending them out to the other ports **Konzentrator**
(d) (in general networking) device where all the cables from nodes are interconnected **Konzentrator**

conceptual model *noun* description of a database or program in terms of the data it contains and its relationships **konzeptionelles Modell**

concertina fold *noun* accordion fold *or* method of folding continuous paper, one sheet in one direction, the next sheet in the opposite direction, allowing the paper to be fed into a printer continuously with no action on the part of the user **Zickzackfaltung**

concurrent *adjective* almost simultaneous (actions *or* sets) **gleichzeitig ablaufend;** *each concurrent process has its own window; three transputers provide concurrent processing cababilitiés for the entire department;* **concurrent operating system** = operating system software that allows several programs *or* activities to be processed at the same time **Parallelbetriebssystem;** **concurrent processing** *see* MULTITASKING; **concurrent programming** = running several programs apparently simultaneously, achieved by executing small sections from each program in turn **mehrere Programme gleichzeitig laufen lassen**

◊ **concurrently** *adverb* running at almost the same time **gleichzeitig ablaufend;** *see also the four categories for processors* SISD, SIMD, MISD, MIMD

QUOTE The system uses parallel-processing technology to allow support for large numbers of concurrent users.
Computing

condenser lens *noun* optical device, usually made of glass, that concentrates a beam of light onto a certain area **Sammellinse**

condition
1 *noun* (i) state of a circuit *or* device *or* register; (ii) series of requirements that have to be met before an action can occur **(i)** Zustand; **(ii) Bedingung; condition code register** = register that contains the state of the CPU after the execution of the last instruction **Anzeigeregister;** *see also* FLAG; **error condition** = state that is entered if an attempt is made to operate on data containing errors **Fehlerbedingung**
2 *verb* to modify data that is to be transmitted so as to meet set parameters **in die richtige Form bringen;** *condition the raw data to a standard format*

◊ **conditional** *adjective*
(a) provided that certain things take place **vorbehaltlich**
(b) (process) which is dependent on the result of another **bedingt; conditional breakpoint** = breakpoint inserted, after which the programmer can jump to one of a number of sections, depending on data *or* program status **bedingter Programmstop; conditional jump** *or* **branch** *or* **transfer** = programming instruction that provides a jump to a section of a program if a certain condition is met **bedingter Sprung** *or* **bedingte Verzweigung** *or* **Übertragung;** *the conditional branch will select routine one if the response is yes and routine two if no;* **conditional statement** = program instruction that will redirect program control according to the outcome of an event **bedingte Anweisung**

conduct *verb* to allow an electrical current to flow through a material **leiten;** *to conduct electricity; copper conducts well*

◊ **conduction** *noun* ability of a material to conduct **Leitfähigkeit;** *the conduction of electricity by gold contacts*

◊ **conductive** *adjective* referring to the ability of a material to conduct **leitfähig**

◊ **conductor** *noun* substance (such as a metal) which conducts electricity **Leiter;** *copper is a good conductor of electricity; see also* SEMICONDUCTOR

conduit *noun* protective pipe *or* channel for wires *or* cables **Kabelrohr;** *the cables from each terminal are channelled to the computer centre by metal conduit*

cone *noun* moving section in most loudspeakers **Konus (Teil der Membran)**

conference *noun* meeting of people to discuss problems **Besprechung, Konferenz; to be in conference** = to be in a meeting in einer Besprechung sein; **conference call** = telephone call which connects together three or more telephone lines allowing each person *or* device to communicate with all the others **Konferenzschaltung; conference phone** = telephone so arranged that several people can speak into it from around a table **Konferenztelefon; conference room** = room where small meetings can take place **Konferenzraum; press conference** = meeting where newspaper and TV reporters are invited to hear news of a new product *or* a change of management, etc. **Pressekonferenz**

◊ **conferencing** *or* **teleconferencing** *noun* discussion between remote users using computers linked by modem or a network **Conferencing, Abhalten einer Konferenz; computer conferencing** = connecting a number of computers *or* terminals together to allow a group of users to communicate **Computerkonferenz;** *the multi-user BBS has a computer conferencing facility*

> QUOTE Small organisations and individuals find it convenient to use online services, offering email, conferencing and information services.
> *Computing*

confidence level *noun* likelihood that a number will lie to within a range of values **statistische Sicherheit, Aussagewahrscheinlichkeit**

CONFIG.SYS (in MS-DOS) configuration text file that contains commands to set parameters and load driver software; this file is read automatically once the PC is switched on and the operating system has loaded **CONFIG.SYS;** *if you add a new adapter card to your PC you will have to add a new command to the CONFIG.SYS file*

configure *verb* to select hardware, software and interconnections to make up a special system **konfigurieren;** *this terminal has been configured to display graphics; you only have to configure the PC once - when you first buy it*

◊ **configuration** *noun* way in which the hardware and software of a computer system are planned and set up **Konfiguration; configuration state** = state of a computer that allows it *or* the system *or* a program to be configured **Konfigurationszustand**

◊ **configured-in** *adjective* (device) whose configuration state indicates it is ready and available for use **betriebsbereit konfiguriert; configured-off** *or* **configured out** = (device) whose configuration state indicates it is not available for use **nicht konfiguriert**

> QUOTE users can configure four of the eight ports to handle links at speeds of 64K bit/sec
> *Computer News*

> QUOTE the machine uses RAM to store system configuration information
> *PC Business World*

> QUOTE several configuration files are provided to assign memory to the program, depending on the available RAM on your system
> *PC Business World*

> QUOTE if you modify a program with the editor, or with a word-processor specified in the configuration file, it will know that the program has changed and will execute the new one accordingly
> *PC Business World*

> QUOTE He said only Banyan Vines had the network configuration and administration capabilities required for implementing an international business plan based on client-server computing.
> *Computing*

confirm *verb* action to indicate that you agree with a particular action **bestätigen;** *click on the OK button to confirm that you want to delete all your files*

conform *verb* to work according to set rules **entsprechen;** *the software will not run if it does not conform to the operating system standards*

congestion *noun* state that occurs when communication *or* processing demands are greater than the capacity of a system **Besetztzustand, Überlastung**

conjunct *noun* one of the variables in an logical AND function **Variable in der logischen UND-Funktion**

◊ **conjunction** *noun* logical function whose output is true if all inputs are true **UND-Funktion**

connect *verb* to link together two points in a circuit *or* communications network **verbinden; connect charge** = (in a commercial on-line system) the cost per minute of time when you are connected to the remote system **Verbindungsgebühren (pl); connect state** = state of a modem in which it is transferring data across a communications line **Verbindungszustand,**

Connect-Status; **connect time** = length of
time a user is logged onto an interactive
system **Dauer der Verbindung**

◊ **connection** *noun* link *or* something
which joins **Verbindung; parallel connection**
= connector on a computer allowing
parallel data to be transferred
Parallelverbindung; *their transmission rate is
60,000 bps through parallel connection*

◊ **connector** *noun* physical device with a
number of metal contacts that allow
devices to be easily linked together
Anschluss(stecker); *the connector at the end
of the cable will fit any standard serial port;*
connector plug = (in an FDDI network)
device at the end of a fibre-optic or copper
cable that connects to a receptacle **Stecker,
Kabelstecker; connector receptacle** = (in an
FDDI network) device mounted on a panel
that connects to a plug **Buchse; card edge
connector** = series of metal tracks ending at
the edge and on the surface of a circuit
board, allowing it to be plugged into an
edge connector to provide electrical path
(for data transmission, etc.)
Kartenrandverbindung; *see also* FEMALE,
MALE

connective *noun* symbol between two
operands that describes the operation to be
performed **Bindewort**

connectivity *noun* ability of a device to
connect with other devices and transfer
information **Connectivity**

conscious error *noun* operator error
that is immediately spotted, but cannot be
prevented in time **bewusster Fehler**

consecutive *adjective* following one
after another **aufeinanderfolgend;** *the
computer ran three consecutive files*

◊ **consecutively** *adverb* one after the
other **aufeinanderfolgend;** *the sections of the
program run consecutively*

consistency check *noun* check to
make sure that objects, data or items
conform to their expected formats
Konsistenzprüfung

console *noun* unit (keyboard and VDU,
and usually a printer) which allows an
operator to communicate with a computer
system **Konsole;** *the console consists of input
device such as a keyboard, and an output
device such as a printer or CRT; see also*
CON

constant
1 *noun* item of data, whose value does not
change (as opposed to a variable) **Konstante**
2 *adjective* which does not change **konstant;**
*the disk drive motor spins at a constant
velocity;* **constant length field** = data field
that always contains the same number of
characters **Datenfeld mit konstanter Länge;
constant ratio code** = character
representation code that has a constant
number of binary ones per word length
gleichgewichteter Code

construct *verb* to build *or* to make (a
device *or* a system) **errichten**

◊ **construction** *noun* building *or* making
of a system **Errichtung;** *construction of the
prototype is advancing rapidly construction
techniques have changed over the past few
years*

consult *verb* to ask an expert for advice
um Rat fragen; *he consulted the maintenance
manager about the disk fault*

◊ **consultancy** *noun* act of giving
specialist advice **Beratung;** *a consultancy
firm; he offers a consultancy service*

◊ **consultant** *noun* specialist who gives
advice **Berater/-in;** *they called in a computer
consultant to advise them on the system
design*

◊ **consulting** *adjective* person who gives
specialist advice **beratend;** *a consulting
engineer*

consumables *plural noun* small cheap
extra items required in the day-to-day
running of a computer system (such as
paper and printer ribbons)
Verbrauchsgüter; *put all the printer leads and
paper with the other consumables*

contact
1 *noun* section of a switch *or* connector that
provides an electrical path when it touches
another conductor **Kontakt;** *the circuit is not
working because the contact is dirty;* **contact
bounce** *see* BOUNCE, DE-BOUNCE
2 *verb* to try to call a user *or* device in a
network **aufrufen**

◊ **contact printing** *noun* photographic
printing process in which the negative
touches the light-sensitive paper
Kontaktdruck

contain *verb* to hold something inside
enthalten; *each carton contains two
computers and their peripherals; we have
lost a file containing important documents*

content *noun* the ideas inside a letter *or*
other document **Inhalt, Gehalt**

◊ **contents** *plural noun*
(a) things contained *or* what is inside something **Inhalt**; *the contents of the bottle poured out onto the computer keyboard; the customs officials inspected the contents of the box;* **the contents of the letter** = the words written in the letter **der Inhalt des Briefes**
(b) list of items in a file **Inhalt**

◊ **content-addressable** *adjective* **content-addressable file** *or* **location** = method of storing data in which each item may be individually accessed **Assoziativdatei**; **content-addressable memory (CAM)** *or* **associative storage** = method of data retrieval which uses part of the data rather than an address to locate the data **Assoziativspeicher (CAM)**

contention *noun* situation that occurs when two or more devices are trying to communicate with the same piece of equipment **Konkurrenzbetrieb**; **contention bus** = communication control system in which a device must wait for a free moment before transmitting data **Konkurrenzbus**; **contention delay** = length of time spent waiting for equipment to become free for use **Verzögerung durch Konkurrenzbetrieb**

context *noun* words and phrases among which a word is used **Zusammenhang, Kontext**; *the example shows how the word is used in context*

◊ **context-sensitive** *adjective* (information) which relates to the particular context **kontextsensitiv**; **context-sensitive help** = help message that gives useful information about the particular function or part of the program you are in rather than general information about the whole program **kontextsensitive Hilfe**

◊ **context-switching** *noun* process in which several programs are loaded in memory, but only one at a time can be executed **Programmwechselbetrieb**

| COMMENT: unlike a true multitasking system which can load several programs into memory and run several programs at once, context-switching only allows one program to be run at a time

contiguous *adjective* which touches the thing next to it **angrenzend**; **contiguous file** = file stored in a series of adjacent disk sectors **angrenzende Datei**; **contiguous graphics** = graphic cells *or* characters that touch each other **zusammenhängende Grafik**; *most display units do not provide contiguous*

graphics: their characters have a small space on each side to improve legibility

> QUOTE If you later edit the file again, some of the new data clusters will not be contiguous with the original clusters but spread around the disk.
>
> *Computing*

contingency plan *noun* secondary plan *or* equipment that will be used if the first fails to work **Plan für unvorhersehbare Zwischenfälle**

continue *verb* to go on doing something *or* to do something which you were doing earlier **fortsetzen**

◊ **continual** *adjective* which happens again and again **ständig**; *the continual system breakdowns have slowed down the processing*

◊ **continually** *adverb* again and again **ständig**

◊ **continuation** *noun* act of continuing **Fortsetzung**; **continuation page** = page *or* screen of text that follows on from a main page **Folge-, Fortsetzungsseite**

◊ **continuity** *noun*
(a) clear conduction path between two points **Kontinuität**
(b) checking that the details of one scene in a film continue into the next scene to be shown, even if the two have been shot at different times **Anschluss**

◊ **continuous** *adjective* with no end *or* with no breaks; which goes on without stopping **andauernd, kontinuierlich**; **continuous data stream** = high speed serial data transmission, in which data words are not synchronized, but follow on immediately from each other **kontinuierlicher Datenstrom**; **continuous feed** = device which feeds continuous stationery into a printer **Endlospapiereinzug**; **continuous loop** = endless piece of recording *or* projection tape **Dauerschleife**; **continuous signal** = analog (continuously variable) signal **Dauerkennzeichen**; **continuous stationery** = paper made as one long sheet, used in computer printers **Endlospapier**; **continuous wave** = high frequency waveform that can be modulated to carry data **kontinuierliche Schwingung**; *see also* CARRIER

◊ **continuously** *adverb* without stopping **ohne Unterbrechung**; *the printer overheated after working continuously for five hours*

contrast
1 *noun*
(a) difference between black and white Kontrast; *the control allows you to adjust brightness and contrast;* contrast enhancement filter = special filter put over a monitor to increase contrast and prevent eye-strain Kontrastverstärkungsfilter **(b)** control knob on a display that alters the difference between black and white tones Kontrasteinstellung **2** *verb* to examine the differences between two sets of information gegenüberstellen, kontrastieren; *the old data was contrasted with the latest information*

◊ **contrasting** *adjective* which show a sharp difference kontrastierend, Kontrast-; *a cover design in contrasting colours*

control
1 *verb* to be in charge of something *or* to make sure that something is kept in check steuern; controlled vocabulary = set of terms *or* words used in an indexing language Regelvokabular NOTE: controlling - controlled
2 *noun*
(a) restricting *or* checking something *or* making sure that something is kept in check Kontrolle; control computer = dedicated computer used to control a process *or* piece of equipment Kontrollrechner; control total = result of summing certain fields in a computer file to provide error detection Kontrollsumme; out of control = not kept in check außer Kontrolle
(b) (i) section of a computer *or* device that carries out instructions and processes signals, etc.; (ii) conditional program statements **(i)** Steuerung; **(ii)** bedingte Anweisungen; control key *or* Ctrl = (on IBM-PC compatible systems) special key (in the lower left corner) that provides a secondary function when pressed with another key Control-Taste, Steuerungstaste, CTRL-Taste, STRG-Taste; *to halt a program, press Ctrl-C - the control key and letter C - at the same time; to reset your PC, press Ctrl-Alt-Del;* control menu = (in Microsoft Windows) menu that allows you to move, resize or close the current window; the menu is accessed by pressing Alt-Space Systemmenü; control panel = (in Windows, Macintosh and OS/2) utility that displays the user-definable options such as keyboard, country-code and type of mouse Systemsteuerung; control statement = program instruction that redirects a program (to another branch etc.) Steueranweisung; control unit (CU) = section of central processor that selects and

executes instructions Steuereinheit; control word = word that defines the actions (in a particular process) that are to be followed Steuerwort; device control character = special code sent in a transmission to a device to instruct it to perform a special function Gerätesteuerzeichen; line control = special code used to control a communications link Übertragungssteuerung
(c) (i) key on a computer keyboard which sends a control character; (ii) data which controls something **(i)** CTRL-Taste; **(ii)** Steuerdaten; control block = reserved area of computer memory that contains control data Steuerblock; control bus = set of connections to a microcomputer that carry the control signals between CPU, memory and input/output devices Steuerbus; control cards = in a punched card system, the first cards which contain the processor control instructions Steuerkarten; control character = special character that provides a control sequence rather than a alphanumeric character Steuerzeichen; control cycle = events required to retrieve, decode and execute an instruction stored in memory Steuerzyklus; control data = data that controls the actions of a device Steuerdaten; control driven = computer architecture where instructions are executed once a control sequence has been received steuerungsgetrieben; control field = storage area for control instructions Kontrollfeld; control instruction = program instruction that controls the actions of a device Steuerbefehl; *the next control instruction will switch to italics;* control language = commands that describe the identification of and resources required by a job that a computer has to process (Job)kontrollsprache; control memory *or* ROM = memory which decodes control instructions into microinstructions which operate the computer *or* microcontroller Mikroprogrammspeicher; control mode = state of a device in which control signals can be received to select options *or* functions Steuermodus; control panel = main computer system control switches and status indicators Bedienerkonsole; control program/monitor *or* control program for microcomputers (CP/M) = old-fashioned but still popular operating system for microcomputers Betriebssystem für Mikrocomputer mit 8-Bit-System (CP/M); control register = storage location only used for control data Steuerregister; control signals = electrical signals transmitted to control the actions of a circuit Steuerungssignale; control sequence =

(series of) codes containing a control character and various arguments, used to carry out a process *or* change mode in a device **Steuerungsablauf; control statement** = program instruction that directs a CPU to provide controlling actions *or* controls the operation of the CPU **Steueranweisung; control token** = special sequence of bits transmitted over a LAN to provide control actions **Steuerkennzeichen, Steuertoken; control transfer** = redirection of the CPU when a jump *or* call instruction is encountered **Steuerungsübergabe**
(d) control group = small group which is used to check a sample group **Kontroll-, Vergleichsgruppe; control systems** = systems used to check that a computer system is working correctly **Kontrollsysteme**

◊ **controllable** *adjective* which can be controlled **kontrollierbar**

◊ **controller** *noun* hardware *or* software device that controls a peripheral (such as a printer) *or* monitors and directs the data transmission over a local area network **Regler; display controller** = device that accepts character *or* graphical codes and instructions, and converts them into dot-matrix patterns that are displayed on a screen **Bildschirmregler; printer's controller** = main device in a printer that translates output from the computer into printing instructions **Druckerregler;** *see also* DEVICE DRIVER

> QUOTE a printer's controller is the brains of the machine. It translates the signals coming from your computer into printing instructions that result in a hard copy of your electronic document
> *Publish*

> QUOTE there are seven print control characters which can be placed in a document
> *Personal Computer World*

convention *noun* well-known standards *or* rules which are followed, allowing hardware *or* software compatibility **Richtlinien, Konvention**

◊ **conventional memory** *or* **RAM** *noun* (in an IBM-PC compatible system) the random access memory region installed in a PC from 0 up to 640Kb; this area of memory can be directly controlled by MS-DOS and it is where most programs are loaded when they are executed **konventioneller Speicher, RAM;** *compare* HIGH MEMORY; EXPANDED MEMORY

conversational (mode) *noun*

computer system that provides immediate responses to a user's input **Dialogbetrieb;** *see also* INTERACTIVE MODE; *compare with* BATCH MODE

conversion *noun* change from one system to another **Umsetzung; conversion equipment** = device that will convert data from one format to another (suitable for another system) without changing the content **Umsetzer; conversion tables** *or* **translation tables** = list of source codes *or* statements and their equivalent in another language *or* form **Übersetzungstabellen;** *conversion tables may be created and used in conjunction with the customer's data to convert it to our systems codes;* **conversion program** = (i) program that converts programs written for one computer into a suitable form for another; (ii) program that converts data format, coding, etc. for use in another program **(i)** & **(ii) Konvertierungsprogramm**

◊ **convert** *verb* to change one thing into another **umsetzen, konvertieren**

◊ **convertibility** *noun* ability to be changed **Konvertierbarkeit**

◊ **convertible** *adjective* which can be converted **konvertierbar**

◊ **converter** *or* **convertor** *noun* device *or* program that translates data from one form to another **Konverter, Umsetzer;** *the convertor allowed the old data to be used on the new system;* **analog to digital converter (ADC)** = device used to convert an analog signal to a digital output form, that can be understood by a computer **Analog-Digital-Umsetzer; digital to analog converter (DAC)** = circuit that outputs an analog signal that is proportional to the input digital number **Digital-Analog-Umsetzer**

convey *verb* to cárry *or* import information **vermitteln, klarmachen;** *the chart conveyed the sales problem graphically*

◊ **conveyor** *noun* method of carrying paper using a moving belt **Förderband**

cooperative processing *noun* system in which two or more computers in a distributed network can each execute a part of a program or work on a particular set of data **kooperative Verarbeitung**

coordinate
1 *noun* **coordinates** = values used to locate a point on a graph *or* map **Koordinaten; coordinate graph** = means of displaying one point on a graph, using two values referring

to axes which are usually at right angles to each other **Koordinatenbild; polar coordinates** = use of a distance and a direction to locate a point **Polarkoordinaten; rectangular coordinates** = two numbers referring to distances along axes at right angles from an origin **rechtwinklige Koordinaten**
2 *verb* to organize complex tasks, so that they fit together efficiently **koordinieren, aufeinander abstimmen;** *she has to coordinate the keyboarding of several parts of a file in six different locations*

◊ **coordination** *noun* organizing complex tasks; synchronizing two *or* more processes **Koordinierung**

copier = COPYING MACHINE, PHOTOCOPIER

copper *noun* red-coloured soft metal, a good conductor of electricity, used in wires and as connecting tracks on PCBs **Kupfer**

◊ **copperplate printing** *noun* printing method that uses a copper plate on which the image is etched **Kupferdruck**

coprocessor *noun* extra, specialized processor, such as an array *or* numerical processor that can work with a main CPU to increase execution speed **Co-, Zusatzprozessor; graphics coprocessor** = high speed display adapter that is dedicated to graphics operations such as line drawing, plotting, etc. **Grafik-Coprozessor; maths coprocessor** = dedicated processor that provides results to mathematical operations much faster than the ALU section of a CPU **Rechen-Coprozessor**

QUOTE Inmos is hiring designers to create highly integrated transputers and co-processors for diverse computer and telecoms systems.

Computing

copy
1 *noun*
(a) document which looks the same as another; duplicate of an original **Kopie; file copy** = copy of a document which is filed in an office for reference **Dateikopie**
(b) document **Exemplar; clean copy** = copy which is ready for keyboarding and does not have many changes to it **Reinkopie; fair copy** *or* **final copy** = document which is written *or* typed with no changes *or* mistakes **Reinschrift; hard copy** = printout of text *or* data which is stored in a computer **(Computer)ausdruck; rough copy** = draft of a

program which, it is expected, will have changes made to it before it is complete **Rohprogramm; top copy** = first *or* top sheet of a document which is typed with carbon copies **Original**
(c) text of material ready to be keyboarded **Text;** *Tuesday is the last date for copy for the advertisement;* **copy reader** = person who checks copy before printing **Korrekturleser**
(d) a book *or* a newspaper **Ausgabe, Exemplar;** *I kept yesterday's copy of "The Times"; I read it in the office copy of "Fortune"; where is my copy of the telephone directory?*
2 *verb* to make a second document which is like the first; to duplicate original data **kopieren;** *he copied all the personnel files at night and took them home; there is a memory resident utility which copies the latest files onto backing store every 40 minutes*

◊ **copier** *or* **copying machine** *noun* machine which makes copies of documents **Kopiergerät**

◊ **copy protect**
1 *noun* switch to prevent copies of a disk being made **Kopierschutz**
2 *verb* to move a switch to prevent copies of a disk being made **Kopierschutz aktivieren;** *the program is not copy protected*

◊ **copy protection** *noun* preventing copies being made **Kopierschutz;** *a hard disk may crash because of copy protection; the new program will come without copy protection*

◊ **COPY** *noun* (operating system command) that copies the contents of one file to another file on a storage device **COPY;** *make a copy of your data using the COPY command before you edit it*

copyright
1 *noun* legal right (lasting for fifty years after the death of an artist whose work has been published) which a writer *or* programmer has in his own work, allowing him not to have it copied without the payment of royalties **Urheberrecht; Copyright Act** = Act of Parliament making copyright legal, and controlling the copying of copyright material **Urheberrechtsgesetz; work which is out of copyright** = work by a writer, etc., who has been dead for fifty years, and which anyone can publish **freigewordenes/nicht mehr urheberrechtlich geschütztes Werk; work still in copyright** = work by a living writer, or by a writer who has not been dead for fifty years **urheberrechtlich geschütztes Werk; infringement of copyright** *or* **copyright**

infringement = act of illegally copying a work which is in copyright **Verletzung des Urheberrechts; copyright notice** = note in a book showing who owns the copyright and the date of ownership **Urheberrechtsvermerk; copyright owner** = person who owns the copyright in a work **Urheber/-in**
2 *verb* to state the copyright of a written work by printing a copyright notice and publishing the work **urheberrechtlich schützen**
3 *adjective* covered by the laws of copyright **urheberrechtlich geschützt;** *it is illegal to take copies of a copyright work*

◊ **copyrighted** *adjective* in copyright **urheberrechtlich geschützt**

CORAL = COMMON REAL-TIME APPLICATIONS LANGUAGE computer programming language used in a real-time system **CORAL (Programmiersprache)**

cord *noun* wire used to connect a device to a socket **Kabel**

◊ **cordless telephone** *noun* telephone which is not connected to a line by a cord, but which uses a radio link **drahtloses Telefon**

core *noun*
(a) central conducting section of a cable **Kern**
(b) core memory *or* **store** = (i) central memory of a computer; (ii) non-volatile magnetic storage method used in old computers **(i) Hauptspeicher; (ii) Magnetkernspeicher; core program** = computer program stored in core memory **Kernprogramm**

coresident *adjective* (two or more programs) stored in main memory at the same time **co-resident**

corona *noun* electric discharge that is used to charge the toner within a laser printer **Korona; corona wire** = thin wire that charges the powdered toner particles in a laser printer as they pass across it **Koronadraht;** *if your printouts are smudged, you may have to clean the corona wire*

coroutine *noun* section of a program *or* procedure that can pass data and control to another coroutine then halt itself **Co-Routine**

correct
1 *adjective* accurate *or* right **richtig**

2 *verb* to remove mistakes from something **korrigieren; error correcting code** = coding system that allows bit errors occurring during transmission to be rapidly corrected by logical deduction methods rather than retransmission **Fehlerkorrekturcode**

◊ **correction** *noun* making something correct; change which makes something correct **Korrektur**

◊ **corrective maintenance** *noun* actions to trace, find and repair a fault after it has occurred **fehlerbedingte Wartung**

correspond *verb*
(a) to correspond with someone = to write letters to someone **mit jdm korrespondieren**
(b) to correspond with something = to fit *or* to match something **einer Sache entsprechen, mit etwas übereinstimmen**

◊ **correspondence** *noun*
(a) letters and messages sent from one person to another **Korrespondenz, Schreibwechsel; business correspondence** = letters concerned with a business **Geschäftskorrespondenz; to be in correspondence with someone** = to write letters to someone and receive letters back **mit jdm in Briefwechsel stehen; correspondence print quality** = quality of print from a computer printer that is acceptable for business letters (that is daisy-wheel rather than dot-matrix printing) **Korrespondenzfähigkeit** NOTE: no plural
(b) way in which something fits in with something **Entsprechung**

◊ **correspondent** *noun*
(a) person who writes letters **Briefschreiber**
(b) journalist who writes articles for a newspaper on specialist subjects **Korrespondent/-in;** *the computer correspondent; the "Times" business correspondent; he is the Paris correspondent of the "Telegraph"*

corrupt
1 *adjective* data *or* program that contains errors **fehlerhaft**
2 *verb* to introduce errors into data *or* a program **verfälschen, verstümmeln;** *power loss during disk access can corrupt the data*

◊ **corruption** *noun* **data corruption** = errors introduced into data, due to noise *or* faulty equipment **Datenverfälschung;** *acoustic couplers suffer from data corruption more than the direct connect form of modem; data corruption on the disk has made one file unreadable*

coulomb *noun* SI unit of electrical charge **Coulomb** ⇨**APPENDIX**

> COMMENT: a coulomb is measured as the amount of charge flowing in a conductor when one amp of current is present for one second

count *verb* to make a total of a number of items **zählen**

◊ **counting perforator** *noun* paper tape punch, used in typesetting, that keeps a record of the characters, their widths, etc., to allow justification operations **Zählperforator**

counter *noun* (i) device which counts; (ii) register *or* variable whose contents are increased *or* decreased by a set amount every time an action occurs **(i) & (ii) Zähler;** *the loop will repeat itself until the counter reaches 100 the number of items changed are recorded with the counter;* **instruction** *or* **program counter** = register in a CPU that contains the location of the next instruction to be processed **Befehlszähler**

◊ **counter-** *prefix* turning the opposite way to normal **Gegen-; counter-rotating ring** = two signal paths transmitted in opposite directions around a ring network **gegenläufiger Ring**

◊ **counterprogramming** *noun* running a popular TV programme at the same time as another station is running a popular series, to try to steal viewers **ein Konkurrenzprogramm senden**

country file *noun* file within an operating system that defines the parameters (such as character set and keyboard layout) for different countries **Länderdatei**

couple *verb* to join together **verbinden, koppeln;** *the two systems are coupled together*

◊ **coupler** *noun* mechanical device used to connect three or more conductors **Koppler; acoustic coupler** = device that connects to a telephone handset, converting binary computer data into sound signals to allow it to be transmitted down a telephone line **Akustikkoppler**

Courier *noun* fixed-space *or* monospace typeface that is similar to the type produced by an office typewriter **Courier**

coverage *noun* size of the potential audience capable of receiving a broadcast **Erfassungsbereich; press coverage** *or* **media coverage** = reports about something in the newspapers *or* on TV, etc. **Berichterstattung;** *the company had good media coverage for the launch of its new model*

CP = CARD PUNCH

◊ **cp** UNIX command to make a copy of a file **cp**

cpi = CHARACTERS PER INCH

CP/M = CONTROL PROGRAM/MONITOR popular operating system for microcomputers **CP/M**

CPM = CRITICAL PATH METHOD

cps = CHARACTERS PER SECOND number of characters printed *or* processed every second **Zeichen pro Sekunde**

CPU = CENTRAL PROCESSING UNIT group of circuits which perform the basic functions of a computer made up of three parts, the control unit, the arithmetic and logic unit and the input/output unit **CPU; CPU bound** = performance of a computer which is limited by the number of instructions the CPU can carry out effectively, the memory and I/O devices can transfer data faster than the CPU can produce it **CPU-abhängig; CPU cycle** = period of time taken to fetch and execute an instruction (usually a simple ADD instruction) used as a measure of computer speed **CPU-Zyklus; CPU elements** = main sections that make up a CPU, including ALU, control unit, I/O bus, memory and various registers **CPU-Teile; CPU handshaking** = interfacing signals between a CPU and a peripheral *or* I/O device **CPU-Quittungsbetrieb; CPU time** = total period of time that a CPU is used to actually process instructions **CPU-Zeit**

> COMMENT: in a file handling program CPU time might be minimal, since data retrieval (from disk) would account for a large part of the program run; in a mathematical program, the CPU time could be much higher in proportion to the total run time

CR = CARRIAGE RETURN, CARD READER

crash
1 *noun* failure of a component *or* a bug in a program during a run, which halts and prevents further use of the system **Absturz, Programmabbruch; disk crash** = fault caused by the read/write head touching the surface of the disk **Plattenabsturz**

2 *verb (of a computer or program)* to come to an sudden stop **abstürzen;** *the disk head has crashed and the data may have been lost*

◊ **crash-protected** *adjective* (disk) which uses a head protection *or* data corruption protection system **absturzgesichert;** *if the disk is crash-protected, you will never lose your data*

COMMENT: it is sometimes possible to recover data from a crashed hard disk before reformatting, if the crash was caused by a bad sector on the disk rather than contact between the r/w head and disk surface

crawl *noun* mechanical device that moves television *or* film titles down in front of a camera, to give the impression that they are moving up the screen **Crawleffekt**

CRC = CAMERA-READY COPY, CYCLIC REDUNDANCY CHECK

create *verb* to make **erstellen;** *a new file was created on disk to store the document; move to the CREATE NEW FILE instruction on the menu*

credit *noun*
(a) time given to a customer before he has to pay **(Kunden)kredit;** *they have asked for six months' credit;* **credit card** = plastic card which allows the owner to borrow money and buy goods without paying for them immediately **Kreditkarte**
(b) money received and placed in an account *or* in the balance sheet **Kredit**
(c) credits = text at the end of a film, giving the names of the actors *or* technical staff **Nachspann**

crew *noun* group of technical staff who work together (as on filming a TV programme, recording an outside broadcast, etc.) **Team; camera crew** = group of people who man a TV camera **Kamerateam;** *the camera crew had to film all day in the snow*

crippled leapfrog test *noun* standard leapfrog test that uses a single memory location rather than a changing location **Teilprüfung im Bocksprungprogramm**

criterion *noun* specification that has to be met **Kriterium**
NOTE: plural is **criteria**

critical error *noun* error that stops processing or crashes the computer **kritischer Fehler**

◊ **critical fusion frequency** *noun* the rate of display of frames of graphics *or* text that makes them appear continuous **kritische Fusionsfrequenz**

◊ **critical path analysis** *noun* the definition of tasks *or* jobs and the time each requires arranged in order to achieve certain goals **Analyse des kritischen Weges** NOTE: also called PERT (Program Evaluation and Review Techniques) **critical path method (CPM)** = use of analysis and projection of each critical step in a large project to help a management team **CPM (Methode der Netzplantechnik);** **critical resource** = resource that can only be used by one process at a time **kritische Betriebsmittel**

QUOTE Surprisingly, critical path analysis and project management, frequently the next career step for engineers, did not seem to warrant a mention.
Computing

CR/LF = CARRIAGE RETURN/LINE FEED

crop *verb* to reduce the size or margins of an image *or* to cut out a rectangular section of an image **beschneiden**

◊ **crop mark** *noun* (in DTP software) printed marks that show the edge of a page or image and allow it to be cut accurately **Beschnittzeichen**

◊ **cropping** *noun* removal of areas of artwork *or* of a photograph which are not needed **Beschneiden;** *the photographs can be edited by cropping, sizing, touching up, etc.*

cross- *prefix* running from one side to another **Quer-; cross fade** = to fade out one signal while bringing in another **ausblenden; cross modulation** = two *or* more modulated signals on one channel interfering with each other **Quermodulation**

◊ **cross-assembler** *noun* assembler that produces machine-code code for one computer whilst running on another **Kreuzassemblierer**

◊ **cross-check** *noun* validation of an answer by using a different method of calculation **Gegenprobe**

◊ **cross-compiler** assembler *or* compiler that compiles programs for one computer whilst running on another **Kreuzkompilierer**

COMMENT: cross-compilers and assemblersare used to compile programs for micros, but are run on larger computers to make the operation faster

◊ **cross-linked files** *plural noun* (in MS-DOS) error in which two files claim to be using the same cluster on disk **Crosslinks, Crosslinkdateien**

◊ **cross-reference generator** *noun* section of an assembler *or* compiler *or* interpreter that provides a list of program labels, variables *or* constants with their location within the program **Verweisgenerator**

crossfire *noun see* CROSSTALK

◊ **crossover** *noun* change from one system to another **Umstellung;** *the crossover to computerized file indexing was difficult*

◊ **cross-reference**
1 *noun* reference in a document to another part of the document **Querverweis**
2 *verb* to make a reference to another part of the document **einen Querverweis machen;** *the SI units are cross-referenced to the appendix*

◊ **cross-section** *noun* view of a material *or* object cut across its centre **Querschnitt;** *the cross-section of the optical fibre showed the problem*

crosstalk *noun* interference between two communication cables or channels **Nebensprechen;** *the crosstalk was so bad, the signal was unreadable* .

CRT = CATHODE RAY TUBE device used for displaying characters *or* figures *or* graphical information, similar to a TV set **Kathodenstrahlröhre, Bildröhre**

COMMENT: cathode ray tubes are used in television sets, computer monitors and VDUs; a CRT consists of a vacuum tube, one end of which is flat and coated with phosphor, the other end containing an electron beam source. Characters *or* graphics are visible when the controllable electron beam strikes the phosphor causing it to glow

cruncher, crunching *see* NUMBER

crushing *noun* reduced contrast range on a TV image due to a fault **Kompression**

cryogenic memory *noun* storage medium operating at very low temperatures (4°K) to use the superconductive properties of a material **supraleitender Speicher** .

cryptanalysis *noun* study and methods of breaking ciphers **Kryptoanalyse**

cryptography *noun* study of encryption and decryption methods and techniques **Kryptographie**

◊ **cryptographic** *adjective* referring to cryptography **kryptographisch; cryptographic algorithm** = rules used to encipher ׀ and decipher data **Chiffrieralgorithmus; cryptographic key** = number *or* code that is used with a cipher algorithm to personalize the encryption and decryption of data **Chiffrierschlüssel**

crystal *noun* small slice of quartz crystal which vibrates at a certain frequency, used as a very accurate clock signal for computer *or* other high precision timing applications **Kristall; liquid crystal display (LCD)** = liquid crystals, that turn black when a voltage is applied, used in many watch, calculator and digital displays **Flüssigkristallanzeige (LCD); crystal microphone** = microphone that uses a piece of piezoelectric crystal which produces a signal when sound waves distort it **piezoelektrisches Mikrofon; crystal oscillator** = small piece of crystal that resonates at a certain frequency when a voltage is applied across it; this can be used as a high precision clock **Quarzoszillator; crystal shutter printer** = page printer that uses a powerful light controlled by a liquid crystal display to produce an image on a photo-sensitive drum **LCD-Drucker;** *see also* LASER PRINTER

CSDC = CIRCUIT SWITCHED DIGITAL CIRCUITRY

CSM = COMBINED SYMBOL MATCHING effecient optical character recognition system **CSM (wirkungsvolles optisches Zeichenerkennungssystem)**

CSMA-CD = CARRIER SENSE MULTIPLE ACCESS-COLLISION DETECTION method of controlling access to a network used in Ethernet networks **CSMA-CD**

CTR *or* **CTRL** = CONTROL control key *or* key on a computer terminal that sends a control character to the computer when pressed **CTRL-Taste**

CTS = CLEAR TO SEND RS232C signal that a line *or* device is ready for data transmission **sendebereit**

CU = CONTROL UNIT

cue *noun* prompt *or* message displayed on a screen to remind the user that an input is expected **Aufruf**

CUG = CLOSED USER GROUP to restrict the entry to a database *or* bulletin board system (on a certain topic *or* subject) to certain known and registered users usually by means of a password **geschlossener Benutzerkreis**

cumulative index *noun* index made up from several different indexes **Kumulativindex**

◊ **cumulative trauma disorder** *see* RSI

current
1 *adjective* referring to the present time **aktuell; current address** = address being used (accessed) at this time **aktuelle Adresse; current address register (CAR)** = CPU register that stores the address that is currently being accessed **aktuelles Adressregister; current directory** = directory within the directory tree which is currently being used **aktuelles Verzeichnis; current drive** = disk drive that is currently being used or has been selected **aktuelles Laufwerk; current instruction register (CIR)** = CPU register that stores the instruction that is currently being executed **aktuelles Befehlsregister**
2 *noun* movement of charge-carrying particles in a conductor **(elektrischer) Strom; direct current (DC)** = constant value electrical current supply that flows in one direction **Gleichstrom; alternating current (AC)** = electrical current whose value varies with time in a regular sinusoidal way (changing direction of flow each half cycle) **Wechselstrom**

COMMENT: mains electricity provides a 240v AC supply at 50Hz in the U.K. and 110v at 60Hz in the USA

cursor *noun* marker on a display device which shows where the next character will appear **Cursor, Positionsanzeiger; cursor control keys** = keys on a keyboard that allow the cursor to be moved in different directions **Cursortasten; cursor home** = movement of the cursor to the top left hand corner of the screen **Cursorausgangsstellung; cursor pad** = group of cursor control keys **Cursortasten; addressable cursor** = cursor whose position on the screen can be defined by a program **adressierbarer Cursor**

COMMENT: cursors can take several forms, such as a square of bright light, a bright underline or a flashing light

QUOTE above the cursor pad are the insert and delete keys, which when shifted produce clear and home respectively
Computing Today

QUOTE further quick cursor movements are available for editing by combining one of the arrow keys with the control function
Personal Computer World

QUOTE Probably the most exciting technology demonstrated was ScreenCam, which allows users to combine voice, cursor movement and on-screen activities into a movie which can be replayed.
Computing

customer *noun* person who buys *or* uses a computer system *or* any peripherals **Kunde/Kundin; customer engineering** = maintenance and repair of a customer's equipment **technischer Außendienst; customer service department** = department which deals with customers and their complaints and orders **Kundendienst(abteilung)**

◊ **custom-built** *adjective* made specially for one customer **kundenspezifisch, auf Bestellung angefertigt**

◊ **custom ROM (PROM)** *noun* ROM produced (usually in small numbers) by a manufacturer to suit a customer's requirements **kundenspezifischer ROM (PROM)**

◊ **customize** *verb* to modify a system to the customer's requirements **individuell anpassen;** *we used customized computer terminals*

cut
1 *noun* removing a piece from a file *or* text; piece removed from a file *or* text **Kürzen; Kürzung;** *the editors have asked for cuts in the first chapter*
2 *verb*
(a) to divide something into parts, using scissors *or* knife *or* guillotine **schneiden; cut in notes** = printed notes in the outer edge of a paragraph of a page **eingezogene Marginalien; cut sheet feeder** mechanism that automatically feeds single sheets of paper into a printer **automatischer Einzelblatteinzug**
(b) to remove pieces of text *or* file to make it

shorter **kürzen**; *the author was asked to cut his manuscript to 250 pages* NOTE: **cuts - cutting - has cut**

◊ **cut and paste** *noun* action of taking pieces of text from one point and inserting them at another (often used in dtp packages for easy page editing) **Textumstellung**

◊ **cut off** *verb*
(a) to remove part of something **abschneiden;** *six metres of paper were cut off the reel*
(b) to stop something flowing **unterbrechen;** *the electricity supply was cut off*

◊ **cutoff frequency** *noun* frequency at which the response of a device drops off **Grenzfrequenz; cutoff point** = point at which (something) stops **Unterbrechungspunkt**

◊ **cutting** *noun* action of cutting **Schneiden; cutting room** = room in a film studio where the unedited film is cut and joined together **Schneideraum; press cuttings** = pieces cut from newspapers *or* magazines which refer to someone *or* to a company **Zeitungsausschnitte**

CWP = COMMUNICATING WORD PROCESSOR

cybernetics *noun* study of the mechanics of human *or* electronic machine movements, and the way in which electronic devices can be made to work and imitate human actions **Kybernetik**

cycle
1 *noun* (i) period of time when something leaves its original position and then returns to it; (ii) one completed operation in a repeated process **(i) & (ii) Zyklus; action cycle** = all the steps required to carry out a process *or* operation on data, (such as reading, processing, output and storage) **Aktionszyklus; clock cycle** = period of time between two consecutive clock pulses **Taktzyklus; cycle availability** = period of time in a cycle, during which data can be accessed *or* transmitted **Zyklusverfügbarkeit; cycle count** = number of times a cycle has been repeated **Gangzahl; cycle index** = number of times a series of instructions have been *or* have to be repeated **Schleifenindex; cycle shift** = to shift a pattern of bits within a word, with the bit(s) that are shifted off the end being inserted at the beginning of the word **zyklische Stellenverschiebung; cycle stealing** = memory access operation by a peripheral that halts a CPU for one *or* more clock

cycles whilst data is being transferred from memory to the device **direkter Speicherzugriff; cycle time** = time between start and stop of an operation, especially between addressing a memory location and receiving the data, and then ending the operation **Zykluszeit;** *compare* ADDRESS TIME
2 *verb* to repeat an operation *or* series of instructions until instructed to stop **immer wieder ausführen**

◊ **cyclic** *adjective* (operation) that is repeated regularly **zyklisch; cyclic access** = access to stored information that can only occur at a certain point in a cycle **zyklischer Zugriff; cyclic check** = error detection method that uses *or* examines a bit of data every n bits (one bit examined then n bits transmitted, then another bit examined, etc.) **zyklische Fehlerprüfung; cyclic code** *see* GRAY CODE; **cyclic decimal code** = cyclic code that refers to decimal digits **zyklischer Dezimalcode; cyclic redundancy check (CRC)** = error detection code for transmitted data **zyklische Blockprüfung, CRC-Prüfung; cyclic shift** = rotation of bits in a word with the previous last bit inserted in the first bit position **zyklische Bitverschiebung**

cylinder *noun* (i) group of tracks on a disk; (ii) the tracks in a multi-disk device that can be accessed without moving the read/write head **(i) & (ii) Zylinder**

cypher = CIPHER

Dd

D hexadecimal figure equivalent to decimal number 13 **D**

3D = THREE-DIMENSIONAL

QUOTE the software can create 3D images using data from a scanner or photographs from an electronic microscope
PC Business World

DA = DESK ACCESSORY

DAC *or* **D/A converter** = DIGITAL TO ANALOG CONVERTER circuit that outputs an analog number that is proportional to the input digital signal, and so converts a digital input to an analog form **Digital-Analog-Umsetzer**; *speech is output from the computer via a D/A converter; the D/A converter on the output port controls the analog machine*

| COMMENT: a D/A converter allows the computer to work outside the computer environment, by driving a machine, imitating speech, etc.

DAD = DIGITAL AUDIO DISK method of recording sound by converting and storing signals in a digital form on magnetic disk **digitale Tonplatte**

daemon *noun* (in a UNIX system) utility program that performs its job automatically without the knowledge of the user **Dämon-Prozess**

dagger *noun* printing sign (†) used to mark a special word **Kreuz**; **double dagger** = printing sign (‡) used to give a second reference level **Doppelkreuz**

daisy chain *noun* method of connecting equipment with a single cable passing from one machine *or* device to the next (rather than separate cables to each device) **Verkettung**; **daisy chain bus** = communications bus that joins one device to the next, each device being able to receive *or* transmit *or* modify data as it passes through to the next device in line **verkettete Busstruktur**; **daisy chain interrupt** = line joining all the interrupt outputs of a number of devices to a CPU **verkettete Unterbrechungsleitung**; **daisy chain recursion** = subroutines in a program that call another in the series, (the first routine calls the second routine which calls the third routine, etc.) **verkettete Rekursion**

◊ **daisy-chain** *verb* to connect equipment using the daisy chain method **verketten**

| QUOTE you can often daisy-chain cards or plug them into expansion boxes
| *Byte*

daisy-wheel *noun* wheel-shaped printing head, with characters on the end of spokes, used in a serial printer **Typenrad**; **daisy-wheel printer** *or* **daisy-wheel typewriter** = serial character printer *or* typewriter with characters arranged on interchangeable wheels **Typenraddrucker**; **Typenradschreibmaschine**; *a daisy-wheel*

printer produces much better quality text than a dot-matrix, but is slower

DAMA = DEMAND ASSIGNED MULTIPLE ACCESS

damage
1 *noun* harm done to things **Schaden**; **to suffer damage** = to be harmed **Schaden erleiden**; **to cause damage** = to harm something **Schaden zufügen**; *the breakdown of the electricity supply caused damage estimated at £100,000* NOTE: no plural
2 *verb* to harm **beschädigen**; *the faulty read/write head appears to have damaged the disks the hard disk was damaged when it was dropped*

◊ **damaged** *adjective* which has suffered damage *or* which has been harmed **beschädigt**; *is it possible to repair the damaged files?*

D to A converter = DIGITAL TO ANALOG CONVERTER circuit that outputs an analog signal that is proportional to an input digital number **Digital-Analog-Umsetzer**

dark current *noun* amount of electrical current that flows in an optoelectrical device when there is no light falling on it **Dunkelstrom**

◊ **dark trace tube** *noun* CRT with a dark image on a bright background **Dunkelschriftröhre**

darkroom *noun* special room with no light, where photographic film can be developed **Dunkelkammer**

DAS = DUAL ATTACHMENT STATION

DASD = DIRECT ACCESS STORAGE DEVICE storage medium whose memory locations can be directly read *or* written to **Direktzugriffsspeicher**

dash *noun* short line in printing **Gedankenstrich**; **em dash** *or* **em rule** = line as long as an em, used to separate one section of text from another **Gedankenstrich von zwei Gevierten, Trennstrich**; **en dash** *or* **en rule** = line as long as an en, used to link two words *or* parts of words **Gedankenstrich von einem Geviert, Bindestrich**

DAT = DIGITAL AUDIO TAPE system of recording sound as digital information onto magnetic tape that provides very high-quality reproduction; also used as a high-capacity tape backup system **DAT**; **DAT drive** = mechanical drive that records data onto a DAT tape and retrieves data from a tape **DAT-Laufwerk**; *we use a DAT drive as the backup device for our network*

data *noun* collection of facts made up of numbers, characters and symbols, stored on a computer in such a way that it can be processed by the computer **Daten**; *programs act upon data files; data is input at one of several workstations; the company stores data on customers in its main computer file; a user needs a password to access data;* **raw data** = (i) pieces of information which have not been input into a computer system; (ii) data (in a databank) which has to be processed to provide information to the user; (iii) unprocessed data **(i)-(iii) Ursprungsdaten; data above voice (DAV)** = data transmission in a frequency range above that of the human voice **Datenübertragung über Sprachfrequenz; data access management** = regulating the users who can access stored data **Datenzugriffsverwaltung; data acquisition** = gathering data about a subject **Datenerfassung; data adapter unit** = device that interfaces a CPU to one or more communications channels **Datenanschlusseinheit; data administrator** = control section of a database management system **Datenverwalter; data aggregate** = collection of items of data that are related **Datengruppierung; data analysis** = extracting information and results from data **Datenanalyse; data area** = amount of storage space that contains data (rather than instructions) **Datenbereich; databank** = collection of data (usually on one theme) **Datenbank; data block** = all the data required for *or* from a process **Datenblock; data break** = memory access operation by a peripheral that halts a CPU for one or more cycles whilst data is being transferred from memory to the device **Datenunterbrechung; data buffer** = temporary storage location for data received by a device that is not yet ready to accept it **Datenpuffer; data bus** = bus carrying the data between a CPU and memory and peripheral devices **Datenübertragungsweg; data capture** = act of obtaining data (either by keyboarding or by scanning, or often automatically from a recording device *or* peripheral) **Datenerfassung; data carrier** = (i) any device *or* medium capable of storing data; (ii) a waveform used as a carrier for data signals **(i) & (ii) Datenträger; data carrier detect (DCD)** = RS232C signal from a modem to a computer indicating a carrier wave is

being received **Datenempfangssignal;** *the call is stopped if the software does not receive a DCD signal from the modem;* **data cartridge** = cartridge that contains stored data **Datenregister; data chaining** = one stored record that holds the address of the next in the list **Datenadresskettung; data channel** = communication link able to carry data signals **Datenkanal; data check** = error in reading data due to a fault with the magnetic medium **Datenprüfung; data circuit** = circuit which allows bi-directional data communications **Datenverbindung; data cleaning** = removing errors from data **Datenkorrektur; data collection** = act of receiving data from various sources (either directly from a data capture device *or* from a cartridge) and inserting correctly in order into a database **Datenerfassung; data collection platform** = station that transmits collected data to a central point (usually via satellite) **Datenerfassungsstation; data communications** = transmission and reception of data rather than speech *or* images **Datenaustausch; data communications buffer** = buffer on a receiver that allows a slow peripheral to accept data from a fast computer, without slowing either down **Datenaustauschpuffer; data communications equipment (DCE)** = equipment (such as a modem) which receives *or* transmits data **Datenaustauschgerät; data communications network** = number of computers, terminals, operators and storage units connected together to allow data transmission between devices *or* files *or* users **Datenkommunikationsnetzwerk; data compacting** = reducing the space taken by data by coding it in a more efficient way **Datenverdichtung;** *all the files were stored on one disk with this new data compacting routine;* **data compression** = means of reducing size of data by removing spaces, empty sections and unused material from the blocks of data **Datenverdichtung;** *scanners use a technique called data compression which manages to reduce, even by a third, the storage required;* **data concentrator** = data which combines intermittent data from various lines and sends it along a single line in one go **Datenkonzentrator; data connection** = link which joins two devices and allows data transmission **Datenverbindung; data control** = data management to and from a database *or* processing system **Datenverwaltung; data corruption** = errors introduced into data due to noise *or* faulty equipment **Datenkorruption;** *data corruption occurs each time the motor is switched on;* **data delimiter**

= special symbol *or* character that marks the end of a file *or* data item **Datenbegrenzungszeichen; data description language (DDL)** = part of database system software which describes the structure of the system and data **Datenbeschreibungssprache; data dictionary/directory (DD/D)** = software which gives a list of types and forms of data contained in a database **Datenwörterbuch, Feldnamenerklärung; data division** = part of a (COBOL) program giving full definitions of the data types and structures **Datenteil; data-driven** = (computer architecture) in which instructions are executed, once the relevant data has been received **datengesteuert; data element** *see* DATA ITEM; **data element chain** = more than one data element treated as a single element **Datenelementkette; data encryption** = encrypting data using a cipher system **Datenverschlüsselung; data encryption standard (DES)** = standard for a block data cipher system **Datenverschlüsselungsnorm; data entry** = method of entering data into a system (usually using a keyboard but also direct from disks after data preparation) **Datenerfassung, Dateneingabe; data error** = error due to incorrect *or* illegal data **Datenfehler; data field** = part of a computer instruction that contains the location of the data **Datenfeld; data file** = file with data in it (as opposed to a program file) **Datei;** *the data file has to be analysed;* **data flow** = movement of data through a system **Datenfluss; data flowchart** = diagram used to describe a computer *or* data processing system **Datenflussplan;** *the data flowchart allowed us to improve throughput, by using a better structure;* **data flow diagram (DFD)** = diagram used to describe the movement of data through a system **Datenflussdiagramm; data format** = rules defining the way in which data is stored *or* transmitted **Datenformat; data hierarchy** = data structure organized hierarchically **Datenhierarchie; data highway** = bus carrying data signals between a CPU and peripherals **Datenübertragungsweg;** *see also* BUS; **data independence** = structure of a database which can be changed without affecting what the user sees **Datenunabhängigkeit; data input** = data transferred into a computer (from an I/O port or peripheral) **Dateneingabe; data input bus (DIB)** = bus used when transferring data from one section of a computer to another, such as between memory and CPU **Dateneingabebus; data integrity** = protection of data against damage *or* errors **Datensicherheit; data interchange format**

(DIF) = de facto standard method of storing spreadsheet formula and data in a file **Data Interchange Format (DIF); data in voice (DIV)** = digital data transmission in place of a voice channel **Datenübertragung auf Sprachfrequenz; data item** = one unit of data such as the quantity of items in stock, a person's name, age or occupation **Datenfeld; data level** = position of a data item within a database structure **Datenebene; data link** = connection between two devices to allow the transmission of data **Datenübertragungsabschnitt; data link control** = protocol and rules used to define the way in which data is transmitted *or* received **Datenleitungssteuerung; data link layer** = one layer in the ISO/OSI defined network that sends packets of data to the next link and deals with error correction **Sicherungsschicht; data logging** = automatic data collection **Datenerfassung; data management** = maintenance and upkeep of a database **Datenpflege; data manipulation language (DML)** = database software that allows the user to access, store and change data **Datenbehandlungssprache; data medium** = medium which allows data to be stored *or* displayed (such as a VDU *or* magnetic disk *or* screen) **Datenträger; data migration** = data transfer (by a user's instruction) from an on-line device to an off-line device **Datenumlagerung; data name** = group of characters used to identify one item of data **Datenname;** *problems occur if an ambiguous data name is chosen;* **data network** = networking system which transmits data **Datennetz; data origination** = conversion of data from its original form to one which can be read by a computer **Datenerstellung; data path** = bus *or* connections over which data is transmitted **Datenweg; data pointer** = register containing the location of the next item of data **Datenzeiger; data preparation** = conversion of data into a machine-readable form (usually by keyboarding) before data entry **Datenvorbereitung; data processing (DP *or* dp)** = selecting and operating on data to produce useful information; sorting *or* organizing data files **Datenverarbeitung; data processing manager** = person who runs a computer department **Datenverarbeitungsmanager; data protection** = means of making sure that data is private and secure **Datensicherung; Data Protection Act** = legislation passed in 1984 in the UK that means any owner of a database that contains personal details must register **Data Protection Act (britisches Datenschutzgesetz); data rate** = maximum rate at which data is processed *or* transmitted in a synchronous system, usually equal to the system clock rate **Datenübertragungsgeschwindigkeit; data record** = one record containing data for use with a program **Datensatz; data reduction** = production of compact, useful data from raw data **Datenverdichtung; data register** = area within a CPU used to store data temporarily before it is processed **Datenregister; data reliability** = measure of the number of data words with errors compared to the total number of words **Datenzuverlässigkeit; data retrieval** = process of searching, selecting and reading data from a stored file **Datenwiedergewinnung; data routing** = defining the path to be taken by a message in a network **Datenleitweg; data security** = protection of data against corruption *or* unauthorized users **Datensicherung; data services** = public services (such as the telephone system) which allow data to be transmitted **Datenservice; data set ready (DSR)** = signal from a device that is ready to accept data, this signal occurs after a DTR signal is received **Betriebsbereitschaft; data sharing** = one file *or* set of data that can be accessed by several users **gemeinsame Datenbenutzung; data signals** = electrical *or* optical pulses *or* waveforms that represent binary data **Datensignale; data signalling rate** = total amount of data that is transmitted through a system per second **Datenübertragungsgeschwindigkeit; data sink** = device in a data terminal which receives data **Datensenke; data source** = device in a data terminal which sends data **Datenquelle; data station** = point that contains a data terminal and a data circuit **Datenstation; data storage** = medium able to store large quantities of data **Datenspeicher;** *see also* BACKING STORE; **data stream** = data transmitted serially one bit *or* character at a time **Datenstrom; data strobe** = signal (in the control bus) that indicates that valid data is on the data bus **Datenimpulseingang, Datenstrobe; data structure** = number of related items that are treated as one by the computer (in an address book record, the name, address and telephone number form separate entries which would be processed as one by the computer) **Datenstruktur; data switching exchange** = device used to direct and switch data between lines **Datenaustauschvermittlung; data tablet** *see* GRAPHICS TABLET; **data terminal** = device that is able to display and transmit *or* receive data **Datenstation;** *a printer is a data terminal for computer output;* **data terminal equipment (DTE)** = device at which a communications path starts *or* finishes

Datenendeinrichtung; data terminal ready (DTR) = signal from a device that indicates that it is ready to send data **Betriebsbereitsignal; data transaction** = one complete operation on data **Datenbewegung; data transfer rate** = rate at which data is moved from one point to another **Datenübertragungsgeschwindigkeit, Transfergeschwindigkeit; data translation** = conversion of data from one system format to another **Datenumsetzung; data transmission** = process of sending data from one location to another over a data link **Datenübertragung; data type** = sort of data which can be stored in a register (such as string, number, etc.) **Datentyp; data under voice (DUV)** = data transmission in a frequency range lower than that of a human voice **Datenübertragung unter Sprachfrequenz; data validation** = process of checking data for errors and relevance in a situation **Datenprüfung; data vetting** = process of checking data as it is input for errors and validity **Datenprüfung; data word** = piece of data stored as a single word **Datenwort; data word length** = number of bits that make up a word in a computer **Datenwortlänge; master data** = reference data which is stored in a master file **Hauptdaten; optical data link** = connection between two devices to allow the transmission of data using light (either line-of-sight or using fibre optics) **optische Datenverbindung; variable data** = data which can be modified, and is not write protected **variable Daten**

COMMENT: Data is different from information in that it is facts stored in machine-readable form. When the facts are processed by the computer into a form which can be understood by people, the data becomes information

◊ **databank** *noun* (i) large amount of data stored in a structured form; (ii) personal records stored in a computer **(i) & (ii) Datenbank**

◊ **database** *noun* integrated collection of files of data stored in a structured form in a large memory, which can be accessed by one or more users at different terminals **Datenbank; database administrator (DBA)** = person in charge of running and maintaining a database system **Datenbankverwalter; database engine** = program that provides an interface between a program written to access the functions of a DBMS and the DBMS **Datenbanksteuerprogramm; database language** = series of languages, such as data description language, that make up a database management system **Datenbanksprache; database machine =** hardware and software combination designed for the rapid processing of database information **Datenbankmaschine; database management system (DBMS)** or **database manager =** series of programs that allow the user to create and modify databases easily **Datenbankverwaltungssystem; database mapping =** description of the way in which the records and fields in a database are related **Datenbankaufgliederung; database schema =** way in which a database is organized and structured **Datenbankschema; database system =** series of programs that allows the user to create, modify, manage and use a database (often includes features such as a report writer or graphical output of data) **Datenbanksystem; on-line database =** interactive search, retrieve and update of database records using an on-line terminal **Datenbank mit Direktanschluss**

◊ **datagram** *noun* packet of information in a packet switching system that contains its destination address and route **Datagramm**

◊ **dataline** *noun* one line of broadcast TV signal that contains the teletext signals and data (usually transmitted at the start of the image and identified with a special code) **Datenleitung**

◊ **dataplex** *noun* multiplexing of data signals **Datenmultiplexmethode**

◊ **dataset** *noun (US)* modem **Modem; dataset ready (DSR) =** RS232C signal from a modem to a computer indicating it is ready for use **Betriebsbereitschaftssignal**

QUOTE Zenith's new notebook models use the power-saving Intel 486 SL microprocessor which offers 32-bit internal and data bus operation.
Computing

QUOTE data compression is the art of squeezing more and more information into fewer and fewer bytes
Practical Computing

QUOTE a database is a file of individual records of information which are stored in some kind of sequential order
Which PC?

QUOTE This information could include hypertext references to information held within a computer database, or spreadsheet formulae.
Computing

date
1 *noun* number of day, month and year **Datum;** *I have received your message of yesterday's date; the date of creation for the file was the 10th of June*
2 *verb* to put a date on a document **datieren**

◊ **out of date** *adjective & adverb* old-fashioned **veraltet;** *their computer system is years out of date; they are still using out-of-date equipment*

◊ **up to date** *adjective & adverb* current or recent or modern **auf dem neuesten Stand;** *an up-to-date computer system;* **to bring** or **keep something up to date =** to add the latest information to something **etwas auf den neuesten Stand bringen/halten;** *we spend a lot of time keeping our files up to date* NOTE: when used as adjectives before a noun, out-of-date and up-to-date are hyphenated

daughter board *noun* add-on board that connects to a system mother board **Tochterplatine**

DAV = DATA ABOVE VOICE

db *see* DECIBEL

DBA = DATABASE ADMINISTRATOR person in charge of running and maintaining a database system **Datenbankverwalter**

dBASE ™ popular database software that includes a built-in programming language **dBASE ™**

COMMENT: dBASE has several versions, II, III and IV; the software development is currently carried out by Borland International. There have been several versions of dBASE, and files created in dBASE can normally be imported into other database programs

DB connector = DATA BUS CONNECTOR D-shape connector normally with two rows of pins used to connect devices that transfer data **DB-Stecker;** *the most common DB connectors are DB-9, DB-25 and DB-50 with 9, 25 and 50 connections respectively*

DBMS = DATABASE MANAGEMENT SYSTEM series of programs that allow the user to create and modify databases **Datenbankverwaltungssystem**

DC = DIRECT CURRENT; **DC signalling =** method of communications using pulses of current over a wire circuit, like a telegraph system **Gleichstromsignal**

DCA = DOCUMENT CONTENT ARCHITECTURE document format defined by IBM that allows documents to be exchanged between computer systems **DCA**

DCD = DATA CARRIER DETECT RS232C signal from a modem to a computer indicating a carrier is being received **Datenempfangssignal**

DCE = DATA COMMUNICATIONS EQUIPMENT

DD = DOUBLE DENSITY

DDC = DIRECT DIGITAL CONTROL machine operated automatically by machine **direkte Digitalsteuerung**

DD/D = DATA DICTIONARY/DIRECTORY software which gives a list of types and forms of data contained in a database **Datenwörterbuch, Feldnamenerklärung**

DDE = DIRECT DATA ENTRY keying in data directly onto magnetic tape *or* disk **direkte Dateneingabe**

DDL = DATA DESCRIPTION LANGUAGE; *many of DDL's advantages come from the fact that it is a second generation language*

DDP = DISTRIBUTED DATA PROCESSING operations to derive information from data which is kept in different places **verteilte Datenverarbeitung**

dead *adjective*
(a) not working; (computer *or* piece of equipment) that does not function **tot; dead halt** *or* **drop dead halt** = program instruction from the user *or* an error, that causes the program to stop without allowing recovery **Unterbrechungshalt;** *the manual does not say what to do if a dead halt occurs;* **dead keys =** keys on a keyboard that cause a function rather than a character to occur, such as the shift key **Tot-, Funktionstasten; dead matter** = type that has been used for printing and is no longer required **Ablegesatz; dead time** = period of time between two events, in which nothing happens, to ensure that they do not interfere with each other **Totzeit, Verlustzeit;** *efficient job management minimises dead time*
(b) (room *or* space) that has no acoustical reverberation **schalldicht**

◊ **deaden** *verb* to make a sound *or* colour

less sharp **dämpfen;** *acoustic hoods are used to deaden the noise of printers*

◊ **deadline** *noun* date by which something has to be done **Termin, Stichtag; to meet a deadline** = to finish something in time **den Termin einhalten;** *we've missed our October 1st deadline*

◊ **deadlock** *noun* situation when two users want to access two resources at the same time, one resource is assigned to each user but neither can use the other **gegenseitiges Sperren**

◊ **deadly embrace** *noun* = DEADLOCK

deal
1 *noun* business agreement *or* contract **Geschäft, Abmachung; package deal** = agreement where several different items are agreed at the same time **Pauschalangebot;** *they agreed a package deal, which involves the development of software, customizing hardware and training of staff*
2 *verb* **to deal with** = to organize **sich befassen mit, erledigen;** *leave it to the DP manager - he'll deal with it*

◊ **dealer** *noun* person who buys and sells **Händler;** *always buy hardware from a recognized dealer*

deallocate *verb* to free resources previously allocated to a job *or* process *or* peripheral **freigeben;** *when a reset button is pressed all resources are deallocated*

debit *noun* bit transmission rate that is twice the baud rate **Bitübertragungsgeschwindigkeit**

deblock *verb* to return a stored block of data to its original form (of individual records) **entblocken**

de-bounce *noun* preventing a single touch on a key giving multiple key contact **Entprellen; de-bounce circuit** = electronic circuit that prevents a key contact producing more than one signal when pressed **Entprellungsstromkreis**

debug *verb* to test a program and locate and correct any faults *or* errors **korrigieren, bereinigen (Programmfehler);** *they spent weeks debugging the system; debugging takes up more time than construction;* **debugged program** = software that works correctly and in which all the mistakes have been removed *or* corrected **korrigiertes Programm**

◊ **DEBUG** *noun* (in MS-DOS) software

utility that allows a user to view the contents of binary files and assemble small assembly-language programs **DEBUG**

◊ **debugger** *noun* software that helps a programmer find faults *or* errors in a program **Debugger, Fehlersuchprogramm**

> QUOTE the debug monitor makes development and testing very easy
> *Electronics & Wireless World*

> QUOTE Further questions, such as how you debug an application built from multisourced software to be run on multisourced hardware, must be resolved at this stage.
> *Computing*

decade *noun* ten items *or* events **Dekade; decade counter** = electronic device able to count actions *or* events from 0-9 before resetting to zero and starting again **Dekadenzähler**

decay
1 *noun* rate at which the electronic impulse *or* the amplitude of a signal fades away **Signalabfall; decay time** = time taken for an impulse to fade **Signalabfallzeit**
2 *verb* to decrease gradually in amplitude *or* size **abfallen, abnehmen;** *the signal decayed rapidly*

deceleration time *noun* time taken for an access arm to come to a stop after it has moved to the correct location over the surface of a hard disk **Verzögerungsdauer**

decentralized computer network *noun* network where the control is shared between several computers **dezentralisiertes Computernetz**

◊ **decentralized data processing** *noun* data processing and storage carried out at each location rather than in one central location **dezentralisierte Datenverarbeitung**

deci- *prefix* meaning one tenth of a number **dezi-, Dezi-**

◊ **decibel** *noun* unit of measurement of noise **Dezibel (dB); decibel meter** = signal power measuring device **Dezibelmeter**

decile *noun* one of a series of nine figures below which one tenth *or* several tenths of the total fall **Dezile, Zehntelwert**

decimal (notation) *noun* arithmetic and number representation using the

decimal system **dezimale (Zahlendarstellung); correct to three places of decimals** = correct to three figures after the decimal point (e.g. 3.485) **auf drei Dezimalstellen genau berechnet; decimal point** = dot which indicates the division between the whole unit digits and the smaller (fractional) parts of a decimal number (such as 4.75) **Dezimalstelle; decimal system** = number system using the digits 0 - 9 **Dezimalsystem; decimal tabbing** = adjusting a column of numbers so that the decimal points are vertically aligned **mit Dezimaltabulator einrichten; decimal tab key** = key for entering decimal numbers (using a word processor) so that the decimal points are automatically vertically aligned **Dezimaltabulatortaste; decimal-to-binary conversion** = converting a decimal (base ten) number into a binary (base two) number **Dezimal-Binär-Umwandlung**

◊ **decimalization** *noun* changing to a decimal system **Dezimalisierung**

◊ **decimalize** *verb* to change to a decimal system **dezimalisieren**

decimonic ringing *noun* selecting one telephone by sending a certain ringing frequency **dezimonisches Läuten**

decipher *verb* to convert an encrypted *or* encoded message (ciphertext) into the original message (plaintext) **entschlüsseln**

decision *noun* making up one's mind to do something **Entscheidung, Entschluss;** *to come to a decision or to reach a decision;* **decision box** = graphical symbol used in a flowchart to indicate that a decision is to be made and a branch *or* path *or* action carried out according to the result **Blockdiagrammsymbol: Entscheidung; decision circuit** *or* **element** = logical circuit that operates on binary inputs, providing an output according to the operation **Verknüpfungsglied; decision** *or* **discrimination instruction** = conditional program instruction that directs control by providing the location of the next instruction to be executed if a condition is met **logische Entscheidung; decision support system** = suite of programs that help a manager reach decisions using previous decisions, information and other databases **Entscheidungsunterstützungssystem; decision table** = chart which shows the relationships between certain variables and actions available when various conditions are met **Entscheidungstabelle; decision tree** = graphical representation of a decision table showing possible paths and actions if different conditions are met **Entscheidungsbaum**

deck *noun*
(a) tape deck = drive for magnetic tape **Bandlaufwerk**
(b) pile of punched cards **Lochkartensatz**

deckle edge *noun* rough edge of paper made by hand **Büttenrand**

declare *verb* to define a computer program variable *or* to set a variable equal to a number **benennen**; *he declared at the start of the program that X was equal to nine*

◊ **declaration** *or* **declarative statement** *noun* statement within a program that informs the compiler *or* interpreter of the form, type and size of a particular element, constant or variable **Vereinbarung; procedure declaration** = to write and declare the variable types used and (if any) the routine name and location **Prozedurvereinbarung**

decode *verb* to translate encoded data back to its original form **entschlüsseln**

◊ **decoder** *noun* program *or* device used to convert data into another form **Decodierer; instruction decoder** = hardware that converts a machine-code instruction (in binary form) into actions **Befehlsdecodierer**

◊ **decoding** *noun* converting encoded data back into its original form **Entschlüsselung**

decollate *verb* to separate continuous stationery into single sheets; to split two-part *or* three-part stationery into its separate parts (and remove the carbon paper) **trennen**

◊ **decollator** *noun* machine used to separate continuous stationery into single sheets *or* to split 2-part or 3-part stationery into separate parts **Trennmaschine**

decompilation *noun* conversion of a compiled program in object code into a source language **Rückumsetzung**; *fast incremental compilation and decompilation*

decrease
1 *noun* fall *or* reduction **Verminderung, Abfall**; *decrease in price; decrease in value; decrease in sales sales show a 10% decrease on last year*
2 *verb* to fall *or* to become less **abnehmen,** *nachlassen; sales are decreasing; the value of the pound has decreased by 5%*

decrement *verb* to subtract a set number from a variable **Dekrement;** *the register contents were decremented until they reached zero*

decrypt *verb* to convert encrypted data back into its original form **entschlüsseln;** *decryption is done using hardware to increase speed*

◊ **decryption** *noun* converting of encrypted data back into its original form **Entschlüsselung**

> QUOTE typically a file is encrypted using a password key and decrypted using the same key. A design fault of many systems means the use of the wrong password for decryption results in double and often irretrievable encryption
>
> *PC Business World*

dedicated *adjective* (program *or* procedure *or* system) reserved for a particular use **ausschließlich zugeordnet, dediziert;** *there's only one dedicated graphics workstation in this network;* **dedicated channel** = communications line reserved for a special purpose **dedizierter Kanal; dedicated computer** = computer which is only used for a single special purpose **dedizierter Computer; dedicated line** = telephone line used only for data communications **festgeschaltete Leitung; dedicated logic** = logical function implemented in hardware designed (usually for only one task *or* circuit **dedizierte Logik;** *the person appointed should have a knowledge of micro-based hardware and dedicated logic; the dedicated logic cuts down the chip count;* **dedicated word processor** = computer which has been configured specially for word processing and which cannot run any other programs **dedizierter Textverarbeitungscomputer**

> QUOTE the server should reduce networking costs by using standard networking cable instead of dedicated links
>
> *PC Business World*

> QUOTE The PBX is changing from a dedicated proprietary hardware product into an open application software development platform
>
> *Computing*

deduct *verb* to remove something from a total **abziehen**

de facto standard *noun* a design *or* method *or* system which is so widely used that it has become a standard but it has not been officially recognised by any committee **De-facto-Standard**

default *noun* predefined course of action *or* value that is assumed unless the operator alters it **Vorgabe; default drive** = disk drive that is accessed first in a multi-disk system (to try and load the operating system or a program) **Standardlaufwerk;** *the operating system allows the user to select the default drive;* **default option** = preset value *or* option that is to be used if no other value has been specified **Standardannahme; default rate** = baud rate (in a modem) that is used if no other is selected **vorgegebene Schrittgeschwindigkeit; default response** = value which is used if the user does not enter new data **Standardwert; default value** = value which is automatically used by the computer if no other value has been specified **Standardvorgabe;** *screen width has a default value of 80*

> QUOTE The default values of columns cannot be set in the database schema, so different applications can trash the database
> *Computing*

defect *noun* something which is wrong *or* which stops a machine from working properly **Fehler;** *a computer defect or; a defect in the computer*

◊ **defective** *adjective* faulty *or* not working properly **defekt;** *the machine broke down because of a defective cooling system;* **defective sector** = fault with a hard disk in which data cannot be correctly read from a particular sector; it could be caused by a damaged disk surface or faulty head alignment **fehlerhafter Sektor**

◊ **defect skipping** *noun* means of identifying and labelling defective magnetic tracks during manufacture so that they will not be used, instead pointing to the next good track to be used **fehlerhaftes Springen**

defensive computing *noun* method of programming that takes into account any problems *or* errors that might occur **defensives Programmieren**

deferred addressing *noun* indirect addressing, where the location accessed contains the address of the operand to be processed **indirekte/ausgesetzte Adressierung**

define *verb* (i) to assign a value to a variable; (ii) to assign the characteristics of processes *or* data to something **(i) definieren; (ii) zuweisen;** *all the variables were defined at initialization*

◊ **definition** *noun* (i) ability of a screen to display fine detail; (ii) value *or* formula assigned to a variable *or* label **(i) Auflösung; (ii) Zuweisung; macro definition** = description (in a program *or* to a system) of the structure, function and instructions that make up a macro operation **Makrodefinition**

deflect *verb* to change the direction of an object *or* beam **ablenken**

◊ **deflection** *noun* **deflection yoke** = magnetic coils around a cathode ray tube used to control the position of the picture beam on the screen **Ablenkjoch**

defocus *verb* to move the point of focus of an optical system from an object, so that it appears out of focus **defokussieren**

DEFRAG (in MS-DOS) defragmentation utility supplied with MS-DOS **DEFRAG**

defragmentation *noun* reorganisation of files scattered across non-contiguous sectors on a hard disk **Defragmentierung; defragmentation utility** = software utility that carries out the process of defragmentation on a hard disk **Hilfsprogramm zur Defragmentierung, Defragmentierer**

> COMMENT: when a file is saved to disk, it is not always saved in adjacent sectors; this will increase the retrieval time. Defragmentation moves files back into adjacent sectors so that the read head does not have to move far across the disk, and it increases performance

degauss *verb* to remove unwanted magnetic fields and effects from magnetic tape, disks *or* read/write heads **entmagnetisieren;** *the r/w heads have to be degaussed each week to ensure optimum performance*

◊ **degausser** *noun* device used to remove unwanted magnetic fields from a disk *or* tape *or* recording head **Entmagnetisierungsgerät**

degradation *noun*
(a) loss of picture *or* signal quality **Verschlechterung; image degradation** = loss of picture contrast and quality due to signal distortion *or* bad copying of a video signal **Bildverschlechterung**

(b) loss of processing capacity because of a malfunction **Verschlechterung; graceful degradation** = allowing some parts of a system to continue to function after a part has broken down **kontrollierter Leistungsrückgang**

DEL = DELETE (in MS-DOS) command to delete a file **DEL;** *to delete all files with the extension BAK, use the command DEL or. BAK;* **DEL key** = key on a keyboard that moves the cursor back one character space and deletes any character at that position **Taste DEL, Taste Entf;** *to remove a word from the screen, press the DEL key repeatedly*

delay
1 *noun* time when something is later than planned **Verspätung, Verzögerung;** *there was a delay of thirty seconds before the printer started printing; we are sorry for the delay in supplying your order, but the computer was not working;* **delay distortion** = signal corruption due to echoes **Laufzeitverzerrung; delay equalizer** = electronic circuit used to compensate for delays caused by a communications line **Laufzeitentzerrer; delay line** = device that causes a signal to take a certain time in crossing it **Verzögerungsleitung; delay line store** = (old) method of storing serial data as sound *or* pulses in a delay line, the data being constantly read, regenerated and fed back into the input **Laufzeitspeicher; delay vector** = time that a message will take to pass from one packet switching network node to another **Verzögerungsvektor**
2 *verb* to cause something to have a delay **aufhalten**

delete *verb*
(a) to cut out words in a document **streichen**
(b) to remove text *or* data from a storage device **löschen;** *the word-processor allows us to delete the whole file by pressing this key;* **undelete** = to restore a file *or* text *or* data that was accidentally deleted **wiederherstellen;** *thankfully, we could undelete the files;* **delete character** = special code used to indicate data *or* text to be removed **Löschzeichen**

◊ **deletion** *noun* (i) making a cut in a document; (ii) text removed from a document **(i) & (ii) Streichung;** *the editors asked the author to make several deletions in the last chapter;* **deletion record** = record containing new data which is to be used to update *or* delete data in a master record **Löschsatz; deletion tracking** = method of allowing deleted files to be undeleted; when

a file is deleted, the sectors on disk are monitored for a period of time in case the file was deleted by mistake **Löschverfolgung**

┃ COMMENT: when you delete a file, you are
┃ not actually erasing it but you are making its
┃ space on disk available for another file by
┃ instructing the operating system to ignore the
┃ file by inserting a special code in the file header
┃ and deleting the entry from the directory

delimit *verb* to set up the size of data using delimiters **begrenzen; comma delimited** = file in which each item *or* field of data is separated by a comma **mit Kommaabgrenzung, Comma-delimited**

◊ **delimiter** *noun* (i) character *or* symbol used to indicate to a language *or* program the start *or* end of data *or* a record *or* information; (ii) the boundary between an instruction and its argument **(i) Begrenzungssymbol; (ii) Abgrenzung**

delta *noun* type of connection used to connect the three wires in a 3-phase electrical supply **Dreieckschaltung; delta clock** = clock that provides timing pulses to synchronize a system, and will restart (with an interrupt signal) a computer *or* circuit that has had an error *or* entered an endless loop *or* faulty state **Delta-Uhr; delta-delta** = connection between a delta source and load **Delta-Delta-Verbindung; delta modulation** = differential pulse coded modulation that uses only one bit per sample **Deltamodulation; delta routing** = means of directing data around a packet switching network **Dreiecksleitweg**

demagnetize *verb* to remove stray *or* unwanted magnetic fields from a disk *or* tape *or* recording head **entmagnetisieren**

◊ **demagnetizer** *noun* device which demagnetizes something **Entmagnetisierer;** *he used the demagnetizer to degauss the tape heads*

demand
1 *noun* asking for something to be done **Bitte, Forderung; demand assigned multiple access (DAMA)** = means of switching in circuits as and when they are required **bedarfsbestimmter Mehrfachzugriff; demand multiplexing** = time division multiplexing method which allocates time segments to signals according to demand **bedarfsmäßige Multiplexmethode; demand paging** = system software that retrieves pages in a virtual memory system from backing store when it is required **Seitenabrufmethode; demand processing** = processing data when it

appears, rather than waiting **unmittelbare Verarbeitung; demand protocol architecture (DPA)** = technique of loading protocol stacks in memory only if they are required for a particular session **Abrufprotokollarchitektur, (DPA, Demand Protocol Architecture); demand reading/writing** = direct data transfer between a processor and storage **unmittelbares Lesen/Schreiben; demand staging** = moving files *or* data from a secondary storage device to a fast access device when required by a database program **bedarfsmäßiges Einspeichern 2** *verb* to ask for something and expect to get it **fordern;** *she demanded her money back; the suppliers are demanding immediate payment*

demarcation *noun* showing the difference between two areas **Abgrenzung; demarcation strip** = device that electrically isolates equipment from a telephone line (to prevent damage) **Demarkationsstreifen**

demo = DEMONSTRATION

democratic network *noun* synchronized network where each station has equal priority **gleichberechtigtes Netz**

demodulation *noun* recovery of the original signal from a received modulated carrier wave **Demodulation**

◊ **demodulator** *noun* circuit that recovers a signal from a modulated carrier wave **Demodulator**

demonstrate *verb* to show how something works **vorführen;** *he demonstrated the file management program*

◊ **demonstration** *noun* act of showing how something works **Vorführung; demonstration model** = piece of equipment in a shop, used to show customers how the equipment works **Vorführgerät; demonstration software** = software that shows what an application is like to use and what it can do, without implementing all the functions **Demoprogramm, Demosoftware;** *the company gave away demonstration software that lets you do everything except save your data*

demultiplex *verb* to split one channel into the original signals that were combined at source **entmultiplexieren**

◊ **demultiplexor** *noun* device that separates out the original multiplexed signals from one channel **Entmultiplexor**

denary notation *noun* number system in base ten, using the digits 0 to 9 **Dezimaldarstellung**

denial *noun* **alternative denial** = logical function whose output is false if all inputs are true, and true if any input is false **NAND-Funktion; joint denial** = logical function whose output is false if any input is true **NOR-Funktion**

dense index *noun* database index containing an address *or* entry for every item *or* entry in the database **Gesamtindex; dense list** = list that has no free space for new records **vollständige Liste**

◊ **densitometer** *noun* photographic device used to measure the density of a photograph **Dichtemesser, Densitometer**

◊ **density** *noun*
(a) amount of light that a photographic negative blocks **Dichte**
(b) darkness of a printed image *or* text **Schwärzungsgrad; density dial** = knob that controls the density of a printed image **Schwärzungsskala;** *when fading occurs, turn the density dial on the printer to full black*
(c) amount of data that can be packed into a space on a disk *or* tape **Speicherkapazität; double density** = system to double the storage capacity of a disk drive by doubling the number of bits which can be put on the disk surface **doppelte Speicherkapazität; double density disk (DD)** = disk that can store two bits of data per unit area compared to a standard disk, using a modified write process **Platte mit doppelter Speicherkapazität; packing** *or* **recording density** = number of bits that can be stored in a unit area on a magnetic disk *or* tape **Zeichendichte; single density disk (SD)** = standard magnetic disk able to store data **Platte mit einfacher Speicherkapazität**

COMMENT: scanner software produces various shades of grey by using different densities *or* arrangements of black and white dots and/or different sized dots

QUOTE diode lasers with shorter wavelengths will make doubling of the bit and track densities possible
Byte

deny access *verb* to refuse access to a circuit *or* system for reasons of workload *or* security **den Zugriff verwehren**

dependent *adjective* which is variable because of something **abhängig;** *a process which is dependent on the result of another* *process; the output is dependent on the physical state of the link;* **machine dependent** = not standardized *or* which cannot be used on hardware *or* software from a different manufacturer without modification **maschinenabhängig**

deposit
1 *noun* thin layer of a substance which is put on a surface **Schicht**
2 *verb*
(a) to print out the contents of all *or* a selected area of memory **darlegen**
(b) to coat a surface with a thin layer of a substance **mit einer Schicht überziehen**
(c) to write data into a register *or* storage location **ablegen**

◇ **deposition** *noun* process by which a surface (of a semiconductor) is coated with a thin layer of a substance **Überzugsverfahren**

depth of field *noun* amount of a scene that will be in focus when photographed with a certain aperture setting **Tiefenbereich; depth of focus** = position of film behind a camera lens that will result in a sharp image **Tiefenschärfe**

deque *noun* = DOUBLE-ENDED QUEUE queue in which new items can be added to either end **nach beiden Seiten offene Warteschlange**

derive *verb* to come from **sich ableiten von; derived indexing** = library index entries produced only from material in the book *or* document **abgeleitete Indizierung; derived sound** = sound signal produced by mixing the left and right hand channels of a stereo signal **monophones Tonsignal**

◇ **derivation graph** *noun* structure within a global database that provides information on the rules and paths used to reach any element *or* item of data **Ableitungsgraph**

DES = DATA ENCRYPTION STANDARD standardized popular cipher system for data encryption **Datenverschlüsselungsnorm**

descender *noun* part of a character that goes below the line (such as the 'tail' of a 'g' or 'p') **Unterlänge;** *compare* ASCENDER

de-scramble *verb* to reassemble an original message *or* signal from its scrambled form **entschlüsseln**

◇ **de-scrambler** *noun* device which

changes a scrambled message back to its original, clear form **Decodierer**

describe *verb* to say what someone *or* something is like **beschreiben;** *the leaflet describes the services the company can offer; the specifications are described in greater detail at the back of the manual*

◇ **description** *noun* words which show what something is like **Beschreibung; description list** = list of data items and their attributes **Erklärungsliste; data description language (DDL)** = part of a database system which describes the structure of the system and data **Datenbeschreibungssprache; page description programming language** = programming language that accepts commands to define the size, position and typestyle for text *or* graphics on a page **Seitenbeschreibungssprache**

◇ **descriptor** *noun* code used to identify a filename *or* program name *or* pass code to a file **Beschreiber, Deskriptor**

design
1 *noun* planning *or* drawing of a product before it is built *or* manufactured **Entwurf; circuit design** = layout of components and interconnections in a circuit **Schaltungsentwurf; industrial design** = design of products made by machines (such as cars and refrigerators) **Industriedesign; product design** = design of products **Produktdesign; design department** = department in a large company which designs the company's products *or* its advertising **Designabteilung; Werbeabteilung; design parameters** = specifications for the design of a product **Designparameter; design studio** = independent firm which specializes in creating designs **Designstudio, Grafikerbüro**
2 *verb* to plan *or* to draw something before it is built *or* manufactured **entwerfen;** *he designed a new chip factory; she designs typefaces*

◇ **designer** *noun* person who designs **Designer/-in;** *she is the designer of the new computer*

desk *noun* writing table in an office, usually with drawers for stationery **Schreibtisch;** *desk diary; desk drawer; desk light;* **desk accessory (DA)** = (in an Apple Macintosh system) add-in utility that enhances the system **Schreibtischzubehör;** *we have installed several DAs that help us manage our fonts;* **desk check** = dry run of a program **Probelauf**

◊ **desktop** *adjective*
(a) which sits on top of a desk; which can be done on a desk **Tisch-; desktop computer (system)** = small microcomputer system that can be placed on a desk **Tischcomputer; Desktop file** = (in an Apple Macintosh system) system file used to store information about all the files on a disk *or* volume (such as version, date, size, author) **Schreibtischdatei; desktop publishing (DTP)** = design, layout and printing of documents using special software, a small computer and a printer **Desktop publishing, Publizieren am Schreibtisch**
(b) (in a GUI) workspace that is a graphical representation of a real-life desktop, with icons for telephone, diary, calculator, filing cabinet **Schreibtischoberfläche, Arbeitsoberfläche**

QUOTE desktop publishing or the ability to produce high-quality publications using a minicomputer, essentially boils down to combining words and images on pages

Byte

COMMENT: a desktop makes it easier for a new user to operate a computer, they do not have to type in commands, instead they can point at icons on the desktop using a mouse

despool *verb* to print out spooled files **übertragen**

despotic network *noun* network synchronized and controlled by one single clock **zwangssynchronisiertes Netz**

de-spun antenna *noun* satellite aerial that always points to the same place on the earth **raumfeste Antenne**

DESQview ™ *noun* software which provides multitasking functionality for an MS-DOS system and allows more than one program to run at the same time **DESQview ™**

destination *noun* place to which something is sent *or* to which something is going; location to which a data is sent **Bestimmungsort**

destructive addition *noun* addition operation in which the result is stored in the location of one of the operands used in the sum, so overwriting it **Überschreibung**

◊ **destructive cursor** *noun* cursor that erases the text as it moves over it **löschender Cursor;** *reading the screen becomes difficult*

without a destructive cursor; **destructive read** = read operation in which the stored data is erased as it is retrieved **löschendes Lesen; destructive readout** = form of storage medium that loses its data after it has been read **löschendes Auslesen**

detail
1 *noun* small part of a description **Detail; detail file** = file containing records that are to be used to update a master file **Detaildatei; in detail** = giving many particulars **im Detail;** *the catalogue lists all the products in detail;* **detail paper** = thin transparent paper used for layouts and tracing **Pauspapier**
2 *verb* to list in detail **genau auflisten;** *the catalogue details the shipping arrangements for customers; the terms of the licence are detailed in the contract*

◊ **detailed** *adjective* in detail **im Detail; detailed account** = account which lists every item **detaillierte Aufzeichnung** *or* **Rechnung**

detect *verb* to sense something (usually something very slight) **erkennen, aufdecken;** *the equipment can detect faint signals from the transducer;* **detected error** = error noticed during a program run, but not corrected **erkannter Fehler; error detecting code** = coding system that allows errors occurring during transmission to be detected, but is not complex enough to correct the errors **Fehlererkennungscode**

◊ **detection** *noun* process of detecting something **Erkennung;** *the detection of the cause of the fault is proving difficult*

◊ **detector** *noun* device which can detect **Detektor; metal detector** = device which can sense hidden metal objects **Metalldetektor**

deterministic *adjective* (result of a process) that depends on the initial state and inputs **deterministisch**

develop *verb*
(a) to plan and produce **entwickeln;** *to develop a new product*
(b) to apply a chemical process to photographic film and paper to produce an image **entwickeln**

◊ **developer** *noun*
(a) property developer = person who plans and builds a group of new houses *or* new factories **Immobilienmakler, Erschließer; software developer** = person *or* company which writes software **Software-Entwickler**
(b) chemical solution used to develop exposed film **Entwickler(flüssigkeit)**

◊ **development** *noun* planning the production of a new product **Entwicklung; research and development** = investigating new products and techniques **Forschung und Entwicklung; development software** = suite of programs that help a programmer write, edit, compile and debug new software **Programmentwicklungssoftware; development time** = amount of time required to develop a new product **Entwicklungszeit**

device *noun* small useful machine *or* piece of equipment **Bauelement, Gerät; device address** = location within the memory area that is used by a particular device; the CPU can control the device by placing instructions at this address **Geräteadresse; device character control** = device control using various characters *or* special combinations to instruct the device **Gerätezeichensteuerung; device code** = unique identification and selection code for each peripheral **Gerätekennung; device control (character)** = special code sent in a transmission to a device to instruct it to perform a special function **Gerätesteuerzeichen; device driver** = program *or* routine used to interface and manage an I/O device *or* peripheral **Gerätetreiber; device flag** = one bit in a device status word, used to show the state of one device **Gerätekennung; device independent** = programming technique that results in a program that is able to run with any peripheral hardware **geräteunabhängig; device name** = abbreviation that denotes a port or I/O device, such as COM for serial port, PRN for printer port, CON for keyboard and monitor **Gerätebezeichnung; device priority** = the importance of a peripheral device assigned by the user *or* central computer which dictates the order in which the CPU will serve an interrupt signal from it **Einheitenvorrangliste;** *the master console has a higher device priority than the printers and other terminals;* **device queue** = list of requests from users *or* programs to use a device **Warteschlange; device status word (DSW)** = data word transmitted from the device that contains information about its current status **Einheitenstatuswort;** *this routine checks the device status word and will not transmit data if the busy bit is set;* **I/O device** = peripheral (such as a terminal) which can be used for inputting or outputting data to a processor **Ein-/Ausgabeeinheit; output device** = device (such as a monitor *or* printer) which allows information to be displayed **Ausgabegerät**

devise *verb* to plan *or* build a system **sich ausdenken;** *they devised a cheap method of avoiding the problem*

Dewey decimal classification *noun* library cataloguing system using classes and subclasses that are arranged in groups of ten **deweysche Dezimalklassifikation**

DFD = DATA FLOW DIAGRAM diagram used to describe the movement of data through a system **Datenflussdiagramm**

D-type flip-flop *noun* flip-flop device with one input and two outputs **Einheit mit bistabiler Schaltung**

Dhrystone benchmark *noun* benchmarking system developed to try and measure and compare the performance of computers **Dhrystone-Benchmark;** *see also* BENCHMARK

diacritic *noun* accent above *or* below a letter **diakritisches Zeichen**

diagnose *verb* to find the cause and effect of a fault in hardware or error in software **diagnostizieren**

◊ **diagnosis** *noun* finding of a fault *or* discovering the cause of a fault (results of diagnosing faulty hardware or software) **Diagnose**

diagnostic
1 *noun* **diagnostic aid** = hardware *or* software device that helps to find faults **Diagnosehilfsmittel; diagnostic chip** = chip that contains circuits to carry out tests on other circuits *or* chips **Diagnosechip; diagnostic message** = message that appears to explain the type, location and probable cause of a software error *or* hardware failure **Diagnosemeldung; diagnostic program** = software that helps find faults in a computer system **Diagnoseprogramm; diagnostic routine** = routine in a program which helps to find faults in a computer system **Diagnostikprogramm; diagnostic test** = means of locating faults in hardware and software by test circuits *or* programs **Diagnosetest; self-diagnostic** = computer that runs a series of diagnostic programs (usually when the computer is switched on)

to ensure that all circuits, memory and peripherals are working correctly **selbstdiagnostizierend**

◊ **diagnostics** *noun* functions *or* tests that help a user find faults in hardware *or* software **Diagnostik; compiler diagnostics =** function in a compiler that helps a programmer find faults in the program code **Kompilirererdiagnostik;** *thorough compiler diagnostics make debugging easy;* **error diagnostics =** information and system messages displayed when an error is detected to help a user debug and correct it **Fehlerdiagnostik**

QUOTE the implementation of on-line diagnostic devices that measure key observable parameters

Byte

QUOTE to check for any hardware problems, a diagnostic disk is provided

Personal Computer World

---

diagonal cut *noun* method of joining two pieces of film *or* magnetic tape together by cutting the ends at an angle so making the join less obvious **Schrägschnitt**

diagram *noun* drawing which shows something as a plan *or* a map **Diagramm; flow diagram =** diagram showing the arrangement of work processes in a series **Flussdiagramm**

◊ **diagrammatic** *adjective* in **diagrammatic form =** in the form of a diagram **diagrammatisch, in einem Schaubild dargestellt;** *the chart showed the sales pattern in diagrammatic form*

◊ **diagramatically** *adverb* using a diagram **diagrammatisch;** *the chart shows the sales pattern diagramatically*

dial
1 *verb* to call a telephone number on a telephone **wählen;** *to dial a number; to dial the operator; he dialled the code for the USA; you can dial New York direct from London;* **to dial direct =** to contact a phone number without asking the operator to do it for you **durchwählen; auto-dial =** modem that can automatically dial a number (under the control of a computer) **Selbstwähler; to dial into =** to call a telephone number, which has a modem and computer at the other end **anwählen;** *with the right access code it is possible to dial into a customer's computer to extract the files needed for the report* NOTE: GB English is **dialling - dialled,** but US spelling is **dialling - dialed**

2 *noun* (i) circular mechanical device which is turned to select something; (ii) round face on an instrument, with numbers which indicate something (such as the time on a clock) **(i) Rundskala, Wählscheibe; (ii) Zifferblatt;** *to tune into the radio station, turn the dial;* **dial conference =** facility on a private exchange that allows one user to call a number of other extensions for a teleconference **Telekonferenzschaltung; dial pulse =** pulse-coded signals transmitted to represent numbers dialled **Wählimpuls; dial tone =** sound made by a telephone that indicates that the telephone system is ready for a number to be dialled **Wählton, Freizeichen; dial-in modem =** auto-answer modem that can be called at any time **Einwählmodem; density dial =** knob that controls the density of a printed image **Schwärzungsskala;** *if the text fades, turn the density dial on the printer to full black*

◊ **dialling** *noun* act of calling a telephone number **Wählen; dialling code =** special series of numbers which you use to make a call to another town *or* country **Vorwahl; dialling tone =** sound made by a telephone that indicates that the telephone system is ready for a number to be dialled **Wählton; international direct dialling (IDD) =** calling telephone numbers in other countries direct **internationale Durchwahl** NOTE: no plural

◊ **dialup** *or* **dial-up service** *noun* online information service that is accessed by dialling into the central computer **Onlinedienst**

QUOTE Customers will be able to choose a wide variety of telephony products, from basic auto-dial programs to call-centre applications.

Computing

---

dialect *noun* slight variation of a standard language **Dialekt;** *this manufacturer's dialect of BASIC is a little different to the one I'm used to*

dialogue *noun* speech *or* speaking to another person; communication between devices such as computers **Dialog; dialog box =** on-screen message from a program to the user **Dialog, Dialogfeld, Dialogfenster**

diameter *noun* distance across a round object **Durchmesser**

DIANE = DIRECT INFORMATION ACCESS NETWORK FOR EUROPE services offered over the Euronet network

DIANE (direktes Informationsanschaltnetz für Europa)

diaphragm *noun*
(a) mechanical device in a camera that varies the aperture size **Membran**
(b) moving part in a loudspeaker *or* microphone **Membran;** *the diaphragm in the microphone picks up sound waves*

diapositive *noun* positive transparency **Diapositiv**

diary *noun* book in which you can write notes *or* appointments for each day of the week **Terminkalender; diary management =** part of an office computer program, which records schedules and appointments **Terminverwaltung**

diascope *noun* slide projector *or* device that projects slide images onto a screen **Diaprojektor**

diazo (process) *noun* method for copying documents (using sensitized paper exposed to the original) **Diazokopie**

DIB = DATA INPUT BUS bus used when transferring data from one section of a computer to another, such as between memory and CPU **Dateneingabebus**

dibit *noun* digit made up of two binary bits **Dibit**

dichotomizing search *noun* fast search method for use on ordered lists of data (the search key is compared with the data in the middle of the list and one half is discarded, this is repeated with the half remaining until only one data item remains) **eliminierende Suche, Einstichverfahren**

dichroic *noun* chemical coating on the surface of a lens **Dichroise**

dictate *verb* to say something to someone who then writes down your words **diktieren;** *to dictate a letter to a secretary; he was dictating orders into his pocket dictating machine;* **dictating machine =** small tape recorder that is used to record notes *or* letters dictated by someone, which a secretary can play back and type out the text **Diktiergerät**

◊ **dictation** *noun* act of dictating **Diktat; to take dictation =** to write down what someone is saying **ein Diktat aufnehmen; dictation speed =** number of words per minute which a secretary can write down in shorthand **Diktiertempo; Silbenzahl pro Minute**

dictionary *noun* (i) book which lists words and meanings; (ii) data management structure which allows files to be referenced and sorted; (iii) part of a spelling checker program: the list of correctly spelled words against which the program checks a text (i) **Wörterbuch;** (ii) **Verzeichnis;** (iii) **Wörterbuch;** *see also* SPELL-CHECKER

dielectric *noun* insulating material that allows an electric field to pass, but not an electric current **Dielektrikum, Nichtleiter**

differ *verb* not to be the same as something else **sich unterscheiden;** *the two products differ considerably - one has an external hard disk, the other has internal hard disk and external magnetic tape drive*

◊ **difference** *noun* way in which two things are not the same **Unterschied;** *what is the difference between these two products? differences in price or price differences;* **symmetric difference =** logical function whose output is true if either of the inputs is true, and false if both inputs are the same **symmetrische Differenz**

◊ **different** *adjective* not the same **anders, unterschiedlich;** *our product range is quite different in design from the Japanese models; we offer ten models each in six different colours*

◊ **differential** *adjective* which shows a difference **verschieden; differential PCM =** DIFFERENTIAL PULSE CODED MODULATION pulse coded modulation that uses the difference in size of a sample value and the previous one, requiring fewer bits when transmitting **Differenzialpulscodemodulation**

DIF file = DATA INTERCHANGE FORMAT de facto standard that defines the way a spreadsheet, its formula and data are stored in a file **DIF-Datei**

diffuse *verb* to move *or* insert something over an area *or* through a substance **diffundieren;** *the smoke from the faulty machine rapidly diffused through the building; the chemical was diffused into the substrate*

◊ **diffusion** *noun* means of transferring doping materials into an integrated circuit substrate **Diffusion**

digipulse telephone *noun* push button

telephone dialling method using coded pulses **Tastentelefon**

digit *noun* symbol *or* character which represents an integer that is smaller than the radix of the number base used **Ziffer;** *a phone number with eight digits or; an eight-digit phone number; the decimal digit 8; the decimal number system uses the digits 0123456789;* **check digit** = additional digit inserted into transmitted text to monitor and correct errors **Prüfziffer; digit place** *or* **position** = position of a digit within a number **Ziffernstelle;** *see also* RADIX

◊ **digital** *adjective* which represents data *or* physical quantities in numerical form (especially using a binary system in computer related devices) **digital; digital audio disk (DAD)** = method of recording sound by converting and storing signals in a digital form on magnetic disk, providing very high quality reproduction **digitale Tonplatte;** *see also* COMPACT DISK; **digital audio tape (DAT)** = method of recording sound by converting and storing signals in a digital form on magnetic tape, providing very high quality reproduction **digitales Tonband; digital camera** = camera that uses a bank of CCD units to capture an image and store it digitally on to a miniature disk *or* in RAM in the camera's body **Digitalkamera, digitale Kamera; digital cassette** = high quality magnetic tape housed in a standard size cassette with write protect tabs, and a standard format leader **Digitalkassette; digital circuit** = electronic circuit that operates on digital information providing logical functions *or* switching **digitaler Stromkreis; digital clock** = clock which shows the time as a series of digits (such as 12:22:04) **Digitaluhr; digital computer** = computer which processes data in digital form (that is data represented in discrete digital form) **Digitalrechner;** *compare* ANALOG; **digital data** = data represented in (usually binary) numerical form **digitale Daten; digital display** = video display that can only show a fixed number of colours *or* shades of grey **Digitalanzeige; digital logic** = applying Boolean algebra to hardware circuits **digitale Logik; digital multimeter (DMM)** = multimeter that uses a digital readout (giving better clarity than an AMM) **digitales Multimeter; digital optical recording (DOR)** = recording signals in binary form as small holes in the surface of an optical *or* compact disk which can then be read by laser **digitale optische Aufzeichnung; digital output** = computer output in digital form **Digitalausgabe;** *compare with* ANALOG OUTPUT; **digital plotter** = plotter whose pen position is controllable in discrete steps, so that drawings in the computer can be output graphically **digitaler Plotter; digital read-out** = data displayed in numerical form, such as numbers on an LCD in a calculator **digitale Sichtanzeige; digital recording** = conversion of sound signals into a digital form and storing them on magnetic disk *or* tape usually in binary form **Digitalaufnahme; digital representation** = data *or* quantities represented using discrete quantities (digits) **digitale Darstellung; digital resolution** = smallest number that can be represented with one digit, the value assigned to the least significant bit of a word *or* number **digitale Auflösung; digital signal** = electric signal that has only a number of possible states, as opposed to analog signals which are continuously variable **digitales Signal; digital signalling** = control and dialling codes sent down a (telephone line) in digital form **digitale Signalisierung; digital signal processing (DSP)** = special integrated circuit used to manipulate digital signals **digitale Signalverarbeitung, Digital Signal Processing (DSP); digital signature** = unique identification code sent by a terminal *or* device in digital form **digitale Signatur; digital speech** *see* SPEECH SYNTHESIS; **digital system** = system that deals with digital signals **Digitalsystem; digital switching** = operating communications connections and switches only by use of digital signals **digitale Vermittlung; digital to analog converter** *or* **D to A converter (DAC)** = circuit that converts a digital signal to an analog one (the analog signal is proportional to an input binary number) **Digital-Analog-Umsetzer; digital transmission system** = communications achieved by converting analog signals to a digital form then modulating and transmitting this (the signal is then converted back to analog form at the receiver) **digitales Übertragungssystem; digital video interactive (DV-I)** = system that defines how video and audio signals should be compressed and displayed on a computer **Digital Video Interactive (DV-I)**

◊ **digitally** *adverb* (quantity represented) in digital form **digital;** *the machine takes digitally recorded data and generates an image*

QUOTE Xerox Parc's LCD breakthrough promises the digital equivalent of paper, by producing thin, low-cost flat displays with a 600dpi resolution.

Computing

digitize *verb* to change analog movement *or* signals into a digital form which can be processed by computers, etc. **digitalisieren;** *we can digitize your signature to allow it to be printed with any laser printer;* **digitized photograph** = image *or* photograph that has been scanned to produce an analog signal which is then converted to digital form and stored *or* displayed on a computer **digitalisierte photographische Aufnahme; digitizing pad** = sensitive surface that translates the position of a pen into numerical form, so that drawings can be entered into a computer **Digitalisierblock**

◊ **digitizer** *noun* analog to digital converter *or* device which converts an analog movement *or* signal to a digital one which can be understood by a computer **Digitalisierer**

> QUOTE The contract covers fibre optic cable and Synchronous Digital Hierarchy transmission equipment to be used to digitize the telecommunications network.
> *Computergram*

DIL = DUAL-IN-LINE PACKAGE standard layout for integrated circuit packages using two parallel rows of connecting pins along each side **DIL-Gehäuse, Doppelreihengehäuse**

dimension *noun* measurement of size **Dimension, Ausmaß;** *the dimensions of the computer are small enough for it to fit into a case*

◊ **dimensioning** *noun* definition of the size of something (usually an array *or* matrix) **Dimensionierung;** *array dimensioning occurs at this line*

diminished radix complement *noun* number representation in which each digit of the number is subtracted from one less than the radix **B1-Komplement;** *see also* ONE'S, NINE'S COMPLEMENT

DIN = DEUTSCHE INDUSTRIENORM German industry standards organization **DIN (deutsche Industrienorm)**

Dingbat ™ *noun* font that contains stars, bullets, symbols, images and drawings in place of characters **Dingbat ™;** *to insert a copyright symbol, use the Dingbat font*

diode *noun* electronic component that allows an electrical current to pass in one direction and not the other **Diode; light-emitting diode (LED)** = semiconductor diode that emits light when a current is applied (used in clock and calculator displays, and as an indicator) **lichtaussendende Diode**

> QUOTE Sullivan would not reveal the launch power of the diode, except that it was twice that of existing LEDs because of the higher efficiency of electron injection in the part.
> *Electronic Times*

diopter *or* **dioptre** *noun* unit of measurement for the power of an optical lens **Dioptrie; diopter lens** = optical device that is placed in front of a standard camera lens when close up shots are required **Nahlinse**

DIP = DUAL-IN-LINE PACKAGE standard layout for integrated circuit packages using two parallel rows of connecting pins along each side **DIL-Gehäuse, Doppelreihengehäuse**

diplex *noun* simultaneous transmission of two signals over the same line **Diplex**

dipole *noun* (i) material *or* molecule *or* object that has two potentials, one end positive and the other negative, due to electron displacement from an applied electric field; (ii) short straight radio aerial that receives a signal from a central connector **(i) Dipol; (ii) Dipolantenne**

DIR = DIRECTORY (in MS-DOS) system command that displays a list of files stored on a disk **DIR**

direct
1 *verb* to manage *or* to organize **leiten; directed scan** = file *or* array search method in which a starting point and a direction of scan is provided, either up *or* down from the starting point (an address *or* record number) **gerichtete Suchmethode**
2 *adjective* straight *or* with no processing *or* going in a straight way **direkt; direct access** = storage and retrieval of data without the need to read other data first **Direktzugriff; direct (access) address** = ABSOLUTE ADDRESS; **direct access storage device (DASD)** = storage medium whose memory locations can be directly read *or* written to **Direktzugriffsspeicher; direct addressing** = method of addressing where the storage location address given in the instruction is the location to be used **direkte Adressierung; direct broadcast satellite (DBS)** = TV and

radio signal broadcast over a wide area from an earth station via a satellite, received with a dish aerial **direktstrahlender Satellit; direct change-over** = switching from one computer to another in one go **Direktumschaltung; direct code** = binary code which directly operates the CPU, using only absolute addresses and values **Direktcode; direct coding** = program instructions written in absolute code **direkte Codierung; direct connect** = (modem) which plugs straight into the standard square telephone socket **Direktanschluss; direct current (DC)** = constant value electric current that flows in one direction **Gleichstrom; direct data entry (DDE)** = keying in data directly onto a magnetic disk or tape **direkte Dateneingabe; direct dialling** = calling a telephone number without passing through an internal exchange **Durchwählen; direct digital control (DDC)** = machine operated automatically by computer **direkte Digitalsteuerung; direct image film** = photographic film that produces a positive image **Umkehrfilm; direct impression** = use of a typewriter to compose a piece of text that is to be printed **Direktsatz; direct information access network for Europe (DIANE)** = services offered over the Euronet network **DIANE (direktes Informationsanschaltnetz für Europa); direct-insert routine** or **subroutine** = routine which can be directly copied (inserted) into a larger routine or program without the need for a call instruction **offenes Programm od Unterprogramm; direct instruction** = program command that contains an operand and the code for the operation to be carried out **Direktanweisung; direct inward dialling** = automatic routing of telephone calls in a private exchange **Durchwahl; direct mail** = selling a product by sending publicity material to possible customers through the post **Direktwerbung; Direktversand;** *these calculators are only sold by direct mail; the company runs a successful direct-mail operation;* **direct-mail advertising** = advertising by sending leaflets to people through the post **Direktwerbung; direct memory access (DMA)** = direct, rapid link between a peripheral and a computer's main memory which avoids the use of accessing routines for each item of data required **direkter Speicherzugriff;** *direct memory access transfer between the main memory and the second processor;* **direct memory access channel** = high speed data transfer link **direkter Speicherzugriffskanal; direct mode** = typing in a command which is executed once return is pressed **Direktmodus; direct outward dialling** =

automatic access to a telephone network form a private exchange **Amtswahl; direct page register** = register that provides memory page access data when a CPU is carrying out a direct memory access, to allow access to any part of memory **direktes Seitenregister; direct reference address** = virtual address that can only be altered by indexing **direkte Bezugsadresse; direct transfer** = bit for bit copy of the contents of one register into another register (including any status bits, etc.) **Direktübertragung**
3 *adverb* straight or with no third party involved **direkt; to dial direct** = to contact a phone number yourself without asking the operator to do it for you **durchwählen;** *you can dial New York direct from London if you want*

◊ **direction** *noun*
(a) organizing or managing **Leitung;** *he took over the direction of a software distribution group*
(b) directions for use = instructions showing how to use something **Gebrauchsanweisung** NOTE: no plural for (a)

◊ **directional** *adjective* which points in a certain direction **gerichtet; directional antenna** = aerial that transmits or receives signals from a single direction **Richtantenne; directional pattern** = chart of the response of an aerial or microphone to signals from various directions **Richtdiagramm**

◊ **directive** *noun* programming instruction used to control the language translator, compiler, etc. **Übersetzungsanweisung**

◊ **directly** *adverb*
(a) immediately **sofort**
(b) straight or with no third party involved **direkt;** *we deal directly with the manufacturer, without using a wholesaler*

◊ **director** *noun*
(a) person appointed by the shareholders to help run a company **Direktor/-in; managing director** = director who is in charge of the whole company **geschäftsführender Direktor; board of directors** = all the directors of a company **Vorstand; Aufsichtsrat**
(b) person who is in charge of a project, an official institute, etc. **Leiter/-in;** *the director of the government computer research institute she was appointed director of the organization*
(c) person who controls the filming of a film or TV programme **Regisseur/-in; casting director** = person in charge of choosing the actors for a film or TV programme **(Rollen)besetzungsdirektor; lighting director**

= person in charge of lighting in a film *or* TV studio **Beleuchtungstechniker; technical director** = person in charge of the technical equipment (especially the cameras) in a TV studio **technischer Direktor** *or* **Leiter; Studioleiter**

QUOTE directives are very useful for selecting parts of the code for particular purposes
Personal Computer World

directory *noun* method of organising the files stored on a disk; a directory contains a group of files or further sub-directories **Verzeichnis, Ordner; change directory (CD)** = (in MS-DOS, OS/2 and UNIX) system command to move to a directory **change directory (CD); make directory (MD)** = (in MS-DOS and OS/2) system command to create a new directory on the disk **make directory (MD); remove directory (RD)** = (in MS-DOS and OS/2) system command to remove an empty directory from disk **remove directory (RD); root directory** = directory at the top of the directory tree structure **Stammverzeichnis; sub-directory** = directory within a directory **Unterverzeichnis, Unterordner;** *see also* TREE STRUCTURE

COMMENT: a directory is best imagined as a folder within a draw of a filing cabinet; the folder can contain files or other folders

dirty bit *noun* flag bit set by memory-resident programs (a utility *or* the operating system) to indicate that they have already been loaded into main memory **Kennbit**

disable *verb* to prevent a device *or* function from operating **ausschalten, sperren;** *he disabled the keyboard to prevent anyone changing the data;* **disable interrupt** = command to the CPU to ignore any interrupt signals **unwirksame Unterbrechung**

disarm *verb* to prevent an interrupt having any effect **desaktivieren; disarmed state** = state of an interrupt that has been disabled, and cannot accept a signal **Desaktivierung**

disassemble *verb* to translate machine code instructions back into assembly language mnemonics **rückassemblieren**

◊ **disassembler** *noun* software that translates a machine code program back into an assembly language form **Rückassemblierer, Disassembler**

disaster dump *noun* program and data dump just before *or* caused by a fatal error *or* system crash **Programm- und Datennotausdruck**

disc *noun* disc refers only to compact disc, magnetic media uses the spelling 'disk' **Disc;** *see* COMPACT DISC, DISK

discard *verb* to throw out something which is not needed **verwerfen**

disclose *verb* to reveal details of something which were supposed to be secret **enthüllen**

◊ **disclosure** *noun* act of telling details about something **Offenlegung**

disconnect *verb* to unplug *or* break a connection between two devices **trennen, abschalten;** *do not forget to disconnect the cable before moving the printer*

discrete *adjective* (values *or* events *or* energy *or* data) which occur in small individual units **diskret, einzeln;** *the data word is made up of discrete bits*

discretionary *adjective* which can be used if wanted *or* not used if not wanted **benutzerbestimmbar; discretionary hyphen** *or* **soft hyphen** = hyphen which is inserted to show that a word is broken (as at the end of a line), but which is not present when the word is written normally **weiches Trennungszeichen**

discrimination instruction *noun* conditional program instruction that directs control by providing the location of the next instruction to be executed (if a condition is met) **logische Entscheidung;** *see also* BRANCH, JUMP, CALL

dish aerial *noun* circular concave directional aerial used to pick up long distance transmissions **Parabolantenne;** *we use a dish aerial to receive signals from the satellite*

disjointed *adjective* (set of information *or* data) that has no common subject **unzusammenhängend**

disjunction *noun* logical function that produces a true output if any input is true **Disjunktion**

◊ **disjunctive search** *noun* search for data items that match at least one of a number of keys **disjunktive Suche**

disk *noun* flat circular plate coated with a

substance that is capable of being magnetized (data is stored on this by magnetizing selective sections to represent binary digits) **Platte; disk access** = operations required to read from or write to a magnetic disk, including device selection, sector and track address, movement of read/write head to the correct location, access location on disk **Plattenzugriff; disk-based (operating system)** = (operating system) held on floppy *or* hard disk **auf Platten basierend; disk cartridge** = protective case containing a removable hard disk **Plattenkassette; disk controller** = IC *or* circuits used to translate a request for data by the CPU into control signals for the disk drive (including motor control and access arm movement) **Plattensteuereinheit; disk-controller card** = add-on card that contains all the electronics and connectors to interface a disk drive to a CPU **Plattensteuereinheitskarte; disk crash** = fault caused by the read/write head touching the surface of the disk **Plattenabsturz; disk drive** = device that spins a magnetic disk and controls the position of the read/write head **Plattenlaufwerk; disk file** = number of related records *or* data items stored under one name on disk **Plattendatei; disk formatting** = initial setting up of a blank disk with track and sector markers and other control information **Plattenformatierung; disk index holes** = holes around the hub of a disk that provide rotational information to a disk controller *or* number of holes providing sector location indicators on a hard-sectored disk **Plattenindexlöcher; disk map** = display of the organization of data on a disk **Plattendarstellung; disk mirroring** *or* **duplexing** = data protection system in which all or part of a hard disk is duplicated onto another, separate, disk drive; any changes made to the data on the original drive are duplicated on the mirrored drive **Festplattenspiegelung, Festplattenduplizierung; disk operating system (DOS)** = section of the operating system software that controls disk and file management **DOS, Plattenbetriebssystem; MS disk operating system** *or* **Microsoft DOS (MS-DOS)** = popular DOS for microcomputers **MS-DOS; disk pack** = number of disks on a single hub, each with its own read/write head **Plattenstapel; disk sector** = smallest area on a magnetic disk that can be addressed by a computer **Plattensektor; disk storage** = using disks as a backing store **Plattenspeicher; disk track** = one of a series of (thin) concentric rings on a magnetic disk, which the read/write head

accesses and along which data is stored in separate sectors **Plattenspur; disk unit** = disk drive **Platteneinheit; backup disk** = disk which contains a copy of the information from other disks, as a security precaution **Datensicherungsplatte; fixed disk** = magnetic disk which cannot be removed from the disk drive **Festplatte; floppy disk** = small disk for storing information which can be removed from a computer **Diskette; hard disk** = solid disk which will store a large amount of computer information in a sealed case, and cannot usually be removed from the computer **Festplatte; optical disk** = disk which contains binary data in the form of small holes which are read by a laser beam (also called WORM (write one, read many) when used on computers) **optische Platte; Winchester disk** = hard disk with a large storage capacity sealed in a computer **Winchesterplatte**

COMMENT: the disk surface is divided into tracks and sectors which can be accessed individually; magnetic tapes cannot be accessed in this way

◊ **diskette** *noun* light, flexible disk that can store data in a magnetic form, used in most personal computers **Diskette**

◊ **diskless** *adjective* which does not use disks for data storage **plattenlos;** *diskless system; they want to create a diskless workstation*

disorderly close-down *noun* system crash that did not provide enough warning to carry out an orderly close-down **unplanmäßiger Abschluss**

dispatch *or* **despatch** *noun* action of sending material *or* information *or* messages to a location **Senden**

dispenser *noun* device which gives out something **Spender, Automat; cash dispenser** = device which gives money when a card is inserted and special instructions keyed in **Bargeldautomat**

dispersion *noun*
(a) separation of a beam of light into its different wavelengths **Dispersion, Streuung**
(b) logical function whose output is false if all inputs are true, and true if any input is false **NAND-Funktion**

displacement *noun* offset used in an indexed address **Distanz(adresse)**

display
1 *noun* device on which information *or*

images can be presented visually Datensichtgerät, Bildschirm; **display adapter** = device which allows information in a computer to be displayed on a CRT (the adapter interfaces with both the computer and CRT) **Bildschirmanschluss; display attribute** = variable which defines the shape *or* size *or* colour of text *or* graphics displayed **Bildschirmvariable; display character** = graphical symbol which appears as a printed *or* displayed item, such as one of the letters of the alphabet *or* a number **Zeichen auf dem Bildschirm; display character generator** = ROM that provides the display circuits with a pattern of dots which form the character **Zeichengenerator; display colour** = colour of characters in a (videotext) display system **Bildschirmfarbe; display controller** = device that accepts character *or* graphics codes and instructions, and converts them into dot-matrix patterns that are displayed on a screen **Bildschirmsteuereinheit; display format** = number of characters that can be displayed on a screen, given as row and column lengths **Bildschirmformat; display highlights** = emphasis of certain words *or* paragraphs by changing character display colour **Intensivanzeige; display line** = horizontal printing positions for characters in a line of text **Bildzeile; display mode** = way of referring to the character set to be used, usually graphics *or* alphanumerics **Anzeigemodus; display processor** = processor that changes data to a format suitable for a display controller **Bildschirmprozessor; display register** = register that contains character *or* control *or* graphical data that is to be displayed **Anzeigeregister; display resolution** = number of pixels per unit area that a display can clearly show **Bildschirmauflösung; display screen** = the physical part of a Visual Display Unit *or* terminal *or* monitor, which allows the user to see characters *or* graphics (usually a Cathode Ray Tube, but sometimes LCD *or* LED displays are used) **Bildschirm; display scrolling** = movement of a screenful of information up or down one line or pixel at a time **Bildschirmblättern; display size** = character size greater than 14 points, used in composition and headlines rather than normal text **Bildschirmgröße; display space** = memory *or* amount of screen available to show graphics *or* text **Darstellungsfläche; display unit** = computer terminal *or* piece of equipment that is capable of showing data *or* information, usually by means of CRT **Bildschirm; composite display** = video display unit that accepts a single composite

video signal and can display an infinite number of colours *or* shade of grey **Kombinationsbildschirm; digital display** = video display unit that can only show a fixed number of colours *or* shades of grey **Digitalanzeige; gas discharge** *or* **plasma** *or* **electroluminescent display** = flat lightweight display screen that is made up of two flat pieces of glass covered with a grid of conductors, separated by a thin layer of gas which luminesces when a point of the grid is selected by two electrical signals **Plasmabildschirm;** *see also* VISUAL DISPLAY UNIT

2 *verb* to show information **anzeigen;** *the customer's details were displayed on the screen; by keying HELP, the screen will display the options available to the user*

> QUOTE the review machine also came with a monochrome display card plugged into one of the expansion slots
> *Personal Computer World*

> QUOTE Barco Chromatics is to supply colour display monitors to the IBM/Siemens Plessey consortium, which is installing the New En Route Centre for air-traffic control.
> *Computing*

distant *adjective* which is located some way away **entfernt;** *the distant printers are connected with cables*

distinguish *verb* to tell the difference between two things **unterscheiden;** *the OCR has difficulty in distinguishing certain characters*

distort *verb* to introduce unwanted differences between a signal input and output from a device **verzerren**

◊ **distortion** *noun* unwanted differences in a signal before and after it has passed through a piece of equipment **Verzerrung; distortion optics** = special photographic lens used to produce a distorted image for special effects **Verzerrungsobjektiv; image distortion** = fault in an optical lens causing the image to be distorted **Bildverzerrung**

distribute *verb*
(a) to send out data *or* information to users in a network *or* system **verteilen; distributed adaptive routing** = directing messages in a packet network switching system by an exchange of information between nodes **verteilte adaptive Verkehrslenkung; distributed database system** = data system where the data is kept on different disks in

different places **verteiltes Datenbanksystem; distributed file system** = system that uses files stored in more than one location *or* backing store but are processed at a central point **verteiltes Dateisystem; distributed intelligence** = decentralized system in which a number of small micros *or* mini-computers carry out a set of fixed (tasks rather than one large computer) **verteilte Intelligenz; distributed (data) processing** = system of processing in a large organization with many small computers at different workstations instead of one central computer **verteilte Datenverarbeitung; distributed system** = computer system which uses more than one processor in different locations, all connected to a central computer **Verbundsystem**

◊ **distribution** *noun* act of sending information out, especially via a network **Verteilung; distribution network** *see* LAN, WAN; **distribution point** = point from which cable television *or* telephone signals are split up from a main line and sent to individual users' homes **Verzweigungseinrichtung**

QUOTE CORBA sets out a standard for how objects in applications, repositories or class libraries should make requests and receive responses across a distributed computing network
Computing

dither *verb* to create a curve or line that looks smoother by adding shaded pixels beside the pixels that make up the image **weichzeichnen, glätten**

dittogram *noun* printing error caused by repeating the same letter twice **Dittographie**

DIV = DATA IN VOICE digital satellite data transmission in place of a voice channel **Datenübertragung auf Sprachfrequenz**

divergence *noun* failure of light *or* particle beams to meet at a certain point **Abweichung, Divergenz**

diversity *noun* coming from more than one source; being aimed at more than one use **Vielfalt; beam diversity** = using a single frequency communications band for two different sets of data **Frequenzbandaufteilung**

diverter *noun* circuit *or* device that redirects a message *or* signal from one path or route to another **Umleiter; call diverter** = device which, on receiving a telephone call,

contacts another point and re-routes the call **Anrufumleiter**

divide *verb*
(a) to divide a number by four = to find out how many fours can be contained in the other number **eine Zahl durch vier teilen;** *twenty-one divided by three gives seven*
(b) to cut *or* to split into parts **trennen;** *in the hyphenation program, long words are automatically divided at the end of lines*

◊ **divider** *noun* **frequency divider** = circuit which divides the frequency of a signal by a certain amount to change the pitch **Frequenzteiler**

◊ **division** *noun* act of dividing **Division; Trennung**

dividend *noun* operand that is divided by a divisor in a division operation **Dividend**

COMMENT: the dividend is divided by the divisor to form the quotient and a remainder

divisor *noun* operand used to divide a dividend in a division operation **Divisor**

DLL = DYNAMIC LINK LIBRARY (in Microsoft Windows and OS/2) library of utility programs that can be called from a main program **DLL;** *the word-processor calls a spell-check program that is stored as a DLL;* **DLL file** = file containing a library of routines that can be used by another program **DLL-Datei**

DMA = DIRECT MEMORY ACCESS direct rapid link between a peripheral and a computer's main memory, which avoids the use of accessing routines for each item of data read **direkter Speicherzugriff; DMA controller** = interface IC that controls high-speed data transfer between a high-speed peripheral and main memory, usually the controller will also halt *or* cycle steal from the CPU **DMA-Controller; DMA cycle stealing** = CPU allowing the DMA controller to send data over the bus during clock cycles when it performs internal *or* NOP instructions **DMA-Zyklusraub**

QUOTE A 32-bit DMA controller, 16-bit video I/O ports and I/O filters complete the chip
Computing

DML = DATA MANIPULATION LANGUAGE

DMM = DIGITAL MULTIMETER

do-nothing (instruction) *noun*

programming instruction that does not carry out any action (except increasing the program counter to the next instruction address **Leerbefehl**

docket *noun (US)* record of an official proceeding **(Vorgehens)erklärung**

document
1 *noun* piece of paper with writing on it *or* file containing text **Schriftstück, Beleg; document assembly** *or* **document merge** = creating a new file by combining two or more sections *or* complete documents **Zusammenstellung eines Schriftstücks; document image processing (DIP)** = process of scanning paper documents, performing OCR on the contents and storing this on disk so that it can be searched for **Dokumentbildverarbeitung, Document Image Processing (DIP); document processing** = processing of documents (such as invoices) by a computer **Belegbearbeitung; document reader** = device which converts written *or* typed information to a form that a computer can understand and process **Beglleser; document recovery** = program which allows a document which has been accidentally deleted to be recovered **Belegwiederherstellung; document retrieval system** = information storage and retrieval system that contains complete documents rather than just quotes *or* references **System zum Dokumentenretrieval**
2 *verb* to write a description of a process **beschreiben**

◊ **documentation** *noun*
(a) all documents referring to something **Dokumentation;** *please send all documentation concerning the product*
(b) information, notes and diagrams that describe the function, use and operation of a piece of hardware *or* software **(Programm)unterlagen**
NOTE: no plural

dollar sign *noun* printed *or* written character ($) used in some languages to identify a variable as a string type **Dollarzeichen**

domain *noun* area *or* group of nodes in a network **Domäne; domain name system (DNS)** = distributed database used in an Internet system to map names to addresses **Domänenbezeichnungssystem, Domain Name System (DNS)**

domestic *adjective* referring to the home market *or* the market of the country where the business is based **Inlands-, Binnen-;** **domestic consumption** = consumption on the home market **Inlandskonsum; domestic market** = market in the country where a company is based **Binnenmarkt;** *they produce goods for the domestic market;* **domestic production** = production of goods for domestic consumption **Binnenproduktion; domestic satellite** = satellite used for television *or* radio transmission, rather than research *or* military applications **Radio- und Fernsehsatellit**

dongle *noun* coded circuit *or* chip that has to be present in a system before a piece of copyright software will run **Dongle, Key**

dope *verb* to introduce a dopant into a substance **dotieren**

◊ **dopant** *noun* chemical substance that is diffused *or* implanted onto the substrate of a chip during manufacture, to provide it with n- or p-type properties **Dotierungsstoff**

◊ **doped** *adjective* (chip) which has had a dopant added **dotiert**

◊ **doping** *noun* adding of dopant to a chip **Dotierung**

DOR = DIGITAL OPTICAL READING recording signals in binary form as small holes in the surface of an optical *or* compact disk which can then be read by laser **digitales optisches Lesen**

DOS = DISK OPERATING SYSTEM section of the operating system software, that controls the disk and file access **DOS, Plattenbetriebssystem;** *boot up the DOS after you switch on the PC;* **DR-DOS ™** = operating system developed by Digital Research for the IBM PC **DR-DOS ™; MS-DOS ™** = operating system developed by Microsoft for the IBM PC **MS-DOS ™**

dot *noun* small round spot **Punkt; dot command** = method of writing instructions with a full stop followed by the command, used mainly for embedded commands in word-processor systems **Punktbefehl; dot matrix** = forming characters by use of dots inside a rectangular matrix **Punktmatrix; dots per inch** *or* **d.p.i.** *or* **dpi** = standard method used to describe the resolution capabilities of a page printer *or* scanner **Punkte pro Inch;** *some laser printers offer high resolution printing: 400 dpi*

◊ **dot-matrix printer** *noun* printer in which the characters are made up by a series of closely spaced dots (it produces a page line by line; a dot-matrix printer can be used either for printing using a ribbon *or* for thermal *or* electrostatic printing) **Matrixdrucker**

> QUOTE the characters are formed from an array of dots like in a dot-matrix printer, except that much higher resolution is used
>
> *Practical Computing*

> QUOTE Star predicts that 500,000 customers will buy a dot-matrix printer in the UK in the next 12 months.
>
> *Computing*

double *adjective* twice; twice as large; twice the size **doppelt; double buffering** = use of two buffers, allowing one to be read while the other is being written to **doppelte Pufferung; double-click** = to click twice, rapidly, on a mouse button to start an action **doppelklicken;** *move the pointer to the icon then start the program with a double-click;* **double dagger** = typeset character used as a second reference mark **Doppelkreuz; double density** = system to double the storage capacity of a disk drive by doubling the number of bits which can be put on the disk surface **doppelte Speicherkapazität; double-density disk** = disk that can store two bits of data per unit area, compared to a standard disk **Platte mit doppelter Speicherkapazität; double document** = error in photographing documents for microfilm, where the same image appears consecutively **Doublette, Doppelbild; double ended queue (deque)** = queue in which new items can be added to either end **nach beiden Seiten offene Warteschlange; double exposure** = two images exposed on the same piece of photographic film, usually used for special effects **Doppelbelichtung; double-length** *or* **double precision arithmetic** = use of two data words to store a number, providing greater precision **Rechnen mit doppelter Stellenzahl; double sideband** = modulation technique whose frequency spectrum contains two modulated signals above and below the unmodulated carrier frequency **doppeltes Seitenband; double-sided disk** = disk which can store information on both sides **beidseitig beschreibbare Platte; double-sided disk drive** = disk drive which can access data on double-sided disks **doppelseitiges Plattenlaufwerk; double-sided printed circuit board** = circuit board with conducting tracks on both sides **beidseitig gedruckte Schaltkarte; double-sided suppressed carrier (DSBSC)** = modulation technique that uses two modulated signal sidebands, but no carrier signal **beidseitig unterdrückter Träger; double word** = two bytes of data handled as one word, often used for address data **Doppelwort**

doublet *or* **dyad** *noun* word made up of two bits **Diade, Zwei-Bit-Byte**

down *adverb (of computers or programs)* not working **ausgefallen;** *the computer system went down twice during the afternoon;* **down stroke** = wide heavy section of a character written with an ink pen **Abstrich; down time** = period of time during which a computer system is not working *or* usable **Ausfallzeit** (NOTE: opposite is **up**)

download *verb* (i) to load a program *or* section of data from a remote computer via a telephone line; (ii) to load data from a mainframe to a small computer; (iii) to send printer font data stored on a disk to a printer (where it will be stored in temporary memory *or* RAM) **(i) fernladen; (ii) hinunterladen; (iii) Zeichensätze laden;** *there is no charge for downloading public domain software from the BBS*

◊ **downloadable** *adjective* which can be downloaded **fernladbar, hinunterladbar; downloadable fonts** = fonts *or* typefaces stored on a disk, which can be downloaded *or* sent to a printer and stored in temporary memory *or* RAM **zusätzlich ladbare Zeichensätze, Downloadfonts**

> QUOTE The cards will also download the latest version of the network drivers from the server.
>
> *Computing*

downsize *verb* to move a company from a computer system based around a central mainframe computer to a networked environment (usually using PCs as workstations) in which the workstations are intelligent **downsizen;** *downsizing is more cost effective and gives more processing power to the end-user*

downward *adjective* towards a lower position **abwärts; downward compatibility** = ability of a complex computer system to work with a simple computer **Abwärtskompatibilität;** *the mainframe is downward compatible with the micro*

dp *or* **DP** = DATA PROCESSING operating on data to produce useful information *or* to sort and organize data files **DV, Datenverarbeitung**

DPA = DEMAND PROTOCOL ARCHITECTURE technique of loading protocol stacks in memory only if they are required for a particular session **DPA**; *see also* PROTOCOL STACK

d.p.i. *or* **dpi** = DOTS PER INCH standard method used to describe the resolution capabilities of a dot-matrix *or* laser printer *or* scanner **Punkte pro Inch**; *a 300 d.p.i. black and white A4 monitor; a 300 dpi image scanner*

‖ COMMENT: 300 d.p.i. is the normal industry standard for a laser printer

DPM = DATA PROCESSING MANAGER

draft
1 *noun* rough copy of a document before errors have been corrected **Entwurf; draft printing** = low quality, high speed printing **Drucken mit geringerer Druckqualität**
2 *verb* to make a rough copy *or* drawing **einen Entwurf machen, entwerfen**; *he drafted out the details of the program on a piece of paper*

drag *verb* to move (a mouse) with a control key pressed, so moving an image on screen **(ver)schieben**; *you can enlarge a frame by clicking inside its border and dragging to the position wanted;* **drag and drop** = to drag a section of text *or* icon *or* object onto another program icon which starts this program and inserts the data **ziehen und ablegen**; *drag and drop the document icon onto the word-processor icon and the system will start the program and load the document*

QUOTE press the mouse button and drag the mouse: this produces a dotted rectangle on the screen

QUOTE you can easily enlarge the frame by dragging from any of the eight black rectangles round the border, showing that it is selected
Desktop Publishing

drain
1 *noun* electrical current provided by a battery *or* power supply connection to a FET **Drain(strom)** ⇨APPENDIX
2 *verb* to remove *or* decrease power *or* energy from a device such as a battery **Strom entnehmen**

DRAM = DYNAMIC RANDOM ACCESS MEMORY

QUOTE cheap bulk memory systems are always built from DRAMs
Electronics & Power

DR-DOS operating system for the IBM PC developed by Digital Research **DR-DOS**

D-region *noun* section of the ionosphere 50-90km above the earth's surface **D-Schicht der Ionosphäre**; *the D-region is the main cause of attenuation in transmitted radio signals*

drift *noun* changes in the characteristics of a circuit with time *or* changing temperature **Drift, Abwanderung**

drive
1 *noun* part of a computer which operates a tape *or* disk **Laufwerk; drive letter** *or* **designator** = letter that denotes the disk drive currently being used; A and B are normally floppy disks, C is normally the hard disk in a personal computer **Laufwerksbuchstabe; disk drive** = device which spins a magnetic disk and controls the position of the read/write head **Plattenlaufwerk; tape drive** = mechanism that carries magnetic tape over the drive heads **Bandlaufwerk**
2 *verb* to make a tape *or* disk work **antreiben**; *the disk is driven by a motor*

◊ **driven** *adjective* operated by something **angetrieben; control driven** = computer architecture where instructions are executed once a control sequence has been received **kontrollgesteuert; event-driven** = computer program *or* process where each step of the execution relies on external actions **ereignisgesteuert**

driver *or* **device driver** *or* **device handler** *noun* program *or* routine used to interface and manage an input/output device *or* other peripheral **Treiber; printer driver** = dedicated software that controls and formats users' commands ready for a printer **Druckertreiber**

DRO = DESTRUCTIVE READOUT form of storage medium that loses its data after it has been read **löschendes Auslesen**

drop *noun* fall to a lower position **abfallen, hinunterfallen; drop cable** = section of cable that links an adapter fitted in a workstation to the main network cable (sometimes to a transceiver or T-connector in the main network cable) **Zuführungskabel; drop cap** = first letter in a sentence, printed in a larger typeface than the rest of the sentence **Initiale (in einer großen Schriftgröße); drop dead halt** *or* **dead halt** = program instruction from the user *or* an error that causes the program to stop without allowing recovery **von außen**

herbeigeführte Programmunterbrechung; **drop-down list box** = list of options for an entry that appears when you move the cursor to the entry field **Einblendliste, Dropdownliste; drop-down menu** = menu that appears below a menu title when it is selected **Einblendmenü, Dropdownmenü; drop line** = cable television line, running from a feeder cable to a users home **Stichleitung**

◊ **drop in** *noun* small piece of dirt that is on a disk *or* tape surface, which does not allow data to be recorded on that section **Störsignal**

◊ **drop out** *noun*
(a) failure of a small piece of tape *or* disk to be correctly magnetized for the accurate storage of data **Ausfall**
(b) loss of transmitted signals due to attenuation *or* noise **Signalausfall**

drum *noun* early type of magnetic computer storage **Trommelspeicher; magnetic drum** = cylindrical magnetic storage device **Magnettrommelspeicher; drum plotter** = computer output device that consists of a movable pen and a piece of paper around a drum that can be rotated, creating patterns and text when both are moved in various ways **Trommelplotter**

dry cell *noun* battery that cannot be recharged **Trockenelement;** *compare with* RECHARGEABLE BATTERY

◊ **dry circuit** *noun* voice signal transmitting circuit that contains no DC signals *or* levels **trockener Schaltkreis**

◊ **dry contact** *noun* faulty electrical connection, often causing an intermittent fault **trockener Kontakt**

◊ **dry joint** *noun* faulty *or* badly made electrical connection **trockene Verbindung**

◊ **dry run** *noun* running a program with test data to check everything works **Probelauf**

DSBSC = DOUBLE SIDEBAND SUPPRESSED CARRIER

DSE = DATA SWITCHING EXCHANGE

DSP = DIGITAL SIGNAL PROCESSING special integrated circuit used to manipulate digital signals **DSP**

DSR = DATA SET READY signal from a device that it is ready to accept data, this signal occurs after a DTR signal is received **Betriebsbereitschaft (zum Empfang)**

DSW = DEVICE STATUS WORD data word transmitted from a device that contains information about its current status **Einheitenstatuswort**

DTE = DATA TERMINAL EQUIPMENT device at which a communications path starts *or* finishes **Datenendeinrichtung**

DTMF = DUAL TONE MULTI-FREQUENCY method of dialling in a telephone system in which each number on the telephone handset generates a tone **Mehrfrequenzwählverfahren (MWV), Tonwahl;** *compare with* PULSE DIALLING

DTP = DESKTOP PUBLISHING the design, layout and printing of documents using special software, a desktop computer and a printer **Desktop publishing, Publizieren am Schreibtisch**

DTR = DATA TERMINAL READY signal from a device that indicates that it is ready to send data **Betriebsbereitschaft (zum Senden)**

D-type connector *noun* connector that is shaped like an elongated letter D, which prevents the connector being plugged in upside down **D-Stecker;** *the serial port on a PC uses a 9-pin D-type connector*

dual *adjective* using two *or* a pair **doppelt; dual attachment station (DAS)** = (in an FDDI system) station that allows two connections to the FDDI ring **DAS, Dual Attachment Station; dual channel** = two separate audio recording paths, as found in stereo equipment **Zweikanalsystem; dual clocking** = multiplexed data, each set of data is available and valid on a different clock pulse *or* edge **doppelte Taktgabe; dual column** = two separate parallel lists of information **Doppelreihe; dual-in-line package (DIL** *or* **DIP)** = standard layout for integrated circuit packages using two parallel rows of connecting pins along each edge **Doppelreihengehäuse, DIL-Gehäuse; dual port memory** = memory with two sets of data and memory lines to allow communications between CPUs **Dual-Port-Speicher; dual processor** = computer system with two processors for faster program execution **Dualprozessor(system); dual systems** = two computer systems, working in parallel on the same data, with the same instructions, to ensure high reliability **Doppelsystem; dual tone multi-frequency (DTMF)** = method of dialling in a telephone system in which each number on the telephone handset generates a tone **Mehrfrequenzwählverfahren (MWV), Tonwahl;** *compare with* PULSE DIALLING

dub *verb* to add sound to a film after the film has been shot (usually to add a sound version in another language) **synchronisieren; dubbed sound** = sound effects added after the film has been shot **einsynchronisierter Toneffekt**

◊ **dubbing** *noun* action of adding sound to a film after the film has been shot **Synchronisation**

duct *noun* pipe containing cables, providing a tidy and protective surrounding for a group of cables **Kabelkanal**

dumb terminal *noun* peripheral that can only transmit and receive data from a computer, but is not capable of processing data **nichtprogrammierbare Datenstation;** *compare* INTELLIGENT TERMINAL

dummy *noun* imitation product to test the reaction of potential customers to its design **Versuchsmuster; dummy instruction** = instruction in a program that is only there to satisfy language syntax *or* to make up a block length **leere Anweisung; dummy variable** = variable set up to satisfy the syntax of a language, but which is replaced when the program is executed **Scheinvariable**

dump
1 *noun* (i) data which has been copied from one device to another for storage; (ii); *(US)* printout of the contents of all *or* selected data in memory (i) **Sicherungskopie;** (ii) **Speicherauszug; binary dump** = sections of memory dumped onto another medium *or* printed out in binary form **binärer Speicherauszug; change dump** = printout of all the locations whose contents have been changed during a program run **Speicherauszug der Änderungen; dump and restart** = software that will stop a program execution, dump any relevant data or program status then restart the program **ausgeben und neu anfangen; dump point** = point in a program where the program and its data are saved onto backing store to minimize the effects of any future faults **Speicherauszugspunkt; screen dump** = outputting the text *or* graphics displayed on a screen to a printer **Bildschirmausdruck**
2 *verb* to move data from one device *or* storage area to another **kopieren;** *the account results were dumped to the backup disk*

duodecimal number system *noun* number system with a radix of twelve **Duodezimalsystem**

duplex *noun*
(a) photographic paper that is light sensitive on both sides **Duplexpapier**
(b) simultaneous transmission of two signals on one line **Duplexübertragung; duplex circuit** = electronic circuit used to transmit data in two directions simultaneously **Gegenverkehrsverbindung; duplex computer** = two identical computer systems used in an on-line application, with one used as a backup in case of failure of the other **Duplexsystem; duplex operation** = transmission of data in two directions simultaneously **Duplexbetrieb;** *see also* HALF-DUPLEX, FULL DUPLEX, SIMPLEX

duplicate
1 *noun* copy **Duplikat, Zweitschrift, Kopie;** *he sent me the duplicate of the contract;* **duplicate receipt** *or* **duplicate of a receipt** = copy of a receipt **Quittungsduplikat; in duplicate** = with a copy in **doppelter Ausfertigung; receipt in duplicate** = two copies of a receipt **Quittung in doppelter Ausfertigung;** *to print an invoice in duplicate*
2 *verb* to copy **kopieren; to duplicate a letter** = to make a copy of a letter **einen Brief kopieren**

◊ **duplicating** *noun* copying **Kopieren; duplicating machine** = machine which makes copies of documents **Kopierer; duplicating paper** = special paper to be used in a duplicating machine **Kopierpapier**

◊ **duplication** *noun* copying of documents **Vervielfältigung; duplication of work** = work which is done twice without being necessary **Arbeitswiederholung**

◊ **duplicator** *noun* machine which produces multiple copies from a master **Vervielfältiger; duplicator paper** = absorbent paper used in a duplicator **Umdruckpapier**

durable *adjective* which will not be destroyed easily **dauerhaft;** *durable cartridge*

duration *noun* length of time for which something lasts **Dauer; pulse duration modulation (PDM)** = pulse modulation where the pulse width depends on the input signal **Impulsdauermodulation**

dustcover *noun* protective cover for a machine **Abdeckhaube**

duty-rated *adjective* referring to the

maximum number of operations which a device can perform in a set time to a certain specification **bezogen auf die Nutzleistung**

QUOTE the laser printer can provide letter-quality print on ordinary cut-sheet paper and is duty-rated at up to 3,000 pages per month

Minicomputer News

DUV = DATA UNDER VOICE data transmission in a frequency range or channel lower than that of a human voice **Datenübertragung unter Sprachfrequenz**

DV-I = DIGITAL VIDEO INTERACTIVE system that defines how video and audio signals should be compressed and displayed on a computer **DV-I**

DVORAK keyboard *noun* keyboard layout that is more efficient to use than a normal QWERTY keyboard layout **DVORAK-Tastatur**

dyadic operation *noun* binary operation using two binary operands **dyadische Operation**

dye-polymer recording *noun* (in optical disks) recording method which creates minute changes in a thin layer of dye imbedded in the plastic optical disk; dye-polymer recording has one big advantage - that the data stored on the optical disk using this method can be erased **Farbpolymeraufzeichnung**

◊ **dye-sublimation printer** *noun* high-quality colour printer that produces images by squirting tiny drops of coloured ink onto paper **Farbsublimationsdrucker;** *the new dye-sublimation printer can produce colour images at a resolution of 300dpi*

dynamic *adjective* referring to data which can change with time **dynamisch; dynamic allocation** = system where resources are allocated during a program run, rather than being determined in advance **dynamische Zuteilung; dynamic buffer** = buffer whose size varies with demand **dynamische Puffer; dynamic data structure** = structure of a data management system which can be changed or adapted **dynamische Datenstruktur; dynamic dump** =dump that is carried out periodically during a program run **dynamischer Speicherauszug; dynamic memory** or **dynamic RAM** = random access memory that requires its contents to be updated regularly **dynamischer Speicher; dynamic**

microphone = microphone using a coil that moves and induces a voltage according to sound pressure **dynamisches Mikrophon; dynamic multiplexing** = time division multiplexing method which allocates time segments to signals according to demand **dynamische Multiplexmethode; dynamic range** = range of softest to loudest sounds that a device or instrument can produce **Lautstärkeumfang, Aussteuerbereich; dynamic relocation (program)** = program that is moved from one section of memory to another during its run-time without affecting it or its data **dynamische Verschiebung; dynamic routing** = process of selecting the shortest or most reliable path for data through exchanges at the time of the connection **dynamische Weiterleitung; dynamic stop** = stop in a process where the system tells the user that some action must be taken before the processing will continue **bedingter Programmstop; dynamic storage allocation** = to allocate memory to a program when it needs it rather than reserving a block before it has run **dynamische Speicherplatzzuordnung; dynamically redefinable character set** = computer or videotext character set that can be changed when required **dynamisch neu definierbarer Zeichensatz; dynamic subroutine** = subroutine whose function must be defined each time it is called **dynamisches Unterprogramm;** *compare* STATIC

◊ **dynamic data exchange (DDE)** *noun* (in Microsoft Windows and OS/2) method in which two active programs can exchange data; one program asks the operating system to create a link between the two programs **dynamischer Datenaustausch, DDE**

◊ **dynamic link library (DLL)** (in Microsoft Windows and OS/2) library of utility programs that can be called from a main program **dynamische Verknüpfungsbibliothek, DLL;** *the word-processor calls a spell-check program that is stored as a DLL*

Ee

E hexadecimal number equivalent to decimal number 14 **E**

e-mail = ELECTRONIC MAIL

EAN = EUROPEAN ARTICLE NUMBER numbering system for bar codes (European version of UPC) **EAN (Europäische Artikelnummer bei Streifencodes)**

EAPROM = ELECTRICALLY ALTERABLE PROGRAMMABLE READ-ONLY MEMORY version of EAROM which can be programmed **EAPROM (elektrisch veränderbarer, programmierbarer Festwertspeicher)**

early token release *noun* (in a Token-Ring or FDDI network) system that allows two tokens to be present on a ring network, useful when traffic is very busy **frühzeitige Tokenfreigabe**

EAROM = ELECTRICALLY ALTERABLE READ-ONLY MEMORY

earth
1 *noun*
(a) the planet on which we live **Erde; earth coverage** = area of the earth's surface able to pick up a satellite's transmissions **Empfangsbereich; earth station** = dish antenna and circuitry used to communicate with a satellite **Bodenstation**
(b) connection in a circuit representing zero potential **Erde;** *all loose wires should be tied to earth;* **earth wire** = connecting wire between an electrical device and the earth, representing zero potential **Erdung**
2 *verb* to connect an electrical device to the earth **erden;** *all appliances must be earthed*
NOTE: US English is **ground**

easy-to-use *adjective* that is simple to understand and operate **einfach zu benutzen**

> QUOTE it is a really easy-to-use, menu-driven program that allows you to produce presentation quality graphics with little or no training
> *Soft*

EAX = ELECTRONIC AUTOMATIC EXCHANGE

EBCDIC = EXTENDED BINARY CODED DECIMAL INTERCHANGE CODE eight bit binary character coding system **EBCDIC-Code**

EBNF = EXTENDED BACKUS-NAUR FORM more flexible way of defining the syntax of a language **EBNF (erweiterte Backus-Naur-Form);** *see also* BNF

EBR = ELECTRON BEAM RECORDING (i) production of microfilm images by means of an electron beam; (ii) recording the output from a computer directly onto microfilm using an electron beam (i) & (ii) **Elektronenstrahlaufzeichnung(smethode)**

echo
1 *noun* return of a signal back to the source from which it was transmitted **Echo; echo chamber** = acoustic *or* electronic device used to increase the echo of a sound **Hallraum; echo check** = each character received at a terminal is returned to the transmitter and checked to ensure accurate data transmission **Echoprüfung; echo suppressor** = device used on long-distance speech lines to prevent echoing effects **Echosperre**
2 *verb* to return a received signal along the same transmission path **widerhallen**

ECL = EMITTER COUPLED LOGIC high-speed logic circuit design using the emitters of the transistors as output connections to other stages **emittergekoppelte Logik**

ECMA = EUROPEAN COMPUTER MANUFACTURERS ASSOCIATION; **ECMA symbols** = standard set of symbols used to draw flowcharts **Normen der ECMA (Zusammenschluss europäischer Computerhersteller)**

EDAC = ERROR DETECTION AND CORRECTION forward error correction system for data communications **Fehlererkennung und -korrektur**

edge *noun* side of a flat object *or* signal *or* clock pulse **Kante, Rand; edge board** *or* **card** = printed circuit board that has a series of contact strips along one edge allowing it to be inserted into an edge connector **gedruckte Schaltungen; edge connector** = long connector with a slot containing metal contacts to allow it to make electrical contact with an edge card **Randstecker; edge detection** = algorithm and routines used in image recognition to define the edges of an object **Randauswertung; edge notched card** = paper card which has punched holes along an edge to represent data **Kerblochkarte; edge-triggered** = process *or* circuit which is clocked *or* synchronized by the changing level (edge) of a clock signal rather than the level itself **taktflankengesteuert**

> QUOTE Connections to the target board are made via IC test clips or the edge connector
> *Electronics Today*

EDI = ELECTRONIC DATA INTERCHANGE system of sending orders, paying invoices or transferring company information over a network or telephone line using an electronic mail system; often used to send instructions to pay money direct from one company to another, or from one bank to a company **elektronischer Datenaustausch**

edit verb to change, correct and modify text or programs **aufbereiten, edieren; edit commands** = sequence of characters or keys that must be pressed to accomplish a function in an editor **EDIT-Befehle; edit key** = key that starts a function that makes an editor easier to use **EDIT-Taste**; there are several special edit keys - this one will reformat the text; **edit window** = area of the screen in which the user can display and edit text or graphics **EDIT-Fenster; editing plan** = detailed plan of how a film or TV programme is to be edited before being shown **Schnittliste; editing run** = processing to check that new data meets certain requirements before actually analysing the data and its implications **Aufbereitungslauf; editing symbol** = character on microfilm to aid positioning, cutting and editing of the frames **Aufbereitungssymbol; editing terms** = command words and instruction sequences used when editing **EDIT-Befehle; linkage editing** = combining separate programs together, and standardizing the calls and references within them **Binderprogramm, Linkage-Editierung**

◊ **edition** noun all the copies of a book or newspaper printed at one time **Auflage;** the second edition has had some changes to the text; did you see the late edition of the evening paper?

◊ **editor** noun
(a) person who edits a film or book **Editor, Herausgeber**
(b) editor program = software that allows the user to select sections of a file and alter, delete or add to them **EDITOR, Textaufbereitungsprogramm; line editor** = software in which only one line of a source program can be edited at a time **Zeileneditor; text editor** = piece of software used to enter and correct text or modify programs under development **Texteditor**
(c) person in charge of a newspaper or a section of a newspaper **Chefredakteur;** the editor of "The Times"; the paper's computer editor

◊ **editorial**
1 adjective referring to an editor or to editing **redaktionell, Redaktions-;** editorial

processing centre = number of small publishers that share a single computer to provide cheaper computing power **Redaktionstextverarbeitungszentrale**
2 noun main article in a newspaper, written by the editor **Leitartikel**

QUOTE an object orientated graphics editor enables you to add text to graphics
Byte

QUOTE while it has many formatting facilities, it does not include an editor with which to create the template for the report
Personal Computer World

QUOTE The Smartbook authoring system is a software product that integrates text and fractally compressed images, using any word-processor line editor
Computing

EDLIN (in MS-DOS) system utility that allows a user to make changes to a file on a line-by-line basis **EDLIN**

EDP = ELECTRONIC DATA PROCESSING data processing using computers and electronic devices **EDV; EDP capability** = word processor that is able to carry out certain data processing functions **Leistungen eines Datenverarbeitungssystems** NOTE: **EDP** is more common in US English

EDS = EXCHANGEABLE DISK STORAGE disk drive using removable disk pack (as opposed to a fixed disk) **auswechselbarer Plattenspeicher**

educational adjective referring to education; which is used to teach **Bildungs-, Erziehungs-, Lehr-; educational TV** = television programme that is in some way educational **Bildungsprogramm (im Fernsehen)**

EEMS = ENHANCED EXPANDED MEMORY SYSTEM (in an IBM PC) development of EMS; standard method of expanding the main memory fitted into a PC **EEMS;** see also EMS

EEPROM = ELECTRICALLY ERASABLE PROGRAMMABLE READ-ONLY MEMORY

EEROM = ELECTRICALLY ERASABLE READ-ONLY MEMORY

QUOTE conventional EEPROM requires two transistors to store each bit of data
Electronics & Power

effective *adjective* which can be used to produce a certain result **effektiv, wirkungsvoll; effective address** = address resulting from the modification of an address **effektive Adresse; effective bandwidth** = usable frequency range of a system **effektive Bandbreite; effective instruction** = the resulting instruction executed after the modification of an original instruction **endgültiger Befehl; effective search speed** = rate of finding a particular section of information from a storage device **tatsächliche Suchgeschwindigkeit; effective throughput** = average throughput of a processor **effektive Verarbeitungsmenge**

◊ **effective aperture** *noun*
(a) received signal power at the output of an aerial **effektive Apertur**
(b) lens aperture after taking into account camera faults and lens defects **effektive Öffnung**

| COMMENT: the effective aperture is measured as the ratio of focal length of the lens to the diameter of the diaphragm

efficient *adjective* which works well **leistungsfähig;** *the program is highly efficient at sorting files*

◊ **efficiently** *adverb* in an efficient way **leistungsfähig;** *the word-processing package has produced a series of labelled letters very efficiently*

◊ **efficiency** *noun* working well **Leistungsfähigkeit;** *he is doubtful about the efficiency of the new networking system*

EFT = ELECTRONIC FUNDS TRANSFER (SYSTEM) system where computers are used to transmit money to and from banks **elektronischer Zahlungsverkehr**

◊ **EFTPOS** = ELECTRONIC FUNDS TRANSFER POINT-OF-SALE terminal at a POS that is linked to a central computer which automatically transfers money from the customer's account to the shop's **elektronische Kasse**

EGA = ENHANCED GRAPHICS ADAPTER popular microcomputer high-resolution colour display standardized system **EGA (erweiterte Graphikkarte)**

EHF = EXTREMELY HIGH FREQUENCY radio frequencies from 30 - 300GHz **(extremhohe) Frequenz zwischen 30GHz und 300GHz**

EIA = ELECTRONIC INDUSTRY ASSOCIATION; **EIA interface** = standard defining interface signals, transmission rate and power, usually used to connect terminals to modems **Schnittstellennorm des Elektronikindustrieverbandes**

eight-bit (system) *noun* referring to an (old) small, low cost, low power home computer in which the CPU can process eight-bit words **8-Bit-System; eight-bit byte** *or* **octet** = byte made up of eight binary digits **Acht-Bit-Byte, Oktett;** *compare with* SIXTEEN, THIRTY-TWO BIT

◊ **eight-inch disk** *noun* high-capacity floppy disk which is eight inches in diameter **8-Zoll-Diskette; eight-inch drive** = disk drive for a eight-inch disk **8-Zoll-Laufwerk**

◊ **eighty-column screen** *noun* screen that can display eighty characters horizontally **80-Spalten-Bildschirm**

◊ **eighty-track disk** *noun* disk formatted to contain eighty tracks **Platte mit 80 Spuren**

EIS = EXECUTIVE INFORMATION SYSTEM easy-to-use software providing information to a manager or executive about his company **EIS;** *the EIS software is very easy to use; with this EIS software, we can see how every part of the company performs*

EISA = ELECTRONICS INDUSTRY STANDARDS ASSOCIATION group of PC manufacturers who formed an association to promote a 32-bit expansion bus standard as a rival to the MCA bus standard from IBM **EISA**

| COMMENT: the EISA expansion bus standard is backwards compatible with the older ISA standard of expansion cards, but also features 32-bit data path and allows bus mastering.

either-or operation *noun* logical function that produces a true output if any input is true **ODER-Funktion**

◊ **either-way operation** *noun* data transmission in one direction at a time over a bidirectional channel **wechselseitige Datenübermittlung**

elapsed time *noun* time taken by the user to carry out a task on a computer **Gesamtverarbeitungszeit**

elastic banding *noun* method of defining the limits of an image on a computer screen by stretching a boundary around it **elastische Grenzen**

◊ **elastic buffer** *noun* buffer size that changes according to demand **elastischer Puffer**

electret *noun* piece of dielectric that keeps an electronic charge after a voltage has been applied at manufacture **(Ferro)dielektrikum; electret microphone** = microphone using a section of dielectric as a transducer that provides an electric signal with varying sound pressure **Elektretmikrophon**

electric *adjective* worked by electricity **elektrisch; electric current** = mass movement of electric charge in a conductor **elektrischer Strom; electric charge** = a number of atoms that are charged (due to excess *or* deficiency of electrons) **elektrische Ladung; electric typewriter** = typewriter whose keys are switches which control motors and solenoids to perform all the functions **elektrische Schreibmaschine**

◊ **electrical** *adjective* referring to electricity **elektrisch, Elektro-;** *the engineers are trying to repair an electrical fault*

◊ **electrically** *adverb* referring to electricity **elektrisch;** *an electrically-powered motor;* **electrically alterable, programmable read-only memory (EAPROM)** = version of EAROM that can be programmed **EAPROM (elektrisch veränderbarer, programmierbarer Festwertspeicher); electrically alterable read-only memory (EAROM)** = read-only memory chip whose contents can be programmed by applying a certain voltage to a write pin, and can be erased by light *or* a reverse voltage **EAROM (elektrisch veränderbarer Festwertspeicher); electrically erasable programmable read-only memory (EEPROM)** = ROM storage chip which can be programmed and erased using an electrical signal **EEPROM (elektrisch löschbarer, programmierbarer Festwertspeicher); electrically erasable read-only memory (EEROM)** = EAROM

memory chip whose contents can be programmed by applying a certain voltage to a write pin, and can be erased by light *or* a reverse voltage **EEROM (elektrisch löschbarer Festwertspeicher)**

electricity *noun* electric current used to provide light *or* heat *or* power **Elektrizität;** *the electricity was cut off, and the computers crashed electricity prices are an important factor in the production costs*

electrode *noun* part of an electric circuit *or* device that collects, controls or emits electrons **Elektrode**

electrographic printer *noun* *see* ELECTROSTATIC PRINTER

electroluminescence *noun* light emitted from a phosphor dot when it is struck by an electron *or* charged particle **Elektrolumineszenz**

◊ **electroluminescing** *adjective* (object) which is emitting light due to electroluminescence **elektrolumineszierend**

◊ **electroluminescent** *adjective* capable of emitting light due to electroluminescence **elektrolumineszent;** *the screen coating is electroluminescent;* **electroluminescent display** = flat, lightweight display screen that is made up of two pieces of glass covered with a grid of conductors, separated by a thin layer of gas which luminesces when a point of the grid is selected by two electric signals **Elektrolumineszenzanzeige**

electromagnet *noun* device that consists of a core and a coil of wire that produces a magnetic field when current is passed through the coil **Elektromagnet**

◊ **electromagnetic** *adjective* generating a magnetic field *or* magnetic effect when supplied with electrical power **elektromagnetisch; electromagnetic interference** = corruption of data due to nearby electrically generated magnetic fields **elektromagnetische Störung; electromagnetic spectrum** = frequency range of electromagnetic radiation (from light to radio wave) **elektromagnetisches Spektrum**

◊ **electromagnetically** *adverb* working due to electromagnetic effects **elektromagnetisch**

◊ **electromagnetic radiation** *noun* energy wave consisting of electric and/or magnetic fields **elektromagnetische Strahlung**

COMMENT: electromagnetic radiation requires no medium to support it, travels approximately at the speed of light and can support frequency ranges from light to radio waves

electromechanical switching *noun* connection of two paths by an electrically operated switch *or* relay **elektromechanische Schaltung**

electromotive force (EMF) *noun* difference in electrical potential across a source of electric current **elektromotorische Kraft (EMK)**

electron *noun* elementary particle with an elementary negative charge **Elektron;** **electron beam** = narrow, focussed stream of electrons moving at high speed in the same direction (often in a vacuum) **Elektronenstrahl;** *the electron beam draws the image on the inside of a CRT screen;* **electron beam recording (EBR)** = (i) production of microfilm images by means of an electron beam; (ii) recording the output from a computer directly onto microfilm using an electron beam **(i) & (ii) Elektronenstrahlaufzeichnung(smethode);** **electron gun** = part of a CRT that produces a beam of electrons **Elektronenkanone**

COMMENT: mass of 9.109 x 10^{-31}kg, and charge of 1.602 x 10^{-19}C

electronic *adjective* referring to something which is controlled by *or* controls electron flow **elektronisch;** **electronic automatic exchange** = telephone routing system that uses electronic circuits to switch signals **elektronische Wählvermittlungsstelle;** **electronic blackboard** = means of transmitting handwritten text and diagrams over a telephone line **elektronische Anzeigetafel;** **electronic composition** = text manipulation by computer before typesetting **elektronischer Schriftsatz;** **electronic data interchange (EDI)** = system of sending orders, paying invoices or transferring company information over a network *or* telephone line using an electronic mail system; often used to send instructions to pay money direct from one company to another, or from one bank to a company **elektronischer Datenaustausch;** **electronic data processing (EDP)** = data processing using computers and electronic devices **elektronische Datenverarbeitung (EDV);** **electronic data processing capability** =

ability of a word processor to carry out certain data processing functions **Leistungen eines Datenverarbeitungssystems;** **electronic digital computer** = digital computer constructed with electronic components (the basic form uses a CPU, main memory, backing storage and input/output devices; these are all implemented with electronic components and integrated circuits) **elektronischer Digitalrechner;** **electronic editing** = video film editing using computers, image storage, etc., rather than physically cutting the tape **elektronische Redaktion; electronic engineer** = person who specializes in work on electronic devices **Elektronikingenieur;** **electronic industry association interface (EIA)** = standard defining interface signals, transmission rate and power usually used to connect terminals to modems **Schnittstellennorm des Elektronikindustrieverbandes;** **electronic filing** = system of storage of documents which can be easily retrieved **elektronisches Ablagesystem; electronic funds transfer (EFT)** = using a computer to transfer money to and from banks **elektronischer Zahlungsverkehr; electronic funds transfer point of sale (EFTPOS)** = terminal at a POS that is linked to a central computer which automatically transfers money from the customer's account to the shop's **elektronische Kasse; electronic keyboard** = keyboard that generates characters electronically in response to a switch making contact when pressed, rather than by mechanical means **elektronische Tastatur; electronic lock** = security device, usually in the form of a password (used to protect a file *or* piece of equipment from unauthorized use) **elektronische Sperre; electronic mail** *or* **email** = sending and receiving messages over a telephone network, usually using a bulletin board **elektronische Post, E-Mail;** *when I log onto the network, I always check my electronic mailbox for new messages;* **electronic mailbox** = system for holding messages sent by electronic mail until the person to whom they were sent is ready to accept them **elektronischer Briefkasten; electronic money** = smart cards *or* phonecards, etc., which take the place of money **Plastikgeld; electronic news gathering (ENG)** = method of reporting news items for TV news programmes, where the reporter has a cameraman with a portable video camera which can transmit live pictures direct to the studio **elektronische Berichterstattung;**

electronic office = office where all the work is done using computers, which store information, communicate with different workstations, etc. **elektronisches Büro; electronic pen** or **stylus** or **wand** = light pen or wand; stylus used to draw on a graphics tablet **Lichtgriffel, Lichtstift; electronic point-of-sale (EPOS)** = system that uses a computer terminal at a point-of-sale site for electronic funds transfer or stock control as well as product identification, etc. **elektronische Kasse; electronic publishing** = (i) use of desktop publishing packages and laser printers to produce printed matter; (ii) using computers to write and display information, such as viewdata **(i) elektronisches Publizieren; (ii) Bildschirmtextverfahren; electronic pulse** = short voltage pulse **elektronischer Impuls; electronic shopping** = system of shopping from the home, using computerized catalogues and paying by credit card, all by means of a home computer terminal **Teleshopping; electronic signature** = special code which identifies the sender of a coded message **elektronische Signatur; electronic smog** = excessive stray electromagnetic fields and static electricity generated by large numbers of electronic equipment (this can damage equipment or a person's health) **elektronischer Smog; electronic stylus** or **wand** see LIGHT PEN; **electronic switching system** = telephone routing using a computer system to control the line switching circuits **elektronisches Vermittlungssystem; electronic traffic** = data transmitted in the form of electronic pulses **elektronischer Datenverkehr; electronic typewriter** = typewriter using an electronic keyboard linked, via a buffer, to an electrically driven printing mechanism, also with the facility to send or receive character data from a computer **elektronische Schreibmaschine; electronic viewfinder** = miniature cathode ray tube in a television or video camera that allows the camera operator to see the images being recorded **elektronischer Sucher**

◊ **electronically** adverb referring to operations using electronic methods **elektronisch;** *the text is electronically transmitted to an outside typesetter*

◊ **electronics** noun science of applying the study of electrons and their properties to manufactured products, such as components, computers, calculators or telephones **Elektronik;** *the electronics industry; an electronics specialist* NOTE: takes a singular verb

electro-optic effect noun changes in the refractive index of a material due to a nearby electric field **elektrooptischer Effekt**

◊ **electrophotography** noun forming an image using electrical and optical effects **Elektrofotografie**

◊ **electrosensitive** adjective **electrosensitive paper** = metal-coated printing paper, which can display characters using localized heating with a special dot-matrix print head **elektrosensitives Papier; electrosensitive printing** = printing using electrosensitive paper **elektrosensitives Drucken**

◊ **electrostatic** adjective referring to devices using the properties of static electrical charge **elektrostatisch; electrostatic printer** = type of printer which forms an image on the paper by charging certain regions to provide character shapes, etc., and using ink with an opposite charge which sticks to the paper where required **elektrostatischer Drucker; electrostatic screen** = metal cage surrounding sensitive equipment (and connected to ground) to protect it from interference **elektrostatischer Schirm; electrostatic speaker** = loudspeaker containing two large charged plates, one flexible which moves when a signal is applied, creating sound signals **elektrostatischer Lautsprecher; electrostatic storage** = data stored in the form of small electric charged regions on a dielectric material **elektrostatischer Speicher**

◊ **electrostatically** adverb using properties of static charge **elektrostatisch**

◊ **electrothermal printer** noun printer that uses a printing head with a dot-matrix of heating elements to form characters on electrosensitive paper **Thermodrucker**

elegant adjective **elegant programming** = writing a well-structured program using the minimum number of instructions **elegantes Programmieren**

element *noun*
(a) small part of an object which is made up of many similar parts **Element; logic element** = gate *or* combination of gates **logisches Element, Verknüpfungsglied; picture element** *or* **pixel** = smallest single unit *or* point on a display whose colour *or* brightness can be controlled **Bildelement; signal element** = smallest basic unit used when transmitting digital data **Schritt**
(b) one number *or* cell of a matrix *or* array **Punkt; array element** = one individual piece of data within an array **Matrixelement**
(c) coil of resistive wire to which an electric current is applied to generate heat **Brennelement**
(d) substance in which all the atoms have the same number of electrons and charge **Element**

◊ **elementary** *adjective* made of many similar small sections *or* objects **elementar; elementary cable section** = model of the characteristics of a short length of transmission cable that can be applied to the whole length of cable **elementarer Kabelausschnitt**

ELF = EXTREMELY LOW FREQUENCY communications frequencies of less than 100Hz **Niederfrequenz (niedriger als 100Hz)**

eliminate *verb* to remove something completely **ausschließen, eliminieren;** *using a computer should eliminate all possibility of error in the address system; the spelling checker does not eliminate all spelling mistakes*

◊ **elimination** *noun* removing of something completely **Eliminierung; elimination factor** = during a search, the section of data that is not used **Eliminierungsfaktor**

QUOTE pointing with the cursor and pressing the joystick button eliminates use of the keyboard almost entirely
Soft

elite *noun* typewriter typeface **Elite**

ellipse *noun* oval shaped; like an elongated circle **Ellipse**

◊ **elliptical orbit** *noun* path of a satellite around the earth that is in the shape of an ellipse **elliptische Umlaufbahn**

else rule *noun* program logical rule used

with an IF-THEN instruction to provide an alternative if the IF-THEN condition is not met **ELSE-Regel;** *IF X=20 THEN PRINT 'X is 20' ELSE PRINT 'X not 20'*

ELT = ELECTRONIC TYPEWRITER

em *noun* space taken by an 'm' in a given typeface (equal to 12 point *or* pica) **Em; em quad** = space printed of a size equal to an em **Geviert (in der Größe eines m); em dash** *or* **em rule** = dash as long as an 'm', showing that words are separated **Em-Strich, Gedankenstrich; ems per hour** = rate of production of characters from a machine *or* operator **Ems pro Stunde;** *see also* EN

EM = END OF MEDIUM

E-mail *or* **email** = ELECTRONIC MAIL system of sending messages to and receiving messages from other users on a network **E-Mail**

QUOTE The main uses for a link are to deliver work, to exchange email or take part in a conference
Computing

embedded code *noun* sections *or* routines written in machine code, inserted into a high-level program to speed up *or* perform a special function **eingebetteter Code; embedded command** = printer command (such as indicating that text should be in italic) inserted into the text and used by a word-processing system when producing formatted printed text **eingebetteter Befehl; embedded computer** *or* **system** = dedicated computer controlling a machine; dedicated computer within a larger system that performs one fixed function **eingebettetes System**

emboldening *noun* making a word print in bold type **halbfettes Drucken**

embrace *see* DEADLY

emf = ELECTROMOTIVE FORCE

EMI = ELECTROMAGNETIC INTERFERENCE corruption of data due to nearby electrically generated magnetic fields **elektromagnetische Störung**

emission *noun* sending out (of a signal *or* radiation, etc.); *the emission of the electron beam; the receiver picked up the radio emission* **Emission**

◊ **emit** *verb* to send out **ausstrahlen, aussenden**

◊ **emitter** *noun* connection to a bipolar transistor Emitter; **emitter-coupled logic (ECL)** = *noun* high-speed logic circuit design using the emitters of the transistors as output connections to other stages **emittergekoppelte Logik**

EMM = EXPANDED MEMORY MANAGER utility that manages the extra expanded memory fitted in an IBM PC and makes it available for programs to use **EMM**

empty *adjective* with nothing inside **leer; empty** *or* **null list** = list with no elements **Leerliste; empty medium** = blank but formatted storage medium that is ready to receive data **unbeschrifteter Datenträger; empty** *or* **null** *or* **void set** = reserved area for related data items, containing no data **leerer Bereich; empty slot** = (i) packet of data in a packet-switching LAN that is carrying no information; (ii) unused expansion edge connector on a motherboard **(i) freier Platz; (ii) freier Steckerplatz; empty** *or* **null string** = variable containing no characters **Leerstring**

EMS *or* **LIM EMS** = EXPANDED MEMORY SYSTEM *or* LOTUS-INTEL-MICROSOFT EXPANDED MEMORY SYSTEM (in an IBM PC) standard that defines extra memory added above the 640Kb limit of conventional memory; this memory can only be used by specially-written programs **EMS** *or* **LIM EMS;** *see also* LIM

emulate *verb* to copy *or* behave like something else **emulieren;** *laser printer which emulates a wide range of office printers*

◊ **emulation** *noun* behaviour by one computer *or* printer which is exactly the same as another, which allows the same programs to be run and the same data to be processed **Emulation; emulation facility** = feature of hardware *or* software which emulates another system **Emulationsfähigkeit**

◊ **emulator** *noun* software *or* hardware that allows a machine to behave like another **Emulator**

emulsion *noun* light-sensitive coating on photographic film *or* paper **Beschichtung, Emulsion; emulsion laser storage** = digital storage technique using a laser to expose lightsensitive material **Schichtlaserspeicher**

en *noun* unit of measure equal to half the width of an em **En; en dash** *or* **en rule** = line as long as an en, showing that two words *or* parts of words are joined together **En-Strich, Bindestrich; en quad** = space that is half the width of an em quad space **Halbgeviert (in der Größe eines n);** *see also* EM

enable *verb*
(a) to allow something to happen **erlauben;** *a spooling program enables editing work to be carried out while printing is going on*
(b) to use an electronic signal to start a process *or* access a function (on a chip *or* circuit) **einschalten, aktivieren; enabling signal** = signal that starts a process *or* allows one to take place **Betriebsbereitschaftssignal**

encapsulated *adjective* (something) contained within something else **verkapselt; encapsulated PostScript** = PostScript commands that describe an image *or* page contained within a file that can be placed within a graphics *or* DTP program **Encapsulated Postscript; encapsulated PostScript file (EPSF)** = file that contains encapsulated PostScript instructions **EPS-Datei, Encapsulated-Postscript-Datei**

◊ **encapsulation** *noun* (in a network) system of sending a frame of data in one format within a frame of another format **Kapselung**

encipher *verb* to convert plaintext into a secure coded form by means of a cipher system **verschlüsseln;** *our competitors cannot understand our files - they have all been enciphered*

enclose *verb* to surround with

something; to put something inside something else **umgeben; beilegen**

◊ **enclosure** *noun* protective casing for equipment **Gehäuse**

encode *verb* to apply the rules of a code to a program *or* data **codieren**

◊ **encoder** *noun* device that can translate data from one format to another **Codeumsetzer; colour encoder** = device that produces a standard TV signal from separate Red, Green and Blue signals **Farbumsetzer**

◊ **encoding** *noun* translation of a message *or* text according to a coding system **Umsetzung; binary encoding** = representing a character *or* element with a unique combination *or* pattern of bits in a word **binäre Umsetzung; encoding format** = method of coding data stored on a magnetic disk (to avoid a series of similar bits) **Codierungsformat; magnetic encoding** = storage of binary data signals on a magnetic medium **magnetische Speicherung**

encrypt *verb* to convert plaintext to a secure coded form, using a cipher system **verschlüsseln;** *the encrypted text can be sent along ordinary telephone lines, and no one will be able to understand it*

◊ **encryption** *noun* conversion of plaintext to a secure coded form by means of a cipher system **Verschlüsselung; data encryption standard (DES)** = standard for a block data cipher system **Datenverschlüsselungsnorm**

end
1 *noun*
(a) final point *or* last part **Ende;** *at the end of the data transmission;* **end product** = manufactured product, made at the end of a production process **Endprodukt;** *after six months' trial production, the end product is still not acceptable;* **in the end** = at last *or* after a lot of problems **schließlich;** *in the end the company had to pull out of the US market; in the end the company had to call in a consultant engineer*
(b) statement *or* character to indicate the last word of a source file **Ende; end about carry** = most significant digit is added into the least significant place (used in BCD arithmetic) **Endübertrag; end about shift** = data movement to the left *or* right in a word, the bits falling outside the word boundary are discarded and replaced with zeros **Ringschieben; end key** = (on an IBM PC keyboard) key that moves the cursor to the

end of the current line **Endetaste; end of address (EOA)** = transmitted code which indicates that address data has been sent **Adressenende; end of block (EOB)** = code which shows that the last byte of a block of data has been sent through a communications link **Blockende; end of data (EOD)** = code which shows that the end of a stored data file has been reached **Datenende; end of document** *or* **end of file (EOF)** = marker after the last record in a file **EOF, Dateiende; end of job (EOJ)** = code used in batch processing to show that a job has been finished **Jobende; end of medium (EM)** = code that indicates the end of usable physical medium **Datenträgerende; end of message (EOM)** = code used to separate the last character of one message from the first of another message **Nachrichtenende; end of page indicator** = indicator on a typewriter to show that a page is nearly finished **Seitenendeanzeiger; end of record (EOR)** = code used to show the end of a record **Satzende; end of run routine** = routine carried out before a program run finishes to perform certain system housekeeping functions **Ende der Laufroutine; end of tape** = code used to indicate the end of a magnetic tape **Bandende; end of text (EOT** *or* **ETX)** = code sent after last character of text **Textende; end of transmission (EOT)** = sequence of characters that indicate that all the data from a terminal *or* peripheral has been transmitted **Übertragungsende**
2 *verb* to finish *or* to stop something **beenden**

◊ **ending** *noun*
(a) action of coming to an end *or* of stopping something **Abschluss**
(b) end part of something **Ende; line endings** = last words on each line of text, which may be hyphenated **Zeilenenden**

◊ **endless** *adjective* with no end **endlos; endless loop** = continuous piece of recording tape *or* number of computer instructions that are continuously repeated **Endlosschleife**

◊ **end user** *noun* person who will use the device *or* program *or* product **Endverbraucher;** *the company is creating a computer with a specific end user in mind*

energy *noun*
(a) force *or* strength; ability of a body *or* object to do work **Energie**
(b) power from electricity *or* petrol, etc. **Energie;** *we try to save energy by switching off the lights when the rooms are empty; if*

you reduce the room temperature to eighteen degrees, you will save energy NOTE: no plural for (b)

◊ **energy-saving** *adjective* which saves energy **energiesparend;** *the company is introducing energy-saving measures*

ENG = ELECTRONIC NEWS GATHERING

enhance *verb* to make better *or* clearer **verbessern, erweitern; enhanced dot matrix** = clearer character *or* graphics printout (using smaller dots and more dots per inch) **verbesserte Punktmatrix; enhanced expanded memory specification (EEMS)** = (in an IBM PC) a development of EMS, standard method of expanding the main memory fitted into a PC **Enhanced Expanded Memory Specification (EEMS); enhanced graphics adapter (EGA)** = popular standardized system of high-resolution colour display for microcomputers **erweiterte Grafikkarte (EGA); enhanced graphics adapter screen** = high-resolution colour monitor that can display EGA system signals and graphics **EGA-Bildschirm; enhanced keyboard** = (in an IBM PC) keyboard with 101 or 102 keys and a row of 12 function keys arranged along the top of the keyboard, with a separate numeric keypad on the right **erweiterte Tastatur; enhanced mode** = (in an IBM PC with an Intel 80386 CPU) operation of software which uses the CPU's protected mode to allow several MS-DOS programs to run in a multitasking environment **erweiterter Modus; enhanced small device interface (ESDI)** = interface standard between a CPU and peripherals such as disk drives **erweiterte Kleingerätschnittstelle**

◊ **enhancement** *noun* add-on facility which improves the output *or* performance of equipment **Erweiterung**

◊ **enhancer** *noun* device *or* software which enhances a process *or* product **Erweiterer**

> QUOTE the typefaces are fairly rudimentary, especially if you are not using an enhanced graphics adapter screen
>
> *Desktop Publishing*

enlarge *verb* to make (a photograph) larger **vergrößern**

◊ **enlargement** *noun* making larger; a larger version of a photograph **Vergrößerung;** *an enlargement of the photograph was used to provide better detail*

ENQ = ENQUIRY

enquiry *noun* request for data *or* information from a device *or* database accessing data in a computer memory without changing the data **An-, Aufforderung; enquiry character** = special control code that is a request for identification *or* status *or* data from a device **Stationsaufforderung**

ensure *verb* to make sure **sicherstellen;** *pushing the write-protect tab will ensure that the data on the disk cannot be erased*

enter *verb* to type in information on a terminal *or* keyboard **eingeben;** *to enter a name on a list; the data has been entered on data capture forms;* **enter key** = key pressed to indicate the end of an input *or* line of text **Eingabetaste;** *see also* CARRIAGE RETURN KEY

◊ **entering** *noun* act of typing in data *or* writing items in a record **Eingabe** NOTE: no plural

enterprise network *noun* network which connects all the workstations *or* terminals *or* computers in a company; it can be within one building or linking several buildings in different countries **Unternehmensnetzwerk**

entity *noun* subject to which the data stored in a file *or* database refers **Dateneinheit**

entry *noun*
(a) single record *or* data about one action *or* object in a database *or* library **Eintrag**
(b) place where you can enter **Eingabe; Eingang; entry condition** = condition that must be satisfied before a routine can be entered **Eingabebedingung; entry instruction** = first instruction executed in a called subroutine **Einsprungbefehl; entry point** = address from which a program *or* subroutine is to be executed **Einsprungstelle; entry time** = point in time when a program *or* job *or* batch will be executed by the operating system scheduler **Eingabezeit**

enumerated type *noun* data storage *or* classification using numbers to represent chosen convenient labels **Nummerierungstyp**

> COMMENT: if 'man', 'horse', 'dog', 'cat' are the items of data, stored by the machine simply as 0, 1, 2, 3, they can still be referred to in the program as man, horse, etc., to make it easier for the user to recognize them

envelope *noun*
(a) transmitted packet of data containing error-detection and control information **Datenpaket**
(b) (in multimedia) shape of the decay curve of a sound **Hüllkurve**
(c) (in electronic mail) name for the data which contains a mail message with the destination address information **Envelope**
(d) paper packet that contains a letter **Briefhülle, Briefumschlag; envelope feeder =** special add-on to a printer used to print on an envelope instead of a sheet of paper **Briefhüllenzufuhr; envelope printer =** special printer used to print the address on an envelope **Briefhüllendrucker**

environment *noun*
(a) condition in a computer system of all the registers and memory locations **Umgebung; environment space =** the amount of memory free to be used by a program **Umgebungsspeicher; environment variable =** variable set by the system *or* by a user at the system command line which can be used by any program **Umgebungsvariable**
(b) surroundings *or* physical conditions **Umgebung**

QUOTE one of the advantages of working in a PC-based environment is the enormous range of software which can run on the same computer
ESL Newsletter

EOA = END OF ADDRESS

EOB = END OF BLOCK

EOD = END OF DATA

EOF = END OF FILE

EOJ = END OF JOB

EOL = END OF LINE

EOM = END OF MESSAGE

EOR = END OF RECORD

EOT = END OF TEXT *or* TRANSMISSION

episcope *noun* projector that can display opaque material and documents onto a screen **Epidiaskop**

epitaxy *noun* method of depositing very thin layers of materials onto a base, for use in chip manufacture **Epitaxie**

◊ **epitaxial layer** *noun* very thin layer of material *or* doped semiconductor deposited onto a substrate base **epitaxiale Schicht**

EPOS = ELECTRONIC POINT-OF-SALE system that uses a computer terminal at a point-of-sale site for electronic funds transfer *or* stock control as well as product identification **elektronische Kasse**

EPROM *noun*
(a) = ELECTRICALLY PROGRAMMABLE READ-ONLY MEMORY
(b) = ERASABLE PROGRAMMABLE READ-ONLY MEMORY

QUOTE the densest EPROMs commercially available today are at the 1Mbit level
Electronics & Power

EPS = ENCAPSULATED POSTSCRIPT

◊ **EPSF** = ENCAPSULATED POSTSCRIPT FILE

equal
1 *adjective* exactly the same **gleich**
2 *verb* to be the same as **gleichkommen;** *production this month has equalled our best month ever* NOTE: **equalling - equalled** but US: **equaling - equaled**

◊ **equality** *noun* logical function whose output is true if either of two inputs is true, and false if both inputs are the same **Gleichheit**

◊ **equalize** *verb* to make equal (to preset values) **gleichmachen, ausgleichen;** *the received signal was equalized to an optimum shape*

◊ **equalization** *noun* process of making a signal equal (to preset values) **Entzerrung**

◊ **equalizer** *noun* device which changes the amplitude of various parts of a signal according to preset values **Entzerrer; frequency equalizer =** device that changes the amplitude of various frequency components of a signal according to preset values **Frequenzentzerrer**

◊ **equally** *adverb* in the same way **gleich;** *they were both equally responsible for the successful launch of the new system*

equate *verb* to make the same as **gleichsetzen;** *the variable was equated to the input data*

◊ **equation** *noun* formula **Gleichung; machine equation =** formula which an analog computer has been programmed to solve **Maschinengleichung**

equator noun imaginary line running round the middle of the earth **Äquator**

◊ **equatorial orbit** noun satellite flight path that follows the earth's equator **äquatoriale Umlaufbahn**

equip verb to provide with machinery or equipment **ausstatten**

◊ **equipment** noun machinery and furniture required to make a factory or office work **Ausstattung, Anlage, Einrichtung**; office equipment or business equipment; computer equipment supplier; office equipment catalogue; **equipment failure** = hardware fault, rather than a software fault **Gerätefehler**
NOTE: no plural

equivalent adjective **to be equivalent to** = to have the same value as or to be the same as **gleichwertig sein**; the total characters keyboarded so far is equivalent to one day's printing time

◊ **equivalence** noun
(a) being equivalent **Gleichheit, Gleichwertigkeit**
(b) logical operation that is true if all the inputs are the same **Äquivalenz; equivalence function** or **operation** = (i) AND function; (ii) logical function whose output is true if both inputs are the same **(i) UND-Funktion; (ii) Äquivalenz-Funktion; equivalence gate** = gate which performs an equivalence function **Äquivalenzglied; non-equivalence function (NEQ)** = logical function where the output is true if the inputs are not the same, otherwise the output is false **Antivalenzfunktion**

| COMMENT: output is 1 if both inputs are 1 or if both are 0 if the two inputs are different, the output is 0

erase verb
(a) to set all the digits in a storage area to zero **auf Null setzen**
(b) to remove any signal from a magnetic medium **löschen; erase head** = small magnet that clears a magnetic tape or disk of recorded signals **Löschkopf**

◊ **erase character** noun character which means do nothing **Nullzeichen**

◊ **erasable** adjective which can be erased **löschbar; erasable storage** or **erasable memory** = (i) storage medium that can be re-used; (ii) temporary storage **(i) löschbarer Speicher; (ii) Zwischenspeicher; erasable programmable read-only memory (EPROM)** = read-only memory chip that

can be programmed by a voltage applied to a write pin and data applied to its output pins, usually erasable with ultraviolet light **löschbarer, programmierbarer Festwertspeicher (EPROM)**

◊ **eraser** noun device that erases the contents of an EPROM (usually using UV light) **Löscheinrichtung; eraser tool** = (in a graphics program) function that allows areas of an image to be erased, or set to the background colour **Radierer**

ERCC = ERROR CHECKING AND CORRECTING memory which checks and corrects errors **Fehlerprüfung und -korrektur**

E-region or **Heaviside-Kennelly layer** noun section of the ionosphere that is 90-150 km above the earth's surface **E-Schicht der Ionosphäre**

ergonomics noun science of designing software or hardware so that it is comfortable and safe to use **Ergonomie**

◊ **ergonomist** noun scientist who studies people at work and tries to improve their working conditions **Ergonom**

EROM = ERASABLE READ-ONLY MEMORY; (same as EAROM)

erratum noun correction on a separate slip of paper to an error or omission from a document **Erratum; Schreib-, Druckfehler**
NOTE: plural is **errata**

error noun mistake due to an operator; mistake caused by a hardware or software fault; mistake in a program that prevents a program or system running correctly **Fehler**; he made an error in calculating the total; the secretary must have made a typing error; **in error** or **by error** = by mistake **aus Versehen; margin of error** = number of mistakes which are acceptable in a document or in a calculation **Fehlermarge, Fehlertoleranz; ambiguity error** = error due to an incorrect selection from ambiguous data **Mehrdeutigkeitsfehler; error burst** = group of several consecutive errors (in a transmission) **Fehlerhäufung; error checking code** = general term used to describe all error correcting and error detecting codes **Fehlerprüfcode; error code** = code that indicates that a particular type of error has occurred **Fehlercode; error condition** = state that is entered if an attempt is made to operate on data containing errors **Fehlerbedingung; error control** = routines that ensure that errors are minimised and any errors that occur are detected and dealt with rapidly **Fehlerüberwachung; error correcting code** = coding system that allows bit errors occurring during transmission to be rapidly corrected by logical deduction methods rather than re-transmission **Fehlerkorrekturcode;** see also GRAY CODE; **error correction** = hardware or software that can detect and correct an error in a transmission **Fehlerkorrektur; error detecting code** = coding system that allows errors occurring during transmission to be detected but is not complex enough to correct the errors **Fehlererkennungscode; error detection** = using special hardware or software to detect errors in a data entry or transmission, then usually ask for re-transmission **Fehlererkennung; error detection and correction (EDAC)** = forward error correction system for data communications **Fehlererkennung und -korrektur; error diagnosis** = finding the cause of an error **Fehlerdiagnose; error diagnostics** = information and system messages displayed when an error is detected to help a user diagnose and correct an error **Fehlerdiagnostik; error handling** or **management** = routines and procedures that diagnose and correct errors or minimise the effects of errors, so that a system will run when an error is detected **Fehlerbehebung; error interrupts** = interrupt signals sent due to an error in hardware or software **Fehlerunterbrechungen; error logging** = recording errors that have occurred **Fehlererfassung;** features of the program include error logging; **error message** = report that an error has occurred **Fehlermeldung; error propagation** = one error causing another **Fehlerfortpflanzung; error rate** = (i) number of mistakes per thousand entries or per page; (ii) number of corrupt bits of data in relation to the total transmission length **(i) Fehlerhäufigkeit; (ii) Fehlerquote;** the error rate is less than 1%; **error recovery** = software or hardware that can continue after an error has occurred **Fehlerbehebung; error routine** = short routine within a main program that handles any errors when they occur **Fehlerroutine; error trapping** = detecting and correcting errors before they cause any problems **Fehlerbehebung; compilation error** = error occurring during program compilation time **Kompilierfehler; diagnostic error message** = explanatory line of text displayed when an error has been found **diagnostische Fehlermeldung; execution error** = error occurring during program execution, due to bad inputs or a faulty program **Ausführungsfehler; logical error** =

fault in a program design causing incorrect branching or operation **logischer Fehler; permanent error** = error in a system which cannot be repaired **dauerhafter Fehler; quantization error** = error in converting an analog signal into a numerical form due to limited accuracy or a rapidly changing signal **Quantisierungsfehler; recoverable error** = error that does not cause complete system shut-down, and allows the user to restart the program **wiederherstellbarer Fehler; rejection error** = error by the scanner which is unable to read a character and leaves a blank **Rückweisungsfehler; scanning error** = error introduced while scanning an image **Abtastfehler;** a wrinkled or torn page may be the cause of scanning errors; **substitution error** = error made by a scanner which mistakes one character or letter for another **Substitutionsfehler; syntax error** = error resulting from incorrect use of programming language syntax **Syntaxfehler; transient read error** = error which can be recovered from (caused by bad data recording) **transienter Lesefehler; undetected error** = error which is not detected by a coding system **unentdeckter Fehler**

> QUOTE syntax errors, like omitting a bracket, will produce an error message from the compiler
> *Personal Computer World*

> QUOTE Microcom has launched a new version of its MNP proprietary error correction protocol, MNP10, which automatically slows down the transmission rate when it detects line interference and speeds up again when conditions improve
> *Computing*

ESC escape character code or key on a computer **ESC-Taste**

escape character noun character used to represent an escape code **ESC-Zeichen, Codeumschaltung; escape codes** = transmitted code sequence which informs the receiver that all following characters represent control actions **ESC-Codes; escape key** = key on a keyboard which allows the user to enter escape codes to control the computer's basic modes or actions **ESC-Taste, Codeumschaltungstaste**

◊ **escapement** noun preset vertical movement of a sheet of paper in a printer or in a typewriter **Schrittschaltung**

ESDI = ENHANCED SMALL DEVICE

INTERFACE interface standard between a CPU and peripherals such as disk drives **erweiterte Kleingerätschnittstelle**

ESS = ELECTRONIC SWITCHING SYSTEM

establish verb (i) to discover and prove something; (ii) to define the use or value of something **(i) erweisen; (ii) festsetzen;** they established which component was faulty

etch verb to use an acid to remove selected layers of metal from a metal printing plate or printed circuit board **ätzen; etch type** = type for printing produced from an etched plate **Ätztype**

Ethernet (refers to IEEE 802.3 standard) standard defining the protocol and signalling method of a local area network **Ethernet; thick-Ethernet** = network implemented using thick coaxial cable and transceivers to connect branch cables; can stretch long distances **Thickwire-Ethernet; thin-Ethernet** = (the most popular type of Ethernet) network implemented using thin coaxial cable and BNC connectors; it is limited to distances of around 1000m **Thinwire-Ethernet;** compare ARCNET, TOKEN-RING

COMMENT: Ethernet has several implementations: 10Base5 (the most common) is a bus-based topology running over coaxial cable; 10BaseT uses unshielded-twisted-pair cable in a ring-based topology; Ethernet normally has a data transmission rate of 10Mbps

◊ **EtherTalk** (in Apple Macintosh systems) variation of the standard Ethernet network developed to connect Macintoshes together as an alternative to the slower AppleTalk **EtherTalk**

ETV = EDUCATIONAL TELEVISION

ETX = END OF TEXT

Euronet noun telephone connected network, covering the EC countries, that provides access to each country's scientific and economic information **Euronet**

evaluate verb to calculate a value or a quantity **auswerten, bewerten**

◊ **evaluation** noun action of calculating a value or a quantity **Auswertung**

◊ **evaluative abstract** noun library abstract that contains details of the value

and usefulness of the document **gewertete Kurzdarstellung**

even adjective (quantity or number) that is a multiple of two **gerade;** the first three even numbers are 2, 4, 6; **even parity check** = error checking method that only transmits an even number of binary ones in each word **Prüfung auf gerade Parität;** compare ODD PARITY; **even working** = section of printed material in 16, 32 or 64 page format **Drucken ohne Restbogen**

event noun an action or activity **Ereignis, Anreiz**

◊ **event-driven** adjective (computer program or process) where each step of the execution relies on external actions **anreizgesteuert**

QUOTE Forthcoming language extensions will include object-oriented features, including classes with full inheritance, as well as event-driven programming

Computing

except preposition & conjunction not including **außer;** all the text has been keyboarded, except the last ten pages; **except gate** = logical function whose output is true if either (of two) inputs is true, and false if both inputs are the same **exklusiv-ODER-Gatter**

◊ **exception** noun thing which is different from all others **Ausnahme; exception dictionary** = store of words and their special word-break requirements, for word-processing and photocomposition **Ausnahmelexikon; exception handling** or **error handling** = routines and procedures that diagnose and correct errors or minimise the effects of errors, so that a system will run when an error is detected **Ausnahmebehandlung, Fehlerbehandlung; exception report** = report which only gives items which do not fit in the general rule or pattern **Ausnahmebericht**

◊ **exceptional** adjective not usual or different **außergewöhnlich; exceptional items** = items in a balance sheet which do not appear there each year **Sonderposten**

excess noun too much of something **Überschuss; excess-3 code** = code in which decimal digits are represented by the binary equivalent of three greater than the number **3-Überschusscode, Stibitz-Code;** the excess-3 code representation of 6 is 1001

◊ **excessive** adjective too much or too

large **überschüssig**; *the program used an excessive amount of memory to accomplish the job*

exchange

1 *noun*
(a) giving of one thing for another **Austausch; part exchange** = giving an old product as part of the payment for a new one in **Zahlung geben**
(b) telephone equipment required to connect incoming and outgoing calls **Telefonzentrale; exchange line** = LOCAL LOOP
2 *verb*
(a) to exchange one article for another = to give one thing in place of something else **einen Artikel gegen einen anderen umtauschen; exchange selection** = sorting method which repeatedly exchanges various pairs of data items until they are in order **Sortiermethode**
(b) to swap data between two locations **austauschen**

◊ **exchangeable** *adjective* which can be exchanged **austauschbar, auswechselbar; exchangeable disk storage (EDS)** = disk drive using a removable disk pack (as opposed to a fixed disk) **auswechselbarer Plattenspeicher**

exclamation mark *noun* printed *or* written sign (!), which shows surprise **Ausrufezeichen**

exclude *verb* to keep out *or* not to include **ausschließen**; *the interest charges have been excluded from the document the password is supposed to exclude hackers from the database*

◊ **excluding** *preposition* not including **außer, ausgenommen;** *all salesmen, excluding those living in London, can stay at hotels during the sales conference*

◊ **exclusion** *noun*
(a) act of not including **Ausschluss, Ausschließung; exclusion clause** = section of an insurance policy *or* warranty which says which items are not covered **Ausschluss-, Freizeichnungsklausel**
(b) restriction of access to a telephone line *or* system **Ausschluss**

◊ **exclusive** *adjective* which excludes **ausschließlich; exclusive agreement** = agreement where a person is made sole agent for a product in a market **Exklusivvertrag, Alleinvertretungsvereinbarung; exclusive NOR (EXNOR)** = logical function whose

output is true if all inputs are the same level, and false if any are different **exklusiv-NOR-Funktion; exclusive NOR gate** = electronic implementation of the EXNOR function **exklusiv-NOR-Gatter; exclusive OR (EXOR)** = logical function whose output is true if any input is true, and false if all the inputs are the same **exklusiv-ODER-Funktion; exclusive OR gate** = electronic implementation of the EXOR function **exklusiv-ODER-Gatter**

executable file *noun* file that contains a program rather than data **ausführbare Datei**

executable form *noun* program translated *or* compiled into a machine code form that a processor can execute **ausführbare Form**

execute *verb* to run *or* carry out a computer program *or* process **aktivieren, ausführen; execute cycle** = events required to fetch, decode and carry out an instruction stored in memory **Ausführungszyklus; execute mode** = state of a computer that is executing a program **Ausführungsmodus;** *compare with* DIRECT MODE; **execute phase** = section of the execute cycle when the instruction is carried out **Ausführungsphase; execute signal** = signal that steps the CPU through the execute cycle **Ausführungssignal; execute statement** = basic operating system command to start a program run **Ausführungsbestimmung; execute time** = EXECUTION TIME; **fetch-execute cycle** = EXECUTE CYCLE

◊ **execution** *noun* carrying out of a computer program *or* process **Verarbeitung, Ausführung; execution address** = location in memory at which the first instruction in a program is stored **Ausführungsadresse; execution cycle** = period of time during which the instruction is executed **Ausführungszyklus; execution error** = error detected while a program is being run **Ausführungsfehler; execution phase** = EXECUTE PHASE; **execution time** = (i) time taken to run *or* carry out a program *or* series of instructions; (ii) time taken for one execution cycle (i) & (ii) **Ausführungszeit**

QUOTE fast execution speed is the single most important feature of a compiler
.EXE

executive

1 *adjective* normally refers to the operating system of a computer **Executive-; executive program** *or* **supervisor program** = master

program in a computer system that controls the execution of other programs **Supervisor; executive control program =** OPERATING SYSTEM; **executive instruction** = instruction used to control and execute programs under the control of an operating system **Ausführungsbefehl;** *see also* SUPERVISOR INSTRUCTION
2 *noun* person in a business who takes decisions (such as a manager *or* director) **leitende(r) Angestellte(r), Führungskraft; executive producer** = person who organizes and arranges for the finance for a film *or* TV programme but does not play an active part in making the film **Produzent; executive terminal** = terminal which is specially adapted for use by company executives **Datenstation der Firmenleitung**

◊ **executive information system (EIS)** *noun* easy-to-use software providing information to a manager or executive about his company **Executive Information System (EIS);** *the EIS software is very easy to use; with this EIS software, we can see how every part of the company performs*

EXE file *noun* (in an operating system) three-letter extension to a filename which indicates that the file contains binary data of a program; the file can be executed directly by the operating system **EXE-Datei;** *in DOS, to start a program type in its EXE file name*

exerciser *noun* tester for a device **Testgerät**

exhaustive search *noun* search through every record in a database **erschöpfende Suche**

exit *verb* to stop program execution *or* to leave a program and return control to the operating system *or* interpreter **beenden; exit point** = point in a subroutine where control is returned to the main program **Ausgangsstelle;** *you have to exit to another editing system to add headlines*

◊ **EXIT** (in MS-DOS) system command to stop and leave a child process and return to the parent process **EXIT**

exjunction *noun* logical function whose output is true if either (of two) inputs is true, and false if both inputs are the same **exklusiv-ODER-Funktion**

EXNOR = EXCLUSIVE NOR logical function whose output is true if all inputs are the same level, false if any are different

exklusiv-NOR-Funktion; EXNOR gate = electronic implementation of the EXNOR function **exklusiv-NOR-Gatter;** *see also* NOR

EXOR = EXCLUSIVE OR logical function whose output is true if any input is true, and false if the all inputs are the same **exklusiv-ODER-Funktion; EXOR gate =** electronic implementation of the EXOR function **exklusiv-ODER-Gatter;** *see also* OR

expand *verb* to make larger **expandieren, vergrößern;** *if you want to hold so much data, you will have to expand the disk capacity*

◊ **expandable** *adjective* which can be expanded **expandierbar; expandable system** = computer system that is designed to be able to grow (in power *or* memory) by hardware *or* software additions **expandierbares System**

◊ **expanded memory (EMS)** *noun* (in an IBM PC) standard that defines extra memory added above the 640Kb limit of conventional memory; this memory can only be used by specially-written programs **Expansionsspeicher;** *see also* LIM; **expanded memory board** = expansion card used to add extra memory to an IBM PC; the memory follows the EMS standard **Expansionsspeicherkarte; expanded memory manager (EMM)** = utility which manages the extra expanded memory fitted in an IBM PC and makes it available for programs to use **Expansionsspeichermanager (EMM)**

◊ **expander** *noun* **video expander** = device that stores one frame of a video image as it is slowly received over a voice grade communications link, with a video compressor used at the transmitting end **Videoexpander**

◊ **expansion** *noun* increase in computing power *or* storage size **Kapazitätsausweitung; expansion box** = device that plugs into an expansion bus and provides several more free expansion slots **Erweiterungsbox; expansion bus** = data and address lines leading to a connector and allowing expansion cards to control and access the data in main memory **Erweiterungsbus; expansion card** *or* **expansion board** = printed circuit board that is connected to a system to increase its functions *or* performance **Erweiterungsplatine; expansion slot** = connector inside a computer into which an expansion card can be plugged **Erweiterungsposition;** *insert the board in the expansion slot;* **macro expansion** = process in which a macro call is replaced with the instuctions in the macro **Makroumwandlung**

> QUOTE it can be attached to mast kinds of printer, and, if that is not enough, an expansion box can be fitted to the bus connector
>
> *Personal Computer World*

expert *noun* person who knows a lot about something **Sachverständige(r), Experte/Expertin;** *he is a computer expert; she is an expert in programming languages;* **expert system** = software that applies the knowledge, advice and rules defined by experts in a particular field to a user's data to help solve a problem **Expertensystem**

expire *verb* to come to an end *or* to be no longer valid **ungültig werden, ablaufen**

◊ **expiration** *noun* coming to an end **Verfall, Ablauf; expiration date** = (i) last date at which photographic film *or* paper can be used with good results; (ii) date when a computer file is no longer protected from deletion by the operating system. **(i) Verfallsdatum; (ii) Dateiverfallsdatum**

explicit address *noun* address provided in two parts, one is the reference point, the other a displacement *or* index value **absolute Adresse**

exponent *noun* number indicating the power to which a base number is to be raised **Exponent; binary exponent** = one word that contains the sign and exponent of a binary number (expressed in exponent and mantissa form) **Binärexponent;** *see also* MANTISSA

◊ **exponentiation** *noun* raising a base number to a certain power **Potenzierung**

export *verb* to save data in a different file format from the default **exportieren;** *to use this data with dBASE, you will have to export it as a DBF file*

express *verb* to state *or* to describe **ausdrücken;** *express the formula in its simplest form; the computer structure was expressed graphically*

◊ **expression** *noun*
(a) mathematical formula *or* relationship **Ausdruck**
(b) definition of a value *or* variable in a program **Ausdruck**

extend *verb* to make longer **verlängern, erweitern; extended arithmetic element** = section of a CPU that provides hardware implementations of various mathematical

functions **erweitertes Rechenelement; extended binary coded decimal interchange code (EBCDIC)** = 8-bit character coding system **EBCDIC-Code; extended BNF (EBNF)** = more flexible way of defining the syntax of a language **erweiterte Backus-Naur-Form; extended graphics array (XGA)** = high resolution graphics standard developed by IBM; capable of displaying resolutions of up to 1024x768 pixels **Extended Graphics Array (XGA); extended industry standard architecture (EISA)** = group of PC manufacturers who formed an association to promote a 32-bit expansion bus standard as a rival to the MCA bus standard from IBM **Extended Industry Standard Architecture (EISA); extended memory** = (in an IBM PC) most popular standard method of adding extra memory above 1Mb which can be used directly by many operating systems *or* programs **Erweiterungsspeicher; extended memory manager** = software utility that configures extra memory fitted in a PC to conform to the extended memory standard **Speichermanager, Erweiterungsspeichermanager; extended memory specification (XMS)** = rules that define how a program should access extended memory fitted in a PC **Extended Memory Specification (XMS); extending serial file** = file that can be added to *or* that has no maximum size **erweiterbare serielle Datei**

◊ **extensible** *adjective* which can be extended **erweiterbar; extensible language** = computer programming language that allows the user to add his own data types and commands **erweiterbare Sprache**

◊ **extension** *noun* making longer; thing which makes something longer **Verlängerung, Erweiterung; extension cable** = cable that allows a device located at some distance to be connected **Verlängerungskabel; extension memory** = storage which is located outside the main computer system but which can be accessed by the CPU **Nebenspeicher; extension tube** = device that moves photographic lens away from the camera to allow close-up shots **Teleobjektiv; filename extension** = additional information after a filename, indicating the type *or* use of the file **Extension beim Dateinamen**

◊ **extent** *noun* number of pages in a printed document, such as a book **Umfang;** *by adding the appendix, we will increase the page extent to*

external *adjective* outside a program *or* device **extern, außerhalb; external clock** =

clock *or* synchronizing signal supplied from outside a device **externer Taktgeber; external data file** = file containing data for a program that is stored separately from it **externe Datei; external device** = (i) item of hardware (such as terminals, printers, etc.) which is attached to a main computer; (ii) any device that allows communications between the computer and itself, but which is not directly operated by the main computer **(i) Hardwareteil; (ii) Peripheriegerät; external disk drive** = device not built into the computer, but which is added to increase its storage capabilities **externes Plattenlaufwerk; external interrupt** = interrupt signal from a peripheral device indicating that attention is required **externe Unterbrechung; external label** = identifying piece of paper stuck to the outside of a device *or* disk **Aufkleber, Etikett; external memory** = memory which is located outside the main computer system confines but which can be accessed by the CPU **externer Speicher; external modem** = modem which is self-contained with its own power supply unit that connects to a serial port of a computer **externes Modem; external registers** = user's registers that are located in main memory rather than within the CPU **externe Register; external schema** = user's view of the structure of data *or* a program **externes Schema; external sort** = method of sorting which uses a file stored in secondary memory, such as a disk, as its data source and uses the disk as temporary memory during sorting **externe Sortierung; external storage** *or* **external store** = storage device which is located outside the main computer system but which can be accessed by the CPU **Zubringerspeicher**

extra
1 *adjective* added *or* which is more than usual **zusätzlich**
2 *noun*
(a) item which is additional to the package **ein Extra;** *the mouse and cabling are sold as extras*
(b) mark at the end of a telegraphic transmission, induced by noise **Störstrom; extra-terrestrial noise** = random noise coming from the air, space and planets **außerirdisches Rauschen**

◊ **extracode** *noun* short routines within the operating system that emulate a hardware function **Extracode**

extract *verb* to remove required data *or* information from a database **herausnehmen;** *we can extract the files required for typesetting;* **extract instruction**

= instruction to select and read required data from a database *or* file **Ausblendbefehl**

◊ **extractor** *noun see* MASK

extrapolation *noun* process of predicting future quantities *or* trends by the analysis of current and past data **Extrapolation, Hochrechnung**

extremely *adverb* to a very high degree **besonders, äußerst;** **extremely high frequency (EHF)** = radio frequencies from 30-300GHz **extremhohe Frequenz (EHF); extremely low frequency (ELF)** = communication frequencies of less than 100Hz **Frequenz niedriger als 100Hz**

eyepiece *noun* camera viewfinder **Sucher**

◊ **eye-strain** *noun* pain in the eyes, caused by looking at bright lights *or* at a VDU for too long **Überanstrengung der Augen**

QUOTE to minimize eye-strain, it is vital to have good lighting conditions with this LCD system
Personal Computer World

Ff

F
(a) hexadecimal number equivalent to decimal number 15 **F**
(b) = FARAD

f = FEMTO- *prefix* equal to one thousandth of a million millionth (10^{-15}) **f**

face *see* TYPEFACE

facet *noun* one surface *or* plane **Facette**

◊ **faceted code** *noun* code which indicates various details of an item, by assigning each one a value **Facettencode**

facility *noun*
(a) being able to do something easily **Möglichkeit, Fazilität;** *we offer facilities for processing a customer's own disks*
(b) facilities = equipment *or* buildings which make it easy to do something **Einrichtungen, Möglichkeiten;** *storage facilities*

(c) communications path between two or more locations, with no ancillary line equipment **Verbindungsweg**
(d) *(US)* single large building **Betriebsanlage;** *we have opened our new data processing facility*

facsimile *noun* exact copy of an original **Faksimile; facsimile character generator** = means of displaying characters on a computer screen by copying preprogrammed images from memory **Faksimilezeichengenerator; facsimile copy** = exact copy of a document **Kopie; facsimile transmission (FAX)** = method of sending and receiving images in digital form over a telephone *or* radio link **Bildfunk, Bildtelegraphie (FAX)**

factor *noun*
(a) thing which is important *or* which has an influence on something else **Faktor; deciding factor** = most important factor which influences someone's decision **entscheidender Faktor;** *the deciding factor was the superb graphics;* **elimination factor** = during a search, the section of data that is not used **Eliminierungsfaktor**
(b) any number in a multiplication that is the operand **Faktor; by a factor of ten** = ten times **zehnmal, mit dem Faktor zehn**

◊ **factorial** *noun* the product of all the numbers below a number **Fakultät;** *example: 4 factorial (written 4!) = 1x2x3x4 = 24*

◊ **factorize** *verb* to break down a number into two whole numbers which when multiplied will give the original number **in Faktoren zerlegen;** *when factorized, 15 gives the factors 1, 15 or 3, 5*

factory *noun* building where products are manufactured **Fabrik;** *computer factory; they have opened a new components factory;* **factory price** *or* **price ex factory** = price not including transport from the maker's factory **Fabrikpreis, Preis ab Werk**

fade *verb (of radio or electrical signal)* to become less strong **schwächer werden, nachlassen;** *(of colour or photograph)* to become less dark **verblassen, verbleichen; to fade out** = to reduce the strength of an audio signal to create an effect **abblenden**

◊ **fading** *noun* (i) variation in strength of radio and television broadcast signals; (ii) *(of photograph or colour)* becoming less dark (i) **Schwund;** (ii) **Verblassen;** *when fading occurs turn the density dial on the printer to full black*

fail *verb* not to do something which should be done; not to work properly **ausfallen, versäumen, versagen;** *the company failed to carry out routine maintenance of its equipment; the prototype disk drive failed its first test; a computer has failed if you turn on the power supply and nothing happens;* **fail safe system** = system that has a predetermined state it will go to if a main program *or* device fails, so avoiding a total catastrophe that a complete system shutdown would produce **ausfallsicheres System; fail soft system** = system that will still be partly operational even after a part of the system has failed **System mit reduziertem Betrieb;** *see also* GRACEFUL DEGRADATION

◊ **failure** *noun* breaking down *or* stopping; not doing something which should be done **Ausfall, Versäumnis; failure logging** = section of the operating system that automatically saves the present system states and relevant data when an error *or* fault is detected **Störungsaufzeichnung; failure rate** = number of a certain type of failure within a specified period of time **Ausfallrate; failure recovery** = resuming a process *or* program after a failure has occurred and has been corrected **Fehlerwiederherstellung; induced failure** = failure of a device due to external effects **induzierter Ausfall; mean time between failures (MTBF)** = average period of time that a piece of equipment will operate for between breakdowns **mittlerer Ausfallabstand; power failure** = loss of the electric power supply **Stromausfall;** *see also* BLACKOUT, BROWN OUT

> QUOTE if one processor system fails, the other takes recovery action on the database, before taking on the workload of the failed system
>
> *Computer News*

> QUOTE The DTI is publishing a new code of best practice which covers hardware reliability and fail-safe software systems
>
> *Computing*

fall back *noun* special *or* temporary instructions *or* procedures *or* data used in the event of a fault *or* failure **Wiederholungsanlauf; fall back recovery** = resuming a program after a fault has been fixed, from the point at which fall back routines were called **Programmwiederaufnahme; fall back routines** = routines that are called *or* procedures which are executed by a user when a machine *or* system has failed **Wiederanlaufroutine**

false *adjective* (i) wrong; not true *or* not correct; (ii) a logical term, equal to binary 0, opposite of true (i) **falsch**; (ii) **FALSE; false code** = code that contains values not within specified limits **FALSE-Code; false drop** *or* **retrieval** = unwanted files retrieved from a database through the use of incorrect search codes **falsches Wiederauffinden; false error** = error warning given when no error has occurred **falsche Fehlermeldung**

FAM = FAST ACCESS MEMORY

family *noun*
(a) range of different designs of a particular typeface **(Schriften)familie**
(b) range of machines from one manufacturer that are compatible with other products in the same line from the same manufacturer **Familie**

fan
1 *noun* (i) mechanism that circulates air for cooling; (ii) a spread of data items *or* devices (i) **Ventilator**; (ii) **Auffächerung**; *if the fan fails, the system will rapidly overheat*
2 *verb* (i) to cool a device by blowing air over it; (ii) to spread out a series of items *or* devices (i) **mit Luft kühlen**; (ii) **auffächern; fan antenna** = antenna whose elements are arranged in a semicircle **Fächerantenne; fan-in** = maximum number of inputs that a circuit *or* chip can deal with **Eingangslastfaktor; fan-out** = maximum number of outputs that a circuit *or* chip can drive without exceeding its power dissipation limit **Ausgangslastfaktor; fanning strip** = cable supporting insulated strip **Drahtführungskamm**

◊ **fanfold** *or* **accordion fold** *noun* method of folding continuous paper, one sheet in one direction, the next sheet in the opposite direction, allowing the paper to be stored conveniently and fed into a printer continuously **Zickzackfaltung**

> QUOTE a filtered fan maintains positive air pressure within the cabinet, to keep dust and dirt from entering
> *Personal Computer World*

> QUOTE Intel is investigating other options to solve the Pentium system overheating problems, including selling the chip with its own miniature fan
> *Computing*

farad (F) *noun* SI unit of capacitance, defined as coulombs over volts **Faraday** ⇨APPENDIX

Faraday cage *noun* wire *or* metal screen, connected to ground, that completely encloses sensitive equipment to prevent any interference from stray electromagnetic radiation **Faradaykäfig**

far end *see* RECEIVING END

fascia plate *noun* front panel on a device **Frontplatte**; *the fascia plate on the disk drive of this model is smaller than those on other models*

fast *adjective*
(a) which moves quickly; which works quickly; (storage *or* peripheral device) that performs its functions very rapidly **schnell**; *fast program execution; this hard disk is fast, it has an access time of 28mS;* **fast access memory (FAM)** = storage locations that can be read from *or* written to very rapidly **Schnellzugriffsspeicher; fast core** = high speed, low access time working memory for a CPU **Schnellspeicher**; *the fast core is used as a scratchpad for all calculations in this system;* **fast line** = special telecommunications line which allows data to be transmitted at 48K *or* 96K baud rates **Schnelleitung; fast peripheral** = peripheral that communicates with the computer at very high speeds, limited only by the speed of the electronic circuits, as opposed to a slow peripheral such as a card reader, where mechanical movement determines speed **schnelles Peripheriegerät; fast time-scale** = operation in which the time-scale factor is less than one **Zeitraffung**
(b) (photographic lens) with a very wide aperture; highly lightsensitive photographic film **lichtstark; hochempfindlich**

FAT = FILE ALLOCATION TABLE (in a PC operating system) data file stored on disk that contains the names of each file stored on the disk, together with its starting sector position, date and size **FAT**

fatal error *noun* fault in a program *or* device that causes the system to crash **unkorrigierbarer Abbruchfehler**

father file *noun* backup of the previous version of a file **Vaterdatei**; *see also* GRANDFATHER, SON

fault *noun* situation where something has gone wrong with software *or* hardware, causing it to malfunction **Fehler;** *the technical staff are trying to correct a programming fault; we think there is a basic fault in the product design; see also* BUG, ERROR; **fault detection** = (automatic) process which logically *or* mathematically determines that a fault exists in a circuit **Fehlerentdeckung; fault diagnosis** = process by which the cause of a fault is located **Fehlerdiagnose; fault location program** = routine that is part of a diagnostic program that identifies the cause of faulty data *or* equipment **Fehlerlokalisierungsprogramm; fault time** = period of time during which a computer system is not working *or* usable **Ausfallzeit; fault trace** = program that checks and records the occurrences of faults in a system **Fehlerprotokoll**

◊ **fault tolerance** *noun* ability of a system to continue functioning even when a fault has occurred **Fehlertoleranz**

◊ **fault-tolerant** *adjective* (system *or* device) that is able to continue functioning even when a fault occurs **fehlertolerant;** *they market a highly successful range of fault-tolerant minis*

◊ **faulty** *adjective* which does not work properly **fehlerhaft;** *there must be a faulty piece of equipment in the system; they traced the fault to a faulty cable;* **faulty sector** = sector of a magnetic disk that cannot be written to *or* read from correctly **fehlerhafter Sektor**

fax *or* **FAX** *noun & verb informal* = FACSIMILE COPY, FACSIMILE TRANSMISSION **(Tele)fax; (tele)faxen;** *we will send a fax of the design plan; I've faxed the documents to our New York office; the fax machine is next to the telephone switchboard;* **fax card** *or* **board** *or* **adapter** = adapter card which plugs into an expansion slot and allows a computer to send or receive fax data **Faxkarte; fax server** = computer connected to a network and fitted with a fax card that is shared by all users on the network **Faxserver**

FCB = FILE CONTROL BLOCK area of memory (used by the operating system) that contains information about the files in use *or* those stored on a disk drive **FCB**

fd *or* **FD**
(a) = FULL DUPLEX data transmission down a channel in two directions simultaneously **Duplex**
(b) = FLOPPY DISK

fdc = FLOPPY DISK CONTROLLER

FDDI = FIBRE DISTRIBUTED DATA INTERFACE ANSI standard for high-speed networks which use fibre optic cable in a dual ring topology; data is transmitted at 100Mbps **FDDI; FDDI II** = extension to FDDI standard to allow transmission of analog data in digital form **FDDI II**

FDISK (in MS-DOS) system utility that configures the partitions on a hard disk **FDISK**

FDM = FREQUENCY DIVISION MULTIPLEXING assigning a number of different signals to different frequencies (or bands) to allow many signals to be sent along one channel **FDM, Frequenzmultiplex;** *using FDM we can transmit 100 telephone calls along one main cable*

fdx *or* **FDX** = FULL DUPLEX

feasibility *noun* ability to be done **Durchführbarkeit;** *he has been asked to report on the feasibility of a project;* **feasibility report** = report saying if something can be done **Durchführbarkeitsbericht; feasibility study** = examination and report into the usefulness and cost of a new product that is being considered for purchase **Projektstudie; to carry out a feasibility study on a project** = to carry out an examination of costs and profits to see if the project should be started **eine Projektstudie durchführen**
NOTE: no plural

feature *noun* special function *or* ability *or* design of hardware *or* software **Einrichtung; key feature** = most important feature **Haupteinrichtung;** *the key features of this system are: 20Mb of formatted storage with an access time of 60ms*

FEDS = FIXED AND EXCHANGEABLE DISK STORAGE magnetic disk storage system that contains some removable disks, such as floppy disks and some fixed *or* hard disk drives **System mit Festplatten und flexiblen Disketten**

feed

1 *noun* device which puts paper *or* tape into and through a machine, such as a printer *or* photocopier **Zuführung; continuous feed** = device which feeds in continuous computer stationery into a printer **Endlospapiereinzug; front feed** *or* **sheet feed attachment** = device which can be attached to a line printer to allow individual sheets of paper to be fed in automatically **Einzelblatteinzug; feed holes** = punched sprocket holes along the edge of continuous paper **Führungslöcher; feed horn** = microwave channelling device used to direct transmitted signals **Speisehornstrahler; feed reel** = reel of tape which is being fed into a machine **Rollenzuführung; paper feed** = mechanism which pulls paper through a printer **Papiertransport; sheet feed** = device which puts in one sheet at a time into a printer **Einzelblatteinzug; tractor feed** = method of feeding paper into a printer, sprocket wheels on the printer connect with sprocket holes on each edge of the paper **Papiertraktor**

2 *verb* to put paper into a machine *or* information into a computer **zuführen;** *this paper should be manually fed into the printer; data is fed into the computer* NOTE: **feeding - fed**

◊ **feedback** *noun*

(a) adding part of the output of a circuit to the input **Rückführung; feedback loop** = path from output to input by which feedback occurs **Rückführungsschleife; negative feedback** = subtraction of part of the output from a device from its input signal **negative Rückführung; positive feedback** = addition of part of the output from a device to its input **positive Rückführung;** *see also* ACOUSTICAL

(b) information from one source which can be used to modify something *or* provide a constructive criticism of something **Rückkopplung; Reaktion, Rückinformation;** *we are getting customer feedback on the new system; they asked the sales teams for feedback on the reception of the new model; have you any feedback from the sales force about the customers' reaction to the new model?;* **feedback control** = information about the effects of a controlling signal on a machine *or* device, returned to the

controlling computer **Rückführungskreis** NOTE: no plural

| COMMENT: negative or positive feedback can be accidental (when it may cause severe overloading of the circuit) or designed into the circuit to make it more stable

feeder *noun*

(a) channel that carries signals from one point to another **Zubringer; feeder cable** = (i) main transmission line that carries signals from a central point for distribution; (ii) cable from an antenna to a circuit **(i) Zubringerkabel; (ii) Verbindungskabel**

(b) mechanism that automatically inserts the paper into a printer **automatischer Papierzuführer**

feevee *noun (US) informal* paycable *or* form of cable TV where the viewer pays an extra fee for extra channels **extra zu bezahlendes Kabelfernsehen**

feint *noun* very light lines on writing paper **Feinlinierung**

female *adjective* **female connector** = connector with connecting sockets into which the pins *or* plugs of a male connector can be inserted **Anschlussbuchse; female socket** = hole into which a pin *or* plug can be inserted to make a connection **Steckdose**

femto- **(f)** *prefix* equal to ten exponent minus fifteen (10^{-15}) **Femto-; femto second** = thousandth of a picosecond **Femtosekunde**

FEP = FRONT END PROCESSOR processor placed between an input source and the central computer, whose function is to preprocess received data to relieve the workload of the main computer **Vorschaltrechner**

ferric oxide *or* **ferrite** *noun* substance (iron oxide) used as tape *or* disk coating that can be magnetized to store data *or* signals **Eisenoxid**

◊ **ferrite core** *noun* small bead of magnetic material that can hold an electromagnetic charge, used in (old) core memory **Ferritkern, Magnetkern**

◊ **ferromagnetic material** *noun* any ferrite material that can be magnetized **ferromagnetisches Material**

FET = FIELD EFFECT TRANSISTOR electronic device that can act as a variable current flow control, an external signal varies the resistance of the device and current flow by changing the width of a conducting channel **Feldeffekttransistor**

fetch *noun* command that retrieves the next instruction from memory **Abruf;** **demand fetching** = virtual page management system in which the pages are selected as required **Abruf auf Anforderung;** **fetch cycle** = events that retrieve the next instruction to be executed from memory (by placing the program counter contents on the address bus) **Abrufzyklus; fetch-execute cycle** = events required to retrieve, decode and carry out an instruction stored in memory **Abruf-Ausführ-Zyklus; fetch instruction** = computer instruction to select and read the next instruction or data to be processed **Abrufbefehl; fetch phase** = section of the fetch-execute cycle that retrieves and decodes the instructions from memory **Abrufphase; fetch protect** = to restrict access to a section of memory **Lesesperre; fetch signal** = signal that steps the CPU through the fetch cycle **Abrufsignal**

FF
(a) = FORM FEED
(b) = FLIP-FLOP

fibre distributed data interface (FDDI) *noun* ANSI standard for high-speed networks that uses fibre optic cable in a dual ring topology; data is transmitted at 100Mbps **FDDI-Schnittstelle, FDDI**

QUOTE Honeywell has won a contract worth £380,000 to cable Abbey National's Milton Keynes-based administration offices. The installation will be based on copper wire and fibre optics and will be carried out by Honeywell's PDS Group
Computing

fibre optics *noun* light transmission through thin strands of glass or plastic, which allows data to be transmitted **Faseroptik; fibre optic cable** or **connection** = fine strands of glass or plastic protected by a surrounding material, used for transmission of light signals **Lichtwellenleiterkabel;** *fibre optic connections enabling nodes up to one kilometre apart to be used*

◊ **fibre ribbon** *noun* fabric-based ribbon used in printers **Gewebeband**

fiche *see* MICROFICHE

fidelity *noun* ability of an audio system to reproduce sound correctly **Klangtreue; high**

fidelity system (hi fi) = high-quality equipment for playing records or compact disks or tapes or for listening to the radio (tape recorder, turntable, amplifier and speakers) **Hi-Fi-Anlage;** *see also* HI FI

field *noun*
(a) area of force and energy distribution, caused by magnetic or electric energy sources **Feld; field effect transistor (FET)** = electronic device that can act as a variable current flow control, an external signal varies the resistance of the device and current flow by changing the width of a conducting channel **Feldeffekttransistor; field programmable device** *see* PLA; **field programming** = writing data into a PROM **Feldprogrammierung;** *see also* BLOW; **field strength** = amplitude of the magnetic or electric field at one point in that field **Feldstärke**
(b) section containing individual data items in a record **Feld;** *the employee record has a field for age;* **address** or **operand field** = part of a computer instruction that contains the location of the operand **Adressfeld od Operandenfeld; card field** = part of a card column reserved for one type of data or record **Lochkartenfeld; data field** = part of a computer instruction that contains the location of the data **Datenfeld; field label** = series of characters used to identify a field or its location **Feldkennung; field length** = number of characters that a field can contain **Feldlänge; field marker** or **separator** = code used to indicate the end of one field and the start of the next **Feldmarkierungszeichen, Trennzeichen; protected field** = storage or display area that cannot be altered by the user **geschütztes Feld**
(c) method of building up a picture on a television screen **Halbbild; field blanking** = interval when television signal field synchronizing pulses are transmitted **(Halb)bildaustastung; field frequency** = number of field scans per second **Feldfrequenz; field flyback** = return of electron beam to top left hand corner of a screen **Bildrücklauf; field sweep** = vertical electron beam movement over a television screen **(Halb)bildabtastung; field sync pulse** = pulse in a TV signal that makes sure that the receiver's field sweep is in sync **Bildsynchronisierpuls**
(d) section of an image that is available after the light has passed through the camera and lens **Feld**
(e) in the field = outside an office or factory **im Außendienst; field engineer** = engineer who does not work at one single company,

but travels between customers carrying out maintenance on their computers **Außendiensttechniker; field sales manager** = manager in charge of a group of salesmen working in a particular area of the country **Außendienstverkaufsleiter; field tested** = product tested outside a company *or* research laboratory, in a real situation **praxisgetestet; field work** = examining the situation among several potential customers **Feldforschung, Außenarbeit**

◊ **fielding** *noun* arrangement of field allocations inside a record and file **Feldanordnung**

FIFO = FIRST IN FIRST OUT storage read/write method in which the first item stored is the first read **FIFO (zuerst Abgelegtes wird als erstes bearbeitet); FIFO memory** = memory using a FIFO access scheme **FIFO-Speichermethode;** *the two computers operate at different rates, but can transmit data using a FIFO memory;* **FIFO queue** = temporary (queue) storage, in which the first item written to the queue is the first to be read **FIFO-Warteschlange;** *compare* LIFO

fifth generation computers *noun* next stage of computer system design using fast VLSI circuits and powerful programming languages to allow human interaction **Computer der fünften Generation**

figure *noun*
(a) printed line illustration in a book **Abbildung;** *see figure 10 for a chart of ASCII codes*
(b) printed number **Zahl; figures case** = characters in a telegraphic transmission that are mainly numbers *or* signs **Ziffern- und Zeichenfeld; figures shift** = (i) transmitted code that indicates to the receiver that all following characters should be read as upper case; (ii) mechanical switch which allows a typewriter to print *or* keyboard to produce special characters and symbols located on the same keys as the numbers **(i) & (ii) Zeichenumschaltung; in round figures** = not totally accurate, but correct to the nearest 10 or 100 **auf-, abgerundet;** *they have a workforce of 2,500 in round figures*

file
1 *noun*
(a) cardboard holder for documents, which can fit in the drawer of a filing cabinet **Aktenordner;** *put these letters in the customer file; look in the file marked "Scottish sales";* **box file** = cardboard box for holding documents **kastenförmiger Aktenordner**

(b) documents kept for reference **Akte; to place something on file** = to keep a record of something **etwas zu den Akten tun; to keep someone's name on file** = to keep someone's name on a list for reference **jdn in den Akten führen; file copy** = copy of a document which is kept for reference in an office **Aktenkopie; card-index file** = information kept on filing cards **Kartei**
(c) section of data on a computer (such as payroll, address list, customer accounts), in the form of individual records which may contain data, characters, digits *or* graphics **Datei; file activity ratio** = ratio of the number of different records accessed within a file compared to the total number in store **Bewegungshäufigkeit der Dateien; file allocation table (FAT)** = (in a PC operating system) data file stored on disk containing the names of each file stored on the disk, together with its starting sector position, date and size **Dateizuordnungstabelle (FAT); file attributes** = control bits of data stored with each file which control particular functions or aspects of the file such as read-only, archived or system file **Dateiattribute; file cleanup** = tidying and removing out of date *or* unnecessary data from a file **Dateisäuberung; file collating** = putting the contents of a file into order **Dateisortierung; file control block** = list (in main memory) of files in use within the system **Dateiverwaltungsblock; file conversion** = change of format *or* structure of a file system, usually when using a new program *or* file handling routine **Dateiumsetzung; file creation** = writing file header information onto a disk and writing an entry into the directory **Dateierstellung; file defragmentation** *see* DEFRAGMENTATION; **file deletion** = erasing a file from storage **Dateilöschung;** *see also* DELETE; **file descriptor** = code *or* series of characters used to identify a file **Dateibeschreibung; file directory** = list of names and information about files in a backing storage device **Dateiverzeichnis; file extent** = actual area *or* number of tracks required to store a file **Dateiumfang; file fragmentation** = file that is stored in non contiguous sectors on a disk **Dateifragmentierung; file gap** = section of blank tape *or* disk that indicates the end of a file **Dateizwischenraum; file handle** = number by which an open file is identified within a program **Dateinummer, Filehandle;** *the new data is written to the file identified by file handle 1;* **file handling routine** = short computer program that manages the reading/writing and organization of stored files **Dateiverwaltungsroutine; file header** =

information about the file stored at the beginning of the file **Dateikennsatz;** *the file header in the database file shows the total number of records and lists the index fields;* **file identification** = unique label *or* name used to identify and locate a file stored on baking store **Dateiname; file index** = sorted table of the main entries in a file, with their address, allowing the rapid location of entries **Datei-Index; file label** = character(s) used to identify a file **Dateikennsatz;** file **layout** = set of rules defining internal file structure **Dateiaufbau; file locking** = software mechanism that prevents data in a file being updated by two different users at the same time; only one user can change the particular information at any one time **Dateisperrung; file maintenance** = process of updating a file by changing, adding *or* deleting entries **Dateiwartung, Fortschreibung; file management (system)** = section of a DOS that allocates disk space to files, keeping track of the sections and their sector addresses **Dateiverwaltung(ssystem); file manager** = routines used to create, locate and maintain files on backing store **Dateiverwalter; file merger** = (i) to combine two data files, but still retaining an overall structure; (ii) one file created from more than one file written one after the other (no order preserved) **(i) & (ii) Mischen von Dateien; file name** = word used to identify a particular stored file **Dateiname; file organization** *see* FILE LAYOUT; **file processing** = applying a set of rules *or* search limits to a file, in order to update *or* find information **Dateiverarbeitung; file protection** = software *or* physical device used to prevent any accidental deletion *or* modification of a file *or* its records **Dateischutz; file protect tab** = plastic tab on a disk which prevents accidental erasure of a file **Schreibschutz; file purge** = erasing the contents of a file **Dateilöschung; file-recovery utility** = software that allows files that have been accidentally deleted *or* damaged to be read again **Dateiwiederherstellungsprogramm;** *a lost file cannot be found without a file-recovery utility;* **file security** = hardware *or* software organization of a computer system to protect users' files from unauthorized access **Dateischutz; file server** = small microcomputer and large backing store device that is used for the management and storage of a user's files in a net work **Controller für Speicherzugriff; file set** = number of related files treated as one unit **Dateimenge; file sharing** = one file that can be used by two or more users *or* programs in a network (often using

file locking) **gemeinsame Dateinutzung; file size** = the number of bytes a file occupies on disk **Dateigröße; file sort** = to put the contents of a file into order **Dateisortierung; file storage** = physical means of preserving data in a file, such as a disk drive *or* tape machine **Dateispeicherung; file store** = files that are available in main memory at any time **Dateispeicher; file structure** = way in which a (data) file is organized **Dateistruktur; file transfer** = moving a file from one area of memory to another *or* to another storage device **Dateitransfer; file transfer access and management (FTAM)** = standard method of transferring files between different computer systems **File Transfer Access and Management (FTAM); file transfer protocol (FTP)** = TCP/IP standard for transferring files between computers; it is a file sharing protocol that operates at layers 5, 6 and 7 of an OSI model network **Dateiübertragungsprotokoll, File Transfer Protocol (FTP); file transfer utility** = software utility that links two computers together (normally via a physical serial cable) and allows files to be transferred between the computers **Dateiübertragungsdienstprogramm; file type** = method of classifying what a file contains; (in an MS-DOS system this is often by the filename extension) **Dateityp;** *files with the extension EXE are file types that contain program code;* **file update** = (i) recent changes *or* transactions to a file; (ii) new version of software which is sent to users of an existing version **(i) Fortschreibung; (ii) neueste Softwareversion; file validation** = checking that a file is correct **Dateiprüfung; data file** = file containing data (as opposed to a program file) **Datei; disk file** = number of related records *or* data items stored under one name on disk **Plattendatei; distributed file system** = system that uses files stored in more than one location *or* backing store, but which are processed at a central point **verteiltes Dateisystem; hidden file** = important system file which is not displayed in a directory and cannot normally be read by a user **versteckte Datei; indexed file** = sequential file with an index of all the entries and their addresses **indizierte Datei; inverted file** = file with an index entry for every data item **invertierte Datei; output file** = set of records that have been completely processed according to various parameters **Ausgabedatei; program file** = file containing a program rather than data **Programmdatei; text file** = file that contains text rather than digits *or* data

Textdatei; **threaded file** = file in which an entry will contain data and an address to the next entry that contains the same data (allowing rapid retrieval of all identical entries) **gekettete Datei; transaction** *or* **change** *or* **detail** *or* **movement file** = file containing recent changes to records *or* transactions used to update a master file **Bewegungsdatei 2** *verb* **to file documents** = to put documents in order so that they can be found easily **Dokumente ablegen;** *the correspondence is filed under "complaints"; he filed the new papers in chronological order*

◊ **filename** *noun* unique identification code allocated to a program **Dateiname;** *in MS-DOS, a filename can be up to eight characters long together with a three character filename extension;* **filename extension** = (in MS-DOS) additional three-character name that is used together with a filename, indicating the type *or* use of the file **Dateinamenerweiterung;** *the filename extension SYS indicates that this is a system file*

filing *noun* (i) putting documents in order; (ii) documents which have to be put in order (i) **Sortierung;** (ii) **zu sortierende Dokumente;** *there is a lot of filing to do at the end of the week; the manager looked through the week's filing to see what letters had been sent;* **filing basket** *or* **filing tray** = container kept on a desk for documents which have to be filed **Ablagekorb; filing cabinet** = metal box with several drawers for keeping files **Aktenschrank; filing card** = card with information written on it, used to classify information into the correct order **Karteikarte** NOTE: no plural

◊ **filing system** *noun*
(a) way of putting documents in order for reference **Ablagesystem**
(b) software which organizes files **Software, die Dateien verwaltet**

fill *verb*
(a) to make something full **füllen;** *the screen was filled with flickering images*
(b) to put characters in gaps in a field so that there are no spaces left **auffüllen; fill character** = character added to a string of characters to make up a required length **Füllzeichen; filled cable** = cable which uses a substance to fill any gaps between outer and conductors, so preventing water getting in **ausgegossenes Kabel**
(c) to draw an enclosed area in one colour *or* shading **ausfüllen**

◊ **fill up** *verb* to make something completely full **voll machen;** *the disk was quickly filled up*

film
1 *noun*
(a) transparent strip of plastic, coated with a light-sensitive compound and used to produce photographs with the aid of a camera **Film; film advance** = (i) lever on a camera used to wind on a roll of film to the next frame; (ii) the distance the film in a phototypesetting machine has to move prior to the next line being set (i) **Filmtransporthebel;** (ii) **Filmtransport; film assembly** = correct arrangement of photographs *or* negatives prior to the production of a printing plate **Bildanordnung; film base** = thin transparent roll of plastic used as a supporting material for photographic film **Filmträger; film chain** = all the necessary equipment needed when showing film *or* slides on television, such as a projector, TV camera and synchronizer **Filmvorführaggregat; film optical scanning device for input into computers (FOSDIC)** = storage device for computer data using microfilm **optische Filmleseeinheit; film pickup** = transmission of a motion picture film by television by electronically scanning each frame **Filmabtaster; film strip** = set of related images on a reel of film, usually for educational purposes **Filmstreifen; photographic film** = light-sensitive film used in a camera to record images **fotografischer Film**
(b) projection at high speed of a series of still images that creates the impression of movement **Film**
2 *verb* to expose a photographic film to light by means of a camera, and so to produce images **fotografieren**

◊ **filming** *noun* shooting of a cinema film *or* TV film **Drehen, Dreharbeiten;** *filming will start next week if the weather is fine*

◊ **filmsetting** *noun* photocomposition **Fotosatz**

filter
1 *noun*
(a) electronic circuit that allows certain frequencies to pass while stopping others **Filter; bandpass filter** = circuit that allows a certain band of frequencies to pass while stopping any that are higher or lower **Bandfilter; high pass filter** = circuit that allows frequencies above a certain limit to pass, but blocks those below that limit **Hochpassfilter; low pass filter** = circuit that blocks signals above a certain frequency **Tiefpassfilter**
(b) optical coloured glass, which stops certain frequencies of light **Filter; absorption filter** = filter that blocks certain colours **Absorptionsfilter; character enhancement filter** = filter placed over a monitor to increase contrast, and also to prevent eyestrain **Linienanhebungsfilter; filter factor** = indicator of the amount of light that an optical filter absorbs when light passes through it **Siebfaktor**
(c) pattern of binary digits used to select various bits from a binary word (a one in the filter retains that bit in the source word) **Filter**
2 *verb*
(a) to remove unwanted elements from a signal *or* file **glätten**
(b) to select various bits *or* records from a word *or* file **herausfiltrieren**

final *adjective* last *or* coming at the end of a period **letzte(r,s);** *to keyboard the final data files; to make the final changes to a document*

find
1 *verb* to get something back which has been lost **finden;** *it took a lot of time to find the faulty chip; the debugger found the error very quickly* NOTE: **finding - found**
2 *noun* command to locate a piece of information **Suchen; find and replace** = feature on a word-processor that allows certain words *or* sections of text to be located and replaced with others **Suchen und Ersetzen**

◊ **Finder ™** *noun* (in an Apple Macintosh system) graphical user interface to the Macintosh; allowing a user to view files and folders and start applications using a mouse **Finder ™**

fine *adjective*
(a) very thin *or* very small **fein;** *the engraving has some very fine lines*
(b) excellent *or* of very high quality **fein**

◊ **fine tune** *verb* to adjust by small amounts the features *or* parameters of hardware *or* software to improve performance **fein abstimmen** *or* **fein einstellen;** *fine-tuning improved the speed by ten per cent*

finish
1 *noun*
(a) final appearance **Finish, Aussehen;** *the product has an attractive finish*
(b) end of a process *or* function **Ende**
2 *verb*
(a) to do something *or* to make something completely **beenden, abschließen;** *the order was finished in time; she finished all the keyboarding before lunch*
(b) to come to an end **fertig sein, (be)enden, auslaufen;** *the contract is due to finish next month*

◊ **finished** *adjective* which has been completed **fertig; finished document** = document which is typed, and is ready to be printed **fertiges Schriftstück, Reinschrift; finished goods** = manufactured goods which are ready to be sold **Fertigerzeugnisse**

finite-precision numbers *noun* use of a fixed number of bits to represent numbers **Zahl mit endlicher Genauigkeit**

firmware *noun* computer program *or* data that is permanently stored in a hardware memory chip, such as a ROM *or* EPROM **Firmware;** *compare with* HARDWARE, SOFTWARE

first fit *noun* routine *or* algorithm that selects the first, largest section of free memory in which to store a (virtual) page **First Fit**

◊ **first generation computer** *noun* original computer made with valve based electronic technology, started around 1951 **Computer der ersten Generation; first generation image** = master copy of an original image, text *or* document **Quelldokument, Ursprungsdokument**

◊ **first in first out (FIFO)** *noun* temporary queue where the first item stored is the first read **FIFO-Methode;** *see also* FIFO

◊ **first-level address** *noun* computer storage address that directly, without any modification, accesses a location *or* device **Erstadresse**

◊ **first party release** *noun* ending of a

telephone connection as soon as either party puts his phone down *or* disconnects his modem **Auslösung einer Verbindung durch zuerst einhängenden Teilnehmer**

fisheye lens *noun* extremely wide angle photographic lens that has a field of view of 180 degrees and produces a distorted circular image **Fischauge**

fit *verb* to plot or calculate a curve that most closely approximates a number of points *or* data **anpassen**

fix
1 *noun* chemical stage in processing a film that sets permanently the developed image on a film *or* paper **Fixierung**
2 *verb*
(a) to make something permanent *or* to attach something permanently **festsetzen, fixieren;** *the computer is fixed to the workstation;* **fixed and exchangeable disk storage (FEDS)** = magnetic disk storage system that contains some removable disks, such as floppy disks and some fixed *or* hard disk drives **System mit Festplatten und flexiblen Disketten; fixed cycle operation** = (i) process in which each operation is allocated a certain, fixed time limit; (ii) actions within a process that are synchronized to a clock **(i) & (ii) Arbeitsweise mit festem Takt; fixed data** = data written to a file *or* screen for information *or* identification purposes and which cannot be altered by the user **Festdaten; fixed disk storage** = hard disk *or* magnetic disk which cannot be removed from the disk drive **Festplattenspeicher; fixed field** = area in a stored record that can only contain a certain amount of data **festes Feld; fixed head disk (drive)** = use of a separate immovable read/write head over each disk track making access time very short **Schnellzugriffsplatte(nlaufwerk); fixed-length record** = record whose size cannot be changed **Satz mit fester Länge; fixed-length word** = preset number of bits that make up a computer word **Wort mit fester Länge; fixed program computer** = (hardwired) computer program that cannot be altered and is run automatically **Festprogrammcomputer; fixed routing** = communications direction routing that does not consider traffic *or* efficient paths **feste Verkehrslenkung; fixed word length** = computer whose word size (in bits) cannot be changed **feste Wortlänge**
(b) to mend **reparieren;** *the technicians are trying to fix the switchboard; can you fix the photocopier?*

◊ **fixed-point notation** *noun* number

representation that retains the position of the digits and decimal points in the computer, so limiting the maximum manageable numbers **Festkommaschreibweise;** *storage of fixed point numbers has two bytes allocated for the whole number and one byte for the fraction part;* **fixed-point arithmetic** = arithmetic rules and methods using fixed-point numbers **Festkommarechnung;** *compare with* FLOATING POINT

flag
1 *noun* (i) way of showing the end of field *or* of indicating something special in a database; (ii) method of reporting the status of a register after a mathematical *or* logical operation **(i) Anzeiger; (ii) Flag;** *if the result is zero, the zero flag is set;* **carry flag** = indicator that a carry has occurred after a subtraction *or* addition **Übertragsanzeiger; device flag** = one bit in a device status word, used to show the state of a device **Geräteanzeiger; overflow bit** *or* **flag** = single bit in a word that is set to one (1) if a mathematical overflow has occurred **Überlaufanzeiger; zero flag** = indicator that the contents of a register *or* result is zero **Nullkennzeichnung; flag bit** = single bit of a word used as a flag for certain operations **Synchronisationszeichen; flag code** = code sequence which informs the receiver that following characters represent control actions **Steuerzeichenkennzeichnung; flag event** = process *or* state *or* condition that sets a flag **Ereignis zum Kennzeichen setzen; flag register** = register that contains the status and flag bits of a CPU **Kennzeichenregister; flag sequence** = sequence of codes sent on a packet switching network as identification of the start and finish of a frame of data **Blockbegrenzung**
2 *verb* to attract the attention of a program while it is running to provide a result *or* to report an action *or* to indicate something special **markieren**

◊ **flagging** *noun*
(a) putting an indicator against an item so that it can be found later **Markieren**
(b) picture distortion from a video recorder due to incorrect synchronization of tape playback head **Markierung**

flare *noun* unwanted light due to internal lens *or* camera reflections causing bright spots on a photographic film **Lichtreflexe**

◊ **flared** *adjective* (image) with unwanted bright spots *or* lines due to internal lens *or* camera reflections **reflektierend**

flash *verb* to switch a light on and off; to

increase and lower the brightness of a cursor to provide an indicator **blinken; flash A/D** = parallel high speed A/D converter **Hochgeschwindigkeits-analog-digital-Umsetzer; flash card** = card containing indexing information photographed with a document **Indexkarte; flashing character** = character intensity that is switched on and off (as an indicator) **blinkendes Zeichen; flash memory** = nonvolatile memory similar to an EEPROM device but that operates with blocks of data rather than single bytes; most often used as an alternative to a disk drive **Flash Memory, Flash-Speicher**

flat *adjective*
(a) lacking contrast (in an image *or* photograph) **kontrastarm; flat address space** = area of memory in which each location has a unique address (OS/2, Macintosh use a flat address space, MS-DOS does not) **linearer Adressraum;** *compare* SEGMENTED ADDRESS SPACE; **flat file database** = database program that does not allow relational data; it can only access data stored in one file at a time **unstrukturierte Datenbank**
(b) smooth (surface) **eben; flat file** = two-dimensional file of data items **Flachdatei; flat pack** = integrated circuit package whose leads extend horizontally, allowing the device to be mounted directly onto a PCB without the need for holes **Flachgehäuse**
(c) fixed *or* not changing **pauschal; flat rate** = set pricing rate that covers all the uses of a facility **Pauschaltarif**

◊ **flatbed** *noun* printing *or* scanning machine that holds the paper *or* image on a flat surface while processing **Flachbettscanner;** *scanners are either flatbed models or platen type, paper-fed models; paper cannot be rolled through flatbed scanners;* **flatbed plotter** = movable pen that draws diagrams under the control of a computer onto a flat piece of paper **Flachbettplotter; flatbed press** = mechanical printing machine where the inked printing plate lies flat on the bed of the machine **Flachbettpresse; flatbed transmitter** = device that keeps a document flat while it is being scanned before being transmitted by facsimile means **Flachbettgerät; horizontaler Belichtungswagen**

flex *noun* wire *or* cable used to connect an appliance to the mains electricity supply **Kabel**
NOTE: no plural: **a piece of flex**

flexible *adjective* which can be altered *or*

changed **flexibel; flexible array** = array whose size and limits can be altered **flexible Feldgruppe; flexible disk** = FLOPPY DISK; **flexible disk cartridge** = FLOPPY DISK; **flexible machining system (FMS)** = computer numeric control (CNC) *or* control of a machine by a computer **flexibles Maschinensteuerungssystem; flexible manufacturing system (FMS)** = use of CNC machines, robots and other automated devices in manufacturing **flexibles Fertigungssystem; flexible working hours** = system where workers can start *or* stop working at different hours of the morning or evening, provided that they work a certain number of hours per week **gleitende Arbeitszeit**

◊ **flexibility** *noun* ability of hardware *or* software to adapt to various conditions *or* tasks **Flexibilität**

flicker
1 *noun*
(a) random variation of brightness in a television picture **Flimmern**
(b) effect that occurs when a frame from a video disk is frozen and two different pictures are displayed alternately at high speed due to the incorrect field matching **Flimmern**
(c) computer graphic image whose brightness alternates due to a low image refresh rate *or* signal corruption **Flimmern**
2 *verb* to move very slightly **flimmern, flackern;** *the image flickers when the printer is switched on*

◊ **flicker-free** *adjective* (display) that does not flicker **flimmerfrei**

> QUOTE the new 640 by 480 pixel standard, coupled with the flicker-free displays on the four new monitors and a maximum of 256 colours from a palette of more than quarter of a million
>
> *PC User*

flier *noun* small advertising leaflet designed to encourage customers to ask for more information about a product *or* service **Hand-, Werbezettel**

flip-flop (FF) *noun* electronic circuit *or* chip whose output can be one of two states, which is determined by one or two inputs, can be used to store one bit of digital data **Flipflop, bistabile Schaltung; JK-flip-flop** = flip-flop device with two inputs (J and K) and two outputs whose states are always complementary and dependent on the inputs **JK-Flipflop** ⇨APPENDIX;

D-flip-flop = flip-flop device with one input and two outputs **D-Flipflop**

flippy *noun* disk that is double-sided but used in a single-sided drive, so it has to be turned over to read the other side **Flippy (doppelseitig beschreibbare, umzudrehende Diskette)**

float *noun* addition of the origin address to all indexed *or* relative addresses to check the amount of memory a program will require **Speicherauszug des gesamten Systems; float factor** = location in memory at which the first instruction of a program is stored **Startadresse; float relocate** = to convert floating addresses to absolute addresses **Umsetzung relativer in absolute Adressen**

◊ **floating** *adjective* not fixed; character which is separate from the character it should be attached to **fließend; floating accent** = method of printing an accent in text where the accent is separate from the letter above which it is printed (on a typewriter, an accented letter may need three keystrokes, one for the accent, then backspace, then key the letter) **gleitender Akzent; floating address** = location specified in relation to a reference address **symbolische Adresse; floating head** = FLYING HEAD; **floating point arithmetic** = arithmetic operations on floating point numbers **Fließkommaarithmetik; floating point (notation)** = numerical notation in which a fractional number is represented with a point after the first digit and a power of ten, so that any number can be stored in a standard form **Fließkommaschreibweise;** *the fixed number 56.47 in floating-point arithmetic would be 0.5647 and a power of 2;* **floating point number** = number represented using floating point notation **Fließkommazahl; floating point operation (FLOP)** = mathematical operation carried out on a floating point number **Fließkommaoperation; floating point unit** *or* **processor (FPU)** = specialized CPU that can process floating point numbers very rapidly **Fließkommaprozessor;** *the floating point processor speeds up the processing of the graphics software; this model includes a built-in floating point processor;* **floating symbolic address** = symbol *or* label that identifies a particular instruction *or* word, regardless of its location **symbolische Adresse; floating voltage** = voltage in a network *or* device that has no related ground *or* reference plane **Schwebspannung**

flooding *noun* rapid, reliable but not very efficient means of routing packet-switched data, in which each node sends the data received to each of its neighbours **paketvermittelte Datenübertragungsmethode**

FLOP = FLOATING POINT OPERATION; **FLOPs per second** = measure of computing power as the number of floating point operations that a computer can execute every second **Fließkommarechnungen pro Sekunde**

floppy disk *or* **floppy** *or* **FD** *noun* secondary storage device, in the form of a flat, circular flexible disk onto which data can be stored in a magnetic form (a floppy disk cannot store as much data as a hard disk, but is easily removed, and is protected by a flexible paper *or* plastic sleeve) **Diskette; floppy disk controller (FDC)** = combination of hardware and software devices that control and manage the read/write operations of a disk drive from a computer **Diskettensteuerelemente; floppy disk sector** = smallest area on a magnetic (floppy) disk that can be individually addressed by a computer **Diskettensektor; floppy disk drive** *or* **unit** = disk drive for floppy disks and ancillary electronics as a separate assembly **Diskettenlaufwerk; floppy tape** *or* **tape streamer** = continuous loop of tape, used for backing storage **Band;** *see also* MICROFLOPPY

| COMMENT: floppies are available in various sizes: the commonest are 3.5 inch, 5.25 inch and 8 inch. The size refers to the diameter of the disk inside the sleeve

flow

1 *noun* regular movement **Fluss;** *automatic text flow across pages; the device controls the copy flow; current flow is regulated by a resistor;* **flow control** = management of the flow of data into queues and buffers, to prevent spillage *or* lost data **Fluss-Steuerung; flow diagram** = FLOWCHART; **flow direction** = order in which events occur in a flowchart **Ablaufrichtung; flowline** = lines connecting flowchart symbols, showing the direction of flow within a flowchart **Ablauflinie; data flow** = movement of data through a system **Datenfluss**
2 *verb* to move smoothly **fließen;** *work is flowing normally again after the breakdown of the printer;* **flow text** = to insert text into a page format in a DTP system; the text fills all the space around pictures, and between set margins **Text einfließen lassen**

◊ **flowchart** *or* **flow diagram**
1 *noun* chart which shows the arrangement of the steps in a process *or* program

Flussdiagramm; flowchart symbols = special symbols used to represent devices, decisions and operations in a flowchart **Sinnbild für Datenflussläufe; flowchart template** = plastic sheet with template symbols cut out, to allow symbols to be drawn quickly and clearly **Zeichenschablone; data flowchart** = diagram used to describe a computer or data processing system structure **Datenflussplan; logical flowchart** = diagram showing where the logical decisions occur in a structure and their effects on program execution **logisches Flussdiagramm 2** verb to describe a process, its control and routes graphically **im Flussdiagramm darstellen**

fluctuate verb to move up and down **schwanken;** the electric current fluctuates between 1 Amp and 1.3 Amp fluctuating signal strength

◊ **fluctuation** noun up and down movement **Schwankung;** voltage fluctuations can affect the functioning of the computer system

flush
1 verb to clear or erase all the contents of a queue, buffer, file or section of memory **löschen; flush buffers** = to erase any data remaining in a buffer, ready for a new job or after a job has been aborted **Speicher löschen**
2 adjective level or in line with **auf gleicher Ebene, glatt beschnitten;** the covers are trimmed flush with the pages; **flush left** or **flush right** see JUSTIFY LEFT, JUSTIFY RIGHT

flutter noun fluctuations of tape speed due to mechanical or circuit problems, causing signal distortion **Gleichlaufschwankung, Jaulen;** wow and flutter are common faults on cheap tape recorders

fly verb to move through the air **fliegen; flying spot scan** = method of transferring a frame of film to television by scanning it with a light beam **Lichtpunktabtastung**

◊ **flyback** noun electron picture beam return from the end of a scan to the beginning of the next **Rücklauf**

flying head noun hard disk read/write head that is wing-shaped to fly just above the surface of the spinning disk **fliegender Lese-/Schreibkopf**

FM = FREQUENCY MODULATION

FMS = FLEXIBLE MANUFACTURING SYSTEM use of CNC machines, robots and other automated devices in manufacturing **FMS**

FNP = FRONT END NETWORK PROCESSOR

f-number noun measurement of the amount of light that an optical lens can collect, measured as the ratio of focal length to maximum aperture **Blendenöffnungsverhältnis, Brennzahl**

focal length noun distance between the centre of an optical lens and the focusing plane, when the lens is focused at infinity **Brennweite**

focus
1 noun image or beam that is clear and well defined **Schärfe; the picture is out of focus** or **is not in focus** = the picture is not clear **das Bild ist unscharf**
2 verb to adjust the focal length of a lens or beam deflection system so that the image or beam is clear and well defined **scharfstellen;** the camera is focused on the foreground; they adjusted the lens position so that the beam focused correctly

fog noun effect on photographic material which has been accidentally exposed to unwanted light, causing a loss of picture contrast **(Grau)schleier**

fold verb to bend a flat thing, so that part of it is on top of the rest **falten;** she folded the letter so that the address was clearly visible; **accordion fold** or **fanfold** = method of folding continuous stationery, one sheet in one direction, the next sheet in the opposite direction, allowing the paper to be stored conveniently and fed into a printer continuously **Zickzackfaltung**

◊ **-fold** suffix times **-fach; four-fold** = four times **vierfach**

folder noun (in an Apple Macintosh) group of files stored together under a name, similar to a directory under MS-DOS **Ordner;** see also DIRECTORY

◊ **folding** noun hashing method (that generates an address by splitting the key into parts and adding them together) **Streuspeichermethode**

◊ **folding machine** noun machine which automatically folds sheets of paper **Falzmaschine**

folio
1 *noun* page with a number, especially two facing pages in an account book which have the same number **nummerierte Seite**
2 *verb* to put a number on a page **paginieren**

font *or* **fount** *noun* set of characters all of the same style, size and typeface **Schriftart, Zeichensatz, Font; font card** = ROM device that fits into a socket on a printer and adds another resident font **Schriftartenkarte; font change** = function on a computer to change the style of characters used on a display screen **Zeichensatzänderung; Font/DA Mover** = (in an Apple Macintosh system) system utility that allows a user to add fonts and DA files to the system environment **Font/DA-Mover; font disk** = (i) transparent disk that contains the master images of a particular font, used in a phototypesetting machine; (ii) magnetic disk that contains the data to drive a character generator to make up the various fonts on a computer display **(i) Schriftenplatte; (ii) Schriftdatenplatte; downloadable fonts** *or* **resident fonts** = fonts *or* typefaces which are stored on a disk and can be downloaded to a printer and stored in temporary memory **verfügbare Zeichensätze**

QUOTE laser printers store fonts in several ways: as resident, cartridge and downloadable fonts
Desktop Publishing Today

QUOTE Word Assistant is designed to help word-processing users produce better-looking documents. It has style templates and forms providing 25 TrueType fonts, 100 clip-art images and two font utility programs
Computing

foolscap *noun* large size of writing paper, longer than A4; *entspricht* **Kanzleipapier;** *the letter was on six sheets of foolscap;* **a foolscap envelope** = large envelope which takes foolscap paper **Umschlag für Kanzleipapier**
NOTE: no plural

foot *noun* bottom part **Fuß;** *he signed his name at the foot of the letter*

◊ **foot candle** *noun* amount of light illumination in one square foot when the incident flux is one lumen **Fußkerze (= 1 Lumen pro sq.ft.)**

◊ **footer** *or* **footing** *noun* message at the bottom of all the pages in a printed document (such as the page number) **Fußzeile**

◊ **footnote** *noun* note at the bottom of a page, which refers to the text above it, usually using a superior number as a reference **Fußnote**

◊ **footprint** *noun*
(a) area covered by a transmitting device such as a satellite *or* antenna **Erfassungsbereich**
(b) area that a computer takes up on a desk **Installationsfläche**

QUOTE Acer has overhauled its desktop PC range with the launch of 16 new models ranging from small-footprint, single-processing systems to large multiprocessing boxes
Computing

for-next loop *noun* loop or routine that is repeated until a condition no longer occurs **FOR-NEXT-Schleife;** *for X=1 to 5: print X: next X - this will print out 1 2 3 4 5*

forbid *verb* to say that something must not be done **verbieten;** *the contract forbids sale of the goods to the USA;* **forbidden character** *or* **combination** = bit combination in a computer word that is not allowed according to the rules defined by the programmer *or* system designer **verbotenes Zeichen; verbotene Zeichenkombination**
NOTE: **forbidding - forbade - forbidden**

force
1 *noun* strength **Kraft; to come into force** = to start to operate *or* work **in Kraft treten;** *the new regulations will come into force on January 1st*
2 *verb* to make someone do something **zwingen;** *competition has forced the company to lower its prices;* **forced page break** = embedded code which indicates a new page start **erzwungener Seitenumbruch**

foreground *noun*
(a) front part of an illustration (as opposed to the background) **Vordergrund; foreground colour** = colour of characters and text displayed on a screen **Vordergrundfarbe**
(b) high priority task done by a computer **Prioritätsaufgabe; foreground/background modes** = computer system in which two modes for program execution are possible: foreground mode for interactive user programs, background mode for housekeeping and other necessary system programs **Vorder-/Hintergrundmodus; foreground processing** *or* **foregrounding** = execution of high priority jobs *or* programs in a multitasking operating system

Vordergrundverarbeitung; foreground processing memory = region of a multitasking operating system in which high priority jobs or programs are executed Vordergrundverarbeitungsspeicher; foreground program = high priority program in a multitasking system, whose results are usually visible to the user Vordergrundprogramm, Prioritäts-, Vorrangprogramm; compare BACKGROUND

QUOTE This brighter - but still anti-glare - type of screen is especially useful for people using colourful graphic applications, where both the background and foreground are visually important
Computing

forest *noun* number of interconnected data structure trees **Wald**

form

1 *noun*
(a) (i) preprinted document with blank spaces where information can be entered; (ii) graphical display that looks like an existing printed form and is used to enter data into a database (i) **Vordruck, Formular;** (ii) **Formular;** *it's been easy to train the operators to use the new software since its display looks like the existing printed forms* (b) complete plate or block of type, ready for printing **Druckform** (c) page of computer stationery **Formularseite; form feed** = command to a printer to move to the next sheet of paper **Formularvorschub; form flash** = text heading held in store and printed out at the same time as the text **Formulareinblendung; form handling equipment** = peripherals (such as decollator) which deal with output from a printer **Papiernachbereitungsmaschine; form letter** = standard letter into which personal details of each addressee are inserted, such as name, address and job **Formbrief; form mode** = display method on a data entry terminal, the form is displayed on the screen and the operator enters relevant details **Formularmodus; form overlay** = heading or other matter held in store and printed out at the same time as the text **Formmaske, Formschablone; form stop** = sensor on a printer which indicates when the paper has run out **Papierendesensor**
2 *verb* to create a shape; to construct **bilden;** *the system is formed of five separate modules*

format

1 *noun*
(a) size and shape of a book **Format;** *the printer can deal with all formats up to quarto*

(b) specific method of arranging text or data; way of arranging data on disk **Format; address format** = way in which address data is stored including which bits select pages, memory protect, etc. **Adressformat; card format** = way in which columns and rows are arranged to represent data or characters in a punched card **Lochkartenformat; data format** = rules defining the way in which data is stored or transmitted **Datenformat; display format** = number of characters that can be displayed on a screen, given as row and column lengths **Anzeigeformat; format mode** = use of protected display fields on a screen to show a blank form or page which cannot be altered, but into which a user can enter information **Formatmodus; instruction format** = rules defining the way the operands, data and address are arranged in an instruction **Befehlsstruktur; local format storage** = format of a empty form or repeated page stored in a terminal rather than being repeatedly transmitted **Schablonenspeicherung; variable format** = changing method of arranging data or text within an area **variables Format** (c) precise syntax of instructions and arguments **Format; symbolic-coding format** = assembly language instruction syntax, using a label, operation and operand fields **Format zur symbolischen Codierung** (d) way of arranging a TV programme **Struktur; magazine format** = type of information programme which contains several different items linked together **Magazinformat**
2 *verb*
(a) to arrange text as it will appear in printed form on paper **anordnen;** *style sheets are used to format documents;* **formatted dump** = text or data printed in a certain format **formatisierter Speicherauszug** (b) **to format a disk** = (i) to set up a blank disk so that it is ready for data, by writing control and track location information on it; (ii) to define the areas of a disk reserved for data and control (i) & (ii) **formatieren; disk formatting** = setting up a blank disk by writing control and track location information on it **Formatierung;** *disk formatting has to be done before you can use a new floppy disk;* **low-level format** = process that defines the physical pattern and arrangement of tracks and sectors on a disk **Low-Level-Formatierung**

◊ **formatter** *noun* hardware or software that arranges text or data according to certain rules **Formatierungsprogramm; print formatter** = software that converts embedded codes and print commands to printer control signals **Druckformatierer; text formatter** = program that converts text to a new form or layout according to parameters or embedded codes (such as line width, page size, justification, etc.) **Textformatierer**

QUOTE there are three models, offering 53, 80 and 160 Mb of formatted capacity
Minicomputer News

QUOTE As an increasing amount of information within businesses is generated in word-processed format, text retrieval tools are becoming a highly attractive pragmatic solution
Computing

formula *noun* set of mathematical rules applied to solve a problem **Formel; formula portability** = feature in a spreadsheet program to find a value in a single cell from data in others, with the possibility of using the same formula in other cells **Werteaustauschbarkeit; formula translator** = FORTRAN
NOTE: plural is **formulae**

FORTH computer programming language mainly used in control applications **FORTH (Programmiersprache)**

QUOTE the main attraction of FORTH over other computer languages is that it is not simply a language, rather it is a programming tool in which it is possible to write other application specific languages
Electronics & Power

FORTRAN = FORMULA TRANSLATOR programming language developed in the first place for scientific use **FORTRAN (Programmiersprache)**

forty-track disk *noun* floppy disk formatted to contain forty tracks of data **Diskette mit 40 Spuren**

forward
1 *adjective* moving in advance *or* in front **vorwärts; forward channel** = communications line containing data transmitted from the user to another party **Hauptvermittlungskanal; forward clearing** = switching telephone systems back to their clear state, starting from the point where the call was made and travelling forward towards the destination **Weitervermittlung; forward error correction** = method of

detecting and correcting certain error conditions with the use of redundant codes **Vorwärtsfehlerkorrektur; forward pointer** = (in a linked list) pointer that contains the address of the next item in the list **Vorwärtszeiger; forward reference** = reference to something which has not yet been established **Verweis nach vorne; forward scatter** = scattered sections of wave travelling in the same direction as the incident **Vorwärtsstreuung**
2 *verb* to pass a call on to another point **weitervermitteln**

◊ **forward mode** *noun* to add a number *or* index *or* displacement to an origin **Vorwärtsmodus**

FOSDIC = FILM OPTICAL SCANNING DEVICE FOR INPUT INTO COMPUTERS storage device for computer data using microfilm **optische Filmleseeinheit**

fount = FONT set of characters all of the same style, size and typeface **Schriftart, Zeichensatz**

four-address instruction *noun* program instruction which contains four addresses within its address field, usually the location of the two operands, the result and the location of the next instruction **Vieradressbefehl; four-plus-one address** = instruction that contains the locations of four registers and the location of the next instruction **Vier-plus-eins-Adressbefehl**

Fourier series *noun* mathematical representation of waveforms by a combination of fundamental and harmonic components of a frequency **Fourier-Serie**

fourth generation computers *noun* computer technology using LSI circuits, developed around 1970 and still in current use **Computer der vierten Generation; fourth generation languages** = languages that are user-friendly and have been designed with the non-expert in mind **Programmiersprachen der vierten Generation**

four-track recorder *noun* tape recorder that is able to record and play back four independent audio tracks at once **Vierspurrekorder**

fps = FRAMES PER SECOND

FPU = FLOATING POINT UNIT

fractal *noun* geometric shape that repeats

itself within itself and always appears the same, however much you magnify the image **Fraktal**

fraction *noun* (i) part of a whole unit, expressed as one figure above another (such as ¼, ¾, etc.); (ii) mantissa of a floating point number **(i) Bruch; (ii) Mantisse (einer Fließkommazahl)**

◊ **fractional** *adjective* made of fractions; referring to fractions **gebrochen, Bruch-, bruch-;** *the root is the fractional power of a number;* **fractional part** = mantissa of a floating point number **Stellen hinter dem Komma einer Zahl; fractional services** = allocation of parts of a bandwidth to different signals or customers **Frequenzbereichsdienste;** *the commercial carrier will sell you fractional services that provide 64Kbps data transmission*

fragmentation *noun*
(a) (in main memory) memory allocation to a number of files, which has resulted in many small, free sections *or* fragments that are too small to be of any use, but waste a lot of space **Fragmentierung**
(b) (on a disk drive) files stored scattered across non-contiguous sectors on a hard disk **Fragmentierung; defragmentation utility** = software utility that carries out the process of defragmentation on a hard disk **Entfragmentierungsprogramm**

> COMMENT: when a file is saved to disk, it is not always saved in adjacent sectors; this will increase the retrieval time. Defragmentation moves files back into adjacent sectors so that the read head does not have to move far across the disk, so it increases performance.

frame *noun*
(a) (i) space on magnetic tape for one character code; (ii) packet of transmitted data including control and route information **(i) Rahmen; (ii) Datenübertragungsblock; frame error** = error due to a faulty bit within a frame on magnetic tape **Rahmenfehler; frame relay** = communications protocol (similar to X.25 and fast packet switching) that operates at OSI level 2 and routes data packets directly to the destination **Frame-Relay-Protokoll**
(b) one complete television *or* photographic image **Rasterfeld; Einzelbild; video frame** = one image on a video film **Videoeinzelbild;** *with the image processor you can freeze a video frame;* **frame flyback** = electron beam return from the bottom right to the top left corner of the screen to start building up a new field **Rahmenrücklauf; frame frequency**

= number of television frames transmitted per second **Bildfrequenz;** *in the UK the frame frequency is 25 fps;* **frame grabber** = high speed digital sampling circuit that stores a television picture frame in memory so that it can then be processed by a computer **Bildgrabber; frame store** = digital storage of analog TV signals on disk **Bildspeicher;** *the image processor allows you to store a video frame in a built-in 8-bit frame store; the frame store can be used to display weather satellite pictures*

◊ **frames per second (fps)** *noun*
(a) speed of single frames of a motion picture through a projector *or* camera every second **Bilder pro Sekunde**
(b) number of television picture frames transmitted per second **Bilder pro Sekunde**

◊ **framing** *noun*
(a) positioning of a camera's field of view for a required image **Einstellung**
(b) synchronization of time division multiplexed frames of data **Bildlageeinstellung; framing bit** = sync bit *or* transmitted bit used to synchronize devices **Rahmenbit; framing code** = method of synchronizing a receiver with a broadcast teletext stream of data **Rahmencode**

◊ **framework** *noun* basic structure of a database *or* process *or* program **Grundstruktur;** *the program framework was designed first*

fraud *noun* making money by tricking people *or* by making them believe something which is not true **Betrug; computer fraud** = theft of data *or* dishonest use *or* other crimes involving computers **Computerkriminalität**

> QUOTE the offences led to the arrest of nine teenagers who were all charged with computer fraud
> *Computer News*

free
1 *adjective* available for use *or* not currently being used; (spare bytes) available on disk *or* in memory **frei; free form database** = database that can store any type of data and does not have a fixed record structure **Datenbank mit freiem Format; free indexing** = library entries having references to documents which the indexer considers useful, even if they do not appear in the text **freie Indizierung; free line** = telephone line that is not connected and so is available for use **freie Telefonleitung; free running mode** = interactive computer mode that allows more than one user to have simultaneous

use of a program **freier Durchlaufbetrieb; free space loss** = measure of the loss of transmitted signals from a satellite antenna to an earth station **Freiraumdämpfung; free space media** = empty space between a transmitter and a receiving aerial which is used for transmission **freier Raum; free wheeling** = transmission protocol where the computer transmitting receives no status signals from the receiver **Freilaufprotokoll 2** *verb* to erase *or* remove *or* backup programs *or* files to provide space in memory **löschen**

◊ **freedom** *noun* being free to do something without restriction **Freiheit; freedom of information** = being able to examine computer records (referring both to government activities and to records kept about individuals) **Informationsfreiheit; freedom of the press** = being able to write and publish in a newspaper what you wish without being afraid of prosecution, provided that you do not break the law **Pressefreiheit; freedom of speech** = being able to say what you want without being afraid of prosecution, provided that you do not break the law **Redefreiheit**

◊ **freely** *adverb* with no restrictions **frei, unbeschränkt**

◊ **freeware** *noun* software that is in the public domain and can be.used by anyone without having to pay **Freeware**

freeze *verb* to freeze (frame) = to stop and display a single frame from a film *or* TV *or* video disk *or* video tape machine **einfrieren;** *the image processor will freeze a single TV frame; see* HANG, CRASH

F-region section of the ionosphere that is 150 - 400Km from the earth's surface **F-Schicht der Ionosphäre**

frequency *noun* number of cycles *or* periods of a regular waveform that are repeated per second **Frequenz; frequency changer** = electronic circuit that shifts the frequency of a signal up *or* down **Frequenzverschieber; frequency divider** = electronic circuit that reduces the frequency of a signal by a multiple of two **Frequenzteiler; frequency division multiplexing (FDM)** = to assign a number of different signals to different frequencies (or bands) to allow many signals to be sent along one channel **Frequenzmultiplex (FDM);** *using FDM we can transmit 100 telephone calls along one main cable;* **frequency domain** = effects of a certain circuit on the frequency range of a signal **Frequenzebene;**

frequency modulation (FM) = varying the frequency of a carrier waveform according to a signal amplitude **Frequenzmodulation (FM); frequency range** = range of allowable frequencies, between two limits **Frequenzbereich; frequency response** = electronic circuit parameter given as the ratio of output to input signal amplitudes at various frequencies **Frequenzgang, Übertragungsbereich; frequency shift keying (FSK)** = transmission system using the translation of two state binary data into two different frequencies, one for on, one for off **Frequenzumtastung; frequency variation** = change of frequency of a signal from normal **Frequenzvariation; clock frequency** = frequency of the main clock that synchronizes a computer system **Taktfrequenz;** *the main clock frequency is 10MHz;* **line frequency** = (in a CRT) the number of times that the picture beam scans a horizontal row of pixels in a monitor **Horizontalfrequenz**

◊ **frequent** *adjective* which comes *or* goes *or* takes place often **häufig;** *we send frequent telexes to New York; how frequent are the planes to Birmingham?*

◊ **frequently** *adverb* often **häufig;** *the photocopier is frequently out of use; we telex our New York office very frequently - at least four times a day*

friction feed *noun* printer mechanism where the paper is advanced by holding it between two rollers (as opposed to tractor feed) **Friktionsantrieb**

friendly front-end *noun* design of the display of a program that is easy to use and understand **gelungene Benutzerführung**

FROM = FUSIBLE READ ONLY MEMORY

front *noun* part of something which faces away from the back **Vorderseite, Front;** *the disks are inserted in slots in the front of the terminal;* **front panel** = main computer system control switches and status indicators **vordere Verkleidungsplatte; front porch** = section of television signal between the line blanking pulse and the line sync pulse **vordere Schwarztreppe; front projection** = projection of background images onto a screen located behind a person **Aufprojektion**

◊ **front-end** *adjective* **(a)** located at the start *or* most important point of a circuit *or* network **Eingangs-; front-end processor (FEP)** = processor

placed between an input source and the central computer whose function is to preprocess received data to relieve the workload of the main computer **Vorschaltrechner; front-end system** = typesetting system, where text is keyboarded on a terminal directly connected to the typesetting computer **Vorverarbeitungssystem**
(b) display presented by a program that is seen by an end user **Benutzeroberfläche;** *the program is very easy to use thanks to the uncomplicated front-end*

FSK = FREQUENCY SHIFT KEYING

FTP = FILE TRANSFER PROTOCOL TCP/IP standard for transferring files between computers; it is a file sharing protocol that operates at layers 5, 6 and 7 of an OSI model network **FTP**

full *adjective*
(a) with as much inside as possible **voll;** *the disk is full, so the material will have to be stored on another disk*
(b) complete *or* including everything **vollständig; full adder** = binary addition circuit that can produce the sum of two inputs and can also accept a carry input, producing a carry output if necessary **Volladdierer; full duplex** = data transmission down a channel in two directions simultaneously **Duplex;** *see also* DUPLEX, HALF-DUPLEX, SIMPLEX; **full-frame time code** = standard method of counting video frames rather than using a time check signal for synchronization with music and effects **Zeitcode zum Zählen von Videovollbildern; full motion video adapter** = computer fitted with a digitising card that is fast enough to capture and display moving video images (at a rate of 25 or 30 frames per second) **Videoadapter; full path** = description of the position of a directory (in relation to the root directory) in which a file is stored **vollständige Pfadangabe; full-screen** = (program display) that uses all the available screen; it is not displayed within a window **Vollbilddarstellung, Vollbildmodus; full-size display** = large screen VDU which can display a whole page of text **Anzeige in voller Größe; full subtractor** = binary subtractor circuit that can produce the difference of two inputs and can also accept a carry input, producing a carry output if necessary **Subtrahierwerk; full-text search** = to carry out a search for something through all the text in a file or database rather than limiting the search to an area or block **Volltextsuche**

◊ **fully** *adverb* completely **vollständig; fully connected network** = situation where each node in a network is connected with every other **vollverbundenes Netz; fully formed characters** = characters produced by a printer in a single action **Volltypen;** *a daisy wheel printer produces fully formed characters;* **fully populated board** = circuit board which has all components in place, including any optional or extra components **komplett bestückte Platine**

function
1 *noun*
(a) mathematical formula, where a result is dependent upon several other numbers **Funktion**
(b) sequence of computer program instructions in a main program that perform a certain task **Funktion; function call** = program instruction that moves execution to a predefined function *or* named sequence of instructions **Funktionsaufruf; function digit** = code used to instruct a computer as to which function *or* branch in a program to follow **Funktionscode; function library** = collection of functions that can be used by a program **Funktionsbibliothek; function table** = list that gives the relationship between two sets of instructions *or* data **Funktionstabelle**
(c) special feature available on a computer *or* word-processor **Funktion;** *the word-processor had a spelling-checker function but no built-in text-editing function;* **function code** = printing codes that control an action rather than representing a character **Funktionscode**
2 *verb* to operate *or* perform correctly **funktionieren;** *the new system has not functioned properly since it was installed*

◊ **functional** *adjective* which refers to the way something works **Funktions-, funktions-; functional diagram** = drawing of the internal workings and processes of a machine *or* piece of software **Funktionsdiagramm; functional specification** = specification which defines the results which a program is expected to produce **Funktionsbeschreibung; functional unit** = hardware *or* software that works as it should **Funktionseinheit**

◊ **function key** *or* **programmable function key** *noun* key *or* switch that has been assigned a particular task *or* sequence of instructions **Funktionstaste;** *tags can be allocated to function keys; hitting F5 will put you into insert mode*

> COMMENT: function keys often form a separate group of keys on the keyboard, and have specific functions attached to them. They may be labelled F1, F2, etc.

> QUOTE they made it clear that the PC was to take its place as part of a much larger computing function that comprised of local area networks, wide area networks, small systems, distributed systems and mainframes
> *Minicomputer News*

> QUOTE if your computer has a MOD function, you will not need the function defined in line 3010
> *Computing Today*

> QUOTE the final set of keys are to be found above the main keyboard and comprise 5 function keys, which together with shift, give 10 user-defined keys
> *Computing Today*

fundamental frequency *noun* most prominent frequency in a complex signal **Grundfrequenz**

> COMMENT: almost all signals contain parts of other frequencies (harmonics) at lower amplitudes to the fundamental, which often causes distortion

fuse
1 *noun* electrical protection device consisting of a small piece of metal, which will melt when too much power passes through it **Sicherung; to blow a fuse** = to melt a fuse by passing too much current through it **eine Sicherung durchbrennen lassen**
2 *verb* to draw too much current, causing a fuse to melt **durchbrennen;** *when the air-conditioning was switched on, it fused the whole system*

◊ **fusible link** *noun* small link in a PLA that can be blown to program the device permanently **Sicherung, die durch Durchbrennen programmiert**

◊ **fusible read only memory (FROM)** *noun* PROM that is made up of a matrix of fusible links which are selectively blown to program it **FROM (spezielle ROMs, die durch den Einbau · und das spätere Durchbrennen von Sicherungen programmiert werden)**

◊ **fusion** *noun* combining two hardware

devices *or* programs *or* chemical substances to create a single form **Verschmelzung, Fusion**

fuzzy *noun* not clear **verschwommen;** *top quality paper will eliminate fuzzy characters;* **fuzzy logic** *or* **fuzzy theory** = type of logic applied to computer programming, which tries to replicate the reasoning methods of the human brain **verschwommene Theorie**

Gg

G = GIGA *prefix* meaning one thousand million **G; GHz** = gigahertz **GHz** ⇨APPENDIX

> COMMENT: in computing G refers to 2^{30}, equal to 1,073,741,824

GaAs = GALLIUM ARSENIDE

gain
1 *noun* increase *or* becoming larger; amount by which a signal amplitude is changed as it passes through a circuit, usually given as a ratio of output to input amplitude **Verstärkungsgrad; gain control** = variable control that sets the amount of gain a circuit *or* amplifier will provide **Verstärkungsregelung**
2 *verb* to obtain *or* to get **erhalten; to gain access to a file** = to be able to access a file **Zugang zu einer Datei erhalten;** *the user cannot gain access to the confidential information in the file without a password*

galactic noise *noun* random electrical noise which originates from planets and stars in space **galaktisches Rauschen**

gallium arsenide (GaAs) *noun* semiconductor compound, a new material for chip construction, that allows faster operation than silicon chips **GaAs (Galliumarsenid)**

galley proof *or* **slip** *noun* rough initial proof of a column *or* section of text, printed on a long piece of paper **Korrekturfahne**

game *noun* something which is played for enjoyment *or* relaxation **Spiel; computer game** = game played on a computer, using special software **Computerspiel; game**

cartridge = ROM device that contains the program code for a computer game, and which is plugged into a game console **Spielesteckmodul; game console** = dedicated computer, joystick and display adapter that is designed to be only used to play games **Spielkonsole; game paddle** = device held in the hand to move a cursor *or* graphics in a computer game **Steuerknüppel; game port** = connection that allows a joystick to be plugged into a computer **Gameport**

gamma *noun* (i) measure of the development of a photographic image, and so its contrast range; (ii) logarithm of the luminescence of the image on a TV screen, in relation to that of the original scene when filmed (i) **Kontrastgrad;** (ii) **Gamma**

ganged *adjective* mechanically linked (devices) that are operated by a single action **zusammengefasst, gruppiert; ganged switch** = series of switches that operate on different parts of a circuit, but which are all switched by a single action **Gruppenschalter;** *a ganged switch is used to select which data bus a printer will respond to*

gap *noun*
(a) space between recorded data **Spalt, Zwischenraum; block** *or* **interblock gap (IBG)** = blank magnetic tape between the end of one block of data and the start of the next in backing store **Blockzwischenraum; gap character** = an extra character added to a group of characters (for parity or another purpose, but not data *or* instructions) **Füllzeichen; gap digit** = an extra digit added to a group of data (for parity or another purpose, but not data *or* instructions) **Füllziffer; record gap** = blank section of magnetic tape between two consecutive records **Satzzwischenraum**
(b) space between a read head and the magnetic medium **Spalt; gap loss** = signal attenuation due to incorrect alignment of the read/write head with the storage medium **Signaldämpfung durch unkorrekte Lese-/Schreibkopfausrichtung; air** *or* **head gap** = narrow gap between a recording *or* playback head and the magnetic medium **Luftspalt**
(c) method of radio communications using a carrier signal that is switched on and off, as in a telegraphic system **Funkübertragungssystem**

garbage *noun*
(a) radio interference from adjacent channels **Rauschen**

(b) data *or* information that is no longer required because it is out of date *or* contains errors **Müll; Schrott; garbage in garbage out (GIGO)** = expression meaning that the accuracy and quality of information that is output depends on the quality of the input **GIGO (Unsinn rein Unsinn raus)**

| COMMENT: GIGO is sometimes taken to mean "garbage in gospel out": i.e. that whatever wrong information is put into a computer, people will always believe that the output results are true

gas discharge display *or* **gas plasma display** *noun* flat, lightweight display screen that is made of two flat pieces of glass covered with a grid of conductors, separated by a thin layer of a gas which luminesces when one point of the grid is selected by two electric signals **Plasmabildschirm**

| COMMENT: mainly used in modern portable computer displays, but the definition is not as good as in cathode ray tube displays

gate *noun*
(a) logical electronic switch whose output depends on the states of the inputs and the type of logical function implemented **Gatter; AND gate** = gate that performs a logical AND function **UND-Gatter; coincidence gate** = gate that produces a logical output depending on various input coincidences (an AND gate requires the coincidence in time of all logically true inputs) **Koinzidenzgatter; EXNOR gate** = electronic implementation of the EXNOR function **exklusiv-NOR-Gatter; EXOR gate** = electronic implementation of the EXOR function **exklusiv-ODER-Gatter; NAND gate** = electronic circuit that provides a NAND function **NAND-Gatter; negation** *or* **NOT gate** = single input gate whose output is equal to the logical inverse of the input **NICHT-Gatter; NOR gate** = electronic circuit which performs a NOR function **NOR-Gatter; OR gate** = electronic circuit that provides the OR function **ODER-Gatter; gate array** = number of interconnected logic gates built into an integrated circuit to perform a complex function **Gatteranordnung; gate delay** *or* **propagation time** = time taken for a gate to produce an output after it has received inputs **Schaltverzögerung; gate circuit** = electronic components that implement a logical function **Schaltkreis**
(b) connection pin of a FET device **Torschaltung**
(c) mechanical film *or* slide frame aligner in a camera *or* projector **Justiervorrichtung**

◊ **gateway** *noun*
(a) (i) device that links two dissimilar networks; (ii) software protocol translation device that allows users working in one network to access another **(i) & (ii) Gateway;** *we use a gateway to link the LAN to WAN* **(b)** (in electronic mail) software that allows mail messages to be sent via a different route *or* to another network **Gateway;** *to send messages by fax instead of across the network, you'll need to install a fax gateway;* **fax gateway** = computer or software that allows users to send information as a fax transmission instead of as a file stored on a disk **Fax-Gateway**

gather *verb* to receive data from various sources (either directly from a data capture device or from a cartridge) and sort and insert in correct order into a database **sammeln; gather write** = to write a group of separate records as one block of data **sammelnd (auf)schreiben**

gauge
1 *noun* device which measures thickness *or* width **Messlehre**
2 *verb* to measure the thickness *or* width of something **messen**

gender changer *noun (informal)* device for changing a female connection to a male or vice versa **Geschlechtsumwandler**

general *adjective*
(a) ordinary *or* not special **allgemein; general office** = main administrative office **Hauptbüro**
(b) dealing with everything **universal; general purpose computer** = computer whose processing power may be applied to many different sorts of applications, depending on its hardware *or* software instructions **Universalcomputer; general purpose interface bus (GPIB)** = standard for an interface bus between a computer and laboratory equipment **IEC-Bus, Universalschnittstellenbus; general purpose program** = program *or* device able to perform many different jobs *or* applications **Universalprogramm; general register** *or* **general purpose register (gpr)** = data register in a computer processing unit that can store items of data for many different mathematical *or* logical operations **Mehrzweckregister**

generate *verb* to use software *or* a device to produce codes *or* a program automatically **generieren, erzeugen;** *to generate an image from digitally recorded*

data; *the graphics tablet generates a pair of co-ordinates each time the pen is moved;* **computer-generated** = produced using a computer **computergeneriert;** *they analyzed the computer-generated image;* **generated address** = location used by a program that has been produced by instructions within the program **errechnete Adresse; generated error** = error occurring due to inaccuracies in data used (such as a sum total error due to a series of numbers which are rounded up) **generierter Fehler**

◊ **generation** *noun*
(a) producing data *or* software *or* programs using a computer **Generierung;** *the computer is used in the generation of graphic images code generation is automatic;* **program generation** *see* GENERATOR
(b) state *or* age of the technology used in the design of a system **Generation; first generation** = earliest type of technology **erste Generation; first generation computers** = original computers made with valve-based electronic technology, started around 1951 **Computer der ersten Generation; first generation image** = master copy of an original image, text *or* document **erste Kopie vom Original; second generation computers** = computers which used transistors instead of valves **Computer der zweiten Generation; third generation computers** = computers which used integrated circuits instead of transistors **Computer der dritten Generation; fourth generation computers** = computer technology using LSI circuits, developed around 1970 and still in current use **Computer der vierten Generation; fourth generation languages** = languages that are user-friendly and have been designed with the non-expert in mind **Computersprachen der vierten Generation; fifth generation computers** = next stage of computer system design using fast VLSI circuits and powerful programming languages to allow human interaction **Computer der fünften Generation**
(c) distance between a file and the original version, used when making backups **Generation;** *the father file is a first generation backup*

◊ **generator** *noun*
(a) (program) that generates new programs according to rules *or* specifications set out by the user **Generierungsprogramm**
(b) device which generates electricity **Generator;** *the computer centre has its own independent generator, in case of mains power failure*

generic *adjective* (something) that is compatible with a whole family of hardware *or* software devices from one manufacturer **auswählbar**

genuine *adjective* real *or* correct **echt**; *authentication allows the system to recognize that a sender's message is genuine*

geometric distortion *noun* linear distortion of a television picture, which can be caused by video tape speed fluctuations **lineare Verzerrung**

geostationary satellite *noun* satellite which moves at the same velocity as the earth, so remains above the same area of the earth's surface, and appears stationary when viewed from the earth **geostationärer Satellit**

germanium *noun* semiconductor material, used as a substrate in some transistors instead of silicon **Germanium**

get *noun* instruction to obtain a record from a file *or* database **Holanweisung**

GHz = GIGAHERTZ

ghost *noun* effect on a television image where a weaker copy of the picture is displayed to one side of the main image, caused by signal reflections **Geisterbild**; **ghost cursor** = second cursor which can be used in some programs **Zusatzcursor**

gibberish *noun* useless and meaningless information **Unsinn**

GIF file *noun* graphics file format of a file containing a bit-mapped image **GIF-Datei**

giga- *or* **G** *prefix* meaning one thousand million **Giga** *or* **G**; **gigabyte** = 10^9 bytes **Gigabyte**; **gigaflop** = one thousand million floating-point operations per second **Gigaflop**; **gigahertz (GHz)** = frequency of one thousand million cycles per second **Gigahertz (GHz)**

COMMENT: in computing giga refers to 2^{30}, which is equal to 1,073,741,824

GIGO = GARBAGE IN GARBAGE OUT expression meaning that the accuracy and quality of information that is output depends on the quality of the input **GIGO (Unsinn rein Unsinn raus)**

COMMENT: GIGO is sometimes taken to mean "garbage in gospel out": i.e. that whatever wrong information is put into a computer, people will always believe that the output results are true

GINO = GRAPHICAL INPUT OUTPUT graphical control routine written in FORTRAN **GINO**

GKS = GRAPHICS KERNEL SYSTEM standard for software command and functions describing graphical input/output to provide the same functions etc. on any type of hardware **Grafikkernsystem**

glare *noun* very bright light reflections, especially on a VDU screen **Blendung**; *the glare from the screen makes my eyes hurt* NOTE: no plural **glare filter** = coated glass or plastic sheet placed in front of a screen to cut out bright light reflections **Blendschutz**

glitch *noun* *(informal)* anything which causes the sudden unexpected failure of a computer *or* equipment **Störimpuls**

global *adjective* covering everything **global, umfassend**; **global backup** = (i) backup of all data stored on all nodes *or* workstations connected to a network; (ii) backup of all files on a hard disk *or* file server **(i) globale Datensicherung, globales Backup; (ii) Gesamtsicherung, Gesamtbackup**; **global exchange** = replace function which replaces one piece of text (such as a word) with another throughout a whole text **globale Austauschfunktion**; **global knowledge** = all the knowledge about one problem *or* task **globale Kenntnis**; **global search and replace** = word-processor search and replace function covering a complete file *or* document **globales Suchen und Ersetzen**; **global variable** = variable *or* number that can be accessed by any routine *or* structure in a program **globale Variable**; *compare* LOCAL VARIABLE

QUOTE In an attempt to bring order to an electronic Tower of Babel, pharmaceutical giant Rhone-Poulenc has assembled an X.400-based global messaging network and a patchwork directory system that will be used until a single email system is deployed worldwide

Computing

glossy
1 *adjective* shiny (paper) **glänzend, Glanz-;** *the illustrations are printed on glossy art paper*
2 *noun (informal)* **the glossies** = expensive magazines **die Hochglänzenden**

GND = GROUND electrical circuit connection to earth *or* to a point with a zero voltage level **Masse, Erde**

go ahead *noun* signal to indicate that a receiver *or* device is ready to accept information **Startsignal**

goal *noun* (i) aim *or* what you are trying to do; (ii) final state reached when a task has been finished *or* has produced satisfactory results **(i) & (ii) Ziel**

gofer *noun (US) informal* person who does all types of work in an office *or* studio, etc. **Mädchen für alles, Faktotum**

gold contacts *noun* electrical contacts, (usually for low-level signals) that are coated with gold to reduce the electrical resistance **Goldkontakte**

golf-ball *noun* metal ball with characters on its surface, which produces printed characters by striking a ribbon onto paper **Kugelkopf; golf-ball printer** = computer printer using a golf-ball as a printing head **Kugelkopfdrucker**

COMMENT: a golf-ball contains all the characters of a single typeface; to change the face, the ball is taken out and replaced by another. The main defect of a golf-ball typewriter when used as a printer, is that it is slower than a dot-matrix printer

GOSIP = GOVERNMENT OPEN SYSTEMS INTERCONNECT PROFILE standards defined by the government of a country to ensure that computers and communications systems can interact **GOSIP**

gospel *see note at* GARBAGE

GOSUB programming command which executes a routine then returns to the following instruction **GOSUB**

GOTO programming command which instructs a jump **Sprunganweisung;** *GOTO 105 instructs a jump to line 105*

COMMENT: GOTO statements are frowned upon by software experts since their use discourages set, structured programming techniques

GPIB = GENERAL PURPOSE INTERFACE BUS standard for an interface bus between a computer and laboratory equipment **IEC-Bus, Universalschnittstellenbus**

gpr = GENERAL PURPOSE REGISTER data register in a computer processing unit that can store items of data for many different mathematical *or* logical operations **Mehrzweckregister**

grab *verb* to take something and hold it **greifen, packen**

◊ **grabber** *noun* **frame grabber** = high speed digital sampling circuit that stores a TV picture in memory so that it can then be processed by a computer **Bildgrabber**

QUOTE sometimes a program can grab all the available memory, even if it is not going to use it

Byte

QUOTE the frame grabber is distinguished by its ability to acquire a TV image in a single frame interval
Electronics & Wireless World

graceful degradation *noun* allowing some parts of a system to continue to function after a part has broken down **kontrollierter Leistungsrückgang**

grade *noun* level *or* rank **Grad, Niveau, (Güte)klasse;** *a top-grade computer expert;* **grade of service** = quality of telephone service at a given time, defined by the likelihood of a successful connection via a telephone network at its busiest time **Servicequalität**

◊ **graduated** *adjective* which has a scale *or* measurements marked on it **mit Maßeinteilung versehen**

grain *noun* spotted effect on fast photographic films due to the size of the light-sensitive silver halide crystals **Korn**

gram _or_ **gramme** _noun_ unit of measurement of weight, one thousandth of a kilogram **Gramm**; _the book is printed on 70 gram paper_

◊ **grammage** _noun_ weight of paper, calculated as grams per square metre **Papiergewicht** NOTE: usually shown as **gsm : 80 gsm paper**

grammar _noun_ rules for the correct use of language **Grammatik**; **grammar checker** = software utility used to check a document or letter to make sure it is grammatically correct **Grammatikprüfung, Grammatikprüfprogramm**

◊ **grammatical error** _noun_ incorrect use of a computer programming language syntax **Syntaxfehler**

grandfather file _noun_ third most recent version of a backed up file, after father and son files **Großvaterdatei**; **grandfather cycle** = period in which the grandfather file is retrieved and updated to produce a new father file, the old father file becoming the new grandfather file **Großvaterzyklus**

granularity _noun_ size of memory segments in a virtual memory system **Körnung**

graph _noun_ diagram showing the relationship between two _or_ more variables as a line _or_ series of points **Diagramm, Graph**; **graph paper** = paper with many little squares, used for drawing graphs **Millimeterpapier**; **graph plotter** = printing device with a pen which takes data from a computer and plots it in graphic form **Plotter, Kurvenschreiber**

◊ **graphic** _adjective_ (representation of information) in the form of pictures _or_ plots instead of by text **grafisch, zeichnerisch**; **graphic data** = stored data that represents graphical information (when displayed on a screen) **grafische Daten**; **graphic display** = computer screen able to present graphical information **grafischer Bildschirm**; **graphic display resolution** = number of pixels that a computer is able to display on the screen **grafisches Auflösungsvermögen des Bildschirms**; **graphic language** = computer programming language with inbuilt commands that are useful when displaying graphics **Computersprache zum Programmieren von Grafiken**; _this graphic language can plot lines, circles and graphs with a single command_

◊ **graphical** _adjective_ referring to something represented by graphics **grafisch**

◊ **graphically** _adverb_ using pictures **grafisch**; _the sales figures are graphically represented as a pie chart_

◊ **graphical user interface (GUI)** _noun_ interface between an operating system _or_ program and the user; it uses graphics _or_ icons to represent functions _or_ files and allow the software to be controlled more easily; system commands do not have to be typed in **grafische Benutzeroberfläche, Graphical User Interface (GUI)**; _compare_ COMMAND LINE INTERFACE

COMMENT: GUIs normally use a combination of windows, icons and a mouse to control the operating system. In many GUIs, such as Microsoft Windows, Apple Macintosh System 7 and DR-GEM, you can control all the functions of the operating system just using the mouse. Icons represent programs and files; instead of entering the file name, you select it by moving a pointer with a mouse.

◊ **graphics** _noun_ pictures _or_ lines which can be drawn on paper _or_ on a screen to represent information **Grafik**; _graphics output such as bar charts, pie charts, line drawings, etc.;_ **graphics adapter** = electronic device (normally on an expansion card) in a computer that converts software commands into electrical signals that display graphics on a connected monitor **Grafikadapter**; _the new graphics adapter is capable of displaying higher resolution graphics;_ **graphics art terminal** = typesetting terminal that is used with a phototypesetter **Grafikterminal für Fotosatz**; **graphics character** = preprogrammed shape that can be displayed on a non-graphical screen instead of a character, used extensively in videotext systems to display simple pictures **grafisches Zeichen**; **graphics coprocessor** _see_ GRAPHICS PROCESSOR; **graphics file** = (binary) file which contains data describing an image **Grafikdatei**; _there are many standards for graphics files including TIFF, IMG and EPS;_ **graphics file format** = method in which data describing an image is stored **Grafikformat, Grafikdateiformat**; **graphics kernel system (GKS)** = standard for software command and functions describing graphical input/output to provide the same functions etc. on any type of hardware **Grafikkernsystem**; **graphics library** = number of routines stored in a library file that can be added to any user program to simplify the task of writing graphics programs **Grafikbibliothek**; **graphics light pen** = high-accuracy light pen used for drawing onto a graphics display screen **grafischer Lichtstift**; **graphics mode** =

videotext terminal whose displayed characters are taken from a range of graphics characters instead of text **Grafikmodus; graphics pad** *or* **tablet** = flat device that allows a user to input graphical information into a computer by drawing on its surface **Grafikblock; graphics primitive** = basic shape (such as an arc, line or filled square) that is used to create other shapes or objects **Grafikelement; graphics printer** = printer capable of printing bit-mapped images **Grafikdrucker; graphics processor** *or* **graphics coprocessor** = secondary processor used to speed up the display of graphics: it calculates the position of pixels that form a line *or* shape and display graphic lines *or* shapes **Grafikprozessor, Grafikbeschleuniger, Grafikchip;** *this graphics adapter has a graphics coprocessor fitted and is much faster;* **graphics software** = prewritten routines that perform standard graphics commands such as line drawing, plotting, etc., that can be called from within a program to simplify program writing **Grafiksoftware; graphics terminal** = special terminal with a high-resolution graphic display and graphics pad *or* other input device **Grafikterminal; graphics VDU** = special VDU which can display high-resolution *or* colour graphics as well as text **Grafik-VDU**

QUOTE one interesting feature of this model is graphics amplification, which permits graphic or text enlargement of up to 800 per cent

QUOTE the custom graphics chips can display an image that has 640 columns by 400 rows of 4-bit pixel

QUOTE several tools exist for manipulating image and graphical data: some were designed for graphics manipulation

Byte

gravure *see* PHOTOGRAVURE

Gray code *noun* coding system in which the binary representation of decimal numbers changes by only one bit at a time from one number to the next **Gray-Verschlüsselung**

COMMENT: used in communications systems to provide error detection facilities

greeked *adjective* (in a DTP program) font with a point size too small to display accurately, shown as a line rather than individual characters **stilisiert**

green phosphor *noun* most commonly used phosphor for monochrome screen coating, which displays green characters on a black background **grüner Phosphor**

COMMENT: a new popular screen type is paper-white, using a white phosphor to display black characters on a white background

gremlin *noun* (*informal*) unexplained fault in a system **Maschinenteufelchen; line gremlin** = unexplained fault when data is lost during transmission **unerklärlicher Datenverlust**

grey scale *noun*
(a) shades of grey that are used to measure the correct exposure when filming **Grauskala**
(b) shades which are produced from displaying what should be colour information on a monochrome monitor **Grauschattierung, Grauwerte**

grid *noun* system of numbered squares used to help when drawing; matrix of lines at right angles allowing points to be easily plotted *or* located **Raster, Koordinatennetz; grid snap** = (in a graphics program) patterns *or* lines drawn on screen limited to the points of a grid **Magnetraster;** *if you want to draw accurate lines, you'll find it easier with grid snap turned on*

grip
1 *noun* person who works on the stage in a film *or* TV studio **Bühnenarbeiter**
2 *verb* to hold something tightly **greifen;** *in friction feed, the paper is gripped by the rollers*

ground *noun*
(a) electrical circuit connection to earth *or* to a point with a zero voltage level **Masse, Erde** NOTE: **ground** is more common in US English; the U.K. English is **earth**
(b) the earth's surface **Boden; ground absorption** = loss of transmitted power in radio waves that are near the ground **Absorptionsverlust; ground station** = equipment and antenna on the earth used to communicate with an orbiting satellite **Bodenfunkstelle**

group
1 *noun*
(a) set of computer records that contain related information **Verbund; group mark** *or* **marker** = code used to identify the start and end of a group of related records *or* items of data **Gruppenmarke, Trennungsmarke; group poll** = polling a number of devices at once **Gruppenaufruf, Gruppenabruf**

(b) six-character word used in telegraphic communications **Gruppe**
(c) (in a GUI) collection of icons of files *or* programs displayed together in a window **Programmgruppe;** *all the icons in this group are to do with painting;* **group icon** = (in a GUI) icon that represents a window which contains a collection of icons of files *or* programs **Programmgruppensymbol, Gruppensymbol**
(d) (in a network) collection of users conveniently identified by one name **Benutzergruppe;** *the group ACCOUNTS contains all the users who work in the accounts department*
2 *verb* to bring several things together **gruppieren, in einer Gruppe zusammenfassen**

◊ **groupware** *noun* (on a network) software specially written to be used by a group of people connected to a network and help them carry out a particular task; it provides useful functions such as a diary or electronic mail that can be accessed by all users **Groupware**

gsm *or* **g/m²** = GRAMS PER SQUARE METRE (PER SHEET) way of showing the weight of paper used in printing **Gramm pro Quadratmeter;** *the book is printed on 70 gsm coated paper*

guarantee *noun* legal document promising that a machine will work properly *or* that an item is of good quality **Garantie;** *the system is still under guarantee and will be repaired free of charge*

guard band *noun*
(a) frequency gap between two communication bands to prevent data corruption due to interference between each other **Schutzabstand**
(b) section of magnetic tape between two channels recorded on the same tape **Schutzabstand**

◊ **guard bit** *noun* one bit within a stored word that indicates to the computer whether it can be altered or if it is protected **Schutzbit**

◊ **guarding** *noun* joining a single sheet to a book *or* magazine **Einkleben eines Einsteckbogens**

GUI = GRAPHICAL USER INTERFACE interface between an operating system *or* program and the user; it uses graphics *or* icons to represent functions or files and allow the software to be controlled more easily; system commands do not have to be typed in **GUI;** *compare* COMMAND LINE INTERFACE (pronounced 'gooey')

COMMENT: GUIs normally use a combination of windows, icons and a mouse to control the operating system. In many GUIs, such as Microsoft Windows, Apple Macintosh System 7 and DR-GEM, you can control all the functions of the operating system just using the mouse. Icons represent programs and files; instead of entering the file name, you select it by moving a pointer with a mouse.

guide bars *noun* special lines in a bar code that show the start and finish of the code **Leitlinien;** *the standard guide bars are two thin lines that are a little longer than the coding lines*

guillotine *noun* office machine for cutting paper **Papierschneidemaschine**

gulp *noun* a group of words, usually two bytes **Zwei-Byte-Wortgruppe;** *see also* BYTE, NIBBLE

gun *or* **electron gun** *noun* source of an electron beam located inside a cathode ray tube **Elektronenkanone**

COMMENT: black and white monitors have a single beam gun, while colour monitors contain three, one for each primary colour (Red, Green and Blue) used

gutter *noun* (in a DTP system) blank space or inner margin between two facing pages **Bundsteg**

Hh

H & J = HYPHENATION AND JUSTIFICATION

hack *verb*
(a) to experiment and explore computer software and hardware **Hard- und Software untersuchen**
(b) to break into a computer system for criminal purposes **Hard- und Software illegal untersuchen**

◊ **hacker** *noun* person who hacks **Hacker**

QUOTE software manufacturers try more and more sophisticated methods to protect their programs and the hackers use equally clever methods to break into them
Electronics & Wireless World

QUOTE the hackers used their own software to break into the credit card centre

Computer News

QUOTE any computer linked to the system will be alerted if a hacker uses its code number

Practical Computing

QUOTE The two were also charged with offences under the Computer Misuse Act and found guilty of the very actions upon which every hacker is intent

Computing

hairline rule *noun* (in a DTP system) very thin line **Haarlinie**

halation *noun* photographic effect seen as a dark region with a very bright surround, caused by pointing the camera into the light **Lichthofbildung**

half *noun* one of two equal parts **Hälfte**; *half the data was lost in transmission; the second half of the program contains some errors;* **half adder** = binary adder that can produce the sum of two inputs, producing a carry output if necessary, but cannot accept a carry input **Halbaddierer**; **half card** = expansion card that is half full length **Halbkarte**; **half duplex** = data transmission in one direction at a time over a bidirectional channel **Halbduplex(übertragung)**; **half-duplex modem** = modem which works in one mode at a time (either transmitting *or* receiving) **Halbduplexmodem**; *some modems can operate in half-duplex mode if required; see also* DUPLEX; **half-height drive** = disk drive whose front is half the height of a standard drive (half height drives, usually 5.25 inches are now the norm on PCs) **halbhohes Laufwerk**; **half-intensity** = character *or* graphics display at half the usual display brightness **halbe Intensität**; **half space** = paper movement in a printer by a half the amount of a normal character **halber Abstand**; **half title** = first page of a book, with the title, but not the publisher's colophon *or* details of the author **Schmutztitel**; **half wave rectifier** = circuit that allows current to pass in one direction only **Einweggleichrichter**; **half word** = sequence of bits occupying half a standard computer word, but which can be accessed as a single unit **Halbwort**

◊ **halftone** *adjective* photograph *or* image that originally had continuous tones, displayed *or* printed by a computer using groups of dots to represent the tones **Halbton-, Raster-**

halide *noun* silver compound that is used to provide a light-sensitive coating on photographic film and paper **(Silber)halogenid**

hall effect *noun* description of the effect of a magnetic field on electron flow **Halleffekt**; **hall effect switch** = solid state electronic switch operated by a magnetic field **Halleffektschalter**

halo *noun* photographic effect seen as a dark region with a very bright line around it, caused by pointing the camera into the light **Lichthof**

halt
1 *noun* computer instruction to stop a CPU carrying out any further instructions until restarted, or until the program is restarted, usually by external means (such as a reset button) **Halt, Stop**; **dead** *or* **drop-dead halt** = program instruction from the user *or* an error that causes the program to stop without allowing recovery **Unterbrechungshalt**; **halt instruction** = program instruction that causes a CPU to halt, suspending operations, usually until it is reset **Haltbefehl**; **programmed halt** = instruction within a program which when executed, halts the processor (to restart the program, a reset is usually required) **programmierter Halt**; **halt condition** = operating state reached when a CPU reaches a fault or faulty instruction *or* halt instruction *or* halt instruction in the program that is being run **Haltbedingung**
2 *verb* to stop **anhalten**; *hitting CTRL S will halt the program*

ham *noun* **radio ham** = private radio operator who works especially with a short-wave transceiver **Funkamateur**

◊ **Hamming code** *noun* coding system that uses check bits and checksums to detect and correct errors in transmitted data, mainly used in teletext systems **Hammingcode**; **Hamming distance** = the number of digits that are different in two equal length words **Hammingabstand**

hand *noun* **hands off** = working system where: (i) the operator does not control the operation which is automatic; (ii) the operator does not need to touch the device in use **(i) & (ii) automatisches System**; **hands on** = working system where the operator controls the operations by keying instructions on the keyboard **operatorbedientes System;** *the sales representatives have received hands-on experience of the new computer; the computer firm gives a two day hands-on training course;* **hand portable sets** *or* **handy talkies** *or* **HT's** = small low-range portable transceivers **Sprechfunkgeräte; hand receiver** = hand-held device containing all necessary electronics to allow reception of broadcast radio signals **Kofferradio; hand viewer** = hand-held magnifying lens with a mount to allow photographic slides to be viewed **Diabetrachter, Gucki**

◊ **hand-held** *adjective* which can be held in the hand **tragbar; hand-held computer** *or* **programmable** = very small computer which can be held in the hand, useful for basic information input, when a terminal is not available **Taschencomputer**

◊ **handler** *or* **driver** *noun* section of the operating system *or* program which controls a peripheral **Treiber**

◊ **hand off** *verb* to pass control of a communications channel from one transmitter to another **übergeben**

◊ **handset** *noun* telephone receiver, with both microphone and loudspeaker **Telefonhörer;** *see also* ACOUSTIC COUPLER

QUOTE A year ago the hand-held computer business resembled that of PCs a decade ago, with a large number of incompatible models, often software incompatible and using proprietary displays, operating systems and storage media

Computing

QUOTE all acquisition, data reduction, processing, and memory circuitry is contained in the single hand-held unit

Byte

handle *noun*
(a) (in programming) number used to identify an active file within the program that is accessing the file **Dateinummer, Handle**
(b) (in a GUI) small square displayed that can be dragged to change the shape of a window or graphical object **Anfasser;** *to stretch the box in the DTP program, select it once to display the handles then drag one handle to change its shape*

◊ **handler** *noun* special software routine that controls a device or function **Handler,**

Unterprogramm; *the disk drive handler code is supplied in the library; see also* DEVICE DRIVER; **error handler** = software routine that controls and reports on an error when it occurs **Fehlerbehandlungsroutine**

handshake *or* **handshaking** *noun* standardized signals between two devices to make sure that the system is working correctly, equipment is compatible and data transfer is correct (signals would include ready to receive, ready to transmit, data OK) **Quittungsbetrieb; full handshaking** = signals transmitted between two communicating devices indicating ready-to-transmit, ready-to-receive, received, transmitted, etc. **Vollquittungsbetrieb; handshake I/O control** = use of handshake signals meaning ready-to-send and ready-to-receive, that allow a computer to communicate with a slower peripheral **Ein-/Ausgabequittungsbetrieb**

QUOTE if a line is free, the device waits another 400ms before reserving the line with a quick handshake process

Practical Computing

handwriting *noun* words written by hand **Handschrift;** *the keyboarders are having difficulty in reading the author's handwriting;* **handwriting recognition** = software that is capable of recognising handwritten text and converting it into ASCII characters **Handschrifterkennung;** *the new PDA has excellent handwriting recognition*

◊ **handwritten** *adjective* written by hand, using a pen or pencil, not typed **handgeschrieben;** *the author sent in two hundred pages of handwritten manuscript*

hang *verb* to enter an endless loop and not respond to further instruction **aufhängen**

◊ **hangover** *noun*
(a) effect on a TV screen where the previous image can still be seen when the next image appears **Auftreten von Fahnen**
(b) sudden tone change on a document that is transmitted over a fax machine as a gradual change, caused by equipment faults **Farbtonänderung**

◊ **hang up** *verb* to cut off a communications line **auflegen;** *after she had finished talking on the telephone, she hung up*

◊ **hangup** *noun* sudden stop of a working program (often due to the CPU executing an illegal instruction *or* entering an endless loop) **Abbruch**

hard *adjective*
(a) solid, as opposed to soft; (parts of a computer system) that cannot be programmed *or* altered **hart; hard card** = board containing a hard disk drive and the required interfacing electronics, which can be slotted into a system's expansion connector **Festplattenlaufwerksplatine; hard copy** = printed document *or* copy of information contained in a computer *or* system, in a form that is readable (as opposed to soft copy) **Hartkopie; hard copy interface** = serial *or* parallel interface used to transmit data between a computer and a printer **Druckerschnittstelle; hard disk** = rigid magnetic disk that is able to store many times more data than a floppy disk, and usually cannot be removed from the disk drive **Festplatte; hard disk drive** = unit used to store and retrieve data from a spinning hard disk (on the commands of a computer) **Festplattenlaufwerk; hard disk model** = model of computer with a hard disk **Festplattenmodell; hard error** = error which is permanent in a system **andauernder Fehler; hard failure** = fault (in hardware) that must be mended before a device will function correctly **Hardwarefehler;** *the hard failure was due to a burnt-out chip;* **hard return** = code in a word-processing document that (normally) indicates the end of a paragraph **Hard Return**
(b) high contrast (photographic paper *or* film) **scharf, kontrastreich**

◊ **hardbound** *adjective* (book) with a hard cased cover, as opposed to a paperback **steif gebunden**

◊ **hardcover** *noun & adjective* version of a book with a cased binding (as opposed to paperback) **Hardcover(-);** *we printed 4,000 copies of the hardcover edition, and 10,000 of the paperback*

◊ **hard-sectoring** *noun* method of permanently formatting a disk, where each track is split into sectors, sometimes preformatted by a series of punched holes around the central hub, where each hole marks the start of a sector **Hartformatierung**

hardware *noun* physical units, components, integrated circuits, disks and mechanisms that make up a computer *or* its peripherals **Hardware, Maschinenausrüstung; hardware compatibility** = architecture of two different computers that allows one to run the programs of the other without changing any device drivers *or* memory locations, or the ability of one to use the add-on boards of the other **Hardwarekompatibilität; hardware**

configuration = way in which the hardware of a computer system is connected together **Geräteanordnung; hardware dependent** = something which will only work with a particular model *or* brand of hardware **hardwareabhängig;** *the communications software is hardware dependent and will only work with Hayes-compatible modems;* **hardware failure** = fault with a hardware device *or* hardware that has stopped working properly **Hardwarefehler; hardware interrupt** = interrupt signal generated by a piece of hardware rather than by software **Hardwareunterbrechung; hardware platform** = standard of a particular computer (such as IBM PC, Apple Macintosh) **Hardwareplattform; hardware reliability** = ability of a piece of hardware to function normally over a period of time **Maschinenzuverlässigkeit; hardware reset** = switch that generates an electrical signal to reset the CPU and all devices, equivalent to turning a computer off and back on again **Reset-Taste; hardware security** = making a system secure by means of hardware (such as keys, cards, etc.) **Hardwaresicherheit** NOTE: no plural *compare* SOFTWARE

COMMENT: computer hardware can include the computer itself, the disks and disk drive, printer, VDU, etc.

QUOTE Sequent's Platform division will focus on hardware and software manufacture, procurement and marketing, with the Enterprise division concentrating on services and client-server implementation
Computing

hardwired connection *noun* permanent phone line connection, instead of a plug and socket **festverdrahtete Verbindung**

◊ **hardwired logic** *noun* logical function *or* program, which is built into the hardware, using electronic devices, such as gates, rather than in software **festverdrahtete Logik**

◊ **hardwired program** *noun* computer program built into the hardware, and which cannot be changed **festverdrahtetes Programm**

harmonic *noun* frequency of an order of magnitude greater *or* smaller than a fundamental **harmonische Oberschwingung; harmonic distortion** = unwanted harmonics produced by a non-linear circuit from an input signal **Klirrverzerrung; harmonic telephone ringer** = telephone that will only detect a certain range of ringing frequencies, this allows many telephones on a single line to be rung individually **harmonisches Telefonklingeln**

hartley *noun* unit of information, equal to 3.32 bits, or the probability of one state out of ten equally probable states **Hartley**

hash
1 *verb* to produce a unique number derived from the entry itself, for each entry in a database **mit Hilfe der Streuspeichertechnik abbilden; hashing function** = algorithm used to produce a hash code for an entry and ensure that it is different from every other entry **Hashfunktion (Algorithmus, um einen Hashcode zu erzeugen)**
2 *noun*
(a) *see* HASHMARK
(b) **hash code** = coding system derived from the ASCII codes, where the code numbers for the first three letters are added up, giving a new number used as hash code **Hashcode (Algorithmus zur Adressberechnung); hash-code system** = coding system using hash codes **Hash-Code-System; hash index** = list of entries according to their hashed numbers **Hashindex; hash table** = list of all entries in a file with their hashed key address **Hashtabelle; hash total** = total of a number of hashed entries used for error detection **Kontrollsumme; hash value** = number arrived at after a key is hashed **Hashwert**

◊ **hashmark** *or* **hash mark** *noun* printed sign (#) used as a hard copy marker *or* as an indicator **Hashzeichen**
NOTE: in US usage (#) means number; # 32 = number 32 (apartment number in an address, paragraph number in a text, etc.). In computer usage, the pound sign (£) is often used in the US instead of the hash to avoid confusion

Hayes Corporation ™ modem manufacturer who developed standard control language for modems **Hayes Corporation™; Hayes AT command set** = set of commands to control a modem prefixed with the letters AT **Hayes AT-Befehlssatz;** *to dial the number 1234, use the Hayes AT command ATD1234;* **Hayes compatible** = modem that is compatible with the Hayes AT command set **Hayes-kompatibel**

hazard *noun* fault in hardware due to incorrect signal timing **Gefahr; hazard-free implementation** = logical function design that has taken into account any hazards that could occur, and solved them **gefahrfreie Ausführung**

HD = HALF DUPLEX data transmission in one direction only, over a bidirectional channel **Halbduplex(übertragung)**

HDLC = HIGH LEVEL DATA LINK CONTROL

HDVS = HIGH DEFINITION VIDEO SYSTEM proposed new television format made up of 1125 lines and requiring a wide screen and high bandwidth equipment to view it on, so limited at present to satellite and cable television installations **HD-Videosystem, hochauflösendes Videosystem**

HDX = HALF DUPLEX

head
1 *noun*
(a) **combined head** *or* **read/write head** = transducer that can read *or* write data from the surface of a magnetic storage medium, such as a floppy disk **Lese-/Schreibkopf; head alignment** = (i) correct position of a tape *or* disk head in relation to the magnetic surface, to give the best performance and correct track location; (ii) location of the read head in the same position as the write head was (in relation to the magnetic medium) **(i) & (ii) Kopfausrichtung; head cleaning disk** = special disk which is used to clean the disk read/write heads **Kopfreinigungsdiskette; head crash** = component failure in a disk drive, where the head is allowed to hit the surface of the spinning disk, causing disk surface damage and data corruption **fehlerhafte Funktion des (Lese-/Schreib)kopfes; head demagnetizer** = device used to remove any stray magnetic effects that might have built up on the tape head **Kopfentmagnetisierer; head park** = to move the read/write head in a (hard) disk drive to a safe position, not over the disk, so that if the unit is knocked *or* jarred the head will not damage the disk surface **Kopfparken; head positioning** = moving the read/write head to the correct track on a disk **Kopfpositionierung; head wheel** = wheel that keeps video tape in contact with the head **Kopfrad; disk head** = head which reads *or* writes on a floppy disk **Festkopf; flying head** = hard disk read/write head that uses a 'wing' to fly just over the surface of the spinning disk **fliegender Kopf; playback head** = transducer that reads signals recorded on a storage medium and usually converts them to an electrical signal **Hörkopf; read head** = transducer that can read data from a magnetic storage medium such as a floppy disk **Lesekopf; tape head** = head which reads *or* writes signals on a magnetic tape

Bandkopf; **write head** = transducer that can write data onto a magnetic medium **Schreibkopf**
(b) data that indicates the start address of a list of items stored in memory **Kopf**
(c) top edge of a book *or* of a page **Kopf**; **head of form** = first line on a form *or* sheet of paper that can be printed on **oberste Zeile**
(d) start of a reel of recording tape *or* photographic film **Anfang**
(e) top part of a device, network *or* body **Kopf**; **head end** = interconnection equipment between an antenna and a cable television network **Kopfstelle**
2 *verb* to be the first item of data in a list **anführen**; *the queue was headed by my file*

◊ **header** *noun*
(a) in a local area network, a packet of data that is sent before a transmission to provide information on destination and routing **Vorsatz**
(b) information at the beginning of a list of data relating to the rest of the data **Kopfzeile, Anfangskennsatz; header block** = block of data at the beginning of a file containing data about file characteristics **Vorsatzblock; header card** = punched card containing information about the rest of the cards in the set **Leitkarte; header label** = section of data at the beginning of a magnetic tape, that contains identification, format and control information **Anfangskennsatz; tape header** = identification information at the beginning of a tape **Bandvorsatz**
(c) words at the top of a page of a document (such as title, author's name, page number, etc.) **Kopfzeile, Spitzmarke;** *see also* FOOTER

◊ **heading** *noun*
(a) title *or* name of a document or file **Überschrift**
(b) header *or* words at the top of each page of a document (such as the title, the page numbers, etc.) **Kopfzeile, Spitzmarke**

◊ **headlife** *noun* length of time that a video *or* tape head can work before being serviced *or* replaced **Lebensdauer eines Kopfes**

◊ **headline** *noun* = HEADING

◊ **headset** *or* **headphones** *noun* small speakers with padding, worn over a person's ears (used for private listening, instead of loudspeakers) **Kopfhörer**

◊ **headword** *noun* main entry word in a printed dictionary **Stichwort**

heap *noun*
(a) temporary data storage area that allows random access **Freispeicher;** *compare with* STACK
(b) binary tree **binärer Baum**

heat sensitive paper *noun see* ELECTROSTATIC PRINTING

heat sink *noun* metal device used to conduct heat away from an electronic component to prevent damage **Kühlkörper**

Heaviside-Kennelly layer *see* E-REGION

helical scan *noun* method of accessing data stored on video tape which is stored at an angle to the tape edge **Schrägspurverfahren**

helios noise *noun* noise originating from the sun that is picked up by an earthbased antenna when it points in the direction of the sun **Sonnenrauschen**

help *noun*
(a) thing which makes it easy to do something **Hilfe**; *he finds his word-processor a great help in the office; they need some help with their programming*
(b) function in a program *or* system that provides useful information about the program in use **HILFE-Funktion**; *hit the HELP key if you want information about what to do next;* **context-sensitive help** = help message that gives useful information about the particular function or part of the program you are in, rather than general information about the whole program **kontextsensitive Hilfe; help key** = (i) (on an Apple Macintosh) special key that displays help information; (ii) (on an IBM PC) F1 function key used to display help information (i) **Hilfetaste;** (ii) **F1-Taste; help screen** = display of information about a program or function **Hilfebildschirm, Hilfeseite**

COMMENT: most software applications for IBM PCs have standardized the use of the F1 function key to display help text explaining how something can be done

Hercules graphics adapter (HGA) *noun* standard for high-resolution mono graphics adapter developed by Hercules Corporation **Hercules-Grafikadapter (HGA)**

Hertz *noun* SI unit of frequency, defined as the number of cycles per second of time **Hertz**

COMMENT: Hertz rate is the frequency at which mains electricity is supplied to the consumer. The Hertz rate in the USA and Canada is 60; in Europe it is 50

heterodyne *noun* circuit producing two outputs equal to the sum and difference in frequency of two inputs **Überlagerung**

heterogeneous network *noun* computer network joining computers of many different types and makes **heterogenes Netz;** **heterogeneous multiplexing** = communications multiplexing system that can deal with channels with different transmission rates and protocols **heterogene Multiplexmethode**

heuristic *adjective.* which learns from past experiences **heuristisch;** *a heuristic program learns from its previous actions and decisions*

Hewlett Packard ™ manufacturer of computers, test equipment, and printers **Hewlett Packard** ™; **Hewlett Packard Graphics Language (HPGL)** = standard set of commands used to describe graphics **Hewlett Packard Graphics Language (HPGL);** **Hewlett Packard Interface Bus (HPIB)** = standard method of interfacing peripheral devices *or* test equipment and computers **Hewlett Packard Interface Bus (HPIB);** **Hewlett Packard LaserJet** *or* **HP LaserJet**= laser printer manufactured by Hewlett Packard that uses its PCL language to describe a page **Hewlett Packard LaserJet** *or* **HP LaserJet;** **Hewlett Packard Printer Control Language (HP-PCL)** = standard set of commands developed by Hewlett Packard to allow a software application to control a laser printer's functions **Hewlett Packard Printer Control Language (HP-PCL)**

hex *or* **hexadecimal notation** *noun* number system using base 16 and digits 0-9 and A-F **Hexadezimalschreibweise;** **hex dump** = display of a section of memory in hexadecimal form **hexadezimale Darstellung;** **hex pad** = keypad with keys for each hexadecimal digit **hexadezimale Tastatur**

HF = HIGH FREQUENCY radio communications range of frequencies from 3 - 30 MHz **Hochfrequenz**

HFS = HIERARCHICAL FILING SYSTEM (in an Apple Macintosh system) method used to store and organise files on a disk **HFS, hierarchische Dateistruktur**

HGA = HERCULES GRAPHICS ADAPTER

hidden *adjective* which cannot be seen **versteckt, verborgen;** **hidden defect in a program** = defect which was not seen when the program was tested **verborgener Programmfehler;** **hidden files** = important system files which are not displayed in a directory listing and cannot normally be read by a user **verborgene Dateien;** *it allows users to backup or restore hidden system files independently;* **hidden lines** = lines which make up a three-dimensional object, but are obscured when displayed as a two-dimensional image **versteckte Linien; hidden line algorithm** = mathematical formula that removes hidden lines from a two-dimensional computer image of a 3-D object **Hidden-Line-Algorithmus;** **hidden line removal** = erasure of lines which should not be visible when looking at a two-dimensional image of a three-dimensional object **Entfernung verdeckter Linien**

hierarchy *noun* way in which objects *or* data *or* structures are organized, usually with the most important *or* highest priority *or* most general item at the top, then working down a tree structure **Hierarchie;** **data hierarchy** = data structure organized hierarchically **Datenhierarchie**

hierarchical classification *noun* library classification system where the list of subjects is divided down into more and more selective subsets **hierarchische Einteilung;** **hierarchical communications system** = network in which each branch has a number of separate minor branches dividing from it **hierarchisches Kommunikationssystem;** **hierarchical computer network** = method of allocating control and processing functions in a network to the computers which are most suited to the task **hierarchisches Computernetz;** **hierarchical database** = database in which records can be related to each other in a defined structure **hierarchische Datenbank;** **hierarchical directory** = directory listing of files on a disk, showing the main directory and its files, branches and any sub-directories **hierarchisches Verzeichnis;** **hierarchical filing system** = (in an Apple Macintosh system) method used to store and organise files on a disk **hierarchische Dateistruktur**

hi fi *or* **hifi** = HIGH FIDELITY accurate reproduction of audio signals by equipment such as a record player and amplifier **Hi-Fi;** **a hi fi system** *or* **a hi fi** = equipment for playing records *or* compact discs *or* tapes *or* listening to the radio (including tape recorder, turntable, amplifier and speakers) **eine Hi-Fi-Anlage**

high *adjective*
(a) large *or* very great **hoch; high density storage** = very large number of bits stored per area of storage medium **Speicher mit hoher Dichte;** *a hard disk is a high density storage medium compared to paper tape;* **high-end** = expensive or high-performance device **High-End; high fidelity** *or* **hifi** *or* **hi fi** = accurate reproduction of audio signals by equipment such as a record player and amplifier **Highfidelity, Klangtreue; high frequency** = radio communications range of frequencies between 3-30 Mhz **Hochfrequenz; high-level data link control (HLDLC)** = ISO defined communications interface protocol which allows several computers to be linked **codeunabhängiges Steuerungsverfahren; high-level data link control station** = equipment and programs which correctly receive and transmit standard HLDLC data frames **Station für codeunabhängige Steuerungsverfahren; high-level (programming) language (HLL)** = computer programming language that is easy to learn and allows the user to write programs using words and commands that are easy to understand and look like English words, the program is then translated into machine code, with one HLL command often representing a number of machine code instructions **höhere Programmiersprache;** *programmers should have a knowledge of high-level languages, particularly PASCAL; compare* LOW-LEVEL LANGUAGE; **high memory** = (on an IBM PC) memory area between 640Kb and 1Mb **hoher Speicher, High Memory; high memory area (HMA)** = (in an IBM PC) first 64Kb of extended memory above 1Mb that can be used by programs **hoher Speicherbereich, HMA-Bereich; high order** = (digit) with the greatest weighting within a number **(Ziffer) mit höchster Wertigkeit; high-order language** = HIGH-LEVEL LANGUAGE; **high pass filter** = circuit that allows frequencies above a certain limit to pass, while blocking those below that frequency limit **Hochpassfilter; high performance equipment** = very good quality *or* high specification equipment **Hochleistungsausrüstung; high performance filing system (HPFS)** = (in OS/2 operating system) method of storing file information that is faster and more flexible than MS-DOS FAT **HPFS-Dateisystem, High Performance Filing System (HPFS); high priority program** = program that is important *or* urgent and is processed before

others **Programm mit hoher Priorität; high reduction** = reduction of text *or* graphics for use in micrographics, usually reduced by 30 to 60 times **starke Verkleinerung; high specification** *or* **high spec** = giving a high degree of accuracy *or* having a large number of features **hohe Spezifikation;** *high spec cabling needs to be very carefully handled;* **high speed carry** = single operation in which a carry into an adder results in a carry out **Schnellübertrag; high usage trunk** = main communications line that carries a large number of calls **Querleitung**
(b) logical high = equal to logic TRUE state or 1 **logischer Pegel H;** *compare* LOGICAL LOW; FALSE

◊ **highlight**
1 *noun* **highlights** = characters *or* symbols treated to make them stand out from the rest of the text, often by using bold type **Hervorhebungen**
2 *verb* to make part of the text stand out from the rest **hervorheben;** *the headings are highlighted in bold*

◊ **high-resolution** *or* **hi-res** *noun* ability to display *or* detect a very large number of pixels per unit area **hohe Auflösung;** *high-resolution graphics; this high-resolution monitor can display 640 x 320 pixels; the new hi-res optical scanner can detect 300 dots per inch*

◊ **high Sierra specification** *noun* industry standard method of storing data on a CD-ROM disc **High-Sierra-Spezifikation**

◊ **high-speed** *adjective* which operates faster than normal data transmission *or* processing **Hochgeschwindigkeits-; high-speed duplicator** = machine that copies video *or* audio tapes by running them at a faster speed than normal **Hochgeschwindigkeitskopierer; high-speed skip** = rapid movement in a printer to miss the perforations in continuous stationery **schneller Sprung**

◊ **high-tech** *or* **high technology** *adjective* technologically advanced **High-Tech-**

◊ **highway** *or* **bus** *noun* communications link consisting of a set of leads *or* wires which connect different parts of a computer hardware system and over which data is transmitted and received by various circuits inside the system **Vielfachleitung; address highway** = physical connections that carry the address data in a parallel form between the central processing unit and memory *or* external devices

Adressenvielfachleitung; data highway = bus carrying the data signals in parallel form between the central processing unit and memory *or* external devices **Datenvielfachleitung**

QUOTE they have proposed a standardized high-level language for importing image data into desktop publishing and other applications programs

QUOTE the computer is uniquely suited to image processing because of its high-resolution graphics

Byte

hill climbing *noun* method of achieving a goal in an expert system **Problemlösungsmethode in einem Expertensystem**

hi-res = HIGH RESOLUTION; *hi-res graphics; this hi-res monitor can display 640 x 320 pixels; the new hi-res optical scanner can detect 300 dots per inch*

hiss *noun* high-frequency noise mixed with a signal **Nebengeräusch**

histogram *noun* graph on which values are represented as vertical *or* horizontal bars **Histogramm**

hit
1 *noun* successful match *or* search of a database **Treffer**; *there was a hit after just a few seconds; there are three hits for this search key;* cache hit = data retrieved from cache memory rather than from the storage device; indicates that time was saved and the cache was useful **Cache-Hit; hit on the line** = short period of noise on a communications line, causing data corruption **Störung der Übertragungsleitung**
2 *verb* to press a key **anschlagen;** *to save the text, hit ESCAPE S*

QUOTE the cause of the data disaster is usually due to your finger hitting the wrong key
PC Business World

HLDLC = HIGH-LEVEL DATA LINK CONTROL

HLL = HIGH-LEVEL LANGUAGE

HMA = HIGH MEMORY AREA (in an IBM PC) first 64Kb of extended memory above 1Mb that can be used by programs **HMA**

HMI = HUMAN-MACHINE INTERFACE facilities provided to improve the interaction betweeen a user and a computer system **Mensch-Maschine-Schnittstelle**

HOF = HEAD OF FORM

hold
1 *noun* synchronization timing pulse for a television time base signal **Halteimpuls**
2 *verb* to retain *or* keep a value *or* communications line *or* section of memory **anhalten; hold current** = amount of electrical current that has to be supplied to keep a device in its operating state, but not operating **Haltestrom; holding line** = boundary line indicating the limits of an area of artwork *or* tone **Haltelinie; holding loop** = section of program that loops until it is broken by some action, most often used when waiting for a response from the keyboard *or* a device **Warteschleife; holding time** = time spent by a communications circuit on call **Haltezeit**

◊ **holdup** *noun* (i) time period over which power will be supplied by a UPS (ii) pause in a program *or* device due to a malfunction **(i) Aufrechterhaltung der Spannung durch eine USV (unterbrechungsfreie Stromversorgung); (ii) Verzögerung, Stockung**

COMMENT: the hold feature keeps the picture steady and central on the screen; some televisions have horizontal and vertical hold controls to allow the picture to be moved and set up according to various conditions

hole *noun*
(a) punched gap in a punched paper tape *or* card, representing data **Loch; index hole** = hole in the edge of a hard-sectored disk **Indexloch**
(b) method of describing the absence of an electron from an atomic structure **Defektelektron**

COMMENT: a hole may move, but in the opposite direction to the flow of electrons in a material; it is also considered to have a positive charge as compared to a electron. This concept is mostly used in semiconductor physics, where the bulk movement of holes and electrons in an electronic device are studied

Hollerith code *noun* coding system that uses punched holes in a card to represent characters and symbols, the system uses two sets of twelve rows to provide possible positions for each code **Hollerith-Code**

hologram *noun* imagined three-dimensional image produced by the interference pattern when a part of a coherent light beam is reflected from an object and mixed with the main beam **Hologramm**

◊ **holograph** *noun* handwritten manuscript, as written by the author using a pen *or* pencil, but not typed **handschriftliches Manuskript, Holographum**

◊ **holographic image** *noun* hologram of a three-dimensional object **Hologramm; holographic storage** = storage of data as a holographic image which is then read by a bank of photocells and a laser (a new storage medium with massive storage potential) **holographische Speicherung**

◊ **holography** *noun* science and study of holograms and their manufacture **Holographie**

home *noun*
(a) place where a person lives **Zuhause; home banking** = method of examining and carrying out bank transactions via a terminal and modem in the user's home **Homebanking (Abwicklung von Bankgeschäften durch Bildschirmtext); home computer** = microcomputer designed for home use, whose applications might include teaching, games, personal finance and word-processing **Heimcomputer**
(b) starting point for printing on a screen, usually taken as the top left hand corner **Ausgangsstellung; home key** = (on an IBM PC keyboard) key that moves the cursor to the beginning of a line of text **Pos1-Taste; home record** = first *or* initial data record in a file **Anfangssatz**

◊ **homing** *noun* location of the source of a transmitted signal *or* data item **Quellenfindung**

homogeneous computer network *noun* network made up of similar machines, that are compatible *or* from the same manufacturer **homogenes Computernetz; homogeneous multiplexing** = switching multiplexer system where all the channels contain data using the same protocol and transmission rate **homogene Multiplexmethode**

hood *noun* cover which protects something **Hülle, Haube; acoustic hood** = soundproof cover put over a line printer to cut down its noise **Schallschluckhaube**

hook *noun* point in a program at which a programmer can insert test code or debugging code **Hook**

hooking *noun* distortion of a video picture caused by tape head timing errors **Störung des Videobildes (am oberen Bildrand) hervorgerufen durch Zeitfehler**

hop *noun* direct transmission path, using the reflections from only the ionosphere, not the earth, to propagate the signal from one point on the earth to another **Funkfeld**

hopper *noun* device which holds punched cards and feeds them into the reader **Kartenmagazin**

horizontal *adjective* lying flat *or* going from side to side, not up and down **horizontal; horizontal blanking** = prevention of a picture signal reaching a television beam during the time it contains no picture information on its return trace **Teilbildunterdrückung; horizontal check** = error detection method for transmitted data **Horizontalprüfung;** *see also* CYCLIC CHECK; **horizontal scrollbar** = (in a GUI) bar along the bottom of a window that indicates that the page is wider than the window; a user can move horizontally across the page by dragging the indicator bar on the scrollbar **horizontale Bildlaufleiste, horizontaler Rollbalken; horizontal scrolling** = to move across a page, horizontally **horizontales Blättern** *or* **Rollen** *or* **Scrollen, Durchführen eines horizontalen Bildlaufs; horizontal synchronization pulse** = pulse in a television broadcast signal that synchronizes the receiver sweep circuitry **Horizontalsynchronisationsimpuls; horizontal wraparound** = movement of a cursor on a computer display from the end of one line to the beginning of the next **Zeilenumlauf**

horn *noun* directional radio device with a wider open end leading to a narrow section, used for the reception and transmission of radio waves **Hornstrahler; feed horn** = microwave channelling device used to direct transmitted signals **Speisehornstrahler**

host *noun & adjective* **host adapter** = adapter which connects to a host computer **Adapter zum Hauptrechner;** *the cable to connect the scanner to the host adapter is included*

◊ **host computer** *noun*
(a) main controlling computer in a multi-user *or* distributed system **Hauptrechner**
(b) computer used to write and debug software for another computer, often using a cross compiler **Leitrechner**

(c) computer in a network that provides special services *or* programming languages to all users **Spezialcomputer**

> QUOTE you select fonts manually or through commands sent from the host computer along with the text
>
> *Byte*

hot chassis *noun* metal framework *or* case around a computer that is connected to a voltage supply rather than being earthed **nichtgeerdetes Gehäuse; hot fix** = detection and repair of a fault (normally a corrupt sector on a hard disk) without affecting normal operations **Hot-Fix; hot key** = special key or key combination which starts a process or activates a program **Hotkey, Tastaturabkürzung, Tastenkombination; hot frame** = very bright film frame caused by over exposure **heller Bildrahmen hervorgerufen durch Überbelichtung; hot metal composition** = old method of producing typeset pages from individual metal letters which were cast from hot liquid metal, now mainly replaced by phototypesetting **gegossener Hartbleisatz; hot spot** = region of high brightness on a film *or* display screen **intensiver Lichtfleck;** *the image of the trumpet is a hotspot and will play a sound when you move the pointer over it;* **hot standby** = piece of hardware that is kept operational at all times and is used as backup in case of system failure **Hot-Standby-System (mitlaufendes Reservesystem); hot type** = characters cast from hot liquid metal **Bleisatz; hot zone** = text area to the left of the right margin in a word-processed document (if a word does not fit in completely, a hyphen is automatically inserted) **Ausschließzone**

◊ **hotspot** *noun* special area on an image or display that does something when the cursor is moved onto it **Hotspot, Detailpunkt**

house

1 *noun* company (especially a publishing company) **Firma; Verlag;** *one of the biggest software houses in the US;* **house corrections** = printing *or* composition errors, caused by and corrected by the printers of a document **Hauskorrekturen; house style** = (i) style of spelling and layout, used by a publishing company in all its books; (ii) method *or* design of a company's products, used to identify them from the products of competitors **(i) Verlagsstil; (ii) Hausstil**
2 *verb* to put a device in a case **einbauen;** *the magnetic tape is housed in a solid plastic case*

◊ **housekeeping** *noun* tasks that have

to be regularly carried out to maintain a computer system (checking backups, deleting unwanted files, etc.) **Systemverwaltung; housekeeping routine** = set of instructions executed once, at the start of a new program to carry out system actions such as clear memory, configure function keys or change screen display mode **Systemverwaltungsroutine;** *see also* IN-HOUSE

◊ **housing** *noun* solid case **Gehäuse;** *the computer housing was damaged when it fell on the floor*

howler *noun*
(a) buzzer that indicates to a telephone exchange operator that a user's telephone handset is not on the receiver **Summer**
(b) very bad and obvious mistake; *what a howler, no wonder your program won't work* **grober Schnitzer, 'Hammer'**

HPFS = HIGH PERFORMANCE FILING SYSTEM (in OS/2 operating system) method of storing file information that is faster and more flexible than MS-DOS FAT **HPFS-Dateisystem**

HPGL = HEWLETT PACKARD GRAPHICS LANGUAGE

◊ **HPIB** = HEWLETT PACKARD INTERFACE BUS

◊ **HP-PCL** = HEWLETT PACKARD PRINTER CONTROL LANGUAGE

HRG = HIGH RESOLUTION GRAPHICS ability to display a large number of pixels per unit area **Grafik mit hoher Auflösung;** *the HRG board can control up to 300 pixels per inch*

HT = HANDY TALKIES small portable transceivers **Sprechfunkgeräte**

hub *noun*
(a) (in a floppy disk) central part of a disk, usually with a hole and ring which the disk drive grips to spin the disk **Nabe, Hub**
(b) (in a star-topology network) central ring *or* wiring cabinet where all circuits meet (and form an electrical path for signals) **Netzknoten**

huffman code *noun* data compression code, where frequent characters occupy less bit space than less frequent ones **Huffman-Code**

huge model *noun* (in programming) memory model of an Intel processor that allows data and program code to exceed 64Kb (but the total of both must be less than 1Mb) **Hugemodell**

hum *noun* low frequency electrical noise *or* interference on a signal **Brummen**

human-computer *or* **human-machine interface (HMI)** *noun* facilities provided to improve the interaction between a user and a computer system **Mensch-Maschine-Schnittstelle**

hung *see* CRASH

hunting *noun* process of searching out a data record in a file **Suchen**

hybrid circuit *noun* connection of a number of different electronic components such as integrated circuits, transistors, resistors and capacitors in a small package, which since the components are not contained in their own protective packages, requires far less space than the individual discrete components **Hybridschaltung; hybrid computer** = combination of analog and digital circuits in a computer system to achieve a particular goal **Hybridrechner; hybrid interface** = one-off interface between a computer and a piece of analog equipment **Hybridschnittstelle; hybrid system** = combination of analog and digital computers and equipment to provide an optimal system for a particular task **Hybridanlage**

HyperCard ™ *noun* database system controlled by HyperTalk programming language used to produce hypertext documents **HyperCard** ™

◊ **hypermedia** *noun* hypertext document that is also capable of displaying images and sound **Hypertextdokument**

◊ **HyperTalk** ™ *noun* programming language used to control a HyperCard database **HyperTalk** ™

◊ **hypertext** *adjective* system of organising information; certain words in a document link to other documents and display the text when the word is selected **Hypertext;** *in this hypertext page, click once on the word 'computer' and it will tell you what a computer is*

hyphen *noun* printing sign (-) to show that a word has been split **Bindestrich, Trennungszeichen; soft** *or* **discretionary hyphen** = hyphen which is inserted when a word is split at the end of a line in word-processed text, but is not present when the word is written normally **weiches Trennungszeichen**

◊ **hyphenated** *adjective* written with a hyphen **mit Bindestrich geschrieben;** *the word 'high-level' is usually hyphenated*

◊ **hyphenation** *noun* splitting of a word (as at the end of a line, when the word is too long to fit) **Silben-, Worttrennung; hyphenation and justification** *or* **H & J** = justifying lines to a set width, splitting the long words correctly at the end of each line **Trennung und Randausgleich;** *an American hyphenation and justification program will not work with British English spellings*

> QUOTE the hyphenation program is useful for giving a professional appearance to documents and for getting as many words onto the page as possible
> *Micro Decision*

hypo *abbreviation* photographic fixing solution **Hypo**

Hz = HERTZ

Ii

IAM = INTERMEDIATE ACCESS MEMORY memory storage that has an access time between that of main memory and a disk based system **Speicher mit mittlerer Zugriffszeit**

IAR = INSTRUCTION ADDRESS REGISTER register in a CPU that contains the location of the next instruction to be processed **Befehlsadressregister**

IAS = IMMEDIATE ACCESS STORE high-speed main memory area in a computer system **Schnellspeicher**

I-beam *noun* cursor shaped like the letter 'I' used (in a GUI) to edit text *or* indicate text operations **Einfügemarke, Schreibbalken**

IBG = INTERBLOCK GAP

IBM = INTERNATIONAL BUSINESS MACHINES largest computer company in the world; developed the first PC based on the Intel processor **IBM; IBM AT** = personal computer based on the Intel 80286 16-bit processor and featured an ISA expansion bus **IBM AT; IBM AT keyboard** = keyboard layout that features 12 function keys in a row along the top of the keyboard, with a separate numeric keypad **IBM AT-Tastatur; IBM compatible** = generic term for a personal computer that is hardware and software compatible with the IBM PC regardless of which Intel processor it uses; it features an ISA, EISA or MCA expansion bus **IBM-kompatibel; IBM PC** = personal computer based on the Intel 8088 8-bit processor **IBM PC; IBM PC keyboard** = keyboard layout that features 10 function keys arranged to the left of the main keys, with no separate numeric keypad **IBM-PC-Tastatur; IBM PS/2** or **IBM Personal System/2** = range of personal computers based on the Intel 8086, 80286 and 80386 processors that feature an MCA expansion bus **IBM PS/2** or **IBM Personal System/2; IBM XT** = personal computer based on the IBM PC but with an internal hard disk drive and featuring an ISA expansion bus **IBM XT**

IC = INTEGRATED CIRCUIT
NOTE: plural is **ICs**

icand *noun* = MULTIPLICAND

icon or **ikon** *noun* graphic symbol or small picture displayed on screen, used in an interactive computer system to provide an easy way of identifying a function **ikonisches Zeichen, Piktogramm;** *the icon for the graphics program is a small picture of a palette; click twice over the wordprocessor icon - the picture of the typewriter*

QUOTE the system has on-screen icons and pop-up menus and is easy to control using the mouse
Electronics & Power

QUOTE an icon-based system allows easy use of a computer without the need to memorize the complicated command structure of the native operating system
Micro Decision

QUOTE Despite (or because of?) the swap file, loading was slow and the hourglass icon of the mouse pointer frequently returned to the arrow symbol well before loading was complete.
Computing

ID = IDENTIFICATION; **ID card** = card which identifies a person **Kennkarte; Personalausweis; ID code** = password or word that identifies a user so that he can access a system **Identifizierungscode;** *after you wake up the system, you have to input your ID code then your password*

IDA = INTEGRATED DIGITAL ACCESS

IDD = INTERNATIONAL DIRECT DIALLING

IDE = INTEGRATED DRIVE ELECTRONICS or INTELLIGENT DEVICE ELECTRONICS popular standard for hard disk drive unit that includes the control electronics on the drive **IDE;** *IDE drives are the standard fitted to most PCs*

ideal *adjective* perfect or very good for something **ideal;** *she is the ideal designer for children's books;* **ideal format** = standard large format for photographic negatives, used mainly in professional equipment **Idealformat**

identical *adjective* exactly the same **identisch;** *the two systems use identical software; the performance of the two clones is identical*

identify *verb* to establish who someone is or what something is **identifizieren;** *the user has to identify himself to the system by using a password before access is allowed; the maintenance engineers have identified the cause of the system failure*

◊ **identification** *noun* procedure used by a host computer to establish the identity and nature of the calling computer or user (this could be for security and access restriction purposes or to provide transmission protocol information) **Identifikation; identification character** = single character sent to a host computer to establish the identity and location of a remote computer or terminal **Identifikationszeichen; identification division** = section of a COBOL program source code, in which the identifiers and formats for data and variables to be used within the program are declared **Erkennungsteil**

◊ **identifier** *noun* set of characters used to distinguish between different blocks of data or files **Kennzeichen, Name; identifier word** = word that is used as a block or file identifier **Kennwort**

◊ **identity** *noun* who someone or what something is **Identität; identity burst** = pattern of bits before the first block of data on a magnetic tape that identifies the tape format used **Identitätsblock; identity gate** *or* **element** = logical gate that provides a single output that is true if the inputs are both the same **Identitätsgatter; identity number** = unique number, used usually with a password to identify a user when logging into a system **Kennnummer;** *don't forget to log in your identity number;* **identity operation** = logical function whose output is true only if all the operands are of the same value **Identitätsfunktion**

idiot tape *noun* tape containing unformatted text, which cannot be typeset until formatting data, such as justification, line width, and page size, has been added by a computer **nicht justiertes Band**

idle *adjective* (machine *or* telephone line *or* device) which is not being used, but is ready and waiting to be used **bereit; idle character** = symbol *or* code that means 'do nothing' *or* a code that is transmitted when there is no data available for transmission at that time **Leerzeichen, Synchronisierzeichen; idle time** = period of time when a device is switched on but not doing anything **Leerlaufzeit**

IDP = INTEGRATED DATA PROCESSING

IEC connector *noun* standard for a three-pin connector used on sockets that carry mains electricity to the computer **IEC-Stecker;** *all PCs use a male IEC connector and a mains lead with a female IEC connector*

IEE *(UK)* = INSTITUTION OF ELECTRICAL ENGINEERS

IEEE *(USA)* = INSTITUTE OF ELECTRICAL AND ELECTRONIC ENGINEERS; **IEEE bus** = interface that conforms to IEEE standards **IEEE-Bus; IEEE-488** = interfacing standard as laid down by the IEEE, where only data and handshaking signals are used, mainly used in laboratories to connect computers to measuring equipment **IEEE-488-Norm; IEEE-802.2** = standard defining data links used with 802.3, 802.4 and 802.5 **IEEE-802.2; IEEE-802.3** = standard defining Ethernet network system (CSMA/CD access using a bus-topology) **IEEE-802.3; IEEE-802.4** = standard defining Token Bus **IEEE-802.4; IEEE-802.5** = standard defining IBM Token-Ring network system (access using a token passed around a ring network) **IEEE-802.5**

ier *noun* = MULTIPLIER

IF *or* **if** = INTERMEDIATE FREQUENCY

IF statement *noun* computer programming statement, meaning do an action IF a condition is true (usually followed by THEN) **IF-Anweisung, WENN-Anweisung; IF-THEN-ELSE** = high-level programming language statement, meaning IF something cannot be done, THEN do this, or ELSE do that **IF-THEN-ELSE-Anweisung, WENN-DANN-SONST-Anweisung**

ignore *verb* not to recognize *or* not to do what someone says **übergehen;** *this command instructs the computer to ignore all punctuation;* **ignore character** = null *or* fill character **Ungültigkeitszeichen**

IH = INTERRUPT HANDLER

IIL = INTEGRATED INJECTION LOGIC

IKBS = INTELLIGENT KNOWLEDGE-BASED SYSTEM

ikon *or* **icon** *noun* graphic symbol *or* picture displayed on screen, used in an interactive computer system to provide an easy way of identifying a function **ikonisches Zeichen, Piktogramm;** *see also* ICON

ILF = INFRA LOW FREQUENCY

ILL = INTER-LIBRARY LOAN

illegal *adjective* which is not legal *or* which is against the law *or* against rules of syntax **illegal; unzulässig; illegal character** = invalid combination of bits in a computer word, according to preset rules **unzulässiges Zeichen; illegal instruction** = instruction code not within the repertoire of a language **unzulässiger Befehl; illegal operation** = instruction *or* process that does not follow the computer system's protocol *or* language syntax **unzulässige Operation**

◊ **illegally** *adverb* against the law *or* against rules **illegal; unzulässig;** *the company has been illegally copying copyright software*

illegible *adjective* which cannot be read **unleserlich;** *if the manuscript is illegible, send it back to the author to have it typed*

illiterate *adjective* (person) who cannot read **analphabetisch; computer illiterate** =

person who does not understand computer-related expressions *or* operations **jemand, der sich mit Computern nicht auskennt;** *see also* LITERATE

QUOTE three years ago the number of people who were computer illiterate was much higher than today

Minicomputer News

illuminate *verb* to shine a light on something **beleuchten;** *the screen is illuminated by a low-power light*

◊ **illumination** *noun* lighting **Beleuchtung; aperture illumination** = pattern generated from an aperture antenna **Ausleuchtung**

◊ **illuminance** *noun* measurement of the amount of light that strikes a surface, measured in lux **Beleuchtungsstärke** ⇨APPENDIX

illustrate *verb* to add pictures to a text **illustrieren, bebildern;** *the book is illustrated in colour; the manual is illustrated with charts and pictures of the networking connections*

◊ **illustration** *noun* picture (in a book) **Illustration;** *the book has twenty-five pages of full-colour illustrations*

image *noun*
(a) exact duplicate of an area of memory **Abbild**
(b) copy of an original picture *or* design **Abbild; image area** = region of microfilm *or* display screen on which characters *or* designs can be displayed **Bildbereich; image carrier** = storage medium containing data that defines the typefaces used in a phototypesetter **Bildträger; image compression** = compressing the data that forms an image **Bildkomprimierung; image degradation** = picture contrast and quality loss due to signal distortion *or* bad copying of a video signal **Bildverschlechterung; image distortion** = optical lens fault causing an image to be distorted **Bildverzerrung; image enhancer** = electronic device that improves the clarity of an image **Vorrichtung zur Qualitätsverbesserung eines Bildes; image master** = data describing fonts and character shapes in a phototypesetter **Imagemaster; image plane** = region where the photographic film is located in a camera, where a sharp image of a scene is formed when the lens is correctly focused **Filmebene; image processing** = analysis of information contained in an image, usually by electronic means *or* using a computer

which provide the analysis *or* recognition of objects in the image, etc. **Bildverarbeitung; image processor** = electronic *or* computer system used for image processing, and to extract information from the image **Bildverarbeiter; image retention** = time taken for a TV image to disappear after it has been displayed, caused by long persistence phosphor **Bildkonservierung; image scanner** = input device which converts documents *or* drawings *or* photographs into a digitized, machine-readable form **Bildabtaster; image sensor** = photoelectric device that produces a signal related to the amount of light falling on it (this scans horizontally over an image, reading in one line at a time) **Bildsensor; image stability** = ability of a display screen to provide a flicker-free picture **Bildbeständigkeit; image storage space** = region of memory in which a digitized image is stored **Bildspeicherplatz; image table** = two bit-mapped tables used to control input and output devices *or* processes **Bild(wiederholungs)speicher**

◊ **imaging** *noun* technique for creating pictures on a screen (in medicine used to provide pictures of sections of the body, using scanners attached to computers) **Bildgestaltungstechnik; magnetic resonance imaging** = scanning technique, using magnetic fields and radio waves **Kernspintomographie; X-ray imaging** = showing X-ray pictures of the inside of part of the body on a screen **Röntgenbildprojektion auf dem Bildschirm**

QUOTE The Max FX also acts as a server to a growing number of printers, including a Varityper 5300 with emerald raster image processor and a Canon CLC 500 colour photocopier

Computing

immediate *adjective* which happens at once **sofort, schnell; immediate access store (IAS)** = high-speed main memory area in a computer system **Schnellspeicher; immediate addressing** = accessing data immediately because it is held in the address field of an instruction **unmittelbare Adressierung; immediate instruction** = computer instruction in which the operand is included within the instruction, rather than an address of the operand location **Direktbefehl; immediate mode** = mode in which a computer executes an instruction as soon as it is entered **Direktmodus; immediate operand** = operand which is fetched at the same time as the instruction (within an immediate addressing operation) **Direktoperand; immediate**

processing = processing data when it appears, rather than waiting for a synchronizing clock pulse *or* time **unmittelbare Verarbeitung;** *compare with* BATCH

immunity *see* INTERFERENCE

impact *noun* hitting *or* striking something **Auftreffen, Auswirkung; impact printer** = printer that prints text and symbols by striking an ink ribbon onto paper with a metal character, such as a daisy-wheel printer (as opposed to a non-impact printer like a laser printer) **mechanischer Drucker;** *see also* DAISY-WHEEL PRINTER, DOT MATRIX PRINTER

QUOTE Lexmark is shipping the Wheelwriter family of typewriters that can be connected to a PC using the parallel printer port, making it act like a PC impact printer

Computing

impedance *noun* measurement of the effect an electrical circuit has on signal current magnitude and phase when a steady voltage is applied **Impedanz, Scheinwiderstand; impedance matching** = means of making the best signal power transfer between two circuits by making sure that their output and input impedances are the same as the transmission line **Scheinwiderstandsanpassung;** *impedance matching a transmitter and receiver minimizes power losses to transmitted signals;* **impedance mismatch** = situation where the impedance of the transmission *or* receiving end of a system does not match the other, resulting in loss of signal power (due to increased attenuation effects of the two different impedances) **fehlerhafte Scheinwiderstandsanpassung;** *see also* OHM

implant *verb* to fix deeply into something; to bond one substance into another chemically **implantieren;** *the dopant is implanted into the substrate*

implement *verb* to carry out *or* to put something into action **realisieren, implementieren**

◊ **implementation** *noun* version of something that works **Realisierung, Implementierung;** *the latest implementation of the software runs much faster*

implication *noun* logical operation that uses an IF-THEN structure, if A is true and

if B is true this implies that the AND function of A and B will be true **Implikation**

implied addressing *noun* assembler instruction that operates on only one register (this is preset at manufacture and the user does not have to specify an address **Fortschaltungsadressierung;** *implied addressing for the accumulator is used in the instruction LDA,16*

import *verb*
(a) to bring goods into a country for sale **importieren**
(b) (i) to bring something in from outside a system; (ii) to convert a file stored in one format to the default format used by a program **(i) importieren; (ii) importieren, konvertieren;** *you can import images from the CAD package into the DTP program;* **imported signal** = broadcast television signal from outside a normal reception area, that is routed into and distributed over a cable network **importiertes Signal**

◊ **importation** *noun* the act of importing something into a system from outside **Fremdübernahme**

QUOTE text and graphics importation from other systems is possible

Publish

QUOTE At the moment, Acrobat supports only the sending and viewing of documents. There are legal implications associated with allowing users to edit documents in the style of the original application, without having the tool itself on their desks, and there is no import facility back into applications

Computing

impression *noun* number of books *or* documents printed all on the same printrun **Auflage; impression cylinder** = roller in a printing press that presses the sheets of paper against the inked type **Druckzylinder**

imprint *noun* publisher's *or* printer's name which appears on the title page *or* in the bibliographical details of a book **Impressum; imprint position** = on a sheet of paper, place where the next letter *or* symbol is to be printed **Andruckposition**

impulse *noun* (voltage) pulse which lasts a very short time **Impuls**

◊ **impulsive** *adjective* lasting a very short time **impulsiv; impulsive noise** = interference on a signal caused by short periods of noise **Impulsstörung**

inaccurate *adjective* not correct *or* wrong falsch; *he entered an inaccurate password*

◊ **inaccuracy** *noun* mistake *or* error Fehler, Ungenauigkeit; *the bibliography is full of inaccuracies*

inactive *adjective* not working *or* running nicht aktiv; **inactive window** = (in a GUI) window still displayed, but not currently being used **inaktives Fenster**

in-band signalling *noun* use of a normal voice grade channel for data transmission **Imband-Signalisierung**

inbuilt *adjective* (feature *or* device) included in a system eingebaut; *this software has inbuilt error correction*

in camera process *noun* film processing which takes place inside the camera **Sofortbildentwicklung**

incandescence *noun* generation of light by heating a wire in an inert gas (as in a light bulb) **Weißglut**

◊ **incandescent** *adjective* shining because of heat produced in an inert gas weißglühend; *current passing through gas and heating a filament in a light bulb causes it to produce incandescent light*

inches-per-second (ips) way of showing the speed of tape past the read/write heads **Inches pro Sekunde**

in-circuit emulator *noun* (circuit) that emulates a device *or* integrated circuit and is inserted into a new or faulty circuit to test it working correctly **Emulationsadapter von eingebauten Schaltungen**; *this in-circuit emulator is used to test the floppy disk controller by emulating a disk drive*

inclined orbit *noun* orbit that is not polar *or* equatorial **geneigte Umlaufbahn**

inclusion *noun* logical operation that uses an IF-THEN structure, if A is true and if B is true this implies that the AND function of A and B will be true **Inklusion**

◊ **inclusive** *adjective* which counts something in with other things **inklusiv**; *prices are inclusive of VAT;* **inclusive OR** *see* OR

incoming *adjective* which is coming in from outside **ankommend**; **incoming message** = message received in a computer eingehende Nachricht; **incoming traffic** = amount of data *or* messages received **ankommender Verkehr**

incompatible *adjective* not compatible *or* which cannot work together **nicht kompatibel**; *they tried to link the two systems, but found they were incompatible*

incorrect *adjective* not correct *or* with mistakes **falsch**; *the input data was incorrect, so the output was also incorrect*

◊ **incorrectly** *adverb* not correctly *or* with mistakes **falsch**; *the data was incorrectly keyboarded*

increment
1 *noun*
(a) addition of a set number, usually one, to a register, often for counting purposes **Zuwachs**; *an increment is added to the counter each time a pulse is detected*
(b) value of the number added to a register **Inkrement**; *increase the increment to three*
2 *verb*
(a) to add something *or* to increase a number **hochzählen**; *the counter is incremented each time an instruction is executed*
(b) to move forward to the next location **inkrementieren**
(c) to move a document *or* card forward to its next preset location for printing *or* reading **inkrementieren**

◊ **incremental backup** *noun* backup procedure that only backs up the files which have changed since the last full *or* incremental backup **Differenzialsicherung**

◊ **incremental computer** *noun* computer that stores variables as the difference between their actual value and an absolute initial value **Inkrementalrechner**; **incremental data** = data which represents the difference of a value from an original value **Inkrementdaten**; **incremental plotter** = graphical output device that can only move in small steps, with input data representing the difference between present position and the position required, so drawing lines and curves as a series of short straight lines **Stufenformplotter**

indent
1 *noun* space *or* series of spaces from the left margin, when starting a line of text **Einrückung, Einzug**
2 *verb* to start a line of text with a space in from the left margin einrücken; *the first line of the paragraph is indented two spaces*

◊ **indentation** *noun* leaving a space at the beginning of a line of text **Einrücken**

independent *adjective* free *or* not controlled by anyone **unabhängig**

◊ **independently** *adverb* freely *or* without being controlled *or* without being connected **unabhängig**; *in spooling, the printer is acting independently of the keyboard*

indeterminate system *noun* system whose logical (output) state cannot be predicted **unbestimmtes System**

index
1 *noun*
(a) list of items in a computer memory, usually arranged alphabetically **Index**; **index build** = creation of an ordered list from the results of a database *or* file search **Indexerstellung**; **index page** = videotext page that tells the user the locations of other pages *or* areas of interest **Indexseite**; **index register** = computer address register that is added to a reference address to provide the location to be accessed **Indexregister**
(b) alphabetical list printed, usually at the back of a book, giving references to items in the main part of the book **Index**
(c) list of terms classified into groups *or* put in alphabetical order **Index, Stichwortverzeichnis**; **index card** = small card used for storing information **Karteikarte**; **index letter** *or* **index number** = letter *or* number which identifies an item in an index **Indexbuchstabe**; **Indexzahl**
(d) address to be used that is the result of an offset value added to a start location **Index**; *see* INDEXED ADDRESSING; **index value** = offset value added to an address to produce a usable address **Indexwert**
(e) guide marks along the edge of a piece of film *or* strip of microfilm **Index**; **index hole** = hole in the edge of a hand-sectored disk **Indexloch**
2 *verb*
(a) to write an index (for a book) **ein Register zusammenstellen**; *the book was sent out for indexing; the book has been badly indexed*
(b) to put marks against items, so that they will be selected and sorted to form an index **indizieren**; **indexed address** = address of the location to be accessed which is found in an index register **indizierte Adresse**; **indexed addressing** = method of addressing where the storage location is addressed with a start address and an offset word, which is added to give the destination address **indizierte Adressierung**; **indexed file** = sequential file with an index of all entries and their addresses **indizierte Datei**; **indexed instruction** = instruction that contains an

origin and offset that are added to provide the location to be accessed **indizierter Befehl**; **indexed sequential access method (ISAM)** = data retrieval method using a list containing the address of each stored record, where the list is searched, then the record is retrieved from the address in the list **indexsequenzielle Zugriffsmethode**; **indexed sequential storage** = method of storing records in a consecutive order, but in such a way that they can be accessed rapidly **Speicher mit indexsequenziellem Zugriff**

◊ **indexer** *noun* person who writes an index **Person, die ein Register zusammenstellt**

◊ **indexing** *noun*
(a) use of indexed addressing methods in a computer **Spezialindizierung**
(b) process of building and sorting a list of records **Indizieren**; **indexing language** = language used in building library *or* book indexes **Indiziersprache**
(c) writing an index for a book **Registererstellung**; **computer indexing** = using a computer to compile an index for a book by selecting relevant words *or* items from the text **Registererstellung mit Hilfe eines Computers**

> QUOTE in microcomputer implementations of COBOL, indexed files are usually based on some type of B-tree structure which allows rapid data retrieval based on the value of the key being used
> *PC-User*

indicate *verb* to show **anzeigen**

◊ **indication** *noun* sign *or* thing which shows **Anzeigen**

◊ **indicator** *noun* something which shows the state of a process, usually a light *or* buzzer **Anzeiger** *or* **Melder**; **indicator chart** = graphical representation of the location and use of indicator flags within a program **Anzeigerdiagramm**; **indicator flag** = register *or* single bit that indicates the state of the processor and its registers, such as a carry or overflow **Anzeigebit**; **indicator light** = light used to warn *or* to indicate the condition of equipment **Anzeigelicht**

indirect *adjective* not direct **indirekt**; **indirect addressing** = way of addressing data, where the first instruction refers to an address which contains a second address **indirekte Adressierung**; **indirect ray** = transmission path of a radio wave that does not take the shortest route, such as a reflection **indirekter Strahl**

individual
1 *noun* single person **Individuum, Einzelperson**; *each individual has his own password to access the system*
2 *adjective* single *or* belonging to a single person **individuell**; *the individual workstations are all linked to the mainframe*

induce *verb* (i) to generate an electrical current in a coil of wire by electromagnetic effects; (ii) to prove (something) mathematically (i) **induzieren**; (ii) **beweisen**; **induced failure** = failure of a device due to external effects **induziertes Versagen**; **induced interference** = electrical noise on a signal due to induced signals from nearby electromagnetic sources **induzierte Störung**

◊ **inductance** *noun* measurement of the amount of energy a device can store in its magnetic field **Induktivität**

◊ **induction** *noun* (i) generation of an electrical current due to electromagnetic effects from a nearby source; (ii) mathematically proving a formula *or* fact (i) **Induktion**; (ii) **Beweis**; **induction coil** = transformer consisting of two nearby coils of insulated wire, one inducing a signal in the other; is often used either to isolate a signal supply from a some equipment *or* as a method of stepping up *or* down a voltage **Induktionsspule**; *see also* TRANSFORMER

◊ **inductive coordination** *noun* agreement between electrical power suppliers and communication providers on methods of reducing induced interference **Kooperation zum Abbau induzierter Störungen**

◊ **inductor** *noun* electrical component consisting of a coil of wire used to introduce inductance effects into a circuit (by storing energy in its magnetic field) **Spule**

Industry Standard Architecture (ISA) *noun* standard used for the 16-bit expansion bus in an IBM PC or compatible **Industry Standard Architecture (ISA)**; *compare* EISA, MCA

inequality operator *noun* symbol used to indicate that two variables *or* quantities are not equal **Ungleichheitsoperator**; *the C programming language uses the symbol '!=' as its inequality operator*

inequivalence *noun* logical function where the output is true if the inputs are not the same, otherwise the output is false **Inäquivalenzfunktion**

inert *adjective* (chemical substance *or* gas) that does not react with other chemicals **inert, (reaktions)träge**

❙❙ COMMENT: inert gas is used to protect a filament from oxidizing

infected computer *noun* computer that carries a virus program **infizierter** *or* **befallener Computer**

inference *noun*
(a) deduction of results from data according to certain rules **Inferenz, logisches Schließen**; **inference engine** *or* **machine** = set of rules used in an expert system to deduce goals *or* results from data **Regelsatz in einem Expertensystem**
(b) method of deducing a result about confidential information concerning an individual by using various data related to groups of people **Inferenz**; **inference control** = determining which information may be released without disclosing personal information about a single individual **Inferenzkontrolle**

inferior figures *noun* smaller numbers *or* characters that are printed slightly below normal characters, used in mathematical and chemical formulae **tiefgestellte Zahlen, Indizes**; *see also* SUBSCRIPT, SUPERSCRIPT, SUPERIOR
NOTE: used in formulae: CO_2

infinite *adjective* with no end **unendlich**; **infinite loop** = loop which has no exit (except by ending the running of the program by switching off the machine *or* resetting) **Endlosschleife**

◊ **infinity** *noun*
(a) very large incomprehensible quantity even bigger than the biggest you can think of **Unendlichkeit**
(b) distance of an object from a viewer where beams of light from the object would be seen to be parallel (i.e. very far away) **Unendlicheinstellung**

infix notation *noun* method of computer programming syntax where operators are embedded inside operands (such as C - D or X + Y) **Infixschreibweise**; *compare with* PREFIX, POSTFIX NOTATION

informatics *noun* science and study of ways and means of information processing and transmission **Informatik**
NOTE: no plural

information *noun*
(a) knowledge presented to a person in a form which can be understood **Information**

(b) data that has been processed *or* arranged to provide facts which have a meaning **information; information bearer channel** = communications channel that is able to carry control and message data, usually at a higher rate than a data only channel **Informationsträgerkanal; information content** = measurement of the amount of information conveyed by the transmission of a symbol *or* character, often measured in shannons **Informationsgehalt; information flow control** = regulation of access to certain information **Steuerung des Informationsflusses; information input** = information received from an input device **Informationseingabe; information line** = line running across the screen which gives the user information about the program running *or* the file being edited, etc. **Informationszeile; information management system** = computer program that allows information to be easily stored, retrieved, searched and updated **Informationsverwaltungssystem; information network** = number of databases linked together, usually by telephone lines and modems, allowing a large amount of data to be accessed by a wider group of users **Datenbanknetz; information output** = display of information on an output device **Informationsausgabe; information processing** = organizing, processing and extracting information from data **Informationsverarbeitung; information processor** = machine that processes a received signal, according to a program, using stored information to provide an output (this is an example of a computer that is not dealing with mathematical functions) **informationsverarbeitende Maschine; information provider (IP)** = company *or* user that provides an information source for use in a videotext system (such as the company providing weather information *or* stock market reports) **Informationsanbieter; information rate** = amount of information content per character multiplied by the number of characters transmitted per second **mittlerer Informationsfluss; information retrieval (IR)** = locating quantities of data stored in a database and producing useful information from the data **Wiederauffinden von Informationen, Informationswiedergewinnung; information retrieval centre** = information search system, providing specific information from a database for a user **Zentrale für Informationsanbieter und Benutzer; information storage** = storing data in a form which allows it to be processed at a later

date **Informationsspeicherung; information storage and retrieval (ISR)** = techniques involved in storing information and retrieving data from a store **Informationsspeicherung und -wiederauffindung; information structure** *see* DATA STRUCTURE; **information system** = computer system which provides information according to a user's requests **Informationssystem; information technology (IT)** = technology involved in acquiring, storing, processing and distributing information by electronic means (including radio, television, telephone, computers) **Informationstechnik; information theory** = formulae and mathematics concerned with data transmission equipment and signals **Informationstheorie; information transfer channel** = connection between a data transmitter and a receiver **Nachrichtenübertragungskanal;** *see also* DATA TERMINAL EQUIPMENT

QUOTE Information Technology is still too young to be an established discipline. However, the national and international IT research programmes are reasonably agreed that it comprises electronics, computing and telecommunications

Electronics and Power

QUOTE Racal-Datacom has picked up a {1.5 million order for its ISDN digital access multiplexers from financial information provider Telerate, its second from the company this year

Computing

infra- *prefix* meaning below *or* less than **Infra-, infra-; infra-low frequency (ILF)** = range of audio frequencies between 300Hz-3KHz **Frequenz zwischen 300Hz und 3KHz**

infrared *adjective* section of the electromagnetic radiation spectrum extending from visible red to microwaves **infrarot; infrared communications** = line of sight of communications path using a modulated infrared light beam rather than electrical signals down a cable **Infrarotnachrichtenübermittlung; infrared detector** = photoelectric cell that is sensitive to the infrared region of the electromagnetic spectrum **Infrarotdetektor; infrared photography** = type of photography that uses a special film which is sensitive to infrared radiation and so can be used in situations where the light level is very low **Infrarotfotografie; infrared sights** = camera and specialized optical equipment that can be used in situations where the light level is low, providing bright, enhanced images **Infrarotsichtgeräte**

◊ **infrasonic frequency** *noun* sound wave frequency that is in the range below that audible by the human ear **Infraschallfrequenz**

◊ **infrastructure** *noun* basic structure *or* basic services **Infrastruktur**

infringement *noun* breaking the law *or* a rule **Übertretung; copyright infringement** = illegally making a copy of a book *or* program which is in copyright **Verletzung des Urheberrechts**

inherent addressing *noun* instruction that contains all the data required for the address to be accessed with no further operation **Anfangsadressierung;** *compare with* EXTENDED, INDEXED

inherit *verb* (in object-oriented programming) one class *or* data type that acquires the characteristics of another **übernehmen**

◊ **inheritance** *noun* (in object-oriented programming) to pass the characteristics of one class *or* data type to another (called its descendant) **Übernahme**

inherited error *noun* error that is the result of a fault in a previous process *or* action **mitgeschleppter Fehler**

inhibit *verb* to stop a process taking place *or* to prevent an integrated circuit *or* gate from operating, (by means of a signal *or* command) **sperren; inhibiting input** = one input of a gate which blocks the output signal **Sperreingang**

in-house *adverb & adjective* working inside a company **innerbetrieblich;** *all the data processing is done in-house; the in-house maintenance staff deal with all our equipment*

initial
1 *adjective* first *or* at the beginning **Anfangs-,; initial address** = address at which the first instruction of a program is stored **Anfangsadresse; initial condition** = condition that must be satisfied before a routine can be entered **Anfangsbedingung; initial error** = error in data that is the difference between the value of the data at the start of processing and its present actual value **Anfangsfehler; initial instructions** = routine that acts as an initial program

loader **Startbefehle; initial program header** = small machine-code program usually stored in a read-only memory device that directs the CPU to load a larger program *or* operating system from store into main memory (such as a boot up routine that loads the operating system when a computer is switched on) **Startprogramm; initial program loader (IPL)** = short routine that loads a program (the operating system) from backing store into main memory **Urlader; initial value** = starting point (usually zero) set when initializing variables at the beginning of a program **Anfangswert**
2 *noun* first letter of a word, especially of a name **Anfangsbuchstabe, Initiale;** *what do the initials IBM stand for?*

◊ **initialization** *noun* process of initializing **Initialisierung;** *initialization is often carried out without the user knowing*

◊ **initialize** *verb* to set values *or* parameters *or* control lines to their initial values, to allow a program *or* process to be re-started **initialisieren**

injection laser *noun* solid state laser device used to transmit data as pulses of light down an optic fibre **Injektionslaser**

◊ **injection logic** *see* INTEGRATED

ink
1 *noun* dark liquid used to mark *or* write with **Tinte; ink-jet printer** = computer printer that produces characters by sending a stream of tiny drops of electrically charged ink onto the paper (the movement of the ink drops is controlled by an electric field this is a non-impact printer with few moving parts) **Tintenstrahldrucker;** *colour ink-jet technology and thermal transfer technology compete with each other*
2 *verb* to draw lines on paper with a pen *or* using a plotter device **mit Tinte zeichnen/schreiben**

QUOTE ink-jet printers work by squirting a fine stream of ink onto the paper
Personal Computer World

inlay card *noun* identification card inside a tape *or* disk box **Begleitkarte**

inline
1 *noun* connection pins on a chip arranged in one or two rows **gereihte Anschlussstifte**
2 *adverb* way in which unsorted *or* unedited data is processed **schritthaltend; in-line program** = program that contains no loops **gestrecktes Programm; in-line processing** =

processing data when it appears rather than waiting for a synchronizing *or* clock pulse **schritthaltende Verarbeitung**

inner loop *noun* loop contained inside another loop **Innenschleife;** *see also* NESTED LOOP

in phase *adverb*
(a) (two electrical signals) that have no phase difference between them, i.e. there is no delay *or* a delay of one complete cycle between them **phasengleich**
(b) synchronization of film frames and projector shutter timing **Projektorsynchronisation**

input (i/p *or* **I/P)**
1 *verb* to transfer data *or* information from outside a computer to its main memory **eingeben;** *the data was input via a modem*
2 *noun*
(a) action of inputting information **Eingeben**
(b) data *or* information that is transferred into a computer **Eingabe; input area** = section of main memory that holds data transferred from backing store until it is processed *or* distributed to other sections **Eingabespeicherbereich; input block** = block of data transferred to an input area **Eingebeblock; input buffer register** = temporary store for data from an input device before it is transferred to main *or* backing store **Eingabepufferregister; input device** = device such as a keyboard *or* bar code reader, which converts actions *or* information into a form which a computer can understand and transfers the data to the processor **Eingabegerät; input lead** = lead which connects an input device to a computer **Kabel zwischen Eingabegerät und Computer; input limited (program)** = (program) which is not running as fast as it could, due to limiting input rate from a slower peripheral **eingabebegrenzt(es Programm); input mode** = computer which is receiving data **Eingabemodus; input port** = circuit *or* connector that allows a computer to receive data from other external devices **Eingabeanschluss; input register** = temporary store for data received at slow speeds from an I/O device, the data is then transferred at high speed to main memory **Eingaberegister; input routine** = set of instructions which control an I/O device and direct data received from it to the correct storage location **Eingabeprogramm; input section** = (i) input routine; (ii) input area **(i) Eingabeprogramm; (ii) Eingabespeicherbereich; input statement** =

computer programming command that waits for data entry from a port *or* keyboard **Eingabeanweisung; input storage** *see* INPUT AREA; **input unit** = an input device **Eingabeeinheit; input work queue** = list of commands to be carried out in the order they were entered (or in order by priority) **Eingabewarteschlange**
(c) electrical signals which are applied to relevant circuits to perform the operation **Eingang**

◊ **input-bound** *or* **limited** *adjective* (program) which is not running as fast as it could due to limiting input rate from a slower peripheral **eingabebegrenzt**

◊ **input/output (I/O)** *noun* receiving *or* transmitting data between a computer and its peripherals, and other points outside the system **Ein-/Ausgabe; input/output buffer** = temporary storage area for data waiting to be output *or* data input **Ein-/Ausgabepuffer; input/output bus** = links allowing data and control signal transfer between a CPU and memory *or* peripheral devices **Ein-/Ausgabebus; input/output channel** = link between a processor and peripheral allowing data transfer **Ein-/Ausgabekanal; input/output control program** = monitoring and control of I/O operations and data flow by a section of the operating system *or* supervisory program **Ein-/Ausgabesteuerprogramm; input/output controller** = intelligent device that monitors, directs and controls data flow between a CPU and I/O devices **Ein-/Ausgabesteuereinheit; input/output device** *or* **unit** = peripheral (such as a terminal in a workstation) which can be used both for inputting and outputting data to a processor **Ein-/Ausgabeeinheit; input/output executive** = master program that controls all the I/O activities of a computer **Ein-/Ausgabesteuerprogramm; input/output instruction** = programming instruction that transfers data from memory to an input/output port **Input-/Output-Anweisung, Ein-/Ausgabe-Anweisung; input/output interface** = circuit allowing controlled data input and output from a CPU, consisting usually of: input/output channel, parallel input/output port and a DMA interface **Ein-/Ausgabeschnittstelle; input/output interrupt** = interrupt signal from a peripheral device *or* to indicate that an input or output operation is required **Ein-/Ausgabeunterbrechung; input/output library** = set of routines that can be used by the programmer to help simplify input/output tasks (such as printer drivers *or* port control routines) **Ein-/Ausgabebibliothek; input/output port =** circuit *or* connector that provides an input/output channel to another device **Ein-/Ausgabeanschluss;** *the joystick can be connected to the input/output port;* **input/output processor (IOP) =** processor that carries out input/output transfers for a CPU, including DMA and error correction facilities **Ein-/Ausgabeprozessor; input/output referencing =** use of labels to refer to specific input/output devices, the actual address of the device being inserted at run-time **Ein-/Ausgabebezugnahme; input/output register =** temporary store for data received from main memory before being transferred to an I/O device (or data from an I/O device to be stored in main memory *or* processed) **Ein-/Ausgaberegister; input/output request (IORQ) =** request signal from the CPU for data input or output **Ein-/Ausgabeanforderung; input/output status word =** word whose bits describe the state of peripheral devices (busy, free, etc.) **Ein-/Ausgabestatuswort; parallel input/output (PIO) =** data input *or* output from a computer **parallele Ein-/Ausgabe**

> QUOTE inputs include raster scan files and ASCII files
> *Byte*

> QUOTE In fact, the non-Qwerty format of the Maltron keyboard did cause a few gasps when it was first shown to the staff, but within a month all the Maltron users had regained normal input speeds
> *Computing*

inquiry *noun* (i) asking a question; (ii) accessing data held in a computer system **(i) Anfrage; (ii) Abfrage; inquiry character (ENQ) =** code transmitted by a computer to a remote terminal, asking for a response **Anfragecode; inquiry station =** terminal that is used to access and interrogate files stored on a remote computer **Abfragestation; inquiry/response =** interactive computer mode, in which a user's commands and enquiries are responded to very quickly **Frage-Antwort-System**

Ins *or* **insert key** *noun* key that switches a word-processor or editor program into insert mode rather than overwrite mode **Einfügetaste**

insert *verb*
(a) to put something into something **hineinstecken;** *first insert the system disk in the left slot*

(b) to add new text inside a word *or* sentence **einfügen; insert key** *or* **Ins key =** key that switches a word-processor or editor program into insert mode rather than overwrite mode **Einfügetaste; inserted subroutine =** series of instructions that are copied directly into the main program where a call instruction appears *or* where a user requires **eingefügtes Unterprogramm**

◊ **insertion loss** *noun* attenuation to a signal caused by adding a device into an existing channel *or* circuit **Einfügungsdämpfung**

◊ **insert mode** *noun* interactive computer mode used for editing and correcting documents **Einfügemodus**

> COMMENT: this is a standard feature on most word-processing packages where the cursor is placed at the required point in the document and any characters typed will be added, with the existing text moving on as necessary

install *verb* to put a machine into an office *or* factory; to set up a new computer system to the user's requirements *or* to configure a new program to the existing system capabilities **installieren;** *the system is easy to install and simple to use;* **install program =** software utility that transfers program code from the distribution disks onto a computer's hard disk and configures the program **Installationsprogramm**

◊ **installable device driver** *noun* device driver that is loaded into memory and remains resident, replacing a similar function built-into the operating system **installierbarer Gerätetreiber** *or* **Einheitentreiber**

◊ **installation** *noun*
(a) computer and equipment used for one type of work and processing **(Computer)anlage;** *the engineers are still testing the new installation*
(b) setting up a new computer system **Montage;** *the installation of the equipment took only a few hours*

instance *noun* (in object-oriented programming) an object *or* duplicate object that has been created **Exemplar**

instantaneous access *noun* extremely short access time to a random access device **Sofortzugriff**

instant replay *noun* feature found in video recording systems that allows the action that has just been recorded to be viewed immediately **sofortige Wiedergabe**

instruct *verb* to tell someone *or* a computer what to do **befehlen**

◊ **instruction** *noun* word used in a programming language that is understood by the computer to represent an action **Befehl** *or* **Anweisung**; *the instruction PRINT is used in this BASIC dialect as an operand to display the following data;* **absolute instruction** = instruction which completely describes the operation to be performed (i.e. no other data is required) **endgültiger Maschinenbefehl; arithmetic instruction** = instruction to perform an arithmetic operation on data rather than a logical function **Rechenbefehl; blank** *or* **null** *or* **dummy instruction** = instruction in a program that is only there to satisfy language syntax *or* to make up a block length **leere Anweisung; breakpoint instruction** = halt command inserted in a program to temporarily stop execution, allowing the programmer to examine data and registers whilst debugging a program **Stoppbefehl; decision** *or* **discrimination instruction** = conditional program instruction that directs control by providing the location of the next instruction to be executed (if a condition is met) **logische Entscheidung; dummy instruction** = instruction in a program that is only there to satisfy language syntax *or* to make up a block length **leere Anweisung; executive instruction** = instruction used to control and execute programs under the control of an operating system **Ausführungsbefehl; four-address instruction** = program instruction which contains four addresses within its address field, usually the location of the two operands, the result and the location of the next instruction **Vieradressbefehl; indexed instruction** = instruction that contains an origin and location of an offset that are added together to provide the address to be accessed **indizierter Befehl; input/output instruction** = computer programming instruction that allows data to be input *or* output from a processor **Ein-/Ausgabebefehl; jump instruction** = program command to end one set of instructions and direct the processor to another section of the program **Sprungbefehl; macro instruction** = one programming instruction that refers to a number of instructions within a routine *or* macro **Makrobefehl; no-op instruction** = instruction that does not carry out any functions, but increments the program counter **Befehl „keine Operation"; n-plus-one instruction** = instruction made up of a number (n) of addresses and one other address that is the location of the next instruction to be executed **n-plus-Eins-**

Befehl; supervisory instruction = instruction used to control and execute programs under the control of an operating system **Überwachungsbefehl; three-address-instruction** = instruction format which contains the addresses of two operands and the location where the result is to be stored **Dreiadressbefehl; two-address-instruction** = instruction format containing the locations of two operands, the result being stored in one of the operand locations **Zweiadressbefehl; two-plus-one-address instruction** = instruction containing locations of two operands and an address for the storage of the result **Zwei-plus-Eins-Adressbefehl; instruction address** = location of an instruction **Befehlsadresse; instruction address register (IAR)** register in a CPU that contains the location of the next instruction to be processed **Befehlsadressregister; instruction area** = section of memory that is used to store instructions **Befehls(speicher)bereich; instruction cache** = area of high-speed memory which stores the next few instructions to be executed by a processor **Befehlsschnellspeicher; instruction character** = special character that provides a control sequence rather than an alphanumeric character **Befehlszeichen; instruction codes** = set of symbols *or* codes that a CPU can directly understand and execute **Befehlscodes; instruction counter** *or* **instruction address register (IAR)** *or* **program counter** = register in a CPU that contains the location of the next instruction to be processed **Befehlszähler; Befehlsadressregister; instruction cycle** = sequence of events and their timing that is involved when fetching and executing an instruction stored in memory **Befehlsablauf; instruction cycle time** = amount of time taken for one instruction cycle **Befehlsablaufzeit; instruction decoder** = program which decodes instructions in machine code **Befehlsdecodierer; instruction execution time** = time taken for a central processing unit to carry out a complete instruction **Befehlsausführungszeit; instruction format** = rules defining the way the operands, data and addresses are arranged in an instruction **Befehlsformat; instruction modification** = altering a part of an instruction (data *or* operator) so that it carries out a different function when next executed **Befehlsänderung; instruction pipelining** = beginning processing a second instruction while still processing the present one (this increases program speed of execution) **Pipelineverarbeitung der Befehle; instruction pointer** = register in a

CPU that contains the location of the next instruction to be processed **Instruktionszeiger; instruction processor** = section of the central processing unit that decodes the instruction and performs the necessary arithmetic and logical functions **Befehlsprozessor; instruction register (IR)** = register in a central processing unit that stores an instruction during decoding and execution operations **Befehlsregister; instruction repertoire** *or* **set** = total number of instructions that a processor can recognize and execute **Befehlsvorrat; instruction storage** *see* INSTRUCTION AREA; **instruction word** = fixed set of characters used to initiate an instruction **Befehlswort;** *the manufacturers of this CPU have decided that JMP will be the instruction word to call the jump function*

COMMENT: in a high level language the instructions are translated by the compiler *or* interpreter to a form that is understood by the central processing unit

QUOTE A Taos kernel, typically 15Kb in size, resides at each processing node to 'translate', non-native instructions - on the fly when needed. This kernel contains the only code which has to be written in the processor's native instruction set
Computing

instrumentation *noun* equipment for testing, display or recording signals **Instrumentierung;** *we've improved the instrumentation on this model to keep you better informed of the machine's position*

insufficient *adjective* not enough **ungenügend;** *there is insufficient time to train the keyboarders properly*

insulate *verb* to prevent a voltage *or* energy from a conductor reaching another point by separating the two points with an insulation material **isolieren**

◊ **insulation material** *noun* substance that is a very bad conductor, used to prevent a voltage *or* energy reaching a point **Isoliermaterial**

◊ **insulator** *noun* material that does not conduct electricity **Isolator, Isoliermaterial;** *plastic is a good insulator*

integer *noun* mathematical term to describe a whole number (it may be positive *or* negative *or* zero) **ganze Zahl; double-precision integer** = two computer words used to store an integer **ganze Zahl doppelter Wortlänge; integer BASIC** = faster version

of BASIC that uses only integer mathematics and cannot support fractions **Integer-BASIC**

◊ **integral** *noun & adjective* add-on device *or* special feature that is already built into a system **eingebaut(e Einheit);** *the integral disk drives and modem reduced desk space*

QUOTE an integral 7 inch amber display screen, two half-height disk drives and terminal emulation for easy interfacing with mainframes
Computing Today

integrated *adjective* (system) that contains many peripherals grouped together in order to provide a neat, complete system **integriert; integrated database** = database that is able to provide information for varied requirements without any redundant data **integrierte Datenbank; integrated data processing (IDP)** = organizational method for the entry and retrieval of data to provide maximum efficiency **integrierte Datenverarbeitung; integrated device** = device that is part of another machine *or* device **integriertes Bauelement;** *our competitor's computer doesn't have an integrated disk drive like this model;* **integrated device electronics (IDE)** = popular standard for hard disk drive unit that combines the drive and control electronics in one device **Integrated Device Electronics (IDE); integrated digital access (IDA)** = system where subscribers can make two telephone calls and be linked (from their office *or* home) to a database, and send material by fax, all at the same time **integrierter Digitalzugriff; integrated digital network** = communications network that uses digital signals to transmit data **integriertes Digitalnetz; integrated emulator** = emulator program run within a multitasking operating system **integrierter Emulator; integrated injection logic (IIL)** = type of circuit design able to produce very small, low-power components **Integrated Injection Logic (IIL); integrated modem** = modem that is a internal part of the system **Einbaumodem; integrated office** = office environment in which all operations are carried out using a central computer (to store information, print, etc.) **im Rechnerverband arbeitendes Büro; integrated optical circuit** = optoelectronic circuit that can generate, detect and transmit light for communications over optical fibres **integrierter optischer Schaltkreis; integrated services digital network (ISDN)** = international digital communications network which can transmit sound, fax and data over the same channel **integriertes Sprach- und Datennetz (ISDN); integrated software** = software such as an operating system *or* word-processor that is stored in the computer system and has been tailored to the requirements of the system **integrierte Software**

◊ **integrated circuit (IC)** *noun* circuit where all the active and passive components are formed on one small piece of semiconductor, by means of etching and chemical processes **integrierter Schaltkreis (IC)**

◊ **integration** *noun* bringing several operations together **Integration;** *small scale integration (SSI); medium scale integration (MSI); large scale integration (LSI); very large scale integration (VLSI); super large scale integration (SLSI)*

COMMENT: integrated circuits can be classified as follows: Small Scale Integration (SSI): 1 to 10 components per IC; Medium Scale Integration (MSI): 10 to 500 components per IC; Large Scale Integration (LSI): 500 to 10,000 components per IC; Very Large Scale Integration (VLSI): 10,000 to 100,000 components per IC Super Large Scale Integration (SLCI): more than 100,000 components per IC

integrity *noun* reliability of data (when being processed *or* stored on disk) **Integrität, Vollständigkeit; integrity of a file** = the fact that a file that has been stored on disk is not corrupted *or* distorted in any way **Vollständigkeit einer Datei; the data in this file has integrity** = the data has not been corrupted **die Daten in dieser Datei sind vollständig**

| QUOTE it is intended for use in applications demanding high data integrity, such as archival storage or permanent databases |
| *Minicomputer News* |

Intel ™ company which developed the first commercially available microprocessor (the 4004); they also developed the range of processors that is used in IBM PCs and compatible computers **Intel** ™; **Intel 8086** = microprocessor that uses a 16-bit data bus and can address up to 1Mb of RAM **Intel 8086; Intel 8088** = microprocessor that uses a 16-bit data bus internally, but uses an 8-bit data bus externally; used in the first IBM PC computers **Intel 8088; Intel 80286** = microprocessor that uses a 16-bit data bus and can address up to 16Mb of RAM **Intel**

80286; Intel 80386 = microprocessor that uses a 32-bit data bus and can address up to 4Gb of RAM **Intel 80386; Intel 80486** = microprocessor that uses a 32-bit data bus and can address up to 64Gb of RAM **Intel 80486; Intel Pentium** ™ = latest, most advanced microprocessor that uses 32-bit data bus **Intel Pentium** ™

intelligence *noun* (i) ability to reason; (ii) ability of a device to carry out processing *or* run a program (i) & (ii) **Intelligenz; artificial intelligence (AI)** = the design of computer programs and systems that attempt to imitate human intelligence and decision-making functions, providing basic reasoning and human characteristics **künstliche Intelligenz**

◊ **intelligent** *noun (of a machine)* (program *or* device) that is capable of limited reasoning facilities, giving it human-like responses **intelligent; intelligent device** = peripheral device that contains a central processing unit allowing it to process data **intelligentes Gerät; intelligent knowledge-based system (IKBS)** *or* expert system = software that applies the knowledge, advice and rules defined by an expert in a particular field to a user's data to help solve a problem **intelligentes, wissensbasiertes System; Expertensystem (XPS); intelligent spacer** = facility on a word-processing system used to prevent words from being hyphenated *or* separated at the wrong point **intelligentes Trennprogramm; intelligent terminal** = computer terminal which contains a CPU and memory, usually with a facility to allow the user to program it independently of the main CPU **intelligentes Terminal** (NOTE: the opposite is **dumb terminal) intelligent tutoring system** = computer-aided learning system that provides responsive and interactive teaching facilities for users **intelligentes Lernsystem; intelligent wiring hub** = wiring hub that can be controlled from a workstation to direct which circuits to connect to each other **intelligenter Schaltknoten**

INTELSAT = INTERNATIONAL TELECOMMUNICATIONS SATELLITE ORGANIZATION international group that deals with the design, construction and allocation of space to various communications satellite projects **internationaler Fernmeldesatellit**

intensity *noun* measure of the strength of

a signal *or* the brightness of a light source *or* the loudness of a noise **Intensität; Helligkeit; Lautstärke**

║ COMMENT: sound intensity is usually measured in decibels

inter- *prefix* meaning between **zwischen; interblock** = between blocks **zwischen Blöcken**

interact *verb (of two things)* to act on each other **aufeinander wirken**

◊ **interaction** *noun* action of two things on each other **Interaktion, Wechselwirkung**

◊ **interactive** *adjective* (system *or* piece of software) that allows communication between the user and the computer (in conversational mode) **interaktiv, im Dialogbetrieb; interactive cable television** = cable television system that allows the viewer to transmit signals such as program choice, teleshopping *or* answers to game questions back to the television transmission centre **dialogfähiges Kabelfernsehen; interactive debugging system** = software development tool that allows the user to run a program under test, set breakpoints, examine source and object code, examine registers and memory contents and trace the instruction execution **integriertes Dialogtestsystem; interactive graphics** = display system that is able to react to different inputs from the user **dialogfähige Grafikverarbeitung;** *the space invaders machine has great interactive graphics, the player controls the position of his spaceship on the screen with the joystick;* **interactive media** = communication between a group of people using different transmission means **interaktive Medien; interactive mode** *or* **processing** = computer mode that allows the user to enter commands *or* programs *or* data and receive immediate responses **(Verarbeitung im) Dialogbetrieb;** *see also* INQUIRY/RESPONSE; **interactive multimedia** = multimedia system in which a user can issue a command and the program responds *or* the user can control actions and control the way a program works **interaktives Multimedia;** *this interactive multimedia title allows a user to make music with a synthesizer program;* **interactive routine** = computer program that can accept data from an operator, process it and provide a real-time reaction to it **Dialogprogramm; interactive system** = system which provides an immediate response to the user's commands *or* programs *or* data **Dialogsystem; interactive**

terminal = terminal in an interactive system which sends and receives information **dialogfähige Datenstation; interactive videotext** = viewdata service that allows the operator to select pages, display them, ask questions use a service such as teleshopping **Bildschirmtextsystem**

◊ **interactive video** *noun* system that uses a computer linked to a video disk player to provide processing power and real images *or* moving pictures **interaktives Videosystem**

║ COMMENT: this system is often used in teaching to ask a student questions, which if answered correctly will provide him with a filmed sequence from the videodisk

QUOTE soon pupils will be able to go shopping in a French town from the comfort of their classroom - carried to their destination by interactive video, a medium which combines the power of the computer with the audiovisual impact of video

Electronics & Power

QUOTE interactivity is a buzzword you've been hearing a lot lately. Resign yourself to it because you're going to be hearing a lot more of it

Music Technology

QUOTE Oracle today details its interactive information superhighway aims, endorsed by 17 industry partners. The lynchpin to the announcement will be software based on the Oracle Media Server, a multimedia database designed to run on massively parallel computers

Computing

interblock gap (IBG) *noun* blank magnetic tape between the end of one block of data and the start of the next in backing store **Blockzwischenraum**

intercarrier noise *noun* interference caused by two different signal carriers getting mixed **Zwischenträgerrauschen;** *television intercarrier noise is noticed when the picture and the sound signal carriers clash*

interchange
1 *noun* exchange of one thing for another **Austausch;** *the machine allows document interchange between it and other machines without reformatting*
2 *verb* to exchange one thing for another **austauschen**

◊ **interchangeable** *adjective* which can be exchanged **austauschbar**

intercharacter spacing *noun* word-processor feature that provides variable spacing between words to create a justified line **variable Zeichenlücken**

intercom *noun* short-range voice communications system **(Gegen)sprechanlage**

> COMMENT: used mainly in offices *or* in automatic door systems where room-to-room communication of voice signals is required

interconnect *verb (of several things)* to connect together **verbinden;** *a series of interconnected terminals*

◊ **interconnection** *noun*
(a) section of connecting material between two devices **Verbindung**
(b) connection between a telephone set and a telephone network **Verbindung**

interface
1 *noun* (i) point at which one computer system ends and another begins; (ii) circuit *or* device *or* port that allows two or more incompatible units to be linked together in a standard communication system, allowing data to be transferred between them; (iii) section of a program which allows transmission of data to another program (i)(ii)(iii) **Schnittstelle; EIA interface** = standard defining interface signals, transmission rate and power usually used to connect terminals to modems **EIA-Schnittstelle; general purpose interface adapter (GPIA)** = usually used to interface a processing unit to a IEEE-488 bus **Mehrzweckschnittstelle; general purpose interface bus (GPIB)** = standard for an interface bus between a computer and laboratory equipment **Mehrzweckschnittstellenbus (IEC-Bus); input/output interface** = circuit allowing controlled data input and output from a CPU, consisting usually of: input/output channel, parallel input/output port and a DMA interface **Ein-/Ausgabeschnittstelle; interface card** = add-on board that allows a computer to interface to certain equipment *or* conform to a certain standard **Schnittstellenkarte; interface message processor** = computer in a packet switching network that deals with the flow of data, acting as an interface processor **Schnittstellenprozessor in einem Schaltnetzwerk; interface processor** = computer that controls data transfer between a processor and a terminal *or* network **Schnittstellenprozessor; interface routines** = software that allows programs *or* data for one system to run on another **Schnittstellenprogramm; parallel interface** = computer circuit *or* connector that allows parallel data to be transmitted *or* received **parallele Schnittstelle** NOTE: parallel interfaces are usually used to drive printers **serial interface** = circuit that converts parallel data in a computer to and from a serial form, allowing serial data to be transmitted *or* received from other equipment **serielle Schnittstelle** NOTE: the most common serial interface is RS232C
2 *verb* (i) to modify a device by adding a circuit *or* connector to allow it to conform to a standard communications system; (ii) to connect two or more incompatible devices together with a circuit, to allow them to communicate **(i) anpassen; (ii) zusammenschalten**

◊ **interfacing** *noun* hardware *or* software used to interface two computers *or* programs *or* devices **Anschlussteil**

> QUOTE The original release of ODBC only included a driver for Microsoft's own SQL Server database. Microsoft has subsequently published the ODBC application program interface enabling third-party vendors to create drivers for other databases and tools
>
> *Computing*

interfere *verb* **to interfere with something** = to stop something working properly *or* to get in the way **etwas stören**

◊ **interference** *noun*
(a) unwanted addition of signals *or* noise to a transmitted signal **Störung**
(b) effect seen when two signals are added, creating constructive interference when both signals are in phase *or* destructive interference when they are out of phase **Überlagerung; interference fading** = effect in radio reception when destructive interference occurs **Interferenzschwund; interference immunity** = ability of a system (i) to ignore interference signals; (ii) to function correctly even with interference **(i) & (ii) Störfestigkeit; interference pattern** = effect seen when light *or* radio *or* x-ray waves interact and produce destructive and constructive interference, causing patterns **Störmuster, Interferenzbild; constructive interference** = increase in peak and trough amplitude when two in phase signals are added **Verstärkung; destructive interference** = cancellation of peaks and troughs when

two out of phase signals are added (if the signals are exactly out of phase, they completely cancel out each other) **Auslöschung; electromagnetic interference** = corruption of data due to nearby electrically generated magnetic fields **elektromagnetische Störung; induced interference** = electrical noise on a signal due to induced signals from nearby electromagnetic sources **induzierte Störung**

COMMENT: interference can be due to electrical noise (such as from a relay), natural galactic noise or two signals mixing due to insufficient insulation

interior label *noun* identification label stored on a storage medium (magnetic tape *or* disk) rather than an exterior *or* physical label stuck to the case **Innenkennung**

interlace *verb* to build up an image on a television screen using two passes, each displaying alternate lines **sich verflechten, ineinandergreifen**

COMMENT: this system uses two picture fields made up of alternate lines to reduce picture flicker effects

interleave factor *noun* ratio of sectors skipped between access operations on a hard disk **Interleavefaktor, Versatzfaktor**

COMMENT: in a hard disk with an interleave of 3, the first sector is read, then three sectors are skipped and the next sector is read. This is used to allow hard disks with slow access time to store more data on the disk

interleaved *adjective*
(a) (thin sheets of paper) which are stuck between the pages of a book **durchschossen;** *blank paper was interleaved with the newly printed text to prevent the ink running*
(b) sections of two programs executed alternately to give the impression that they are running simultaneously **verzahnt; interleaved memory** = two separate banks of memory used together in sequence **verschränkter Speicher**

◊ **interleaving** *noun*
(a) processor dealing with slices *or* sections of processes alternately, so that they appear to be executed simultaneously **Verzahnung**
(b) addition of blank paper between printed sheets to prevent the ink from making other sheets dirty **Durchschießen**
(c) dividing data storage into sections so that each can be accessed separately **Überlappung**

QUOTE there are two separate 40-bit arrays on each card to allow interleaved operation, achieving data access every 170ns machine cycle
Minicomputer News

inter-library loan (ILL) *noun* lending of books *or* documents between from one library to another **Fernleihe**

interlinear spacing *noun (on a phototypesetter)* insertion of spaces between lines of text **Einrichten des Zeilenabstands**

interlock
1 *noun*
(a) security device which is part of the logon prompt and requires a password **Verriegelung**
(b) method of synchronizing audio tape with a video *or* filmed sequence (this can be achieved by using a frame counter *or* a timer *or* by running both audio and visual tapes on the same motor) **Synchronisierungsmechanismus; interlock projector** = film display machine that can also provide synchronized sound **Synchronisierungsprojektor**
2 *verb* to prevent a device from performing another task until the present one has been completed **verriegeln**

interlude *noun* small initial routine at the start of a program that carries out housekeeping tasks **Vorprogramm**

intermediate *adjective* which is at a stage between two others **Zwischen-, zwischen-; intermediate access memory (IAM)** = memory storage that has an access time between that of main memory and disk based systems **Hilfszugriffsspeicher; intermediate code** = code used by a computer *or* assembler during the translation of a high-level code to machine code **Zwischencode; intermediate file** = series of records that contain partially processed data, that will be used at a later date to complete that task **Zwischendatei; intermediate materials** = medium *or* format used for recording prior to the transfer to another format **Zwischenmedien;** *those slides, photographs, video and film are the intermediate materials to be mastered onto the video disk;* **intermediate storage** = temporary area of memory for items that are currently being processed **Zwischenspeicher**

◊ **intermediate frequency (IF** *or* **if)***noun* frequency in a radio receiver to which the incoming received signal is transformed **Zwischenfrequenz**

COMMENT: this is to allow high frequency signals to be converted to a lower intermediate frequency so that they can be processed with standard components, rather than more expensive high-frequency versions

intermittent error *noun* error which apparently occurs randomly in a computer *or* communications system due to a program fault *or* noise **zeitweise auftretender Fehler**

COMMENT: these errors are very difficult to trace and correct due to their apparent random appearance

internal *adjective* which is inside **intern; internal arithmetic** = arithmetic operations performed by the ALU **interner Rechenvorgang; internal character code** = representation of characters in a particular operating system **interner Zeichencode; internal command** = command that is part of the operating system, rather than a separate utility program **interner Befehl;** *in MS-DOS, the internal command DIR is used frequently;* **internal** *or* **resident font** = font that is stored on a ROM in a printer **interne** *or* **residente Schriftart; internal format** = way in which data and instructions are represented within a CPU *or* backing store **internes Format; internal hard disk** = hard disk drive mounted inside the main case of a computer **interne Festplatte; internal language** = language used in a computer system that is not under the direct control of the operator **interne Sprache**

COMMENT: many compiled languages are translated to an internal language

◊ **internal memory** *or* **store** *noun* section of RAM and ROM to which the central processing unit is directly connected without the use of an interface (as in external memory devices such as disk drives) **interner Speicher**

◊ **internal modem** *noun* modem on an expansion card that fits into an expansion connector and transfers information to the processor through the bus rather than connecting to a serial port **internes Modem**

◊ **internal sort** *noun* sorting program using only the main memory of a system **interne Sortierung**

◊ **internally stored program** *noun* computer program code that is stored in a ROM device in a computer system (and does not have to be loaded from backing store) **intern gespeichertes Programm**

international *adjective* referring to different countries **international; international direct dialling (IDD)** = system using an international dialling code that allow a user to telephone any country without going through an operator **internationale Durchwahl; international dialling code** = INTERNATIONAL PREFIX CODE; **international number** = digits to be dialled after the international prefix code to reach a subscriber in another country **internationale Nummer; international prefix code** = code number to be dialled at the start of a number to select another country's exchange system **internatonale Zugangskennzahl; international standard book number (ISBN)** = ten-digit identifying number allocated to every new book published **ISBN; international standard serial number (ISSN)** = identifying number allocated to every journal *or* magazine published **ISSN**

◊ **International Standards Organization (ISO)** *noun* organization which regulates standards for many types of product **internationale Normenorganisation; International Standards Organization Open System Interconnection (ISO/OSI)** = standardized ISO network design which is constructed in layered form, with each layer having a specific task, allowing different systems to communicate if they conform to the standard **ISO-Norm**

internet *noun* wide area network formed of many local area networks **Internet; internet protocol (IP)** = TCP/IP standard that defines how data is transferred **Internetprotokoll, Internet Protocol (IP); internet protocol address (IP Address)** = unique, 32-bit number which identifies computers that want to connect to a TCP/IP network **Internetprotokolladresse, Internet Protocol Address (IP Address)**

◊ **Internet** *noun* international wide area network that provides file and data transfer, together with electronic mail functions for millions of users around the world; anyone can use the Internet **Internet**

interpolation *noun* calculation of intermediate values between two points **Interpolierung**

interpret *verb* to translate what is said in one language into another **übersetzen,**

auswerten; interpreted language = programming language that is executed by an interpreter Übersetzersprache

◊ **interpreter** *noun* software that is used to translate (at the time of execution) a user's high-level program into machine code Übersetzer(programm), Interpretierer; *compare with* COMPILER

|| COMMENT: a compiler translates the high-
|| level language into machine code and then
|| executes it, rather than the real-time translation
|| by an interpreter

◊ **interpretative** *adjective* interpretative code = code used with an interpretative program Interpretiercode; interpretative program = software that translates (at run-time) high level interpretative code into machine code instructions Interpretierprogramm

interrecord gap = INTERBLOCK GAP

interrogation *noun* asking questions (Ab)frage; file interrogation = questions asked to select various records *or* data items from a file Dateiabfrage

interrupt
1 *verb* to stop something happening while it is happening unterbrechen
2 *noun*
(a) stopping of a transmission due to an action at the receiving end of a system Unterbrechung
(b) signal which diverts a central processing unit from one task to another which has higher priority, allowing the CPU to return to the first task later Programmunterbrechung; *this printer port design uses an interrupt line to let the CPU know it is ready to receive data;* armed interrupt = interrupt line which has been made active (using an interrupt mask) absichtliche Unterbrechung; interrupt disable = to disable an interrupt (by resetting a bit in the interrupt mask to zero) eine Unterbrechung unmöglich machen; interrupt enable = to arm an interrupt (by setting a bit in the interrupt mask) eine Unterbrechung herbeiführen; interrupt handler (IH) = software that accepts interrupt signals and acts on them (such as running a special routine *or* sending data to a peripheral) Unterbrechungssteuerungsprogramm; interrupt level = priority assigned to the interrupt from a peripheral Unterbrechungsebene; interrupt line = connection to a central processing unit from outside the system that allows

external devices to use the CPU's interrupt facility Unterbrechungsleitung; interrupt mask = term in computer programming that selects which interrupt lines are to be activated Unterbrechungsmaske; interrupt priorities = deciding which interrupt is given highest priority Unterbrechungsprioritäten; *see also* NON-MASKABLE INTERRUPT; interrupt request = signal from a device that indicates to the CPU that it requires attention Unterbrechungsanforderung; interrupt servicing = carrying out some action when an interrupt is detected, such as running a routine Unterbrechungsservice; interrupt signal *see* INTERRUPT; interrupt stacking = storing interrupts in a queue and processing according to priority Unterbrechungsschichtung; maskable interrupt = interrupt line that can be disabled and ignored using an interrupt mask maskierbare Unterbrechung; non-maskable interrupt (NMI) = high priority interrupt signal that cannot be blocked and overrides all other commands nichtmaskierbare Unterbrechung (mit höchster Priorität); polled interrupt = interrupt signal determined by polling Unterbrechung auf Abruf; priority interrupt table = list of peripherals and their priorities when they send an interrupt signal (used instead of a hardware priority scheduler) Interrupt-Prioritätstabelle; transparent interrupt = mode in which if an interrupt occurs, all machine and program states are saved, the interrupt is serviced then the system restores all previous states and continues normally transparente Unterbrechung; vectored interrupt = interrupt which directs the CPU to transfer to a particular location zeigergesteuerte Unterbrechung

intersection *noun* logical function whose output is only true if both its inputs are true UND-Funktion; Schnittmenge

interstation muting *noun* ability of a radio receiver to prevent the noise found between radio stations from being amplified and heard by the user geräuschfreie Abstimmung

interval *noun* short pause between two actions Pause; *there was an interval between pressing the key and the starting of the printout*

intervention *noun* acting to make a change in a system Eingriff

interword spacing *noun* variable

spacing between words in a text, used to justify lines **variabler Wortzwischenraum**

intimate *noun* software that operates and interacts closely with hardware in a system **hardwaregeeichte Software**

intrinsic *adjective* pure (substance) which has had no other chemicals (such as dopants) added **spezifisch, rein;** *the base material for ICs is an intrinsic semiconductor which is then doped*

introduce *verb* to put something into something **einführen;** *errors were introduced into the text at keyboarding*

intruder *noun* person who is not authorized to use a computer or connect to a network **Eindringling**

intrusion *noun* action by a telephone operator to allow both parties on each end of the telephone line to hear his *or* her message **Mitsprechanlage**

invalid *adjective* not valid **ungültig;** *he tried to use an invalid password; the message was that the instruction was invalid*

inverse *noun* changing the logical state of a signal *or* device to its logical opposite **Umkehrung, Gegenteil;** *the inverse of true is false; the inverse of 1 is 0;* **inverse video** = television effect created by swapping the background and foreground text display colours **invertiertes Videobild**

◊ **inversion** *noun* changing over the numbers in a binary word (one to zero, zero to one) **Umkehrung;** *the inversion of a binary digit takes place in one's complement*

◊ **invert** *verb* to change all binary ones to zeros and zeros to ones **umkehren; inverted commas** = printing sign (") which is usually used to indicate a quotation **Anführungszeichen; inverted file** = file with an index entry for all the data items **invertierte Datei**

◊ **inverter** *noun*
(a) logical gate that provides inversion facilities **Inverter**
(b) circuit used to provide alternating current supply from a DC battery source **Gleichstromumrichter; inverter (AC/DC)** = device which changes alternating current to direct current, or direct current to alternating current **Wechselrichter**

invitation *noun* action by a processor to contact another device to allow it to send a message **Aufruf; invitation to send (ITS)** = special character transmitted to indicate to a device that the host computer is willing to receive messages **Sendeaufruf**

◊ **invite** *verb* to ask someone to do something **aufrufen, auffordern**

invoke *verb* to start *or* run a program (often a memory resident utility) **aufrufen**

QUOTE when an error is detected, the editor may be invoked and positioned at the statement in error
Personal Computer World

involve *verb* to have to do with; to include (something) in a process **betreffen;** *backing up involves copying current working files onto a separate storage disk*

I/O = INPUT/OUTPUT referring to the receiving *or* transmitting of data **Ein-/Ausgabe; I/O address** = the memory location that is used by an I/O port to transfer data with the CPU **I/O-Adresse, E/A-Adresse; I/O bound** = processor that is doing very little processing since its time is taken up reading *or* writing data from a I/O port **ein-/ausgabeabhängig; I/O buffer** = temporary storage area for data waiting to be input *or* output **Ein-/Ausgabepuffer; I/O bus** = links allowing data and control signal transfer between a CPU and memory *or* peripheral devices **Ein-/Ausgabebus; I/O channel** = link between a processor and peripheral, allowing data transfer **Ein-/Ausgabekanal; I/O device** = peripheral (such as a terminal in a workstation) which can be used for both inputting and outputting data to a processor **Ein-/Ausgabegerät; I/O file** = file whose contents have been *or* will be transferred from storage to a peripheral **Ein-/Ausgabedatei; I/O instruction** = computer programming instruction that allows data to be input *or* output from a processor **Ein-/Ausgabebefehl; I/O mapping** = method of assigning a special address to each I/O port that does not use any memory locations **Ein-/Ausgabemapping;** *compare with* MEMORY MAPPING; **I/O port** = circuit *or* connector that provides an input/output channel from a CPU to another device **Ein-/Ausgabeanschlussstelle;** *see also* SERIAL PORT, PARALLEL PORT

ion *noun* charged particle **Ion**

COMMENT: an ion is an atom that has gained *or* lost an extra electron, producing a negative *or* positive ion

◊ **ionosphere** *noun* layer of charged particles surrounding the earth **Ionosphäre**

|| COMMENT: the ionosphere extends from 50km above the surface of the earth

IOP = INPUT/OUTPUT PROCESSOR

IORQ = INPUT/OUTPUT REQUEST

i/p *or* **I/P** = INPUT

ip = INFORMATION PROVIDER company *or* user that provides an information source for use in a videotext system **Informationsanbieter, Btx-Anbieter; ip terminal** = special visual display unit that allows users to create and edit videotext pages before sending to the main videotext page database **Btx-Datenstation**

◊ **IP** = INTERNET PROTOCOL TCP/IP standard that defines how data is transferred **IP; IP Address** = unique, 32-bit number which identifies computers that want to connect to a TCP/IP network **IP-Adresse; IP Datagram** = packet of data transferred across a TCP/IP network **IP-Datagramm**

IPL = INITIAL PROGRAM LOADER

ips = INCHES PER SECOND

IPSE = INTEGRATED PROJECT SUPPORT ENVIRONMENT

> QUOTE one of the first aims of an IPSE is to provide a centralized information base into which all project data can be deposited in a form which enables all tools to exchange data
>
> *Electronics & Power*

IR
(a) = INFORMATION RETRIEVAL
(b) = INDEX REGISTER
(c) = INSTRUCTION REGISTER

◊ **IRC** = INFORMATION RETRIEVAL CENTRE

irretrievable *adjective* which cannot be retrieved **nicht wiederauffindbar;** *the files are irretrievable since the computer crashed*

irreversible process *noun* process which, once carried out, cannot be reversed **irreversibler Prozess**

IS = INDEXED SEQUENTIAL

ISA = INDUSTRY STANDARD ARCHITECTURE standard used for the 16-bit expansion bus in an IBM PC or compatible **ISA;** *compare* EISA, MCA

ISAM = INDEXED SEQUENTIAL ACCESS METHOD

ISBN = INTERNATIONAL STANDARD BOOK NUMBER

ISDN = INTEGRATED SERVICES DIGITAL NETWORK

ISO = INTERNATIONAL STANDARDS ORGANIZATION **ISO/OSI** = INTERNATIONAL STANDARDS ORGANIZATION OPEN SYSTEM INTERCONNECTION

◊ **ISO/OSI model** = INTERNATIONAL STANDARDS ORGANIZATION/OPEN SYSTEM INTERCONNECTION layered architecture that defines how computers and networks should interact **ISO/OSI-Modell**

isolate *verb* (i) to separate something from a system; (ii) to insulate (something) electrically **(i) trennen; (ii) isolieren; isolated adaptive routing** = method of controlling message transmission path **isolierte adaptive Verkehrslenkung; isolated location** = (hardware) storage location which cannot be directly accessed by a user's program, protecting it against accidental erasure **geschützter Speicherplatz**

◊ **isolation** *noun* being isolated **Isolation; isolation transformer** = transformer used to isolate equipment from direct connection with the mains electricity supply, in case of voltage spikes etc. **Trennübertrager**

◊ **isolator** *noun* device *or* material which isolates **Isolator**

isotropic *adjective* with the same properties in all dimensions and directions **isotrop; isotropic radiator** = antenna that transmits in all directions **Kugelantenne**

ISR = INFORMATION STORAGE AND RETRIEVAL

ISSN = INTERNATIONAL STANDARD SERIAL NUMBER

IT = INFORMATION TECHNOLOGY

italic *adjective & noun* type of character font in which the characters slope to the right **kursiv; Kursive;** *the headline is printed in italic and underlined;* **italics** = italic characters **Kursivschrift;** *all the footnotes are printed in italics; hit CTRL I to print the text in italics*

item *noun* single thing among many **Element, (Daten)feld;** *a data item can be a word or; a series of figures or; a record in a file;* **item size** = number of characters *or* digits in an item of data **Feldgröße**

iterate *or* **iterative routine** *noun* loop *or* series of instructions in a program which repeat over and over again until the program is completed **Iterationsschleife**

◊ **iteration** *noun* repeated application of a program to solve a problem **Iteration**

◊ **iterative process** *noun* process that is continuously repeated until a condition is met **iterative Operation**

ITS = INVITATION TO SEND

Jj

jabber *noun* continuous random signal transmitted by a faulty adapter card *or* node on a network **Störsignal, Jabber-Signal**

jack *noun* plug which consists of a single pin **Stecker, Buchse;** **data jack** = plug that allows a modem to be connected directly to the telephone system **Modembuchse**

jacket *noun* cover for a book *or* disk **Umschlag, Hülle;** *the book jacket has the author's name on it*

jaggies *plural noun* jagged edges which appear along diagonal or curved lines displayed on a computer screen, caused by the size of each pixel **gezackte Ränder;** *see also* ALIASING, ANTI-ALIASING

jam
1 *noun* process *or* mechanism which has stopped working due to a fault **Stau;** *a jam in the paper feed*
2 *verb*
(a) *(of a device)* to stop working because something is blocking the functioning **sich stauen;** *the recorder's not working because the tape is jammed in the motor; lightweight copier paper will feed without jamming*

(b) to prevent a transmission from being correctly received by transmitting a strong noise at the same frequency (often used to prevent unauthorized transmission) **stören;** *the TV signals are being jammed from that tower*

jar *verb* to give a sharp shock to a device **schlagen, stoßen;** *you can cause trouble by turning off or jarring the PC while the disk read heads are moving; hard disks are very sensitive to jarring*

JCL = JOB CONTROL LANGUAGE commands that describe the identification of and resources required by a job that a computer has to process **Jobkontrollsprache**

jet *see* INK-JET

jingle *noun* short easily-remembered tune used to advertise a product on television **Werbemelodie, Bimmeln, Jingle**

jitter *noun* fault where there is rapid small up-and-down movement of characters *or* pixels on a screen of image bits in a facsimile transmission **Flattern;** *looking at this screen jitter is giving me a headache*

JK-flip-flop *noun* flip-flop device with two inputs (J and K) and two complementary outputs that are dependent on the inputs **JK-Flipflop**

job *noun* task *or* number of tasks *or* work to be processed as a single unit **Job, Arbeitsauftrag;** *the next job to be processed is to sort all the records;* **job control file** = file which contains instructions in a JCL **Jobkontrolldatei; job control language (JCL)** = commands that describe the identification of and resources required by a job that a computer has to process **Jobbetriebssprache; job control program** = short program of job control instructions loaded before a particular application is run, that sets up the system as required by the application **Jobsteuerprogramm; job file** = file containing jobs *or* job names waiting to be processed **Jobdatei; job mix** = the jobs being executed at any one time in a system **Jobmischung; job number** = number which is given to a job in a queue, waiting to be processed **Jobnummer; job orientated language** = computer programming language that provides specialized instructions relating to job control tasks and processing **aufgabenorientierte Programmiersprache; job orientated terminal** = computer terminal designed for and used for a particular task **aufgabenorientierte Außenstation; job priority** = importance of a job compared to others **Jobpriorität; job processing** = to read in job control instructions from an input source and execute them **Jobverarbeitung; job queue** or **job stream** = number of tasks arranged in an order waiting to be processed in a multitasking or batch system **Jobwarteschlange; job scheduling** = arranging the order in which jobs are processed **Joborganisation; job statement control** = use of instructions and statements to control the actions of the operating system of a computer **Jobanweisungssteuerung; job step** or **step** = one unit of processing involved in a task **Jobschritt; Jobfolge; remote job entry (RJE)** = use of an interactive user terminal to enter job control instructions **Jobferneingabe; stacked job control** = queue of job control instructions that are processed in the order in which they were received **sequenzielle Jobbearbeitung**

◊ **jobbing printer** noun person who does small printing jobs, such as printing business cards **Akzidenzdrucker**

jog verb to advance a video tape by one frame at a time **Videoband um 1 Bild weiterstellen**

joggle verb to align a stack of punched cards or sheets of paper **rütteln**

join verb
(a) to put several things together **verbinden**
(b) to combine two or more pieces of information to produce a single unit of information **zusammenfügen; join files** = instruction to produce a new file consisting of one file added to the end of another **Dateien zusammenfügen**
(c) logical function that produces a true output if any input is true **ODER-Funktion**

joint denial noun logical function whose output is false if any input is true **NOR-Funktion**

journal noun
(a) record of all communications to and from a terminal **Protokoll; journal file** = stored record of every communication between a user and the central computer, used to help retrieve files after a system crash or fault **Protokolldatei**
(b) list of any changes or updates to a file **Protokoll;** the modified records were added to the master file and noted in the journal
(c) learned journal = specialized magazine **Fachzeitschrift**

◊ **journalist** noun person who writes for a newspaper **Journalist/-in**

joystick noun device that allows a user to move a cursor around the screen by moving an upright rod connected to an I/O port on the computer **Joystick, Steuerknüppel; joystick port** = circuit and connector used to interface a joystick with a computer **Joystickanschlussstelle;** a joystick port is provided with the home computer

‖ COMMENT: mostly used for computer games ‖ or CAD or desktop publishing packages

judder noun unwanted movement in a printing or facsimile machine that results in a distorted picture **Ungleichförmigkeit, Verwacklung**

jumbo chip noun integrated circuit made using the whole of a semiconductor wafer **Jumbochip;** see also WAFER SCALE INTEGRATION

‖ COMMENT: these devices are very new and ‖ proving rather difficult to manufacture without ‖ faults to any of the thousands of gates on the ‖ surface; when working, these devices will be ‖ extremely powerful

jump (instruction)
1 noun programming command to end one set of instructions and direct the processor to another section of the program **Sprungbefehl; conditional jump** = situation where the processor is directed to another section of the program only if a condition is met **bedingter Sprungbefehl; jump operation** = situation where the CPU is sent from the instruction it is currently executing to another point in the program **Sprungoperation; unconditional jump** = instruction which transfers control from one point in the program to another, without requiring any condition to be met **unbedingter Sprungbefehl**
2 verb
(a) to direct a CPU to another section of a program **springen; jump on zero** = conditional jump executed if a flag or register is zero **Sprungbefehl bei Null**
(b) to miss a page or a line or a space when printing **überspringen;** the typewriter jumped two lines; the paging system has jumped two folio numbers

◊ **jumper** noun temporary wire connection on a circuit board **Brücke; jumper-selectable** = circuit or device whose options can be selected by positioning various wire connections **wählbare Brücke;** the printer's typeface was jumper-selectable

junction *noun*
(a) connection between wires *or* cables Zusammenführung (von Leitungen); **junction box** = small box where a number of wires can be interconnected **Verteilerkasten**
(b) region between two areas of semiconductor which have different doping levels (such as a p-type and n-type area), resulting in a potential difference between them **Zonenübergang; bipolar junction transistor (BJT)** = transistor constructed of 3 layers of alternating types of doped semiconductor (p-n-p *or* n-p-n), each layer having a terminal labelled as emitter, base and collector; usually the base controls the current flow between emitter and collector **bipolarer Sperrschichttransistor**

junk
1 *noun* information *or* hardware which is useless *or* out-of-date *or* non-functional **Unsinn, Schrott; junk mail** = form letters containing special offers *or* advertisements **Postwurfsendungen; space junk** = satellites and hardware that are out of action and no longer used, but are still in orbit in space **Weltraumabfall**
2 *verb* to get rid of a file; to make a file *or* piece of hardware redundant **löschen; to junk a file** = to erase *or* delete from storage a file that is no longer used **eine Datei löschen**

justify *verb*
(a) to change the spacing between words *or* characters in a document so that the left and right margins will be straight **ausschließen (der Zeile), Rand ausgleichen; justify inhibit** = to prevent a word processor justifying a document **das Ausschließen verbieten; justify margin** *see* LEFT *or* RIGHT JUSTIFY; **hyphenate and justify** = to break long words correctly where they split at the ends of lines, so as to give a straight right margin **trennen und ausgleichen; left justify** = to print with a straight left-hand margin **linksbündig ausrichten; right justify** = to print with a straight right-hand margin **rechtsbündig ausrichten**
(b) to shift the contents of a computer register by a set amount **verschieben**

◊ **justification** *noun* moving data bits *or* characters to the left *or* right so that the lines have straight margins **Randausgleich; hyphenation and justification** *or* **H & J** = justifying lines to a set width, splitting the long words correctly at the end of each line **Trennung und Randausgleich;** *an American hyphenation and justification program will not work with British English spellings*

juxtaposition *noun* arranging *or* placing items next to or adjacent to each other **Nebeneinanderstellung**

Kk

K *prefix*
(a) = KILO symbol used to represent one thousand **k**
(b) symbol used to represent 1,024, equal to 2^{10} **K**

◊ **Kb** *or* **Kbit** = KILOBIT measure of 1,024 bits **Kb** *or* **Kbit**

◊ **KB** *or* **Kbyte** = KILOBYTE unit of measure for high capacity storage devices meaning 1,024 bytes **KB** *or* **Kbyte;** *the new disk drive has a 100KB capacity; the original PC cannot access more than 640K bytes of RAM*

COMMENT: 1,024 is the strict definition in computer or electronics applications, being equal to a convenient power of two; these abbreviations can also be taken to equal approximately one thousand, even in computing applications. 1KB is roughly equal to 1,000 output characters in a PC

Karnaugh map *noun* graphical representation of states and conditions in a logic circuit **Karnaugh-Diagramm;** *the prototype was checked for hazards with a Karnaugh map*

Kermit *noun* file transfer protocol usually used when downloading data with a modem **Kermit**

kern *verb* to adjust the space between pairs of letters so that they are printed closer together **die Laufweite verkleinern;** *we have kerned 'T' and 'o' so they are closer together*

◊ **kerning** *noun* slight overlapping of certain printed character areas to prevent large spaces between them, giving a neater appearance **Kerning**

kernel *noun* basic essential instruction routines required as a basis for any operations in a computer system **Kernroutine; graphics kernel system (gks)** = number of basic commands required to illuminate in various shades and colours the pixels on a screen (these are then used to provide more complex functions such as line *or* shape plotting) **Graphikkernsystem**

COMMENT: kernel routines are usually hidden from the user they are used by the operating system for tasks such as loading a program or displaying text on a screen

key

1 *noun*

(a) button on a keyboard that operates a switch **Taste**; *there are 64 keys on the keyboard;* key click = sound produced by a computer to allow the operator to know that the key he pressed has been registered **Anschlagsklicken; key force =** pressure required to close the switch in a key **Tastenwiderstand; key matrix** = design of interconnections between keys on a keyboard **Tastenmatrix; key number** = numeric code used to identify which key has been pressed **Tastennummer; key overlay** = paper placed over the keys on a keyboard describing their functions for a particular application **Tastenschablone**; *without the key overlay, I would never remember which function key does what;* key **punch** = machine used for punching data into punched cards by means of a keyboard **Kartenlocher; key rollover** = use of a buffer between the keyboard and computer to provide rapid key stroke storage for fast typists who hit several keys in rapid succession **überlappende Tastung; key strip** = piece of paper above certain keys used to remind the operator of their special functions **Tastenerklärungsstreifen; key travel** = distance a key has to be pressed before it registers **Tastenweg**

(b) *(names of keys)* alphanumeric key *or* character key = key which produces a character (letter *or* symbol *or* figure) **Zeichentaste; carriage return key** = key which moves a cursor *or* printhead to the beginning of the next line on screen *or* on a typewriter *or* in printing **Wagenrücklauftaste; function key** = key which has a specific task *or* sequence of instructions **Funktionstaste**; *tags can be allocated to function keys;* shift **key** = key which provides a second function for a key (usually by moving the output into upper case) **Umschalttaste**

(c) important object *or* group of characters in a computer system, used to represent an instruction *or* set of data **Schlüssel; key plate** = initial printing plate used when printing colour images **Konturplatte, Klatsch; key terminal** = most important terminal in a computer system *or* one with the highest priority **Hauptdatenstation**

(d) special combination of numbers *or* characters that are used with a cipher to encrypt *or* decrypt a message **Schlüssel;** *type this key into the machine, that will decode the last message;* key **management** = the selection, protection and safe transmission of cipher keys **Schlüsselverwaltung**

(e) identification code *or* word used for a stored record *or* data item **Schlüssel;** *we selected all the records with the word DISK in their keys;* index key = one field which is used to index a record **Indexschlüssel; key field** = field which identifies entries in a record **Schlüsselfeld; keyed sequential access method (KSAM)** = file structure that allows data to be accessed using key fields or key field content **sequenzieller Zugriff in Schlüsselfolge**

2 *verb* **to key in** = to enter text *or* commands via a keyboard **eingeben;** *they keyed in the latest data*

◊ keyboard

1 *noun* number of keys fixed together in some order, used to enter information into a computer *or* to produce characters on a typewriter **Tastatur; keyboard to disk entry** = system where information entered on a keyboard is stored directly on to disk with no processing **Eingabe von der Tastatur direkt auf die Platte; ANSI keyboard** = standard for a keyboard that provides either upper case or upper and lower case characters on a typewriter style keyboard **ANSI-Tastatur; ASCII keyboard** = keyboard that provides a key for every ASCII code **ASCII-Tastatur; ASR keyboard** = communications console keyboard that has all the characters and punctuation keys and special control, send and receive keys **ASR-Tastatur; AZERTY keyboard** = non-English language key layout (the first six letters on the top left row of the keyboard being AZERTY) **AZERTY-Tastatur; interactive keyboard** = keyboard that helps to direct the user *or* prompts for an input by lighting up certain keys on the keyboard (under program control) **interaktive Tastatur; keyboard contact bounce** = multiple signals from a key pressed just once, due to a faulty switch and key bounce **Tastaturkontaktprellen; keyboard encoder** = way in which each key generates a unique word when pressed **Tastaturcodierer; keyboard layout** = way in which various function and character keys are arranged **Tastenanordnung; keyboard overlay** = paper placed over the keys on a keyboard describing their special functions for a particular application **Tastaturschablone; keyboard scan** = method for a computer to determine if a key has

been pressed by applying a voltage across each key switch (if the key is pressed a signal will be read by the computer) **Tastenabtaster; keyboard send/receive (KSR)** = terminal which has a keyboard and monitor, and is linked to a CPU **KSR (Datenstation mit Tastatur und seriellem Drucker mit Bildschirmfunktion); keyboard to disk entry** = system where information entered on a keyboard is stored directly onto disk with no processing **Eingabe von der Tastatur direkt auf die Platte; QWERTY keyboard** = standard English language key layout (the first six letters on the top left row of keys are QWERTY) **QWERTY-Tastatur; touch sensitive keyboard** = thin, flat membrane type keyboard whose keys are activated by touching the particular key, with no movement involved (often used for heavy duty or dirty environments where normal keys would not function correctly) **Folientastatur**
2 *verb* to enter information by using a keyboard **eingeben;** *it was cheaper to have the manuscript keyboarded by another company*

◊ **keyboarder** *noun* person who enters data via a keyboard **Dateneingeber**

◊ **keyboarding** *noun* action of entering data using a keyboard **Eingeben;** *the cost of keyboarding is calculated in keystrokes per hour*

◊ **keypad** *noun* group of special keys used for certain applications **Tastenblock;** *you can use the numeric keypad to enter the figures;* **hex keypad** = keypad with 16 keys (0-9 and A-F) for all the hexadecimal digits **hexadezimale Tastatur; numeric keypad** = set of ten keys with figures (0-9), included in most computer keyboards as a separate group, used for entering large amounts of data in numeric form **numerische Tastatur**

◊ **keystroke** *noun* action of pressing a key **Tastenanschlag;** *he keyboards at a rate of 3500 keystrokes per hour;* **keystroke count** = counting of each keystroke made, often used to calculate keyboarding costs **Anschlagzahl; keystroke verification** = check made on each key pressed to make sure it is valid for a particular application **Anschlagbestätigung**

◊ **key-to-disk** *noun* system where data is keyed in and stored directly on disk without any processing **Eingabe von der Tastatur direkt auf die Platte**

◊ **keyword** *noun* (i) command word used in a programming language to provide a function; (ii) important *or* informative word

in a title *or* document that describes its contents; (iii) word which is relevant *or* important to a text **(i) Kennwort; (ii) & (iii) Schlüsselwort;** *the BASIC keyword PRINT will display text on the screen computer is a keyword in IT;* **keyword and context (KWAC)** = library index system using important words from the text and title as index entries **KWAC-Index; keyword in context (KWIC)** = library index system that uses keywords from the title *or* text of a book *or* document as an indexed entry, followed by the title *or* text it relates to **KWIC-Index; keyword out of context (KWOC)** = library index system that indexes book *or* document titles under any relevant keywords **KWOC-Index**

QUOTE where large orders are being placed over the telephone it is easy to key them into the micro
Micro Decision

QUOTE the new keyboard is almost unchanged, and features sixteen programmable function keys
Micro Decision

QUOTE it uses a six button keypad to select the devices and functions
Byte

QUOTE the main QWERTY typing area is in the centre of the keyboard with the 10 function keys on the left
Personal Computer World

KHz = KILOHERTZ

kill *verb* to erase a file *or* stop a program during execution **löschen, stoppen; kill file** = command to erase a stored file completely **Datei löschen; kill job** = command to halt a computer job while it is running **Stopbefehl**

kilo *prefix*
(a) meaning one thousand **Kilo-; kilobaud** = 1,000 bits per second **Kilobaud; kilohertz (KHz)** = frequency of one thousand cycles per second **Kilohertz (KHz); kilo instructions per second (KIPS)** = one thousand computer instructions processed every second, used as a measure of computer power **tausend Anweisungen pro Sekunde; kilo-ohm** = resistance of one thousand ohms **Kiloohm; kiloVolt-ampere output rating (KVA)** = method of measuring the power rating of a device **Anschlusswerte-Messmethode; kilowatt** *or* **kW** = power measurement equal to one thousand watts **Kilowatt**

(b) meaning 1,024 units, equal to 2^{10} (used only in computer and electronics applications) **Kilo-; kilobit** *or* **Kb** = 1,024 bits of data **Kilobit; kilobyte** *or* **KB** *or* **Kbyte** = unit of measurement for high capacity storage devices meaning 1,024 bytes of data **Kilobyte** *or* **KB** *or* **Kbyte; kiloword** *or* **KW** = unit of measurement of 1,024 computer words **Kilowort, KWort**

kimball tag *noun* coded card attached to a product in a shop, containing information about the product that is read by a scanner when the product is sold **Kimball-Etikett**

KIPS = KILO INSTRUCTIONS PER SECOND one thousand computer instructions processed every second, used as a measure of computer power **tausend Anweisungen pro Sekunde**

kludge *or* **kluge** *noun informal* (i) temporary correction made to a badly written *or* constructed piece of software *or* to a keyboarding error; (ii) hardware which should be used for demonstration purposes only **(i) Flickschusterei; (ii) Vorführgerät**

◊ **kluged** *adjective* temporarily repaired **zusammengeflickt**

knob *noun* round button (such as on a monitor), which can be turned to control some process **Knopf;** *turn the on/off knob; the brightness can be regulated by turning a knob at the back of the monitor*

knowledge *noun* what is known **Wissen; intelligent knowledge-based system (IKBS)** = software that applies the knowledge, advice and rules defined by experts in a particular subject, to a user's data to help solve a problem **intelligentes, wissensbasiertes System; knowledge-based system** = computer system that applies the stored reactions, instructions and knowledge of experts in a particular field to a problem **wissensbasiertes System;** *see also* EXPERT SYSTEM; **knowledge engineering** = designing and writing expert computer systems **Wissenstechnik**

KSAM = KEYED SEQUENTIAL ACCESS METHOD file structure that allows data to be accessed using key fields or key field content **KSAM**

KSR = KEYBOARD SEND/RECEIVE terminal which has a keyboard and monitor, and is linked to a CPU **KSR (Datenstation mit Tastatur und seriellem**

Drucker mit Bildschirmfunktion); *compare with* ASR

KVA = KILOVOLT-AMPERE OUTPUT RATING

KW = KILOWORD

KWAC = KEYWORD AND CONTEXT library indexing system using important words from the text and title as indexed entries **KWAC-Index**

◊ **KWIC** = KEYWORD IN CONTEXT library indexing system that uses keywords from the title *or* text of a book *or* document as an indexed entry followed by the text it relates to **KWIC-Index**

◊ **KWOC** = KEYWORD OUT OF CONTEXT library indexing system that indexes books *or* document titles under any relevant keywords **KWOC-Index**

Ll

label
1
(a) *noun* (i) word *or* other symbol used in a computer program to identify a routine *or* statement; (ii) character(s) used to identify a variable *or* piece of data *or* a file **(i) Bezeichnung, Marke; (ii) Kennung;** *BASIC uses many program labels such as line numbers;* **label field** = an item of data in a record that contains a label **Kennungsfeld; label record** = record containing identification for a stored file **Kennsatz**
(b) piece of paper *or* card attached to something to show instructions for use *or* an address **Hinweisschildchen; Etikett; continuous labels** = removable adhesive labels attached to a backing sheet that can be fed into a printer **Endlosetiketten; external label** = identifying piece of paper stuck to the outside of a device *or* disk **Etikett; label printer** = special printer used to print addresses onto continuous labels **Etikettendrucker**
2 *verb* (i) to put a label on something; (ii) to print an address on a label; **(i) etikettieren; (ii) beschriften**
NOTE: **labelling - labelled** but US **labeling - labeled**

◊ **labelling** *noun* (i) putting a label on

something; (ii) printing labels (i) Etikettierung; (ii) Etikettendruck; *the word-processor has a special utility allowing simple and rapid labelling*

laboratory *noun* place where scientists work on research and development of new products Labor; *the new chip is being developed in the university laboratories*

lag *noun*
(a) time taken for a signal to pass through a circuit, such that the output is delayed compared to the input Verzögerung; *time lag is noticeable on international phone calls*
(b) time taken for an image to be no longer visible after it has been displayed on a CRT screen (this is caused by long persistence phosphor) Kurzzeitnachleuchten

laminate *verb* to cover a paper with a thin film of plastic, to give it a glossy look beschichten, zellglasieren; *the book has a laminated cover*

LAN *or* **lan** = LOCAL AREA NETWORK network where various terminals and equipment are all within a short distance of one another (at a maximum distance of about 500m, for example in the same building), and can be interconnected by cables LAN, Lokalnetz; LAN segment = part of a network separated from the rest by a bridge LAN; LAN server = computer which runs a network operating system and controls the basic network operations; all the workstations in a LAN are connected to the central network server and users log onto the network server LAN-Server; *see also* PEER-TO-PEER; *compare* WAN

◊ **LAN Manager** ™ *noun* network operating system developed for the PC by Microsoft LAN-Manager ™

◊ **LAN Server** ™ *noun* network operating system for the PC developed by IBM LAN-Server ™

> QUOTE The opportunities to delete and destroy data are far greater on our LAN than in the days when we had a mainframe. PC people are culturally different from mainframe people. You really don't think about security problems when you can physically lock your system up in a closet
> *Computing*

> QUOTE since most of the LAN hardware is already present, the installation costs are only $50 per connection
> *Practical Computing*

landing zone *noun* area of a hard disk which does not carry data, the head can come into contact with the disk in this area without damaging the disk or data Landezone; *see also* PARKING

landline *noun* communications link that uses cable to physically and electrically link two devices Landleitung

landscape *noun* orientation of a page *or* piece of paper where the longest edge is horizontal Querformat; *compare* PORTRAIT

language *noun*
(a) spoken *or* written words which are used to communicate with other people Sprache; *he speaks several European languages;* foreign language = language which is spoken by people of another country Fremdsprache
(b) system of words *or* symbols which allows communication with computers (such as one that allows computer instructions to be entered as words which are easy to understand, and then translates them into machine code) Programmiersprache; assembly language *or* assembler language = programming language using mnemonics to code instructions which will then be converted to machine code Assemblersprache; command language = programming language made up of procedures for various tasks, that can be called up by a series of commands Befehlssprache; control language = commands that identify and describe the resources required by a job that a computer has to perform (Job)steuerungssprache; graphic language = computer programming language with inbuilt commands that are useful when displaying graphics Programmiersprache zur Erstellung von Grafiken; high-level language (HLL) = computer programming language that is easy to learn and allows the user to write programs using words and commands that are easy to understand and look like English words, the program is then translated into machine code, with one HLL instruction often representing more than one machine code instruction höhere Programmiersprache; low-level language (LLL) = language which is fast, but long and complex to program in, where each instruction represents a single machine code instruction maschinenorientierte Programmiersprache; machine language = programming language that consists of commands in binary code form that can be directly understood by the CPU

Maschinensprache; programming language = software that allows a user to enter a program in a certain language and then to execute it **Programmiersprache; query language** = language in a database management system that allows a database to be easily searched and queried **Abfragesprache; source language** = original language in which a program is written prior to processing by a computer **Ursprungssprache; language assembler** = program used to translate and assemble a source code program into a machine executable binary form **Assembler; language compiler** = software that converts an encoded source program into another (machine code) form, and then executes it **Umsetzungsprogramm; language interpreter** = any program that takes each consecutive line of source program and translates it into another (machine code) language at run-time **Übersetzungsprogramm; language processor** = language translator from one language to machine code (there are three types of language processor: assembler, compiler and interpreter) **Sprachverarbeiter; language rules** = syntax and format for instructions and data items used in a particular language **Sprachregeln; language support environment** = hardware and software tools supplied to help the programmer write programs in a particular language **Programmierungshilfe; language translation** = using a computer to translate text from one language to another **Computerübersetzung; language translator** = program that converts code written in one language into equivalent instructions in another language **Übersetzungsprogramm**

COMMENT: There are three main types of computer languages: machine code, assembler and high-level language. The higher the level the language is, the easier it is to program and understand, but the slower it is to execute. The following are the commonest high-level languages: ADA, ALGOL, APL, BASIC, C, COBOL, COMAL, CORAL, FORTH, FORTRAN, LISP, LOGO, PASCAL, PL/1, POP-2, PROLOG. Assembly language uses mnemonics to represent machine code instructions; machine code is the basic binary patterns that instruct the processor to perform various tasks

lap *noun*
(a) a person's knees, when he is sitting down **Schoß**; *he placed the computer on his lap and keyboarded some orders while sitting in his car*
(b) overlap of printed colours which prevents any gaps showing **Überlappung**

◊ **lapheld (computer)** *or* **laptop (computer)** *noun* computer that is light enough to carry but not so small as to fit in a pocket, usually containing a screen, keyboard and disk drive **Laptopcomputer, Laptop**

QUOTE in our summary of seven laphelds we found features to admire in every machine

QUOTE the idea of a hard disk in a lapheld machine which runs on batteries is not brand new
PC Business World

QUOTE Michael Business Systems has provided research company BMRB with 240 Toshiba laptop computers in a deal valued at {300,000. The deal includes a three-year maintenance contract
Computing

LAP = LINK ACCESS PROTOCOL CCITT standard protocol used to start and maintain links over an X.25 network **LAP; LAP-B** = CCITT standard setup routine to establish a link between a DCE and DTE (such as a computer and modem) **LAP-B; LAP-M** = LINK ACCESS PROTOCOL FOR MODEMS variation of LAP-B protocol used in V.42 error correcting modems **LAP-M**

lapel microphone *noun* small microphone that is pinned to someone's jacket **Ansteckmikrofon**

large model *noun* (in an Intel processor) memory model in which both code and data can exceed 64Kb in size, but combined size should be less than 1Mb **Largemodell**

large-scale computer *noun* high-powered (large word size) computer system that can access high capacity memory and backing storage devices as well as multiple users **Großrechner**

◊ **large-scale integration (LSI)** *noun* integrated circuit with 500 to 10,000 components **Großintegration**

laser *noun* = LIGHT AMPLIFICATION BY STIMULATED EMISSION OF RADIATION device that produces coherent light of a single wavelength in a narrow beam, by exciting a material so that it emits photons of light **Laser; laser beam recording** = production of characters on a light-sensitive film by a laser beam controlled directly from a computer

Laserstrahlaufzeichnung; laser beam communications = use of a modulated laser beam as a line-of-sight communications medium Laserstrahlkommunikation; laser disc = COMPACT DISC; laser disk = plastic disk containing binary data in the form of small etched dots that can be read by a laser, used to record high quality TV images or sound in digital form Laserbildplatte; laser emulsion storage = digital storage technique using a laser to expose light-sensitive material Speicher mit Laserschicht; laser printer = high-resolution computer printer that uses a laser source to print high-quality dot matrix character patterns on paper (these have a much higher resolution than normal printers, usually 300 dpi) Laserdrucker; injection laser = solid-state laser device used to transmit data as pulses of light down an optic fibre Injektionslaser

LaserJet ™ or **Hewlett Packard LaserJet** or **HP LaserJet** noun laser printer manufactured by Hewlett Packard that uses its PCL language to describe a page LaserJet ™ or Hewlett Packard LaserJet or HP LaserJet

LaserWriter ™ noun laser printer manufactured by Apple that uses the PostScript page description language LaserWriter ™

last in first out (LIFO) noun queue system that reads the last item stored, first LIFO (zuletzt Abgelegtes wird als erstes bearbeitet); this computer stack uses a last in first out data retrieval method; compare with FIRST IN FIRST OUT

latch
1 noun electronic component that maintains an output condition until it receives an input signal to change elektronischer Schalter; see also FLIP-FLOP
2 verb to set an output state verriegeln; the output latched high until we reset the computer

QUOTE other features of the device include a programmable latch bypass which allows any number of latches from 0 to 8 so that this device may be used as latched or combinatorial
Electronics & Power

latency noun time delay between the moment when an instruction is given to a computer and the execution of the instruction or return of a result (such as the

delay between a request for data and the data being transferred from memory) Wartezeit

◊ **latent image** noun image formed before developing on light sensitive film after it has been exposed latentes Bild

lateral reversal noun creating the mirror image of a picture by swapping left and right Kontern

launch
1 noun (i) putting a new product on the market; (ii) putting a satellite in space (i) Einführung, Lancierung; (ii) Abschuss; the launch of the new PC has been put back six months; the launch date for the network will be September
2 verb
(a) (i) to put a new product on the market; (ii) to put a satellite into space (i) einführen, lancieren; (ii) abschießen; the new PC was launched at the Personal Computer Show launching costs for the computer range were calculated at $250,000
(b) to start or run a program starten, ausführen; you launch the word-processor by double-clicking on this icon

◊ **launch amplifier** noun amplifier used to boost the television signals before they are transmitted over a cable network Fernsehsignalverstärker

◊ **launch vehicle** noun spacecraft used to transport a satellite from earth into space Trägerrakete

layer noun
(a) division of sections of space at certain distances from the earth into separate regions used for various radio communications (these are: D-Region from 50 - 90km above earth's surface, E-Region from 90 - 150km above earth's surface, F-Region from 150 - 400km above earth's surface) Schicht
(b) ISO/OSI standards defining the stages a message has to pass through when being transmitted from one computer to another over a network Schicht; application layer = the program that requests a transmission Anwendungsschicht; data link layer = layer that sends packets of data to the next link, and deals with error correction Sicherungsschicht; network layer = layer that decides on the routes to be used, the costs, etc. Vermittlungsschicht; physical layer = layer that defines the rules for bit rate, power, medium for transmission, etc. Bitübertragungsschicht; presentation layer = section that agrees on format, codes and

request for start/end of a connection **Darstellungsschicht; session layer** = layer that makes the connection/disconnection between a transmitter and receiver **Sitzungsschicht; transport layer** = layer that checks and controls the quality of the connection **Transportschicht**

◊ **layered** *adjective* consisting of layers **geschichtet;** *the kernel has a layered structure according to user priority*

◊ **lay in** *verb* to synchronize a frame of film with the music *or* sound tracks **(Tonspur) anlegen**

◊ **layout** *noun*
(a) mock-up of a finished piece of printed work showing the positioning and sizes of text and graphics **Entwurf, Montage;** *the design team is working on the layouts for the new magazine*
(b) rules governing the data input and output from a computer **Aufbau**

◊ **lay out** *verb* to plan and design the positions and sizes of a piece of work to be printed **entwerfen;** *the designers have laid out the pages in A4 format*

LBR = LASER BEAM RECORDING producing characters on a light sensitive film by laser directly controlled from a computer **Laserstrahlaufzeichnung**

LC circuit *noun* simple inductor-capacitor circuit that acts as a filter *or* oscillator **LC-Oszillator**

LCD = LIQUID CRYSTAL DISPLAY liquid crystal that turns black when a voltage is applied, used in many watches, calculators and other small digital displays **LCD-Anzeige, Flüssigkristallanzeige; LCD shutter printer** = page printer that uses an LCD panel in front of a bright light to describe images onto the photosensitive drum; the LCD panel stops the light passing through, except at pixels that describe the image **LCD-Drucker**

QUOTE LCD screens can run for long periods on ordinary or rechargeable batteries
Micro Decision

LCP = LINK CONTROL PROCEDURE rules defining the transmission of data over a channel **Verbindungssteuerungsverfahren**

LDS = LOCAL DISTRIBUTION SERVICE TV signal relay station that transmits signals to another point from which they are distributed over cable **lokaler Verteilerservice**

lead *noun*
(a) electrical conducting wire **Netzkabel**
(b) thin piece of metal used to give extra space between lines of type before printing **Durchschuss**

◊ **lead in page** *noun* videotext page that directs the user to other pages of interest **Einführungsseite**

◊ **leader** *noun*
(a) section of magnetic tape *or* photographic film that contains no signal *or* images, used at the beginning of the reel for identification and to aid the tape machine to pick up the tape **(Streifen)vorspann; leader record** = initial record containing information (such as titles, format, etc.) about following records in a file **Vorlaufsatz**
(b) row of printed dots **Führungspunkte**

◊ **leading** *noun* extra space between lines of print **Durchschuss**

◊ **leading edge** *noun* first edge of a punched card that enters the card reader **Führungskante**

◊ **leading zero** *noun* zero digit used to pad out the beginning of a stored number **führende Null**

leaf *noun*
(a) page of a book (printed on both sides) **Blatt**
(b) final node in a data tree structure **Blatt**

◊ **leaflet** *noun* small publicity sheet (usually one page folded in half) **Hand-, Reklamezettel**

leak
1 *noun*
(a) loss of secret documents *or* a breach of security **Leck;** *a leak informed the press of our new designs*
(b) gradual loss of charge from a charged component due to imperfect insulation **undichte Stelle**
2 *verb*
(a) to provide secret information to unauthorized people **etwas durchsickern lassen, zuspielen;** *the details of our new software package have been leaked to the press*
(b) to lose electric charge gradually **entweichen;** *in this circuit, the capacitor charge leaks out at 10% per second*

◊ **leakage** *noun* loss of signal strength **Leck**

QUOTE signal leakages in both directions can be a major problem in co-axial cable systems

Electronics & Wireless World

leapfrog test *noun* memory location test, in which a program skips from one location to another random location, writing data then reading and comparing for faults, until all locations have been tested **Bocksprungtest, sprungweise Durchprüfung; crippled leapfrog test** = standard leapfrog test that uses a single memory location rather than a changing location **Teilprüfung im Bocksprungprogramm**

learning curve *noun* graphical description of how someone can acquire knowledge (about a product) over time **Lernkurve; steep learning curve** = means that a product is very difficult to use **steile Lernkurve**

lease
1 *noun* written contract for letting *or* renting a piece of equipment for a period against payment of a fee **Leasingvertrag**
2 *verb*
(a) to let *or* rent equipment for a period **mieten;** *the company has a policy of only using leased equipment;* **leased circuit** = electronic circuit *or* communications channel rented for a period **Mietleitung; leased line** = communications channel, such as a telephone line, which is rented for the exclusive use of the subscriber **Mietleitung**
(b) to use equipment for a time and pay a fee **mieten;** *the company leases all its computers*

least cost design *noun* best money-saving use of space *or* components **Niedrigstkostenplan;** *the budget is only £1000, we need the least cost design for the new circuit*

◊ **least recently used algorithm** *noun* algorithm which finds the page of memory that was last accessed before any other, and erases it to make room for another page **LRU-Algorithmus (am längsten nicht benutzter Algorithmus)**

◊ **least significant digit (LSD)** *noun* digit which occupies the right hand position in a number and so carries the least power (equal to the number radix raised to zero = 1) **niederwertigste Ziffer; least significant bit (LSB)** = binary digit occupying the right hand position of a

word and carrying the least power of two in the word (usually equal to two raised to zero = 1) **niederwertigstes Bit**

leaving files open *phrase* meaning that a file has not been closed *or* does not contain an end of text marker (this will result in the loss of data since the text will not have been saved) **Offenlassen von Dateien**

LED = LIGHT EMITTING DIODE semiconductor diode that emits light when a current is applied **LED (Leuchtdiodenanzeige); LED printer** = page printer (similar to a laser printer) that uses an LED light source instead of a laser **LED-Drucker**

COMMENT: LED displays are used to display small amounts of information, as in pocket calculators, watches, indicators, etc.

left justification *noun*
(a) shifting a binary number to the left hand end of the word containing it **Stellenverschiebung nach links**
(b) making the left hand margin of the text even **Linksausrichtung, Linksbündigkeit**

◊ **left justify** *verb* printing command that makes the left hand margin of the text even **linksbündig ausrichten**

◊ **left shift** *noun* left arithmetic shift by one bit of data in a word, a binary number is doubled for each left shift **Linksverschiebung**

leg *noun* one possible path through a routine **Zweig einer Schaltung**

legal *adjective* statement or instruction that is acceptable within language syntax rules **gültig**

legible *adjective* which can be read easily **lesbar;** *the manuscript is written in pencil and is hardly legible*

◊ **legibility** *noun* being able to be read **Lesbarkeit;** *the keyboarders find the manuscript lacks legibility*

length *noun* how long something is; the number of data items in a variable *or* list **Länge; block length** = number of records *or* fields *or* characters in a block of data **Blocklänge; buffer length** = number of data items that can be stored in a buffer while waiting for the processor to attend to them **Pufferlänge; field length** = number of characters stored in a field **Feldlänge; file length** = number of characters *or* bytes in a stored file **Dateilänge; length of filename** = number of characters allowed for identification of a file **Länge des Dateinamens; line length** = number of characters which can be displayed horizontally on one line of a display (CRT displays often use an 80 character line length) **Zeilenlänge; record length** = total number of characters contained in the various fields within a stored record **Satzlänge; register length** = number of bits that make up a register **Registerlänge**

lens *noun* shaped glass that changes the path of a light beam **Linse; concave lens** = lens that is thinner in the centre than at the edges, bending light out **konkave Linse; convex lens** = lens that is thicker in the centre than the edges, bending light in **konvexe Linse; lens speed** = the maximum aperture of a lens, relating to the amount of light that can enter the lens **Öffnungsverhältnis; lens stop** = lens aperture size **Blende**

letter *noun*
(a) piece of writing sent from one person to another *or* from a company to another, to give information, to send instructions, etc. **Brief; form letter** *or* **standard letter** = letter sent to several addressees by name without any change to the text **Formbrief**
(b) written *or* printed sign, which goes to make a word (such as A, B, C, etc.) **Buchstabe;** *his name was written in capital letters*

◊ **letterhead** *noun* name and address of a company printed at the top of the company's notepaper **Briefkopf;** *business forms and letterheads can now be designed on a PC*

◊ **letter-quality (LQ) printing** *noun* feature of some dot-matrix printers to provide characters of the same quality as a typewriter by using dots which are very close together **LQ (Schönschriftdruck); near-letter-quality (NLQ) printing** = printing by a dot-matrix printer that provides higher quality type, which is almost as good as a typewriter, by decreasing the space between the dots **NLQ (korrespondenzfähiges Schriftbild)**

QUOTE the printer offers reasonable speeds of printing in both draft and letter-quality modes
Which PC?

level *noun*
(a) strength *or* power of an electrical signal

Pegel; *turn the sound level down, it's far too loud;* **sound pressure level (SPL)** = measurement of the magnitude of the pressure wave conveying sound **Schalldruckpegel**
(b) quantity of bits that make up a digital transmitted signal **Stufe; quatenary level quantization** = use of four bits of data in an A/D conversion process **quaternäre Stufenquantisierung**

lexical analysis *noun* stage in program translation when the compiling *or* translating software replaces program keywords with machine code instructions **lexikalische Analyse**

lexicographical order *noun* order of items, where the words are listed in the order of the letters of the alphabet, as in a dictionary **lexikographische Anordnung**

LF
(a) = LOW FREQUENCY range of audio frequencies between 5 - 300Hz *or* range of radio frequencies between 30 - 300KHz **Niederfrequenz**
(b) = LINE FEED

library *noun*
(a) collection of files *or* documents *or* books *or* records, etc., which can be consulted *or* borrowed by the public, usually kept in a public place **Bibliothek;** *the editors have checked all the references in the local library; a copy of each new book has to be deposited in the British Library; look up the bibliographical details in the library catalogue*
(b) collection of programs *or* books belonging to a person **Bibliothek;** *he has a large library of computer games;* **library function** = software routine that a user can insert into his program to provide the function with no effort **Bibliotheksfunktion; library program** = (i) number of specially written *or* relevant software routines, which a user can insert into his own program, saving time and effort; (ii) group of functions which a computer needs to refer to often, but which are not stored in main memory **(i) & (ii) Bibliotheksprogramm;** *the square root function is already in the library program;* **macro library** = number of useful, independent routines that can be incorporated into any program to ease program writing **Makrobibliothek; library routine** = prewritten routine that can be inserted into a main program and called up when required **Bibliotheksroutine; library subroutine** = tried and tested subroutine

stored in a library, and which can be inserted into a user's program when required **Bibliotheks(unter)programm; library track** = one track on a magnetic disk *or* tape used to store information about the contents (such as titles, format and index data) **Hinweisspur**

◊ **librarian** *noun* person who works in a library **Bibliothekar/-in**

> QUOTE a library of popular shapes and images is supplied
> *Practical Computing*

licence *noun* permission given by one manufacturer to another manufacturer to make copies of his products against payment of a fee **Lizenz;** *the software is manufactured in this country under licence*

lifetime *noun* period of time during which a device is useful *or* not outdated **Lebensdauer;** *this new computer has a four-year lifetime*

LIFO = LAST IN FIRST OUT queue system that reads the last item stored, first **LIFO (zuletzt Abgelegtes wird als erstes bearbeitet);** *this computer stack uses a LIFO data retrieval method; see also* FIFO

lifter *noun* mechanical device that lifts magnetic tape away from the heads when rewinding the tape **Anheber**

ligature *noun* two characters printed together to form a combined character *or* a short line connecting two characters **Ligatur**

light
1 *noun* perception of brightness due to electromagnetic effects in the frequency range 400 - 750 nm, which allows a person to see **Licht;** *the VDU should not be placed under a bright light;* **light conduit** = fibre optics used to transmit light from one place to another rather than for the transmission of data **Lichtleitung; light emitting diode (LED)** = semiconductor diode that emits light when a current is applied (used in calculators and clock displays and as indicators) **LED (lichtaussendende Diode); light guide** = fine strands of glass *or* plastic protected by a surrounding material, used for the transmission of light **Lichtwellenleiter; light pen** = computer accessory in the shape of a pen that contains a light-sensitive device that can detect pixels on a video screen (often used with suitable software to draw graphics on a screen *or* position a cursor) **Lichtstift; light**

pipe = LIGHT GUIDE; **coherent light** = light beam in which all the waveforms are in phase **kohärentes Licht; infrared light (IR light)** = electromagnetic radiation just below visible red (often used for communications purposes such as remote control) **Infrarotlicht (IR-Licht); ultraviolet light (UV light)** = electromagnetic radiation with wavelengths just greater than the visible spectrum, from 200 to 4,000 angstroms (often used to erase data from EPROMs) **ultraviolettes Licht (UV-Licht); visible light** = range of light colours that can be seen with the human eye **sichtbares Licht 2** *adjective* not dark **hell; light face** = typeface with thin lines, which appears light on the page **magere Schrift**

◊ **light-sensitive** *adjective* which is sensitive to light **lichtempfindlich;** *the photograph is printed on light-sensitive paper;* **light-sensitive device** = device (such as a phototransistor) which is sensitive to light, and produces a change in signal strength *or* resistance **Fotozelle**

◊ **lightweight** *adjective* which is not heavy **leicht(gewichtig);** *a lightweight computer which can easily fit into a suitcase*

LIM EMS = LOTUS, INTEL, MICROSOFT EXPANDED MEMORY SYSTEM (in an IBM PC) standard that defines extra memory added above the 640Kb limit of conventional memory; this memory can only be used by specially-written programs **LIM EMS**

limits *noun* predefined maximum ranges for numbers in a computer **Grenzwerte**

◊ **limited distance modem** *noun* data transmission device with a very short range that sends pure digital data rather than a modulated carrier **Modem für begrenzte Entfernungen**

◊ **limiter** *noun* electronic circuit that prevents a signal from going above a certain level **Begrenzer**

◊ **limiting resolution** *noun* maximum number of lines that make up a television picture **Grenzauflösung**

line *noun*
(a) physical connection for data transmission (such as a cable between parts of a system *or* a telephone wire) **Leitung; access line** = permanently connected communications line between a terminal and a DSE **Anschlussleitung; fast line** = special communications link that allows data to be transmitted at 48K *or* 96K baud

Schnellleitung; telephone line = cable used to connect a telephone handset with a central exchange Telefonleitung; line adapter = electronic circuit that matches the correct signal voltage and impedance for a particular line Leitungsadapter; line analyzer = test equipment that displays the characteristics of a line *or* the signals carried on the line Leitungsprüfgerät; line busy tone = signal generated to indicate that a connection *or* telephone line is already in use Besetztzeichen; line communications = signal transmission using a cable link *or* telegraph wire drahtgebundene Übertragung; line conditioning = (techniques) used to keep the quality of data transmissions *or* signals on a line to a certain standard Leitungsaufbereitung; line control = special codes used to control a communications channel Übertragungssteuerung; line driver = high power circuit and amplifier used to send signals over a long distance line without too much loss of signal Kabeltreiber; line extender = circuit used to boost a television signal Nebenleitung; line impedance = impedance of a communications line *or* cable (equipment should have a matching load to minimize power loss) Leitungsimpedanz; line level = amplitude of a signal transmitted over a cable Leitungsstufe; line load = number of messages transmitted over a line compared to the maximum capacity Leitungsbelastung; line speed = rate at which data is sent along a line Übertragungsgeschwindigkeit; line switching = communications line and circuit established on demand and held until no longer required Durchschaltevermittlungstechnik; line transient = large voltage spike on a line Wanderwelle
(b) single long thin mark drawn by a pen *or* printed on a surface Linie, Strich; *the printer has difficulty in reproducing very fine lines;* line art = black and white graphics, with no shades of grey Schwarz-Weiß-Grafik; line drawings = drawings made of lines drawn by the artist Strichzeichnungen; *the book is illustrated with line drawings and halftones*
(c) one trace by the electron picture beam on a screen *or* monitor Zeile; line blanking interval = period of time when the picture beam is not displayed, this is during line flyback Zeilenaustastlücke; line drive signal = signal to start the scanning procedure in a television camera Zeilentreibersignal; line flyback = electron beam returning from the end of one line to the beginning of the next Zeilenrücklauf; line frequency = number of picture lines that are scanned per second Zeilenfrequenz
(d) row of characters (printed on a page *or* displayed on a computer screen *or* printer) Zeile; *each page has 52 lines of text; several lines of manuscript seem to have been missed by the keyboarder; can we insert an extra line of spacing between the paragraphs?;* command line = program line that contains a command Kommandozeile; information line = line running across the screen which gives the user information about the program being executed *or* the file being edited Informationszeile; line editor = piece of software that allows the operator to modify one line of text from a file at a time Zeileneditor; line ending = character which shows that a line has ended (instructed by pressing the carriage return key) Zeilenende; line feed (LF) = control on a printer *or* computer terminal that moves the cursor down by one line Zeilenvorschub; line folding = move a section of a long line of text onto the next row Zeilenumbruch; line increment = minimum distance between two lines of type, which can be as small as one eighteenth of a point (kleinster) Zeilenschritt; line length = number of characters contained in a displayed line (on a computer screen this is normally 80 characters, on a printer often 132 characters) Zeilenlänge; line spacing = distance between two rows of characters Zeilenabstand; lines per minute (LPM) = number of lines printed by a line printer per minute Zeilen pro Minute
(e) series of characters received as a single input by a computer Zeile; line input = command to receive all characters including punctuation entered up to a carriage return code Zeileneingabe
(f) one row of commands *or* arguments in a computer program Zeile; line number = number that refers to a line of program code in a computer program Zeilennummer

> COMMENT: the programming language will sort out the program into order according to line number

> QUOTE straight lines are drawn by clicking the points on the screen where you would like the line to start and finish
> *Personal Computer World*

> QUOTE while pixel editing is handy for line art, most desktop scanners have trouble producing the shades of grey or half-tones found in black and white photography
> *Publish*

line of sight *noun* clear transmission path for radio communications in a straight line **Sichtverbindung**

> COMMENT: line of sight paths are used with a very directional transmission medium such as a laser beam rather than a uni-directional one such as radio

line printer *noun* device for printing draft quality information at high speeds, typical output is 200 to 3000 lines per minute **Zeilendrucker**

> COMMENT: line printers print a whole line at a time, running from right to left and left to right, and are usually dot matrix printers with not very high quality print. Compare page printers, which print a whole page at a time

linear *adjective* (circuit output) that varies directly with the input signal so that the output to input characteristics are a straight line (in practice this is never achieved since all components have maximum and minimum output limits at which points the signal becomes distorted) **linear; linear array** = antenna whose elements lie in a straight line **Dipolzeilenantenne; linear function** = mathematical expression where the input is not raised to a power above one and contains no multiplications other than by a constant **lineare Funktion;** *the expression $Y = 10 + 5X - 3W$ is a linear function; the expression $Y = (10 + 5X^2)$ is not a linear function;* **linear integrated circuit** = electronic device whose output varies linearly with its input over a restricted range (device usually used to provide gain to an analog signal) **analoge integrierte Schaltung; linear list** = list that has no free space for new records within its structure **lineare Liste; linear program** = computer program that contains no loops *or* branches **lineares Programm; linear programming** = method of mathematically breaking down a problem so that it can be solved by computer **lineare Programmierung; linear search** = search method which compares each item in a list with the search key until the correct entry is found (starting with the first item and working sequentially towards the end) **lineare Suche**

link

1 *noun*
(a) communications path *or* channel between two components *or* devices **Verbindungsstrecke;** *to transmit faster, you can use the direct link with the mainframe;* **data link layer** = ISO/OSI layer that sends packets of data to the next link, and deals with error correction **Sicherungsschicht; link control procedure (LCP)** = rules defining the transmission of data over a channel **Verbindungssteuerungsverfahren; link loss** = attenuation of signals transmitted over a link **Signaldämpfung; satellite link** = use of a satellite to allow the transmission of data from one point on earth to another **Satellitenstrecke**
(b) software routine that allows data transfer between incompatible programs **Verbindungsprogramm; link trials** = testing computer programs so as to see if each module works in conjunction with the others **Verbindungsüberprüfung**
2 *verb* to join *or* interface two pieces of software *or* hardware **verbinden;** *the two computers are linked;* **link files** = command to merge together a list of separate files **Dateien verschmelzen; linked list** = list of data where each entry carries the address of the next consecutive entry **verbundene Liste; linked subroutine** = number of computer instructions in a program that can be called at any time, with control being returned on completion to the next instruction in the main program **verbundenes Unterprogramm**

◊ **linkage** *noun* act of linking two things **Verbindung; linkage editing** = combining separate programs together, and standardizing the calls *or* references within them **Binderprogramm, Linkage-Editierung; linkage software** = special software which links sections of program code with any library routines *or* other code **Programmverbindungssoftware;** *graphics and text are joined without linkage software*

◊ **linking** *noun* merging of a number of small programs together to enable them to run as one unit **Programmverbindung; linking loader** = short software routine that merges sections of programs to allow them to be run as one **Bindelader**

LIPS = LOGICAL INFERENCES PER SECOND standard for the measurement of processing power of an inference engine **logische Schlussfolgerungen pro Sekunde**

> COMMENT: one inference often requires thousands of computer instructions

liquid crystal display (LCD) *noun* liquid crystals that turn black when a voltage is applied, used in many watch, calculator and digital displays **Flüssigkristallanzeige (LCD); liquid crystal display shutter printer** *see* LCD SHUTTER PRINTER

COMMENT: LCDs do not generate light and so cannot be seen in the dark without an external light source (as opposed to LEDs)

LISP = LIST PROCESSING high-level language used mainly in processing lists of instructions *or* data and in artificial intelligence work **LISP (Programmiersprache)**

list
1 *noun* series of ordered items of data **Liste; chained list** = list in which each element contains data and an address to the next element in the list **gekettete Liste; linear list** = list that has no free space for new records within its structure **lineare Liste; linked list** = list of data where each entry carries the address of the next consecutive entry **gekettete Liste; pushdown list** = temporary storage, in a LIFO format, for a list of items of data **Rückstellliste; reference list** = list of routines *or* instructions and their location within a program **Verweisliste; stop list** = list of words that are not to be used *or* are not significant for a file search **Liste der verbotenen Wörter; list processing** = (i) computation of a series of items of data such as adding *or* deleting *or* sorting *or* updating entries; (ii) LISP *or* a high-level language used mainly in processing lists of instructions *or* data, and in artificial intelligence work **(i) Listenbearbeitung; (ii) LISP (Programmiersprache)**
2 *verb* to print *or* display certain items of information **auflisten; to list a program** = to display a program line by line in correct order **ein Programm auflisten**

◊ **listing** *noun*
(a) program lines printed *or* displayed in an ordered way **Auflistung; computer listing** = printout of a list of items, taken from data stored in a computer **Computerauflistung; a program listing** = a printed copy of the lines of a program **eine (gedruckte) Programmauflistung; listing paper** = continuous stationery **Endlospapier**
(b) **listings** = series of information items (such as cinema times, etc.) listed in a newspaper **Programm**

literal *noun*
(a) (operand) computer instruction that contains the actual number *or* address to be used, rather than a label *or* its location **Literal**
(b) printing error when one character is replaced by another *or* when two characters are transposed **Druckfehler**

literate *adjective* (person) who can read and write **des Lesens und Schreibens kundig; computer-literate** = able to understand expressions relating to computers and how to use a computer **computersachverständig**

◊ **literacy** *noun* being able to read and write **Kenntnis des Lesens und Schreibens; computer literacy** = understanding the basic principles of computers, related expressions and being able to use computers for programming *or* applications **Fähigkeit, sich mit Computern auszukennen**

lith film *noun* high quality and contrast photographic film used in lithographic printing **lithographischer Film**

◊ **lithography** *or* (*informal*) **litho** *noun* offset lithography = printing process used for printing books, where the ink sticks to dry areas on the film and is transferred to rubber rollers from which it is printed on to the paper **Offsetlithographie**

◊ **lithographic** *adjective* referring to lithography **lithographisch; lithographic film** = LITH FILM

liveware *noun* the operators and users of a computer system (as opposed to the hardware and software) **EDV-Personal**

LLC = LOGICAL LINK CONTROL IEEE 802.2 standard defining the protocol for data-link-level transmissions **LLC**

LLL = LOW-LEVEL LANGUAGE

load
1 *noun*
(a) job *or* piece of work to be done **Aufgabe, Belastung; load sharing** = use of more than one computer in a network to even out the work load on each processor **Belastungsverteilung; line load** = number of messages transmitted over a line compared to the maximum capacity of the line **Leitungsbelastung; work load** = number of tasks that a machine has to complete **Arbeitsbelastung**
(b) impedance presented to a line *or* device **Belastung; load life** = length of time an impedance can operate with a certain power before it is no longer usable **Lebensdauer bei Belastung; matched load** = load that is the same as the impedance of the transmission line *or* device connected to it **angepasste Belastung**
2 *verb*
(a) to transfer a file *or* program from disk *or* tape to main memory **laden; scatter load** =

to load sequential data into various non-continuous locations in memory **gestreut laden; load and run** or **load and go** = computer program that is loaded into main memory and then starts to execute itself automatically **Laden und Ausführen; load high** = (using MS-DOS on a PC) to transfer a program into high or expanded memory **in den hohen Speicherbereich laden**
(b) to put a disk or tape into a computer, so that it can be run **laden**
(c) to place an impedance or device at the end of a line **belasten**

◊ **loading** noun action of transferring a file or program from disk to memory **Laden;** loading can be a long process

◊ **load point** noun start of a recording section in a reel of magnetic tape **Ladepunkt**

◊ **loader** noun program which loads another file or program into computer memory **Ladeprogramm; absolute loader** = program that loads a section of code into main memory **Ladeprogramm für absolute Programme;** compare BOOTSTRAP; **binary loader** = short section of program code that allows programs in binary form (such as object code from a linker or assembler) to be loaded into memory **binäres Ladeprogramm; card loader** = short program that transfers data from a punched card into main memory **Kartenlader; initial program loader (IPL)** = short routine that loads the first section of a program, after which it continues the loading process itself **Urlader**

> QUOTE this windowing system is particularly handy when you want to load or save a file or change directories
> *Byte*

lobe noun section of a response curve around an antenna or microphone **(Strahlungs)keule**

local adjective & noun
(a) (variable or argument) that is only used in a certain section of a computer program or structure **lokal, Lokal-, lokal-; local bridge** = bridge that links two local networks **lokale Brücke;** we use a local bridge to link the two LANs in the office; **local bus** = direct link or bus between a device and the processor; with no logic circuits or buffers or decoders in between **Localbus, lokaler Bus;** the fastest expansion cards fit into this local bus connector; **local declaration** = assignment of a variable that is only valid in a section of a computer program or structure **lokale Erklärung; local drive** = disk drive that is physically attached to a computer rather

than a resource being accessed across a network **lokales Laufwerk; local memory** = high speed RAM that is used instead of a hardware device to store bit streams or patterns **Lokalspeicher; local printer** = printer physically attached to a computer rather than a shared resource available on a network **lokaler Drucker; local variable** = variable which can only be accessed by certain routines in a certain section of a computer program **lokale Variable;** compare GLOBAL VARIABLE
(b) referring to a system with limited access **lokal;** (of a terminal) **on local** = not working with a CPU, but being used as a stand-alone terminal **stationärer Betrieb; local mode** = operating state of a computer terminal that does not receive messages **stationärer Betrieb**

◊ **local area network (LAN** or **lan)** noun network where various terminals and equipment are all a short distance from one another (at a maximum distance of about 500m, for example in the same building) and can be interconnected by cables **Lokalnetz (LAN);** compare with WAN; **local area network server** = computer which runs a network operating system and controls the basic network operations; all the workstations in a LAN are connected to the central network server and users log onto the network server **LAN-Server**

COMMENT: LANs use cables or optical fibre links; WANs use modems, radio and other long distance transmission methods

◊ **LocalTalk** ™ noun cabling system and connectors used in Apple's AppleTalk network **LocalTalk** ™

◊ **locate** verb (i) to be situated; (ii) to find (i) **sich befinden;** (ii) **lokalisieren;** the computer is located in the main office building; have you managed to locate the programming fault?

◊ **location** noun
(a) number or absolute address which specifies the point in memory where a data word can be found and accessed **Speicherstelle**
(b) on location = filming in real situations, and not in the studio **vor Ort; location shots** = sections of a film which are shot on location **Außenaufnahmen**

lock verb to prevent access to a system or file **sperren; locking a file** = the action of preventing any further writing to a file **eine Datei sperren; to lock onto** = to synchronize an internal clock with a received signal **einstellen auf**

◊ **lockout** *noun* preventing a user sending messages over a network by continuously transmitting data **Aussperrung**

◊ **lock up** *noun* faulty operating state of computer that cannot be recovered from without switching off the power **Sperre**

|| COMMENT: this can be caused by an infinite program loop *or* a deadly embrace

log
1 *noun* record of computer processing operations **Protokoll**
2 *verb*
(a) to record a series of actions **protokollieren; to log calls** = to keep a record of telephone calls **Anrufe protokollieren**
(b) to log in *or* **log on** = to make a connection and start using a remote device such as a network server **im System anmelden, einloggen; automatic log on** = telephone number, password and user number transmitted when requested by a remote system to automate logon **automatische Anmeldung; log on script** = series of batch instructions that are automatically executed when you connect *or* log on to a network *or* server **Logonskript, Anmeldeskript; log on server** = computer that checks user identification and password data against a user database to authorize connection to a network *or* server **Logonserver, Anmeldeserver; to log off** *or* **log out** = to enter a symbol *or* instruction at the end of a computing session to close all files and break the channel between the user's terminal and the main computer **sich abmelden** NOTE: the verbs can be spelled **log on, log-on,** or **logon; log off, log-off** or **logoff**

◊ **logger** *noun* **call logger** = device which logs telephone calls (and notes the number called, the time when the call was made, and the length of the call) **Anrufaufzeichner**

◊ **logging** *noun* input of data into a system **Aufzeichnen; logging on** *or* **logging off** = process of opening *or* ending operations with a system **Anmelden; Abmelden; call logging** = system of monitoring telephone calls **Anrufaufzeichnung; error logging** = recording errors met **Fehlererfassung;** *features of the program include error logging*

> QUOTE logging on and off from terminals is simple, requiring only a user name and password

> QUOTE once the server is up and running it is possible for users to log-on
> *Micro Decision*

> QUOTE facilities for protection against hardware failure and software malfunction include log files
> *Computer News*

logarithm *noun* mathematical operation that gives the power a number must be raised to, to give the required number **Logarithmus;** *decimal logarithm of 1,000 is 3 (= 10 x 10 x 10)*

◊ **logarithmic** *adjective* referring to variations in the logarithm of a scale **logarithmisch;** *bel is a unit in the logarithmic scale;* **logarithmic graph** = graph whose axes have a scale that is the logarithm of the linear measurement **logarithmische Darstellung**

logic *noun*
(a) science which deals with thought and reasoning **Logik; formal logic** = treatment of form and structure, ignoring content **formale Logik**
(b) mathematical treatment of formal logic operations such as AND, OR, etc., and their transformation into various circuits **Art der Schaltungstechnik;** *see also* BOOLEAN ALGEBRA; **logic map** = graphical representation of states and conditions in a logic circuit **logische Map; logic state** = one out of two possible levels in a digital circuit, the levels being 1 and 0 or TRUE and FALSE **logischer Zustand; logic state analyzer** = test equipment that displays the logic states of a number of components *or* circuits **Logikanalysator; logic symbol** = graphical symbol used to represent a type of logic function **logisches Symbol**
(c) system for deducing results from binary data **Logik; logic bomb** = section of code that performs various unpleasant functions such as system crash when a number of conditions are true (the logic bomb is installed by unpleasant hackers *or* very annoyed programmers) **programmierte Zeitbombe; logic level** = voltage used to represent a particular logic state (this is often five volts for a one and zero volts for a zero) **Logikpegel; logic operation** = computer operation *or* procedure in which a decision is made **logische Operation**
(d) components of a computer *or* digital system **Logik; sequential logic** = logic circuit whose output depends on the logic state of the previous inputs **sequenzielle Logik; logic card** *or* **logic board** = printed circuit board containing binary logic gates rather than analog components **Schaltkreisplatine; logic circuit** = electronic circuit made up of

various logical gates such as AND, OR and EXOR **logischer Schaltkreis; logic element =** gate *or* combination of logic gates **Verknüpfungsglied; logic flowchart =** graphical representation of logic elements, steps and decisions and the interconnections **logisches Flussdiagramm; logic gate =** electronic circuit that applies a logical operator to an input signal and produces an output **logisches Steuerelement;** *see also* GATE

◊ **logical** *adjective* that uses logic in its operation **logisch;** *logical reasoning can be simulated by an artificial intelligence machine;* **logical channel =** electronic circuit between a terminal and a network node in a packet switching system **logischer Kanal; logical chart =** graphical representation of logic elements, steps and decisions and their interconnections **logisches Diagramm; logical comparison =** function to see if two logic signals are the same **Identitätsvergleich; logical decision =** one of two paths chosen as a result of one of two possible answers to a question **logische Entscheidung; logical drive =** letter assigned to a disk drive *or* storage area on a disk drive that can be used as if it were a local drive **logisches Laufwerk;** *the logical drive F: actually stores data on part of the server's disk drive;* **logical error =** fault in a program design causing incorrect branching *or* operations **logischer Fehler; logical expression =** function made up from a series of logical operators such as AND and OR **logischer Ausdruck; logical high =** equal to logic true state *or* 1 **logischer Pegel H; logical inferences per second (LIPS) =** standard for the measurement of processing power of an inference engine **logische Schlussfolgerungen pro Sekunde, Logical Inferences Per Second (LIPS); logical link control (LLC) =** IEEE 802.2 standard defining the protocol for data-link-level transmissions **logische Verknüpfungssteuerung, Logical Link Control (LLC); logical low =** equal to logic false state *or* 0 **logischer Pegel L; logical operator =** character *or* word that describes the logical action it will perform (the most common logical operators are AND, NOT, and OR) **logischer Operator; logical record =** unit of information ready for processing that is not necessarily the same as the original data item in storage, which might contain control data, etc. **logischer Satz; logical ring =** (in a Token-Ring or FDDI network) the path a token follows through the layers of each node; in FDDI the physical topology

does not effect the logical ring **logischer Ring; logical shift =** data movement to the left *or* right in a word, the bits falling outside the word boundary are discarded, the free positions are filled with zeros **logisches Verschieben;** *compare with* ARITHMETIC SHIFT

◊ **logic-seeking** *adjective* (printer) that can print the required information with the minimum head movement, detecting ends of lines, justification commands, etc. **logisch(er Drucker)**

QUOTE a reduction in the number of logic gates leads to faster operation and lower silicon costs

QUOTE the removal of complex but infrequently used logic makes the core of the processor simpler and faster, so simple operations execute faster
Electronics & Power

login = LOGGING IN

LOGO *noun* high-level programming language used mainly for educational purposes, with graphical commands that are easy to use **LOGO (Programmiersprache)**

◊ **logo** *noun* special printed set of characters *or* symbols used to identify a company *or* product **Logo**

logoff = LOG OFF, LOGGING OFF

◊ **logon =** LOG ON, LOGGING ON

◊ **logout =** LOGGING OUT

long haul network *noun* communications network between distant computers that usually uses the public telephone system **Überlandnetz**

◊ **long integer** *noun* (in programming languages) an integer represented by several bytes of data **lange Ganzzahl**

long persistence phosphor *noun* television screen coating that retains the displayed image for a period of time longer than the refresh rate, reducing flicker effects **Bildschirmbeschichtung mit langer Nachleuchtdauer**

look ahead *noun* action by some CPUs to fetch instructions and examine them before they are executed (to speed up operations) **Vorgriff; carry look ahead =** high speed adder that can predict if a carry will be generated by a sum and add it in, removing the delay found in a ripple through carry adder **Addierer mit Parallelübertrag**

◊ **binary look-up** *noun* fast search method for use on ordered lists of data; the search key is compared with the data in the middle of the list and one half is discarded, this is repeated with remaining half until only one data item remains **binäre Abfragemethode**

◊ **look-up table** *or* **LUT** *noun* collection of stored results that can be accessed very rapidly by a program without the need to calculate each result whenever needed **Nachschlagetabelle**; *lookup tables are preprogrammed then used in processing so saving calculations for each result required*

> QUOTE a lookup table changes a pixel's value based on the values in a table
> **Byte**

loop
1 *noun*
(a) procedure *or* series of instructions in a computer program that are performed again and again until a test shows that a specific condition has been met *or* until the program is completed **Schleife; closed loop** = computer control operation in which data is fed back from the output of the controlled device to the controlling loop **geschlossener Regelkreis; endless loop** *or* **infinite loop** = loop which has no end, except when the program is stopped **Endlosschleife; holding loop** = section of program that loops until it is broken by some action, most often used when waiting for a response from the keyboard *or* a device **Warteschleife; modification loop** = instructions within a loop that change other instructions *or* data within a program **Modifikationsschleife; nested loop** = loop contained inside another **Schleife in der Schleife; loopback** = diagnostic test that returns the transmitted signal to the sending device after it has passed through a device *or* across a link **Prüfschleife; loop body** = main section of instructions within a loop that carry out the primary function rather than being used to enter or leave or setup the loop **Schleifenrumpf; loop check** = check that data has been correctly transmitted down a line by returning the data to the transmitter **Schleifenprüfung; loop counter** = register that contains the number of times a loop has been repeated **Schleifenzähler; loop program** = sequence of instructions that are repeated until a condition is met **Schleifenprogramm**
(b) (i) long piece of tape with the two ends

joined; (ii) communications channel that is passed via all receivers and is terminated where it started from (i) **Schlaufe**; (ii) **Schleife; loop film** = endless piece of magnetic *or* photographic film that plays continuously **Endlosfilm**
(c) length of wire coiled in the shape of a circle **Schlinge; loop antenna** = aerial in the shape of a circle **Rahmenantenne; loop network** = communications network that consists of a ring of cable joining all terminals **Ringnetz**
2 *verb* to make a piece of wire *or* tape into a circle **eine Schlinge machen; looping program** = computer program that runs continuously **Schleifenprogramm**

lose *verb* not to have something any more **verlieren**; *we have lost the signal in the noise; all the current files were lost when the system crashed and we had no backup copies;* **lost call** = telephone call that cannot be established **Verlustbelegung; lost cluster** = number of sectors on a disk whose identification bits have been corrupted; the operating system has marked this area of disk as being used by a file, but the data they contain can no longer be identified with a particular file **verlorene Zuordnungseinheit, verlorenes Cluster; lost time** = period of a transmitted facsimile signal when the image is being scanned, that contains no image data **Verlustzeit**

◊ **loss** *noun* the power of a signal that is lost when passing through a circuit **Dämpfung; Verlust**

Lotus ™ software company best known for its spreadsheet program, 1-2-3 ™ **Lotus** ™

loudness *noun* volume of a signal which you can hear **Lautstärke**

loudspeaker *noun* electromagnetic device that converts electrical signals into audible noise **Lautsprecher**

low end *noun* hardware *or* software that is not very powerful or sophisticated and is designed for beginners **Low-End**

◊ **lower case** *noun* small characters (such as a, b, c, as opposed to upper case A, B, C) **Kleinbuchstaben**

◊ **low frequency (LF)** *noun* range of audio frequencies between 5-300Hz *or* range of radio frequencies between 30-300kHz **Niederfrequenz**

◊ **low-level format** *noun* process that

defines the physical pattern and arrangement of tracks and sectors on a disk **Low-Level-Formatierung**

◊ **low-level language (LLL)** *noun* programming language similar to assembler and in which each instruction has a single equivalent machine code instruction (the language is particular to one system *or* computer) **niedere Programmiersprache;** *see also* HIGH-LEVEL LANGUAGE

◊ **low-memory** *noun* (in a PC) memory locations up to 640Kb **niedriger Speicherbereich;** *compare* HIGH MEMORY

◊ **low-order digit** *noun* digit in the position within a number that represents the lowest weighting of the number base **niederwertige Ziffer;** *the number 234156 has a low-order digit of 6*

◊ **low pass filter** *noun* electronic circuit that blocks signals above a certain frequency **Durchgangsfilter für niedrige Frequenzen**

◊ **low-priority work** *noun* task which is not particularly important **Aufgabe niedriger Priorität**

◊ **low-resolution graphics** *or* **low-res graphics** *noun* ability to display character-sized graphic blocks *or* preset shapes on a screen rather than using individual pixels **Grafik mit niedriger Auflösung;** *compare* HIGH-RESOLUTION

◊ **low speed communications** *noun* data transmission at less than 2400 bits per second **normale Übertragungsgeschwindigkeit**

LPM = LINES PER MINUTE

LPT1 (in a PC) name given to the first, main parallel printer port in the system **LPT1**

LQ = LETTER QUALITY

LRU = LEAST RECENTLY USED ALGORITHM *noun* algorithm which finds the page of memory that was last accessed before any other, and erases it to make room for another page **LRU-Algorithmus**

LSB = LEAST SIGNIFICANT BIT binary digit occupying the right hand position of a word and carrying the least power of two in the word, usually equal to two raised to zero = 1 **niederwertigstes Bit**

LSD = LEAST SIGNIFICANT DIGIT digit

which occupies the right hand position in a number and so carries least power (equal to the number radix raised to zero = 1) **niederwertigste Ziffer**

LSI = LARGE SCALE INTEGRATION system with between 500 and 10,000 circuits on a single IC **LSI (Großintegration)**

luggable *noun* *(informal)* personal computer that is just about portable and usually will not run off batteries (it is much heavier and less compact than a lap-top or true transportable machine) **Koffercomputer**

lumen *noun* SI unit of illumination, defined as the amount of flux emitted from a candela into an angle of one steradion **Lumen** ⇨APPENDIX

luminance *noun* amount of light radiated from a source **Leuchtdichte; luminance signal** = part of television signal providing luminance data **Leuchtdichtsignal**

LUT =LOOK-UP TABLE

QUOTE an image processing system can have three LUTs that map the image memory to the display device
Byte

lux *noun* SI unit of measurement of one lumen per square metre **Lux** ⇨APPENDIX

Mm

m *prefix* = MILLI one thousandth **m**

◊ **mA** = MILLIAMPERE electrical current measure equal to one thousandth of an ampere **mA**

M *prefix* = MEGA
(a) one million **M; Mbps** = MEGA BITS PER SECOND number of million bits transmitted every second **Mbps; MFLOPS** = MEGA FLOATING POINT OPERATIONS PER SECOND measure of computing power and speed, equal to one million floating point operations per second **Millionen Fließkommaoperationen pro Sekunde (MFLOPS)**
(b) symbol for 1,048,576, used only in computer and electronic related

applications, equal to 2^{20} **M; Mbyte (MB)** = measurement of mass storage equal to 1,048,576 bytes **Mbyte (MB)**; *the latest model has a 30Mbyte hard disk*

MAC
(a) = MULTIPLEXED ANALOG COMPONENTS standard television broadcast signal format **MAC**
(b) = MESSAGE AUTHENTICATION CODE special code transmitted at the same time as a message as proof of its authenticity **Nachrichtenberechtigungscode**

◊ **Mac** *see* Macintosh

◊ **MacBinary** ™ *noun* file storage and transfer system that allows Macintosh files, together with their icons and long file names, to be stored on other computer systems **MacBinary** ™

machine *noun*
(a) number of separate moving parts *or* components, acting together to carry out a process **Maschine; copying machine** *or* **duplicating machine** = machine which makes copies of documents **Kopiergerät; dictating machine** = recording machine which records what someone dictates, so that the text can be typed **Diktiergerät; machine proof** = proof of sheets of a book, taken from the printing machine **Maschinenabzug**
(b) computer *or* system *or* processor made of various components connected together to provide a function *or* perform a task **Computer; clean machine** = computer that contains only the minimum of ROM based code to boot its system from disk, any languages required must be loaded separately **Computer mit minimalem ROM-basiertem Code; source machine** = computer which can compile source code **Quellcomputer, Sourcecomputer; virtual machine** = simulated machine and its operations **virtuelle Maschine; machine address** = number *or* absolute address which specifies the point in memory where a data word can be found and accessed **Maschinenadresse, absolute Adresse; machine check** = fault caused by equipment failure **Maschinenprüfung; machine code** *or* **machine language** = programming language that consists of commands in binary code that can be directly understood by the central processing unit without the need for translation **Maschinencode; Maschinensprache; machine code format** = a machine code instruction is usually made up of 1, 2 or 3 bytes for operand, data and address **Maschinencodeformat; machine code**

instruction = instruction that directly controls the CPU and is recognized without the need for translation **Maschinencodebefehl; machine cycle** = minimum period of time taken by the CPU for the execution of an instruction **Maschinenzyklus; machine dependent** = not standardized *or* which cannot be used on hardware *or* software from a different manufacturer without modifications **maschinenabhängig; machine equation** = formula which an analog computer has been programmed to solve **Maschinengleichung; machine error** = error caused by a hardware malfunction **Hardwarefehler, Maschinenfehler; machine independent** = (computer software) that can be run on any computer system **maschinenunabhängig; machine independent language** = programming language that can be translated and executed on any computer that has a suitable compiler **maschinenunabhängige Programmiersprache; machine instruction** = an instruction which can be recognized by a machine and is part of its limited set of commands **Maschinenbefehl; machine intelligence** = the design of computer programs and devices that attempt to imitate human intelligence and decision-making functions, providing basic reasoning and other human characteristics **künstliche Intelligenz; machine intimate** = software that operates and interacts closely with the hardware in a system **hardwarenah; machine language** = (i) the way in which machine code is written; (ii) MACHINE CODE (i) **Maschinensprache;** (ii) **Maschinencode; machine language compile** = to generate a machine code program from a HLL program by translating and assembling each HLL instruction **die Maschinensprache umsetzen; machine language programming** = slowest and most complex method of programming a CPU, but the fastest in execution, achieved by entering directly into RAM or ROM the binary representation for the machine code instructions to be carried out (rather than using an assembler with assembly language programs *or* a compiler with HLL programs) **Programmieren in Maschinensprache; machine-readable** = (commands *or* data) stored on a medium that can be directly input to the computer **maschinenlesbar;** *the disk stores data in machine-readable form;* **machine run** = action of processing instructions in a program by a computer **Computerlauf; machine translation** = computer system that is used to translate text and commands from one language and syntax to another **Maschinenübersetzung**; **machine word** = number of bits of data operated on simultaneously by a CPU in one machine cycle, often 8, 16 or 32 bits **Maschinenwort**

◊ **machinery** *noun* machines **Maschinerie** NOTE: no plural

◊ **machining** *noun* making a product using a machine; printing the sheets of a book **maschinelle Fertigung; Druckgang**

◊ **machinist** *noun* person who works a machine **Maschinist/-in**

Macintosh ™ *noun* range of personal computers designed by Apple Corporation; the Macintosh uses the Motorola family of processors, the 68000, and offers similar computing power to a PC. The Macintosh is best known for its graphical user interface which allows a user to control the computer using icons and a mouse. **Macintosh** ™; *Macintosh computers are not compatible with an IBM PC unless you use special emulation software*

macro- *prefix* very large *or* applying to the whole system **Makro-**

◊ **macro** *noun* program routine *or* block of instructions identified by a single word *or* label **Makro**; **macro assembler** *or* **assembly program** = assembler program that is able to decode macro instructions **Makroassemblierer**; **macro call** = use of a label in an assembly language program to indicate to an assembler that the macro routine is to be inserted at that point **Makroaufruf**; **macro code** *or* **macro command** *or* **macro instruction** = one word that is used to represent a number of instructions, simplifying program writing **Makrobefehl**; **macro definition** = description (in a program *or* to the operating system) of the structure, function and instructions that make up a macro operation **Makrodefinition**; **macro expansion** = process in which a macro call is replaced with the instructions in the macro **Makroauflösung**; **macro flowchart** = graphical representation of the logical steps, stages and actions within a routine **Makroflussdiagramm**; **macro language** = programming language that allows the programmer to define and use macro instructions **Makrosprache**; **macro programming** = writing a program using macro instructions *or* defining macro instructions **Makroprogrammierung**

◊ **macroelement** *noun* number of data items treated as one element **Makroelement**

◊ **macroinstruction** *noun* one programming instruction that refers to a number of instructions within a routine *or* macro **Makrobefehl**

> QUOTE Microsoft has released a developer's kit for its Word 6.0 for Windows word-processing package. The 900-page kit explains how to use the WordBasic macro language supplied with the software
>
> *Computing*

magazine *noun* (a) paper, usually with illustrations which comes out regularly, every month or every week **Zeitschrift**; *a weekly magazine; he edits a computer magazine* (b) number of pages in a videotext system **Magazin** (c) container for photographic film **Magazin**

magnet *noun* something that produces a magnetic field **Magnet**

◊ **magnetic** *adjective* which has a magnetic field associated with it **magnetisch**; **magnetic bubble memory** = method of storing large amounts of binary data as small magnetized areas in the medium (made of certain pure materials) **Magnetblasenspeicher**; **magnetic card** = plastic card with a strip of magnetic recording material on its surface, allowing data to be stored (used in automatic cash dispensers) **Magnetkarte**; **magnetic card reader** *or* **magnetic strip reader** = machine that can read data stored on a magnetic card **Magnetkartenleser; Magnetstreifenleser**; **magnetic cartridge** *or* **cassette** = small box containing a reel of magnetic tape and a pick up reel **Magnetbandkassette**; **magnetic cell** = small piece of material whose magnetic field can be altered to represent the two states of binary data **Magnetzelle**; **magnetic core** = early main memory system for storing data in the first types of computer, each bit of data was stored in a magnetic cell **Magnetkern**; **magnetic disk** = flat circular piece of material coated with a substance, allowing signals and data to be stored magnetically **Magnetplatte**; *see also* FLOPPY DISK, HARD DISK; **magnetic disk unit** = computer peripheral made up of a disk drive and necessary control electronics **Magnetplatteneinheit**; **magnetic drum** = computer data storage peripheral that uses a coated cylinder to store data magnetically(not often used now) **Magnettrommelspeicher**; **magnetic encoding** = storage of (binary) data signals on a magnetic medium **magnetische Codierung**; **magnetic field** = description of the polarity and strength of magnetic effects at a point **Magnetfeld; magnetic flux** = measure of magnetic field strength per unit area **magnetischer Fluss; magnetic focusing** = use of magnetic field to focus a beam of electrons (in a television) **magnetische Fokussierung; magnetic head** = electromagnetic component that converts electrical signals into a magnetic field, allowing them to be stored on a magnetic medium **Magnetkopf; magnetic ink** = printing ink that contains a magnetic material, used in some character recognition systems **Magnettinte; magnetic ink character recognition (MICR)** = system that identifies characters by sensing the magnetic ink patterns (as used on bank cheques) **Magnetschriftzeichenerkennung; magnetic master** = original version of a recorded tape *or* disk **Original; magnetic material** *or* **medium** = substance that will retain a magnetic flux pattern after a magnetic field is removed **Magnetträger; magnetic media** = magnetic materials used to store signals, such as disk, tape, etc. **magnetische Medien; magnetic memory** *or* **store** = storage that uses a medium that can store data bits as magnetic field changes **Magnetspeicher; magnetic recording** = transferring an electrical signal onto a moving magnetic tape *or* disk by means of a magnetic field generated by a magnetic head **magnetische Aufzeichnung; magnetic screen** = metal screen used to prevent stray magnetic fields affecting electronic components **Magnetschirm; magnetic storm** = disturbance in the earth's magnetic fields affecting radio and cable communications **(erd)magnetischer Sturm; magnetic strip** = layer of magnetic material on the surface of a plastic card, used for recording data **Magnetstreifen; magnetic thin film storage** = high-speed access RAM device using a matrix of magnetic cells and a matrix of read/write heads to access them **Dünnschichtspeicher; magnetic transfer** = copy signals stored on one type of magnetic medium to another **magnetische Übertragung**

◊ **magnetic tape** *noun* narrow length of thin plastic coated with a magnetic material used to store signals magnetically **Magnetband; magnetic tape cartridge** *or* **cassette** = small box containing a reel of magnetic tape and a pick up reel, used in a cassette player *or* tape drive **Magnetbandkassette; magnetic tape encoder** = device that directly writes data entered at a keyboard onto magnetic tape

Magnetbandcodierer; magnetic tape reader = machine that can read signals stored on magnetic tape and convert them to an electrical form that can be understood by a computer **Magnetbandleser; magnetic tape recorder** = device with a magnetic head, motor and circuitry to allow electrical signals to be recorded onto *or* played back from a magnetic tape **Magnetbandgerät; magnetic tape transport** = computer-controlled magnetic tape drive mechanism **Magnetbandtransport**

◊ **magnetize** *verb* to convert a material *or* object into a magnet **magnetisieren**

COMMENT: magnetic tape is available on spools of between 200 and 800 metres. The tape is magnetized by the read/write head. Tape is a storage medium which only allows serial access, that is, all the tape has to be read until the required location is found (as opposed to disk storage, which can be accessed randomly)

◊ **magneto-optical disc** *noun* optical disc that is used in a magneto-optical recording device **magnetooptische Platte**

◊ **magneto-optical recording** *noun* storage media that uses an optical disc **magnetooptische Speicherung, magnetooptische Aufzeichnung**

COMMENT: the optical disk has a thin layer of magnetic film which is heated by a laser, the particles are then polarised by a weak magnetic field. Magneto-optical media has very high capacity (over 600Mb) and is re-writable

magnify *verb* to make something appear larger **vergrößern;** *the photograph has been magnified 200 times*

◊ **magnification** *noun* amount by which something has been made to appear larger **Vergrößerung;** *the lens gives a magnification of 10 times*

magnitude *noun* level *or* strength of a signal *or* variable **Ausmaß; signal magnitude** = strength of an electrical current and voltage *or* power signal **Signalgröße**

mag tape *noun informal* = MAGNETIC TAPE

mail
1 *noun*
(a) system of sending letters and parcels from one place to another **Post**
(b) letters sent *or* received **Post**
(c) electronic messages to and from users of a bulletin board *or* network **Post; electronic mail** *or* **email** *or* **e-mail** = messages sent

between users of a bulletin board *or* interconnecting network **elektronische Post, E-Mail; mail-enabled** = application that has access to an electronic mail system without leaving the application **mit E-Mail-Anbindung;** *this word-processor is mail-enabled - you can send messages to other users from within it*

2 *verb* to send something by post **mit der Post schicken;** *to mail a letter; we mailed our order last Wednesday*

◊ **mailbox** *or* **mail box** *noun* electronic storage space with an address in which a user's incoming messages are stored **Briefkasten**

◊ **mailing** *noun* sending something using the post **Verschicken;** *the mailing of publicity material;* **direct mailing** = sending of publicity material by post to possible buyers **Direktwerbung; mailing list** = list of names and addresses of people who might be interested in a product *or* list of names and addresses of members of a society **Adressliste;** *his name is on our mailing list; to build up a mailing list;* **to buy a mailing list** = to pay a society, etc. money to buy the list of members so that you can use it to mail publicity material **eine Adressliste erwerben; mailing piece** = leaflet suitable for sending by direct mail **Postwurfsendung, Mailer; mailing shot** = leaflets sent by mail to possible customers **Rundschreiben, Briefwerbeaktion**

◊ **mail-merge** *noun* word-processing program which allows a standard form letter to be printed out to a series of different names and addresses **Mailmerge**

QUOTE Spreadsheet views for data and graphical forms for data entry have been added to the Q&A database, with the traditional reporting, mailmerge, and labels improved through Windows facilities

Computing

main *adjective* most important **Haupt-; main beam** = direction of the central most powerful region of an antenna's transmission pattern **Hauptstrahl; main body (of a program)** = set of instructions that form the main part of a program and from which other subroutines are called **Hauptprogrammteil; main clock** = clock signal that synchronizes all the components in a system **Haupttaktgeber; main distributing frame** = racks of termination circuits for the cables in a telephone network **Hauptverteiler; main entry** = entry in a catalogue under which is contained the

most important information about the document **Haupteintrag; main index** = more general index that directs the user gradually to more specific index areas **Generalindex; main loop (of a program)** = series of instructions performed repeatedly that carry out the main action of a program; this loop is often used to wait for user input before processing the event **Hauptprogrammschleife; main memory** *or* **main storage** = fast access RAM whose locations can be directly and immediately addressed by the CPU **Hauptspeicher;** *the 16-bit system includes up to 3Mb of main memory;* **main routine** = section of instructions that make up the main part of a program (a program often consists of a main routine and several subroutines, which are called from the main routine) **Hauptprogramm**

◊ **mainframe (computer)** *noun* large-scale high power computer system that can handle high capacity memory and backing storage devices as well as a number of operators simultaneously **Großrechner; mainframe access** = using microcomputers to access a mainframe computer **Großrechnerzugang**

mains electricity *noun* normal domestic electricity supply to consumers **öffentliches Versorgungsnetz**

COMMENT: in UK this is 240 volts at 50Hz; in the USA, it is 120 volts at 60Hz

maintain *verb* to ensure a system is in good condition and functioning correctly **warten; well maintained** = well looked after **gut gewartet**

◊ **maintainability** *noun* the ability to have repairs carried out quickly and efficiently if a failure occurs **Wartbarkeit**

◊ **maintenance** *noun* (i) keeping a machine in good working condition; (ii) tasks carried out in order to keep a system running, such as repairing faults, replacing components, etc. (i) **Instandhaltung;** (ii) **Wartung; file maintenance** = process of updating a file by changing *or* adding *or* deleting entries **Dateiwartung; preventive maintenance** = regular inspection and cleaning of a system to prevent faults occurring **vorbeugende Wartung; maintenance contract** = arrangement with a repair company that provides regular checks and special repair prices in the event of a fault **Wartungsvertrag; maintenance release** = program revision that corrects a minor problem or bug but does not offer any major new features **Bugfix, überarbeitete Version;** *the maintenance release of the database program, version 2.01, corrects the problem with the margins;* **maintenance routine** = software diagnostic tool used by an engineer during preventative maintenance operations **Wartungsroutine**

major cycle *noun* minimum access time of a mechanical storage device **Hauptzyklus**

majuscule *noun* capital letter **Großbuchstabe, Majuskel**

make-ready time *noun* time taken by a printer to prepare the machines and film for printing **Vorbereitungs-, Zurichtungszeit**

◊ **make up** *verb* to arrange type into the correct page formats before printing **umbrechen**

◊ **make up** *or* **makeup** *noun* arrangement and layout of type into correct page formats before printing **Umbruch;** *corrections after the page makeup are very expensive*

male connector *noun* plug with conducting pins that can be inserted into a female connector to provide an electrical connection **Stecker**

malfunction
1 *noun (of hardware or software)* not working correctly **Störung;** *the data was lost due to a software malfunction;* **malfunction routine** = software routine used to find and help diagnose the cause of an error or fault **Fehlererkennungsroutine**
2 *verb* not to work properly **nicht richtig funktionieren;** *some of the keys on the keyboard have started to malfunction*

◊ **malfunctioning** *noun* not working properly **Störung**

MAN = METROPOLITAN AREA NETWORK network extending over a limited area (normally a city) **MAN;** *compare* LAN, WAN

man-machine interface (MMI) *noun* hardware and software designed to make it easier for users to communicate effectively with a machine **Mensch-Maschine-Schnittstelle**

◊ **man-made** *adjective* not natural, produced by man **künstlich; man-made noise** = electrical interference caused by machines *or* motors **technische Funktionsstörung;** *compare* GALACTIC NOISE

manage *verb* to direct *or* to be in charge of **leiten**

◊ **manageable** *adjective* which can be dealt with easily **zu bewältigen;** *processing problems which are still manageable; the problems are too large to be manageable; data should be split into manageable files*

◊ **management** *noun* directing *or* organizing (work *or* a business) **Leitung, Verwaltung; network management** = organization, planning, running and upkeep of a network **Netzführung; product management** = directing the making and selling of a product as an independent item **Produktmanagement; management training** = training managers by making them study problems and work out ways of solving them **Managementtraining** NOTE: no plural

◊ **management information service (MIS)** *noun* department within a company that is responsible for information and data processing; in practice, this department is often responsible for the computer system in a company **Management Information Service (MIS)**

◊ **management information system (MIS)** *noun* software that allows managers in a company to access and analyse data **Management-Informationssystem, Management Information System (MIS)**

◊ **manager** *noun*
(a) user-friendly front end software that allows easy access to operating system commands **benutzerfreundliche Eingangssoftware; file manager** = section of a disk operating system that allocates disk space to files, keeping track of the file sections (if it has to be split) and their sector addresses **Dateimanager; queue manager** = software which orders tasks waiting to be processed **Warteschlangenverwaltung; records manager** = program which maintains records and can access and process them **Satzverwaltungssystem; text manager** = facilities that allow text to be written, stored, retrieved, edited and printed **Textverwaltungssystem**
(b) head of a department in a company **Leiter/-in;** *a department manager; data processing manager; production manager*

◊ **managerial** *adjective* referring to managers **Management-;** *managerial staff*

Manchester coding *noun* method of encoding data and timing signals that is used in communications; the first half of the bit period indicates the value of the bit (1 or 0) and the second half is used as a timing signal **Richtungstaktschrift**

Mandlebrot set *noun* mathematical equation that is called recursively to generate a set of values; when plotted these form a fractal image **Mandlebrot-Gleichung;** *see also* FRACTAL

manipulate *verb* to move, edit and change text *or* data **bearbeiten;** *an image processor that captures, displays and manipulates video images*

◊ **manipulation** *noun* moving *or* editing *or* changing text *or* data **Bearbeitung;** *the high-speed database management program allows the manipulation of very large amounts of data*

mantissa *noun* fractional part of a number **Mantisse;** *the mantissa of the number 45.897 is 0.897*

manual
1 *noun* document containing instructions about the operation of a system *or* piece of software **Handbuch;** *the manual is included with the system;* **installation manual** = booklet showing how a system should be installed **Installationshandbuch; instruction manual** = document describing how to use a system *or* software **Handbuch mit Anweisungen; user's manual** = booklet showing how a device *or* system should be used **Benutzerhandbuch**
2 *adjective* (work) done by hand; (process) carried out by the operator without the help of a machine **manuell, von Hand; manual data processing** = sorting and processing information without the help of a computer **manuelle Datenverarbeitung; manual entry** *or* **manual input** = act of entering data into a computer, by an operator via a keyboard **Eingeben von Hand**

◊ **manually** *adverb* done by hand, not automatically **manuell, von Hand;** *the paper has to be fed into the printer manually*

manufacture *verb* to make in a factory **herstellen;** *the company manufactures diskettes and magnetic tape*

◊ **manufacturer** *noun* company which manufactures a product **Hersteller;** *if the system develops a fault it should be returned to the manufacturer for checking; the manufacturer guarantees the system for 12 months*

manuscript *or* **MS** *noun* original draft copy of a book written *or* typed by the author **Manuskript;** *this manuscript was all written on computer*

map
1 *noun* diagram representing the internal layout of a computer's memory *or* communications regions **Abbild, Map; memory map** = diagram indicating the allocation of address ranges to various memory devices, such as RAM, ROM and memory-mapped input/output devices **Hauptspeicherabbild**
2 *verb* to retrieve data and display it as a map **abbilden; database mapping** = description of the way in which the records and fields in a database are related **Datenbankaufgliederung; I/O mapping** = method of assigning a special address to each (I/O) port in a microcomputer rather than a memory location **Ein-/Ausgabeadressierung; to map out** = to draw *or* set down the basic way in which something should be done **entwerfen; memory-mapped** = with addresses allocated to a computer's input *or* output devices to allow them to be accessed as if they were a memory location **speicherorientiert;** *a memory-mapped screen has an address allocated to each pixel, allowing direct access to the screen by the CPU;* **memory-mapped I/O** *or* **memory-mapped input/output** = an I/O port which can be accessed as if it were a memory location within the CPU's normal address range **speicherorientierte Ein-/Ausgabe;** *see also* BIT-MAP, BIT-MAPPED

MAR = MEMORY ADDRESS REGISTER register within the CPU that contains the next location to be accessed **Speicheradressregister**

marching display *noun* display device that contains a buffer to show the last few characters entered **wandernde Anzeige**

margin *noun*
(a) blank space around a section of printed text **Rand;** *when typing the contract leave wide margins; the left margin and right margin are the two sections of blank paper on either side of the page;* **to set the margin** = to define the size of a margin **den Rand setzen**
(b) extra time *or* space **Spielraum; safety margin** = time *or* space allowed for something to be safe **Sicherheitsspielraum; margin of error** = number of mistakes which are accepted in a document *or* in a calculation **Fehlerspanne**

◊ **margination** *noun* giving margins to a printed page **Marginierung, Umrandung**

mark
1 *noun*
(a) sign put on a page to show something **Zeichen; proof correction marks** = special marks used to show changes to a proof **Korrekturzeichen**
(b) transmitted signal that represents a logical one *or* true condition **Marke; mark hold** = continuously transmitted mark signal that indicates there are no messages on the network **Freizeichensignal; mark space** = two-state transmission code using a mark and a space (without a mark) as signals **Code bestehend aus einem Zeichen und einem Abstand**
2 *verb* to put a mark on something **kennzeichnen, markieren; mark block** = to put a block marker at the beginning and end of a block of text **Blockmarkierungszeichen setzen; marking interval** = time when a mark signal is being carried out **Markierungszeit; mark sense** = to write characters with conductive *or* magnetic ink so that they are then machine readable **für Zeichenabfühlung lesbar machen; mark sense device** *or* **reader** = device that reads data from special cards containing conductive *or* magnetic marks **Markierungsleser; mark sensing card** = preprinted card with spaces for mark sense characters **Zeichenlochkarte**

◊ **marker** *noun*
(a) marker pen = coloured pen used to indicate *or* highlight sections of text **Markierstift, Textmarker**
(b) code inserted in a file *or* text to indicate a special section **Markierung; block markers** = two markers inserted at the start and finish of a section of data *or* text to indicate a special block which can then be moved *or* deleted *or* copied as a single unit **Blockmarkierungszeichen; field marker** = code used to indicate the end of one field and the start of the next **Feldmarkierungszeichen; word marker** = symbol indicating the start of a word in a variable word length machine **Wortmarkierungszeichen**

◊ **mark up** *verb* to prepare copy for the compositor to set, by showing on the copy the typeface to be used, the line width, and other typesetting instructions **Satzanweisungen machen, auszeichnen**

MASER = **MICROWAVE AMPLIFICATION BY STIMULATED EMISSION OF RADIATION** low noise amplifier, formerly used for microwave signals from satellites **Maser**

mask
1 *noun*
(a) integrated circuit layout stencil that is used to define the pattern to be etched *or* doped onto a slice of semiconductor **Schablone;** *a mask or stencil is used to transfer the transistor design onto silicon*
(b) photographic device used to prevent light reaching selected areas of the film **Maske**
(c) pattern of binary digits used to select various bits from a binary word (a one in the mask retains that bit in the word) **Maske; mask bit** = one bit used to select the required bit from a word *or* string **Maskenbit; mask register** = storage location in a computer that contains the pattern of bits used as a mask **Maskenregister; interrupt mask** = data word in a computer that selects which interrupt lines are to be activated **Abbruchmaske**
2 *verb* to cover an area of (something) with (something) **maskieren; masked ROM** = read-only memory device that is programmed during manufacture, by depositing metal onto selected regions dictated by the shape of a mask **maskierter Festspeicher**

◊ **maskable** *adjective* which can be masked **maskierbar; maskable interrupt** = interrupt which can be activated by using an interrupt mask **maskierbare Unterbrechung; non-maskable interrupt (NMI)** = high priority interrupt signal that cannot be deactivated **nichtmaskierbare Unterbrechung (mit höchster Priorität)**

◊ **masking** *noun* operation used to select various bits in a word **Maskierung**

QUOTE the device features a maskable interrupt feature which reduces CPU overheads
Electronics & Power

mass media *noun* media which aim to reach a large public (such as television, radio, mass-market newspapers) **Massenmedien**

◊ **mass storage** *noun* storage and retrieval of large amounts of data **Massenspeicher; mass storage device** = computer backing store device that is able to store large amounts of data **Massenspeichereinheit;** *the hard disk is definitely a mass storage device;* **mass storage system** = data storage system that can hold more than one million million bits of data **Massenspeichersystem**

mast *noun* radio mast *or* TV mast = tall structure used to position an aerial above natural obstacles (such as houses, hills, etc.) **Mast**

master

1 *adjective (& noun)* main *or* most important **Haupt-, Leit-, Original-, Stamm-;** *the master computer controls everything else;* **master antenna television system (MATV)** = single main receiving antenna that provides television signals to a number of nearby receivers **Gemeinschaftsantennenanlage; master card** = first punched card in a pack that provides information about the rest of the pack **Leitkarte; master clock** = timing signal to which all components in a system are synchronized **Haupttaktgeber; master computer** = computer in a multiprocessor system that controls the other processors and allocates jobs, etc. **Hauptrechner; master control program (MCP)** = software that controls the operations in a system **Steuerprogramm; master data** = reference data which is stored in a master file **Leitdaten; master disk** = (i) disk containing all the files for a task; (ii) disk containing the code for a computer's operating system that must be loaded before the system will operate (i) **Hauptplatte;** (ii) **Betriebssystemplatte; master file** = set of all the reference data required for an application, which is updated periodically **Stammdatei; master/master computer system** = system in which each processor is a master, dedicated to one task **Leitrechner(system); master program file** = magnetic medium which contains all the programs required for an application **Hauptprogrammdatei; master proof** = final proof of a section of text before it is printed **Korrekturbogen mit Pressrevision; master/slave computer system** = system with a master controlling computer and a slave that takes commands from the master **Computersystem, in dem der eine dem anderen übergeordnet ist; master tape** = magnetic tape which contains all the vital operating system routines, loaded once when the computer is switched on (by the initial program loader) **System-Urband; master terminal** = one terminal in a network that has priority over any other, used by the system manager to set up the system *or* carry out privileged commands **Hauptbedienerstation; image master** = data describing fonts and character shapes in a phototypesetter **Imagemaster**
2 *verb* to learn and understand a language *or* process **beherrschen;** *we mastered the new word-processor quite quickly; the user-friendly package is easier to master*

match *verb*
(a) to search through a database for a similar piece of information **vergleichen**
(b) to set a register *or* electrical impedance equal to another **abgleichen; matched load** = impedance of the same value as the cable across which it is connected, so minimizing signal reflections **angepasste Belastung; matching transformer** = transformer used to connect and match two lines of differing impedance, while isolating them electrically **Anpassungstransformator; impedance matching** = means of making the best signal power transfer between two circuits by making sure that their output and input impedances are the same **Scheinwiderstandsanpassung**

material *noun*
(a) substance which can be used to make a finished product **Material;** *gold is the ideal material for electrical connections;* **synthetic materials** = substances made as products of a chemical process **Kunststoffe; materials control** = system to check that a company has enough materials in stock to do its work **Materialsteuerung; materials handling** = storing and moving materials from one part of a factory to another in an efficient way **innerbetriebliches Transport- und Lagerwesen**
(b) display material = posters, photographs, etc., which can be used to attract attention to goods which are for sale **Ausstellungsmaterial**

mathematics *noun* study of the relationship between numbers, their manipulation and organization to (logically) prove facts and theories **Mathematik;** *see also* ALGEBRA

◊ **mathematical** *adjective* referring to mathematics **mathematisch; mathematical model** = representation of a system using mathematical ideas and formulae **mathematisches Modell; mathematical subroutines** = library routines that carry out standard mathematical functions, such as square root, logarithm, cosine, sine, etc. **mathematische Unterprogramme**

◊ **maths** *or (US)* **math** *informal* = MATHEMATICS; **maths chip** *or* **coprocessor** = dedicated IC that can be added to a system to carry out mathematical functions far more rapidly than a standard CPU, speeding up the execution of a program **mathematischer Zusatzprozessor**

matrix *noun*
(a) array of numbers *or* data items arranged in rows and columns **Matrix; matrix rotation** = swapping the rows with the columns in an array (equal to rotating by 90 degrees) **Matrixdrehung**
(b) array of connections between logic gates providing a number of possible logical functions **Matrix; key matrix** = way in which the keys of a keyboard are arranged as an array of connections **Schlüsselmatrix**
(c) pattern of the dots that make up a character on a computer screen *or* dot-matrix *or* laser printer **Matrix; matrix printer** *or* **dot-matrix printer** = printer in which the characters are made up by a series of dots printed close together, producing a page line by line; a dot-matrix printer can be used either for printing using a ribbon or for thermal *or* electrostatic printing **Matrixdrucker; character matrix** = pattern of dots that makes up a displayed character **Zeichenmatrix**

matt *or* **matte**
1 *noun*
(a) addition of an image onto a film of a background **Aufprojektion, Mattaufnahme**
(b) mask used to prevent light reaching certain areas on a film **Lichthofschutzschicht**
2 *adjective* (print) which is not shiny **matt**

matter *noun*
(a) question *or* problem to be discussed **Angelegenheit, Sache, Thema; it is a matter of concern to the members of the committee** = the members of the committee are worried about it **es ist eine Angelegenheit, die den Mitgliedern des Komittees Sorge macht;** *the most important matter on the agenda; we shall consider first the matter of last month's fall in prices*
(b) main section of text on a page as opposed to titles *or* headlines **Satzspiegel, Text; printed matter** = printed books, newspapers, publicity sheets, etc. **Drucksache; publicity matter** = sheets *or* posters *or* leaflets used for publicity **Werbematerial**
NOTE: no plural for (b)

MATV = MASTER ANTENNA TELEVISION SYSTEM

maximize *verb* (in MS-Windows) to expand an application icon back to its original display window **als Vollbild darstellen, maximieren;** *compare* MINIMIZE

COMMENT: you maximize a window by clicking once on the up arrow in the top right hand corner

maximum *adjective & noun* highest value used *or* which is allowed **maximal, Höchst-, höchst-; Maximum; maximum capacity** = greatest amount of data that can be stored **Höchstleistungsgrenze; maximum reading** = greatest signal magnitude recorded **Vollaussteuerung; maximum transmission rate** = greatest number of data that can be transmitted every second **höchste Übertragungsgeschwindigkeit; maximum usable frequency** = highest signal frequency which can be used in a circuit without distortion **höchste Nutzfrequenz; maximum users** = greatest number of users that a system can support at any one time **höchstmögliche Benutzerzahl**

Mb = MEGABIT equal to 1,048,576 bits of storage, equal to 131,072 bytes **M-Bit; Mbps** = MEGA BITS PER SECOND

MB *or* **Mbyte** = MEGABYTE equal to 1,048,576 bytes of storage, equal to 2^{20} bytes **MB, Megabyte**

QUOTE the maximum storage capacity is restricted to 8 Mbytes
Micro Decision

MBR = MEMORY BUFFER REGISTER register in a CPU that temporarily buffers all inputs and outputs **Speicherpufferregister**

mC = MILLICOULOMB

MCA = MICROCHANNEL ARCHITECTURE design of the expansion bus within IBM's PS/2 range of personal computers that has taken over from the older ISA/AT bus; MCA is a 32-bit bus that supports bus master devices **MCA; MCA chipset** = number of electronic components required to manage the timing and data signals over an MCA expansion bus **MCA-Chipset, MCA-Chipsatz**

MCGA = MULTICOLOR GRAPHICS ADAPTER colour graphics adapter standard fitted in low-end IBM PS/2 computers **MCGA**

MCP = MASTER CONTROL PROGRAM

MD *or* **MKDIR** = MAKE DIRECTORY DOS command used to create a new directory on a disk **MD** *or* **MKDIR**

MDA = MONOCHROME DISPLAY ADAPTER video adapter standard used in early PC systems that could display text in 25 lines of 80 columns **MDA**

MDR = MEMORY DATA REGISTER register in a CPU that holds data before it is processed *or* moved to a memory location **Speicherdatenregister**

mean
1 *noun & adjective* average value of a set of numbers *or* values **Mittelwert, Durchschnitt; Mittel-, mittlere(r,s), durchschnittlich; mean time between failures (MTBF)** = average period of time that a piece of equipment will operate between failures **mittlerer Ausfallabstand; mean time to failure (MTF)** = average period of time for which a device will operate (usually continuously) before failing **mittlere Lebensdauer; mean time to repair** = average period of time required to repair a faulty piece of equipment **mittlere Reparaturdauer**
2 *verb* to signify something **bedeuten**; *the message DISK FULL means that there is no more room on the disk for further data*

measure
1 *noun*
(a) way of calculating size *or* quantity **Maß; square measure** = area in square feet *or* metres, calculated by multiplying width and length **Flächenmaß**
(b) tape measure = long tape with centimetres *or* inches marked on it, used to measure how long something is **Bandmaß**
(c) total width of a printed line of text (shown in picas) **Satzbreite**
(d) type of action **Maßnahme, Vorkehrung; to take measures to prevent something happening** = to act to stop something happening **Vorkehrungen treffen, um etwas zu verhindern; safety measures** = actions to make sure that something is safe **Sicherheitsvorkehrungen**
2 *verb* (i) to find out the size *or* quantity of something; (ii) to be of a certain size *or* quantity (i) **messen**; (ii) **betragen**

◊ **measurement** *noun*
(a) measurements = size **Maße**; *to write down the measurements of a package*
(b) way of judging something **Maßstab**; *performance measurement or; measurement of performance is carried out by running a benchmark program*

mechanical *adjective* referring to machines **mechanisch**

◊ **mechanical mouse** *noun* pointing device that is operated by moving it across a flat surface; as the mouse is moved, a ball inside spins and turns two sensors that feed the horizontal and vertical movement back to the computer **mechanische Maus**; *compare* OPTICAL MOUSE

◊ **mechanical paper** *noun* paper (such as newsprint) made from rough wood, which has not been processed **Holzschliffpapier**

◊ **mechanism** *noun* piece of machinery **Mechanismus**; *the printer mechanism is very simple; the drive mechanism appears to be faulty*

media *plural noun*
(a) means of communicating information to the public (such as television, radio, newspapers) **Medien**; *the product attracted a lot of interest in the media or; a lot of media interest;* **media analysis** *or* **media research** = examining different types of media (such as the readers of newspapers, television viewers) to see which is best for advertising a certain type of product **Medienforschung; media coverage** = number of reports about an event *or* product in newspapers, magazines and on TV **Berichterstattung durch die Medien**; *we got good media coverage for the launch of the new model*
NOTE: **media** is followed by a singular or plural verb
(b) any physical material that can be used to store data **Medien, Datenträger**; *computers can store data on a variety of media, such as disk, punched card or CD-ROM;* **magnetic media** = magnetic materials used to store signals, such as disk, tape, etc. **magnetische Medien; media conversion** = to copy data from one type of storage media to another **Datenträgerkonvertierung**; *to transfer from magnetic tape to floppy disk, you need a media conversion device;* **media error** = fault in the storage media that corrupts data **Datenträgerfehler**

> QUOTE The Kontron IN Lite notebook, said to continue working even when fully immersed in a metre of liquid, includes an Intel i386 25MHz processor, between 4Mb and 20Mb of RAM, a 80Mb or 200Mb hard disk and a 40Mb removable media option
> *Computing*

medium
1 *adjective* middle *or* average **Mittel-, mittel-**; *a medium-sized computer system;* **medium model** = memory model of the Intel 80x86 processor family that allows 64Kb of data and up to 1MB of code **Mediummodell**
2 *noun*
(a) way of doing something *or* means of doing something **Mittel; advertising medium** = type of advertisement (such as a TV

commercial) **Werbeträger**; *the product was advertised through the medium of the trade press*
(b) storage medium = any physical material that can be used to store data for a computer application **Datenträger**; *data storage mediums such as paper tape, magnetic disk, magnetic tape, paper, card and microfiche are available;* **data medium** = medium which allows data to be stored *or* displayed such as magnetic disk *or* a VDU **Datenträger**; **empty medium** = blank but formatted storage medium that is ready to accept data **unbeschrifteter Datenträger**; **magnetic medium** *or* **material** = substance that will retain a magnetic flux pattern after a magnetic field is removed **Magnetträger** NOTE: plural is **mediums** or **media**

◊ **medium frequency** *noun* radio frequency range between 300 to 3000KHz (often referred to as medium wave (MW), especially on radio receivers) **Mittelfrequenz**

◊ **medium lens** *noun* optical photographic lens that has a focal length near the standard for the film size **mittlere Linse**

◊ **medium scale integration (MSI)** *noun* integrated circuit with 10 to 500 components **mittlere Integrationstechnik**

◊ **medium speed** *noun* data communication speed between 2400 and 9600 bits per second **mittlere Geschwindigkeit**

| COMMENT: medium speed transmission describes the maximum rate of transfer for a normal voice grade channel

◊ **medium wave (MW)** *see* MEDIUM FREQUENCY

meet *noun* logical function whose output is true if both inputs are true **UND/ODER-Funktion**

meg *abbreviation (informal)* = MEGABYTE; *this computer has a ninety-meg hard disk*

mega- *prefix*
(a) meaning one million **Mega-, mega-**; **megabits per second (Mbps)** = number of million bits transmitted every second **Megabits pro Sekunde**; **megaflops (MFLOPS)** measure of computing power and speed equal to one million floating point instructions per second **Millionen Fließkommaoperationen pro Sekunde (MFLOPS)**; **megahertz (MHz)** = measure of frequency equal to one million cycles per

second **Megahertz (MHz)**; **Megastream** ™ = data link provided by British Telecom that offers data transfer at rates up to 8Mbits/second **Megastream** ™
(b) meaning 1,048,576 (equal to 2^{20}) and used only in computing and electronic related applications **Mega-, mega-**; **megabit (Mb)** = equal to 1,048,576 bits **Megabit**; **megabyte (MB)** equal to 1,048,576 bytes of storage **Megabyte (MB)**; **megapixel display** = display adapter and monitor that are capable of displaying over one million pixels; this means a resolution of at least 1,024x1,024 pixels **Megapixelanzeige**

| QUOTE adding multiple megabytes of memory is a simple matter of plugging memory cards into the internal bus
| *Byte*

| QUOTE The component manufacturers sell flash memory at an average price of $30 a megabyte. By comparison, the hard-disk components sell at $3 a megabyte
| *Computing*

member *noun* individual record *or* item in a field **Glied**

membrane keyboard *noun* keyboard that uses a thin plastic or rubber sheet with key shapes moulded into it; when the user presses on a key, it activates a pressure sensor **Folientastatur**

| COMMENT: the keys in a membrane keyboard have less travel than normal mechanical keys, but since they have no moving parts, they are more robust and reliable

memo field *noun* field in a database *or* text window in an application that allows a user to add comments or a memo about the entry **Memofeld, Kommentarfeld**

memomotion *noun* method of filming an action by taking one frame every few seconds **Memomotion**

memory *noun* storage space in a computer system *or* medium that is capable of retaining data *or* instructions **(Haupt)speicher**; **associative memory** = method of data retrieval that uses part of the data rather than an address to locate data **Assoziativspeicher**; **backing memory** = any data storage medium, such as a magnetic tape *or* floppy disk, that is not the main high speed memory **Zusatzspeicher**; **bootstrap memory** = permanent memory within a terminal *or* microcomputer, that allows a user to customize the attributes, booting the system and loading programs **Urladerprogrammspeicher; bubble memory** = method of storing large amounts of binary data, as small magnetized areas in the medium (certain pure materials) **Blasenspeicher; cache memory** = section of high-speed memory which stores data that the CPU needs to access quickly **Cache-Speicher (schneller Pufferspeicher); charge coupled device (CCD) memory** = volatile, low-cost, high-storage capability memory device **ladungsgekoppelter Speicher; content-addressable memory** = memory that is addressed and accessed by its contents rather than a location **Assoziativspeicher; control memory** = memory which decodes control instructions into microinstructions which operate the computer *or* microcontroller **Mikroprogrammspeicher; core memory** *or* **primary memory** = central fast-access memory which stores the programs and data currently in use **Kernspeicher; disk memory** = data stored on magnetic disk, not on tape **Plattenspeicher; dynamic memory** = random access memory that requires its contents to be updated regularly **dynamischer Speicher; external memory** = memory which is located outside the main computer system confines, but which can be accessed by the CPU **externer Speicher; fast access memory (FAM)** = storage locations that can be read from *or* written to very rapidly **Schnellzugriffsspeicher; FIFO memory** *or* **first in first out memory** = memory using a FIFO access scheme **FIFO-Speichermethode; internal memory** = storage available within and under the direct control of the main computer, such as main memory **Hauptspeicher; magnetic memory** = storage that uses a medium that can store data bits as magnetic field changes **Magnetspeicher; main memory** = fast access RAM whose locations can be directly and immediately addressed by a CPU **Zentralspeicher; nonvolatile memory** = storage medium that retains data even when power has been switched off **nichtflüchtiger Speicher; random access memory (RAM)** = memory that allows access to any location in any order without having to access the rest of memory **Direktzugriffsspeicher (RAM); read only memory (ROM)** = memory device that has had data written into it at manufacture, which can only be read **Festspeicher (ROM); scratchpad memory** = workspace *or* area of high-speed memory that is used for the temporary storage of data currently in use

Notizblockspeicher; serial memory = storage whose locations can only be accessed in a serial way, locating one item requires a search through every location **Speicher mit seriellem Zugriff;** *magnetic tape is a high capacity serial memory;* **static memory** = non-volatile memory that does not require refreshing **statischer Speicher; virtual memory** = system where the workspace is held in both backing store and memory at the same time **virtueller Speicher; volatile memory** = memory *or* storage medium which loses data stored in it when its power supply is switched off **flüchtiger Speicher; memory access time** = time delay between requesting access to a location and being able to do so **Speicherzugriffszeit; memory address register (MAR)** = register within the CPU that contains the address of the next location to be accessed **Speicheradressregister; memory bank** = number of smaller storage devices connected together to form one large area of memory **Speicherbank; memory board** = printed circuit board containing memory chips **Speicherplatine; memory buffer register (MBR)** = register in a CPU that temporarily buffers all inputs and outputs **Speicherpufferregister; memory capacity** = number of bits *or* bytes that can be stored within a memory device **Speicherkapazität; memory cell** = smallest location that can be individually accessed **Speicherelement; memory chip** = electronic component that is able to store binary data **Speicherchip; memory cycle** = period of time from when the CPU reads *or* writes to a location and the action being performed **Operationszyklus; memory data register (MDR)** = register in a CPU which holds data before it is processed *or* moved to a memory location **Speicherdatenregister; memory diagnostic** = software routine that checks each memory location in main memory for faults **Speicherdiagnose; memory dump** = printout of all the contents of an area of memory **Speicherauszug; memory edit** = to change (selectively) the contents of various memory locations **Speicheraufbereitung; memory hierarchy** = the different types (capacity and access time) of memory available in a system **Speicherhierarchie; memory-intensive software** = software that uses large amounts of RAM or disk storage during run-time, such as programs whose entire code has to be in main memory during execution **speicherintensive Software; memory management** = software that controls and regulates the flow and position in memory of files and data **Speicherverwaltung; memory management unit (MMU)** = electronic logic circuits that generate the memory refresh signals and manage the mapping of virtual memory addresses to physical memory locations; the MMU is normally integrated into the processor chip **Speicherverwaltungseinheit, Memory Management Unit (MMU); memory map** = diagram indicating the allocation of address ranges to various devices such as RAM, ROM and memory-mapped input/output devices **Hauptspeicherabbild; memory-mapped** = with addresses allocated to a computer's input *or* output devices to allow them to be accessed as if they were a memory location **speicherorientiert;** *a memory-mapped screen has an address allocated to each pixel, allowing direct access to the screen by the CPU;* **memory-mapped I/O** = an I/O port which can be accessed as if it were a memory location within the CPU's normal address range **speicherorientierte Ein-/Ausgabe; memory model** = method used in a program to address the code and data that is used within that program; the memory model defines how much memory is available for code and data; processors with a segmented address space (like the Intel 80x86 range) can support multiple memory models **Speichermodell; memory page** = one section of main store which is divided into pages, which contains data *or* programs **Speicherseite; memory protect** = feature on most storage systems to prevent the accidental overwriting of data **Speicherschutz; memory-resident** = (program) that is held permanently in memory **speicherresident;** *the system can bomb if you set up too many memory-resident programs at the same time;* **memory switching system** = system which communicates information, stores it in memory and then transmits it according to instructions **Speicherschaltersystem; memory workspace** = amount of extra memory required by a program to store data used during execution **Speicherarbeitsbereich**

◊ **memorize** *verb* to remember *or* to retain in the memory **sich erinnern**

QUOTE when a program is loaded into memory, some is used for the code, some for the permanent data, and some is reserved for the stack which grows and shrinks for function calls and local data
Personal Computer World

QUOTE The lower-power design, together with an additional 8Kb of on-board cache memory, will increase the chip's performance to 75 million instructions per second
Computing

menu *noun* list of options *or* programs available to the user **Menü; menu-bar** = (in a GUI) list of options available to a user which are displayed on a horizontal line along the top of the screen or window: each menu option activates a pull-down menu **Menüleiste; menu-driven software** = program where commands *or* options are selected from a menu by the operator **menügesteuerte Software; menu item** = one of the choices in a menu **Menüoption, Menüeintrag; menu selection** = choosing commands from a list of options presented to the operator **Auswahl; main menu** = list of primary options available **Hauptmenü; pop-up menu** = set of options that are displayed in the centre of the screen **Einblendmenü; pull-down menu** = set of options that are displayed below the relevant entry on a menu-bar **Pulldown-Menü, Einklappmenü;** *the pull-down menu is viewed by clicking on the menu bar at the top of the screen*

QUOTE when the operator is required to make a choice a menu is displayed
Micro Decision

QUOTE The London Borough of Hackney has standardised on terminal emulator software from Omniplex to allow its networked desktop users to select Unix or DOS applications from a single menu
Computing

mercury delay line *noun* (old) method of storing serial data as pulses in a length of mercury, the data was constantly read, regenerated and fed back into the input **Quecksilberverzögerungsleitung**

merge *verb* to combine two data files, but still retaining an overall order **mischen;** *the system automatically merges text and illustrations into the document;* **merge sort** = software application in which the sorted files are merged into a new file **mischendes Sortieren;** *see also* MAIL-MERGE

mesh *noun* any system with two *or* more possible paths at each interconnection **Vermaschung; mesh network** = method of connecting several machines together, where each pair of devices has two *or* more connections **vermaschtes Netz**

message *noun*
(a) information sent from one person to another **Nachricht**
(b) certain defined amount of information **Nachricht; message format** = predetermined rules defining the coding, size and speed of transmitted messages **Nachrichtenformat; message header** = sequence of data at the beginning of a message that contains routing and destination information **Nachrichtenkopf; message numbering** = identification of messages by allocating a number to each one **Nachrichtennummerierung; message routing** = selection of a suitable path between the source and destination of a message in a network **Nachrichtenvermittlung; message slot** = number of bits that can hold a message which circulates around a ring network **Nachrichtenschlitz; message switching** = storing, arranging and making up batches of convenient sizes of data to allow for their economical transmission over a network **Nachrichtenvermitteln; message text** = information that concerns the user at the destination without routing *or* network control data **Nachrichtentext**

metabit *noun* extra identifying bit for each data word **Metabit**

◊ **metacompilation** *noun* compiling a program that will compile other programs when executed **Metakompilierung**

◊ **metafile** *noun* (i) file that contains other files; (ii) file that defines or contains data about other files **(i) & (ii) Metadatei;** *the operating system uses a metafile to hold data that defines where each file is stored on disk*

◊ **metalanguage** *noun* language which describes a programming language **Metasprache**

metal oxide semiconductor (MOS) *noun* production and design method for a certain family of integrated circuits using patterns of metal conductors and oxide deposited onto a semiconductor **Metalloxidhalbleiter; metal oxide semiconductor field effect transistor (MOSFET)** = high-powered and high-speed field effect transistor manufactured using MOS techniques **Feldeffekttransistor mit Metalloxidhalbleiteraufbau MOS-Transistor; complementary metal oxide semiconductor (CMOS)** = integrated circuit design and construction method, using a pair of complementary p- and n-type transistors **Halbleiterelement; Kombination von PMOS- und NMOS-Technik (CMOS)**

meter
1 *noun* device which counts *or* records something **Zähler;** *an electricity meter; a meter attached to the photocopier records the number of copies made; see also* MULTIMETER
2 *verb* to record and count **zählen;** *the calls from each office are metered by the call logger*

metropolitan area network (MAN) *noun* network extending over a limited area (normally a city) **Ortsnetz, Metropolitan Area Network (MAN);** *compare* LAN, WAN

MF = MEDIUM FREQUENCY

MFLOPS = MEGA FLOATING POINT INSTRUCTIONS PER SECOND measure of computing speed calculated as the number of floating point instructions that can be processed each second **MFLOPS**

MFM = MODIFIED FREQUENCY MODULATION method of storing data on magnetic media (such as a magnetic disk) that encodes the data bit according to the state of the previous bit; MFM is more efficient than FM, but less efficient than RLL encoding **MFM**

MFS = MACINTOSH FILING SYSTEM

MHz = MEGAHERTZ one million cycles per second **MHz**

MICR = MAGNETIC INK CHARACTER RECOGNITION system that identifies characters by sensing magnetic ink patterns (as used on bank cheques) **Magnetschriftzeichenerkennung**

micro *noun* = MICROCOMPUTER

micro- *prefix*
(a) meaning one millionth of a unit **Mikro-, mikro; micrometre** = one millionth of a metre **Mikrometer; microsecond** = one millionth of a second **Mikrosekunde**
(b) meaning very small **mikro; microcassette** = small format audio cassette used mainly in pocket dictating equipment **Mikrokassette; microchip** = circuit in which all the active and passive components are formed on one small piece of semiconductor, by means of etching and chemical processes **Mikrochip; microcircuit** = complex integrated circuit **Mikroschaltung; microcode** = ALU control instructions implemented as hardwired software **Mikrobefehlscode**

Micro Channel Architecture (MCA)
design of the expansion bus within IBM's
PS/2 range of personal computers that has
taken over from the older ISA/AT bus;
MCA is a 32-bit bus that supports bus
master devices **Micro Channel Architecture
(MCA); Micro Channel Architecture chipset**
= number of electronic components that
are required to manage the timing and data
signals over an MCA expansion bus **Micro-
Channel-Architecture-Chipsatz**

◊ **Micro Channel Bus** *noun*
proprietary 32-bit expansion bus defined
by IBM in its Micro Channel Architecture
Micro-Channel-Bus

**Microcom Networking Protocol ™
(MNP)** error detection and correction
system developed by Microcom Inc. used
in modems and some communications
software **Microcom Networking Protocol ™
(MNP)**

microcomputer *or* **micro** *noun*
complete small-scale, cheap, low-power
computer system based around a
microprocessor chip and having limited
memory capacity **Mikrocomputer;
microcomputer architecture** = layout and
interconnection of a microcomputer's
internal hardware
**Mikrocomputerarchitektur; microcomputer
backplane** = main printed circuit board of a
system, containing most of the components
and connections for expansion boards, etc.
**Mikrocomputerrückwandplatine;
microcomputer bus** = main data, address
and control buses in a microcomputer
**Mikrocomputerbus; microcomputer
development kit** = basic computer based
around a new CPU chip that allows
hardware and software designers to
experiment with the new device
**Mikrocomputerentwicklungsbausatz; single-
board microcomputer** = microcomputer
whose components are all contained on a
single printed circuit board
Einzelplatinenmikrocomputer

◊ **microcomputing** *adjective & noun*
referring to microcomputers and their use
Mikrocomputer-; Mikrocomputing; *the
microcomputing industry*

‖ COMMENT: micros are particularly used as
‖ home computers *or* as small office computers

microcontroller *noun* small self-
contained microcomputer for use in
dedicated control applications
Mikrocontroller; single-chip microcontroller
= one integrated circuit that contains a

CPU, I/O ports, RAM and often a basic
programming language
Einchipmikrocontroller

◊ **microcycle** *noun* unit of time (usually
a multiple of the system clock period) used
to give the execution time of instructions
Mikrozyklus

◊ **microdevice** *noun* very small device,
such as a microprocessor **Mikrogerät**

◊ **microelectronics** *noun* design and
manufacture of electronic circuits with
integrated circuits and chips **Mikroelektronik**

◊ **microfiche** *noun* sheet of text and
graphics in highly reduced form on a
photographic film **Mikrofiche**

◊ **microfilm**
1 *noun* reel of film containing a sequence of
very small images used for document
storage **Mikrofilm;** *we hold all our records on
microfilm*
2 *verb* to take very small photographs **auf
Mikrofilm aufnehmen;** *the 1985 records have
been sent away for microfilming*

◊ **microfloppy** *noun* small size magnetic
floppy disk (usually refers to 3.5 inch disks)
Mikrodiskette

◊ **microform** *noun* medium used for
storing information in microimage form
Mikroform

◊ **micrographics** *noun* images and
graphics stored as microimages **Mikrografie**

◊ **microimage** *noun* graphical image too
small to be seen with the naked eye
Mikrobild

◊ **microinstruction** *noun* one
hardwired instruction (part of a
microcode) that controls the actions of the
ALU **Mikrobefehl**

◊ **micron** *noun* one millionth of a metre
Mikron

◊ **microphone** *noun* device that converts
sound waves into an electrical signal
Mikrofon; dynamic microphone =
microphone using a coil that moves and
induces a voltage according to sound
pressure **dynamisches Mikrofon; lapel
microphone** = small microphone that is
pinned to someone's jacket
Ansteckmikrofon; moving coil microphone =
microphone that uses a coil of wire moved
by sound waves to generate an electrical
signal **Tauchspulenmikrofon**

◊ **microphotography** *noun*
photographic production of microimages
(too small to be seen with the naked eye)
Mikrofotografie

◊ **microprocessor** *noun* central processing unit elements, often contained on a single integrated circuit chip, which when combined with other memory and I/O chips will make up a microcomputer **Mikroprozessor; bit-slice microprocessor** = large word size CPU constructed by joining a number of smaller word size blocks **Slice-Mikroprozessor;** *the bit-slice microprocessor uses four 4-bit processors to make a 16-bit word processor;* **microprocessor addressing capabilities** = highest address that a CPU can directly address, without special features (this depends on the address word size - the bigger the word the greater the addressing capacity) **Mikroprozessoradressleistungen; microprocessor architecture** = layout of the basic parts within a CPU (I/O, ALU, etc.) **Mikroprozessoraufbau; microprocessor chip** = integrated circuit that contains all the elements of a central processing unit, connected with other memory and I/O chips to make a microcomputer **Mikroprozessorchip; microprocessor unit (MPU)** = unit containing the main elements of a microprocessor **Mikroprozessor (MIP)**

◊ **microprogram** *noun* series of microinstructions **Mikroprogramm; microprogram assembly language** = each assembly language instruction of a computer is carried out by a microprogram **Mikroprogrammassembliersprache; microprogram counter** = register that stores the address of the next microinstruction to be carried out (the microprogram counter is the same as the memory address register) **Mikroprogrammzähler; microprogram instruction set** = complete set of basic microinstructions available in a CPU **Mikroprogrammbefehlsvorrat; microprogram store** = storage device used to hold a microprogram **Mikroprogrammspeicher**

◊ **microprogramming** *noun* writing microcode using microinstructions **Mikroprogrammierung**

◊ **microsecond** *noun* one millionth of a second **Mikrosekunde**

◊ **microsequence** *noun* series of microinstructions **Mikrosequenz**

◊ **microwave** *noun* radio frequency range from 1 to 3000GHz **Mikrowelle; microwave communications link** = use of a microwave beam to transmit data between two points **Mikrowellenübertragung; microwave relay** = radiocommunications equipment used to receive microwave signals, then boost and retransmit them

Mikrowellenrelais; microwave transmission = communication using modulated microwaves allowing high data rates, used for international telephone and satellite communications **Mikrowellenübertragung**

◊ **microwriter** *noun* portable keyboard and display, used for keyboarding when travelling **Mikroschreiber**

Microsoft ™ the biggest developer and publisher of software for the PC and Macintosh; Microsoft developed the MS-DOS operating system for the IBM PC and later Windows together with a range of application software **Microsoft** ™; **Microsoft DOS (MS-DOS)** = operating system for IBM PC range of personal computers that manages data storage onto disks, display output and user input; MS-DOS is a single-user, single-tasking operating system that is controlled by a command-line interface **Microsoft-DOS (MS-DOS); Microsoft Windows** = multi-tasking graphical user interface designed to be easy to use; Windows uses icons to represent files and devices and can be controlled using a mouse, unlike MS-DOS which requires commands to be typed in **Microsoft Windows**

MIDI = MUSICAL INSTRUMENT DIGITAL INTERFACE serial interface that connects electronic instruments; the MIDI interface carries signals from a controller or computer that instructs the different instruments to play notes **MIDI**

mid-user *noun* operator who retrieves relevant information from a database for a customer *or* end user **Vermittler**

middleware *noun* system software that has been customized by a dealer for a particular user **Middleware**

migration *noun* moving users from one hardware platform to another **Migration**

milk disk *noun* disk used to transfer data from a small machine onto a larger computer, which provides greater processing power **Datenübertragungsplatte**

◊ **milking machine** *noun* portable machine which can accept data from different machines, then transfer it to another larger computer **Datenübertragungsmaschine**

milli- *prefix* meaning one thousandth **Milli-, milli-; milliampere** *or* **mA** = electrical current measure equal to one thousandth of an ampere **Milliampere, mA; millisecond** or **ms** = one thousandth of a second **Millisekunde, ms**

MIMD = MULTIPLE INSTRUCTION STREAM - MULTIPLE DATA STREAM architecture of a parallel processor that uses a number of ALUs and memory devices in parallel to provide high speed processing **Mehrfachbefehlsstrom · Mehrfachdatenstrom**

mini- *prefix* meaning small **Mini-, mini-; miniaturization** = making something very small **Miniaturisierung; minidisk** = magnetic disk smaller than the 5.25 inch standard, usually 3.5 inch **Miniplatte; minifloppy** = magnetic disk (usually refers to the 5.25 inch standard) **Minidiskette;** *(slang)* **miniwinny** = small Winchester hard disk **Mini-Winchesterplatte**

minicomputer *or* **mini** *noun* small computer, with a greater range of instructions and processing power than a microcomputer, but not able to compete with the speed *or* data handling capacity of a mainframe computer **Minicomputer**

minimal latency coding *see* MINIMUM ACCESS CODE

◊ **minimal tree** *noun* tree whose nodes are organized in the optimum way, providing maximum efficiency **Kleinstbaum**

minimum *noun* the smallest amount of something **Minimum; minimum access code** *or* **minimum delay code** = coding system that provides the fastest access and retrieval time for stored data items **Bestzeitcode; minimum weight routing** = method of optimizing the transmission path of a message through a network **optimaler Nachrichtenübertragungsleitweg**

◊ **minimize** *verb*
(a) to make as small as possible **minimieren;** *we minimized costs by cutting down the number of components*
(b) (in MS-Windows) to shrink an application window to an icon **auf Symbolgröße verkleinern, minimieren;** *compare* MAXIMIZE

COMMENT: the application can continue to run in the background; you minimize a window by clicking once on the down arrow in the top right hand corner

minmax *noun* method used in artificial intelligence to solve problems **Minimaxmethode**

minuend *noun* number from which another is subtracted **Minuend**

minus *or* **minus sign** *noun* printed *or* written sign (like a small dash) to indicate subtraction *or* to show a negative value **Minuszeichen**

minuscule *noun* lower case printed character **Kleinbuchstabe, Minuskel**

MIPS = MILLION INSTRUCTIONS PER SECOND measure of processor speed **MIPS**

QUOTE ICL has staked its claim to the massively parallel market with the launch of the Goldrush MegaServer, providing up to 16,000 Unix MIPS of processing power
Computing

mirror
1 *noun* glass with a metal backing, which reflects an image **Spiegel; mirror image** = image produced that is equivalent to that which would be seen in a mirror **Spiegelbild**
2 *verb*
(a) to create an identical copy **abbilden, spiegeln**
(b) to duplicate all disk operations onto a second disk drive that can be used if the first breaks down **spiegeln;** *there's less chance of losing our data now that we have mirrored the server's disk drive*

QUOTE they also offer mirror-disk protection against disk failure, providing automatic backup of a database

QUOTE disks are also mirrored so that the system can continue to run in the event of a disk crash

QUOTE mirroring of the database is handled automatically by systems software
Computer News

MIS = MANAGEMENT INFORMATION SYSTEM

MISD = MULTIPLE INSTRUCTION STREAM - SINGLE DATA STREAM architecture of a parallel computer that has a single ALU and data bus with a number of control units **Mehrfachbefehlsstrom · Einfachdatenstrom**

mismatch *noun* situation occurring when two things are not correctly matched **Fehlanpassung; impedance mismatch** =

situation where the impedance of the transmission *or* receiving end of a system does not match the other, resulting in loss of signal power **fehlerhafte Scheinwiderstandsanpassung**

mission-critical *adjective* (application or hardware) on which your company depends **unverzichtbar; mission-critical application** = software program without which your company cannot function **unverzichtbare Anwendung**

mix
1 *noun* way in which different signals have been combined to form a single signal (usually audio) **Mischung**
2 *verb* to combine several separate signals into a single signal **mischen; to mix down** = to combine the signals from several sources such as a number of recorded audio tracks *or* instruments into a single signal **vermischen**

◊ **mixed highs** *noun* fine colour detail that is in monochrome in a TV signal **gemischte Höhen**

◊ **mixer** *noun* electronic circuit used to combine two *or* more separate signals into a single output **Mischer**

◊ **mixing** *noun*
(a) combining several audio signals into a single signal **Mischen; mixing studio** = room with audio mixers and sound processors used when recording music **Tonmischstudio**
(b) printing a line of text with several different typefaces **Typenmischung, Mischsatz**

MKS = METRE KILOGRAM SECOND widely used measurement system based on the metre, kilogram and second **mks-System;** *see also* SI UNITS

MMI = MAN MACHINE INTERFACE hardware and software designed to make it easier for users to communicate effectively with a machine **Mensch-Maschine-Schnittstelle**

MMU = MEMORY MANAGEMENT UNIT electronic logic circuits that generate the memory refresh signals and manage the mapping of virtual memory addresses to physical memory locations; the MMU is normally integrated into the processor chip **MMU**

mnemonic(s) *noun* shortened form of a word *or* function that is helpful as a reminder (such as INCA for increment

register A) **Mnemonik; assembler mnemonics** *or* **mnemonic operation codes** = standard word abbreviations used when writing a program for a particular CPU in assembly language (such as LDA for load register A) **symbolische Operationsschlüssel**

MNP ™ = MICROCOM NETWORKING PROTOCOL error detection and correction system developed by Microcom Inc., used in modems and some communications software **MNP** ™

mobile *adjective & noun* (i) which can move about; (ii) *informal* a travelling radio base such as a car transceiver **(i) beweglich; (ii) mobiler Funkempfänger; mobile earth terminal** = satellite communications equipment that is mobile **mobile Erdstation; mobile unit** = complete set of television filming and editing equipment carried in a vehicle (for outside broadcasts) **mobile Einheit; mobile radiophone** = radio telephone linked to a main telephone system, which uses a network of stations, each covering a certain area, to provide a service over a large area **mobiles Funktelefon**

mock-up *noun* model of a new product for testing *or* to show to possible customers **Attrappe**

mode *noun*
(a) way of doing something; method of operating a computer **Art und Weise; Betriebsart;** *when you want to type in text, press this function key which will put the terminal in its alphanumeric mode;* **burst mode** = data transmission using intermittent bursts of data **Stoßbetrieb; byte mode** = data transmitted one byte at a time **Bytemodus; control mode** = state of a device in which control signals can be received to select options *or* functions **Steuermodus; deferred mode** = entering a command as a program line, then executing the program **verzögerter Modus; direct mode** = typing in a command which is executed once carriage return has been pressed **Direktmodus; execute mode** = entering a command in direct mode to start a program run **Ausführungsmodus; form mode** = display method on a data entry terminal, the form is displayed on the screen and the operator enters relevant details **Formularmodus; input mode** = mode in which a computer is receiving data **Eingabebetrieb; insert mode** = interactive computer mode in which new text is entered within the previous text, which adjusts to make room for it **Einfügungsmodus; interactive mode** = mode

in which a computer allows the user to enter commands *or* programs *or* data and receive an immediate response **Dialogbetrieb; noisy mode** = floating point arithmetic in which a digit other than a zero is deliberately added in the least significant position during the normalization of a floating point number **Fließkommabetriebsart; replace mode** = interactive computer mode in which new text entered replaces any previous text **Überschreibmodus; sequential mode** = each instruction in a program is stored in consecutive locations **Sequenzmodus**
(b) number of paths taken by light when travelling down an optical fibre **Moden; mode dispersion** = loss of power in a light signal transmitted down an optic fibre due to dispersion from transmission paths that are not directly along the axis of the fibre **Modenstreuung;** *see* MONOMODE, MULTIMODE
(c) number that occurs most frequently in a series of samples **häufigster Wert**

◊ **modal** *adjective* referring to modes **modal**

QUOTE the printer gives print quality in three modes: high speed, data processing and letter-quality
Minicomputer News

QUOTE The approach being established by the Jedec committee provides for burst mode data transfer clocked at up to 100MHz.
Computing

model
1 *noun*
(a) small copy of something to show what it will look like when finished **Modell;** *he showed us a model of the new computer centre building*
(b) style *or* type of product; version of a product **Modell;** *the new model B has taken the place of model A; this is the latest model; the model on display is last year's; they are selling off the old models at half price;* **demonstration model** = piece of equipment used in demonstrations (and then sold cheaply) **Demonstrationsmodell**
2 *adjective* which is a perfect example to be copied **Modell-, modellhaft, Muster-, vorbildlich;** *a model agreement*
3 *verb* to make a computerized model of a new product *or* of the economic system, etc. **ein Modell erstellen** NOTE: **modelling - modelled** but US **modeling - modeled**

◊ **modelling** *noun* creating computer models **Erstellen von Computermodellen**

modem *or* **MODEM** *noun* = MODULATOR/DEMODULATOR device that allows data to be sent over telephone lines by converting binary signals from a computer into analog sound signals which can be transmitted over a telephone line **Modem; dial-in modem** = auto-answer modem that can be called at any time to access a system **Modem bereit für ankommende Rufe; null modem** = circuit *or* cable that allows two computers to communicate via their serial ports **Nullmodemkabel;** *this cable is configured as a null modem, which will allow me to connect these 2 computers together easily;* **modem eliminator** = cable *or* device that allows two computers to communicate via their serial ports without using modems **Modemeliminator;** *see also* STANDARD; *compare* ACOUSTIC COUPLER

COMMENT: the process of converting binary signals to analog is called "modulation". When the signal is received, another modem reverses the process (called "demodulation"). Both modems must be working according to the same standards

QUOTE AST Research has bundled together a notebook PC with a third-party PCMCIA fax modem technology for a limited-period special offer
Computing

modify *verb* to change something *or* to make something fit a different use **abändern;** *the keyboard was modified for European users; we are running a modified version of the mail-merge system; the software will have to be modified to run on a small PC*

◊ **modification** *noun* change made to something **Abänderung;** *the modifications to the system allow it to be run as part of a LAN;* **modification loop** = instructions within a loop that changes other instructions *or* data within a program **Modifikationsschleife**

◊ **modified frequency modulation (MFM)** *noun* method of storing data on magnetic media (such as a magnetic disk) that encodes the data bit according to the state of the previous bit; MFM is more efficient than FM, but less efficient than RLL encoding **modifizierte Frequenzmodulation (MFM)**

◊ **modifier** *noun* programming instruction that alters the normal action of a command **Modifizierer**

Modula-2 *noun* high-level programming

language derived from Pascal that supports modular programming techniques and data abstraction **Modula-2**

modular *adjective* (method of constructing hardware *or* software products) by connecting several smaller blocks together to produce a customized product **nach dem Baukastenprinzip, modular; modular programming** = programming small individually written sections of computer code that can be made to fit into a structured program and can be called up from a main program **modulare Programmierung**

◊ **modularity** *noun* being made up from modules **Modularität;** *the modularity of the software or hardware allows the system to be changed*

◊ **modularization** *noun* designing programs from a set of standard modules **Modularisierung**

modulate *verb* to change a carrier wave so that it can carry data **modulieren; modulated signal** = constant frequency and amplitude carrier signal that is used in a modulated form to transmit data **moduliertes Signal; modulating signal** = signal to be transmitted that is used to modulate a carrier **Modulationssignal**

◊ **modulation** *noun* process of varying a carrier's amplitude *or* frequency *or* phase according to an applied signal **Modulation** ⇨APPENDIX; **amplitude modulation (AM)** = system that varies the amplitude of a constant carrier signal according to an external signal **Amplitudenmodulation (AM); frequency modulation (FM)** = system that varies the frequency of a constant amplitude carrier signal according to an external signal **Frequenzmodulation (FM)**

◊ **modulator** *noun* electronic circuit that varies a carrier signal according to an applied signal **Modulator, Sendersignalumsetzer; modulator/demodulator** = MODEM

module *noun*
(a) small section of a large program that can if required function independently as a program in its own right **Programm-Modul**
(b) self-contained piece of hardware that can be connected with other modules to form a new system **Baustein;** *a multifunction analog interface module includes analog to digital and digital to analog converters*

modulo arithmetic *noun* branch of

arithmetic that uses the remainder of one number when divided by another **Moduloarithmetik; modulo-N** = modulo arithmetic using base N **Modulo N; modulo-N check** = error detection test using the remainder from a modulo arithmetic operation on data **Modulo-N-Prüfung**

modulus *or* **MOD** *noun* the remainder after the division of one number by another **Rest;** *7 mod 3 = 1*

momentary switch *noun* switch that only conducts while it is being pressed **federnder Schalter, Taster**

monadic (Boolean) operator *noun* logical operator with only one operand **monadischer Operator;** *the monadic operator NOT can be used here;* **monadic operation** = operation that uses one operand to produce one result **monadische Operation**

monitor
1 *noun*
(a) visual display unit used to display high quality text *or* graphics, generated by a computer **Monitor, Bildschirm; multi-scan** *or* **multi-sync monitor** = monitor which has circuitry to lock onto the required scanning frequency for any type of graphics card **Multiscanmonitor; monitor unit** *see* VDU
(b) (i) loudspeaker used to listen to the sound signals produced during recording *or* mixing; (ii) TV screen in a TV studio control room, which shows the image being filmed by one of the cameras **(i) Kontroll-Lautsprecher; (ii) Kontrollschirm**
(c) **monitor program** = computer program that allows basic commands to be entered to operate a system (such as load a program, examine the state of devices, etc.) **Monitorprogramm;** *see also* OPERATING SYSTEM; **firmware monitor** = monitor program that is resident in a ROM device, used to load in the operating system when a machine is switched on **residentes Festspeichermonitorprogramm**
(c) system that watches for faults *or* failures in a circuit **Überwachungssystem; power monitor** = circuit that shuts off the electricity supply if it is faulty *or* likely to damage equipment **Netzspannungsüberwachung**
2 *verb* (i) to check *or* to examine how something is working; (ii) to look after and supervise a process *or* experiment to make sure it is operating correctly **(i) & (ii) überwachen;** *he is monitoring the progress of the trainee programmers; the machine monitors each signal as it is sent out*

mono- *prefix* meaning single *or* one **mono-, ein-**

◊ **monoaural** *adjective* single audio channel presented to only one ear **einohrig**

◊ **monochrome** *adjective & noun* (image) in one colour, usually shades of grey and black and white **einfarbig, monochrom, schwarzweiß; einfarbiges Bild; monochrome display adapter (MDA)** = video adapter standard used in early PC systems that could display text in 25 lines of 80 columns **Monochrombildschirmadapter, Monochrome Display Adapter (MDA); monochrome monitor** = computer monitor that displays text and graphics in black, white and shades of grey instead of colours **Schwarz-Weiß-Monitor**

◊ **monolithic** *adjective* (integrated circuit) manufactured on a single crystal of semiconductor **monolithisch**

◊ **monomode fibre** *noun* optical fibre that only allows light to travel along its axis without any internal reflections, as the result of having a very fine core diameter **Monomodefaser;** *see also* MODE

◊ **monophonic** *adjective* system where one audio signal is used to feed one *or* more loudspeakers **monophon;** *compare with* STEREOPHONIC

◊ **monoprogramming system** *noun* computer batch processing system that executes one program at a time **Einprogrammsystem;** *compare with* MULTIPROGRAMMING SYSTEM

◊ **monospacing** *noun* system of printing where each character occupies the same amount of space, as on a typewriter (as opposed to proportional spacing) **gleichbleibender Schaltschritt (Schriftart, bei der die Drucktypen die gleiche Dickte haben)**

◊ **monostable** *adjective & noun* (electronic circuit) that produces an output pulse for a predetermined period when it receives an input signal **monostabil(er Stromkreis)**

Monte Carlo method *noun* statistical analysis technique **Monte-Carlo-Methode**

Morse code *noun* system of signalling using only two symbols: dots and dashes **Morsealphabet; morse key** = switch used to send morse messages by hand **Morsetaste**

MOS = METAL OXIDE SEMICONDUCTOR production and design method for a certain family of integrated circuits using patterns of metal conductors and oxide deposited onto a semiconductor **MOS (Metalloxidhalbleiterelement);** *see also* MOSFET; **MOS memory** = solid-state memory using MOSFETs to store binary data **MOS-Speicher; CMOS** = COMPLEMENTARY METAL OXIDE SEMICONDUCTOR integrated circuit design and construction method (using a pair of complementary p- and n- type transistors) **CMOS (Halbleiterelement, Kombination von PMOS- und NMOS-Technik)**

> QUOTE integrated circuits fall into one of two distinct classes, based either on bipolar or metal oxide semiconductor (MOS) transistors
> *Electronics & Power*

mosaic *noun* display character used in videotext systems that is made up of small dots **Mosaik**

MOSFET = METAL OXIDE SEMICONDUCTOR FIELD EFFECT TRANSISTOR high power and high speed field effect transistor manufactured using MOS techniques **Feldeffekttransistor mit Metalloxidhalbleiteraufbau MOS-Transistor**

most significant bit *or* **msb** *or* **MSB** *noun* bit in a word that represents the greatest value *or* weighting (usually the bit which is furthest to the left) **wichtigstes Bit;** *the most significant bit in an eight bit binary word represents 128 in decimal notation*

◊ **most significant character** *or* **most significant digit (MSD)** *noun* digit at the far left of a number, that represents the greatest power of the base **wichtigstes Zeichen; wichtigste Ziffer** NOTE: the opposite is **LSB, LSD**

motherboard *noun* main printed circuit board of a system, containing most of the components and connections for expansion boards, etc. **Grundplatine**

motion picture *noun* projection at high speed of a series of still images that creates the impression of movement **Film**

motor *noun* electromagnetic machine that converts an electrical supply into (rotary) motion (by means of a magnetic field) **Motor**

Motorola ™ manufacturer of electronic components, including the 68000 range of processors used in Apple Macintosh computers **Motorola** ™; **Motorola 68000** =processor that can manage 32-bit words internally, but transfers data externally via a 16-bit data bus; used in the Apple Macintosh SE and Macintosh Plus **Motorola 68000**; **Motorola 68020** = processor similar to the 68000 that uses full internal and external 32-bit architecture **Motorola 68020**; **Motorola 68030** = processor similar to the 68020, that can manage 32-bit words internally and externally, but can run at much faster clock rates than the 68020 **Motorola 68030**

mount *verb*
(a) to fix a device *or* a circuit onto a base **einstecken, sockeln**; *the chips are mounted in sockets on the PCB*
(b) to insert a disk in a disk drive or inform an operating system that a disk drive is ready to be used **einlegen**

mouse *noun* small hand-held input device moved on a flat surface to control the position of a cursor on the screen **Maus; bus mouse** = mouse that connects to a special expansion card plugged into the computer's expansion bus **Busmaus**; **mechanical mouse** = pointing device that is operated by moving it across a flat surface; as the mouse is moved, a ball inside spins and turns two sensors that feed the horizontal and vertical movement back to the computer **mechanische Maus; optical mouse** = pointing device that is operated by moving it across a special flat mat; on the mat is printed a grid of lines, as the mouse is moved, two light sensors count the number of lines that have been passed to produce a measure of the distance and direction of travel; an optical mouse has fewer moving parts than a mechanical mouse and so is more reliable, but requires an accurately printed mat **optische Maus; serial mouse** = mouse that connects to the serial port of a PC and transfers positional data via the serial port **serielle Maus; mouse-driven** = (software) which uses a mouse rather than a keyboard for input **mausgesteuert; mouse driver** = program which converts data from a mouse to a standard form that can be used by any software **Maustreiber; mouse pointer** = small arrow displayed on screen that moves around as the mouse is moved **Mauszeiger** (NOTE: the plural is **mice**)

QUOTE This project has now borne fruit, with the announcement last week of Windots, a project which allows users to 'see' Windows screens in a Braille form of Ascii. Other areas of research include a sound system which allows a sound to 'move', mirroring the movement of a mouse
Computing

QUOTE a powerful new mouse-based editor:- you can cut, paste and copy with the mouse
Personal Computer World

QUOTE you can use a mouse to access pop-up menus and a keyboard for a word-processor
Byte

mouth *noun* open end of an antenna **(Trichter)öffnung**

M out of N code *noun* coding system providing error detection, each valid character which is N bits long must contain M binary "one" bits **Codiersystem**

move *verb* to change the place of something **bewegen; move block** = command which changes the place of a block of text identified by block markers **Blockbewegungsbefehl; moving coil microphone** = microphone which uses a coil of wire moved by sound waves to generate an electrical signal **Tauchspulenmikrofon**

◊ **movable** *adjective* which can be moved **beweglich; movable head disk** = magnetic disk head assembly that moves across the disk until the required track is reached **Platte mit beweglichem Kopf**

◊ **movement** *noun* changing the place of something **Bewegung; movement file** = file containing recent changes *or* transactions to records, which is then used to update a master file **Bewegungsdatei**

MPS = MICROPROCESSOR SYSTEM

MPU = MICROPROCESSOR UNIT

ms = MILLISECOND one thousandth of a second **ms**

MS = MANUSCRIPT
NOTE: plural is **MSS**

msb *or* **MSB** = MOST SIGNIFICANT BIT bit in a word that represents the greatest value *or* weight (usually the bit furthest to the left) **wichtigstes Bit**

MSD = MOST SIGNIFICANT DIGIT

MS-DOS = MICROSOFT DOS operating system for IBM PC range of personal computers that manages data storage onto disks, display output and user input; MS-DOS is a single-user, single-tasking operating system that is controlled by a command-line interface **MS-DOS**

MSI = MEDIUM SCALE INTEGRATION

M signal *noun* signal produced from the sum of left and right signals in a stereophonic system **M-Signal, Mittensignal**

MS-Windows = MICROSOFT WINDOWS

MSX *noun* hardware and software standard for home computers that can use interchangeable software **MSX-Norm**

MTBF = MEAN TIME BETWEEN FAILURES average period of time that a piece of equipment will operate between failures **mittlerer Ausfallabstand**

MTF = MEAN TIME TO FAILURE average period of time for which a device will operate (usually continuously) before failing **mittlere Lebensdauer**

multi- *prefix* meaning many *or* more than one **mehrfach, Multi-, multi-;** *multimegabyte memory card; a multistandard unit;* **multi-access system** = computer system that allows several users to access one file *or* program at the same time **System mit mehrfachem Zugriff;** *see also* MULTI-USER; **multi-address** *or* **multi-address instruction** = instruction that contains more than one address (of data *or* locations *or* input/output) **Mehradressbefehl**

◊ **multi-board computer** *noun* computer which has several integrated circuit boards connected to a mother board **Mehrplatinencomputer**

◊ **multiburst signal** *noun* television test signal **Multiburstsignal**

◊ **multi-bus system** *noun* computer architecture that uses a high speed bus between CPU and main memory and a slower bus between CPU and other peripherals **Mehrbussystem**

◊ **multicasting** *noun* broadcasting to a number of receivers *or* nodes, with an address in each message to indicate the node required **Mehrfachausstrahlung**

◊ **multichannel** *adjective* with more than one channel **Mehrkanal-**

◊ **multicolour** *adjective* with several colours **mehrfarbig**

◊ **multidimensional** *adjective* with features in more than one dimension **mehrdimensional; multidimensional array** = number of arrays arranged in parallel, providing depth **mehrdimensionale Feldgruppe; multidimensional language** = programming language that can be represented in a number of ways **mehrdimensionale Programmiersprache**

◊ **multi-disk** *adjective* referring to several types of disk **Mehrplatten-; multi-disk option** = system that can have disk drives installed in a number of sizes **Mehrplattenoption; multi-disk reader** = device which can read from various sizes and formats of disk **Mehrplattenleser**

◊ **multidrop circuit** *noun* network allowing communications between a number of terminals and a central computer, but not directly between terminals **Übertragungsleitung mit mehreren Stationen**

◊ **multifrequency** *noun* dual tone, multifrequency (DTMF) = communication signalling system using two different frequencies to transmit binary data **Mehrfrequenzwählverfahren (MFV)**

◊ **multifunction** *adjective* which has several functions **Mehrfunktions-, multifunktional;** *a multifunction analog interface module includes analog to digital and digital to analog converters;* **multifunction card** = add-on circuit board that provides many features to upgrade a computer **Mehrfunktionskarteneinheit; multifunction workstation** = workstation where several tasks can be carried out **Mehrfunktionsdatenstation**

◊ **multifunctional** *adjective* which has several functions **Mehrfunktions-, multifunktional;** *a multifunctional scanner*

◊ **multilayer** *noun* printed circuit board that has several layers *or* interconnecting conduction tracks **Mehrschichtplatine**

◊ **multilevel** *adjective* (signal) with a number of possible values (quaternary signals have four levels) **mehrstufig**

◊ **multilink system** *noun* system where there is more than one connection between two points **Mehrfachverbindungssystem**

◊ **multimedia** *adjective* referring to several forms of media **multimedial;**

multimedia mail = messages that can contain voice, sound, images or data **multimediale Post**

◊ **multimeter** *noun* testing equipment that provides an indication of the voltage *or* current *or* impedance at a point or of a component **Multimeter; analog multimeter (AMM)** = testing equipment using a moving needle to indicate voltage, current *or* impedance levels **Analogmultimeter; digital multimeter (DMM)** = multimeter that uses a digital readout to indicate voltage, current *or* impedance levels **Digitalmultimeter**

◊ **multimode fibre** *noun* optical fibre that allows many different paths in addition to the direct straight path for light beams, causing pulse stretching and interference on reception of the signal **Multimodefaser**

◊ **multi-part stationery** *noun* continuous stationery with two or more sheets together, either with carbons between *or* carbonless **Vordrucksatz**

◊ **multipass overlap** *noun* system of producing higher quality print from a dot matrix printer by repeating the line of characters but shifted slightly, so making the dots less noticeable **Mehrfachüberschreibung**

◊ **multiphase program** *noun* program that requires more than one fetch operation before execution is complete **Mehrphasenprogramm**

MultiFinder ™ version of Apple Macintosh Finder that supports multitasking **MultiFinder** ™

multimedia *adjective* the combination of sound, graphics, animation, video and text within an application **Multimedia; multimedia PC** = computer that can run multimedia application; normally equipped with a sound card, CD-ROM drive and high-resolution colour monitor **Multimedia-PC**

> QUOTE The Oracle Media Server is a multimedia database designed to run on massively parallel computers, running hundreds of transactions per second and managing multiple data types, such as video, audio and text
>
> *Computing*

multiple *adjective* having many parts *or* acting in many ways **mehrfach; multiple access** *see* MULTI-ACCESS; **multiple**

address code = instruction with more than one address for the operands, result and the location of the next instruction to be executed **Mehrfachzugriffscode;** *see also* THREE-PLUS-ONE; FOUR-PLUS-ONE ADDRESS; **multiple bus architecture** = computer architecture that uses a high speed bus between CPU and main memory and a slower bus between CPU and other peripherals **Mehrfachbusarchitektur; multiple instruction stream - multiple data stream (MIMD)** = architecture of a parallel processor that uses a number of ALUs and memories in parallel to provide high speed processing **Mehrfachbefehlsstrom - Mehrfachdatenstrom; multiple instruction stream - single data stream (MISD)** = architecture of a parallel computer that has a single ALU and data bus with a number of control units **Mehrfachbefehlsstrom - Einfachdatenstrom; multiple precision** = use of more than one byte of data for number storage to increase possible precision **Mehrfachgenauigkeit**

multiplex *verb* to combine several messages in the same transmission medium **vielfach ausnutzen; multiplexed analog components (MAC)** = standard television broadcast signal format **MAC; multiplexed bus** = one bus used to carry address, data and control signals at different times **Multiplexbus**

◊ **multiplexing** *noun* combining several messages in the same transmission medium **Multiplexmethode (Unterteilung eines Übertragungskanals in mehrere Kanäle); dynamic multiplexing** = multiplexing method which allocates time segments to signals according to demand **dynamische Multiplexmethode;** homogeneous **multiplexing** = switching multiplexor system where all the channels contain data using the same protocol and transmission rate **homogene Multiplexmethode; optical multiplexing** = sending several light beams down a single path *or* fibre **optisches Multiplexing**

◊ **multiplexor (MUX)** *noun* circuit that combines a number of inputs into a smaller number of outputs **Multiplexor;** *compare with* DEMULTIPLEXOR; *a 4 to 1 multiplexor combines four inputs into a single output*

> QUOTE the displays use BCD input signals and can be multiplexed to provide up to six digits
>
> *Electronics & Power*

multiply *verb* to perform the

multiplication of a number (the multiplicand) by another number (the multiplier) **multiplizieren**

◊ **multiplicand** *noun* number which is multiplied by another number **Multiplikant**

◊ **multiplication** *noun* mathematical operation that adds one number to itself a number of times **Multiplikation;** *the multiplication of 5 and 3 = 15;* **multiplication sign** = printed *or* written sign (x) used to show that numbers are multiplied **Multiplikationszeichen**

◊ **multiplier** *noun* number which multiplies a multiplicand **Multiplikator**

multipoint *adjective* (connection) with several lines, attaching several terminals to a single line to a single computer **Mehrpunkt-**

◊ **multiprecision** *noun* use of more than one data word to represent numbers (increasing the range *or* precision possible) **Mehrfachgenauigkeit**

◊ **multiprocessing system** *noun* system where several processing units work together sharing the same memory **Simultanverarbeitungssystem**

◊ **multiprocessor** *noun* number of processing units acting together *or* separately but sharing the same area of memory **Mehrprozessorsystem; multiprocessor interleaving** = each processor in a multiprocessor system dealing with a section of one or more processes **Mehrprozessorenverschachtelung**

◊ **multi-programming** *noun* operating system used to execute more than one program apparently simultaneously (each program being executed a little at a time) **Mehrprogrammbetrieb**

◊ **multi-scan monitor** *noun* monitor which contains circuitry to lock onto the required scanning frequency of any type of graphics card **Multiscanmonitor**

◊ **multi-statement line** *noun* line from a computer program that contains more than one instruction *or* statement **Mehrfachanweisungszeile**

◊ **multi-strike printer ribbon** *noun* inked ribbon in a printer that can be used more than once **mehrfach benutzbares Farbband**

multitasking *or* **multi-tasking** *noun* ability of a computer system to run two or more programs at the same time **Multitasking;** *the system is multi-user and*

multi-tasking; **real-time multitasking** = executing several (real-time) tasks simultaneously without slowing the execution of any of the processors **Echtzeitmultitasking**

COMMENT: few small systems are capable of simultaneous multitasking, since each program would require its own processor this is overcome by allocating to each program an amount of processing time, executing each a little at a time so that they will appear to run simultaneously due to the speed of the processor and the relatively short gaps between programs

QUOTE this is a true multi-tasking system, meaning that several computer applications can be running at the same time
Which PC?

QUOTE page management programs are so greedy for memory that it is not a good idea to ask them to share RAM space with anything else, so the question of multi-tasking does not arise here
Desktop Publishing

QUOTE X is the underlying technology which allows Unix applications to run under a multi-user, multitasking GUI. It has been adopted as the standard for the Common Open Software Environment, proposed recently by top Unix vendors including Digital, IBM and Sun
Computing

multi-terminal system *noun* system where several terminals are linked to a single CPU **System mit mehreren Datenstationen**

◊ **multithread** *noun* program design using more than one logical path through it, each path being concurrently executed **Mehrpfadprogramm**

◊ **multi-user system** *noun* computer system that can support more than one user at a time **Mehrplatzsystem;** *the program runs on a standalone machine or a multi-user system*

◊ **multivibrator** *noun* electronic circuit that switches continuously between two output states, often used for clock generation **Multivibrator; astable multivibrator** = electronic circuit that repeatedly switches an output between two voltage levels **astabiler** *or* **instabiler Multivibrator**

◊ **multi-window editor** *noun* program

used for creating and editing a number of applications programs independently, each in a separate window on screen at the same time **Mehrfenster-Editor**

mung up *verb (informal)* to distort data *or* to ruin a file **versauen**

Murray code *noun* code used for teleprinters that uses only 5 bits **Murray-Code**

mush *noun* distortion and loss of signal **Störung; mush area** = distortion and loss of signal due to two transmissions interfering **Störungsgebiet**

musical instrument digital interface (MIDI) *noun* serial interface that connects electronic instruments **Musical Instrument Digital Interface (MIDI)**

> COMMENT: the MIDI interface carries signals from a controller or computer that instructs the different instruments to play notes

music chip *noun* integrated circuit capable of generating musical sounds and tunes **Musikchip; music synthesizer** = device able to generate musical notes which are similar to those made by musical instruments **Synthesizer**

muting *noun* **interstation muting** = ability of a radio receiver to prevent the noise found between radio stations from being amplified and heard by the user **geräuschfreie Abstimmung**

MUX = MULTIPLEXOR circuit that combines a number of inputs into a smaller number of outputs **Multiplexor;** *compare* DEMULTIPLEXOR

MW = MEDIUMWAVE

Nn

n *prefix* meaning nano- **n**

n-channel metal oxide semiconductor *noun* transistor design, with MOS techniques, that uses an n-type region for conduction **N-Kanal-Metalloxidhalbleiter**

N-key rollover *noun* facility on a keyboard where each keystroke (up to a maximum of N) is registered in sequence even if they are struck very fast **Tastatur mit überlappender Eingabe über mehr als 2 Tasten**

NAK = NEGATIVE ACKNOWLEDGEMENT

name *noun*
(a) word used to call a thing *or* a person **Name; brand name** = name of a particular make of product **Markenname; corporate name** = name of a large corporation **Firmenname;** *the company buys computer parts from several suppliers, and packages them together to make their own name product*
(b) ordinary word used to identify an address in machine language **Name; file name** = word used to identify a particular stored file **Dateiname; program name** = identification name for a stored program file **Programmname; name table** *or* **symbol table** = list of reserved words *or* commands in a language and the addresses in the computer that refer to them **Namen-, Symboltabelle; variable name** = word used to identify a variable in a program **Variablenname**

NAND function *noun* logical function whose output is false if all inputs are true, and true if any input is false **NAND-Funktion; NAND gate** = electronic circuit that provides a NAND function **NAND-Gatter** NOTE: the NAND function is equivalent to an AND function with a NOT function at the output

> COMMENT: the output is 0 only if both inputs are 1; if one input is 1 and the other 0, or if both inputs are 0, then the output is 1

nano- *or* **n** *prefix* meaning one thousand millionth *or (US)* one billionth **nano-** *(US)* **ein milliardstel; nanocircuit** *or* **nanosecond circuit** = electronic and logic circuits that can respond to impulses within nanoseconds **Nanoschaltung; nanometre** *or* **nm** one thousand millionth of a metre **Nanometer; nanosecond** *or* **ns** = one thousand millionth of a second **Nanosekunde** NOTE: US billion is the same as UK one thousand million (10 to the power of nine); UK billion is one million million (10 to the power of 10)

> QUOTE the cache's internal RAM is accessed in under 70ns from address strobe to ready signal
> *Electronics & Power*

narrative *noun* explanatory notes or comments to help a user operate a program **Erklärung**

◊ **narrative statement** *noun* statement which sets variables and allocates storage at the start of a program **erklärende Festlegung**

narrow band *noun* communication method that uses a bandwidth less than that of a voice channel **Schmalband; narrow band FM (NBFM)** = frequency modulation system using very small bandwidth (with only one pair of sidebands) **Schmalbandfrequenzmodulation;** *compare* WIDE BAND

National Television Standards Committee (NTSC) *noun* official body that defines television and video formats *or* standards used mainly in the USA and in Japan **NTSC;** *see also* VIDEO STANDARDS

‖ COMMENT: NTSC standards are based on ‖ 525 horizontal lines and 60 frames per second

◊ **National Television System Committee** *see* NTSC

native *adjective* **native compiler** = compiler that produces code that will run on the same system on which it is running (a cross-compiler produces code that will run on another hardware platform) **systemeigener Compiler; native file format** = (normally proprietary) default file format that is used by an application to store its data on disk **ursprüngliches** *or* **systemeigenes Dateiformat; native format** = first *or* basic format **Ausgangsformat, Ursprungsformat; native language** = language that can be executed by a processor without the need for any special software (normally this means the processor's native machine code) **systemeigene Sprache, Maschinensprache**

natural *adjective* occurring in nature *or* not created artificially **natürlich; natural binary coded decimal (NBCD)** = representation of single decimal digits as a pattern of 4 bits **natürliche binärcodierte Dezimale; natural language** = language that is used *or* understood by humans **natürliche Sprache;** *the expert system can be programmed in a natural language*

QUOTE there are two main types of natural-language interface: those based on menus, and those where the user has to discover what questions the computer will respond to by trial and error
Electronics & Power

NBCD = NATURAL BINARY CODED DECIMAL

NBFM = NARROW BAND FREQUENCY MODULATION

NC = NUMERICAL CONTROL machine operated automatically by computer *or* circuits controlled by a stored program *or* data **NC (Computer, die zur numerischen Steuerung von Werkzeugmaschinen dienen)**

NCR paper = NO CARBON REQUIRED special type of paper impregnated with chemicals and used in multipart forms; when NCR paper is printed on by an impact printer, the writing also appears on the sheets below **Durchschlagpapier**

NDIS = NETWORK DRIVER INTERFACE SPECIFICATION standard command interface (defined by Microsoft) between network driver software and network adapter cards **NDIS**

NDR = NON DESTRUCTIVE READOUT display system that continues to display previous characters when new ones are displayed **nichtlöschendes Auslesen**

near letter-quality (NLQ) *noun* printing by a dot-matrix printer that provides higher quality type, which is almost as good as a typewriter, by decreasing the spaces between the dots **korrespondenzfähiges Schriftbild, NLQ-Druckmodus;** *switch the printer to NLQ for these form letters*

needle *noun* tiny metal pin on a dot matrix printer which prints one of the dots **Nadel**

negate *verb* to reverse the sign of a number **negieren;** *if you negate 23.4 the result is −23.4*

◊ **negation** *noun* reversing the sign of a number (such as from 5 to −5) **Negierung**

◊ **negative**
1 *adjective* meaning "no" **negativ; negative acknowledgement (NAK)** = signal sent by a receiver to indicate that data has been incorrectly *or* incompletely received **negative Rückmeldung; negative feedback** = loop around a circuit in which part of the output signal is subtracted from the input signal **negative Rückkopplung; negative number** = number which represents the number subtracted from zero, indicated by a minus sign in front of the number **negative**

Zahl; negative-true logic = use of a lower voltage level to represent binary 1 than for binary 0 negative Logik

2 noun normal photographic film where the colours are reversed (black is white and white is black) Negativfilm; contact negative = film which can be used to produce a print without any reduction or enlargement Kontaktstreifen

neither-nor function noun logical function whose output is false if any input is true NOR-Funktion

NEQ = NON-EQUIVALENCE; NEQ function = logical function where the output is true if the inputs are not the same, otherwise the output is false Inäquivalenzfunktion; NEQ gate = electronic implementation of an NEQ function Inäquivalenzgatter

nest verb (i) to insert a subroutine within a program or another routine; (ii) to use a routine that calls itself recursively (i) & (ii) verschachteln; nested loop = loop inside another loop in the same program verschachtelte Schleife; nested macro call = a macro called from within another macro verschachtelter Makroaufruf; nested structure = section of a program in which one control loop or subroutine is used within another verschachtelte Struktur; nesting level = number of subroutines within a subroutine Verschachtelungsgrad; nesting store = hardware stack (normally stacks are implemented with software) Stapelspeicher

NetBIOS = NETWORK BASIC INPUT OUTPUT SYSTEM commonly used standard set of commands (originally developed by IBM) that allow application programs to carry out basic operations over a network (operations such as file sharing and transferring data between nodes) Net-BIOS; this software uses NetBIOS calls to manage file sharing

network

1 noun any system made of a number of points or circuits that are interconnected Netz; communications network = group of devices such as terminals and printers that are interconnected with a central computer allowing the rapid and simple transfer of data Nachrichtennetz; computer network = shared use of a series of interconnected computers, peripherals and terminals Computernetz; information network = number of databases linked together, usually using telephone lines and modems,

allowing a large amount of data to be accessed by a wider number of users Informationsnetz; local area network (LAN) = network where the various terminals and equipment are all within a short distance of one another (at a maximum distance of 500m, for example in the same building) and can be interconnected by cables Lokalnetz; long haul network = communications network between distant computers that usually uses the public telephone system Überlandnetz; neural network = system running an artificial intelligence program that attempts to simulate the way the brain works, how it learns and remembers neurales Netz; radio or television network = series of local radio or TV stations linked to a main central station Funk- od Fernsehnetz; wide area network (WAN) = network where the various terminals are far apart and linked by radio or satellite Weitverkehrsnetz; network adapter = add-in board that connects a computer to a network; the board converts the computer's data into electrical signals that are then transmitted along the network cable Netzwerkadapter; network administrator = individual who is responsible for looking after a network; responsibilities include installing, configuring and maintaining the network Netzwerkadministrator, Netzwerkverwalter; network analysis = study of messages, destinations and routes in a network to provide a better operation Netzplantechnik; network architecture = method in which a network is constructed, such as layers in an OSI system Netzwerkarchitektur; Network Basic Input Output System see NetBIOS; network control program = software that regulates the flow of and channels for data transmitted in a network Netzwerksteuerprogramm; network controller = network user responsible for allocating disk space, answering queries and solving problems from other users of the same network Netzüberwacher; network database = database structure in which data items can be linked together Datenbanknetz; network device driver = software which controls and manages a network adapter card to ensure that it functions correctly with other hardware and software in the computer Netzwerkgerätetreiber; network diagram = graphical representation describing the interconnections between points Netzwerkplan; network directory = directory that is stored on a disk drive on another computer in the network, but it can be accessed by anyone on the network; not on the local disk drive **Netzwerkverzeichnis; network drive** = disk drive that is part of another computer on a network, but it can be used by anyone on the network **Netzlaufwerk; network hardware** = physical links, computers and control equipment that make up a network **Netzwerkhardware; network interface card (NIC)** = add-in board that connects a computer to a network; the board converts the computer's data into electrical signals that are then transmitted along the network cable **Netzwerkschnittstellenkarte, Netzwerkkarte; network layer** = ISO/OSI standard layer that decides on the routes to be used, the costs, etc. **Vermittlungsschicht;** *see also* LAYER; **network management** = organization, planning, running and upkeep of a network **Netzführung; network operating system (NOS)** = operating system running on a (normally dedicated) server computer that controls access to the network resources, manage network links, printing, and users **Netzwerkbetriebssystem, Network Operating System (NOS); network printer** = printer attached to a server or workstation that can be used by any user connected to the network **Netzwerkdrucker; network processor** = signal multiplexer controlled by a microprocessor in a network **Netzwerkprozessor; network protocol** = set of handshaking signals that defines how a workstation sends data over a network without clashing with other data transmissions **Netzwerkprotokoll; network redundancy** = extra links between points allowing continued operation in the event of one failing **Netzwerkredundanz; network server** = computer which runs a network operating system and controls the basic network operations; all the workstations in a LAN are connected to the central network server and users log onto a network server **Netzwerkserver; network software** = software which is used to establish the link between a user's program and the network **Netzwerksoftware; network structure** = data structure that allows each node to be connected to any of the others **Netzstruktur; network timing** = signals that correctly synchronize the transmission of data **Netzsynchronisation; network topology** = arrangement of nodes and links within a network; a bus network topology; ring network topology **Netzwerktopologie, Netztopologie;** *see also* BUS, MESH, PROTOCOL, RING, STAR, TOPOLOGY **2** *verb* to link points together in a network **vernetzen;** *they run a system of networked micros; the workstations have been networked together rather than used as*

standalone systems; **networked TV programme** = programme which is broadcast (usually simultaneously) by all the stations in a TV network **vernetztes Fernsehprogramm**

◊ **networking** *noun*
(a) broadcasting a prime-time TV programme over several local stations at the same time **Netzwerkausstrahlung**
(b) (i) working *or* organization of a network; (ii) interconnecting two *or* more computers either in the same room *or* different buildings, in the same town *or* different towns, allowing them to exchange information (i) **Netzwerkbetrieb;** (ii) **Netzwerkverlegung; networking hardware** *or* **network hardware** = physical links, computers and control equipment that make up a network **Netzwerkhardware; networking software** *or* **network software** = software which is used to establish the link between a user's program and the network **Netzwerksoftware; networking specialist** = company *or* person who specializes in designing and setting up networks **Netzwerkspezialist;** *this computer firm is a UK networking specialist*

> COMMENT: networking allows a machine with a floppy disk drive to use another PC's hard disk when both machines are linked by a cable and are using networking software

neutral *adjective* with no state *or* bias *or* voltage **neutral; neutral transmission** = (transmission) system in which a voltage pulse and zero volts represent the binary digits 1 and 0 **neutrale Übertragung**

new *adjective* recent *or* not old **neu;** *they*

have installed a new computer system; the new programmer does not seem as efficient as the old one; **new (command)** = program command that clears main memory of the present program ready to accept a new program to be entered **NEW (zu Beginn einer neuen Programmeingabe); new line character** = character that moves a cursor *or* printhead to the beginning of the next line **Zeilenvorschubzeichen;** *see also* CARRIAGE RETURN (CR); LINEFEED (LF); **new technology** = electronic instruments which have recently been invented **neue Technologie**

◊ **news** *noun* information about things which have happened **Nachrichten;** *business news; financial news; financial markets were shocked by the news of the collapse of the computer company;* **news agency** = office which distributes news to newspapers and television companies **Nachrichtenagentur; news release** = sheet giving information about a new event which is sent to newspapers and TV and radio stations so that they can use it **Nachrichtenveröffentlichung;** *the company sent out a news release about the new managing director*

◊ **newsletter** *noun* **company newsletter** = printed sheet *or* small newspaper giving news about a company **Firmeninformationsblatt**

◊ **newsprint** *noun* mechanical paper used for printing newspapers **Zeitungspapier**
NOTE: no plural

next instruction register *noun* register in a CPU that contains the location where the next instruction to be executed is stored **Befehlsfolgeregister;** *see also* REGISTER

nexus *noun* connection point between units in a network **Verknüpfung**

nibble *or* **nybble** *noun* half the length of a standard byte **Vier-Bit-Byte**
NOTE: a nibble is normally 4 bits, but can vary according to different micros or people

NIC = NETWORK INTERFACE CARD add-in board that connects a computer to a network; the board converts the computer's data into electrical signals that are then transmitted along the network cable **NIC-Karte**

nil pointer *noun* pointer used to indicate the end of a chained list of items **Nullanzeiger**

nine's complement *noun* decimal complement (equivalent to the binary one's complement) formed by subtracting each digit in the number from nine **Neunerkomplement;** *see also* TEN'S COMPLEMENT

n-key rollover *noun* use of a buffer between the keyboard and computer to provide key stroke storage (up to 'n' keys can be stored) for fast typists who hit several keys in rapid succession **Tastaturpuffer**

n-level logic *noun* logic gate design in which no more than n gates occur in a series **n-stufige Logik**

NLQ = NEAR LETTER-QUALITY

NMI = NON-MASKABLE INTERRUPT

NMOS = N-CHANNEL METAL OXIDE SEMICONDUCTOR

no-address operation *noun* instruction which does not require an address within it **Anweisung ohne Adresse**

◊ **no op** *or* **no operation instruction** = NO OPERATION programming instruction which does nothing „**keine Operation"**

◊ **no parity** *noun* data transmission which does not use a parity bit **keine Parität**

node *noun* interconnection point in a structure *or* network **Netzknoten;** *a tree is made of branches that connect together at nodes this network has fibre optic connection with nodes up to one kilometre apart*

noise *noun* random signal present in addition to any wanted signal, caused by static, temperature, power supply, magnetic or electric fields and also from stars and the sun **Rauschen, Störungen; noise immunity** = ability of a circuit to ignore *or* filter out *or* be protected from noise **Störfestigkeit; noise margin** = maximum amplitude of noise that will affect a device, such as switch a logic gate **Störabstand; noise temperature** = temperature of a component for it to produce the same thermal noise as a source **Rauschtemperatur; galactic noise** = electrical noise which originates from planets and stars in space **galaktisches Rauschen; impulsive noise** =

interference on a signal caused by short periods of noise **Impulsstörung; thermal noise** = background noise signal caused by temperature variations in components **thermisches Rauschen**

◊ **noisy mode** *noun* floating point arithmetic system, in which a digit other than a zero is deliberately added in the least significant position during the normalization of a floating point number **Fließkommabetriebsart; noisy digit** = digit, usually not zero, added during the normalization of a floating point number when in noisy mode **Normierungsbit**

> QUOTE the photographs were grainy, out of focus, and distorted by signal noise
>
> *Byte*

nomenclature *noun* predefined system for assigning words and symbols to represent numbers or terms **Nomenklatur**

nomogram *or* **nomograph** *noun* graphical system for solving one value given two others **Nomogramm, Funktionsnetz**

non- *prefix* meaning not **nicht**

◊ **nonaligned** *adjective* two devices that are not correctly positioned in relation to each other, for optimum performance **nicht richtig ausgerichtet; nonaligned read head** = read head that is not in the same position on a magnetic medium as the write head was, producing a loss of signal quality **nicht richtig ausgerichteter Lesekopf**

◊ **non-arithmetic shift** *see* LOGICAL SHIFT

◊ **non-breaking space** *noun* (in word-processing or DTP software) space character that prevents two words being separated by a line break **geschütztes Leerzeichen**

◊ **noncompatibility** *noun* two or more pieces of hardware *or* software that cannot exchange data *or* use the same peripherals **fehlende Kompatibilität**

◊ **noncounting keyboard** *noun* entry keyboard on a phototypesetter that does not allow page format instructions to be entered **nicht zählende Tastatur**

◊ **non-dedicated server** *noun* computer that runs a network operating system in the background and can also be used to run normal applications at the same time **nicht dedizierter Server**

◊ **non-destructive cursor** *noun*

cursor on a display that does not erase characters already displayed as it passes over them **nichtlöschender Cursor;** *the screen quickly became unreadable when using a non-destructive cursor;* **non-destructive readout (NDR)** = display device that retains previous characters when displaying new characters **nichtlöschendes Auslesen; non-destructive test** = series of tests carried out on a piece of equipment without destroying it **nichtlöschender Test;** *I will carry out a number of non-destructive tests on your computer; if it passes, you can start using it again;* **non-scrollable** = part of the screen display which is always displayed (in a WP, the text can scroll whilst instructions, etc., are non-scrollable) **nicht umblätterbar;** *see also* STATUS LINE

◊ **non-equivalence function (NEQ)** *noun* logical function where the output is true if the inputs are not the same, otherwise the output is false **Antivalenzfunktion; non-equivalence gate** = electronic implementation of an NEQ function **Antivalenzglied**

◊ **nonerasable storage** *noun* storage medium that cannot be erased and re-used **nichtlöschbarer Speicher;** *paper tape is a nonerasable storage*

◊ **non-impact printer** *noun* printer (like an ink-jet printer) where the character form does not hit a ribbon onto the paper **nichtmechanischer Drucker; (Laserdrucker)**

◊ **non-interlaced** *adjective* (in a monitor, system) in which the picture electron beam scans each line of the display once during each refresh cycle; the beam in an interlaced display scans every alternate line **Non-Interlaced-**

◊ **nonlinear** *adjective* electronic circuit whose output does not change linearly in proportion to its input **nichtlinear**

◊ **non-maskable interrupt (NMI)** *noun* high priority interrupt signal that cannot be blocked by software and overrides other commands **nichtmaskierbare Unterbrechung**

◊ **non-operable instruction** *noun* instruction that does not carry out any function, but increments the program counter **nicht ausführbare Anweisung**

◊ **non-printing codes** *noun* codes that represent an action of the printer rather than a printed character **Druckanweisungscodes;** *the line width can be set using one of the non-printing codes, .LW, then a number*

◊ **non return to zero (NRZ)** *noun* signalling system in which a positive voltage represents one binary digit and a negative voltage the other; representation of binary data in which the signal changes when the data changes state, and does not return to zero volts after each bit of data **ohne Rückkehr zu Null**

◊ **non-volatile** *adjective* **non-volatile memory** *or* **non-volatile store** *or* **storage** = storage medium *or* memory that retains data even when the power has been switched off **nichtflüchtiger Speicher;** *bubble memory is a non-volatile storage; using magnetic tape provides non-volatile memory* NOTE: opposite is **volatile**

| COMMENT: disks (both hard and floppy) and tapes are non-volatile memory stores; solid-state memory, such as RAM chips are volatile unless battery backed

| QUOTE 100 sets of test results can be stored in non-volatile memory for later hard-copy printout
| *Computing*

NOR function *noun* logical function whose output is false if either input is true **NOR-Funktion; NOR gate** = electric circuit *or* chip which performs a NOR function **NOR-Gatter**

| COMMENT: the output is 1 only if both inputs are 0; if the two inputs are different or if both are 1, the output is 0

normal *adjective* usual *or* which happens regularly **normal;** *the normal procedure is for backup copies to be made at the end of each day's work;* **normal form** = method of structuring information in a database to avoid redundancy and improve storage efficiency **Normalform; normal format** = standardized format for data storage **Normalformat; normal range** = expected range for a result *or* number, any outside this range are errors **Normalbereich**

◊ **normalize** *verb*
(a) to convert data into a form which can be read by a particular computer system **normalisieren, standardisieren**
(b) to convert characters into just capitals or into just a lower case form **normalisieren**
(c) to store and represent numbers in a pre-agreed form, usually to provide maximum precision **normieren;** *all the new data has been normalized to 10 decimal places;* **normalized form** = floating point number that has been normalized so that its mantissa is within a certain range **Standardform**

◊ **normalization** *noun* process of normalizing data **Normalisierung, Standardisierung; normalization routine** = routine that normalizes a floating point number and adds extra (noisy) digits in the least significant position **Standardisierungsroutine**

NOS = NETWORK OPERATING SYSTEM

NOT function *noun* logical inverse function where the output is true if the input is false **NICHT-Funktion; NOT-AND** = equivalent to the NAND function **NAND-Funktion; NOT gate** = electronic circuit *or* chip which performs a NOT function **NICHT-Gatter**

| COMMENT: if the input is 1, the output is 0; if the input is 0, the output is 1

notation *noun* method of writing *or* representing numbers **Schreibweise; binary notation** = base two numerical system using only the digits 0 and 1 **Binärschreibweise; decimal notation** = number representation in base 10, using the digits 0-9 **Dezimalschreibweise; hexadecimal notation** = number system using base 16 and the digits 0-9 and A-F **hexadezimale Schreibweise; infix notation** = mathematical syntax where operators are embedded inside operands (such as C - D or X + Y) **Infixschreibweise; octal notation** = number system using base 8 and the digits 0-7 **oktale Schreibweise; postfix notation** = mathematical operations written in a logical way, so that the operator appears after the operands, this removes the need for brackets **Postfixschreibweise;** *normal notation: (x-y) + z, but using postfix notation: xy - z +;* **prefix notation** = mathematical operations written in a logical way, so that the operator appears before the operands, this removes the need for brackets **Präfixschreibweise;** *normal notation: (x-y) + z, but using prefix notation: - xy + z*

notched *see* EDGE NOTCHED CARD

notepad *noun* **screen notepad** = part of the screen used to store information even when the terminal is switched off **Bildschirmnotizblock**

notice board *noun* (i) board fixed to a wall where notices can be pinned up (ii) type of bulletin board on which messages to all users can be left **(i) Schwarzes Brett; (ii) Anschlagetafel**

Novell ™ large company that produces network software; it is best known for its NetWare ™ range of network operating system software that runs on a PC server **Novell** ™

n-plus-one address instruction *noun* instruction made up of a number (n) of addresses and one other address that is the location of the next instruction **n-plus-Eins-Adressbefehl**

npn transistor *noun* bipolar transistor design using p-type semiconductor for the base and n-type for the collector and emitter **bipolarer Transistortyp**; *see also* TRANSISTOR, BIPOLAR

NRZ = NON RETURN TO ZERO

ns *abbreviation* nanosecond **ns**

NTSC = NATIONAL TELEVISION STANDARDS (or SYSTEM) COMMITTEE official body that defines television and video formats *or* standards used mainly in the USA and in Japan **NTSC**; *see also* VIDEO STANDARDS

‖ COMMENT: the NTSC standard is based on ‖ 525 horizontal lines and 60 frames per seconds

QUOTE the system has a composite video output port that conforms to the NTSC video specification

Byte

n-type material *or* **N-type material** *or* **n-type semiconductor** *noun* semiconductor that has been doped with a substance that provides extra electrons in the material, giving it an overall negative charge compared to the intrinsic semiconductor **Material vom N-Typ; N-Halbleiter**; *see also* NPN TRANSISTOR

NuBus ™ *noun* high-speed 96-pin expansion bus used within Apple Macintosh II computers **NuBus** ™

null *noun* nothing **nichts; null character** = character which means nothing (usually code 0) **Nullzeichen; null instruction** = program instruction that does nothing **leere Anweisung; null list** = list which contains nothing **Leerliste; null modem** = emulator circuit that allows two pieces of equipment that normally require modems to communicate, to be connected together over a short distance **Nullmodem**; *this cable is configured as a null modem, which will allow me to connect these 2 computers*

together easily; **null set** = set that only contains zeros **Nullsatz; null string** = string that contains no characters **Zeichenfolge der Länge Null; null terminated string** = string of characters that has a null character to indicate the end of the string **String mit Nullzeichenabschluss**

QUOTE you have to connect the two RS232 ports together using a crossed cable, or null modem

PC Business World

number
1 *noun*
(a) representation of a quantity **Zahl; number cruncher** = dedicated processor used for high-speed calculations **'Zahlenfresser', Supercomputer; number crunching** = performing high-speed calculations **'Zahlenfressen'**; *a very powerful processor is needed for graphics applications which require extensive number crunching capabilities;* **number range** = set of allowable values **Zahlenbereich**
(b) written figure **Nummer**; *each piece of hardware has a production number; please note the reference number of your order;* **box number** = reference number used when asking for mail to be sent to a post office *or* to a newspaper, in reply to advertisements **Postfachnummer; check number** = number produced from data for parity *or* error detection **Prüfnummer**
2 *verb*
(a) to put a figure on a document **nummerieren**; *the pages of the manual are numbered 1 to 395*
(b) to assign digits to a list of items in an ordered manner **durchnummerieren**

◊ **numeral** *noun* character *or* symbol which represents a number **Ziffer, Numeral; Arabic numerals** = figures written 1, 2, 3, 4, etc. **arabische Ziffern; Roman numerals** = figures written I, II, III, IV, etc. **römische Ziffern**

◊ **numeric** *adjective* (i) referring to numbers; (ii) (field, etc.) which contains only numbers **(i) & (ii) numerisch; numeric array** = array containing numbers **numerische Matrix; numeric character** = letter used in some notations to represent numbers (for example in hex the letters A-F are numeric characters) **numerisches Zeichen; numeric keypad** = set of ten keys with figures, included in most computer keyboards as a separate group, used for entering large amounts of data in numeric form **numerischer 10er-Block; numeric operand** = operand that only uses numerals numerischer Operand; numeric pad = numeric keypad **numerische Tastatur, numerischer 10er-Block**; numeric punch = punched hole in rows 0-9 of a punched card **numerische Lochung**

◊ **numerical** *adjective* referring to numbers **numerisch; numerical analysis** = study of ways of solving mathematical problems **numerische Analyse; numerical control (NC)** *or* **computer numerical control (CNC)** = machine operated automatically by computer *or* circuits controlled by stored data **NC (Computer, die zur numerische Steuerung von Werkzeugmaschinen dienen)**

> QUOTE Hewlett-Packard's 100LX Palmtop PC weighs 11oz and has a separate numeric keypad
> *Computing*

Num Lock key *noun* (on a keyboard) key that switches the function of a numeric keypad from cursor control to numeric entry **Num-Lock-Taste, Num-Taste, Ziffernfeststelltaste**

nybble *or* **nibble** *noun (informal)* half the length of a standard byte **Vier-Bit-Byte** NOTE: a nybble is normally 4 bits, but can vary according to different micros

Oo

OA = OFFICE AUTOMATION

object *noun*
(a) the data that makes up a particular image *or* sound **Objekt**
(b) data in a statement which is to be operated on by the operator **Objekt**; *see also* ARGUMENT, OPERAND; **object** *or* **object-orientated architecture** = structure where all files, outputs, etc., in a system are represented as objects **objektorientierter Aufbau; object code** = binary code which directly operates a central processing unit (a program code after it has been translated, compiled or assembled into machine code) **Objektcode, Maschinensprache; object computer** = computer system for which a program has been written and compiled **Programmablaufanlage; object deck** = punched cards that contain a program

Objektprogrammkartensatz; object file = file that contains object code for a routine *or* program **Objektdatei; object language** = the language of a program after it has been translated **Maschinensprache;** *compare with* SOURCE LANGUAGE; **object program** = computer program in object code form, produced by a compiler *or* assembler **Zielprogramm**

◊ **objective** *noun*
(a) something which someone tries to do **Absicht, Ziel**
(b) optical lens nearest the object viewed **Objektiv**

◊ **object linking and embedding (OLE)** *noun* (in Microsoft Windows) method of sharing data between applications; an object (such as an image or sound) can be linked to a document or spreadsheet **Objekte verknüpfen und einbetten (OLE)**

◊ **object-oriented** *adjective* (system or language) that uses objects **objektorientiert; object-oriented graphics** = image which uses vector definitions (lines, curves) to describe the shapes of the image rather than pixels in a bit-map image **objektorientierte Grafik;** *this object-oriented graphics program lets you move shapes around very easily;* **object-oriented language** = programming language that is used for object-oriented programming, such as C++ **objektorientierte Sprache; object-oriented programming (OOP)** = method of programming, such as C++, in which each element of the program is treated as an object that can interact with other objects within the program **objektorientierte Programmierung (OOP);** *see also* OBJECT

> QUOTE UK PC-maker Elonex has signed a strategic agreement with NeXT Computer designed to create a volume market in Europe for NeXT's pioneering object based operating system
> *Computing*

obtain *verb* to get *or* to receive **erhalten;** *to obtain data from a storage device; a clear signal is obtained after filtering*

OCCAM computer programming language, used in large multiprocessor *or* multi-user systems **OCCAM (Programmiersprache)**

| COMMENT: this is the development language for transputer systems

occur *verb* to happen *or* to take place

geschehen; *data loss can occur because of power supply variations*

OCP = ORDER CODE PROCESSOR; *(in a multiprocessor system)* a processor which decides and performs the arithmetic and logical operations according to the program code **OCP (Anweisungscodeprozessor)**

OCR
(a) = OPTICAL CHARACTER READER device which scans printed *or* written characters, recognizes them, and converts them into machine-readable form for processing in a computer **(maschineller) optischer Leser**
(b) = OPTICAL CHARACTER RECOGNITION process that allows printed *or* written characters to be recognized optically and converted into machine-readable code that can be input into a computer, using an optical character reader **(maschinelle) optische Zeichenerkennung; OCR font** = character design that can be easily read using an OCR reader **OCR-Zeichensatz**

COMMENT: there are two OCR fonts in common use: OCR-A, which is easy for scanners to read, and OCR-B, which is easier for people to read than the OCR-A font

QUOTE In 1986, Calera Recognition Systems introduced the first neural-network-based OCR system that could read complex pages containing any mixture of non-decorative fonts without manual training.
Computing

octal (notation) *noun* number notation using base 8, with digits 0 to 7 **Oktalsystem; octal digit** = digit (0 to 7) used in the octal system **Oktalziffer; octal scale** = power of eight associated with each digit position in a number **Oktalskala**

COMMENT: in octal, the digits used are 0 to 7; so decimal 9 is octal 11

octave *noun* series of 8 musical notes, each a semitone higher than the previous one **Oktave**

octet *noun* a group of eight bits treated as one unit; word made up of eight bits **Oktett;** *see also* BYTE

odd *adjective* (number, such as 5 or 7) which cannot be divided by two **ungerade; odd-even check** = method of checking that

transmitted binary data has not been corrupted **Paritätsprüfung; odd parity (check)** = error checking system in which any series of bits transmitted must have an odd number of binary ones **Prüfung auf ungerade Parität** (NOTE: opposite is **even**)

ODI = OPEN DATALINK INTERFACE standard interface, defined by Novell, between a network driver and network interface card **ODI-Schnittstelle;** *compare* NDIS

OEM = ORIGINAL EQUIPMENT MANUFACTURER company which produces equipment using basic parts made by other manufacturers, and customizes the product for a particular application **Hersteller von Fremdfabrikaten**

QUOTE IBM UK has appointed Steve Wainwright as regional sales manager, northern Europe, for micro-electronics products. He was previously OEM sales manager, north Europe, for Harris Corporation
Computing

off-cut *noun* scrap paper that is left when a sheet is trimmed to size **Beschnitt**

off-hook *adverb* condition in a modem similar to picking up a telephone receiver; a modem goes off-hook to answer a call and remains off-hook whilst connected **ausgehängt**

office *noun* room *or* building where a company works *or* where business is done **Büro; office automation (OA)** = use of machines and computers to carry out normal office tasks **Textverarbeitung, Büroautomatisierung; office computer** = small computer (sometimes with a hard disk and several terminals) suitable for office use **Bürocomputer; office copier** = copying machine in an office **Bürokopierer; office equipment** = desks, typewriters, and other furniture and machines needed in an office **Büroausstattung; office of the future** = design of an office that is completely coordinated by a computer **Büro der Zukunft;** *see also* PAPERLESS OFFICE

off-line *adverb & adjective* (i) (processor *or* printer *or* terminal) that is not connected to a network *or* central computer (usually temporarily); (ii) (peripheral) connected to a network, but not available for use (i) **systemunabhängig, offline;** (ii) **offline;** *before changing the paper in the printer, switch it* *off-line;* **off-line printing** = printout operation that is not supervised by a computer **Offlinedrucken; off-line processing** processing by devices not under the control of a central computer **Offlineverarbeitung; off-line storage** = storage that is not currently available for access, such as a magnetic tape that must first be loaded into the tape machine **Offlinespeicherung, systemunabhängige Speicherung** NOTE: opposite is **on-line**

offprint *noun* section of a journal reprinted separately **Sonderdruck**

off screen *adverb* TV action that is taking place off the screen, outside the viewer's field of vision **außerhalb des Bildschirms**

offset
1 *noun*
(a) **offset lithography** = printing process used for printing books, where the ink sticks to dry areas on the film and is transferred to rubber rollers from which it is printed on to the paper **Offsetlithographie; offset printing** = printing method that transfers the ink image to the paper via a second roller **Offsetdruck**
(b) quantity added to a number *or* address to give a final number **Ausgleichszahl; offset value** *or* **offset word** = value to be added to a base address to provide a final indexed address **Relativzeigerwert**

ohm *noun* unit of measurement of electrical resistance **Ohm;** *this resistance has a value of 100 ohms;* **kilo-ohm** = one thousand ohms **Kiloohm** ⇨APPENDIX

◊ **Ohm's Law** *noun* definition of one ohm as: one volt drop across a resistance of one ohm when one amp of current is flowing **ohmsches Gesetz**

O.K. used as a prompt in place of 'ready' in some systems **Bereit-Signal; OK button** = (in a GUI) button with 'OK' label that is used to start or confirm an action **Schaltfläche ‚OK'**

OLE = OBJECT LINKING AND EMBEDDING (in Microsoft Windows) method of sharing data between applications; an object (such as an image or sound) can be linked to a document or spreadsheet **OLE**

omega wrap *noun* system of threading video tape around a video head **Omegawicklung**

| COMMENT: the tape passes over most of the circular head and is held in place by two small rollers

omission factor *noun* number of relevant documents that were missed in a search **Vermisstenfaktor**

omnidirectional *adjective* device that can pick up signals from all directions **mit Kugel(charakteristik);** *omnidirectional aerial; omnidirectional microphone*

OMR
(a) = OPTICAL MARK READER device that can recognize marks *or* lines on a special form (such as on an order form *or* a reply to a questionnaire) and that inputs them into a computer **optischer Markierungsleser**
(b) = OPTICAL MARK RECOGNITION process that allows certain marks *or* lines on special forms (such as on an order form *or* a reply to a questionnaire) to be recognized by an optical mark reader, and input into a computer **optische Markierungserkennung**

on-board *adjective* (feature *or* circuit) which is contained on a motherboard *or* main PCB **auf der Platine**

QUOTE the electronic page is converted to a printer-readable video image by the on-board raster image processor

QUOTE the key intelligence features of these laser printers are emulation modes and on-board memory
Byte

on chip *noun* circuit constructed on a chip **Schaltung auf dem Chip**

◊ **on-chip** *adjective* (circuit) constructed on a chip **auf dem Chip;** *the processor uses on-chip bootstrap software to allow programs to be loaded rapidly*

one address computer *noun* computer structure whose machine code only uses one address at a time **Einadresscomputer; one address instruction** = instruction made up of an operator and one address **Einadressbefehl**

◊ **one element** *noun* logical function that produces a true output if any input is true **eingliedriges Element**

◊ **one for one** *noun* programming language, usually assembler, that produces one machine code instruction for each instruction *or* command word in the language **One-for-one (Assembliersprache)**

COMMENT: compilers and interpreters are usually used for translating high-level languages which use more than one machine code instruction for each high-level instruction

◊ **one-level address** *noun* storage address that directly, without any modification, accesses a location *or* device **direkte Adresse; one-level code** = binary code which directly operates the CPU, using only absolute addresses and values (this is the final form of a program after a compiler *or* assembler pass) **Direktcode; one-level store** = organization of storage in which each different type of storage device is treated as if it were the same **einschichtiger Speicher; one-level subroutine** = subroutine which does not call another subroutine during its execution **einstufiges Unterprogramm**

◊ **one's complement** *noun* inverse of a binary number **Einerkomplement;** *the one's complement of 10011 is 01100; see also* COMPLEMENT; TWO'S COMPLEMENT

◊ **one-pass assembler** *noun* assembler program that translates the source code in one action **Assemblierer mit einem Durchlauf;** *this new one-pass assembler is very quick in operation*

◊ **one-plus-one address** *noun* address format that provides the location of one register and the location of the next instruction **Eins-plus-Eins-Adresse**

◊ **one-time pad** *noun* coding system that uses a unique cipher key each time it is used **hochspezielles Codiersystem**

COMMENT: two identical pieces of paper with an encrypted alphabet printed on each one are used, one by the sender, one by the receiver; this is one of the most secure cipher systems

◊ **one to zero ratio** *noun* ratio between the amplitude of a binary one and zero output **Eins-zu-Null-Verhältnis**

on-hook *adverb* condition similar to replacing a telephone receiver; a modem goes on-hook when it has finished a call **eingehängt**

onion skin architecture *noun* design of a computer system in layers, according to function *or* priority **Zwiebelschalenarchitektur;** *the onion skin architecture of this computer is made up of a kernel at the centre, an operating system, a low-level language and then the user's program*

◊ **onion skin language** *noun* database

manipulation language that can process hierarchical data structures **Zwiebelschalensprache**

on-line *adverb & adjective* (terminal *or* device) connected to and under the control of a central processor **im Dialogbetrieb, online;** *the terminal is on-line to the mainframe;* **on-line database** = interactive search, retrieve and update of database records, with a terminal that is on-line **Onlinedatenbank; on-line help** = text screen displayed from within an application that explains how to use the application **Onlinehilfe; on-line information retrieval** = system that allows an operator of an on-line terminal to access, search and display data held in a main computer **Online-Informationswiedergewinnung; on-line processing** = processing by devices connected to and under the control of the central computer (the user remains in contact with the central computer while processing) **Onlineverarbeitung; on-line storage** = data storage equipment that is directly controlled by a computer **rechnerabhängiger Speicher; on-line system** = computer system that allows users who are on-line to transmit and receive information **Onlinesystem, Dialogbetrieb; on-line transaction processing** = interactive processing in which a user enters commands and data on a terminal which is linked to a central computer, with results being displayed on the screen **Onlinetransaktionsverarbeitung**

on-screen *adjective* (information) that is displayed on a computer screen rather than printed out **am Bildschirm**

◊ **on-site** *adjective* at the place where something is **am Einsatzort;** *the new model has an on-site upgrade facility*

on the fly *adverb* (to examine and modify data) during a program run without stopping the run **fliegend**

OOP = OBJECT ORIENTED PROGRAMMING

O/P *or* **o/p** = OUTPUT

opacity *noun* measure of how opaque an optical lens is **Lichtundurchlässigkeit, Opazität**
NOTE: opposite is **transmittance**

op amp = OPERATIONAL AMPLIFIER term for a versatile electronic component that provides amplification, integration, addition, subtraction and many other functions on signals depending on external components added **Operationsverstärker**

> COMMENT: usually in the form of an 8 pin IC package with 2 inputs (inverting and noninverting), output, power supply and other control functions

op code = OPERATION CODE part of the machine code instruction that defines the action to be performed **Operationscode, Operationsschlüssel**

> QUOTE the subroutine at 3300 is used to find the op code corresponding to the byte whose hex value is in B
> *Computing Today*

opaque *adjective* will not allow light to pass through it **undurchsichtig, opak;** *the screen is opaque - you cannot see through it;* **opaque projector** = device that is able to project an image of an opaque object **Epidiaskop**

open
1 *adjective*
(a) command to prepare a file before reading *or* writing actions can occur **eröffnet;** *you cannot access the data unless the file is open;* **open file** = file that can be read from or written to; the application opens the file which locates the file on disk and prepares it for an operation **offene Datei** **(b)** not closed **offen; open access** = system where many workstations are available for anyone to use **offener Zugang; open architecture** = computer with a published expansion interface that has been designed to allow add-on hardware to be plugged in **offene Architektur; open code** = extra instructions required in a program that mainly uses macroinstructions **Open Code; open datalink interface** *see* ODI; **open-ended program** = program designed to allow future expansion and easy modification **Programm mit offenem Ende; open loop** = control system whose input is free of feedback **offener Regelkreis;** *see also* FEEDBACK; **open reel** = magnetic tape on a reel that is not enclosed in a cartridge *or* cassette **offene Spule; open routine** = routine which can be inserted into a larger routine *or* program without using a call instruction **Open-Routine, Dateieröffnungsroutine; open subroutine** = code for a subroutine which is copied into memory whenever a call instruction is found, rather than executing a jump to the subroutine's address **offenes Unterprogramm; open system** = system which is constructed in such a way that different operating systems can work together **offenes System; Open System Interconnection (OSI)** = standardized ISO network which is constructed in layered form, with each layer having a specific task, allowing different systems to communicate if they conform to the standard **Kommunikation offener Systeme (OSI);** *see also* ISO/OSI LAYERS, INTERNATIONAL
2 *verb*
(a) to take the cover off *or* to make a door open **öffnen;** *open the disk drive door; open the top of the computer by lifting here* **(b)** to prepare a file before accessing *or* editing *or* carrying out other transactions on stored records **eröffnen;** *you cannot access the data unless the file has been opened*

> QUOTE X.400 messaging company Isocor has appointed Steve McDaniel to the position of sales director. Steve previously worked for Retix, where he was European sales manager for the company's OSI products
> *Computing*

operand *noun* data (in a computer instruction) which is to be operated on by the operator **Rechengröße, Operand;** *in the instruction ADD 74, the operator ADD will add the operand 74 to the accumulator;* **immediate operand** = within an immediate addressing operation, the operand is fetched at the same time as the instruction **Direktoperand; literal operand** = actual number *or* address to be used rather than a label *or* its location **aktueller Operand; numeric operand** = operand that only contains numerals **numerischer Operand; operand field** = space allocated for an operand in a program instruction **Operandenfeld;** *see also* ARGUMENT, MACHINE-CODE INSTRUCTION

operate *verb* to work *or* to make a machine work **arbeiten, bedienen;** *do you know how to operate the telephone switchboard?;* **disk operating system (DOS)** = section of the operating system software that controls disk and file management **Betriebssystem; operating code (op code)** = part of the machine code instruction that defines the action to be performed **Operationsschlüssel; operating console** = terminal in an interactive system which sends and receives information **Bedienerkonsole; operating instructions** = commands and instructions used to operate a computer **Bedienungsanweisung; operating system (OS)** = software that controls the basic, low-level hardware operations, and file management, without the user having to operate it (the operating system is usually supplied with the computer as part of the bundled software or in ROM) **Betriebssystem; operating time** = total time required to carry out a task **Betriebszeit**

◊ **operation** *noun* working (of a machine) **Operation, Arbeitsgang; arithmetic operation** = mathematical function carried out on data **Rechenoperation; binary operation** = (i) operation on two operands; (ii) operation on an operand in binary form **(i) duale Operation; (ii) Binäroperation; block operation** = process carried out on a block of data **Blockoperation; Boolean operation** = logical operation on a number of operands, conforming to Boolean algebra rules **boolesche Operation; complete operation** = operation that retrieves the necessary operands from memory, performs the operation and returns the results and operands to memory, then reads the next instruction to be processed **vollständige Operation; dyadic Boolean operation** = logical operation that produces an output from two inputs **dyadische boolesche Operation; no-address operation** = instruction which does not require an address within it **adressfreie Operation; no-operation instruction (no-op)** = programming instruction which does nothing **Befehl: „keine Operation"; operation code (op code)** = part of a machine-code instruction that defines the action to be performed **Operationsschlüssel; operation cycle** = section of the machine cycle during which the instruction is executed **Operationszyklus;** *see also* FETCH-EXECUTE CYCLE, MACHINE CYCLE; **operation decoder** = hardware that converts a machine-code instruction (in binary form) into actions **Operationsumwandler; operation field** = part of an assembly language statement that contains the mnemonic or symbol for the op code **Operationsfeld; operation priority** = the sequence order in which the operations within a statement are carried out **Arbeitsgangpriorität; operation register** = register that contains the op code during its execution **Operationsregister; operation time** = period of time that an operation requires for its operation cycle **Operationszeit; operation trial** = series of tests to check programs and data preparation **Betriebsuntersuchung; operations manual** *see* INSTRUCTION MANUAL

◊ **operational** *adjective* which is working

or which refers to the way a machine works **funktionsfähig; operational information** = information about the normal operations of a system **Betriebsinformation**

◊ **operational amplifier (op amp)** *noun* versatile electronic component that provides amplification, integration, addition, subtraction and many other functions on signals depending on external components added **Operationsverstärker**

| COMMENT: usually in the form of an 8 pin IC package with 2 inputs (inverting and non-inverting) output, power supply and other control functions

operator *noun*
(a) person who makes a machine *or* process work **Bediener, Operator;** *the operator was sitting at his console;* **computer operator** = person who operates a computer **Computeroperator; operator's console** = input and output devices used by an operator to control a computer (usually consisting of a keyboard and VDU) **Bedienerkonsole; operator overloading** = assigning more than one function to a particular operator (the function often depends on the type of data being operated on and is used in the C++ and Ada programming languages) **Operatorenüberladung; operator precedence** = order in which a number of mathematical operations will be carried out **Operatorvorrang; operator procedure** = set of actions that an operator has to carry out to work a machine *or* process **Vorgehensweise des Operatoren**
(b) character *or* symbol *or* word that defines a function *or* operation **Operator;** *x is the multiplication operator;* **arithmetic operator** = symbol which indicates an arithmetic function (such as + for addition, x for multiplication) **Rechenzeichen**

op register *noun* register that contains the operating code for the instruction that is being executed **Operationsschlüsselregister**

optic fibres = OPTICAL FIBRES; **fibre optics** = using optical fibres (fine strands of glass *or* plastic protected by a surrounding material) for the transmission of light signals which can carry data **Faseroptik**

optical *adjective* referring to *or* making use of light **optisch;** *an optical reader uses a light beam to scan characters or patterns or lines;* **optical bar reader** *or* **bar code reader** *or* **optical wand** = optical device that reads data from a bar code **Balkencodeleser; optical character reader (OCR)** = device which scans printed *or* written characters, recognizes them, and converts them into machine-readable code for processing in a computer **optischer Zeichenleser; optical character recognition (OCR)** = process that allows printed *or* written characters to be recognized optically and converted into machine-readable code that can be input into a computer, using an optical character reader **optische Zeichenerkennung; optical communication system** = communication system using fibre optics **optisches Nachrichtenübertragungssystem; optical data link** = connection between two devices to allow the transmission of data using light signals (either line-of-sight or optic fibre) **optische Datenverbindung; optical disk** = disk that contains binary data in the form of small holes in the surface which are read with a laser beam **Laserplatte, VLP-Bildplatte** (NOTE: also called WORM (write once, read many times, for computers) which can be programmed once, or compact disk (CD) and video disk which are programmed at manufacture) **optical fibre** = fine strand of glass *or* plastic protected by a surrounding material, that is used for the convenient transmission of light signals **Glasfaser; optical font** *or* **OCR font** = character design that can be easily read using an OCR reader **OCR-Zeichensatz; optical mark reader (OMR)** = device that can recognize marks *or* lines on a special forms (such as on an order form *or* a reply to a questionnaire) and convert them into a form a computer can process **optischer Markierungsleser; optical mark recognition (OMR)** = process that allows certain marks *or* lines on special forms (such as on an order form *or* a reply to a questionnaire) to be recognized by an optical mark reader, and input into a computer **optische Markierungserkennung; optical memory** = optical disks **Laserplatte, VLP-Bildplatte; optical mouse** = pointing device that is operated by moving it across a special flat mat; on the mat is printed a grid of lines, as the mouse is moved, two light sensors count the number of lines that have been passed to produce a measure of the distance and direction of travel; an optical mouse has fewer moving parts than a mechanical mouse and so is more reliable, but requires an accurately printed mat **optische Maus; optical scanner** = equipment that converts an image into electrical signals which can be stored in and displayed on a computer **optischer Abtaster, Scanner; optical storage** = data storage using mediums such as

optical disk, etc. **optischer Speicher; optical transmission** = use of fibre optic cables, laser beams and other light sources to carry data, in the form of pulses of light **optische Übertragung; optical wand** = OPTICAL BAR READER

optimization *noun* making something work as efficiently as possible **Optimierung**

◊ **optimize** *verb* to make something work as efficiently as possible **optimieren; optimized code** = program that has been passed through an optimizer to remove any inefficient code *or* statements **Optimierungscode; optimizing compiler** = compiler that analyses the machine code it produces in order to improve the speed or efficiency of the code **Optimierungscompiler**

◊ **optimizer** *noun* program which adapts another program to run more efficiently **Optimierer**

optimum *noun & adjective* best possible **Optimum, optimal; optimum code** *or* **minimum access code** *or* **minimum delay code** = coding system that provides the fastest access and retrieval time for stored data items **Bestzeitcode**

option *noun* action which can be chosen **Auswahlmöglichkeit, Option;** *there are usually four options along the top of the screen the options available are described in the main menu*

◊ **optional** *adjective* which can be chosen **wahlfrei;** *the system comes with optional 3.5 or 5.25 disk drives*

QUOTE with the colour palette option, remarkable colour effects can be achieved on an RGB colour monitor
Electronics & Wireless World

optoelectrical *adjective* which converts light to electrical signals *or* electrical signals into light **optoelektrisch**

◊ **optoelectronic** *adjective* (microelectronic component) that has optoelectrical properties **optoelektronisch**

◊ **optoelectronics** *noun* electronic components that can generate *or* detect light, such as phototransistors, light-emitting diodes **Optoelektronik**

optomechanical mouse *see* MECHANICAL MOUSE

OR function *noun* logical function that produces a true output if any input is true

ODER-Funktion; OR gate = electronic implementation of the OR function **ODER-Gatter**

COMMENT: the result of the OR function will be 1 if either or both inputs is 1; if both inputs are 0, then the result is 0

orbit
1 *noun* path in space that a satellite follows around the earth **Umlaufbahn;** *the satellite's orbit is 100km from the earth's surface;* **elliptical orbit** = path of a satellite around the earth that is in the shape of an ellipse **elliptische Umlaufbahn; geostationary orbit** = satellite which moves at the same velocity as the earth, so remains above the same area of the earth's surface, and appears stationary when viewed from earth **geostationäre Umlaufbahn; polar orbit** = satellite flight path that goes over the earth's poles **polare Umlaufbahn**
2 *verb* to follow a path in space around the earth **umkreisen;** *the weather satellite orbits the earth every four hours*

order
1 *noun*
(a) instruction **Anweisung, Befehl; order code** = operation code **Befehlscode; order code processor (OCP)** = *(in a multiprocessor system)* a processor which decodes and performs the arithmetic and logical operations according to the program code **Befehlscodeprozessor (OCP)**
(b) an arrangement of things in sequence **Reihenfolge, Ordnung;** *in alphabetical order*
2 *verb*
(a) to direct *or* instruct **anweisen**
(b) to sort according to a key **sortieren; ordered list** = list of data items which has been sorted into an order **geordnete Liste**

organize *verb* to arrange something so that it works efficiently **organisieren**

◊ **organization** *noun*
(a) way of arranging something so that it works efficiently **Organisation;** *the chairman handles the organization of the sales force; the organization of the group is too centralized to be efficient; the organization of the head office into departments;* **organization and methods** = examining how an office works, and suggesting how it can be made more efficient **Organisation und Durchführung; organization chart** = list of people working in various departments, showing how a company *or* office is organized **Organigramm, Stellenbesetzungsplan**
(b) group of people which is arranged for efficient work **Organisation; a government organization** = official body, run by the government **eine staatliche Organisation; an employers' organization** = group of employers with similar interests **ein Arbeitgeberverband**
NOTE: no plural for (a)

◊ **organizational** *adjective* referring to the way in which something is organized **organisatorisch**

orientated *adjective* aimed towards **orientiert; problem-orientated language (POL)** = high-level programming language that allows caertain problems to be expressed easily **problemorientierte Programmiersprache**

◊ **orientation** *noun* (i) direction *or* position of an object; (ii) (in word-processing or DTP software) direction of a page, either landscape (long edge horizontal) or portrait (long edge vertical) **(i) Ausrichtung, Orientierung; (ii) Ausrichtung**

origin *noun*
(a) position on a display screen to which all coordinates are referenced, usually the top left hand corner of the screen **Anfang**
(b) location in memory at which the first instruction of a program is stored **Programmbeginn;** *see also* INDEXED

original
1 *adjective* used *or* made first **original;** *this is the original artwork for the advertisement*
2 *noun*
(a) first document, from which a copy is made **Original(vorlage);** *did you keep the original of the letter? the original document is too faint to photocopy well*
(b) (first) master data disk *or* photographic film *or* sound recording used, from which a copy can be made **Original**

◊ **original equipment manufacturer (OEM)** *noun* company which produces equipment using basic parts made by other manufacturers, and customizes the product for a particular application **Fremdhersteller;** *one OEM supplies the disk drive, another the monitor; he started in business as a manufacturer of PCs for the OEM market*

◊ **originate** *verb* to start *or* come from **stammen von;** *the data originated from the new computer;* **originate modem** = modem that (normally) makes a call to another modem that is waiting to answer calls; the originate modem emits a carrier in response to an answertone from the remote modem **anrufendes Modem**

◊ **origination** *noun* work involved in creating something **Herstellung, Anfertigung;** *the origination of the artwork will take several weeks*

orphan *noun* first line of a paragraph of text printed alone at the bottom of a column, with the rest of the paragraph at the top of the next column; an orphan makes a page look ugly **Schusterjunge;** *see also* WIDOW

ortho *or* **orthochromatic film** *noun* photographic black and white film that is not sensitive to red light **orthochromatischer Film**

orthogonal *adjective* (instruction) made up of independent parameters *or* parts **orthogonal**

OS = OPERATING SYSTEM software that controls the basic, low-level hardware operations, and file management, without the user having to operate it (the operating system is usually supplied with the computer as part of the bundled software in ROM) **Betriebssystem**

◊ **OS/2 ™** multitasking operating system for PC computers developed by IBM and Microsoft **OS/2 ™**

oscillator *noun* electronic circuit that produces a pulse *or* signal at a particular frequency **Oszillator**

oscilloscope *noun* electronic test equipment that displays on a CRT the size and shape of an electrical signal **Oszilloskop**

OSI = OPEN SYSTEM INTERCONNECTION; *see also* ISO/OSI

out of band signalling *noun* transmission of signals outside the frequency limits of a normal voice channel **Außerbandsignalisierung**

◊ **out of phase** *adverb* situation where a waveform is delayed in comparison to another **phasenverschoben**

◊ **out of range** *adjective* (number *or* quantity) that is outside the limits of a system **außer Reichweite**

outage *noun* time during which a system is not operational **Ausfall**

outdent *verb* to move part of a line of text into the margin **ausrücken**
NOTE: opposite is **indent**

outlet *noun* connection *or* point in a circuit *or* network where a signal *or* data can be accessed **Ausgang**

outline *noun* the main features of something **Gliederung; outline flowchart** = flowchart of the main features, steps and decisions in a program *or* system **Gliederungsdiagramm; outline font** = printer or display font (collection of characters) stored as a set of outlines that mathematically describe the shape of each character (which are then used to draw each character rather than actual patterns of dots); outline fonts can be easily scaled, unlike bit-map fonts **Outlinefont, Konturenschriftart;** *see also* BIT-MAP FONTS

◊ **outliner** *noun* (utility program) used to help a user order sections and sub-sections of a list of things to do or parts of a project **Outliner**

output (o/p *or* **O/P)**
1 *noun*
(a) information *or* data that is transferred from a CPU *or* the main memory to another device such as a monitor *or* printer *or* secondary storage device **Ausgabe; computer output** = data *or* information produced after processing by a computer **Computerausgabe** NOTE opposite is **input**
(b) action of transferring the information *or* data from store to a user **Ausgabe; output area** *or* **block** = section of memory that contains data to be transferred to an output device **Ausgabebereich; output bound** *or* **limited** = processor that cannot function at normal speed because of a slower peripheral **ausgabegebunden; output buffer register** = temporary store for data that is waiting to be output **Ausgabepufferregister; output device** = device (such as a monitor *or* printer) which allows information to be displayed **Ausgabegerät; output file** = set of records that have been completely processed according to various parameters **Ausgabedatei; output formatter** = (i) software used to format data *or* programs (and output them) so that they are compatible with another sort of storage medium (ii) part of a word processor program that formats text according to embedded commands **(i)** & **(ii) Ausgabeformatierer; output mode** = computer mode in which data is moved from internal storage *or* the CPU to external devices **Ausgabemodus; output port** = circuit and connector that allow a computer to output *or* transmit data to other .devices *or* machines

Ausgabeschnittstelle; *connect the printer to the printer output port;* **output register** = register that stores data to be output until the receiver is ready *or* the channel is free **Ausgaberegister; output stream** = communications channel carrying data output to a peripheral **Ausgabestrom; output port** = circuit and connector that allow a computer to output *or* transmit data to other devices *or* machines **Ausgabeanschlusspunkt;** *connect the printer to the printer output port;* **input/output (I/O)** = (i) receiving *or* transmitting of data between a computer and its peripherals and other points outside the system; (ii) all data received *or* transmitted by a computer **(i) & (ii) Ein-/Ausgabe;** *see also* INPUT
2 *verb* to transfer data from a computer to a monitor *or* printer **ausgeben;** *finished documents can be output to the laser printer*
NOTE: **outputting - output**

> QUOTE most CAD users output to a colour plotter
> *PC Business World*

OV = OVERFLOW

overflow *or* OV *noun*
(a) mathematical result that is greater than the limits of the computer's number storage system **Überlauf; overflow bit** *or* **flag** *or* **indicator** = single bit in a word that is set to one (1) if a mathematical overflow has occurred **Überlaufbit; Überlaufanzeiger; overflow check** = examining an overflow flag to see if an overflow has occurred **Überlaufprüfung**
(b) situation in a network when the number of transmissions is greater than the line capacity and are transferred by another route **Kapazitätsüberschreitung**

overhead *noun*
(a) extra code that has to be stored to organize the program **Zusatzcode;** *the line numbers in a BASIC program are an overhead;* **overhead bit** = single bit used for error detection in a transmission **Zusatzbit; polling overhead** = amount of time spent by a computer calling and checking each terminal in a network **Sendeaufrufzeit**
(b) overhead projector = projector which projects an image of transparent artwork onto a screen **Tageslichtprojektor**

overheat *verb* to become too hot **überhitzen;** *the system may overheat if the room is not air-conditioned*

overink *verb* to put on too much ink when

printing **zu stark einfärben;** *two signatures were spoilt by overinking*

overlap
1 *noun* two things where one covers part of the other *or* two sections of data that are placed on top of each other **überlappen; multipass overlap** = system of producing higher quality print from a dot matrix printer by repeating the line of characters but shifted slightly, so making the dots less noticeable (used to produce NLQ print) **Mehrfachüberschreibung**
2 *verb* to cover part of an item with another **überdecken**

overlay *noun*
(a) keyboard overlay = strip of paper that is placed above keys on a keyboard to indicate their function **Tastaturschablone**
(b) small section of a program; the entire program is bigger than the main memory capacity of a computer, and so the overlay is loaded into memory when required, so that main memory only contains the sections it requires **Overlay, Overlayprogramm, Überlagerungsmodul; form overlay** = heading *or* other matter held in store and printed out at the same time as the text **Formmaske, Formschablone; overlay manager** = system software that manages (during run-time) the loading and execution of sections of a program when they are required **Overlaysystemprogramm; overlay region** = area of main memory that can be used by the overlay manager to store the current section of the program being run **Überlagerungsbereich; overlay segments** = short sections of a long program that can be loaded into memory when required, and executed **Overlaysegmente, Überlagerungssegmente;** *contrast with* VIRTUAL MEMORY MANAGEMENT

◊ **overlay network** *noun* two communications networks that have some common interconnections **Überlagerungsnetz**

◊ **overlaying** *noun* putting an overlay into action **Überlagern**

> QUOTE Many packages also boast useful drawing and overlay facilities which enable the user to annotate specific maps
> *Computing*

overload *verb* to demand more than the device is capable of **überlasten;** *the computer is overloaded with that amount of processing;* **channel overload** = transmission of data at a rate greater than the channel capacity **Kanalüberlastung**

overmodulation *noun* situation where an amplitude modulated carrier signal is reduced to zero by excessive input signal **Übermodulation**

overpunching *noun* altering data on a paper tape by punching additional holes **Überlochung**

overscan *noun* period when the television picture beam is outside the screen limits **Nutzflächenüberschreitung**

overstrike *verb* to print on top of an existing character to produce a new one **überschreiben**

overtones *noun see* HARMONICS

overrun *verb* data that was missed by a receiver because it was not synchronized with the transmitter *or* because it operates at a slower speed than the transmitter and has no buffer **überlaufen**

overwrite *verb* to write data to a location (memory *or* tape *or* disk) and, in doing so, to destroy any data already contained in that location **überschreiben;** *the latest data input has overwritten the old information*

over-voltage protection *noun* safety device that prevents a power supply voltage exceeding certain specified limits **Überspannungsschutz**

oxide *noun* chemical compound of oxygen **Oxid; ferric oxide** = iron oxide used as a coating for magnetic disks and tapes **Eisenoxid; metal oxide semiconductors (MOS)** = production and design method for a certain family of integrated circuits using patterns of metal conductors and oxide deposited onto a semiconductor **Metalloxidhalbleiterelemente;** *see also* MOSFET, CMOS

Pp

p = PICO-
◊ **P** = PETA equal to one quadrillion (2^{50}) **P**

◊ **PB** = PETABYTE one quadrillion bytes **PB**

PA = PUBLIC ADDRESS

p-channel *noun* section of semiconductor that is p-type **p-Kanal; p-channel MOS** = MOS transistor that conducts via a small region of p-type semiconductor **p-Kanal-MOS;** *see also* MOS, P-TYPE SEMICONDUCTOR

P-code *noun* intermediate code produced by a compiler that is ready for an interpreter to process, usually from PASCAL programs **p-Code**

PABX = PRIVATE AUTOMATIC BRANCH EXCHANGE

pack
1 *noun* number of punched cards or magnetic disks **Stapel; disk pack** = number of magnetic disks on a single spindle, either fixed or removable (from the drive) **Plattenstapel**
2 *verb*
(a) to put things into a container for selling *or* sending **packen;** *to pack goods into cartons; the diskettes are packed in plastic wrappers; the computer is packed in expanded polystyrene before being shipped*
(b) to store a quantity of data in a reduced form, often by representing several characters of data with one stored character **verdichten; packed decimal** = way of storing decimal digits in a small space, by using only four bits for each digit **gepackte Dezimalzahl; packed format** = two binary coded decimal digits stored within one computer word *or* byte (usually achieved by removing the check *or* parity bit) **gepacktes Format, verdichtete Datenanordnung**
NOTE: opposite is **padding**

package *noun*
(a) group of different items joined together in one deal **Komplex, Paket; package deal** = agreement where several different items are agreed at the same time **Pauschalangebot;** *we are offering a package deal which includes the whole office computer system, staff training and hardware maintenance*
(b) applications package = set of computer programs and manuals that cover all aspects of a particular task (such as payroll, stock control, invoicing, etc.) **Anwendungssoftwarepaket; packaged** *or* **canned software** *or* **software package** = computer programs and manuals designed for a special purpose **Softwarepaket;** *the computer is sold with accounting and word-processing packages*

◊ **packaging** *noun*
(a) material used to protect goods which are being packed; attractive material used to wrap goods for display **Verpackung;** *airtight packaging; packaging material* (b) creating books for publishers **Packaging** NOTE: no plural

◊ **packager** *noun* person who creates a book for a publisher **Packager**

packet *noun* group of bits of uniform size which can be transmitted as a group, using a packet switched network **Datenpaket;** **packet assembler/disassembler (PAD)** = dedicated computer that converts serial data from asynchronous terminals to a form that can be transmitted along a packet switched (synchronous) network **Konzentrator, der Datenpakete zusammenstellt bzw. auseinandernimmt;** *the remote terminal is connected to a PAD device through which it accesses the host computer;* **packet switched data service** *or* **packet switched network (PSN)** = service which transmits data in packets of a set length **paketweiser Datenservice; Netz im Datenpaketbetrieb; packet switching** = method of sending messages *or* data in uniform-sized packets, and processing and routing packets rather than bit streams **Datenpaketvermittlung; packet switching service (PSS)** = commercial data transmission service that sends data over its WAN using packet switching **Paketvermittlungsdienst, Packet Switching Service (PSS);** *compare* STORE-AND-FORWARD

> QUOTE The network is based on Northern Telecom DPN data switches over which it will offer X.25 packet switching, IBM SNA, and frame-relay transmission
> *Computing*

packing *noun*
(a) action of putting goods into boxes and wrapping them for shipping **(Ver)packen;** *what is the cost of the packing? packing is included in the price* (b) putting large amounts of data into a small area of storage **Verdichtung; packing density** = amount of bits of data which can be stored in a unit area of a disk *or* tape **Zeichendichte; packing routine** = program which packs data into a small storage area **Verdichtungsprogramm** (NOTE: opposite is **padding**) (c) material used to protect goods **Verpackung(smaterial);** *packed in airtight packing;* **non-returnable packing** = packing which is to be thrown away when it has

been used and not returned to the sender **Einwegverpackung** NOTE: no plural

PAD = PACKET ASSEMBLER/DISASSEMBLER

pad
1 *noun* number of keys arranged together **Block; cursor pad** = group of four arrowed cursor control keys, used to move the cursor up and down or to the right or left **Richtungstastenfeld; keypad** = group of special keys used for certain applications **Tastatur; hex keypad** = set of sixteen keys, with all the figures (0-9, A-F) needed to enter hexadecimal numbers **hexadezimale Tastatur; numerical keypad** = set of ten keys with figures (0-9), included on most computer keyboards as a separate group, used for entering large amounts of data in numeric form **numerische Tastatur 2** *verb* to fill out **auffüllen; pad character** = extra character added to a string *or* packet *or* file until it is a required size **Auffüllzeichen**

◊ **padding** *noun* characters or digits added to fill out a string *or* packet until it is the right length **Auffüllen** (NOTE: opposite is **packing**)

paddle *noun* computer peripheral consisting of a knob *or* device which is turned to move a cursor *or* pointer on the screen **Konsole; game paddle** = device held in the hand to move a cursor *or* graphics in a computer game **Spielkonsole, Steuerknüppel**

page *noun*
(a) sheet of paper **Blatt** (b) (i) one side of a printed sheet of paper in a book *or* newspaper *or* magazine *or* catalogue, etc.; (ii) text held on a computer monitor screen (which if printed out will fill a page of paper *or* which fills the screen) (i) & (ii) **Seite; page break** = (i) point at which a page ends and a new page starts (in continuous text); (ii) marker used when word-processing to show where a new page should start (i) **Seitenwechsel;** (ii) **Umbruch; page description language (PDL)** = software that controls a printer's actions to print a page of text to a particular format according to a user's instructions **Seitenbeschreibungssprache; page display** = showing on the screen a page of text as it will appear when printed out **Seitenanzeige; page down key** = (on a keyboard) key that moves the cursor position down by the number of lines on one screen **Taste "Bild nach unten", Taste zum Vorwärtsblättern; page image buffer** = memory in a page

printer that holds the image as it is built up before it is printed **Seitenabbildpuffer; page layout** = arrangement of text and pictures within a page of a document **Seitenlayout, Seitenaufbau;** *we do all our page layout using desktop publishing software;* **page length** = length of a page (in word-processing) **Seitenlänge; page makeup** = action of pasting images and text into a page ready for printing **Seitengestaltung, Seitenaufbereitung; page orientation** = direction of the long edge of a piece of paper **Seitenausrichtung;** *see* PORTRAIT, LANDSCAPE; **pages per minute (ppm)** = number of pages that a printer can print in one minute; measurement of the speed of a printer shown as the number of pages of text printed every minute **Seiten pro Minute;** *this laser printer can output eight pages per minute;* **page preview** = (in WP or DTP software) graphical representation of how a page will look when printed, with different type styles, margins, and graphics correctly displayed **Druckvorschau, Seitenansicht; page printer** = printer which composes one page of text within memory and then prints it in one pass (normally refers to laser printers) **Seitendrucker;** *this dot-matrix printer is not a page printer, it only prints one line at a time;* **page reader** = device which converts written *or* typed information to a form that a computer can understand and process **Seitenlesegerät, Seitenleser; page setup** = (within software) options that allow a user to set up how the page will look when printed - normally setting the margins, size of paper, and scaling of a page **Seiteneinrichtung, Seitenaufbau; page up key** = (on a keyboard) key that moves the cursor position up by the number of lines in one screen **Taste „Bild nach oben", Taste zum Rückwärtsblättern**

(c) section of main store, which contains data *or* programs **Seite; multiple base page** = multi-user system in which each user and the operating system have one page of main memory, which can then call up other pages within main memory **Gemeinschaftscomputersystem; page addressing** = main memory which has been split into blocks, with a unique address allocated to each block of memory which can then be called up and accessed individually, when required **Seitenadressierung(sspeicher); page boundary** = point where one page ends and the next starts **Seitengrenze; page frame** = physical address to which a page of virtual (or logical) memory can be mapped **Seitenrahmen; page-mode RAM** = dynamic RAM designed to access sequential memory locations very quickly **dynamischer RAM, RAM mit Seitenzugriff;** *the video adapter uses page-mode RAM to speed up the display;* **page protection** = software controls to ensure that pages are not overwritten by accident or copied into a reserved section of memory **Seitenschutz; page table** = list of all the pages and their locations within main memory, used by the operating system when accessing a page **Seitentabelle**

(d) one section of a main program which can be loaded into main memory when required **Seite**

2 *verb*

(a) to **page someone** = to try to find someone in a building (using a PA *or* radio pager) **jemanden ausrufen lassen;** *see also* RADIO PAGING

(b) to make up a text into pages **Seitenumbruch machen**

(c) to divide computer backing store into sections to allow long programs to be executed in a small main memory **umlagern**

◊ **paged address** *noun* (in a paged-memory scheme) actual physical memory address that is calculated from a logical address and its page address **Seitenadresse; paged-memory scheme** = way of dividing memory into areas (pages) which are then allocated a page number; memory addresses are relative to a page which is then mapped to the real, physical memory (this system is normally used to implement virtual memory) **Speicherseitenprinzip; paged-memory management unit** = electronic logic circuit that manages the translation between logical addresses that refer to a particular page and the real physical address that is being referenced **Speicherseitenmanager**

◊ **pager** *noun* small device carried by someone, which allows him to be called from a central office, by using a radio signal **Piepser, Mobilfunk**

◊ **pagination** *noun* process of dividing text into pages; arrangement of pages in a book **Paginierung, Seitenumbruch**

◊ **paging** *noun* virtual memory technique that splits main memory into small blocks (pages) which are allocated an address and which can be called up when required **Aufteilung in Speicherseiten; paging algorithm** = formula by which the memory management allocates memory to pages, also covering the transfer from backing storage to main memory in the most efficient way **Algorithmus zur Aufteilung von Speicherseiten**

COMMENT: a virtual memory management system stores data as pages in memory to provide an apparently larger capacity main memory by storing unused pages in backing store, copying them into main memory only when required

QUOTE Mannesmann Tally has launched the T9005, a five-page-a-minute page printer designed to handle over 3,000 pages a month

Computing

paint
1 *noun* (in a graphics program) colour and pattern used to fill an area **Füllfarbe, Füllmuster**
2 *verb* (in a graphics program) to fill an enclosed graphics shape with a colour **ausfüllen**

◊ **paint program** *noun* software that allows a user to draw pictures on screen in different colours, with different styles of brush and special effects **Malprogramm;** *I drew a rough of our new logo with this paint program*

COMMENT: paint programs normally operate on bitmap images; drafting or design software normally works with vector-based images

paired register *noun* two basic word size registers used together as one large word size register (often used for storing address words) **gepaartes Register;** *the 8-bit CPU uses a paired register to provide a 16-bit address register*

PAL = PHASE ALTERNATING LINE standard that defines television and video formats, using 625 horizontal scan lines and 50 frames per second **PAL-System**

COMMENT: mainly used in Western Europe, Australia, some parts of the Middle East and Africa

palette *noun* range of colours which can be used (on a printer *or* computer display) **Palette**

QUOTE the colour palette option offer sixteen colours from a range of over four thousand
Electronics & Wireless World

palmtop *noun* personal computer that is small enough to be held in one hand and operated with the other **Taschencomputer, Palmtop;** *this palmtop has a tiny keyboard and twenty-line LCD screen*

PAM = PULSE AMPLITUDE MODULATION pulse modulation in which the height of the pulse varies with the input signal **PAM (Pulsamplitudenmodulation) APPENDIX**

pan *verb* (in computer graphics) to move a viewing window horizontally across an image that is too wide to display all at once **schwenken**

panel *noun* flat section of a casing with control knobs *or* sockets **Konsole; back panel** = panel at the rear of a computer which normally holds the connectors to peripherals such as keyboard, printer, video display unit, and mouse **Rückwand;** *the socket is on the back panel;* **control panel** = panel with indicators and switches which allows an operator to monitor and control the actions of a computer *or* peripheral **Bedienerkonsole; front panel** = main computer system control switches and status indicators **vordere Verkleidungsplatte**

Pantone Matching System ™ (PMS) standard method of matching ink colours on screen and on printed output using a book of pre-defined colours **Pantone Matching System ™ (PMS)**

paper *noun* thin material used for making books *or* newspapers *or* stationery items **Papier;** *the book is printed on 80gsm paper; glossy paper is used for printing half-tones; bad quality paper gives too much show-through;* **paper feed** = mechanism which pulls paper through a printer **Papiertransport;** *(US)* **paper slew** = PAPER THROW; **paper tape** = long strip of paper on which data can be recorded, usually in the form of punched holes (**ungelochter**) **Lochstreifen; paper tape feed** = method by which paper tape is passed into a machine **Lochstreifenzuführung; paper tape punch** = device which punches holes in paper tape to carry data **Lochstreifenstanzer; paper tape reader** = device which accepts punched paper tape and converts the punched information stored on it into signals which a computer can process **Lochstreifenleser; paper throw** = rapid vertical movement of paper in a printer **schneller Papiervorschub; paper tray** = container used to hold paper to be fed into a printer **Papierbehälter; paper weight** = weight of paper used in printing (usually measured in gsm *or* grams per square metre) **Papiergewicht**

◊ **paperback** *noun* book which has a paper cover **Paperback, Taschenbuch;** *we are publishing the book as a hardback and as a paperback*

◊ **paperbound** *adjective* (book) bound with a paper cover (as opposed to hardbound) **broschiert**

◊ **paper-fed** *adjective* (device) which is activated when paper is introduced into it **durch Papiereinschub aktiviert(es Gerät);** *a paper-fed scanner*

◊ **paperless** *adjective* without using paper **ohne Papier; paperless office** = electronic office *or* office which uses computers and other electronic devices for office tasks and avoids the use of paper **computerisiertes Büro**

◊ **paper-white monitor** *noun* monitor that normally displays black text on a white background, rather than the normal illuminated text on a black background **Paperwhite-Monitor**

QUOTE Indeed, the concept of the paperless office may have been a direct attack on Xerox and its close ties to the paper document. Yet, as we all know, the paperless office has so far been an empty promise

Computing

paragraph *noun*
(a) (in a document) section of text between two carriage return characters **Absatz; paragraph marker** = (in a document) non-printing character that shows where a carriage return is within a document **Absatzmarke**
(b) (in a memory map) 16-byte section of memory which starts at a hexadecimal address that can be evenly divided by 16 **Absatz**

parallel *adjective* (i) (computer system) in which two or more processors operate simultaneously on one or more items of data; (ii) two or more bits of a word transmitted over separate lines at the same time **(i) simultan; (ii) parallel; parallel access** = data transfer between two devices with a number of bits (usually one byte wide) being sent simultaneously **Parallelzugriff; parallel adder** = number of adders joined together in parallel, allowing several digits to be added at once **Paralleladdierer; parallel computer** = computer with one or more logic *or* arithmetic units, allowing parallel processing **Simultanrechner; parallel connection** = transmission link that handles parallel data **Parallelschaltung;** *their average transmission rate is 60,000 bps through parallel connection;* **parallel data transmission** = transmission of bits of data simultaneously along a number of data

lines **parallele Datenübertragung; parallel input/output (PIO)** = data input *or* output from a computer in a parallel form **parallele Ein-/Ausgabe; parallel input/output chip** = dedicated integrated circuit that performs all handshaking, buffering, etc., needed when transferring parallel data to and from a CPU **paralleler Ein-/Ausgabe-Chip; parallel input/parallel output (PIPO)** = device that can accept and transmit parallel data **parallele Eingabe/parallele Ausgabe; parallel input/serial output (PISO)** = device that can accept parallel data and transmit serial data **parallele Eingabe/serielle Ausgabe; parallel interface** *or* **port** = circuit and connector that allows parallel data to be received *or* transmitted **paralleler Schnittstellenanschluss; parallel operation** = number of processes carried out simultaneously on a number of inputs **Parallelbetrieb; parallel port** *see* PARALLEL INTERFACE; **parallel priority system** = number of peripherals connected in parallel to one bus, if they require attention, they send their address and an interrupt signal, which is then processed by the computer according to device priority **paralleles Rangsystem; parallel printer** = printer that accepts character data in parallel form **Paralleldrucker; parallel processing** = computer operating on several tasks simultaneously **Simultanverarbeitung; parallel running** = running an old and a new computer system together to allow the new system to be checked before it becomes the only system used **Parallellauf; parallel search storage** = data retrieval from storage that uses part of the data other than an address to locate the data **Parallelabfragespeicher; parallel transmission** = data transmitted over a number of data lines carrying all the bits of a data word simultaneously **Parallelübertragung**
NOTE: opposite is **serial transmission**

parameter *noun* information which defines the limits *or* actions of something, such as a variable *or* routine *or* program **Parameter;** *the X parameter defines the number of characters displayed across a screen; the size of the array is set with this parameter;* **parameter-driven software** = software whose main functions can be modified and tailored to a user's needs by a number of variables **parametergesteuerte Software; parameter passing** = (in a program) value passed to a routine or program when it is called **Parameterübergabe; parameter testing** = using a program to examine the parameters and set up the system *or* program accordingly **Parameterprüfung; parameter word** = data word that contains information defining the limits *or* actions of a routine or program **Parameterwort; physical parameter** = description of the size, weight, voltage or power of a system **physikalischer Parameter**

◊ **parametric (subroutine)** *noun* subroutine that uses parameters to define its limits *or* actions **parametrisches Unterprogramm**

◊ **parameterization** *noun* action of setting parameters for software **Parametrisierung**

parent directory *noun* (in DOS filing system) the directory above a sub-directory **Elternverzeichnis**

◊ **parent folder** *noun* (in Macintosh filing system) one folder that contains other folders **übergeordneter Ordner**

◊ **parent program** *noun* program that starts another program (a child program), whilst it is still running; control passes back to the parent program when the child program has finished **Elternprogramm**

parity *noun* being equal **Parität, Gleichheit; block parity** = parity check on a block of data **Blockparitätsprüfung; column parity** = parity check on every punched card *or* tape column **Spaltenparitätsprüfung; even parity check** = error checking system in which any series of bits transmitted must have an even number of binary ones **Prüfung auf gerade Parität; no parity** = data transmission which does not use a parity bit **keine Parität; odd parity (check)** = error checking system in which any series of bits transmitted must have an odd number of binary ones **Prüfung auf ungerade Parität; parity bit** = extra bit added to a data word as a parity checking device **Prüfbit; parity check** = method of checking (odd *or* even parity check) for errors and that transmitted binary data has not been corrupted **Paritätsprüfung; parity flag** = indicator that shows if data has passed a parity check or if data has odd or even parity **Paritätsanzeiger; parity interrupt** = interrupt signal from an error checking routine that indicates that received data has failed a parity check and is corrupt **Paritätsprüfungsabbruch; parity track** = one track on magnetic *or* paper tape that carries the parity bit **Prüfspur**

QUOTE The difference between them is that RAID level one offers mirroring, whereas level five stripes records in parity across the disks in the system

Computing

park *verb* to move the read/write head of a hard disk drive over a point on the disk where no data is stored **parken;** *when parked, the disk head will not damage any data if it touches the disk surface*

parse *verb* to break down high-level language code into its element parts when translating into machine code **parsen, syntaktisch analysieren**

◊ **parsing** *noun* operation to break down high-level language code into its element parts when translating into machine code **Parsing (Syntaxanalyse)**

part *noun*
(a) section of something **Teil; part page display** = display of only a section of a page, and not the whole page **Teilseitenanzeige**
(b) **spare part** = small piece of a machine which is needed to replace a piece which is broken *or* missing **Ersatzteil;** *the printer won't work - we need to get a spare part*
(c) one of a series **Teil; two part stationery** = stationery (invoices, receipts, etc.) with a top sheet and a copy sheet **Vordruck in zweifacher Ausführung; four-part invoice** = invoice with four sheets (a top sheet and three copies) **Rechnung in vierfacher Ausführung;** *see also* MULTI-PART

partial carry *noun* temporary storage of all carries generated by parallel adders rather than a direct transfer **Teilübertrag**

◊ **partial RAM** *noun* RAM chip in which only a certain area of the chip functions correctly, usually in newly released chips (partial RAM's can be used by employing more than one to make up the capacity of one fully functional chip) **Teil-RAM**

particle *noun* very small piece of matter **Teilchen**

partition
1 *noun*
(a) area of a hard disk that is treated as a logical drive and can be accessed as a separate drive **Partition;** *I defined two partitions on this hard disk - called drive C: and D:*
(b) section of computer memory set aside as foreground *or* background memory **Arbeitsspeicherbereich; partitioned file** = one file made up of several smaller sequential files, each part can be accessed individually by the control program **untergliederte Datei**
2 *verb*
(a) to divide a hard disk into two or more

logical drives that can be accessed as separate drives **partitionieren**
(b) to divide a large file *or* block into several smaller units which can be accessed and handled more easily **aufteilen**

party line *or* **shared line** *noun* one telephone line shared by a number of subscribers **Gemeinschaftsleitung**

PASCAL high-level structured programming language used both on micros and for teaching programming **PASCAL (Programmiersprache)**

pass
1 *noun* (i) the execution of a loop, once; (ii) single operation **(i) Durchlauf; (ii) Arbeitsgang; single-pass assembler** = assembler program that translates the source code in one action **Assemblierer mit einem Durchlauf; sorting pass** = single run through a list of items to put them into order **Sortierlauf**
2 *verb* action of moving the whole length of a magnetic tape over the read/write heads **ablaufen**

password *noun* word *or* series of characters which identifies a user so that he can access a system **Kennwort, Passwort;** *the user has to key in the password before he can access the database;* **password protection** = computer *or* software that requires the user to enter a password before he can gain access **Passwortschutz, Kennwortschutz**

> QUOTE the system's security features let you divide the disk into up to 256 password-protected sections
>
> *Byte*

paste *verb* to insert text or graphics that has been copied or cut into a file **einfügen;** *now that I have cut this paragraph from the end of the document, I can paste it in here;* **cut-and-paste** = action of taking a section of text *or* data from one point and inserting it at another (often used in word-processors and DTP packages for easy page editing) **Cut-and-Paste, Ausschneiden und Einfügen**

patch *noun* (temporary) correction made to a program; small correction made to software by the user, on the instructions of the software publisher **Korrektur**

◇ **patchboard** *noun* board with a number of sockets connected to devices, into which plugs can be inserted to connect other devices *or* functions **Schalttafel; patch cord** = short cable with a connector at each

end, used to make an electrical connection on a patch panel **Verbindungskabel; patch panel** = electrical terminals that can be interconnected using short patch cords, allowing quick and simple re-configuration of a network **Stecktafel**

path *noun* possible route or sequence of events *or* instructions within the execution of a program **Pfad**
(b) route from one point in a communications network to another **Strecke**
(c) (in the DOS operating system) list of subdirectories where the operating system should look for a named file **Suchpfad, Pfadanweisung;** *you cannot run the program from the root directory until its directory is added to the path;* **pathname** = location of a file with a listing of the subdirectories leading to it **Pfadname;** *the pathname for the letter file is* \FILES\SIMON\DOCS\LETTER.DOC

pattern *noun* series of regular lines *or* shapes which are repeated again and again **Struktur, Muster; pattern recognition** = algorithms *or* program functions that can identify a shape from a video camera, etc. **Strukturerkennung**

◇ **patterned** *adjective* with patterns **strukturiert**

pause key *noun* (in a keyboard) key that temporarily stops a process, often a scrolling screen display, until the key is pressed a second time **Pause-Taste**

pay TV *noun* form of cable television, where the viewer pays for programs *or* channels watched **Fernsehen mit Extragebühr**

◇ **paycable** *noun* (*US*) form of cable television where the viewer pays an extra fee for extra channels **Kabelfernsehen mit Extragebühr**

PAX = PRIVATE AUTOMATIC EXCHANGE

PBX = PRIVATE BRANCH EXCHANGE

PC
(a) = PERSONAL COMPUTER (originally referring to a microcomputer specification with an 8086-based low-power computer); now normally used to refer to any computer that uses an Intel 80x86 processor and is based on the IBM PC-style architecture **PC; PC-compatible** =

computer that is compatible with the IBM PC **PC-kompatibel, IBM-kompatibel; PC/AT** = (IBM PC compatible) computer that used an Intel 80286 processor and was fitted with 16-bit ISA expansion connectors **PC/AT; PC/AT keyboard** = keyboard that features twelve function keys arranged in one row along the top of the keyboard **PC/AT-Tastatur; PC/XT** = (IBM PC compatible) computer that was fitted with a hard disk drive and used a 8086 Intel processor **PC/XT; PC/XT keyboard** = keyboard that features ten function keys arranged in two columns along the left hand side of the keyboard **PC/XT-Tastatur** **(b)** = PRINTED CIRCUIT (BOARD) **(c)** = PROGRAM COUNTER

QUOTE in the UK, the company is known not for PCs but for PC printers
Which PC?

PCB = PRINTED CIRCUIT BOARD

PC-DOS ™ version of MS-DOS that is sold by IBM **PC-DOS** ™

PCI = PERIPHERAL COMPONENT INTERCONNECT specification produced by Intel defining a type of fast local bus that allows high-speed data transfer between the processor and the PCI-compatible expansion cards **PCI**

PCL ™ = PRINTER CONTROL LANGUAGE standard set of commands, defined by Hewlett Packard, that allow a computer to control a printer **PCL** ™

PCM **(a)** = PULSE CODE MODULATION pulse stream that carries data about a signal in binary form **PCM (Pulscodemodulation)** ⇨APPENDIX; *see also* PULSE AMPLITUDE, PULSE DURATION, PULSE POSITION **(b)** = PLUG-COMPATIBLE MANUFACTURER company that produces add-on boards which are compatible with another manufacturer's computer **steckerkompatibler Anbieter**

PCMCIA = PERSONAL COMPUTER MEMORY CARD INTERNATIONAL ASSOCIATION specification for add-in expansion cards that are the size of a credit card with a connector at one end **PCMCIA;** *the extra memory is stored on this PCMCIA card and I use it on my laptop;* **PCMCIA card** = memory *or* peripheral which complies with the PCMCIA standard **PCMCIA-Karte; PCMCIA connector** = 68-pin connector that is inside a PCMCIA slot and on the end of a PCMCIA card **PCMCIA-Anschluss; PCMCIA slot** = expansion slot (normally on a laptop) that can accept a PCMCIA expansion card **PCMCIA-Steckplatz**

PCU = PERIPHERAL CONTROL UNIT device that converts input and output signals and instructions to a form that a peripheral device will understand **periphere Steuereinheit**

PDA = PERSONAL DIGITAL ASSISTANT lightweight palmtop computer that provides the basic functions of a diary, notepad, address-book and to-do list together with fax or modem communications; current PDA designs do not have a keyboard, but use a touch-sensitive screen with a pen and handwriting-recognition to control the software **PDA**

PDL = PAGE DESCRIPTION LANGUAGE, PROGRAM DESIGN LANGUAGE

PDM = PULSE DURATION MODULATION pulse width modulation system where the pulse width varies with the magnitude of the input signal **PDM (Pulsdauermodulation)** ⇨APPENDIX

PDN = PUBLIC DATA NETWORK

peak
1 *noun* highest point; maximum value of a variable *or* signal **Spitze;** *keep the peak power below 60 watts or the amplifier will overheat; the marker on the thermometer shows the peak temperature for today;* **peak and trough** = maximum and minimum points of a waveform **Wellenberg und Wellental; peak period** = time of the day when most power is being used **Hauptbelastungszeit; time of peak demand** = time when something is being used most **Spitzenbedarfszeit; peak output** = highest output **Höchstleistung**
2 *verb* to reach the highest point **den Höchststand erreichen;** *the power peaked at 1,200 volts; sales peaked in January*

peek *noun* BASIC computer instruction that allows the user to read the contents of a memory location **PEEK-Anweisung (Blick in den Speicher);** *you need the instruction PEEK 1452 here to examine the contents of memory location 1452; compare* POKE

peer *noun* any two similar devices

operating on the same network protocol level **Peer**

◊ **peer-to-peer network** *noun* local area network (normally using network adapter cards in each computer) that does not use a central dedicated server, instead each computer in the network shares the jobs **Peer-zu-Peer-Netzwerk**; *we have linked the four PCs in our small office using a peer-to-peer network*

peg *verb* sudden swing of an analog meter to its maximum readout due to a large signal **ausschlagen**; *after he turned up the input level, the signal level meter was pegging on its maximum stop*

pel *see* PIXEL

pen *see* LIGHT PEN; **pen computer** = type of computer that uses a pen instead of a keyboard for input; the computer has a touch-sensitive screen and uses handwriting recognition software to interpret the commands written on the screen using the pen **Schreibstiftcomputer**; **pen plotter** = plotter that uses removable pens to draw on paper **Stiftplotter**; **pen recorder** = peripheral which moves a pen over paper according to an input (a value or coordinate) **Tintenschreiber**

Pentium ™ *noun* processor developed by Intel; it is backwards compatible with the 80x86 family used in IBM PCs; the processor uses a 32-bit address bus and a 64-bit data bus **Pentium** ™

per *preposition*
(a) as per = according to **gemäß**; as per sample = as shown in the sample **gemäß dem Muster**; as per specification = according to the details given in the specification **wie angegeben**
(b) at a rate of; **per hour** *or* **per day** *or* **per week** *or* **per year** = for each hour *or* day *or* week *or* year **pro Stunde; pro Tag; pro Woche; pro Jahr**
(c) out of **von, pro**; *the rate of imperfect items is about twenty-five per thousand; the error rate has fallen to twelve per hundred*

◊ **per cent** *noun, adjective & adverb* out of each hundred *or* for each hundred **Prozent; prozentual**; **10 per cent** = ten in every hundred **10 Prozent, 10%**; *what is the increase per cent? fifty per cent of nothing is still nothing*

◊ **percentage** *noun* amount shown as part of one hundred **Prozentsatz**; **percentage increase** = increase calculated on the basis

of a rate for one hundred **prozentualer Anstieg**; **percentage point** = one per cent **Prozentpunkt**

◊ **percentile** *noun* one of a series of ninety-nine figures below which a certain percentage of the total falls **Perzentil**

perfect
1 *adjective* completely correct *or* with no mistakes **perfekt, vollkommen**; *we check each batch to make sure it is perfect; she did a perfect typing test*
2 *verb* to make something which is completely correct **vervollkommnen**; *he perfected the process for making high grade steel*

◊ **perfect binding** *noun* method of binding paperback books, where the pages are trimmed at the spine, and glued to the cover **Klebebindung**

◊ **perfect bound** *adjective* (book, usually a paperback) bound without sewing, where the pages are trimmed at the spine and glued to the cover with strong glue **(Buch) mit Klebebindung**

◊ **perfectly** *adverb* with no mistakes *or* correctly **fehlerfrei, perfekt**; *she typed the letter perfectly*

◊ **perfector** *noun* printing machine that prints on both sides of a sheet of paper **Perfektor, Schön- und Widerdruckmaschine**

perforations *noun* line of very small holes in a sheet of paper *or* continuous stationery, to help when tearing **Perforationen**

◊ **perforated tape** *noun* paper tape *or* long strip of tape on which data can be recorded in the form of punched holes **Lochstreifen**

◊ **perforator** *noun* machine that punches holes in a paper tape **Locher**

perform *verb* to do well *or* badly **abschneiden, aus-, durchführen**

◊ **performance** *noun* way in which someone *or* something acts **Leistung(sniveau)**; **as a measure of the system's performance** = as a way of judging if the system is working well **als Maßstab für das Leistungsniveau des Systems**; *in benchmarking, the performances of several systems or devices are tested against a standard benchmark*; **high performance** = high quality *or* high specification equipment **Hochleistung**

perigee *noun* point during the orbit of a

satellite when it is closest to the earth **Perigäum, erdnächster Punkt**

period *noun*
(a) length of time **Zeitraum;** *for a period of time or for a period of months or for a six-year period; sales over a period of three months* (b) *(US)* full stop *or* printing sign used at the end of a piece of text **Punkt** (NOTE: GB English is **full stop)**

◊ **periodic** *or* **periodical**
1 *adjective*
(a) from time to time **periodisch;** *a periodic review of the company's performance* (b) **periodic** = (signal *or* event) that occurs regularly **regelmäßig;** *the clock signal is periodic*
2 *noun* **periodical** = magazine which comes out regularly **Zeitschrift, Periodika**

◊ **periodically** *adverb* from time to time **regelmäßig**

peripheral
1 *adjective* which is not essential *or* which is attached to something else **peripher, Zusatz-, zusatz-**
2 *noun* (i) item of hardware (such as terminals, printers, monitors, etc.) which is attached to a main computer system; (ii) any device that allows communication between a system and itself, but is not directly operated by the system **(i) Anschlussgerät; (ii) Peripheriegerät;** *peripherals such as disk drives or printers allow data transfer and are controlled by a system, but contain independent circuits for their operation;* **fast peripheral** = peripheral that communicates with the computer at very high speeds, limited only by the speed of the electronic circuits **schnelles Peripheriegerät; slow peripheral** = peripheral such as a card reader, where mechanical movement determines speed **langsames Peripheriegerät; peripheral control unit (PCU)** = device that converts the input/output signals and instructions from a computer to a form and protocol which the peripheral will understand **periphere Steuereinheit; peripheral driver** = program *or* routine used to interface, manage and control an input/output device *or* peripheral **Treiberroutine; peripheral equipment** = (i) external devices that are used with a computer, such as a printer *or* scanner; (ii) (communications) equipment external to a central processor that provides extra features **(i) Anschlussgeräte; (ii) Peripheriegeräte; peripheral interface adapter (PIA)** = circuit that allows a

computer to communicate with a peripheral by providing serial and parallel ports and other handshaking signals required to interface the peripheral **peripherer Schnittstellenadapter; peripheral limited** = CPU that cannot execute instructions at normal speed because of a slow peripheral **durch Peripheriegeräte in der Geschwindigkeit eingeschränkt; peripheral memory** = storage capacity available in a peripheral **peripherer Speicher; peripheral processing unit (PPU)** = device used for input, output or storage which is controlled by the CPU **periphere Verarbeitungseinheit; peripheral software driver** = short section of computer program that allows a user to access and control a peripheral easily **Gerätesteuerprogramm;** *same as* DEVICE DRIVER; **peripheral transfer** = movement of data between a CPU and peripheral **periphere Übertragung; peripheral unit** = (i) item of hardware (such as terminal, printer, monitor, etc.) which is attached to a main computer system; (ii) any device that allows communication between a system and itself, but is not operated only by the system **(i) Anschlussgerät; (ii) Peripheriegerät**

permanent *adjective* which will last for a very long time *or* for ever **dauerhaft, ständig; permanent dynamic memory** = storage medium which retains data even when power is removed **dynamischer Dauerspeicher; permanent error** = error in a system which cannot be mended **ständiger Fehler; permanent file** = data file that is stored in a backing storage device such as a disk drive **permanente Datei; permanent memory** = computer memory that retains data even when power is removed **Dauerspeicher;** *see also* NON-VOLATILE MEMORY; **permanent swap file** = file on a hard disk, made up of contiguous disk sectors, which stores a swap file for software that implements virtual memory, such as Microsoft's Windows **permanente Auslagerungsdatei**

◊ **permanently** *adverb* done in a way which will last for a long time **dauerhaft, ständig;** *the production number is permanently engraved on the back of the computer casing*

permeability *noun* measure of the ratio of the magnetic flux in a material to the size of the generating field **magnetische Durchlässigkeit, Permeabilität**

permission *noun* authorization given to a particular user to access a certain shared resource or area of disk **Berechtigung;** *this* *user cannot access the file on the server because he does not have permission; see also* RIGHTS

permutation *noun* number of different ways in which something can be arranged **Permutation;** *the cipher system is very secure since there are so many possible permutations for the key*

persistence *noun* length of time that a CRT will continue to display an image after the picture beam has stopped tracing it on the screen **Nachleuchtdauer;** *slow scan rate monitors need long persistence phosphor to prevent the image flickering*

person *noun* human being **Person; person-to-person call** = telephone call placed through an operator, where the caller will only speak to a certain person **Gespräch mit namentlicher Voranmeldung**

◊ **personal** *adjective* referring to one person **persönlich; personal computer (PC)** = low-cost microcomputer intended mainly for home and light business use **Personalcomputer (PC); personal digital assistant (PDA)** = lightweight palmtop computer that provides the basic functions of a diary, notepad, address-book and to-do list together with fax or modem communications; current PDA designs do not have a keyboard, but use a touch-sensitive screen with a pen and handwriting-recognition to control the software **Personal Digital Assistant (PDA); personal identification device (PID)** = device (such as a card) connected *or* inserted into a system to identify *or* provide authorization for a user **Kennkarte; personal identification number (PIN)** = unique sequence of digits that identifies a user to provide authorization to access a system (often used on automatic cash dispensers *or* with a PID or password to enter a system) **persönliche Identifikationsnummer; personal information manager (PIM)** = software utility that stores and manages a user's everyday data, such as diary, telephone numbers, address book and notes **Personal Information Manager (PIM)**

◊ **personalize** *verb* to customize *or* to adapt a product specially for a certain user **individuell anfertigen**

PERT = PROGRAM EVALUATION AND REVIEW TECHNIQUE definition of tasks *or* jobs and the time each requires, arranged in order to achieve a goal **Netzplantechnik zur Terminüberwachung von komplexen Projekten**

peta (P) equal to one quadrillion (2^{50}) **Peta- (P)**

◊ **petabyte (PB)** *noun* one quadrillion bytes **Petabyte (PB)**

petal printer = DAISY WHEEL PRINTER

pF = PICOFARAD unit of measurement of capacitance equal to one million millionth of a farad **Picofarad**

phantom ROM *noun* duplicate area of read-only memory that is accessed by a special code **Phantom-ROM**

phase
1 *noun*
(a) one part of a larger process **Phase; run phase** = period of time when a program is run **Ausführungsphase; compile phase** = period of time during which a program is compiled **Kompilierphase**
(b) delay between two similar waveforms **Phase; in phase** = two signals that have no time delay between them **phasengleich; out of phase** = one signal that has a time delay when compared to another **phasenverschoben; phase alternating line (PAL)** = method of providing colour information in a television signal, used in standard receivers in certain countries **PAL-System; phase angle** = measurement of the phase difference between two signals, where a phase angle of 0 degrees represents signals that are in phase **Phasenwinkel; phase equalizer** = circuit that introduces delays into signal paths to produce a phase angle of zero degrees **Phasenentzerrer; phase modulation** = modulation method in which the phase of a carrier signal varies with the input **Phasenmodulation**
2 *verb* **to phase in** *or* **to phase out** = to introduce something gradually *or* to reduce something gradually **allmählich einführen; auslaufen lassen; phased change-over** = new device that is gradually introduced as the old one is used less and less **schrittweise Umstellung**

COMMENT: when two signals are in phase there is no time delay between them, when one is delayed they are said to be out of phase by a certain phase angle

phon *noun* measure of sound equal to a one thousand Hertz signal at one decibel **Phon**

phone
1 *noun* telephone *or* machine used for

speaking to someone over a long distance **Telefon;** *we had a new phone system installed last week;* **house phone** *or* **internal phone** = telephone for calling from one office to another **Haustelefon; by phone** = using the telephone **per Telefon; to be on the phone** = to be speaking to someone on the telephone **telefonieren;** *she has been on the phone all morning; he spoke to the manager on the phone;* **card phone** = public telephone that accepts a phonecard instead of money **Kartentelefon; phone book** = book which lists names of people and companies with their addresses and phone numbers **Telefonbuch;** *look up his address in the phone book;* **phone call** = speaking to someone on the phone **Telefonanruf; to make a phone call** = to speak to someone on the telephone **telefonieren; to answer the phone** *or* **to take a phone call** = to reply to a call on the phone **das Telefon abnehmen; phonecard** = special plastic card which allows the user to use a card phone for a certain length of time **Telefonkarte; phone number** = set of figures for a particular telephone **Telefonnummer;** *he keeps a list of phone numbers in a little black book; the phone number is on the company notepaper; can you give me your phone number?*
2 *verb* **to phone someone** = to call someone by telephone **jemanden anrufen;** *don't phone me, I'll phone you; his secretary phoned to say he would be late; he phoned the order through to the warehouse;* **to phone for something** = to make a phone call to ask for something **wegen etwas anrufen; etwas telefonisch bestellen;** *he phoned for a taxi;* **to phone about something** = to make a phone call to speak about something **wegen etwas anrufen;** *he phoned about the order for computer stationery*

◊ **phone back** *verb* to reply by phone **zurückrufen;** *the chairman is in a meeting, can you phone back in about half an hour? Mr Smith called while you were out and asked if you would phone him back*

phoneme *noun* single item of sound used in speech **Phonem;** *the phoneme "oo" is present in the words too and zoo*

◊ **phonetic** *adjective* referring to phonetics **phonetisch;** *the pronunciation is indicated in phonetic script*

◊ **phonetics** *noun* written symbols that are used to represent the correct pronunciation of a word **Phonetik**

phosphor *noun* substance that produces light when excited by some form of energy, usually an electron beam, used for the coating inside a cathode ray tube **Phosphor;** *see* TELEVISION; **phosphor coating** = thin layer of phosphor on the inside of a CRT screen **Phosphorbeschichtung; phosphor dots** = individual dots of red, green and blue phosphor on a colour CRT screen **Phosphorpunkte; phosphor efficiency** = measure of the amount of light produced in ratio to the energy received from an electron beam **Phosphorwirksamkeit; long persistence phosphor** = television screen coating that retains the displayed image for a period of time longer than the refresh rate, so reducing flicker effects **langleuchtender Phosphor**

COMMENT: a thin layer of phosphor is arranged in a pattern of small dots on the inside of a television screen which produces an image when scanned by the picture beam

phosphorescence *noun* ability of a material to produce light when excited by some form of energy **Postlumineszenz, Phosphoreszenz**

photo
1 *prefix* referring to light **Photo-, Foto-**
2 *abbreviation of* PHOTOGRAPH

◊ **photocell** *noun* electronic device that produces *or* varies an electrical signal according to the amount of light shining on it **Photozelle**

◊ **photocomposition** *noun* composition of typeset text direct onto film **Fotosatz**

◊ **photoconductivity** *noun* material which varies its resistance according to the amount of light striking it **Photoleitfähigkeit**

◊ **photoconductor** *noun* photocell whose resistance varies with the amount of light shining on it **Photoleiter**

◊ **photocopier** *noun* machine which makes a copy of a document by photographing and printing it **Fotokopierer**

◊ **photocopy**
1 *noun* copy of a document made by photographing and printing it **Fotokopie;** *make six photocopies of the contract*
2 *verb* to make a copy of a document by photographing and printing it **fotokopieren;** *she photocopied the contract*

◊ **photocopying** *noun* making photocopies **Fotokopieren;** *photocopying costs are rising each year;* **photocopying bureau** = office which photocopies documents for companies which do not possess their own photocopiers

Fotokopierbüro; **there is a mass of photocopying to be done** = there are many documents waiting to be photocopied **es gibt eine Menge zu fotokopieren**.
NOTE: no plural

◊ **photodigital memory** *noun* computer memory system that uses a LASER to write data onto a piece of film which can then be read many times but not written to again **Laserspeicher** NOTE: also called WORM (Write Once Read Many times memory)

◊ **photodiode** *noun* electronic component displaying the electrical properties of a diode but whose resistance varies with the amount of light that shines on it **Photodiode**; *see also* AVALANCHE

◊ **photoelectric** *adjective* (material) that generates an electrical signal when light shines on it **photoelektrisch**; **photoelectric cell** = component which produces *or* varies an electrical signal when a light shines on it **Photozelle**; *the photoelectric cell detects the amount of light passing through the liquid*

◊ **photoelectricity** *noun* production of an electrical signal from a material that has light shining on it **Photoelektrizität**

◊ **photoemission** *noun* material that emits electrons when light strikes it **Photoemission**

photograph *noun* image formed by light striking a light-sensitive surface, usually coated paper **Fotografie**; *colour photograph; black and white photograph; it's a photograph of the author; he took six photographs of the set; we will be using a colour photograph of the author on the back of the jacket*

◊ **photographic** *adjective* referring to photography *or* photographs **fotografisch**; *the copier makes a photographic reproduction of the printed page*

◊ **photographically** *adverb* using photography **fotografisch**; *the text film can be reproduced photographically*

◊ **photography** *noun* method of creating images by exposing light-sensitive paper to light, using a camera **Fotografie**

photogravure *noun* printing method in which the paper is pressed directly onto the etched printing plate **Foto-, Heliogravüre**

◊ **photolithography** *noun* printing using a lithographic printing plate formed photographically **Fotolithographie**

◊ **photomechanical transfer (PMT)** *noun* system for transferring line drawings and text onto film before printing **fotomechanische Übertragung**

◊ **photometry** *noun* study and measurement of light **Photometrie**

◊ **photon** *noun* packet of electromagnetic radiation **Photon**

◊ **photoprint** *noun* (*in typesetting*) final proof **druckfertige Vorlage**

◊ **photoresist** *noun* chemical *or* material that hardens into an etch resistant material when light is shone on it **Fotoresist, Fotolack**; *to make the PCB, coat the board with photoresist, place the opaque pattern above, expose, then develop and etch, leaving the conducting tracks*; **positive photoresist** = method of forming photographic images where exposed areas of photoresist are removed, used in making PCBs **positives Fotoresistverfahren**

◊ **photosensor** *noun* component *or* circuit that can produce a signal related to the amount of light striking it **Photosensor**

◊ **photostat**
1 *noun* type of photocopy **Fotokopie**
2 *verb* to make a photostat of a document **fotokopieren**

◊ **phototelegraphy** *noun* transmission of images over a telephone line **Bildtelegrafie**; *see also* FACSIMILE TRANSMISSION

◊ **phototext** *noun* characters and text that have been produced by a phototypesetter **Fotosatz**

◊ **phototransistor** *noun* electronic component that can detect light and amplify the generated signal *or* vary a supply according to light intensity **Phototransistor, Photozelle**

phototypesetter *noun* company which specializes in phototypesetting **Fotosetzer**

◊ **phototypesetting** *noun* method of typesetting that creates characters using a computer and exposing a sensitive film in front of a mask containing the required character shape **Fotosatz**

COMMENT: this is the method by which most new publications are typeset, superseding metal type, since it produces a good quality result in a shorter time

photovoltaic *adjective* which produces a voltage across a material due to light shining on it **photovoltaisch**

physical *adjective* solid *or* which can be touched **physisch, wirklich; physical address** = memory address that corresponds with a hardware memory location in a memory device **physische Adresse; physical database** = organization and structure of a stored database **physische Datenbank; physical layer** = the ISO/OSI defined network layer that defines rules for bit rate, power and medium for signal transmission **Bitübertragungsschicht;** *see also* LAYER; **physical memory** = memory fitted in a computer **physischer Speicher;** *compare* VIRTUAL MEMORY; **physical record** = (i) maximum unit of data that can be transmitted in a single operation; (ii) all the information, including control data for one record stored in a computer system **(i) & (ii) physischer Satz; physical topology** = actual arrangement of the cables in a network **physische Topologie**

PIA = PERIPHERAL INTERFACE ADAPTER circuit that allows a computer to communicate with a peripheral by providing serial and parallel ports and other handshaking signals required to interface the peripheral **peripherer Schnittstellenadapter**

pica *noun*
(a) method of measurement used in printing and typesetting (equal to twelve point type) **Pica**
(b) typeface used on a printer, giving ten characters to the inch **Pica**

PICK TM *noun* multiuser, multitasking operating system that runs on mainframe, mini or PC computers **PICK** TM

pickup *noun* arm and cartridge used to playback music from a record **Tonarm**

◊ **pickup reel** *noun* empty reel used to take the tape as it is played from a full reel **Aufnahmespule**

pico- **(p)** *prefix* representing one million millionth of a unit **Pico-, pico-; picofarad (pF)** = measure of capacitance equal to one million millionth of a farad **Picofarad; picosecond (ps)** = one million millionth of a second **Picosekunde**

picture
1 *noun* printed *or* drawn image of an object or scene **Bild;** *this picture shows the new design;* **picture beam** = moving electron beam in a TV, that produces an image on the screen by illuminating the phosphor coating and by varying its intensity

according to the received signal **Strahlstrom;** **picture element** *or* **pixel** = smallest single unit *or* point on a display whose colour *or* brightness can be controlled **Bildelement;** *see also* PIXEL; **picture phone** = communications system that allows sound and images of the user to be transmitted and received **Bildtelefon;** **picture processing** = analysis of information contained in an image, usually by computer *or* electronic methods, providing analysis *or* recognition of objects in the image **Bildverarbeitung;** **picture transmission** = transmission of images over a telephone line **Bildübertragung;** *see also* FACSIMILE TRANSMISSION
2 *verb* to visualize an object *or* scene **sich vorstellen;** *try to picture the layout before starting to draw it in*

PID = PERSONAL IDENTIFICATION DEVICE device (such as a card) connected *or* inserted into a system to identify or provide authorization for a user **Kennkarte**

piece accent *noun* floating accent **gleitender Akzent**

◊ **piece fractions** *noun* printed fractions contained in one character space **fertige Bruchzifferntypen (mit waagerechtem Bruchstrich)**

pie chart *noun* diagram where ratios are shown as slices of a circle **Kreisdiagramm**

piezoelectric *adjective (of certain crystals)* being able to change their electrical properties when a force is applied *or* to change their physical dimensions when an electrical signal is applied **piezoelektrisch**

piggyback *verb* to connect two integrated circuits in parallel, one top of the other to save space **huckepack verbinden;** *piggyback those two memory chips to boost the memory capacity;* **piggyback entry** = to gain unauthorized access to a computer system by using an authorized user's password *or* terminal **Huckepackzugang**

◊ **piggybacking** *noun* using transmitted messages to carry acknowledgements from a message which has been received earlier **Huckepackübertragung**

PILOT computer programming language that uses a text-based format and is mainly used in computer-aided learning **PILOT (Programmiersprache)**

pilot

1 *adjective* used as a test, which if successful will then be expanded into a full operation **Pilot-;** *the company set up a pilot project to see if the proposed manufacturing system was efficient; the pilot factory has been built to test the new production process;* **pilot system** = system constructed to see if it can be manufactured, if it works and if the end-user likes it **Pilotsystem**
2 *verb* to test **testen;** *they are piloting the new system*

PIM = PERSONAL INFORMATION MANAGER software utility that stores and manages a user's everyday data, such as diary, telephone numbers, address book and notes **PIM**

PIN = PERSONAL IDENTIFICATION NUMBER unique sequence of digits that identifies   the   user   **persönliche Identifikationsnummer**

COMMENT: the PIN is commonly used in automatic cash machines in banks, along with a card (PID) which allows the user to be identified

pin *noun*

(a) one of several short pieces of wire attached to an integrated circuit package that allows the IC to be connected to a circuit board **Kontaktstift; pin compatible** = an electronic chip that can directly replace another because the arrangement of the pins is the same and they carry the same signals **Pin-kompatibel;** *it's easy to upgrade the processor because the new one is pin-compatible*
(b) short piece of metal, part of a plug which fits into a hole in a socket **Kontaktstift;** *use a three-pin plug to connect the printer to the mains;* **three-pin mains plug** = plug with three pins (one neutral, one live and one earthed) **Netzstecker mit drei Kontaktstiften; two-pin mains plug** = plug with two pins (one neutral, one live) **Netzstecker mit zwei Kontaktstiften**

◊ **pin cushion distortion** *noun* optical image distortion in which objects are seen with stretched corners due to lens aberration **Nadelkissenverzerrung**

◊ **pinfeed** *noun see* TRACTOR FEED

◊ **pinout** *noun* description of the position of all the pins on an integrated circuit together with their function and signal **Pinbelegungsplan**

◊ **pin photodiode** *noun* electronic photodiode that can detect light, made up of layers of P-type, Intrinsic and N-type semiconductor **PIN-Photodiode**

pinchwheel *noun* small rubber wheel in a tape machine that holds the tape in place and prevents flutter **Andruckrad**

PIO = PARALLEL INPUT/OUTPUT; *see also* PIPO, PISO

pipe *noun* (in DOS and UNIX) symbol, normally (ø), that tells the operating system to send the output of one command to another command, instead of displaying it **Pipe-Symbol, Verkettungszeichen**

pipeline (computer)

1 *noun* CPU or ALU that is constructed in blocks and executes instructions in steps, each block dealing with one part of the instruction, so speeding up program execution **Leitung**
2 *verb*
(a) to schedule inputs to arrive at the microprocessor when nothing else is happening, so increasing apparent speed **im Pipelinesystem verarbeiten**
(b) to begin processing of a second instruction while still processing the present one to increase speed of execution of a program **im Pipelinesystem verarbeiten**
◊ **pipelining** *noun*
(a) method of scheduling inputs to arrive at the microprocessor when nothing else is happening, so increasing apparent speed **Pipelining-Methode**
(b) beginning the processing of a second instruction while still processing the present one to increase speed of execution of a program **Pipelining**

PIPO = PARALLEL INPUT/PARALLEL OUTPUT

pirate

1 *noun* person who copies a patented invention *or* a copyright work and sells it **Patenträuber, Markenpirat; Hersteller von Raubdrucken;** *the company is trying to take the software pirates to court*
2 *adjective* **pirate copy** = copy of software or other copyright material which has been made illegally **Raubkopie;** *a pirate copy of a computer program*
3 *verb* to manufacture copies of an original copyrighted work illegally **unerlaubt nachahmen/nachbauen/nachdrucken;**   *a pirated tape or a pirated design; the designs for the new system were pirated in the Far East; he used a cheap pirated disk and found the program had bugs in it*

◊ **piracy** *noun* copying of patented inventions *or* copyright works **Patentraub; Raubdruck, Raubpressung** NOTE: no plural

COMMENT: the items most frequently pirated are programs on magnetic disks and tapes which are relatively simple to copy

PISO = PARALLEL INPUT/SERIAL OUTPUT

pitch *noun*
(a) number of characters which will fit into one inch of line, when the characters are typed in single spacing (used on line printers, the normal pitches available being 10, 12 and 17 characters per inch) **Zeichendichte**
(b) actual frequency of a sound **Tonhöhe**; **pitch envelope** = shape that defines how the frequency of a sound will vary with time **Hüllkurve**
(c) satellite *or* antenna movement about the horizontal axis **Nicken**
(d) **sales pitch** = talk by a salesman to persuade someone to buy **Verkaufsgespräch**

pix *noun* picture *or* pictures **Bilder**

◊ **pix lock** *noun* synchronization of a video playback circuit by an external signal **Bildsynchronisation**

◊ **pixel** *or* **picture element** *noun* smallest single unit *or* point of a display whose colour *or* brightness can be controlled **Bildelement**

COMMENT: in high resolution display systems the colour or brightness of a single pixel can be controlled; in low resolution systems a group of pixels are controlled at the same time

QUOTE an EGA display and driver give a resolution of 640 x 350 pixels and support sixteen colours
PC Business World

QUOTE adding 40 to each pixel brightens the image and can improve the display's appearance
Byte

PL/1 = PROGRAMMING LANGUAGE/1 high level programming language mainly used in commercial and scientific work on large computers, containing features of ALGOL, COBOL and FORTRAN **PL/1 (Programmiersprache)**

PLA = PROGRAMMABLE LOGIC ARRAY IC that can be permanently programmed to perform logic operations on data **programmierbares logisches Feld**

COMMENT: a PLA consists of a large matrix of paths between input and output pins, with logic gates and a fusible link at each connection point which can be broken or left to conduct when programming to define a function from input to output

place *noun* position of a digit within a number **Platz, Stelle**

plaintext *noun* text *or* information that has not been encrypted *or* coded **Klartext**; *the messages were sent as plaintext by telephone; enter the plaintext message into the cipher machine*

PLAN low-level programming language **PLAN (Programmiersprache)**

plan
1 *noun*
(a) organized way of doing something **Plan**
(b) drawing which shows how something is arranged *or* how something will be built **Plan; floor plan** = drawing of a floor in a building, showing where different departments are **Grundriss**; **street plan** *or* **town plan** = map of a town showing streets and buildings **Stadtplan**
2 *verb* to organize carefully how something should be done **planen** NOTE: **planning - planned**

planar *noun*
(a) method of producing integrated circuits by diffusing chemicals into a slice of silicon to create the different components **Planartechnik**
(b) graphical objects or images arranged on the same plane **planare Anordnung**

planchest *noun* piece of furniture with wide flat drawers, in which large plans *or* artwork can be kept **Graphik-, Planschrank**

planner *noun*
(a) software program that allows appointments and important meetings to be recorded and arranged in the most efficient way **Planprogramm**
(b) **desk planner** *or* **wall planner** = book *or* chart which shows days *or* weeks *or* months so that the work of an office can be shown by diagrams **Terminplaner**

◊ **planning** *noun* organizing how something should be done **Planung**; *long-term planning or short-term planning* NOTE: no plural

planet *noun* large body in space (such as the earth), moving in orbit round the sun **Planet**

◊ **planetary camera** *noun* microfilm camera in which the film and article being photographed are stationary **(Mikrofilm)schrittkamera**

plant *verb* to store a result in memory for later use **zwischenspeichern**

plasma display *or* **gas plasma display** *noun* display screen using the electroluminescing properties of certain gases to display text **Plasmabildschirm**

‖ COMMENT: this is a modern thin display ‖ usually used in small portable computers

> QUOTE the disadvantage of using plasma technology is that it really needs mains power to work for any length of time

> QUOTE the plasma panel came out of the extended use test well
> *Micro Decision*

plastic bubble keyboard *noun* keyboard whose keys are small bubbles in a plastic sheet over a contact which when pressed completes a circuit **Plastikblasentastatur**

‖ COMMENT: these are very solid and cheap ‖ keyboards but are not ideal for rapid typing

plate *noun*
(a) illustration in a book, usually printed separately and on better quality paper than the text **Abbildung, Tafel**
(b) etched *or* patterned printing surface that carries the ink to the paper **Platte, Druckform**
(c) photographic image using a sheet of glass as the backing material **Platte; plate camera** = camera which takes pictures on glass plates **Plattenkamera**

‖ COMMENT: photographic plates are now ‖ used mainly in high quality, large-format ‖ professional cameras while the most popular ‖ backing material is still plastic as in a film

platen *noun*
(a) roller which supports the paper in a printer *or* typewriter **Walze; platen press** = printing press where the paper passes under a flat printing plate **Tiegeldruckpresse**
(b) device that keeps film in a camera in the correct position **Filmandruckplatte**

platform *noun* standard type of hardware that makes up a particular range of computers **Plattform**; *this software will only work on the IBM PC platform*; **platform independence** = software or a network that can work with or connect to different types of incompatible hardware **Plattformunabhängigkeit**

platter *noun* one disk within a hard disk drive **Platte**

‖ COMMENT: the disks are made of metal or ‖ glass and coated with a magnetic compound; ‖ each platter has a read/write head that moves ‖ across its surface to access stored data

play back *verb* to read data *or* a signal from a recording medium **abspielen, wiedergeben**; *after you have recorded the music, press this button to play back the tape and hear what it sounds like*

◊ **playback head** *noun* transducer that reads signals recorded on a storage medium and usually converts them to an electrical signal **Hör-/Lesekopf**; *disk playback head; tape playback head*

player missile graphics *see* SPRITES

PLD = PROGRAMMABLE LOGIC DEVICE

plex database *noun* database structure in which data items can be linked together **komplexe Datenbank**

◊ **plex structure** *noun* network structure *or* data structure in which each node is connected to all the others **komplexe Netzwerkstruktur**

PL/M = PROGRAMMING LANGUAGE FOR MICROPROCESSORS high level programming language derived from PL/1 for use on microprocessors **PL/M (Programmiersprache)**

plot
1 *noun* graph *or* map **Zeichnung**
2 *verb* to draw an image (especially a graph) based on information supplied as a series of coordinates **grafisch darstellen; plotting mode** = ability of some word-processors to produce graphs by printing a number of closely spaced characters rather than individual pixels (this results in a broad low-resolution line) **Grafikmodus**

◊ **plotter** *noun* computer peripheral that draws straight lines between two coordinates **Kurvenschreiber, Plotter; plotter driver** = dedicated software that converts simple instructions issued by a user into complex control instructions to direct the plotter **Plottertreiber; plotter pen** = instrument used in a plotter to mark the paper with ink as it moves over the paper

Plotterschreibkopf; **digital plotter** = plotter
which receives the coordinates to plot to in
a digital form **Digitalplotter; drum plotter** =
computer output device that consists of a
movable pen and a piece of paper wrapped
around a drum that rotates, creating
patterns and text **Trommelplotter;
incremental plotter** = plotter which receives
positional data as increments to its current
position rather than separate coordinates
Stufenformplotter; pen plotter = plotter that
uses removable pens to draw an image on
paper **Stiftplotter; printer-plotter** = high-
resolution printer that is able to mimic a
plotter and produce low-resolution plots
Drucker-Plotter; x-y plotter *or* **graph plotter** =
plotter which plots to coordinates supplied,
by moving the pen in two planes while the
paper remains stationary **Plotter,
Kurvenzeichner**

COMMENT: plotters are used for graph and
diagram plotting and can plot curved lines as a
number of short straight lines

plug
1 *noun*
(a) connector with protruding pins that is
inserted into a socket to provide an
electrical connection **Stecker;** *the printer is
supplied with a plug;* **adapter plug** = plug
which allows devices with different plugs
(two-pin, three-pin, etc.) to be fitted into
the same socket **Zwischenstecker; plug-
compatible** = equipment manufactured to
operate with another system when
connected to it by a connector *or* cable
steckerkompatibel; *this new plug-compatible
board works much faster than any of its
rivals, we can install it by simply plugging it
into the expansion port*
(b) to give a plug to a new product = to
publicize a new product **für ein neues
Produkt die Werbetrommel rühren**
2 *verb*
(a) to plug in = to make an electrical
connection by pushing a plug into a socket
einstecken; *no wonder the computer does
nothing, you have not plugged it in at the
mains;* **plug-in unit** = small electronic circuit
that can be simply plugged into a system to
increase its power **Steckeinheit** NOTE:
opposite is **unplug**
(b) to publicize *or* to advertise **Werbung
betreiben;** *they ran six commercials plugging
holidays in Spain*

◊ **plugboard** *or* **patchboard** *noun*
board with a number of sockets connected
to devices into which plugs can be inserted
to connect various other devices **Schalttafel**

plus *or* **plus sign** *noun* printed *or* written
sign (+) showing that figures are added *or*
showing a positive value **Pluszeichen**

PMBX = PRIVATE MANUAL BRANCH
EXCHANGE small telephone exchange
inside a company where all calls coming in
or going out have to be placed through the
switchboard **private Handvermittlungsanlage**

PMOS = P-channel METAL OXIDE
SEMICONDUCTOR metal oxide
semiconductor transistor that conducts via
a small region of p-type semiconductor **p-
Kanal-MOS**

PMR = PRIVATE MOBILE RADIO

PMT = PHOTOMECHANICAL
TRANSFER

pn-junction *noun* area where regions of
p-type and n-type semiconductor meet,
resulting in a diode characteristic **pn-
Übergang; diffused pn-junction** = practical
result of doping one section of
semiconductor as p-type and an adjacent
section as n-type, where the doping
concentration drops gradually over a short
distance between the two areas **diffundierter
pn-Übergang; step pn-junction** = ideal
junction between p-type and n-type areas in
a semiconductor where the doping changes
occur suddenly **pn-Stufenübergang**

◊ **pnp transistor** *noun* layout of a
bipolar transistor whose collector and
emitter are of p-type semiconductor and
whose base is n-type semiconductor **pnp-
Transistor**

pocket *noun* **pocket calculator** *or* **pocket
diary** = calculator *or* diary which can be
carried in the pocket **Taschenrechner;
Taschenkalender**

point
1 *noun*
(a) place *or* position **Punkt; access point** =
point on a circuit board *or* in software,
allowing an engineer to check signals *or*
data **Zugriffspunkt; breakpoint** = symbol

inserted into a program which stops its execution at that point to allow registers, variables and memory locations to be examined (used when debugging a program) **bedingter Programmstop; re-entry point** = point in a program *or* routine where it is re-entered **Wiedereinstiegspunkt; starting point** = place where something starts **Startpunkt**
(b) **binary point** = dot which indicates the division between the bits for the numbers' whole units and the fractional part of the binary number **Binärstelle; decimal point** = dot (in a decimal number) which indicates the division between a whole unit and its fractional parts (such as 4.25) **Dezimalstelle; percentage point** = 1 per cent **Prozentpunkt**
(c) measurement system used in typesetting (one point is equal to 0.351 mm) **(typografischer) Punkt;** *the text of the book is set in 9 point Times; if we increase the point size to 10, will the page extent increase?* NOTE: usually written **pt** after figures: **10pt Times Bold**
2 *verb* **to point out** = to show **hinweisen**

◊ **pointer** *noun*
(a) variable in a computer program that contains the address to a data item *or* instruction **Hinweisadresse;** *increment the contents of the pointer to the address of the next instruction;* **pointer file** = file of pointers referring to large amounts of stored data **Verweisungsdatei**
(b) graphical symbol used to indicate the position of a cursor on a computer display **Zeiger;** *desktop publishing on a PC is greatly helped by the use of a pointer and mouse*

◊ **pointing device** *noun* input device that controls the position of a cursor on screen as it is moved by the user **Zeigevorrichtung, Zeigereinheit;** *see also* MOUSE

◊ **point-of-sale (POS)** *noun* the place where goods in a shop are paid for **Kasse; point-of-sale material** = display material (such as posters, dump bins) to advertise a product where it is being sold **Werbematerial an der Kasse; point-of-sale terminal** *or* **POS terminal** = computer terminal at a point-of-sale, used to provide detailed product information and connected to a central computer to give immediate stock control information **Computerkasse; electronic point-of-sale (EPOS)** = system that uses a computer terminal at a point-of-sale site for electronic funds transfer, as well as for product identification and stock control **elektronische Kasse**

◊ **point to point** *noun* communications network where every point is connected to every other **Punkt zu Punkt**

> COMMENT: this provides rapid reliable transmissions but is very expensive and wasteful in cabling

> QUOTE the arrow keys, the spacebar or the mouse are used for pointing, and the enter key or the left mouse button are to pick
> *PC User*

> QUOTE pointing with the cursor and pressing the joystick button eliminates use of the keyboard entirely
> *Soft*

poke *noun* computer instruction that modifies an entry in a memory by writing a number to an address in memory **POKE-Anweisung (Übertragung eines Byte an eine bestimmte Stelle im aktuellen Arbeitsspeichersegment);** *poke 1423,74 will write the data 74 into location 1423 compare with* PEEK

POL = PROBLEM-ORIENTATED LANGUAGE

polar *adjective* referring to poles **polar; polar coordinates** = system of defining positions as an angle and distance from the origin **Polarkoordinaten;** *compare with* CARTESIAN COORDINATES; **polar diagram** = graphical representation of polar coordinates **Polardiagramm; polar orbit** = satellite flight path that flies over the earth's poles **polare Umlaufbahn; polar signal** = signal that uses positive and negative voltage levels **Doppelstromsignal; unipolar signal** = signal that uses only positive voltage levels **Einfachstrom-Signal**

◊ **polarity** *noun* definition of direction of flow of flux *or* current in an object **Polarität; electrical polarity** = definition of whether an electrical signal is positive *or* negative, indicating if a point is a source or collector of electrical current (positive polarity terminals are usually marked red, negative are black) **elektrische Polarität; magnetic polarity** = method of indicating if a point is a source *or* collector of magnetic flux patterns **magnetische Polarität; polarity test** = check to see which electrical terminal is positive and which negative **Polaritätsprüfung; reverse polarity** = situation where positive and negative terminals have been confused, resulting in the equipment not functioning **umgekehrte Polarität (durch Umpolung)**

◊ **polarized** *adjective*
(a) broadcast signal waveforms are all aligned in one plane **polarisiert; vertically polarized** = signal whose waveforms travel horizontally while alternating vertically **vertikal polarisiert**
(b) polarized plug = plug which has a feature (usually a peg *or* a special shape) so that it can only be inserted into a socket in one way **polarisierter Stecker; polarized edge connector** = edge connector that has a hole or key to prevent it being plugged in the wrong way round **polarisierter Randstecker**

polaroid filter *noun* photographic filter that only allows light in one plane, vertical *or* horizontal, to be transmitted **Polaroidfilter**

║ COMMENT: often used to remove glare by
║ placing in front of a camera lens or as glasses in
║ front of a person's eyes

Polish notation *see* REVERSE

poll *verb (of computer)* to determine the state of a peripheral in a network **abrufen; polled interrupt** = interrupt signal determined by a polling device **Unterbrechung auf Abruf**

◊ **polling** *noun* system of communication between a controlling computer and a number of networked terminals (the computer checks each terminal in turn to see if it is ready to receive *or* transmit data, and takes the required action) **Sendeaufruf; polling characters** = special sequence of characters for each terminal to be polled (when a terminal recognises its sequence, it responds) **Sendeabrufzeichen; polling interval** = period of time between two polling operations **Sendeaufrufintervall; polling list** = order in which terminals are to be polled by a computer **Aufrufliste; polling overhead** = amount of time spent by a computer in calling and checking each terminal in a network **Aufrufzeitaufwand**

║ COMMENT: the polling system differs from
║ other communications systems in that the
║ computer asks the terminals to transmit or
║ receive, not the other way round

polynomial code *noun* error detection system that uses a set of mathematical rules applied to the message before it is transmitted and again when it is received to reproduce the original message **Polynomcode**

POP 2 high level programming language used for list processing applications **POP 2 (Programmiersprache)**

pop *verb* (instruction to a computer) to read and remove the last piece of data from a stack **letzten Eintrag lesen und löschen; pop-down menu** *or* **pop-up menu** = menu that can be displayed on the screen at any time by pressing the appropriate key, usually displayed over material already on the screen **Hervorholmenü, Einblendmenü; to pop off** *or* **pop on** = to remove *or* add suddenly an image *or* section of image from a frame **wegnehmen; hervorholen;** *this is the last frame of the film so pop on the titles*

◊ **pop filter** *noun* electronic circuit used when recording voices to attenuate signals caused by wind *or* breathing **Pop-Filter;** *every time you say a 'p' you overload the tape recorder, so put this pop filter in to stop it*

║ QUOTE you can use a mouse to access
║ pop-up menus and a keyboard for word
║ processing
║   *Byte*

populate *verb* to fill the sockets on a printed circuit board with components **bestücken; fully-populated** = (i) all the options or memory is fitted into a computer; (ii) printed circuit board that has components in all free sockets **(i) komplett ausgestattet; (ii) vollständig bestückt**

porch *see* FRONT PORCH

port *noun* socket *or* physical connection allowing data transfer between a computer's internal communications channel and another external device **Anschlussstelle; asynchronous port** = connection to a computer allowing asynchronous data communications **Asynchronanschlussstelle; input port** = circuit *or* connector that allows a computer to receive data from other external devices **Eingabeanschluss; joystick port** = socket and interfacing circuit into which a joystick can be plugged **Joystickanschlussstelle; output port** = circuit *or* connector that allows a computer to output *or* transmit data to another machine *or* device **Ausgabeanschluss; parallel port** = circuit and connector that allows parallel data to be received *or* transmitted **Parallelanschlussstelle; printer port** = output port of a computer with a standard connector to which a printer is connected to receive character data (either serial *or* parallel) **Druckeranschluss; serial port** = circuit that converts parallel data in a computer to and from a serial form, allowing serial data access **serielle Anschlussstelle; port selector** = switch that allows the user to choose which peripheral a computer (via its o/p port) is connected to **Anschlusswahlschalter; port sharing** = device that is placed between one I/O port and a number of peripherals, allowing the computer access to all of them **Gemeinschaftsanschluss**

QUOTE the 40 Mbyte hard disk model is provided with eight terminal ports
Micro Decision

portable
1 *noun* compact self-contained computer that can be carried around and used either with a battery pack *or* mains power supply **tragbarer Computer, Aktentaschencomputer**
2 *adjective* (any hardware *or* software *or* data files) that can be used on a range of different computers **übertragbar, kompatibel; portable software** *or* **portable programs** = programs that can be run on several different computer systems **übertragbare Programme**

◊ **portability** *noun* extent to which software *or* hardware can be used on several systems **Übertragbarkeit**

QUOTE although portability between machines is there in theory, in practice it just isn't that simple
Personal Computer World

POS = POINT-OF-SALE place in a shop where goods are paid for **Kasse; EPOS** = ELECTRONIC POINT-OF-SALE system that uses a computer terminal at a point-of-sale site for electronic fund transfer *or* stock control as well as product pricing, etc. **elektronische Kasse**

position
1 *noun* place where something is **Stelle, Position;** *this is the position of that chip on the PCB*
2 *verb* to place something in a special place **setzen;** *the VDU should not be positioned in front of a window position this photograph at the top right-hand corner of the page;* **positioning time** = amount of time required to access data stored in a disk drive *or* tape machine, including all mechanical movements of the read head and arm **Einstellzeit**

◊ **positional** *adjective* referring to position; in a certain position **Stellen-, stellen-**

positive *adjective*
(a) meaning "yes" **positiv; positive response**

= communication signal that indicates correct reception of a message **positive Antwort; positive terminal** = connection to a power supply source that is at a higher electrical potential than ground and supplies current to a component **positive Klemme**
(b) (image) which shows objects as they are seen **Positiv-; positive display** = (screen) where the text and graphics are shown as black on a white background to imitate a printed page **schwarz auf weiß Anzeige; positive presentation** = screen image which is coloured on a white background **farbig auf weiß Anzeige;** *compare* NEGATIVE
(c) of electrical voltage greater than zero **positiv; positive logic** = logic system in which a logical one is represented by a positive voltage level, and a logical zero represented by a zero or negative voltage level **positive Logik**

◊ **positive feedback** *noun* part of an output signal that is added into the input of a device **positive Rückkopplung;** *make sure the microphone is not too close to the loudspeaker or positive feedback will occur and you will overload the amplifier*

COMMENT: positive feedback is often accidental, resulting in a stronger output which provides a bigger positive feedback signal which rapidly overloads the system

POSIX = PORTABLE OPERATING SYSTEM INTERFACE IEEE standard that defines a set of services provided by an operating system; software that works to the POSIX standard can be easily ported between hardware platforms **POSIX**

post
1 *verb* to enter data into a record in a file **eintragen**
2 *prefix* action that occurs after another **nachträglich, Nach-, nach-; post-editing** = editing and modifying text after it has been compiled *or* translated by a machine **nachträgliches Modifizieren von Daten; post-formatted** = (text) arranged at printing time rather than on screen **nachträglich bearbeitet; post mortem** = examination of a computer program *or* piece of hardware after it has failed to try to find out why the failure took place **Post-Mortem-Fehlersuche**

◊ **postbyte** *noun* in a program instruction, the data byte following the op code that defines the register to be used **Postbyte**

◊ **postfix** *noun* word *or* letter written after another **Postfix; postfix notation** =

mathematical operations written in a logical way, so that the operator appears after the operands, this removes the need for brackets **Postfixschreibweise;** *normal notation: (x-y) + z, but using postfix notation: xy - z+* NOTE: often referred to as **reverse Polish notation**

◊ **postprocessor** *noun*
(a) microprocessor that handles semi-processed data from another device **Postprozessor**
(b) program that processes data from another program, which has already been processed **Postprozessorprogramm**

poster *noun* large printed sheet, used to advertise something **Plakat**

PostScript ™ standard page description language developed by Adobe Systems; PostScript offers flexible font sizing and positioning; it is most often found in laser printers **PostScript** ™; *if you do a lot of DTP work, you will benefit from a PostScript printer;* **Display PostScript** = graphics language system that allows a user to see on the screen exactly what would appear on the printer **Display PostScript**

pot = POTENTIOMETER

potential *noun* ability of energy to carry out work (by transformation) **Potenzial, Spannung; potential difference** = voltage difference between two points in a circuit **Potenzialunterschied**

◊ **potentiometer** *noun* mechanical variable resistance component consisting of a spindle which is turned to move a contact across a resistance track to vary the resistance of the potentiometer **Potenziometer;** *see also* VARIABLE RESISTOR APPENDIX

power
1 *noun*
(a) unit of energy in electronics equal to the product of voltage and current, measured in Watts **(Netz)strom, Leistung; automatic power off** = equipment that will switch itself off if it has not been used for a certain time **automatische Stromabschaltung; power dump** = to remove all power from a computer **den Strom abschalten; power failure** = stoppage of the electrical power supply (for a long *or* very short period of time) which will cause electrical equipment to stop working or malfunction, unless they are battery backed **Stromausfall; power loss** = amount of power lost (in transmission *or* due to

connection equipment) **Spannungsverlust;** "**power off**" = switching off *or* disconnecting an electrical device from its power supply **Netz aus;** "**power on**" = indication that a voltage is being supplied to a piece of electrical equipment **Netz ein; power-on reset** = automatic reset of a CPU to a known initial state immediately after power is applied (some CPUs will not automatically start with clear registers, etc., but might contain garbage) **Netz Ein-Grundstellung; power on self test (POST)** = series of hardware tests that a computer carries out when it is first switched on **Einschalt-Selbsttest, Selbsttest beim Einschalten; power pack** = self-contained box that will provide a voltage and current supply for a circuit **Netzteil; power supply** *or* **power supply unit (PSU)** = electrical circuit that provides certain direct current voltage and current levels from an alternating current source for use in other electrical circuits (a PSU will regulate, smooth and reduce the mains voltage level for use in low power electronic circuits) **Stromversorgungseinheit; power up** = to switch on *or* apply a voltage to a electrical device **den Strom einschalten; uninterruptable power supply (UPS)** = power supply that can continue to provide a regulated supply to equipment even after mains power failure **unterbrechungslose Stromversorgungsanlage (UPS)**
(b) mathematical term describing the number of times a number is to be multiplied by itself **Potenz;** *5 to the power 2 is equal to 25* NOTE: written as small figures in superscript: 10^5: say: "ten to the power five"
(c) **power user** = user who needs the latest, fastest model of computer because he runs complex or demanding applications **Power-User**
2 *verb* to provide electrical or mechanical energy to a device **mit Strom versorgen;** *the monitor is powered from a supply in the main PC;* **power down** *or* **off** = to turn off the power to a device **ausschalten, herunterfahren;** *once you have shut down the software, you can power off the server*

◊ **powered** *adjective* driven by a type of energy **angetrieben**

PowerBook ™ *noun* laptop version of a Macintosh computer, designed by Apple Corp. **PowerBook** ™

PPM = PULSE POSITION MODULATION pulse modulation method that varies the time between pulses in relation to the magnitude of an input signal

Pulslagenmodulation; *see also* PULSE MODULATION

ppm = PAGES PER MINUTE

PR = PUBLIC RELATIONS; *a PR firm is handling all our publicity; he is working in PR the PR people gave away 100,000 leaflets*

pre- *prefix* meaning before **vorher, prä-;** **pre-agreed** = which has been agreed in advance **vorher abgesprochen; preallocation** = execution of a process which does not begin until all memory and peripheral requirements are free for use **Vorab-Zuordnung; pre-fetch** = instructions read and stored in a short temporary queue with a CPU that contains the next few instructions to be processed, increasing the speed of execution **Befehlsvorauslese**

◊ **pre-amplifier** *noun* low noise electronic circuit that increases the magnitude of very small signals, used before a power amplifier **Vorverstärker**

precede *verb* to come before **vorangehen;** *instruction which cancels the instruction which precedes it*

◊ **precedence** *noun* computational rules defining the order in which mathematical operations are calculated (usually multiplications are done first, then divisions, additions, and subtractions last) **Vorrang; operator precedence** = order in which a number of mathematical operations will be carried out **Bedienungsreihenfolge**

precise *adjective* very exact **genau, präzis;** *the atomic clock will give the precise time of starting the process*

◊ **precision** *noun* being very accurate **Genauigkeit, Präzision; double precision** = using two data words to store a number, providing greater precision **doppelte Genauigkeit; multiple precision** = using more than one byte of data for number storage to increase possible precision **Mehrfachgenauigkeit; precision of a number** = number of digits in a number **Zahlengenauigkeit; single precision** = number stored in one word **einfache Genauigkeit;** *compare with* MULTIPLE, DOUBLE

precompiled code *noun* code that is output from a compiler, ready to be executed **vorkompilierter Code**

precondition *verb* to condition data before it is processed **Vorbedingung**

predefined *adjective* which has been defined in advance **vordefiniert**

◊ **predesigned** *adjective* (graphic material) provided to the customer already designed **vorher entworfen;** *a wide selection of predesigned layouts help you automatically format typical business and technical documents*

◊ **predetermined** *adjective* which has already been determined **vorherbestimmt**

predicate *noun* function *or* statement used in rule-based programs such as expert systems **Prädikat**

> QUOTE we should stick to systems which we know are formally sound, such as predicate logic
>
> *Personal Computer World*

pre-edit *verb* to change text before it is run through a machine to make sure it is compatible **vorher bearbeiten**

◊ **pre-emphasise** *verb* to boost certain frequencies of a signal before transmission *or* processing to minimize noise (signals are de-emphasised on reception) **vorverzerren, anheben**

preemptive multitasking *noun* form of multitasking in which the operating system executes a program for a period of time, then passes control to the next program so preventing any one program using all the processor time **präemptives Multitasking**

prefix *noun*
(a) code *or* instruction *or* character at the beginning of a message *or* instruction **Vorspann**
(b) word attached to the beginning of another word to give it a special meaning **Präfix, Vorsilbe**

◊ **prefix notation** *noun* mathematical operations written in a logical way, so that the operator appears before the operands, this removes the need for brackets **Präfixschreibweise;** *normal notation: (x-y) + z, but using prefix notation: - xy + z*

preformatted *adjective* which has been formatted already **vorformatiert;** *a preformatted disk*

premix *noun* combination of a number of signals before they have been processed in any way **Vormischung**

preparation *noun* getting something

ready **Erstellung, Vorbereitung, Programmodifikation; data preparation** = conversion of data into a machine-readable form (usually by keyboarding) before data entry **Datenaufbereitung**

preprinted *adjective* already printed *or* printed in advance **vorgedruckt; preprinted form** = paper used for printing databases *or* applications programs that already contain some information printed **vorgedrucktes Formular; preprinted stationery** = computer stationery (such as invoices) which has already been printed with the company's logo and address as well as the blank columns, etc. **Vordruck**

preprocessor *noun*
(a) software that partly processes *or* prepares data before it is compiled *or* translated **Vorkompilierer**
(b) small computer that carries out some initial processing of raw data before passing it to the main computer **Vorprozessor**
◊ **preprocess** *verb* to carry out initial organization and simple processing of data **vorübersetzen**

QUOTE the C preprocessor is in the first stage of converting a written program into machine instructions

QUOTE the preprocessor can be directed to read in another file before completion, perhaps because the same information is needed in each module of the program
Personal Computer World

preproduction *noun* organization of the filming *or* recording of a video *or* compact disk, taking the form of diagrams and scene descriptions **Vorproduktion**

preprogrammed *adjective* (chip) which has been programmed in the factory to perform one function **vorprogrammiert**

prerecord
1 *verb* to record something which will be played back later *or* to record sound effects that are added to a film at a later date **voraufzeichnen;** *the answerphone plays a prerecorded message*
2 *noun* section of text stored in a word-processor system which will be used as the basis for a form letter **Voraufzeichnung**

presentation graphics *noun* graphics used to represent business information or data **Präsentationsgrafik;** *the sales for last*

month looked even better thanks to the use of presentation graphics

◊ **presentation layer** *noun* ISO/OSI standard network layer that agrees on formats, codes and requests for start and end of a connection **Darstellungsschicht;** *see also* ISO/OSI, LAYER

◊ **Presentation Manager** ™ *noun* graphical user interface supplied with the OS/2 operating system **Presentation Manager** ™

preset *verb* to set something in advance **voreinstellen;** *the printer was preset with new page parameters*
NOTE: **presetting - preset**

press
1 *noun*
(a) newspapers and magazines **Presse; the local press** = newspapers which are sold in a small area of the country **die Lokalpresse; the national press** = newspapers which sell in all parts of the country **die überregionale Presse;** *the new car has been advertised in the national press; we plan to give the product a lot of press publicity; there was no mention of the new product in the press;* **press conference** = meeting where reporters from newspapers are invited to hear news of a new product *or* of a takeover bid, etc. **Pressekonferenz; press coverage** = reports about something in the press **Pressebericht;** *we were very disappointed by the press coverage of the new car;* **press cutting** = piece cut out of a newspaper *or* magazine, which refers to an item which you find interesting **Zeitungsausschnitt;** *we have kept a file of press cuttings about the new software package;* **press release** = advance publicity material about a new product given out to newspapers and other media **Presseverlautbarung;** *the company sent out a press release about the launch of the new scanner* NOTE: no plural
(b) printing press = machine which prints **Druckerpresse; the book is on the press** = the book is being printed **das Buch ist im Druck**
2 *verb* to push with the fingers **drücken;** *to end the program press ESCAPE*

pressure pad *noun* transducer that converts pressure changes into an electrical signal **Druckumwandler;** *the pressure pad under the carpet will set off the burglar alarm if anyone steps on it*

prestore *verb* to store data in memory before it is processed **vorweg speichern**

presumptive address *noun* initial

address in a program, used as a reference for others unmodifizierte Adresse

◊ **presumptive instruction** *noun* unmodified program instruction which is processed to obtain the instruction to be executed unmodifizierter Befehl

prevent *verb* to stop something happening verhindern; *the police prevented anyone from leaving the building; we have changed the passwords to prevent hackers getting into the database*

◊ **preventive** *or* **preventative** *adjective* which tries to stop something happening vorbeugend; **preventive maintenance** = regular checks on equipment to correct and repair any small faults before they cause a major problem vorbeugende Wartung; *we have a preventive maintenance contract for the system*

◊ **prevention** *noun* preventing something happening Vorbeugung

preview *verb* to display text *or* graphics on a screen as it will appear when it is printed out das Layout kontrollieren

◊ **previewer** *noun* feature that allows a user to see on screen what a page will look like when printed Layoutkontrolle; *the built-in previewer allows the user to check for mistakes*

previous *adjective* which happens earlier vorherig; *copy data into the present workspace from the previous file*

◊ **previously** *adverb* happening earlier vorherig; *the data is copied onto previously formatted disks*

primary *adjective* first *or* basic *or* most important Primär-, primär-, Haupt-, haupt-; **primary channel** = channel that carries the data transmission between two devices Primärkanal; *compare* SECONDARY CHANNEL; **primary colours** = colours (red, yellow and blue) from which all other colours can be derived Grundfarben; **primary group** = number of signals that are merged into one signal (which may be merged with others) prior to transmission Primärgruppe; **primary key** = unique identifying word that selects one entry from a database Primärschlüssel; **primary memory** *or* **storage** *or* **main memory** = (i) small fast-access internal memory of a computer system (whose main memory is slower secondary storage) which stores the program currently being used; (ii) main internal memory of a computer system (i)

Primärspeicher; (ii) Hauptspeicher; *compare* SECONDARY STORAGE; **primary station** = the single station in a data network that can select a path and transmit the primary station status is temporary and is transferred from one station to another Primärstation

◊ **primarily** *adverb* mainly hauptsächlich

prime
1 *adjective* very important Haupt-, haupt-; **prime attribute** = most important feature *or* design of a system Hauptattribut; **prime time** = (i) time when there are the greatest number of TV viewers (ii) most expensive advertising time for TV commercials (i) & (ii) Hauptsendezeit (Sendezeit mit den höchsten Einschaltquoten); *we are putting out a series of prime-time commercials*
2 *noun* number that can only be divided by itself and by one Primzahl; *the number seven is a prime*

primer *noun* manual *or* simple instruction book with instructions and examples to show how a new program *or* system operates Elementarbuch

primitive *noun* (i) (in programming) basic routine that can be used to create more complex routines; (ii) (in graphics) simple shape (such as circle, square, line, curve) used to create more complex shapes in a graphics program (i) Grundroutine, Elementarroutine; (ii) Grafikelement

print
1 *noun*
(a) image produced using an etched printing plate Druck; *he collects 18th century prints; the office is decorated with Japanese prints*
(b) positive photographic image in which black is black and white is white Abzug; *compare with* NEGATIVE; **print contrast ratio** = difference between the brightest and darkest areas of an image Kontrastverhältnis
(c) characters made in ink on paper Gedrucktes; *he was very pleased to see his book in print; the print from the daisy-wheel printer is clearer than that from the line printer;* **print control character** = special character sent to a printer that directs it to perform an action *or* function (such as change font), rather than print a character Drucksteuerzeichen; **print format** = way in which text is arranged when printed out, according to embedded codes, etc., used to set the margins, headers, etc. Druckformat; **print hammer** = moving arm in a daisy-wheel printer that presses the metal

character form onto the printer ribbon leaving a mark on the paper **Druckhammer; print job** = file in a print queue that contains all the characters and printer control codes needed to print one document *or* page **Druckjob, Druckauftrag; print life** = number of characters a component can print before needing to be replaced **Druckerlebensdauer;** *the printhead has a print life of over 400 million characters;* **print modifiers** = codes in a document that cause a printer to change mode, i.e. from bold to italic **Druckanweisungen; printout** = final printed page **Ausdruck; print pause** = temporarily stopping a printer while printing (to change paper, etc.) **Druckpause; print quality** = the quality of the text *or* graphics printed; normally measured in dots per inch **Druckqualität;** *a desktop printer with a resolution of 600dpi provides good print quality;* **print queue** = area of memory that stores print jobs ready to send to the printer when it has finished its current work **Druckwarteschlange; print server** = computer in a network that is dedicated to managing print queues and printers **Druckserver; print spooling** = automatic printing of a number of different documents in a queue at the normal speed of the printer, while the computer is doing some other task **SPOOL-Funktion; print style** = typeface used on a certain printer *or* for a certain document **Drucktype, Schriftart**
2 *verb*
(a) to put letters *or* figures in ink on paper **drucken;** *printed agreement; printed regulations; the printer prints at 60 characters per second*
(b) to put letters *or* illustrations onto sheets of paper so that they form a book **drucken;** *the book was printed in Hong Kong; the book is printing at the moment, so we will have bound copies at the end of the month*
(c) to write in capital letters **in Druckschrift schreiben;** *please print your name and address on the top of the form*

◊ **printed circuit** *or* **printed circuit board (PCB)** *noun* flat insulating material that has conducting tracks of metal printed *or* etched onto its surface which complete a circuit when components are mounted on it **gedruckte Schaltkarte**

◊ **printer** *noun*
(a) device that converts input data in an electrical form into a printed readable form **Drucker; barrel printer** = type of printer where characters are located around a rotating barrel **Typenwalzendrucker; bi-directional printer** = printer which is able to print characters from left to right *or* from

right to left as the head moves backwards and forwards across the paper **Zweirichtungsdrucker; bubble-jet printer** = printer that produces characters by sending a stream of tiny drops of ink onto the paper **Tintenstrahldrucker, Bubble-Jet-Drucker; chain printer** = printer whose characters are located on a continuous belt **Kettendrucker; computer printer** = machine which prints information from a computer **Computerdrucker; daisy-wheel printer** = printer with characters arranged on interchangeable daisy-wheels **Typenraddrucker; dot-matrix printer** = printer which forms characters from a series of tiny dots printed close together **Matrixdrucker, Nadeldrucker; impact printer** = printer that prints text and symbols by striking an inked ribbon onto paper with a metal character **Anschlagdrucker, mechanischer Drucker; ink-jet printer** = printer that produces characters by sending a stream of tiny drops of electrically charged ink onto the paper (the movement of the ink drops is controlled by an electric field) **Tintenstrahldrucker; laser printer** = high-resolution printer that uses a laser source to print high quality dot-matrix characters **Laserdrucker; line printer** = printer which prints draft-quality information at high speed (typical output is 200 - 3000 lines per minute) **Zeilendrucker; page printer** = printer which composes one page of text, then prints it rapidly **Seitendrucker, Blattschreiber; thermal printer** = printer where the character is formed on thermal paper with a printhead containing a matrix of small heating elements **Thermodrucker; printer buffer** = temporary store for character data waiting to be printed (used to free the computer before the printing is completed making the operation faster) **Druckerpuffer; printer control characters** = command characters in a text which transmit printing commands to a printer **Druckersteuerzeichen; printer control language (PCL)** = standard set of commands, defined by Hewlett Packard, that allow a computer to control a printer **Printer Control Language (PCL); printer driver** = dedicated software that converts and formats users' commands ready for a printer **Druckertreiber; printer emulation** = printer that is able to interpret the standard set of commands used to control another brand of printer **Druckeremulation;** *this printer emulation allows my NEC printer to emulate an Epsom;* **printer-plotter** = high resolution printer that is able to operate as a low resolution plotter **Drucker-Plotter;**

printer port = output port of a computer to which a printer is connected to receive character data (either parallel or serial) **Druckeranschlussstelle; printer quality** = standard of printed text from a particular printer (high resolution dot-matrix printers produce near letter-quality, daisy-wheel printers produce letter-quality text) **Druckqualität; printer ribbon** = roll of inked material which passes between a printhead and the paper **Farbband**
(b) company which prints books *or* newspapers **Druckerei;** *the book will be sent to the printer next week; we are using Japanese printers for some of our magazines*

◊ **printhead** *noun* (i) row of needles in a dot-matrix printer that produce characters as a series of dots; (ii) metal form of a character that is pressed onto an inked ribbon to print the character on paper **(i) Druckerkopf; (ii) Typenkopf**

◊ **printing** *noun* action of printing **Drucken**

◊ **print out** *verb* to print information stored in a computer with a printer **ausdrucken**

◊ **printout** *noun* **computer printout** = printed copy of information from a computer **Computerausdruck;** *the sales director asked for a printout of the agents' commissions*

◊ **printrun** *noun* number of copies of a book which are printed at one time **Auflage**

◊ **print shop** *noun* shop where jobbing printing takes place **Akzidenzdruckerei**

◊ **printwheel** *noun* daisy-wheel *or* the wheel made up of a number of arms, with a character shape at the end of each arm, used in a daisy-wheel printer **Typenrad**

prior *adjective* happening before **vorherig**
2 *adverb* **prior to** = before **bevor;** *the password has to be keyed in prior to accessing the system*

◊ **priority** *noun* importance of a device *or* software routine in a computer system **Vorrang, Priorität;** *the operating system has priority over the application when disk space is allocated; the disk drive is more important than the printer, so it has a higher priority;* **job priority** = importance of a job compared to others **Jobvorrangigkeit; priority interrupt** = signal to a computer that takes precedence over any other task **Vorrangunterbrechung;** *see also* INTERRUPT, NON-MASKABLE INTERRUPT; **priority interrupt table** = list

of peripherals and their priority when they send an interrupt signal (used instead of a hardware priority scheduler) **Vorrangunterbrechungstabelle; priority sequence** = the order in which various devices that have sent an interrupt signal are processed, according to their importance or urgency (a disk drive will usually come before a printer in a priority sequence) **Prioritätsreihenfolge; priority scheduler** = system that organizes tasks into correct processing priority (to improve performance) **Prioritätsplaner**

privacy *noun* the right of an individual to limit the extent of and control the access to the data that is stored about him **(Daten)schutz; privacy of data** = rule that data is secret and must not be accessed by users who have not been authorized **Datenschutz; privacy of information** = rule that unauthorized users cannot obtain data about private individuals from databases *or* that each individual has the right to know what information is being held about him *or* her on a database **Informationsschutz; privacy transformation** = encryption of messages *or* data to ensure that it remains private **Schutzverschlüsselung**

private *adjective* belonging to an individual *or* to a company, not to the public **privat; private address space** = memory address range that is reserved for a single user, not for public access **privater Adressbereich; private automatic branch exchange (PABX)** = small telephone exchange in a company that handles all internal and external calls to the main public network **Nebenstellenanlage; private automatic exchange (PAX)** = small telephone exchange in a company that only allows internal calls within the company to be made **private Fernsprechvermittlung; private branch exchange (PBX)** = small manual *or* automatic exchange in a company that can handle internal *or* external calls **private Vermittlungsanlage; private dial port** = unlisted telephone number that connects one user to a packet network system **privater Wählanschluss; private line** = special telephone line, rented from the telephone company and used only by the user **Privatleitung; private manual branch exchange (PMBX)** = small telephone exchange inside a company where all telephone calls coming in *or* going out have to be placed through a switchboard **private Handvermittlungsanlage; private mobile radio (PMR)** *see* MOBILE;

private telephone system = telephone system in a company that cannot be accessed from a public telephone system **privates Telefonsystem**

privilege *noun* status of a user referring to the type of program he can run and the resources he can use **Zugriffsrecht; privileged account** = computer account that allows special programs *or* access to sensitive system data **bevorrechtigter Bereich;** *the system manager can access anyone else's account from his privileged account;* **privileged instructions** = computer commands which can only be executed via a privileged account, such as delete another account *or* set up a new user *or* examine passwords **bevorrechtigte Befehle; privileged mode** = mode of an Intel 80286 processor that is in protected mode and allows a program to modify vital parts of the operating environment **privilegierter Modus**

PRN = PRINTER acronym used in MS-DOS to represent the standard printer port **PRN**

problem *noun*
(a) question to which it is difficult to find an answer **Problem; to solve a problem** = to find an answer to a problem **ein Problem lösen; problem definition** = the clear explanation, in logical steps, of a problem that is to be solved **Problemdarstellung; problem-orientated language (POL)** = high-level programming language that allows certain problems to be expressed easily **problemorientierte Programmiersprache**
(b) malfunction *or* fault with hardware or software **Fehler; problem diagnosis** = finding the cause and method of repairing a fault *or* error **Fehlererkennung**

procedure *noun*
(a) small section of computer instruction code that provides a frequently used function and can be called upon from a main program **Prozedur;** *this procedure sorts all the files into alphabetic order, you can call it from the main program by the instruction SORT; see also* SUBROUTINE
(b) method *or* route used when solving a problem **Vorgehensweise;** *you should use this procedure to retrieve lost files; the procedure is given in the manual;* **procedure-orientated language** = high-level programming language that allows procedures to be programmed easily **verfahrensorientierte Programmiersprache**

◊ **procedural** *adjective* using a procedure (to solve a problem) **Prozedur-, prozedur-, prozedural; procedural language** =

high-level programming language in which the programmer enters the actions required to achieve the result wanted **verfahrensorientierte Programmiersprache**

proceed *verb* to move forward **fortfahren;** *after spellchecking the text, you can proceed to the printing stage*

process
1 *noun* a number of tasks that must be carried out to achieve a goal **Verfahren, Prozess;** *the process of setting up the computer takes a long time there are five stages in the process;* **process bound** = program that spends more time executing instructions and using the CPU than in I/O operations **prozessgebunden; process camera** = camera designed for the stages required in printing, such as tone and colour separation **Reprokamera; process chart** = diagram that shows each step of the computer procedures needed in a system **Verfahrensdiagramm; process control** = automatic control of a process by a computer **Prozesssteuerung; process control computer** = dedicated computer that controls and manages a process **Prozessrechner; process control system** = complete input, output modules, a CPU with memory and a program (usually stored in ROM) and control and feedback devices such as A/D and D/A converters that completely monitors, manages and regulates a process **Prozess-Steuersystem**
2 *verb* to carry out a number of tasks to produce a result (such as sorting data *or* finding the solution to a problem) **verarbeiten;** *we processed the new data; processing all the information will take a long time*

◊ **processing** *noun* sorting of information; using a computer to solve a problem *or* organize data **Verarbeitung;** *page processing time depends on the complexity of a given page; see also* CPU; **batch processing** = computer system, where information is collected into batches before being loaded into the computer **Stapelverarbeitung, Batch-Betrieb; data processing** *or* **information processing** = selecting and examining data in a computer to produce information in a special form **Datenverarbeitung, Informationsverarbeitung (EDV); distributed processing** = using many small computers at different workstations instead of one central computer **verteilte Verarbeitung; image processing** = analysis of information contained in an image (usually by electronic means or by using a computer to provide the analysis or for recognition of objects in the image) Abbildungsverarbeitung; immediate processing = processing data when it appears, rather than waiting for a certain clock pulse or time **unmittelbare Verarbeitung; off-line processing** = processing by devices not under the control of a central computer **Verarbeitung unabhängig von der DV-Anlage; on-line processing** = processing by devices connected to and under the control of the central computer (the user remains in contact with the central computer while processing) **Verarbeitung abhängig von der DV-Anlage; query processing** = processing of queries, either by extracting information from a database *or* translating query commands from a query language **Anfrageverarbeitung; real-time processing** = processing operations that take a time of the same order of magnitude as the problem to be solved **Echtzeitbetrieb; serial processing** = executing one instruction at a time **Serienverarbeitung;** *compare with* PARALLEL PROCESSING; **word-processing** *or* text processing = working with words, using a computer to produce, check and change texts, reports, letters, etc. **Textverarbeitung** NOTE: no plural

COMMENT: the central processing unit is a hardware device that allows a computer to manipulate and modify data; a compiler is a software language processor that translates data and instructions in one language into another form

processor *noun* hardware *or* software device that is able to manipulate *or* modify data according to instructions **Prozessor; array processor** = computer that can act upon several arrays of data simultaneously for very fast mathematical applications **Vektorenrechner, Array-Prozessor; associative processor** = processor that uses associative storage **Assoziativprozessor; attached processor** = separate microprocessor in a system that performs certain functions under the control of a central processor **Anschlussprozessor; auxiliary processor** = extra, specialized processor, such as an array or numerical processor, that can work with a main processor to improve performance **Hilfsprozessor; back-end processor** = special purpose auxiliary processor **Nachschaltrechner; bit-slice processor** = construction of a large word size CPU by joining a number of smaller word size blocks **Slice-Prozessor, Bitscheibenprozessor; dual processor** = computer system with two processors for faster program execution **Computer mit zwei Prozessoren; front-end processor (FEP)** = processor placed between an input source and the central computer, whose function is to preprocess received data to reduce the main computer's workload **Vorschaltrechner; image processor** = electronic *or* computer system used for image processing **Image-Prozessor; input/output processor** = processor that handles data communications, including DMA and error correcting functions **Ein-/Ausgabeprozessor; language processor** = program that translates from one language to machine code (there are three type of translator: (i) assembler; (ii) compiler; (iii) interpreter) **(i) Assemblierer; (ii) Kompilierer; (iii) Übersetzer; network processor** = signal multiplexer controlled by a microprocessor in a network **Netzwerkprozessor;** *(in a multiprocessor system)* **order code processor** = a processor which decodes and performs the arithmetic and logical operations according to the program code **Anweisungscodeprozessor; word-processor** = small computer which is used for working with words, to produce texts, reports, letters, etc. **Textverarbeitungscomputer; processor controlled keying** = data entry by an operator which is prompted and controlled by a computer **prozessorgesteuerte Eingabe; processor interrupt** = to send an interrupt signal to a processor requesting attention, that will usually cause it to stop what it is doing and attend to the calling device **Prozessorabbruchsignal; processor status word (PSW)** = word which contains a number of status bits, such as carry flag, zero flag and overflow flag **Prozessor-Statuswort; processor-limited** = (operation *or* execution time) that is set by the speed of the processor rather than a peripheral **durch den Prozessor begrenzt**

QUOTE each chip will contain 128 processors and one million transistors
Computer News

produce *verb* to make *or* manufacture **herstellen**

◊ **producer** *noun*
(a) person *or* company *or* country which manufactures **Hersteller;** *country which is a producer of high quality computer equipment; the company is a major magnetic tape producer*
(b) person who is in charge of a film *or* TV show, who has the idea for the show, and organizes the filming, the actors, etc **Produzent**

◊ **producing** *adjective* which produces produzierend; **producing capacity** = capacity to produce **Produktionskapazität**

product *noun*
(a) item which is made *or* manufactured **Produkt, Erzeugnis; basic product** = main product made from a raw material **Ausgangsprodukt; end product** *or* **final product** *or* **finished product** = product made at the end of a production process **Endprodukt**
(b) manufactured item for sale **Produkt, Erzeugnis; product advertising** = advertising a particular named product, not the company which makes it **Produktwerbung; product analysis** = examining each separate product in a company's range to see why it sells *or* who buys it, etc. **Produktanalyse; product design** = design of consumer products **Produktdesign, Produktgestaltung; product development** = improving an existing product line to meet the needs of the market **Produktentwicklung; product engineer** = engineer in charge of the equipment for making a product **Fertigungsingenieur; product line** *or* **product range** = series of different products made by the same company which form a group (such as printers in different models *or* different colours, etc.) **Produktgruppe, Sortiment; product management** = directing the making and selling of a product as an independent item **Produktmanagement; product mix** = group of quite different products made by the same company **Warenmischung, Produktmix**
(c) result after multiplication **Produkt**

◊ **production** *noun* making *or* manufacturing of goods for sale **Produktion, Herstellung;** *production will probably be held up by industrial action; we are hoping to speed up production by installing new machinery;* **batch production** = production in batches **Stapelherstellung, Serienfertigung; mass production** = manufacturing of large quantities of goods **Massenproduktion;** *mass production of monitors or of calculators;* **rate of production** *or* **production rate** = speed at which items are made **Produktionsrate; production control** = control of the manufacturing of a product (using computers) **Fertigungssteuerung; production cost** = cost of making a product **Produktionskosten; production department** = section of a company which deals with the making of the company's products **Fertigungsabteilung; production line** = system of making a product, where each item (such as a TV set) moves slowly through the factory with new sections added to it as it goes along **Fließband;** *he works on the production line; she is a production line worker; a typical use of an image processor includes production line control;* **production manager** = person in charge of the production department **Produktionsleiter; production run** = manufacturing a product *or* running a program, as opposed to a test run **Produktionslauf; production unit** = separate small group of workers producing a certain product **Produktionseinheit**
NOTE: no plural

◊ **productive** *adjective* during *or* in which something useful is produced **produktiv; productive time** = period of time during which a computer can run error-free tasks **Bearbeitungszeit**

PROFS ™ electronic mail system developed by IBM that runs on mainframe computers **PROFS** ™

program
1 *noun* complete set of instructions which direct a computer to carry out a particular task **Programm; assembly program** = number of assembly code instructions which perform a task **Assemblerprogramm; background program** = computer program with a very low priority **Hintergrundprogramm; blue-ribbon program** = perfect program that runs first time with no errors **erstklassiges Programm; control program/monitor** *or* **control program for microcomputers (CP/M)** = popular operating system for microcomputers **Steuerprogramm (CP/M); diagnostic program** = software that helps find faults in a computer system **Diagnostikprogramm; executive program** = master program in a computer system that controls the execution of other programs **Organisationsprogramm; foreground program** = high priority program in a multitasking system **Vordergrundprogramm, Prioritäts-, Vorrangprogramm; hardwired program** = computer program built into the hardware (and which cannot be changed) **festverdrahtetes Programm; job control program** = short program of job control instructions loaded before a particular application is run, that sets up the system as required by the application **Jobsteuerprogramm; library program** = (i) number of specially written *or* relevant software routines, which a user can insert into his own program, saving time and effort; (ii) group of functions which a computer needs to refer to often, but which are not stored in main memory **(i) & (ii)**

Bibliotheksprogramm; linear program = computer program that contains no loops or branches **lineares Programm; user program** = program written by a user (often in a high-level language) **Benutzerprogramm; program address counter** = register in a CPU that contains the location of the next instruction to be processed **Adressregister; program branch** = one or more paths that can be followed after a conditional statement **Programmzweig; program cards** = punched cards that contain the instructions that make up a program **Programmkarten; program coding sheet** = specially preprinted form on which computer instructions can be written, simplifying program writing **Programmierblatt; program compatibility** = ability of two pieces of software to function correctly together **Programmkompatibilität; program compilation** = translation of an encoded source program into machine code **Programmübersetzung; program counter (PC)** or **instruction address register (IAR)** = register in a CPU that contains the location of the next instruction to be processed **Programmzähler; Befehlsadressregister;** see also INSTRUCTION ADDRESS REGISTER; SEQUENCE CONTROL REGISTER; **program crash** = unexpected failure of a program due to a programming error or a hardware fault **Programmabsturz;** I forgot to insert an important instruction which caused a program to crash, erasing all the files on the disk!; **program design language (PDL)** = programming language used to design the structure of a program **Programmentwurfssprache; program development** = all the operations involved in creating a computer program from first ideas to initial writing, debugging and the final product **Programmentwicklung; program development system** = all the hardware and software needed for program development on a system **Programmentwicklungssystem; program documentation** = set of instruction notes, examples and tips on how to use a program **Programmunterlagen;** see also MANUAL; **program editor** = software that allows the user to alter, delete and add instructions to a program file **Programm-Editor; program execution** = instructing a processor to execute in sequence the instructions in a program **Programmausführung; program file** = file containing a program rather than data **Programmdatei; program flowchart** = diagram that graphically describes the various steps in a program **Programmablaufplan; program generator** = software that allows users to write complex programs using a few simple instructions **Programmgenerator; program icon** = (in a GUI) icon that represents an executable program file **Programmsymbol;** to run the program, double-click on the program icon; **program information file (PIF)** = (in Microsoft Windows) file that contains the environment settings for a particular program **Programminformationsdatei, Program Information File (PIF); program instruction** = single word or expression that represents one operation (in a high level program each program instruction can consist of a number of low level machine code instructions) **Programmanweisung; program item** = (in a GUI) an icon that represents a program **Programmsymbol; program library** = collection of useful procedures and programs which can be used for various purposes and included into new software **Programmbibliothek; program line** = one row of commands or arguments in a computer program **Programmzeile; program line number** = number that refers to a line of program code in a computer program **Zeilennummer; program listing** = list of the set of instructions that make up a program (program listings are displayed in an ordered manner, BASIC listings by line number, assembly listings by memory location they do not necessarily represent the order in which the program will be executed, since there could be jumps or subroutines) **Programmauflistung; program maintenance** = keeping a program free of errors and up to date **Programmwartung; program name** = identification name for a stored program file **Programmname; program origin** = address at which the first instruction of a program is stored **Programmbeginn; program register** = register in a CPU that contains an instruction during decoding and execution operations **Programmregister; program relocation** = moving a stored program from one area of memory to another **Programmverschiebung; program report generator** = software that allows users to create reports from files, databases and other stored data **Programmlistengenerator; program run** = executing (in correct order) the instructions in a program **Programmlauf; program segment** = section of a main program that can be executed in its own right; without the rest of the main program being required **Programmabschnitt;** see also OVERLAY; **program specification** = document that contains details on all the functions and abilities of a computer program **Programmbeschreibung; program**

stack = section of memory reserved for storing temporary system *or* program data **Programmkellerspeicher; program statement** = high level program instruction that is made up of a number of machine code instructions **Programmanweisung; program step** = one operation within a program, usually a single instruction **Programmschritt; program storage** = section of main memory in which programs (rather than operating system or data) can be stored **Programmspeicher; program structure** = the way in which sections of program code are interlinked and operate **Programmstruktur; program testing** = testing a new program with test data to ensure that it functions correctly **Programmprüfung; program verification** = number of tests and checks performed to ensure that a program functions correctly **Programmprüfung**

2 *verb* to write *or* prepare a set of instructions which direct a computer to perform a certain task **programmieren; programmed halt** = instruction within a program that when executed, halts the processor (to restart the CPU a reset action is required) **programmierter Stop; programmed learning** = using educational software which allows a learner to follow a course of instruction **programmiertes Lernen** NOTE: **programs - programming - programmed**

◊ **programmable** *adjective (& noun)* (device) that can accept and store instructions then execute them **programmierbar; programmable calculator** = small calculator which can hold certain basic mathematical calculating programs **programmierbarer Rechner; programmable logic array (PLA)** *or* **programmable logic device (PLD)** = integrated circuit that can be permanently programmed to perform logic operations on data using a matrix of links between input and output pins **programmierbares logisches Feld /Gerät; programmable interrupt controller** = circuit *or* chip which can be programmed to ignore certain interrupts, accept only high priority interrupts and select the priority of interrupts **programmierte Unterbrechungssteuerung; programmable key** = special key on a computer terminal keyboard that can be programmed with various functions *or* characters **programmierbare Taste; programmable memory (PROM)** = electronic device in which data can be stored **programmierbarer Speicher;** *see also* EAROM; EEPROM; EPROM; ROM; **programmable read only**

memory (PROM) = memory integrated circuit that can be programmed with data by a user (some PROMs provide permanent storage, others such as EPROMs are erasable) **programmierbarer Festwertspeicher; hand-held programmable** = very small computer, which can be held in the hand, used for inputting information when a larger terminal is not available (as by a salesman on a call) **Handcomputer**

◊ **programmer** *noun* **(a)** person who is capable of designing and writing a working program **Programmierer/-in;** *the programmer is still working on the new software;* **applications programmer** = programmer who writes applications software **Anwendungsprogrammierer; systems programmer** = programmer who specializes in writing systems software **Systemprogrammierer (b)** device that allows data to be written into a programmable read only memory **Programmiergerät**

◊ **programming** *noun* **(a)** writing programs for computers **Programmieren; programming in logic** = PROLOG; **programming language** = software that allows a user to write a series of instructions to define a particular task, which will then be translated to a form that is understood by the computer **Programmiersprache; programming standards** = rules to which programs must conform to produce compatible code **Programmiernormen (b)** writing data into a PROM device **Programmieren** ·

COMMENT: programming languages are grouped into different levels: the high-level languages such as BASIC and PASCAL are easy to understand and use, but offer slow execution time since each instruction is made up of a number of machine code instructions; low-level languages such as assembler are more complex to read and program in but offer faster execution time

programme or *(US)* **program** *noun*
TV or radio broadcast which is separate
from other broadcasts, and has its own
producer, director, etc **Programm, Sendung;**
*they were filming a wild life programme;
children's programmes are scheduled for
early evening viewing*

project
1 *noun* planned task **Projekt;** *his latest
project is computerizing the sales team; the
design project was entirely worked out on
computer; CAD is essential for accurate
project design*
2 *verb* to forecast future figures from a set
of data **vorausplanen, projektieren;** *the
projected sales of the new PC*

◊ **projection** *noun*
(a) forecast of a situation from a set of data
Vorausplanung; *the projection indicates that
sales will increase*
(b) showing pictures on a screen **Projektion;
projection room** = room in a cinema where
the projectors which show the films are
housed **Vorführraum**

◊ **projector** *noun* **film projector** or **slide
projector** = mechanical device that displays
films or slides on a screen **Filmprojektor;
Diaprojektor;** *see also* OVERHEAD

PROLOG = PROGRAMMING IN LOGIC
high-level programming language using
logical operations for artificial intelligence
and data retrieval applications **PROLOG
(Programmiersprache)**

PROM
(a) = PROGRAMMABLE READ-ONLY
MEMORY read-only memory which can be
programmed by the user (as opposed to
ROM, which is programmed by the
manufacturer) **PROM (programmierbarer
Festwertspeicher); PROM burner** or
programmer = electronic device used to
program a PROM **PROM-Programmiergerät;**
see also EPROM
(b) = PROGRAMMABLE MEMORY
electronic memory in which data can be
stored **programmierbarer Speicher**

prompt *noun* message or character
displayed to remind the user that an input is
expected **Eingabeaufforderung;** *the prompt
READY indicates that the system is
available to receive instructions;* **command
prompt** = symbol displayed to indicate a
command is expected **Befehlsaufforderung;**
*MS-DOS normally displays the command
prompt C:\> to indicate that it is ready to
process instructions typed in by a user*

proof
1 *noun* printed matter from a printer that
has to be checked and corrected
Korrekturabzug; galley proofs = proofs in the
form of long pieces of text, not divided into
pages, printed on long pieces of paper
Korrekturfahnen; page proofs = proofs which
are divided into pages, but may not have
page numbers or headings inserted
Umbruchfahnen, Bogenkorrekturen
2 *verb* to produce proofs of a text **einen
Korrekturabzug anfertigen**

◊ **proofer** *noun* printer which produces
proofs, as opposed to finished printed
pages **Andruckpresse;** *output devices such as
laser proofers and typesetters*

◊ **proofing** *noun* producing proofs of text
which have to be read and corrected
Anfertigung von Korrekturabzügen

◊ **proofread** *verb* to correct spelling and
printing errors in a printed text **Korrektur
lesen;** *has all the text been proofread yet?*

◊ **proofreader** *noun* person who reads
and corrects proofs **Korrektor/-in,
Korrekturleser/-in**

> COMMENT: the stages of full proofing are
> galley proofs, page on galley (where the pages
> are indicated, but the proofs are still printed on
> long pieces of paper), and page proofs. It is
> usual to miss out some of these stages, and
> many books are proofed in pages from the start

propagate *verb* to travel or spread **sich
ausbreiten; propagated error** = one error in a
process that has affected later operations
mitgelaufener Fehler; propagating error = an
error that occurs in one place or operation
and affects another operation or process
mitlaufender Fehler

◊ **propagation delay** *noun* time taken
for a signal to travel through a circuit; time
taken for an output to appear in a logic gate
after the input is applied **Schaltverzögerung;**
*propagation delay in the transmission path
causes signal distortion*

proportion *noun* size of something as
compared to others **Proportion**

◊ **proportional spacing** *noun* printing
system where each letter takes a space
proportional to the character width ('i'
taking less space than 'm')
**Proportionalschrittschaltung (Schriftart, bei
der die Drucktypen verschiedene Dickte
haben);** *compare* MONOSPACING

proprietary file format *noun* method
of storing data devised by a company for its

products and incompatible with other products **herstellerspezifisches Dateiformat;** *you cannot read this spreadsheet file because my software saves it in a proprietary file format*

protect *verb* to stop something being damaged **schützen; protected location =** memory location that cannot be altered *or* cannot be accessed without authorization **geschützter Speicherplatz; protected storage =** section of memory that cannot be altered **geschützter Speicher; copy protect =** switch used to prevent copies of a disk being made **Kopierschutz;** *all the disks are copy protected;* **crash protected =** (disk) which uses a head protection *or* data corruption protection system **absturzgeschützt;** *if the disk is crash protected, you will never lose your work*

◊ **protection** *noun* action of protecting **Schutz; protection key =** signal checked to see if a program can access a section of memory **Speicherschutzschlüssel; protection master =** spare copy of a master film *or* tape **Schutzkopie; copy protection =** preventing copies being made **Kopierschutz;** *a hard disk may crash because of faulty copy protection; the new product will come without copy protection;* **data protection =** making sure that data is not copied by an unauthorized user **Datenschutz; Data Protection Act =** act which prevents confidential data about people being copied without authority (also every organization that keeps information subject to the act on a computer, must protect it adequately) **Datenschutzgesetz**

◊ **protective** *adjective* which protects **Schutz-, schützend;** *the disks are housed in hard protective cases*

protocol *noun* pre-agreed signals, codes and rules to be used for data exchange between systems **Leistungsprozedur, Protokoll; protocol converter** device used for converting protocols from one computer system to another, such as for converting data from a micro to a phototypesetter; **protocol standards =** standards laid down to allow data exchange between any computer systems conforming to the standard **Leistungsprozedurnormen**

QUOTE there is a very simple protocol that would exclude hackers from computer networks using the telephone system

Practical Computing

prototype *noun* first working model of a device *or* program, which is then tested and adapted to improve it **Prototyp**

◊ **prototyping** *noun* making a prototype **Herstellung eines Prototyps**

provider *noun* **information provider (ip) =** company *or* user that provides an information source for use in a videotext system (such as the company providing weather information *or* stock exchange reports) **jd, der Informationen zur Verfügung stellt**

PrtSc = PRINT SCREEN (on an IBM PC keyboard) key that sends the contents of the current screen to the printer **Druck-Taste**

ps = PICOSECOND

PS/2 ™ range of IBM PC computers that are software compatible with the original IBM PC, but use a different MCA expansion bus **PS/2** ™; *see also* MCA

PSA = PUBLIC SERVICE ANNOUNCEMENT advertisement for a public service *or* charity, which is shown on TV, but for which the TV company is not paid **kostenlose Werbeansage zur Information der Öffentlichkeit/für gemeinnützige Institutionen**

pseudo- *prefix* meaning similar to something, but not genuine **Pseudo-, pseudo-**

◊ **pseudo-code** *noun* English sentence structures, used to describe program instructions which are translated at a later date into machine code **Pseudocode**

◊ **pseudo-digital** *adjective* (modulated analog signals) produced by a modem and transmitted over telephone lines **pseudodigital**

◊ **pseudo-instruction** *noun* label (in an assembly language program) that represents a number of instructions **Pseudobefehl**

◊ **pseudo-operation** *noun* command in an assembler program that controls the assembler rather than producing machine code **Pseudooperation**

◊ **pseudo-random** *noun* generated sequence that appears random but is repeated over a long period **pseudozufällig; pseudo-random number generator =** hardware *or* software that produces pseudo-random numbers **Pseudozufallszahlengenerator**

PSN = PACKET SWITCHED NETWORK

PSS = PACKET SWITCHING SYSTEM

PSTN = PUBLIC SWITCHED TELEPHONE NETWORK

PSU = POWER SUPPLY UNIT electrical circuit that provides certain direct current voltage and current levels from an alternating current source to other electrical circuits **Stromversorgungseinheit**

COMMENT: a PSU will regulate, smooth and step down a higher voltage supply for use in small electronic equipment

PSW = PROCESSOR STATUS WORD

PTR = PAPER TAPE READER

p-type semiconductor *noun* semiconductor material that has been doped with a chemical to provide extra holes (positive charge carriers), giving it an overall positive potential compared to intrinsic semiconductor **p-Halbleiter;** *see also* HOLES, INTRINSIC SEMICONDUCTOR

public *adjective* open to anyone to use; made for the use of everyone **öffentlich; public address system (PA)** = microphone, amplifier and loudspeaker set up to allow one person to be heard by a group of people **Lautsprecheranlage; public data network** = data transmission service for the public **öffentliches Datennetz; public dial port** = port connecting a packet network to a public telephone system **öffentlicher Wählanschluss; public domain (PD)** = documents *or* text *or* program that has no copyright and can be copied by anyone **Gemeingut; Public Domain Software (ohne Kopierschutz);** *compare* SHAREWARE; **public key cipher system** = cipher that uses a public key to encrypt messages and a secret key to decrypt them (conventional cipher systems use one secret key to encrypt and decrypt messages) **Verschlüsselungssystem mit bekanntem Chiffrierschlüssel;** *see also* CIPHER, KEY; **public switched telephone network (PSTN)** = national telephone system *or* country and world-wide exchanges, lines and telephone sets that are all interconnected and can be used by the public **öffentliches Telefonnetz**

publication *noun*
(a) making something public **Veröffentlichung;** *the publication of the report on data protection; the publication date of the book is November 15th*

(b) printed book *or* leaflet, etc. which is sold to the public *or* which is given away **Veröffentlichung;** *government publications can be bought at special shops; the company specializes in publications for the business reader*

publicity *noun* attracting the attention of the public to products *or* services by mentioning them in the media *or* by advertising them **Werbung, Publicity; publicity bureau** = office which organizes publicity for companies **Werbebüro, Werbeagentur; publicity campaign** = period when planned publicity takes place **Werbekampagne; publicity department** = department in a company which organizes the publicity for the company's products **Werbeabteilung; publicity matter** = leaflets *or* posters, etc., which publicize a product *or* service **Werbematerial**

◊ **publicize** *verb* to attract people's attention to a product *or* service **bekannt machen, Werbung durchführen;** *they are publicizing their low prices for computer stationery; the new PC has been publicized in the press*

publish *verb* to print a text (such as a book *or* newspaper *or* catalogue) and then sell *or* give it to the public **veröffentlichen;** *the institute has published a list of sales figures for different home computers; the company specializes in publishing reference books*

◊ **publisher** *noun* company which prints books *or* newspapers and sells *or* gives them to the public **Verlag**

◊ **publishing** *noun* the business of printing books *or* newspapers and selling them *or* giving them to the public **Verlagswesen; desktop publishing (DTP)** = design, layout and printing of documents using special software, a small computer and a printer **Desktop Publishing; electronic publishing** = (i) use of desktop publishing packages and laser printers to produce printed matter; (ii) using computers to write and display information (such as viewdata) **(i) elektronisches Publizieren; (ii) Bildschirmtextverfahren; professional publishing** = publishing books on law, accountancy, and other professions **Verlegen von Fachliteratur**

QUOTE desktop publishing or the ability to produce high-quality publications using a minicomputer, essentially boils down to combining words and images on pages
Byte

pull *verb* to remove data from a stack **herausnehmen;** *compare with* PUSH

pull-down menu *noun* set of options that are displayed below the relevant entry on a menu-bar **Menüliste, Aktionsfenster, Pulldown-Menü;** *the pull-down menu is viewed by clicking on the menu bar at the top of the screen; compare* POP-UP MENU

◊ **pull up** *verb* **to pull up a line** = to connect *or* set a line to a voltage level **eine Leitung unter Spannung setzen;** *pull up the input line to a logic one by connecting it to 5 volts*

> QUOTE the gated inputs lower the standby current and also eliminate the need for input pull-up or pull-down resistors
>
> **Electronics & Power**

pulse
1 *noun* short rush of electricity; short period of a voltage level **Impuls APPENDIX; pulse amplitude modulation (PAM)** = pulse modulation where the height of the pulse depends on the input signal **Impulsamplitudenmodulation; pulse code modulation (PCM)** = pulse stream that carries data about a signal in binary form **Pulscodemodulation (PCM); pulse-dialling** = telephone dialling that dials a telephone number by sending a series of pulses along the line **Impulswahl, Impulswählverfahren;** *pulse-dialling takes longer to dial than the newer tone-dialling system;* **pulse duration modulation (PDM)** = pulse modulation where the pulse width depends on the input signal **Impulsdauermodulation; pulse generator** = electronic test equipment used to produce different size pulses **Zeichengeber; pulse modulation** = use of a series of short pulses which are modified by an input signal, to carry information **Impulsmodulation; pulse position modulation (PPM)** = pulse modulation where the time between pulses depends on the input signal **Pulslagenmodulation; pulse stream** = continuous series of similar pulses **Impulsstrom; pulse width modulation (PWM)** = pulse modulation where the pulse width depends on the input signal **Impulsbreitenmodulation**
2 *verb* to apply a short-duration voltage level to a circuit **einen Impuls geben;** *we pulsed the input but it still would not work*

> COMMENT: electric pulse can be used to transmit information, as the binary digits 0 and 1 correspond to 'no pulse' and 'pulse' (the voltage level used to distinguish the binary digits 0 and 1, is often zero and 5 or 12 volts,

with the pulse width depending on transmission rate)

punch
1 *noun* device for making holes in punched cards **Locher**
2 *verb* to make a hole **lochen; punch** *or* **punched card** = small piece of card which contains holes which represent various instructions *or* data **Lochkarte; punched card reader** = device that transforms data on a punched card to a form that can be recognized by a computer **Lochkartenleser; punched tag** = card attached to a product in a shop, with punched holes containing data about the product **gelochtes Etikett; punched (paper) tape** = strip of paper tape that contains holes to represent data **Lochstreifen**

◊ **punch-down block** *noun* device used in a local area network to connect UTP cable **Punchdown-Block**

punctuation mark *noun* printing symbol, which cannot be spoken, but which helps to understand the text **Satzzeichen**

> COMMENT: the main punctuation marks are the question mark and exclamation mark; inverted commas (which show the type of text being written); the comma, full stop, colon and semicolon (which show how the words are broken up into sequences); the apostrophe (which shows that a letter or word is missing); the dash and hyphen and brackets (which separate or link words)

pure *adjective* clean *or* not mixed with other things **rein; pure code** = code that does not modify itself during execution **reiner Code; pure semiconductor** = semiconductor material that has not had extra doping substances added **reiner Halbleiter;** *see also* INTRINSIC; **pure tone** = single frequency containing no harmonics **reiner Ton**

purge *verb* to remove unnecessary *or* out of date data from a file or disk **löschen;** *each month, I purge the disk of all the old email messages*

push *verb* to press something *or* to move something by pressing on it **drücken; push-down list** *or* **stack** = temporary storage queue system where the last item added is at the top of the list **Umkehrliste; Umkehrstapel;** *see also* LIFO; **push instruction** *or* **operation** = computer instruction that stores data on a LIFO list *or* stack **Befehl zur Speicherung nach dem LIFO-Prinzip; push-up list** *or* **stack** =

temporary storage queue system where the last item added is at the bottom of the list **Eingangsfolgeliste;** *see also* FIFO

◊ **pushbutton** *adjective* which works by pressing on a button **Drucktasten-; pushbutton dialling** = using buttons rather than a dial on a telephone to dial a number **Drucktastenwählen; pushbutton telephone** = telephone operated with buttons rather than a dial **Drucktastentelefon**

put *verb* to push *or* place data onto a stack **schreiben**

PWM = PULSE WIDTH MODULATION

Qq

QAM = QUADRATURE AMPLITUDE MODULATION

QBE = QUERY BY EXAMPLE simple language used to retrieve information from a database management system by, normally, entering a query with known values, which is then matched with the database and used to retrieve the correct data **QBE;** *in most QBE databases, the query form looks like the record format in the database - retrieving data is as easy as filling in a form*

QISAM = QUEUED INDEXED SEQUENTIAL ACCESS METHOD indexed sequential file that is read item by item into a buffer **QISAM (erweiterte indizierte Zugriffsmöglichkeit für sequenzielle Dateien)**

QSAM = QUEUED SEQUENTIAL ACCESS METHOD queue of blocks that are waiting to be processed, retrieved using a sequential access method **QSAM (erweiterte Zugriffsmöglichkeit für sequenzielle Dateien)**

QL = QUERY LANGUAGE

quad *noun*
(a) sheet of paper four times as large as a basic sheet **Quartblatt**
(b) meaning four times **vierfach; quadbit** = four bits that are used by modems to increase transmission rates when using

QAM **Vierbit; quad density** = four bits of data stored in the usual place of one **vierfache Schreibdichte**
(c) **em quad** = space printed that is equal in size to an em **Geviert (in der Größe eines m); en quad** = space that is half the width of an em quad space **Halbgeviert (in der Größe eines n)**

◊ **quadding** *noun* insertion of spaces into text to fill out a line **Zeilenfüllen, Ausschließen**

QUOTE in this case, interfacing is done by a single quad-wide adapter
Minicomputer News

quadr- *prefix* meaning four **quadro-**

◊ **quadrophonic** *adjective* (audio music system) using four speakers **quadrophon**

◊ **quadruplex** *noun* four signals combined into a single one **Quadruplex**

◊ **quadruplicate** *noun* in quadruplicate = with the original and three copies in **vierfacher Ausfertigung;** *the statements are printed in quadruplicate*
NOTE: no plural

quadrature *noun* video playback error due to the heads being wrongly aligned to the edge of the tape **Quadratur**

quadrature amplitude modulation (QAM) *noun* data encoding method used by high-speed modems (transmitting at rates above 2,400bps); QAM combines amplitude modulation and phase modulation to increase the data transmission rate **Quadratur-Amplituden-Modulation (QAM)**

◊ **quadrature encoding** *noun* system used to determine the direction in which a mouse is being moved; in a mechanical mouse, two sensors send signals that describe its horizontal and vertical movements - these signals are transmitted using quadrature encoding **Quadraturencodierung**

quality *noun* what something is like *or* how good or bad something is **Qualität;** *there is a market for good quality secondhand computers;* **high quality** *or* **top quality** = very best quality **beste Qualität, Spitzenqualität;** *the store specializes in high quality imported items;* **printer quality** = standard of printed text from a particular printer (high-resolution dot-matrix printers produce near-letter quality, daisy-wheel printers produce letter-quality text) **Druckqualität;**

see also LETTER, NEAR-LETTER, DRAFT; **quality control** = checking that the quality of a product is good **Qualitätskontrolle; quality controller** = person who checks the quality of a product **Qualitätsprüfer** NOTE: no plural

QUOTE the computer operates at 120cps in draft quality mode and 30cps in near letter-quality mode

Minicomputer News

quantify *verb* to quantify the effect of something = to show the effect of something in figures **die Auswirkungen von etwas in Zahlen ausdrücken;** *it is impossible to quantify the effect of the new computer system on our production*

◊ **quantifiable** *adjective* which can be quantified **in Zahlen ausdrückbar;** *the effect of the change in the pricing structure is not quantifiable*

◊ **quantifier** *noun* sign *or* symbol which indicates the quantity *or* range of a predicate **Quantor**

quantity *noun*
(a) amount *or* number of items **Menge;** *a small quantity of illegal copies of the program have been imported; he bought a large quantity of spare parts*
(b) large amount **große Menge;** *the company offers a discount for quantity purchases*

quantize *verb* to convert an analog signal into a numerical representation **quantisieren;** *the input signal is quantized by an analog to digital converter;* **quantizing noise** = noise on a signal due to inaccuracies in the quantizing process **Quantisierungsgeräusch**

◊ **quantizer** *noun* device used to convert an analog input signal to a numerical form, that can be processed by a computer **Quantisierer, Größenwandler**

◊ **quantization** *noun* conversion of an analog signal to a numerical representation **Quantisierung; quantization error** = error in converting an analog signal into a numerical form due to limited accuracy *or* rapidly changing signal **Quantisierungsfehler;** *see also* A/D

quantum *noun*
(a) smallest unit of energy of an electromagnetic radiation at a certain frequency **Quant**
(b) (in communications) a packet of data that is the result of a signal being quantized **Quantum**

quartile *noun* one of three figures below which 25%, 50% *or* 75% of a total falls **Quartil**

quarto *noun* paper size, made when a sheet is folded twice to make eight pages **Quarto**

quartz (crystal) clock *noun* small slice of quartz crystal which vibrates at a certain frequency when an electrical voltage is supplied, used as a very accurate clock signal for computers and other high precision timing applications **Quarzuhr**

quasi- *prefix* almost *or* which seems like **quasi-; quasi-instruction** = label (in an assembly program) that represents a number of instructions **Quasibefehl**

quaternary *adjective* referring to four bits *or* levels *or* objects **quaternär**

query
1 *noun* question **Abfrage; query by example (QBE)** = simple language used to retrieve information from a database management system by, normally, entering a query with known values, which is then matched with the database and used to retrieve the correct data **Abfrage mittels Beispiel, Query By Example (QBE); query facility** = program (usually a database *or* retrieval system) that allows the user to ask questions and receive answers *or* access certain information according to the query **Abfragemöglichkeit; query language (QL)** = language in a database management system, that allows a database to be searched and queried easily **Abfragesprache, Datenbanksprache; query processing** = processing of queries, either by extracting information from a database *or* by translating query commands from a query language **Abfragebearbeitung**
2 *verb* to ask a question about something *or* to suggest that something may be wrong **in Frage stellen, bezweifeln**

QUOTE The Query By Example features now found on some database packages, Foxpro in particular, are easy to use and very powerful

Computing

question
1 *noun*
(a) words which need an answer **Frage;** *the managing director refused to answer questions about faulty keyboards; the market research team prepared a series of questions to test the public's reactions to colour and price*

(b) problem **Frage;** *he raised the question of moving to less expensive offices; the main question is that of cost; the board discussed the question of launching a new business computer*
2 *verb*
(a) to ask questions **(be)fragen;** *the police questioned the accounts staff for four hours; she questioned the chairman on the company's sales in the Far East*
(b) to query *or* to suggest that something may be wrong **bezweifeln;** *we all question how accurate the computer printout is*

◊ **question mark** *noun* the character (?) which is often used as a wildcard to indicate that any single character in the position will produce a match **Fragezeichen;** *to find all the letters, use the command DIR LETTER?.DOC which will list LETTER1.DOC, LETTER2.DOC and LETTER3.DOC; see also* ASTERISK

◊ **questionnaire** *noun* printed list of questions, especially used in market research **Fragebogen;** *to send out a questionnaire to test the opinions of users of the system; to answer or to fill in a questionnaire about holidays abroad*

queue
1 *noun*
(a) line of people waiting one behind the other **(Warte)schlange;** *to form a queue or to join a queue*
(b) list of data *or* tasks that are waiting to be processed; series of documents (such as orders, application forms) which are dealt with in order **Warteschlange; channel queue** = (i) queue of requests to use a channel; (ii) queue of data that has yet to be sent over a channel **(i)** & **(ii) Kanalwarteschlange; file queue** = number of files temporarily stored in order before being processed **Dateiwarteschlange;** *output devices such as laser printers are connected on-line with an automatic file queue;* **job queue** = number of tasks arranged in order waiting to be processed in a batch system **Jobwarteschlange; his order went to the end of the queue** = his order was dealt with last **sein Auftrag kam ans Ende der Warteschlange; queue discipline** = method used as the queue structure, either LIFO or FIFO **Warteschlangenstruktur; queue management** *or* **queue manager** = software which orders tasks to be processed **Warteschlangenverwaltung;** *this is a new software spooler with a built-in queue management*
2 *verb* to add more data *or* tasks to the end of a queue **in die Warteschlange einreihen; queued access method** = programming

method which minimises input/output delays by ensuring that data transferred between software and an I/O device is synchronised with the I/O device **erweiterte Zugriffsmethode; queued indexed sequential access method** (QISAM) = indexed sequential file that is read item by item into a buffer **erweiterte indizierte Zugriffsmöglichkeit für sequenzielle Dateien (QISAM); queued sequential access method** (QSAM) = queue of blocks that are waiting to be processed, retrieved using a sequential access method **erweiterte Zugriffsmöglichkeit für sequenzielle Dateien (QSAM); queuing time** = period of time messages have to wait before they can be processed *or* transmitted **Wartezeit**

quick *adjective* fast *or* not taking any time **schnell;** *the company made a quick recovery; he is looking for a quick return on his investment; we are hoping for a quick sale*

◊ **quickly** *adverb* without taking much time **schnell**

◊ **QuickDraw** ™ (in an Apple Macintosh) graphics routines built into the Macintosh's operating system that control displayed text and images **QuickDraw ™**

◊ **quicksort** *noun* very rapid file sorting and ordering method **Quicksort, Schnellsortierer**

◊ **QuickTime** ™ (in an Apple Macintosh) graphics routines built into the Macintosh's operating system that allow windows, boxes and graphic objects (including animation and video files) to be displayed **QuickTime ™**

quiescent *adjective* state of a process *or* circuit *or* device when no input signal is applied **ruhig**

quiet *adjective* not making very much noise **leise;** *laser printers are much quieter than dot-matrix*

quintet *noun* byte made up of five bits **Fünf-Bit-Byte**

quit *verb* to leave a system *or* a program **beenden;** *do not forget to save your text before you quit the system*
NOTE: **quitting - quit**

quote
1 *verb*
(a) to repeat words used by someone else; to repeat a reference number **zitieren;** *he quoted figures from the newspaper report; in reply please quote this number; when making a complaint please quote the batch number printed on the computer case; he replied, quoting the number of the account*
(b) to estimate *or* to say what costs may be **einen Preis angeben/nennen;** *to quote a price for supplying stationery; their prices are always quoted in dollars; he quoted me a price of £1,026; can you quote for supplying 20,000 envelopes?*
2 *noun*
(a) quotation **Zitat**
(b) quotes = quotation marks *or* inverted commas **Anführungszeichen; single quotes** = single inverted commas **einfache Anführungszeichen; double quotes** = double inverted commas **(doppelte) Anführungszeichen;** *the name of the company should be put in double quotes*
◊ **quotation** *noun* part of a text borrowed from another text **Zitat; quotation marks** = inverted commas *or* signs printed at the beginning and end of text to show that it has been quoted from another source **Anführungszeichen**

quotient *noun* result of one number divided by another **Quotient**

COMMENT: when two numbers are divided, the answer is made up of a quotient and a remainder (the fractional part), 16 divided by 4 is equal to a quotient of 4 and zero remainder, 16 divided by 5 is equal to a quotient of 3 and a remainder of 1

QWERTY *noun* **QWERTY keyboard** = English language keyboard for a typewriter *or* computer, where the top line of letters are Q-W-E-R-T-Y **QWERTY-Tastatur;** *the computer has a normal QWERTY keyboard; see also* AZERTY

QUOTE the keyboard does not have a QWERTY layout but is easy to use
Micro Decision

Rr

R & D = RESEARCH AND DEVELOPMENT; **R & D department** =

department in a company that investigates new products, discoveries and techniques **Forschungs- und Entwicklungsabteilung**

race *noun* error condition in a digital circuit, in which the state *or* output of the circuit is very dependent on the exact timing between the input signals (faulty output is due to unequal propagation delays on the separate input signals at a gate) **Zeitbedingung**

rack *noun*
(a) frame to hold items for display **Ständer;** *a display rack; a rack for holding mag tapes*
(b) metal supporting frame for electronic circuit boards and peripheral devices such as disk drives **Rahmen; rack mounted** = system consisting of removable circuit boards in a supporting frame **Konsole**

radar *noun* method of finding the position of objects such as aircraft, by transmitting radio waves which are reflected back if they hit an object and are displayed on a screen **Radar**

radial transfer *noun* data transfer between two peripherals *or* programs that are on different layers of a structured system (such as an ISO/OSI system) **Radialübertragung**

radiant *adjective* which radiates **strahlend, Strahlungs-, strahlungs-; radiant energy** = amount of energy radiated by an aerial **Strahlungsenergie**
◊ **radiate** *verb*
(a) to go out in all directions from a central point **ausstrahlen**
(b) (i) to send out rays; (ii) to convert electrical signals into travelling electromagnetic waves **(i) ausstrahlen; (ii) aussenden; radiating element** = single basic unit of an antenna that radiates signals **Primärstrahler**
◊ **radiator** *noun* single basic unit of an antenna *or* any device that radiates signals **Radiator**
◊ **radiation** *noun* (i) sending out of waves of energy from certain substances (ii) conversion of electrical signals in an antenna into travelling electromagnetic waves **(i) Strahlung; (ii) Ausstrahlung**

radio *noun* medium used for the transmission of speech, sound and data over long distances by radio frequency electromagnetic waves **Funk; radio**

frequency (RF) = electromagnetic spectrum that lies between the frequency range 10KHz and 3000GHz **Hochfrequenz, Funkfrequenz;** *the radio frequency range extends from a few hertz to hundreds of gigahertz;* **radio microphone** = audio microphone with a small radio transmitter attached allowing the transmission of sound signals without wires **Funkmikrofon; radio pager** *or* **radio paging device** = small pocket receiver that responds to a certain unique transmitted code to alert the user **Piepser, Mobilfunk;** *you could contact your salesman if he had a radio pager;* **radio paging** = calling someone by transmitting a code to their radio pager **über einen Piepser aufrufen; radio phone** *or* **radio telephone** = mobile two-way radio communications system that can access the public telephone network **Funktelefon; radio receiver** = device that can receive signals broadcast on one radio frequency and convert them into their original audio form **Empfangsgerät; radio spectrum** = range of radio frequencies **Funkspektrum; radio telegraphy** = telegraph codes transmitted via radio **Funktelegrafie; radio transmission of data** = sending data by radio **Datenübertragung per Funk; radio waves** = electromagnetic radiation waves **Funkwellen** ·

◊ **radio button** *noun* (in a GUI) circle displayed beside an option that, when selected, has a dark centre; radio buttons are a method of selecting one of a number of options, only one radio button can be selected at one time (select another and the first is deselected) **Optionsfeld**

◊ **radiocommunications** *noun* transmission and reception of sound and data by radio waves **Funkverkehr**

radix *noun* the value of the base of the number system being used **Basis, Radix;** *the hexadecimal number has a radix of 16;* **radix complement** *see* TEN'S, TWO'S COMPLEMENT; **radix notation** = numbers represented to a certain radix **Radixschreibweise;** *see also* BASE (e); **radix point** = dot which indicates the division between a whole unit and its fractional parts **Radixpunkt**

ragged *adjective* not straight *or* with an uneven edge **ausgefranst; ragged left** = printed text with a flush right-hand margin and uneven left-hand margin **rechtsbündiger Flattersatz; ragged right** = printed text with a flush left-hand margin and uneven right-hand margin **linksbündiger Flattersatz; ragged text** =

unjustified text, text with a ragged right margin **Text im Flattersatz**

RAID = REDUNDANT ARRAY of INEXPENSIVE DISKS fast, fault-tolerant disk drive system that uses multiple drives which would, typically, each store one byte of a word of data, so allowing the data to be saved faster; one drive in the array would also store a check byte for error detection **RAID-Technik**

> QUOTE A Japanese investor group led by system distributor Technography has pumped $4.2 million ($2.8 million) into US disk manufacturer Storage Computer to help with the development costs of RAID 7 hard disk technology
> *Computing*

RAM = RANDOM ACCESS MEMORY memory that allows access to any location in any order, without having to access the rest first **Direktzugriffsspeicher, RAM;** *compare* SEQUENTIAL ACCESS MEMORY; **dynamic RAM** = most common RAM ICs, which use capacititive charge to retain data but which must be refreshed (read from and rewritten to) every few thousandths of a second **dynamischer RAM; partial RAM** = RAM chip in which only a certain area of the chip functions correctly, usually in newly released chips (partial RAM's can be used by employing more than one to make up the capacity of one fully functional chip) **Teil-RAM; static RAM** = RAM ICs that do not have to be refreshed but cannot store as much data per chip as dynamic RAM **statischer RAM; RAM cache** = section of high-speed RAM that is used to buffer data transfers between the (faster) processor and a (slower) disk drive **RAM-Cache; RAM card** = expansion card which contains RAM chips; it is plugged into a computer *or* device to increase the main memory capacity **Speichererweiterungskarte, RAM-Karte; RAM cartridge** = plug-in device that contains RAM chips and increases a computer *or* device's memory **Speichermodul, RAM-Modul;** *you can increase the printer's memory by plugging in another RAM cartridge;* **RAM chip** = chip which stores data, allowing random access **RAM-Chip; RAM disk** = section of RAM that is made to look like and behave as a high-speed disk drive (using special software) **RAM-Platte; RAM loader** = routine that will transfer a program from external backing store into RAM **RAM-Lader; RAM refresh** = signals used to update the contents of dynamic RAM chips every few thousandths of a second, involving reading and rewriting the contents, needed to retain data **RAM-Regenerierer**; **RAM refresh rate =** number of times every second that the data in a dynamic RAM chip has to be read and rewritten **RAM-Regenerationsgeschwindigkeit**; **RAM resident program** or **TSR =** program that loads itself into main memory and carries out a function when activated **speicherresidentes Programm, TSR-Programm**; *when you hit Ctrl-F5, you will activate the RAM resident program and it will display your day's diary;* **self-refreshing RAM =** dynamic RAM chip that has built-in circuitry to generate refresh signals, allowing data to be retained when the power is off by using a battery **selbstregenerierender RAM**; *see also* CHIP, ROM NOTE: there is no plural for RAM, and it often has no article: **512K of RAM; the file is stored in RAM**

> COMMENT: dynamic RAM which uses a capacitor to store a bit of data (as a charge) needs to have each location refreshed from time to time to retain the data, but is very fast and can contain more data per unit area than static RAM which uses a latch to store the state of a bit, and has the advantage of not requiring to be refreshed to retain its data, and will keep data for as long as power is supplied

> QUOTE in addition the board features 512K of video RAM, expandable up to a massive 1MB
> *PC Business World*

> QUOTE fast memory is RAM that does not have to share bus access with the chip that manages the video display
> *Byte*

> QUOTE The HP Enterprise Desktops have hard-disk capacities of between 260Mb and 1Gb, with RAM ranging from 16Mb up to 128Mb
> *Computing*

random *adjective* (event) that cannot be anticipated **zufällig, willkürlich**; **pseudo-random =** generated sequence that appears random but is repeated over a long period **pseudozufällig**; **random number =** number that cannot be predicted **Zufallsnummer, Zufallszahl**; **random number generation =** method of creating a sequence of numbers which appears to be random so that no number appears more often than another **Zufallszahlgenerierung**; **random number generator =** program which generates

random numbers (used in lotteries, games, etc.) **Zufallszahlgenerator**; **random process =** system whose output cannot be related to its input or internal structure **unkalkulierbarer Vorgang**

◊ **random access** *noun* direct acces or ability to access immediately memory locations in any order **wahlfreier Zugriff**; *disk drives are random access, magnetic tape is sequential access memory;* **random access device =** device whose access time to retrieve data is not dependent on the location or type of data **Vorrichtung für wahlfreien Zugriff**; **random access files =** file in which each item or record can be immediately accessed by its address, without searching through the rest of the file, and is not dependent on the previous location **Direktzugriffsdatei**; **random access memory (RAM) =** memory that allows access to any location in any order, usually in the form of ICs **Direktzugriffsspeicher (RAM)**; **random access storage =** storage medium that allows access to any location in any order **Direktzugriffsspeicher**

◊ **random processing** *noun* processing of data in the order required rather than the order in which it is stored **wahlfreie Verarbeitung**

range
1 *noun*
(a) series of items from which the customer can choose **Bereich, Auswahl**; *a wide range of products; the catalogue lists a wide range of computer stationery*
(b) set of allowed values between a maximum and minimum **Wertebereich**; *the telephone channel can accept signals in the frequency range 300 - 3400Hz; magnetic tape is stable within a temperature range of 0° to 40°C;* **number range =** set of allowable values **Wertebereich**; **frequency range =** range of allowable frequencies, between two limits **Frequenzbereich**
2 *verb*
(a) to vary or to be different **sich bewegen, rangieren**; *the company's products range from a cheap lapheld micro to a multistation mainframe*
(b) to put text in order to one side **ausrichten, verschieben**; **range left =** move text to align it to the left margin; to move the contents of a word to the left edge **links ausrichten, nach links verschieben**

rank *verb* to sort data into an order, usually according to size or importance **ordnen, einstufen**

rapid *adjective* fast **schnell**; **rapid access =**

device *or* memory whose access time is very short **Schnellzugriff(sspeicher)**; **rapid access memory** *or* **fast access memory** (**FAM**) = storage locations that can be read from *or* written to very quickly **Schnellzugriffsspeicher**

raster *noun* system of scanning the whole of a CRT screen with a picture beam by sweeping across it horizontally, moving down one pixel *or* line at a time **Raster; raster graphics** = graphics where the picture is built up in lines across the screen *or* page **Rastergrafik; raster image processor** = raster which translates software instructions into an image *or* complete page which is then printed by the printer **Rasterbildverarbeiter;** *an electronic page can be converted to a printer-readable video image by an on-board raster image processor;* **raster scan** = one sweep of the picture beam horizontally across the front of a CRT screen **Zeilenabtastung**

rate
1 *noun* quantity of data *or* tasks that can be processed in a set time **Rate;** *the processor's instruction execution rate is better than the older version;* **error rate** = number of errors that occur within a certain time **Fehlerrate; information rate** = amount of information content per character multiplied by the number of characters transmitted per second **mittlerer Informationsfluss**
2 *verb* to evaluate how good something is *or* how large something is **abschätzen; rated throughput** = maximum throughput of a device that will still meet original specifications **Nenndurchlauf**

◊ **ratings** *noun* calculation of how many people are watching a TV programme **Einschaltquote; ratings battle** *or* **war** = fight between two TV companies to increase their share of the market **Kampf um die Einschaltquote**

ratio *noun* proportion of one number to another **Verhältnis;** *the ratio of 10 to 5 is 2:1; the ratio of corrupt bits per transmitted message is falling with new technology*

◊ **rational number** *noun* number that can be written as the ratio of two whole numbers **rationale Zahl;** *24 over 7 is a rational number; 0.333 can be written as the rational number ⅓*

raw *adjective* in the original state *or* not processed **roh, unbearbeitet; raw data** = (i) pieces of information that have not yet been input into a computer system; (ii) data

in a database which has to be processed to provide information to the user (i) **Ausgangsdaten;** (ii) **Ursprungsdaten;** *this small computer collects raw data from the sensors, converts it and transmits it to the mainframe;* **raw mode** = (in DOS and UNIX operating systems) method of accessing a file which, when data is read from the file, does not carry out any data translation or filtering **Rohdatenmodus, Raw Mode**

ray *noun* one line of light *or* radiation in a beam *or* from a source **Strahl;** *the rays of light pass down the optical fibre*

◊ **ray tracing** *noun* (in graphics) method of creating life-like computer-generated graphics which correctly show shadows and highlights on an object as if coming from a light source; ray tracing software calculates the direction of each ray of light, its reflection and how it looks on an object **Strahlverfolgung;** *to generate this picture with ray tracing will take several hours on this powerful PC*

RD = REMOVE DIRECTORY (in DOS) command to remove an empty subdirectory **RD**

RDBMS = RELATIONAL DATABASE MANAGEMENT SYSTEM

react *verb* **to react to something** = to act in response to something **auf etwas reagieren; to react with something** = to change because a substance is present **mit etwas reagieren**

◊ **reactance** *noun* impedance associated with a component (capacitor *or* inductor) **Reaktanz, Blindwiderstand**

◊ **reaction** *noun* action which takes place because of something which has happened earlier **Reaktion**

◊ **reactive mode** *noun* computer operating mode in which each entry by the user causes something to happen but does not provide an immediate response **Reaktionsmodus;** *compare with* INTERACTIVE; BATCH

read *verb*
(a) to look at printed words and understand them **lesen;** *conditions of sale are printed in such small characters that they are difficult to read; can the OCR read typeset characters?*
(b) to retrieve data from a storage medium **lesen;** *this instruction reads the first record of a file; access time can be the time taken to*

read from a record; **destructive read** = read operation in which the stored data is erased as it is retrieved **löschendes Lesen; read back check** = system to ensure that data was correctly received, in which the transmitted data is sent back and checked against the original for any errors **Leseprüfung; read cycle** = period of time between address data being sent to a storage device and the data being returned **Lesezyklus; read error** = error that occurs during a read operation, often because the stored data has been corrupted **Lesefehler; read head** = transducer that reads signals stored on a magnetic medium and converts them back to their original electrical form **Lesekopf; read only** = device *or* circuit whose stored data cannot be changed **nur zum Lesen; read only attribute** = attribute bit of a file that, if set, prevents new data being written to the file or its contents edited **Nur-Lesen-Attribut, Schreibschutzattribut; read only memory (ROM)** = memory device that has had data written into it at the time of manufacture, and now its contents can only be read **Festwertspeicher;** *the manufacturer provided the monitor program in two ROM chips;* **read rate** = number of bytes *or* bits that a reader can read in a certain time **Lesegeschwindigkeit; read/write channel** = channel that can carry signals travelling in two directions **Lese-/Schreibkanal; read/write cycle** = sequence of events used to retrieve and store data **Lese-/Schreibzyklus; read/write head** = transducer that can read *or* write data from the surface of a magnetic storage medium, such as a floppy disk **Lese-/Schreibkopf; read/write memory** = storage medium that can be written to and read from **Lese-/Schreibspeicher;** *compare with* READ ONLY

◊ **readable** *adjective* that can be read *or* understood by someone *or* an electronic device **lesbar;** *the electronic page is converted to a printer-readable video image;* **machine readable** = (commands *or* data) stored on a medium that can be directly input to the computer **maschinenlesbar**

◊ **reader** *noun* device that reads data stored on one medium and converts it into another form **Leser; card reader** = device that transforms data on a punched card to a form that can be recognized by the computer **Lochkartenleser; tape reader** = machine that reads punched holes in paper tape *or* signals on magnetic tape **Magnetbandleser;** *see also* OPTICAL

◊ **read-in** *or* **read in** *verb* to transfer data from an external source to main memory

einlesen; *the computer automatically read-in thirty values from the A/D converter*

◊ **reading** *noun* note taken of figures *or* degrees, especially of degrees on a scale **Ablesewert**

◊ **readout** *noun* display of data **Anzeige;** *the readout displayed the time; the clock had a digital readout;* **destructive readout** = display device that erases previous characters when displaying new ones **löschendes Auslesen; readout device** = device that allows information (numbers *or* characters) to be displayed **Anzeigevorrichtung**

> QUOTE some OCR programs can be taught to read typefaces that are not in their library
> *Publish*

> QUOTE the machine easily reads in text from typewriters and daisy-wheel printers
> *PC Business World*

ready *adjective* fit to be used *or* sold; (equipment) that is waiting and able to be used **bereit;** *the green light indicates the system is ready for another program; the programming will not be ready until next week; the maintenance people hope that the system will be ready for use in 24 hours;* **ready state** = communications line *or* device that is waiting to accept data **Bereitzustand**

real address *noun* absolute address that directly accesses a memory location **reale Adresse;** *compare* PAGED ADDRESS

◊ **real memory** *noun* actual physical memory that can be addressed by a CPU **Realspeicher;** *compare with* VIRTUAL MEMORY

◊ **real mode** *noun* (in an IBM PC) the default operating mode for an IBM PC and the only mode in which DOS operates; real mode normally means a single-tasking operating system in which software can use any available memory *or* I/O device **Real Mode, realer Modus**

◊ **real number** *noun* (in computing) number that is represented with a fractional part (sometimes refers to numbers represented in a floating-point form) **reelle Zahl**

◊ **real time** *noun* actions *or* processing time that is of the same order of magnitude as the problem to be solved (i.e. the processing time is within the same time as the problem to be solved, so that the result can influence the source of the data) **Echtzeit, Real Time;** *a navigation system needs to be able to process the position of a ship in real time and take suitable action before it hits a rock (US)* **program shown in real time** = TV program which is broadcast live **Livesendung; real-time animation** = animation in which objects appear to move at the same speed as they would in real life; real-time animation requires display hardware capable of displaying a sequence with tens of different images every second **Echtzeitanimation; real-time clock** = clock in a computer that provides the correct time of day **Uhrzeitgeber;** *compare* RELATIVE-TIME CLOCK; **real-time input** = data input to a system as it happens *or* is required **Echtzeiteingabe; real-time multi-tasking** = executing several real-time tasks simultaneously without slowing the execution of any of the processes **Echtzeitmultitasking; real-time operating system** = operating system designed to control a real-time system *or* process-control system **Echtzeitbetriebssystem; real-time processing** = processing operation that takes a time of the same order of magnitude as the problem to be solved **Echtzeitbetrieb; real-time simulation** = computer model of a process where each process is executed in a similar time to the real process **Echtzeitsimulation**

◊ **real-time system** *noun* system whose processing time is within that of the problem, so that it can influence the source of the data **Echtzeitsystem;** *in a -real-time system, as you move the joystick left, the image on the screen moves left. If there is a pause for processing it is not a true real-time system*

QUOTE a real-time process is one which interacts with a real external activity and respects deadlines imposed by that activity
.EXE

QUOTE define a real-time system as any system which is expected to interact with its environment within certain timing constraints
British Telecom Technology Journal

QUOTE Quotron provides real-time quotes, news and analysis on equity securities through a network of 40,000 terminals to US brokers and investors
Computing

reboot *verb* to reload an operating system

during a computing session **erneut laden;** *we rebooted and the files reappeared; see also* BOOT

recall
1 *noun* bringing back text *or* files from store **Aufruf**
2 *verb* to bring back text *or* files from store for editing **aufrufen**

QUOTE automatic recall provides the facility to recall the last twenty commands and to edit and re-use them
Practical Computing

receive *verb* to accept data from a communications link **empfangen;** *the computer received data via the telephone line;* **receive only** = computer terminal that can only accept and display data (but not transmit) **Empfänger**

◊ **receiver** *noun* electronic device that can detect transmitted signals and present them in a suitable form **Empfänger; radio receiver** = device that detects signals broadcast on one radio frequency and converts them into their original audio form **Empfangsgerät;** *the radio receiver picked up your signal very strongly;* **receiver register** = temporary storage register for data inputs, before processing **Empfangsregister**

reception *noun* quality of a radio *or* TV signal received **Empfang;** *signal reception is bad with that aerial*

re-chargeable *adjective* (battery) which can be charged again with electricity when it is flat **wiederaufladbar**

recode *verb* to code a program which has been coded for one system, so that it will work on another **umcodieren**

recognition *noun* (i) being able to recognize something; (ii) process that allows something to be recognized, such as letters on a printed text *or* bars on bar codes, etc. **(i) & (ii) (Wieder)erkennung; recognition logic** = logical software used in OCR, AI, etc. **Erkennungslogik; optical character recognition** = process that allows printed *or* written characters to be recognized optically (using an optical character reader), and converted into a form that can be input into a computer **optische Zeichenerkennung; optical mark recognition** = process that allows certain marks *or* lines *or* patterns to be recognized optically (using an optical character reader), and converted into a form that can be input into a computer **optische Markierungserkennung**

◊ **recognize** verb to see something and remember that it has been seen before **(wieder)erkennen;** *the scanner will recognize most character fonts*

◊ **recognizable** *adjective* which can be recognized **erkennbar**

recompile verb to compile a source program again, usually after changes *or* debugging **neu kompilieren**

reconfigure verb to alter the structure of data in a system **rekonfigurieren**

◊ **reconfiguration** *noun* altering the structure of data in a system **Rekonfiguration;** *I reconfigured the field structure in the file; this program allows us to reconfigure the system to our own requirements; see also* CONFIGURE, SET UP

reconnect verb to connect again **wiederanschließen;** *the telephone engineers are trying to reconnect the telephone*

reconstitute verb to return a file to a previous state, usually to restore a file after a crash *or* corruption **rekonstituieren, wiederherstellen**

record
1 *noun*
(a) set of items of related data **(Daten)satz;** *your record contains several fields that have been grouped together under the one heading; this record contains all their personal details;* **chained record** = data record in a chained file **geketteter Satz; change** *or* **transaction record** = record containing new data which is to be used to update a master record **Änderungssatz; logical record** = number of items of related data that are held in temporary memory ready to be processed **logischer Satz; physical record** = record and control data combination stored on a backing device **physischer Satz; record count** = number of records within a stored file **Satzanzahl; record format** *or* **layout** = organization and length of separate fields in a record **Satzformat; record length** = quantity of data in a record **Satzlänge; record locking** = (in a multiuser system) software method of preventing more than one user writing data to a record at the same time; the first user's software sets a locked flag for the record during write operations, preventing other users from corrupting data by also writing

data **Datensatzsperrung; records management/manager** = program which maintains records and can access and process them to provide information **Satzverwaltungsprogramm; record structure** = list of the fields which make up a record, together with their length and data type **Datensatzstruktur, Satzstruktur**
(b) plastic disk on the surface of which music *or* other sounds are recorded **Schallplatte**
2 *verb* to store data *or* signals on tape *or* on disk *or* in a computer **aufzeichnen;** *record the results in this column; this device records signals onto magnetic tape; digitally recorded data are used to generate images;* **record button** = key pressed on a recorder when ready to record signals onto a medium **Aufnahmetaste; record gap** *see* BLOCK GAP; **record head** *or* **write head** = transducer that converts an electrical signal into a magnetic field to write the data onto a magnetic medium **Schreibkopf**

QUOTE you can echo the previous record if a lot of replication is involved

QUOTE records may be sorted before the report is created, using up to nine sort fields
Byte

QUOTE file and record-locking procedures have to be implemented to make sure that files cannot be corrupted when two users try to read or write to the same record simultaneously
Micro Decision

QUOTE Micro Focus provides Fileshare 2, which it claims substantially reduces network traffic, and provides features such as full record locking, update logging and roll-forward recovery
Computing

recorder *noun* equipment able to transfer input signals onto a storage medium **Aufnahmegerät; magnetic tape recorder** = device with a motor, read/write head and circuitry to allow electrical signals to be recorded onto *or* played back from magnetic tape **Magnetbandgerät**

COMMENT: the signal recorded is not always in the same form as the input signal: many recorders record a modulated carrier signal for better quality. A recorder is usually combined with a suitable playback circuit since the read and write heads are often the same physical device

recording *noun*
(a) action of storing signals *or* data on tape *or* in a computer **Aufzeichnen; recording density** = number of bits of data that can be stored in a unit area on a magnetic disk *or* tape **Zeichendichte; recording trunk** = telephone line between a local and long distance exchange for operator use **Verbindungsleitung**
(b) signal (especially music) which has been recorded on tape *or* disk **Aufnahme;** *a new recording of Beethoven's quartets*

> QUOTE file and record-locking procedures have to be implemented to make sure that files cannot be corrupted when two users try to read or write to the same record simultaneously
> *Micro Decision*

recover *verb* to get back something which has been lost **wiederherstellen;** *it is possible to recover the data but it can take a long time*

◊ **recoverable error** *noun* error type that allows program execution to be continued after it has occurred **wiederherstellbarer Fehler**

◊ **recovery** *noun* (i) returning to normal operating after a fault; (ii) getting back something which has been lost (i) **Wiederaufnahme;** (ii) **Zurückgewinnung; recovery procedure** = processes required to return a system to normal operation after an error **Wiederherstellungsverfahren;** *the recovery of lost files can be carried out using the recovery procedure;* **automatic recovery program** = software that is automatically run when a piece of equipment fails, to ensure that the system continues to operate **automatisches Wiederanlaufprogramm; failure recovery** = resuming a process *or* program after a failure has occurred and has been corrected **Wiederaufnahme nach Abbruch; fall back recovery** = resuming a program after a fault has been fixed, from a point at which the fall back routines were called **Programmwiederaufnahme; sense recovery time** = time that a RAM device takes to switch from read to write mode **Lese-Erholzeit**

rectangular waveguide *noun* microwave channel that is rectangular in cross section **rechteckige Wellenleitung**

rectify *verb*
(a) to correct something *or* to make something right **berichtigen;** *they had to rectify the error at the printout stage*
(b) to remove the positive *or* negative sections of a signal so that it is unipolar **gleichrichten**

◊ **rectifier** *noun* electronic circuit that converts an alternating current supply into a direct current supply **Gleichrichter**

recto *noun* right hand page of a book (usually given an odd number) **Rekto**

recursion *or* **recursive routine** *noun* subroutine in a program that calls itself during execution **Rekursion; rekursives Unterprogramm; recursive call** = subroutine that calls itself when it is run **rekursiver Aufruf**

redefine *verb* to change the function *or* value assigned to a variable *or* object **neu definieren;** *we redefined the initial parameters;* **to redefine a key** = to change the function of a programmable key **eine Taste neu definieren;** *I have redefined this key to display the figure five when pressed*

◊ **redefinable** *adjective* which can be redefined **neu definierbar**

> QUOTE the idea of the packages is that they enable you to redefine the keyboard
> *Practical Computing*

> QUOTE one especially useful command lets you redefine the printer's character-translation table
> *Byte*

red, green, blue (RGB) *noun*
(a) high-definition monitor system that uses three separate input signals controlling red, green and blue colour picture beams **Rot-Grün-Blau-System**
(b) the three colour picture beams used in a colour TV **Rot-Grün-Blau**

> COMMENT: there are three colour guns producing red, green and blue beams acting on groups of three phosphor dots at each pixel location

redirect *verb*
(a) to send a message to its destination by another route **umleiten**
(b) (in DOS and UNIX operating systems) to treat the output of one program as input for another program **umleiten;** *you can sort the results from a DIR command by redirecting to the SORT command;* **redirect** *or* **redirection operator** = character used by an operating system to indicate that the output of one program is to be sent as input to another; in DOS, the '>' character is used **Umleitungssymbol**

◊ **redirection** *noun* sending a message to its destination by another route **Umleiten;**

call forwarding is automatic redirection of calls

redliner *noun* feature of workgroup or word-processor software that allows a user to highlight text in a different colour **farbliche Hervorhebung**

redo *verb* to do something again **neu anfangen; redo from start** = start again from the beginning **nochmals von vorne anfangen**

redraw *verb* to draw again **erneut zeichnen;** *can the computer redraw the graphics showing the product from the top view?*

reduce *verb*
(a) to make smaller **verringern**
(b) to convert raw data into a more compact form which can then be easily processed **reduzieren**

◊ **reduced instruction set computer (RISC)** *noun* CPU design whose instruction set contains a small number of simple fast-executing instructions, that makes program writing more complex, but increases speed **Computer mit reduziertem Befehlsvorrat;** *compare with* WISC

◊ **reduction** *noun* act of reducing; proportion by which something is made smaller **Verringerung;** *we need a 25% reduction to fit the halftone in the space*

redundant *adjective*
(a) (data) that can be removed without losing any information **überflüssig, redundant;** *the parity bits on the received data are redundant and can be removed;* **redundant array of inexpensive disks (RAID)** = fast, fault-tolerant disk drive system that uses multiple drives which would, typically, each store one byte of a word of data, so allowing the data to be saved faster; one drive in the array would also store a check byte for error detection **RAID-Anordnung; redundant character** = character added to a block of characters for error detection or protocol purposes, and carries no information **redundantes Zeichen; redundant code** = check bit or data added to a block of data for error detection purposes, and carries no information **redundanter Code**
(b) (extra piece of equipment) kept ready for a task in case of faults **redundant**

◊ **redundancy** *noun* providing extra components in a system in case there is a breakdown **Redundanz; longitudinal**

redundancy check = check on received blocks of data to detect any errors **Blockprüfung; network redundancy** = extra links between points allowing continued operation in the event of one failing **Netzwerkredundanz; vertical redundancy check** = (odd) parity check on each character of a block received, to detect any errors **Querprüfung; redundancy checking** = checking of received data for correct redundant codes to detect any errors **Redundanzprüfung**

reel *noun* holder round which a tape is rolled **Spule;** *he dropped the reel on the floor and the tape unwound itself;* **pick-up reel** = empty reel used to store tape as it is played from a full reel **Leerspule**

◊ **reel to reel** *noun* copying one tape of data onto another magnetic tape **von Band auf Band (kopieren); reel to reel recorder** = magnetic tape recording machine that uses tape held on one reel and feeds it to a pick-up reel **Magnetbandgerät mit zwei Rollen**

re-entrant program *or* **code** *or* **routine** *noun* one program *or* code shared by many users in a multi-user system (it can be interrupted *or* called again by another user before it has finished its previous run, and returns to the point at which it was interrupted when it has finished that run) **wiederverwendbares Programm; wiederverwendbarer Code**

◊ **re-entry** *noun* calling a routine from within that routine; running a program from within that program **Rücksprung; re-entry point** = point in a program *or* routine where it is re-entered **Rücksprungstelle**

refer *verb* to mention *or* to deal with *or* to write about something **sich beziehen auf;** *the manual refers to the serial port, but I cannot find it*

◊ **reference**
1 *noun*
(a) value used as a starting point for other values, often zero **Bezugspunkt; reference address** = initial address in a program used as an origin *or* base for others **Bezugsadresse; reference level** = signal level to which all others are calibrated **Bezugspegel**
(b) mentioning *or* dealing with something **Bezug; reference file** = file of data which is kept so that it can be referred to **Zuordnungsdatei; reference instruction** = command that provides access to sorted *or* stored data **Zuordnungsbefehl; reference list** = list of routines *or* instructions and their

location within a program **Verweisliste; reference mark** = printed symbol to indicate the presence of a note *or* reference not in the text **Verweiszeichen; reference retrieval system** = index which provides a reference to a document **Wiederauffindungssystem; reference table** = list of ordered items **Bezugstabelle; reference time** = point in time that is used as an origin for further timings *or* measurements **Bezugszeit**

2 *verb* to access a location in memory **zugreifen auf;** *the access time taken to reference an item in memory is short*

> QUOTE a referencing function dynamically links all references throughout a document
>
> *Byte*

reflect *verb* to send back (light *or* image) from a surface **reflektieren;** *in a reflex camera, the image is reflected by an inbuilt mirror*

◊ **reflected code** *noun* coding system in which the binary representation of decimal numbers changes by only one bit at a time from one number to the next **Gray-Verschlüsselung**

◊ **reflectance** *noun* difference between the amount of light *or* signal incident and the amount that is reflected back from a surface **Remission, Reflexionsgrad** NOTE: the opposite is **absorptance**

◊ **reflection** *noun* light *or* image which is reflected **Reflexion, Spiegelung; signal reflection** = amount of transmitted signal that is reflected at the receiver due to an impedance mismatch *or* fault **Signalreflexion**

◊ **reflective disk** *noun* video disk that uses a reflected laser beam to read the data etched into the surface **reflektierende Platte**

reflex (camera) *noun* camera with an optical mirror that allows a scene to be viewed through the camera lens so that the user sees what he is photographing **Spiegelreflexkamera**

reformat *verb* to format a disk that already contains data, and erasing the data by doing so **neu formatieren;** *do not reformat your hard disk unless you can't do anything else*

◊ **reformatting** *noun* act of formatting a disk which already contains data **Neuformatierung;** *reformatting destroys all the data on a disk; see also* FORMAT

refract *verb* to change the direction of

light as it passes through a material (such as water *or* glass) **brechen**

◊ **refraction** *noun* change in direction of light rays as they pass through a material **Brechung**

◊ **refractive index** *noun* measure of the angle that light is refracted by, as it passes through a material **Brechungsindex**

refresh *verb*
(a) to update regularly the contents of dynamic RAM by reading and rewriting stored data to ensure data is retained **wiederauffrischen;** *memory refresh signal;* **refresh cycle** = period of time during which a controller updates the contents of dynamic RAM chips **Auffrischzyklus, Auffrischrate; RAM refresh rate** = number of times every second that the data in a dynamic RAM chip has to be read and rewritten **RAM-Regenerationsgeschwindigkeit; self-refreshing RAM** = dynamic RAM chip that has built-in circuitry to generate refresh signals, allowing data to be retained when the power is off, using a battery backup **selbstregenerierender RAM**
(b) screen refresh = to update regularly the images on a CRT screen by scanning each pixel with a picture beam to make sure the image is still visible **Bildwiederholung; refresh rate** = number of times every second that the image on a CRT is redrawn **Bildwiederholfrequenz**

> QUOTE Philips autoscan colour monitor, the 4CM6099, has SVGA refresh rates of 72Hz (800 x 600) and EVGA refresh rates of 70Hz (1,024 x 768)
>
> *Computing*

regenerate *verb* (i) to redraw an image on a screen many times a second so that it remains visible; (ii) to receive distorted signals, process and error check them, then retransmit the same data **(i) & (ii) regenerieren**

◊ **regeneration** *noun* process of regenerating a signal **Regeneration**

◊ **regenerative memory** *noun* storage medium whose contents need to be regularly refreshed to retain its contents **Regenerationsspeicher;** *dynamic RAM is regenerative memory - it needs to be refreshed every 250ns; the CRT display can be thought of as regenerative memory, it requires regular refresh picture scans to prevent flicker;* **regenerative reading** = reading operation that automatically regenerates and rewrites the data back into memory **regeneratives Lesen**

◊ **regenerator** *noun* device used in communications that amplifies or regenerates a received signal and transmits it on regenerators are often used to extend the range of a network **Regenerator**

region *noun* special *or* reserved area of memory or program **Region, Bereich; region fill** = to fill an area of a the screen or a graphics shape with a particular colour **Bereichsauffüllung**

◊ **regional breakpoint** *noun* breakpoint that can be inserted anywhere within a program that is being debugged **regionaler Programmstop;** *see also* BREAKPOINT, DEBUGGING

register
1 *noun*
(a) (i) special location within a CPU (usually one or two words wide) that is used to hold data and addresses to be processed in a machine code operation; (ii) reserved memory location used for special storage purposes **(i)** & **(ii)** **Register; accumulator register** = most important internal storage register in a CPU, containing the data to be processed **Akkumulatorregister; address register** = register in a computer that is able to store all the bits of an address which can then be processed as a single unit **Adressregister; base register** = register in a CPU (not usually in small computers) that contains the address of the start of a program **Basisregister; buffer register** = temporary storage for data being written to *or* read from memory **Pufferregister; circulating register** = shift register whose output is fed back into its input (to form a closed loop) **Ringschieberegister; control register** = storage location for control data **Steuerregister; data register** = area within a CPU used to store data temporarily before it is processed **Datenregister; external register** = registers which are located outside the main CPU, in locations within main memory, allowing the user to access them easily **externes Register; index register** = computer address register that is added to a reference address to provide the location to be accessed **Indexregister; input/output register** = temporary storage for data received from memory before being transferred to an I/O device *or* data from an I/O device waiting to be stored in main memory or to be processed **Ein-/Ausgaberegister; instruction register** = temporary storage for the instruction that

is being executed **Befehlsregister; instruction address register (IAR)** = register in a CPU that stores the location of the next instruction to be processed **Befehlsadressregister; memory address register (MAR)** = register within the CPU that contains the address of the next location to be accessed **Speicheradressregister; next instruction register** = register in the CPU that contains the address of the next instruction to be processed **Befehlsfolgeregister; program status word register (PSW register)** = register which contains a number of status bits, such as carry flag, zero flag, overflow flag **Programmstatuswortregister (PSW-Register); sequence control register (SCR)** = CPU register that contains the address of the next instruction to be processed **Befehlsfolgeregister;** *see also* NEXT INSTRUCTION REGISTER; **shift register** = temporary storage into which data can be shifted **Schieberegister; register addressing** = instruction whose address field contains the register in which the operand is stored **Registeradressierung; register file** = number of registers used for temporary storage **Registerdatei; register length** = size (in bits) of a register **Registerlänge;** *in this small micro, the data register is eight bits wide, an address register is sixteen bits wide;* **register map** = display of the contents of all the registers **Registerinhaltsverzeichnis**
(b) superimposing two images correctly **Register; the two colours are out of register** = the colours are not correctly printed one on top of the other **die zwei Farben halten nicht Register**
2 *verb*
(a) to react to a stimulus **ansprechen auf;** *light-sensitive films register light intensity*
(b) to correctly superimpose two images **Registerhalten; register marks** = marks at the corners of a film used to help in lining up two images **Passmarken**

regulate *verb* to control a process (usually using sensors and a feedback mechanism) **regeln; regulated power supply** = constant, controlled voltage *or* current source whose output will not vary with input supply variation **Konstantstromversorgung**

│ COMMENT: a regulated power supply is
│ required for all computers where components
│ cannot withstand voltage variations

rehyphenation *noun* changing the hyphenation of words in a text after it has been put into a new page format *or* line width **erneute Worttrennung**

reject *verb* to refuse to accept something zurückweisen; *the computer rejects all incoming data from incompatible sources*

◊ **rejection** *noun* refusing to accept something Zurückweisung; **rejection error** = error by a scanner which cannot read a character and so leaves a blank Zurückweisungsfehler

relational database *or* **relational database management system (RDBMS)** *noun* database in which all the items of data can be interconnected; data is retrieved by using one item of data to search for a related field RDBMS-System; *if you search the relational database for the surname, you can pull out his salary from the related accounts database;* **relational operator** *or* **logical operator** symbol that compares two items Vergleichsoperator; **relational query** = database query that contains relational operators kombinierte Abfrage; *the relational query 'find all men under 35 years old' will not work on this system*

◊ **relationship** *noun* way in which two similar things are connected Beziehung

> QUOTE Data replication is the process of duplicating data on, or distributing it between, databases, usually on different servers. It is not new, having been around for many years: nor is it confined to relational databases
>
> *Computing*

relative *adjective* which is compared to something relativ; **relative address** *or* **indirect address** = location specified in relation to a reference or base address relative Adresse; **relative coding** = writing a program using relative address instructions relative Codierung; **relative coordinates** = positional information given in relation to a reference point relative Koordinaten; **relative data** = data that gives new coordinate information relative to previous coordinates relative Daten; **relative error** = difference between a number and its correct value (caused by rounding off) relativer Fehler; **relative pointing device** = input device (such as a mouse) in which the movement of a pointer on screen is relative to the movement of the input device relative Zeigereinheit, relative Zeigevorrichtung; **relative-time clock** = regular pulses that allow software in a computer to calculate the real time Relativzeitgeber

relay *noun* electromagnetically controlled switch Relais; *there is a relay in the circuit; it is relay-rated at 5 Amps;* **microwave relay** = radiocommunications equipment used to receive microwave signals, then boost and retransmit them Mikrowellenrelais 2 *verb* to receive data from one source and then retransmit it to another point (weiter)übertragen; *all messages are relayed through this small micro*

release
1 *noun*
(a) version of a product Version; *the latest software is release 5;* **release number** = number of the version of a product Versionsnummer; *see also* VERSION
(b) putting a new product on the market Freigabe; **new releases** = new records put on the market Neuerscheinungen; **on general release** = (i) available to the public; (ii) (film) shown at many cinemas (i) allgemein zugänglich; (ii) überall angelaufen
(c) **press release** = sheet giving news about a news item which is sent to newspapers and TV and radio stations so that they can use the information in it Presseverlautbarung
2
(a) to put a new product on the market zum Verkauf freigeben, herausbringen
(b) (of software) to relinquish control of a block of memory *or* file freigeben

relevant *adjective* which has an important connection relevant, sachdienlich

◊ **relevance** *noun* (i) way in which something has a connection with something else; (ii) importance of something in a situation *or* process (i) & (ii) Relevanz

reliability *noun* the ability of a device to function as intended, efficiently and without failure Zuverlässigkeit; *it has an excellent reliability record; the product has passed its reliability tests*

◊ **reliable** *adjective* which can be trusted to work properly zuverlässig; *the early versions of the software were not completely reliable*

relief printing *noun* printing process in which the ink is held on a raised image Hochdruckverfahren, Reliefdruck

reload *verb* to load again neu laden; *we reloaded the program after the crash see also* LOAD

relocate *verb* to move data from one area of storage to another verschieben; *the data* *is relocated during execution;* **self-relocating program** = program that can be loaded into any part of memory (that will modify its addresses depending on the program origin address) **selbstverschiebliches Programm**

◊ **relocatable** *adjective* which can be moved to another area of memory without affecting its operation **verschiebbar; relocatable program** = computer program that can be loaded into and executed from any area of memory **relativierbares Programm;** *the operating system can load and run a relocatable program from any area of memory*

◊ **relocation** *noun* moving to another area in memory **Verschiebung; dynamic relocation** = moving data *or* coding *or* assigning absolute locations during a program execution **dynamische Verschiebung; relocation constant** = quantity added to all addresses to move them to another section of memory, (equal to the new base address) **Verschiebungskonstante; static relocation** = moving data *or* coding *or* assigning absolute locations before a program is run **statische Verschiebung**

REM = REMARK statement in a BASIC program that is ignored by the interpreter, allowing the programmer to write explanatory notes **REM**

remainder
1 *noun* number equal to the dividend minus the product of the quotient and divider **Rest;** *7 divided by 3 is equal to 2 remainder 1; compare with* QUOTIENT
2 *verb* to sell products below cost price **verramschen;** *this computer model is out of date so we have to remainder the rest of the stock*

remark (REM) statement in a BASIC program that is ignored by the interpreter, allowing the programmer to write explanatory notes **Kommentar (REM)**

remedial maintenance *noun* maintenance to repair faults which have developed in a system **Bedarfswartung**

remote *adjective* (communications) with a computer at a distance from the systems centre **entfernt, fern-, Fern-;** *users can print reports on remote printers;* **remote access** = link that allows a user to access a computer from a distance (normally using a modem) **Fernzugriff; remote console** *or* **device** = input/output device located away from the computer (sending data to it by line *or* modem) **Außenstelle; remote control** = system that allows a remote user to control (run programs, copy files, control resources) a computer from a distance; the remote user has the impression of using the remote computer locally **Fernsteuerung; remote control software** = software that runs on a local computer and a remote computer allowing a user to control the remote computer **Fernsteuerungssoftware;** *this remote control software will work with Windows and lets me operate my office PC from home over a modem link;* **remote job entry (RJE)** = batch processing system where instructions are transmitted to the computer from a remote terminal **Jobferneingabe; remote station** = communications station that can be controlled by a central computer **Gegenstelle; remote terminal** = computer terminal connected to a distant computer system **entfernt stehende Datenstation**

remove *verb* to take away *or* to move to another place **entfernen;** *the file entry was removed from the floppy disk directory*

◊ **removable** *adjective* which can be removed **auswechselbar;** *a removable hard disk*

◊ **removal** *noun* taking away **Beseitigung;** *the removal of this instruction could solve the problem*

rename *verb* to give a new name to a file **neu benennen;** *save the file and rename it* CUSTOM

renumber *noun* feature of some computer languages that allows the programmer to allocate new values to all *or* some of a program's line numbers **neu nummerieren;** *see also* LINE NUMBER

reorganize *verb* to organize again **neu organisieren;** *wait while the spelling checker database is being reorganized*

repaginate *verb* to change the lengths of pages of text before they are printed **einen Seitenumbruch durchführen;** *the text was repaginated with a new line width*

◊ **repagination** *noun* action of changing pages lengths **Seitenumbruch;** *the dtp package allows simple repagination*

repeat *verb* to do an action again **wiederholen; repeat counter** = register that holds the number of times a routine *or* task has been repeated **Wiederholungszähler;**

repeat key = key on a keyboard which repeats the character pressed **Dauertaste**

◊ **repeater** *noun* device used in communications that amplifies or regenerates a received signal and transmits it on regenerators are often used to extend the range of a network **Relaisstelle**

◊ **repeating group** *noun* pattern of data that is duplicated in a bit stream **Wiederholungsgruppe**

reperforator *noun* machine that punches paper tape according to received signals **Lochstreifenempfänger;** **reperforator transmitter** = reperforator and a punched tape transmitter connected together **Lochstreifensender mit Empfangslocher**

repertoire *noun* the range of functions of a/device *or* software **Repertoire;** *the manual describes the full repertoire;* **character repertoire** = list of all the characters that can be displayed *or* printed **Zeichenvorrat;** **instruction repertoire** = all the commands that a system can recognise and execute **Befehlsvorrat;** *see also* RESERVED WORD

> QUOTE the only omissions in the editing repertoire are dump, to list variables currently in use, and find
> *Computing Today*

repetitive letter *noun* form letter *or* standard letter into which the details of each addressee (such as name and address) are inserted **Formbrief**

◊ **repetitive strain injury** *or* **repetitive stress injury (RSI)** *noun* pain in the arm felt by someone who performs the same movement many times over a certain period, as when operating a computer terminal **Dauerbelastungssyndrom, Repetitive Strain Injury (RSI);** *RSI can be avoided by adjusting your chair so that you do not excessively flex your wrists when typing*

replace *verb*
(a) to put something back where it was before; to put something in the place of something else **ersetzen;** *the printer ribbons need replacing after several thousand characters*
(b) instruction to a computer to find a certain item of data and put another in its place **austauschen;** *see also* SEARCH AND REPLACE

replay
1 *noun*
(a) playback *or* reading back data *or* a signal from a recording **Wiedergabe**

(b) repeating a short section of filmed action, usually in slow motion **Wiederholung;** *the replay clearly showed the winner;* *this video recorder has a replay feature;* **instant replay** = feature of video recording systems that allows an action that has just been recorded to be viewed immediately **sofortige Wiedergabe**
2 *verb* to play back (something which has been recorded) **wiedergeben;** *he replayed the tape; she recorded the TV programme on video tape and replayed it the next evening*

replenish *verb* to charge a battery with electricity again **wieder aufladen**

replicate *verb* to copy **wiederholen;** *the routine will replicate your results with very little effort*

◊ **replication** *noun* (i) extra components in a system in case there is a breakdown *or* fault in one; (ii) copying a record *or* data to another location **(i) Replikation; (ii) Kopie**

report generator *noun* software that allows data from database files to be merged with a document (in the form of graphs or tables) to provide a complete report **Listengenerator**

◊ **report program generator (RPG)** *noun* programming language used mainly on personal computers for the preparation of business reports, allowing data in files, databases, etc., to be included **Listenprogrammgenerator**

represent *verb*
(a) to act as a symbol for something **darstellen;** *the hash sign is used to represent a number in a series*
(b) to act as a salesman for a product **repräsentieren, vertreten**

◊ **representation** *noun* action of representing something **Darstellung;** **character representation** = combination of bits used for each character code **Zeichendarstellung**

◊ **representative**
1 *adjective* typical example of something **repräsentativ**
2 *noun* salesman who represents a company **Vertreter, Beauftragter;** *the representative called yesterday about the order*

reprint
1 *verb* to print more copies of a document *or* book **nachdrucken**

2 *noun* printing of copies of a book after the first printing **Nachdruck, Neuauflage;** *we ordered a 10,000 copy reprint*

repro *noun (informal)* finished artwork *or* camera-ready copy, ready for filming and printing **Repro; repro proof** = perfect proof ready to be reproduced **Reproabzug**

reproduce *verb* to copy data *or* text from one material *or* medium to another similar one **kopieren**

◊ **reproduction** *noun* action of copying **Kopieren**

reprogram *verb* to alter a program so that it can be run on another type of computer **neu programmieren**

request
1 *noun* thing which someone asks for **Anforderung; request to send signal (RTS)** = signal sent by a transmitter to a receiver asking if the receiver is ready to accept data (used in the RS232C serial connection) **Sendeanforderung**
2 *verb* to ask for something **anfordern**

require *verb* to need something *or* to demand something **erfordern;** *delicate computer systems require careful handling*

◊ **required hyphen** *or* **hard hyphen** *noun* hyphen which is always in a word, even if the word is not split (as in co-administrator) **unveränderlicher Bindestrich;** *see also* SOFT

◊ **requirements** *noun* things which are needed **Erfordernisse, Voraussetzungen;** *memory requirements depend on the application software in use*

re-route *verb* to send by a different route **umsteuern;** *the call diverter re-routes a call*

rerun *verb* to run a program *or* a printing job again **wiederholen; rerun point** = place in the program from where to start a running again after a crash *or* halt **Wiederanlaufpunkt**

res *see* RESOLUTION; **hi-res** = HIGH RESOLUTION; **lo-res** = LOW RESOLUTION

resave *verb* to save again **nochmals abspeichern;** *it automatically resaves the text*

rescue dump *noun* data saved on disk automatically when a computer fault occurs (it describes the state of the system at that time, used to help in debugging) **Notspeicherauszug**

research *noun* scientific investigation to learn new facts about a field of study **Forschung; research and development (R & D)** = investigation of new products, discoveries and techniques **Forschung und Entwicklung;** *the company has spent millions of dollars on R & D*

reserved character *noun* special character which is used by the operating system *or* which has a particular function to control an operating system and cannot be used for other uses **reserviertes Zeichen;** *in DOS, the reserved character \ is used to represent a directory path*

◊ **reserved sector** *noun* area of disk space that is used only for control data storage **reservierter Sektor**

◊ **reserved word** *noun* word *or* phrase used as an identifier in a programming language (it performs a particular operation *or* instruction and so cannot be used for other uses by the programmer *or* user) **festgelegtes Wort**

QUOTE sometimes a process will demand cache space when the only free cache space is reserved for higher priority processes
.EXE

reset *verb*
(a) to return a system to its initial state, to allow a program *or* process to be started again **zurückstellen; reset button** *or* **key** = switch that allows a program to be terminated and reset manually **Rückstelltaste; hard reset** = electrical signal that usually returns the system to its initial state when it was switched on, requiring a reboot **harte Rückstellung; soft reset** = instruction that terminates any program execution and returns the user to the monitor *or* BIOS **weiche Rückstellung**
(b) to set a register *or* counter to its initial state **in Grundstellung bringen;** *when it reaches 999 this counter resets to zero*
(c) to set data equal to zero **auf Null stellen**

COMMENT: hard reset is similar to soft reset but with a few important differences: it is a switch that directly signals the CPU, while soft reset signals the operating system; hard reset clears all memory contents, a soft reset does not affect memory contents; hard reset should always reset the system, a soft reset does not always work (if, for example, you have really upset the operating system a soft reset will not work)

resident *adjective* (data *or* program) that is always in a computer **ständig vorhanden, resident**; **resident engineer** = engineer who works permanently for one company **fest angestellter Ingenieur**; **resident font** = font data which is always present in a printer *or* device and which does not have to be downloaded **residente Schriftart, Druckerschriftart**; **resident software** *or* **memory-resident software** = program that is held permanently in memory (whilst the machine is on) **speicherresidentes Programm**; **terminate and stay resident software (TSR)** = program that is started from the command line, then loads itself into memory, ready to be activated by an action, and passes control back to the command line **speicherresidentes Programm, TSR-Programm**

residual *adjective* which remains behind **Rest-, rest-**; **residual error rate** = ratio between incorrect and undetected received data and total data transmitted **Restfehlerhäufigkeit**

◊ **residue check** *noun* error detection check in which the received data is divided by a set number and the remainder is checked against the required remainder **Modulo-N-Prüfung**

resist
1 *verb* to fight against something *or* to refuse to do something **Widerstand leisten**
2 *noun* substance used to protect a pattern of tracks on a PCB, that is not affected by etching chemicals **Abdeckmittel**; *see also* PHOTORESIST

◊ **resistance** *noun* measure of the voltage drop across a component with a current flowing through it **Widerstand**; *see also* OHM'S LAW

◊ **resistor** *noun* electronic component that provides a known resistance **Widerstand** ⇨APPENDIX; **resistor transistor logic (RTL)** = circuit design method using transistors and resistors **Widerstand-Transistor-Logik**; **variable resistor** = component whose resistance can be changed by turning a knob **Regelwiderstand**

resolution *noun* number of pixels that a screen *or* printer can display per unit area **Auflösungsvermögen**; *the resolution of most personal computer screens is not much more than 70 dpi (dots per inch)*; **graphic display resolution** = number of pixels that a computer is able to display on the screen **Auflösungsvermögen eines Grafikbildschirms**; **high resolution (hi-res)** =

ability to display *or* detect a very large number of pixels per unit area **hohe Auflösung**; *the high resolution screen can display 640 by 450 pixels*; **limiting resolution** = maximum number of lines that make up an image on a CRT screen **Auflösungsgrenze**; **low resolution (low-res)** = ability of a display system to control a number of pixels at a time rather than individual pixels **niedrige Auflösung**

QUOTE the resolution is 300 dots per inch and the throughput is up to eight pages per minute
Practical Computing

QUOTE Group IV fax devices can send a grey or colour A4 page in about four seconds, at a maximum resolution of 15.7 lines per millimetre over an Integrated Services Digital Network circuit
Computing

resolving power *noun* measurement of the ability of an optical system to detect fine black lines on a white background (given as the number of lines per millimetre) **Auflösungsvermögen**

resonance *noun* situation where a frequency applied to a body being the same as its natural frequency, causes it to oscillate with a very large amplitude **Resonanz**

resource *noun* products *or* programs which are useful **Betriebsmittel**; **resource allocation** = dividing available resources in a system between jobs **Betriebsmittelzuteilung**; **resource fork** = (in an Apple Macintosh) one of two forks of a file; the resource fork contains the resources that the file needs (fonts, code or icons) **Ressourcenzweig**; **resource sharing** = the use of one resource in a network *or* system by several users **gemeinsame Betriebsmittelbenutzung**

respond *verb* to reply *or* to react because of something **beantworten**

◊ **response** *noun* reaction caused by something **Antwort**; **response frame** = page in a videotext system that allows a user to enter data **Antwortrahmen**; **response position** = area of a form that is to be used for optical mark reading data **Markierungsstelle**; **response time** = (i) time which passes between the user starting an action (by pressing a key) and the result appearing on the screen; (ii) speed with which a system responds to a stimulus **(i)** Beantwortungszeit; **(ii) Antwortzeit;** *the response time of this flight simulator is very good*

restart *verb* to start again **wiederanlaufen;** *first try to restart your system*

restore *verb* to put back into an earlier state **rückstellen**

QUOTE first you have to restore the directory that contains the list of deleted files

Personal Computer World

.**restrict** *verb* to keep something within a certain limit; to allow only certain people to access information **einschränken;** *the document is restricted, and cannot be placed on open access*

◊ **restriction** *noun* something which restricts (data flow *or* access) **Einschränkung**

result *noun* answer *or* outcome of an arithmetic *or* logical operation **Ergebnis; result code** = message sent from a modem to the local computer indicating the state of the modem **Ergebniscode**

resume *verb* to restart the program from the point where it was left, without changing any data **wiederaufnehmen**

retain *verb* to keep **festhalten**

◊ **retention** *noun* keeping **Zurückhalten; image retention** = time taken for a TV image to disappear after it has been displayed, caused by long persistence phosphor **Bildkonservierung**

retouch *verb* to change a print *or* photograph slightly by hand, to make it clearer *or* to remove any blemishes **retuschieren;** *I retouched the scratch mark on the last print; the artwork for the line drawings needs retouching in places*

retrain *verb* to re-establish a better quality connection when the quality of a line is very bad **resynchronisieren**

retransmit *verb* to transmit again (a received signal) **erneut übertragen**

◊ **retransmission** *noun* signal *or* data that has been retransmitted **nochmalige Übertragung**

retrieval *noun* the process of searching, locating and recovering information from a

file *or* storage device **Wiederauffinden; information retrieval** = locating quantities of data stored in a database and producing information from the data **Informationswiedergewinnung; information retrieval centre** = research system, providing specific information from a database for a user **Datenbankzentrale; text retrieval** = information retrieval system that allows the user to examine complete documents rather than just a reference to a document **Wiederauffinden eines Textes**

◊ **retrieve** *verb* to extract information from a file *or* storage device **herausfinden;** *these are the records retrieved in that search; this command will retrieve all names beginning with S*

retro- *prefix* meaning going back; progress backwards **Rück-, rück-; retrofit** = device *or* accessory added to a system to upgrade it **Nachrüstung**

retrospective parallel running *noun* running a new computer system with old data to check if it is accurate **rückweisender Parallellauf**

◊ **retrospective search** *noun* search of documents on a certain subject since a certain date **rückwärtsgerichtete Suche**

return *noun*
(a) instruction that causes program execution to return to the main program from a subroutine **Rücksprung;** *the program is not working because you missed out the return instruction at the end of the subroutine;* **return address** = address to be returned to after a called routine finishes **Rücksprungadresse**
(b) key on a keyboard used to indicate that all the required data has been entered **Eingabetaste;** *you type in your name and code number then press return*
(c) indication of an end of line (in printing) **Zeilenbruch; carriage return (CR)** = code *or* key to indicate the end of an input line and to move the cursor to the start of the next line **Rücklauftaste**

◊ **return to zero signal** recording reference mark taken as the level of unmagnetized tape **Rückkehr-nach-Null-Signal** NOTE: opposite is **non return to zero**

COMMENT: the return address is put on the stack by the call instruction and provides the address of the instruction after the call, which is to be returned to after the called routine has finished

reveal *verb* to display previously hidden

information once a condition has been met **aufdecken**

reverse

1 *adjective* going in the opposite direction **rückwärts; reverse channel** = low speed control data channel between a receiver and transmitter **Rückkanal, Hilfskanal; reverse characters** = characters which are displayed in the opposite way to other characters for emphasis (as black on white *or* white on black, when other characters are the opposite) **invertierte Zeichen, umgekehrte Schrift; reverse engineering** = method of product design in which the finished item is analysed to determine how it should be constructed **Umkehrentwurf, Reverse Engineering; reverse index** = movement of a printer head up half a line to print superscripts **rückläufiger Index; reverse interrupt** = signal sent by a receiver to request the termination of transmissions **Betriebsunterbrechungsanfrage; reverse polarity** = situation where the positive and negative terminals have been confused, resulting in the equipment not functioning **umgekehrte Polarität (durch Umpolung); reverse Polish notation (RPN)** = mathematical operations written in a logical way, so that the operator appears after the numbers to be acted upon, this removes the need for brackets **Postfixschreibweise;** *three plus four, minus two is written in RPN as 3 4 + 2 - = 5; normal notation: (x-y) + z, but using RPN: xy - z+; same as* POSTFIX NOTATION; **reverse video** = screen display mode where white and black are reversed (colours are complemented) **invertierte Darstellung**
2 *verb* to go *or* travel in the opposite direction; to send (control) data from a receiver to a transmitter **umkehren**

QUOTE the options are listed on the left side of the screen, with active options shown at the top left in reverse video
PC User

revert *verb* to return to a normal state **zurückfallen in;** *after the rush order, we reverted back to our normal speed;* **revert command** = command (in text) that returns a formatted page to its original state **Rücknahmebefehl**

review *verb* to see again *or* replay and check **überprüfen;** *the program allows the user to review all wrongly spelled words*

revise *verb* to update *or* correct a version of a document *or* file **überarbeiten, revidieren;** *the revised version has no mistakes*

rewind *verb* to return a tape *or* film *or* counter to its starting point **zurückspulen;** *the tape rewinds onto the spool automatically*

rewrite

1 *verb* to write something again **neu schreiben;** *see also* REGENERATE
2 *noun* act of writing something again **erneuter Schreibvorgang;** *the program is in its second rewrite*

RF = RADIO FREQUENCY electromagnetic spectrum that lies between the frequency range 10KHz and 3000GHz **HF; RF modulator** *or* **radio frequency modulator** = electronic circuit that modulates a high frequency carrier signal with a video signal to enable it to be displayed on a domestic TV **Hochfrequenzmodulator; RF shielding** = thin metal foil wrapped around a cable that prevents the transmission of radio frequency interference signals **HF-Abschirmung;** *without RF shielding, the transmitted signal would be distorted by the interference*

RGB = RED, GREEN, BLUE method of producing colours by mixing the light made up of three primary colours red, green and blue **RGB**

◊ **RGB display** *or* **monitor** *noun* high-definition monitor system that uses three separate input signals controlling red, green and blue colour picture beams **RGB-Bildschirm**

rheostat *noun* resistance with a movable wiper that will provide a variable output voltage **Regelwiderstand, Rheostat** NOTE: also called **variable potential divider**

RI = RING INDICATOR

ribbon *noun* long thin flat piece of material **Band; printer ribbon** = roll of inked material which passes between a printhead and the paper **Farbband; ribbon cable** = number of insulated conductors arranged next to each other forming a flat cable **Bandkabel**

right *adjective* not left **rechts; right justify** = to align the right margin so that the text is straight **rechts ausrichten; right justification** = aligning the text and spacing characters so that the right margin is straight **Rechtsausrichtung; right shift** = to move a section of data one bit to the right **nach**

rechts verschieben; *see also* LOGICAL SHIFT, ARITHMETIC SHIFT

rightsizing *noun* process of moving a company's information technology structure to the most cost-effective hardware platform; often used to mean moving from a mainframe-based network to a PC-based network **Rightsizing**

rigid *adjective* hard *or* which cannot bend **starr; rigid disk** = rigid magnetic disk that is able to store many times more data than a floppy disk, and usually cannot be removed from the disk drive **Festplatte**

ring
1 *noun*
(a) data list whose last entry points back to the first entry **Ring; ring (data) network** = type of network where each terminal is connected one after the other in a circle **Ringnetz;** *see also* CHAINED LIST
(b) topology of a network in which the wiring sequentially connects one workstation to another **Ringtopologie; Token Ring network** = IEEE 802.5 standard that uses a token passed from one workstation to the next in a ring network a workstation can only transmit data if it captures the token (Token Ring networks, although logically a ring, are often physically wired in a star topology) **Token-Ring-Netzwerk;** *Token Ring networks are very democratic and retain performance against increasing load; compare* BUS NETWORK, ETHERNET
2 *verb* to telephone **anrufen; ring back system** = remote computer system in which a user attempting to access it phones once, allows it to ring a number of times, disconnects, waits a moment, then redials (usually in a bulletin board system) **Rückrufsystem; ring down** = to call a number of users in a telephone network **einen Rundruf machen; ring indicator (RI)** = signal from a line answering device that it has detected a call to the DTE and has answered by going into an off-hook state **Anrufsignal**

◊ **ring counter** *noun* electronic counter in which any overflow from the last digit is fed into the input **Ringzählwerk**

◊ **ring shift** *noun* data movement to the left *or* right in a word, the bits falling outside the word boundary are discarded, the free positions are filled with zeros **Ringverschiebung**

RIP = RASTER IMAGE PROCESSOR

ripple *noun* small alternating current voltage apparent on a badly regulated direct current output supply **Brummspannung**

◊ **ripple-through carry** *noun* one operation producing a carry out from a sum and a carry in **Schnellübertrag**

◊ **ripple-through effect** *noun* (in a spreadsheet) results *or* changes *or* errors appearing in a spreadsheet as a result of the value in one cell being changed **Schneeballeffekt**

RISC REDUCED INSTRUCTION SET COMPUTER CPU design whose instruction set contains a small number of simple fast-executing instructions, that makes program writing more complex, but increases speed **Computer mit reduziertem Befehlsvorrat;** *see also* WISC

rise time *noun* time taken for a voltage to increase its amplitude (from 10 to 90 per cent or zero to RMS value of its final amplitude) **Anlaufzeit; the circuit has a fast rise time** = electronic circuit that is able to handle rapidly changing signals such as very high frequency signals **der Schaltkreis hat eine schnelle Anlaufzeit**

RJ11 connector *noun* popular standard of four-wire modular connector **RJ11-Anschluss**

◊ **RJ45 connector** *noun* popular name for an eight-pin modular connector used in 10BaseT networks to connect UTP cables **RJ45-Anschluss**

RJE = REMOTE JOB ENTRY batch processing system where instructions are transmitted to the computer from a remote terminal **Jobferneingabe**

RLL encoding = RUN-LENGTH LIMITED ENCODING fast and efficient method of storing data onto a disk in which the changes in a run of data bits is stored **RLL-Codierung**

rm (in UNIX) command to remove an empty subdirectory **rm**

◊ **RMDIR** *or* **RD** = REMOVE DIRECTORY (in DOS) command to remove an empty subdirectory **RMDIR** *or* **RD**

RMS = ROOT MEAN SQUARE; **RMS line current** = the root mean square of the electrical current on a line **Effektivstrom**

RO = RECEIVE ONLY computer terminal

that can only accept and display data, not transmit **Empfänger**

roam *verb* (in wireless communications) to move around freely and still be in contact with a wireless communications transmitter **roamen**

robot *noun* device which can be programmed to carry out certain manufacturing tasks which are similar to tasks carried out by people **Roboter**

◊ **robotics** *noun* study of artificial intelligence, programming and building involved with robot construction **Robotik**

> QUOTE so far no robot sensor has been devised which can operate quickly enough to halt the robot if a human being is in its path of work
>
> *IEE News*

robust *adjective* solid *or* (system) which can resume working after a fault **robust, widerstandsfähig**; *this hard disk is not very robust*

◊ **robustness** *noun*
(a) strength of a system's casing and its ability to be knocked *or* dropped **Widerstandsfähigkeit**
(b) system's ability to continue functioning even with errors *or* faults during a program execution **Gutmütigkeit**

rogue indicator *noun* special code used only for control applications such as end of file marker **Endmarke**

◊ **rogue value** *or* **terminator** *noun* item in a list of data, which shows that the list is terminated **Endmarke**

role indicator *noun* symbol used to show the role of a index entry in its particular context **Funktionsanzeiger**

roll
1 *noun* length of film *or* tape wound around itself **Rolle**; *he put a new roll of film into the camera*
2 *verb*
(a) to rotate a device about its axis **rollen**
(b) to start filming **die Kameras laufen lassen; roll in/roll out** = the transfer of one process (in a multiprogramming system) from storage to processor then back once it has had its allocated processing time **ein-/ausspeichern**

◊ **rollback** *noun* reloading software after the master software has been corrupted **Neuladen**

◊ **roll-in** *verb* to transfer data from backing store into main memory **einspeichern**

◊ **rolling headers** *noun* titles *or* headers of (teletext) pages displayed as they are received **rollende Kopfzeilen**

◊ **roll-out** *verb* to save the contents of main memory onto backing store **ausspeichern**

◊ **rollover** *noun* keyboard with a small temporary buffer so that it can still transmit correct data when several keys are pressed at once **Tastatur mit überlappender Eingabe; key rollover** = use of a buffer between the keyboard and computer to provide rapid keystroke storage for fast typists **Tastenüberlappungspuffer**

◊ **roll scroll** *verb* displayed text that moves up *or* down the computer screen one line at a time **zeilenweises Blättern**

ROM = READ ONLY MEMORY; **CD-ROM** *or* **compact disk-ROM** = small plastic disk which is used as a high capacity ROM device; data is stored in binary form as holes etched on the surface which are then read by a laser **CD-ROM; ROM BIOS** = code which makes up the BIOS routines stored in a ROM chip (normally executed automatically when the computer is switched on) **ROM-BIOS; ROM cartridge** = software stored in a ROM mounted in a cartridge that can be easily plugged into a computer **ROM-Kassette**

◊ **romware** *noun* software which is stored in ROM **ROM-Software**

roman *noun* ordinary typeface, neither italic nor bold **Antiqua**; *the text is set in Times Roman*

◊ **Roman numerals** *noun* figures written I, II, III, IV, etc. (as opposed to Arabic numerals such as 1, 2, 3, 4, etc.) **römische Zahlen**

root *noun*
(a) starting node from which all paths branch in a data tree structure **Stamm; root directory** = (in a disk filing system) the topmost directory from which all other directories branch **Stammverzeichnis;** *in DOS, the root directory on drive C: is called C:*
(b) fractional power of a number **Wurzel; square root** = number raised to the power one half **Quadratwurzel;** *the square root of 25 is 5;* **root mean square (RMS)** = measure of the amplitude of a signal (equal to the square root of the mean value of the signal)

Effektivwert; *the root mean square of the pure sinusoidal signal is 0.7071 of its amplitude*

rotary *adjective* which works by turning **rotierend, Dreh-; rotary camera** = camera able to photograph microfilm as it is moved in front of the lens by moving the film at the same time **Rotationskamera; rotary press** = printing press whose printing plate is cylindrical **Rotationspresse**

◊ **rotate** *verb* to move data within a storage location in a circular manner **rotieren**

◊ **rotation** *noun* amount by which an object has been rotated **Rotation; bit rotation** *or* **rotate operation** = shifting a pattern of bits in a word to the left or right, the old last bit moving to the new first bit position **Rotationsoperation; matrix rotation** = swapping the rows with the columns in an array (equal to rotating by 90 degrees) **Matrixdrehung;** *see also* SHIFT (CYCLIC)

round

1 *adjective* which goes in a circle **rund; round robin** = way of organizing the use of a computer by several users, who each use it for a time and then pass it on the next in turn **Ringmodell, Reihum-Methode**

2 *verb* **to round down** = to approximate a number to a slightly lower one of lower precision **abrunden;** *we can round down 2.651 to 2.65;* **to round off** = to approximate a number to a slightly larger *or* smaller one of lower precision **auf-, abrunden;** *round off 23.456 to 23.46;* **round off errors** = inaccuracies in numbers due to rounding off **Auf-, Abrundungsfehler; to round up** = to approximate a number to a slightly larger one of lower precision **aufrunden;** *we can round up 2.647 to 2.65*

◊ **rounding** *noun*
(a) approximation of a number to a slightly larger *or* smaller one of lower precision **Runden; rounding error** = error in a result caused by rounding off the number **Rundungsfehler**
(b) giving graphics a smoother look **Abrundung; character rounding** = making a displayed character more pleasant to look at (within the limits of pixel size) by making sharp corners and edges smooth **Zeichenrundungen**

route *noun* path taken by a message between a transmitter and receiver in a network **Leitweg;** *the route taken was not the most direct since a lot of nodes were busy*

◊ **router** *noun* (i) communications device that receives data packets in a particular protocol and forwards them to their correct location via the most efficient route; (ii) (in a LAN) device that connects two or more LANs and allows data to be transmitted between each network **(i) Leitwegprogramm; (ii) Router**

◊ **routing** *noun* determining a suitable route for a message through a network **Wegewahl;** *there is a new way of routing data to the central computer;* **routing overheads** = actions that have to be taken when routing messages **Maßnahmen zur Leitwegbestimmung;** *the information transfer rate is very much less once all routing overheads have been accommodated;* **routing page** = videotext page describing the routes to other pages **Leitwegseite; routing table** = list of preferred choices for a route for a message **Leitwegtabelle**

routine *noun* a number of instructions that perform a particular task, but are not a complete program; they are included as part of a program **Programm, Routine;** *the routine copies the screen display onto a printer; the RETURN instruction at the end of the routine sends control back to the main program;* **closed routine** *or* **closed subroutine** = one section of code at a location, that is used by all calls to the routine **geschlossenes Programm; abgeschlossenes Unterprogramm; fall back routines** = routines that are called *or* processes which are executed by a user when a machine *or* system has failed **Wiederanlaufroutine; floating-point routines** = set of routines that allow floating-point numbers to be handled and processed **Gleitkommaprogramm; input routine** = short section of code that accepts data from an external device, such as reading an entry from a keyboard **Eingabeprogramm; open routine** *or* **open subroutine** = set of instructions in a routine, that are copied to whichever part of the program requires them **offenes Programm; offenes Unterprogramm; packing routine** = program which packs data into a small storage area **Verdichtungsprogramm;** *see also* CALL, RETURN

COMMENT: routines are usually called from a main program to perform a task, control is then returned to the part of the main program from which the routine was called once that task is complete

QUOTE Hewlett Packard has announced software which aims to reduce PC-network downtime and cut support costs by automating housekeeping routines such as issuing alerts about potential problems

Computing

row *noun*
(a) (i) line of printed *or* displayed characters; (ii) horizontal line on a punched card **(i) Zeile; (ii) Lochzeile;** *the figures are presented in rows, not in columns; each entry is separated by a row of dots*
(b) horizontal set of data elements in an array *or* matrix **Sprosse**

RPC = REMOTE PROCEDURE CALL method of communication between two programs running on two separate, but connected, computers

RPG = REPORT PROGRAM GENERATOR

RS-232C EIA approved standard used in serial data transmission, covering voltage and control signals **RS-232C; RS-422** = EIA approved standard that extends the RS-232's 50ft limit; **RS-423** = EIA approved standard that extends the RS-232's 50ft limit, introduced at the same time as the RS-422 standard, but less widely used

COMMENT: the RS-232C has now been superceeded by the RS-422 and RS-423 interface standards, similar to the RS-232, but allowing higher transmission rates

RSA cipher system the Rivest, Shamir and Adleman public key cipher system **Kryptosystem RSA**

RS-flip-flop = RESET-SET FLIP-FLOP electronic bistable device whose output can be changed according to the Reset and Set inputs **RS-Kippstufe;** *see also* FLIP-FLOP

RSI = REPETITIVE STRAIN INJURY

RTE = REAL TIME EXECUTION

RTL = RESISTOR-TRANSISTOR LOGIC

RTS = REQUEST TO SEND SIGNAL

rubber banding *see* ELASTIC BANDING

rubout *see* ERASE

rubric *noun* printed headings of a book chapter *or* section **Rubrik, Überschrift**

rule *noun*
(a) set of conditions that describe a function **Regel;** *the rule states that you wait for the clear signal before transmitting;* **rule-based system** = software that applies the

rules and knowledge defined by experts in a particular field to a user's data to solve a problem **auf Regeln beruhendes System**
(b) thin line in printing **Linie; em rule** = dash as long as an em, used to show that words are separated **Trennstrich (in der Größe eines m); en rule** = dash as long as an en, used to show that words are joined **Bindestrich (in der Größe eines n)**

◊ **ruler** *noun* bar displayed on screen that indicates a unit of measurement; often used in DTP or word-processor software to help with layout **Lineal**

run
1 *noun* execution by a computer of a set of instructions *or* programs *or* procedures **Ablauf;** *the next invoice run will be on Friday;* **program run** = executing (in correct order) the instructions in a program **Programmablauf; run indicator** = indicator bit *or* LED that shows that a computer is currently executing a program **Ablaufanzeiger**
2 *verb* to be in operation **in Betrieb sein;** *the computer has been running ten hours a day; do not interrupt the spelling checker while it is running; the new package runs on our PC;* **parallel running** = running old and new computer systems together to allow the new system to be checked before it becomes the only system used **Parallellauf; run around** = to fit text around an image on a printed page **umlaufen; run in** = to operate a system at a lower capacity for a time in case of any faults **mit reduzierter Kraft laufen**

◊ **runaway** *noun* uncontrolled operation of a device *or* computer (due to a malfunction *or* error) **Weglaufen**

◊ **run-length limited encoding (RLL)** fast and efficient method of storing data onto a disk in which the changes in a run of data bits is stored **RLL-Codierung**

◊ **running head** *noun* title line of each page in a document **lebender Kolumnentitel**

◊ **run on** *verb*
(a) to make text continue without a break **ohne Absatz drucken;** *the line can run on to the next without any space*
(b) to print more copies to add to a print run **fortdrucken;** *we decided to run on 3,000 copies to the first printing;* **run-on price** = price of extra copies printed after a fixed print run **Preis für zusätzliche Auflagen**

◊ **run-time** *or* **run-duration**
1 *noun*
(a) period of a time a program takes to run **Durchlaufzeit**

(b) time during which a computer is executing a program **Laufzeit**
2 *adjective* (operation) carried out only when a program is running **Laufzeit-; run-time error** = fault only detected when a program is run *or* error made while a program is running **Laufzeitfehler;** *see also* EXECUTION ERROR; **run-time system** = software that is required in main storage while a program is running (to execute instructions to peripherals, etc.) **Laufzeitsystem**

R/W = READ/WRITE
◊ **R/W cycle** = READ/WRITE CYCLE sequence of events used to retrieve *or* store data **Lese-/Schreibzyklus**

◊ **R/W head** = READ/WRITE HEAD electromagnetic device that allows data to be read from *or* written to a storage medium **Lese-/Schreibkopf**

RX = RECEIVE, RECEIVER; *the RXed signal needs to be amplified*

Ss

S100 bus *or* **S-100 bus** *noun* IEEE-696 standard bus, a popular 8 and 16 bit microcomputer bus using 100 lines and a 100-pin connector **S-100-Bus;** *see also* BUS NOTE: say "S one hundred bus"

SAA = SYSTEMS APPLICATION ARCHITECTURE standard developed by IBM which defines the look and feel of an application regardless of the hardware platform; SAA defines which keystrokes carry out standard functions (such as F1 to display help), the application's display and how the application interacts with the operating system **SAA**

SAFE = SIGNATURE ANALYSIS USING FUNCTIONAL ANALYSIS signature validation technique **Unterschriftsbestätigungsmethode (mit Hilfe von Funktionsanalyse)**

safe area *noun* area of a TV image that will be seen on a standard television set **Rahmen**

◊ **safe format** *noun* format operation

that does not destroy the existing data and allows the data to be recovered in case you formatted the wrong disk **sichere Formatierung**

◊ **safety net** *noun* software *or* hardware device that protects the system *or* files from excessive damage in the event of a system crash **Sicherheitsvorrichtung;** *if there is a power failure, we have a safety net in the form of a UPS*

salami technique *noun* computer fraud involving many separate small transactions that are difficult to detect and trace **Salamitechnik**

SAM = SERIAL ACCESS MEMORY storage where a particular data item can only be accessed by reading through all the previous items in the list (as opposed to random access) **serieller Zugriffsspeicher**

| COMMENT: magnetic tape is a form of SAM; you have to go through the whole tape to access one item, while disks provide random access to stored data

sample
1 *noun* measurement of a signal at a point in time **Stichprobe;** *the sample at three seconds showed an increase;* **sample and hold circuit** = circuit that freezes an analog input signal for long enough for an A/D converter to produce a stable output **Abtast- und Haltekreis**
2 *verb* to obtain a number of measurements of a signal that can be used to provide information about the signal **abtasten; sampling interval** = time period between two consecutive samples **Abtastintervall; sampling rate** = number of measurements of a signal recorded every second **Abtastgeschwindigkeit;** *see also* ANALOG/DIGITAL CONVERSION, QUANTIZE

◊ **sampler** *noun*
(a) electronic circuit that takes many samples of a signal and stores them for future analysis **Abtaster**
(b) electronic circuit used to record audio signals in digital form and store them to allow future playback **Abfrageschalter**

| COMMENT: if the sampling is on a music signal and the sampling frequency is great enough, digitally stored signals sound like the original analog signal. For analog signals, a sampling rate of at least two times the greatest frequency is required to provide adequate detail

sans serif *noun* typeface whose letters

have no serifs **serifenlose Schrift, Groteskschrift**

sapphire *noun* blue-coloured precious stone used as a substrate for certain chips **Saphir**

SAR = STORE ADDRESS REGISTER register within the CPU that contains the address of the next location to be accessed **Speicheradressregister**

SAS = SINGLE ATTACHMENT STATION

satellite *noun*
(a) device that orbits the earth receiving, processing and transmitting signals *or* generating images *or* data to be transmitted back to earth, such as weather pictures **Satellit; communications satellite** = satellite that relays radio *or* TV signals from one point on the earth's surface to another **Nachrichtensatellit; direct broadcast satellite (DBS)** = TV and radio signal broadcast over a wide area from an earth station via a satellite to homes (received with a dish aerial) **direktstrahlender Satellit; weather satellite** = device that orbits the earth, transmitting images of the weather systems above the earth's surface **Wettersatellit; satellite broadcasting** = sending public radio and TV signals from one part of the earth to another, using a communications satellite **Satellitenrundfunk; satellite link** = use of a satellite to allow the transmission of data from one point on earth to another **Satellitenstrecke; satellite network** = series of satellites which provide wide coverage of an area **Satellitennetz**
(b) small system that is part of a larger system **Satellit; satellite computer** = computer doing various tasks under the control of another computer **Satellitenrechner; satellite terminal** = computer terminal that is outside the main network **Satellitendatenstation**

> COMMENT: in a network the floppy disk units are called 'satellites' and the hard disk unit the 'server'. In a star network each satellite is linked individually to a central server

saturation *noun* point where a material cannot be further magnetized **Sättigung; saturation noise** = errors due to saturation of a magnetic storage medium **Sättigungsstörung; saturation testing** = testing a communications network, by transmitting large quantities of data and messages over it **Sättigungstesten**

save *verb* to store data *or* a program on an

auxiliary storage device **speichern, sichern;** *this WP saves the text every 15 minutes in case of a fault don't forget to save the file before switching off;* **save area** = temporary storage area of main memory, used for registers and control data **Zwischenspeicherbereich; save as** = option in an application that allows the user to save the current work in a file with a different name **Speichern unter**

sawtooth waveform *noun* waveform that regularly rises to a maximum and drops to a minimum in a linear way **Sägezahnschwingung**

SBC = SINGLE BOARD COMPUTER computer whose main components such as processor, input/output and memory are all contained on one PCB **Einplatinenrechner**

S-box *noun* matrix transformation process used in certain cipher systems **S-Box-Verfahren**

scalable font *noun* method of describing a font so that it can produce characters of different sizes **skalierbare Schriftart;** *see also* OUTLINE FONT

◊ **scalable software** *noun* groupware application that can easily accommodate more users on a network without having to invest in new software **skalierbare Software**

scalar *noun* variable that has a single value assigned to it **Skalar;** *a scalar has a single magnitude value, a vector has two or more positional values;* **scalar data** = data type containing single values which are predictable and follow a sequence **skalare Daten; scalar processor** = processor designed to operate at high-speed on scalar values **skalarer Prozessor; Scalar Processor Architecture (SPARC)** ™ = RISC processor designed by Sun Microsystems and used in its range of workstations **Scalar Processor Architecture (SPARC)** ™; **scalar variable** = variable which can contain a single value rather than a complex data type (such as an array or record) **skalare Variable; scalar value** = single value rather than a matrix or record (scalar values are not normally floating-point numbers) **Skalarwert**

scale
1 *noun* ratio of two values **Maßstab; large scale** *or* **small scale** = working with large *or* small amounts of data **im großen/kleinen Maßstab; large scale integration (LSI)** =

integrated circuit with 500 - 10,000 components **Großintegration; medium scale integration (MSI)** = integrated circuit with 10 - 500 components **mittlere Integration; small scale integration (SSI)** = integrated circuit with 1 - 10 components **Kleinintegration; super large scale integration (SLSI)** = integrated circuit with more than 100,000 components **Größtintegration; very large scale integration (VLSI)** = integrated circuit with 10,000 - 100,000 components **Übergroßintegration**
2 *verb* **to scale down** *or* **scale up** = to lower *or* increase in proportion **verkleinern; vergrößern**

scan
1 *noun* examination of an image *or* object *or* list of items to obtain data **Abtastung;** *the heat scan of the computer quickly showed which component was overheating; the scan revealed which records were now out of date;* **raster scan** = one sweep of the picture beam horizontally across the front of the CRT screen **Rasterabtastung; scan area** = section of an image read by a scanner **Abtastbereich; scan code** = number transmitted from the keyboard to an IBM PC compatible computer to indicate that a key has been pressed and to identify the key **Suchcode; scan head** = device used in scanners, photocopiers and fax machines, which uses photo-electric cells to turn an image into a pattern of pixels **Abtastkopf;** *this model uses a scan head that can distinguish 256 different colours;* **scan length** = number of items in a file *or* list that are examined in a scan **Abtastlänge; scan line** = one of the horizontal lines of phosphor (or phosphor dots) on the inside of a CRT or monitor; *the monitor's picture beam sweeps along each scan line to create the image on the screen* **Abtastzeile; scan rate** = number of times every second that the image on a CRT is redrawn **Abtastfrequenz**
2 *verb* to examine and produce data from the shape *or* state of an object *or* drawing *or* file *or* list of items **abtasten, durchsuchen;** *the facsimile machine scans the picture and converts this to digital form before transmission; the machine scans at up to 300 dpi resolution*
◊ **scanner** *noun* (usual term for) a device which uses photo-electric cells to convert an image *or* drawing *or* photograph *or* document into graphical data which can be manipulated by a computer; a scanner is connected and controlled by a computer which can then display or process the image data **Scanner, Abtaster;** *a scanner reads the bar-code on the product label using a laser*

beam and photodiode; **scanner memory** = memory area allocated to store images which have been scanned **Abtastspeicherbereich; flatbed scanner** = device with a flat sheet of glass on which the image *or* photograph *or* document is placed; the scan head moves below the glass and converts the image into data which can be manipulated by a computer **Flachbettscanner; hand-held scanner** = device that is held in your hand and contains a row of photo-electric cells which, when moved over an image, convert it into data which can be manipulated by a computer **Handscanner; image scanner** = input device that converts documents *or* drawings *or* photographs into digitized machine-readable form **Bildabtaster; optical scanner** = equipment that converts an image into electrical signals which can be stored in and displayed on a computer **optisches Abtastgerät**

> COMMENT: a scanner can be a device using photoelectric cells as in an image digitizer, or a device that samples data from a process

scanning *noun* action of examining and producing data from the shape of an object *or* drawing **Abtasten; scanning device** = device that allows micrographic images to be selected rapidly from a reel of film **Abtastgerät; scanning error** = error introduced while scanning an image **Abtastfehler; scanning radio receiver** = radio receiver that can check a range of frequencies to find a strong signal *or* a particular station **abtastender Funkempfänger; scanning line** = path traced on a CRT screen by the picture beam **Abtastzeile; scanning rate** = time taken to scan one line of a CRT image **Abtastgeschwindigkeit; scanning resolution** = ability of a scanner to distinguish between small points (usual resolution is 300 dpi) **Abtastauflösungsvermögen; scanning software** = dedicated program that controls a scanner and allows certain operations (rotate *or* edit *or* store, etc.) to be performed on a scanned image **Scannerprogramm; scanning speed** = how fast a line *or* image is scanned **Abtastgeschwindigkeit;** *throughput is 1.3* inches per second scanning speed; its scanning speed is 9.9 seconds for an 8.5 inch by 11 inch document; (of modem) **auto-baud scanning** or **auto-baud sensing** = circuit that can automatically sense and select the correct baud rate for a line **automatischer Baudratenabfühler**

COMMENT: a modem with auto-baud scanning can automatically sense which baud rate to operate on and switches automatically to that baud rate

◊ **scanning spot** noun
(a) small area of an image that is being read by a facsimile machine that moves over the whole image **Abtastfleck**
(b) small area covered by the picture beam on a TV screen that moves to follow a scanning line to write the whole of an image onto the screen **Abtastfleck**; **scanning spot beam** = satellite transmission to a number of areas, as the satellite passes over them **punktförmige Abtastung**

QUOTE scanning time per page ranged from about 30 seconds to three minutes
PC Business World

scatter noun part of a beam that is deflected or refracted **Streuung**; **scatter graph** = individual points or values plotted on a two axis graph **Korrelationsdiagramm**; **scatter proofs** = proofs showing several illustrations, not arranged in any order, prior to PMT **gemischte Fahnen mit Illustrationen**; see also BACKSCATTER

◊ **scatter load** verb to load sequential data into various (non-continuous) locations in memory **gestreut laden**; **scatter read** = to access and read sequential data stored in various (non-continuous) locations **gestreut lesen**

scavenge verb to search through and access database material without permission **unerlaubt durchsuchen**

schedule noun
1 noun order in which tasks are to be done or order in which CPU time will be allocated to processes in a multi-user system **(Zeit)plan**
2 verb to organize the broadcasting of TV or radio programmes at certain times **(zeitlich) planen**

◊ **scheduled circuits** noun telephone lines for data communications only **Datenübertragungsleitungen**

◊ **scheduler** noun
(a) program which organizes use of a CPU or of peripherals which are shared by several users **Zeitplanungsprogramm**
(b) utility software that helps users organise their meetings, appointments or use of a resources (such as a boardroom) **Terminplaner, Scheduler**

◊ **scheduling** noun
(a) method of working which allows several users to share the use of a CPU **Zeitablaufplanung**; **job scheduling** = arranging the order in which jobs are to be processed **Joborganisation**
(b) **programme scheduling** = organizing the broadcasting of radio or TV programmes at certain times **Programmplanung**

schema noun graphical description of a process or database structure **Schema**

◊ **schematic** adjective & noun (diagram) showing system components and how they are connected **schematisch**; **Schema**

scientific adjective referring to science **wissenschaftlich**; **scientific calculator** = specially adapted calculator which has several scientific functions built into it **technisch-wissenschaftlicher Rechner**

scissor verb to remove the areas of text or graphics that lie outside a page's limits **beschneiden**

SCR = SEQUENCE CONTROL REGISTER

scramble verb to code speech or data which is transmitted in such a way that it cannot be understood unless it is decoded **verwürfeln**

◊ **scrambler** noun
(a) device that codes a data stream into a pseudorandom form before transmission to eliminate any series of one's or zero's or alternate one's and zero's that would cause synchronization problems at the receiver and produce unwanted harmonics **Verwürfler**
(b) device that codes speech or other signals prior to transmission so that someone who is listening in without authorization cannot understand what is being transmitted (the scrambled signals are de-scrambled on reception to provide the original signals) **Verwürfler, Scrambler**; he called the President on the scrambler telephone

scrapbook noun utility (on an Apple Macintosh) that stores frequently used graphic images **Album**; we store our logo in the scrapbook

scratch

1 *noun*
(a) area of memory *or* file used for temporary storage of data **Arbeitsbereich**
(b) mark on the surface of a disk **Kratzer;** *this scratch makes the disk unreadable*
2 *verb* to delete *or* move an area of memory to provide room for other data **löschen**

◊ **scratch file** *or* **work file** *noun* work area which is being used for current work **Arbeitsdatei, ungeschützte Datei; scratch tape** = magnetic tape used for a scratch file **Arbeitsband**

◊ **scratchpad** *noun* workspace *or* area of high speed memory that is used for temporary storage of data currently in use **Notizblockspeicher; scratchpad memory** = cache memory used to buffer data being transferred between a fast processor and a slow I/O device (such as a disk drive) **Arbeitspuffer**

> QUOTE Mathcad is described as an easy-to-use 'handy scratchpad for quick number crunching', which is positioned as an alternative to popular spreadsheets
> *Computing*

screen

1 *noun*
(a) display device capable of showing a quantity of information, such as a CRT *or* VDU **Bildschirm;** *see also* READOUT **screen attribute** = (in some operating systems, including DOS) attribute bits which define how each character will be displayed on screen; they set background and foreground colour and bold, italic or underline **Bildschirmattribut; screen border** = margin around text displayed on a screen **Bildschirmrand; screen buffer** = temporary storage area for characters *or* graphics before they are displayed **Bildschirmpuffer; screen dump** = outputting the text *or* graphics displayed on a screen to a printer **Bildschirmausdruck; screen editor** *or* **text editor** = software that allows the user to edit text on-screen, with one complete screen of information being displayed at a time **Bildschirmtexteditor; screen flicker** = (on a display) image that moves slightly or whose brightness alternates due to a low image refresh rate *or* signal corruption **Bildschirmflimmern; screen font** = (in a GUI) typeface and size designed to be used to display text on screen rather than be printed out **Bildschirmschriftart;** *the screen font is displayed at 72dpi on a monitor, rather than printed at 300dpi on this laser printer;* **screen format** = way in which a

screen is laid out **Bildschirmanzeigeformat; screen grab** = (i) digitizing a single frame from a display *or* television; (ii) capturing what is displayed on a monitor and storing it as a graphics file **(i) Herausgreifen eines Bildes; (ii) Screenshot; screen memory** = in a memory-mapped screen, the area of memory that represents the whole screen, usually with one byte representing one *or* a number of pixels **Bildschirmspeicher; screen saver** = software which, after a predetermined period of user inactivity, replaces the existing image on screen and displays objects moving upon screen to protect against screen burn **Bildschirmschoner; on-screen** = information displayed on a screen **am Bildschirm;** *the dtp package offers on-screen font display;* **text screen** = area of a computer screen that has been set up to display text **Textbereich; touch screen** = computer display that allows the user to control the cursor position by touching the screen **Tastbildschirm**
(b) thing which protects **Schirm; magnetic screen** = metal screen to prevent stray magnetic fields affecting electronic components **magnetische Abschirmung;** *without the metal screen over the power supply unit, the computer just produced garbage*
2 *verb*
(a) to protect something with a screen **abschirmen;** *the PSU is screened against interference*
(b) to display *or* show information **vorführen;** *the film is now being screened*
(c) to select **aussortieren**

◊ **screenful** *noun* complete frame of information displayed on a screen **kompletter Bildschirminhalt**

> QUOTE the screen memory is, in fact a total of 4K in size, the first 2K hold the character codes, of which 1K is displayed. Scrolling brings the remaining area into view
> *Computing Today*

script *noun* set of instructions which carry out a function, normally used with a macro language or batch language **Skript;** *I log in automatically using this script with my communications software;* **scripting language** = simple programming language (normally proprietary to an application) that allows a user to automate the application's functions **Skriptsprache;** *this communications software has a scripting language that lets me dial and log in automatically*

scroll *verb* to move displayed text vertically up *or* down the screen, one line *or* pixel at a time **auf-, abrollen, blättern; roll scroll** = displayed text that moves up *or* down the screen one line at a time **zeilenweises Blättern; smooth scroll** = text that is moved up a screen pixel by pixel rather than line by line, which gives a smoother movement **punktweises Blättern; scroll arrows** = (in a GUI) arrows that when clicked, move the contents of the window up or down or sideways **Bildlaufpfeile, Schiebepfeile; scroll bar** = (in a GUI) bar displayed along the side of a window with a marker which indicates how far you have scrolled **Bildlaufleiste, Schiebeleiste;** *the marker is in the middle of the scroll bar so I know I am in the middle of the document;* **Scroll Lock key** = key (on an IBM PC keyboard) that changes how the cursor control keys operate; their function is dependent on the application **Taste „Rollen", Rolltaste; scroll mode** = terminal mode that transmits every key press and displays what is received **Bilddurchlaufmodus**

scrub *verb* to wipe information off a disk *or* remove data from store **löschen;** *scrub all files with the .BAK extension*

SCSI = SMALL COMPUTER SYSTEM INTERFACE standard high-speed parallel interface used to connect computers to peripheral devices (such as disk drives and scanners) **SCSI; Fast-SCSI** = development that allows data to be transferred at a higher rate than with the original SCSI specification **Fast-SCSI; SCSI-2** = newer standard that provides a wider data bus and transfers data faster than the original SCSI specification **SCSI-2; Wide-SCSI** = development that provides a wider data bus than the original SCSI specification, so can transfer more data at a time **Wide-SCSI**

COMMENT: SCSI is the current standard used to interface high-capacity, high-performance disk drives to computers, smaller disk drives are connected with an IDE interface, which is slower, but cheaper. SCSI replaced the older ESDI interface and allows several (normally eight) peripherals to be connected, in a daisy-chain, to one controller

SD = SINGLE DENSITY (DISK)

SDI = SELECTIVE DISSEMINATION OF INFORMATION

SDLC = SYNCHRONOUS DATA LINK CONTROL data transmission protocol most often used in IBM's Systems Network Architecture (SNA) and defines how synchronous data is transmitted **SDLC**

SDR = STORE DATA REGISTER register in a CPU which holds data before it is processed *or* moved to memory location **Speicherdatenregister**

seal *verb* to close something tightly so that it cannot be opened **versiegeln;** *the hard disk is in a sealed case*

seamless integration *noun* the process of including a new device or software into a system without any problems **reibungslose Integration;** *it took a lot of careful planning, but we succeeded in a seamless integration of the new application*

search
1 *noun* process of looking for and identifying a character *or* word *or* section of data in a document *or* file **Suche; chaining search** = searching a file of elements arranged as a chained list **Suche in verknüpfter Liste; linear search** = search method which compares each item in a list with the search key until the correct entry is found (starting with the first item and working sequentially towards the end) **lineare Suche; retrospective search** = search of documents on a certain subject since a certain date **rückwärtsgerichtete Suche; sequential search** = search where each item in a list (starting at the beginning) is checked until the required one is found **sequenzielle Suche; search key** = (i) word *or* phrase that is to be found in a text; (ii) field and other data used to select various records in a database **(i) Suchbegriff; (ii) Suchkriterium; search memory** = method of data retrieval that uses part of the data rather than an address to locate the data **Direktsuche**
2 *verb* to look for an item of data **suchen**

◊ **search and replace** *noun* feature on

word-processors which allows the user to find certain words *or* phrases, then replace them with another word *or* phrase **Suchen und Ersetzen, Ersetzungsfunktion; global search and replace** = word-processor search and replace function covering a complete file *or* document **globales Suchen und Ersetzen**

◊ **searching storage** *noun* method of data retrieval that uses part of the data rather than an address to locate the data **Direktsuche**

QUOTE a linear search of 1,000 items takes 500 comparisons to find the target, and 1,000 to report that it isn't present. A binary search of the same set of items takes roughly ten divisions either to find or not to find the target
Personal Computer World

SECAM *short for* SYSTEME ELECTRONIQUE COULEUR AVEC MEMOIRE standard which defines TV and video formats in France, the USSR and Saudi Arabia. It is similar to PAL, and uses 625 horizontal scan lines and 50 frames per second **SECAM**

second *adjective* (thing) which comes after the first **zweite(r,s)**; *we have two computers, the second one being used if the first is being repaired;* **second generation computers** = computer which used transistors instead of valves **Computer der zweiten Generation; second-level addressing** = instruction that contains an address at which the operand is stored **indirekte Adressierung; second sourcing** = granting a licence to another manufacturer to produce an electronic item *or* component when production capacity is not great enough to meet demand **einen Zweitlieferanten ernennen; second user** *or* **second hand** = (old equipment) that has already been used and is to be sold again **Gebrauchtgerät**

◊ **secondary** *adjective* second in importance *or* less important than the first **zweitrangig, Sekundär-, sekundär-; secondary channel** = second channel containing control information transmitted at the same time as data **Zweitkanal; secondary colour** = colour produced from two primary colours **Sekundärfarbe; secondary station** = temporary status of a station that is receiving data **Folgestation; secondary storage** = any data storage medium (such as magnetic tape *or* floppy disk) that is not the main, high-speed computer storage (RAM) **Sekundärspeicher**

COMMENT: this type of storage is usually of a higher capacity, lower cost and slower access time than main memory

section *noun* part of a main program that can be executed in its own right, without the rest of the main program being required **Abschnitt**

sector
1 *noun* smallest area on a magnetic disk that can be addressed by a computer; the disk is divided into concentric tracks, and each track is divided into sectors which, typically, can store 512 bytes of data **Sektor; bad sector** = sector which has been identified as faulty and cannot be used to reliably store data (bad sectors are stored in a sector map) **schadhafter** *or* **defekter Sektor; sector interleave** = ratio of sectors skipped between access operations on a hard disk; in a hard disk with an interleave of 3, the first sector is read, then three sectors are skipped and the next sector is read; this is used to allow hard disks with slow access time to store more data on the disk. **Sektorenversatz; sector map** = table which contains the addresses of unusable sectors on a hard disk **Sektorentabelle**
2 *verb* to divide a disk into a series of sectors **sektorieren, in Sektoren unterteilen; (disk) sector formatting** = dividing a disk into a series of addressable sectors (a table of their addresses is also formed, allowing each sector to be accessed) **(Platten)sektorformatierung; sectoring hole** = hole in the edge of a disk to indicate where the first sector is located **Sektorierungsloch; hard-sectored** = disk with sector start locations described by holes *or* other physical marks on the disk, which are set when the disk is manufactured **hartsektoriert; soft-sectored** = disk where sectors are described by an address and start code data written onto it when the disk is formatted **weichsektoriert;** *see also* FORMAT

COMMENT: a disk is divided into many tracks, each of which is then divided into a number of sectors which can hold a certain number of bits

secure system *noun* system that cannot be accessed without authorization **Sicherheitssystem**

◊ **secured** *adjective* (file) that is protected against accidental writing *or* deletion *or* against unauthorized access **gesichert**

◊ **security** *noun* being protected *or* being secret **Sicherheit;** *the system has been* *designed to assure the security of the stored data;* security backup = copy of a disk *or* tape *or* file kept in a safe place in case the working copy is lost *or* damaged **Sicherheitskopie;** security check = identification of authorized users (by a password) before granting access **Sicherheitsprüfung**

seed *noun* starting value used when generating random or pseudorandom numbers **Startwert**

seek *verb* to try to find **suchen; seek area =** section of memory that is to be searched for a particular item of data *or* a word **Suchbereich; seek time =** time taken by a read/write head to find the right track on a disk **Positionierzeit;** *the new hard disk drive has a seek time of just 35mS*

segment
1 *noun* section of a main program that can be executed in its own right, without the rest of the main program being required **(Programm)segment; LAN segment =** (i) (in a bus network) an electrically continuous piece of cable; (ii) part of a network separated from the rest by a bridge **(i) & (ii) LAN-Segment**
2 *verb* to divide a long program into shorter sections which can then be called up when required **segmentieren, in Abschnitte unterteilen;** *see also* OVERLAY; **segmented address space =** memory address space divided into areas called segments; to address a particular location, the segment and offset values must be specified **segmentierter Adressraum**

QUOTE you can also write in smaller program segments. This simplifies debugging and testing
                Personal Computer World

select *verb* to find and retrieve specific information from a database **auswählen; chip select (CS) =** single line on a chip that will enable it to function when a signal is present (often ICs do not function even when power is applied, until a CS signal is provided) **Bausteinauswahl**

◊ **selectable** *adjective* which can be selected **auswählbar; jumper-selectable =** circuit *or* device whose options can be selected by positioning various wire connections **Brückenauswahlschaltung; selectable attributes =** the function *or* attributes of a device which can be chosen by the user **Auswahlfunktion; user-selectable** = which can be chosen or selected by the

user **vom Benutzer auswählbar; this modem has user-selectable baud rates =** the receive and transmit baud rates of the modem can be chosen by the user, and are not preset **dieses Modem hat vom Benutzer wählbare Schrittgeschwindigkeiten**

◊ **selection** *noun* action *or* process of selecting **Auswahl;** *selection of information from a large database may take some time*

◊ **selective** *adjective* which chooses certain items **wahlweise, selektiv; trennscharf; selective calling =** calling a remote station from a main site **selektiver Abruf; selective dump =** display *or* printout of a selected area of memory **selektiver Speicherauszug; selective sort =** sorting a section of data items into order **Auswahlsortierung**

◊ **selectivity** *noun* ability of a radio receiver to distinguish between two nearby carrier frequencies **Trennschärfe**

◊ **selector** *noun* mechanical device that allows a user to choose an option *or* function **Selektor, Wähler;** *the selector knob for the amplification is located there turn the selector control;* **selector channel =** communications link that operates with only one transmitter/receiver at a time **Selektorkanal**

self- *prefix* referring to oneself **Selbst-, selbst-; self-adapting system =** system that can adapt itself to various tasks **selbstanpassendes System; self-checking system =** system that carries out diagnostic tests on itself usually at switch on **automatisches Prüfungssystem; self-checking code =** character coding system that can detect an error *or* bad character but not correct it **Fehlererkennungscode; self-correcting code =** character coding system that can detect and correct an error *or* bad character **selbstkorrigierender Code; self-diagnostic =** computer that runs a series of diagnostic programs (usually when it is switched on) to ensure that it is all working correctly, often memory, peripherals and disk drives are tested **selbstdiagnostisch; self-documenting program =** computer program that provides the user with operating instructions as it runs **selbstdarstellendes Programm; self-learning =** (expert system) that adds each new piece of information or rule to its database, improving its knowledge, expertise and performance as it is used **selbstlernendes (Computer)system; self-refreshing RAM =** dynamic RAM chip that has built in circuitry to generate refresh signals, allowing data to be retained when the power is off, using battery back-up **selbstregenerierender RAM; self-relocating program** = program that can be loaded into any part of memory (that will modify its addresses depending on the program origin address) **selbstverschiebliches Programm; self-resetting** or **self-restoring loop** = loop that returns any locations or registers accessed during its execution to the state they were in **selbstrücksetzende Schleife**

semantics noun (i) part of language which deals with the meaning of words, parts of words or combinations of words; (ii) (in computing) meanings of words or symbols used in programs **(i) & (ii) Semantik; semantic error** = error due to use of an incorrect symbol within a program instruction **Semantikfehler**

semaphore noun
(a) coordination of two jobs and appropriate handshaking to prevent lock-outs or other problems when both require a peripheral or function **Semaphor**
(b) signalling system that uses two flags held in different positions by two mechanical or human arms **Winkeralphabet, Semaphor**

semi- prefix meaning half or partly **Semi-, semi-, Halb-, halb-; semi-processed data** = raw data which has had some processing carried out, such as sorting, recording, error detection, etc. **halbverarbeitete Daten**

semicolon noun printing sign (;) which indicates a separation between parts of a sentence or marks the end of a program line or statement in some languages (such as C and Pascal) **Strichpunkt**

semicompiled adjective (object code) program converted from a source code program, but not containing the code for functions from libraries, etc., that were used in the source code **halbkompiliert**

semiconductor noun material that has conductive properties between those of a conductor (such as a metal) and an insulator **Halbleiter; semiconductor device** = electronic component that is constructed on a small piece of semiconductor (the components on the device are constructed using patterns of insulator or conductor or semiconductor material whose properties have been changed by doping) **Halbleiterbauelement; semiconductor memory** = storage using capacitors

(dynamic memory) or latches and bistables (static memory) constructed as a semiconductor device to store bits of data **Halbleiterspeicher; semiconductor** or **solid-state laser** = piece of semiconductor bar that has a polished end, and a semi-silvered mirror, generating pulses of photons that reflect inside the bar until they have enough power to leave via the semi-silvered end **Halbleiterlaser; Festkörperlaser**

COMMENT: semiconductor material (such as silicon) is used as a base for manufacturing integrated circuits and other solidstate components, usually by depositing various types of doping substances on or into its surface

sender noun person who sends a message **Absender**

◊ **send-only device** noun device such as a terminal which cannot receive data, only transmit it **Sendegerät**

sense verb to examine the state of a device or electronic component **prüfen;** the condition of the switch was sensed by the program; this device senses the holes punched in a paper tape; **auto-baud sensing** see SCANNING; **sense recovery time** = time that a RAM takes to switch from read to write mode **Lese-Erholzeit; sense switch** = switch on a computer front panel whose state can by examined by the computer **Programmschalter**

◊ **sensitive** adjective which can sense even small changes **sensibel, empfindlich;** the computer is sensitive even to very slight changes in current; light-sensitive film changes when exposed to light

◊ **sensitivity** noun
(a) being sensitive to something **Empfindlichkeit;** the scanner's sensitivity to small objects
(b) minimum power of a received signal that is necessary for a receiver to distinguish the signal **Empfindlichkeit**

◊ **sensor** noun electronic device that produces an output dependent upon the condition or physical state of a process **Messwertgeber, Sensor;** see also TRANSDUCER; the sensor's output varies with temperature; the process is monitored by a bank of sensors; **image sensor** = photoelectric device that produces a signal related to the amount of light falling on it **Lichtsensor**

sentinel noun (i) marker or pointer to a special section of data; (ii) a flag that reports the status of a register after a mathematical *or* logical operation **(i) & (ii) Markierung**

separate
1 *adjective* not together **getrennt; separate channel signalling** = use of independent communications channel *or* bands in a multichannel system to send the control data and messages **getrennte Kanalsignalisierung**
2 *verb* to divide **trennen; separated graphics** = displayed characters that do not take up the whole of a character matrix, resulting in spaces between them **einzeln gestellte Zeichen**

◊ **separation** *noun* act of separating **Trennung; colour separation** = process by which colours are separated into primary colours **Farbauszug, Farbseparation; colour separations** = different artwork *or* film for the various colours to be used in multicolour printing **Farbauszüge**

◊ **separator** *noun* symbol used to distinguish parts of an instruction line in a program, such as command and argument **Trennzeichen;** *see also* DELIMITER

septet *noun* word made up of seven bits **Sieben-Bit-Byte**

sequence *noun* number of items *or* data arranged as a logical, ordered list **Folge, Sequenz;** *the sequence of names is arranged alphabetically; the program instructions are arranged in sequence according to line numbers;* **binary sequence** = series of binary digits **Binärsequenz; control sequence** = (series of) codes containing a control character and various arguments, used to carry out a process *or* change mode in a device **Steuerzeichenfolge; sequence check** = check to ensure that sorted data is in the correct order **Folgekontrolle; sequence control register (SCR)** *or* **sequence counter** *or* **sequence register** *or* **instruction address register** = CPU register that contains the address of the next instruction to be processed **Befehlsfolgeregister; Adressfolgeregister; logon sequence** = order in which user number, password and other authorization codes are to be entered when attempting to access a system **Anmeldesequenz**

◊ **sequencer** *noun* section within a bit-slice microprocessor that contains the next microprogram address **Ablaufsteuerung**

◊ **sequential** *adjective* arranged in an ordered manner **sequenziell, aufeinanderfolgend; queued indexed sequential access method (QISAM)** = indexed sequential file that is read item by item into a buffer **erweiterte indizierte Zugriffsmöglichkeit für sequenzielle Dateien (QISAM); queued sequential access method (QSAM)** = queue of blocks waiting to be processed, retrieved using a sequential access method **erweiterte Zugriffsmöglichkeit für sequenzielle Dateien (QSAM); sequential batch processing** = completing one job in a batch before the next can be started **sequenzielle Stapelverarbeitung; sequential computer** = type of computer, for which each instruction must be completed before the next is started, and so cannot handle parallel processing **sequenzieller Computer; sequential file** *or* **serial file** = stored file whose records are accessed sequentially **sequenzielle Datei; sequential logic** = logical circuit whose output depends on the logic state of the previous inputs **sequenzielle Logik;** *if the input sequence to the sequential logic circuit is 1101 the output will always be zero (0); compare with* COMBINATIONAL CIRCUIT; **sequential mode** = each instruction in a program is stored in consecutive locations **sequenzieller Modus; sequential operation** = operations executed one after the other **sequenzielle Arbeitsweise; sequential processing** = data *or* instructions processed sequentially, in the same order as they are accessed **sequenzielle Verarbeitung;** *see also* INDEXED; **sequential search** = each item in a list (starting at the beginning) is checked until the required one is found **sequenzielle Suche**

◊ **sequentially** *adverb* (done) one after the other, in sequence **sequenziell**

◊ **sequential access** *noun* method of retrieving data from a storage device by starting at the beginning of the medium (such as tape) and reading each record until the required data is found **sequenzieller Zugriff; sequential access storage** = storage medium in which the data is accessed sequentially **Speicher mit sequenziellem Zugriff**

COMMENT: a tape storage system uses sequential access, since the tape has to be played through until the section required is found. The access time of sequential access storage is dependent on the position in the file of the data, compared with random access that has the same access time for any piece of data in a list

Séquentiel à Mémoire (SECAM) standards that define TV and video formats, mainly in France, USSR and Saudi Arabia, using 625 horizontal scan lines and 50 frames per second (similar to PAL) SECAM

serial *adjective* (data *or* instructions) ordered sequentially (one after the other) and not in parallel **seriell, in Reihe; serial access** = one item of the data accessed by reading through all the data in a list until the correct one is found (as on a tape) **serieller Zugriff; serial-access memory (SAM)** = storage where a particular data item can only be accessed by reading all the previous items in the list (as opposed to random access) **Speicher mit seriellem Zugriff; serial adder** = addition circuit that acts on one digit at a time from a larger number **Serienaddierer; serial computer** = computer system that has a single ALU and carries out instructions one at a time **serieller Computer;** *see also* SEQUENTIAL COMPUTER; **serial data transmission** *or* **communications** = transmission of the separate bits that make up data words, one at a time down a single line **serielle Datenübertragung; serial file** = stored file whose records are accessed sequentially **serielle Datei; serial input/output (SIO)** *see* SERIAL TRANSMISSION; **serial input/parallel output (SIPO)** *or* **serial to parallel converter** = device that can accept serial data and transmit parallel data **serielle Eingabe/parallele Ausgabe; Serien-Parallel-Umsetzer; serial input/serial output (SISO)** = *see* SERIAL TRANSMISSION; **serial interface** *or* **port** = circuit that converts parallel data in a computer to and from a serial form that allows serial data to be transmitted and received from other equipment (the most common form is the RS232C interface) **serielle Schnittstelle;** *parallel connections are usually less trouble to set up and use than serial interfaces, but are usually limited to 20 feet in length;* **serial memory** = memory in which data is stored sequentially, only allowing sequential access **serieller Speicher; serial mouse** = mouse which connects to the serial port of a PC and transfers positional data via the serial port **serielle Maus; serial operation** = working of a device on data in a sequential manner **serielle Operation; serial printer** = printer that prints characters one at a time **Seriendrucker, Zeichendrucker; serial processing** = data *or* instructions processed sequentially, in the same order as they are retrieved **serielle Verarbeitung; serial storage** = storage which only allows sequential access **Serienspeicher; serial to parallel**

converter = electronic device that converts data from a serial form to a parallel form **Serien-Parallel-Umsetzer; serial transmission** *or* **serial input/output** = data transmitted one bit at a time (this is the normal method of transmission over long distances, since although slower it uses fewer lines and so is cheaper than parallel transmission) **serielle Übertragung; serielle Ein-/Ausgabe; word serial** = data words transmitted one after the other, along a parallel bus **Wortserie**

◊ **serially** *adverb* one after the other *or* in a series **seriell, in Reihe;** *their transmission rate is 64,000 bits per second through a parallel connection or 19,200 serially*

◊ **series** *noun* group of related items ordered sequentially **Reihe, Serie; series circuit** = circuit in which the components are connected serially **Reihenschaltung**

COMMENT: in a series circuit the same current flows through each component; in a parallel circuit the current flow is dependent upon the component impedance

serif *noun* small decorative line attached to parts of characters in certain typefaces **Serife; sans serif** = typeface without serifs **serifenlose Schrift**

server *noun* dedicated computer *or* peripheral that provides a function to a network **Server; file server** = computer connected to a network which runs a network operating system software to manage user accounts, file sharing and printer sharing **Fileserver; LAN server** = dedicated computer and backing storage facility used by terminals and operators of a LAN **LAN-Server; LAN Server ™** = network operating system for the PC developed by IBM **LAN-Server ™; print server** = computer in a network which is dedicated to managing print queues and printers **Druckserver; server-based application** = application program, stored on a server's hard disk, which can be accessed (and executed) by several users at one time **Serveranwendung; server message block (SMB)** = system (developed by Microsoft) which allows a user to access another computer's files and peripherals over a network as if they were local resources **Server Message Block (SMB)**

COMMENT: in a network the hard disk machine is called the 'server' and the floppy disk units the 'satellites'. In a star network each satellite is linked individually to a central server

> QUOTE Sequent Computer Systems'
> Platform division will focus on hardware
> and software manufacture, procurement
> and marketing, with the Enterprise
> division concentrating on services and
> server implementation
>
> *Computing*

service

1 *verb* to check *or* repair *or* maintain a system warten, instandhalten; *the disk drives were serviced yesterday and are working well* 2 maintenance Wartung; service bureau = company which provides a specialist service, such as outputting DTP files to a typesetter, converting files or creating slides from graphics files Dienst; service bit = transmitted bit that is used for control rather than data Hilfsbit; service contract = agreement that an engineer will service equipment if it goes wrong Wartungsvertrag; service program = useful program that is used for routine activities such as file searching, copying, sorting, debugging, etc. Wartungsprogramm

◊ **services** *noun* (i) set of functions provided by a device; (ii) (in an OSI network model) set of functions provided by one OSI layer for use by a higher layer (i) Funktionen; (ii) Dienste

servo *or* servomechanism *noun*

mechanical device whose position *or* state can be accurately controlled Folgesteuerungsmechanismus

session *noun* (i) period of work; (ii) time

during which a program *or* process is running *or* active (i) Arbeitsabschnitt; (ii) Sitzung; session key = cipher key used for a particular session Verschlüsselung für einen bestimmten Arbeitsabschnitt; session layer = layer in the ISO/OSI standard model that makes the connection/disconnection between transmitter and receiver Sitzungsschicht

set

1 *noun*
(a) number of related data items Gruppe, Satz; character set = all the characters that can be displayed *or* printed Zeichensatz; set theory = mathematics related to numerical sets Mengenlehre
(b) width of a printed typeface Set; set size = measurement of horizontal dimensions in sets (one set equals one point) Setmaß; set width = width of the body of a printed character Kegelbreite
(c) radio *or* television receiver Radio-,

Fernsehgerät; set-top converter = device that converts TV signals from a network *or* satellite into a form that can be displayed Kopfumsetzer
(d) physical layout of a stage *or* filming studio including props and background Bühnenbild; Filmkulisse
2 *verb*
(a) (i) to make one variable equal to a value; (ii) to define a parameter value (i) setzen; (ii) einstellen; *we set the right-hand margin at 80 characters;* set breakpoints = to define the position of breakpoints within a program being debugged Unterbrechungspunkte setzen
(b) to give a bit the value of 1 setzen
(c) to compose a text into typeset characters setzen; *the page is set in 12 point Times Roman; see also* TYPESET

◊ **setting** *noun*
(a) action of fixing *or* arranging something Einstellung; brightness setting = TV brightness control position Helligkeitseinstellung; contrast setting = TV contrast control position Kontrasteinstellung; tab settings = preset points along a line, where the printing head *or* cursor will stop for each tabulation command Tabulatorschritte
(b) action of composing text into typeset characters Setzen; *the MS has been sent to the typesetter for setting; setting charges have increased since last year;* computer setting = typesetting using a computerized typesetting machine Computersatz

set up *verb* to configure *or* initialize *or*

define *or* start an application *or* system einrichten, konfigurieren; *the new computer worked well as soon as the engineer had set it up;* setup option = the choices available when setting up a system Einrichtungsoption, Setup-Option; setup time = period of time between a signal to start an operation and the start Vorbereitungszeit

sexadecimal *see* HEXADECIMAL

◊ **sextet** *noun* byte made up of six bits Sechs-Bit-Byte, Sextett

sex changer *noun* device for changing a

female connection to a male or vice versa Zwischenstück, Adapter

sf signalling = SINGLE FREQUENCY SIGNALLING

SGML = STANDARD GENERALIZED

MARKUP LANGUAGE hardware-independent standard which defines how documents should be marked up to indicate bolds, italics, margins and so on SGML

shade *noun* (i) variation in a printed colour due to added black; (ii) quantity of black added to a colour to make it darker **(i) Schattierung, Farbtönung; (ii) Bildschwarz**

◊ **shading** *noun* showing darker sections of a line drawing by adding dark colour *or* by drawing criss-cross lines **Schraffur, Schattierung**

shadow *noun* area where broadcast signals cannot be received because of an obstacle that blocks the transmission medium **Schatten;** *the mountain casts a shadow over those houses, so they cannot receive any radio broadcasts*

◊ **shadowmask** *noun* sheet with holes placed just behind the front of a colour monitor screen to separate the three-colour picture beams **Lochmaske**

◊ **shadow memory** *or* **page** *noun* duplicate memory locations accessed by a special code **Schattenspeicher; shadow page table** = conversion table that lists real memory locations with their equivalent shadow memory locations **Seitentabelle für Schattenspeicher;** *see also* VIRTUAL

◊ **shadow ROM** *noun* read-only shadow memory **Schatten-ROM**

shannon *noun* measure of the information content of a transmission **Shannon**

◊ **Shannon's Law** *noun* law defining the maximum information carrying capacity of a transmission line **shannonsches Gesetz**

COMMENT: Shannon's Law is defined as B lg(1 + S/N) where B = Bandwidth, lg is logarithm to the base two and S/N is Signal to Noise ratio

share *verb* to own *or* use something together with someone else **gemeinsam benutzen;** *the facility is shared by several independent companies;* **shared access** = computer *or* peripheral used by more than one person *or* system **gemeinsam benutzter Zugang;** *see also* TIME-SHARING SYSTEM, MULTI-USER; **shared bus** = one bus used (usually) for address and data transfer between the CPU and a peripheral **Gemeinschaftsbus; shared directory** = directory (on a file server or workstation) which can be accessed by several users connected to a network **gemeinsames**

Verzeichnis, gemeinsam benutztes Verzeichnis; shared file = stored file that can be accessed by more than one user *or* system **Gemeinschaftsdatei; shared line** *or* **party line** = one telephone line shared by a number of subscribers **Gemeinschaftsleitung; shared logic system** = one computer and backing storage device used by a number of people in a network for an application **zentralisiertes System; shared logic text processor** = word-processing available to a number of users of a shared logic system **gemeinsam benutztes Textverarbeitungssystem; shared memory** = memory that can be accessed by more than one CPU **Gemeinschaftsspeicher; shared network directory** = directory (on a file server or workstation) which can be accessed by several users connected to a network **gemeinsames Netzverzeichnis, gemeinsam benutztes Netzverzeichnis; shared resources system** = system where one peripheral *or* backing storage device *or* other resource is used by a number of users **Mehrplatzsystem; share level security** = network operating system which assigns passwords to resources rather than setting up user accounts to limit access **Sicherheit auf Freigabeebene; time-sharing** = computer system that allows several independent users to use it *or* be on-line at the same time **Gemeinschaftsbetrieb**

◊ **shareware** *noun* software that is available free to try, but if kept the user is expected to pay a fee to the writer (often confused with public domain software which is completely free) **Shareware**

QUOTE Bulletin board users know the dangers of 'flaming' (receiving hostile comments following a naive or ridiculous assertion) and of being seen 'troughing' (grabbing every bit of shareware on the network)
Computing

sheet *noun* large piece of paper **Blatt; (single) sheet feed** = paper feed system which puts single sheets of paper into a printer, one at a time **Einzelblattzufuhr; sheet feed attachment** = device which can be attached to a printer to allow single sheets of paper to be fed in automatically **Einzelblattzuführung**

shelf life *noun* maximum storage time of a product before it is no longer guaranteed good to use **Dauer der Lagerfähigkeit;** *the developer has a shelf life of one year*

shell *noun* software which operates

between the user and the operating system, often to try and make the operating system more friendly or easier to use Shell; *MS-DOS's COMMAND.COM is a basic shell that interprets commands typed in at the prompt; the Macintosh Finder is a sophisticated shell with a GUI front-end*

◊ **shell out** *verb* (when running an application) to exit to the operating system, whilst the original application is still in memory; the user then returns to the application **zur Shell wechseln;** *I shelled out from the word-processor to check which files were on the floppy, then went back to the program*

◊ **shell sort** *noun* algorithm for sorting data items, in which items can be moved more than one position per sort action **"Shell"-Sortierung**

SHF = SUPER HIGH FREQUENCY

shield

1 *noun* metal screen connected to earth, that prevents harmful voltages *or* interference reaching sensitive electronic equipment **Abschirmung**
2 *verb* to protect a signal *or* device from external interference *or* harmful voltages **abschirmen; shielded cable** = cable made up of a conductive core surrounded by an insulator, then a conductive layer to protect the transmitted signal against interference **Isolierkabel; shielded twisted pair (STP) cable** = cable consisting of two insulated copper wires twisted around each other (to reduce induction and so interference), the pair of wires are then wrapped in an insulated shielding layer to further reduce interference **abgeschirmtes verdrilltes Adernpaar; unshielded twisted pair (UTP) cable** = cable made of two insulated copper wires twisted around each other (to reduce induction and so interference), unlike STP cable the pair of wires are not wrapped in any other layer **unabgeschirmtes verdrilltes Adernpaar**

shift *verb*

(a) to move a bit *or* word of data left or right by a certain amount (usually one bit) **verschieben; arithmetic shift** = word *or* data moved one bit to the right *or* left inside a register, losing the bit shifted off the end **arithmetische Stellenverschiebung; cyclic shift** = rotation of bits in a word with the previous last bit inserted in the first bit position **zyklische Stellenverschiebung; logical shift** = data movement to the left *or* right in a word, the bits falling outside the

word boundary are discarded, the free positions are filled with zeros **logische Stellenverschiebung; shift instruction** = computer command to shift the contents of a register to the left or right **Verschiebebefehl; shift left** = left arithmetic shift of data in a word (the number is doubled for each left shift) **Linksverschiebung;** *0110 left shifted once is 1100;* **shift register** = temporary storage into which data can be shifted **Verschieberegister; shift right** = right arithmetic shift of data in a word (the number is halved for each right shift) **Rechtsverschiebung**
(b) to change from one character set to another, allowing other characters (such as capitals) to be used **umschalten; shift character** = transmitted character code that indicates that the following code is to be shifted **Umschaltzeichen; shift code** = method of increasing total possible bit combinations by using a number of bits to indicate the following code is to be shifted **Umschaltcode**

◊ **shift key** *noun* key on a keyboard that switches secondary functions for keys, such as another character set, by changing the output to upper case **Umschalttaste**

shoot *verb* to take a film **aufnehmen, drehen;** *they shot hundreds of feet of film, but none of it was any good; the programme was shot on location in Spain*
NOTE: **shooting - shot**

short *adjective* not long **kurz; short card** = add-on expansion board that is shorter than a standard size **Kurzlochkarte; short haul modem** = modem used to transmit data over short distances (often within a building), usually without using a carrier **Nahbereichsmodem**

short circuit

1 *noun* electrical connection of very low resistance between two points **Kurzschluss**
2 *verb* to connect two points together with a (very low resistance) link **kurzschließen; short-circuited** = two points that are electrically connected, usually accidentally **kurzgeschlossen**

┃ COMMENT: short circuits can be accidental, due to bad circuit design or used as a protective ┃ measure

shorten *verb* to make shorter **kürzen;** *we had to shorten the file to be able to save it on one floppy*

short-run *adjective* with a printrun of

only a few hundred copies **kleine Auflage;** *a printer specializing in short-run printing; the laser printer is good for short-run leaflets*

short wave (SW) *noun* radio communications frequency below 60 metres **Kurzwelle; short-wave receiver** = radio receiver able to pick up broadcasts on the short wave bands **Kurzwellenempfänger**

shotgun microphone *noun* long, highly directional microphone **besonders empfindliches Richtmikrofon**

show-through *noun* text printed on one side of a piece of paper that can be seen from the other **durchscheinender Druck**

shrink *verb* to become smaller **schrumpfen;** *the drawing was shrunk to fit the space*
NOTE: **shrinks - shrank - has shrunk**

shut down *verb* to switch off and stop the functions of a machine *or* system **abschalten**

◊ **shut-off mechanism** *noun* device which stops a process in case of fault **Abschaltmechanismus**

COMMENT: most hard disks have an automatic shut-off mechanism to pull the head back from the read position when the power is turned off

shutter *noun* device on a camera which opens and shuts rapidly allowing light from an object to fall on the film **Verschluss**

SI units = SYSTEME INTERNATIONAL UNITS international measurement units such as candela, lumen, and ampere **internationale Maßeinheiten;** *see also* MKS ⇨APPENDIX

sibilance *noun* excess signal recorded when certain letters such as 's' are spoken **Zischen**

sideband *noun* frequency band of a modulated signal, a little above or below the carrier frequency **Seitenband;** *upper sideband; lower sideband;* **double sideband =** modulation technique whose frequency spectrum contains two modulated signals above and below the unmodulated carrier frequency **Zweiseitenbandübertragung; double sideband suppressed carrier (DSBSC) =** modulation technique that uses two modulated signal sidebands, but no carrier signal **Zweiseitenbandübertragung mit unterdrückter Trägerwelle; single sideband** = modulated signal filtered to leave just one sideband, usually the upper (this is very economical on bandwidth but requires more complex circuitry) **Einseitenband**

side lobe *noun* side sections of an aerial's response pattern **Nebenzipfel**

sideways ROM *noun* software which allows selection of a particular memory bank *or* ROM device **Seiten-ROM-Programm**

SIG = SPECIAL INTEREST GROUP group of people (within a larger club) who are interested in a particular aspect of software or hardware **Fachgruppe;** *our local computer club has a SIG for comms and networking*

sign
1 *noun* polarity of a number *or* signal (whether it is positive *or* negative) **Vorzeichen; sign and modulus** = way of representing numbers, where one bit shows if the number is positive *or* negative (usually 0 = positive, 1 = negative) **Absolutzahl mit Vorzeichen(ziffer); sign bit** *or* **sign indicator** = single bit that indicates if a binary number is positive *or* negative (usually 0 = positive, 1 = negative) **Vorzeichenbit; sign digit** = one digit that indicates if a number is positive *or* negative **Vorzeichenziffer; sign and magnitude** *or* **signed magnitude** = number representation in which the most significant bit indicates the sign of the number, the rest of the bits its value **Größendarstellung mit Vorzeichen; sign position** = digit *or* bit position that contains the sign bit *or* digit **Vorzeichenposition; signed field** = storage field which can contain a number and a sign bit **Feld mit Vorzeichen**
2 *verb* to identify oneself to a computer using a personalized signature **unterschreiben; to sign off** = to logoff a system **sich abmelden; to sign on** = to logon to a system **sich anmelden**

signal
1 *noun* (i) generated analog *or* digital waveform used to carry information; (ii) short message used to carry control codes **(i) & (ii) Signal;** *the signal received from the computer contained the answer;* **interrupt signal** = voltage pulse from a peripheral sent to the CPU requesting attention **Unterbrechungssignal; signal conditioning** = converting *or* translating a signal into a form that is accepted by a device **Signalaufbereitung; signal conversion** = processing, changing or modulating a

signal **Signalumwandlung; signal converter** = device that converts signals from one format to another, usually from UHF to VHF for TV signals **Signalumsetzer; signal distance** = number of bit positions with different contents in two data words **Hammingabstand;** *see also* HAMMING; **signal element** = smallest basic unit used when transmitting digital data **Schritt;** *the signal element in this system is a short voltage pulse, indicating a binary one; the signal elements for the radio transmission system are 10mS of 40KHz and 10mS of 60KHz for binary 0 and 1 respectively;* **signal generator** = device that can produce various signals of varying amplitude, frequency and shape **Zeichengeber; signal to noise ratio (S/N)** = difference between the power of the transmitted signal and the noise on the line **Störabstand, Rauschabstand; signal processing** = processing of signals to extract the information contained **Signalverarbeitung;** *the system is used by students doing research on signal processing techniques; the message was recovered by carrier signal processing* **2** *verb* to send a radio signal *or* a message to a computer **melden;** *signal to the network that we are busy*

◊ **signalling** *noun* (i) method used by a transmitter to warn a receiver that a message is to be sent; (ii) communication to the transmitter about the state of the receiver **(i) & (ii) Signalisierung; in-band signalling** = use of a normal voice grade channel for data transmission **Imband-Signalisierung**

signature *noun*
(a) name written in a special way by someone **Unterschrift;** *do you recognize the signature on the cheque?*
(b) series of printed and folded pages in a book (usually 8, 16 or 32 pages) **Signatur**
(c) special authentication code, such as a password, which a user gives prior to access to a system *or* prior to the execution of a task (to prove identity) **Signatur**

COMMENT: in some systems this can be written by the user or determined from the user in some way (such as fingerprint or eye scan: these are very advanced and secure systems)

signify *verb* to mean **bedeuten;** *a carriage return code signifies the end of an input line*

◊ **significance** *noun* special meaning **Bedeutung**

◊ **significant** *adjective* which has a special meaning **bedeutsam; significant digit**

codes *or* **faceted codes** = codes which indicate various details of an item, by assigning each one a value **bedeutsame Zifferncodes, Facettencodes**

silicon *noun* element with semiconductor properties, used in crystal form as a base for IC manufacture **Silizium; silicon chip** = small piece of silicon in and on the surface of which a complete circuit *or* logic function has been produced (by depositing other substances *or* by doping) **Siliziumchip; silicon disk** *or* **RAM disk** = section of RAM that is made to look and behave like a high speed disk drive **Siliziumplatte; silicon foundry** = machine used to create crystals of silicon, then slice them into silicon wafers **Chip-Produktionsanlage; silicon gate** = type of MOS transistor gate that uses doped silicon regions instead of a metal oxide to provide the function **Siliziumgatter;** *see also* MOS, GATE; **silicon on sapphire (SOS)** = manufacturing technique that allows MOS devices to be constructed onto a sapphire substrate for high speed operation **Silizium-Saphir-Technologie; Silicon Glen** = area of Scotland where many Scottish IT companies are based **Silicon Glen; silicon transistor** = microelectronic transistor manufactured on a silicon semiconductor base **Siliziumtransistor; Silicon Valley** = area in California where many US semiconductor device manufacturers are based **Silicon Valley; silicon wafer** = thin slice of a pure silicon crystal, usually around 4 inches in diameter on which integrated circuits are produced (these are then cut out of the wafer to produce individual chips) **Siliziumscheibe**

COMMENT: silicon is used in the electronics industry as a base material for integrated circuits. It is grown as a long crystal which is then sliced into wafers before being etched or treated, producing several hundred chips per wafer. Other materials, such as germanium and gallium arsenide, are also used as a base for ICs

silk *noun* fine white material used to diffuse light when photographing a subject **Seide**

SIMD = SINGLE INSTRUCTION STREAM MULTIPLE DATA STREAM architecture of a parallel computer that has a number of ALUs and data buses with one control unit **SIMD**

SIMM = SINGLE IN-LINE MEMORY MODULE small, compact circuit board with an edge connector along one edge that carries densely-packed memory chips

SIMM; *you can expand the main memory of your PC by plugging in two more SIMMs*

simple *adjective* not complicated, not difficult **einfach; simple to use** = (machine *or* software) easy to use and operate **einfach zu benutzen**

◊ **simple mail transfer protocol** ™ **(SMTP)** standard protocol which allows electronic mail messages to be transferred from one system to another **Simple Mail Transfer Protocol** ™ **(SMTP)**

◊ **simple network management protocol (SNMP)** network management system which defines how status data is sent from monitored nodes back to a control station; SNMP is able to work with virtually any type of network hardware and software **Simple Network Management Protocol (SNMP)**

simplex *noun* data transmission in only one direction **Simplex** NOTE: opposite is **duplex**

simplify *verb* to make something simpler **vereinfachen;** *function keys simplify program operation*

simulate *verb* to copy the behaviour of a system *or* device with another **nachvollziehen, simulieren;** *this software simulates the action of an aeroplane*

◊ **simulator** *noun* device that simulates another system **Simulator; flight simulator** = computer program which allows a user to pilot a simulated plane, showing a realistic control panel and moving scenes (either as training programme *or* computer game) **Flugsimulator**

◊ **simulation** *noun* operation where a computer is made to imitate a real life situation *or* a machine, and shows how something works *or* will work in the future **Nachahmung, Simulation;** *simulation techniques have reached a high degree of sophistication*

simultaneity *adjective* in which the CPU and the I/O sections of a computer can handle different data *or* tasks at the same time **Gleichzeitigkeit**

simultaneous *adjective* which takes place at the same time as something else **gleichzeitig, Simultan-, simultan-;** simultaneous processing = two or more processes executed at the same time **Simultanverarbeitung; simultaneous**

transmission = transmission of data *or* control codes in two directions at the same time **Simultanübertragung** NOTE: same as duplex

◊ **simultaneously** *adverb* at the same time **gleichzeitig, simultan**

║ COMMENT: true simultaneous processing requires two processors, but can be imitated by switching rapidly between two tasks with a single processor

sin *or* **sine** *noun* mathematical function defined as: the sine of an angle (in a right-angled triangle) is equal to the ratio of opposite to hypotenuse sides **Sinus**

◊ **sine wave** *noun* waveform that is the sine function with time (classic wave shape, changing between a maximum and minimum with a value of zero at zero time) **Sinuswelle**

║ COMMENT: sine waves are usually the basic carrier waveform shape in modulation systems

single *adjective* only one **einfach, einzeln;** **single address code** *or* **instruction** = machine code instruction that contains one operator and one address **Einadresscode; single address message** = message with a single destination **Einfachadresse; single attachment station (SAS)** = (in an FDDI network) station with only one port through which to attach to the network; SAS stations are connected to the FDDI ring through a concentrator **SAS, Single Attachment Station; single board computer (SBC)** = micro *or* mini computer whose components are all contained on a single printed circuit board **Einplatinenrechner; single density disk (SD)** = standard magnetic disk and drive able to store data **Platte mit einfacher Schreibdichte; single frequency signalling** *or* **sf signalling** = use of various frequency signals to represent different control codes **Einfrequenztonwahl; single function software** = applications program that can only be used for one kind of task **auf einen Anwendungsbereich beschränktes Programm; single in-line memory module (SIMM)** = small, compact circuit board with an edge connector along one edge that carries densely-packed memory chips **SIMM-Modul; single in-line package (SIP)** = electronic component which has all its leads on one side of its package **SIP-Gehäuse; single instruction stream multiple data stream (SIMD)** = architecture of a parallel computer that has a number of ALUs and data buses with one control unit **SIMD-Rechner (Parallelrechner);**

single instruction stream single data stream (SISD) = architecture of a serial computer, that has one ALU and data bus, with one control unit **SISD-Rechner (serieller Rechner)**; **single key response** = software that requires only one key to be pressed (no CR required) to select an option **Einzelanschlag-Programm**; **single length precision** = number stored in one word **einfache Genauigkeit**; *compare with* DOUBLE, MULTIPLE; **single length working** = using numbers that can be stored within a single word **Arbeiten mit einfacher Wortlänge**; **single line display** = small screen which displays a single line of characters at a time **Einzeilenanzeige**; **single mode** *or* **monomode** = optic fibre which allows the light signal to travel along only one path **Singlemodefaser, Monomodefaser**; **single operand instruction** *see* SINGLE ADDRESS INSTRUCTION; **single operation** = communications system that allows data to travel in only one direction at a time (controlled by codes S/O = send only, R/O = receive only, S/R = send or receive) **Einzeloperation**; *see also* SIMPLEX; **single pass operation** = software that produces the required result *or* carries out a task after one run **Einschrittoperation**; **single pole** = switch that connects two points **einseitiger Schalter**; **single precision** = number stored in one word **einfache Genauigkeit**; **single scan non segmented** = video tape system that allows freeze framing by recording one complete television picture field at a time **(Halb)bildabtastung**; **single sheet feed** = device attached to a printer to allow single sheets of paper to be used instead of continuous stationery **Einzelblatteinzug**; **single sideband** = modulated signal filtered to leave just one sideband, usually the upper (this is very economical on bandwidth, but needs more circuitry) **Einseitenband**; **single-sided disk (SSD)** = floppy disk that can only be used to store data on one side, because of the way it is manufactured *or* formatted **Diskette mit einfacher Schreibdichte**; **single step** = the execution of a program one instruction at a time **Einzelschritt**; **single-strike ribbon** = printer ribbon which can only be used once **Einmalfarbband**; *compare* MULTI-STRIKE; **single-user system** = computer system which can only be used by a single user at a time (as opposed to a multi-user system) **Einzelplatzsystem**

sink *noun* receiving end of a communications line **(Nachrichten)senke**; **heat sink** = metal device used to conduct heat away from an electronic component to

prevent damage **Wärmeableitung, Kühlkörper**; **sink tree** = description in a routing table of all the paths in a network to a destination **Baumdiagramm** NOTE: the opposite of sink is **source**

sinusoidal *adjective* waveform *or* motion that is similar to a sine wave **sinusförmig**; *the carrier has a sinusoidal waveform*

SIO = SERIAL INPUT/OUTPUT

SIP = SINGLE IN-LINE PACKAGE

siphoning *noun* transmission of a direct broadcast TV programme over a cable network **Hebern**

SIPO = SERIAL INPUT/PARALLEL OUTPUT

SISD = SINGLE INSTRUCTION STREAM SINGLE DATA STREAM

SISO = SERIAL INPUT/SERIAL OUTPUT

site *noun* place where something is based **Gelände**

◊ **site licence** *noun* licence between a software publisher and a user which allows any number of users in that site to use the software **Standortlizenz**; *we have negotiated a good deal for the site licence for our 1200 employees in our HQ*

◊ **site poll** *verb* to poll all the terminals *or* devices in a particular location *or* area **global aufrufen**; *see also* POLLING

sixteen-bit *adjective* (microcomputer system *or* CPU) that handles data in sixteen bit words, providing much faster operation than older eight bit systems **16-Bit-CPU**

sixteenmo *or* **16mo** *noun* size of a book page, where the sheet of paper has been folded four times to make a signature of 32 pages **Sedezformat**

size
1 *noun* physical dimensions of an image *or* object *or* page **Größe**; *the size of the print has been increased to make it easier to read*; **page size** = physical dimensions of a printed page **Seitengröße**; *our page sizes vary from 220 x 110 to 360 x 220*; **screen size** = (i) number of characters a computer display can show horizontally and vertically; (ii) size of a monitor screen based on international paper sizes (i) **Bildschirmformat**; (ii) **Bildschirmgröße**

2 *verb* to calculate the resources available, and those required to carry out a particular job **abschätzen**

◊ **sizing** *noun* reducing *or* enlarging a picture to fit **Einpassen, Skalieren**; *photographs can be edited by cropping, sizing, etc*

skeletal code *noun* program which is not complete, with the basic structure coded **Rahmencodierung**

sketch
1 *noun* rough drawing made rapidly **Skizze**
2 *verb* to make a rough rapid drawing **skizzieren**

skew
1 *noun* the amount by which something which is not correctly aligned **Schräglauf**
2 *verb* to align something incorrectly **schräg ausrichten**; *this page is badly skewed*

skip *verb*
(a) to transmit radio waves over an abnormally long distance due to the reflective properties of the atmosphere **(eine Strecke) überspringen**
(b) to ignore an instruction in a sequence of instructions **überspringen**; *the printer skipped the next three lines of text;* **skip capability** = feature of certain word-processors to allow the user to jump backwards *or* forwards by a quantity of text in a document **Überspringfähigkeit; skip instruction** = null computer command which directs the CPU to the next instruction **Überspringbefehl; high-speed skip** = rapid movement of paper in a printer, ignoring the normal line advance **schneller Papiervorschub**

slash *or* **oblique stroke** *noun* printing sign (/) like stroke sloping to the right **Schrägstrich**

◊ **slashed zero** *noun* a printed *or* written sign (∅) to distinguish a zero from the letter O **durchgestrichene Null**

slave *noun* remote secondary computer *or* terminal controlled by a central computer **Nebencomputer; bus slave** = data sink which receives data from a bus master **untergeordneter Bus; slave cache** *or* **store** = section of high-speed memory which stores data that the CPU can access quickly **Nebenspeicher; slave processor** = dedicated processor that is controlled by a master processor **untergeordneter Prozessor; slave terminal** = terminal controlled by a main computer *or* terminal **untergeordnete Datenstation; slave tube** = second CRT display connected to another so that it shows exactly the same information **Zweitröhre**

sleep *noun* the state of a system that is waiting for a signal (log-on) before doing anything **bereitstehendes System;** *see also* **WAKE UP**

sleeve *noun* cover for a magnetic disk *or* for a record **Schutzhülle**

slew *noun* rapid movement of paper in a printer, ignoring the normal line advance **schneller Papiervorschub**

slice *noun* section *or* piece of something **Scheibe, Slice; bit-slice architecture** = construction of a large word size CPU by joining a number of smaller word size blocks **(Bit-)Slice-Aufbau;** *the bit-slice design uses four four-bit word processors to make a sixteen-bit processor;* **time slice** = period of time allocated for a user *or* program *or* job within a multitasking system; amount of time allowed for a single task in a time-sharing system *or* in multiprogramming **Zeitscheibe**

◊ **slicing** *noun* cutting thin round wafers from a bar of silicon crystal **In-Scheiben-Schneiden**

slide
1 *noun* positive transparent photographic image **Dia(positiv); slide projector** = device that projects slide images onto a screen **Diaprojektor; slide/sync recorder** = audio tape recorder that can control a slide projector in sync with music *or* commentary **Diaprojektor mit Tonspur**
2 *verb* to move smoothly across a surface **gleiten;** *the disk cover slides on and off easily*

slip pages *or* **slip proofs** *noun* proofs, where each page of text is printed on a separate piece of paper **Bogenkorrekturen**

slot
1 *noun*
(a) long thin hole **Schlitz;** *the system disk should be inserted into the left-hand slot on the front of the computer;* **expansion slot** = connector inside a computer into which an expansion card can be plugged **Erweiterungssteckplatz;** *there are two free slots in the micro, you only need one for the add-on board*
(b) **message slot** = number of bits that can hold a message which circulates round a ring network **Nachrichtenschlitz**

2 *verb* to insert an object into a hole **hineinstecken;** *the disk slots into one of the floppy drive apertures*

slow motion *noun* playing back of a video tape *or* disk sequence slower than recorded **Zeitlupe;** *the film switched to slow motion; play the film again in slow motion*

◊ **slow scan television** *noun* television images transmitted line by line over a transmission link at a slow rate **Schmalbandfernsehen**

SLSI = SUPER LARGE SCALE INTEGRATION

slug *noun* line of metal type, cast in hot metal setting **Zeilenguss**

slur *noun* (i) printed image which is blurred because of movement during printing; (ii) distortion of voice during transmission **(i) Schmitz; (ii) Verzerrung**

small *adjective* not large **klein; small caps** = printing style, with capital letters which are the same size as ordinary letters **Kapitälchen; small scale integration (SSI)** = integrated circuit with 1 to 10 components **Kleinintegration**

◊ **small computer systems interface (SCSI)** *noun* standard high-speed parallel interface used to connect computers to peripheral devices (such as disk drives and scanners) **SCSI**

Smalltalk ™ object-oriented programming language developed by Xerox **Smalltalk ™**

smart *adjective* intelligent **intelligent; smart card** = plastic card with a memory and microprocessor embedded in it, so that it can be used for direct money transfer *or* for identification of the user **Chipkarte;** *see also* PID; **smart terminal** *or* **intelligent terminal** = computer terminal that is able to process information **intelligente Datenstation; smart wiring hub** = network hub *or* concentrator which can transmit status information back to a managing station and allows management software to configure each port remotely **intelligenter Knoten;** *using this management software, I can shut down Tom's port on the remote smart wiring hub*

SMB = SERVER MESSAGE BLOCK system (developed by Microsoft) which allows a user to access another computer's files and peripherals over a network as if they were local resources **SMB**

smog *noun* **electronic smog** = excessive stray electromagnetic fields and static electricity generated by large numbers of electronic equipment (this can damage equipment and a person's health) **elektronischer Smog**

smoke test *noun* *(informal)* casual test that indicates that the machine must be working if no smoke appears when it is switched on **Feuerprobe**

SMT = SURFACE-MOUNT TECHNOLOGY method of manufacturing circuit boards in which the electronic components are bonded directly onto the surface of the board rather than being inserted into holes and soldered into place **SMD-Technik, Oberflächenmontagetechnik;** *surface-mount technology is faster and more space-efficient than soldering*

SMTP = SIMPLE MAIL TRANSFER PROTOCOL standard protocol allowing electronic mail messages to be transferred from one system to another **SMTP**

SNA = SYSTEMS NETWORK ARCHITECTURE design methods developed by IBM which define how communications in a network should occur and allow different hardware to communicate **SNA**

snapshot *noun* (i) recording of all the states of a computer at a particular instant; (ii) storing in main memory the contents of a screen full of information at an instant **(i) selektives Protokollprogramm; (ii) selektives Bildschirmspeichern; snapshot dump** = printout of all the registers and a section of memory at a particular instant, used when debugging a program **dynamischer Speicherauszug**

SNMP = SIMPLE NETWORK MANAGEMENT PROTOCOL

SNOBOL = STRING ORIENTATED SYMBOLIC LANGUAGE high-level programming language that uses string processing methods **SNOBOL (Programmiersprache)**

snow *noun* interference displayed as flickering white flecks on an monitor **Schnee**

s/n ratio = SIGNAL TO NOISE RATIO

ratio of the amplitude of the transmitted signal to the noise on the received signal **Rauschabstand**

soak *verb* to run a program *or* device continuously for a period of time to make sure it functions correctly **ununterbrochen laufen lassen;** *the device was soak-tested prior to delivery*

socket *noun* device with a set of holes, into which a plug fits **Steckdose; female socket** = hole into which a pin *or* plug can be inserted to make an electrical connection **Steckdose**

> QUOTE the mouse and keyboard sockets are the same, and could lead to the kind of confusion that arose with the early PCs when the keyboard could be connected to the tape socket
> *PC User*

soft *adjective*
(a) (material) that loses its magnetic effects when removed from a magnetic field **weich, soft**
(b) (data) that is not permanently stored in hardware (soft usually refers to data stored on magnetic medium) **weich; soft copy** = text listed on screen (as opposed to hard copy on paper) **Bildschirmaufzeichnung; soft error** = random error caused by software or data errors (this type of error is very difficult to trace and identify since it only appears under certain conditions) **Fehler durch Fremdkörpereinwirkung;** *compare with* HARD ERROR; **soft-fail** = (system) that is still partly operational even after a part of the system has failed **Softfail-; soft font** = fonts *or* typefaces stored on a disk, which can be downloaded *or* sent to a printer and stored in temporary memory *or* RAM **Softfont, externe Schriftart; soft hyphen** = hyphen which is inserted when a word is split at the end of a line, but is not present when the word is written normally **weiche Trennfuge; soft keys** = keys which can be changed by means of a program **frei belegbare Funktionstasten; soft keyboard** = keyboard where the functions of the keys can be changed by programs **frei belegbare Tastatur; soft reset** = instruction that terminates any program execution and returns the user to the monitor program *or* BIOS **weiche Rückstellung;** *compare with* HARD RESET; **soft-sectored disk** = disk where the the sectors are described by an address and start code data written onto it when the disk is formatted **weichsektorierte Platte; soft zone** = text area to the left of the

right margin in a word-processed document, where if a word does not fit completely, a hyphen is automatically inserted **Bereich um die weiche Trennfuge; Ausschließzone**

software *noun* any program *or* group of programs which instructs the hardware on how it should perform, including operating systems, word processors and applications programs **Software, Programmausrüstung; applications software** = programs which are used by the user to perform a certain task **Anwendungssoftware; bundled software** = software which is included in the price of the system **im Preis eingeschlossene Software; common software** = useful routines that can be used by any program **Allgemeinsoftware; network software** = software which is used to establish the link between a users' program and a network **Netzsoftware; pirate software** = illegal copy of a software package **Raubkopie; system software** = programs which direct the basic functions, input-output control, etc., of a computer **Systemsoftware; unbundled software** = software which is not included in the price of a system **im Preis nicht eingeschlossene Software; user-friendly software** = program that is easy for a non-expert to use and interact with **benutzerfreundliche Software; software compatible** = (computer) which will load and run programs written for another computer **softwarekompatibel, softwareverträglich; software development** = processes required to produce working programs from an initial idea **Software-Entwicklung; software documentation** = information, notes and diagrams that describe the function, use and operation of a piece of software **Softwaredokumentation; software engineer** = person who can write working software to fit an application **Softwareingenieur; software engineering** = field of study covering all software-related subjects **Software-Engineering; software house** = company which develops and sells computer programs **Softwarehaus; software interrupt** = high priority program generated signal, requesting the use of the central processor **Softwareunterbrechung; software library** = number of specially written routines, stored in a library file which can be inserted into a program, saving time and effort **Softwarebibliothek; software licence** = agreement between a user and a software house, giving details of the rights of the user to use *or* copy the software **Softwarelizenz; software life cycle** = period of time when a piece of software exists, from its initial design to the moment when it becomes out of date **Lebensdauer einer Software; software maintenance** = carrying out updates and modifications to a software package to make sure the program is up to date **Softwarewartung; software package** = complete set of programs (and the manual) that allow a certain task to be performed **Softwarepaket; software piracy** = illegal copying of software for sale **Softwarepiraterie; software quality assurance (SQA)** = making sure that software will perform as intended **Softwarequalitätssicherung; software reliability** = ability of a piece of software to perform the task required correctly **Softwarezuverlässigkeit; software specification** = detailed information about a piece of software's abilities, functions and methods **Softwarespezifikation; software system** = all the programs required for one or more tasks **Softwaresystem; software tool** = program used in the development of other programs **Programmentwicklungswerkzeug** NOTE: no plural for **software** for the plural say **pieces of software**

solar *adjective* referring to the sun **solar, Sonnen-, sonnen-; solar cell** = component that converts the light of the sun into electrical energy **Solarzelle; solar power** = (electrical) power derived from the sun **Sonnenenergie; solar-powered calculator** = calculator with a battery powered by light **Solarrechner**

solder
1 *noun* soft lead which, when melted, forms a solid electrical connection to join wires, pins and metal components **Lötmetall** NOTE: no plural
2 *verb* to join two pieces of metal with molten solder **löten**

◊ **solderless** *adjective* which does not use solder; (board, such as a breadboard) which does not need solder **lötstellenfrei**

solenoid *noun* mechanical device operated by an electromagnetic field **Solenoid**

solid *adjective* (printed text) with no spaces between the lines **kompress; solid error** = error that is always present when certain equipment is used **bleibender Fehler; solid font printer** = printer which uses a whole character shape to print in one movement, such as a daisy wheel printer **Festzeichendrucker**

◊ **solid-state** *adjective* referring to semiconductor devices **Halbleiter-, Festkörper-; solid-state device** = electronic device that operates by using the effects of electrical *or* magnetic signals in a solid semiconductor material **Halbleiterbauteil;** solid-state memory device = solid-state memory storage device (usually in the form of RAM or ROM chips) **Festkörperspeicher**

solve *verb* to find the answer to a problem **lösen**

◊ **solution** *noun* answer to a problem **Lösung**

son file *noun* latest working version of a file **Sohndatei;** *compare with* FATHER FILE, GRANDFATHER FILE

sonar *noun* device that uses sound waves to determine the state and depth of water **Echolot**

◊ **sonic** *adjective* referring to sound; (sound signals) within the human hearing range (20 - 20,000Hz) **akustisch; ultrasonic** = (sound pressure waves) at a frequency above the audio band (above 20kHz) **Ultraschall-**

sophisticated *adjective* technically advanced **hochentwickelt;** *a sophisticated desktop publishing program*

◊ **sophistication** *noun* being technically advanced **hoher Entwicklungsstand;** *the sophistication of the new package is remarkable*

sort *verb* to put data into order, according to a system, on the instructions of the user **sortieren;** *to sort addresses into alphabetical order; to sort orders according to account numbers;* **bubble sort** = sorting method which repeatedly exchanges various pairs of data items until they are in order **Bubblesort, Blasensortierung; shell sort** = algorithm for sorting data items, in which items can be moved more than position per sort action „Shell"-Sortierung; sort/merge = program which allows new files to be sorted and then merged in correct order into existing files **Sortier-/Mischprogramm; tree selection sort** = rapid form of selection where the information from the first sort pass is used in the second pass to speed up selection **Auswahlsortierverfahren**

◊ **sortkey** *or* **sort field** *noun* field in a stored file that is used to sort the file **Sortierschlüssel; Sortierfeld;** *the orders were sorted according to dates by assigning the date field as the sortkey*

SOS = SILICON ON SAPPHIRE

sound *noun* noise **Klang; sound advance** = distance between a film frame and its sound track on a film due to the difference in position of the sound head and camera aperture **Vorrücken der Tonspur; sound capture** = conversion of an analog sound into a digital form that can be used by a computer **Klangdigitalisierung;** *see also* ANALOG TO DIGITAL CONVERSION; **sound card** = expansion card which produces analog sound signals under the control of a computer **Soundkarte;** *this software lets you create almost any sound - but you can only hear them if you have a sound card fitted;* **sound chip** = electronic device that can generate sound signals **Tonchip; sound effects** = artificially produced sounds used when recording to give the impression of real sounds **Klangeffekte, Geräuschkulisse;** *all the sound effects for the film were produced electronically;* **sound head** = device that converts to or from a magnetic signal stored on tape **Tonkopf; sound hood** = cover which cuts down the noise from a noisy printer **Lärmschutzhaube; sound pressure level (SPL)** = measurement of the magnitude of the pressure wave conveying sound **Schalldruckpegel; sound synthesizer** = device able to produce complex real sounds by the combination of various generated signals **Synthesizer; sound track** = track on a film on which the sound is recorded **Tonspur**

◊ **soundproof** *adjective* which does not allow sound to pass through **schalldicht;** *the telephone is installed in a soundproof booth*

source *noun*
(a) point where a transmitted signal enters a network **Quelle** NOTE: opposite is **sink**
(b) name of a terminal on a FET device **Quelle** ⇨APPENDIX
(c) original *or* initial point **Ursprung(spunkt); source address filtering** = feature of some bridges which detects a particular address in the received packet and either rejects or forwards the data **Source Address Filtering, Quelladressfilterung; source code** = set of codes written by the programmer which cannot be directly executed by the computer, but has to be translated into an object code program by a compiler *or* interpreter **Ausgangscode; source deck** *or* **pack** = set of punched cards that contain the source code for a program **Ursprungskartensatz; source document** = form *or* document from which data is extracted prior to entering it into a database **Originaldokument; source editor** =

software that allows the user to alter, delete or add instructions in a program source file **Ursprungsdatei-Editor; source file** = program written in source language, which is then converted to machine code by a compiler **Ursprungsdatei; source language** = (i) language in which a program is originally written; (ii) language of a program prior to translation **(i) & (ii) Ursprungssprache** NOTE: opposite is **object** *or* **target language**; **source listing** = (i) listing of a text in its original form; (ii) listing of a source program **(i) Quellenliste; (ii) Quellcodelisting; source machine** = computer which can compile source code **Übersetzungsanlage;** *compare with* OBJECT MACHINE; **source program** = program, prior to translation, written in a programming language by a programmer **Quellprogramm; source routing** = method (originally developed by IBM for its Token Ring networks) of moving data between two networks which examines the data within the token and passes the data to the correct station **Source-Routing; source transparent routing (SRT)** = standard developed by IBM and the IEEE; it allows IBM networks and non-IBM Token Ring networks to be bridged and so exchange data **SRT-Weiterleitung, Source Transparent Routing (SRT)**

SP = STACK POINTER

space
1 *noun*
(a) gap between characters or lines **Leerschritt, Leerzeichen; space character** = character code that prints a space **Leerzeichen; space bar** = long bar at the bottom of a keyboard, which inserts a space into the text when pressed **Leertaste**
(b) transmitted signal representing a binary zero **Leerzeichen** NOTE: opposite is **mark**
(c) region extending out and around from the earth's atmosphere **Weltraum; space craft** = vehicle that travels in space **Raumfahrzeug; space station** = space craft which remains in orbit for a long time, and can be visited by other space vehicles **Weltraumstation**
2 *verb* to spread out text **spationieren;** *the line of characters was evenly spaced out across the page*

◊ **spacer** *noun* **intelligent spacer** = facility on a word-processing system used to prevent words from being hyphenated *or* separated at the wrong point **intelligentes Trennprogramm**

◊ **spacing** *noun* way in which spaces are inserted in a printed text **Wortabstände** (einrichten); *the spacing on some lines is very uneven*

span *noun* set of allowed values between a maximum and minimum **Bereich**

◊ **spanning tree** *noun* method of creating a logical topology for a widely-spread network that does not contain any loops **aufspannender Baum**

SPARC ™ = SCALAR PROCESSOR ARCHITECTURE RISC processor designed by Sun Microsystems which is used in its range of workstations **SPARC ™**

spark printer *noun* thermal printer which produces characters on thermal paper by electric sparks **Funkendrucker**

sparse array *noun* data matrix structure containing mainly zero *or* null entries **schwach besetzte Matrix**

speaker *see* LOUDSPEAKER

spec *informal* = SPECIFICATION; **high-spec** = high specification **hochspezifiziert**

special *adjective* which is different *or* not usual **speziell, Sonder-, sonder-**; **special character** = character which is not a normal one in a certain font (such as a certain accent *or* a symbol) **Sonderzeichen; special effects** = way of making strange things happen in films (such as monsters *or* explosions, etc.) **Tricks, optische Effekte; special interest group (SIG)** = group (within a larger club) which is interested in a particular aspect of software or hardware **Fachgruppe;** *our local computer club has a SIG for comms and networking;* **special sort** = extra printing character not in the standard font range **Sonderzeichen**

◊ **specialize** *verb* to study and be an expert in a subject **sich spezialisieren;** *he specializes in the design of CAD systems*

◊ **specialist** *noun* expert in a certain field of study **Spezialist/-in, Fachmann;** *you need a specialist programmer to help devise a new word-processing program*

specify *verb* to state clearly what is needed **angeben**

◊ **specification** *noun* detailed information about what is to be supplied *or* about a job to be done **Spezifikation; to work to standard specifications** = to work to specifications which are accepted anywhere in the same industry **nach anerkannten**

Normen arbeiten; the work is not up to specification *or* does not meet the customer's specifications = the product was not manufactured in the way which was detailed in the specifications **die Arbeit entspricht nicht den vorgegebenen Normen; high specification** *or* **high spec** = high degree of accuracy *or* large number of features **hoher Qualitätsmaßstab;** *high spec cabling needs to be very carefully handled;* **program specification** = detailed information about a program's abilities, features and methods **Programmspezifizierung**

specific address *noun* storage address that directly, without any modification, accesses a location *or* device **absolute Adresse**

◊ **specific code** *noun* binary code which directly operates the central processing unit, using only absolute addresses and values **absoluter Code; specific coding** = program code that has been written so that it only uses absolute addresses and values **absolute Adressierung**

◊ **specificity** *noun* ratio of non-relevant entries not retrieved to the total number of non-relevant entries contained in a file, database or library **Spezifität**

spectrum *noun* range of frequencies; range of colours **Spektrum; spectrum analyzer** = electronic test equipment that displays the amplitudes of a number of frequencies in a signal **Spektralanalysator**

speech *noun* speaking *or* making words with the voice **Sprache; speech chip** = integrated circuit that generates sounds (usually phonemes) which when played together sound like human speech **Sprach-Chip; speech plus** = method of transmitting a bandlimited speech signal and a number of low speed data signals in a voice grade channel **Einlagerungstelegrafie; speech processor** = device that alters speech, such as a scrambler **Sprachprozessor; speech recognition** = analysing spoken words in such a way that a computer can recognize spoken words and commands **Spracherkennung; speech signal** = signal which transmits spoken words **Sprachsignal; speech synthesis** = production of spoken words by a speech synthesizer **Sprachsynthese; speech synthesizer** = device which takes data from a computer and outputs it as spoken words **Sprachsynthesizer**

> QUOTE speech conveys information, and
> the primary task of computer speech
> processing is the transmission and
> reception of that information
> *Personal Computer World*

speed *noun*
(a) measure of the sensitivity of a
photographic material (film *or* paper) to
light **Lichtempfindlichkeit**; *high speed film is
very sensitive to light*
(b) time taken for a movement divided by
the distance travelled **Geschwindigkeit**;
speed of loop = method of benchmarking a
computer by measuring the number of
loops executed in a certain time
Schleifendurchgangsgeschwindigkeit;
playback speed = rate at which tape travels
past a playback head
Wiedergabegeschwindigkeit

spellcheck *verb* to check the spelling in a
text by comparing it with a dictionary held
in the computer **auf Schreibfehler prüfen**

◊ **spellchecker** *or* **spelling checker**
noun dictionary of correctly spelled words,
held in a computer, and used to check the
spelling of a text **Orthographie-,
Rechtschreibprüfprogramm**; *the program will
be upgraded with a word-processor and a
spelling checker*

spherical aberration *noun* optical
distortion causing lines to appear curved
sphärische Aberration

spike *noun* very short duration voltage
pulse **Überschwingspitze**

spillage *noun* situation when too much
data is being processed and cannot be
contained in a buffer **Überlauf**

spin *verb* to turn round fast **sich (schnell)
drehen**; *the disk was spun by the drive; the
disk drive motor spins at a constant velocity*
NOTE: spinning - span - spun

spindle *noun* object which grips and spins
a disk in the centre hole **(Antriebs)spindel**

◊ **spindling** *noun* turning a disk by hand
Umdrehen

spine *noun* back edge of the book which is
covered by the binding **Rücken**; *the author's
name and the title usually are shown on the
spine as well as on the front cover*

spirit duplication *noun* short-run
printing method using spirit to transfer ink

onto the paper **Umdruckverfahren,
Hektographieren**

SPL = SOUND PRESSURE LEVEL

splice *verb* to join two lengths of magnetic
tape *or* film, forming a continuous length
verspleißen, zusammenkleben; *you can use
glue or splicing tape to splice the ends;*
splicing block = device used to correctly
position the ends of two lengths of tape *or*
film that are to be spliced **Klebeeinrichtung**;
splicing tape = non-magnetic tape which is
applied to the back of the two ends of tape
to be spliced **Klebeband**

split screen *noun* software which can
divide the display into two or more
independent areas, to display two text files
or a graph and a text file **geteilte Anzeige**; *we
use split screen mode to show the text being
worked on and another text from memory
for comparison*

◊ **splitter** *noun* device which allows a
number of other devices to be plugged into
one supply *or* line **Verteiler; beam splitter** =
optical device to redirect part of a light
beam **Strahlteiler**

spool
1 *noun* reel on which a tape *or* printer ribbon
is wound **Spule**
2 *verb* to transfer data from a disk to a tape
spulen

◊ **spooler** *or* **spooling device** *noun*
device which holds a tape and which
receives information from a disk for
storage **Spulgerät**

◊ **spooling** *noun* transferring data to a
disk from which it can be printed at the
normal speed of the printer, leaving the
computer available to do something else
Spulbetrieb, SPOOL-Betrieb

sporadic fault *noun* error that occurs
occasionally **sporadischer Fehler**

spot *noun* point on a CRT screen that is
illuminated by the electron beam **Punkt,
Spurelement**

◊ **spot beam** *noun* narrow (satellite)
antenna coverage of a select region (on
earth) **scharfbündelnde Antenne**

spreadsheet *noun* (i) program which
allows calculations to be carried out on
several columns of numbers; (ii) printout of
calculations on wide computer stationary
(i) **elektronische Kalkulationstabelle**; (ii)
Kalkulationstabellendruck

sprite *noun* object which moves round the screen in computer graphics **Kobold**

sprocket *or* **sprocket wheel** *noun* wheel with teeth round it which fit into holes in continuous stationery *or* punched tape **Stachelradwalze**

◊ **sprocket feed** *noun* paper feed, where the printer pulls the paper by turning sprocket wheels which fit into a series of holes along each edge of the sheet **Stachelbandführung**; *see also* TRACTOR FEED

◊ **sprocket holes** *noun* series of small holes on each edge of continuous stationery, which allow the sheet to be pulled through the printer **Führungslöcher**

spur *noun* connection point into a network **Netzanschlusspunkt**

SPX = SIMPLEX

SQA = SOFTWARE QUALITY ASSURANCE

square wave *noun* waveform with a square shape **Rechteckwelle**

SQL = STRUCTURED QUERY LANGUAGE simple, commonly used, standard database programming language that is only used to create queries to retrieve data from the database **SQL**

SRT = SOURCE TRANSPARENT ROUTING

SS = SINGLE-SIDED

SSBSC = SINGLE SIDEBAND SUPPRESSED CARRIER

SSD = SINGLE-SIDED DISK

SSI = SMALL SCALE INTEGRATION

ST connector *noun* connector used to terminate optical fibres **ST-Anschluss**

ST506 standard *noun* (old) disk interface standard used in early IBM PCs, developed by Seagate **ST506-Standard**; *the ST506 standard has now been replaced by IDE and SCSI*

stable *adjective* not moving *or* not changing **stabil**; **stable state** = the state of a system when no external signals are applied **Ruhezustand, Grundzustand**

◊ **stability** *noun* being stable **Stabilität**;

image stability = ability of a display screen to provide a flicker-free picture **Bildstabilität**

stack *noun* temporary storage for data, registers *or* tasks where items are added and retrieved from the same end of the list **Kellerspeicher**; *see also* LIFO; **pushdown stack** *or* **pushdown list** = method of storing data, where the last item stored is always at the same location, the rest of the list being pushed down by one address **Rückstellstapel**; **virtual memory stack** = temporary store for pages in a virtual memory system **virtueller Matrixblock**; **stack address** = location pointed to by the stack pointer **Stapeladresse**; **stack base** = address of the origin *or* base of a stack **Anfangsadresse**; **stack job processing** = storing a number of jobs to be processed in a stack and automatically executing one after the other **Stapeljobverarbeitung**; **stack pointer (SP)** = address register containing the location of the most recently stored item of data *or* the location of the next item of data to be retrieved **Stapelzeiger**

stage *noun* one of several points in a process **Stufe**; *the text is ready for the printing stage; we are in the first stage of running in the new computer system*

◊ **staged** *adjective* carried out in stages, one after the other **Schritt für Schritt**; **staged change-over** = change between an old and a new system in a series of stages **schrittweises Überwechseln**

stand-alone *or* **standalone** *adjective & noun* (device *or* system) which can operate without the need of any other devices **selbständig(es), autonom(es System)**; *the workstations have been networked together rather than used as stand-alone systems*; **stand-alone terminal** = computer terminal with a processor and memory which can be directly connected to a modem, without being a member of a network *or* cluster **autonome Datenstation**

standard *adjective* normal *or* usual **standardmäßig**; **standard document** *or* **standard form** *or* **standard paragraph** *or* **standard text** = normal printed document *or* form *or* paragraph which is used many times (with different names and addresses often inserted - as in a form letter) **Standardformular** *or* **Standardtext**; **standard function** = special feature included as normal in a computer system **Standardfunktion**; **Standard Generalized Markup Language** *see* SGML; **standard interface** = interface between two or more systems that conforms to pre-defined standards **Standardschnittstelle; standard letter** = letter which is sent without any change to the main text, but being personalised by inserting the names and addresses of different people **Standard-, Formbrief; standard mode** = (in an IBM PC) mode of operation of Microsoft Windows which uses extended memory but does not allow multitasking of DOS applications **Standardmodus; standard subroutine** = routine which carries out an often used function, such as keyboard input or screen display **Standardunterprogramm**

◊ **standardize** verb to make a series of things conform to a standard **normalisieren, standardisieren;** the standardized control of transmission links

◊ **standards** noun normal quality or normal conditions which are used to judge other things **Normen; production standards** = quality of production **Produktionsnormen, Produktionsstandards; up to standard** = of an acceptable quality **den Anforderungen entsprechend;** this batch of disks is not up to standard; **standards converter** = device to convert received signals conforming to one standard into a different standard **Normenumsetzer;** the standards converter allows us to watch US television broadcasts on our UK standards set; **video standards** see VIDEO; **modem standards** = rules defining transmitting frequencies, etc., which allow different modems to communicate **Modemnormen**

COMMENT: modem standards are set by the CCITT in the UK, the Commonwealth and most of Europe, while the USA and part of South America use modem standards set by Bell

standby noun **standby equipment** = secondary system identical to the main system, to be used if the main system breaks down **Reserveausrüstung; cold standby** = backup system that will allow the equipment to continue running but with the loss of any volatile data **Cold-Standby-System; hot standby** = backup equipment that is kept operational at all times in case of system failure **Hot-Standby-System (mitlaufendes Reservesystem)**

QUOTE before fault-tolerant systems, users had to rely on the cold standby, that is switching on a second machine when the first developed a fault; the alternative was the hot standby, where a second computer was kept running continuously

Computer News

star network noun network of several machines where each terminal or floppy disk unit or satellite is linked individually to a central hard disk machine or server **Sternnetz;** compare BUS NETWORK, RING NETWORK

◊ **star program** noun perfect program that runs (first time) with no errors or bugs **fehlerloses Programm**

start adjective beginning or first part **Start; cold start** = switching on a computer or to run a program from its original start point **Kaltstart; warm start** = restarting a program which has stopped, without losing any data **Warmstart; start bit** or **element** = transmitted bit used (in asynchronous communications) to indicate the start of a character **Startbit** NOTE: opposite is **stop bit start of header** = transmitted code indicating the start of header (address or destination) information for a following message **Anfang des Kopfes; start of text (SOT** or **STX)** = transmitted code indicating the end of control or address information and the start of the message **Textanfang**

◊ **startup disk** noun floppy disk which holds the operating system and system configuration files which can, in case of hard disk failure, be used to boot the computer **Startdiskette**

stat informal = PHOTOSTAT

state noun the way something is **Zustand, Status; active state** = state in which an action can or does occur **aktiver Status; steady state** = circuit or device or program state in which no action is occurring but can accept an input **Dauerbetrieb**

statement noun (i) expression used to convey an instruction or define a process; (ii) instruction in a source language which is translated into several machine code instructions **(i) & (ii) Anweisung; conditional statement** = program instruction that will redirect program control according to the outcome of an event **bedingte Anweisung; control statement** = (i) program instruction that directs a program (to another branch, etc.); (ii) program instruction that directs a CPU to provide controlling actions or controls the actions of the CPU **(i) & (ii) Steueranweisung; directive statement** = program instruction used to control the language translator, compiler, etc. **Übersetzungsanweisung; input statement** = computer programming command that waits for data entry from a port *or* keyboard **Eingabeanweisung; multi-statement line** = line from a computer program that contains more than one instruction *or* statement **Mehrfachanweisungszeile; narrative statement** = statement which sets variables and allocates storage **erklärende Festlegung, Setzanweisung; statement number** = number assigned (in a sequential way) to a series of instruction statements **Anweisungsnummer;** *see also* LINE NUMBER

state-of-the-art *adjective* very modern *or* technically as advanced as possible **auf dem neuesten Stand der Technik**

> QUOTE the main PCB is decidedly non-state-of-the-art
> *Personal Computer World*

static
1 *noun*
(a) (i) loud background noise *or* interference in a radio broadcast due to atmospheric conditions; (ii) background noise in a recorded signal **(i) atmosphärische Störungen; (ii) Rauschen**
(b) charge that does not flow **Reibungselektrizität, statische Aufladung** NOTE: no plural
2 *adjective* (i) (data) which does not change with time; (ii) (system) that is not dynamic **(i) fest; (ii) statisch; static dump** = printout of the state of a system when it has finished a process **statischer Speicherauszug; static memory** = non-volatile memory that does not require refreshing **statischer Speicher; static RAM** = RAM which retains data for as long as the power supply is on, and where the data does not have to be refreshed **statischer RAM;** *compare with* DYNAMIC RAM; **static subroutine** = subroutine that uses no variables apart from the operand addresses **statisches Unterprogramm**

> COMMENT: static RAM uses bistable devices such as flip-flops to store data; these take up more space on a chip than the capacititive storage method of dynamic RAM but do not require refreshing

station *noun*
(a) point in a network *or* communications system that contains devices to control the input and output of messages, allowing it to be used as a sink *or* source **Station; station management (SMT)** = software and hardware within the FDDI specification which provides control information **Stationsmanagement (SMT);** secondary

station = temporary status of the station that is receiving data **Sekundärstation; workstation** = desk with computer, keyboard, monitor, printers, etc., where a person works **Arbeitsplatz**
(b) earth station = dish antenna and circuitry used to communicate with a satellite **Erdfunkstelle; radio station** = broadcast signal booster *or* relay point consisting of a receiver and transmitter linked with ancillary equipment **Funkstation;** *the signal from this radio station is very weak; we are trying to jam the signals from that station*

stationary *adjective* not moving **stationär; geostationary orbit** = orbit of a satellite which keeps it above the same part of the earth **geostationäre Umlaufbahn**

stationery *noun* office supplies for writing, especially paper, envelopes, labels, etc. **Büromaterial, Schreibwaren; computer stationery** = paper specially made for use in a computer printer **Computerdruckerpapier; continuous stationery** = printer stationery which takes the form of a single long sheet **Endlospapier; preprinted stationery** = computer stationery (such as invoices) which is preprinted with the company heading and form layout onto which the details will be printed by the computer **vorgedrucktes Briefpapier, Vordruck** NOTE: no plural

statistics *noun* (study of) facts in the form of figures **Statistik**

◊ **statistical** *adjective* based on statistics **statistisch; statistical time division multiplexing (STDM)** = time division multiplexing system that allocates time slots when they are required, allowing greater flexibility and a greater number of devices to transmit **statistische Zeitmultiplexmethode;** *see also* TIME DIVISION MULTIPLEXING

◊ **statistician** *noun* person who analyses statistics **Statistiker/-in**

status *noun* importance *or* position **Status, Zustand; status bit** = single bit in a word used to provide information about the state *or* result of an operation **Zustandsbit; status line** = line at the top *or* bottom of a screen which gives information about the task currently being worked on (number of lines, number of columns, filename, time, etc.) **Statuszeile; status poll** = signal from a computer requesting information on the current status of a terminal **Statusabfrage;**

status register = register containing information on the status of a peripheral device **Statusregister; program status word (PSW)** = word which contains a number of status bits, such as carry flag, zero flag, overflow bit, etc. **Programmstatuswort**

STD = SUBSCRIBER TRUNK DIALLING

STDM = STATISTICAL TIME DIVISION MULTIPLEXING

steady state *noun* circuit *or* device *or* program state in which no action is occurring but can accept an input **Dauerbetrieb**

stencil *noun* material with component shapes and symbols already cut out, allowing designers to draw components and other symbols rapidly **Schablone;** *the stencil has all the electronic components on it; the schematic looks much neater if you use a stencil;* **flowchart stencil** *or* **template** = plastic sheet with template symbols cut out, to allow flowcharts to be quickly and clearly drawn **Zeichenschablone**

step
1 *noun* a single unit **Schritt; single step** = executing a computer program one instruction at a time, used for debugging **Einzelschritt**
2 *verb* to move forwards *or* backwards by one unit **(einen Schritt vorwärts) gehen;** *we stepped forward through the file one record at a time; we stepped forward the film one frame at a time*

◊ **stepper motor** *or* **stepping motor** *noun* motor which turns in small steps as instructed by a computer (used in printers, disk drives and robots) **Schrittmotor**

steradian *noun* unit of solid angle **Sterad(iant)** ⇨APPENDIX

stereo *informal* = STEREOPHONIC

stereophonic *adjective* using two audio signals recorded from slightly different positions to provide a three-dimensional sound effect when replayed through two separate loudspeakers **stereophon, Stereo-, stereo-; stereophonic microphone** = one device containing two microphones allowing stereo signals to be recorded **Stereomikrofon; stereophonic recorder** = tape recorder that records two audio signals onto magnetic tape **Stereorekorder**

still frame *noun* one single video *or* film frame displayed by itself **Stillstandprojektion**

stochastic model *noun* mathematical representation of a system that includes the effects of random actions **Zufallsmodell**

stock control program *noun* software designed to help manage stock in a business **Programm zur Lagerbestandsführung**

stop
1 *verb* to cease doing something **stoppen, beenden**
2 *noun* not doing any action **Stillstand; tab stop** = preset point along a line, where the printing head *or* cursor will stop for each tabulation command **Tabulatorstop; stop and wait protocol** = communications protocol in which the transmitter waits for a signal from the receiver that the message was correctly received before transmitting further data **Anhalt- und Warteprotokoll**

◊ **stop bit** *or* **stop element** *noun* transmitted bit used in asynchronous communications to indicate the end of a character **Stoppbit; stop code** = instruction that temporarily stops a process to allow the user to enter data **Haltecode; stop instruction** = computer programming instruction that stops program execution **Haltebefehl; stop list** = list of words that are not to be used *or* not significant for a file *or* library search **Stoppliste; stop time** = time taken for a spinning disk to come to a stop after it is no longer powered **Abbremszeit**

storage *noun* memory *or* part of the computer system in which data *or* programs are kept for further use **Speicher; archive storage** = storage of data for a long period of time **Archivspeicherung; auxiliary storage** = any data storage medium (such as magnetic tape *or* disk) that is not the main, high speed memory **Zusatzspeicher, peripherer Speicher; dynamic storage** *or* **memory** = memory that requires its contents to be updated regularly **dynamischer Speicher; external storage** = storage device which is located outside the main computer system but which can be accessed by the CPU **externer Speicher; information storage** = storing data in a form which allows it to be processed at a later date **Informationsspeicherung; instruction storage** = section of memory that is used to store instructions **Befehlsspeicher; intermediate storage** = temporary area of memory for items that are currently being processed **Zwischenspeicher; mass storage system** = data storage that can hold more than one million million bits of data **Großspeicher; nonerasable storage** = storage medium that cannot be erased and re-used nicht löschbarer Speicher; **primary storage** = (i) small fast-access internal memory of a system which contains the program currently being executed; (ii) main internal memory of a system **(i) & (ii) Hauptspeicher, Primärspeicher; secondary storage** = any data storage medium (such as magnetic tape*or* floppy disk) that is not the main, high-speed computer storage **Zusatzspeicher; static storage** = non-volatile memory that does not require refreshing **statischer Speicher; temporary storage** = storage which is not permanent **Zwischenspeicher; volatile storage** = memory *or* storage medium that loses data stored when the power supply is switched off **flüchtiger Speicher; storage allocation** = how memory is allocated for different uses, such as programs, variables, data, etc. **Speicherplatzzuteilung; storage capacity** = amount of space available for storage of data **Speicherkapazität; storage density** = number of bits that can be recorded per unit area of storage medium **Aufzeichnungsdichte; storage device** = any device that can store data and then allow it to be retrieved when required **Speicher; storage disk** = disk used to store data **Speicherplatte; storage dump** = printout of all the contents of an area of storage space **Speicherauszug; storage media** = various materials which are able to store data **Speichermedien, Datenträger; storage tube** = special CRT used for computer graphics that retains an image on screen without the need for refresh actions **Speicherröhre;** *see also* REFRESH

◊ **store**

1 *noun* memory *or* part of the computer system in which data *or* programs are kept for further use **Speicher; store address register (SAR)** = register in a CPU that contains the address of the next location to be accessed **Speicheradressregister; store data register (SDR)** = register in a CPU which holds data before it is proceesed *or* moved to a memory location **Speicherdatenregister; store location** *or* **cell** = unit in a computer system which can store information **Speicherzelle**
2 *verb* to save data, which can then be used again as necessary **speichern;** *storing a page of high resolution graphics can require 3 Mb;* **store and forward** = electronic mail communications system which stores a number of messages before retransmitting them **Speichervermittlung; stored program** = computer program that is stored in memory (if it is stored in dynamic RAM it

will be lost when the machine is switched off, if stored on disk or tape (backing store) it will be permanently retained) **gespeichertes Programm; stored program signalling** = system of storing communications control signals on computer in the form of a program **speicherprogrammgesteuertes Signal**

> COMMENT: storage devices include hard and floppy disk, RAM, punched paper tape and magnetic tape

straight-line coding *noun* program written to avoid the use of loops and branches, providing a faster execution time **lineare Codierung**

stray *adjective* lost *or* wandering; (something) which has avoided being stopped **vereinzelt, verstreut, verirrt;** *the metal screen protects the CPU against stray electromagnetic effects from the PSU*

streaking *noun* horizontal television picture distortion **Nachzieheffekt, Fahnen**

stream *noun* long flow of serial data **Strom; job stream** = number of tasks arranged in order waiting to be processed in a batch system **Jobfolge, Programmablauffolge**

◊ **streamer** *noun* tape streamer *or* **streaming tape drive** = (device containing a) continuous loop of tape, used as backing storage **Magnetbandstreamer**

> QUOTE the product has 16Mb of memory, 45Mb of Winchester disk storage and 95Mb streaming tape storage
> *Minicomputer News*

string *noun* any series of consecutive alphanumeric characters *or* words that are manipulated and treated as a single unit by the computer **Zeichenfolge, Zeichenkette; alphanumeric** *or* **character string** = storage allocated for a series of alphanumeric characters **alphanumerische Zeichenfolge; numeric string** = string which contains only numbers **numerische Zeichenfolge; null** *or* **blank string** = string that contains nothing **Nullstring, Zeichenfolge der Länge Null; string area** = section of memory in which strings of alphanumeric characters are stored **Stringbereich; string concatenation** = linking a series of strings together **Zeichenfolgenverkettung; string function** = program operation which can act on strings **Zeichenfolgenfunktion; string length** = the number of characters in a string **Länge der**

Zeichenfolge, Stringlänge; **string name** = identification label assigned to a string **Name der Zeichenfolge, Stringname; string orientated symbolic language (SNOBOL)** = high-level programming language that uses string processing methods **SNOBOL (Programmiersprache); string variable** = variables used in a computer language that can contain alphanumeric characters as well as numbers **Stringvariable**

◊ **stringy floppy** *or* **tape streamer** *noun* continuous loop of tape, used for backing storage **Magnetbandstreamer**

strip
1 *noun* long thin piece of material **Streifen; strip window** = display which shows a single line of text **Einzeilenfenster; magnetic strip** = layer of magnetic material on the surface of a plastic card, used for recording data **Magnetstreifen**
2 *verb* to remove the control data from a received message, leaving only the relevant information **strippen**

stripe *noun* long thin line of colour **Streifen; balance stripe** = thin magnetic strip on a cine film on the opposite side to the sound track, so that the whole film will lie flat when played back **Ausgleichsstreifen**

strobe
1 *verb* to send a pulse (usually on the selection line) of an electronic circuit **einen Impuls geben**
2 *noun* pulse of an electric circuit **Impuls; address strobe** = signal indicating that a valid address is on the address bus **Adressimpulseingang; data strobe** = signal indicating that valid data is on the data bus **Datenimpulseingang**

◊ **stroboscope** *or* **strobe** *noun* light source which produces flashes of light **Stroboskop**

stroke *noun* basic curved *or* straight line that makes up a character **Strich**

strowger exchange *noun* telephone exchange worked by electromechanical switches **strowgersches Fernsprechamt**

structure
1 *noun* way in which something is organized *or* formed **Struktur; network structure** = data structure that allows each node to be connected to any of the others **Netzwerkstruktur**
2 *verb* to organize *or* to arrange in a certain way **strukturieren;** *you first structure a*

document to meet your requirements and then fill in the blanks; **structured cabling** = (organisation which is cabled) using UTP cable feeding into hubs designed in such a way that it is easy to trace and repair cable faults and also to add new stations or more cable **strukturierte Verkabelung; structured design** = problem solved by a number of interconnected modules **strukturierte Entwicklung; structured programming** = well-ordered and logical technique of assembling programs **strukturierte Programmierung; structured query language (SQL)** = simple, commonly used, standard database programming language which is only used to create queries to retrieve data from the database **Structured Query Language (SQL)**

stub *noun* short program routine which contains comments to describe the executable code that will, eventually, be inserted into the routine **Stubroutine**

stuck beacon *noun* (error condition in which) a station continuously transmits beacon frames **Endlosfehlersignal**

studio *noun* place where a designer draws; place where recordings take place; place where films are made **Studio**

STX = START OF TEXT

style sheet *noun* (i) sheet giving the style which should be followed by an editor; (ii) template that can be preformatted to generate automatically the style *or* layout of a document such a a manual, a book, a newsletter, etc. **(i) Merkblatt zur Manuskriptgestaltung; (ii) Schablone**

stylus *noun*
(a) (transducer) needle which converts signals on an audio record into electrical signals **Stift, Abspielnadel**
(b) pen-like device that is used in computer graphics systems to dictate cursor position on the screen **(Licht)stift;** *use the stylus on the graphics tablet to draw*
(c) (transducer) that detects data stored on a video disk **Anzeigenadel; stylus printer** *see* DOT MATRIX PRINTER

sub- *prefix* meaning less (important) than *or* lower than **Unter-, unter-; subaddress** = peripheral identification code, used to access one peripheral (this is then followed by address data to access a location within the peripheral's memory) **Subadresse; subaudio frequencies** = frequencies below the audio range (below 20Hz) **Frequenzen unterhalb des Hörbereichs; subclass** = number of data items to do with one item in a master class **Unterklasse; subbing** *or* **sub-editing** = editing of a manuscript before it is sent for typesetting **Redigieren; subrange** = below the normal range **unterhalb der normalen Reichweite**

subdirectory *noun* directory of disk *or* tape contents contained within the main directory **Unterverzeichnis**

> QUOTE if you delete a file and then delete the subdirectory where it was located, you cannot restore the file because the directory does not exist
> *Personal Computer World*

subprogram *noun* (i) subroutine in a program; (ii) program called up by a main program **(i) & (ii) Unterprogramm**

subroutine *noun* section of a program which performs a required function and that can be called upon at any time from inside the main program **Unterprogramm; subroutine call** = computer programming instruction that directs control to a subroutine **Aufruf eines Unterprogramms; closed** *or* **linked subroutine** = number of computer instructions in a program that can be called at any time, with control being returned on completion to the next instruction after the call **abgeschlossenes/verbundenes Unterprogramm; open subroutine** = code for a subroutine which is copied into memory whenever a call instruction is found **offenes Unterprogramm; static subroutine** = subroutine that uses no variables apart from the operand addresses **statisches Unterprogramm; two-level subroutine** = subroutine containing another subroutine **zweistufiges Unterprogramm; subroutine call** = computer programming instruction that directs control to a subroutine **Aufruf eines Unterprogramms**

> COMMENT: a subroutine is executed by a call instruction which directs the processor to its address; when finished it returns to the instruction after the call instruction in the main program

subscriber *noun* (i) person who has a telephone; (ii) person who pays for access to a service such as a BBS **(i) & (ii) Teilnehmer/-in; subscriber trunk dialling (STD)** = system where a person can dial direct from one telephone to another, without referring to the operator **Selbstwählferndienst**

subscript *noun* small character which is printed below the line of other characters **(tiefstehender) Index;** *see also* SUPERSCRIPT (NOTE: used in chemical formulae: CO_2) **subscripted variable** = element in an array, which is identified by a subscript **indizierte Variable**

◊ **subset** *noun* small set of data items which forms part of another larger set **Untermenge**

◊ **subsegment** *noun* small section of a segment **Subsegment**

substance *noun* any matter whose properties can be described **Materie, Substanz**

substitute *verb* to put something in the place of something else **ersetzen; substitute character** = character that is displayed if a received character is not recognized **Ersatzzeichen** NOTE: you substitute one thing **for** another

◊ **substitution** *noun* replacing something by something else **Austausch, Substitution; substitution error** = error made by a scanner which mistakes one character *or* letter for another **Substitutionsfehler; substitution table** = list of characters *or* codes that are to be inserted instead of received codes **Substitutionstabelle**

substrate *noun* base material on which an integrated circuit is constructed **Substrat, Trägermaterial;** *see also* INTEGRATED CIRCUIT

subsystem *noun* one smaller part of a large system **Subsystem**

◊ **subtotal** *noun* total at the end of a column, which when added to others makes the grand total **Zwischensumme**

subtraction *noun* taking one number away from another **Subtraktion**

◊ **subtrahend** *noun* in a subtraction operation, the number to be subtracted from the minuend **Subtrahend**

subvoice grade channel *noun* communications channel using frequencies (240 - 300Hz) below a voice channel, used for low speed data transmission **Nachrichtenkanal für Frequenzen zwischen 240Hz und 300Hz**

successive *adjective* which follow one after the other **aufeinanderfolgend;** *each successive operation adds further characters to the string*

suffix notation *noun* mathematical operations written in a logical way, so that the symbol appears after the numbers to be acted upon **Suffixschreibweise**; *see also* POSTFIX NOTATION

suitcase *noun* (in the Apple Macintosh environment) icon which contains a screen font and allows fonts to be easily installed onto the system **Koffer**

suite of programs *noun* (i) group of programs which run one after the other; (ii) number of programs used for a particular task **(i) Programmfolge; (ii) Programmgruppe;** *the word-processing system uses a suite of three programs, editor, spelling checker and printing controller*

sum *noun* total of a number of items added together **Summe**

◊ **summation check** *noun* error detection check performed by adding together the characters received and comparing with the required total **Summenprüfung**

sun outage *noun* length of time during which a satellite does not operate due to the position of the moon *or* earth, causing a shadow over the satellite's solar cells **Ausfallzeit mangels Sonnenlicht**

super- *prefix* meaning very good *or* very powerful **besonders gut/groß;** **supercomputer** = very powerful mainframe computer used for high speed mathematical tasks **Größtrechner;** **supergroup** = a number (60) of voice channels collected together into five adjacent channels for simultaneous transmission **Übergruppe, Sekundärgruppe;** **super VGA (SVGA)** = enhancement to the standard VGA graphics display system which allows resolutions of up to 800 x 600 pixels with 16 million colours **Super VGA (SVGA);** **super high frequency (SHF)** = frequency range between 3 - 30GHz **Frequenz zwischen 3GHz und 30GHz;** **super large scale integration (SLSI)** = integrated circuit with more than 100,000 components **Größtintegration;** **super master group** = collection of 900 voice channels **Quartärgruppe**

superheterodyne radio *noun* radio receiver that converts a received signal by means of a heterodyne process to an intermediate frequency for easier processing **Superüberlagerungsfunkempfänger**

superimpose *verb* to place something on top of something else **überlagern**

superior number *noun* superscript figure **Hochzahl, Index**

superscript *noun* small character printed higher than the normal line of characters **hochgestelltes Zeichen, Index;** *compare with* SUBSCRIPT NOTE: used often in mathematics: 10^5 (say: ten to the power five)

supersede *verb* to take the place of something which is older *or* less useful **ablösen;** *the new program supersedes the earlier one, and is much faster*

superstation *noun* (*US*) TV system, where a single TV station broadcasts many programmes simultaneously via satellite and cable **Superstation**

supervise *verb* to watch carefully to see if work is well done **überwachen;** *the manufacture of circuit boards is very carefully supervised*

◊ **supervision** *noun* being supervised **Überwachung**

◊ **supervisor** *noun* (i) person who makes sure that equipment is always working correctly; (ii) section of a computer operating system that regulates the use of peripherals and the operations undertaken by the CPU **(i) Aufsichtsperson; (ii) Supervisor**

◊ **supervisory** *adjective* as a supervisor **Überwachungs-, überwachungs-;** **supervisory program** *or* **executive program** = master program in a computer system that controls the execution of other programs **Überwachungsprogramm, Supervisor;** **supervisory sequence** = combination of control codes that perform a controlling function in a data communications network **Steuerzeichenfolge;** **supervisory signal** = (i) signal that indicates if a circuit is busy; (ii) signal that provides an indication of the state of a device **(i) & (ii) Überwachungssignal**

supply
1 *noun* providing goods *or* products *or* services **Versorgung;** *the electricity supply has failed; they signed a contract for the supply of computer stationery*
2 *verb* to provide something which is needed (for which someone will pay) **versorgen;** *the computer was supplied by a recognized dealer; they have signed a contract to supply on-line information*

◊ **supplier** *noun* company which supplies Lieferant; *a supplier of computer parts; a supplier of disk drives or; a disk drive supplier; Japanese suppliers have set up warehouses in the country*

support *verb* to give help to *or* to help to run unterstützen; *the main computer supports six workstations;* **support chip** = dedicated IC that works with a CPU, and carries out an additional function *or* a standard function very rapidly, so speeding up the processing time Unterstützungschip; *the maths support chip can be plugged in here*

> QUOTE enhanced screen and I/O handling, and supporting up to 80 screens
> *PC User*

suppress *verb* to remove unterdrücken; *the filter is used to suppress the noise due to static interference;* **suppressed carrier modulation** = modulated waveform where the carrier signal has been suppressed prior to transmission, leaving only the modulated sidebands Modulation mit unterdrückter Trägerwelle; **double sideband suppressed carrier (DSBSC)** = amplitude modulation that has a suppressed carrier, leaving only two sidebands Zweiseitenbandübertragung mit unterdrückter Trägerwelle; **single sideband suppressed carrier (SSBSC)** = amplitude modulation that has a suppressed carrier, and only one sideband for data transmission Einseitenbandübertragung mit unterdrückter Trägerwelle

‖ COMMENT: single sideband suppressed carrier modulation allows a greater number of channels in a frequency range, since each one is narrower

◊ **suppression** *noun* act of suppressing Unterdrückung

◊ **suppressor** *noun* device which suppresses interference Unterdrücker; **echo suppressor** = device used on long-distance speech lines to prevent echoing effects Echosperre

surface-mount technology (SMT) *noun* method of manufacturing circuit boards in which the electronic components are bonded directly onto the surface of the board rather than being inserted into holes and soldered into place SMD-Technik, Oberflächenmontagetechnik; *surface-mount technology is faster and more space-efficient than soldering*

surge *noun* sudden increase in electrical

power in a system, due to a fault *or* noise *or* component failure Stromstoß; **surge protector** = electronic device that cuts off the power supply to sensitive equipment if it detects a power surge that could cause damage Überspannungsableiter

‖ COMMENT: power surges can burn out circuits before you have time to pull the plug; a surge protector between your computer and the wall outlet will help prevent damage

sustain *verb* to keep a voltage at a certain level for a period of time (Spannung) aufrechterhalten

SVGA = SUPER VGA enhancement to the standard VGA graphics display system which allows resolutions of up to 800 x600 pixels with 16 million colours SVGA

SW = SHORT WAVE

swap
1 *noun* = SWAPPING
2 *verb* to stop using one program, put it into store temporarily, run another program, and when that is finished, return to the first one austauschen

◊ **swapping** *or* **swap** *noun* system where a program is moved to backing storage while another program is being used wechselndes Heraus- und Hereinholen

sweep *noun* movement of the electron beam over the area of a television screen in regular horizontal and vertical steps, producing the image Hin- und Rücklauf, Zeitablenkung

swim *noun* computer graphics that move slightly due to a faulty display unit Schwimmen

switch
1 *noun*
(a) (in some command-line operating systems) an additional character entered on the same line as the program command and which affects how the program runs Befehlszeilenschalter; *add the switch '/W' to the DOS command DIR and the directory listing will be displayed across the screen*
(b) point in a computer program where control can be passed to one of a number of choices Verzweigung
(c) mechanical *or* solid state device that can electrically connect *or* isolate two or more lines Verteiler; **switch train** = series of switches between a caller and a receiver in a telephone network Schaltfolge

2 *verb* to connect *or* disconnect two lines by activating a switch **einschalten** *or* **ausschalten; to switch on** = to start to provide power to a system by using a switch to connect the power supply lines to the circuit **einschalten; to switch off** = to disconnect the power supply to a device **ausschalten; to switch over** = to start using an alternative device when the primary one becomes faulty **umschalten; switched network backup** = user's choice of a secondary route through a network if the first is busy **Wählleitungsausweichverfahren; switched star** = cable television distribution system **sternförmiges Verteilungssystem; switched virtual call** = connection between two devices in a network that is only made when required, after a request signal **Verbindung auf Anfrage**

◊ **switchboard** *noun* central point in a telephone system, where the lines from various telephone handsets meet, where calls can be directed to any other telephone **Telefonzentrale, Vermittlung; switchboard operator** = person who works a central telephone switchboard, by connecting incoming and outgoing calls to various lines **Telefonist/-in**

◊ **switching** *noun* constant update of connections between changing sinks and sources in a network **Vermittlung; switching centre** = point in a communications network where messages can be switched to and from the various lines and circuits that end there **Vermittlungszentrale; switching circuit** = electronic circuit that can direct messages from one line *or* circuit to another in a switching centre **Umschaltnetzwerk; line switching** = communication line and circuit established on demand and held until no longer required **Durchschaltetechnik**

symbol *noun* sign *or* picture which represents something **Symbol;** *this language uses the symbol ? to represent the print command;* **logic symbol** = graphical symbol used to represent a type of logic function in a diagram **logisches Symbol; symbol table** *or* **library** = list of labels *or* names in a compiler *or* assembler, which relate to their addresses in the machine code program **Symboltabelle**

◊ **symbolic** *adjective* which acts as a symbol *or* which uses a symbol name *or* label **symbolisch; symbolic address** = address represented by a symbol *or* name **symbolische Adresse; symbolic code** *or* **instruction** = instruction that is in mnemonic form rather than a binary number **symbolischer Code** *or* **Befehl; symbolic debugging** = debugger that allows

symbolic representation of variables *or* locations **symbolische Austestung; symbolic language** = (i) any computer language where locations are represented by names; (ii) any language used to write source code **(i) & (ii) symbolische Programmiersprache; symbolic logic** = study of reasoning and thought (formal logic) **mathematische Logik; symbolic name** = name used as a label for a variable *or* location **(symbolischer) Name; symbolic programming** = writing a program in a source language **symbolisches Programmieren**

symmetric difference *noun* logical function whose output is true if either (of 2) inputs is true, and false if both inputs are the same **Antivalenz**

sync *noun* (*informal*) = SYNCHRONIZATION; **sync bit** = transmitted bit used to synchronize devices **Synchronisierungsbit; sync character** = transmitted character used to synchronize devices **Synchronisierungszeichen; sync** *or* **synchronization pulses** = transmitted pulses used to make sure that the receiver is synchronized with the transmitter **Synchronisierungsimpulse; in sync** = synchronized **synchronisiert; the two devices are out of sync** = the two devices are not properly synchronized **die beiden Geräte sind nicht synchronisiert**

◊ **synchronization** *noun* action of synchronizing two or more devices **Synchronisieren**

◊ **synchronize** *verb* to make sure that two or more devices *or* processes are coordinated in time or action **synchronisieren**

◊ **synchronizer** *noun* device that will perform a function when it receives a signal from another device **Synchronisierer**

◊ **synchronous** *adjective* which runs in sync with something else (such as a main clock) **synchron; synchronous computer** = computer in which each action can only take place when a timing pulse arrives **Synchronrechner; synchronous data link control (SDLC)** = data transmission protocol most often used in IBM's Systems Network Architecture (SNA) and defines how synchronous data is transmitted **SDLC; synchronous data network** = communications network in which all the actions throughout the network are controlled by a single timing signal **synchrones Datennetz; synchronous detection** = method of obtaining the signal from an amplitude modulation carrier **Synchronisationsdemodulation; synchronous idle character** = character transmitted by a DTE to ensure correct synchronization when no other character is being transmitted **Synchronisierungszeichen; synchronous mode** = system mode in which operations and events are synchronized with a clock signal **Synchronverfahren; synchronous network** = network in which all the links are synchronized with a single timing signal **Synchronnetz; synchronous system** = system in which all devices are synchronized to a main clock signal **Synchronsystem; synchronous transmission** = transmission of data from one device to another, where both devices are controlled by the same clock, and the transmitted data is synchronized with the clock signal **Synchronübertragung**

synonym *noun* word which means the same thing as another word **Synonym**

◊ **synonymous** *adjective* meaning the same **synonym;** *the words "error" and "mistake" are synonymous*

syntactic error *noun* programming error in which the program statement does not follow the syntax of the language **syntaktischer Fehler**

syntax *noun* grammatical rules that apply to a programming language **Syntax; syntax analysis** = stage in compilation where statements are checked to see if they obey the rules of syntax **Syntaxanalyse; syntax error** = programming error in which the program statement does not follow the syntax of the language **Syntaxfehler**

synthesis *noun* producing something artificially (from a number of smaller elements) **Synthese**

◊ **synthesize** *verb* to produce something artificially (from a number of smaller elements) **synthetisieren**

◊ **synthesizer** *noun* device which generates something (signals *or* sound *or* speech) **Synthesizer; music synthesizer** = device which makes musical notes which are similar to those made by musical instruments **Musiksynthesizer; speech synthesizer** = device which generates sounds which are similar to the human voice **Sprachsynthesizer**

◊ **synthetic address** *noun* location used by a program that has been produced by instructions within the program

errechnete Adresse; **synthetic language** = programming language in which the source program is written **synthetische Sprache**

> QUOTE despite the fact that speech can now be synthesized with very acceptable quality, all it conveys is linguistic information
>
> *Personal Computer World*

sysgen = SYSTEM GENERATION

system *noun* any group of hardware *or* software *or* peripherals, etc., which work together **System; adaptive system** = system which is able to alter its responses and processes according to inputs *or* situations **anpassungsfähiges System; computer system** = central processor with storage and associated peripherals which make up a working computer **Computersystem; expert system** = software which applies the knowledge, advice and rules followed by experts in a particular field to a user's data to help solve a problem **Expertensystem; information system** = computer system which provides information according to a user's requests **Informationssystem; interactive system** = system which provides an immediate response to the user's commands *or* programs *or* data **interaktives System; operating system (op sys)** = basic software that controls the running of the hardware and the management of data files, without the user having to operate it **Betriebssystem; secure system** = system that cannot be accessed without authorization **Sicherheitssystem; system check** = running diagnostic routines to ensure that there are no problems **Systemprüfung; system console** = main terminal or control centre for a computer which includes status lights and control switches **Systemkonsole; system control panel** = main computer system control switches and status indicators **Bedienungspult; system crash** = situation where the operating system stops working and has to be restarted **Systemabsturz; system design** = identifying and investigating possible solutions to a problem, and deciding upon the most appropriate system to solve the problem **Systemplanung; system diagnostics** = tests, features and messages that help find hardware *or* software faults **Systemdiagnose; system disk** = disk which holds the system software **Systemplatte; system firmware** = basic operating system functions and routines in a ROM device **im Festspeicher implementierte Systemsoftware; system flowchart** = diagram that shows each step of the computer procedures needed in a system **Systemablaufplan; system folder** = (in the Apple Macintosh environment) folder that contains the program files for the operating system and Finder **Systemordner; system generation** or **sysgen** = process of producing an optimum operating system for a particular task **Systemgenerierung; system library** = stored files that hold the various parts of a computer's operating system **Systembibliothek; system life cycle** = time when a system exists, between its initial design and its becoming out of date **Lebensdauer eines Systems; system log** = record of computer processor operations **Systemprotokoll; system prompt** = prompt which indicates the operating system is ready and waiting for the user to enter a system command **Eingabeaufforderung; system security** = measures, such as password, priority protection, authorization codes, etc., designed to stop browsing and hackers **Systemsicherheit; system software** = software which makes applications run on hardware **Systemsoftware; system specifications** = details of hardware and software required to perform certain tasks **Pflichtenheft; system support** = group of people that maintain and operate a system **Einsatzunterstützung; system unit** = main terminal or control centre for a computer which includes status lights and control switches **Systemeinheit**

◊ **System 7** ™ version of the operating system for the Apple Macintosh personal computer that introduces multitasking, virtual memory and peer-to-peer file sharing **System 7** ™

◊ **systems analysis** noun (i) analysing a process or system to see if it could be more efficiently carried out by a computer; (ii) examining an existing system with the aim of improving or replacing it **(i) & (ii) Systemanalyse; systems analyst** = person who undertakes system analysis **Systemanalytiker; systems integration** = combining different products from different manufacturers to create a system **Systemintegration; systems program** = program which controls the way in which a computer system works **Systemprogramm; systems programmer** = person who writes system software **Systemprogrammierer**

◊ **Systems Application Architecture (SAA)** noun standard developed by IBM which defines the look and feel of an application regardless of the hardware platform; SAA defines which

keystrokes carry out standard functions (such as F1 to display help), the application's display and how the application interacts with the operating system **Systemanwendungsarchitektur (SAA)**

◊ **Systems Network Architecture (SNA)** noun design methods developed by IBM which define how communications in a network should occur and allow different hardware to communicate **Systemnetzwerkarchitektur (SNA)**

QUOTE the core of an expert system is its database of rules
Personal Computer World

Tt

T = TERA- prefix meaning 10^{12}; one million million **T**

T carrier noun US standard for digital data transmission lines, such as T1, T1C, and corresponding signal standards DS1, DS1C **T-Träger**

T connector noun coaxial connector, shaped like the letter 'T', which connects two thin coaxial cables using BNC plugs and provides a third connection for another cable or network interface card **T-Anschluss**

◊ **T junction** noun connection at right angles with a main signal or power carrying cable **T-Verbindung**

◊ **T network** noun simple circuit network with three electronic components connected in the shape of a letter T **T-Netz**

T1 committee noun ANSI committee which sets digital communications standards for the US, particularly ISDN services **T1-Kommittee**

T1 link noun long distance data transmission link (not related to the T1 committee) that can carry data at 1.544Mbits per second **T1-Verbindung**

TAB = TABULATE

tab verb to tabulate or to arrange text in columns with the cursor automatically

tab 366 **takedown**

running from one column to the next in keyboarding **tabellieren**; *the list was neatly lined up by tabbing to column 10 at the start of each new line*; **tab character** = ASCII character 09hex which is used to align text at a preset tab stop **Tabulatorzeichen**; **tab key** = key on a keyboard, normally positioned on the far left, beside the 'Q' key, with two arrows pointing opposite horizontal directions, used to insert a tab character into text and so align the text at a preset tab stop **Tabulatortaste**; **tab memory** = ability of a editing program (usually a word-processor) to store details about various tab settings **Tabulatorspeicher**; **tab rack** *or* **ruler line** = graduated scale, displayed on the screen, showing the position of tabulation columns **Tabulatorraster**; *the tab rack shows you the left and right margins*; **tab stop** = preset points along a line, where the printing head *or* cursor will stop for each tabulation command **Tabulatorstop**

◊ **tabbing** *noun* movement of the cursor in a word-processing program from one tab stop to the next **Tabellieren**; *tabbing can be done from inside the program*; **decimal tabbing** = adjusting a column of numbers so that the decimal points are aligned vertically **mit Dezimaltabulator einrichten**

table *noun* list of data in columns and rows on a printed page *or* on the screen **Tabelle**; **decision table** = list of all possible events *or* states that could happen and the actions taken (sometimes used instead of a flowchart) **Entscheidungstabelle**; **look-up table** = collection of stored results that can be accessed very rapidly **Nachschlagetabelle**; *this is the value of the key pressed, use a look-up table to find its ASCII value*; **table lookup** = using one known value to select one entry in a table, providing a secondary value **Tabellensuchen**; **reference program table** = list produced by a compiler *or* system of the location, size and type of the variables, routines and macros within a program **Programmreferenzliste**; **symbol table** = list of all the symbols which are accepted by a language *or* compiler and their object code translation **Symboltabelle**; **table of contents** = list of the contents of a book, usually printed at the beginning **Inhaltsverzeichnis**

tablet *noun* **graphics tablet** = graphics pad *or* flat device that allows a user to input graphical information into a computer by drawing on its surface **Grafiktablett**; *it is much easier to draw accurately with a tablet than with a mouse*

tabulate *verb* to arrange text in columns, with the cursor moving to each new column automatically as the text is keyboarded **tabellieren**

◊ **tabular** *adjective* **in tabular form** = arranged in a table **in Tabellenform**

◊ **tabulating** *noun* processing punched cards, such as a sorting operation **Tabellieren**

◊ **tabulation** *noun* (i) arrangement of a table of figures; (ii) moving a printing head *or* cursor a preset distance along a line (i) **tabellarische Aufstellung**; (ii) **Tabulieren**; **tabulation markers** = symbols displayed to indicate the position of tabulation stops **Tabulatormarkierer**; **tabulation stop** = preset point along a line at which a printing head *or* cursor will stop for each tabulation command **Tabulatorstop**

◊ **tabulator** *noun* part of a typewriter *or* word-processor which automatically sets words *or* figures into columns **Tabulator**

TACS = TOTAL ACCESS COMMUNICATION SYSTEM UK standard for cellular radio systems **Nachrichtensystem**

tactile *adjective* using the sense of touch **fühlbar**; **tactile feedback** = information provided by using the sense of touch **taktile Information**; **tactile keyboard** = keyboard that provides some indication that a key has been pressed, such as a beep **taktile Tastatur**

tag *noun*
(a) one section of a computer instruction **Tag**
(b) identifying characters attached to a file *or* item (of data) **Identifizierungskennzeichen**; *each file has a three letter tag for rapid identification*

◊ **tag image file format (TIFF)** *noun* standard file format used to store graphic images **TIFF-Format, Tag Image File Format (TIFF)**

tail *noun*
(a) data recognized as the end of a list of data **Schluss**
(b) control code used to signal the end of a message **Endcode**

takedown *verb* to remove paper *or* disks *or* tape from a peripheral after one job and prepare it for the next **entfernen**; **takedown time** = amount of time required to takedown a peripheral ready for another job **Vorbereitungszeit**

take-up reel *noun* reel onto which magnetic tape is collected **Aufwickelspule;** *put the full reel on this spindle, and feed the tape into the take-up reel on the other spindle*

talk *verb* to speak *or* to communicate **sprechen**

◊ **talkback** *noun* speech communications between a control room and a studio **Anweisungen im Hintergrund**

QUOTE a variety of technologies exist which allow computers to talk to one another

Which PC?

tandem *noun* working in tandem = situation where two things are working together **im Gespann arbeiten; tandem processor** = two processors connected so that if one fails, the second takes over **Tandemprozessor; tandem switching** = one switch controlling another switch in the same exchange by means of a secondary switch **Durchgangsvermittlung**

tape *noun* long thin flat piece of material **Band; cassette tape** = tape stored on two small reels protected by a solid casing **Kassettenband;** *cassette tape is mainly used with home computers;* **(magnetic) tape** = narrow length of thin plastic coated with a magnetic material used to store signals magnetically **Magnetband; master tape** = magnetic tape which contains all the vital operating system routines, loaded by the initial program loader once when the computer is switched on *or* hard reset **Hauptband; (paper) tape** *or* **punched tape** = strip of paper on which information can be recorded in the form of punched holes **Lochstreifen; (video cassette) tape** = magnetic tape used in a video recorder to store pictures and sound **Videoband; open reel tape** = tape on a reel which is not enclosed in a cassette *or* cartridge **Wickelrolle; streaming tape drive** = device containing a continuous loop of tape, used as backing store **Endlosbandbetrieb; tape back-up** = to use (usually magnetic) tape as a medium for storing back-ups from faster main *or* secondary storage (such as RAM *or* hard disk) **Sicherung auf Band; tape cable** *or* **ribbon cable** = number of insulated conductors arranged next to each other forming a flat cable **Bandkabel; tape cartridge** = cassette box containing magnetic tape (on a reel) **Magnetbandkassette; tape cassette** = small box containing a reel of magnetic tape and a pickup reel **(Magnetband)kassette; tape**

code = coding system used for punched data representation on paper tape **Bandcode; tape counter** = indication (on a tape recorder) of the amount of tape that has been used **Bandzählwerk; tape deck** = device which plays back and records data onto magnetic tape **Magnetbandgerät; tape drive** = mechanism which controls magnetic tape movement over the tape heads **Magnetbandlaufwerk;** *our new product has a 96Mb streaming tape drive;* **tape format** = way in which blocks of data, control codes and location data is stored on tape **Bandformat; tape guide** = method by which the tape is correctly positioned over the tape head **Bandführung;** *the tape is out of alignment because one of the tape guides has broken;* **tape head** = transducer that can read and write signals onto the surface of magnetic tape **Bandleseschreibkopf; tape header** = identification information at the beginning of a tape **Vorspann; tape label** = tape header and trailer containing information about the contents of a tape **Bandkennzeichnung; tape library** = (i) secure area for the storage of computer data tapes; (ii) series of computer tapes kept in store for reference **(i) & (ii) Bandbibliothek; tape loadpoint** = position on a magnetic tape at which reading should commence to load a file **Bandladepunkt; tape punch** = machine that punches holes into paper tape **Streifenlocher; tape reader** = machine that reads punched holes in paper tape *or* signals on magnetic tape **Lochstreifenleser; tape recorder** = machine that records data and signals onto magnetic tape **Magnetbandgerät; tape streamer** = continuous loop of tape used for backing storage **Magnetbandstreamer; tape timer** = device that displays the total time left *or* amount of playing time used on a reel of magnetic tape **Bandzeitgeber; tape to card converter** = device that reads data from magnetic tape and stores it on punched cards **Lochstreifen-in-Lochkarte-Umsetzer; tape transmitter** = device that reads data from paper tape and transmits it to another point **Magnetband für Datenfernverarbeitung; tape trailer** = identification information at the beginning of a tape **Vorsatz; tape transport** = method (in a magnetic tape recorder) by which the tape is moved smoothly from reel to reel over the magnetic heads **Bandtransport; tape unit** = device with tape deck, amplifier, circuitry, etc. for recording and playing back tapes **Bandgerät**

COMMENT: cassettes *or* reels of tape are easy to use and cheaper than disks, the cassette casing usually conforms to a standard size. They are less adaptable and only provide sequential access, usually being used for master copies *or* making back-ups

target *noun* goal which you aim to achieve **Ziel; target computer** = computer on which software is to be run (but not necessarily written on, e.g. using a cross-assembler) **Zielcomputer; target disk** = disk onto which a file is to be copied **Zieldatenträger;; target language** = language into which a language will be translated from its source language **Objektsprache;** *the target language for this PASCAL program is machine code*

◊ **target level** = interpretive processing mode for program execution **Zielebene; target** *or* **run phase** = period of time during which the target program is run **Bearbeitungszeit; target program** = object program *or* computer program in object code form, produced by a compiler **Zielprogramm**

QUOTE the target board is connected to the machine through the in-circuit emulator cable
Electronics & Wireless World

tariff *noun* charge incurred by a user of a communications *or* computer system **Gebühr;** *there is a set tariff for logging on, then a rate for every minute of computer time used*

TASI = TIME ASSIGNED SPEECH INTERPOLATION method of using a voice channel for other signals during the gaps and pauses in a normal conversation **TASI (Verfahren zur Mehrfachausnutzung von Sprachkanälen bei Transatlantikkabeln)**

task *noun* job which is to be carried out by a computer **Aufgabe; multitasking** = ability of a computer system to run two or more programs at the same time **Multitasking;** *this operating system provides a multitasking environment, but not a multi-user one;* **task management** = system software that controls the use and allocation of resources to programs **Aufgabensteuerung, Tasksteuerung; task queue** = temporary storage of jobs waiting to be processed **Taskwarteschlange; task swapping** *or* **switching** = exchanging one program in memory for another which is temporarily stored on disk; task switching is not the same as multitasking which can execute several programs at once **Taskwechsel;** *see also* MULTITASKING

TAT = TURNAROUND TIME

TCP = TRANSMISSION CONTROL PROTOCOL standard data transmission protocol that provides full duplex transmission, the protocol bundles data into packets and checks for errors **TCP**

◊ **TCP/IP** = TRANSMISSION CONTROL PROTOCOL/INTERFACE PROGRAM data transfer protocol used in networks and communications systems (often used in Unix-based networks) **TCP/IP**

TDM = TIME DIVISION MULTIPLEXING method of combining several signals into one high-speed transmission carrier; each input signal is sampled in turn and the result transmitted, the receiver reconstructs the signals **Zeitmultiplextechnik, TDM**

TDR = TIME DOMAIN REFLECTOMETRY test that identifies where cable faults lie by sending a signal down the cable and measuring how long it takes for the reflection to come back **Impulsreflektometrie, TDR**

TDS = TRANSACTION-DRIVEN SYSTEM computer system that will normally run batch processing tasks until interrupted by a new transaction, at which point it allocates resources to the new transaction **vorganggesteuertes System**

tearing *noun* distortion of a television image due to bad sweep synchronization **Zerreißen, Zeilenausreißen**

technical *adjective* referring to a particular machine *or* process **technisch;** *the document gives all the technical details on the new computer;* **technical support** = (person who provides) technical advice to a user to explain how to use software *or* hardware or explain why it might not work **Technical Support, technischer Support, technische Unterstützung**

◊ **technician** *noun* person who is specialized in industrial work **Techniker/-in;** *the computer technicians installed the new system;* **laboratory technician** = person who deals with practical work in a laboratory **Labortechniker/-in**

◊ **technique** *noun* skilled way of doing a job **Technik;** *the company has developed a new technique for processing customers' disks; he has a special technique for answering complaints from users of the software*

technology *noun* applying scientific knowledge to industrial processes **Technologie; information technology (IT) =** technology involved in acquiring, storing, processing, and distributing information by electronic means (including radio, TV, telephone and computers) **Informationstechnik; the introduction of new technology =** putting new electronic equipment into a business *or* industry **die Einführung neuer Technologien**

◊ **technological** *adjective* referring to technology **technologisch; the technological revolution =** changing of industrial methods by introducing new technology **die technologische Revolution**

tel = TELEPHONE

tele- *prefix* (i) meaning long distance; (ii) referring to television **(i) Fern-, (ii) Tele-; telebanking =** system by which an account holder can carry out transactions with his bank via a terminal and communications network **Homebanking; telecine =** method of displaying a cine film on television **Film-Fernsehbetrieb-Methode; telecommunications =** technology of passing and receiving messages over a distance (as in radio, telephone, telegram, satellite broadcast, etc.) **Fernmeldewesen; telecommuting =** practice of working on a computer in one place (normally from home) that is linked by modem to the company's central office allowing messages and data to be transferred **Telecommuting; teleconferencing =** to link video, audio and computer signals from different locations so that distant people can talk and see each other, as if in a conference room **Videokonferenztechnik, Telekonferenz; telecontrol =** control of a remote device by a telecommunications link **Nachrichtenübertragungssteuerung; telegram =** message sent to another country by telegraph **Telegramm;** *to send an international telegram*

telegraph
1 *noun* message transmitted using a telegraphy system **Telegramm; telegraph office =** office from which telegrams can be sent **Telegrafenamt**
2 *verb* to send a telegram to another person; to send printed *or* written *or* drawn material by long-distance telegraphy **telegrafieren;** *they telegraphed their agreement; the photographs were telegraphed to New York*

◊ **telegraphic** *adjective* referring to a telegraph system **telegrafisch; telegraphic**
address = short address to which a telegram is sent **Telegrammadresse**

◊ **telegraphy** *noun* system of sending messages along wires using direct current pulses **Telegrafie; carrier telegraphy =** system of transmitting telegraph signals via a carrier signal **Trägerfrequenztelegrafie**

teleinformatic services *noun* any data only service, such as telex, facsimile, which uses telecommunications **Datenfernübertragungsservice**

telematics *noun* interaction of all data processing and communications devices (computers, networks, etc.) **Telematik**

telemessage *noun (GB)* message sent by telephone, and delivered as a card **Fernnachricht**

telemetry *noun* data from remote measuring devices transmitted over a telecommunications link **Fernmessung**

teleordering *noun* book ordering system, in which the bookseller's orders are entered into a computer which then puts the order through to the distributor at the end of the day **Bestellelektronik**

telephone
1 *noun* machine used for speaking to someone over a long distance **Telefon;** *we had a new telephone system installed last week;* **to be on the telephone =** to be speaking to someone using the telephone **telefonieren;** *the managing director is on the telephone to Hong Kong; she has been on the telephone all day;* **by telephone =** using the telephone **über das Telefon, per Telefon;** *to place an order by telephone; to reserve a room by telephone;* **conference telephone =** telephone specially made to be used in a teleconference **Konferenztelefon; house telephone** *or* **internal telephone =** telephone for calling from one room to another in an office *or* hotel **Haustelefon; telephone answering machine =** device that answers a telephone, plays a prerecorded message and records any response **automatischer Anrufbeantworter; telephone book** *or* **telephone directory =** book which lists people and businesses in alphabetical order with their telephone numbers **Telefonbuch;** *he looked up the number of the company in the telephone book;* **telephone call =** speaking to someone on the telephone **Telefonanruf; to make a telephone call =** to dial a number and speak to someone on the telephone **telefonieren; to answer the**

telephone *or* **to take a telephone call** = to speak in reply to a call on the telephone **das Telefon abnehmen; ein Telefongespräch annehmen; telephone (data carrier)** = using a modem to send binary data as sound signals over a telephone line **Telefonübertragung; telephone exchange** = central office where the telephones of a whole district are linked **Fernsprechamt; telephone number** = set of figures for a particular telephone subscriber **Telefonnummer;** *can you give me your telephone number?;* **telephone operator** = person who operates a telephone switchboard **Telefonist/-in; telephone orders** = orders received by telephone **telefonische Bestellungen;** *since we mailed the catalogue we have received a large number of telephone orders;* **telephone repeater** = receiver, transmitter and associated circuits that boost a telephone signal **Telefonsignalverstärker; telephone subscriber** = person who has a telephone connected to the main network **Teilnehmer/-in; telephone switchboard** = central point in a private telephone system where all internal and external lines meet **(Telefon)zentrale** **2** *verb* **to telephone a person** = to call a person by telephone **jemanden anrufen;** *his secretary telephoned to say he would be late;* **he telephoned the order through to the warehouse** = he telephoned the warehouse to place an order **er hat die Bestellung ans Lager durchtelefoniert; to telephone about something** = to make a telephone call to speak about something **wegen etwas anrufen;** *he telephoned about the order for computer stationery;* **to telephone for something** = to make a telephone call to ask for something **wegen etwas anrufen, etwas telefonisch bestellen;** *he telephoned for a taxi*

◊ **telephonist** *noun* person who works a telephone switchboard **Telefonist/-in**

◊ **telephony** *noun* data *or* signal transmission over a telephone using audio frequencies **Fernsprechwesen**

teleprinter *noun* device that is capable of sending and receiving data from a distant point by means of a telegraphic circuit, and printing out the message on a printer **Fernschreiber;** *you can drive a teleprinter from this modified serial port;* **teleprinter interface** = terminal interface *or* hardware and software combination required to control the functions of a terminal **Fernschreiberschnittstelle; teleprinter roll** = roll of paper onto which messages are printed **Fernschreiberpapier**

teleprocessing (TP) *noun* processing

of data at a distance (as on a central computer from outside terminals) **Datenfernverarbeitung**

telesales *noun* sales made by telephone **telefonischer Verkauf**

◊ **teleshopping** *noun* use of a telephone-based data service such as viewdata to order products from a shop **Teleshopping**

telesoftware (TSW) *noun* software which is received from a viewdata *or* teletext service **Bildschirmtextsystem;** *the telesoftware was downloaded yesterday*

teletext *noun* method of transmitting text and information with a normal television signal, usually as a serial bit stream that can be displayed using a special decoder **Teletext**

teletype (TTY) *noun* term used for teleprinter equipment **Fernschreiber**

◊ **teletypewriter** *noun* keyboard and printer attached to a computer system which can input data either direct *or* by making punched paper tape **Fernschreiber**

◊ **teletypesetting** *noun* typesetter operated from a punched paper tape **Fernsatz**

television (TV) *noun* (i) system for broadcasting pictures and sound using high-frequency radio waves, captured by a receiver and shown on a screen; (ii) device that can receive (modulated) video signals from a computer *or* broadcast signals with an aerial and display images on a CRT screen with sound **(i) Fernsehen; (ii) Fernsehgerät; television camera** = optical lenses in front of an electronic device which can convert images into electronic signals in a form that can be transmitted *or* displayed on a TV **Fernsehkamera; television monitor** = device able to display signals from a computer without sound, but not broadcast signals (this is usually because there is no demodulator device which is needed for broadcast signals) **Fernsehmonitor; television projector** = device that projects a TV image onto a large screen **Fernsehprojektor; television receiver** = device able to display with sound, broadcast signals *or* other modulated signals (such as signals from a video recorder) **Fernsehempfänger; television receiver/monitor** = device able to act as a TV receiver *or* monitor **Fernsehempfänger/-monitor; television scan** = horizontal movement of the picture beam over the screen, producing one line of an image **Abtastung; television tube** = CRT with electronic devices that provide the line by line horizontal and vertical scanning movement of the picture beam **Fernsehröhre;** *see also* CRT, RGB

> COMMENT: in a colour TV there are three electron guns corresponding to red, green and blue signals. In the UK the TV screen has 625 lines to be scanned; this is normally done in two sweeps of alternate lines, providing a flicker-free image

telex
1 *noun*
(a) system for sending messages using telephone lines, which are printed out at the receiving end on a special printer **Telex;** *to send information by telex; the order came by telex;* **telex line** = wire linking a telex machine to the telex system **Telexverbindung;** *we cannot communicate with our Nigerian office because of the breakdown of the telex lines;* **telex operator** = person who operates a telex machine **Telexoperator; telex subscriber** = company which has a telex **Telexteilnehmer**
(b) a telex = (i) a machine for sending and receiving telex messages; (ii) a message sent by telex **(i) ein Fernschreiber; (ii) ein Telex;** *he sent a telex to his head office; we received his telex this morning*
2 *verb* to send a message using a teleprinter **ein Telex schicken;** *can you telex the Canadian office before they open? he telexed the details of the contract to New York*

template *noun* (i) plastic *or* metal sheet with cut-out symbols to help the drawing of flowcharts and circuit diagrams; (ii) *(in text processing)* standard text (such as a standard letter *or* invoice) into which specific details (company address *or* prices *or* quantities) can be added **(i) & (ii) Schablone; template command** = command that allows functions *or* other commands to be easily set **Schablonenbefehl;** *a template paragraph command enables the user to specify the number of spaces each paragraph should be indented; see also* STANDARD, FORM LETTER

temporary register *noun* register used for temporary storage for the results of an ALU operation **Zwischenregister; temporary storage** = storage which is not permanent **Zwischenspeicher; temporary swap file** = file on a hard disk which is used by software to store data temporarily or for

software that implements virtual memory, such as Microsoft's Windows **temporäre Auslagerungsdatei**

◊ **temporarily** *adverb* for a certain time *or* not permanently **vorübergehend**

10Base2 IEEE standard specification for running Ethernet over thin coaxial cable **10Base2**

◊ **10Base5** IEEE standard specification for running Ethernet over thick coaxial cable **10Base5**

◊ **10BaseT** IEEE standard specification for running Ethernet over unshielded twisted pair cable **10BaseT**

ten's complement *noun* formed by adding one to the nine's complement of a decimal number **Zehnerkomplement**

tera- (T) *prefix* prefix meaning 10^{12}; one million million **Tera- (T)**

◊ **terabyte** *noun* one thousand gigabytes or one million megabytes of data **Terabyte**

terminal
1 *noun*
(a) device usually made up of a display unit and a keyboard which allows entry and display of information when on-line to a central computer system (computer terminals can be intelligent, smart or dumb according to the inbuilt processing capabilities) **Terminal; addressable terminal** = terminal that will only accept data if it has the correct address and identification data in the message header **adressierbare Datenstation;** *all the messages go to all the terminals since none are addressable terminals;* **applications terminal** = terminal (such as at a sales desk) which is specifically configured to carry out certain tasks **Anwendungsterminal; dumb terminal** = peripheral that can only receive and transmit data, and is not capable of processing data **nicht programmierbarer Terminal (zum Drucken-Sichern-Kopieren); central terminal** = terminal which controls communications between a central *or* host computer and remote terminals **Zentraldatenstation; intelligent terminal** *or* **smart terminal** = computer terminal which contains a CPU and memory, allowing basic data processing to be carried out, usually with the facility to allow the user to program it independently of the host computer **intelligente Datenstation;** *the new intelligent terminal has a built-in text editor;* **master terminal** = one terminal in a

network that has priority over any other, used by the system manager to set-up the system *or* carry out privileged commands **Hauptbedienerstation;** *the system manager uses the master terminal to restart the system;* **remote terminal** = computer terminal connected to a distant computer system **entfernt stehende Datenstation; slave terminal** = terminal controlled by a main computer *or* terminal **abhängige/untergeordnete Datenstation; terminal area** = part of a printer circuit board at which edge connectors can be connected **Anschlussstelle für eine Datenstation; terminal character set** = range of characters available for a particular type of terminal, these might include graphics *or* customized characters **Zeichensatz einer Datenstation; terminal controller** = hardware device *or* IC that controls a terminal including data communications and display **Terminalsteuerelement; terminal emulation** = ability of a terminal to emulate the functions of another type of terminal so that display codes can be correctly decoded and displayed and keystrokes correctly coded and transmitted **Terminalemulation; terminal identity** = unique code transmitted by a viewdata terminal to provide identification and authorization of a user **Stationsidentifikationscode; terminal interface** = hardware and software combination required to control the functions of a terminal from a computer **Geräteschnittstelle;** *the network controller has 16 terminal interfaces;* (*slang*) **terminal junky (TJ)** = person (a hacker) who is obsessed with computers **Computerfreak;** *my son has turned into a real terminal junky;* **terminal keyboard** = standard QWERTY *or* special keyboard allowing input at a terminal **Tastatur einer Datenstation**
(b) an electrical connection point; **terminal block** = strip of insulated connection points for wires **Anschlussblock; terminal strip** = row of electrical connectors that allow pairs of wires to be electrically connected using a screw-down metal plate **Klemmleiste**
(c) point in a network where a message can be transmitted *or* received **Netzstation;** *see also* SOURCE, SINK
2 *adjective* fatal *or* which cannot be repaired **endgültig;** *the computer has a terminal fault*

QUOTE The London Borough of Hackney has standardised on terminal emulator software from Omniplex to allow its networked desktop users to select Unix or DOS applications from a single menu
Computing

terminate *verb* to end **abbrechen, beenden**
◊ **terminate and stay resident (TSR) program** *noun* program which loads itself into main memory and carries out a function when activated **speicherresidentes Programm, TSR-Programm;** *when you hit Ctrl-F5, you will activate the TSR program and it will display your day's diary*

◊ **termination** *noun* ending *or* stopping **Abbruch; abnormal termination** = unexpected stoppage of a program which is being run, caused by a fault *or* power failure **abnormaler Abbruch**

◊ **terminator** *noun*
(a) (i) (in a LAN) resistor that fits onto the each end of a coaxial cable in a bus network to create an electrical circuit; (ii) (in a SCSI installation) resistor that fits onto the last SCSI device in the daisy-chain, creating an electrical circuit (i) **Abschlusswiderstand;** (ii) **Terminator, Abschlussstecker**
(b) item in a list of data, which indicates the end of a list **Endezeichen**

ternary *adjective* (number system) with three possible states **ternär**

test
1 *noun* action carried out on a device *or* program to establish whether it is working correctly, and if not, which component *or* instruction is not working **Prüfung, Test; test bed** = (software) environment used to test programs **Testumgebung; test data** = data with known results prepared to allow a new program to be tested **Prüfdaten; test equipment** = special equipment which tests hardware *or* software **Prüfgerät;** *the engineer has special test equipment for this model;* **test numeric** = check to ensure that numerical information is numerical **Prüfung auf numerisch; test pattern** = graphical pattern displayed on a TV screen to test its colour, balance, horizontal and vertical linearity and contrast **Testmuster;** *see also* BENCHMARK; **test run** = program run with test data to ensure that the software is working correctly **Testlauf;** *a test run will soon show up any errors*
2 *verb* to carry out an examination of a device *or* program to see if it is working correctly **prüfen, testen; saturation testing** = testing a communications network by transmitting large quantities of data and messages over it **Sättigungsprüfung**

text *noun* alphanumeric characters that convey information **Text; ragged text** = unjustified text, text with a ragged right margin **Flattersatz**; **start-of-text (SOT** *or* **STX)** = transmitted code indicating the end of control and address information and the start of the message **Anfang des Textes**; **text compression** = reducing the space required by a section of text, by using one code to represent more than one character, by removing spaces and punctuation marks, etc. **Textkomprimierung**; **text-editing facilities** = word-processing system that allows the user to add, delete, move, insert and correct sections of text **Textverarbeitungssystem, Editierprogramm**; **text-editing function** = option in a program that provides text-editing facilities **Textverarbeitungs-, Editierfunktion**; *the program includes a built-in text-editing function;* **text editor** = piece of software that provides the user with text-editing facilities **Texteditor**; *the text editor will only read files smaller than 64Kbytes long;* **text file** = stored file on a computer that contains text rather than digits *or* data **Textdatei**; **text formatter** = program that arranges a text file according to preset rules, such as line width and page size **Textformatierer**; *people use the text formatter as a basic desk-top publishing program;* **text management** = facilities that allow text to be written, stored, retrieved, edited and printed **Textanwendungen**; **text manipulation** = facilities that allow text editing, changing, inserting and deleting **Textbearbeitung**; **text processing** = word-processing *or* using a computer to keyboard, edit and output text, in the forms of letters, labels, etc. **Textverarbeitung**; **text register** = temporary computer storage register for text characters only **Textregister**; **text retrieval** = information retrieval system that allows the user to examine complete documents rather than just a reference to one **Textretrieval, Textwiederauffindung**; **text screen** = area of computer screen that has been set up to display text **Textbereich**; **text-to-speech converter** = electronic device that uses a speech synthesizer to produce the spoken equivalent of a piece of text that has been entered **Text-in-Sprache-Umwandler**

◊ **textual** *adjective* referring to text **Text-**; *the editors made several textual changes before the proofs were sent back for correction*

TFT screen = THIN FILM TRANSISTOR SCREEN method of creating a high-quality LCD display often used in laptop computers **Dünnfilmtransistorbildschirm, TFT-Bildschirm**

thermal *adjective* referring to heat **Thermo-**; **thermal inkjet printer** = computer printer which produces characters by sending a stream of tiny drops, (created by heating the ink) of electrically charged ink onto the paper (the movement of the ink drops is controlled by an electric field; this is a non-impact printer with few moving parts) **Thermotintenstrahldrucker**; **thermal paper** = special paper whose coating turns black when heated, allowing characters to be printed by using a matrix of small heating elements **Thermopapier, wärmeempfindliches Spezialpapier**; **thermal printer** = type of printer where the character is formed on thermal paper with a printhead containing a matrix of small heating elements **Thermodrucker**

|| COMMENT: this type of printer is very quiet in operation since the printing head does not strike the paper

◊ **thermal transfer** *or* **thermal wax** *or* **thermal wax transfer printer** *noun* method of printing where the colours are produced by melting coloured wax onto the paper **Thermotransferdrucker**; *thermal wax transfer technology still provides the best colour representation on paper for PC output*

thermistor *noun* electronic device whose resistance changes with temperature **Thermistor (temperaturabhängiger Widerstand)**

thermo-sensitive *adjective* which is sensitive to heat **wärmeempfindlich**

thesaurus *noun* file which contains synonyms that are displayed as alternatives to a misspelt word during a spell-check **Thesaurus**

thick *adjective* with a large distance between two surfaces **dick**; **thick film** = miniature electronic circuit design in which miniature components are mounted on an insulating base, then connected as required **Dickschicht**

|| COMMENT: this provides a package that is larger but cheaper for short runs than chips

◊ **thick-Ethernet** *noun* network implemented using thick coaxial cable and transceivers to connect branch cables; can stretch long distances **Thickwire-Ethernet**; *see also* ETHERNET; THIN-ETHERNET

thimble printer *noun* computer printer using a printing head similar to a daisy wheel but shaped like a thimble **Fingerhutdrucker**

thin *adjective* with only a small distance between two surfaces **dünn; thin film** = method of constructing integrated circuits by depositing in a vacuum very thin patterns of various materials onto a substrate to form the required interconnected components **Dünnschicht;** *see also* CHIP, SUBSTRATE; **thin film memory** = high-speed access RAM device using a matrix of magnetic cells and a matrix of read/write heads to access them **Dünnschichtspeicher; thin film transistor screen** *see* TFT screen; **thin window** = single line display window **Einzeilenfenster**

◊ **thin-Ethernet** *noun* (the most popular type of Ethernet) network implemented using thin coaxial cable and BNC connectors; it is limited to distances of around 1000m **Thinwire-Ethernet**

third *adjective* **third generation computers** = range of computers where integrated circuits were used instead of transistors **Computer der dritten Generation; third party** = company which supplies items *or* services for a system sold by one party (the seller) to another (the buyer) **Fremdhersteller**

COMMENT: a third party might supply computer maintenance *or* might write programs, etc.

QUOTE they expect third party developers to enhance the operating systems by adding their own libraries
PC Business World

thirty-two bit system *noun* microcomputer system *or* CPU that handles data in thirty-two bit words **32-Bit-System**

thrashing *noun* (i) excessive disk activity; (ii) configuration *or* program fault in a virtual memory system, that results in a CPU wasting time moving pages of data between main memory and disk *or* backing store (i) **Festplattenüberlastung;** (ii) **Flattern**

thread *noun* program that consists of many independent smaller sections or beads **gekettetes Programm; threaded file** = file in which an entry will contain data and an address to the next entry that has the same data content (allowing rapid retrieval of all identical records) **gekettete Datei; threaded language** = programming language that allows many small sections of code to be written then used by a main program **gekettete Programmiersprache; threaded tree** = structure in which each node contains a pointer to other nodes **gekettete Baumstruktur**

QUOTE WigWam makes it easier for a user to follow a thread in a bulletin-board conference topic by ordering responses using a hierarchical indent similar to that found in outline processor
Computing

three-address instruction *noun* instruction which contains the addresses of two operands and the location where the result is to be stored **Dreiadressbefehl**

◊ **three-dimensional** *or* **3D** *adjective* (image) which has three dimensions (width, breadth and depth), and therefore gives the impression of being solid **dreidimensional; 3D**

◊ **three input adder** *see* FULL ADDER

three-pin plug *noun* standard plug with three connections, to connect an electric device to the mains electricity supply **Stecker mit drei Kontaktstiften**

COMMENT: the three pins are for the live, neutral and earth connections

three state logic *noun* logic gate *or* IC that has three possible output states (rather than the usual two): logic high, logic low and high impedance **Dreizustandslogik, Tri-State-Logik**

throughput *noun* rate of production by a machine *or* system, measured as total useful information processed in a set period of time **Datendurchlauf;** *for this machine throughput is 1.3 inches per second (ips) scanning speed;* **rated throughput** = maximum throughput of a device that will still meet original specifications **maximale Durchsatzrate**

thyristor *noun* semiconductor device that will allow the control of an AC voltage according to an input signal **Thyristor**

tie line *or* **tie trunk** *noun* communications link between switchboards *or* PBX systems **Querverbindungsleitung**

TIFF = TAG IMAGE FILE FORMAT standard file format used to store graphic images **TIFF**

tilde *noun* printed accent (˜), commonly used over the letter "n" in Spanish, vowels in Portuguese, etc. **Tilde**

tile *verb* (in a GUI) to arrange a group of

windows so that they are displayed side by side without overlapping **nebeneinander anordnen**

tilt and swivel *adjective* (monitor) which is mounted on a pivot so that it can be moved to point in the most convenient direction for the operator **kippbar und schwenkbar**

time
1 *noun* period expressed in hours, minutes, seconds, etc. **Zeit; addition time** = time an adder takes to carry out an addition operation **Additionszeit; cycle time** = time between start and stop of an operation, especially between addressing a memory location and receiving the data **Zykluszeit; queuing time** = period of time messages have to wait before they are processed *or* transmitted **Wartezeit; real time** = actions *or* processing time that is of the same order of magnitude as the problem to be solved (i.e. the processing time is within the same time as the problem to be solved, so that the result can influence the source of the data) **Echtzeit; response time** = (i) time which passes between the user starting an action (by pressing a key) and the result appearing on the screen; (ii) speed with which a system responds to a stimulus **(i) & (ii) Antwortzeit; stop time** = time taken for a spinning disk to come to rest after it is no longer powered **Stoppzeit; time address code** = signal recorded on a video tape to display time elapsed when editing **Zeitadresscode; time base** = (i) signal used as a basis for timing purposes; (ii) regular sawtooth signal used in an oscilloscope to sweep the beam across the screen **(i) & (ii) Zeitbasis; time coded page** = teletext page that contains additional text which is displayed after a period of time **zeitcodierte Seite; time derived channel** = communications channel using time division multiplexing techniques **Zeitmultiplexkanal; time display** = digits *or* dial which show the current time **Zeitanzeige; time division multiple access** = time division multiplexing system that allocates time slots to various users according to demand **zeitmultiplexe Zugriffsmethode; time division multiplexing (TDM)** = method of combining several signals into one high-speed transmission carrier; each input signal is sampled in turn and the result transmitted, the receiver reconstructs the signals **Zeitmultiplextechnik, TDM; time division switching** = moving data from one time slot to another **Zeitmultiplexdurchschaltung; time domain analysis** = signal analysis as it varies with time **Zeitbereichsanalyse; time domain reflectometry (TDR)** = test which identifies where cable faults lie by sending a signal down the cable and measuring how long it takes for the reflection to come back **Impulsreflektometrie, TDR; time shift viewing** = use of a video recorder to record programs which are then replayed at a more convenient time **zeitversetztes Anschauen; time slice** = amount of time allowed for a single task in a time-sharing system *or* in multiprogramming; period of time allocated for a user *or* program *or* job within a multitasking system **Zeitscheibe; time slot** = period of time that contains an amount of data about one signal in a time division multiplexing system **Zeitkanal**
2 *verb* to measure the time taken by an operation **die Zeit messen; timed backup** = backup which occurs automatically after a period of time, or at a particular time each day **(automatische) Datensicherung nach Zeitplan; microprocessor timing** = correct selection of system clock frequency to allow for slower peripherals etc. **Zeitberechnung mit Mikroprozessoren; network timing** = signals that correctly synchronize the transmission of data **Netzsynchronisation; timing loop** = computer program loop that is repeated a number of times to produce a certain time delay **Taktschleife; timing master** = clock signal that synchronizes all the components in a system **Haupttaktgeber**

◊ **timeout** *noun* (i) logoff procedure carried out if no data is entered on an on-line terminal; (ii) period of time reserved for an operation **(i) Zeitsperre; (ii) Zeitauslösung**

◊ **time out** *verb* (of an event or option) to become no longer valid after a period of time **bei Zeitüberschreitung abbrechen;** *if you do not answer this question within one minute, the program times out and moves onto the next question*

◊ **timer** *noun* device which records the time taken for an operation to be completed **Zeitnehmer**

◊ **time-sharing** *noun* computer system that allows several independent users to use it *or* be on-line at the same time **Gemeinschaftsbetrieb, Timesharing**

COMMENT: in time-sharing, each user appears to be using the computer all the time, when in fact each is using the CPU for a short time slice only; the CPU processing one user for a short time then moving on to the next

tiny model *noun* memory model of the Intel 80x86 processor family that allows a combined total of 64Kb for data and code **Tiny-Modell**

title *noun* identification name given to a file *or* program *or* disk **(externer) Name; title of disk** = identification of a disk, referring to its contents **Plattenname; title page** = first main page of a book, with the title, the name of the author and the name of the publisher **Titelseite**

toggle *verb* to switch between two states **kippen; toggle switch** = electrical switch that has only two positions **Kippschalter**

> QUOTE the symbols can be toggled on or off the display
>
> *Micro Decision*

token *noun*
(a) internal code which replaces a reserved word *or* program statement in a high-level language **Kennzeichen, Token**
(b) (in a local area network) control packet which is passed between workstations to control access to the network **Token; control token** = special sequence of bits transmitted over a LAN to provide control actions **Steuertoken**

◊ **token bus network** *noun* IEEE 802.4 standard for a local area network formed with a bus-topology cable; workstations transfer data by passing a token **Token-Bus-Netzwerk**

◊ **token passing** *noun* method of controlling access to a local area network by using a token packet: a workstation cannot transmit data until it receives the token **Tokenweitergabe**

◊ **token ring network** *noun* IEEE 802.5 standard that uses a token passed from one workstation to the next in a ring network, a workstation can only transmit data if it captures the token (Token Ring networks, although logically a ring, are often physically wired in a star topology) **Token-Ring-Netzwerk;** *Token Ring networks are very democratic and retain performance against increasing load*

tomo- *prefix* meaning a cutting *or* section **Tomo-**

◊ **tomogram** *noun* picture of part of the body taken by tomography **Tomogramm**

◊ **tomography** *noun* scanning of a particular part of the body using X-rays *or* ultrasound **Tomographie; computerized axial tomography (CAT)** = X-ray examination where a computer creates a picture of a section of a patient's body **Computertomographie**

tone *noun*
(a) sound at one single frequency **Ton; dial(ling) tone** = sound made by a telephone to show that it is ready for the number to be dialled **Wählton; engaged tone** = sound made by a telephone showing that the number dialled is busy **Besetztzeichen; ringing tone** = sound made by a telephone showing that the number dialled is not busy and is just waiting for the call to be answered **Freizeichen** *or* **Rufzeichen; tone dialling** = telephone dialling system that uses different frequency tones to represent the dialled number **Tonwählsystem; tone signalling** = tones used in a telephone network to convey control *or* address signals **Tonsignalsystem**
(b) shade of a colour **Farbton, Schattierung;** *the graphics package can give several tones of blue*

toner *noun* finely powdered ink (usually black) that is used in laser printers; the toner is transferred onto the paper by electrical charge, then fixed permanently to the paper by heating **Toner;** *if you get toner on your hands, you can only wash it off with cold water;* **toner cartridge** = plastic container which holds powdered toner for use in a laser printer **Tonerkassette, Tonerbehälter, Tonerpatrone**

toolbox *noun*
(a) box containing instruments needed to repair *or* maintain *or* install equipment **Werkzeugkasten**
(b) set of predefined routines *or* functions that are used when writing a program **Toolbox, Werkzeugsammlung**

◊ **Toolbox** ™ *noun* (in an Apple Macintosh) set of utility programs stored in ROM to provide graphic functions **Toolbox** ™

◊ **toolkit** *noun* series of functions which help a programmer write *or* debug programs **Werkzeug(ausrüstung)**

◊ **tools** *noun* set of utility programs (backup, format, etc.) in a computer system **Hilfsprogramme**

top *noun* part which is the highest point of something **Spitze; top down programming** *or* **structured programming** = method of writing programs where a complete system is divided into simple blocks *or* tasks, each block unit is written and tested before proceeding with the next one **strukturierte**

Programmierung; **top of stack** = the newest data item added to a stack **Spitze des Stapels**; **top space** = number of blank lines left at the top of a printed text **Durchschuss am oberen Rand**

topology *noun* way in which the various elements in a network are interconnected **Topologie**; **bus topology** = network topology in which all devices are connected to a single cable which has terminators at each end **Bustopologie**; *Ethernet is a network that uses the bus topology*; *token ring uses a ring topology*; **network topology** = layout of machines in a network (such as a star network *or* a ring network *or* a bus network) which will determine what cabling and interfaces are needed and what possibilities the network can offer **Netzwerktopologie**; **star topology** = network topology in which all devices are connected by individual cable to a single central hub **Sterntopologie**; *if one workstation cable snaps in a star topology, the rest continue, unlike a bus topology*

TOPS ™ software that allows IBM PCs and Apple Macintoshes to share files on a network **TOPS** ™

torn tape *noun* communications switching method, in which the received message is punched onto a paper tape which is fed by hand into the appropriate tape reader for transmission to the required destination **Lochstreifen**

total *noun* **hash total** = total of a number of hashed entries, used for error detection **Kontrollsumme**

touch *verb* to make , contact with something with the fingers **berühren**; **touch pad** = flat device that can sense where on its surface and when it is touched, used to control a cursor position *or* switch a device on or off **Cursorsteuerungsfeld**; **touch screen** = computer display that has a grid of infrared transmitters and receivers, positioned on either side of the screen used to control a cursor position (when a user wants to make a selection *or* move the cursor, he points to the screen, breaking two of the beams, which gives the position of his finger) **Sensorbildschirm**

◊ **touch up** *verb* to remove scratches *or* other marks from a photograph *or* image **retuschieren**

TP = TELEPROCESSING, TRANSACTION PROCESSING

TPI = TRACKS PER INCH

trace *noun* method of verifying that a program is functioning correctly, in which the current status and contents of the registers and variables used are displayed after each instruction step **Programmablaufverfolgung**; **trace program** = diagnostic program that executes a program that is being debugged, one instruction at a time, displaying the states and registers **Programm zur Programmablaufverfolgung**; **trace trap** = selective breakpoint where a tracing program stops, allowing registers to be examined **Unterbrechung während einer Ablaufverfolgung**

track
1 *noun* one of a series of thin concentric rings on a magnetic disk *or* thin lines on a tape, which the read/write head accesses and along which the data is stored in separate sectors **(Magnet)spur**; **address track** = track on a magnetic disk containing the address of files, etc., stored on the other tracks **Adressenspur**; **track address** = location of a particular track on a magnetic disk **Spuradresse**; **tracks per inch (TPI)** = number of concentric data tracks on a disk surface per inch **Spuren pro Inch**
2 *verb* to follow a path *or* track correctly **spurgenau laufen**; *the read head is not tracking the recorded track correctly*

COMMENT: the first track on a tape is along the edge and the tape may have up to nine different tracks on it, while a disk has many concentric tracks around the central hub; the track and sector addresses are set-up during formatting

trackball *noun* device used to move a cursor on-screen, which is controlled by turning a ball contained in a case **Steuerungsball, Maus**

tractor feed *noun* method of feeding paper into a printer, where sprocket wheels on the printer connect with the sprocket holes on either edge of the paper to pull the paper through **Stachelbandführung**

QUOTE the printer is fairly standard with both tractor and cut sheet feed system
Which PC?

traffic *noun* term covering all the messages and other signals processed by a system *or* carried by a communications link **(Daten)verkehr**; *our Ethernet network begins to slow down if the traffic reaches 60 per cent* *of the bandwidth;* **traffic analysis** = study of the times, types and quantities of messages and signals being processed by a system **Datenverkehrsanalyse; traffic density** = number of messages and data transmitted over a network *or* system in a period of time **Datenverkehrsdichte; traffic intensity** = ratio of messages entering a queue against those leaving the queue within a certain time **Datenverkehrsquote; incoming traffic** = data and messages received **eingehende Daten** NOTE: no plural

trail *noun* line followed by something **Spur; audit trail** = recording details of the use made of a system by noting transactions carried out (used for checking on illegal use *or* malfunction) **Prüfprotokoll**

◊ **trailer** *noun*
(a) leader *or* piece of non magnetic tape to the start of a reel of magnetic tape to make loading easier **Vorspannband**
(b) final byte of a file containing control *or* file characteristics **Nachsatz; trailer record** = last record in a file containing control *or* file characteristics **Nachsatz**

transaction *noun* one single action which affects a database (a sale, a change of address, a new customer, etc.) **Datenbewegung, Transaktion; transaction-driven system (TDS)** = computer system that will normally run batch processing tasks until interrupted by a new transaction, at which point it allocates resources to the transaction **bewegungsgesteuertes System; transaction file** *or* **change file** *or* **detail file** *or* **movement file** = file containing recent changes *or* transactions to records which is then used to update a master file **Bewegungsdatei; transaction processing (TP)** = interactive processing in which a user enters commands and data on a terminal which is linked to a central computer, with results being displayed on-screen **Transaktionsverarbeitung; transaction record** *or* **change record** = record containing new data which is to be used to update a master record **Bewegungssatz**

transborder data flow *noun* passing of data from one country to another using communications links such as satellites *or* land lines **grenzüberschreitender Datenfluss**

transceiver *noun* transmitter and receiver *or* device which can both transmit and receive signals (such as a terminal *or* modem) **Fernkopierersender/-empfänger; radio transceiver** = radio transmitter and receiver in a single housing **Funkgerät**

transcoder *noun* electronic device used to convert television signal standards **Umwandler;** *use the transcoder to convert PAL to SECAM*

transcribe *verb* to copy data from one backing storage unit *or* medium to another **umschreiben**

◊ **transcription** *noun* action of transcribing data **Umschreibung**

transducer *noun* electronic device which converts signals in one form into signals in another **Messwertwandler;** *the pressure transducer converts physical pressure signals into electrical signals*

transfer
1 *verb* (i) to change command *or* control; (ii) to copy a section of memory to another location **(i) & (ii) übertragen;** *all processing activities have been transferred to the mainframe*
2 *noun* (i) changing command or control; (ii) copying a section of memory to another location **(i) & (ii) Übertragung, Transfer; conditional transfer** = programming instruction that provides a jump to a section of a program if a certain condition is met **bedingte Übertragung; radial transfer** = data transfer between two peripherals *or* programs that are on different layers of a structured system (such as an OSI/ISO system) **radiale Übertragung; transfer check** = check that a data transfer is correct according to a set of rules **Übertragungskontrolle; transfer command** = instruction that directs processor control from one part of a program to another **Übertragungsbefehl;** *see also* JUMP, CALL; **transfer control** = when a branch *or* jump instruction within a program is executed, control is transferred to another point in the program **Übertragungssteuerung; transfer rate** = speed at which data is transferred from backing store to main memory *or* from one device to another **Übertragungsgeschwindigkeit, Übertragungsrate;** *with a good telephone line, this pair of modems can achieve a transfer rate of 14.4Kbps;* **transfer time** = time taken

to transfer data between devices *or* locations **Übertragungszeit**

transform *verb* to change something from one state to another **umwandeln, transformieren**

◊ **transformation** *noun* action of changing **Umwandlung, Transformation**

◊ **transformational rules** *noun* set of rules that are applied to data that is to be transformed into coded form **Transformationsregeln**

◊ **transformer** *noun* device which changes the voltage *or* current amplitude of an AC signal **Transformator**

COMMENT: a transformer consists of two electrically insulated coils of wire; the AC signal in one induces a similar signal in the other which can be a different amplitude according to the ratio of the turns in the coils of wire

transient
1 *adjective* which is present for a short period of time **kurzzeitig, Übergangs-; transient area** = section of memory for user programs and data **Übergangsbereich; transient error** = temporary error which occurs for a short period of time **kurzzeitiger Fehler**
2 *noun* something which is present for a short period **Übergangs-; power transient** = very short duration voltage pulse *or* spike **Übergangsstrom; voltage transient** = sudden surge in voltage **Spannungsspitze, Spannungssprung; transient suppressor** = device which suppresses voltage transients **Spannungssprungunterdrücker**

transistor *noun* electronic semiconductor device which can control the current flow in a circuit (there are two main types of transistors: bipolar and unipolar) **Transistor; bipolar (junction) transistor (BJT)** = transistor constructed of three layers of alternating types of doped semiconductor (p-n-p or n-p-n), each layer has a terminal labelled emitter, base and collector, usually the base controls the current flow between emitter and collector **bipolarer Sperrschichttransistor; field effect transistor (FET)** = electronic device that can act as a variable current flow control (an external signal varies the resistance of the device and current flow by changing the width of a conducting channel by means of a field. It has three terminals: source, gate and drain) **Feldeffekttransistor (FET); transistor-resistor logic (TRL)** = early logic gate design method using bipolar

transistors and resistors **Aufbau von Schaltelementen durch Transistoren und Widerstände; transistor-transistor logic (TTL)** = most common family of logic gates and high-speed transistor circuit design, in which the bipolar transistors are directly connected (usually collector to base) to provide the logic function **Aufbau von Schaltelementen durch Transistoren (TTL); unipolar transistor** = FIELD EFFECT TRANSISTOR

transition *noun* change from one state to another **Übergang; transition point** = point in a program *or* system where a transition occurs **Übergangsstelle**

translate *verb* to convert data from one form into another **übersetzen**

◊ **translation tables** *or* **conversion tables** *noun* lookup tables *or* collection of stored results that can be accessed very rapidly by a process without the need to calculate each result when needed **Übersetzungstabellen**

◊ **translator (program)** *noun* program that translates a high level language program into another language (usually machine code) **Übersetzerprogramm;** *see also* INTERPRETER, COMPILER

transmit *verb* to send information from one device to another, using any medium, such as radio, cable, wire link, etc. **senden**

◊ **transmission** *noun* sending of signals from one device to another **Übertragung; neutral transmission** = (transmission) in which a voltage pulse and zero volts represent the binary digits 1 and 0 **neutrale Übertragung; parallel transmission** = number of data lines carrying all the bits of a data word simultaneously **Parallelübertragung; serial transmission** = data transmission one bit at a time (this is the normal method of transmission over longer distances, since although slower, it uses fewer lines and so is cheaper than parallel) **serielle Übertragung; synchronous transmission** = transmission of data from one device to another, where both devices are controlled by the same clock, and the transmitted data is synchronized with the clock signal **Synchronübertragung; transmission channel** = physical connection between two points that allows data to be transmitted (such as a link between a CPU and a peripheral) **Übertragungskanal; transmission control protocol (TCP)** = standard data transmission protocol that provides full duplex transmission, the protocol bundles data into packets and checks for errors **Übertragungskontrollprotokoll (TCP); transmission control protocol/interface program (TCP/IP)** = data transfer protocol used in networks and communications systems (often used in Unix-based networks) **Übertragungskontrollprotokoll/ Schnittstellenprogramm (TCP/IP); transmission errors** = errors due to noise on the line **Übertragungsfehler; transmission media** = means by which data can be transmitted, such as radio, light, etc. **Übertragungsmedien; transmission rate** = measure of the amount of data transmitted in a certain time **Übertragungsgeschwindigkeit;** *their average transmission is 64,000 bits per second (bps) through a parallel connection or 19,200 bps through a serial connection;* **transmission window** = narrow range of wavelengths to which a fibre optic cable is most transparent **Übertragungsfenster**

◊ **transmissive disk** *noun* optical data storage disk in which the reading laser beam shines through the disk to a detector below **Übertragungsplatte;** *compare with* REFLECTIVE DISK

◊ **transmittance** *noun* amount of light transmitted through a material in ratio to the total light incident on the surface of the material **Transmittanz, (Licht)durchlassgrad**

◊ **transmitter (TX)** *noun* device that will take an input signal, process it (modulate *or* convert to sound, etc.) then transmit it by some medium (radio, light, etc.) **Sender**

QUOTE an X-ray picture can be digitized and transmitted from one hospital to a specialist at another for diagnosis
Electronics & Business World

QUOTE modern high-power transmitters are much reduced in size and a simple and uncluttered appearance
Electronics & Power

transparent *noun*
(a) computer program which is not obvious to the user *or* which cannot be seen by the user when it is running **transparent; transparent interrupt** = mode in which, if an interrupt occurs, all program and machine states are saved, the interrupt is serviced and then the system is restored to its previous states **transparente Unterbrechung; transparent paging** = software that allows the user to access any memory location in a paged memory system as if it were not paged **Transparentpaginierung**

(b) device *or* network that allows signals to pass through it without being altered in any way **durchsichtiges System**

◊ **transparency** *noun* transparent positive film, which can be projected onto a screen *or* to make film for printing **Diapositiv, Transparentkopie**

transphasor *noun* optical transistor, that is constructed from a crystal which is able to switch a main beam of light according to a smaller input signal **Transphasor**

COMMENT: this is used in the latest research for an optical computer which could run at very high speeds, i.e., at the speed of light

transponder *noun* communications device that receives and retransmits signals **Transponder**

transport *verb* to carry from one place to another **befördern, transportieren; transport layer** = layer in the ISO/OSI standard that checks and controls the quality of the connection **Transportschicht;** *see also* LAYER

◊ **transportable** *adjective* which can be carried **transportierbar;** *a transportable computer is not as small as a portable or a laptop*

QUOTE WSL has potential as the repository's 'meta transport layer for program objects', claims Healey, but it would need to be significantly extended. 'It only handles a 10th of the translation problem,' says Healey
Computing

transposition *noun* changing the order of a series of characters (as "comupter" for "computer" *or* "1898" for "1988" **Umstellung, Vertauschung;** *a series of transposition errors caused faulty results*

transputer *noun* single large very powerful chip containing a 32-bit microprocessor running at around 10 MIPS, that can be connected together to form a parallel processing system (running OCCAM) **Transputer**

QUOTE TAOS kernels are now available from TKS for the Intel 486 and Pentium, the Apple/Olivetti ARM, the Inmos T800/T9000 transputer and the Mips R3000 series
Computing

transverse mode noise *noun*

interference which is apparent between power supply lines **Rauschen durch transversale Eigenschwingung**

◊ **transverse scan** *noun* method of reading data from a video tape in which the playback head is at right angles to the tape **Querabtastung**

trap *noun* device, software or hardware that will catch something, such as a variable, fault or value **Fangstelle; trace trap** = selective breakpoint where a tracing program stops, allowing registers to be examined **Unterbrechung während einer Ablaufverfolgung; trap handler** = software that accepts interrupt signals and acts on them (such as running a special routine *or* sending data to a peripheral) **Traphandler, Trapabfangprogramm**

◊ **trapdoor** *noun* way of getting into a system to change data *or* browse *or* hack **Fangstelle**

trashcan *noun* (in a GUI) icon which looks like a dustbin or trash can; it deletes any file that is dragged onto it **Papierkorb**

tree *noun* tree (structure) = data structure system where each item of data is linked to several others by branches (as opposed to a line system where each item leads on to the next) **Baum(struktur); tree and branch network system** = system of networking where data is transmitted along a single output line, from which other lines branch out, forming a tree structure that feeds individual stations **Baumnetzsystem; tree selection sort** = rapid form of selection where the information from the first sort pass is used in the second pass to speed up selection **Auswahlsortierverfahren; binary tree** = data system where each item of data *or* node has only two branches **binärer Baum**

trellis coding *noun* method of modulating a signal that uses both amplitude and phase modulation to give a greater throughput and lower error rates for data transmission speeds of over 9600bits per second **Trelliscodierung**

tremendously high frequency (THF) *noun* radio frequency between 300GHz and 3000GHz **Frequenz zwischen 300GHZ und 3000GHz**

triad *noun* (i) three elements *or* characters *or* bits; (ii) triangular shaped grouping of the red, green and blue colour phosphor spots at each pixel location on the screen of a colour RGB monitor **(i) Triade; (ii) Dreier**

trial *noun* test for new equipment to see if it works **Probe; trials engineer** = person who designs, runs and analyses trials of new equipment **Ingenieur in der Versuchsabteilung**

tributary station *noun* any station on a multilink network other than the main control station **Außenstelle**

trim *verb* to cut off the edge of something **beschneiden;** *the printed pages are trimmed to 198 x 129mm; you will need to trim the top part of the photograph to make it fit*

TRL = TRANSISTOR-RESISTOR LOGIC

Trojan Horse *noun* program inserted into a system by a hacker that will perform a harmless function while copying information in a classified file into a file with a low priority, which the hacker can then access without the authorized user knowing **Trojanisches Pferd**

troposphere *noun* region of space extending up to six miles above the earth's surface, causing radio wave scatter **Troposphäre;** *see also* IONOSPHERE

troubleshoot *verb* (i) to debug computer software; (ii) to locate and repair faults in hardware **(i) Softwarefehler bereinigen; (ii) Hardwarefehler suchen und beseitigen**

◊ **troubleshooter** *noun* person who troubleshoots hardware *or* software **jd, der Computerfehler beseitigt**

trough *noun* lowest point in a waveform **(Wellen)tal;** *compare* PEAK

TRUE *noun* logical condition (representing binary one) **WAHR;** *compare* FALSE

TrueType ™ outline font technology introduced by Apple and Microsoft as a means of printing exactly what is displayed on screen **TrueType ™**

truncate *verb*
(a) to cut short **abschneiden**
(b) to give an approximate value to a number by reducing it to a certain number of digits **abstreichen**

◊ **truncation** *noun* removal of digits from a number so that it is a certain length **Abschneiden;** *3.5678 truncated to 3.56;* **truncation error** = error caused when a number is truncated **Abschneidefehler**

trunk *noun* bus *or* communication link consisting of wires *or* leads, which connect different parts of a hardware system **Fernverbindungskabel**

◊ **trunk call** *noun (GB)* long-distance telephone call **Ferngespräch**

◊ **trunk exchange** *noun (GB)* telephone exchange that only handles trunk calls **Fernvermittlungsstelle**

truth table *noun* method of defining a logic function as the output state for all possible inputs **Wahrheitstabelle; truth value** = two values (true *or* false, T *or* F, 1 *or* 0) used in Boolean algebra **Wahrheitswert**

TSR = TERMINATE AND STAY RESIDENT (PROGRAM)

TSW = TELESOFTWARE

TTL = TRANSISTOR-TRANSISTOR LOGIC most common family of logic gates and high-speed transistor circuit design in which the bipolar transistors are directly connected (usually collector to base) **TTL (Aufbau von Schaltelementen durch Transistoren); TTL compatible** = MOS or other electronic circuits *or* components that can directly connect to and drive TTL circuits **TTL-kompatibel; TTL logic** = use of TTL design and components to implement logic circuits and gates **TTL-Logik; TTL monitor** = design of monitor which can only accept digital signals, so can only display monochrome images or a limited range of colours **TTL-Bildschirm, TTL-Monitor**

TTY = TELETYPE

tune *verb*
(a) to set a system at its optimum point by careful adjustment **optimal einstellen; to fine tune** = to adjust by small amounts the parameters of hardware *or* software to improve performance **fein abstimmen** *or* **fein einstellen**
(b) (i) to adjust a radio receiver's frequency until the required station is received clearly; (ii) to adjust a transmitter to the correct frequency **(i) einstellen; (ii) abstimmen**

Turing machine *noun* mathematical model of a device that could read and write data to a controllable tape storage while altering its internal states **Turingmaschine**

◊ **Turing test** *noun* test to decide if a computer is "intelligent" **Turingtest**

turn off *verb* to switch off *or* to disconnect

the power supply to a machine **ausschalten; turn off the power before unplugging the monitor**

◊ **turn on** *verb* to switch on *or* to connect the power supply to a machine **einschalten**

◊ **turnaround document** *noun* document which is printed out from a computer, sent to a user and returned by the user with new notes *or* information written on it, which can be read by a document reader **Kreisverkehrdokument**

◊ **turnaround time (TAT)** *noun*
(a) length of time it takes to switch data flow direction in a half duplex system **Verweilzeit**
(b) time taken for a product to be constructed and delivered after an order has been received **Fertigungs- und Lieferzeit**
(c) *(US)* time taken to activate a program and produce the result which the user has asked for **Durchlaufzeit**

◊ **turnkey system** *noun* complete system which is designed to a customer's needs and is ready to use (to operate it, the user only has to switch it on or turn a key) **schlüsselfertiges System**

turtle *noun* device whose movement and position are controllable, which is used to draw graphics (with instructions in the computer language LOGO), either a device which works on a flat surface (floor turtle) *or* which draws on a VDU screen (screen turtle), used as a teaching aid **Schildkröte; turtle graphics** = graphic images created using a turtle and a series of commands **Schildkrötengrafik;** *the charts were prepared using turtle graphics*

TV = TELEVISION

tweak *verb* to make small adjustments to a program *or* hardware to improve performance **trimmen**

tweening *noun* (in computer graphics) calculating the intermediate images that lead from a starting image to a different finished image **Tweening;** *using tweening, we can show how a frog turns into a princess in five steps*

tweeter *noun (informal)* small loudspeaker used for high frequency sounds only **Hochtonlautsprecher;** *compare* WOOFER

twisted-pair cable *noun* cable which consists of two insulated copper wires twisted around each other (to reduce induction and so interference) **verdrilltes Adernpaar; shielded twisted pair (STP) cable** = cable which consists of two insulated copper wires twisted around each other (to reduce induction and so interference), the pair of wires are then wrapped in an insulated shielding layer to further reduce interference **abgeschirmtes verdrilltes Adernpaar, STP-Draht; unshielded twisted pair (UTP) cable** = cable which consists of two insulated copper wires twisted around each other (to reduce induction and so interference), unlike STP cable the pair of wires are not wrapped in any other layer **unabgeschirmtes verdrilltes Adernpaar, UTP-Draht**

two-address instruction *noun* instruction format containing the location of two operands, the result being stored in one of the operand locations **Eins-plus-Eins-Adressbefehl; two-plus-one instruction** = instruction containing the locations of two operands and an address for the result **Zwei-plus-Eins-Adressbefehl**

◊ **two-dimensional** *adjective* which has two dimensions (that is, flat, with no depth) **zweidimensional; two-dimensional array** = array which locates items both vertically and horizontally **zweidimensionale Feldgruppe**

◊ **two input adder** *see* HALF ADDER

◊ **two-level subroutine** *noun* subroutine containing another subroutine **zweischichtiges Unterprogramm**

◊ **two-part** *noun* paper (for computers *or* typewriters) with a top sheet for the original and a second sheet for a copy **zweilagiges Papier**; *two-part invoices; two-part stationery*

◊ **two-pass assembler** *noun* assembler that converts an assembly language program into machine code in two passes - the first pass stores symbolic addresses, the second converts them to absolute addresses **Assemblierer mit zwei Durchläufen**

two's complement *noun* formed by adding one to the one's complement of a binary number, often used to represent negative binary numbers **Zweierkomplement**

two way cable *noun* (*US*) system of cable TV, where the viewer can take which programmes he wants by selecting them *or* where the viewer can respond to broadcast questions by sending his response down the cable **Gegenkabelfernsehbetrieb**

two way radio *noun* radio transmitter and receiver in a single housing, allowing duplex communication with another user **Gegenradiobetrieb**

two wire circuit *noun* two insulated wires used to carry transmitted and received messages independently **Zweidrahtleitung**

TX = TRANSMITTER

type
1 *noun*
(a) metal bars with a raised characters used for printing **Type**
(b) characters used in printing *or* characters which appear in printed form **Buchstaben, Schrift**; *they switched to italic type for the heading;* **type size** = size of a font, measured in points **Schriftgröße; type style** = weight and angle of a font, such as bold or italic **Schriftstil, Schriftformat**
(c) definition of the processes *or* sorts of data which a variable in a computer can contain (this can be numbers, text only, etc.) **Typ; variable data type** = variable that can contain any sort of data, such as numerical, text, etc. **variabler Datentyp; string type** = variable that can contain alphanumeric characters only **Typ der Zeichenfolge**
2 *verb* to enter information via a keyboard **eingeben**; *I typed in the command again, but it still didn't work*

◊ **typeface** *noun* set of characters in a particular design and particular weight **Schriftbild**; *most of this book is set in the Times typeface*

typeset *verb* to set text in type for printing **setzen**; *in desktop publishing, the finished work should look almost as if it had been typeset*

◊ **typesetter** *noun* (i) company which typesets; (ii) machine which produces very high-quality text output using a laser to create an image on photosensitive paper (normally at a resolution of 1275 or 2450dpi) **(i) Setzerei; (ii) Setzmaschine;** *the text is ready to be sent to the typesetter*

◊ **typesetting** *noun* action of setting text in type **Setzen**; *typesetting costs can be reduced by supplying the typesetter with prekeyed disks; see also* PHOTOTYPESETTING

typewriter *noun* machine which prints letters *or* figures on a piece of paper when a key is pressed by striking an inked ribbon onto the paper with a character type **Schreibmaschine;** *she wrote the letter on her portable typewriter; he makes fewer mistakes now he is using an electronic typewriter;* **typewriter faces** = spacing, size and font of characters available on a typewriter **Schrifttypen der Schreibmaschine**

◊ **typewritten** *adjective* written on a typewriter **maschinengeschrieben;** *he sent in a typewritten job application*

◊ **typing** *noun* writing letters with a typewriter **Maschineschreiben; typing error** = mistake made when using a typewriter **Tippfehler;** *the secretary must have made a typing error;* **typing pool** = group of typists, working together in a company, offering a secretarial service to several departments **zentraler Schreibdienst; copy typing** = typing documents from originals, not from dictation **Abtippen von Dokumenten** NOTE: no plural

◊ **typist** *noun* person whose job is to write letters using a typewriter **Schreibkraft; copy typist** = person who types documents from originals, not from dictation **Schreibkraft (ohne Diktat); shorthand typist** = typist who takes dictation in shorthand and then types it **Stenotypist/-in**

typo *noun (informal)* typographical error which is made while typesetting **typographischer Fehler**

◊ **typographer** *noun* person who designs a typeface *or* text to be printed **Typograph**

◊ **typographic** *or* **typographical** *adjective* referring to typography *or* to typesetting **typographisch;** *no typographical skills are required for this job; a typographical error made while typesetting is called a "typo";* **typographical error** = mistake made while typesetting **typographischer Fehler**

◊ **typography** *noun* art and methods used in working with type **Typographie**

Uu

UART = UNIVERSAL ASYNCHRONOUS RECEIVER/TRANSMITTER chip which converts asynchronous serial bit streams to a parallel form *or* parallel data to a serial bit stream **UART (universelle Schnittstelle für die Umsetzung von bitparalleler in bitserielle Übertragung und umgekehrt im Asynchronverfahren); UART controller** = circuit that uses a UART to convert (serial) data from a terminal into a parallel form, then transmits it over a network **UART-Steuereinheit;** *see also* USART

UBC = UNIVERSAL BLOCK CHANNEL

UHF = ULTRA HIGH FREQUENCY range of frequencies normally used to transmit television signals **UHF**

ULA = UNCOMMITTED LOGIC ARRAY chip containing a number of unconnected logic circuits and gates which can then be connected by a customer to provide a required function **nicht festgeschriebene logische Anordnung**

ultra- *prefix* meaning very large *or* further than **ultra-; ultra high frequency (UHF)** = range of frequencies normally used to transmit television signals **Ultrahochfrequenz (UHF), Dezimeterwellen; ultrafiche** = microfiche with images that have been reduced by more than ninety times **Ultramikrofiche; ultrasonic waves** = sound pressure waves at a frequency above the audio band, above 20KHz **Ultraschallwellen; ultrasound** = sound emitted at a frequency above the audio band **Ultraschall; ultraviolet (UV) light** = electromagnetic radiation with wavelength just greater than the visible spectrum, from 200 to 4000 angstroms **Ultraviolettstrahlung; ultraviolet erasable PROM** = EPROM whose contents are erased by exposing to UV light **mit Ultraviolett löschbarer Festwertspeicher**

umlaut *noun* accent consisting of two dots over a German a, o or u **Umlaut**

unallowable digit *noun* illegal combination of bits in a word, according to predefined rules **unzulässige Zahl**

unary operation *noun* computing operation on only one operand, such as the logical NOT operation **einstellige Operation**

unattended operation *noun* system that can operate without the need for a person to supervise **automatischer Betrieb**

unauthorized *adjective* which has not been authorized **unbefugt;** *the use of a* *password is to prevent unauthorized access to the data*

unbundled software *noun* software which is not included in the price of the equipment **im Kaufpreis nicht inbegriffene Software**

unclocked *adjective* electronic circuit *or* flip-flop that changes state as soon as an input changes, not with a clock signal **ohne Taktgeber**

uncommitted logic array (ULA) *noun* chip containing a number of unconnected logic circuits and gates which can then be connected by a customer to provide a required function **nicht festgeschriebenes logisches Feld; uncommitted storage list** = table of the areas of memory in a system that are free *or* have not been allocated **nicht festgeschriebene Speicherliste**

unconditional *adjective* which does not depend on any condition being met **unbedingt; unconditional branch** *or* **jump** *or* **transfer** = instruction which transfers control from one point in the program to another, without depending on any condition being met **unbedingte Verzweigung; unbedingter Sprungbefehl; unbedingte Übertragung** NOTE: opposite is **CONDITIONAL**

undelete *verb* to restore deleted information *or* a deleted file **wiederherstellen;** *don't worry, this function will undelete your cuts to the letter*

underexposed *adjective* (photograph) that is too dark because it did not receive a long enough exposure **unterbelichtet**

underflow *noun* result of a numerical operation that is too small to be represented with the given accuracy of a computer **Unterlauf**

underline *or* **underscore** **1** *noun* line drawn *or* printed under a piece of text **Unterstreichung;** *the chapter headings are given a double underline and the paragraphs a single underline* **2** *verb* to print *or* write a line under a piece of text **unterstreichen; underlining** = word-processing command which underlines text **Unterstreichen**

undertake *verb* to agree to do something **sich bereit erklären;** *he has undertaken to reprogram the whole system*

undetected *adjective* which has not been detected **unentdeckt;** *the programming error was undetected for some time*

undo *verb* (option in a program) to reverse the previous action, normally an editing command **rückgängig machen;** *you've just deleted the paragraph, but you can undo it from the option in the Edit menu*

unedited *adjective* which has not been edited **nicht redigiert, unediert, unredigiert;** *the unedited text is with the publisher for editing*

unformatted *adjective* (i) (disk) which has not been formatted; (ii) (text file) which contains no formatting commands, margins or typographical commands **(i) & (ii) unformatiert;** *it is impossible to copy to an unformatted disk; the cartridge drive provides 12.7Mbyte of unformatted storage*

uni- *prefix* meaning one *or* single **Ein-, ein-;** *compare* POLAR

◊ **unidirectional microphone** *noun* microphone that is most sensitive in one direction only **Richtmikrofon;** *compare with* OMNIDIRECTIONAL

◊ **union** *noun* logical function that produces a true output if any input is true **Union**

◊ **unipolar** *adjective*
(a) (transistor) that can act as a variable current flow control an external signal varies the resistance of the device **unipolar;** *see also* FET, TRANSISTOR
(b) (transmission system) in which a positive voltage pulse and zero volts represents the binary bits 1 and 0 **unipolar;** *compare with* POLAR; **unipolar signal** = signal that uses only positive voltage levels **unipolares Signal**

uninterruptable power supply (UPS) *noun* power supply that can continue to provide a regulated supply to equipment even after a mains power failure (using a battery) **unterbrechungslose Stromversorgungsanlage**

unique *adjective* which is different from everything else **eindeutig, einzigartig;** *each separate memory byte has its own unique address*

unit *noun*
(a) smallest element **Einheit; unit buffer** = buffer that is one character long **Einheitenpuffer** (NOTE: usually used to

mean that there are no buffering facilities)
unit record = single record of information
einzelner (Daten)satz
(b) single machine (possibly with many
different parts) **einzelne Maschine;
arithmetic and logic unit (ALU)** = section of
the CPU that performs all the
mathematical and logical functions
Rechenwerk; central processing unit (CPU)
= group of circuits which perform the basic
functions of a computer, made up of three
main parts: the control unit, the arithmetic
and logic unit and the input/output unit
CPU, Zentraleinheit; control unit = section of
the CPU that selects and executes
instructions **Steuereinheit; desk top unit** =
computer that will fit onto a desk
Tischcomputer; input/output unit or **device** =
peripheral (such as a terminal in a
workstation) which can be used both for
inputting and outputting data to a
processor **Ein-/Ausgabeeinheit**

universal *adjective* which applies
everywhere *or* which can be used
everywhere *or* used for a number of tasks
**allgemein, universell; universal asynchronous
receiver/transmitter (UART)** = chip which
converts an asynchronous serial bit stream
to a parallel form *or* parallel data to a serial
bit stream **universelle Schnittstelle für die
Umsetzung von bitparalleler in bitserielle
Übertragung und umgekehrt im
Asynchronverfahren; universal block channel
(UBC)** = communications channel
allowing high speed transfer of blocks of
data to and from high speed peripherals
universeller Blockkanal; universal device = (i)
UART; (ii) USRT; (iii) USART **(i) UART;
(ii) USRT; (iii) USART; universal product code
(UPC)** = standard printed bar coding
system used to identify products in a shop
(using a bar code reader *or* at a EPOS)
Balkencode; *see also* EAN; **universal
programming** = writing a program that is
not specific to one machine, so that it can
run on several machines **universelles
Programmieren; universal set** = complete set
of elements that conform to a set of rules
universeller Satz; *the universal set of prime
numbers less than ten and greater than two is
3,5,7;* **universal synchronous asynchronous
receiver-transmitter (USART)** = chip that
can be instructed by a CPU to
communicate with asynchronous or
synchronous bit streams *or* data lines
**universelle Schnittstelle für die Umsetzung
von bitparalleler in bitserielle Übertragung und
umgekehrt im Synchronverfahren und im
Asynchronverfahren (USART);** universal
synchronous receiver/transmitter (USRT) =

single integrated circuit that can carry out
all the serial to parallel and interfacing
operations required between a computer
and transmission line **universelle
Schnittstelle für die Umsetzung von
bitparalleler in bitserielle Übertragung und
umgekehrt im Synchronverfahren (USRT)**

UNIX *noun* popular multiuser,
multitasking operating system developed
by AT&T Bell Laboratories to run on
almost any computer, · from a PC, to
minicomputers and large mainframes **UNIX;
UNIX-to-UNIX copy (UUCP)** = software
utilities that help make it easier for a user to
copy data from one computer (running
UNIX) via a serial link to another
computer (running UNIX) **UNIX-to-UNIX-
Copy (UUCP)**

QUOTE Hampshire fire brigade is
investing {2 million in a command and
control system based on the new SeriesFT
fault-tolerant Unix machine from
Motorola
Computing

unjustified *adjective* (text) which has not
been justified **im Flattersatz, nicht
ausgerichtet; unjustified tape** *or* **idiot tape** =
tape containing unformatted text, which
cannot be printed until formatting data
(such as justification, line width and page
size) has been added by a computer **nicht
justiertes Band**

unlock *verb* action to allow other users to
write to a file *or* access a system **freigeben,
entsperren**

unmodified instruction *noun*
program instruction which is directly
processed without modification to obtain
the operation to be performed
unmodifizierter Befehl

unmodulated *adjective* (signal) which
has not been modulated **unmoduliert;** *see
also* BASE BAND

unmount *verb* (i) to remove a disk from a
disk drive; (ii) (instruction) to inform the
operating system that a disk drive is no
longer in active use **(i) entnehmen; (ii)
abmelden, unmounten**

unpack *verb* to remove packed data from
storage and expand it to its former state
auspacken; *this routine unpacks the archived
file*

unplug *verb* to take a plug out of a socket

den Stecker herausziehen; *do not move the system without unplugging it; simply unplug the old drive and plug-in a new one*

unpopulated *adjective* printed circuit board which does not yet contain any components *or* whose sockets are empty unbestückt; *you can buy an unpopulated RAM card and fit your own RAM chips*

unprotected *adjective* (data) that can be modified and is not protected by a security measure ungeschützt; **unprotected field** = section of a computer display that a user can modify ungeschütztes Feld

unrecoverable error *noun* computer hardware *or* software error that causes a program to crash nicht korrigierbarer Fehler

unshielded twisted-pair (UTP) cable *noun* cable consisting of two insulated copper wires twisted around each other (to reduce induction and so interference), unlike STP cable the pair of wires are not wrapped in any other layer unabgeschirmtes verdrilltes Adernpaar

COMMENT: UTP is normally used for telephone cabling, but is also the cabling used in the IEEE 802.3 (10BaseT) standard that defines Ethernet running over UTP at rates of up to 10Mbits per second

unsigned *adjective* (number system) that does not represent negative numbers ohne Vorzeichen

unsorted *adjective* (data) which has not been sorted unsortiert; *it took four times as long to search the unsorted file*

unwanted *adjective* which is not needed unerwünscht, störend; *use the global delete command to remove large areas of unwanted text*

up *adverb* *(of computer or program)* working *or* running laufend; *they must have found the fault - the computer is finally up and running;* **up time** *or* **uptime** = time during which a device is operational and error free Nutzzeit
NOTE: opposite is **down**

◊ **up and down propagation time** *noun* total length of time that a transmission takes to travel from earth to a satellite and back to an earth station Gesamtlaufzeit

UPC = UNIVERSAL PRODUCT CODE

update
1 *noun* (i) master file which has been made up-to-date by adding new material; (ii) printed information which is an up-to-date revision of earlier information; (iii) new version of a system which is sent to users of the existing system (i) aktuelle Datei; (ii) aktuelle Information; (iii) neueste Version; **update file** *or* **transaction file** = file containing recent changes *or* transactions to records which is used to update the master file Fortschreibungsdatei
2 *verb* to change *or* add to specific data in a master file so as to make the information up-to-date auf den neuesten Stand bringen; *he has the original and updated documents on disks*

QUOTE it means that any item of data stored in the system need be updated only once
Which PC?

up/down counter *noun* electronic counter that can increment *or* decrement a counter with each input pulse Auf-/Abzähler

upgrade *verb* to make (a system) more powerful *or* more up-to-date by adding new equipment aufrüsten, verbessern; *they can upgrade the printer; the single processor with 2Mbytes of memory can be upgraded to 4Mbytes; all three models have an on-site upgrade facility*

QUOTE the cost of upgrading a PC to support CAD clearly depends on the peripheral devices added
PC Business World

upkeep *noun* keeping data up-to-date; keeping devices in working order Instandhaltung; *the upkeep of the files means reviewing them every six months*

uplink *noun* transmission link from an earth station to a satellite Uplink

upload *verb* (i) to transfer data files *or* programs from a small computer to a main CPU; (ii) to transfer a file from one computer to a BBS or host computer (i) & (ii) hochladen, uploaden NOTE: the opposite is **download**

◊ **uploading** *noun* action of transferring files to a main CPU Hochladen; *the image can be manipulated before uploading to the host computer*

upper case *noun* series of capital letters and other symbols on a typewriter *or* keyboard, which are accessed by pressing the shift key **Großbuchstaben, Versalien**

upper memory *noun* (in an IBM PC) 384Kb of memory located between the 640Kb and 1Mb limits; upper memory is after the 640Kb conventional memory but before the high memory areas above the 1Mb range **oberer Speicherbereich, Upper Memory**

UPS = UNINTERRUPTABLE POWER SUPPLY power supply that can continue to provide a regulated supply to equipment even after a mains power failure (using a battery) **unterbrechungslose Stromversorgungsanlage**

QUOTE Magnum Power Systems has launched a new UPS for PCs. The BI-UPS prevents loss of data due to power dips or 'brown-outs' - voltage drops because of circuit overload

Computing

uptime *noun* time when a computer is functioning correctly (as opposed to downtime) **Nutzzeit**

upwards compatible *or* *(US)* **upward compatible** *adjective* (hardware *or* software) designed to be compatible either with earlier models *or* with future models which have not yet been invented **aufwärts kompatibel**

usable *adjective* which can be used *or* which is available for use **nutzbar**; *the PC has 512K of usable memory;* **maximum usable frequency** = highest signal frequency which can be used in a circuit without distortion **höchste Nutzfrequenz**

◊ **usability** *noun* the ease with which hardware *or* software can be used **Usability, Bedienerfreundlichkeit**; *we have studied usability tests and found that a GUI is easier for new users than a command line*

USART = UNIVERSAL SYNCHRONOUS ASYNCHRONOUS RECEIVER-TRANSMITTER chip that can be instructed by a CPU to communicate with asynchronous *or* synchronous bit streams *or* parallel data lines **universelle Schnittstelle für die Umsetzung von bitparalleler in bitserielle Übertragung und umgekehrt im Synchronverfahren und im Asynchronverfahren (USART)**

USASCII *(US)* = USA STANDARD CODE FOR INFORMATION INTERCHANGE; *see* ASCII

use
1 *noun*
(a) way in which something can be used **Benutzung, Gebrauch;** *the printer has been in use for the last two hours; the use of that file is restricted;* **to make use of something** = to use something **etwas benutzen**
(b) value; being useful **Nutzen;** *what use is an extra disk drive? it's no use, I cannot find the error;* **in use** = already in operation in **Betrieb/Gebrauch;** *sorry, the printer is already in use*
2 *verb*
(a) to operate something **benutzen, verwenden;** *if you use the computer for processing the labels, it will be much quicker; the computer is used too often by the sales staff*
(b) to consume heat, light, etc. **verbrauchen;** *it's using too much electricity*

◊ **used** *adjective* which is not new **benutzt, gebraucht;** *special offer on used terminals*

user *noun* (i) person who uses a computer *or* machine *or* software; (ii) especially, a keyboard operator **(i) & (ii) Benutzer;** **user account** = (in a network *or* multiuser system) record which identifies a user, contains his password and holds his rights to use resources **Benutzeraccount, Useraccount;** *I have a new user account on this LAN but I cannot remember my password;* **user area** = part of the memory which is available for the user, and does not contain the operating system **Benutzerspeicher; user-definable** = feature *or* section of a program that a user can customize as required **benutzerdefinierbar;** *the style sheet contains 125 user-definable symbols;* **user-defined characters** = characters which are created by the user and added to the standard character set **benutzerdefinierte Zeichen; user documentation** = documentation provided with a program which helps the user run it **Benutzerdokumentation;** *using the package was easy with the excellent user documentation;* **user group** = association *or* club of users of a particular system *or* computer **Benutzergruppe;** *I found how to solve the problem by asking people at the user group meeting;* **user guide** = manual describing how to use a software package *or* system **Benutzerhandbuch; user ID** = unique identification code that allows a computer to recognize a user **Benutzerkennzeichen;** *if you forget your user ID, you will not be able to logon;* **user interface** = hardware *or* software designed to make it easier for a user to communicate with the machine **Benutzerschnittstelle; user name** = (in a network *or* multiuser system) name by which a user is known to the system and which opens the correct user account **Benutzername; user-operated language** = high-level programming language that allows certain problems *or* procedures to be easily expressed **benutzerorientierte Programmiersprache; user port** = socket which allows peripherals to be connected to a computer **Benutzeranschluss; user's program** = computer software written by a user rather than a manufacturer **Benutzerprogramm; user-selectable** = which can be chosen *or* selected by the user **vom Benutzer auswählbar;** *the video resolution of 640 by 300, 240 or, 200 pixels is user-selectable*

◊ **user-friendly** *adjective* (language *or* system *or* program) that is easy to use and interact with **benutzerfreundlich;** *it's such a user-friendly machine; compared with the previous version this one is very user-friendly*

QUOTE the user's guides are designed for people who have never seen a computer, but some sections have been spoiled by careless checking

PC User

QUOTE the first popular microcomputer to have a user-friendly interface built into its operating system

Micro Decision

QUOTE ModelMaker saves researchers a great deal of time and effort, and provides a highly user-friendly environment using menus and 'buttons', instant output, and instant access to a wide variety of mathematical techniques built into the system

Computing

USRT = UNIVERSAL SYNCHRONOUS RECEIVER/TRANSMITTER

utility (program) *noun* useful program that is concerned with such routine activities as file searching, copying files, file directories, sorting and debugging and various mathematical functions **Dienstprogramm;** *a lost file cannot be found without a file-recovery utility on the disk is a utility for backing up a hard disk*

UTP cable = UNSHIELDED TWISTED-PAIR CABLE

UUCP = UNIX-TO-UNIX COPY

UV light = ULTRAVIOLET LIGHT

V = VOLTAGE

V & V = VERIFICATION AND VALIDATION

V format *noun* data organization, in which variable length records are stored with a header which contains their length **V-Format, variables Format**

V series *noun* CCITT (UK-European) standards for data transmission using a modem **V-Serie (Steckernorm)**

COMMENT:
V.21 = 300 bits/second transmit and receive, full duplex
V.22 = 1200 bits/second transmit and receive, half duplex
V.22 BIS = 1200 bits/second transmit and receive, full duplex
V.23 = 75 bits/second transmit, 1200 bits/second receive, half duplex
V.24 = interchange circuits between a DTE and a DCE
V.25 BIS = automatic calling and answering equipment on a PSTN
V.26 = 2400 bits/second transmission over leased lines
V.26 BIS = 2400 bits/second transmit, 1200 bits/second receive, half duplex for use on a PSTN
V.26 TER = 2400 bits/second transmit, 1200 bits/second receive, full duplex for use on a PSTN
V.27 = 4800 bits/second modem for use on a leased line
V.27 BIS = 4800 bits/second transmit, 2400 bits/second receive for use on a leased line
V.27 TER = 4800 bits/second transmit, 2400 bits/second receive for use on a PSTN
V.29 = 9600 bits/second modem for use on a PSTN or leased line
V.42 = error control and correction protocol
V.42 BIS = data compression used with V.42 error control

V20, V30 processor chips made by NEC, which are compatible with the Intel 8088 and 8086 **V20, V30**

vaccine *noun* software utility used to check a system to see if any viruses are present, and remove any that are found **Impfprogramm**

vacuum *noun* state with no air **Vakuum**; *there is a vacuum in the sealed CRT;* **vacuum tube** = electronic current flow control device consisting of a heated cathode and an anode in a sealed glass tube with a vacuum inside it **Vakuumröhre**

|| COMMENT: used in the first generation of computers, now replaced by solid state current control devices such as the transistor

valid *adjective* correct, according to a set of rules **gültig**; **valid memory address** = signal on control bus indicating that an address is available on the address bus **gültige Speicheradresse**

◊ **validate** *verb* to check that an input *or* data is correct according to a set of rules **für gültig erklären**

◊ **validation** *noun* check performed to validate data **Gültigkeitsprüfung**

◊ **validity** *noun* correctness of an instruction *or* password **Gültigkeit**; **validity check** = check that data *or* results are realistic **Gültigkeitsprüfung**

value *noun* what something is worth (either in money *or* as a quantity) **Wert**; **absolute value** = value of a number regardless of its sign **Absolutwert**; *the absolute value of −62.34 is 62.34;* **initial value** = starting point (usually zero) set when initializing variables at the beginning of a program **Anfangswert**

◊ **value-added** *adjective* (something) with extra benefit for a user **Mehrwert-**; **value-added network (VAN)** = commercial network which offers information services, such as stock prices, weather, email or advice as well as basic file transfer **Onlinedienst, Mehrwertnetzwerk**; **value-added reseller (VAR)** = company that buys hardware *or* software and adds another feature, customizes or offers an extra service to attract customers **Mehrwerthändler**

valve *noun* electronic current flow control device consisting of a heated cathode and an anode in a sealed glass vacuum tube **Ventil**

|| COMMENT: used in the first generation of computers, now replaced by solid state current control devices such as a transistor

VAN = VALUE-ADDED NETWORK

vapourware *noun* (*informal*) products which exist in name only **nur auf dem Papier existierende Ware**

| QUOTE Rivals dismissed the initiative as IBM vapourware, designed to protect its installed base of machines running under widely differing operating systems *Computing* |

VAR = VALUE-ADDED RESELLER

variable
1 *adjective* able to change **veränderlich, variabel**; **variable data** = data which can be modified, and is not write-protected **variable Daten**; **variable length record** = record which can be of any length **Satz mit variabler Länge**; **variable word length computer** = computer in which the number of bits which make up a word is variable, and varies according to the type of data **Computer mit variabler Wortlänge**
2 *noun* (computer program identifier for a) register *or* storage location which can contain any number *or* characters and which may vary during the program run **Variable**; **global variable** = number that can be accessed by any routine *or* structure in a program **globale Variable**; **local variable** = number which can only be accessed by certain routines in a certain section of a computer program **lokale Variable**

◊ **vary** *verb* to change **sich verändern**; *the clarity of the signal can vary with the power supply*

VCR = VIDEO CASSETTE RECORDER

VDT *or* **VDU** = VISUAL DISPLAY TERMINAL, VISUAL DISPLAY UNIT terminal with a screen and a keyboard, on which text *or* graphics can be viewed and information entered **Bildschirmgerät**

> QUOTE it normally consists of a keyboard to input information and either a printing terminal or a VDU screen to display messages and results
> *Practical Computing*

> QUOTE a VDU is a device used with a computer that displays information in the form of characters and drawings on a screen
> *Electronics & Power*

vector *noun*
(a) address which directs a computer to a new memory location **Vektor**
(b) coordinate that consists of a magnitude and direction **Vektor; vector graphics** *or* **vector image** *or* **vector scan** = computer drawing system that uses line length and direction from an origin to plot lines **Vektorbild; vector processor** = coprocessor that operates on one row or column of an array at a time **Vektorprozessor**

◊ **vectored interrupt** *noun* interrupt signal which directs the processor to a routine at a particular address **zeigergesteuerte Unterbrechung**

> QUOTE the great advantage of the vector-scan display is that it requires little memory to store a picture
> *Electronics & Power*

Veitch diagram *noun* graphical representation of a truth table **Veitch-Diagramm**

velocity *noun* speed **Geschwindigkeit;** *the disk drive motor spins at a constant velocity*

vendor *noun* person who manufactures *or* sells *or* supplies hardware *or* software products **Händler; vendor independent** = hardware *or* software that will work with hardware and software manufactured by other vendors **händlerunabhängig;** *opposite is* PROPRIETARY

Venn diagram *noun* graphical representation of the relationships between the states in a system *or* circuit **Venn-Diagramm**

verify *verb* to check that data recorded *or* entered is correct **überprüfen, bestätigen**

◊ **verification** *noun* checking that data has been keyboarded correctly *or* that data

transferred from one medium to another has been transferred correctly **Verifikation; keystroke verification** = check made on each key pressed to make sure it is valid for a particular application **Tastenanschlagsprüfung; verification and validation (V & V)** = testing a system to check that it is functioning correctly and that it is suitable for the tasks intended **Funktions- und Eignungsprüfung**

◊ **verifier** *noun* special device for verifying input data **Prüfer**

version *noun* copy *or* program *or* statement which is slightly different from others **Version;** *the latest version of the software includes an improved graphics routine;* **version control** = utility software that allows several programmers to work on a source file and monitors the changes that have been made by each programmer **Versionsprüfung, Versionskontrolle; version number** = number of the version of a product **Versionsnummer**

verso *noun* left hand page of a book (usually given an even number) **Rückseite, Verso**

vertical *adjective* at right angles to the horizontal **vertikal, senkrecht; vertical application** = application software that has been designed for a specific use, rather than for general use **Spezialanwendung;** *your new software to manage a florist's is a good vertical application;* **vertical blanking interval** *see* RASTER; **vertical format unit (VFU)** = part of the control system of a printer which governs the vertical format of the document to be printed (such as vertical spacing, page length) **vertikale Formatsteuerungseinheit; vertical justification** = adjustment of the spacing between lines of text to fit a section of text into a page **vertikale Texteinrichtung, vertikaler Zeilenausgleich; vertical parity check** = error detection test in which the bits of a word are added and compared with a correct total **Querparitätsprüfung; vertical redundancy check (VRC)** = (odd) parity check on each character of a block received, to detect any errors **Querprüfung; vertical scrolling** = displaying text so that it moves up or down the computer screen one line at a time **vertikales Blättern; vertical sync signal** = (in a video signal) signal which indicates the end of the last trace at the bottom of the display **Vertikalsynchronsignal; vertical tab** = number of lines that should be skipped before printing starts again **Vertikaltabulator**

◊ **vertically** *adverb* from top to bottom *or* going up and down at right angles to the horizontal **vertikal;** *the page has been justified vertically;* **vertically polarized signal** = signal whose waveforms are all aligned in one vertical plane **vertikal polarisiertes Signal**

very high frequency (VHF) *noun* range of radio frequencies between 30-300 MHz **Ultrakurzwellenbereich**

very large scale integration (VLSI) *noun* integrated circuit with 10,000 to 100,000 components **Übergroßintegration**

very low frequency (VLF) *noun* range of radio frequencies between 3-30 KHz **Niederfrequenz**

VESA = VIDEO ELECTRONICS STANDARDS ASSOCIATION; **VESA local bus** *or* **VL-bus** = (in an IBM PC) standard defined by VESA which allows up to three special expansion slots that provide direct, bus-master control of the central processor and allow very high speed data transfers between main memory and the expansion card without using the processor **VESA-Local-Bus, VL-Bus;** *for a high-performance PC, choose one with a VESA local bus*

vestigial sideband *noun* single sideband transmission with a small part of the other sideband kept to provide synchronization data, often used in TV transmissions **Restseitenband**

vf band = VOICE FREQUENCY BAND

VFU = VERTICAL FORMAT UNIT

VGA = VIDEO GRAPHICS ARRAY (in an IBM PC) standard of video adapter developed by IBM that can support a display with a resolution up to 640x480 pixels in up to 256 colours, superseded by SVGA **VGA; super VGA (SVGA)** = enhancement to the standard VGA graphics display system that allows resolutions of up to 800 x 600 pixels with 16 million colours **Super-VGA (SVGA)**

VHD = VERY HIGH DENSITY video disk able to store very large quantities of data **VHD**

VHF = VERY HIGH FREQUENCY radio frequency between 30MHz and 300MHZ (used for broadcasting radio and TV programmes) **Ultrakurzwellenbereich**

via *preposition* going through something *or* using something to get to a destination **über, via;** *the signals have reached us via satellite; you can download the data to the CPU via a modem*

video *noun* text *or* images *or* graphics viewed on television *or* a monitor **Video; video adapter** *or* **board** *or* **controller** = add-in board which converts data into electrical signals to drive a monitor and display text and graphics **Videoadapter, Videocontroller, Videokarte; video buffer** = memory in a video adapter that is used to store the bit-map of the image being displayed **Videopuffer; video conferencing** = linking video, audio and computer signals from different locations so that distant people can talk and see each other, as if in a conference room **Videokonferenztechnik; video digitiser** = high speed digital sampling circuit which stores a TV picture in memory so that it can then be processed by a computer **Videodigitizer; videodisk** = optical disk used to store television pictures and sound **Videospeicherplatte; video graphics array (VGA)** = (in an IBM PC) standard of video adapter developed by IBM that can support a display with a resolution up to 640x480 pixels in up to 256 colours, superseded by SVGA **Video Graphics Array (VGA); video interface chip** = chip that controls a video display allowing information stored in a computer (text, graphics) to be displayed **Videoschnittstellenchip; video lookup table** = collection of pre-calculated values of the different colours that are stored in memory and can be examined very quickly to produce an answer without the need to recalculate **Bildschirmreferenztabelle; video memory** *or* **video RAM (VRAM)** = high speed random access memory used to store computer-generated *or* digitized images **Video-RAM; video monitor** = device able to display, without sound, signals from a computer **Video-, Sichtmonitor; video phone** = two way voice and image transmission **Bildschirmtelefon; video port** = connection on a video recorder allowing the data read from the tape to be used in other ways, such as being stored in a computer **Videoanschluss; video scanner** = device which allows images of objects *or* pictures to be entered into a computer **Bildscanner, Bildabtaster;** *new video scanners are designed to scan three-dimensional objects;* **video signal** = signal which provides line picture information and synchronization pulses **BAS-Signal**

◊ **videotext** *or* **videotex** *noun* system

for transmitting text and displaying it on a screen **Bildschirm-, Videotext**

> COMMENT: this covers information transmitted either by TV signals (teletext) *or* by signals sent down telephone lines (viewdata)

> QUOTE Vision Dynamics has upgraded its video capture and display boards for PCs. Elvis II will now display TV pictures on a VGA screen at a resolution of 1,024 x 768 square pixels and 2 million colours to provide enhanced picture quality from PAL, NTSC and S-VHS sources
> *Computing*

view *verb* to look at something, especially something displayed on a screen **einsehen, ansehen;** *the user has to pay a charge for viewing pages on a bulletin board*

◊ **viewdata** *noun* interactive system for transmitting text *or* graphics from a database to a user's terminal by telephone lines, providing facilities for information retrieval, transactions, education, games and recreation **Bildschirmtextsystem**

> COMMENT: the user calls up the page of information required, using the telephone and a modem, as opposed to teletext, where the pages of information are repeated one after the other automatically

◊ **viewer** *noun*
(a) person who watches television **Zuschauer**
(b) device with an eyepiece through which a person can look at film *or* transparencies **Leuchtkasten, Dia-, Bildbetrachter, Gucki**

◊ **viewfinder** *noun* eyepiece in a camera that allows a user to see what is being filmed **Sucher; electronic viewfinder** = miniature cathode ray tube in a television *or* video camera, that allows the camera operator to see the images being recorded **elektronischer Sucher**

virgin *adjective* (tape) that has not been recorded on before **unbespielt**

virtual *adjective* feature *or* device which does not actually exist but which is simulated by a computer and can be used by a user as if it did exist **virtuell; virtual address** = an address referring to virtual storage **virtuelle Adresse; virtual circuit** = link established between a source and sink (in a packet-switching network) for the duration of the call **virtuelle Verbindung; virtual disk** = section of RAM used with a short controlling program as if it were a fast disk storage system **virtuelle Platte; virtual**

machine = simulated machine and its operations **virtuelle Maschine; virtual memory** *or* **virtual storage (VS)** = large imaginary main memory made available by loading smaller pages from a backing store into the available main memory only as and when they are required **virtueller Speicher; virtual reality** = simulation of a real-life scene or environment by computer **Virtual Reality, virtuelle Realität;** *this new virtual reality software can create a three-dimensional room that you can navigate around;* **virtual terminal** = ideal terminal specifications used as a model by a real terminal **virtueller Terminal**

> QUOTE Autodesk suggests that anyone wishing to build Virtual Reality applications with the Cyberspace Developer's Kit should have solid knowledge of programming in C++ along with general knowledge of computer graphics
> *Computing*

virus *noun* program which adds itself to an executable file and copies (or spreads) itself to other executable files each time an infected file is run; a virus can corrupt data, display a message or do nothing **Virus;** *if your PC is infected with a virus, your data is at risk;* **anti-virus software** = software which removes a virus from a file **Antivirussoftware; virus detector** = utility software which checks executable files to see if they contain (have been infected) with a known virus **Virensuchprogramm, Virenprüfprogramm**

> COMMENT: viruses are spread by downloading unchecked files from a bulletin board system or via unregulated networks or by inserting an unchecked floppy disk into your PC - always use a virus detector

visible *adjective* which can be seen **sichtbar; visible light** = range of light colours that can be seen with the human eye **sichtbares Licht**

visual
1 *adjective* which can be seen *or* which is used by sight **visuell; visual programming** = method of programming a computer by showing it or taking it through the processes of what it has to do rather than writing a series of instructions **visuelles Programmieren**
2 *noun* **visuals** = graphics *or* photographs *or* illustrations, used as part of a printed output **Abbildungen, Bildmaterial**

◊ **visual display terminal (VDT)** *or* **visual display unit (VDU)** *noun* terminal with a screen and a keyboard, on which text *or* graphics can be viewed and information entered **Sicht(anzeige)gerät; Datensicht-, Videoterminal**

◊ **visualize** *verb* to imagine how something will appear, even before it has been created **sich vorstellen**

VL-bus *or* **VL local bus** *noun* standard defined by VESA which allows up to three special expansion slots that provide direct, bus-master control of the central processor and allow very high speed data transfers between main memory and the expansion card without using the processor **VL-Bus, VESA-Local-Bus;** *for a high-performance PC, choose one with a VL-bus*

VLF = VERY LOW FREQUENCY radio frequency between 30Hz and 30KHz **Niederfrequenz**

VLSI = VERY LARGE SCALE INTEGRATION system with between 10,000 and 100,000 components on a single IC **Größtintegration**

voice *noun* sound of human speech **Stimme; voice answer back** = computerized response service using a synthesized voice to answer enquiries **Sprachantwort; voice band** = minimum bandwidth required for recognizable transmission of speech (usually 300 - 3400Hz) **Sprechfrequenzband; voice data entry** *or* **input** = input of information into a computer using a speech recognition system and the user's voice **Spracheingabedaten; voice grade channel** = communications channel (bandwidth usually equal to voice band), able to carry speech and some data (such as facsimile) **Sprechkanal; voice mail** = computer linked to a telephone exchange that answers a person's telephone when they are not there and allows messages to be recorded (in digital form) **Voicemail;** *I checked my voice mail to see if anyone had left me a message;* **voice messaging** = device for recording a caller's spoken message if the number he calls does not reply **Anrufaufzeichnung; voice output** = production of sounds which sound like human speech, made as a result of voice synthesis **Sprachausgabe; voice print** = identification of a person by registering tones and signals in that person's speech **Stimmabdruck; voice recognition** = ability of a computer to recognize certain words in a human voice and provide a suitable response **Spracherkennung; voice response** = VOICE

OUTPUT; **voice synthesis** = reproduction of sounds similar to those of the human voice **Sprachsynthese; voice synthesizer** = device which generates sounds which are similar to the human voice **Sprachsynthesizer**

◊ **voice-over** *noun* spoken commentary by an actor who does not appear on the screen (as the text of a TV commercial) **Hintergrundkommentar**

◊ **voice unit** *noun* unit of signal measurement equal to a one millivolt signal across a 600 ohm resistance **Sprecheinheit**

> QUOTE the technology of voice output is reasonably difficult, but the technology of voice recognition is much more complex
> *Personal Computer World*

volatile memory *or* **volatile store** *or* **volatile dynamic storage** *noun* memory *or* storage medium which loses data stored in it when the power supply is switched off **flüchtiger Speicher** NOTE: opposite is **non-volatile memory**

◊ **volatility** *noun* number of records that are added *or* deleted from a computer system compared to the total number in store **Flüchtigkeit**

volt *noun* SI unit of electrical potential, defined as voltage across a one ohm resistance when one amp is flowing **Volt**

◊ **voltage** *noun* electromotive force expressed in volts **elektrische Spannung; voltage dip** *or* **dip in voltage** = sudden fall in voltage which may last only a very short while, but which can affect the operation of a computer system **Spannungsabfall; voltage regulator** = device which provides a steady output voltage even if the input supply varies **Spannungsregler; voltage transient** = spike of voltage that is caused by a time delay in two devices switching *or* by noise on the line **Übergangsspannung**

> COMMENT: electricity supply can have peaks and troughs of current, depending on the users in the area. Fluctuations in voltage can affect computers; a voltage regulator will provide a steady supply of electricity

volume *noun*
(a) total space occupied by data in a storage system **Volumen, Gesamtraum**
(b) measure of sound pressure **(Klang)volumen, Lautstärke; volume control** = knob which turns to increase the volume from a radio, TV or amplifier **Lautstärkeregler**

VRAM = VIDEO RANDOM ACCESS MEMORY high speed random access memory used to store computer-generated or digitized images **Video-RAM**

VRC = VERTICAL REDUNDANCY CHECK (odd) parity check on each character of a block received, to detect any errors **Querprüfung**

VS = VIRTUAL STORAGE

V series series of CCITT recommendations for data communications **V-Serie**

VT-terminal emulation *noun* standard set of codes developed by Digital Equipment Corporation to control how text and graphics are displayed on its range of terminals **VT-Terminalemulation; VT-52** = popular standard of a terminal that defines the codes used to display text and graphics **VT-52**

VTR = VIDEO TAPE RECORDER

VU = VOICE UNIT

Ww

wafer *noun* thin round slice of a large single crystal of silicon onto which hundreds of individual integrated circuits are constructed, before being cut into individual chips **Halbleiterscheibe**

◊ **wafer scale integration** *noun* one large chip, the size of a wafer, made up of smaller integrated circuits connected together (these are still in the research stage) **Integrationstechnikplättchen**

> QUOTE Rockwell International has signed a letter of intent to buy Western Digital's silicon wafer fabrication facility in Irvine, California for a proposed price of $115 million ({77 million)
> *Computing*

wait condition *or* **state** *noun* state where a processor is not active, but waiting for input from peripherals **Wartestatus**

◊ **wait loop** *noun* processor that repeats one loop of program until some action occurs **Warteschleife**

◊ **wait time** *noun* time delay between the moment when an instruction is given and the execution of the instruction *or* return of a result (such as the delay between a request for data and the data being transferred from memory) **Wartezeit**

◊ **waiting list** *noun see* QUEUE

◊ **waiting state** *noun* computer state, in which a program requires an input *or* signal before continuing execution **Wartestatus**

wake up *verb* to switch on *or* start *or* initiate **einschalten; wake-up code** = code entered at a remote terminal to indicate to the central computer that someone is trying to log-on at that location **Wake-up-Code**

walk through *verb* to examine each step of a piece of software **durchgehen**

wallpaper *noun* (in a GUI) image or pattern used as a background in a window **Hintergrundbild**

WAN = WIDE AREA NETWORK

wand *noun* bar code reader *or* optical device which is held in the hand to read bar codes on products in a store **Lesestift**

warm boot *noun* system restart which normally reloads the operating system but does not reset or check the hardware **Warmstart;** *compare* HARD RESET

◊ **warm standby** *noun* secondary backup device that can be switched into action a short time after the main system fails **Warm-Stand-by-System;** *compare with* COLD STANDBY, HOT STANDBY

◊ **warm start** *noun* restarting a programme which has stopped, but without losing any data **Warmstart;** *compare* COLD START

◊ **warm up** *verb* to allow a machine to stand idle for a time after switching on, to reach the optimum operating conditions **anwärmen**

> QUOTE warm-up time measures how long each printer takes to get ready to begin printing
> *Byte*

warn *verb* to say that something dangerous is about to happen; to say that there is a possible danger **warnen;** *he warned the keyboarders that the system might become overloaded* NOTE: you warn someone **of** something, or **that** something may happen

◊ **warning** *noun* notice of possible danger **Warnung;** *to issue a warning; warning notices were put up around the high powered laser;* **warning light** = (small light) which lights up to show that something dangerous may happen **Warnlicht;** *when the warning light on the front panel comes on, switch off the system*

warrant *verb* to guarantee **garantieren;** *all the spare parts are warranted*

◊ **warrantee** *noun* person who is given a warranty **Garantieinhaber, Garantieempfänger**

◊ **warrantor** *noun* person who gives a warranty **Garantiegeber, Garant**

◊ **warranty** *noun*
(a) guarantee *or* legal document which promises that a machine will work properly *or* that an item is of good quality **Garantie;** *the printer is sold with a twelve-month warranty; the warranty covers spare parts but not labour costs*
(b) promise in a contract **Gewähr; breach of warranty** = failing to do something which is a part of a contract **Verletzung der Gewährleistungspflicht**

wash PROM *verb* to erase the data from a PROM **einen Festwertspeicher löschen**

waste instruction *noun* instruction that does not carry out any action (except increasing the program counter to the location of next instruction) **leere Anweisung**

Watt *noun* SI unit of measurement of electrical power, defined as power produced when one amp of current flows through a load that has one volt of voltage across it **Watt**

wave *noun* signal motion that rises and falls periodically as it travels through a medium **Welle; microwave** = high frequency, short wavelength signals used for communication links, such as an earth station to satellite link **Mikrowelle; sound wave** = pressure wave that carries sound **Schallwelle**

◊ **waveform** *noun* shape of a wave **Schwingungsverlauf, Wellenform; waveform digitization** = conversion and storing a waveform in numerical form using an A/D converter **Wellenformdigitalisierung**

◊ **waveguide** *noun* physical system used to direct waves in a particular direction (usually metal tubes for microwave signals *or* optical fibres for light signals) **Hohlleiter**

◊ **wavelength** *noun* distance between two corresponding points of adjacent waves in a periodic waveform; defined as the speed of the wave divided by the frequency **Wellenlänge**

WBFM = WIDEBAND FREQUENCY MODULATION

weigh *verb*
(a) to measure how heavy something is **wiegen (lassen);** *he weighed the packet at the post office*
(b) to have a certain weight **wiegen;** *the packet weighs twenty-five grams*

◊ **weighing machine** *noun* machine which measures how heavy a thing *or* a person is **Waage**

◊ **weight** *noun* measurement of how heavy something is **Gewicht; gross weight** = weight of both the container and its contents **Bruttogewicht; net weight** = weight of goods after deducting the packing material and container **Nettogewicht; paper weight** = amount which a certain quantity of paper weighs **Papiergewicht;** *our paper weight is 70 - 90 gsm*

◊ **weighted** *adjective* sorted according to importance *or* priority **gewichtet; weighted average** = average calculated taking several factors into account, giving some more value than others **gewichteter Durchschnitt, Bewertungsdurchschnitt; weighted bit** = each bit having a different value depending on its position in a word **gewichtetes Bit**

◊ **weighting** *noun*
(a) sorting of users, programs or data by their importance or priority **Gewichtung**
(b) additional salary *or* wages paid to compensate for living in an expensive part of the country **Zulage;** *salary plus a London weighting*

well-behaved *adjective* (program) that does not make any non-standard system calls, using only the standard BIOS input/output calls rather than directly addressing peripherals *or* memory **gut funktionierend(es Programm)**

| COMMENT: if well-behaved, the software should work on all machines using the same operating system

wetware *noun* (*US*) *informal* the human brain *or* intelligence which writes software to be used with hardware **Wetware**

What-You-See-Is-All-You-Get (WYSIAYG) *noun* program where the output on screen cannot be printed out in any other form (that is, it cannot contain hidden print *or* formatting commands) **Was-man-sieht-ist-alles-was-man-bekommen-kann (WYSIAYG)**

What-You-See-Is-What-You-Get (WYSIWYG) *noun* program where the output on the screen is exactly the same as the output on printout, including graphics and special fonts **Was-man-sieht-ist-was-man-bekommt (WYSIWYG)**

while-loop *noun* conditional program instructions that carries out a loop while a condition is true **WHILE-Schleife**

white *adjective & noun* the colour of snow **weiß, das Weiße; white flag** = signal indicating a new frame on a video disk **Signal, das ein neues Videovollbild anzeigt; white level** = maximum TV signal strength corresponding to maximum brightness on the screen **Weißpegel; white noise** = random noise that is of equal power at all frequencies **weißes Rauschen; white writer** = laser printer which directs its laser beam on the points that are not printed **spezieller Laserdrucker** NOTE: the opposite is **black writer**

| COMMENT: with a white writer, the black areas are printed evenly but edges and borders are not so sharp

wide-angle lens *noun* lens which has a large acceptance angle **Weitwinkelobjektiv**

◊ **wide area network (WAN)** *noun* network where the various terminals are far apart and linked by radio, satellite and cable **Weitverkehrsnetz, Breitnetz;** *compare with* LAN

| COMMENT: WANs use modems, radio and other long distance transmission methods; LANs use cables or optical fibre links

wideband *noun* (in local area networks or communications) transmission method that combines several channels of data onto a carrier signal and can carry the data over long distances **Breitband; wideband frequency modulation (WBFM)** = frequency modulation that uses a large frequency bandwidth and has more than one pair of sidebands **Breitbandfrequenzmodulation;** *compare* BASEBAND

widow *noun* last line of a paragraph which is printed by itself at the top of a column **Hurenkind;** *compare* ORPHAN

width *noun* size of something from edge to edge **Breite; page width** *or* **line width** = number of characters across a page *or* line **Seitenbreite; Zeilenbreite**

wildcard character *noun* symbol used when searching for files *or* data which represents all files **Platzhalterzeichen, Stellvertreterzeichen, Jokerzeichen;** *a wildcard character can be used to find all files names beginning DIC*

| COMMENT: in DOS, UNIX and PC operating systems, the wildcard character '?' will match any single character in this position; the wildcard character '*' means match any number of any characters

WIMP = WINDOW, ICON, MOUSE, POINTERS description of an integrated software system that is entirely operated using windows, icons and a mouse controlled pointer **WIMP (Fenster, Ikon, Maus, Zeiger)**

| COMMENT: WIMPs normally use a combination of windows, icons and a mouse to control the operating system. In many GUIs, such as Microsoft Windows, Apple Macintosh System 7 and DR-GEM, you can control all the functions of the operating system just using the mouse. Icons represent programs and files; instead of entering the file name, you select it by moving a pointer with a mouse *see also* ENVIRONMENT, GUI; *compare* COMMAND LINE INTERFACE

Winchester disk *or* **drive** *noun* compact high-capacity hard disk which is usually built into a computer system and cannot be removed **Winchesterplatte, Festplatte; removable Winchester** = small hard disk in a sealed unit, which can be detached from a computer when full *or* when not required **herausnehmbare Winchesterplatte**

window
1 *noun* (i) reserved section of screen used to display special information, that can be selected and looked at at any time and which overwrites information already on the screen; (ii) part of a document currently displayed on a screen; (iii) area of memory *or* access to a storage device **(i) & (ii) Fenster; (iii) Ausschnitt;** *several remote stations are connected to the network and each has its own window onto the hard disk; the operating system will allow other programs to be displayed on-screen at the same time in different windows;* **active window** = area of the display screen where the operator is

currently working **aktives Fenster;** **command window** = area of the screen that always displays the range of commands available **Befehlsfenster;** *the command window is a single line at the bottom of the screen;* **edit window** = area of the screen in which the user can display and edit text *or* graphics **Editier-, Aufbereitungsfenster; text window** = window in a graphics system, where the text is held in a small space on the screen before being allocated to a final area **Textfenster;** **window, icon, mouse, pointer (WIMP)** = program display which uses graphics *or* icons to control the software and make it easier to use system commands do not have to be typed in **WIMP-Umgebung (window, icon, mouse, pointer)** **2** *verb* to set up a section of screen by defining the coordinates of its corners, that allows information to be temporarily displayed, overwriting previous information but without altering information in the workspace **als Fenster einrichten**

◊ **windowing** *noun* (i) action of setting up a window to show information on the screen; (ii) displaying *or* accessing information via a window **(i) & (ii) Fenstertechnik**

QUOTE when an output window overlaps another, the interpreter does not save the contents of the obscured window
Personal Computer World

QUOTE for instance, if you define a screen window using PowerBuilder, you can build a whole family of windows, which automatically inherit the characteristics of the first
Computing

QUOTE you can connect more satellites to the network, each having its own window onto the hard disk
PC Plus

QUOTE windowing facilities make use of virtual screens as well as physical screens
Byte

QUOTE the functions are integrated via a windowing system with pull-down menus used to select different operations
Byte

QUOTE the network system uses the latest windowing techniques
Desktop Publishing

Windows ™ multitasking graphical user

interface for the IBM PC developed by Microsoft Corp. that is designed to be easy to use; Windows uses icons to represent files and devices and can be controlled using a mouse, unlike MS-DOS which requires commands to be typed in **Windows** ™; **Windows for Workgroups** ™ = version of Windows that includes basic peer-to-peer file-sharing functions and email, fax and scheduler utilities **Windows for Workgroups** ™; **Windows NT** ™ = high-performance GUI derived from Windows that does not use DOS as an operating system and features 32-bit code **Windows NT** ™

wipe *verb* to clean data from a disk **löschen;** *by reformatting you will wipe the disk clean*

◊ **wiper** *noun* movable arm in a potentiometer, a variable resistor *or* selector switch that can be turned to select a new resistance *or* function **Abstreifer**

wire
1 *noun*
(a) thin metal conductor **Draht; wire printer** = dot-matrix printer; *Nadeldrucker* **wire wrap** = simple method of electrically connecting component terminals together using thin insulated wire wrapped around each terminal which is then soldered into place, usually used for prototype systems **Drahtwickeln**
2 *verb* to install wiring **verkabeln;** *the studio is wired for sound;* **wired** *or* **hardwired program computer** = computer with a program built into the hardware which cannot be changed **verbindungsprogrammierter Computer;** *see also* HARDWIRED

◊ **wireless**
1 *noun (old use)* device that can receive radio broadcasts **Radio**
2 *adjective* communication system that does not require wires to carry signals **drahtlos; wireless microphone** = audio microphone with a small transmitter attached allowing the transmission of signals without interconnecting wires **drahtloses Mikrofon**

◊ **wire tap** *noun* unauthorized connection to a private communications line in order to listen to conversations *or* obtain private data **Abhöranlage**

◊ **wiring** *noun* series of wires **elektrische Leitungen;** *the wiring in the system had to be replaced;* **wiring closet** = box in which the cabling for a network or part of network is terminated and interconnected **Schaltschrank, Schaltkasten; wiring frame** = metal structure used to support incoming cables and provide connectors to allow cables to be interconnected **Verdrahtungsrahmen**

WISC = WRITABLE INSTRUCTION SET COMPUTER CPU design that allows a programmer to add extra machine code instructions using microcode, to customize the instruction set **beschreibbare CPU**

woofer *noun (informal)* large loudspeaker used to produce low frequency sounds **Tieftonlautsprecher**

word *noun*
(a) separate item of language, which is used with others to form speech *or* writing which can be understood **Wort; words per minute (wpm** *or* **WPM)** = method of measuring the speed of a printer **Wörter pro Minute; word break** = division of a word at the end of a line, where part of the word is left on one line with a hyphen, and the rest of the word is taken over to begin the next line **Worttrennung; word count** = number of words in a file *or* text **Wortzahl; word wrap** *or* **wraparound** = system in word processing where the operator does not have to indicate the line endings, but can keyboard continuously, leaving the program to insert word breaks and to continue the text on the next line **Umlaufsystem**
(b) separate item of data on a computer, formed of a group of bits, stored in a single location in a memory **Wort; word length** = length of a computer word, counted as the number of bits **Wortlänge; word mark** = symbol indicating the start of a word in a variable word length machine **Wortmarke; word serial** = data words transmitted along a parallel bus one after the other **Wortserie; word time** = time taken to transfer a word from one memory area *or* device to another **Wort(takt)zeit**

◊ **WordPerfect** ™ popular word-processing application developed by WordPerfect Corp. to run on a wide range of hardware platforms and operating systems **WordPerfect** ™

◊ **word-process** *verb* to edit, store and manipulate text using a computer **Text verarbeiten;** *it is quite easy to read word-processed files*

◊ **wordprocessing** *or* **word-processing (WP)** *noun* using a computer to keyboard, edit, and output text, in the form of letters, labels, address lists, etc. **Textverarbeitung;** *load the word-processing program before you start keyboarding;* **word-processing bureau** = office which specializes in word-processing for other companies **Textverarbeitungsbüro, Textbüro, Schreibbüro**

◊ **word-processor** *noun*
(a) small computer *or* typewriter with a computer in it, used for word-processing text and documents **Textverarbeitungscomputer**
(b) word-processing package *or* program for a computer which allows the editing and manipulation and output of text, such as letters, labels, address lists, etc. **Textverarbeitungssystem**

◊ **WordStar** ™ popular word-processing application developed by MicroPro International for CP/M and IBM PC computers **WordStar** ™

work
1 *noun* things done using the hands *or* brain **Arbeit; work area** = memory space which is being used by an operator **Arbeitsbereich; work disk** = disk on which current work is stored **Arbeitsplatte; work file** *or* **scratch file** temporary work area which is being used for current work **Arbeitsdatei, ungeschützte Datei; working store** *or* **scratch pad** = area of high-speed memory used for temporary storage of data in current use **Arbeitsspeicher; Notizblockspeicher**
2 *verb* to function **arbeiten, funktionieren;** *the computer system has never worked properly since it was installed*

◊ **workflow** *noun* network software designed to improve the flow of electronic documents around an office network, from user to user **Workflow, Arbeitsablauf**

◊ **workgroup** *noun* small group of users who are working on a project *or* connected with a local area network **Arbeitsgruppe, Workgroup; workgroup enabled** = feature added to standard software package to give it more appeal to a group of networked users **workgroupfähig;** *this word-processor is workgroup enabled which adds an email gateway from the standard menus;* **workgroup software** = application designed to be used by many users in a group to improve productivity - such as a diary or scheduler **Workgroupsoftware, Arbeitsgruppensoftware**

◊ **working** *adjective* (something) which is operating correctly **funktionierend, in Betrieb**

◊ **workload** *noun* amount of work which a person *or* computer has to do

Arbeitsbelastung; *he has difficulty in dealing with his heavy workload*

◊ **workplace** *noun* place where you work Arbeitsplatz

◊ **work-sharing** *noun* system where two part-timers share one job Arbeitsteilung

◊ **worksheet** *noun* (in a spreadsheet program) a two-dimensional matrix of rows and columns that contains cells which can, themselves, contain equations Arbeitsblatt

◊ **workspace** *noun* space in memory, which is available for use *or* is being used currently by an operator Arbeitsbereich

◊ **workstation** *noun* place where a computer user works, with a terminal, printer, modem, etc. Arbeitsplatz; *the system includes five workstations linked together in a ring network; the archive storage has a total capacity of 1200 Mb between seven workstations*

QUOTE an image processing workstation must provide three basic facilities: the means to digitize, display and manipulate the image data
Byte

WORM = WRITE ONCE READ MANY TIMES MEMORY

WOW *noun* fluctuation of the frequency of a recorded signal at playback, (usually caused by uneven tape movement) Gleichlaufschwankung, Jaulen

WP = WORD-PROCESSING

WPM *or* **wpm** = WORDS PER MINUTE

wrap *noun* **omega wrap** = system of threading video tape round a video head (the tape passes over most of the circular head and is held in place by two small rollers Omegawicklung

◊ **wraparound** *or* **word wrap** *noun* system in word-processing where the operator does not have to indicate the line endings, but can keyboard continuously, leaving the program to insert word breaks and to continue the text on the next line Umlaufsystem; **horizontal wraparound** = movement of a cursor on a computer display from the end of one line to the beginning of the next Zeilenumlauf

writable instruction set computer (WISC) *noun* CPU design that allows a programmer to add extra machine code instructions using microcode, to customize the instruction set WISC-Computer

write *verb*
(a) to put words *or* figures on to paper schreiben; *she wrote a letter of complaint to the manager; the telephone number is written at the bottom of the notepaper*
(b) to put text *or* data onto a disk *or* tape schreiben; *access time is the time taken to read from or; write to a location in memory;* **write** *or* **write-back** *or* **write-behind cache** = temporary storage used to hold data intended for a storage device until the device is ready Write-Behind-Cache; *write-back cacheing improves performance, but can be dangerous; see also* CACHE, READ CACHE; **write error** = error reported when trying to save data onto a magnetic storage medium Schreibfehler; **write head** = transducer that can write data onto a magnetic medium Schreibkopf; **write once, read many times memory (WORM)** = optical disk storage system that allows one writing action but many reading actions in its life einmal beschreibbarer, mehrfach lesbarer Speicher; **writing pad** = special device which allows a computer to read in handwritten characters which have been written onto a special pad Sensor(schreib)block; *see* OCR; **write time** = time between requesting data transfer to a storage. location and it being written Schreibzeit NOTE: you write data to a file. Note also: **writing - wrote - has written**

◊ **write black printer** *noun* printer where toner sticks to the points hit by the laser beam when the image drum is scanned Schwarzdrucker; *compare* WHITE WRITER

COMMENT: a write black printer produces sharp edges and graphics, but large areas of black are muddy

◊ **write-permit ring** *noun* ring on a reel of magnetic tape which allows the tape to be overwritten *or* erased Schreiberring

◊ **write protect** *verb* to make it impossible to write to a floppy disk *or* tape by moving a special write-protect tab einen Schreibschutz anbringen; **write-protect tab** = tab on a floppy disk which if moved, prevents any writing to *or* erasing from the disk Schreibschutzetikett

◊ **writer** *noun see* BLACK, WHITE

◊ **writing** *noun* something which has been written Schrift; *to put the agreement in*

writing; he has difficulty in reading my writing
NOTE: no plural

WYSIAYG = WHAT YOU SEE IS ALL YOU GET

WYSIWYG = WHAT YOU SEE IS WHAT YOU GET

X = EXTENSION

X.25 CCITT standard that defines the connection between a terminal and a packet-switching network **X.25**

◊ **X.400** CCITT standard that defines an electronic mail transfer method **X.400**

◊ **X.500** CCITT standard that defines a method of global naming that allows every individual user to have a unique identity and allows any user to address an electronic mail message to any other user **X.500**

x-axis *noun* horizontal axis of a graph **x-Achse, Abszisse(nachse)**

◊ **x-coordinate** *noun* horizontal axis position coordinate **x-Koordinate, Abszisse**

◊ **x-direction** *noun* movement horizontally **x-Richtung**

◊ **x-distance** *noun* distance along an x-axis from an origin **Entfernung auf der x-Achse**

xerographic printer printer (such as a photocopier) where charged ink is attracted to areas of a charged picture **xerographischer Drucker**

◊ **xerography** *noun* copying method that relies on ink being attracted to dark regions of a charged picture **Xerographie**

Xerox
1 *noun*
(a) trademark for a type of photocopier **Xerox (Xerokopiergerät);** *to make a xerox copy of a letter; we must order some more xerox paper for the copier; we are having a new xerox machine installed tomorrow*
(b) photocopy made with a xerox machine **Xerokopie;** *to send the other party a xerox of the contract; we have sent xeroxes to each of the agents*

2 *verb* to make a photocopy with a xerox machine **xerokopieren;** *to xerox a document; she xeroxed all the files*

XMODEM standard file transfer and error-detecting protocol used in asynchronous (modem) data transmissions **XMODEM; XMODEM 1K** = version of XMODEM that transfers 1024-byte blocks of data **XMODEM 1K; XMODEM CRC** = enhanced version of XMODEM that includes error checking **XMODEM CRC**

XMS = EXTENDED MEMORY SPECIFICATION rules that define how a program should access extended memory fitted in a PC **XMS**

XNS = XEROX NETWORKING SYSTEM proprietary protocol developed by Xerox and used in many local area networks **XNS**

XON/XOFF asynchronous transmission protocol in which each end can regulate the data flow by transmitting special codes **XON/XOFF**

X/OPEN group of vendors that are responsible for promoting open systems **X/OPEN**

x punch *noun* card punch for column 11, often used to represent a negative number **x-Lochung**

X-ray *noun*
(a) ray with a very short length, which is invisible, but can go through soft tissue and register as a photograph on a film **Röntgenstrahl; X-ray imaging** = showing images of the inside of a body using X-rays **Röntgen**
(b) photograph taken using X-rays **Röntgenbild;** *the medical text is illustrated with X-ray photographs*

X-series *noun* recommendations for data communications over public data networks **x-Serie**

XT version of the original IBM PC, developed by IBM, that used an 8088 processor and included a hard disk **XT; XT keyboard** = keyboard used with the IBM PC which had ten function keys running in two columns along the left-hand side of the keyboard **XT-Tastatur**

X-Window System *or* **X-Windows** standard set of API commands and display handling routines, that provides a hardware-independent programming interface for applications; originally developed for UNIX workstations, it can also run on a PC or minicomputer terminals **X-Window-System** *or* **X-Windows**

> QUOTE X is the underlying technology which allows Unix applications to run under a multi-user, multitasking GUI. It has been adopted as the standard for the Common Open Software Environment, proposed recently by top Unix vendors including Digital, IBM and Sun
> *Computing*

x-y *noun* coordinates for drawing a graph, where x is the horizontal and y the vertical value **x/y-Koordinaten**; **x-y plotter** = device for drawing lines on paper between given coordinates **Koordinatenschreiber, Plotter**

Yy

yaw *noun* rotation of satellite about a vertical axis with the earth **Gieren**

y-axis *noun* vertical axis of a graph **y-Achse, Ordinate(nachse)**

◊ **y-coordinate** *noun* vertical axis position coordinate **y-Koordinate, Ordinate**

◊ **y-direction** *noun* vertical movement **y-Richtung**

◊ **y-distance** *noun* distance along an y-axis from an origin **Entfernung auf der y-Achse**

YMCK = YELLOW, MAGENTA, CYAN, BLACK colour definition based on these four colours used in DTP software when creating separate colour film to use for printing **YMCK**

YMODEM variation of the XMODEM file transfer protocol that uses 1024-byte blocks and can send multiple files **YMODEM**

yoke *noun* **deflection yoke** = magnetic coils around a TV tube used to control the position of the picture beam **Ablenkjoch**

y punch *noun* card punch for column 12 (often used to indicate a positive number) **y-Lochung**

Zz

Z = IMPEDANCE

Z80 8-bit processor developed by Zilog, used in many early popular computers **Z80**

zap *verb* to wipe off all data currently in the workspace **löschen**; *he pressed CONTROL Z and zapped all the text*

z-axis *noun* axis for depth in a three-dimensional graph *or* plot **z-Achse**

zero
1 *noun* (i) the digit 0; (ii) equivalent of logical off or false state **(i) & (ii) Null**; *the code for international calls is zero one zero (010)*; **jump on zero** = conditional jump executed if a flag *or* register is zero **Sprungbefehl bei Null**; **zero compression** *or* **zero suppression** = shortening of a file by the removal of unnecessary zeros **Nullenunterdrückung**; **zero flag** = indicator that the contents of a register *or* result is zero **Nullkennzeichnung**; *the jump on zero instruction tests the zero flag*; **zero-level address** *or* **immediate address** = instruction in which the address is the operand **virtuelle Adresse**
2 *verb* to erase *or* clear a file **löschen**; **to zero a device** = to erase the contents of a programmable device **einen Zusatz löschen**; **to zero fill** = to fill a section of memory with zero values **mit Nullen auffüllen**

◊ **zero insertion force (ZIF)** *noun* chip socket that has movable connection terminals, allowing the chip to be inserted with no force, then a small lever is turned to grip the legs of the chip **Nullkraftstecker**

◊ **zero slot LAN** *noun* local area network that does not use internal expansion adapters, instead it uses the serial port (or sometimes an external pocket network adapters connected to the printer port) **Rechnerdirektverbindung**

◊ **zero wait state** *noun* state of a device (normally processor *or* memory chips) that is fast enough to run at the same speed as the other components in a computer, so does not have to be artificially slowed down by inserting wait states **Wartestatus Null, Zero-Waitstate**

ZIF = ZERO INSERTION FORCE

zip code *noun (US)* numbers used to indicate a postal delivery area in an address on an envelope **Postleitzahl**
NOTE: the GB English for this is **post code**

ZMODEM enhanced version of the XMODEM file transfer protocol that includes error detection and the ability to re-start a transfer where it left off if the connection is cut **ZMODEM**

zone *noun* region *or* part of a screen defined for specialized printing **Zone; hot zone** = text area to the left of the right margin in a word-processed document, if a word does not fit completely into the line, a hyphen is automatically inserted **Ausschließzone, Bereich um die weiche Trennfuge**

zoom *verb* (i) to change the focal length of a lens to enlarge (or reduce) the object in the viewfinder; (ii) to enlarge an area of text (to make it easier to work on) **(i) zoomen; (ii) vergrößern**

◊ **zooming** *noun* enlarging an area of text *or* graphics **Vergrößern;** *variable zooming from 25% to 400% of actual size*

◊ **zoom lens** *noun* lens whose focal length can be varied to make an object larger in the viewfinder **Zoom(objektiv)**

QUOTE there are many options to allow you to zoom into an area for precision work
Electronics & Wireless World

QUOTE any window can be zoomed to full-screen size by pressing the F-5 function key
Byte

Deutsch-Englisches
Register

10 Prozent: *10 per cent*
16-Bit-CPU: *sixteen-bit*
32-Bit-System: *thirty-two bit system*
3-Überschusscode: *excess-3 code*
80-Spalten-Bildschirm: *eighty-column screen*
80-Spalten-Drucker: *80-column printer*
8-Bit-System: *eight-bit (system)*
8-Zoll-Diskette: *eight-inch disk*
8-Zoll-Laufwerk: *eight-inch drive*

Aa

abändern: *to alter or modify*
Abänderung: *modification*
AB-Ausblendung: *AB roll*
Abbild: *image*
abbilden: *to map; to mirror*
Abbildung: *figure; chart; plate*
Abbildungen: *visuals*
Abbildungsverarbeitung: *image processing*
abblenden: *to fade out*
abbrechen: *to abandon or abort or cancel or terminate*
Abbremszeit: *stop time*
Abbruch: *hangup; termination; aborted connection*
Abbruchcode: *abend code*
Abbruchmaske: *interrupt mask*
Abbruchsequenz: *abort sequence*
Abdeckhaube: *dustcover*
Abdeckmittel: *resist*
Abenteuerspiel: *adventure game*
Aberration: *aberration*
Abfall: *decrease*
abfallen: *to decay; to drop*
Abfrage: *inquiry; interrogation*
Abfrage mittels Beispiel: *Query By Example (QBE)*
Abfrageschalter: *sampler*
Abfragesprache: *query language*
Abfragestation: *inquiry station*

abgekürzte Installation: *abbreviated installation*
abgeleitete Indizierung: *derived indexing*
abgerundet: *rounded down or in round figures*
abgeschirmtes verdrilltes Adernpaar: *shielded twisted pair (STP) cable*
abgeschlossen: *complete*
abgeschlossenes Unterprogramm: *closed subroutine*
abgleichen: *to match*
Abgrenzung: *delimiter; demarcation*
abhängig: *dependent*
abhängig von Groß-/Kleinschreibung: *case sensitive*
abhängige Datenstation: *slave terminal*
Abhöranlage: *wire tap*
Abkürzung: *abbreviation*
Ablagekorb: *filing basket or filing tray*
Ablagesystem: *filing system*
Ablation: *ablation*
Ablauf: *expiration; run*
Ablaufanzeiger: *run indicator*
ablaufen: *to pass; to expire*
Ablauflinie: *flowline*
Ablaufrichtung: *flow direction*
Ablaufsteuerung: *sequencer*
ablegen: *to deposit*
Ablegesatz: *dead matter*
Ableitungsgraph: *derivation graph*
ablenken: *to deflect*
Ablenkjoch: *deflection yoke*
Ablesewert: *reading*
ablösen: *to supersede*
Abmachung: *deal*
abmelden: *to unmount*
Abmelden: *logging off*
abmelden: sich ~: *to log off or log out; to sign off*
Abnahme: *acceptance*
Abnahmeprüfung: *acceptance test or testing*
abnehmen: *to decay; to decrease*
abnormaler Abbruch: *abnormal termination*
abnormales Ende: *abend*
abrollen: *to scroll down*
Abruf: *fetch*
Abruf auf Anforderung: *demand fetching*
Abruf-Ausführ-Zyklus: *fetch-execute cycle*

Abrufbefehl: *fetch instruction*
Abrufcode: *attention code*
abrufen: *to poll; to call up*
Abrufphase: *fetch phase*
Abrufprotokollarchitektur: *demand protocol architecture (DPA)*
Abrufsignal: *fetch signal*
Abruftaste: *attention key*
Abrufunterbrechung: *attention interruption*
Abrufzyklus: *fetch cycle*
abrunden: *to round down or off*
Abrundung: *rounding*
Abrundungsfehler: *round off errors*
Absatz: *paragraph*
Absatzmarke: *paragraph marker*
abschalten: *to disconnect; to shut down*
Abschaltmechanismus: *shut-off mechanism*
abschätzen: *to rate*
abschießen: *to launch*
abschirmen: *to screen; to shield*
Abschirmung: *shield*
abschließen: *to finish*
Abschluss: *completion; ending*
Abschlussstecker: *terminator*
Abschlusswiderstand: *terminator*
Abschneidefehler: *truncation error*
Abschneiden: *truncation*
abschneiden: *to cut off; to truncate; to perform*
Abschnitt: *section*
Abschuss: *launch*
abschwächen: *to attenuate*
Abschwächung: *attenuation*
Absender: *sender*
Absicht: *objective*
absichtliche Unterbrechung: *armed interrupt*
absolute Adresse: *absolute or actual or direct or explicit or machine or specific address*
absolute Adressierung: *absolute addressing*
absolute Bezugszelle: *absolute cell reference*
absolute Einheit: *absolute device*
absolute Instruktion: *absolute instruction*
absolute Koordinaten: *absolute coordinates*
absolute Maximumwerte: *absolute maximum rating*
absolute Priorität: *absolute priority*
absoluter Assemblierer: *absolute assembler*
absoluter Ausdruck: *absolute expression*
absoluter Code: *absolute or actual or specific code*
absoluter Fehler: *absolute error*
absolutes Programm: *absolute program*

Absolutwert: *absolute value*
Absolutzahl mit Vorzeichen(ziffer): *sign and modulus*
absorbieren: *to absorb*
Absorption: *absorption*
Absorptionsfilter: *absorption filter*
Absorptionskonstante: *absorptance*
Absorptionsverlust: *ground absorption*
abspielen: *to play back*
Abspielnadel: *stylus*
abstimmen: *to adjust or tune*
Abstimmung: *adjustment*
abstrakter Datentyp: *abstract*
Abstreifer: *wiper*
Abstrich: *down stroke*
Absturz: *crash*
abstürzen: *to bomb or crash*
absturzgeschützt *or* **absturzgesichert:** *crash-protected*
Abszisse: *X-coordinate*
Abszissenachse: *horizontal axis or X-axis*
Abtast- und Haltekreis: *sample and hold circuit*
Abtastauflösungsvermögen: *scanning resolution*
Abtastbereich: *scan area*
Abtasten: *scanning*
abtasten: *to sample; to scan*
abtastender Funkempfänger: *scanning radio receiver*
Abtaster: *sampler; scanner*
Abtastfehler: *scanning error*
Abtastfleck: *scanning spot*
Abtastfrequenz: *scan rate*
Abtastgerät: *scanning device*
Abtastgeschwindigkeit: *sampling rate or scanning rate or speed*
Abtastintervall: *sampling interval*
Abtastkopf: *scan head*
Abtastlänge: *scan length*
Abtastspeicherbereich: *scanner memory*
Abtastung: *scan*
Abtastzeile: *scan(ning) line*
Abtippen von Dokumenten: *copy typing*
Abtretende(r): *assignor*
Abtretung: *assignment*
Abwanderung: *drift*
abwärts: *downward*
Abwärtskompatibilität: *downward compatibility*
abwechselnd: *alternate(ly)*
Abweichung: *divergence*
abziehen: *to deduct*
Abzug: *print*
ACD-System: *ACD*
achromatisch: *achromatic*
achromatische Farbe: *achromatic colour*
Achse: *axis*

Acht-Bit-Byte: *eight-bit byte*
Achtung Unterbrechung: *attention interruption*
Ackermann-Funktion: *Ackerman's function*
Acrobat: *Acrobat*
Adapter: *adapter or adaptor*
Adapter zum Hauptrechner: *host adapter*
adaptive differenzielle Pulscodemodulation (ADPCM): *adaptive differential pulse code modulation (ADPCM)*
adaptive Kanalzuordnung: *adaptive channel allocation*
adaptive Paketierung: *adaptive packet assembly*
adaptiver Leitweg: *adaptive routing*
Addier-/Subtrahiereinrichtung: *adder-subtractor*
Addiereinrichtung: *adder*
addieren: *to add*
Addierer für binär codierte Dezimalzahlen: *BCD adder*
Addierer mit Parallelübertrag: *carry look ahead*
Addition ohne Übertrag: *addition without carry*
Addition: *addition*
Additionsregister: *add register*
Additionszeit: *add(ition) time*
additives Farbmischen: *additive colour mixing*
adjunktives Register: *adjunct register*
Administrator: *administrator*
Adressabbild: *address mapping*
Adressänderung: *address modification*
Adressat/-in: *addressee*
Adressauflösungsprotokoll: *address resolution protocol (ARP)*
Adressbasis: *address base*
Adressbuch: *address book*
Adressbus: *address bus*
Adressbusleitung: *bus address lines*
Adresse: *address*
Adressendecodierer: *address decoder*
Adressenende: *end of address (EOA)*
Adressenliste: *address list*
Adressenregister: *address register*
Adressenspur: *address track*
Adressenvielfachleitung: *address highway*
Adressenzugriffszeit: *address access time*
Adressfeld: *address field*
Adressfolgeregister: *sequence control register (SCR) or sequence counter or instruction address register*
Adressformat: *address format*
adressfreie Operation: *no-address operation*
adressierbar: *addressable*

adressierbare Datenstation: *addressable terminal*
adressierbarer Cursor or **Positionsanzeiger:** *addressable cursor*
adressierbarer Punkt: *addressable point*
adressierbarer Terminal: *addressable terminal*
Adressierbarkeit: *addressability*
Adressierebene: *addressing level*
adressieren: *to address*
Adressierkapazität: *addressing capacity*
Adressiermaschine: *addressing machine*
Adressiermethode: *addressing method*
Adressierung: *addressing*
Adressierungsart: *addressing mode*
Adressierungscode: *address*
Adressimpulseingang: *address strobe*
Adressliste: *mailing list*
Adressmarke: *address mark*
Adressmodifikation: *address modification*
Adressraum: *address space*
Adressrechnung: *address computation*
Adressregister: *address register*
Adressumsetzung: *address translation*
Adresswort: *address word*
Advanced Peer-to-Peer Networking: *advanced peer-to-peer networking (APPN)*
Advanced Run-Length Limited (ARLL): *advanced run-length limited (ARLL)*
affirmativ: *affirmative*
Agent: *agent*
Aggregat: *aggregate*
aggregierte Bandbreite: *aggregate bandwidth*
Akkumulator(register): *accumulator or ACC (register)*
Akkumulatoradresse: *accumulator address*
akkurat: *accurate(ly)*
Akronym: *acronym*
Akte: *file*
Aktenkopie: *file copy*
Aktenordner: *file*
Aktenschrank: *filing cabinet*
Aktentaschencomputer: *portable*
aktinisches Licht: *actinic light*
Aktion: *action*
Aktionscode: *action code*
Aktionsfeld: *action field*
Aktionsfenster: *pull-down menu or action bar pull-down*
Aktionsleiste: *action bar*
Aktionsliste: *action list*
Aktionsnachricht: *action message*
Aktionsobjekt: *action object*
Aktionsrahmen: *action frame*
Aktionszyklus: *action cycle*
aktiv: *active*

aktive Anwendung: *active application*
aktive Codeseite: *active code page*
aktive Datei: *active file*
aktive Datenbank: *active database*
aktive Leitung: *active line*
aktive Verbindungsstrecke: *active link*
aktive Zelle: *active or current cell*
aktiver Bereich: *active area*
aktiver Datensatz: *active record*
aktiver Drucker: *active printer*
aktiver Gateway: *active gateway*
aktiver Hub: *active hub*
aktiver Knoten: *active node*
aktiver Speicher: *active storage*
aktiver Status: *active state*
aktives Fenster: *active window*
aktives Programm: *active program*
aktivieren: *to activate or enable or execute*
aktiviertes Tabellenfeld: *active cell*
Aktivität: *activity*
Aktivitätenprotokoll: *activity trail*
Aktivvorrichtung: *active device*
Aktualisierungsdatenstation für große
Datenmengen: *bulk update terminal*
aktuell: *current*
aktuelle Adresse: *current address*
aktuelle Datei *or* Information: *update*
aktueller Operand: *literal operand*
aktuelles Adressregister: *current address
register (CAR)*
aktuelles Befehlsregister: *current
instruction register (CIR)*
aktuelles Laufwerk: *current drive*
aktuelles Verzeichnis: *current directory*
Akustik: *acoustics*
Akustikkoppler: *acoustic coupler*
akustisch: *acoustic*
akustische Rückmeldung: *acoustical
feedback*
akustische Verzögerungsleitung:
acoustic delay line
akustischer Speicher: *acoustic store or
memory*
Akut: *acute accent*
Akzentzeichen: *accent*
akzeptabel: *acceptable*
akzeptieren: *to accept*
Akzidenzdrucker: *jobbing printer*
Akzidenzdruckerei: *print shop*
Alarmzustand: *alert condition*
Album: *scrapbook*
Albumin: *albumen plate*
Algebra: *algebra*
algebraische Sprache: *algebraic language*
algorithmisch: *algorithmic*
algorithmische Sprache: *algorithmic
language*

Algorithmus zur Aufteilung von
Speicherseiten: *paging algorithm*
Algorithmus: *algorithm*
Aliasing: *aliasing*
Aliasname: *alias (name)*
Alleinvertretungsvereinbarung: *exclusive
agreement*
allgemein zugänglich: *on general release*
allgemein: *general*
allgemeiner Speicherbereich: *common
storage area*
Allgemeinsoftware: *common software*
allmählich einführen: *to phase in*
Allofon: *allophone*
Alphabet: *alphabet*
Alpha-Beta-Technik: *alpha beta technique*
alphabetisch: *alphabetically*
alphabetisch ordnen: *to alphasort or
alphabetize*
alphabetische Reihenfolge: *alphabetical
order*
alphafotografisch: *alphaphotographic*
alphageometrisch: *alphageometric*
Alphakanal: *alpha channel*
alphamosaik: *alphamosaic*
alphanumerische Anzeige: *alphanumeric
display*
alphanumerische Daten: *alphanumeric
data*
alphanumerische Feldgruppe:
alphanumeric array
alphanumerische Tastatur: *alphanumeric
keyboard*
alphanumerische Zeichen: *alphanumeric
characters or alphanumerics*
alphanumerische Zeichenfolge *or*
Zeichenkette: *alphanumeric or character
string*
alphanumerischer Operand: *alphanumeric
operand*
Alphastrahlen: *alpha radiation*
Alphateilchen: *alpha particle*
Alphateilchenempfindlichkeit: *alpha-
particle sensitivity*
Alphatest: *alpha test*
Alphawindung: *alpha wrap*
alte Ausgabe: *back number*
alternativ: *alternative*
Alternative: *alternative*
alternativer Zeichensatz: *alternate
character set*
Alternativmodus: *alternate mode*
Alternativschlüssel: *alternate key*
Alternativweg: *alternate route*
alternieren: *to alternate*
alternierend: *alternate(ly)*
Alt-Taste: *Alt key*

am Bildschirm: *on-screen*
am Einsatzort: *on-site*
Ampere: *amp or ampere (A)*
Amplitude: *amplitude*
Amplitudenmodulation (AM): *amplitude modulation (AM)*
Amplituden-Quantisierung: *amplitude quantization*
Amplitudenverzerrung: *amplitude distortion*
Amtswahl: *direct outward dialling*
Analoganzeige: *analog display*
Analogaufzeichnung: *analog recording*
Analogbildschirm: *analog monitor*
Analogdarstellung: *analog representation*
Analogdaten: *analog data*
Analog-Digital-Umsetzer: *analog to digital converter (ADC or A to D converter)*
Analog-Digital-Umwandlung: *analog to digital (A to D or A/D)*
analoge Ausgabekarte: *analog output card*
analoge Eingabekarte: *analog input card*
analoge integrierte Schaltung: *linear integrated circuit*
analoge Übertragung: *analog transmission*
analoges Signal: *analog signal*
Analogkanal: *analog channel*
Analogleitung: *analog line*
Analogmultimeter: *analog multimeter (AMM)*
Analogrechner: *analog computer*
Analogschaltelement: *analog gate*
Analogschleife (mit Selbsttest): *analog loopback (with selftest)*
analphabetisch: *illiterate*
Analysator: *analyzer*
Analyse: *analysis*
Analyse des kritischen Weges: *critical path analysis*
analysieren: *to analyse or analyze*
Analytiker/-in: *analyst*
analytische Maschine: *analytical engine*
anastigmatische Linse: *anastigmat*
andauernd: *continuous*
andauernder Fehler: *hard error*
ändern: *to alter*
anders: *different*
anders formatierte Diskette: *alien disk*
Änderung: *alteration*
Änderungsband: *change tape*
Änderungsdatei: *change file*
Änderungssatz: *amendment or change or transaction record*
andeuten: *to block in*
Andruckposition: *imprint position*
Andruckpresse: *proofer*
Andruckrad: *pinchwheel*

Anerkennung: *acknowledgements*
Anerkennungsurkunde: *certificate of approval*
Anfang: *beginning; head; origin*
Anfang des Kopfes: *start of header*
Anfang des Textes: *start-of-text (SOT or STX)*
Anfangsadresse: *initial address; stack base*
Anfangsadressierung: *inherent addressing*
Anfangsbedingung: *initial condition*
Anfangsbuchstabe: *initial*
Anfangsfehler: *initial error*
Anfangskennsatz: *header label*
Anfangskurve: *attack envelope*
Anfangssatz: *home record*
Anfangswert: *initial value*
Anfertigung: *origination*
Anfertigung von Korrekturabzügen: *proofing*
anfordern: *to request*
Anforderung: *enquiry; request*
Anfrage: *inquiry*
Anfragecode: *inquiry character (ENQ)*
Anfrageverarbeitung: *query processing*
anfügen: *to append*
anführen: *to head*
Anführungszeichen: *inverted commas*
angeben: *to specify*
angegliedert: *affiliated*
angehängte Datei: *attachment*
angepasste Belastung: *matched load*
angerufene Seite: *called party*
angeschnittener Satzspiegel: *bleed*
angetrieben: *driven or powered*
Angleichung: *adjustment*
angliedern: *to affiliate*
angrenzend: *adjacent or contiguous*
angrenzende Datei: *contiguous file*
Ångström: *angstrom (Å)*
Anhalt- und Warteprotokoll: *stop and wait protocol*
anhalten: *to halt; to hold*
Anhang: *appendix*
anhängen: *to append*
anhäufen: *to accumulate*
anheben: *to boost*
Anheber: *lifter*
Animation: *animation*
animieren: *to animate*
Ankerzelle: *anchor cell*
ankommend: *incoming*
ankommender Verkehr: *incoming traffic*
Anlage: *equipment*
Anlaufzeit: *acceleration time; rise time*
anlegen: *to lay in*
Anmelden: *logging on*
anmelden: *to attach*

anmelden: sich ~: *to sign on*
Anmeldesequenz: *logon sequence*
Anmeldeserver: *log on server*
Anmeldeskript: *log on script*
Anmerkung: *annotation*
Anmerkungszeichen: *annotation symbol*
annähernd: *approximate(ly);*
approximating
Annäherung(swert): *approximation*
Annahmezahl: *accession number*
annehmbar: *acceptable*
annehmen: *to accept*
Anode: *anode*
anomalistischer Zeitraum: *anomalistic*
period
anordnen: *to format*
Anordnung: *array*
Anordnung einer Zeichenkette: *string*
array
anormal: *abnormal(ly)*
anormaler Abbruch: *abnormal end or abend*
or abnormal termination
anpassen: *to fit; to adapt; to interface*
Anpassung: *adaptation*
anpassungsfähiges System: *adaptive*
system
Anpassungsfähigkeit: *adaptation*
Anpassungstransformator: *matching*
transformer
anreizgesteuert: *event-driven*
Anruf: *call*
Anrufablenker: *call diverter*
Anrufaufzeichner: *call logger*
Anrufaufzeichnung: *call logging; voice*
messaging
Anrufbeantworterbüro: *answering service*
Anrufdauer: *call duration*
Anrufe aufzeichnen *or* **protokollieren:** *to*
log calls
Anrufeinplanung: *call scheduling*
anrufen: *to call (in); to ring*
anrufendes Modem: *originate modem*
Anrufer: *caller*
Anrufsignal: *ring indicator (RI)*
Anrufumleiter: *call diverter*
Anrufumleitung: *call forwarding*
Anschlagbestätigung: *keystroke*
verification
Anschlagdrucker: *impact printer*
anschlagen: *to hit*
Anschlagetafel: *notice board*
Anschlagsklicken: *key click*
Anschlagzahl: *keystroke count*
anschließen: *to attach*
Anschluss: *attachment; continuity*
Anschluss(stecker): *connector*
Anschlussblock: *terminal block*
Anschlussbuchse: *female connector*

Anschlussgerät: *peripheral (unit)*
Anschlussgeräte: *peripheral equipment*
Anschlusskarte: *adapter card*
Anschlussleitung: *access line*
Anschlussprozessor: *attached processor*
Anschlussstelle: *port*
Anschlussstelle für eine Datenstation:
terminal area
Anschlussteil: *interfacing*
Anschlusswahlschalter: *port selector*
Anschlusswerte-Messmethode: *kiloVolt-*
ampere output rating (KVA)
ansehen: *to view*
ANSI-Bildschirmsteuerung: *ANSI screen*
control
ANSI-Escapesequenz: *ANSI escape*
sequence
ANSI-Tastatur: *ANSI keyboard*
ANSI-Treiber: *ANSI driver*
ansprechen auf: *to register*
Ansprechzeit: *access*
Ansteckmikrofon: *lapel microphone*
Antenne: *antenna or aerial*
Antennengruppierung: *antenna array*
Antennenverstärkung: *antenna gain*
anthropomorphe Software:
anthropomorphic software
Antialiasing: *anti-aliasing*
antistatische Unterlage: *anti-static mat*
Antivalenz: *symmetric difference*
Antivalenzfunktion: *non-equivalence*
function (NEQ)
Antivalenzglied: *anticoincidence circuit or*
function; non-equivalence gate
Antivirenprogramm: *anti-virus program*
Antivirussoftware: *anti-virus software*
Antrag: *application*
Antragsformular: *application form*
antreiben: *to drive*
Antriebsspindel: *spindle*
Antwort: *answer or response*
Antwortbetrieb: *answer mode*
antworten: *to answer*
Antwortmodem: *answer modem*
Antwortrahmen: *response frame*
Antwortton: *answertone*
Antwortzeit: *response time*
anwählen: *to dial into*
anwärmen: *to warm up*
anweisen: *to assign; to order*
Anweiser: *assignor*
Anweisung: *instruction; order; statement*
Anweisung ohne Adresse: *no-address*
operation
Anweisungen im Hintergrund: *talkback*
Anweisungscodeprozessor: *order code*
processor

Anweisungsnummer: *statement number*
Anwendung: *application*
anwendungsbezogene Schicht:
application layer
anwendungsbezogene Sprache:
application orientated language
Anwendungsdienstelement: *application
service element*
Anwendungsentwickler: *application
developer*
Anwendungsfenster: *application window*
Anwendungsgenerator: *application
generator*
anwendungsorientierte Datenstation:
applications terminal
**anwendungsorientierte
Fachausstellung:** *business efficiency
exhibition*
**anwendungsorientierte
Programmiersprache:** *A programming
language (APL)*
Anwendungsprogramm: *applications
program*
Anwendungsprogrammierer: *applications
programmer*
**Anwendungsprogrammierschnittstelle
(API):** *application programming interface
(API)*
Anwendungsprogrammpaket:
applications package
Anwendungsschicht: *application layer*
Anwendungssoftware: *applications
software*
Anwendungssoftwarepaket: *applications
package*
Anwendungssymbol: *application icon*
Anwendungsterminal: *applications
terminal*
anwesend sein: *to attend*
Anzeige: *annunciator; readout*
Anzeige in voller Größe: *full-size display*
Anzeigebit: *indicator flag*
Anzeigeformat: *display format*
Anzeigelicht: *indicator light*
Anzeigemodus: *display mode*
Anzeigen: *indication*
anzeigen: *to browse; to discharge; to
indicate*
Anzeigenadel: *stylus*
Anzeiger: *flag or indicator*
Anzeigerdiagramm: *indicator chart*
Anzeigeregister: *condition code register;
display register*
Anzeigevorrichtung: *readout device*
Aperturflächenausleuchtung: *aperture
illumination*
apochromatische Linse: *apochromatic
lens*

Apogäum: *apogee*
Apostroph: *apostrophe*
Apple-Desktop-Bus: *Apple-Desktop-Bus*
Apple-Taste: *Apple Key*
Äquator: *equator*
äquatoriale Umlaufbahn: *equatorial orbit*
Äquivalenz: *equivalence*
Äquivalenz-Funktion: *equivalence function
or operation*
Äquivalenzglied: *equivalence gate*
arabische Zahlen: *Arabic numbers or
figures*
arabische Ziffern: *Arabic numerals*
arbeiten: *to work*
Arbeiten mit einfacher Wortlänge: *single
length working*
Arbeitgeberverband: *employers'
organization*
Arbeitsablauf: *workflow*
Arbeitsabschnitt: *session*
Arbeitsband: *scratch tape*
Arbeitsbelastung: *workload*
Arbeitsbereich: *work area or workspace;
scratch*
Arbeitsblatt: *worksheet*
Arbeitsdatei: *work file or scratch file*
Arbeitsgang: *operation; pass*
Arbeitsgangpriorität: *operation priority*
Arbeitsgruppe: *workgroup*
Arbeitsgruppensoftware: *workgroup
software*
Arbeitsplatte: *work disk*
Arbeitsplatz: *workplace; workstation*
Arbeitspuffer: *scratchpad memory*
Arbeitsspeicher: *working store or scratch
pad*
Arbeitsspeicherbereich: *partition*
Arbeitsteilung: *work-sharing*
Arbeitsweise mit festem Takt: *fixed cycle
operation*
Arbeitswiederholung: *duplication of work*
Archetyp: *archetype*
Architektur: *architecture*
Archiv: *archive*
Archivbit: *archive bit*
Archivdatei: *archive file*
archivieren: *to archive*
Archivierungsattribut: *archive attribute*
Archivierungsqualität: *archival quality*
Archivkopie: *archived copy*
Archivspeicherung: *archive storage*
argumentieren: *to argue*
Argumenttrennzeichen: *argument
separator*
Arithmetik: *arithmetic*
arithmetische Fähigkeit: *arithmetic
capability*
arithmetische Funktionen: *arithmetic
functions*

arithmetische Stellenverschiebung: *arithmetic shift*
Array-Prozessor: *array processor*
Art der Schaltungstechnik: *logic*
Artikel: *article*
ASCII-Datei: *ASCII file*
ASCII-Tastatur: *ASCII keyboard*
ASCII-Text: *ASCII text*
ASCII-Zeichen: *ASCII character*
ASCIIZ-String: *ASCIIZ string*
Aspekt: *aspect*
Aspektkarte: *aspect card*
Aspektsystem: *aspect system*
ASR-Tastatur: *ASR keyboard*
Assembler: *language assembler*
Assemblerliste: *assembly listing*
Assemblerprogramm: *assembly program or assembler*
assemblieren: *to assemble*
Assemblierer: *language processor*
Assemblierer mit einem Durchlauf: *one-pass or single-pass assembler*
Assemblierer mit zwei Durchläufen: *two-pass assembler*
Assemblierer-Fehlermeldungen: *assembler error messages*
Assembliersprache: *assembler or assembly language; base language*
Assistent/-in: *assistant*
assistieren: *to assist*
Assoziativadressierung: *associative addressing or content-addressable addressing*
Assoziativdatei: *content-addressable file or location*
Assoziativprozessor: *associative processor*
Assoziativschnitt: *associational editing*
Assoziativspeicher: *associative memory or storage; content-addressable memory or storage*
Assoziativspeicherregister: *associative storage register*
assoziiert: *associate*
astabiler Multivibrator: *astable multivibrator*
Astigmatismus: *astigmatism*
asymmetrische Störung: *common mode noise*
asymmetrische Übertragung: *asymmetric transmission*
asymmetrische Videokompression: *asymmetric video compression*
asymmetrischer Fehlerbereich: *bias*
asynchron: *asynchronous*
Asynchronanschluss(stelle): *asynchronous port*
Asynchronbetrieb: *asynchronous transfer mode (ATM)*

asynchrone Datenübertragung: *asynchronous data transfer*
asynchrone Übertragung: *asynchronous transmission*
asynchroner Kommunikationsschnittstellenanschluss: *asynchronous communications interface adapter (ACIA)*
asynchroner Prozeduraufruf (APC): *asynchronous procedure call (APC)*
asynchroner Übertragungsmodus: *asynchronous transfer mode (ATM)*
asynchroner Zugriff: *asynchronous access*
Asynchronrechner: *asynchronous computer*
Asynchronübertragung: *asynchronous mode*
AT-Befehlssatz: *AT command set*
AT-Bus: *AT-bus*
AT-Modus: *AT mode*
Atmosphäre: *atmosphere*
atmosphärisch: *atmospheric*
atmosphärische Absorption: *atmospheric absorption*
atmosphärische Bedingungen: *atmospheric conditions*
atmosphärische Störungen: *static*
Atom: *atom*
atomar: *atomic*
Atomuhr: *atomic clock*
AT-Tastatur: *AT-keyboard*
Attrappe: *mock-up*
Attribut: *attribute*
ätzen: *to etch*
Ätztype: *etch type*
audioaktiv: *audio active*
Audiokassettenrecorder (ACR): *audio cassette recorder (ACR)*
audiovisuell: *audiovisual (AV)*
audiovisuelle Hilfsmittel: *audiovisual aids*
auf dem Chip: *on-chip*
auf dem neuesten Stand der Technik: *state-of-the-art*
auf dem neuesten Stand: *up to date*
auf den neuesten Stand bringen: *to update*
auf der Platine: *on-board*
Auf-/Abzähler: *up/down counter*
Aufbau: *architecture; layout*
Aufbau von Schaltelementen durch Transistoren (TTL): *transistor-transistor logic (TTL)*
Aufbau von Schaltelementen durch Transistoren und Widerstände: *transistor-resistor logic (TRL)*
aufbereiten: *to edit*
Aufbereitungslauf: *editing run*
Aufbereitungssymbol: *editing symbol*
aufdecken: *to reveal; to detect*
aufeinander wirken: *to interact*

aufeinanderfolgend: *consecutive(ly);*
successive; sequential
auffächern: *to fan*
Auffächerung: *fan*
auffordern: *to invite*
Aufforderung: *enquiry*
Auffrischrate: *refresh cycle*
Auffrischzyklus: *refresh cycle*
auffüllen: *to fill; to pad*
Auffüllen: *padding*
Auffüllzeichen: *pad character*
Aufgabe: *assignment or task*
Aufgabe niedriger Priorität: *low-priority*
work
aufgabenorientierte Außenstation: *job*
orientated terminal
aufgabenorientierte
Programmiersprache: *job orientated*
language
Aufgabensteuerung: *task management*
aufgerundet: *rounded up or in round figures*
aufhalten: *to delay or block*
aufhängen: *to hang*
Aufkleber: *external label*
aufladbar: *chargeable*
Auflage: *edition; impression; printrun*
Auflage(nziffer): *circulation*
auflegen: *to hang up*
auflisten: *to list*
Auflistung: *listing*
Auflösung: *definition*
Auflösungsgrenze: *limiting resolution*
Auflösungsvermögen: *resolving power or*
resolution
Auflösungsvermögen eines
Grafikbildschirms: *graphic display*
resolution
Aufmerksamkeit: *attention*
Aufnahme: *recording*
Aufnahmegerät: *recorder*
Aufnahmespule: *pickup reel*
Aufnahmetaste: *record button*
Aufprojektion: *front projection*
aufrechnen: *to accumulate*
aufrechterhalten: *to sustain*
aufrollen: *to scroll up*
Aufruf: *cue; invitation; recall*
Aufruf eines Unterprogramms: *subroutine*
call
Aufrufbefehl: *call instruction*
aufrufen: *to call; to contact; to invite; to*
invoke; to recall
Aufruffolge von Unterprogrammen:
calling sequence
Aufrufliste: *polling list*
Aufrufzeitaufwand: *polling overhead*
aufrunden: *to round up or off*

Aufrundungsfehler: *round off errors*
aufrüsten: *to upgrade*
aufsaugen: *to absorb*
aufschließen: *to close up*
Aufschwungindustrie: *boom industry*
Aufsichtsperson: *supervisor*
aufspannender Baum: *spanning tree*
aufsteigende Folge: *ascending order*
aufteilen: *to partition*
Aufteilung in Speicherseiten: *paging*
Auftreffen: *impact*
Auftreten von Fahnen: *hangover*
Auftrieb: *boost*
aufwärts kompatibel: *upwards compatible*
or (US) upward compatible
Aufwickelspule: *take-up reel*
Aufzählungszeichen: *bullet*
Aufzeichnen: *logging or recording*
Aufzeichnen des Zugriffspfads: *access*
path journalling
aufzeichnen: *to record*
Aufzeichnungsdichte: *storage density*
Augend: *augend*
AUI-Anschluss: *AUI connector*
aural: *aural*
aus Versehen: *in error or by error*
ausbalancieren: *to balance*
Ausblendbefehl: *extract instruction*
ausblenden: *to cross fade*
ausbreiten: sich ~: *to propagate*
Ausbrennen: *burn out*
ausdenken: sich ~: *to devise*
Ausdruck: *expression; printout*
ausdrücken: *to express*
ausdrucken: *to print out*
Auseinandersetzung: *argument or arg*
Ausfall: *breakdown; drop out; failure;*
outage
ausfallen: *to break down or fail*
Ausfallrate: *failure rate*
ausfallsicheres System: *fail safe system*
Ausfallzeit: *down time or fault time*
Ausfallzeit mangels Sonnenlicht: *sun*
outage
ausführbare Datei: *executable file*
ausführbare Form: *executable form*
ausführen: *to execute; to perform*
Ausführung: *execution*
Ausführungsadresse: *execution address*
Ausführungsbefehl: *executive instruction*
Ausführungsbestimmung: *execute*
statement
Ausführungsfehler: *execution error*
Ausführungsmodus: *execute mode*
Ausführungsphase: *run phase or execute*
phase
Ausführungssignal: *execute signal*
Ausführungszeit: *execution time*

Ausführungszyklus: *execute or execution cycle*
ausfüllen: *to fill; to paint*
Ausgabe: *output (olp or OlP); copy*
Ausgabe auf Mikrofilm: *computer output on microfilm (COM)*
Ausgabe(puffer)register: *output (buffer) register*
Ausgabeanschluss(punkt): *output port*
Ausgabebereich: *output area or block*
Ausgabedatei: *output file*
Ausgabeformatierer: *output formatter*
ausgabegebunden: *output bound or limited*
Ausgabegerät: *output device*
Ausgabemodus: *output mode*
Ausgabeschnittstelle: *output port*
Ausgabestrom: *output stream*
Ausgang: *outlet*
Ausgangscode: *source code*
Ausgangsdaten: *raw data*
Ausgangsformat: *native format*
Ausgangslastfaktor: *fan-out*
Ausgangsprodukt: *basic product*
Ausgangsstelle: *exit point*
Ausgangsstellung: *home*
ausgeben: *to output*
ausgeben und neu anfangen: *to dump and restart*
ausgefallen: *down*
ausgefranst: *ragged*
ausgeglichene Leitungsausnutzung: *balanced routing*
ausgeglichener Stromkreis: *balanced circuit*
Ausgeglichenheit: *balance*
ausgegossenes Kabel: *filled cable*
ausgehängt: *off-hook*
ausgehend von: *based on*
Ausgewogenheit: *balance*
ausgleichen: *to balance; to equalize*
Ausgleichsstreifen: *balance stripe*
Ausgleichszahl: *offset*
Auslandsvorwahl: *international dialling code*
Auslassungszeichen: *caret mark or sign*
Auslastungsgrad: *activity level*
auslaufen: *to finish*
auslaufen lassen: *to phase out*
Ausleuchtung: *aperture illumination*
Auslöschung: *destructive interference*
Ausmaß: *dimension; magnitude*
Ausmerzung von Softwarefehlern: *bug patches*
Ausnahme: *exception*
Ausnahmebehandlung: *exception handling or error handling*
Ausnahmebericht: *exception report*

Ausnahmelexikon: *exception dictionary*
auspacken: *to unpack*
ausrichten: *to align; to range*
ausrichtenbündig ausrichten: *to align*
Ausrichtung: *alignment; orientation*
Ausrichtungsnadel: *alignment pin*
Ausrichtungstransportbahn: *aligner*
ausrücken: *to outdent*
Ausrufezeichen: *exclamation mark*
Aussagewahrscheinlichkeit: *confidence level*
ausschalten: *to turn or switch off; to power down or off; to disable; to peg*
ausschließen (der Zeile): *to justify*
ausschließen: *to bar or exclude; to eliminate*
ausschließlich zugeordnet: *dedicated*
ausschließlich: *exclusive*
Ausschließung: *exclusion*
Ausschließzone: *soft zone or hot zone*
Ausschluss: *exclusion*
Ausschlussklausel: *exclusion clause*
Ausschneiden und Einfügen: *cut-and-paste*
ausschneiden: *to clip*
Ausschnitt: *window*
Aussehen: *aspect*
Außenaufnahmen: *location shots*
aussenden: *to radiate*
Außendiensttechniker: *field engineer*
Außendienstverkaufsleiter: *field sales manager*
Außenstelle: *remote console or device; tributary station*
außer Kontrolle: *out of control*
außer Reichweite: *out of range*
Außerbandsignalisierung: *out of band signalling*
außergewöhnlich: *exceptional*
außerhalb des Bildschirms: *off screen*
außerirdisches Rauschen: *extra-terrestrial noise*
außerordentliche Aufwendungen: *below-the-line expenditure*
aussortieren: *to screen*
ausspeichern: *to roll-out*
Aussperrung: *lockout*
ausstatten: *to equip*
Ausstattung: *equipment*
Ausstellungsmaterial: *display material*
Aussteuerbereich: *dynamic range*
ausstrahlen: *to radiate; to emit*
Ausstrahlung: *radiation; broadcast*
Austasten: *blanking*
Austastlücke: *blanking interval*
Austausch: *exchange; interchange*

austauschbar: *interchangeable;*
exchangeable
austauschen: *to change; to exchange; to*
interchange; to replace; to swap .
Auswahl: *range or selection*
auswählbar: *selectable*
auswählen: *to select*
Auswahlfunktion: *selectable attributes*
Auswahlmöglichkeit: *option*
Auswahlsortierung: *selective sort*
Auswahlsortierverfahren: *tree selection*
sort
auswechselbar: *exchangeable; removable*
auswechselbare Zeichensätze: *cartridge*
fonts
auswechselbarer Plattenspeicher:
exchangeable disk storage (EDS)
Ausweichleitweg: *alternate route*
Ausweichmodus: *alternate mode*
Ausweichpfad: *backup path*
Ausweichserver: *backup server*
Ausweisleser: *badge reader*
auswerten: *to evaluate; to interpret*
Auswertung: *evaluation*
Auswirkung: *impact*
auszeichnen: *to mark up*
authentifizieren: *to authenticate*
Authentifizierung: *authentication*
authentisch: *authentic*
Authoring: *authoring*
Automat: *automatic vending machine;*
dispenser
automatisch: *automatic(ally)*
automatische Anmeldung: *auto-login or*
auto-logon or automatic log on
automatische Anrufaufzeichnung:
automatic message accounting
automatische Anrufbeantwortung:
auto-answer
automatische Anrufeinrichtung:
automatic calling unit (ACU)
automatische Anrufverteilung (ACD):
automatic call distribution (ACD)
automatische Baud-Abtastung: *auto-*
baud scanning
automatische Dateisicherung: *auto save*
automatische Datenaufzeichnung:
automatic data capture
automatische Datenverarbeitung:
automatic data processing (ADP)
automatische
Dezimalstellenausrichtung: *automatic*
decimal adjustment
automatische Fehlererkennung:
automatic error detection
automatische Fehlerkorrektur: *automatic*
error correction

automatische Frequenzumschaltung:
automatic mode or frequency switching
automatische
Geschwindigkeitsangleichung: *automatic*
speed matching
automatische Neuberechnung: *automatic*
recalculation
automatische Programmsteuerung:
automatic sequencing
automatische Prüfeinrichtung: *automatic*
test equipment (ATE)
automatische Prüfung: *automatic checking*
automatische Rufnummernerkennung:
automatic number identification
automatische Selbstprüfung: *built-in*
check
automatische Sicherung: *automatic*
backup
automatische Stromabschaltung:
automatic power off
automatische Verstärkungsregelung:
automatic gain control (AGC)
automatische Wählwiederholung: *auto-*
redial
automatische
Wiederholungsanforderung (ARQ):
automatic repeat request (ARQ)
automatische Zählmaschine:
comptometer
automatische Zeichensatzladung:
automatic font downloading
automatischer Anrufbeantworter:
answering machine or answerphone
automatischer Baudratenabfühler:
auto-baud scanning or auto-baud sensing
automatischer Betrieb: *unattended*
operation
automatischer Einzelblatteinzug: *cut*
sheet feeder
automatischer Papierzuführer: *feeder*
automatischer Sender/Empfänger: ·
automatic send/receive (ASR)
automatischer Start: *auto start*
automatischer Urlader: *auto boot*
automatischer Wagenrücklauf: *automatic*
carriage return
automatischer Zeilenvorschub: *auto*
advance
automatisches
Banküberweisungssystem (BACS):
bankers automated clearance system (BACS)
automatisches Briefschreiben: *automatic*
letter writing
automatisches Ladeprogramm:
automatic loader
automatisches Programmieren:
automatic programming

automatisches Prüfungssystem: *self-checking system*
automatisches System: *hands off*
automatisches Wiederanlaufprogramm: *automatic recovery program*
automatisieren: *to automate*
automatisiertes Büro: *automated office*
Automatisierung: *automation*
autonome Datenstation: *stand-alone terminal*
Autor: *author*
Autorensprache: *authoring language*
Autorensystem: *authoring system*
autorisieren: *to authorize*
autorisiert: *authorized*
Auto-Speichern: *auto save*
Auto-Trace: *auto trace*
Avalanchediode: *avalanche photodiode (APD)*
AZERTY-Tastatur: *AZERTY keyboard*
Azetat: *acetate*
Azimut: *azimuth*

Bb

B1-Komplement: *diminished radix complement*
Backlevel: *back-level*
Backslash: *backslash*
Backup-Utility: *backup utility*
Backus-Naur-Form: *Backus-Naur-Form (BNF)*
Balken: *bar*
Balkencode: *bar code or universal product code (UPC)*
Balkencodeleser: *bar code reader or optical bar reader or optical wand*
Balkendiagramm: *bar chart or bar graph*
Balkenüberschrift: *banner*
Band: *band; ribbon; tape*
Bandanfang: *beginning of tape*
Bandanfangsmarke: *beginning of tape (BOT) marker*
bandbegrenzt: *bandlimited*
Bandbibliothek: *tape library*
Bandbreite: *bandwidth*
Bandcode: *tape code*
Banddrucker: *band printer*
Bandende: *end of tape*
Bandfilter: *bandpass filter*
Bandformat: *tape format*
Bandführung: *tape guide*

Bandgerät: *tape unit*
Bandkabel: *tape cable or ribbon cable*
Bandkennzeichnung: *tape label*
Bandkopf: *tape head*
Bandladepunkt: *tape loadpoint*
Bandlaufwerk: *tape deck or tape drive*
Bandleseschreibkopf: *tape head*
Bandmaß: *tape measure*
Bandpassfilter: *bandpass filter*
Bandtransport: *tape transport*
Bandvorsatz: *tape header*
Bandzählwerk: *tape counter*
Bandzeitgeber: *tape timer*
Bandzuteilung: *band allocation*
Bank: *bank*
Bankauswahl: *bank switching*
Bargeldautomat: *cash dispenser*
Bargeldkarte: *cash card*
Barytpapier: *baryta paper*
Basis: *base; basis*
Basisadresse: *base address*
Basisadressregister: *base address register*
Basisaustauschformat: *basic exchange format*
Basisband: *baseband or base band*
Basisband-Netzwerk: *baseband local area network*
Basisband-Signalgebung: *baseband signalling*
Basisdateien: *base*
Basisdirektzugriffsmethode: *basic direct access method (BDAM)*
Basisgewicht: *basic weight*
Basisregister: *base register*
Basisspeicher: *base memory or conventional memory or base RAM*
Bass(-): *bass*
BAS-Signal: *video signal*
Basslautsprecher: *bass driver or speaker*
Bass-Signal: *bass signal*
Basswiedergabe: *bass response*
Batch-Betrieb: *batch processing*
Batchbetrieb: *batch mode*
Batchdatei: *batch file*
Batchregion: *batch region*
Batterie: *battery*
Batterieaufladen: *battery charging*
Batteriesicherung: *battery backup*
batterieunterstützt: *battery-backed*
Baudot-Code: *Baudot code*
Baudrate: *baud or baud rate*
Baudratengenerator: *baud rate generator*
Bauelement: *device*
Baum(struktur): *tree (structure)*
Baumdiagramm: *sink tree*
Baumnetzsystem: *tree and branch network system*

Baustein: *building block; module*
Bausteinauswahl: *chip select (CS)*
Beacon-Rahmen: *beacon frame*
beantworten: *to answer or respond*
Beantwortungszeit: *answer time or response time*
bearbeiten: *to manipulate*
Bearbeitung: *manipulation*
Bearbeitungsnummer: *batch number*
Bearbeitungszeit: *productive time; target or run phase*
Beauftragte(r): *representative*
bebildern: *to illustrate*
bedarfsbestimmter Mehrfachzugriff: *demand assigned multiple access (DAMA)*
bedarfsmäßige Multiplexmethode: *demand multiplexing*
bedarfsmäßiges Einspeichern: *demand staging*
Bedarfswartung: *remedial maintenance*
bedeuten: *to mean; to signify*
bedeutsam: *significant*
bedeutsame Zifferncodes: *significant digit codes*
Bedeutung: *significance*
bedienen: *to operate*
Bediener: *operator*
Bedienerfreundlichkeit: *usability*
Bedienerkonsole: *control panel; operating or operator's console*
Bedienungsanweisung: *operating instructions*
Bedienungspult: *system control panel*
Bedienungsreihenfolge: *operator precedence*
bedingt: *conditional*
bedingte Anweisung: *conditional statement*
bedingte Übertragung: *conditional transfer*
bedingte Verzweigung: *conditional branch*
bedingter Programmstop: *conditional breakpoint; dynamic stop*
bedingter Sprung(befehl): *conditional jump*
Bedingung: *condition*
beeinflussen: *to affect or influence*
beenden: *to end; to complete; to exit; to finish; to stop; to terminate*
befangen: *biased*
Befehl: *command; instruction; order*
Befehl zur Speicherung nach dem LIFO-Prinzip: *push instruction or operation*
Befehl zur Stellenverschiebung im Akkumulator: *accumulator shift instruction*
Befehl: „keine Operation": *no-operation instruction (no-op)*
befehlen: *to instruct*
Befehls(speicher)bereich: *instruction area*

Befehls(zeilen)argument: *command line argument*
Befehlsablauf: *instruction cycle*
Befehlsablaufzeit: *instruction cycle time*
Befehlsadresse: *instruction address*
Befehlsadressregister: *instruction address register (IAR)*
Befehlsänderung: *instruction modification*
Befehlsaufforderung: *command prompt*
Befehlsausführungszeit: *instruction execution time*
Befehlsbereich: *code area*
Befehlscode: *order code or command code or instruction code*
Befehlscodeprozessor (OCP): *order code processor (OCP)*
Befehlsdatei: *command file*
Befehlsdateiprozessor: *command file processor*
Befehlsdecodierer: *instruction decoder*
Befehlseingabeformat: *command prompt*
Befehlsfenster: *command window*
Befehlsfolgeregister: *sequence control register (SCR) or sequence counter or instruction address register or next instruction register*
Befehlsformat: *instruction format*
befehlsgetriebenes Programm: *command-driven program*
Befehlsinterpreter: *command interpreter*
Befehlskette: *command chain*
Befehlsmodus: *command state*
Befehlsprozessor: *instruction processor*
Befehlsregister: *command register; instruction register (IR)*
Befehlsschnellspeicher: *instruction cache*
Befehlsspeicher: *instruction storage*
Befehlssprache: *command language*
Befehlsstatus: *command state*
Befehlssteuersprache: *command control language*
Befehlsstruktur: *instruction format*
Befehlstaste: *command key*
Befehlsvorauslese: *pre-fetch*
Befehlsvorrat: *instruction repertoire or set*
Befehlswort: *instruction word*
Befehlszähler: *instruction or program counter*
Befehlszeichen: *instruction character*
Befehlszeile: *command line*
Befehlszeilenbetriebssystem: *command line operating system*
Befehlszeilenschalter: *switch*
befestigen: *to attach*
befördern: *to transport*
Befugnis: *authority*
Begleitkarte: *inlay card*

begrenzen: *to delimit*
Begrenzer: *limiter*
Begrenzungssymbol: *delimiter*
Behauptung: *assertion*
beherrschen: *to master*
beidohrig: *binaural*
beidseitig beschreibbare Platte: *double-sided disk*
beidseitig gedruckte Schaltkarte: *double-sided printed circuit board*
beidseitig unterdrückter Träger: *double-sided suppressed carrier (DSBSC)*
beilegen: *to enclose*
bejahend: *affirmative*
bekannt machen: *to publicize*
Bel: *bel*
BEL: *BEL*
belasten: *to load*
Belastung: *load*
Belastungsverteilung: *load sharing*
Beleg: *document*
Belegbearbeitung: *document processing*
Belegleser: *document reader*
belegt: *busy*
Belegwiederherstellung: *document recovery*
beleuchten: *to illuminate*
Beleuchtung: *illumination*
Beleuchtungsstärke: *illuminance*
Beleuchtungstechniker: *lighting director*
Belichtungsreihe: *bracketing*
Bell-kompatibles Modem: *Bell-compatible modem*
Bemerkung: *annotation*
benachbart: *adjacent*
benennen: *to declare*
benutzbarer Punkt: *available point*
benutzen: *to use*
Benutzer: *user*
Benutzeraccount: *user account*
Benutzeranschluss: *user port*
benutzerbestimmbar: *discretionary*
Benutzerdatei: *authority file or list*
benutzerdefinierbar: *user-definable*
benutzerdefinierte Zeichen: *user-defined characters*
Benutzerdokumentation: *user documentation*
benutzerfreundlich: *user-friendly*
benutzerfreundliche Software: *user-friendly software*
Benutzergruppe: *user group*
Benutzerhandbuch: *user guide or user's manual*
Benutzerkennzeichen: *user ID*
Benutzername: *account name or user name*
Benutzeroberfläche: *front-end*

benutzerorientierte Programmiersprache: *user-operated language*
Benutzerprofil: *account*
Benutzerprogramm: *user('s) program*
Benutzerschnittstelle: *user interface*
Benutzerspeicher: *user area*
benutzt: *used*
Benutzung: *use*
beratend: *consulting*
Berater/-in: *consultant*
Beratung: *consultancy*
Beratungssystem: *advisory system*
berechenbar: *computable*
berechnen: *to calculate; to compute*
Berechnung: *calculation; computation*
berechtigen: *to authorize*
berechtigt: *authorized*
berechtigter Benutzer: *authorized user*
Berechtigung: *authority or authorization or clearance or permission*
Berechtigungscode: *authorization code*
Bereich um die weiche Trennfuge: *hot zone or soft zone*
Bereich: *area; range; region; span*
Bereiche freimachen: *to blast*
Bereichs(auf)füllung: *area fill or region fill*
Bereichssuche: *area search*
bereinigen (Programmfehler): *to debug*
bereit: *idle; ready*
Bereit-Signal: *O.K.*
Bereitzustand: *ready state*
Berichterstattung durch die Medien: *media coverage*
berichtigen: *to rectify*
Bernoulli-Box: *Bernoulli box*
berühren: *to touch*
beschädigen: *to damage*
beschädigt: *damaged*
beschäftigt: *busy*
beschichten: *to coat; to laminate*
Beschleunigerkarte: *accelerator board or card*
Beschleunigungszeit: *acceleration time*
Beschneiden: *cropping*
beschneiden: *to crop or scissor or trim*
Beschnitt: *off-cut*
Beschnittzeichen: *crop mark*
beschreiben: *to describe; to document*
Beschreiber: *descriptor*
Beschreibung: *description*
beschriften: *to label*
Beseitigung: *removal*
besetzt: *busy*
Besetztzeichen: *engaged or line busy tone*
Besetztzustand: *congestion*
Besprechung: *conference*

Best Fit: *best fit*
bestätigen: *to acknowledge or confirm; to authenticate or verify*
bestätigte Post: *acknowledged mail*
Bestätigung: *authentication*
Bestätigungsschaltstück: *actuator*
Bestellelektronik: *teleordering*
Bestimmungsort: *destination*
bestücken: *to populate*
Bestzeitcode: *optimum code or minimum access code or minimum delay code*
Betasoftware: *beta software*
Betatest: *beta test*
Betatester: *beta site*
Betaversion: *beta version*
Beteiligungsgesellschaft: *associate company*
Beteuerung: *assertion*
betont: *accented*
betragen: *to amount to; to measure*
betreffen: *to apply; to involve*
Betriebsanlage: *facility*
Betriebsart: *mode*
betriebsbereit konfiguriert: *configured-in*
Betriebsbereitschaft(ssignal) (zum Empfang): *dataset ready (DSR)*
Betriebsbereitschaft(ssignal) (zum Senden): *data terminal ready (DTR)*
Betriebsinformation: *operational information*
Betriebsmittel: *resource*
Betriebsmittelzuteilung: *resource allocation*
Betriebssystem: *operating system (OS or op sys)*
Betriebssystem für Mikrocomputer mit 8-Bit-System (CP/M): *control program/monitor or control program for microcomputers (CPIM)*
Betriebssystemplatte: *master disk*
Betriebsunterbrechungsanfrage: *reverse interrupt*
Betriebsuntersuchung: *operation trial*
Betriebszeit: *operating time*
Betrug: *fraud*
Beutel: *bag*
bevorrechtigte Befehle: *privileged instructions*
bevorrechtigter Bereich: *privileged account*
bewegen: *to move*
beweglich: *mobile or movable*
Bewegung: *movement*
Bewegungen: *activities*
Bewegungsdatei: *transaction file or change file or detail file or movement file*
bewegungsgesteuertes System: *transaction-driven system (TDS)*

Bewegungshäufigkeit der Dateien: *file activity ratio*
Bewegungshäufigkeit: *activity ratio*
Bewegungssatz: *transaction record or change record*
Beweis: *induction*
beweisen: *to induce*
bewerten: *to evaluate*
Bewertungsdurchschnitt: *weighted average*
bewusster Fehler: *conscious error*
Bezeichnung: *label*
Beziehung: *relationship*
Bâzierkurve: *Bâzier curve*
Bezug: *reference*
Bezugsadresse: *base address or reference address*
Bezugsspegel: *reference level*
Bezugspunkt: *reference*
Bezugstabelle: *reference table*
Bezugszeit: *reference time*
Bibliografie: *bibliography*
bibliografisch: *bibliographic(al)*
bibliografische Information: *bibliographical information*
Bibliothek: *library*
Bibliothekar/-in: *librarian*
Bibliotheks(unter)programm: *library subroutine*
Bibliotheksfunktion: *library function*
Bibliotheksprogramm: *library program*
Bibliotheksroutine: *library routine*
bidirektionaler Bus: *bi-directional bus*
Bild: *picture*
Bild(wiederholungs)speicher: *image table*
Bildabtaster: *image scanner or video scanner*
Bildanordnung: *film assembly*
Bildbereich: *image area*
Bildbeständigkeit: *image stability*
Bildbetrachter: *viewer*
Bilddurchlaufmodus: *scroll mode*
Bildelement: *picture element or pixel*
bilden: *to form*
Bilder pro Sekunde: *frames per second (fps)*
Bilder: *pix*
Bilderläuterung: *caption*
Bildfrequenz: *frame frequency*
Bildfunk (FAX): *facsimile transmission (FAX)*
Bildgestaltungstechnik: *imaging*
Bildgrabber: *frame grabber*
Bildkomprimierung: *image compression*
Bildkonservierung: *image retention*
Bildlageeinstellung: *framing*
Bildlaufleiste: *scroll bar*
Bildlaufpfeile: *scroll arrows*
Bildmaterial: *visuals*

Bildröhre: *cathode ray tube (CRT)*
Bildröhrenspeicher: *cathode ray tube storage*
Bildrücklauf: *field flyback*
Bildscanner: *video scanner*
Bildschirm: *(display) screen; monitor*
Bildschirmanschluss: *display adapter*
Bildschirmanzeigeformat: *screen format*
Bildschirmattribut: *screen attribute*
Bildschirmauflösung: *display resolution*
Bildschirmaufzeichnung: *soft copy*
Bildschirmausdruck: *screen dump*
Bildschirmbeschichtung mit langer Nachleuchtdauer: *long persistence phosphor*
Bildschirmblättern: *display scrolling*
Bildschirmfarbe: *display colour*
Bildschirmflimmern: *screen flicker*
Bildschirmformat: *display format*
Bildschirmgerät: *VDT or VDU*
Bildschirmgröße: *display size or screen size*
Bildschirmnotizblock: *screen notepad*
Bildschirmprozessor: *display processor*
Bildschirmpuffer: *screen buffer*
Bildschirmrand: *screen border*
Bildschirmreferenztabelle: *video lookup table*
Bildschirmregler: *display controller*
Bildschirmreinigungsausrüstung: *screen cleaning kit*
Bildschirmschoner: *screen saver*
Bildschirmschriftart: *screen font*
Bildschirmspeicher: *screen memory*
Bildschirmsteuereinheit: *display controller*
Bildschirmtelefon: *video phone*
Bildschirmtexteditor: *screen editor or text editor*
Bildschirmtextsystem: *viewdata*
Bildschirmtextverfahren: *electronic publishing*
Bildschirmvariable: *display attribute*
Bildschwarz: *shade*
Bildsensor: *image sensor*
Bildspeicher: *frame store*
Bildspeicherplatz: *image storage space*
Bildstabilität: *image stability*
Bildsynchronisation: *pix lock*
Bildsynchronisierpuls: *field sync pulse*
Bildtelefon: *picture phone*
Bildtelegrafie: *phototelegraphy*
Bildtelegraphie (FAX): *facsimile transmission (FAX)*
Bildträger: *image carrier*
Bildüberschrift: *caption*
Bildübertragung: *picture transmission*
Bildungsprogramm (im Fernsehen): *educational TV*
Bildunterschrift: *caption*

Bildverarbeiter: *image processor*
Bildverarbeitung: *image or picture processing*
Bildverschlechterung: *image degradation*
Bildverzerrung: *image distortion*
Bildwiederholfrequenz: *refresh rate*
Bildwiederholung: *screen refresh*
Bildzeile: *display line*
billigen: *to approve of*
Billigung: *approval*
Bimmeln: *jingle*
binär: *binary*
binär codierte Dezimalzahl: *binary coded decimal (BCD)*
binär codierte Zeichen: *binary coded characters*
Binärarithmetik: *binary arithmetic*
Binäraufteilung: *binary split*
Binärcode: *binary code*
Binärdatei: *binary file*
Binär-Dezimal-Umwandlung: *binary-to-decimal conversion*
binäre Abfragemethode: *binary look-up*
binäre Mantisse: *binary mantissa*
binäre Umsetzung: *binary encoding*
binäre Variable: *binary variable*
binäre Verschlüsselung: *binary encoding*
binäre Zeichengabe: *binary signalling*
binäre Zelle: *binary cell*
binärer Addierer: *binary adder*
binärer Baum: *binary tree or heap*
binärer Bit: *binary bit*
binärer Bruch: *binary fraction*
binärer Exponent: *binary exponent*
binärer Halbaddierer: *binary half adder*
binärer Speicherauszug: *binary dump*
binares Halbierungsverfahren: *binary chop*
binäres Ladeprogramm: *binary loader*
binäres Suchen: *binary search*
binäres Zahlensystem: *base 2*
Binärexponent: *binary exponent*
Binärkomma: *binary point*
Binärlader: *binary loader*
Binäroperation: *binary operation*
Binärschreibweise: *binary notation*
Binärsequenz: *binary sequence*
Binärskala: *binary scale*
Binärstelle: *binary point*
binär-synchrone Übertragungssteuerung: *binary synchronous communications (BSC)*
Binärsystem: *binary system*
Binärzahl: *binary number*
Binärzähler: *binary counter*
Binärzeichen: *bit*
Binärziffer: *binary digit*

binaural: *binaural*
Bindelader: *linking loader*
Binden: *binding*
binden: *to bind*
Binderprogramm: *linkage editing*
Bindery: *Bindery*
Bindestrich: *hyphen; en dash or en rule*
Bindewort: *connective*
Bindungsprogramm: *binder*
Binnenmarkt: *domestic market*
Binnenproduktion: *domestic production*
Biosensor: *biosensor*
bipolar: *bipolar*
bipolare Codierung: *bipolar coding*
bipolarer Sperrschichttransistor: *bipolar junction transistor (BJT)*
bipolarer Transistor: *bipolar transistor*
bipolares Signal: *bipolar signal*
Biquinärcode: *biquinary code*
bistabil: *bistable*
bistabile Kippschaltung: *bistable circuit or multivibrator*
bistabile Schaltung: *flip-flop (FF)*
Bit: *bit*
Bitadressierung: *bit addressing*
Bitbearbeitung: *bit handling*
Bitbild: *bit image*
Bitblock: *bit block*
Bitblockverschiebung: *bit block transfer or bit blit or bitblt*
Bitdichte: *bit density*
Bitebene: *bit plane*
Bitfehlerrate (BER): *bit error rate (BER)*
Bit-Füllung: *bit stuffing*
Bithantierung: *bit flipping*
Bitmuster: *bit pattern*
bitparallel: *bit parallel*
Bitposition: *bit position*
Bitrate: *bps rate*
Bitreihe: *bit stream*
Bits pro Inch: *bits per inch (bpi)*
Bits pro Pixel (BPP): *bits per pixel (BPP)*
Bits pro Sekunde: *bits per second (bps)*
Bitscheibenaufbau: *bit-slice design*
Bitscheibenprozessor: *bit-slice processor*
bitsignifikant: *bit significant*
Bit-Slice-Aufbau: *bit-slice architecture*
Bitspur: *bit track*
Bitstelle: *bit position*
Bitte: *demand*
Bitübertragungsschicht: *physical layer*
Bitverarbeitung: *bit manipulation*
Bitverschachtelung: *bit interleaving*
bitweise: *bit wise*
Blackbox: *black box*
Blasensortierung: *bubble sort*
Blasenspeicher: *bubble memory*

Blasenspeicherkassette: *bubble memory cassette*
Blatt: *leaf or page or sheet*
blättern: *to scroll*
Blattschreiber: *page printer*
Blaupause: *blueprint*
bleibender Fehler: *solid error*
Bleisatz: *hot type*
Blende: *lens stop*
Blendenöffnungsverhältnis: *f-number*
Blendschutz: *glare filter*
Blendung: *glare*
blind: *blind*
Blindenschrift: *Braille*
blindes Anwählen: *blind dialling*
Blindkopieversand: *blind copy receipt*
Blindwiderstand: *reactance*
blinken: *to blink or flash*
Blinken: *blinking*
blinkendes Zeichen: *flashing character or character blink*
Blitterchip: *blitter*
Blittern: *bit blit or bitblt*
blittern: *to blit or bitblt*
Block: *block; pad*
Blockade (als Maß der Farbintensität): *bullet*
Blockade (in Form einer Linie): *block*
Blockbegrenzung: *flag sequence*
Blockbewegungsbefehl: *move block*
Blockcode: *block code*
Blockcursor: *block cursor*
Blockdatenprüfung: *BCC*
Blockdiagramm: *block diagram*
Blockdiagrammsymbol: Entscheidung: *decision box*
Blockeingabeverarbeitung: *block input processing*
Blockeinheit: *block device*
Blockende: *end of block (EOB)*
Blockfehlerhäufigkeit: *block error rate*
blockieren: *to block*
Blockignorierungszeichen: *block ignore character*
Blockkopf: *block header*
Blocklänge: *block length*
Blockliste: *block list*
Blockmarke: *block mark*
Blockmarkierungszeichen setzen: *to mark block*
Blockmarkierungszeichen: *block markers*
Blockoperation: *block operation*
Blockparitätsprüfung: *block parity*
Blockprüfung: *longitudinal redundancy check*
Blockschrift: *block capitals or block letters*
Blockschutz: *block protection*

Blocksynchronisierung: *block synchronization*
Blocktransfer: *block transfer*
Blockübertragung: *block transfer*
Blockungsfaktor: *blocking factor*
Blockzeichenprüfung: *block character check (BCC)*
Blockzugriff: *block retrieval*
Blockzwischenraum: *(inter)block gap (IBG)*
BNC-Stecker: *BNC connector*
BNC-T-Stecker: *BNC T-piece connector*
Bocksprungtest: *leapfrog test*
Boden: *ground*
Bodenfunkstelle: *ground station*
Bodenstation: *earth station*
Bogenkorrekturen: *slip pages or slip proofs or page proofs*
Bondpapier: *bond paper*
boolesche Algebra: *Boolean algebra or logic*
boolesche Operation: *Boolean operation*
boolesche Variable: *Boolean variable or data type*
boolescher Operator: *Boolean operator or connective*
boolescher Wert: *Boolean value*
Boom: *boom*
Boot-Partition: *boot partition*
borgen: *to borrow*
BOS (Basisbetriebssystem): *BOS (basic operating system)*
Bose-Chandhuri-Hocquenghem-Code: *Bose-Chandhuri-Hocquenghem code (BCH)*
Bottom-Up-Verfahren: *bottom up method*
bps (Bit pro Sekunde): *bps (bits per second)*
bps-Anpassung: *bps rate adjust*
Branchenverzeichnis: *classified directory*
brandneu: *brand new*
brechen: *to break; to refract*
Brechung: *refraction*
Brechungsindex: *refractive index*
B-Register: *B register or B box*
Breitband: *broadband or wideband*
Breitbandfrequenzmodulation: *wideband frequency modulation (WBFM)*
Breitbandradio: *broadband radio*
Breite: *width*
Breitnetz: *wide area network (WAN)*
Brennelement: *element*
Brenner: *burner*
Brennweite: *focal length*
Brennzahl: *f-number*
Brettschaltung: *breadboard*
Brief: *letter*
Briefhülle: *envelope*
Briefhüllendrucker: *envelope printer*
Briefhüllenzufuhr: *envelope feeder*

Briefkasten: *letter box or mail box*
Briefkopf: *letterhead*
Briefschreiber: *correspondent*
Briefumschlag: *envelope*
Briefwerbeaktion: *mailing shot*
brilliant: *brilliant*
Brillianz: *brilliance*
Britisches Normeninstitut: *British Standards Institute (BSI)*
Bromidsilberdruck *or*
Bromidsilberplatte: *bromide or bromide print*
broschiert: *paperbound*
Broschüre: *booklet or brochure*
Brouter: *brouter*
Bruch: *fraction*
Brücke: *bridge or bridging product; jumper*
Brückenauswahlschaltung: *jumper-selectable*
Brummen: *hum*
Brummspannung: *ripple*
Bruttogewicht: *gross weight*
BTAM-Zugriffsmethode: *basic telecommunications access method (BTAM)*
Btx-Datenstation: *ip terminal*
Bubble-Jet-Drucker: *bubble-jet printer*
Bubblesort: *bubble sort*
Buch: *book*
Buchbinder: *binder*
Buchbinderei: *bindery or binder's*
Buchdecke: *case*
Buchdeckenmaschine: *case-making machine*
buchen: *to book*
Bücherstand: *bookstall*
Buchführungsarbeit: *bookwork*
Buchhändler: *bookseller*
Buchhandlung: *bookshop or bookstore*
Buchproduktion: *bookwork*
Buchse: *connector receptacle; jack*
Buchstabe: *letter or alphabetic character (set)*
Buchstabenkette: *alphabetic string*
Buchungskontrolle: *audit trail*
Bugfix: *maintenance release*
Bühnenarbeiter: *grip*
Bühnenbild: *set*
Bullet: *bullet*
Bündel: *bundle*
bundeln: *to bundle*
bündig ausrichten: *to align*
Bundsteg: *gutter*
Büro: *office or bureau*
Büro der Zukunft: *office of the future*
Büroausstattung: *office equipment*
Büroautomatisierung: *office automation (OA)*
Bürocomputer: *office computer*

Bürokopierer: *office copier*
Bus: *bus*
Busdatenübertragungsleitung: *bus data lines*
Buserhöhung: *bus extender or bus extension card (BEC)*
Buserweiterung: *bus extender or bus extension card (BEC)*
Bushauptkontrolle: *bus master*
Buskarte: *bus board*
Buskontroller-Adapter: *bus master adapter*
Busmaus: *bus mouse*
Busnebenstelle: *bus slave*
Busnetzwerk: *bus network*
Busplatine: *bus board*
Bussteuerungsleitung: *bus control line*
Busstruktur: *bus structure*
Bustopologie: *bus topology*
Bustreiber: *bus driver*
Buszuteilung: *bus arbitration*
Büttenrand: *deckle edge*
Byte: *byte*
Byteadresse: *byte address*
Bytemanipulation: *byte manipulation*
Bytemodus: *byte mode*
byteorientiertes Protokoll: *byte-orientated protocol*
Bytes pro Inch: *bytes-per-inch*
byteserielle Übertragung: *byte serial transmission or mode*

Cc

Cache-Controller: *cache controller*
Cache-Hit: *cache hit*
Cache-Speicher: *cache memory*
Callier-Effekt: *callier effect*
calloc: *calloc*
Cambridge-Netz: *Cambridge ring*
Campusumgebung: *campus environment*
Candela: *candela*
Capstan: *capstan*
Caretzeichen: *caret mark or sign*
Cartridge-Laufwerk: *cartridge drive*
Case: *case*
Case-Verzweigung: *case branch*
C-Band: *C band*
CD-ROM-Laufwerk: *CD-ROM player*
CD-Spieler: *compact disk player*
Cedille: *cedilla*
Centronics-Schnittstelle: *Centronics interface*

CEPT-Norm: *CEPT standard*
charakteristisch: *characteristic*
charakteristische Kurve: *characteristic curve*
charakteristischer Überlauf: *characteristic overflow*
Chefredakteur: *editor(-in-chief)*
Chemikalie: *chemical*
chemisch: *chemical*
chemische Reaktion: *chemical reaction*
Chiffrieralgorithmus: *cryptographic algorithm*
Chiffrierschlüssel: *cryptographic key or cipher key*
Chip: *chip*
Chipanzahl: *chip count*
Chiparchitektur: *chip architecture*
Chipkarte: *chip card or smart card*
Chip-Produktionsanlage: *silicon foundry*
Chipsatz: *chip set*
Chipverbindungsstelle: *chip select line*
chromatisch: *chromatic*
chromatische Abweichung: *chromatic aberration*
chromatische Dispersion: *chromatic dispersion*
Chromatizität: *chromaticity*
chronologische Anordnung: *chronological order*
Cinematographie: *cinematography*
Citizen-Band (CB): *citizens band radio (CB)*
Claim Frame: *claim frame*
Client: *client*
Client-Server-Architektur: *client-server architecture*
Client-Server-Netzwerk: *client-server network*
Clip: *clip*
Clipart: *clip-art*
Cluster: *cluster*
Code: *code*
Codebit: *code bit*
Codeelement: *code element*
Codegruppe: *code group*
Codesegment: *code segment*
Codeseite: *code page*
Codeumschaltung: *escape character*
Codeumschaltungstaste: *escape key*
Codeumsetzer: *encoder*
Codeumsetzung: *code conversion*
codeunabhängiges Steuerungsverfahren: *high-level data link control (HLDLC)*
Codieren: *coding*
codieren: *to (en)code*
Codierer: *coder*
Codierer/Decodierer: *CODEC*

Codierungsformat: *encoding format*
Codierzeile: *code line*
Cold-Standby-System: *cold standby*
COM-Datei: *COM file*
Comma-delimited: *comma delimited*
Comma-delimited-Datei: *comma-delimited file*
Compact Disk (CD): *compact disk (CD)*
Computer: *computer*
Computer der ersten/zweiten/dritten/vierten/fünften Generation: *first/second/third/fourth/fifth generation computer(s)*
Computer Graphics Metafile (CGM): *computer graphics metafile (CGM)*
Computer Input Microfilm (CIM): *computer input microfilm (CIM)*
Computer mit reduziertem Befehlsvorrat: *reduced instruction set computer (RISC)*
Computer mit variabler Wortlänge: *variable word length computer*
Computer mit zwei Prozessoren: *dual processor*
Computerabteilung: *computer department*
Computeranimation: *computer animation*
Computeranlage: *installation*
Computeranwendungen: *computer applications*
Computerarchitektur: *computer architecture*
Computerauflistung: *computer listing*
Computerausdruck: *computer printout or hard copy*
Computerausgabe: *computer output*
Computerbediener: *computer operator*
Computerbüro: *computer bureau*
Computerbürosystem: *computer office system*
Computercode: *computer code*
Computerdatei: *computer file*
Computerdrucker: *computer printer*
Computerdruckerpapier: *computer stationery*
Computerfachkenntnis: *computer literacy*
Computerfehler: *computer error*
Computerfreak: *terminal junky (TJ)*
Computergenerationen: *computer generations*
computergeneriert: *computer-generated*
computergesteuertes Fahrzeug: *buggy*
computergesteuertes Fernsprechamt: *automatic telephone exchange*
computergestützt: *computer-aided or computer-assisted*
computergestützte Bildverarbeitung: *computer image processing*

computergestützte Entwurf und Fertigung (CAD/CAM): *CAD/CAM*
computergestützte Entwurf und Konstruktion (CAD): *computer-aided or assisted design (CAD)*
computergestützte Fertigung (CAM): *computer-aided or assisted manufacture (CAM)*
computergestützte, numerische Werkzeugmaschinensteuerung (CNC): *computer numeric control (CNC)*
computergestützter Unterricht (CAI): *computer-aided or assisted instruction (CAI)*
computergestütztes Konstruieren: *computer-aided or assisted engineering (CAE)*
computergestütztes Lernen (CAL): *computer-aided or assisted learning (CAL) or computer-based learning (CBL) or computer-managed learning (CML)*
computergestütztes Nachrichtensystem: *computer-based message system (CBMS)*
computergestütztes Prüfen (CAT): *computer-aided or assisted testing (CAT)*
computergestütztes Training: *computer-aided or assisted training (CAT) or computer-based training (CBT)*
Computergrafik: *computer graphics*
Computeringenieur: *computer engineer*
computerintegrierte Fertigung: *computer-integrated manufacturing (CIM)*
computerintegrierte Systeme: *computer-integrated systems*
computerisieren: *to computerize*
computerisierte Heiratsvermittlung: *computer dating*
computerisiertes Büro: *paperless office*
Computerisierung: *computerization*
Computerkasse: *point-of-sale terminal or POS terminal*
Computerkonferenz: *computer conferencing*
Computerkriminalität: *computer crime or computer fraud*
Computerlauf: *machine run*
Computerleistung: *computer power*
computerlesbar: *computer-readable*
Computerlogik: *computer logic*
Computernetz: *computer network*
Computeroperator: *computer operator*
Computerprogramm: *computer program*
Computer-Programmlauf: *computer run*
computersachverständig: *computer-literate*
Computersatz: *computer setting*
Computerservice: *computer services*

Computerspiel: *computer game*
**Computersprache zum Programmieren
von Grafiken:** *graphic language*
**Computersprachen der vierten
Generation:** *fourth generation languages*
Computerstärke: *computer power*
Computersystem: *computer system*
Computertomographie: *computerized
axial tomography (CAT)*
Computerübersetzung: *language
translation*
**computerunabhängige
Programmiersprache:** *computer
independent language*
Computerverwalter: *computer manager*
Computervirus: *computer virus*
Conferencing: *conferencing or
teleconferencing*
Connectivity: *connectivity*
Connect-Status: *connect state*
Controller für Speicherzugriff: *file server*
Control-Taste: *control key or CTR or Ctrl*
Coprozessor: *coprocessor*
co-resident: *coresident*
Co-Routine: *coroutine*
Coulomb: *coulomb*
Courier: *Courier*
CPU-abhängig: *CPU bound*
CPU-Quittungsbetrieb: *CPU handshaking*
CPU-Teile: *CPU elements*
CPU-Zeit: *CPU time*
CPU-Zyklus: *CPU cycle*
Crawleffekt: *crawl*
CRC-Prüfung: *cyclic redundancy check
(CRC)*
Crosslinks *or* **Crosslinkdateien:** *cross-
linked files*
CTRL-Taste: *control key or CTR or Ctrl*
Cursor: *cursor*
Cursorausgangsstellung: *cursor home*
Cursorsteuerungsfeld: *touch pad*
Cursortasten: *cursor control keys*
Cut-and-Paste: *cut-and-paste*

Dd

Dämon-Prozess: *daemon*
dämpfen: *to attenuate; to deaden*
Dämpfung: *attenuation*
Danksagung: *acknowledgements*
darlegen: *to deposit*

darstellen: *to represent*
Darstellung: *representation*
Darstellungsfläche: *display space*
Darstellungsschicht: *presentation layer*
Data Interchange Format (DIF): *data
interchange format (DIF)*
Datagramm: *datagram*
Datei: *file or data file*
Datei löschen: *kill file*
Datei mit Kommaabgrenzung: *comma-
delimited file*
Datei schließen: *close file*
Dateiabfrage: *file interrogation*
Dateianfang: *beginning of file (bof)*
Dateiattribute: *file attributes*
Dateiaufbau: *file layout*
Dateibeschreibung: *file descriptor*
Dateien verschmelzen: *to link files*
Dateien zusammenfügen: *to join files*
Dateiende: *end of file (EOF)*
Dateierstellung: *file creation*
Dateifragmentierung: *file fragmentation*
Dateigröße: *file size*
Datei-Index: *file index*
Dateikennsatz: *file header; file label*
Dateikopie: *file copy*
Dateilänge: *file length*
Dateilöschung: *file deletion or file purge*
Dateimanager: *file manager*
Dateimenge: *file set*
Dateiname: *file identification or file name*
Dateinamenerweiterung: *filename
extension*
Dateinamenerweiterung BAK: *BAK file
extension*
Dateinummer: *file handle*
Dateiprüfung: *file validation*
Dateisäuberung: *file cleanup*
Dateischutz: *file protection or file security*
Dateisortierung: *file collating or file sort*
Dateispeicher: *file store*
Dateispeicherung: *file storage*
Dateisperrung: *file locking*
Dateistruktur: *file structure*
Dateitransfer: *file transfer*
Dateityp: *file type*
Dateiübertragungsdienstprogramm: *file
transfer utility*
Dateiübertragungsprotokoll: *file transfer
protocol (FTP)*
Dateiumfang: *file extent*
Dateiumsetzung: *file conversion*
Dateiverarbeitung: *file processing*
Dateiverwalter: *file manager*
Dateiverwaltung(ssystem): *file
management (system)*
Dateiverwaltungsblock: *file control block*

Dateiverwaltungsroutine: *file handling routine*
Dateiverzeichnis: *file directory*
Dateivorfahre: *ancestral file*
Dateiwartung: *file maintenance*
Dateiwiederherstellungsprogramm: *file-recovery utility*
Dateizuordnungstabelle (FAT): *file allocation table (FAT)*
Dateizwischenraum: *file gap*
Daten: *data*
Daten(adress)kettung: *data chaining*
Daten(fern)übertragung (DFÜ): *data communications*
Datenadapter: *data adapter unit*
Datenadresskettung: *data chaining*
Datenanalyse: *data analysis*
Datenanschlusseinheit: *data adapter unit*
Datenaufbereitung: *data preparation*
Datenaustausch: *data communications*
Datenaustauschgerät: *data communications equipment (DCE)*
Datenaustauschpuffer: *data communications buffer*
Datenaustauschvermittlung: *data switching exchange*
Datenauswertung: *data analysis*
Datenbank mit Direktanschluss: *on-line database*
Datenbank mit freiem Format: *free form database*
Datenbank: *databank or database*
Datenbankaufgliederung: *database mapping*
Datenbankmaschine: *database machine*
Datenbanknetz: *information network or network database*
Datenbankschema: *database schema*
Datenbanksprache: *database language*
Datenbanksteuerprogramm: *database engine*
Datenbanksystem: *database system*
Datenbankverwalter: *database administrator (DBA)*
Datenbankverwaltungssystem: *database management system (DBMS)*
Datenbankzentrale: *information retrieval centre*
Datenbegrenzungszeichen: *data delimiter*
Datenbehandlungssprache: *data manipulation language (DML)*
Datenbenutzer: *accessor*
Datenbereich: *data area*
Datenbeschreibungssprache: *data description language (DDL)*
Datenbewegung: *data transaction*
Datenblock: *data block*

Datendurchlauf: *throughput*
Datenebene: *data level*
Dateneingabe: *data entry or data input*
Dateneingabebus: *data input bus (DIB)*
Dateneingeber: *keyboarder*
Dateneinheit: *entity*
Datenelementkette: *data element chain*
Datenempfangssignal: *data carrier detect (DCD)*
Datenende: *end of data (EOD)*
Datenendeinrichtung: *data terminal equipment (DTE)*
Datenerfassung: *data acquisition or data capture or data collection or data logging*
Datenerfassungsstation: *data collection platform*
Datenerstellung: *data origination*
Datenfehler: *data error*
Datenfeld: *data field; item*
Datenfeld mit konstanter Länge: *constant length field*
Datenfernübertragungsservice: *teleinformatic services*
Datenfernverarbeitung (DFV): *teleprocessing (TP)*
Datenfluss: *data flow*
Datenflussdiagramm: *data flow diagram (DFD)*
Datenflussplan: *data flowchart*
Datenformat: *data format*
datengesteuert: *data-driven*
Datengruppierung: *data aggregate*
Datenhierarchie: *data hierarchy*
Datenimpulseingang: *data strobe*
Datenkanal: *data channel*
Datenkassette: *data cassette*
Datenkommunikationsnetzwerk: *data communications network*
Datenkomprimierung: *data compacting*
Datenkonzentrator: *data concentrator*
Datenkorrektur: *data cleaning*
Datenkorruption: *data corruption*
Datenleitung: *dataline*
Datenleitungssteuerung: *data link control*
Datenleitweg: *data routing*
Datenmultiplexmethode: *dataplex*
Datenname: *data name*
Datennetz: *data network*
Datenpaket: *packet; envelope*
Datenpaketvermittlung: *packet switching*
Datenpflege: *data management*
Datenprüfung: *data check or data validation or data vetting*
Datenpuffer: *data buffer*
Datenquelle: *data source*
Datenregister: *data register*
Datenreinigung: *data cleaning*

Datensatz: *data record*
Datensatzsperrung: *record locking*
Datensatzstruktur: *record structure*
Datenschutz: *data protection*
Datenschutzgesetz: *Data Protection Act*
Datenschwingungsträger: *data carrier*
Datensenke: *data sink*
Datenservice: *data services*
Datensicherheit: *data integrity*
Datensicherung nach Zeitplan: *timed backup*
Datensicherung: *data security*
Datensicherungsplatte: *backup disk*
Datensicherungsprozedur: *backup procedure*
Datensichtgerät: *display*
Datensichtterminal: *visual display terminal (VDT) or visual display unit (VDU)*
Datensignale: *data signals*
Datenspeicher: *data storage*
Datenstation: *data station or data terminal*
Datenstation der Firmenleitung: *executive terminal*
Datenstation mit allgemeiner Zugriffsberechtigung: *public access terminal*
Datenstrobe: *data strobe*
Datenstrom: *data stream*
Datenstruktur: *data structure*
Datenteil: *data division*
Datenträger: *data carrier or data medium*
Datenträgerende: *end of medium (EM)*
Datenträgerfehler: *media error*
Datenträgerkonvertierung: *media conversion*
Datentyp: *data type*
Datenübertragung auf Sprachfrequenz: *data in voice (DIV)*
Datenübertragung per Funk: *radio transmission of data*
Datenübertragung über Sprachfrequenz: *data above voice (DAV)*
Datenübertragung unter Sprachfrequenz: *data under voice (DUV)*
Datenübertragung: *data transmission*
Datenübertragungsabschnitt: *data link*
Datenübertragungsanschluss: *communications port*
Datenübertragungsblock: *frame*
Datenübertragungseinrichtung: *data communications equipment (DCE)*
Datenübertragungsgeschwindigkeit: *data (signalling) rate or data transfer rate*
Datenübertragungsleitungen: *scheduled circuits*
Datenübertragungsmaschine: *milking machine*

Datenübertragungsplatte: *milk disk*
Datenübertragungsprotokoll: *communications protocol*
Datenübertragungspuffer: *data communications buffer*
Datenübertragungsserver: *communications server*
Datenübertragungssoftware: *communications software*
Datenübertragungsweg: *data bus or data highway*
Datenumlagerung: *data migration*
Datenumsetzung: *data translation*
Datenunabhängigkeit: *data independence*
Datenunterbrechung: *data break*
Datenverarbeitung: *data processing (DP or dp)*
Datenverarbeitungsmanager: *data processing manager*
Datenverbindung: *data circuit; data connection*
Datenverbund: *data aggregate*
Datenverbundfunktion: *aggregate function*
Datenverbundoperator: *aggregate operator*
Datenverdichtung: *data compacting or data compression or data reduction*
Datenverfälschung: *data corruption*
Datenverkehr: *traffic*
Datenverkehrsanalyse: *traffic analysis*
Datenverkehrsdichte: *traffic density*
Datenverkehrsquote: *traffic intensity*
Datenverschlüsselung: *data encryption*
Datenverschlüsselungsnorm: *data encryption standard (DES)*
Datenverwalter: *data administrator*
Datenverwaltung: *data control*
Datenvielfachleitung: *data highway*
Datenvorbereitung: *data preparation*
Datenweg: *data path*
Datenwiedergewinnung: *data retrieval*
Datenwort: *data word*
Datenwörterbuch: *data dictionary/directory (DD/D)*
Datenwortlänge: *data word length*
Datenzeiger: *data pointer*
Datenzugriffsverwaltung: *data access management*
Datenzuverlässigkeit: *data reliability*
datieren: *to date*
DAT-Laufwerk: *DAT drive*
Datum: *date*
Dauer der Lagerfähigkeit: *shelf life*
Dauer der Verbindung: *connect time*
Dauer: *duration*
Dauerbelastungssyndrom: *repetitive strain injury or repetitive stress injury (RSI)*
Dauerbetrieb: *steady state*

Dauerfunktion: *auto(matic) repeat*
dauerhaft: *durable; permanent*
dauerhafter Fehler: *permanent error*
Dauerkennzeichen: *continuous signal*
Dauerschleife: *continuous loop*
Dauerspeicher: *permanent memory*
Dauertaste: *repeat key*
DB-Stecker: *DB connector*
Debugger: *debugger*
Decodierer: *decoder or de-scrambler*
dediziert: *dedicated*
dedizierte Logik: *dedicated logic*
dedizierter Computer: *dedicated computer*
dedizierter Kanal: *dedicated channel*
dedizierter Textverarbeitungscomputer:
dedicated word processor
De-facto-Standard: *de facto standard*
defekt: *defective*
Defektelektron: *hole*
defensives Programmieren: *defensive computing*
definieren: *to define*
defokussieren: *to defocus*
Defragmentierer: *defragmentation utility*
Defragmentierung: *defragmentation*
Dekade: *decade*
Dekadenzähler: *decade counter*
Dekrement: *decrement*
Delta-Delta-Verbindung: *delta-delta*
Deltamodulation: *delta modulation*
Delta-Uhr: *delta clock*
Demarkationsstreifen: *demarcation strip*
Demodulation: *demodulation*
Demodulator: *demodulator*
Demonstrationsmodell: *demonstration model*
Demosoftware: *demonstration software*
Densitometer: *densitometer*
desaktivieren: *to disarm*
Desaktivierung: *disarmed state*
Designabteilung: *design department*
Designer/-in: *designer*
Designparameter: *design parameters*
Designstudio: *design studio*
Deskriptor: *descriptor*
Desktop publishing: *desktop publishing (DTP)*
Detail: *detail*
Detaildatei: *detail file*
detaillierte Rechnung: *detailed account*
Detektor: *detector*
deterministisch: *deterministic*
deweysche Dezimalklassifikation: *Dewey decimal classification*
dezentralisierte Datenverarbeitung:
decentralized data processing

dezentralisiertes Computernetz:
decentralized computer network
Dezibel (dB): *decibel*
Dezibelmeter: *decibel meter*
Dezile: *decile*
Dezimal-Binär-Umwandlung: *decimal-to-binary conversion*
Dezimaldarstellung: *denary notation*
dezimales Zahlensystem: *base 10*
dezimalisieren: *to decimalize*
Dezimalisierung: *decimalization*
Dezimalschreibweise: *decimal notation*
Dezimalstelle: *decimal point*
Dezimalsystem: *decimal system*
Dezimaltabulatortaste: *decimal tab key*
dezimonisches Läuten: *decimonic ringing*
D-Flipflop: *D-flip-flop*
DFÜ-Anschluss: *communications port*
DFÜ-Paket: *communications package*
DFÜ-Server: *communications server*
DFÜ-Software: *communications software*
DFV-Abtaster: *communications scanner*
DFV-Hauptsteuerprogramm:
communications executive
DFV-Netz: *communications network*
DFV-Netz-Prozessor: *communications network processor*
DFV-Puffer: *communications buffer*
DFV-Satellit: *communications satellite*
DFV-Schnittstellenanschluss:
communications interface adapter
DFV-Verbindungsweg: *communications link*
Dhrystone-Benchmark: *Dhrystone benchmark*
Dia(positiv): *slide*
Diabetracter: *viewer*
Diade: *doublet or dyad*
Diagnose: *diagnosis*
Diagnosechip: *diagnostic chip*
Diagnosehilfsmittel: *diagnostic aid*
Diagnosemeldung: *diagnostic message*
Diagnoseprogramm: *diagnostic program*
Diagnosetest: *diagnostic test*
Diagnostik: *diagnostics*
Diagnostikhilfe: *diagnostic aid*
Diagnostikprogramm: *diagnostic program*
diagnostische Fehlermeldung: *diagnostic error message*
diagnostizieren: *to diagnose*
Diagramm: *diagram; chart*
diagrammatisch: *diagramatically*
diakritisches Zeichen: *diacritic*
Dialekt: *dialect*
Dialog: *dialogue*
Dialogbetrieb: *conversational or interactive mode*

dialogfähige Datenstation: *interactive terminal*
dialogfähige Grafikverarbeitung: *interactive graphics*
dialogfähiges Kabelfernsehen: *interactive cable television*
Dialogfeld: *dialog box*
Dialogfenster: *dialog box*
Dialogprogramm: *interactive routine*
Dialogsystem: *interactive system*
Diapositiv: *diapositive or transparency*
Diapositiv mit Tonspur: *audio slide*
Diaprojektor: *diascope*
Diaprojektor: *slide projector or diascope*
Diaprojektor mit Tonspur: *slide/sync recorder*
Diazokopie: *diazo (process)*
Dibit: *dibit*
Dichroise: *dichroic*
Dichte: *density*
Dichtemesser: *densitometer*
dick: *thick*
Dickschicht: *thick film*
Dielektrikum: *dielectric*
Dienstprogramm: *utility (program)*
DIF-Datei: *DIF file*
Differenzialpulscodemodulation: *differential PCM*
Differenzialsicherung: *incremental backup*
diffundieren: *to diffuse*
diffundierter pn-Übergang: *diffused pn-junction*
Diffusion: *diffusion*
Digital Video Interactive (DV-I): *digital video interactive (DV-I)*
digital: *digital(ly)*
Digital-Analog-Umsetzer: *digital to analog converter or D to A converter (DAC)*
Digitalanzeige: *digital display*
Digitalaufnahme: *digital recording*
Digitalausgabe: *digital output*
digitale Auflösung: *digital resolution*
digitale Darstellung: *digital representation*
digitale Daten: *digital data*
digitale Logik: *digital logic*
digitale optische Aufzeichnung: *digital optical recording (DOR)*
digitale Sichtanzeige: *digital read-out*
digitale Signalisierung: *digital signalling*
digitale Signalverarbeitung: *digital signal processing (DSP)*
digitale Signatur: *digital signature*
digitale Tonplatte: *digital audio disk (DAD)*
digitale Vermittlung: *digital switching*
digitaler Plotter: *digital plotter*
digitaler Stromkreis: *digital circuit*

digitales Multimeter: *digital multimeter (DMM)*
digitales Signal: *digital signal*
digitales Tonband: *digital audio tape (DAT)*
digitales Übertragungssystem: *digital transmission system*
Digitalisierblock: *digitizing pad*
digitalisieren: *to digitize*
Digitalisierer: *digitizer*
digitalisierte photographische Aufnahme: *digitized photograph*
Digitalkamera: *digital camera*
Digitalkassette: *digital cassette*
Digitalmultimeter: *digital multimeter (DMM)*
Digitalplotter: *digital plotter*
Digitalrechner: *digital computer*
Digitalschaltung: *digital circuit*
Digitalsystem: *digital system*
Digitaluhr: *digital clock*
Diktat aufnehmen: *to take dictation*
Diktat: *dictation*
diktieren: *to dictate*
Diktiergerät: *dictating machine*
Diktiertempo: *dictation speed*
DIL-Gehäuse: *dual-in-line package (DIL or DIP)*
Dimension: *dimension*
Dimensionierung: *dimensioning*
DIN (deutsche Industrienorm): *DIN*
Diode: *diode*
Dioptrie: *diopter or dioptre*
Diplex: *diplex*
Dipol: *dipole*
Dipolantenne: *dipole*
Dipolzeilenantenne: *linear array*
direkt: *direct(ly)*
Direktanschluss: *direct connect*
Direktanweisung: *direct instruction*
Direktbefehl: *immediate instruction*
Direktcode: *direct or one-level or specific code*
direkte Adresse: *one-level address*
direkte Adressierung: *direct addressing*
direkte Bezugsadresse: *direct reference address*
direkte Codierung: *direct coding*
direkte Dateneingabe: *direct data entry (DDE)*
direkte Digitalsteuerung: *direct digital control (DDC)*
direkter Speicherzugriff: *direct memory access (DMA)*
direkter Speicherzugriffskanal: *direct memory access channel*
direktes Informationsanschaltnetz für

Europa (DIANE): *direct information access network for Europe (DIANE)*
direktes Seitenregister: *direct page register*
Direktmodus: *direct mode or immediate mode*
Direktoperand: *immediate operand*
Direktor/-in: *director*
Direktsatz: *direct impression*
direktstrahlender Satellit: *direct broadcast satellite (DBS)*
Direktsuche: *search memory or searching storage*
Direktübertragung: *direct transfer*
Direktumschaltung: *direct change-over*
Direktversand: *direct mail*
Direktwerbung: *direct mail(ing) or direct-mail advertising*
Direktzugriff: *direct access*
Direktzugriffsdatei: *random access files*
Direktzugriffsspeicher (RAM): *random access memory (RAM) or direct access storage device (DASD)*
Disassembler: *disassembler*
Disc: *disc*
Disjunktion: *disjunction*
disjunktive Suche: *disjunctive search*
Diskette: *diskette or floppy disk or floppy or FD*
Diskette mit 40 Spuren: *forty-track disk*
Diskette mit einfacher Schreibdichte: *single-sided disk (SSD)*
Diskettenlaufwerk: *floppy disk drive or unit*
Diskettensektor: *floppy disk sector*
Diskettensteuerelemente: *floppy disk controller (FDC)*
diskret: *discrete*
diskutieren: *to argue*
Dispersion: *dispersion*
Distanz(adresse): *displacement*
Dittographie: *dittogram*
Divergenz: *divergence*
Dividend: *dividend*
Division: *division*
Divisor: *divisor*
DLL-Datei: *DLL file*
DMA-Controller: *DMA controller*
DMA-Zyklusraub: *DMA cycle stealing*
Dokumentation: *documentation*
Dokumentbildverarbeitung: *document image processing (DIP)*
Dokumente ablegen: *to file documents*
Dollarzeichen: *dollar sign*
Domäne: *domain*
Domänenbezeichnungssystem: *domain name system (DNS)*
Dongle: *dongle*
Doppelbelichtung: *double exposure*

Doppelbild: *double document*
Doppelklick: *double-click*
doppelklicken: *to double-click*
Doppelkreuz: *double dagger*
Doppelpunkt: *colon*
Doppelreihe: *dual column*
Doppelreihengehäuse: *dual-in-line package (DIL or DIP)*
doppelseitiges Plattenlaufwerk: *double-sided disk drive*
Doppelstromsignal: *polar signal*
Doppelsystem: *dual systems*
doppelt: *double or dual*
doppelte Genauigkeit: *double precision*
doppelte Pufferung: *double buffering*
doppelte Speicherkapazität: *double density*
doppelte Taktgabe: *dual clocking*
doppeltes Seitenband: *double sideband*
doppeltes Übertragungswegsystem: *dual bus system*
Doppelwort: *double word*
dotieren: *to dope*
dotiert: *doped*
Dotierung: *doping*
Dotierungsstoff: *dopant*
Doublette: *double document*
Downloadfonts: *downloadable fonts*
downsizen: *to downsize*
Draht: *wire*
Drahtführungskamm: *fanning strip*
drahtgebundene Übertragung: *line communications*
drahtlos: *wireless*
drahtloses Mikrofon: *wireless microphone*
drahtloses Telefon: *cordless telephone*
Drahtwickeln: *wire wrap*
Drain(strom) Strom entnehmen: *to drain*
Dreharbeiten: *filming*
Drehen: *filming*
Dreiadressbefehl: *three-address instruction*
dreidimensional (3D): *three-dimensional (3D)*
dreidimensionale Matrix: *three-dimensional array*
Dreieckschaltung: *delta*
Dreiecksleitweg: *delta routing*
Dreier: *triad*
Dreizustandslogik: *three state logic*
Drift: *drift*
Dropdownliste: *drop-down list box*
Dropdownmenü: *drop-down menu*
Druck: *print*
Druckanweisungen: *print modifiers*
Druckanweisungscodes: *non-printing codes*
Druckauftrag: *print job*
drücken: *to press or push*

drucken: *to print*
Drucken ohne Restbogen: *even working*
Drucken: *printing*
Drucker: *printer*
Druckeranschluss(stelle): *printer port*
Druckerei: *printer's*
Druckeremulation: *printer emulation*
Druckerkopf: *printhead*
Druckerlebensdauer: *print life*
Drucker-Plotter: *printer-plotter*
Druckerpresse: *printing press*
Druckerpuffer: *printer buffer*
Druckerregler: *printer's controller*
Druckerschnittstelle: *hard copy interface*
Druckersteuerzeichen: *printer control characters*
Druckertreiber: *printer driver*
Druckfehler: *literal*
druckfertige Vorlage: *photoprint*
Druckform: *form; plate*
Druckformat: *print format*
Druckformatierer: *print formatter*
Druckhammer: *print hammer*
Druckjob: *print job*
Druckpause: *print pause*
Druckqualität: *print quality*
Drucksache: *printed matter*
Druckserver: *print server*
Drucksteuerzeichen: *print control character*
Drucktastentelefon: *pushbutton telephone*
Drucktastenwählen: *pushbutton dialling*
Drucktype: *print style*
Druckumwandler: *pressure pad*
Druckvorschau: *page preview*
Druckwarteschlange: *print queue*
Druckzylinder: *impression cylinder*
D-Schicht der Ionosphäre: *D-region*
D-Stecker: *D-type connector*
Dual Attachment Station (DAS): *dual attachment station (DAS)*
duale Operation: *binary operation*
Dualkartenverarbeitung: *card image*
Dual-Port-Speicher: *dual port memory*
Dualprozessor(system): *dual processor*
Dualschreibweise: *binary notation or representation*
Dualzahl: *binary number*
Dunkelkammer: *darkroom*
Dunkelschriftröhre: *dark trace tube*
Dunkelstrom: *dark current*
Dünnfilmtransistorbildschirm: *TFT screen*
Dünnschicht: *thin film*
Dünnschichtspeicher: *thin film memory; magnetic thin film storage*
Duodezimalsystem: *duodecimal number system*
Duplex: *full duplex or fd or FD*

Duplexbetrieb: *duplex operation*
Duplexpapier: *duplex (paper)*
Duplexsystem: *duplex computer*
Duplexübertragung: *duplex*
Duplikat: *duplicate*
durchbrennen: *to fuse*
Durchführbarkeit: *feasibility*
Durchführbarkeitsbericht: *feasibility report*
durchführen: *to perform*
Durchgangsfilter für niedrige Frequenzen: *low pass filter*
Durchgangsvermittlung: *tandem switching*
durchgehen: *to walk through*
durchgestrichene Null: *slashed zero*
Durchlauf: *pass*
Durchlaufzeit: *run-time or run-duration*
Durchmesser: *diameter*
durchnummerieren: *to number*
Durchschalte(vermittlungs)technik: *line switching*
Durchschaltevermittlung: *circuit switching*
Durchschaltnetz: *circuit switched network*
durchscheinender Druck: *show-through*
Durchschießen: *interleaving*
Durchschlag: *carbon (copy)*
Durchschlagpapier: *NCR paper*
Durchschnitt: *average or mean*
durchschnittlich betragen: *to average out*
durchschnittlich: *(on an) average or mean*
durchschossen: *interleaved*
Durchschuss am oberen Rand: *top space*
Durchschuss: *lead or leading*
durchsichtiges System: *transparent*
durchsuchen: *to scan*
Durchwahl: *direct inward dialling*
Durchwählen: *direct dialling*
durchwählen: *to dial direct*
DV (Datenverarbeitung): *dp or DP (data processing)*
DVORAK-Tastatur: *DVORAK keyboard*
dyadische (boolesche) Operation: *dyadic (Boolean) operation*
dynamisch neu definierbarer Zeichensatz: *dynamically redefinable character set*
dynamisch: *dynamic*
dynamische Datenstruktur: *dynamic data structure*
dynamische Multiplexmethode: *dynamic multiplexing*
dynamische Puffer: *dynamic buffer*
dynamische Speicherplatzzuordnung: *dynamic storage allocation*
dynamische Verknüpfungsbibliothek (DLL): *dynamic link library (DLL)*

dynamische Verschiebung: *dynamic relocation*
dynamische Weiterleitung: *dynamic routing*
dynamische Zuteilung: *dynamic allocation*
dynamischer Datenaustausch (DDE): *dynamic data exchange (DDE)*
dynamischer Dauerspeicher: *permanent dynamic memory*
dynamischer RAM: *dynamic RAM*
dynamischer Speicher: *dynamic memory or storage*
dynamischer Speicherauszug: *dynamic or snapshot dump*
dynamisches Mikrofon: *dynamic microphone*
dynamisches Unterprogramm: *dynamic subroutine*

Ee

Echo: *echo*
echofrei: *anechoic*
Echolot: *sonar*
Echoprüfung: *echo check*
Echosperre: *echo suppressor*
echt: *genuine*
Echtheitsbestätigung von Meldungen: *authentication of messages*
Echtzeit: *real time*
Echtzeitanimation: *real-time animation*
Echtzeitbetrieb: *real-time processing*
Echtzeitbetriebssystem: *real-time operating system*
Echtzeiteingabe: *real-time input*
Echtzeitmultitasking: *real-time multitasking*
Echtzeitsimulation: *real-time simulation*
Echtzeitsystem: *real-time system*
eckige Klammern: *square brackets*
edieren: *to edit*
EDIT-Befehle: *edit commands*
EDIT-Fenster *or* **Editierfenster:** *edit window*
Editierfunktion: *text-editing function*
Editierprogramm: *text-editing facilities*
Editor: *editor*
EDIT-Taste: *edit key*
EDV: *EDP*
EDV-Personal: *liveware*
effektiv: *effective*
effektive Adresse: *effective address*

effektive Apertur: *effective aperture*
effektive Bandbreite: *effective bandwidth*
effektive Verarbeitungsmenge: *effective throughput*
Effektivstrom: *RMS line current*
Effektivwert: *root mean square (RMS)*
EGA-Bildschirm: *enhanced graphics adapter (EGA) screen*
EIA-Schnittstelle: *EIA interface*
Eichung: *calibration*
Ein-/Ausgabe: *input/output (I/O)*
ein-/ausgabeabhängig: *I/O bound*
Ein-/Ausgabeadressierung: *I/O mapping*
Ein-/Ausgabeanforderung: *input/output request (IORQ)*
Ein-/Ausgabeanschluss(stelle): *input/output (I/O) port*
Ein-/Ausgabeanweisung *or* **Ein-/Ausgabebefehl:** *input/output (I/O) instruction*
Ein-/Ausgabebezugnahme: *input/output referencing*
Ein-/Ausgabebibliothek: *input/output library*
Ein-/Ausgabebus: *input/output (I/O) bus*
Ein-/Ausgabedatei: *I/O file*
Ein-/Ausgabedatenbus: *input/output data bus (I/O bus)*
Ein-/Ausgabeeinheit: *input/output (I/O) unit or device*
Ein-/Ausgabegerät: *I/O device*
Ein-/Ausgabekanal: *input/output (I/O) channel*
Ein-/Ausgabemapping: *I/O mapping*
Ein-/Ausgabeprozessor: *input/output processor (IOP)*
Ein-/Ausgabepuffer: *input/output (I/O) buffer*
Ein-/Ausgabequittungsbetrieb: *handshake I/O control*
Ein-/Ausgaberegister: *input/output register*
Ein-/Ausgabeschnittstelle: *input/output interface*
Ein-/Ausgabestatuswort: *input/output status word*
Ein-/Ausgabesteuereinheit: *input/output controller*
Ein-/Ausgabesteuerprogramm: *input/output control program*
Ein-/Ausgabeunterbrechung: *input/output interrupt*
ein-/ausspeichern: *to roll in/roll out*
Einadressbefehl: *one address instruction*
Einadresscode: *single address code*
Einadresscomputer: *one address computer*
einbauen: *to house*
Einbaumodem: *integrated modem*

Einblattdruck: *broadsheet*
Einblendliste: *drop-down list box*
Einblendmenü: *pop-up menu or drop-down menu*
Einbrennen: *burn-in*
einbrennen: *to blast; to burn in*
Einchipmikrocontroller: *single-chip microcontroller*
Eindringling: *intruder*
Einerkomplement: *one's complement*
einfach zu benutzen: *easy-to-use or simple to use*
einfach: *simple; single*
Einfachadresse: *single address message*
einfache Genauigkeit: *single precision*
Einfachstrom-Signal: *unipolar signal*
Einfangwinkel: *acceptance angle*
einfarbig: *monochrome*
Einfrequenztonwahl: *single frequency signalling or sf signalling*
einfrieren: *to freeze (frame)*
Einfügemarke: *I-beam*
Einfügemodus: *insert mode*
einfügen: *to paste or insert*
Einfügetaste: *insert key or Ins key*
Einfügungsdämpfung: *insertion loss*
Einfügungsmodus: *insert mode*
einführen: *to introduce; to launch*
Einführung: *launch*
Einführungsseite: *lead in page*
Eingabe von der Tastatur direkt auf die Platte: *keyboard to disk entry*
Eingabe: *entering; entry; input (i/p or I/P)*
Eingabeanschluss: *input port*
Eingabeanweisung: *input statement*
Eingabeaufforderung: *(system) prompt*
Eingabebedingung: *entry condition*
eingabebegrenzt: *input-bound or limited*
eingabebegrenztes Programm: *input limited program*
Eingabebereich: *input area*
Eingabebetrieb: *input mode*
Eingabeeinheit: *input unit*
Eingabegerät: *input device*
Eingabemodus: *input mode*
Eingabeprogramm: *input routine*
Eingabepufferregister: *input buffer register*
Eingaberegister: *input register*
Eingabespeicherbereich: *input area or section*
Eingabetaste: *enter key or return*
Eingabewarteschlange: *input work queue*
Eingabezeit: *entry time*
Eingang: *entry; input*
Eingangsfolgeliste: *push-up list or stack*
Eingangslastfaktor: *fan-in*
eingebaut: *built-in or inbuilt*

eingebaut(e Einheit): *integral*
eingebaute Standardfunktion: *built-in function*
Eingebeblock: *input block*
eingeben: *to enter; to input; to keyboard; to key in; to type*
Eingeben von Hand: *manual entry or manual input*
Eingeben: *input (i/p or I/P); keyboarding*
eingebetteter Befehl: *embedded command*
eingebetteter Code: *embedded code*
eingebettetes System: *embedded system*
eingefügtes Unterprogramm: *inserted subroutine*
eingehängt: *on-hook*
eingehende Daten: *incoming traffic*
eingehende Nachricht: *incoming message*
eingeklammert: *bracketed*
eingezogene Marginalien: *cut in notes*
eingliedriges Element: *one element*
Eingriff: *intervention*
Einheit: *unit*
Einheit mit bistabiler Schaltung: *D-type flip-flop*
Einheitenpuffer: *unit buffer*
Einheitenstatuswort: *device status word (DSW)*
Einheitenvorrangliste: *device priority*
einheitliche Maschinensprache: *common language*
einklammern: *to bracket together*
Einklappmenü: *pull-down menu*
Einkleben eines Einsteckbogens: *guarding*
Einlagerungstelegrafie: *speech plus*
einlegen: *to mount*
einlesen: *to capture; to read-in or read in*
einloggen: *to log in or log on; to attach*
Einmalfarbband: *single-strike ribbon*
einohrig: *monoaural*
Einpassen: *sizing*
Einplatinenrechner: *single board computer (SBC)*
Einprogrammsystem: *monoprogramming system*
einrahmen: *to box in*
Einrichten des Zeilenabstands: *interlinear spacing*
einrichten: *to adjust; to set up*
Einrichtung: *equipment; feature*
Einrichtungen: *facilities*
Einrichtungsoption: *setup option*
Einrücken: *indentation*
einrücken: *to indent*
Einrückung: *indent*
Einsatz: *attack*
Einsatzunterstützung: *system support*

einschalten: *to turn on or switch on or wake up or activate or enable*
Einschaltquote: *ratings*
Einschalt-Selbsttest: *power on self test (POST)*
einschichtiger Speicher: *one-level store*
einschränken: *to restrict*
Einschränkung: *restriction*
Einschrittoperation: *single pass operation*
einsehen: *to view*
Einseitenband: *single sideband*
Einseitenbandübertragung mit unterdrückter Trägerwelle: *single sideband suppressed carrier (SSBSC)*
einseitig bedrucktes Blatt: *broadsheet*
einseitiger Schalter: *single pole*
einspeichern: *to roll-in*
Eins-plus-Eins-Adressbefehl: *two-address instruction*
Eins-plus-Eins-Adresse: *one-plus-one address*
Einsprungbefehl: *entry instruction*
Einsprungstelle: *entry point*
einstecken: *to plug in*
einstellen auf: *to lock onto*
einstellen: *to adjust or set or tune; to appoint*
einstellige Operation: *unary operation*
Einstellung: *framing; setting*
Einstellzeit: *positioning time*
Einstichverfahren: *dichotomizing search*
einstufen: *to rank*
einstufiges Unterprogramm: *one-level subroutine*
einsynchronisierter Toneffekt: *dubbed sound*
Eins-zu-Null-Verhältnis: *one to zero ratio*
Eintrag: *attribute; entry*
eintragen: *to post*
Einverständnis: *approval*
Einwählmodem: *dial-in modem*
Einweggleichrichter: *half wave rectifier*
Einwegverpackung: *non-returnable packing*
Einzeilenanzeige: *single line display*
Einzeilenfenster: *strip window or thin window*
Einzelanschlag-Programm: *single key response*
Einzelbild: *frame*
Einzelblatteinzug: *single sheet feed*
Einzelblattzuführung: *sheet feed attachment*
Einzelchipcomputer: *single chip computer*
einzeln: *single*
einzeln gestellte Zeichen: *separated graphics*
einzelne Maschine: *unit*
einzelner (Daten)satz: *unit record*
Einzeloperation: *single operation*

Einzelperson: *individual*
Einzelplatinencomputer: *single board computer (sbc)*
Einzelplatinenmikrocomputer: *single-board microcomputer*
Einzelplatzsystem: *single-user system*
Einzelschritt: *single step*
einzigartig: *unique*
Einzug: *indent*
Eisenoxid: *ferric oxide or ferrite*
elastische Grenzen: *elastic banding*
elastischer Puffer: *elastic buffer*
elegantes Programmieren: *elegant programming*
Elektretmikrophon: *electret microphone*
elektrisch: *electric(al)*
elektrische Ladung: *electric charge*
elektrische Leitungen: *wiring*
elektrische Polarität: *electrical polarity*
elektrische Schreibmaschine: *electric typewriter*
elektrische Spannung: *voltage*
elektrischer Strom: *electric current*
Elektrizität: *electricity*
Elektrode: *electrode*
Elektrofotografie: *electrophotography*
elektrolumineszent: *electroluminescent*
Elektrolumineszenz: *electroluminescence*
Elektrolumineszenzanzeige: *electroluminescent display*
elektrolumineszierend: *electroluminescing*
elektrolytische Kondensatoren: *electrolytic capacitors*
Elektromagnet: *electromagnet*
elektromagnetisch: *electromagnetic(ally)*
elektromagnetische Störung: *electromagnetic interference (EMI)*
elektromagnetische Strahlung: *electromagnetic radiation*
elektromagnetisches Spektrum: *electromagnetic spectrum*
elektromechanische Schaltung: *electromechanical switching*
elektromotorische Kraft (EMK): *electromotive force (EMF)*
Elektron: *electron*
Elektronenkanone: *electron gun*
Elektronenstrahl: *electron beam*
Elektronenstrahlaufzeichnung-(smethode): *electron beam recording (EBR)*
Elektronik: *electronics*
Elektronikingenieur: *electronic engineer*
elektronisch: *electronic(ally)*
elektronische Anzeigetafel: *electronic blackboard*
elektronische Berichterstattung: *electronic news gathering (ENG)*

elektronische Datenverarbeitung (EDV): *electronic data processing (EDP)*
elektronische Kalkulationstabelle: *spreadsheet*
elektronische Kasse: *electronic point-of-sale (EPOS)*
elektronische Post: *computer mail or electronic mail or email*
elektronische Redaktion: *electronic editing*
elektronische Schreibmaschine: *electronic typewriter*
elektronische Setzmaschine: *electronic compositor*
elektronische Signatur: *electronic signature*
elektronische Sperre: *electronic lock*
elektronische Tastatur: *electronic keyboard*
elektronische Wählvermittlungsstelle: *electronic automatic exchange*
elektronischer Briefkasten: *electronic mailbox*
elektronischer Datenaustausch: *electronic data interchange (EDI)*
elektronischer Datenverkehr: *electronic traffic*
elektronischer Digitalrechner: *electronic digital computer*
elektronischer Impuls: *electronic pulse*
elektronischer Schalter: *latch*
elektronischer Schriftsatz: *electronic composition*
elektronischer Smog: *electronic smog*
elektronischer Sucher: *electronic viewfinder*
elektronischer Terminplaner: *electronic agenda*
elektronischer Zahlungsverkehr: *electronic funds transfer (EFT)*
elektronisches Ablagesystem: *electronic filing*
elektronisches Büro: *electronic office*
elektronisches Publizieren: *electronic publishing*
elektronisches Vermittlungssystem: *electronic switching system*
elektrooptischer Effekt: *electro-optic effect*
elektrosensitives Drucken: *electrosensitive printing*
elektrosensitives Papier: *electrosensitive paper*
elektrostatisch: *electrostatic(ally)*
elektrostatischer Drucker: *electrostatic printer*
elektrostatischer Lautsprecher: *electrostatic speaker*
elektrostatischer Schirm: *electrostatic screen*

elektrostatischer Speicher: *electrostatic storage*
Element: *element*
elementar: *elementary*
Elementarbuch: *primer*
elementarer Kabelausschnitt: *elementary cable section*
Elementarroutine: *primitive*
eliminieren: *to eliminate*
eliminierende Suche: *dichotomizing search*
Eliminierung: *elimination*
Eliminierungsfaktor: *elimination factor*
Elite: *elite*
Ellipse: *ellipse*
elliptische Umlaufbahn: *elliptical orbit*
ELSE-Regel: *else rule*
Elternprogramm: *parent program*
Elternverzeichnis: *parent directory*
Em: *em*
E-Mail: *E-mail or email*
Emission: *emission*
Emitter: *emitter*
emittergekoppelte Logik: *emitter-coupled logic (ECL)*
Empfang: *reception*
empfangen: *to receive*
Empfänger: *receiver; addressee*
Empfangs-/Sendegerät: *answer/originate (device)*
Empfangsbereich: *earth coverage*
Empfangsgerät: *radio receiver*
Empfangsregister: *receiver register*
Empfangssignal eines Datenschwingungsträgers: *data carrier detect (DCD)*
Empfangssignal: *carrier detect (CD)*
empfindlich: *sensitive*
Empfindlichkeit: *sensitivity*
Ems pro Stunde: *ems per hour*
Em-Strich: *em dash or em rule*
Emulation: *emulation*
Emulationsadapter von eingebauten Schaltungen: *in-circuit emulator*
Emulationsfähigkeit: *emulation facility*
Emulator: *emulator*
emulieren: *to emulate*
Emulsion: *emulsion*
En: *en*
Encapsulated-Postscript-Datei (EPS-Datei): *encapsulated PostScript file (EPSF)*
Endcode: *tail*
Ende: *end or ending or finish*
Ende der Laufroutine: *end of run routine*
Ende des (Datenübertragungs)blocks: *end of block (EOB)*
enden: *to finish*
Endetaste: *end key*

Endezeichen: *terminator*
endgültiger Maschinenbefehl: *actual or absolute or effective instruction*
endlos: *endless*
Endlosbandbetrieb: *streaming tape drive*
Endlosetiketten: *continuous labels*
Endlosfehlersignal: *stuck beacon*
Endlosfilm: *loop film*
Endlospapier: *continuous stationery; listing paper*
Endlospapiereinzug: *continuous feed*
Endlosschleife: *endless loop or infinite loop*
Endmarke: *rogue indicator or rogue value or terminator*
Endprodukt: *end product or final product or finished product*
Endübertrag: *end about carry*
Endverbraucher: *end user*
Energie: *energy*
energiesparend: *energy-saving*
En-Strich: *en dash or en rule*
entblocken: *to deblock*
entfernen: *to remove; to takedown*
entfernt: *distant or remote*
entfernt stehende Datenstation: *remote terminal*
Entfernung auf der x-Achse: *X distance*
Entfernung auf der y-Achse: *Y-distance*
Entfernung verdeckter Linien: *hidden line removal*
Entfragmentierungsprogramm: *defragmentation utility*
enthalten: *to contain*
enthüllen: *to disclose*
entleihen: *to borrow*
Entleiher: *borrower*
entmagnetisieren: *to demagnetize or degauss*
Entmagnetisierer: *demagnetizer*
Entmagnetisierungsgerät: *degausser*
entmultiplexieren: *demultiplex*
Entmultiplexor: *demultiplexor*
entnehmen: *to capture; to unmount*
entprellen: *to de-bounce*
Entprellungsstromkreis: *de-bounce circuit*
entscheidender Faktor: *deciding factor*
Entscheidung: *decision*
Entscheidungsbaum: *decision tree*
Entscheidungsschaltung: *decision circuit*
Entscheidungstabelle: *decision table*
Entscheidungsunterstützungssystem: *decision support system*
Entschluss: *decision*
entschlüsseln: *to decipher or decode or decrypt or de-scramble*
Entschlüsselung: *decoding or decryption*
entsperren: *to unlock*

entsprechen: *to conform; to corrrespond*
Entsprechung: *correspondence*
entweichen: *to leak*
entwenden: *to abstract*
entwerfen: *to design; to draft; to lay out; to map out*
entwickeln: *to develop*
Entwickler(flüssigkeit): *developer*
Entwicklung: *development*
Entwicklungszeit: *development time*
Entwurf: *design; draft; layout*
Entzerrer: *equalizer*
Entzerrung: *equalization*
Envelope: *envelope*
Epidiaskop: *episcope or opaque projector*
epitaxiale Schicht: *epitaxial layer*
Epitaxie: *epitaxy*
Erde: *earth; ground or GND*
erden: *to earth*
Erdfunkstelle: *earth station*
erdnächster Punkt: *perigee*
Erdung: *earth wire*
Ereignis: *event*
ereignisgesteuert: *event-driven*
erfassen: *to collect*
Erfassungsbereich: *footprint or coverage*
erfordern: *to require*
Erfordernisse: *requirements*
Ergänzung: *appendix*
Ergebnis: *result*
Ergebniscode: *result code*
Ergonom: *ergonomist*
Ergonomie: *ergonomics*
erhalten: *to obtain; to gain*
erhöhen: *to augment*
erkannter Fehler: *detected error*
erkennbar: *recognizable*
erkennen: *to detect*
Erkennung: *detection*
Erkennungslogik: *recognition logic*
Erkennungsteil: *identification division*
erkärende Festlegung: *narrative statement*
Erklärung: *narrative*
Erklärungsliste: *description list*
erlauben: *to enable*
erledigen: *to deal with*
ermächtigen: *to authorize*
Ernannte(r): *appointee*
ernennen: *to appoint*
Ernennung: *appointment*
Ernennungsschreiben: *letter of appointment*
erneut laden: *to reboot*
erneut übertragen: *to retransmit*
erneut zeichnen: *to redraw*
erneute Worttrennung: *rehyphenation*
erneuter Schreibvorgang: *rewrite*

eröffnen: *to open*
eröffnet: *open*
Erratum: *erratum*
errechnete Adresse: *generated or synthetic address*
errichten: *to construct*
Errichtung: *construction*
Ersatz- und Ergänzungsblatt: *cancel page*
Ersatzteil: *spare part*
Ersatzzeichen: *substitute character*
Erscheinung: *aspect*
Erschließer: *property developer*
erschöpfende Suche: *exhaustive search*
ersetzen: *to replace or substitute*
Erstadresse: *first-level address*
erste Generation: *first generation*
erste Kopie vom Original: *first generation image*
Erstellen von Computermodellen: *modelling*
erstellen: *to create*
Erstellung: *preparation*
erstklassiges Programm: *blue-ribbon program*
erweisen: *to establish*
erweiterbar: *extensible*
erweiterbare serielle Datei: *extending serial file*
erweiterbare Sprache: *extensible language*
Erweiterer: *enhancer*
erweitern: *to augment; to enhance; to extend*
erweitert: *advanced*
erweiterte Adressierung: *augmented addressing*
erweiterte Backus-Naur-Form: *extended BNF (EBNF)*
erweiterte Grafikkarte (EGA): *enhanced graphics adapter (EGA)*
erweiterte indizierte Zugriffsmöglichkeit für sequenzielle Dateien (QISAM): *queued indexed sequential access method (QISAM)*
erweiterte Kleingerätschnittstelle: *enhanced small device interface (ESDI)*
erweiterte Programm-zu-Programm-Verbindung (APPC): *advanced program to program communications (APPC)*
erweiterte Tastatur: *enhanced keyboard*
erweiterte Version: *advanced version*
erweiterte Zugriffsmöglichkeit für sequenzielle Dateien (QSAM): *queued sequential access method (QSAM)*
erweiterter Modus: *enhanced mode*
erweitertes Rechenelement: *extended arithmetic element*
Erweiterung: *enhancement; extension*
Erweiterungsbox: *expansion box*
Erweiterungsbus: *expansion bus*

Erweiterungsplatine: *expansion board or card or add on board or daughter board*
Erweiterungsposition: *expansion slot*
Erweiterungsspeicher: *extended memory*
Erweiterungsspeichermanager: *extended memory manager*
Erweiterungssteckplatz: *expansion slot*
Erwerb: *acquisition*
erzeugen: *to generate*
Erzeugnis: *product*
erzwungener Seitenumbruch: *forced page break*
E-Schicht der Ionosphäre: *E-region or Heaviside-Kennelly layer*
ESC-Codes: *escape codes*
ESC-Taste: *escape key*
ESC-Zeichen: *escape character*
Ethernet: *Ethernet*
Etikett: *label*
Etikettendruck: *labelling*
Etikettendrucker: *label printer*
etikettieren: *to label*
Etikettierung: *labelling*
Euronet: *Euronet*
EXE-Datei: *EXE file*
Exemplar: *copy*
exklusiv-NOR-Funktion: *exclusive NOR (EXNOR)*
exklusiv-NOR-Gatter: *exclusive NOR gate*
exklusiv-ODER-Funktion: *exclusive OR (EXOR)*
exklusiv-ODER-Gatter: *exclusive OR gate*
Exklusivvertrag: *exclusive agreement*
expandierbar: *expandable*
expandierbares System: *expandable system*
expandieren: *to expand*
Expansionsspeicher: *expanded memory (EMS)*
Expansionsspeicherkarte: *expanded memory board*
Expansionsspeichermanager (EMM): *expanded memory manager (EMM)*
Experte/Expertin: *expert*
Expertensystem: *expert system*
Exponent: *exponent*
exportieren: *to export*
Extension beim Dateinamen: *filename extension*
extern ausgeführte Rechnung: *external arithmetic*
externe Datei: *external data file*
externe Register: *external registers*
externe Sortierung: *external sort*
externe Unterbrechung: *external interrupt*
externer Name: *title*

externer Speicher: *external memory or external storage*
externer Taktgeber: *external clock*
externes Modem: *external modem*
externes Plattenlaufwerk: *external disk drive*
externes Register: *external register*
externes Schema: *external schema*
Extra: *extra*
Extracode: *extracode*
Extrapolation: *extrapolation*
extremhohe Frequenz (EHF): *extremely high frequency (EHF)*

Ff

F1-Taste: *help key*
Fabrik: *factory*
Fabrikpreis: *factory price*
Facette: *facet*
Facettencode: *faceted code*
Fach: *bin*
Fächerantenne: *fan antenna*
Fachgruppe: *special interest group (SIG)*
Fachzeitschrift: *learned journal*
Fahnen: *streaking*
Faksimile: *facsimile*
Faksimilezeichengenerator: *facsimile character generator*
Faktor: *factor*
Faktotum: *gofer*
Fakultät: *factorial*
falsch: *false or inaccurate or incorrect*
falsche Fehlermeldung: *false error*
falsches Wiederauffinden: *false drop or retrieval*
FALSE-Code: *false code*
falten: *to fold*
Falzmaschine: *folding machine*
Familie: *family*
Fangstelle: *trap(door)*
Faraday: *farad (F)*
Faradaykäfig: *Faraday cage*
Farbaberration: *chromatic aberration*
Farbabstimmung: *colour balance*
Farbabweichung: *chromatic aberration*
Farbauszug: *colour separation*
Farbband: *printer ribbon*
Farbbildschirm: *colour display*
Farbbildsignalgemisch: *composite video*
Farbbits: *colour bits*
Farbcodierer: *colour encoder*
Farbdecodierer: *colour decoder*
Farbdetektor: *chroma detector*
Farbdia: *colour transparency*
Farbdrucker: *colour printer*
Farbe: *colour*

Farbenintensität: *chroma*
Farbenreinheit: *chroma*
Farberkennungssignal: *colour burst*
Farbgrafikadapter: *colour graphics adapter (CGA)*
Farbkontrolle: *chroma control*
farbliche Hervorhebung: *redliner*
Farbmischsignal: *composite video signal*
Farbmonitor: *colour monitor*
Farbpolymeraufzeichnung: *dye-polymer recording*
Farbsättigung: *colour saturation*
Farbseparation: *colour separation*
Farbsignal: *chrominance signal*
Farbsublimationsdrucker: *dye-sublimation printer*
Farbtemperatur: *colour temperature*
Farbton: *tone*
Farbtönung: *shade*
Farbumsetzer: *colour encoder*
Farbverschiebung: *colour shift*
Farbzelle: *colour cell*
Faseroptik: *fibre optics*
Fax-Gateway: *fax gateway*
Faxkarte: *fax card or board or adapter*
Faxserver: *fax server*
Fazilität: *facility*
federnder Schalter: *momentary switch*
Fehlanpassung: *mismatch*
fehlende Kompatibilität: *noncompatibility*
Fehler: *error or fault or defect*
Fehler aufgrund von Uneindeutigkeit: *ambiguity error*
Fehler durch Fremdkörpereinwirkung: *soft error*
Fehler löschen: *to bloop*
fehlerbedingte Wartung: *corrective maintenance*
Fehlerbedingung: *error condition*
Fehlerbehandlung: *exception handling or error handling*
Fehlerbehandlungsroutine: *error handler*
Fehlerbehebung: *error handling or management or recovery or trapping*
Fehlercode: *error code*
Fehlerdiagnose: *fault diagnosis or error diagnosis*
Fehlerdiagnostik: *error diagnostics*
Fehlerentdeckung: *fault detection*
Fehlererfassung: *error logging*
Fehlererkennung und -korrektur: *error detection and correction (EDAC)*
Fehlererkennung: *error detection*
Fehlererkennungscode: *error detecting code or self-checking code*
Fehlererkennungsroutine: *malfunction routine*
Fehlerfortpflanzung: *error propagation*
fehlerfrei: *perfect(ly)*

fehlerhaft: *faulty or corrupt*
fehlerhafte Funktion des
(Lese-/Schreib)kopfes: *head crash*
fehlerhafte
Scheinwiderstandsanpassung:
impedance mismatch
fehlerhafter Sektor: *faulty or bad or*
defective sector
fehlerhaftes Springen: *defect skipping*
Fehlerhäufigkeit: *error rate*
Fehlerhäufung: *error burst*
Fehlerkorrektur: *error correction*
Fehlerkorrekturcode: *error correcting code*
Fehlerlokalisierungsprogramm: *fault*
location program
fehlerloses Programm: *star program*
Fehlermarge: *margin of error*
Fehlermeldung: *error message*
Fehlerprotokoll: *fault trace*
Fehlerprüfcode: *error checking code*
Fehlerprüfung und -korrektur: *ERCC*
Fehlerquote: *error rate*
Fehlerrate: *error rate*
Fehlerroutine: *error routine*
Fehlersignal: *beacon*
Fehlerspanne: *margin of error*
Fehlersuchprogramm: *debugger*
fehlertolerant: *fault-tolerant*
Fehlertoleranz: *fault tolerance*
Fehlerüberwachung: *error control*
Fehlerunterbrechungen: *error interrupts*
Fehlerwiederherstellung: *failure recovery*
fein: *fine*
fein abstimmen *or* **einstellen:** *to fine tune*
Feinlinierung: *feint*
Feld: *field*
Feld mit Vorzeichen: *signed field*
Feldanordnung: *fielding*
Feldeffekttransistor (FET): *field effect*
transistor (FET)
Feldeffekttransistor mit
Metalloxidhalbleiteraufbau MOS-
Transistor: *metal oxide semiconductor field*
effect transistor (MOSFET)
Feldforschung: *field work*
Feldfrequenz: *field frequency*
Feldgröße: *item size*
Feldgruppe: *array*
Feldkennung: *field label*
Feldlänge: *field length*
Feldmarkierungszeichen: *field marker*
Feldnamenerklärung: *data*
dictionary/directory (DD/D)
Feldprogrammierung: *field programming*
Feldstärke: *field strength*
Femtosekunde: *femto second*
Fenster: *window*

Fenstertechnik: *windowing*
Ferndatensteuereinheit: *data adapter unit*
Ferngespräch: *trunk call or long-distance*
call
Fernkopierersender/-empfänger:
transceiver
fernladbar: *downloadable*
fernladen: *to download*
Fernleihe: *inter-library loan (ILL)*
Fernmeldewesen: *telecommunications*
Fernmessung: *telemetry*
Fernnachricht: *telemessage*
Fernsatz: *teletypesetting*
Fernschreiber: *teleprinter or teletypewriter*
Fernschreiberpapier: *teleprinter roll*
Fernschreiberschnittstelle: *teleprinter*
interface
Fernsehempfänger: *television receiver*
Fernsehempfänger/-monitor: *television*
receiver/monitor
Fernsehen: *television (TV)*
Fernsehgerät: *television (TV)*
Fernsehkamera: *television camera*
Fernsehmonitor: *television monitor*
Fernsehnetz: *television network*
Fernsehprojektor: *television projector*
Fernsehqualität: *broadcast quality*
Fernsehröhre: *television tube*
Fernsehsignalverstärker: *launch amplifier*
Fernsprechamt: *telephone exchange*
Fernsprechwesen: *telephony*
Fernsteuerung: *remote control*
Fernsteuerungssoftware: *remote control*
software
Fernverbindungskabel: *trunk*
Fernvermittlungsstelle: *trunk exchange*
Fernzugriff: *remote access*
Ferritkern: *ferrite core*
Ferrodielektrikum: *electret*
ferromagnetisches Material:
ferromagnetic material
fertig: *finished*
fertige Bruchzifferntypen (mit
waagerechtem Bruchstrich): *piece*
fractions
Fertigerzeugnisse: *finished goods*
fertiges Schriftstück: *finished document*
Fertigungs- und Lieferzeit: *turnaround*
Fertigungsabteilung: *production*
department
Fertigungsingenieur: *product engineer*
Fertigungssteuerung: *production control*
fest binden: *to case*
fest eingebaut: *built into*
fest gebundenes Buch: *cased book*
fest: *static*

Fest(wert)speicher: *read only memory (ROM)*
Festdaten: *fixed data*
feste Verkehrslenkung: *fixed routing*
feste Wortlänge: *fixed word length*
fester Einband: *case binding*
festes Feld: *fixed field*
festgelegtes Wort: *reserved word*
festgeschaltete Leitung: *dedicated line*
festhalten: *to retain*
Festkommarechnung: *fixed-point arithmetic*
Festkommaschreibweise: *fixed-point notation*
Festkopf: *disk head*
Festkörperlaser: *solid-state laser*
Festkörperspeicher: *solid-state memory device*
Festplatte: *hard disk or fixed disk or rigid disk*
Festplattenduplizierung: *disk duplexing*
Festplattenkomprimierungssoftware: *disk compression software*
Festplattenlaufwerk: *hard disk drive*
Festplattenlaufwerksplatine: *hard card*
Festplattenmodell: *hard disk model*
Festplattenspeicher: *fixed disk storage*
Festplattenspiegelung: *disk mirroring*
Festplattenüberlastung: *thrashing*
Festprogrammcomputer: *fixed program computer*
festsetzen: *to establish; to fix*
Feststelltaste: *caps lock*
festverdrahtete Logik: *hardwired logic*
festverdrahtete Verbindung: *hardwired connection*
festverdrahtetes Programm: *hardwired program*
Festzeichendrucker: *solid font printer*
Fettdruck: *bold face*
Feuerprobe: *smoke test*
FIFO-Speichermethode: *FIFO memory*
FIFO-Warteschlange: *FIFO queue*
Filehandle: *file handle*
Fileserver: *file server*
Film: *film or motion picture*
Filmabtaster: *film pickup*
Filmandruckplatte: *platen*
Filmebene: *image plane*
Filmempfindlichkeitsangabe: *ASA exposure index*
Film-Fernsehbetrieb-Methode: *telecine*
Filmkamera: *cine camera*
Filmkulisse: *set*
Filmlochkarte: *aperture card*
Filmprojektor: *film projector*
Filmstreifen: *film strip*

Filmträger: *film base*
Filmtransport(hebel): *film advance*
Filmvorführaggregat: *film chain*
Filter: *filter*
Finanzbuchhaltungsprogramm: *accounting or accounts package*
finanzielle Unterstützung: *financial assistance*
finden: *to find*
Fingerhutdrucker: *thimble printer*
Finish: *finish*
Firmeninformationsblatt: *company newsletter*
Firmenname: *corporate name*
Firmware: *firmware*
First Fit: *first fit*
Fischauge: *fisheye lens*
fixieren: *to fix*
Fixierung: *fix*
Flachbettgerät: *flatbed*
Flachbettplotter: *flatbed plotter*
Flachbettpresse: *flatbed press*
Flachbettscanner: *flat-bed scanner*
Flachdatei: *flat file*
Flächenmaß: *square measure*
Flachgehäuse: *flat pack*
flackern: *to flicker*
Flag: *flag*
Flash Memory: *flash memory*
Flash-Speicher: *flash memory*
Flattermarken: *collating marks*
Flattern: *thrashing; jitter*
Flattersatz: *ragged text*
Fleisch: *beard*
flexibel: *flexible*
Flexibilität: *flexibility*
flexible Feldgruppe: *flexible array*
flexibles Fertigungssystem: *flexible manufacturing system (FMS)*
flexibles Maschinensteuerungssystem: *flexible machining system (FMS)*
Flickschusterei: *kludge or kluge*
fliegender Kopf: *flying head*
Fließband: *production line*
fließen: *to flow*
fließend: *floating*
Fließkommaarithmetik: *floating point arithmetic*
Fließkommabetriebsart: *noisy mode*
Fließkommaoperation: *floating point operation (FLOP)*
Fließkommaprozessor: *floating point unit or processor (FPU)*
Fließkommarechnungen pro Sekunde: *FLOPs per second*
Fließkommaschreibweise: *floating point (notation)*

Fließkommazahl: *floating point number*
flimmerfrei: *flicker-free*
Flimmern: *flicker*
flimmern: *to flicker*
Flipflop: *flip-flop (FF)*
Flippy: *flippy*
flüchtiger Speicher: *volatile memory or volatile store or volatile storage*
Flüchtigkeit: *volatility*
Flugblatt: *broadside*
Flugsimulator: *flight simulator*
Fluss: *flow*
Flussdiagramm: *flowchart or flow diagram*
Flüssigkristallanzeige (LCD): *liquid crystal display (LCD)*
Fluss-Steuerung: *flow control*
Folge: *sequence*
Folgekontrolle: *sequence check*
Folgeseite: *continuation page*
Folgestation: *secondary station*
Folgesteuerungsmechanismus: *servo or servomechanism*
Folientastatur: *membrane keyboard or touch sensitive keyboard*
Font: *font or fount*
Förderband: *conveyor*
fordern: *to demand*
Forderung: *demand*
formale Logik: *formal logic*
Format: *format*
Format zur symbolischen Codierung: *symbolic-coding format*
formatieren: *to format*
Formatierung: *formatting*
Formatierungsprogramm: *formatter*
formatisierter Speicherauszug: *formatted dump*
Formatmodus: *format mode*
Formbrief: *form letter or standard letter*
Formel: *formula*
Formmaske: *form overlay*
Formschablone: *form overlay*
Formular: *form*
Formulare mit Kohlepapier: *carbon set*
Formulareinblendung: *form flash*
Formularmodus: *form mode*
Formularseite: *form*
Formularvorschub: *form feed*
FOR-NEXT-Schleife: *for-next loop*
Forschung: *research*
Forschung und Entwicklung: *research and development (R & D)*
Forschungs- und Entwicklungsabteilung: *R & D department*
fortdrucken: *to run on*
fortfahren: *to proceed*
fortgeschritten: *advanced*

Fortschaltungsadressierung: *implied addressing*
Fortschreibung: *file update*
Fortschreibungsdatei: *update file or transaction file*
fortsetzen: *to continue*
Fortsetzung: *continuation*
Fortsetzungsseite: *continuation page*
Fotoapparat: *camera*
Fotografie: *photography*
fotografieren: *to photograph*
fotografisch: *photographic(ally)*
fotografischer Film: *photographic film*
Fotogravüre: *photogravure*
Fotokopie: *photocopy or photostat*
Fotokopierbüro: *photocopying bureau*
Fotokopieren: *photocopying*
fotokopieren: *to photocopy or photostat*
Fotokopierer: *photocopier*
Fotolithographie: *photolithography*
fotomechanische Übertragung: *photomechanical transfer (PMT)*
Fotoresist: *photoresist*
Fotosatz: *photocomposition; phototext; phototypesetting*
Fotosetzer: *phototypesetter*
Fotozelle: *light-sensitive device*
Fourier-Serie: *Fourier series*
Fragmentierung: *fragmentation*
Fraktal: *fractal*
Frame-Relay-Protokoll: *frame relay*
Freeware: *freeware*
frei belegbare Funktionstasten: *soft keys*
frei belegbare Tastatur: *soft keyboard*
freie Indizierung: *free indexing*
freie Telefonleitung: *free line*
freier (Stecker)platz: *empty slot*
freier Durchlaufbetrieb: *free running mode*
freier Raum: *free space media*
Freigabe: *release*
freigeben: *to release or clear or deallocate or unlock*
freihalten: *to assign*
Freiheit: *freedom*
Freilaufprotokoll: *free wheeling*
Freiraumdämpfung: *free space loss*
Freispeicher: *heap*
Freizeichen: *ringing tone*
Freizeichnungsklausel: *exclusion clause*
Fremdhersteller: *original equipment manufacturer (OEM)*
Fremdsprache: *foreign language*
Fremdübernahme: *importation*
Frequenz: *frequency*
Frequenzanalysator: *frequency analyzer*
Frequenzbandaufteilung: *beam diversity*
Frequenzbereich: *frequency range*

Frequenzbereichsdienste: *fractional services*
Frequenzebene: *frequency domain*
Frequenzen unterhalb des Hörbereichs: *subaudio frequencies*
Frequenzentzerrer: *frequency equalizer*
Frequenzgang: *frequency response*
Frequenzmodulation (FM): *frequency modulation (FM)*
Frequenzmultiplex (FDM): *frequency division multiplexing (FDM)*
Frequenzteiler: *frequency divider*
Frequenzumtastung: *frequency shift keying (FSK)*
Frequenzvariation: *frequency variation*
Frequenzverschieber: *frequency changer*
Friktionsantrieb: *friction feed*
Front: *front*
Frontblende: *bezel*
Frontplatte: *fascia plate*
frühzeitige Tokenfreigabe: *early token release*
F-Schicht der Ionosphäre: *F-region*
fühlbar: *tactile*
führende Null: *leading zero*
Führungskante: *aligning or leading edge*
Führungslöcher: *feed holes or sprocket holes*
Führungspunkte: *leader*
Fülldiagramm: *area graph*
füllen: *to fill*
Füllfarbe: *paint*
Füllmuster: *paint*
Füllzeichen: *fill character or gap character*
Füllziffer: *gap digit*
Funk: *radio*
Funkamateur: *radio ham*
Funk-Basisstation: *base station*
Funkendrucker: *spark printer*
Funkfeld: *hop*
Funkfrequenz: *radio frequency (RF)*
Funkgerät: *radio transceiver*
Funkmikrofon: *radio microphone*
Funkspektrum: *radio spectrum*
Funkstation: *radio station*
Funktelefon: *radio (tele)phone*
Funktelegrafie: *radio telegraphy*
Funktion: *function*
funktionieren: *to function or work*
Funktions- und Eignungsprüfung: *verification and validation (V & V)*
Funktionsanzeiger: *role indicator*
Funktionsaufruf: *function call*
Funktionsbeschreibung: *functional specification*
Funktionsbibliothek: *function library*
Funktionscode: *function code*

Funktionsdiagramm: *functional diagram*
Funktionseinheit: *functional unit*
funktionsfähig: *operational*
Funktionstabelle: *function table*
Funktionstaste: *function key*
Funkverkehr: *radiocommunications*
Funkwellen: *radio waves*
Fusion: *fusion*
Fuß: *foot*
Fußkerze: *foot candle*
Fußnote: *footnote*
Fußsteg: *bottom space*
Fußzeile: *footer or footing*

Gg

Gabelung: *bifurcation*
galaktisches Rauschen: *galactic noise*
Galgen: *boom*
Galliumarsenid (GaAs): *gallium arsenide (GaAs)*
Gameport: *game port*
Gamma: *gamma*
Gangzahl: *cycle count*
ganze Zahl doppelter Wortlänge: *double-precision integer*
ganze Zahl: *integer*
Garant: *warrantor*
Garantie: *guarantee or warranty*
Garantieempfänger: *warrantee*
Garantiegeber: *warrantor*
Garantieinhaber: *warrantee*
garantieren: *to guarantee or warrant*
Gateway: *gateway*
Gatter: *gate*
Gatteranordnung: *gate array*
Gebietsleiter: *area manager*
Gebrauch: *use*
Gebrauchsanweisung: *directions for use*
gebrauchsfertiger Computer: *appliance computer*
gebraucht: *used*
gebrochen: *fractional*
Gebühr: *tariff*
Gedankenstrich von einem Geviert: *en dash or en rule*
Gedankenstrich von zwei Gevierten: *em dash or em rule*
Gedankenstrich: *dash*
gedruckte Schaltkarte: *printed circuit board (PCB)*

gedruckte Schaltungen: *edge board or card*
Gedrucktes: *print*
Gefahr: *hazard*
gefahrfreie Ausführung: *hazard-free implementation*
Gegenkabelfernsehbetrieb: *two way cable*
gegenläufiger Ring: *counter-rotating ring*
Gegenprobe: *cross-check*
Gegenradiobetrieb: *two way radio*
gegenseitiges Sperren: *deadlock*
Gegensprechanlage: *intercom*
Gegenstelle: *remote station*
Gegenteil: *inverse*
Gegenverkehrsverbindung: *duplex circuit*
gegossener Hartbleisatz: *hot metal composition*
Gehalt: *content*
Gehäuse: *case; casing; chassis; enclosure; housing*
Geisterbild: *ghost*
gekettete Baumstruktur: *threaded tree*
gekettete Datei: *chained or threaded file*
gekettete Liste: *chain(ed) or linked list*
gekettete Programmiersprache: *threaded language*
geketteter Code: *chain code*
geketteter Satz: *chained record*
gekettetes Programm: *thread*
Gelände: *site*
Geld(ausgabe)automat: *automatic telling machine or automated teller machine (ATM)*
Geldkassette: *cash box*
gelochtes Etikett: *punched tag*
gelungene Benutzerführung: *friendly front-end*
gemäß dem Muster: *as per sample*
Gemeingut: *public domain (PD)*
gemeinsam benutzen: *to share*
gemeinsam benutzter Zugang: *shared access*
gemeinsam benutztes Textverarbeitungssystem: *shared logic text processor*
gemeinsame Betriebsmittelbenutzung: *resource sharing*
gemeinsame Dateinutzung: *file sharing*
gemeinsame Datenbenutzung: *data sharing*
gemeinsames Netzverzeichnis: *shared network directory*
Gemeinschaft: *community*
Gemeinschaftsanschluss: *port sharing*
Gemeinschaftsantennenanlage: *master antenna television system (MATV)*
Gemeinschaftsbetrieb: *time-sharing*
Gemeinschaftsbus: *shared bus*
Gemeinschaftsdatei: *shared file*

Gemeinschaftsleitung: *shared line or party line*
Gemeinschaftsspeicher: *shared memory*
gemischte Höhen: *mixed highs*
Genauigkeit: *accuracy*
Genauigkeitsprüfzeichen: *accuracy control character*
genehmigen: *to authorize*
Genehmigungszertifikat: *certificate of approval*
geneigte Umlaufbahn: *inclined orbit*
Generalindex: *main index*
Generation: *generation*
Generator: *generator*
generieren: *to generate*
generierter Fehler: *generated error*
Generierung: *generation*
Generierungsprogramm: *generator*
geordnete Liste: *ordered list*
geostationäre Umlaufbahn: *geostationary orbit*
geostationärer Satellit: *geostationary satellite*
gepaartes Register: *paired register*
gepackte Dezimalzahl: *packed decimal*
gepacktes Format: *packed format*
gerade: *even*
Gerät: *appliance; device*
Geräteadresse: *device address*
Geräteanordnung: *hardware configuration*
Geräteanzeiger: *device flag*
Gerätebezeichnung: *device name*
Gerätefehler: *equipment failure*
Gerätekennung: *device code or device flag*
Geräteschnittstelle: *terminal interface*
Gerätesteuerprogramm: *peripheral software driver*
Gerätesteuerzeichen: *device control character*
Gerätetreiber: *device driver*
geräteunabhängig: *device independent*
Gerätezeichensteuerung: *device character control*
geräuschfreie Abstimmung: *interstation muting*
Geräuschkulisse: *sound effects*
gereihte Anschlussstifte: *inline*
gereinigt: *clean*
gerichtet: *directional*
gerichtete Suchmethode: *directed scan*
Germanium: *germanium*
Gesamtausfall: *blackout or black out*
Gesamtbackup: *global backup*
Gesamtindex: *dense index*
Gesamtlaufzeit: *up and down propagation time*
Gesamtsicherung: *global backup*

Gesamtverarbeitungszeit: *elapsed time*
Geschäft: *business; deal*
Geschäftsadresse: *business address*
Geschäftscomputer: *business computer*
geschäftsführender Direktor: *managing director*
Geschäftskorrespondenz: *business correspondence*
geschätzter Satzumfang: *cast off*
geschichtet: *layered*
Geschlechtsumwandler: *gender changer*
geschlossener Benutzerkreis: *closed user group (CUG)*
geschlossener Regelkreis: *closed loop*
geschlossener Übertragungsblock: *burst*
geschlossenes Bussystem: *closed bus system*
geschlossenes Programm: *closed routine*
geschützter Speicher: *protected storage*
geschützter Speicherplatz: *protected location*
geschütztes Feld: *protected field*
geschütztes Leerzeichen: *non-breaking space*
geschweifte Klammern: *curly brackets or braces*
Geschwindigkeit: *speed or velocity*
gesichert: *secured*
gespeichertes Programm: *stored program*
Gespräch mit namentlicher Voranmeldung: *person-to-person call*
gestrecktes Programm: *in-line program*
gestreut laden: *to scatter load*
gestreut lesen: *to scatter read*
gestrichenes Papier: *coated paper*
geteilte Anzeige: *split screen*
geteilte Baudrate: *split baud rate*
getrennt: *separate*
getrennte Kanalsignalisierung: *separate channel signalling*
getrenntes Schalten von Ton und Bild: *breezeway*
Geviert (in der Größe eines m): *em quad*
Gewähr: *warranty*
Gewebeband: *fibre ribbon*
gewertete Kurzdarstellung: *evaluative abstract*
Gewicht: *weight*
gewichtet: *weighted*
gewichteter Durchschnitt: *weighted average*
gewichtetes Bit: *weighted bit*
Gewichtung: *weighting*
gezackte Ränder: *jaggies*
Gieren: *yaw*
Gießmaschine: *caster machine*
GIF-Datei: *GIF file*

Gigabyte: *gigabyte*
Gigaflop: *gigaflop*
Gigahertz (GHz): *gigahertz (GHz)*
glänzend: *glossy*
Glasfaser: *optical fibre*
glatt beschnitten: *flush*
glätten: *to dither; to filter*
gleich: *equal(ly)*
gleichberechtigtes Netz: *democratic network*
gleichbleibender Schaltschritt: *monospacing*
gleichgewichteter Code: *constant ratio code*
Gleichheit: *equality or parity*
gleichkommen: *to equal*
Gleichlaufschwankung: *flutter; wow*
gleichmachen: *to equalize*
gleichrichten: *to rectify*
Gleichrichter: *rectifier*
gleichsetzen: *to equate*
Gleichstrom: *direct current (DC)*
Gleichstromsignal: *DC signalling*
Gleichstromumrichter: *inverter*
Gleichung: *equation*
gleichwertig sein: *to be equivalent to*
Gleichwertigkeit: *equivalence*
gleichzeitig (ablaufend): *concurrent(ly) or simultaneous(ly)*
Gleichzeitigkeit: *simultaneity*
gleiten: *to slide*
gleitende Arbeitszeit: *flexible working hours or flexitime*
gleitender Akzent: *floating accent or piece accent*
Gleitkommaprogramm: *floating-point routines*
Gleitpunktexponent: *characteristic*
Glied: *member*
Gliederung: *outline*
Gliederungsdiagramm: *outline flowchart*
global aufrufen: *to site poll*
globale Austauschfunktion: *global exchange*
globale Datensicherung *or* **globales Backup:** *global backup*
globale Kenntnis: *global knowledge*
globale Variable: *global variable*
globales Suchen und Ersetzen: *global search and replace*
Goldkontakte: *gold contacts*
Grad: *grade*
Grafik: *graphics*
Grafik mit hoher Auflösung: *high-resolution or high-res graphics (HRG)*
Grafik mit niedriger Auflösung: *low-resolution or low-res graphics (LRG)*

Grafikadapter: *graphics adapter*
Grafikbibliothek: *graphics library*
Grafikblock: *graphics pad*
Grafik-Coprozessor: *graphics coprocessor*
Grafikdatei: *graphics file*
Grafikdateiformat: *graphics file format*
Grafikdrucker: *graphics printer*
Grafikelement: *graphics primitive*
Grafikerbüro: *design studio*
Grafikkernsystem: *graphics kernel system (GKS)*
Grafikmodus: *graphics mode*
Grafikprozessor: *graphics processor*
Grafiksoftware: *graphics software*
Grafiktablett: *graphics tablet*
Grafikterminal für Fotosatz: *graphics art terminal*
Grafikterminal: *graphics terminal*
Grafik-VDU: *graphics VDU*
grafisch: *graphic or graphical(ly)*
grafisch darstellen: *to plot*
grafische Benutzeroberfläche: *graphical user interface (GUI)*
grafische Daten: *graphic data*
grafischer Bildschirm: *graphic display*
grafischer Lichtstift: *graphics light pen*
grafisches Auflösungsvermögen des Bildschirms: *graphic display resolution*
grafisches Zeichen: *graphics character*
Gramm: *gram or gramme*
Grammatik: *grammar*
Grammatikprüfung *or*
Grammatikprüfprogramm: *grammar checker*
Graph: *graph*
Graphikkernsystem: *graphics kernel system (gks)*
Grauschleier: *fog*
Grauskala: *grey scale*
Gravis: *grave accent*
Gray-Verschlüsselung: *Gray code*
greifen: *to grip or grab*
Grenzauflösung: *limiting resolution*
Grenzen: *boundary or bounds*
Grenzen der Strukturgröße: *array bounds*
Grenzenregister: *boundary register*
Grenzenschutz: *boundary protection*
Grenzfrequenz: *cutoff frequency*
Grenzmarkierung: *boundary punctuation*
grenzüberschreitender Datenfluss: *transborder data flow*
Grenzwerte: *limits*
grobe Berechnung: *rough calculation*
grober Schnitzer: *howler*
Großbuchstaben: *capitals or caps or upper case*

Größe: *size*
Größendarstellung mit Vorzeichen: *sign and magnitude or signed magnitude*
Großintegration: *large-scale integration (LSI)*
Großrechner: *large-scale or mainframe computer or supercomputer*
Großrechnerzugang: *mainframe access*
Großschreibung: *capitalization*
Großspeicher: *mass storage system*
größtes Bit: *most significant bit (MSB)*
Größtintegration: *super large scale integration (SLSI)*
Größtrechner: *supercomputer*
Großvaterdatei: *grandfather file*
Großvaterzyklus: *grandfather cycle*
Groupware: *groupware*
Grundadresse: *base address*
Grundbefehl: *basic instruction*
Grundcode: *basic code*
Grundfarben: *primary colours*
Grundfrequenz: *fundamental frequency*
grundlegend: *basic*
Grundlinie: *base line*
Grundplatine: *motherboard*
Grundposition: *base*
Grundriss: *floor plan*
Grundroutine: *primitive*
Grundsteuereinheit: *basic controller*
Grundstruktur: *framework*
Grundzustand: *stable state*
grüner Phosphor: *green phosphor*
Gruppe: *group*
Gruppenabruf: *group poll*
Gruppenaufruf: *group poll*
Gruppenmarke: *group mark or marker*
Gruppenschalter: *ganged switch*
Gruppensteuereinheit: *cluster controller*
Gruppensymbol: *group icon*
gruppieren: *to group*
gruppiert: *ganged*
Gruppierung: *clustering*
Gucki: *viewer*
gültig: *legal or valid*
gültige Speicheradresse: *valid memory address*
Gültigkeit: *validity*
Gültigkeitsprüfung: *validity check or validation*
Gummituchzylinder: *blanket cylinder*
gut funktionierend: *well-behaved*
gut gewartet: *well maintained*
Güteklasse: *grade*
gutheißen: *to approve of*
Gutmütigkeit: *robustness*

Hh

Haarlinie: *hairline rule*
Hacker: *hacker*
Halbaddierer: *half adder*
Halbbild: *field*
Halbbildabtastung: *field sweep*
Halbbildaustastung: *field blanking*
Halbduplex(übertragung): *half duplex*
Halbduplexmodem: *half-duplex modem*
halbe Intensität: *half-intensity*
halber Abstand: *half space*
halbfettes Drucken: *emboldening*
Halbgeviert (in der Größe eines n): *en
quad*
halbhohes Laufwerk: *half-height drive*
Halbkarte: *half card*
halbkompiliert: *semicompiled*
Halbleiter: *semiconductor*
Halbleiterbauelement: *semiconductor
device*
Halbleiterbauteil: *solid-state device*
Halbleiterlaser: *semiconductor laser*
Halbleiterscheibe: *wafer*
Halbleiterspeicher: *semiconductor memory*
Halbton-: *halftone*
halbverarbeitete Daten: *semi-processed
data*
Halbwort: *half word*
Hälfte: *half*
Halleffekt: *hall effect*
Halleffektschalter: *hall effect switch*
Hallraum: *echo chamber*
Halogenid: *halide*
Halt: *halt or stop*
Haltbedingung: *halt condition*
Haltbefehl: *halt instruction or stop
instruction*
Haltecode: *stop code*
Halteimpuls: *hold*
Haltelinie: *holding line*
Haltestrom: *hold current*
Haltezeit: *holding time*
Hammer: *howler*
Hammingabstand: *Hamming distance*
Hammingcode: *Hamming code*
Handbuch mit Anweisungen: *instruction
manual*
Handbuch: *manual*
Handcomputer: *hand-held programmable*
handgeschrieben: *handwritten*
Handle: *handle*

Händler: *dealer; vendor*
Handler: *handler*
händlerunabhängig: *vendor independent*
Handscanner: *hand-held scanner*
Handschrift: *handwriting*
Handschrifterkennung: *handwriting
recognition*
Handzettel: *leaflet or flier*
Hard Return: *hard return*
Hardware: *hardware*
hardwareabhängig: *hardware dependent*
Hardwarefehler: *hard(ware) failure*
hardwaregeeichte Software: *intimate*
Hardwarekompatibilität: *hardware
compatibility*
hardwarenah: *machine intimate*
Hardwareplattform: *hardware platform*
Hardwaresicherheit: *hardware security*
Hardwareteil: *external device*
Hardwareunterbrechung: *hardware
interrupt*
harmonische Oberschwingung: *harmonic*
harmonisches Telefonklingeln: *harmonic
telephone ringer*
harte Rückstellung: *hard reset*
Hartformatierung: *hard-sectoring*
Hartkopie: *hard copy*
Hartley: *hartley*
hartsektoriert: *hard-sectored*
Hashcode: *hash code*
Hash-Code-System: *hash-code system*
Hashfunktion: *hashing function*
Hashindex: *hash index*
Hashtabelle: *hash table*
Hashwert: *hash value*
Hashzeichen: *hashmark or hash mark*
Haube: *hood*
häufigster Wert: *mode*
Hauptattribut: *prime attribute*
Hauptband: *master tape*
Hauptbedienerstation: *master terminal*
Hauptbelastungszeit: *peak period*
Hauptbüro: *general office*
Hauptdaten: *master data*
Hauptdatenstation: *key terminal*
Haupteinrichtung: *key feature*
Haupteintrag: *main entry*
Hauptmenü: *main menu*
Hauptplatine: *motherboard*
Hauptplatte: *master disk*
Hauptprogramm: *main routine*
Hauptprogrammdatei: *master program file*
Hauptprogrammschleife: *main loop (of a
program)*
Hauptprogrammteil: *main body (of a
program)*
Hauptquartier: *base*

Hauptrechner: *host computer or master computer*
hauptsächlich: *primarily*
Hauptsendezeit: *prime time*
Hauptspeicher: *core or main or primary memory or storage or store*
Hauptspeicherabbild: *memory map*
Hauptstrahl: *main beam*
Haupttaktgeber: *main clock or master clock or timing master*
Hauptterminal: *central terminal*
Haupttextteil: *body*
Hauptübertragungsweg: *A-bus*
Hauptvermittlungskanal: *forward channel*
Hauptverteiler: *main distributing frame*
Hauptzyklus: *major cycle*
Hauskorrekturen: *house corrections*
Hausstil: *house style*
Haustelefon: *house (tele)phone or internal (tele)phone*
Hayes AT-Befehlssatz: *Hayes AT command set*
Hayes-kompatibel: *Hayes compatible*
HD-Videosystem: *HDVS*
Hebern: *siphoning*
heften: *to clip*
Heftrandversatz: *binding offset*
Heimcomputer: *home computer*
Hektographieren: *hectography or spirit duplication*
Holiogravüre: *photogravure*
hell: *bright; light*
Helligkeit: *brightness*
Helligkeitsbereich: *brightness range*
Helligkeitseinstellung: *brightness setting*
herausbringen: *to release*
herausfiltrieren: *to filter (out)*
Herausgreifen eines Bildes: *screen grab*
herauskommentieren: *to comment out*
herausnehmbare Winchesterplatte: *removable Winchester*
herausnehmen: *to extract or pull (out)*
Hercules-Grafikadapter (HGA): *Hercules graphics adapter (HGA)*
herstellen: *to manufacture or produce*
Hersteller: *manufacturer or producer*
herstellerspezifisches Dateiformat: *proprietary file format*
Herstellung: *production; origination*
Herstellung eines Prototyps: *prototyping*
Herstellung eines Schriftsatzes (aus Standardtexten): *boilerplating*
Hertz: *Hertz*
herunterfahren: *to power down or off*
hervorheben: *to highlight*
Hervorhebungen: *highlights*
hervorholen: *to pop on*

Hervorholmenü: *pop-down or pop-up menu*
herzförmige Empfangscharakteristik: *cardioid response*
heterogene Multiplexmethode: *heterogeneous multiplexing*
heterogenes Netz: *heterogeneous network*
heuristisch: *heuristic*
hexadezimale Darstellung: *hex dump*
hexadezimale Schreibweise: *hex(adecimal) notation*
hexadezimale Tastatur: *hex (key)pad*
hexadezimales Zahlensystem: *base 16*
HF-Abschirmung: *RF shielding*
Hidden-Line-Algorithmus: *hidden line algorithm*
Hierarchie: *hierarchy*
hierarchische Datenbank: *hierarchical database*
hierarchische Einteilung: *hierarchical classification*
hierarchisches Computernetz: *hierarchical computer network*
hierarchisches Kommunikationssystem: *hierarchical communications system*
hierarchisches Verzeichnis: *hierarchical directory*
Hi-Fi(-Anlage): *hi fi (system)*
High-End: *high-end*
Highfidelity: *high fidelity or hifi or hi fi*
High-Sierra-Spezifikation: *high Sierra specification*
Hilfe: *help or aid or assistance*
Hilfebildschirm: *help screen*
HILFE-Funktion: *help*
Hilfeseite: *help screen*
Hilfetaste: *help key*
Hilfsbit: *service bit*
Hilfsgeräte: *auxiliary equipment*
Hilfskanal: *backward channel*
Hilfsprogramm: *applet*
Hilfsprogramm zur Defragmentierung: *defragmentation utility*
Hilfsprogramme: *tools*
Hilfsprozessor: *auxiliary processor*
Hilfsspeicher: *auxiliary or backing memory or storage or store*
Hilfszugriffsspeicher: *intermediate access memory (IAM)*
Hin- und Rücklauf: *sweep*
hineinstecken: *to insert or slot*
Hintergrund: *background*
Hintergrundbeleuchtung: *backlight*
Hintergrundbild: *wallpaper or background image*
Hintergrundfarbe: *background colour*
Hintergrundgeräusch: *ambient noise level*
Hintergrundjob: *background job*

Hintergrundkommentar: *voice-over*
Hintergrundprogramm: *background program*
Hintergrundprogrammbetrieb: *background*
Hintergrundprojektion: *background projection or back projection*
Hintergrundprozess: *background operation*
Hintergrundspiegelung: *background reflectance*
Hintergrundtask *background task*
Hintergrundübertragung: *background communication*
Hintergrundverarbeitung: *background*
hinterleuchtete Anzeige: *backlit display*
hinübertragen: *to carry*
hinunterfallen: *to drop*
hinunterladbar: *downloadable*
hinunterladen: *to download*
Hinweisadresse: *pointer*
hinweisen: *to point out*
Hinweisschildchen: *label*
Hinweisspur: *library track*
hinzufügen: *to add*
Histogramm: *histogram*
HMA-Bereich: *high memory area (HMA)*
Hochdruckverfahren: *relief printing*
hochempfindlich: *fast*
hochentwickelt: *sophisticated*
Hochfrequenz: *high frequency (HF)*
Hochfrequenzmodulator: *RF modulator or radio frequency modulator*
Hochgeschwindigkeits-analog-digital-Umsetzer: *flash A/D*
Hochgeschwindigkeitskopierer: *high-speed duplicator*
hochgestelltes Zeichen: *superscript*
Hochladen: *uploading*
hochladen: *to upload*
Hochleistung: *high performance*
Hochleistungsausrüstung: *high performance equipment*
Hochpassfilter: *high pass filter*
Hochrechnung: *extrapolation*
hochspezifiziert: *high-spec*
höchste Nutzfrequenz: *maximum usable frequency*
höchste Übertragungsgeschwindigkeit: *maximum transmission rate*
Höchstleistung: *peak output*
Höchstleistungsgrenze: *maximum capacity*
höchstmögliche Benutzerzahl: *maximum users*
höchstpassend: *best fit*
Hochtonlautsprecher: *tweeter*
Hochzahl: *superior number*

hochzählen: *to increment*
hohe Auflösung: *high resolution or hi-res*
hohe Spezifikation: *high specification or high spec*
hoher Entwicklungsstand: *sophistication*
hoher Qualitätsmaßstab: *high specification or high spec*
hoher Speicher: *high memory*
hoher Speicherbereich: *high memory area (HMA)*
höhere Programmiersprache: *high-level (programming) language (HLL)*
Hohlleiter: *waveguide*
Holanweisung: *get*
Hollerith-Code: *Hollerith code*
Hologramm: *hologram or holographic image*
Holographie: *holography*
holographische Speicherung: *holographic storage*
Holographum: *holograph*
Holzschliffpapier: *mechanical paper*
Homebanking: *home banking or telebanking*
homogene Multiplexmethode: *homogeneous multiplexing*
homogenes Computernetz: *homogeneous computer network*
Hook: *hook*
Hör-/Lesekopf: *playback head*
hörbar: *audible*
horizontale Bildlaufleiste *horizontal scrollbar*
horizontaler Rollbalken: *horizontal scrollbar*
horizontales Blättern or Rollen or Scrollen: *horizontal scrolling*
Horizontalfrequenz: *line frequency*
Horizontalprüfung: *horizontal check*
Horizontalsynchronisationsimpuls: *horizontal synchronization pulse*
Hörkopf *playback head*
Hornstrahler: *horn*
Hörschärfe: *acuity*
Host-Netzwerk: *back-end network*
Hot-Fix: *hot fix*
Hotkey: *hot key*
Hotspot: *hotspot*
Hot-Standby-System: *hot standby*
Hub: *hub*
huckepack verbinden: *to piggyback*
Huckepackübertragung: *piggybacking*
Huckepackzugang: *piggyback entry*
Huffman-Code: *huffman code*
Hugemodell: *huge model*
Hülle: *hood; jacket*
Hüllkurve: *pitch envelope*
Hurenkind: *widow*
Hybridanlage: *hybrid system*

Hybridrechner: *hybrid computer*
Hybridschaltung: *hybrid circuit*
Hybridschnittstelle: *hybrid interface*
Hybridstation: *combined station*
Hypertext: *hypertext*
Hypertextdokument: *hypermedia*
Hypo: *hypo*

Ii

I/O-Adresse: *I/O address*
IBM AT-Tastatur: *IBM AT keyboard*
IBM-kompatibel: *IBM compatible*
IBM-PC-Tastatur: *IBM PC keyboard*
Idealformat: *ideal format*
Identifikation: *identification*
Identifikationszeichen: *identification character*
identifizieren: *to identify*
Identifizierungscode: *ID code*
Identifizierungskennzeichen: *tag*
identisch: *identical*
Identität: *identity*
Identitätsblock: *identity burst*
Identitätsfunktion: *identity operation*
Identitätsgatter: *identity gate or element*
Identitätsvergleich: *logical comparison*
IEC-Bus: *general purpose interface bus (GPIB)*
IEC-Stecker: *IEC connector*
IEEE-Bus: *IEEE bus*
IF-Anweisung: *IF statement*
IF-THEN-ELSE-Anweisung: *IF-THEN-ELSE*
ikonisches Zeichen: *icon or ikon*
illegal: *illegal(ly)*
Illustration: *illustration*
illustrieren: *to illustrate*
Imagemaster: *image master*
Image-Prozessor: *image processor*
Imbandsignalisierung: *in-band signalling*
Immobilienmakler: *property developer*
Impedanz: *impedance*
Impedanzwandler: *balun*
Impfprogramm: *vaccine*
implantieren: *to implant*
implementieren: *to implement*
Implementierung: *implementation*
Implikation: *implication*
importieren: *to import*
importiertes Signal: *imported signal*

Impressum: *imprint*
Impuls: *impulse; strobe*
Impulsamplitudenmodulation: *pulse amplitude modulation (PAM)*
Impulsbreitenmodulation: *pulse width modulation (PWM)*
Impulsdauermodulation: *pulse duration modulation (PDM)*
impulsiv: *impulsive*
Impulsmodulation: *pulse modulation*
Impulsreflektometrie: *time domain reflectometry (TDR)*
Impulsstörung: *impulsive noise*
Impulsstrom: *pulse stream*
Impulswahl *or* **Impulswählverfahren:** *pulse-dialling*
inaktives Fenster: *inactive window*
Inäquivalenzfunktion: *inequivalence or NEQ function*
Inäquivalenzgatter: *NEQ gate*
Inches pro Sekunde: *inches-per-second (ips)*
Index: *index*
Indexbuchstabe: *index letter*
Indexerstellung: *index build*
Indexkarte: *flash card*
Indexloch: *index hole*
Indexregister: *index register*
Indexschlüssel: *index key*
Indexseite: *index page*
indexsequenzielle Zugriffsmethode: *indexed sequential access method (ISAM)*
Indexwert: *index value*
Indexzahl: *index number*
indirekte Adressierung: *indirect or second-level addressing*
indirekter Strahl: *indirect ray*
individuell anfertigen *or* **anpassen:** *to customize or personalize*
individuell: *individual*
Individuum: *individual*
Indizes: *inferior figures*
Indizieren: *indexing*
indizieren: *to index*
Indiziersprache: *indexing language*
indizierte Adresse: *indexed address*
indizierte Adressierung: *indexed addressing*
indizierte Datei: *indexed file*
indizierte Variable: *subscripted variable*
indizierter Befehl: *indexed instruction*
Induktion: *induction*
Induktionsspule: *induction coil*
Induktivität: *inductance*
Industriedesign: *industrial design*
induzieren: *to induce*
induzierte Störung: *induced interference*

induzierter Ausfall *or* **induziertes Versagen:** *induced failure*
inert: *inert*
Inferenz: *inference*
Inferenzkontrolle: *inference control*
Infixschreibweise: *infix notation*
infizierter Computer: *infected computer*
Informatik: *informatics or computer science*
Information: *information*
Informationsanbieter: *information provider (IP)*
Informationsanfangsmarke: *beginning of information mark (bim)*
Informationsausgabe: *information output*
Informationsbüro: *information bureau*
Informationseingabe: *information input*
Informationsfreiheit: *freedom of information*
Informationsgehalt: *information content*
Informationsnetz: *information network*
Informationsschutz: *privacy of information*
Informationsspeicherung und -wiederauffindung: *information storage and retrieval (ISR)*
Informationssystem: *information system*
Informationstechnik: *information technology (IT)*
Informationstheorie: *information theory*
Informationsträgerkanal: *information bearer channel*
informationsverarbeitende Maschine: *information processor*
Informationsverarbeitung: *information processing*
Informationsverwaltungssystem: *information management system*
Informationswiedergewinnung: *information retrieval (IR)*
Informationszeile: *information line*
infrarot: *infrared*
Infrarotdetektor: *infrared detector*
Infrarotfotografie: *infrared photography*
Infrarotlicht (IR-Licht): *infrared light (IR light)*
Infrarotnachrichtenübermittlung: *infrared communications*
Infrarotsichtgeräte: *infrared sights*
Infraschallfrequenz: *infrasonic frequency*
Infrastruktur: *infrastructure*
Ingenieur in der Versuchsabteilung: *trials engineer*
Inhalt: *contents*
Inhaltsverzeichnis: *table of contents*
Initiale: *initial*
initialisieren: *to initialize*
Initialisierung: *initialization*
Injektionslaser: *injection laser*

Inklusion: *inclusion*
inklusiv: *inclusive*
Inkrement: *increment*
Inkrementalrechner: *incremental computer*
Inkrementdaten: *incremental data*
inkrementieren: *to increment*
Inlandskonsum: *domestic consumption*
Innenkennung: *interior label*
Innenschleife: *inner loop*
innerbetrieblich: *in-house*
innerbetriebliches Transport- und Lagerwesen: *materials handling*
Input-/Output-Anweisung: *input/output instruction*
In-Scheiben-Schneiden: *slicing*
instabiler Multivibrator: *astable multivibrator*
Installationsfläche: *footprint*
Installationshandbuch: *installation manual*
Installationsprogramm: *install program*
installierbarer Gerätetreiber *or* **Einheitentreiber:** *installable device driver*
installieren: *to install*
instandhalten: *to service*
Instandhaltung: *maintenance or upkeep*
Instruktionszeiger: *instruction pointer*
Instrumentierung: *instrumentation*
Integer-BASIC: *integer BASIC*
Integration: *integration*
Integrationstechnikplättchen: *wafer scale integration*
integrierte Datenbank: *integrated database*
integrierte Datenverarbeitung: *integrated data processing (IDP)*
integrierte Schaltkreise für bestimmte Funktionen: *applications specific integrated circuits (ASIC)*
integrierte Software: *integrated software*
integrierter Digitalzugriff: *integrated digital access (IDA)*
integrierter Emulator: *integrated emulator*
integrierter optischer Schaltkreis: *integrated optical circuit*
integrierter Schaltkreis (IC): *integrated circuit (IC)*
integriertes Bauelement: *integrated device*
integriertes Dialogtestsystem: *interactive debugging system*
integriertes Digitalnetz: *integrated digital network*
integriertes Sprach- und Datennetz (ISDN): *integrated services digital network (ISDN)*
Integrität: *integrity*
intelligente Datenstation: *intelligent terminal or smart terminal*

intelligenter Schaltknoten: *intelligent or smart wiring hub*
intelligentes Gerät: *intelligent device*
intelligentes Lernsystem: *intelligent tutoring system*
intelligentes Terminal: *intelligent terminal*
intelligentes Trennprogramm: *intelligent spacer*
intelligentes, wissensbasiertes System: *intelligent knowledge-based system (IKBS)*
Intelligenz: *intelligence*
Intensität: *intensity*
Intensivanzeige: *display highlights*
intensiver Lichtfleck: *hot spot*
Interaktion: *interaction*
interaktive Medien: *interactive media*
interaktive Tastatur: *interactive keyboard*
interaktives Multimedia: *interactive multimedia*
interaktives System: *interactive system*
interaktives Videosystem: *interactive video*
Interferenzbild: *interference pattern*
Interferenzschwund: *interference fading*
Interleavefaktor: *interleave factor*
intern gespeichertes Programm: *internally stored program*
internationale Durchwahl: *international direct dialling (IDD)*
internationale Maßeinheiten: *SI units*
internationale Normenorganisation: *International Standards Organization (ISO)*
internationale Nummer: *international number*
Internationale Vorwahl: *international dialling code*
internationale Zugangskennzahl: *international prefix code*
internationaler Fernmeldesatellit: *INTELSAT*
interne Festplatte: *internal hard disk*
interne Schriftart: *internal font*
interne Sortierung: *internal sort*
interne Sprache: *internal language*
interner Befehl: *internal command*
interner Rechenvorgang: *internal arithmetic*
interner Speicher: *internal memory or store*
interner Zeichencode: *internal character code*
internes Format: *internal format*
internes Modem: *internal modem*
Internetprotokoll (IP): *internet protocol (IP)*
Internetprotokolladresse (IP-Adresse): *internet protocol address (IP Address)*
Interpolierung: *interpolation*
Interpretiercode: *interpretative code*

Interpretierer: *interpreter*
Interpretierprogramm: *interpretative program*
Interrupt-Prioritätstabelle: *priority interrupt table*
Inverter: *inverter*
invertierte Darstellung: *reverse video*
invertierte Datei: *inverted file*
invertierte Zeichen: *cameo; reverse characters*
invertiertes Videobild: *inverse video*
Ion: *ion*
Ionosphäre: *ionosphere*
IP-Adresse: *IP Address*
IP-Datagramm: *IP Datagram*
irreversibler Prozess: *irreversible process*
ISO/OSI-Modell: *ISO/OSI model*
Isolation: *isolation*
Isolationseinrichtung für Kanäle: *channel isolation*
Isolator: *isolator; insulator*
isolieren: *to insulate; to isolate*
Isolierkabel: *shielded cable*
Isoliermaterial: *insulation material; insulator*
Isoliersteg: *barrier box*
isolierte adaptive Verkehrslenkung: *isolated adaptive routing*
isotrop: *isotropic*
Iteration: *iteration*
Iterationsschleife: *iterate or iterative routine*
iterative Operation: *iterative process*

Jj

Jabber-Signal: *jabber*
Jaulen: *flutter; wow*
Jingle: *jingle*
JK-Flipflop: *JK-flip-flop*
Job: *job*
Jobanweisungssteuerung: *job statement control*
Jobbetriebssprache: *job control language (JCL)*
Jobdatei: *job file*
Jobende: *end of job (EOJ)*
Jobferneingabe: *remote job entry (RJE)*
Jobfolge: *job stream*
Jobkontrolldatei: *job control file*
Jobkontrollsprache: *JCL*
Jobmischung: *job mix*
Jobnummer: *job number*

Joborganisation: *job scheduling*
Jobpriorität: *job priority*
Jobschritt: *job step*
Jobsteuerprogramm: *job control program*
Jobsteuerungssprache: *control language*
Jobverarbeitung: *job processing*
Jobvorrangigkeit: *job priority*
Jobwarteschlange: *job queue*
Jokerzeichen: *wildcard character*
Journalist/-in: *journalist*
Joystick: *joystick*
Joystickanschlussstelle: *joystick port*
Jumbochip: *jumbo chip*
Justieren des Richtungswinkels: *azimuth alignment*
justieren: *to adjust*
Justierschiene: *aligner*
Justiervorrichtung: *gate*

Kk

Kabel: *cable or cabling; cord; lead*
Kabeladapter: *cable matcher*
Kabelanlage: *cable plant*
Kabelfernsehen: *cable television or cable TV*
Kabelkanal: *duct*
Kabelmessgerät: *cable tester*
Kabelprüfgerät: *cable tester*
Kabelrohr: *conduit*
Kabelstecker: *cable connector*
Kabeltreiber: *line driver*
Kabine: *booth*
Kalkulation: *calculation*
Kalkulationstabellendruck: *spreadsheet*
kalkulieren: *to calculate*
Kalligraphie: *calligraphy*
Kaltfehler: *cold fault*
Kaltstart: *cold boot or cold start*
Kameraaggregat: *camera chain*
Kamerateam: *camera crew*
Kampf um die Einschaltquote: *ratings battle or war*
Kanal: *channel*
Kanalanschluss: *channel adapter*
Kanalbank: *channel bank*
Kanalbefehl: *channel command*
Kanalgruppe: *channel group*
Kanalisierung: *channelling*
Kanalkapazität: *channel capacity*
Kanalsynchronisierer: *channel synchronizer*

Kanalüberlastung: *channel overload*
Kanalwarteschlange: *channel queue*
Kanalzugriffssteuerung: *access channel control*
Kanal-zu-Kanal-Verbindung: *channel-to-channel connection*
kanonisches Schema: *canonical schema*
Kante: *edge*
Kanzleipapier: *foolscap*
Kapazität: *capacitance or capacity*
Kapazitätsausweitung: *expansion*
Kapazitätsüberschreitung: *overflow*
kapazitiv: *capacitive*
Kapitälchen: *small caps*
Kapitel: *chapter*
Kapitelende: *chapter stop*
Kapitelüberschrift: *chapter heading*
kappen: *to clip*
Kapselung: *encapsulation*
Karbonband: *carbon ribbon*
Kardinalzahl: *cardinal number*
Karnaugh-Diagramm: *Karnaugh map*
Karte: *card*
Kartei: *card-index (file)*
Karteikarte: *filing card or index card*
Kartenchassis: *card frame or card chassis*
Kartenformat: *card format*
Kartenhäuschen: *ticket booth*
Kartenlader: *card loader*
Kartenlocher: *card punch (CP)*
Kartenmagazin: *hopper*
Kartenmischer: *collator*
Kartenrandverbindung: *card edge connector*
Kartentelefon: *card phone*
Kartenzeile: *card row*
Kartenzuführung: *card feed*
kartesische Koordinaten: *cartesian coordinates*
kartesische Struktur: *cartesian structure*
Karton: *card; cardboard*
Kaskadensteuerung: *cascade control*
Kaskadenübertrag: *cascade carry*
Kaskadenverbindung: *cascade connection*
Kasse: *point-of-sale (POS)*
Kassette: *cartridge or cassette*
Kassettenband: *cassette tape*
Kassettenfarbband: *cartridge ribbon*
Kassettenrekorder: *cassette recorder*
Kasten: *box*
kastenförmiger Aktenordner: *box file*
Katalog: *catalogue*
Katalogdatei: *card-index file*
katalogisieren: *to card-index or to catalogue*
Katalogisierer: *cataloguer*
Katalogisierung: *card-indexing or cataloguing*

Katastrophe: *catastrophe*
Kathode: *cathode*
Kathodenstrahlröhre: *cathode ray tube*
(CRT)
Kegelbreite: *set width*
keine Parität: *no parity*
Keller: *cellar*
Kellerspeicher: *stack*
Kennbit: *dirty bit*
Kennkarte: *personal identification device*
(PID)
Kennnummer: *identity number*
Kennsatz: *label record*
Kennung: *label*
Kennungsfeld: *label field*
Kennwort: *identifier word or keyword*
Kennzeichen: *identifier*
Kennzeichenregister: *flag register*
kennzeichnen: *to mark*
Keramikkondensatoren: *ceramic capacitors*
keramisch: *ceramic*
Kerblochkarte: *edge notched card*
Kermit: *Kermit*
Kern: *core*
Kerning: *kerning*
Kernprogramm: *core program*
Kernroutine: *kernel*
Kernspeicher: *core memory or primary memory*
Kernspintomographie: *magnetic resonance imaging*
Kette: *catena; chain; chaining*
ketten: *to append*
Kettenbefehl: *chain*
Kettencode: *chain code*
Kettendrucker: *chain printer*
Kettenliefermethode: *chain delivery mechanism*
Kilobaud: *kilobaud*
Kilobit: *kilobit or Kb*
Kilobyte: *kilobyte or KB or Kbyte*
Kilohertz (KHz): *kilohertz (KHz)*
Kiloohm: *kilo-ohm*
Kilowatt: *kilowatt or kW*
Kilowort: *kiloword or KW*
Kimball-Etikett: *kimball tag*
Kino: *cinema*
kippbar und schwenkbar: *tilt and swivel*
kippen: *to toggle*
Kippschalter: *toggle switch*
Kiste: *(packing) case*
Klammer: *bracket*
Klang: *sound*
Klangdatei: *audio file*
Klangdigitalisierung: *sound capture*
Klangeffekte: *sound effects*

Klangtreue: *fidelity*
Klangvolumen: *volume*
Klarheit: *clarity*
klarmachen: *to convey*
Klartext: *plaintext*
Klasse: *class*
Klassenintervall: *class interval*
klassifizieren: *to classify*
Klassifizierung: *classification*
Klatsch: *key plate*
Klebeband: *splicing tape*
Klebebindung: *perfect binding*
Klebebindung: mit Ð: *perfect bound*
Klebeeinrichtung: *splicing block*
Kleinbuchstaben: *lower case*
Kleinintegration: *small scale integration (SSI)*
Kleinstbaum: *minimal tree*
klemmen: *to clamp*
Klemmleiste: *terminal strip*
Klicken: *click*
Klingelzeichen: *bell character*
Klirrverzerrung: *harmonic distortion*
Klon: *clone*
knacken: *to break*
Knopf: *knob*
Koaxialkabel: *co-axial cable*
Kobold: *sprite*
kodierter Exponent: *biased exponent*
Koerzitivkraft: *coercivity*
Koffer: *suitcase*
Koffercomputer: *luggable*
Kofferradio: *hand receiver*
kohärent: *coherent*
kohärentes Bündel: *coherent bundle*
kohärentes Licht: *coherent light*
Kohlemikrofon: *carbon microphone*
Kohlepapier: *carbon (paper)*
Koinzidenzgatter: *coincidence gate*
Koinzidenzschaltung: *coincidence circuit or element*
Kollationierungsfolge: *collating sequence*
Kollege: *associate*
Kolumne: *column*
Kolumnenzentimeter: *column-centimetre*
Koma: *coma*
Kombination: *combination*
Kombinationsbildschirm: *composite display*
Kombinatorik: *combinational logic*
kombinierte Abfrage: *relational query*
kombinierter Lese-/Schreibkopf: *combined head*
kombinierter Schaltkreis: *composite circuit*
Komma: *comma*
Kommandoschnittstelle: *command interface*

Kommandosprache: *command language*
Kommandozeile: *command line*
Kommentar: *comment(ary); remark*
Kommentarfeld: *comment field*
Kommunikation offener Systeme (OSI):
Open System Interconnection (OSI)
kommunizieren: *to communicate*
Kompaktcode: *compact code*
Kompaktkassette: *compact cassette*
Kompaktmodell: *compact model*
Kompandierer: *compandor*
Kompandierung: *companding*
kompatibel: *compatible*
Kompatibilität: *compatibility*
Kompatibilitätsfenster: *compatibility box*
kompilieren: *to compile*
kompilieren und verarbeiten: *to compile and go*
Kompilierer: *compiler (program); language processor*
Kompiliererdiagnostik: *compiler diagnostics*
Kompilierersprache: *compiler language*
Kompilierfehler: *compilation error*
Kompilierphase: *compile phase*
Kompilierung: *compilation*
Kompilierzeit: *compilation time*
Komplement: *complement*
komplementär: *complementary*
Komplementärfarben: *complementary colours*
Komplementbildung: *complementation*
komplementieren: *to complement*
komplementiert: *complemented*
komplett ausgestattet: *fully-populated*
komplett bestückte Platine: *fully populated board*
komplex: *complex*
komplexe Datenbank: *plex database*
komplexe Netzwerkstruktur: *plex structure*
Komplexität: *complexity*
Komplexitätsmaß: *complexity measure*
kompliziert: *complicated*
Komponente: *component*
Komponentendichte: *component density*
Komponentenfehler: *component error*
kompress: *solid*
Kompression: *crushing*
komprimieren: *to compact or compress or concentrate*
Komprimierung: *compression*
Komprimierungsalgorithmus: *compacting algorithm*
Kondensator: *capacitor*
Kondensatormikrofon: *capacitor microphone*
Kondensatorspeicher: *capacitor storage*

Konferenz: *conference*
Konferenzraum: *conference room*
Konferenzschaltung: *conference call*
Konferenztelefon: *conference telephone*
Konfiguration: *configuration*
Konfigurationszustand: *configuration state*
konfigurieren: *to configure or set up*
konkave Linse: *concave lens*
Konkurrenzbetrieb: *contention*
Konkurrenzbus: *contention bus*
Konsistenzprüfung: *consistency check*
Konsole: *console; paddle; panel*
konstant: *constant*
Konstante: *constant*
Konstantstromversorgung: *regulated power supply*
Kontakt: *contact*
Kontaktdruck: *contact printing*
Kontaktstift: *pin*
Kontaktstreifen: *contact negative*
Kontern: *lateral reversal*
Kontext: *context*
kontextsensitive Hilfe: *context-sensitive help*
kontinuierliche Schwingung: *continuous wave*
kontinuierlicher Datenstrom: *continuous data stream*
Kontinuität: *continuity*
Kontrast: *contrast*
kontrastarm: *flat*
Kontrasteinstellung: *contrast (setting)*
Kontrastgrad: *gamma*
kontrastieren: *to contrast*
kontrastierend: *contrasting*
Kontrastverhältnis: *print contrast ratio*
Kontrastverstärkungsfilter: *contrast enhancement filter*
Kontrolle: *control*
Kontrollfeld: *control field*
kontrollgesteuert: *control driven*
Kontrollgruppe: *control group*
kontrollierbar: *controllable*
kontrollierter Leistungsrückgang: *graceful degradation*
Kontroll-Lautsprecher: *monitor unit*
Kontrollleuchte: *activity light*
Kontrollrechner: *control computer*
Kontrollschirm: *monitor unit*
Kontrollsprache: *control language*
Kontrollsumme: *checksum or check total; control total; hash total*
Kontrollsysteme: *control systems*
Konturenglättung: *anti-aliasing*
Konturplatte: *key plate*
Konus: *cone*
Konvention: *convention*

konventioneller Speicher: *conventional memory*
Konverter: *converter or convertor*
konvertierbar: *convertible*
Konvertierbarkeit: *convertibility*
konvertieren: *to convert*
Konvertierungsausdruck: *cast*
Konvertierungsprogramm: *conversion program*
konvexe Linse: *convex lens*
Konzentrator: *concentrator*
konzentrieren: *to concentrate*
konzeptionelles Modell: *conceptual model*
kooperative Verarbeitung: *cooperative processing*
Koordinaten: *coordinates*
Koordinatenbild: *coordinate graph*
Koordinatennetz: *grid*
Koordinatenschreiber: *X-Y plotter*
koordinieren: *to coordinate*
Koordinierung: *coordination*
Kopf: *head*
Kopfausrichtung: *head alignment*
Kopfentmagnetisierer: *head demagnetizer*
Kopfhörer: *headset or headphones*
Kopfparken: *head park*
Kopfpositionierung: *head positioning*
Kopfrad: *head wheel*
Kopfreinigungsdiskette: *head cleaning disk*
Kopfstelle: *head end*
Kopfumsetzer: *set-top converter*
Kopfzeile: *header*
Kopie: *copy*
Kopieren: *duplicating*
kopieren: *to copy or duplicate*
Kopierer: *duplicating machine*
Kopiergenehmigung: *authorization to copy (ATC)*
Kopiergerät: *copier or copying machine or duplicating machine*
Kopierpapier: *duplicating paper*
Kopierschutz: *copy protect(ion)*
koppeln: *to couple*
Koppler: *coupler*
Korn: *grain*
Körnung: *granularity*
Korona: *corona*
Koronadraht: *corona wire*
Korrektor: *proofreader*
Korrektur lesen: *to proofread*
Korrektur: *correction; patch*
Korrekturabzug: *proof*
Korrekturbogen mit Pressrevision: *master proof*
Korrekturfahne: *galley proof or slip*
Korrekturleser/-in: *copy reader or proofreader*

Korrekturzeichen: *proof correction marks*
Korrelationsdiagramm: *scatter graph*
Korrespondent/-in: *correspondent*
Korrespondenz: *correspondence*
Korrespondenzfähigkeit: *correspondence print quality*
korrigieren: *to correct*
korrigiertes Programm: *debugged program*
Kosten über dem Strich: *above-the-line costs*
Kosten unter dem Strich: *below-the-line costs*
Kostenanalyse: *cost analysis*
Kraft: *force*
Kratzer: *scratch*
Kredit: *credit*
Kreditkarte: *charge card or credit card*
Kreisbozug: *circular reference*
Kreisblattschreiber: *chart recorder*
Kreisdiagramm: *pie chart*
kreisen: *to circulate*
kreisförmig: *circular*
Kreislaufregister: *circulating register*
Kreisliste: *circular list*
Kreisumlaufbahn: *circular orbit*
Kreisverkehrdokument: *turnaround document*
Kreuz: *dagger*
Kreuzassemblierer: *cross-assembler*
Kreuzkompilierer: *cross-compiler*
Kristall: *crystal*
Kriterium: *criterion*
kritische Betriebsmittel: *critical resource*
kritische Fusionsfrequenz: *critical fusion frequency*
kritischer Fehler: *critical error*
Kryptoanalyse: *cryptanalysis*
Kryptographie: *cryptography*
kryptographisch: *cryptographic*
Kryptosystem RSA: *RSA cipher system*
Kugelantenne: *isotropic radiator*
Kugelkopf: *golf-ball*
Kugelkopfdrucker: *golf-ball printer*
Kühlkörper: *heat sink*
kumulative Übertragungsgeschwindigkeit: *aggregate line speed*
Kumulativindex: *cumulative index*
Kunde/Kundin: *customer*
Kundendienst(abteilung): *customer service (department)*
kundenspezifisch: *custom-built*
kundenspezifischer ROM: *custom ROM*
künstlich: *artificial or man-made*
künstliche Intelligenz: *artificial intelligence (AI) or machine intelligence*
Kunststoffe: *synthetic materials*

Kupfer: *copper*
Kupferdruck: *copperplate printing*
kursiv: *italic*
Kursivschrift: *italics*
Kurvenschreiber *or* **Kurvenzeichner:** *graph plotter*
Kurzadresse: *abbreviated address*
Kurzadressierung: *abbreviated addressing or abb. add.*
Kurzdarstellung: *abstract*
kürzen: *to cut or shorten*
kurzgeschlossen: *short-circuited*
Kurzlochkarte: *short card*
kurzschließen: *to short circuit*
Kurzschluss: *short circuit*
Kürzung: *cut*
Kurzunterbrechung: *check*
Kurzwelle: *short wave (SW)*
Kurzwellenempfänger: *short-wave receiver*
kurzzeitiger Fehler: *transient error*
KWAC-Index: *keyword and context (KWAC)*
KWIC-Index: *keyword in context (KWIC)*
KWOC-Index: *keyword out of context (KWOC)*
Kybernetik: *cybernetics*

LI

Labor: *laboratory*
Laborplatine: *breadboard*
Labortechniker/-in: *laboratory technician*
Laden und Ausführen: *load and run or load and go*
Laden: *loading or boot up or booting*
laden: *to load or boot (up)*
Ladeprogramm: *loader*
Ladeprogramm für absolute Programme: *absolute loader*
Ladepunkt: *load point*
Ladung: *charge*
ladungsgekoppelter Elektronikbaustein: *charge-coupled device (CCD)*
ladungsgekoppelter Speicher: *charge coupled device (CCD) memory*
lancieren: *to launch*
Lancierung: *launch*
Länderdatei: *country file*
Landezone: *landing zone*
Landleitung: *landline*
Länge: *length*
Länge des Dateinamens: *length of filename*
lange Ganzzahl: *long integer*
Längen- und Seitenverhältnis: *aspect ratio*

langleuchtender Phosphor: *long persistence phosphor*
langsames Peripheriegerät: *slow peripheral*
LAN-Rückkanal: *backward LAN channel*
LAN-Segment: *LAN segment*
LAN-Server: *LAN server*
Laptop(computer): *lapheld (computer) or laptop (computer)*
Largemodell: *large model*
Lärmschutzhaube: *sound hood*
Laser: *laser*
Laserbildplatte: *laser disk*
Laserdrucker: *laser printer*
Laserspeicher: *photodigital memory*
Laserstrahlaufzeichnung: *laser beam recording (LBR)*
Laserstrahlkommunikation: *laser beam communications*
latentes Bild: *latent image*
Laufwerk: *drive*
Laufwerksbuchstabe: *drive letter or designator*
Laufwerksschacht: *bay or drive bay*
Laufzeit: *run-time or run-duration*
Laufzeitentzerrer: *delay equalizer*
Laufzeitfehler: *run-time error*
Laufzeitspeicher: *delay line store*
Laufzeitsystem: *run-time system*
Laufzeitverzerrung: *delay distortion*
Lautsprecher: *loudspeaker*
Lautsprecheranlage: *public address system (PA)*
Lautstärke: *loudness or volume*
Lautstärkeregler: *volume control*
Lautstärkeumfang: *dynamic range*
lautverstärktes Telefon: *amplified telephone*
Lawine: *avalanche*
Lawinendiode: *avalanche photodiode (APD)*
Lay-out: *area composition*
Layoutkontrolle: *previewer*
LCD-Anzeige: *LCD*
LCD-Drucker: *LCD or crystal shutter printer*
LC-Oszillator: *LC circuit*
Leasingvertrag: *lease*
lebender Kolumnentitel: *running head*
Lebensdauer bei Belastung: *load life*
Lebensdauer einer Software: *software life cycle*
Lebensdauer eines Kopfes: *headlife*
Lebensdauer eines Systems: *system life cycle*
Lebensdauer: *lifetime*
Leck: *leak or leakage*
LED-Drucker: *LED printer*
leer: *empty or blank*
Leerbefehl: *do-nothing (instruction)*

leere Anweisung: *blank or null or dummy or waste instruction*
leere Platte: *blank disk*
leere Zeichenfolge: *blank string*
leerer Bereich: *empty or null or void set*
leeres Band: *blank tape*
Leerimpuls: *blanking pulse*
Leerlaufzeit: *idle time*
Leerliste: *empty or null list*
Leerschritt: *space*
Leerspule: *pick-up reel*
Leerstring: *empty or null string*
Leertaste: *space bar*
Leerzeichen: *blank character or space (character)*
Leerzeichenfüllung: *character stuffing*
Leerzelle: *blank cell*
leicht(gewichtig): *lightweight*
Leistung: *power*
Leistung(sniveau): *performance*
Leistungen eines Datenverarbeitungssystems: *electronic data processing (EDP) capability*
leistungsfähig: *capable; efficient*
Leistungsfähigkeit: *capability; efficiency*
Leistungslist: *capability list*
Leistungsprozedur: *protocol*
Leistungsprozedurnormen: *protocol standards*
Leistungsvergleichsaufgabe: *benchmark problem*
Leistungsvermögen eines Stromkreises: *circuit capacity*
Leistungsvermögen: *capacity*
Leitartikel: *editorial*
Leitdaten: *master data*
leiten: *to channel or conduct or direct or manage*
Leiter: *conductor*
Leiter/-in: *director or manager*
leitfähig: *conductive*
Leitfähigkeit: *conduction*
Leitkarte: *header card or master card*
Leitlinien: *guide bars*
Leitrechner: *host*
Leitrechnersystem: *master/master computer system*
Leitung: *direction; management; line*
Leitungsadapter: *line adapter*
Leitungsaufbereitung: *line conditioning*
Leitungsbelastung: *line load*
Leitungsgeräuschpegel: *circuit noise level*
Leitungsimpedanz: *line impedance*
Leitungsprüfgerät: *line analyzer*
Leitungsstufe: *line level*
Leitweg: *route*
Leitwegprogramm: *router*
Leitwegseite: *routing page*

Leitwegtabelle: *routing table*
Leporellofalzung: *accordion fold or fanfold*
Lernkurve: *learning curve*
lesbar: *legible or readable*
Lesbarkeit: *legibility*
Lese-/Schreibkanal: *read/write channel*
Lese-/Schreibkopf: *combined head or read/write head or R/W head*
Lese-/Schreibspeicher: *read/write memory*
Lese-/Schreibzyklus: *read/write cycle or R/W cycle*
Lese-Erholzeit: *sense recovery time*
Lesefehler: *read error*
Lesegeschwindigkeit: *read rate*
Lesekopf: *read head*
lesen: *to read*
Leseprüfung: *read back check*
Leser: *reader*
Leser für anders formatierte Disketten: *alien disk reader*
Lesesperre: *fetch protect*
Lesestift: *wand*
Lesezeichen: *bookmark*
Lesezyklus: *read cycle*
letzten Eintrag lesen und löschen: *to pop*
Leuchtdichte: *luminance*
Leuchtdichtsignal: *luminance signal*
Leuchtkasten: *viewer*
lexikalische Analyse: *lexical analysis*
lexikographische Anordnung: *lexicographical order*
Licht: *light*
lichtaussendende Diode: *light-emitting diode (LED)*
lichtempfindlich: *light-sensitive*
Lichtempfindlichkeit: *(film) speed*
Lichtgriffel: *electronic pen or stylus or wand*
Lichthof: *halo*
Lichthofbildung: *halation*
Lichthofschutzschicht: *matt or matte*
Lichtleitung: *light conduit*
Lichtmaschine: *alternator*
Lichtpunktabtastung: *flying spot scan*
Lichtreflexe: *flare*
Lichtsensor: *image sensor*
lichtstark: *fast*
Lichtstift: *light pen or electronic pen; stylus*
Lichtundurchlässigkeit: *opacity*
Lichtwellenleiter: *light guide*
Lichtwellenleiterkabel: *fibre optic cable or connection*
Lieferant: *supplier*
Ligatur: *ligature*
Lineal: *ruler*
lineare Codierung: *straight-line coding*
lineare Funktion: *linear function*
lineare Liste: *linear list*

lineare Programmierung: *linear programming*
lineare Suche: *linear search*
lineare Verzerrung: *geometric distortion*
linearer Adressraum: *flat address space*
lineares Programm: *linear program*
Linie: *line or rule*
Linienanhebungsfilter: *character enhancement filter*
Linkage-Editierung: *linkage editing*
links ausrichten: *range left*
Linksausrichtung: *left justification*
linksbündig ausrichten: *to left justify*
linksbündiger Flattersatz: *ragged right*
Linksbündigkeit: *left justification*
Linksverschiebung: *left shift or shift left*
Linse: *lens*
LISP (Programmiersprache): *list processing*
Liste: *list*
Liste der verbotenen Wörter: *stop list*
Liste freier Speicherplätze: *available list*
Listenbearbeitung: *list processing*
Listengenerator: *report generator*
Listenprogrammgenerator: *report program generator (RPG)*
Literal: *literal*
Literaturverzeichnis: *bibliography*
lithographisch: *lithographic*
lithographischer Film: *lith film*
Lizenz: *licence*
Localbus: *local bus*
Loch: *hole*
lochen: *to punch*
Locher: *perforator or punch*
Lochkarte: *punch(ed) card*
Lochkartencode: *card code or punched code*
Lochkartenfeld: *card field*
Lochkartenformat: *card format*
Lochkartenleser: *punched card reader*
Lochkartensatz: *deck*
Lochkartenspalte: *card column*
Lochmaske: *shadowmask*
Lochstreifen: *paper tape or perforated tape or punched (paper) tape or torn tape*
Lochstreifenempfänger: *reperforator*
Lochstreifen-in-Lochkarte-Umsetzer: *tape to card converter*
Lochstreifenleser: *paper tape reader*
Lochstreifensender mit Empfangslocher: *reperforator transmitter*
Lochstreifenstanzer: *paper tape punch*
Lochstreifenzuführung: *paper tape feed*
Lochzeile: *row*
logarithmisch: *logarithmic*
logarithmische Darstellung: *logarithmic graph*

Logarithmus: *logarithm*
Logik: *logic*
Logikanalysator: *logic state analyzer*
Logikpegel: *logic level*
Logikplan: *logical chart*
logische Entscheidung: *logical decision or discrimination instruction*
logische Map: *logic map*
logische Operation: *logic operation*
logische Schaltung: *logic circuit*
logische Schlussfolgerungen pro Sekunde: *logical inferences per second (LIPS)*
logische Stellenverschiebung: *logical shift*
logische Verknüpfungssteuerung: *logical link control (LLC)*
logischer Ausdruck: *logical expression*
logischer Drucker: *logic-seeking printer*
logischer Fehler: *logical error*
logischer Kanal: *logical channel*
logischer Operator: *logical operator*
logischer Pegel H: *logical high*
logischer Pegel L: *logical low*
logischer Ring: *logical ring*
logischer Satz: *logical record*
logischer Schaltkreis: *logic circuit*
logischer Zustand: *logic state*
logisches Diagramm: *logical chart*
logisches Element: *logic element*
logisches Flussdiagramm: *logic flowchart*
logisches Laufwerk: *logical drive*
logisches Schließen: *inference*
logisches Steuerelement: *logic gate*
logisches Symbol: *logic symbol*
logisches Verschieben: *logical shift*
Logo: *logo*
Logonserver: *log on server*
Logonskript: *log on script*
lokale Brücke: *local bridge*
lokale Erklärung: *local declaration*
lokale Variable: *local variable*
lokaler Bus: *local bus*
lokaler Drucker: *local printer*
lokaler Verteilerservice: *LDS*
lokales Laufwerk: *local drive*
lokalisieren: *to locate*
Lokalnetz (LAN): *local area network (LAN or lan)*
Lokalspeicher: *local memory*
löschbar: *erasable*
löschbarer Speicher: *erasable storage or erasable memory*
löschbarer, programmierbarer Festwertspeicher (EPROM): *erasable programmable read-only memory (EPROM)*
Löscheinrichtung: *eraser*

löschen: *to clear or delete or erase or flush or free or junk or kill or purge or scratch or scrub or wipe or zap or zero*
löschende Addition: *destructive addition*
löschender Cursor: *destructive cursor*
löschendes Auslesen: *destructive readout (DRO)*
löschendes Lesen: *destructive read*
Löschkopf: *erase head*
Löschsatz: *deletion record*
Löschverfolgung: *deletion tracking*
Löschzeichen: *delete character*
lösen: *to solve*
Lösung: *solution*
löten: *to solder*
Lötmetall: *solder*
lötstellenfrei: *solderless*
Low-End: *low end*
Low-Level-Formatierung: *low-level format*
LRU-(Speicher)methode: *activity loading*
LRU-Algorithmus: *least recently used algorithm*
Luftansicht: *aerial image*
Luftbild: *aerial image*
Luftkabel: *aerial cable*
Luftschalter: *air circuit breaker*
Luftspalt: *air gap or head gap*
Lumen: *lumen*
Lux: *lux*

Mm

Magazin: *magazine*
Magazinformat: *magazine format*
magere Schrift: *light face*
Magnet: *magnet*
Magnetband: *magnetic tape*
Magnetband für Datenfernverarbeitung: *tape transmitter*
Magnetbandcodierer: *magnetic tape encoder*
Magnetbandgerät: *tape deck or (magnetic) tape recorder*
Magnetbandgerät mit zwei Rollen: *reel to reel recorder*
Magnetbandkassette: *(magnetic) tape cartridge or cassette*
Magnetbandkassettenlaufwerk: *cartridge drive*
Magnetbandlaufwerk: *tape drive*
Magnetbandleser: *magnetic tape reader*

Magnetbandstreamer: *stringy floppy or tape streamer or streaming tape drive*
Magnetbandtransport: *magnetic tape transport*
Magnetblasenspeicher: *magnetic bubble memory*
Magnetfeld: *magnetic field*
magnetische Abschirmung: *magnetic screen*
magnetische Aufzeichnung: *magnetic recording*
magnetische Codierung: *magnetic encoding*
magnetische Fokussierung: *magnetic focusing*
magnetische Medien: *magnetic media*
magnetische Polarität: *magnetic polarity*
magnetische Speicherung: *magnetic encoding*
magnetische Übertragung: *magnetic transfer*
magnetischer Fluss: *magnetic flux*
magnetischer Sturm: *magnetic storm*
magnetisieren: *to magnetize*
Magnetkarte: *magnetic card*
Magnetkartenleser: *magnetic card reader*
Magnetkern: *magnetic core*
Magnetkernspeicher: *core memory or store*
Magnetkopf: *magnetic head*
magnetooptische Aufzeichnung: *magneto-optical recording*
magnetooptische Platte: *magneto-optical disc*
Magnetplatte: *magnetic disk*
Magnetplatteneinheit: *magnetic disk unit*
Magnetraster: *grid snap*
Magnetschirm: *magnetic screen*
Magnetschriftzeichenerkennung: *magnetic ink character recognition (MICR)*
Magnetspeicher: *magnetic memory or store*
Magnetstreifen: *magnetic strip*
Magnetstreifenleser: *magnetic strip reader*
Magnettinte: *magnetic ink*
Magnetträger: *magnetic material or medium*
Magnettrommelspeicher: *magnetic drum*
Magnetzelle: *magnetic cell*
Mailer: *mailing piece*
Mailmerge: *mail-merge*
Majuskel: *majuscule*
Makroassemblierer: *macro assembler or assembly program*
Makroauflösung: *macro expansion*
Makroaufruf: *macro call*
Makrobefehl: *macro command or macro instruction*
Makrobibliothek: *macro library*
Makrocode: *macro code*

Makrodefinition: *macro definition*
Makroelement: *macroelement*
Makroflussdiagramm: *macro flowchart*
Makroprogrammierung: *macro programming*
Makrosprache: *macro language*
Makroumwandlung: *macro expansion*
Malprogramm: *paint program*
Management-Informationssystem (MIS): *management information system (MIS)*
Managementtraining: *management training*
Mandlebrot-Gleichung: *Mandlebrot set*
Mantisse: *mantissa or fraction*
manuell: *manual(ly)*
manuelle Datenverarbeitung: *manual data processing*
Manuskript: *manuscript or MS*
Map: *map*
Marginierung: *margination*
Marke: *brand; label; mark*
Markenartikel: *branded goods*
Markenimage: *brand image*
Markenname: *brand name*
Markenpirat: *pirate*
Markieren: *flagging*
markieren: *to flag*
Markierstift: *marker pen*
Markierung: *blip or flagging or marker or sentinel*
Markierungsleser: *mark sense device or reader*
Markierungsstelle: *response position*
Markierungszeit: *marking interval*
Maschine: *machine*
maschinelle Fertigung: *machining*
maschinenabhängig: *machine dependent*
Maschinenabzug: *machine proof*
Maschinenadresse: *machine address*
Maschinenbefehl: *machine instruction*
Maschinencode: *machine code*
Maschinencodebefehl: *machine code instruction*
Maschinencodeformat: *machine code format*
Maschinenfehler: *machine error*
maschinengeschrieben: *typewritten*
Maschinengleichung: *machine equation*
maschinenlesbare Codes: *machine-readable codes*
maschinenorientierte Programmiersprache: *low-level language (LLL)*
Maschinenprüfung: *machine check*
Maschinensprache: *machine language*
Maschinenteufelchen: *gremlin*
Maschinenübersetzung: *machine translation*

maschinenunabhängige Programmiersprache: *machine independent language*
Maschinenwort: *machine word*
Maschinenzuverlässigkeit: *hardware reliability*
Maschinenzyklus: *machine cycle*
Maschinerie: *machinery*
Maschineschreiben: *typing*
Maschinist/-in: *machinist*
Maske: *mask*
Maskenbit: *mask bit*
Maskenregister: *mask register*
maskierbare Unterbrechung: *maskable interrupt*
maskieren: *to mask*
maskierter Festspeicher: *masked ROM*
Maskierung: *masking*
Maß: *measure or measurement*
Masse: *ground or GND*
Massenmedien: *mass media*
Massenproduktion: *mass production*
Massenspeicher: *mass storage*
Massenspeichereinheit: *mass storage device*
Massenspeichermedium: *bulk storage medium*
Massenspeichersystem: *mass storage system*
Maßnahme: *measure*
Maßnahmen zur Leitwegbestimmung: *routing overheads*
Maßstab: *measure or scale*
Mast: *mast*
Material vom N-Typ: *n-type or N-type material*
Materialsteuerung: *materials control*
Materie: *substance*
Mathematik: *mathematics*
mathematisch: *mathematical*
mathematische Logik: *symbolic logic*
mathematische Unterprogramme: *mathematical subroutines*
mathematischer Zusatzprozessor: *maths chip or coprocessor*
mathematisches Modell: *mathematical model*
Matrix: *matrix*
Matrixdimension: *array dimension*
Matrixdrehung: *matrix rotation*
Matrixdrucker: *matrix printer or dot-matrix printer*
Matrixelement: *array element*
Matrixgrenzen: *array bounds*
matt: *matt or matte*
Mattaufnahme: *matt or matte*
Maus: *mouse*

mausgesteuert: *mouse-driven*
Maustreiber: *mouse driver*
Mauszeiger: *mouse pointer*
maximal: *maximum*
maximale Durchsatzrate: *rated throughput*
maximieren: *to maximize*
MCA-Chipset, MCA-Chipsatz: *MCA chipset*
mechanisch: *mechanical*
mechanische Maus: *mechanical mouse*
mechanischer Drucker: *impact printer*
Mechanismus: *mechanism*
Medien: *media*
Medienforschung: *media analysis or media research*
Mediummodell: *medium model*
Megabit: *megabit (Mb)*
Megabits pro Sekunde: *megabits per second (Mbps)*
Megabyte (MB): *megabyte (MB)*
Megahertz (MHz): *megahertz (MHz)*
Megapixelanzeige: *megapixel display*
Mehradressbefehl: *multi-address (instruction)*
Mehrbenutzer-Terminplaner: *multi-user or network calendar program*
Mehrbussystem: *multi-bus system*
mehrdeutig: *ambiguous*
Mehrdeutigkeit: *ambiguity*
Mehrdeutigkeitsfehler: *ambiguity error*
mehrdimensionale Feldgruppe: *multidimensional array*
mehrdimensionale Programmiersprache: *multidimensional language*
mehrfach: *multiple*
mehrfach benutzbares Farbband: *multi-strike printer ribbon*
Mehrfachanweisungszeile: *multi-statement line*
Mehrfachausstrahlung: *multicasting*
Mehrfachbefehlsstrom - Einfachdatenstrom: *multiple instruction stream - single data stream (MISD)*
Mehrfachbefehlsstrom - Mehrfachdatenstrom: *multiple instruction stream - multiple data stream (MIMD)*
Mehrfachbusarchitektur: *multiple bus architecture*
Mehrfachdatenstation: *cluster*
Mehrfachgenauigkeit: *multiple precision or multiprecision*
Mehrfachüberschreibung: *multipass overlap*
Mehrfachverbindungssystem: *multilink system*

Mehrfachzugriffscode: *multiple address code*
mehrfarbig: *multicolour*
Mehrfenster-Editor: *multi-window editor*
Mehrfrequenzwählverfahren (MWV): *dual tone multi-frequency (DTMF)*
Mehrfunktionsdatenstation: *multifunction workstation*
Mehrfunktionskarteneinheit: *multifunction card*
Mehrkanal-: *multichannel*
Mehrpfadprogramm: *multithread*
Mehrphasenprogramm: *multiphase program*
Mehrplatinencomputer: *multi-board computer*
Mehrplattenleser: *multi-disk reader*
Mehrplattenoption: *multi-disk option*
Mehrplatzsystem: *multi-user system or shared resources system*
Mehrprogrammbetrieb: *multi-programming*
Mehrprozessorenverschachtelung: *multiprocessor interleaving*
Mehrprozessorsystem: *multiprocessor*
Mehrpunkt-: *multipoint*
Mehrschichtplatine: *multilayer*
mehrstufig: *multilevel*
Mehrwerthändler: *value-added reseller (VAR)*
Mehrwertnetzwerk: *value-added network (VAN)*
Mehrzweckhardware: *common hardware*
Mehrzweckregister: *general register or general purpose register (gpr)*
Mehrzweckschnittstelle: *general purpose interface adapter (GPIA)*
Mehrzweckschnittstellenbus: *general purpose interface bus (GPIB)*
Mehrzwecksoftware: *common software*
melden: *to signal*
Melder: *indicator*
Membran: *diaphragm*
Memofeld: *memo field*
Memomotion: *memomotion*
Menge: *amount*
Mengenlehre: *set theory*
Mensch-Maschine-Schnittstelle: *human-machine interface (HMI) or man-machine interface (MMI)*
Menü: *menu*
Menüeintrag: *menu item*
Menüfenster: *action bar pull-down*
menügesteuerte Software: *menu-driven software*
Menüleiste: *menu-bar or action bar*
Menüliste: *pull-down menu*

Merkblatt zur Manuskriptgestaltung: *style sheet*
Merkmal: *characteristic*
messen: *to gauge; to measure*
Messlehre: *gauge*
Messwertwandler: *transducer*
Metabit: *metabit*
Metadatei: *metafile*
Metakompilierung: *metacompilation*
Metalldetektor: *metal detector*
Metalloxidhalbleiter: *metal oxide semiconductor (MOS)*
Metasprache: *metalanguage*
Methode der rohen Gewalt: *brute force method*
Micro-Channel-Architecture-Chipsatz: *Micro Channel Architecture chipset*
Micro-Channel-Bus: *Micro Channel Bus*
Middleware: *middleware*
mieten: *to lease*
Mietleitung: *leased circuit or leased line*
Migration: *migration*
Mikrobefehl: *microinstruction*
Mikrobefehlscode: *microcode*
Mikrobild: *microimage*
Mikrochip: *microchip*
Mikrocomputer: *microcomputer or micro*
Mikrocomputerarchitektur: *microcomputer architecture*
Mikrocomputerbus: *microcomputer bus*
Mikrocomputerentwicklungsbausatz: *microcomputer development kit*
Mikrocomputerrückwandplatine: *microcomputer backplane*
Mikrocomputing: *microcomputing*
Mikrocontroller: *microcontroller*
Mikrodiskette: *microfloppy*
Mikroelektronik: *microelectronics*
Mikrofiche: *microfiche*
Mikrofilm: *microfilm*
Mikrofon: *microphone*
Mikroform: *microform*
Mikrofotografie: *microphotography*
Mikrogerät: *microdevice*
Mikrografie: *micrographics*
Mikrokassette: *microcassette*
Mikrometer: *micrometre*
Mikron: *micron*
Mikroprogramm: *microprogram*
Mikroprogrammassembliersprache: *microprogram assembly language*
Mikroprogrammbefehlsvorrat: *microprogram instruction set*
Mikroprogrammierung: *microprogramming*
Mikroprogrammspeicher: *microprogram store*

Mikroprogrammzähler: *microprogram counter*
Mikroprozessor: *microprocessor*
Mikroprozessoradressleistungen: *microprocessor addressing capabilities*
Mikroprozessoraufbau: *microprocessor architecture*
Mikroprozessorchip: *microprocessor chip*
Mikroschaltung: *microcircuit*
Mikroschreiber: *microwriter*
Mikrosekunde: *microsecond*
Mikrosequenz: *microsequence*
Mikrowelle: *microwave*
Mikrowellenrelais: *microwave relay*
Mikrowellenübertragung: *microwave transmission*
Mikrozyklus: *microcycle*
Milliampere (mA): *milliampere (mA)*
Milliarde: *billion*
milliardstel: *nano- or n*
Millimeterpapier: *graph paper*
Millionen Fließkommaoperationen pro Sekunde (MFLOPS): *megaflops (MFLOPS)*
Millisekunde (ms): *millisecond (ms)*
Miniaturisierung: *miniaturization*
Minicomputer: *minicomputer or mini*
Minidiskette: *minifloppy*
Minimaxmethode: *minmax*
minimieren: *to minimize*
Minimum: *minimum*
Miniplatte: *minidisk*
Mini-Winchesterplatte: *miniwinny*
Minuend: *minuend*
Minuskel: *minuscule*
Minuszeichen: *minus or minus sign*
mischen: *to merge or mix*
Mischen: *mixing*
Mischen von Dateien: *file merger*
mischendes Sortieren: *merge sort*
Mischer: *mixer*
Mischsatz: *mixing*
Mischung: *mix*
mitgelaufener Fehler: *propagated error*
mitgelieferte Software: *bundled software*
mitgeschleppter Fehler: *inherited error*
mitlaufender Fehler: *propagating error*
Mitsprechanlage: *intrusion*
Mittel: *medium*
Mittelfrequenz: *medium frequency*
Mittelpunkt: *centre or center*
Mittelwert: *mean*
mittlere Geschwindigkeit: *medium speed*
mittlere Integration: *medium scale integration (MSI)*
mittlere Lebensdauer: *mean time to failure (MTF)*

mittlere Linse: *medium lens*
mittlere Reparaturdauer: *mean time to repair*
mittlere Verzögerung: *average delay*
mittlere Zugriffszeit: *average access time*
mittlerer Ausfallabstand: *mean time between failures (MTBF)*
mittlerer Informationsfluss: *information rate*
mks-System: *MKS*
Mnemonik: *mnemonic(s)*
mobile Einheit: *mobile unit*
mobile Erdstation: *mobile earth terminal*
mobiler Funkempfänger: *mobile*
mobiles Funktelefon: *mobile radiophone*
Mobilfunk: *radio pager or radio paging device*
modal: *modal*
Modell: *model*
modellhaft: *model*
Modem: *modem or MODEM*
Modem bereit für ankommende Rufe: *dial-in modem*
Modem für begrenzte Entfernungen: *limited distance modem*
Modembuchse: *data jack*
Modemeliminator: *modem eliminator*
Modemnormen: *modem standards*
Moden: *mode*
Modenstreuung: *mode dispersion*
Modifikationsschleife: *modification loop*
Modifizierer: *modifier*
modizifierte Frequenzmodulation (MFM): *modified frequency modulation (MFM)*
modular: *modular*
modulare Programmierung: *modular programming*
Modularisierung: *modularization*
Modularität: *modularity*
Modulation: *modulation*
Modulation mit unterdrückter Trägerwelle: *suppressed carrier modulation*
Modulationssignal: *modulating signal*
Modulator: *modulator*
modulieren: *to modulate*
moduliertes Signal: *modulated signal*
Moduloarithmetik: *modulo arithmetic*
Modulo N: *modulo-N*
Modulo-N-Prüfung: *modulo-N check*
Möglichkeiten: *facilities*
monadische boolesche Operation: *monadic Boolean operation*
monadische Operation: *monadic operation*
monadischer Operator: *monadic (Boolean) operator*
Monitor: *monitor*
Monitorprogramm: *monitor program*
monochrom: *monochrome*

Monochrombildschirmadapter: *monochrome display adapter (MDA)*
monolithisch: *monolithic*
Monomodefaser: *monomode fibre*
monophon: *monophonic*
monophones Tonsignal: *derived sound*
monostabil: *monostable*
Montage: *assembly or installation; layout*
Montagewerk: *assembly plant*
Monte-Carlo-Methode: *Monte Carlo method*
Morsealphabet: *Morse code*
Morsetaste: *morse key*
Mosaik: *mosaic*
MOS-Speicher: *MOS memory*
Motor: *motor*
M-Signal: *M signal*
MSX-Norm: *MSX*
Mucken: *bug*
Müll: *garbage*
Multiburstsignal: *multiburst signal*
multifunktional: *multifunctional*
Multimedia: *multimedia*
multimedial: *multimedia*
multimediale Post: *multimedia mail*
Multimedia-PC: *multimedia PC*
Multimeter: *multimeter*
Multimodefaser: *multimode fibre*
Multiplexbus: *multiplexed bus*
Multiplexmethode: *multiplexing*
Multiplexor: *multiplexor (MUX)*
Multiplikant: *multiplicand*
Multiplikation: *multiplication*
Multiplikationszeichen: *multiplication sign*
Multiplikator: *multiplier*
multiplizieren: *to multiply*
Multiscanmonitor: *multi-scan or multi-sync monitor*
Multitasking: *multitasking or multi-tasking*
Multivibrator: *multivibrator*
Murray-Code: *Murray code*
Musikchip: *music chip*
Musiksynthesizer: *music synthesizer*
Muster: *pattern*

Nn

Nabe: *hub*
Nachabbild: *after-image*
Nachahmung: *simulation*
Nachbarbereiche: *adjacent domains*
Nachbarknoten: *adjacent nodes*

Nachdruck: *reprint*
nachdrucken: *to reprint*
nachgeschalteter Server: *back-end server*
nachlassen: *to decrease; to fade*
Nachleuchtdauer: *persistence*
nachrangige Verarbeitung: *background processing*
Nachricht: *message*
Nachrichten: *news*
Nachrichtenagentur: *news agency*
Nachrichtenberechtigungscode: *MAC*
Nachrichtenende: *end of message (EOM)*
Nachrichtenformat: *message format*
Nachrichtenkopf: *message header*
Nachrichtennetz: *communications network*
Nachrichtennummerierung: *message numbering*
Nachrichtensatellit: *communications satellite*
Nachrichtenschlitz: *message slot*
Nachrichtentext: *message text*
Nachrichtenübertragungskanal: *information transfer channel*
Nachrichtenübertragungssteuerung: *telecontrol*
Nachrichtenverbindung: *communication*
Nachrichtenvermittlung: *message routing or switching*
Nachrichtenveröffentlichung: *news release*
Nachrüstung: *retrofit*
Nachsatz: *trailer*
Nachschaltrechner: *back-end processor*
Nachschlagetabelle: *look-up table or LUT*
Nachspann: *credits*
nachträglich bearbeitet: *post-formatted*
nachträgliches Modifizieren von Daten: *post-editing*
Nachzieheffekt: *streaking*
Nadel: *needle*
Nadeldrucker: *dot-matrix printer or wire printer*
Nadeldruckwerk: *clapper*
Nadelkissenverzerrung: *pin cushion distortion*
Nahaufnahme: *close-up*
Nahbereichsmodem: *short haul modem*
Näherungsfehler: *approximation error*
Nahlinse: *diopter lens*
Name: *name*
Namentabelle: *name table*
NAND-Funktion: *NAND function*
NAND-Gatter: *NAND gate*
Nanometer: *nanometre or nm*
Nanoschaltung: *nanocircuit or nanosecond circuit*
Nanosekunde: *nanosecond or ns*

natürliche binärcodierte Dezimale: *natural binary coded decimal (NBCD)*
natürliche Sprache: *natural language*
Nebencomputer: *slave*
nebeneinander anordnen: *to tile*
Nebeneinanderstellung: *juxtaposition*
Nebengeräusch: *hiss or background noise*
Nebenherdrucken: *background printing*
Nebenleitung: *line extender*
Nebenspeicher: *extension memory or slave cache or store*
Nebensprechen: *babble or crosstalk*
Nebenstellenanlage: *private automatic branch exchange (PABX)*
Nebenweg: *bypass*
Nebenzipfel: *side lobe*
negative Logik: *negative-true logic*
negative Rückkopplung: *negative feedback*
negative Rückmeldung: *negative acknowledgement (NAK)*
negative Zahl: *negative number*
Negativfilm: *negative*
Negativsignal: *active low*
negieren: *to negate*
negierte Operation: *complementary operation*
Negierung: *negation*
Nenndurchlauf: *rated throughput*
Net-BIOS: *NetBIOS*
Nettogewicht: *net weight*
Netz: *network*
Netz aus: *"power off"*
Netz ein: *"power on"*
Netz Ein-Grundstellung: *power-on reset*
Netzanschlusspunkt: *spur*
Netzführung: *network management*
Netzkabel: *lead*
Netzknoten: *hub or node*
Netzlaufwerk: *network drive*
Netzplantechnik zur Terminüberwachung von komplexen Projekten: *PERT*
Netzplantechnik: *network analysis*
Netzsoftware: *network software*
Netzspannungsüberwachung: *power monitor*
Netzstation: *terminal*
Netzstecker mit drei Kontaktstiften: *three-pin mains plug*
Netzstecker mit zwei Kontaktstiften: *two-pin mains plug*
Netzsteuerungscomputer: *communications computer*
Netzsteuerungseinheit: *communications control unit*
Netzstrom: *power*
Netzstruktur: *network structure*

Netzsynchronisation: *network timing*
Netzteil: *power pack*
Netztopologie: *network topology*
Netzüberwacher: *network controller*
Netzwerkadapter: *network adapter*
Netzwerkadministrator: *network administrator*
Netzwerkadresse: *network address*
Netzwerkalarm: *network alert*
Netzwerkarchitektur: *network architecture*
Netzwerkausstrahlung: *networking*
Netzwerkbetrieb: *networking*
Netzwerkbetriebssystem: *network operating system (NOS)*
Netzwerkdrucker: *network printer*
Netzwerkgerätetreiber: *network device driver*
Netzwerkhardware: *network(ing) hardware*
Netzwerkplan: *network diagram*
Netzwerkprotokoll: *network protocol*
Netzwerkprozessor: *network processor*
Netzwerkredundanz: *network redundancy*
Netzwerkschnittstellenkarte,
Netzwerkkarte: *network interface card (NIC)*
Netzwerkserver: *network server*
Netzwerksoftware: *network(ing) software*
Netzwerkspezialist: *networking specialist*
Netzwerksteuerprogramm: *network control program*
Netzwerkstruktur: *network structure*
Netzwerktopologie: *network topology*
Netzwerkverlegung: *networking*
Netzwerkverwalter: *network administrator*
Netzwerkverzeichnis: *network directory*
neu benennen: *to rename*
neu definierbar: *redefinable*
neu definieren: *to redefine*
neu formatieren: *to reformat*
neu kompilieren: *to recompile*
neu laden: *to reload*
neu nummerieren: *to renumber*
neu organisieren: *to reorganize*
neu programmieren: *to reprogram*
neu schreiben: *to rewrite*
Neuauflage: *reprint*
Neuberechnung im Hintergrund: *background recalculation*
neue Technologie: *new technology*
Neuerscheinungen: *new releases*
Neuerwerbungen: *accessions*
neueste Version: *update*
Neuformatierung: *reformatting*
Neuladen: *rollback*
Neunerkomplement: *nine's complement*
neurales Netz: *neural network*
neutral: *neutral*

neutrale Übertragung: *neutral transmission*
N-Halbleiter: *n-type or N-type semiconductor*
nicht aktiv: *inactive*
nicht ausführbare Anweisung: *non-operable instruction*
nicht ausgerichtet: *unjustified*
nicht dedizierter Server: *non-dedicated server*
nicht festgeschriebene logische Anordnung: *uncommitted logic array (ULA)*
nicht festgeschriebene Speicherliste: *uncommitted storage list*
nicht justiertes Band: *unjustified tape or idiot tape*
nicht kompatibel: *incompatible*
nicht konfiguriert: *configured-off or configured out*
nicht korrigierbarer Fehler: *unrecoverable error*
nicht löschbarer Speicher: *nonerasable storage*
nicht programmierbarer Terminal: *dumb terminal*
nicht redigiert: *unedited*
nicht richtig ausgerichtet: *nonaligned or out of alignment*
nicht richtig ausgerichteter Lesekopf: *nonaligned read head*
nicht richtig funktionieren: *to malfunction*
nicht umblätterbar: *non-scrollable*
nicht wiederauffindbar: *irretrievable*
nicht zählende Tastatur: *noncounting keyboard*
nichtelektrolytische Kondensatoren: *non-electrolytic capacitors*
nichtflüchtiger Speicher: *non-volatile memory or non-volatile store or storage*
NICHT-Funktion: *NOT function*
NICHT-Gatter: *negation or NOT gate*
nichtgeerdetes Gehäuse: *hot chassis*
Nichtleiter: *dielectric*
nichtlinear: *nonlinear*
nichtlöschbarer Speicher: *nonerasable storage*
nichtlöschender Cursor: *non-destructive cursor*
nichtlöschender Test: *non-destructive test*
nichtlöschendes Auslesen: *non-destructive readout (NDR)*
nichtmaskierbare Unterbrechung: *non-maskable interrupt (NMI)*
nichtmechanischer Drucker: *non-impact printer*
nichtprogrammierbare Datenstation: *dumb terminal*
nichts: *null*

NIC-Karte: *NIC*
Nicken: *pitch*
niedere Programmiersprache: *low-level language (LLL)*
Niederfrequenz: *low frequency (LF)*
niederwertige Ziffer: *low-order digit*
niederwertigste Ziffer: *least significant digit (LSD)*
niederwertigstes Bit: *least significant bit (LSB)*
niedrige Auflösung: *low resolution (low-res)*
niedriger Speicherbereich: *low-memory*
Niedrigstkostenplan: *least cost design*
N-Kanal-Metalloxidhalbleiter: *n-channel metal oxide semiconductor*
NLQ-Druckmodus: *near letter-quality (NLQ)*
nochmalige Übertragung: *retransmission*
nochmals abspeichern: *to resave*
Nomenklatur: *nomenclature*
Nomogramm: *nomogram or nomograph*
NOR-Funktion: *NOR function*
NOR-Gatter: *NOR gate*
Normalbereich: *normal range*
Normalform: *normal form*
Normalformat: *normal format*
normalisieren: *to normalize*
Normalisierung: *normalization*
Normen: *standards*
Normenumsetzer: *standards converter*
normieren: *to normalize*
Normierungsbit: *noisy digit*
Notizblockspeicher: *working store or scratchpad memory*
Notplan: *backup plan*
Notspeicherauszug: *rescue dump*
n-plus-Eins-Adressbefehl: *n-plus-one address instruction*
n-plus-Eins-Befehl: *n-plus-one instruction*
n-stufige Logik: *n-level logic*
Null: *zero*
Nullanzeiger: *nil pointer*
Nullenunterdrückung: *zero compression or zero suppression*
Nullkennzeichnung: *zero flag*
Nullkraftstecker: *zero insertion force (ZIF)*
Nullmodem: *null modem*
Nullsatz: *null set*
Nullstring: *null or blank string*
Nullzeichen: *erase character or null character*
Numeral: *numeral*
numerische Analyse: *numerical analysis*
numerische Lochung: *numeric punch*
numerische Matrix: *numeric array*
numerische Tastatur: *numeric keypad*

numerische Zeichenfolge: *numeric string*
numerischer 10er-Block: *numeric keypad*
numerischer Operand: *numeric operand*
numerisches Zeichen: *numeric character*
Num-Lock-Taste: *Num Lock key*
Nummer: *number*
nummerieren: *to number*
nummerierte Seite: *folio*
Nummerierungstyp: *enumerated type*
Num-Taste: *Num Lock key*
nur zum Lesen: *read only*
Nur-Lesen-Attribut: *read only attribute*
nutzbar: *usable*
Nutzen: *use*
Nutzflächenüberschreitung: *overscan*
Nutzzeit: *up time or uptime*

Oo

oberer Speicherbereich: *upper memory*
Oberflächenmontagetechnik: *surface-mount technology (SMT)*
Oberlänge: *ascender*
oberste Zeile: *head of form*
Objekt: *object*
Objektcode: *object code*
Objektdatei: *object file*
Objekte verknüpfen und einbetten: *object linking and embedding (OLE)*
Objektiv: *objective*
objektorientierte Grafik: *object-oriented graphics*
objektorientierte Programmierung (OOP): *object-oriented programming (OOP)*
objektorientierte Sprache: *object-oriented language*
objektorientierter Aufbau: *object-orientated architecture*
Objektprogrammkartensatz: *object deck*
Objektsprache: *target language*
OCR-Zeichensatz: *optical font or OCR font*
ODER-Funktion: *OR function*
ODER-Gatter: *OR gate*
offene Architektur: *open architecture*
offene Datei: *open file*
offene Spule: *open reel*
offener Regelkreis: *open loop*
offener Zugang: *open access*
offenes Programm: *open routine*
offenes System: *open system*
offenes Unterprogramm: *open subroutine*

Offenlassen von Dateien: *leaving files open*
Offenlegung: *disclosure*
öffentlicher Wählanschluss: *public dial port*
öffentliches Datennetz: *public data network*
öffentliches Telefonnetz: *public switched telephone network (PSTN)*
öffentliches Transportuntermehmen: *common carrier*
offline: *off-line*
Offlinedrucken: *off-line printing*
Offlinespeicherung: *off-line storage*
Offlineverarbeitung: *off-line processing*
öffnen: *to open*
Öffnung: *aperture*
Öffnungsverhältnis: *lens speed*
Offsetdruck: *offset printing*
Offsetlithographie: *offset lithography*
Ohm: *ohm*
ohmsches Gesetz: *Ohm's Law*
ohne Absatz drucken: *to run on*
ohne Papier: *paperless*
ohne Rückkehr zu Null: *non return to zero (NRZ)*
ohne Taktgeber: *unclocked*
ohne Unterbrechung: *continuously*
ohne Vorzeichen: *unsigned*
oktale Schreibweise: *octal notation*
oktales Zahlensystem: *base 8*
Oktalskala: *octal scale*
Oktalsystem: *octal (notation)*
Oktalziffer: *octal digit*
Oktave: *octave*
Oktett: *octet*
Omegawicklung: *omega wrap*
online: *on-line*
Onlinedatenbank: *on-line database*
Onlinedienst: *dialup or dial-up service*
Onlinehilfe: *on-line help*
Online-Informationswiedergewinnung: *on-line information retrieval*
Online-Komprimierer: *disk compression software*
Onlinesystem: *on-line system*
Onlinetransaktionsverarbeitung: *on-line transaction processing*
Onlineverarbeitung: *on-line processing*
opak: *opaque*
Opazität: *opacity*
Open Code: *open code*
Open-Routine: *open routine*
Operand: *operand*
Operandenfeld: *operand field*
Operation: *operation*
Operationscode: *operation code or operating code (op code)*
Operationsfeld: *operation field*

Operationsregister: *operation register*
Operationsschlüssel: *operation code or operating code (op code)*
Operationsschlüsselregister: *op register*
Operationsumwandler: *operation decoder*
Operationsverstärker: *operational amplifier (op amp)*
Operationszeit: *operation time*
Operationszyklus: *operation cycle*
Operator: *operator*
operatorbedientes System: *hands on system*
Operatorenüberladung: *operator overloading*
Operatorvorrang: *operator precedence*
optimale Codierung: *optimum code*
optimaler Nachrichtenübertragungsleitweg: *minimum weight routing*
optimieren: *to optimize*
Optimierer: *optimizer*
Optimierung: *optimization*
Optimierungscode: *optimized code*
Optimierungscompiler: *optimizing compiler*
Optimum: *optimum*
Option: *option*
Optionsfeld: *radio button*
optisch: *optical*
optische Datenverbindung: *optical data link*
optische Effekte: *special effects*
optische Filmleseeinheit: *film optical scanning device for input into computers (FOSDIC)*
optische Markierungserkennung: *optical mark recognition (OMR)*
optische Maus: *optical mouse*
optische Platte: *optical disk*
optische Übertragung: *optical transmission*
optische Zeichenerkennung: *optical character recognition (OCR)*
optischer Abtaster: *optical scanner*
optischer Leser: *bar-code reader*
optischer Markierungsleser: *optical mark reader (OMR)*
optischer Speicher: *optical storage*
optischer Zeichenleser: *optical character reader (OCR)*
optisches Abtastgerät: *optical scanner*
optisches Multiplexing: *optical multiplexing*
optisches Nachrichtenübertragungssystem: *optical communication system*
optoelektrisch: *optoelectrical*
Optoelektronik: *optoelectronics*

optoelektronisch: *optoelectronic*
Ordinatenachse: *vertical axis or Y-axis*
ordnen: *to rank*
Ordner: *directory; folder*
Ordnung: *order*
Organigramm: *organization chart*
Organisation: *organization*
Organisation und Durchführung:
organization and methods
Organisationsprogramm: *executive program*
organisatorisch: *organizational*
organisieren: *to organize*
orientiert: *orientated*
Orientierung: *orientation*
original: *original*
Original: *original; top copy*
Originaldokument: *source document*
orthochromatischer Film: *ortho or orthochromatic film*
orthogonal: *orthogonal*
Orthographieprüfprogramm: *spellchecker or spelling checker*
Ortsgespräch: *local call*
Ortsnetz: *metropolitan area network (MAN)*
Ortsnetzkennzahl: *area code*
Oszillator: *oscillator*
Oszilloskop: *oscilloscope*
Outlinefont: *outline font*
Outliner: *outliner*
Overlay: *overlay*
Overlayprogramm: *overlay*
Overlaysegmente: *overlay segments*
Overlaysystemprogramm: *overlay manager*
Oxid: *oxide*

Pp

Packager: *packager*
Packaging: *packaging*
packen: *to pack*
paginieren: *to folio*
Paginierung: *pagination*
Paket: *package*
**paketvermittelte
Datenübertragungsmethode:** *flooding*
Paketvermittlungsdienst: *packet switching service (PSS)*
paketweiser Datenservice: *packet switched data service*

Palette: *palette*
Palmtop: *palmtop*
PAL-System: *phase alternating line (PAL)*
Paperback: *paperback*
Paperwhite-Monitor: *paper-white monitor*
Papier: *paper*
Papierbehälter: *paper tray*
Papierendesensor: *form stop*
Papiergewicht: *paper weight; grammage*
Papierkorb: *trashcan; bit bucket*
Papiernachbereitungsmaschine: *form handling equipment*
Papierschneidemaschine: *guillotine*
Papiertraktor: *tractor feed*
Papiertransport: *paper feed*
Pappe: *cardboard*
Pappkarton: *cardboard box*
Parabolantenne: *dish aerial*
parallel: *parallel*
Parallelabfragespeicher: *parallel search storage*
Paralleladdierer: *parallel adder*
Parallelanschlussstelle: *parallel port*
Parallelbetrieb: *parallel operation*
Parallelbetriebssystem: *concurrent operating system*
Paralleldrucker: *parallel printer*
parallele Datenübertragung: *parallel data transmission*
parallele Ein-/Ausgabe: *parallel input/output (PIO)*
parallele Eingabe/parallele Ausgabe: *parallel input/parallel output (PIPO)*
parallele Eingabe/serielle Ausgabe: *parallel input/serial output (PISO)*
parallele Schnittstelle: *parallel interface*
paralleler Ein-/Ausgabe-Chip: *parallel input/output chip*
paralleler Schnittstellenanschluss: *parallel interface or port*
paralleler Zugriff: *parallel access*
paralleles Rangsystem: *parallel priority system*
Parallellauf: *parallel running*
Parallelschaltung: *parallel connection*
Parallelübertragung: *parallel transmission*
Parallelverbindung: *parallel connection*
Parallelzugriff: *parallel access*
Parameter: *parameter*
parametergesteuerte Software: *parameter-driven software*
Parameterprüfung: *parameter testing*
Parameterübergabe: *parameter passing*
Parameterwort: *parameter word*
parametrisches Unterprogramm: *parametric (subroutine)*
Parametrisierung: *parameterization*

Parität: *parity*
Paritätsanzeiger: *parity flag*
Paritätsprüfung: *parity check or odd-even check*
Paritätsprüfungsabbruch: *parity interrupt*
parken: *to park*
parsen: *to parse*
Parsing: *parsing*
Partition: *partition*
partitionieren: *to partition*
Partner: *associate*
Passmarken: *register marks*
Passwort: *password*
Passwortschutz: *password protection*
Patentraub: *piracy*
Patenträuber: *pirate*
Pauschalabmachung: *blanket agreement*
Pauschalangebot: *package deal*
Pauschaltarif: *flat rate*
Pause: *interval*
Pause-Taste: *pause key or Break key*
Pauspapier: *detail paper*
PC/AT-Tastatur: *PC/AT keyboard*
PC/XT-Tastatur: *PC/XT keyboard*
PC-kompatibel: *PC-compatible*
PCMCIA-Anschluss: *PCMCIA connector*
PCMCIA-Karte: *PCMCIA card*
PCMCIA-Steckplatz: *PCMCIA slot*
p-Code: *P-code*
PEEK-Anweisung: *peek*
Peer: *peer*
Peer-zu-Peer-Netzwerk: *peer-to-peer network*
Pegel: *level*
per Telefon: *by phone*
perfekt: *perfect(ly)*
Perfektor: *perfector*
Perforationen: *perforations*
Perigäum: *perigee*
Periodika: *periodical*
periodisch: *periodic or periodical*
peripher: *peripheral*
periphere Steuereinheit: *peripheral control unit (PCU)*
periphere Übertragung: *peripheral transfer*
peripherer Schnittstellenadapter: *peripheral interface adapter (PIA)*
peripherer Speicher: *peripheral memory*
Peripheriegerät: *peripheral (unit); external device*
Peripheriegeräte: *peripheral equipment*
Perle: *bead*
permanente Auslagerungsdatei: *permanent swap file*
permanente Datei: *permanent file*
Permeabilität: *permeability*
Permutation: *permutation*

Person: *person*
Personalausweis: *ID card*
Personalcomputer (PC): *personal computer (PC)*
persönlich: *personal*
persönliche Identifikationsnummer: *personal identification number (PIN)*
persönlicher Assistent: *personal assistant*
Perzentil: *percentile*
Petabyte (PB): *petabyte (PB)*
Pfad: *path*
Pfadanweisung: *path*
Pfadname: *pathname*
Pfeiltasten: *arrow keys*
Pflichtenheft: *system specifications*
p-Halbleiter: *p-type semiconductor*
Phantom-ROM: *phantom ROM*
Phase: *phase*
Phasenentzerrer: *phase equalizer*
phasengleich: *in phase*
Phasenmodulation: *phase modulation*
phasenverschoben: *out of phase*
Phasenwinkel: *phase angle*
Phon: *phon*
Phonem: *phoneme*
Phonetik: *phonetics*
phonetisch: *phonetic*
Phosphor: *phosphor*
Phosphorbeschichtung: *phosphor coating*
Phosphoreszenz: *phosphorescence*
Phosphorpunkte: *phosphor dots*
Phosphorwirksamkeit: *phosphor efficiency*
Photodiode: *photodiode*
photoelektrisch: *photoelectric*
Photoelektrizität: *photoelectricity*
Photoemission: *photoemission*
Photoleiter: *photoconductor*
Photoleitfähigkeit: *photoconductivity*
Photometrie: *photometry*
Photon: *photon*
Photosensor: *photosensor*
Phototransistor: *phototransistor*
photovoltaisch: *photovoltaic*
Photozelle: *photoelectric cell or photocell*
physikalischer Parameter: *physical parameter*
physische Adresse: *physical address*
physische Datenbank: *physical database*
physische Topologie: *physical topology*
physischer Satz: *physical record*
physischer Satz: *physical record*
physischer Speicher: *physical memory*
Pica: *pica*
Picofarad: *picofarad (pF)*
Picosekunde: *picosecond (ps)*
piepsen: *to b(l)eep*
Piepser: *bleeper or pager*

Piepton: *b(l)eep*
piezoelektrisch: *piezoelectric*
piezoelektrisches Mikrofon: *crystal microphone*
Pigmentpapier: *carbon tissue*
Piktogramm: *ikon or icon*
Pilotsystem: *pilot system*
Pinbelegungsplan: *pinout*
Pin-kompatibel: *pin compatible*
PIN-Photodiode: *pin photodiode*
Pinsel: *brush*
Pinselform: *brush style*
Pipelineverarbeitung der Befehle: *instruction pipelining*
Pipelining(-Methode): *pipelining*
Pipe-Symbol: *pipe*
p-Kanal: *p-channel*
p-Kanal-MOS: *p-channel MOS*
Plakat: *poster*
Plan: *plan*
planare Anordnung: *planar*
Planartechnik: *planar*
planen: *to plan*
Planet: *planet*
Planprogramm: *planner*
Planschrank: *planchest*
Planung: *planning*
Plasmabildschirm: *gas discharge display or (gas) plasma display*
Plastikblasentastatur: *plastic bubble keyboard*
Plastikgeld: *electronic money*
Platine: *board; card*
Platinenerweiterung: *card extender*
Platinengehäuse: *card cage*
Platte: *disk; plate; platter*
Platte mit 80 Spuren: *eighty-track disk*
Platte mit beweglichem Kopf: *movable head disk*
Platte mit doppelter Speicherkapazität: *double density disk (DD)*
Platte mit einfacher Speicherkapazität: *single density disk (SD)*
Plattenabsturz: *disk crash*
Plattenbetriebssystem: *disk operating system (DOS)*
Plattendarstellung: *disk map*
Plattendatei: *disk file*
Platteneinheit: *disk unit*
Plattenformatierung: *disk formatting*
Plattenindexlöcher: *disk index holes*
Plattenkamera: *plate camera*
Plattenkassette: *disk cartridge*
Plattenlaufwerk: *disk drive*
plattenlos: *diskless*
Plattenname: *title of disk*
Plattensektor: *disk sector*

Plattensektorformatierung: *disk sector formatting*
Plattenspeicher: *disk memory or disk storage*
Plattenspur: *disk track*
Plattenstapel: *disk pack*
Plattensteuereinheit: *disk controller*
Plattensteuereinheitskarte: *disk-controller card*
Plattenverzeichnis: *disk catalogue or directory*
Plattenwechsler: *record changer*
Plattenzugriff: *disk access*
Plattenzugriffsarm: *access arm*
Plattenzugriffsverwaltung: *disk access management*
Plattform: *platform*
Plattformunabhängigkeit: *platform independence*
Platz: *place*
Platzhalterzeichen: *wildcard character*
Plotter: *plotter*
Plotterschreibkopf: *plotter pen*
Plottertreiber: *plotter driver*
Pluszeichen: *plus or plus sign*
pnp-Transistor: *pnp transistor*
pn-Stufenübergang: *step pn-junction*
pn-Übergang: *pn-junction*
POKE-Anweisung: *poke*
Polardiagramm: *polar diagram*
polare Umlaufbahn: *polar orbit*
polarisiert: *polarized*
polarisierter Randstecker: *polarized edge connector*
polarisierter Stecker: *polarized plug*
Polarität: *polarity*
Polaritätsprüfung: *polarity test*
Polarkoordinaten: *polar coordinates*
Polaroidfilter: *polaroid filter*
Polynomcode: *polynomial code*
Pop-Filter: *pop filter*
Pos1-Taste: *home key*
Position: *position*
Positionierzeit: *seek time*
Positionsanzeiger: *cursor*
Positiv: *positive*
positiv: *positive or affirmative*
positive Antwort: *positive response*
positive Klemme: *positive terminal*
positive Logik: *positive logic*
positive Rückkopplung: *positive feedback*
positive Rückmeldung: *acknowledge or affirmative acknowledgement*
positives Fotoresistverfahren: *positive photoresist*
Positivsignal: *active high*
Post: *mail*

Postbyte: *postbyte*
Postfachnummer: *box number*
Postfix: *postfix*
Postfixschreibweise: *postfix notation*
Postleitzahl: *post code or zip code*
Post-Mortem-Fehlersuche: *post mortem*
Postprozessor: *postprocessor*
Postwurfsendung: *mailing piece*
Postwurfsendungen: *junk mail*
Potenz: *power*
Potenzial: *potential*
Potenzialunterschied: *potential difference*
Potenzierung: *exponentiation*
Potenziometer: *potentiometer*
Powor-User: *power user*
Prädikat: *predicate*
präemptives Multitasking: *preemptive multitasking*
Präfix: *prefix*
Präfixschreibweise: *prefix notation*
Präsentationsgrafik: *presentation graphics*
praxisgetestet: *field tested*
präzis: *precise*
Präzision: *precision*
Preis ab Werk: *price ex factory*
Preis für zusätzliche Auflagen: *run-on price*
Preisabsprache: *common pricing*
Prellen: *bounce*
Presse: *press*
Presseausschnittdienst: *clipping service*
Pressebericht: *press coverage*
Pressefreiheit: *freedom of the press*
Pressekonferenz: *press conference*
Presseverlautbarung: *press release*
Primärgruppe: *primary group*
Primärkanal: *primary channel*
Primärschlüssel: *primary key*
Primärspeicher: *primary memory or storage*
Primärstation: *primary station*
Primärstrahler: *radiating element*
Primzahl: *prime*
Priorität: *priority*
Prioritätsaufgabe: *foreground*
Prioritätsplaner: *priority scheduler*
Prioritätsprogramm: *foreground program*
Prioritätsreihenfolge: *priority sequence*
privat: *private*
Privatadresse: *home address*
private Fernsprechvermittlung: *private automatic exchange (PAX)*
private Handvermittlungsanlage: *private manual branch exchange (PMBX)*
private Vermittlungsanlage: *private branch exchange (PBX)*
privater Adressbereich: *private address space*

privater Wählanschluss: *private dial port*
privates Telefonsystem: *private telephone system*
Privatleitung: *private line*
privilegierter Modus: *privileged mode*
pro Stunde/Tag/Woche/Jahr: *per hour/day/week/year*
Probe: *trial*
Probelauf: *dry run; desk check*
Problem: *problem*
Problemdarstellung: *problem definition*
problemorientierte Programmiersprache: *problem-orientated language (POL)*
Produkt: *product*
Produktanalyse: *product analysis*
Produktdesign: *product design*
Produktentwicklung: *product development*
Produktgestaltung: *product design*
Produktgruppe: *product line or product range*
Produktion: *production*
Produktionseinheit: *production unit*
Produktionskapazität: *producing capacity*
Produktionskosten: *production cost*
Produktionslauf: *production run*
Produktionsleiter: *production manager*
Produktionsnormen: *production standards*
Produktionsrate: *rate of production or production rate*
Produktionsstandards: *production standards*
produktiv: *productive*
Produktmanagement: *product management*
Produktmix: *product mix*
Produktwerbung: *product advertising*
Produzent: *producer*
produzierend: *producing*
Programm: *program; programme*
Programm mit hoher Priorität: *high priority program*
Programm mit offenem Ende: *open-ended program*
Programm- und Datennotausdruck: *disaster dump*
Programm zur Lagerbestandsführung: *stock control program*
Programm zur Programmablaufverfolgung: *trace program*
Programmabbruch: *crash*
Programmablauf: *program run*
Programmablaufanlage: *object computer*
Programmablaufplan: *program flowchart*
Programmablaufverfolgung: *trace*
Programmabschnitt: *program segment*
Programmabsturz: *program crash*

Programmanweisung: *program instruction*
Programmauflistung: *program listing*
Programmausführung: *program execution*
Programmbeginn: *program origin*
Programmbeschreibung: *program specification*
Programmbibliothek: *program library*
Programmdatei: *program file*
Programm-Editor: *program editor*
Programmentwicklung: *program development*
Programmentwicklungssystem: *program development system*
Programmentwicklungswerkzeug: *software tool*
Programmentwurfssprache: *program design language (PDL)*
Programmfehler: *bug*
Programmfolge: *suite of programs*
Programmgenerator: *program generator*
programmgesteuerter Zeittaktgeber: *programmable clock*
Programmgruppe: *group or suite of programs*
programmierbare Taste: *programmable key*
programmierbarer Festwertspeicher: *programmable read only memory (PROM)*
programmierbarer Rechner: *programmable calculator*
programmierbarer Speicher: *programmable memory*
programmierbares logisches Feld: *programmable logic array (PLA)*
programmierbares logisches Gerät programmable logic device (PLD)
Programmierblatt: *program coding sheet*
Programmieren: *programming*
Programmieren in Maschinensprache: *machine language programming*
programmieren: *to program*
Programmierer/-in: *programmer*
Programmiergerät: *programmer*
Programmiernormen: *programming standards*
Programmiersprache: *programming language*
Programmiersprache zur Erstellung von Grafiken: *graphic language*
Programmiersprachen der vierten Generation: *fourth generation languages*
programmierte Unterbrechungssteuerung: *programmable interrupt controller*
programmierte Zeitbombe: *logic bomb*
programmierter Halt *or* **Stop:** *programmed halt*

programmiertes Lernen: *programmed learning*
Programmierungshilfe: *language support environment*
Programminformationsdatei: *program information file (PIF)*
Programmkarten: *program cards*
Programmkellerspeicher: *program stack*
Programmkompatibilität: *program compatibility*
Programmlauf: *program run*
Programmlistengenerator: *program report generator*
Programm-Modul: *module*
Programmname: *program name*
Programmplanung: *programme scheduling*
Programmprüfung: *program testing or program verification*
Programmreferenzliste: *reference program table*
Programmregister: *program register*
Programmschalter: *sense switch*
Programmschema: *coding sheet or coding form*
Programmschritt: *program step*
Programmspeicher: *program storage*
Programmspezifizierung: *program specification*
Programmstatuswort: *program status word (PSW)*
Programmstatuswortregister (PSW-Register): *program status word register (PSW register)*
Programmstopsignal: *breakpoint symbol*
Programmstruktur: *program structure*
Programmsymbol: *program icon or program item*
Programmübersetzung: *program compilation*
Programmunterbrechung: *interrupt*
Programmunterlagen: *program documentation*
Programmverbindung: *linking*
Programmverbindungssoftware: *linkage software*
Programmverschiebung: *program relocation*
Programmwartung: *program maintenance*
Programmwechselbetrieb: *context-switching*
Programmwiederaufnahme: *fall back recovery*
Programmzähler: *program counter (PC)*
Programmzeile: *program line*
Programmzweig: *program branch*
Projekt: *project*
projektieren: *to project*

Projektion: *projection*
Projektstudie: *feasibility study*
PROM-Programmiergerät: *PROM burner or programmer*
Proportion: *proportion*
Proportionalschrittschaltung: *proportional spacing*
Protokóll: *protocol; journal or log*
Protokolldatei: *journal file*
Prototyp: *prototype*
Prozedur: *procedure*
prozedural: *procedural*
Prozedurvereinbarung: *procedure declaration*
Prozent: *per cent*
Prozentpunkt: *percentage point*
Prozentsatz: *percentage*
prozentual: *per cent*
prozentualer Anstieg: *percentage increase*
Prozess: *process*
prozessgebunden: *process bound*
Prozessor: *processor*
Prozessorabbruchsignal: *processor interrupt*
prozessorgesteuerte Eingabe: *processor controlled keying*
Prozessor-Statuswort: *processor status word (PSW)*
Prozessrechner: *process control computer*
Prozess-Steuersystem: *process control system*
Prozesssteuerung: *process control*
Prüfanzeiger: *check indicator*
Prüfbit: *check bit*
Prüfdaten: *test data*
prüfen: *to audit; to check; to test*
Prüfer: *verifier*
Prüfgerät: *test equipment*
Prüfnummer: *check number*
Prüfprogramm: *checking program*
Prüfprotokoll: *audit trail*
Prüfpunkt: *check point*
Prüfregister: *check register*
Prüfschleife: *loopback*
Prüfspur: *parity track*
Prüfung: *check; test*
Prüfung auf gerade Parität: *even parity (check)*
Prüfung auf numerisch: *test numeric*
Prüfung auf ungerade Parität: *odd parity (check)*
Prüfzahl: *check number*
Prüfzeichen: *check character*
Prüfziffer: *check digit*
Pseudobefehl: *pseudo-instruction*
Pseudocode: *pseudo-code*
pseudodigital: *pseudo-digital*

Pseudooperation: *pseudo-operation*
pseudozufällig: *pseudo-random*
Pseudozufallszahlengenerator: *pseudo-random number generator*
Publicity: *publicity*
Publikum: *audience*
Puffer: *buffer*
Puffergröße: *buffer size*
Pufferlänge: *buffer length*
Pufferregister: *buffer register*
Pufferspeicher: *buffered memory*
Pufferung: *buffering*
Pulldown-Menü or **Pull-Down-Menü:** *pull-down menu*
Pulscodemodulation (PCM): *pulse code modulation (PCM)*
Pulslagenmodulation: *pulse position modulation (PPM)*
Punchdown-Block: *punch-down block*
Punkt: *point; dot; element; period; spot*
Punkt zu Punkt: *point to point*
punktadressierbarer Modus: *all points addressable (APA) mode*
Punktbefehl: *dot command*
Punkte pro Inch: *dots per inch or d.p.i. or dpi*
punktförmige Abtastung: *scanning spot beam*
Punktmatrix: *dot matrix*
punktweises Blättern: *smooth scroll*

Qq

Quadratur-Amplituden-Modulation (QAM): *quadrature amplitude modulation (QAM)*
Quadraturencodierung: *quadrature encoding*
Quadratwurzel: *square root*
quadrophon: *quadrophonic*
Quadruplex: *quadruplex*
Qualität: *quality*
Qualitätskontrolle: *quality control*
Qualitätskontrolle mittels Stichprobe: *acceptance sampling*
Quant: *quantum*
quantisieren: *to quantize*
Quantisierer: *quantizer*
Quantisierung: *quantization*
Quantisierungsfehler: *quantization error*
Quantisierungsgeräusch: *quantizing noise*
Quantum: *quantum*

Quartärgruppe: *super master group*
Quarzoszillator: *crystal oscillator*
Quarzuhr: *quarz clock*
Quasibefehl: *quasi-instruction*
quaternär: *quaternary*
quaternäre Stufenquantisierung:
quatenary level quantization
Quecksilberverzögerungsleitung:
mercury delay line
Quelladressfilterung: *source address filtering*
Quellcode: *source code*
Quellcodelisting: *source listing*
Quellcomputer: *source machine*
Quelldokument: *first generation image*
Quelle: *source*
Quellenfindung: *homing*
Quellenliste: *source listing*
Quellprogramm: *source program*
Querabtastung: *transverse scan*
Querformat: *landscape*
Querleitung: *high usage trunk*
Quermodulation: *cross modulation*
Querparitätsprüfung: *vertical parity check*
Querprüfung: *vertical redundancy check (VRC)*
Querschnitt: *cross-section*
Querverbindungsleitung: *tie line or tie trunk*
Querverweis: *cross-reference*
Quicksort: *quicksort*
Quittung in doppelter Ausfertigung:
receipt in duplicate
Quittungsbetrieb: *handshake or handshaking*
Quittungsduplikat: *duplicate (of a) receipt*
Quittungszeichen: *acknowledge character*
Quotient: *quotient*
QWERTY-Tastatur: *QWERTY keyboard*

Rr

Radar: *radar*
Radialübertragung: *radial transfer*
Radiator: *radiator*
Radierer: *eraser tool*
Radixpunkt: *radix point*
Radixschreibweise: *radix notation*
Raffinessen: *bells and whistles*
Rahmen: *frame; rack*
Rahmenantenne: *loop antenna*

Rahmenbit: *framing bit*
Rahmencode: *framing code*
Rahmencodierung: *skeletal code*
Rahmenfehler: *frame error*
Rahmenrücklauf: *frame flyback*
RAID-Anordnung: *redundant array of inexpensive disks (RAID)*
RAM mit Seitenzugriff: *page-mode RAM*
RAM-Cache: *RAM cache*
RAM-Chip: *RAM chip*
RAM-Karte: *RAM card*
RAM-Lader: *RAM loader*
RAM-Platte: *RAM disk*
RAM-Regenerationsgeschwindigkeit:
RAM refresh rate
RAM-Regenerierer: *RAM refresh*
Rand: *edge; margin*
Rand ausgleichen: *to justify*
Randausgleich: *justification*
Randauswertung: *edge detection*
Randschärfe: *acutance*
Randstecker: *edge connector*
rangieren: *to range*
Raster: *raster; grid*
Rasterabtastung: *raster scan*
Rasterbildverarbeiter: *raster image processor*
Rastergrafik: *raster graphics*
Rate: *rate*
rationale Zahl: *rational number*
Raubdruck: *piracy*
Raubkopie: *pirate copy or bootleg*
Raubpressung: *piracy*
Raumfahrzeug: *space craft*
raumfeste Antenne: *de-spun antenna*
Rauschabstand: *signal to noise ratio*
rauscharmer Verstärker: *low noise amplifier*
Rauschen: *noise; garbage; static*
Rauschen durch transversale Eigenschwingung: *transverse mode noise*
Rauschtemperatur: *noise temperature*
Read-Only-Attribut: *read-only attribute*
Reaktanz: *reactance*
Reaktion: *reaction; feedback*
Reaktionsmodus: *reactive mode*
Real Time: *real time*
reale Adresse: *real address*
realer Modus: *real mode*
Realspeicher: *real memory*
Rechenbefehl: *arithmetic instruction*
Rechen-Coprozessor: *maths coprocessor*
Rechenfehler: *computational error*
Rechengeschwindigkeit: *computing speed*
Rechenmaschine: *calculator*
Rechenoperation mit zwei Operanden:
binary operation
Rechenoperation: *arithmetic operation*

Rechenprüfung: *arithmetic check*
Rechenregister: *arithmetic register*
Rechenstärke: *computing power*
Rechensystem: *computer system*
Rechenwerk: *arithmetic and logic unit (ALU)*
Rechenzeichen: *arithmetic operator*
Rechenzeit: *computer time*
Rechenzentrumsoperator: *centre operator*
Rechnen mit doppelter Stellenzahl: *double-length or double precision arithmetic*
Rechner mit variabler Wortlänge: *byte machine*
Rechner: *computer*
rechnerabhängiger Speicher: *on-line storage*
Rechnerdirektverbindung: *zero slot LAN*
Rechnung in vierfacher Ausführung: *four-part invoice*
rechteckige Wellenleitung: *rectangular waveguide*
Rechteckwelle: *square wave*
rechts(bündig) ausrichten: *to right justify*
Rechtsausrichtung: *right justification*
rechtsbündiger Flattersatz: *ragged left*
Rechtschreibprüfprogramm: *spellchecker or spelling checker*
Rechtsverschiebung: *shift right*
rechtwinklige Koordinaten: *rectangular coordinates*
redaktionell: *editorial*
Redaktionsausschuss: *editorial board*
Redaktionstextverarbeitungszentrale: *editorial processing centre*
Redefreiheit: *freedom of speech*
Redigieren: *subbing or sub-editing*
redundanter Code: *redundant code*
redundantes Zeichen: *redundant character*
Redundanz: *redundancy*
Redundanzprüfung: *redundancy checking*
reduzieren: *to reduce*
reelle Zahl: *real number*
Referenzprogramm: *benchmark*
reflektieren: *to reflect*
reflektierende Platte: *reflective disk*
Reflexion: *reflection*
Reflexionsgrad: *reflectance*
Regel: *rule*
regelmäßig: *periodic(ally)*
regeln: *to regulate*
Regelvokabular: *controlled vocabulary*
Regelwiderstand: *variable resistor*
Regeneration: *regeneration*
Regenerationsspeicher: *regenerative memory*
regeneratives Lesen: *regenerative reading*
Regenerator: *regenerator*

regenerieren: *to regenerate*
Region: *region*
regionaler Programmstop: *regional breakpoint*
Regisseur/-in: *director*
Register: *register*
Registeradressierung: *register addressing*
Registerdatei: *register file*
Registererstellung: *indexing*
Registerhalten: *register*
Registerinhaltsverzeichnis: *register map*
Registerlänge: *register length*
Regler: *controller*
Reibungselektrizität: *static*
reibungslose Integration: *seamless integration*
Reihenfolge der Lagen: *collating sequence*
Reihenfolge: *order*
Reihenschaltung: *series circuit*
Reihum-Methode: *round robin*
reiner Code: *pure code*
reiner Halbleiter: *pure semiconductor*
reiner Ton: *pure tone*
reinigen: *to clean*
Reinkopie: *clean copy or clean proof*
Reinraum: *clean room*
Reinschrift: *fair copy or final copy or finished document*
Reklamezettel: *leaflet or flier*
Rekonfiguration: *reconfiguration*
rekonfigurieren: *to reconfigure*
rekonstituieren: *to reconstitute*
Rekto: *recto*
Rekursion: *recursion*
rekursiver Aufruf: *recursive call*
rekursives Unterprogramm: *recursive routine*
Relais: *relay*
Relaisstation für Kabelfernsehen: *cable TV relay station*
Relaisstelle: *repeater*
relative Adresse: *relative address*
relative Adressierung: *base addressing*
relative Codierung: *relative coding*
relative Daten: *relative data*
relative Koordinaten: *relative coordinates*
relative Zeigevorrichtung: *relative pointing device*
relativer Fehler: *relative error*
relativierbares Programm: *relocatable program*
Relativzeigerwert: *offset value or offset word*
Relativzeitgeber: *relative-time clock*
relevant: *relevant*
Relevanz: *relevance*
Reliefdruck: *relief printing*

Repertoire: *repertoire*
Replikation: *replication*
repräsentativ: *representative*
repräsentieren: *to represent*
Repro: *repro*
Reproabzug: *repro proof*
Reprokamera: *process camera*
reproreife Vorlage: *camera-ready copy (crc)*
Reprovorlage: *artwork*
Reserveausrüstung: *standby equipment*
reservierter Sektor: *reserved sector*
reserviertes Zeichen: *reserved character*
Reset-Taste: *hardware reset*
resident: *resident*
residente Schriftart: *resident font*
residentes Festspeichermonitorprogramm: *firmware monitor*
Resonanz: *resonance*
Resonanzwand: *baffle*
Ressourcenzweig: *resource fork*
Rest: *remainder*
Restfehlerhäufigkeit: *residual error rate*
Restkapazitäten ausnutzen: *to use up spare or excess capacity*
Restseitenband: *vestigial sideband*
Resultatfeld: *calculated field*
resynchronisieren: *to retrain*
retuschieren: *to touch up or retouch*
revidieren: *to revise*
Revision: *audit*
RGB-Bildschirm: *RGB display or monitor*
Rheostat: *rheostat*
Richt(leistungs)wirkungsgrad: *available power*
Richtantenne: *directional antenna*
Richtdiagramm: *directional pattern*
richtig: *correct*
richtig ausgerichtet: *in alignment*
Richtmikrofon: *unidirectional microphone*
Richtungstastenfeld: *cursor pad*
Rightsizing: *rightsizing*
Ring: *ring*
Ringmodell: *round robin*
Ringnetz: *loop network or ring (data) network*
Ringschieben: *end about shift*
Ringschieberegister: *circulating register*
Ringtopologie: *ring*
Ringverschiebung: *ring shift*
Ringzählwerk: *ring counter*
RJ11-Anschluss: *RJ11 connector*
RJ45-Anschluss: *RJ45 connector*
RLL-Codierung: *RLL encoding*
roamen: *to roam*
Roboter: *robot*
Robotik: *robotics*

robust: *robust*
roh: *raw*
Rohdatenmodus: *raw mode*
Rohprogramm: *rough copy*
Rolle: *roll; coil*
rollen: *to roll*
Rollenbesetzungsdirektor: *casting director*
rollende Kopfzeilen: *rolling headers*
Rollenzuführung: *feed reel*
Rolltaste: *Scroll Lock key*
römische Zahlen or **Ziffern:** *Roman numerals*
ROM-Kassette: *ROM cartridge*
ROM-Software: *romware*
Röntgenbild: *X-ray (picture)*
Röntgenbildprojektion auf dem Bildschirm: *X-ray imaging*
Röntgenstrahl: *X-ray*
Rotation: *rotation*
Rotationskamera: *rotary camera*
Rotationsoperation: *rotate operation*
Rotationspresse: *rotary press*
Rot-Grün-Blau: *red, green, blue (RGB)*
rotieren: *to rotate*
rotierend: *rotary*
Router: *router*
Routine: *routine*
RS-Kippstufe: *RS-flip-flop*
Rubrik: *rubric*
rückassemblieren: *to disassemble*
Rückassemblierer: *disassembler*
Rücken: *spine*
Rückführung: *feedback*
Rückführungskreis: *feedback control*
Rückführungsschleife: *feedback loop*
rückgängig machen: *to undo*
Rückgespräch: *transferred charge call or collect call*
Rückinformation: *feedback*
Rückkanal: *reverse channel*
Rückkehr-nach-Null-Signal: *return to zero signal*
Rückkopplung: *feedback*
Rücklauf: *flyback*
rückläufiger Index: *reverse index*
Rücklauftaste: *carriage return (CR)*
Rücknahmebefehl: *revert command*
Rückrufmodem: *call back modem*
Rückrufsystem: *ring back system*
Rucksack: *backpack*
Rückseite: *back panel*
Rücksetzungszeichen: *backspace character*
Rücksprung: *re-entry; return*
Rücksprungadresse: *return address*
Rücksprungstelle: *re-entry point*
Rückstand: *backlog*

rückstellen: *to restore*
Rückstellliste: *pushdown list*
Rückstellstapel: *pushdown stack*
Rückstelltaste: *reset button or key*
Rückstreuung: *backscatter*
Rücktaste: *backspace key*
Rückumsetzung: *decompilation*
Rückwand: *back panel*
Rückwandplatine: *backplane*
rückwärtige Fehlerkorrektur: *backward error correction*
rückwärts: *backward or backwards; reverse*
rückwärtsgerichtete Suche: *retrospective search*
Rückwärtskettung: *backward chaining*
Rückwärtsmodus: *backward mode*
Rückwärtsschritt: *backspace*
Rückwärtssteuerung: *backwards supervision*
Rückwärtssuche: *backwards search*
Rückwärtszeiger: *back pointer*
rückweisender Parallellauf: *retrospective parallel running*
Rückweisungsfehler: *rejection error*
Rufannahmesignal: *call accept(ed) signal*
Ruhezustand: *stable state*
rund: *round*
Runddatei: *circular file*
runde Klammern: *round brackets*
Runden: *rounding*
Rundfunksatellitentechnik: *broadcast satellite technique*
Rundfunksendestelle: *broadcasting station*
Rundhohlleiter: *circular waveguide*
Rundpuffer: *circular buffer*
Rundschreiben: *mailing shot*
Rundsendenachricht: *broadcast message*
Rundskala: *dial*
Rundspruch: *broadcast message*
Rundspruchnetz: *broadcast network*
Rundungsfehler: *rounding error*
Rundverschiebung: *circular shift*
rütteln: *to joggle*

Ss

S-100-Bus: *S100 bus or S-100 bus*
Sachverständige(r): *expert*
Sägezahnschwingung: *sawtooth waveform*
Salamitechnik: *salami technique*
Sammelfeld: *bucket*

Sammellinse: *condenser lens*
Sammeln: *collection*
sammeln: *to gather*
sammelnd (auf)schreiben: *to gather write*
sammelnd laden: *to collect transfer*
Sammelschiene: *bus*
Sammlung: *collection*
Saphir: *sapphire*
Satellit für Grundsteuerungssysteme: *basic control system satellite (BCS)*
Satellit: *satellite*
Satellitendatenstation: *satellite terminal*
Satellitennetz: *satellite network*
Satellitenrechner: *satellite computer*
Satellitenrundfunk: *satellite broadcasting*
Satellitenstrecke: *satellite link*
Sättigung: *saturation*
Sättigungsprüfung: *saturation testing*
Sättigungsstörung: *saturation noise*
Sättigungstesten: *saturation testing*
Satz: *block; set*
Satz mit fester Länge: *fixed-length record*
Satz mit variabler Länge: *variable length record*
Satzanstalt: *output bureau*
Satzanzahl: *record count*
Satzbreite: *measure*
Satzende: *end of record (EOR)*
Satzformat: *record format or layout*
Satzlänge: *record length*
Satzspiegel: *type area; matter*
Satzstruktur: *record structure*
Satzumfang schätzen: *to cast*
Satzverwaltungssystem: *records manager*
Satzzeichen: *punctuation mark*
Satzzwischenraum: *record gap*
sauber: *clean*
Säulendiagramm: *columnar graph*
S-Box-Verfahren: *S-box*
Scanner: *scanner*
Scannerprogramm: *scanning software*
Schablone: *mask; stencil; template*
Schablonenbefehl: *template command*
Schablonenspeicherung: *local format storage*
Schachtel: *case*
Schaden: *damage*
Schaden erleiden: *to suffer damage*
Schaden zufügen: *to cause damage*
schadhafter Sektor: *bad sector*
Schalldämpfkonsole: *acoustic panel*
schalldicht: *soundproof*
Schalldruckpegel: *sound pressure level (SPL)*
Schallplatte: *record*
Schallschluckhaube: *acoustic hood*
schalltot: *anechoic*

Schallwelle: *sound wave*
Schaltbild: *circuit diagram*
Schaltbrücke: *communications channel*
Schaltfläche ‚OK': *OK button*
Schaltfläche: *button*
Schaltfolge: *switch train*
Schaltkarte: *circuit board or card*
Schaltkasten: *wiring closet*
Schaltkreis: *gate circuit*
Schaltkreisanalysator: *circuit analyzer*
Schaltkreisplatine: *logic card or logic board*
Schaltlogik: *circuitry*
Schaltnetz: *combinational circuit*
Schaltschrank: *wiring closet*
Schalttafel: *plugboard or patchboard*
Schaltung: *circuit*
Schaltungsentwurf: *circuit design*
Schaltverzögerung: *propagation delay*
scharfbündelnde Antenne: *spot beam*
Schärfe: *focus*
scharfstellen: *to focus*
Schatten: *shadow*
Schattenmaske: *aperture mask*
Schatten-ROM: *shadow ROM*
Schattenschwärzung: *black crush*
Schattenspeicher: *shadow memory or page*
Schattierung: *shading or shade or tone*
Schätzen des Satzumfangs: *casting off*
schätzen: *to calculate*
Scheckbuch: *cheque book*
Scheduler: *scheduler*
Scheibe: *slice*
Scheinvariable: *dummy variable*
Scheinwiderstand: *impedance*
Scheinwiderstandsanpassung:
impedance matching
Schema: *schema*
schematisch: *schematic*
Schicht: *deposit; layer*
Schichtlaserspeicher: *emulsion laser storage*
Schiebeleiste: *scroll bar*
Schiebepfeile: *scroll arrows*
Schieberegister: *shift register*
Schildkröte: *turtle*
Schildkrötengrafik: *turtle graphics*
Schlagzeilen: *banner headlines*
schlechtes Manuskript: *bad copy*
Schleife: *loop*
Schleife in der Schleife: *nested loop*
Schleife ohne Ausgang: *closed loop*
Schleifendurchgangsgeschwindigkeit:
speed of loop
Schleifenindex: *cycle index*
Schleifenprogramm: *loop(ing) program*
Schleifenprüfung: *loop check*
Schleifenrumpf: *loop body*

Schleifenzähler: *loop counter*
schließen: *to close*
schlimmer Fehler: *catastrophic error*
Schlinge: *loop*
Schlitz: *slot*
Schluss: *tail*
Schlüssel: *key*
Schlüsselfeld: *key field*
schlüsselfertiges System: *turnkey system*
Schlüsselmatrix: *key matrix*
Schlüsselverwaltung: *key management*
Schlüsselwort: *keyword*
Schmalband: *narrow band*
Schmalbandfernsehen: *slow scan television*
Schmalbandfrequenzmodulation: *narrow band FM (NBFM)*
Schmitz: *blur or slur*
Schmutztitel: *half title*
Schnappschuss: *action shot*
Schnee: *snow*
Schneeballeffekt: *ripple-through effect*
Schneiden: *cutting*
schneiden: *to cut*
Schneideraum: *cutting room*
schnell: *fast or rapid*
schneller Papiervorschub: *paper throw; slew*
schneller Sprung: *high-speed skip*
schnelles Peripheriegerät: *fast peripheral*
Schnellleitung: *fast line*
Schnellsortierer: *quicksort*
Schnellspeicher: *fast core; immediate access store (IAS)*
Schnelltasten: *accelerator key*
Schnellübertrag: *high speed carry; ripple-through carry*
Schnellzugriff: *rapid access*
Schnellzugriffsplatte(nlaufwerk): *fixed head disk (drive)*
Schnellzugriffsspeicher: *rapid access memory or fast access memory (FAM)*
Schnittliste: *editing plan*
Schnittmenge: *intersection*
Schnittstelle zu einem Kassettenrekorder: *ACR interface*
Schnittstelle: *interface*
Schnittstellenkarte: *interface card*
Schnittstellennorm des Elektronikindustrieverbandes: *electronic industry association interface (EIA)*
Schnittstellenprogramm: *interface routines*
Schnittstellenprozessor in einem Schaltnetzwerk: *interface message processor*
Schnittstellenprozessor: *interface processor*
Schön- und Widerdruckmaschine: *perfector*

Schönschriftdruck: *letter-quality (LQ) printing*
Schoß: *lap*
Schraffur: *shading*
schräg ausrichten: *to skew*
Schräglauf: *skew*
Schrägschnitt: *diagonal cut*
Schrägspurverfahren: *helical scan*
Schrägstrich: *slash or oblique stroke*
Schreibbalken: *I-beam*
schreiben: *to write*
Schreiberring: *write-permit ring*
Schreibfehler: *write error*
Schreibkopf: *write head or record head*
Schreibkraft: *typist*
Schreibmaschine: *typewriter*
Schreibschutzattribut: *read only attribute*
Schreibschutzetikett: *write-protect tab*
Schreibstiftcomputer: *pen computer*
Schreibtisch: *desk*
Schreibtischdatei: *Desktop file*
Schreibtischoberfläche: *desktop*
Schreibtischzubehör: *desk accessory (DA)*
Schreibwaren: *stationery*
Schreibwechsel: *correspondence*
Schreibweise: *notation*
Schreibzeit: *write time*
Schrift: *type; writing*
Schriftart: *font or fount or print style*
Schriftartenkarte: *font card*
Schriftbild: *typeface*
Schriftdatenplatte: *font disk*
Schriftenfamilie: *family*
Schriftenplatte: *font disk*
Schriftgröße: *type size*
Schriftsatz (aus Standardtexten): *boilerplate*
Schriftspiegel: *body size*
Schriftstil: *type style*
Schriftstück: *document*
Schrifttypen der Schreibmaschine: *typewriter faces*
Schritt: *step; signal element*
Schritt für Schritt: *staged*
schritthaltende Verarbeitung: *in-line processing*
Schrittkamera: *planetary camera*
Schrittmotor: *stepper motor or stepping motor*
Schrittschaltung: *escapement*
schrittweise Umstellung: *phased change-over*
schrittweises Überwechseln: *staged change-over*
Schrott: *garbage or junk*
schrumpfen: *to shrink*
Schrumpffolienverpackung: *blister pack*

Schuppenstreifen: *chadded tape*
Schusterjunge: *orphan*
Schutz: *protection*
Schutzabstand: *guard band*
Schutzbit: *guard bit*
schützen: *to protect*
schützend: *protective*
Schutzhülle: *sleeve*
Schutzkopie: *protection master*
Schutzverschlüsselung: *privacy transformation*
schwach besetzte Matrix: *sparse array*
schwanken: *to fluctuate*
Schwankung: *fluctuation*
schwarz: *black*
schwarz auf weiß Anzeige: *positive display*
Schwarzdrucker: *write black printer*
Schwarzes Brett: *notice board*
Schwarzes-Brett-System: *bulletin board system (BBS)*
Schwarzpegel: *black level*
Schwärzungsgrad: *density*
Schwärzungsskala: *density dial*
schwarzweiß: *black and white*
Schwarz-Weiß-Grafik: *line art*
Schwarz-Weiß-Monitor: *monochrome monitor*
Schwebspannung: *floating voltage*
schwenken: *to pan*
Schwimmen: *swim*
Schwingungsverlauf: *waveform*
Schwund: *fading*
Scrambler: *scrambler*
Screenshot: *screen grub*
Sechs-Bit-Byte: *sextet*
Sedezformat: *sixteenmo or 16mo*
Segment: *segment*
segmentieren: *to segment*
segmentierter Adressraum: *segmented address space*
Sehschärfe: *acuity*
Seide: *silk*
Seite: *page*
Seiten pro Minute: *pages per minute (ppm)*
Seitenabbildpuffer: *page image buffer*
Seitenabrufmethode: *demand paging*
Seitenadresse: *paged address*
Seitenadressierung(sspeicher): *page addressing*
Seitenansicht: *page preview*
Seitenanzeige: *page display*
Seitenaufbau: *page layout or page setup*
Seitenaufbereitung: *page makeup*
Seitenausrichtung: *page orientation*
Seitenband: *sideband*
Seitenbeschreibungssprache: *page description language (PDL)*

Seitenbreite: *page width*
Seitendrucker: *page printer*
Seiteneinrichtung: *page setup*
Seitenendeanzeiger: *end of page indicator*
Seitengestaltung: *page makeup*
Seitengrenze: *page boundary*
Seitengröße: *page size*
Seitenlänge: *page length*
Seitenlayout: *page layout*
Seitenlesegerät *or* **Seitenleser:** *page reader*
Seitenrahmen: *page frame*
Seiten-ROM-Programm: *sideways ROM*
Seitenschutz: *page protection*
Seitentabelle: *page table*
Seitentabelle für Schattenspeicher: *shadow page table*
Seitenumbruch: *pagination*
Seitenumbruch machen: *to page*
Seitenwechsel: *page break*
Sektor: *sector*
Sektorentabelle: *sector map*
Sektorenversatz: *sector interleave*
sektorieren: *to sector*
Sektorierungsloch: *sectoring hole*
Sekundärfarbe: *secondary colour*
Sekundärspeicher: *secondary storage*
Sekundärstation: *secondary station*
selbst wählen: *to auto-dial*
selbständig(es System): *stand-alone or standalone*
selbstanpassendes System: *self-adapting system*
selbstdarstellendes Programm: *self-documenting program*
selbstdiagnostisch: *self-diagnostic*
selbstdurchschreibend: *carbonless*
selbstdurchschreibendes Papier: *carbonless paper*
selbstkorrigierender Code: *self-correcting code*
selbstlernendes (Computer)system: *self-learning*
Selbstprüfung: *auto verify*
selbstregenerierender RAM: *self-refreshing RAM*
selbstrücksetzende Schleife: *self-resetting or self-restoring loop*
Selbsttest beim Einschalten: *power on self test (POST)*
selbstverschiebliches Programm: *self-relocating program*
Selbstwähler: *auto-dial*
Selbstwählferndienst: *subscriber trunk dialling (STD)*
selektiv: *selective*
selektiver Abruf: *selective calling*
selektiver Speicherauszug: *selective dump*

selektives Bildschirmspeichern: *snapshot*
selektives Protokollprogramm: *snapshot*
Selektor: *selector*
Selektorkanal: *selector channel*
Semantik: *semantics*
Semantikfehler: *semantic error*
Semaphor: *semaphore*
Sendeabrufzeichen: *polling characters*
Sendeanforderung: *request to send signal (RTS)*
Sendeaufruf: *polling; invitation to send (ITS)*
Sendeaufrufintervall: *polling interval*
Sendeaufrufzeit: *polling overhead*
sendebereit: *clear to send (CTS)*
Sendegerät: *send-only device*
Senden: *dispatch or despatch*
senden: *to transmit*
Sender: *transmitter (TX)*
Sendung: *broadcast or programme or (US) program*
Senke: *sink*
senkrecht: *vertical*
sensibel: *sensitive*
Sensor: *sensor*
Sensor(schreib)block: *writing pad*
Sensorbildschirm: *touch screen*
Sequenz: *sequence*
sequenziell: *sequential(ly)*
sequenzielle Arbeitsweise: *sequential operation*
sequenzielle Datei: *sequential file or serial file*
sequenzielle Jobbearbeitung: *stacked job control*
sequenzielle Logik: *sequential logic*
sequenzielle Stapelverarbeitung: *sequential batch processing*
sequenzielle Suche: *sequential search*
sequenzielle Verarbeitung: *sequential processing*
sequenzieller Computer: *sequential computer*
sequenzieller Modus: *sequential mode*
sequenzieller Zugriff in Schlüsselfolge: *keyed sequential access method (KSAM)*
sequenzieller Zugriff: *sequential access*
Sequenzmodus: *sequential mode*
Serie: *series*
seriell: *serial(ly)*
serielle Anschlussstelle: *serial port*
serielle Datei: *serial file*
serielle Datenübertragung: *serial data transmission or communications*
serielle Ein-/Ausgabe: *serial input/output*
serielle Eingabe/parallele Ausgabe: *serial input/parallel output (SIPO)*

serielle Maus: *serial mouse*
serielle Operation: *serial operation*
serielle Schnittstelle: *serial interface or port*
serielle Übertragung: *serial transmission*
serielle Verarbeitung: *serial processing*
serieller Computer: *serial computer*
serieller Speicher: *serial memory*
serieller Zugriff: *serial access*
Serienaddierer: *serial adder*
Seriendrucker: *serial printer*
Serienfertigung: *batch production*
Serien-Parallel-Umsetzer: *serial to parallel converter*
Serienspeicher: *serial storage*
Serienverarbeitung: *serial processing*
Serife: *serif*
serifenlose Schrift: *sans serif*
Server: *server*
Serveranwendung: *server-based application*
Servicequalität: *grade of service*
Set: *set*
Setmaß: *set size*
Setup-Option: *setup option*
Setzanweisung: *narrative statement*
Setzen: *setting; composition; typesetting*
setzen: *to set; to compose; to position; to typeset*
Setzer: *compositor*
Setzerei: *typesetter's*
Setzkasten: *case*
Setzmaschine: *typesetter or typesetting machine*
Setzraum: *composing room*
Sextett: *sextet*
Shannon: *shannon*
shannonsches Gesetz: *Shannon's Law*
Shareware: *shareware*
Shell: *shell*
Shell-Sortierung: *shell sort*
sichere Formatierung: *safe format*
Sicherheit auf Freigabeebene: *share level security*
Sicherheit: *security*
Sicherheitskopie: *security backup*
Sicherheitsprüfung: *security check*
Sicherheitsspielraum: *safety margin*
Sicherheitssystem: *secure system*
Sicherheitsvorkehrungen: *safety measures*
Sicherheitsvorrichtung: *safety net*
sichern: *to back up or save*
sicherstellen: *to ensure*
Sicherung: *fuse*
Sicherung auf Band: *tape back-up*
Sicherungs-Domänen-Controller: *backup domain controller*
Sicherungshilfsprogramm: *backup utility*

Sicherungskondensatorspeicher: *memory backup capacitor*
Sicherungskopie: *backup (copy); dump*
Sicherungsschicht: *data link layer*
Sicherungsversion: *backup version*
sichtbar: *visible*
sichtbares Licht: *visible light*
Sichtmonitor: *video monitor*
Sichtverbindung: *line of sight*
Sieben-Bit-Byte: *septet*
Siebfaktor: *filter factor*
Signal: *signal*
Signalabfall: *decay*
Signalabfallzeit: *decay time*
Signalaufbereitung: *signal conditioning*
Signalausfall: *drop out*
Signaldämpfung durch unkorrekte Lese-/Schreibkopfausrichtung: *gap loss*
Signaldämpfung: *link loss*
Signalgröße: *signal magnitude*
Signalisierung: *signalling*
Signalreflexion: *signal reflection*
Signalumsetzer: *signal converter*
Signalumwandlung: *signal conversion*
Signalverarbeitung: *signal processing*
Signatur: *signature*
Signet: *colophon*
Silbentrennautomatik: *automatic hyphenation*
Silbentrennfehler: *bad break*
Silbentrennung: *hyphenation*
Silizium: *silicon*
Siliziumchip: *silicon chip*
Siliziumgatter: *silicon gate*
Siliziumplatte: *silicon disk*
Silizium-Saphir-Technologie: *silicon on sapphire (SOS)*
Siliziumscheibe: *silicon wafer*
Siliziumtransistor: *silicon transistor*
Simplex: *simplex*
Simulation: *simulation*
Simulator: *simulator*
simulieren: *to simulate*
simultan: *simultaneous(ly)*
Simultanrechner: *parallel computer*
Simultanübertragung: *simultaneous transmission*
Simultanverarbeitung: *parallel or simultaneous processing*
Simultanverarbeitungssystem: *multiprocessing system*
Singlemodefaser: *single mode*
Sinnbild für Datenflussläufe: *flowchart symbols*
Sinus: *sin or sine*
sinusförmig: *sinusoidal*
Sinuswelle: *sine wave*

SIP-Gehäuse: *single in-line package (SIP)*
Sitz: *base*
Sitzung: *session*
Sitzungsschicht: *session layer*
Skalar: *scalar*
skalare Daten: *scalar data*
skalare Variable: *scalar variable*
skalarer Prozessor: *scalar processor*
Skalarwert: *scalar value*
skalierbare Schriftart: *scalable font*
skalierbare Software: *scalable software*
Skalieren: *sizing*
Skizze: *sketch*
skizzieren: *to sketch; to block in*
Skript: *script*
Skriptsprache: *scripting language*
Slice: *slice*
Slice-Mikroprozessor: *bit-slice microprocessor*
Slice-Prozessor: *bit-slice processor*
SMD-Technik: *surface-mount technology (SMT)*
sockeln: *to mount*
Sofortbildentwicklung: *in camera process*
sofortige Wiedergabe: *instant replay*
Sofortzugriff: *instantaneous access*
Softfail-: *soft-fail*
Softfont: *soft font*
Software: *software*
Software im Bundle: *bundled software*
Softwarebibliothek: *software library*
Softwaredokumentation: *software documentation*
Software-Engineering: *software engineering*
Software-Entwickler: *software developer*
Software-Entwicklung: *software development*
Softwarefehler: *bug*
Softwarehaus: *software house*
Softwareingenieur: *software engineer*
softwarekompatibel: *software compatible*
Softwarelizenz: *software licence*
Softwarepaket: *software package*
Softwarepiraterie: *software piracy*
Softwarequalitätssicherung: *software quality assurance (SQA)*
Softwarespezifikation: *software specification*
Softwaresystem: *software system*
Softwareunterbrechung: *software interrupt*
softwareverträglich: *software compatible*
Softwarewartung: *software maintenance*
Softwarezuverlässigkeit: *software reliability*
Sohndatei: *son file*

solange Vorrat reicht: *offer subject to availability*
solar: *solar*
Solarrechner: *solar-powered calculator*
Solarzelle: *solar cell*
Solenoid: *solenoid*
Sonderausgaben: *below-the-line expenditure*
Sonderdruck: *offprint*
Sonderposten: *exceptional items*
Sonderzeichen: *special character or special sort*
Sonnenenergie: *solar power*
Sonnenrauschen: *helios noise*
Sortier-/Mischprogramm: *sort/merge (program)*
sortieren: *to sort or order or collate*
Sortierer: *collator*
Sortierfeld: *sort field*
Sortierlauf: *sorting pass*
Sortiermethode: *exchange selection*
Sortierschlüssel: *sortkey*
Sortierung: *filing*
Sortiment: *product line or product range*
Soundkarte: *sound card*
Sourcecomputer: *source machine*
Source-Routing: *source routing*
Spalt: *gap*
Spalte: *column*
Spaltenanzeige: *column indicator*
Spaltenausgleich: *column balance*
Spaltenlinie: *column guide*
Spaltenparitätsprüfung: *column parity*
spaltenweise: *columnar*
Spannung: *potential*
Spannungsabfall: *voltage dip or dip in voltage; brown-out*
Spannungsebene der Batterie: *battery voltage level*
Spannungsregler: *voltage regulator*
Spannungsspitze or Spannungssprung: *voltage transient*
Spannungssprungunterdrücker: *transient suppressor*
Spannungsverlust: *power loss*
spationieren: *to space; to align text*
Speicher: *memory or storage or storage device or store*
Speicher löschen: *to flush buffers*
Speicher mit hoher Dichte: *high density storage*
Speicher mit indexsequenziellem Zugriff: *indexed sequential storage*
Speicher mit Laserschicht: *laser emulsion storage*
Speicher mit mittlerer Zugriffszeit: *IAM*

Speicher mit sequenziellem Zugriff: *sequential access storage*
Speicher mit seriellem Zugriff: *serial-access memory (SAM)*
Speicheradressregister: *memory address register (MAR) or store address register (SAR)*
Speicherarbeitsbereich: *memory workspace*
Speicheraufbereitung: *memory edit*
Speicherauszug: *memory dump or storage dump*
Speicherauszug der Änderungen: *change dump*
Speicherauszug des gesamten Systems: *float*
Speicherauszug des Programmstops: *check point dump*
Speicherauszugspunkt: *dump point*
Speicherbank: *memory bank*
Speicherbereich: *area*
Speicherbus: *memory bus*
Speicherchip: *memory chip*
Speicherdatenregister: *memory data register (MDR) or store data register (SDR)*
Speicherdiagnose: *memory diagnostic*
Speicherelement: *memory cell*
Speicherhierarchie: *memory hierarchy*
speicherintensive Software: *memory-intensive software*
Speicherkapazität: *memory capacity or storage capacity*
Speicherkondensator: *memory backup capacitor*
Speichermedien: *storage media*
Speichermodell: *memory model*
Speichern unter: *save as*
speichern: *to store or save*
speicherorientiert: *memory-mapped*
speicherorientierte Ein-/Ausgabe: *memory-mapped I/O*
Speicherplatine: *memory board*
Speicherplatte: *storage disk*
Speicherplatzzuteilung: *storage allocation*
speicherprogrammgesteuertes Signal: *stored program signalling*
Speicherpufferregister: *memory buffer register (MBR)*
speicherresident: *memory-resident*
speicherresidentes Programm: *memory-resident software*
Speicherröhre: *storage tube*
Speicherschaltersystem: *memory switching system*
Speicherschutz: *memory protect*
Speicherschutzschlüssel: *protection key*
Speicherseite: *memory page*

Speicherseitenmanager: *paged-memory management unit*
Speicherseitenprinzip: *paged-memory scheme*
Speicherstelle: *location*
Speicherverwaltung: *memory management*
Speicherverwaltungseinheit: *memory management unit (MMU)*
Speicherzelle: *store cell*
Speicherzugriffszeit: *memory access time*
Speicherzuordnung: *memory allocation*
Speisehornstrahler: *feed horn*
Spektralanalysator: *spectrum analyzer*
Spektrum: *spectrum*
Spender: *dispenser*
Sperre: *lock up*
Sperreingang: *inhibiting input*
sperren: *to disable; to inhibit; to lock*
Sperrverhinderung: *advisory lock*
Spezialanwendung: *vertical application*
Spezialindizierung: *indexing*
Spezialist/-in: *specialist*
Spezifikation: *specification*
Spezifität: *specificity*
sphärische Aberration: *spherical aberration*
Spiegel: *mirror*
Spiegelbild: *mirror image*
spiegeln: *to mirror*
Spiegelreflexkamera: *reflex (camera)*
Spiegelung: *reflection*
Spiel: *game*
Spielesteckmodul: *game cartridge*
Spielkonsole: *game console*
Spielraum: *margin*
Spitze: *peak; top*
Spitze des Stapels: *top of stack*
Spitzenbedarfszeit: *time of peak demand*
Spitzmarke: *header*
SPOOL-Funktion: *print spooling*
sporadischer Fehler: *sporadic fault*
Sprachantwort: *voice answer back*
Sprachausgabe: *voice output*
Sprachausgabeeinheit: *audio response unit*
Sprach-Chip: *speech chip*
Sprache: *language; speech*
Spracheingabedaten: *voice data entry or input*
Spracherkennung: *speech recognition or voice recognition*
Sprachkompilierer: *language compiler*
Sprachprozessor: *speech processor*
Sprachregeln: *language rules*
Sprachsignal: *speech signal*
Sprachsynthese: *speech synthesis or voice synthesis*
Sprachsynthesizer: *speech or voice synthesizer*

Sprachverarbeiter: *language processor*
Sprecheinheit: *voice unit*
sprechen: *to talk*
Sprechfrequenzband: *voice band*
Sprechfunkgeräte: *hand portable sets* or *handy talkies* or *HT's*
Sprechkanal: *voice grade channel*
springen: *to jump*
Sprühdose: *airbrush*
Sprunganweisung: *GOTO*
Sprungbefehl: *jump (instruction)*
Sprungbefehl bei Null: *jump on zero*
Sprungoperation: *jump operation*
Spulbetrieb: *spooling*
Spule: *spool; reel; coil; inductor*
spulen: *to spool*
Spulgerät: *spooler* or *spooling device*
Spur: *track; trail*
Spuradresse: *track address*
Spurelement: *spot*
Spuren pro Inch: *tracks per inch (TPI)*
spurgenau laufen: *to track*
SRT-Weiterleitung: *source transparent routing (SRT)*
ST506-Standard: *ST506 standard*
Stabdrucker: *bar printer*
stabil: *stable*
Stabilität: *stability*
Stachelbandführung: *sprocket feed* or *tractor feed*
Stachelradwalze: *sprocket (wheel)*
Stadtplan: *street plan* or *town plan*
Stamm: *root*
Stammdatei: *master file*
stammen von: *to originate from*
Stammverzeichnis: *root directory*
Standardannahme: *default option*
Standardbrief: *standard letter*
Standardform: *normalized form*
Standardformular: *standard form*
Standardfunktion: *standard function*
standardisieren: *to standardize*
Standardisierungsroutine: *normalization routine*
Standardlaufwerk: *default drive*
standardmäßig: *standard*
Standardmodus: *standard mode*
Standardschnittstelle: *standard interface*
Standardschriftart: *base font*
Standardtext: *standard text*
Standardunterprogramm: *standard subroutine*
Standardvorgabe: *default value*
Standardwert: *default response*
Ständer: *rack*
ständig: *continual(ly)* or *permanent(ly)*
ständiger Fehler: *permanent error*

Standort: *base*
Standortlizenz: *site licence*
ST-Anschluss: *ST connector*
Stanzrückstand: *chad*
Stapel: *batch; pack; stack*
Stapeladresse: *stack address*
Stapelbetrieb: *batch mode*
Stapelherstellung: *batch production*
Stapeljobverarbeitung: *stack job processing*
stapeln: *to batch*
Stapelnummer: *batch number*
Stapelregion: *batch region*
Stapelspeicher: *nesting store*
Stapelübertragung: *batched communication*
Stapelverarbeiter: *batch processor*
Stapelverarbeitung: *batch processing*
Stapelverarbeitungsdatei: *batch file*
Stapelverarbeitungssystem: *batch system*
Stapelzeiger: *stack pointer (SP)*
starke Verkleinerung: *high reduction*
starr: *rigid*
Start: *start*
Startadresse: *float factor*
Startbefehle: *initial instructions*
Startbit: *start bit* or *element*
Startdiskette: *startup disk* or *boot disk*
starten: *to start* or *launch*
Startprogramm: *initial program header*
Startpunkt: *starting point*
Startsignal: *go ahead*
Startwert: *seed*
Station: *station*
Station für codeunabhängige Steuerungsverfahren: *high-level data link control station*
stationär: *stationary*
stationärer Betrieb: *local mode*
Stationsaufforderung: *enquiry character*
Stationsidentifikationscode: *terminal identity*
Stationsmanagement (SMT): *station management (SMT)*
statisch: *static*
statische Aufladung: *static*
statische Verschiebung: *static relocation*
statischer RAM: *static RAM*
statischer Speicher: *static memory* or *static storage*
statischer Speicherauszug: *static dump*
statisches Unterprogramm: *static subroutine*
Statistik: *statistics*
Statistiker/-in: *statistician*
statistisch: *statistical*
statistische Sicherheit: *confidence level*
statistische Zeitmultiplexmethode: *statistical time division multiplexing (STDM)*

Status: *status or state*
Statusabfrage: *status poll*
Statusregister: *status register*
Statuszeile: *status line*
Stau: *jam*
Steckdose: *(female) socket*
Steckeinheit: *plug-in unit*
Stecker: *plug; jack; male connector*
Stecker mit drei Kontaktstiften: *three-pin plug*
steckerkompatibel: *plug-compatible*
Stecktafel: *patch panel*
steif gebunden: *hardbound*
steile Lernkurve: *steep learning curve*
Stelle: *appointment; place; position*
Stellenbesetzungsplan: *organization chart*
Stellenverschiebung nach links: *left justification*
stellvertretender Manager: *assistant manager*
Stellvertreterzeichen: *wildcard character*
Stenotypist/-in: *shorthand typist*
Sterad(iant): *steradian*
Stereomikrofon: *stereo(phonic) microphone*
stereophon: *stereophonic*
Stereorekorder: *stereo(phonic) recorder*
Stern(chen): *asterisk*
sternförmiges Netzwerk: *active star*
sternförmiges Verteilungssystem: *switched star*
Sternfüllung: *asterisk fill*
Sternnetz: *star network*
Sterntopologie: *star topology*
Steueranweisung: *control statement*
Steuerbefehl: *control instruction*
Steuerblock: *control block*
Steuerbus: *control bus*
Steuerdaten: *control data*
Steuereinheit: *control unit (CU)*
Steuerelement für DFV-Verbindungswege: *communications link control*
Steuerkarten: *control cards*
Steuerkennzeichen: *control token*
Steuerknüppel: *game paddle or joystick*
Steuermodus: *control mode*
steuern: *to control*
Steuerprogramm: *control program*
Steuerregister: *control register*
Steuertoken: *control token*
Steuerung: *control*
Steuerung des Informationsflusses: *information flow control*
Steuerungsablauf: *control sequence*
Steuerungsball: *trackball*
steuerungsgetrieben: *control driven*
Steuerungssignale: *control signals*

Steuerungstaste: *control key or CTR or Ctrl*
Steuerungsübergabe: *control transfer*
Steuerwort: *control word*
Steuerzeichen: *control character*
Steuerzeichenfolge: *control sequence or supervisory sequence*
Steuerzeichenkennzeichnung: *flag code*
Steuerzyklus: *control cycle*
Stichleitung: *drop line*
Stichprobe: *sample*
Stichtag: *deadline*
Stichwort: *headword*
Stichwortverzeichnis: *index*
Stift: *stylus*
Stiftplotter: *pen plotter*
stilisiert: *greeked*
Stillstand: *stop*
Stillstandprojektion: *still frame*
Stimmabdruck: *voice print*
Stimme: *voice*
stöbern: *to browse*
Stockung: *holdup*
Stopbefehl: *breakpoint instruction or halt or kill job*
Stoppbit: *stop bit or stop element*
stoppen: *to stop*
Stoppliste: *stop list*
Stoppzeit: *stop time*
Störabstand: *noise margin or signal to noise ratio (S/N)*
stören: *to jam*
Störfestigkeit: *interference immunity or noise immunity*
Störimpuls: *glitch*
Störmuster: *interference pattern*
stornieren: *to cancel*
Stornierung: *cancellation*
Störsignal: *drop in*
Störstrom: *extra*
Störung: *interference; malfunction; mush*
Störung der Übertragungsleitung: *hit on the line*
Störungen: *noise*
Störungsaufzeichnung: *failure logging*
Störungsgebiet: *mush area*
Stoßbetrieb: *burst mode*
STP-Draht: *shielded twisted pair (STP) cable*
Strahl: *beam or ray*
Strahl(en)teiler: *beam splitter*
Strahlenablenkung: *beam deflection*
Strahlenbreite: *beam width*
strahlend: *radiant*
Strahlstrom: *picture beam*
Strahlung: *radiation*
Strahlungsenergie: *radiant energy*
Strahlungskeule: *lobe*
Strahlverfolgung: *ray tracing*

Strecke: *path*
streichen: *to delete*
Streichmasse: *coating*
Streichung: *deletion*
Streifen: *strip or stripe*
Streifencode: *bar code*
Streifenlocher: *tape punch*
Streifenvorspann: *leader*
Streuladen: *scatter load*
Streuspeichermethode: *folding*
Streuung: *dispersion; scatter*
STRG-Taste: *control key or CTR or Ctrl*
Strich: *stroke; line*
Strichpunkt: *semicolon*
Strichzeichnungen: *line drawings*
String mit Nullzeichenabschluss: *null terminated string*
Stringbereich: *string area*
Stringlänge: *string length*
Stringname: *string name*
Stringvariable: *string variable*
strippen: *to strip*
Stroboskop: *stroboscope or strobe*
Strom: *current; stream*
Stromausfall: *power failure*
Stromkreis: *circuit*
Stromkreisunterbrecher: *circuit breaker*
Stromstoß: *surge*
Stromversorgungseinheit: *power supply unit (PSU)*
strowgersches Fernsprechamt: *strowger exchange*
Struktur: *structure; pattern*
Strukturerkennung: *pattern recognition*
strukturieren: *to structure*
strukturierte Entwicklung: *structured design*
strukturierte Programmierung: *structured programming*
strukturierte Verkabelung: *structured cabling*
Stubroutine: *stub*
Studio: *studio*
Stufe: *level or stage*
Stufenformplotter: *incremental plotter*
Subadresse: *subaddress*
Subsegment: *subsegment*
Substanz: *substance*
Substitution: *substitution*
Substitutionsfehler: *substitution error*
Substitutionstabelle: *substitution table*
Substrat: *substrate*
Subsystem: *subsystem*
Subtrahend: *subtrahend*
Subtrahierwerk: *full subtractor*
Subtraktion: *subtraction*
Suchbegriff: *search key*

Suchbereich: *seek area*
Suchcode: *scan code*
Suche: *search; find*
Suche in verknüpfter Liste: *chaining search*
Suche mit Berücksichtigung der Groß-/Kleinschreibung: *case sensitive search*
suchen: *to search or seek*
Suchen: *hunting*
Suchen und Ersetzen: *find and replace*
Sucher: *eyepiece or viewfinder*
Suchkriterium: *search key*
Suchpfad: *path*
Suffixschreibweise: *suffix notation*
Summand: *addend*
Summe: *sum*
Summen: *buzz*
summen: *to buzz*
Summenprüfung: *summation check*
Summer: *buzzer; howler*
summieren: *to accumulate*
Superstation: *superstation*
Superüberlagerungsfunkempfänger: *superheterodyne radio*
Supervisor: *executive program or supervisor(y) program or supervisor*
supraleitender Speicher: *cryogenic memory*
Symbol: *symbol*
symbolisch: *symbolic*
symbolische Adresse: *symbolic address*
symbolische Austestung: *symbolic debugging*
symbolische Operationsschlüssel: *assembler mnemonics or mnemonic operation codes*
symbolische Programmiersprache: *symbolic language*
symbolischer Befehl: *symbolic instruction*
symbolischer Code: *symbolic code*
symbolischer Name: *symbolic name*
symbolisches Programmieren: *symbolic programming*
Symboltabelle: *symbol table*
symmetrische Differenz: *symmetric difference*
symmetrische Leitung: *balanced line*
symmetrischer Fehler: *balanced error*
synchron: *synchronous*
synchrones Datennetz: *synchronous data network*
Synchronisation: *dubbing*
Synchronisationsdemodulation: *synchronous detection*
Synchronisieren: *synchronization*
synchronisieren: *to synchronize; to dub*
Synchronisierer; *synchronizer*

synchronisiert: *in sync*
Synchronisierungsbit: *sync bit*
Synchronisierungsimpulse: *sync or synchronization pulses*
Synchronisierungsmechanismus: *interlock*
Synchronisierungsprojektor: *interlock projector*
Synchronisierungszeichen: *sync character*
Synchronnetz: *synchronous network*
Synchronrechner: *synchronous computer*
Synchronsignale: *clocked signals*
Synchronsystem: *synchronous system*
Synchronübertragung: *synchronous transmission*
Synchronverfahren: *synchronous mode*
Synonym: *synonym*
synonym: *synonymous*
syntaktischer Fehler: *syntactic error*
Syntax: *syntax*
Syntaxanalyse: *syntax analysis*
Syntaxfehler: *syntax error*
Synthese: *synthesis*
Synthesizer: *synthesizer*
synthetische Sprache: *synthetic language*
synthetisieren: *to synthesize*
System: *system*
System mit Festplatten und flexiblen Disketten: *fixed and exchangeable disk storage (FEDS)*
System mit mehreren Datenstationen: *multi-terminal system*
System mit mehrfachem Zugriff: *multi-access system*
System mit reduziertem Betrieb: *fail soft system*
System zum Dokumentenretrieval: *document retrieval system*
Systemablaufplan: *system flowchart*
Systemabsturz: *system crash*
Systemanalyse: *systems analysis*
Systemanalytiker: *systems analyst*
Systemanwendungsarchitektur (SAA): *Systems Application Architecture (SAA)*
Systemattribut: *system attribute*
Systembibliothek: *system library*
Systemdiagnose: *system diagnostics*
systemeigene Sprache: *native language*
systemeigener Compiler: *native compiler*
systemeigenes Dateiformat: *native file format*
Systemeinheit: *system unit*
Systemgenerierung: *system generation or sysgen*
Systemintegration: *systems integration*
Systemkonsole: *system console*
Systemmenü: *control menu*

Systemnetzwerkarchitektur (SNA): *Systems Network Architecture (SNA)*
Systemordner: *system folder*
Systemplanung: *system design*
Systemplatte: *system disk*
Systemprogramm: *systems program*
Systemprogrammierer: *systems programmer*
Systemprotokoll: *system log*
Systemprüfung: *system check*
Systemsicherheit: *system security*
Systemsoftware: *system software*
Systemsteuerung: *control panel*
systemunabhängig: *off-line*
System-Urband: *master tape*
Systemverwaltung: *housekeeping*
Systemverwaltungsroutine: *housekeeping routine*

Tt

T1-Kommittee: *T1 committee*
T1-Verbindung: *T1 link*
tabellarische Aufstellung: *tabulation*
Tabelle: *table*
Tabelle der booleschen Operationen: *Boolean operation table*
Tabellensuchen: *table lookup*
Tabellieren: *tabbing or tabulating*
tabellieren: *to tab or tabulate*
Tabulator: *tabulator*
Tabulatormarkierer: *tabulation marker(s)*
Tabulatorraster: *tab rack or ruler line*
Tabulatorschritte: *tab settings*
Tabulatorspeicher: *tab memory*
Tabulatorstop: *tab stop or tabulation stop*
Tabulatortaste: *tab key*
Tabulatorzeichen: *tab character*
Tabulieren: *tabulation*
Tafel: *plate*
Tag: *tag*
Tageslichtprojektor: *overhead projector*
Tagesordnung: *agenda*
Tagesordnungspunkt (TOP): *agenda item*
takten: *to clock*
taktflankengesteuert: *edge-triggered*
Taktfrequenz: *clock frequency*
Taktgeber: *clock*
Taktgeberrate: *clock rate*
taktile Information: *tactile feedback*
taktile Tastatur: *tactile keyboard*

Taktschleife: *timing loop*
Taktsignal: *clock pulse*
Taktspur: *clock track*
Taktverdoppler: *clock doubler*
Taktzyklus: *clock cycle*
Tandemprozessor: *tandem processor*
T-Anschluss: *T connector*
Taschenbuch: *paperback*
Taschencomputer: *hand-held computer or palmtop or programmable*
Taschenkalender: *pocket diary*
Taschenrechner: *pocket calculator*
Tasksteuerung: *task management*
Taskwarteschlange: *task queue*
Taskwechsel: *task swapping or switching*
Tastatur: *keypad or keyboard*
Tastatur einer Datenstation: *terminal keyboard*
Tastatur mit überlappender Eingabe: *rollover*
Tastaturcodierer: *keyboard encoder*
Tastaturkontaktprellen: *keyboard contact bounce*
Tastaturpuffer: *n-key rollover*
Tastaturschablone: *keyboard overlay*
Tastbildschirm: *touch screen*
Taste: *button; key*
Taste DEL *or* **Taste Entf:** *DEL key*
Taste zum Rückwärtsblättern: *page up key*
Taste zum Vorwärtsblättern: *page down key*
Tastenabtaster: *keyboard scan*
Tastenanordnung: *keyboard layout*
Tastenanschlag: *keystroke*
Tastenanschlagsprüfung: *keystroke verification*
Tastenblock: *keypad*
Tastenerklärungsstreifen: *key strip*
Tastenfolge: *chord keying*
Tastenmatrix: *key matrix*
Tastennummer: *key number*
Tastenschablone: *key overlay*
Tastentelefon: *digipulse telephone*
Tastenüberlappungspuffer: *key rollover*
Tastenweg: *key travel*
Tastenwiderstand: *key force*
Tat: *action*
Tätigkeit: *activity*
tatsächliche Adresse: *actual or absolute address*
tatsächliche Datenübertragungsrate: *actual data transfer rate*
tatsächliche Position: *absolute positioning*
tatsächliche Suchgeschwindigkeit: *effective search speed*
Tauchspulenmikrofon: *moving coil microphone*

tausend Anweisungen pro Sekunde: *kilo instructions per second (KIPS)*
Team: *team or crew*
Technik: *technique*
Techniker/-in: *technician*
technisch: *technical*
technische Funktionsstörung: *man-made noise*
technische Unterstützung: *technical support*
technischer Außendienst: *customer engineering*
technischer Direktor: *technical director*
technisch-wissenschaftlicher Rechner: *scientific calculator*
Technologie: *technology*
technologisch: *technological*
Teil: *part*
Teilbauelement: *component*
Teilbildunterdrückung: *horizontal blanking*
Teilchen: *particle*
Teilhaberfirma: *associate company*
Teilnehmer/-in: *subscriber*
Teilprüfung im Bocksprungprogramm: *crippled leapfrog test*
Teil-RAM: *partial RAM*
Teilseitenanzeige: *part page display*
Teilübertrag: *partial carry*
Telecommuting: *telecommuting*
Telefax: *fax or FAX*
telefaxen: *to fax*
Telefon: *(tele)phone*
Telefonanruf: *(tele)phone call*
Telefonbuch: *(tele)phone book*
Telefonhörer: *handset*
telefonieren: *to be on the (tele)phone; to make a (tele)phone call*
telefonische Bestellungen: *telephone orders*
telefonischer Verkauf: *telesales*
Telefonist/-in: *telephonist; telephone operator; switchboard operator*
Telefonkarte: *phonecard*
Telefonleitung: *telephone line*
Telefonnummer: *(tele)phone number*
Telefonsignalverstärker: *telephone repeater*
Telefonübertragung: *telephone (data carrier)*
Telefonvermittlungsstelle: *area exchange*
Telefonzelle: *call box or telephone booth*
Telefonzentrale: *exchange; switchboard*
Telegrafenamt: *telegraph office*
Telegrafie: *telegraphy-*
telegrafieren: *to telegraph or cable*
telegrafisch: *telegraphic*

Telegramm: *telegram or telegraph or cable(gram)*
Telegrammadresse: *cable address or telegraphic address*
Telekonferenz: *teleconferencing*
Telekonferenzschaltung: *dial conference*
Telematik: *telematics*
Teleobjektiv: *extension tube*
Teleshopping: *teleshopping or electronic shopping*
Teletext: *teletext*
Telex: *telex*
Telexoperator: *telex operator*
Telexteilnehmer: *telex subscriber*
Telexverbindung: *telex line*
tomporäre Auslagerungsdatei: *temporary swap file*
tendenziöse Daten: *biased data*
Terabyte: *terabyte*
Termin: *appointment; deadline*
Terminal: *terminal*
Terminalemulation: *terminal emulation*
Terminalsteuerelement: *terminal controller*
Terminator: *terminator*
Terminkalender: *appointments book or diary*
Terminplaner: *scheduler*
Terminverwaltung: *diary management*
ternär: *ternary*
Test: *test*
testen: *to test; to pilot*
Testgerät: *exerciser*
Testlauf: *test run*
Testmuster: *test pattern*
Testprogramm: *benchmark*
Testumgebung: *test bed*
Text: *text; copy; matter*
Text im Flattersatz: *ragged text*
Text verarbeiten: *to word-process*
Textanfang: *start of text (SOT or STX)*
Textanwendungen: *text management*
Textaufbereitungsprogramm: *editor program*
Textbearbeitung: *text manipulation*
Textbereich: *text screen*
Textdatei: *text file*
Texteditor: *text editor*
Textende: *end of text (EOT or ETX)*
Textfenster: *text window*
Textfernverarbeiter: *communicating word-processor*
Textformatierer: *text formatter*
Text-in-Sprache-Umwandler: *text-to-speech converter*
Textkomprimierung: *text compression*
Textlücke: *blank*
Textmarke: *bookmark*
Textmarker: *marker pen*

Textregister: *text register*
Textretrieval: *text retrieval*
Textumstellung: *cut and paste*
Textverarbeitung: *word-processing or text processing*
Textverarbeitungsbüro: *word-processing bureau*
Textverarbeitungscomputer: *word-processor*
Textverarbeitungsfunktion: *text-editing function*
Textverarbeitungssystem: *word-processor*
Textverwaltungssystem: *text manager*
Textwiederauffindung: *text retrieval*
TFT-Bildschirm: *TFT screen*
thermisches Rauschen: *thermal noise*
Thermistor: *thermistor*
Thermodrucker: *thermal printer*
Thermopapier: *thermal paper*
Thermotintenstrahldrucker: *thermal inkjet printer*
Thermotransferdrucker: *thermal transfer printer*
Thesaurus: *thesaurus*
Thickwire-Ethernet: *thick-Ethernet*
Thinwire-Ethernet: *thin-Ethernet*
Thyristor: *thyristor*
Tiefenbereich: *depth of field*
Tiefenregler: *bass control*
Tiefenschärfe: *depth of focus*
tiefgestellte Zahlen: *inferior figures*
Tiefpassfilter: *low pass filter*
tiefstehender Index: *subscript*
Tieftonlautsprecher: *woofer*
Tiegeldruckpresse: *platen press*
Tilde: *tilde*
Timesharing: *time-sharing*
Tinte: *ink*
Tintenkartusche: *ink cartridge*
Tintenschreiber: *pen recorder*
Tintenstrahldrucker: *ink-jet printer*
Tiny-Modell: *tiny model*
Tippfehler: *typing error*
Tischcomputer: *desktop computer*
Titelseite: *title page*
T-Netz: *T network*
Tochterplatine: *daughter board*
Token: *token*
Token-Bus-Netzwerk: *token bus network*
Token-Ring-Netzwerk: *token ring network*
Tokenweitergabe: *token passing*
Tomogramm: *tomogram*
Tomographie: *tomography*
Ton: *tone*
Ton(frequenz)bereich: *audio range*
Ton(frequenz)kompressor: *audio compressor*

Tonarm: *pickup*
Tonbandkassette: *cassette tape*
Tonchip: *sound chip*
Toner: *toner*
Tonerbehälter or **Tonerkassette** or
Tonerpatrone: *toner cartridge*
Tonfrequenz: *audio frequency*
Tonhöhe: *pitch*
Tonkassette: *audio cassette*
Tonkompressor: *audio compressor*
Tonkopf: *sound head*
Tonmischstudio: *mixing studio*
Tonne: *barrel*
Tonnenverzeichnung: *barrel distortion*
Tonsignalsystem: *tone signalling*
Tonspur: *sound track*
Tonteil: *sound chip*
Tonträger-Endabschaltung: *auto stop*
Tonverstärker: *audio amplifier*
Tonwahl: *dual tone multi-frequency
(DTMF)*
Tonwählsystem: *tone dialling*
Toolbox: *toolbox*
Topologie: *topology*
Torschaltung: *gate*
tot: *dead*
Totalausfall: *catastrophic failure*
Tottasten: *dead keys*
Totzeit: *dead time*
tragbar: *hand-held*
tragbarer Computer: *portable*
Träger: *carrier*
Trägerfrequenz: *carrier frequency*
Trägerfrequenzsystem: *carrier system*
Trägerfrequenztelegrafie: *carrier
telegraphy*
Trägerrakete: *launch vehicle*
Trägerschwingung: *carrier wave*
Trägersignal: *carrier signal*
Transaktion: *transaction*
Transaktionsverarbeitung: *transaction
processing (TP)*
Transfer: *transfer*
Transfergeschwindigkeit: *data transfer
rate*
Transformation: *transformation*
Transformationsregeln: *transformational
rules*
Transformator: *transformer*
transformieren: *to transform*
transienter Lesefehler: *transient read error*
Transistor: *transistor*
Transmittanz: *transmittance*
transparente Unterbrechung: *transparent
interrupt*
Transparentkopie: *transparency*
Transparentpaginierung: *transparent
paging*

Transphasor: *transphasor*
Transponder: *transponder*
transportierbar: *transportable*
transportieren: *to transport*
Transportschicht: *transport layer*
Transputer: *transputer*
Traphandler or **Trapabfangprogramm:**
trap handler
Treffer: *hit*
Treiber: *driver* or *handler*
Treiberroutine: *peripheral driver*
Trelliscodierung: *trellis coding*
trennen und ausgleichen: *to hyphenate
and justify*
trennen: *to decollate; to divide; to isolate; to
separate*
Trennmaschine: *decollator*
Trennschärfe: *selectivity*
Trennstrich (in der Größe eines m): *em
dash* or *em rule*
Trennübertrager: *isolation transformer*
Trennung: *division* or *separation*
Trennung und Randausgleich:
hyphenation and justification or *H & J*
Trennungszeichen: *hyphen*
Trennzeichen: *(field) separator*
Triade: *triad*
Trichteröffnung: *mouth*
trimmen: *to tweak*
Tri-State-Logik: *three state logic*
trockene Verbindung: *dry joint*
Trockenelement: *dry cell*
trockener Kontakt: *dry contact*
trockener Schaltkreis: *dry circuit*
Trojanisches Pferd: *Trojan Horse*
Trommelplotter: *drum plotter*
Trommelspeicher: *drum*
Troposphäre: *troposphere*
TSR-Programm: *terminate and stay resident
software (TSR)*
TTL-Bildschirm: *TTL monitor*
TTL-kompatibel: *TTL compatible*
TTL-Logik: *TTL logic*
T-Träger: *T carrier*
Turingmaschine: *Turing machine*
Turingtest: *Turing test*
T-Verbindung: *T junction*
Tweening: *tweening*
Typ: *type*
Typ der Zeichenfolge: *string type*
Type: *type*
Typengröße: *composition size*
Typenkopf: *printhead*
Typenmischung: *mixing*
Typenrad: *printwheel* or *daisy-wheel*
Typenraddrucker: *daisy-wheel printer*

Typenradschreibmaschine: *daisy-wheel typewriter*
Typenwalzendrucker: *barrel printer*
Typograph: *typographer*
Typographie: *typography*
typographisch: *typographic(al)*
typographischer Fehler: *typographical error or typo*

Uu

UART-Steuereinheit: *UART controller*
überall angelaufen: *on general release*
Überanstrengung der Augen: *eye-strain*
überarbeiten: *to revise*
überarbeitete Version: *maintenance release*
überbrücken: *to bridge*
überdecken: *to overlap*
Übereignung: *assignment*
überflüssig: *redundant*
Übergang: *transition*
Übergangsbereich: *transient area*
Übergangsspannung: *voltage transient*
Übergangsstelle: *transition point*
Übergangsstrom: *power transient*
übergeben: *to hand off*
übergehen: *to ignore*
übergeordneter Ordner: *parent folder*
Übergroßintegration: *very large scale integration (VLSI)*
Übergruppe: *supergroup*
überhitzen: *to overheat*
überlagern: *to superimpose*
Überlagern: *overlaying*
Überlagerungsbereich: *overlay region*
Überlagerungsmodul: *overlay*
Überlagerungsnetz: *overlay network*
Überlagerungssegmente: *overlay segments*
Überlandnetz: *long haul network*
überlappen: *to overlap*
überlappende Fenster: *cascading windows*
überlappende Tastung: *key rollover*
Überlappung: *interleaving; lap*
überlasten: *to overload*
Überlastung: *congestion*
Überlauf: *overflow or OV or spillage*
Überlaufanzeiger: *overflow flag or indicator*
Überlaufbit: *overflow bit*
überlaufen: *to overrun*
Überlaufprüfung: *overflow check*
Überlochung: *overpunching*

Übermodulation: *overmodulation*
Übernahme: *inheritance*
übernehmen: *to inherit*
überprüfen: *to review; to verify*
Überprüfung: *checking*
überschreiben: *to overstrike or overwrite*
Überschreibmodus: *replace mode*
Überschreibung: *destructive addition*
Überschrift: *heading*
Überschuss: *excess*
überschüssig: *excessive*
Überschwingspitze: *spike*
übersetzen: *to translate*
Übersetzer: *language processor*
Übersetzer(programm): *interpreter or translator (program)*
Übersetzersprache: *interpreted language*
Übersetzungsanlage: *source machine*
Übersetzungsanweisung: *directive statement*
Übersetzungsprogramm: *language interpreter or language translator*
Übersetzungstabellen: *conversion tables or translation tables*
Überspannungsableiter: *surge protector*
Überspannungsschutz: *over-voltage protection*
Überspringbefehl: *skip instruction*
überspringen: *to jump or skip*
Überspringfähigkeit: *skip capability*
Überstrahlen: *bloom*
Übertrag: *carry*
Übertrag des Überlaufs in die niedere Stelle: *end-around carry*
übertragbar: *portable*
übertragbare Programme: *portable software or portable programs*
Übertragbarkeit: *portability*
übertragen: *to transfer*
Übertragsanzeiger: *carry flag*
Übertragsbit: *carry bit*
Übertragszeit: *carry time*
Übertragung: *transfer; transmission*
Übertragung beendet-Signal: *carry complete signal*
Übertragungsbefehl: *transfer command*
Übertragungsbereich: *frequency response*
Übertragungsende: *end of transmission (EOT)*
Übertragungsfehler: *transmission error(s)*
Übertragungsfenster: *transmission window*
Übertragungsgeschwindigkeit: *transmission or transfer rate; bit rate; line speed*
Übertragungskanal: *transmission channel*
Übertragungskontrolle: *transfer check*

Übertragungskontrollprotokoll (TCP): *transmission control protocol (TCP)*
Übertragungskontrollprotokoll/ Schnittstellenprogramm (TCP/IP): *transmission control protocol/interface program (TCP/IP)*
Übertragungsleitung mit mehreren Stationen: *multidrop circuit*
Übertragungsmedien: *transmission media*
Übertragungsplatte: *transmissive disk*
Übertragungsrate: *transfer rate*
Übertragungssteuerung: *line control or transfer control*
Übertragungsweg: *bus*
Übertragungszeit: *transfer time*
Übertretung: *infringement*
überwachen: *to monitor; to supervise*
überwachter Ablauf: *attended operation*
Überwachung: *supervision*
Überwachungsbefehl: *supervisory instruction*
Überwachungsprogramm: *supervisory program or executive program*
Überwachungssignal: *supervisory signal*
Überwachungssystem: *monitor*
überwechseln: *to change over*
überziehen: *to coat*
Überzug: *coating*
Überzugsverfahren: *deposition*
Uhr: *clock*
Uhrzeitgeber: *real-time clock*
Ultrahochfrequenz (UHF): *ultra high frequency (UHF)*
Ultrakurzwellenbereich: *very high frequency (VHF)*
Ultramikrofiche: *ultrafiche*
Ultraschall: *ultrasound*
Ultraschallwellen: *ultrasonic waves*
ultraviolettes Licht (UV-Licht): *ultraviolet light (UV light)*
umbrechen: *to make up*
Umbruch: *make up or makeup; page break*
Umbruchfahnen: *page proofs*
umcodieren: *to recode*
Umdrehen: *spindling*
Umdruckpapier: *duplicator paper*
Umdruckverfahren: *spirit duplication*
Umfang: *extent*
umgeben: *to enclose*
umgebend: *ambient*
umgebender Schall: *ambisonics*
Umgebung: *environment*
Umgebungsspeicher: *environment space*
Umgebungstemperatur: *ambient temperature*
Umgebungsvariable: *environment variable*

umgekehrte Polarität (durch Umpolung): *reverse polarity*
umgekehrte Schrift: *reverse characters*
Umgrenzung: *border*
umkehren: *to invert or reverse*
Umkehrentwicklung: *autopositive*
Umkehrentwurf: *reverse engineering*
Umkehrfilm: *direct image film*
Umkehrliste: *push-down list*
Umkehrstapel: *push-down stack*
Umkehrung: *inversion*
umkreisen: *to orbit*
umlagern: *to page*
Umlauf: *circulation*
Umlaufbahn: *orbit*
umlaufen: *to run around*
Umlaufspeicher: *circulating storage*
Umlaufsystem: *wraparound or word wrap*
Umlaut: *umlaut*
Umleiten: *redirection*
umleiten: *to redirect*
Umleiter: *diverter*
Umleitungssymbol: *redirect or redirection operator*
Umrandung: *margination*
Umschaltcode: *shift code*
umschalten: *to switch (over)*
Umschaltnetzwerk: *switching circuit*
Umschalttaste: *shift key or case change*
Umschaltzeichen: *shift character*
umschreiben: *to transcribe*
Umschreibung: *transcription*
umsetzen: *to convert*
Umsetzer: *conversion equipment; converter or convertor*
Umsetzung: *conversion; encoding*
Umsetzungsprogramm: *language compiler*
Umstellung: *crossover; transposition*
umsteuern: *to re-route* .
umwandeln: *to transform; to assemble*
Umwandler: *transcoder; changer*
Umwandlung: *assembly; transformation*
Umwandlungscode: *assembly code*
Umwandlungszeit: *assembly time*
unabgeschirmtes verdrilltes Adernpaar: *unshielded twisted pair (UTP) cable*
unabhängig: *independent(ly)*
unbearbeitet: *raw*
unbedingte Übertragung: *unconditional transfer*
unbedingte Verzweigung: *unconditional branch*
unbedingter Sprungbefehl: *unconditional jump*
unbefugt: *unauthorized*
unbeschrifteter Datenträger: *empty medium*

unbespielt: *virgin*
unbestimmtes System: *indeterminate system*
unbestückt: *unpopulated*
unbestückte Leiterplatine: *bare board*
UND-Funktion: *AND or coincidence function*
UND-Funktion: *equivalence function or operation*
UND-Gatter: *AND gate*
undichte Stelle: *leak*
UND-Schaltung: *AND or coincidence gate or circuit or element*
undurchsichtig: *opaque*
UND-Verknüpfung: *AND or coincidence operation*
Und-Zeichen: *ampersand*
unediert: *unedited*
uneindeutig: *ambiguous*
uneindeutiger Dateiname: *ambiguous filename*
unendlich: *infinite*
Unendlicheinstellung: *infinity*
Unendlichkeit: *infinity*
unentdeckt: *undetected*
unentdeckter Fehler: *undetected error*
unerlaubt durchsuchen: *to scavenge*
unerlaubt nachahmen/nachbauen/nachdrucken: *to pirate*
unerwünscht: *unwanted*
unformatiert: *unformatted*
Ungenauigkeit: *inaccuracy*
ungenügend: *insufficient*
ungerade: *odd*
ungeschützt: *unprotected*
ungeschützte Datei: *scratch file or work file*
ungeschütztes Feld: *unprotected field*
Ungleichförmigkeit: *judder*
Ungleichheitsoperator: *inequality operator*
ungültig: *invalid*
ungültig werden: *to expire*
Ungültigkeitszeichen: *ignore character or cancel character*
Union: *union*
unipolar: *unipolar*
unipolares Signal: *unipolar signal*
universal: *general*
Universalcomputer: *general purpose computer*
Universalprogramm: *general purpose program*
Universalschnittstellenbus: *general purpose interface bus (GPIB)*
universell: *universal*
universeller Blockkanal: *universal block channel (UBC)*

universeller Satz: *universal set*
universelles Programmieren: *universal programming*
unkalkulierbarer Vorgang: *random process*
unkorrigierbarer Abbruchfehler: *fatal error*
unleserlich: *illegible*
unmittelbare Adressierung: *immediate addressing*
unmittelbare Verarbeitung: *immediate or demand processing*
unmittelbarer Zugriff: *instantaneous access*
unmittelbares Lesen/Schreiben: *demand reading/writing*
unmodifizierte Adresse: *presumptive address*
unmodifizierter Befehl: *presumptive or unmodified instruction*
unmoduliert: *unmodulated*
unmounten: *to unmount*
unplanmäßiger Abschluss: *disorderly close-down*
unredigiert: *unedited*
unruhig: *busy*
unsichtbar schreibende Tastatur: *blind keyboard*
Unsinn: *gibberish*
unsortiert: *unsorted*
unstrukturierte Datenbank: *flat file database*
unterbelichtet: *underexposed*
unterbrechen: *to interrupt; to cut*
Unterbrechung: *break or interrupt*
Unterbrechung auf Abruf: *polled interrupt*
Unterbrechung während einer Ablaufverfolgung: *trace trap*
Unterbrechungsanforderung: *interrupt request*
Unterbrechungsebene: *interrupt level*
Unterbrechungshalt: *dead halt or drop dead halt*
Unterbrechungsleitung: *interrupt line*
unterbrechungslose Stromversorgungsanlage: *uninterruptable power supply (UPS)*
Unterbrechungsmaske: *interrupt mask*
Unterbrechungsprioritäten: *interrupt priorities*
Unterbrechungspunkt: *cutoff point*
Unterbrechungspunkte setzen: *to set breakpoints*
Unterbrechungsschichtung: *interrupt stacking*
Unterbrechungsservice: *interrupt servicing*
Unterbrechungssignal: *interrupt signal*
Unterbrechungssteuerungsprogramm: *interrupt handler (IH)*

Unterbrechungstaste: *attention key*
unterdrücken: *to suppress*
Unterdrücker: *suppressor*
Unterdrückung des Telefonklingelns:
anti-tinkle suppression
Unterdrückung: *suppression*
untergeordnete Datenstation: *slave
terminal*
untergeordneter Bus: *bus slave*
untergeordneter Prozessor: *slave
processor*
untergliederte Datei: *partitioned file*
Unterklasse: *subclass*
Unterlagen: *documentation*
Unterlänge: *descender*
Unterlauf: *underflow*
Untermenge: *subset*
Unternehmensnetzwerk: *enterprise
network*
Unterordner: *subdirectory*
Unterprogramm: *subprogram or subroutine*
unterscheiden: *to distinguish*
unterscheiden: sich ~: *to differ*
Unterschied: *difference*
unterschiedlich: *different*
unterschreiben: *to sign*
Unterschrift: *signature*
Unterschriftsbestätigungsmethode (mit
Hilfe von Funktionsanalyse): *SAFE*
Unterstreichen: *underlining*
unterstreichen: *to underline or underscore*
Unterstreichung: *underline or underscore*
unterstützen: *to back or support*
Unterstützung: *aid or assistance*
Unterstützungschip: *support chip*
Unterverzeichnis: *subdirectory*
ununterbrochen laufen lassen: *to soak*
unveränderlicher Bindestrich: *required
hyphen or hard hyphen*
unveränderte Speicherseite: *clean page*
unverzichtbare Anwendung: *mission-
critical application*
unvorbereitet: *cold*
unwirksame Unterbrechung: *disable
interrupt*
unzulässige Operation: *illegal operation*
unzulässige Zahl: *unallowable digit*
unzulässiger Befehl: *illegal instruction*
unzulässiges Zeichen: *illegal character*
unzusammenhängend: *disjointed*
Uplink: *uplink*
uploaden: *to upload*
Urheber/-in: *copyright owner*
Urheberrecht: *copyright*
urheberrechtlich geschützt:
copyright(ed)
urheberrechtlich geschütztes Werk:
work still in copyright

urheberrechtlich schützen: *to copyright*
Urheberrechtsgesetz: *Copyright Act*
Urheberrechtsvermerk: *copyright notice*
Urladeprogrammblock: *boot block or
record*
Urlader: *bootstrap (loader) or initial
program loader (IPL)*
Urladerprogrammspeicher: *bootstrap
memory*
Ursprung(spunkt): *source*
ursprüngliches Dateiformat: *native file
format*
Ursprungsdatei: *source file*
Ursprungsdatei-Editor: *source editor*
Ursprungsdaten: *raw data*
Ursprungsdokument: *first generation
image*
Ursprungsformat: *native format*
Ursprungskartensatz: *source deck or pack*
Ursprungssprache: *source language*
Usability: *usability*
Useraccount: *user account*
UTP-Draht: *unshielded twisted pair (UTP)
cable*

Vv

Vakuum: *vacuum*
Vakuumröhre: *vacuum tube*
variabel: *variable*
variable Daten: *variable data*
variable Zeichenlücken: *intercharacter
spacing*
Variable: *variable*
Variablenname: *variable name*
variabler Datentyp: *variable data type*
variabler Kondensator: *variable capacitor*
variabler Wortzwischenraum: *interword
spacing*
variables Format: *variable format*
Vaterdatei: *father file*
Veitch-Diagramm: *Veitch diagram*
Vektor: *vector*
Vektorbild: *vector graphics or vector image
or vector scan*
Vektorprozessor: *vector processor*
Venn-Diagramm: *Venn diagram*
Ventil: *valve*
Ventilator: *fan*
Verabredung: *appointment*
veraltet: *out of date*
veränderbar: *alterable*

veränderlich: *variable*
verändern: *to change*
verändern: sich ~: *to vary*
verarbeiten: *to process*
Verarbeitung: *processing; execution*
Verarbeitung abhängig von der DV-Anlage: *on-line processing*
Verarbeitung im Dialogbetrieb: *interactive mode or processing*
Verarbeitung unabhängig von der DV-Anlage: *off-line processing*
verbergen: *to conceal*
verbessern: *to enhance; to upgrade*
verbesserte Punktmatrix: *enhanced dot matrix*
verbieten: *to forbid or bar*
verbinden: *to combine or connect or couple or join or link*
verbindend: *combinational*
Verbindung: *connection or interconnection or linkage*
Verbindung auf Anfrage: *switched virtual call*
Verbindungsgebühren: *connect charge*
Verbindungskabel: *feeder cable; patch cord*
Verbindungsleitung: *recording trunk*
Verbindungsprogramm: *link*
verbindungsprogrammierter Computer: *wired or hardwired program computer*
Verbindungssteuerungssignal: *call control signal*
Verbindungssteuerungsverfahren: *link control procedure (LCP)*
Verbindungsstrecke: *link*
Verbindungsüberprüfung: *link trials*
Verbindungsweg: *facility*
Verbindungszustand: *connect state*
Verblassen: *fading*
verblassen *or* **verbleichen:** *to fade*
verborgen: *hidden*
verborgene Dateien: *hidden files*
verborgener Programmfehler: *hidden defect in a program*
verbotene Zeichenkombination: *forbidden character combination*
verbotenes Zeichen: *forbidden character*
verbrauchen: *to use*
Verbrauchsgüter: *consumables*
Verbund: *group*
verbunden: *associate*
verbundene Liste: *linked list*
verbundenes Unterprogramm: *linked subroutine*
Verbundsystem: *distributed system*
verdichten: *to pack or compress*
Verdichter: *compressor*
Verdichtung: *packing or compression*

Verdichtungsprogramm: *compressor or packing routine*
Verdrahtungsrahmen: *wiring frame*
verdrilltes Adernpaar: *twisted-pair cable*
Vereinbarung: *declaration or declarative statement*
vereinfachen: *to simplify*
vereinigen: *to coalesce*
vereinzelt: *stray*
Vereinzelungsmaschine: *burster*
Verfahren: *process*
Verfahren der (Daten)übertragungssteuerung: *basic mode link control*
Verfahrensdiagramm: *process chart*
verfahrensorientierte Programmiersprache: *procedural or procedure-orientated language*
Verfall: *expiration*
Verfallsdatum: *expiration date*
verfälschen: *to corrupt*
Verfasser: *author*
Verfassersprache: *author language*
Verfassersystem: *authoring system*
verflechten: sich ~: *to interlace*
verfügbar: *available*
verfügbare Benutzerzeit: *available time*
verfügbare Zeichensätze: *downloadable fonts or resident fonts*
Verfügbarkeit: *availability*
Vergleich: *comparison*
vergleichbar: *comparable*
vergleichen: *to compare or match*
Vergleicher: *comparator*
Vergleichsoperator: *relational operator or logical operator*
Vergleichspunkt: *benchmark*
vergrößern: *to augment; to enlarge; to expand; to magnify; to scale up; to zoom*
Vergrößern: *zooming*
Vergrößerung: *enlargement or magnification*
Verhältnis: *ratio*
verhindern: *to prevent*
Verifikation: *verification*
verirrt: *stray*
verkabeln: *to wire*
Verkabelungsplan: *cabling diagram*
verkapselt: *encapsulated*
Verkäufer/-in: *shop assistant*
Verkaufsgespräch: *sales pitch*
verketten: *to chain; to (con)catenate; to daisy-chain*
verkettete Busstruktur: *daisy chain bus*
verkettete Dateien: *concatenated data set*
verkettete Rekursion: *daisy chain recursion*

verkettete Unterbrechungsleitung: *daisy chain interrupt*
Verkettung: *daisy chain*
Verkettungszeichen: *pipe*
Verkleidung: *cladding*
verkleinern: *to scale down*
verknüpfen: *to bind*
Verknüpfung: *nexus*
Verknüpfungsglied: *decision circuit or element; logic element*
Verknüpfungszeit: *binding time*
Verlag: *publisher*
Verlagsstil: *house style*
Verlagswesen: *publishing*
verlängern: *to extend*
Verlängerung: *extension*
Verlängerungskabel: *extension cable*
Verlaufen: *bleed*
Verlegen von Fachliteratur: *professional publishing*
Verletzung: *breach*
Verletzung der Gewährleistung(spflicht): *breach of warranty*
Verletzung des Urheberrechts: *infringement of copyright or copyright infringement*
verlieren: *to lose*
verlorene Zuordnungseinheit *or*
verlorenes Cluster: *lost cluster*
Verlust: *loss; breakup*
Verlustbelegung: *lost call*
Verlustzeit: *lost time*
vermaschtes Netz: *mesh network*
Vermaschung: *mesh*
vermehren: *to augment*
Verminderung: *decrease*
vermischen: *to mix down*
Vermisstenfaktor: *omission factor*
vermitteln: *to convey*
Vermittler: *mid-user*
Vermittlung: *switchboard; switching*
Vermittlungsschicht: *network layer*
Vermittlungszentrale: *switching centre*
vernetzen: *to network*
vernetztes Fernsehprogramm: *networked TV programme*
veröffentlichen: *to publish*
Veröffentlichung: *publication*
Verpacken: *packing*
Verpackung: *packaging or packing*
verramschen: *to remainder*
verriegeln: *to interlock; to latch*
Verriegelung: *interlock*
verringern: *to reduce*
Verringerung: *reduction*
versagen: *to fail*
Versalien: *upper case*

Versatzfaktor: *interleave factor*
versauen: *to mung up*
versäumen: *to fail*
Versäumnis: *failure*
verschachteln: *to nest*
verschachtelte Schleife: *nested loop*
verschachtelte Struktur: *nested structure*
verschachtelter Makroaufruf: *nested macro call*
Verschachtelungsgrad: *nesting level*
Verschicken: *mailing*
verschiebbar: *relocatable*
Verschiebebefehl: *shift instruction*
verschieben: *to blit or bitblt; to drag; to justify; to range; to relocate; to shift*
Verschieberegister: *shift register*
Verschiebung: *relocation*
Verschiebungskonstante: *relocation constant*
verschieden: *differential*
Verschlechterung: *degradation*
Verschluss: *shutter*
verschlüsseln: *to encipher or encrypt*
verschlüsselter Text: *ciphertext*
Verschlüsselung: *cipher or encryption*
Verschlüsselungssystem mit bekanntem Chiffrierschlüssel: *public key cipher system*
Verschmelzung: *fusion*
verschränkter Speicher: *interleaved memory*
verschwommen: *fuzzy*
verschwommene Theorie: *fuzzy logic or fuzzy theory*
verschwommenes Bild: *blur*
versiegeln: *to seal*
Version: *version or release or build*
Versionskontrolle: *version control*
Versionsnummer: *version number or release number*
Versionsprüfung: *version control*
Verso: *verso*
versorgen: *to supply*
Versorgung: *supply*
Verspätung: *delay*
verspleißen: *to splice*
verstärken: *to amplify; to boost*
Verstärker: *amplifier*
Verstärkerklasse: *amplifier class*
Verstärkung: *amplification*
Verstärkungsgrad: *gain*
Verstärkungsregelung: *gain control*
versteckt: *hidden*
versteckte Datei: *hidden file*
versteckte Linien: *hidden lines*
Verstoß: *breach*
verstreut: *stray*
verstümmeln: *to corrupt*

Versuchsmuster: *dummy*
Vertauschung: *transposition*
verteilen: *to distribute*
Verteiler: *splitter; switch*
Verteilerkasten: *junction box*
verteilte adaptive Verkehrslenkung:
distributed adaptive routing
verteilte Datenverarbeitung: *distributed
data processing (DDP)*
verteilte Intelligenz: *distributed intelligence*
verteiltes Dateisystem: *distributed file
system*
verteiltes Datenbanksystem: *distributed
database system*
Verteilung: *distribution*
Verteilungskanäle: *distribution channels or
channels of distribution*
vertikal: *vertical(ly)*
vertikal polarisiert: *vertically polarized*
vertikal polarisiertes Signal: *vertically
polarized signal*
vertikale Formatsteuerungseinheit:
vertical format unit (VFU)
vertikale Texteinrichtung: *vertical
justification*
vertikaler Zeilenausgleich: *vertical
justification*
vertikales Blättern: *vertical scrolling*
Vertikalsynchronsignal: *vertical sync
signal*
Vertikaltabulator: *vertical tab*
Vertragsbruch: *breach of contract*
vertreten: *to represent*
Vertreter: *representative*
Vervielfältiger: *duplicator*
Vervielfältigung: *duplication*
vervollkommnen: *to perfect*
verwackeln: *to blur*
Verwacklung: *judder*
verwalten: *to account*
Verwalter: *administrator*
Verwaltung: *management*
verwanzen: *to bug*
Verweilzeit: *turnaround time (TAT)*
Verweis nach vorne: *forward reference*
Verweisgenerator: *cross-reference
generator*
Verweisliste: *reference list*
Verweisungsdatei: *pointer file*
Verweiszeichen: *reference mark*
verwenden: *to use*
verwerfen: *to discard*
verwürfeln: *to scramble*
Verwürfler: *scrambler*
verzahnt: *interleaved*
Verzahnung: *interleaving*
Verzeichnis: *directory or dictionary*
Verzeichnung: *anamorphic image*

verzerren: *to distort*
verzerrte Übertragung: *ANAPROP*
Verzerrung: *distortion; slur*
Verzerrungsobjektiv: *distortion optics*
verzögerter Modus: *deferred mode*
Verzögerung: *delay; holdup; lag*
Verzögerung durch Konkurrenzbetrieb:
contention delay
Verzögerungsdauer: *deceleration time*
Verzögerungsleitung: *delay line*
Verzögerungsvektor: *delay vector*
verzweigen: *to branch*
Verzweigung: *branch; switch*
Verzweigungsbefehl: *branch instruction*
Verzweigungseinrichtung: *distribution
point*
Verzweigungspunkt: *branchpoint*
Verzweigungstabelle: *branch table*
VESA-Local-Bus: *VESA local bus*
V-Format: *V format*
Video: *video*
Videoadapter: *video adapter*
Videoanschluss: *video port*
Videoband: *(video cassette) tape*
Videoband um 1 Bild weiterstellen: *to jog*
Videocontroller: *video controller*
Videodigitizer: *video digitiser*
Videoeinzelbild: *video frame*
Videoexpander: *video expander*
Videokarte: *video board*
Videokassette: *video cassette*
Videokonferenztechnik: *video
conferencing*
Videomonitor: *video monitor*
Videopuffer: *video buffer*
Video-RAM: *video memory or video RAM
(VRAM)*
Videoschnittstellenchip: *video interface
chip*
Videospeicherplatte: *videodisk*
Videoterminal: *visual display terminal
(VDT) or visual display unit (VDU)*
Videotext: *videotext or videotex*
vielfach ausnutzen: *to multiplex*
Vielfachleitung: *highway or bus*
Vielfalt: *diversity*
Vieradressbefehl: *four-address instruction*
Vier-Bit-Byte: *nibble or nybble*
vierfach: *four-fold*
Vier-plus-eins-Adressbefehl: *four-plus-
one address*
Vierspurrekorder: *four-track recorder*
Virenscanner: *anti-virus program*
Virensuchprogramm or*
Virenprüfprogramm: *virus detector or
anti-virus program*
virtuelle Adresse: *virtual or zero-level or
immediate address*

virtuelle Maschine: *virtual machine*
virtuelle Platte: *virtual disk*
virtuelle Realität: *virtual reality*
virtuelle Verbindung: *virtual circuit*
virtueller Matrixblock: *virtual memory stack*
virtueller Speicher: *virtual memory or virtual storage (VS)*
virtueller Terminal: *virtual terminal*
Virus: *virus*
Visitenkarte: *business card*
visuell: *visual*
visuelles Programmieren: *visual programming*
VL-Bus: *VL-bus*
VLP-Bildplatte: *optical disk*
Voicemail: *voice mail*
voll: *full*
voll machen: *to fill up*
Volladdierer: *full adder*
Vollaussteuerung: *maximum reading*
Vollbilddarstellung: *full-screen*
Vollbildmodus: *full-screen*
vollkommen: *perfect*
Vollmacht: *authority*
Vollquittungsbetrieb: *full handshaking*
vollständig: *complete(ly); full(y)*
vollständig bestückt: *fully-populated*
vollständig löschen: *to bulk erase*
vollständige Liste: *dense list*
vollständige Operation: *complete operation*
vollständige Pfadangabe: *full path*
Vollständigkeit einer Datei: *integrity of a file*
Volltextsuche: *full-text search*
Volltypen: *fully formed characters*
vollverbundenes Netz: *fully connected network*
Volt: *volt*
Volumen: *volume*
vom Benutzer auswählbar: *user-selectable*
vor Ort: *on location*
Vorab-Zuordnung: *pre-allocation*
Voraltern: *burn-in*
vorangehen: *to precede*
vorangemeldetes Gespräch zu bestimmten Personen: *person-to-person call*
voraufzeichnen: *to prerecord*
vorausplanen: *to project*
Vorausplanung: *projection*
Voraussetzungen: *requirements*
Vorbedingung: *precondition*
vorbehaltlich: *conditional*
vorbereiten: *to arm*
Vorbereitung: *preparation*
Vorbereitungszeit: *make-ready time or setup time*

vorbeugend: *preventive or preventative*
vorbeugende Wartung: *preventive maintenance*
Vorbeugung: *prevention*
vorbildlich: *model*
vordefiniert: *predefined*
Vorder-/Hintergrundmodus: *foreground/background modes*
vordere Schwarztreppe: *front porch*
vordere Verkleidungsplatte: *front panel*
Vordergrund: *foreground*
Vordergrundfarbe: *foreground colour*
Vordergrundprogramm: *foreground program*
Vordergrundverarbeitung: *foreground processing or foregrounding*
Vordergrundverarbeitungsspeicher: *foreground processing memory*
Vorderseite: *front*
Vordruck: *preprinted stationery or form*
Vordruck in zweifacher Ausführung: *two part stationery*
Vordrucksatz: *multi-part stationery*
voreingenommen: *biased*
voreinstellen: *to preset*
vorformatiert: *preformatted*
vorführen: *to demonstrate*
vorführen: *to screen*
Vorführgerät: *demonstration model; kludge or kluge*
Vorführraum: *projection room*
Vorführung: *demonstration*
Vorgabe: *default*
vorgedrucktes Briefpapier: *preprinted stationery*
vorgedrucktes Formular: *preprinted form*
vorgegebene Schrittgeschwindigkeit: *default rate*
Vorgehenserklärung: *docket*
Vorgehensweise: *procedure*
Vorgehensweise des Operatoren: *operator procedure*
Vorgriff: *look ahead*
vorhandenes Licht: *available light*
vorher abgesprochen: *pre-agreed*
vorher bearbeiten: *to pre-edit*
vorher entworfen: *predesigned*
vorherbestimmt: *predetermined*
vorherig: *previous(ly); prior*
Vorkehrung: *measure*
Vorkompilierer: *preprocessor*
vorkompilierter Code: *precompiled code*
Vorlaufsatz: *leader record*
Vormagnetisierung: *bias*
Vormischung: *premix*
Vorproduktion: *preproduction*
Vorprogramm: *interlude*

vorprogrammiert: *preprogrammed*
Vorprozessor: *preprocessor*
Vorrang: *precedence or priority*
Vorrangprogramm: *foreground program*
Vorrangunterbrechung: *priority interrupt*
Vorrangunterbrechungstabelle: *priority interrupt table*
Vorrichtung für wahlfreien Zugriff: *random access device*
Vorrichtung zum Auswählen der Extremsignale: *auctioneering device*
Vorrichtung zur Qualitätsverbesserung eines Bildes: *image enhancer*
Vorrichtung: *appliance*
Vorrücken der Tonspur: *sound advance*
Vorsatz: *header or tape trailer*
Vorsatzblock: *header block*
Vorschaltrechner: *front-end processor (FEP)*
Vorschub: *carriage*
Vorschublöcher: *centre holes*
Vorschubsteuerung: *carriage control*
Vorsilbe: *prefix*
Vorspann: *prefix or tape header*
Vorspannband: *trailer*
Vorspannung: *bias*
vorstellen: sich ~: *to visualize*
vorübergehend: *temporarily*
vorübersetzen: *to preprocess*
Vorverarbeitungssystem: *front-end system*
Vorverstärker: *pre-amplifier*
vorverzerren: *to pre-emphasise*
Vorwahl: *area code or dialling code*
vorwärts: *forward*
vorwärts bewegen: *to advance*
Vorwärtsfehlerkorrektur: *forward error correction*
Vorwärtsmodus: *forward mode*
Vorwärtsstreuung: *forward scatter*
Vorwärtszeiger: *forward pointer*
vorweg speichern: *to prestore*
Vorzeichen: *sign*
Vorzeichenbit: *sign bit*
Vorzeichenposition: *sign position*
Vorzeichenziffer: *sign digit*
V-Serie: *V series*
VT-Terminalemulation: *VT-terminal emulation*

Ww

Waage: *weighing machine*
Wagenrücklauf(taste): *carriage return (CR) key*
wählbare Brücke: *jumper-selectable*
Wählen: *dialling*
wählen: *to dial*
Wähler: *selector*
wahlfrei: *optional*
wahlfreie Verarbeitung: *random processing*
wahlfreier Zugriff: *random access*
Wählimpuls: *dial pulse*
Wählleitungsausweichverfahren: *switched network backup*
Wählscheibe: *dial*
Wählton: *dial(ling) tone*
WAHR: *TRUE*
Wahrheitstabelle: *truth table*
Wahrheitswert: *truth value*
Wake-up-Code: *wake-up code*
Wald: *forest*
Walze: *platen*
wandernde Anzeige: *marching display*
Wanderwelle: *line transient*
Wanze: *bug*
Warencode: *stock code*
Wärmeableitung: *heat sink*
wärmeempfindlich: *thermo-sensitive*
Warm-Stand-by-System: *warm standby*
Warmstart: *warm boot or warm start*
warnen: *to warn*
Warnfeld: *alert box*
Warnlicht: *warning light*
Warnmeldung: *alert*
Warnsignal: *alarm*
Warnung: *warning*
Wartbarkeit: *maintainability*
warten: *to maintain or service*
Warteschlange: *device queue*
Warteschlangenverwaltung: *queue manager*
Warteschleife: *holding loop or wait loop*
Wartestatus: *wait(ing) state*
Wartestatus Null: *zero wait state*
Wartezeit: *queuing time; wait time; latency*
Wartung: *maintenance; service*
Wartungsprogramm: *service program*
Wartungsroutine: *maintenance routine*
Wartungsvertrag: *maintenance or service contract*

Was-man-sieht-ist-alles-was-man-bekommen-kann (WYSIAYG): *What-You-See-Is-All-You-Get (WYSIAYG)*
Was-man-sieht-ist-was-man-bekommt (WYSIWYG): *What-You-See-Is-What-You-Get (WYSIWYG)*
Watt: *Watt*
Wechsel: *alternation*
wechseln: *to alternate*
wechselndes Heraus- und Hereinholen: *swapping or swap*
Wechselrichter: *inverter (AC/DC)*
wechselseitige Datenübermittlung: *either-way operation*
Wechselstrom: *alternating current (AC)*
Wechselstromgenerator: *alternator*
Wechselwirkung: *interaction*
Weg: *channel*
Wegewahl: *routing*
Weglaufen: *runaway*
wegnehmen: *to pop off*
weiche Rückstellung: *soft reset*
weiche Trennfuge: *soft hyphen*
weiches Trennungszeichen: *soft or discretionary hyphen*
weichsektoriert: *soft-sectored*
weichsektorierte Platte: *soft-sectored disk*
weichzeichnen: *to dither*
weißes Rauschen: *white noise*
weißglühend: *incandescent*
Weißglut: *incandescence*
Weißpegel: *white level*
weiterübertragen: *to relay*
weitervermitteln: *to forward*
Weitervermittlung: *forward clearing*
Weitverkehrsnetz: *wide area network (WAN)*
Weitwinkelobjektiv: *wide-angle lens*
Welle: *wave*
Wellenberg und Wellental: *peak and trough*
Wellenform: *waveform*
Wellenformdigitalisierung: *waveform digitization*
Wellenlänge: *wavelength*
Weltraum: *space*
Weltraumabfall: *space junk*
Weltraumstation: *space station*
WENN-Anweisung: *IF statement*
WENN-DANN-SONST-Anweisung: *IF-THEN-ELSE*
Werbeabteilung: *publicity department*
Werbeagentur: *advertising agency*
Werbebüro: *publicity bureau*
Werbekampagne: *publicity campaign*
Werbematerial an der Kasse: *point-of-sale material*
Werbemelodie: *jingle*

Werbespot: *commercial*
Werbeträger: *advertising medium*
Werbezettel: *flier*
Werbung betreiben or **durchführen:** *to plug or publicize*
Werbung: *publicity; commercial*
Werdegang: *background*
Werkzeug(ausrüstung): *toolkit*
Werkzeugkasten: *toolbox*
Wert: *value*
Werteaustauschbarkeit: *formula portability*
Wertebereich: *number range*
Wettersatellit: *weather satellite*
Wetware: *wetware*
WHILE-Schleife: *while-loop*
wichtigste Ziffer: *most significant digit (MSD)*
wichtigstes Bit: *most significant bit or msb or MSB*
wichtigstes Zeichen: *most significant character*
Wickelrolle: *open reel tape*
widerhallen: *to echo*
Widerstand: *resistance; resistor*
Widerstand leisten: *to resist*
widerstandsfähig: *robust*
Widerstandsfähigkeit: *robustness*
Widerstand-Transistor-Logik: *resistor transistor logic (RTL)*
Wide-SCSI: *Wide-SCSI*
wie angegeben: *as per specification*
wieder aufladen: *to replenish*
wiederanlaufen: *to restart*
Wiederanlaufprogramm nach abnormalem Ende: *abend recovery program*
Wiederanlaufpunkt: *rerun point*
Wiederanlaufroutine: *fall back routines*
wiederanschließen: *to reconnect*
Wiederauffinden eines Textes: *text retrieval*
Wiederauffinden von Informationen: *information retrieval (IR)*
Wiederauffinden: *retrieval*
Wiederauffindungssystem: *reference retrieval system*
wiederauffrischen: *to refresh*
wiederaufladbar: *re-chargeable*
wiederaufladbare Batterie: *re-chargeable battery*
Wiederaufnahme nach Abbruch: *failure recovery*
Wiederaufnahme: *recovery*
wiederaufnehmen: *to resume*
Wiedereinschaltautomatik: *auto restart*
Wiedereinstiegspunkt: *re-entry point*
wiedererkennen: *to recognize*

Wiedererkennung: *recognition*
Wiedergabe: *replay*
Wiedergabegeschwindigkeit: *playback speed*
wiedergeben: *to play back or replay*
wiederherstellbarer Fehler: *recoverable error*
wiederherstellen: *to recover; to undelete*
Wiederherstellungsverfahren: *backward recovery; recovery procedure*
wiederholen: *to repeat; to replicate; to rerun*
Wiederholung: *replay*
Wiederholungsanlauf: *fall back*
Wiederholungsgruppe: *repeating group*
Wiederholungszähler: *repeat counter*
wiederverwendbarer Code: *re-entrant code*
wiederverwendbares Programm: *re-entrant program*
wiegen: *to weigh*
willkürlich: *random*
Winchesterplatte: *Winchester disk*
Winkel: *angle*
Winkelzeichen: *caret*
Winkeralphabet: *semaphore*
wirksam: *active*
wirkungsvoll: *effective*
Wissen: *knowledge*
wissensbasiertes System: *knowledge-based system*
wissenschaftlich: *scientific*
Wissenstechnik: *knowledge engineering*
Wölbung: *buckling*
Workflow: *workflow*
Workgroup: *workgroup*
workgroupfähig: *workgroup enabled*
Workgroupsoftware: *workgroup software*
Wort: *word*
Wort mit fester Länge: *fixed-length word*
Wort(takt)zeit: *word time*
Wortabstände: *spacing*
Wörter pro Minute: *words per minute (wpm or WPM)*
Wörterbuch: *dictionary*
Wortlänge: *word length*
Wortmarke: *word mark*
Wortmarkierungszeichen: *word marker*
Wortserie: *word serial*
Worttrennung: *word break or hyphenation*
Wortzahl: *word count*
Write–Behind–Cache: *write or write-back or write-behind cache*
Wurzel: *root*

Xx

x-Achse: *x-axis or horizontal axis*
Xerographie: *xerography*
xerographischer Drucker: *xerographic printer*
Xerokopie: *Xerox*
xerokopieren: *to Xerox*
Xerokopiergerät: *Xerox (machine)*
x-Koordinate: *x-coordinate*
x-Lochung: *x punch*
x-Richtung: *x-direction*
x-Serie: *X-series*
XT-Tastatur: *XT keyboard*
X-Window-System *or* **X-Windows:** *X-Window System or X-Windows*

Yy

y-Achse: *y-axis or vertical axis*
y-Koordinate: *y-coordinate*
y-Lochung: *y punch*
y-Richtung: *y-direction*

Zz

z-Achse: *z-axis*
Zahl: *figure or number*
Zahl der Kettenglieder: *catena*
Zahl mit endlicher Genauigkeit: *finite-precision numbers*
zählen: *to count; to meter*
Zahlenbereich: *number range*
Zahlenfressen: *number crunching*
Zahlenfresser: *number cruncher*
Zahlengenauigkeit: *precision of a number*
Zähler: *counter; meter*
Zählperforator: *counting perforator*
Zedent: *assignor*
Zehnerkomplement: *ten's complement*

Zehntelwert: decile
Zeichen auf dem Bildschirm: display character
Zeichen pro Inch: characters per inch (cpi)
Zeichen pro Sekunde: characters per second (cps)
Zeichen: character or mark
Zeichenanzeige: character display
Zeichenblock: character block
Zeichenbyte: character byte
Zeichencode: character code
Zeichendarstellung: character representation
Zeichendichte: character density; packing or recording density; pitch
Zeichendrucker: character printer
Zeichenerkennung: character recognition
Zeichenfolge aus Leerzeichen: blank string
Zeichenfolge der Länge Null: null string
Zeichenfolge: character string
Zeichenfolgenfunktion: string function
Zeichenfolgenverkettung: string concatenation
Zeichenformatierung im Haupttextteil: body type
Zeichengabe mit gemeinsamem Zeichenkanal: common channel signalling
Zeichengeber: pulse generator or signal generator
Zeichengenerator: character generator
Zeichenkette: string
Zeichenlochkarte: mark sensing card
Zeichenmatrix: character matrix
Zeichenneigung: character skew
zeichenorientiert: character orientated
Zeichenpapier: cartridge paper
Zeichenprüfung: character check
Zeichenrasterung: character assembly
Zeichenrundungen: character rounding
Zeichensatz: character set; font or fount
Zeichensatz einer Datenstation: terminal character set
Zeichensatzänderung: font change
Zeichensätze laden: to download
Zeichenschablone: flowchart stencil or template
Zeichentaste: alphanumeric key or character key
Zeichenumschaltung: figures shift
Zeichenvorrat: character repertoire
zeichnerisch: graphic
Zeichnung: plot
Zeiger: pointer
Zeigereinheit: pointing device
zeigergesteuerte Unterbrechung: vectored interrupt

Zeigevorrichtung: pointing device
Zeile: line; row
Zeilen pro Minute: lines per minute (LPM)
Zeilen(ein)richter: aligner
Zeilenabstand: line spacing
Zeilenabtastung: raster scan
Zeilenanordnung quer (bei Mikrofilmen): cine orientated image
Zeilenausreißen: tearing
Zeilenaustastlücke: line blanking interval
Zeilenbreite: line width
Zeilenbruch: return
Zeilendrucker: line printer
Zeileneditor: line editor
Zeileneingabe: line input
Zeilenende: line ending
Zeilenfrequenz: line frequency
Zeilenguss: slug
Zeilenlänge: line length
Zeilennummer: line number
Zeilenrücklauf: line flyback
Zeilenschritt: line increment
Zeilentreibersignal: line drive signal
Zeilenumbruch: line folding
Zeilenumlauf: horizontal wraparound
Zeilenvorschub: line feed (LF)
Zeilenvorschubzeichen: new line character
zeilenweises Blättern: roll scroll
Zeit: time
Zeitablaufplanung: scheduling
Zeitablenkung: sweep
Zeitadresscode: time address code
Zeitanzeige: time display
Zeitauslösung: timeout
Zeitbasis: time base
Zeitbedingung: race
Zeitberechnung mit Mikroprozessoren: microprocessor timing
Zeitbereichsanalyse: time domain analysis
Zeitbombe: bomb
Zeitcode zum Zählen von Videovollbildern: full-frame time code
zeitcodierte Seite: time coded page
Zeitkanal: time slot
zeitlich planen: to schedule
Zeitlupe: slow motion
Zeitmultiplexdurchschaltung: time division switching
zeitmultiplexe Zugriffsmethode: time division multiple access
Zeitmultiplexkanal: time derived channel
Zeitmultiplextechnik: time division multiplexing (TDM)
Zeitnehmer: timer
Zeitplan: schedule
Zeitplanungsprogramm: scheduler
Zeitraffung: fast time-scale

Zeitraum: *period*
Zeitscheibe: *time slice*
Zeitschrift: *magazine or periodical*
Zeitsperre: *timeout*
Zeitungsausschnitt: *press cutting*
Zeitungspapier: *newsprint*
zeitversetztes Anschauen: *time shift viewing*
zeitweise auftretender Fehler: *intermittent error*
Zelle: *cell*
Zellenadresse: *cell address*
Zellendefinition: *cell definition*
Zellenformat: *cell format*
Zellenschutz: *cell protection*
zellglasieren: *to laminate*
Zellradio: *cellular radio*
Zellreferenzvariable: *cell reference variable*
Zelltelefon: *cell phone*
Zelltelefon-Fernsprechdienst: *cellular service*
Zentimeter: *centimetre*
zentral: *central*
Zentraldatenstation: *central terminal*
zentrale Datenverarbeitung: *centralized data processing*
Zentrale für Informationsanbieter und Benutzer: *information retrieval centre*
Zentraleinheit: *central processing unit (CPU) or central processor*
zentraler Schreibdienst: *typing pool*
zentrales Computernetz: *centralized computer network*
zentralisiert: *centralized*
zentralisiertes System: *shared logic system*
Zentralspeicher: *central memory (CM)*
Zentralverarbeitungseinheit: *central processing element (CPE)*
zentrieren: *to centre or center*
Zentrierung: *centering*
Zero-Waitstate: *zero wait state*
Zerreißen: *tearing*
Zickzackfaltung: *fanfold or accordion fold or concertina fold*
ziehen und ablegen: *to drag and drop*
Ziehen und Klicken: *drag-and-click*
Ziel: *goal or objective or target*
Zieladresse: *destination address*
Zielcomputer: *target computer*
Zieldatenträger;: *target disk*
Zielebene: *target level*
Zielprogramm: *object program or target program*
Zielsymbol: *aiming symbol*
Ziffer: *digit*
Zifferblatt: *dial*
Ziffern- und Zeichenfeld: *figures case*

Ziffernfeststelltaste: *Num Lock key*
Ziffernstelle: *digit place or position*
zirkulierend: *circulating*
Zirkumflex: *circumflex*
Zischen: *sibilance*
Zitat: *quotation*
zitieren: *to quote*
Zone: *zone*
Zonenübergang: *junction*
Zoom(objektiv): *zoom lens*
zoomen: *to zoom*
zu bewältigen: *manageable*
zu stark einfärben: *to overink*
Zubehör(teil): *accessory*
Zubringer: *feeder*
Zubringerkabel: *feeder cable*
Zubringerspeicher: *external storage or external store*
zufällig: *accidental; random*
Zufallsmodell: *stochastic model*
Zufallsnummer or Zufallszahl: *random number*
Zufallszahlgenerator: *random number generator*
Zufallszahlgenerierung: *random number generation*
zuführen: *to feed*
Zuführung: *feed*
Zuführungskabel: *drop cable*
Zugang: *access*
Zugang zu einem System verwehren: *to bar access to a system*
Zugang zu einer Datei erhalten: *to gain access to a file*
zugänglich: *accessible*
Zugangspunkt: *access point*
zugehörig: *associate*
zugeordnete Frequenz: *assigned frequency*
zugreifen auf: *to access; to reference*
Zugriff: *access*
Zugriff verweigert: *access barred*
Zugriffsarm: *access arm*
Zugriffsberechtigte(r): *accessor*
Zugriffsberechtigung: *access authority or permission or authorization*
Zugriffsbezeichnung: *access name*
Zugriffscode: *access code*
Zugriffsebene: *access level*
Zugriffseinheit: *access unit*
Zugriffsgebühr: *access charge*
Zugriffskategorie: *access category*
Zugriffskontrollbyte: *access control byte*
Zugriffskontrolle: *access control*
Zugriffsmechanismus: *access mechanism*
Zugriffsmethode: *access method*
Zugriffsöffnung: *access hole*
Zugriffspfad: *access path*

Zugriffsprivileg: *access privilege*
Zugriffspunkt: *access point*
Zugriffsrechte: *access rights*
Zugriffsroutinen: *access method routines*
Zugriffszeit: *access time*
Zugriffszeitraum: *access period*
Zuhause: *home*
Zuhörer: *audience*
Zulage: *weighting*
zunehmen: *to ascend*
zuordnen: *to assign*
Zuordnung: *assignment*
Zuordnungsänderung: *assignment conversion*
Zuordnungsanweisung: *assignment statement*
Zuordnungsbefehl: *reference instruction*
Zuordnungsdatei: *reference file*
Zuordnungseinheit: *allocation unit*
zuordnungskompatibel: *assignment compatible*
zur Shell wechseln: *to shell out*
Zurichtungszeit: *make-ready time*
zurückfallen in: *to revert*
Zurückgewinnung: *recovery*
Zurückhalten: *retention*
zurückrufen: *to phone back*
zurücksetzen: *to backout*
zurückspulen: *to rewind*
zurückstellen: *to reset*
zurückverfolgen: *to backtrack*
zurückweisen: *to reject*
Zurückweisung: *rejection*
Zurückweisungsfehler: *rejection error*
zusammenfassen: *to abstract*
zusammenfügen: *to add; to join*
Zusammenführung (von Leitungen): *junction*
zusammengefasst: *ganged*
zusammengeflickt: *kluged*
zusammengesetzte Anweisung: *compound statement*
zusammengesetztes logisches Element: *compound logical element*
Zusammenhang: *context*
zusammenhängend: *coherent*
zusammenhängende Grafik: *contiguous graphics*
zusammenkleben: *to splice*
zusammenschalten: *to interface*
zusammensetzen: *to assemble*
Zusammenstellung eines Schriftstücks: *document assembly or document merge*
Zusammenstoßerkennung: *collision detection*
zusammentragen: *to collate*
Zusatz: *add-in or add-on*

Zusatzadressregister: *B register or B-line counter*
Zusatzbit: *overhead bit*
Zusatzcode: *overhead*
Zusatzcursor: *ghost cursor*
Zusatzdatensatz: *addition record*
Zusatzgerät: *attachment*
Zusatzgeräte: *ancillary or auxiliary equipment*
zusätzlich: *additional or extra; auxiliary*
zusätzlicher Eintrag: *added entry*
Zusatzspeicher: *backing or secondary or auxiliary memory or store or storage*
Zuschauer: *audience; viewer(s)*
Zustand: *condition; state; status*
Zustandsbit: *status bit*
zustimmen: *to approve*
Zustimmung: *approval*
zuteilen: *to allocate*
Zuteilungsroutine: *allocation routine*
zuverlässig: *reliable*
Zuverlässigkeit: *reliability*
Zuwachs: *increment*
zuweisen: *to define*
Zuweiser: *assignor*
Zuweisung: *definition*
zwangssynchronisiertes Netz: *despotic network*
Zweiadressbefehl: *two-address-instruction*
Zwei-Bit-Byte: *doublet or dyad*
Zwei-Byte-Wortgruppe: *gulp*
zweideutig: *ambiguous*
Zweideutigkeit: *ambiguity*
zweidimensional: *two-dimensional*
zweidimensionale Feldgruppe or Matrix: *two-dimensional array*
Zweidrahtleitung: *two wire circuit*
Zweierkomplement: *two's complement*
Zweig einer Schaltung: *leg*
Zweikanalsystem: *dual channel*
zweilagiges Papier: *two-part (paper)*
Zwei-plus-Eins-Adressbefehl: *two-plus-one-address instruction*
Zweirichtungsdrucker: *bi-directional printer*
zweischichtiges Unterprogramm: *two-level subroutine*
Zweiseitenbandübertragung mit unterdrückter Trägerwelle: *double sideband suppressed carrier (DSBSC)*
Zweiseitenbandübertragung: *double sideband*
zweiseitig gerichteter Übertragungsweg: *bi-directional bus*
zweistufiges Unterprogramm: *two-level subroutine*
zweiter Summand: *augmenter*

Zweitkanal: *secondary channel*
zweitrangig: *secondary*
Zweitröhre: *slave tube*
Zweitschrift: *duplicate*
Zwiebelschalenarchitektur: *onion skin architecture*
Zwiebelschalensprache: *onion skin language*
zwingen: *to force*
Zwischenablage: *clipboard*
Zwischencode: *intermediate code*
Zwischendatei: *intermediate file*
Zwischenfrequenz: *intermediate frequency (IF or if)*
zwischengespeicherte Ein-/Ausgabe: *buffered input/output*
Zwischenmedien: *intermediate materials*
Zwischenraum: *gap*
Zwischenregister: *temporary register*
Zwischenspeicher: *intermediate or temporary storage or buffer; clipboard*
Zwischenspeicherbereich: *save area*

zwischenspeichern: *to buffer or plant*
Zwischenstecker: *adapter plug*
Zwischenstück: *sex changer*
Zwischensumme: *subtotal*
Zwischensumme pro Stapel: *batch total*
Zwischenträgerrauschen: *intercarrier noise*
zyklische Bitverschiebung: *cyclic shift*
zyklische Blockprüfung: *cyclic redundancy check (CRC)*
zyklische Fehlerprüfung: *cyclic check*
zyklische Stellenverschiebung: *cyclic shift*
zyklischer Code: *cyclic code*
zyklischer Dezimalcode: *cyclic decimal code*
zyklischer Zugriff: *cyclic access*
Zyklus: *cycle*
Zyklusverfügbarkeit: *cycle availability*
Zykluszeit: *cycle time*
Zylinder: *cylinder*

SPECIALIST GERMAN DICTIONARIES

BUSINESS GERMAN DICTIONARY
GERMAN-ENGLISH/ENGLISH-GERMAN

The second edition of this respected dictionary. The dictionary is a fully bilingual edition that has been revised and updated to provide one of the most comprehensive and up-to-date dictionaries available. The dictionary includes accurate translation for over 50,000 terms that cover all aspects of business usage. Each entry includes example sentences, part of speech, grammar notes and comments.

ISBN 0-948549-50-5   hardback   220x153mm   638pages

BUSINESS GERMAN GLOSSARY

A range of bilingual business glossaries that provide accurate translations for over 5,000 business terms. Each glossary is in a convenient paperback format with 196 pages.

English-German/German-English   ISBN 0-948549-53-X
Spanish-German/German-Spanish   ISBN 0-948549-98-X

English-German with German-English Glossary
A range of specialist bilingual dictionaries (different in layout to our main Business German Dictionary or Glossary). The first part includes full translations from English to German together with examples, part of speech, notes and quotations. The second part is organised as a German-English glossary allowing fast cross-referencing.

Title	ISBN	Pages	Format
Dictionary of Agriculture	0-948549-25-4	450	hardback
Dictionary of Banking & Finance	0-948549-25-4	470	hardback
Dictionary of Computing & IT, 2nd ed	1-901659-00-3	530	hardback
Dictionary of Ecology & Environment	0-948549-25-4	320	hardback
Dictionary of Hotels, Tourism, Catering	0-948549-25-4	420	hardback
Dictionary of Law, 2nd ed	1-901659-25-9	520	hardback
Dictionary of Marketing	0-948549-25-4	300	hardback
Dictionary of Medicine	0-948549-25-4	650	hardback
Dictionary of Printing & Publishing	0-948549-25-4	380	hardback

For full details of all our English and bilingual titles, please request a catalogue or visit our web site.
tel: +44 20 7222 1155 fax: +44 20 7222 1551 email: info@petercollin.com
www.petercollin.com